*Cyprus: Conflict
and Conciliation, 1954–1958*

A PUBLICATION OF
THE MERSHON CENTER FOR EDUCATION
IN NATIONAL SECURITY

Conflict and

Conciliation, 1954–1958

STEPHEN G. XYDIS

Cyprus

THE OHIO STATE UNIVERSITY PRESS
COLUMBUS OHIO

✶

This book is dedicated to Mrs. J.C.H.,
whose grand and gracious friendship
has vitally sustained the author
in work and life alike.

✳

"When it comes to the good fight, it is simply impermissible to let one's effort depend on one's calculations as to the prospects for failure or success. In the great issues, it's the struggle itself that counts, not whether one is likely to win."— *George F. Kennan*

✳

"To talk should be only a means for acting. . . . But, as long as one cannot act, to talk is already something."—*Roger Martin du Gard, "L'Eté 1914"*

✳

"Be a craftsman in speech, so that thou mayest be strong. The tongue is a sword, and speech is more valorous than any fighting."—*An Egyptian Pharaoh to His Son, ca. 2100 B.C.*

✳

"It's a mystery . . . a great mystery! So we want liberty in this bad world, we've got to have all those murders, all those lousy tricks, have we?"—*Nikos Kazantzakis, "Zorba the Greek"*

PREFACE

A DISPUTE, by Webster's definition, is a verbal controversy, strife by opposing arguments and by expressions of opposing views. In such a conflict, "the tongue is a sword," as a Pharaoh advised his son four thousand years ago. In this situation words are not used just as tools but as weapons in an effort to achieve control of, or induce changes in, the behavior of other persons, as though words were real objects and, if introduced in the environment of the target person, could effect changes in his conduct.[1]

The Cyprus conflict, to a major extent, constituted a dispute in the sense defined above. But it also included non-verbal, violent forms of combat and thus had features of warfare, albeit of an imperfect nature—waged as it was by proxies in Cyprus, with EOKA (National Organization of Cyprus Fighters) on the one side and the British authorities on the other, with a Turkish anti-Greek Cypriot underground first called Volkan and then TMT (Turkish Defense Organization) appearing on the scene by 1956.[2]

If wars consist of a number of battles fought in various locations or theaters (this, at least, has been the case in the past), disputes one might say, consist of a number of debates fought in various arenas or forums. Thus, in the Cyprus dispute, the debates took place in the closed or open forums of international organizations or at special conferences, or through the diplomatic channel. They also went on, though not through direct confrontation, through official statements at press conferences, editorials in the press, commentaries on the radio, lectures and pamphlets of various kinds, and even the printing of special postage stamps, just as in the case of an election campaign. In the public eye, however, the battle royal—or "debate royal"—in the Cyprus dispute took place in the United Nations, the most important forum in the world for "parliamentary diplomacy" and for face-to-face debate between and among representatives of various states.

It is primarily to this aspect of the Cyprus dispute (i.e., to the verbal controversy and strife by opposing arguments or expressions of opposing views in the United Nations) that this study is devoted. More specifically, this study examines in depth the debate of the Cyprus dispute that took place at the twelfth regular session of the General Assembly in 1957, the third of a series of four full debates on the Cyprus question that took place in the Assembly between 1954–58.

Although the spotlight is directed on this particular debate, during which Greece came closest to its UN goal, the adoption of a resolution referring to self-determination for the population of Cyprus, it turns, too, on the verbal battle that occurred at the Assembly's eleventh session earlier in 1957, when the third recourse of Greece over the Cyprus question, together with a British counter-recourse, was considered in that organ of the United Nations. For, in contrast to the dramatic "dissensus" at the twelfth Assembly that led to the adoption of no resolution, i.e., to failure from the UN viewpoint if resolution-making is regarded as a criterion for UN success, the consensus-building achievements of the Assembly are illustrated in the outcome of the eleventh Assembly's dealings with the Cyprus item in the form of a resolution. That resolution not only remained in force when the next Assembly after another protracted debate failed to adopt any resolution at all, but raised interesting problems of interpretation and compliance for the parties to the dispute and was used especially by Greek foreign policy–makers in several political ways. Thirdly, the first, second, and last Greek recourses to the United Nations, at the Assembly's ninth, tenth, and thirteenth sessions will be illuminated in this study, in introduction, main text, epilogue, and notes, though somewhat more fleetingly than the debates at the eleventh and twelfth sessions. Because the basic arguments of protagonist and antagonist [3] were repeated from session to session, albeit in varying proportions and with shifts in emphasis, which are duly noted, this approach has the advantage of economy without precluding comparisons.

But since the UN debates over Cyprus were but one facet of the Cyprus dispute between 1954–58, they cannot be understood without reference to Greece's Cyprus policy as a whole and the responses it evoked in the international arena on the part of Britain, Turkey, and third-party states, among which the United States, as leader of the West, was pre-eminent. This policy included not only resort to the United Nations, an organization whose unique features are almost universal participation and equality of voting, but also to regional international organizations such as NATO or the Council of Europe, to conventional intergovernmental communications through the diplomatic channel, and to techniques lying within the "black" end of the spectrum of international politics—unavowed, unconventional warfare waged on the island of Cyprus itself. Information, therefore, on these other facets of Greek policy will be provided in this study, through flashbacks, if need be, to negotiations that failed but augured the shape of things to come. Moreover, three of the outstanding Greek or Greek Cypriot personalities that starred during this conflict will be presented in short biographical political sketches. Finally, the even wider circles of the foreign policy of Greece as a country aligned with the West against the East will also be briefly touched upon and viewed against the still wider regional and world backgrounds.

Because of the primary and hitherto unpublished documentation on which this study is mostly based—the personal papers of Mr. Evangelos Averoff-Tossizza, Foreign Minister of Greece almost uninterruptedly between 1956–63—the picture is presented mainly as seen through the eyes of the "External Decision-Maker" of Greece who conducted Greek foreign policy for the "Central Decision-Maker," Premier Constantine Karamanlis and his Cabinet, and periodically had to explain to Parliament this policy, in the face of the criticism from the "Aspiring Decision-Makers," the leaders of the Opposition.[4] The remarks about the psychological reactions of some of the Foreign Minister's conversation partners, it should be noted, are no "romanticizations" invented by the author to make lively reading but are faithfully taken from the minutes the Foreign Minister himself kept of these conversations.

Ideally, of course, one should have had access to British-Turkish, British-American, and Turkish-American diplomatic exchanges over this intricate issue, as well as to the relevant proceedings of NATO Councils and of the European Commission of Human Rights and the subcommission it set up for the specific purpose of examining two applications the Greek government made to it in 1956 and 1957.

Such access unfortunately was not possible. The picture would indeed be rounded up even more perfectly if archival materials on the communications between the British government and the Governor of Cyprus, and those between the Turkish government and Turkish Cypriot leaders and their agitational organizations on the island had become available. However, at the risk of being suspected of a desire to rationalize, the author wishes to point out that the Greek archival materials he presents on Greek-British, Greek-Turkish, and Greek-American diplomatic exchanges, not to mention certain Greek exchanges with NATO's Secretary-General, have a very particular importance. For it had been the Greek government's behavior which had served as a stimulus for the responses of the British, Turkish, and U.S. governments in the Cyprus question. Without this stimulus, no Cyprus question is likely to have existed—on the international level at least—unless some other state had raised the issue of the status of this British Crown Colony in the eastern Mediterranean.

All in all, this is a study of the way in which a state seeks to use the United Nations as an instrument of national policy, of the methods through which it tries to influence the members of the Assembly in the pursuit of a particular national goal, and of the effect the availability of this organization has on diplomacy conducted through conventional chan-nels. Unlike another study,[5] it does not deal with the over-all political influence of a member state in the Assembly, though incidentally it illustrates some of the findings of that study about the particular methods used by another state—the United States, in this instance—in exerting its influence in the United Nations. Nor is it one about the general attitude of a particular member state toward the United Nations [6] or about the UN political process as seen through the eyes of members of Permanent Missions to the United Nations with no special focus on the position of their own governments on the issues discussed, though it, too, corroborates the view that most UN decisions are settled by informal negotiations outside the formal meetings of the UN organs.[7]

Finally, in contrast to two recent books,[8] which approach the Assembly as a quasi-legislature in which blocs or caucusing groups of member states are the equivalents of political parties in domestic politics, and dwell exclusively on the analysis of roll-call votes, i.e., on dissensus decision-making, this study not only discloses the process of consensus-building but also is based on the concept that, in the last analysis, each single member state is the basic political group in the Assembly and that in effect this organ of the United Nations is composed today of 121 interest groups rather than of a smaller number of blocs or caucusing groups. In the future, such an approach would become quite ordinary if the anti-colonial-colonial and East-West polarities were to break down and no new classes of issues were to arise that would lead to new polarities and alignments of a permanent character. Each issue, then, would bring into being merely *ad hoc* alliances among the various member states of the Assembly instead of setting in movement, as is usually the case today, entire blocs or groups of states.

This study which also illustrates the various political textures in the conduct of foreign policy of interacting multiparty political systems, was prepared under a grant from the Mershon Social Science Program, Ohio State University, then under the distinguished directorship of the late Edgar S. Furniss, Jr. The author wishes to express his gratitude for this support, which enabled him both to take a trip to Athens, Ankara, and Nicosia in the summer of 1964, for the purpose of gathering materials for this book, and to devote his undivided attention to writing from October, 1964, to June, 1965. Likewise to be thanked are those Greek, Turkish, and Cypriot officials who were good enough to receive the author and helped him in collecting materials and in understanding the various viewpoints, as well as Dr. Dana Atchley and Mr. George S. Coumantaros, who made possible a new trip by the author to Greece in 1966 for the purpose of clarifying certain problematic points and for gathering materials for a new book. Mr. Averoff-Tossizza's contribution has already been singled out for mention. His graciousness in permitting the author to delve into his personal papers is deeply appreciated. Without it, this book could hardly have been written—at least with its present substance which, among other things, perhaps enables the political scientist better to understand the complex process of resolution-making in the United Nations and the extraordinary intricacies of conflict and conciliation at Turtle Bay and beyond.

STEPHEN G. XYDIS
HUNTER COLLEGE
CITY UNIVERSITY OF NEW YORK

TABLE OF CONTENTS

Introduction: The First Battle over Cyprus in the United Nations   3

PART ONE

  I   February 26, 1957: The UN Expresses "Its Earnest Desire"   39
      A. UN Resolution 1013 (XI)   39
      B. The Greek Parliament and Resolution 1013 (XI)   45

  II   Relaxation and Tension in Point-Counterpoint   66
      A. Grivas' Truce Offer   66
      B. British Moves—Their Immediate Impact   72
      C. New Tensions in Greek-Turkish Relations   78
      D. Greek-Soviet Confrontation over Nuclear Bases   96

  III   Deadlock: Greece Opts for a New UN Battle   101
      A. A Complete Cessation of EOKA Operations?   101
      B. Deadlock   109
      C. The Precedent for Bipartite Talks   114
      D. Makarios Proposes Bipartite Talks   134
      E. Spaak's First Probes Blocked—
         New Greek Recourse to the UN   136
      F. The House of Commons Debate on Cyprus   148

  IV   Greece Avoids a New Tripartite Conference   154
      A. British Probes for a Tripartite Conference   154
      B. The Precedent for a Tripartite Conference   158
      C. The Impact of the British Probes and
         Their Continuation   161
      D. Final Greek Rebuff to the British Probes   181

PART TWO

  V Greece Gets Item 58 Included in the UN Agenda   191
      A. Preliminary Diplomacy on Item 58
         in the UN—The Explanatory Memorandum   191
      B. The General Committee Recommends
         Inclusion of Item 58 in the Agenda   198
      C. Non-UN Diplomacy over Cyprus at the
         UN and Outside   217
      D. The General Assembly Adopts the
         General Committee's Recommendation
         to Place Item 58 on Its Agenda   220
      E. The World Ambience and Item 58
         in the General Debate   224
      F. Phase I of the UN Struggle   233

  VI Vain Greek Initiatives through the Diplomatic Channel   242
      A. Greek Probes with the U.S. and Britain
         for a Solution Outside of the United Nations   242
      B. The Greek Parliament Debates Phase I
         on Item 58 in the United Nations   261
      C. Controlling an Unavowed Instrument of Foreign Policy   263
      D. Continued Deadlock in British and NATO Diplomacy
         on Cyprus   267

  VII The Greek Delegation Prepares for the Main UN Battle   271
      A. The Attitude of Various UN Members toward Item 58   271
      B. The Greek Pro-Arab Stand in the Debate
         on the Syrian Crisis   276
      C. The First Committee Decides When to
         Consider Item 58   278
      D. Backstage Talks with the U.S., British,
         Indian, and Turkish Delegations   279
      E. Preparing the Greek Draft Resolution   295

PART THREE

  VIII December 9: The Battle in the Committee Begins   301
      A. The 927th Meeting of the First Committee   301
      B. The 928th Meeting of the First Committee   329
      C. Backstage Diplomacy in the United Nations
         and in Washington   353

IX   December 10: The Voice of the United States
     Is Heard above Other Voices   356
     A. Backstage Diplomacy in Washington   356
     B. The Debate in the First Committee   358

 X   December 11: Third Parties Take Sides   379
     A. Backstage Diplomacy in the UN
        and Washington   379
     B. The 930th Meeting of the First Committee   381
     C. The 931st Meeting of the First Committee   394
     D. The 932d Meeting of the First Committee   410
     E. Backstage   425

XI   December 12: The Greek Side Wins in the
     Committee Battle and India Comments   427
     A. Backstage   427
     B. The 933d Meeting of the First Committee   428
     C. Interlude Backstage   443
     D. The 934th Meeting of the First Committee   447

XII December 14: Anticlimax in the General Assembly   477
     A. Backstage at the UN   477
     B. The General Assembly Rejects the
        Committee's Recommendation   484
     C. The Greek Mission to the UN Evaluates
        the UN Struggle   495
     D. The Greek Parliament Debates the Handling
        of the Cyprus Question in the UN   500
     E. Coda   505

Epilogue: The Last Battle over Cyprus in the United Nations   511

Conclusions   529

Appendixes

     A. Application, under the Auspices of the
        United Nations, of the Principle of
        Equal Rights and Self-determination of
        Peoples in the Case of the Population
        of the Island of Cyprus   567
     B. Letter Dated 23 July 1955 from the
        Permanent Representative of Greece
        to the Secretary-General   572

C. Greece: Request for the Inclusion of an
   Item in the Provisional Agenda of the
   Eleventh Session   573
D. United Kingdom of Great Britain and
   Northern Ireland: Request for the
   Inclusion of a Supplementary Item in
   the Agenda of the Eleventh Session   579
E. Greece: Request for the Inclusion of an
   Item in the Provisional Agenda of the
   Twelfth Session   581
F. Greece: Request for the Inclusion of a
   Supplementary Item in the Agenda of the
   Thirteenth Session   585

Notes   591

Bibliography   683

Index   691

*Cyprus: Conflict
and Conciliation, 1954—1958*

The First Battle Over Cyprus in the United Nations

Between 1954 and 1958, Greece resorted to the United Nations five times over the Cyprus question. Its ostensible goal in the organization was to get the General Assembly to adopt a resolution that recommended self-determination for the population of Cyprus or, in the case of the fifth recourse, the setting up an independent Cyprus. What was the Assembly's response to these five successive political stimuli?

The first time, the Assembly, at its ninth session, merely debated the question; and on December 17, 1954, in Resolution 814 (IX), it decided not to consider the item further, for the time being. The second time, the Assembly, at its tenth session, decided, on September 23, 1955, not to include the Cyprus item in its agenda. The third time, the Assembly, at its eleventh session, considered both the Greek request and another from Britain entitled "Support from Greece for Terrorism in Cyprus," as a single item. On February 26, 1957, it adopted Resolution 1013 (XI) under which the Assembly, believing that the solution of the question of Cyprus required an atmosphere of peace and freedom of expression, expressed the "earnest desire" that a peaceful, democratic, and just solution could be found in accordance with the purposes and principles of the Charter and the hope that negotiations would be resumed and continued to that end. The fourth time, the Assembly, at its twelfth session, once more considered the issue but failed to adopt any resolution on the matter. The fifth time, at its thirteenth session, it again considered that question. On December 5, 1958, it adopted Resolution 1287 (XIII), which appeared to be a repetition of Resolution 1013 (XI). Under it, the Assembly "expressed its confidence" that continued efforts would be made by the parties to reach a peaceful, democratic, and just solution in accordance with the Charter of the United Nations. This confidence was not misplaced. The issue was settled outside the United Nations by the

Zürich and London agreements of February, 1959, with the establishment of an independent state of Cyprus.

Why did the foreign policy–makers of Greece, a small non-caucusing
state in the United Nations, so persistently resort to the Assembly five
times in succession? What political effects did they actually hope to gain
from such moves? What methods did they use in promoting their Cyprus
recourses through the debating and resolution-making machinery of the
Assembly with its rules and restraints? Were these methods any different
from those resorted to by decision-makers and diplomatic officials of
more influential states in their recourses to the United Nations? What
was their evaluation of these recourses and their outcomes? This study
suggests or supplies certain answers to these questions. It highlights, too,
the specific problems involved in a debate of what might be termed an
imperfect dispute, namely, one in which protagonist and antagonist are,
otherwise, not foes but allies. Incidentally, it also sheds light on the
political authority of the United Nations—at two different phases of its
life—"as an organ of political settlement, of peace-making and peace-
keeping," [1] in dealing with a specific issue that affected only a limited
sector of world society, a dispute among two or more nations [2] which,
both protagonist and antagonist agreed, with varying degrees of emphasis, was connected with the colonial problem.

The rational motivations for, and ostensibly desired gains from, the
recourses to debates in, and negotiations [3] with, the United Nations on
the Cyprus question were basically established at the time the Greek
government first requested the Assembly to consider the problem in a
document dated August 16, 1954, entitled: "Application, under the auspices of the United Nations, of the principle of equal rights and self-
determination of peoples in the case of the population of the island of
Cyprus." This first recourse set a precedent for the four later ones even
though, as already mentioned, the Greek draft resolution tabled at the
thirteenth Assembly in 1958 differed from the earlier ones in proposing
independence for the island rather than self-determination.

The political rationale for resorting to the United Nations as described
by Greek policy–makers of 1954 in their long explanatory memorandum,
which was an integral part of the text of the recourse (see Appendix A),
may be summarized as follows:

The leaders of "four-fifths of the Cypriot population," faced by the
adamant British attitude toward the claim for *enosis* (union with
Greece) expressed in a plebiscite in January, 1950, had in September,
1953, petitioned the Assembly's eighth session to consider this claim
against Britain and to adopt a resolution recommending that Britain
should accept the right of the people of Cyprus to self-determination "in
compliance with . . . resolution 637 (VII) of December 16, 1952." [4]
Since, under the UN Charter, such a petition on the part of a non-state
could not be considered by the United Nations, the Cypriots had asked
the Greek government to sponsor this petition and to request the United

Nations to examine this dispute. In Greece itself, "public opinion" had been exerting pressures in the same direction.[5] Under the circumstances, the Greek government, which since 1949 had tried to approach the British government in order to find a solution to the problem, had since September, 1953, more pressingly than before renewed its efforts to get the British government to agree to engage in negotiations on the matter of the future of Cyprus. Indeed, in the general debate at the previous session of the Assembly, the Greek Delegate, on September 21, 1953, after mentioning the petition of Archbishop Makarios to the United Nations, had indicated that his government preferred the course of bipartite negotiations for dealing with the problem of resorting to the United Nations. At the same time, he had warned that in case the "normal procedure of friendly conversations was inconclusive," an eventual recourse "before this international tribunal" was not to be excluded.[6]

The British government, however, had consistently rejected such overtures for negotiations. As in the past, it not only had declared the matter "closed" but "had added fuel to the fire" by statements to the effect that Cyprus would "never" break away from British rule. And in Cyprus itself, the British authorities had passed certain decrees "prohibiting, under the penalty of excessively severe punishment, every manifestation of the will of the people." This negative policy presaged no good. The Greek government, consequently, "having exhausted every means of achieving an agreement directly," had felt "compelled" to ask the United Nations "to redress this situation by securing acceptance of the solution required by justice, dignity, and the sacred principles set forth in the Charter" and appealed to the Assembly for a constructive solution "conducive to peace and freedom."

In this appeal the Greek government specifically invoked Article 1, paragraph 2 of the Charter, which refers to the development of friendly relations among nations based "on respect for the principle of equal rights and self-determination of peoples . . ."; Article 10, which authorizes the Assembly to "discuss any questions or any matters within the scope of the present Charter . . ."; and Article 14, which empowers the Assembly to recommend measures for the peaceful adjustment of any situation, regardless of origin, which it deems likely to impair the general welfare or friendly relations among nations. . . ." It also reserved the right to invoke, "if it considered such a course to be justified by subsequent events," Article 35, paragraph 1, under which "any member of the United Nations may bring any dispute or any situation" which might lead to international friction or give rise to a dispute, to the attention of the Security Council or of the Assembly. In brief, because of the inflexible British attitude, the Greek government, wishing to act, to do something, and not let matters drift further because of awareness "of both the present and future dangers inherent in this situation," had decided to resort to the Assembly to get at least a public face-to-face debate of what it regarded as an international dispute (without technically labeling it as such) and to place before the world organization certain proposals for dealing with the question.

As against the original goal of getting negotiations of a redistributive character [7] started with the British government over the future of Cyprus, an intermediate goal was now established as a second-best approach to the issue: negotiating with the United Nations to get it to agree to hold a debate on the Cyprus item, consider the Greek proposals, and adopt them as a formal resolution. Recourse to "parliamentary diplomacy," in other words, was a substitute for diplomatic negotiations.

The story of the diplomatic activities that preceded this recourse to "parliamentary diplomacy" [8] shows the subtle escalation-like course of events that led the Greek government in 1954 to take this bold and grave step of raising before the United Nations an issue that the British government regarded as internationally non-negotiable.

Official Greek indications of a desire to negotiate with the British government over the future of Cyprus went further back than 1949, the date mentioned in the explanatory memorandum of the first Greek recourse to the United Nations. At the very nadir of its power, when its members had escaped from Athens and had taken refuge in Crete, in May, 1941, the Greek government, through its Prime Minister, Emmanuel J. Tsouderos, had raised the matter, perhaps stimulated by Anthony Eden's suggestion during his second visit to the Greek capital, in February, 1941, that the future of Cyprus would be settled after the war in talks between the two governments. A year later, in a memorandum on postwar Greek claims addressed to the U.S. government and also communicated to the British government, it had drawn attention to the Cyprus question and had expressed the hope that this issue would be settled directly between Greece and Britain. After the end of World War II, however, Greek governments refrained from pressing it. They were almost exclusively [9] preoccupied with promoting the northward claims of Greece before the Council of Foreign Ministers and at the Paris Peace Conference or with trying to get British and/or American economic aid for reconstruction while internally facing a new Communist-led uprising. It was only the Communist party of Greece that clamored for Cyprus on anti-British, anticolonialist, anti-imperialist grounds.

After the United States appeared on the Greek scene with the "Truman Doctrine," King Paul, in mid-1948, publicly raised the issue of Cyprus in the irredentist terms of *enosis* in an interview with an American journalist. He made it plain that such a change in the island's colonial status would in no way interfere with British bases there and offered to Britain and the United States further bases on Greek soil. Less than three years later, in March, 1951, after the Communist-led unconventional warfare had been stamped out, Premier Sophocles Venizelos not only publicly raised the question in the Greek Parliament but also conferred with Sir

Clifford Norton, the British Ambassador in Athens, on the matter. He reiterated the proposal the King had made about the establishment of British bases on Greek territory. Later that year the Greek government informed the State Department about this offer. All Greek political leaders at this point were agreed that the question of Cyprus should be promoted within the framework of traditional Anglo-Greek friendship and also concurred with the idea of offering to Britain bases in Greece.[10]

Shortly afterward, there were indications that the Greek government had given thought to bringing the United Nations into the picture. The Greek Ambassador in London inquired of the British Foreign Secretary, Herbert S. Morrison, what the British government would do if the General Assembly were to adopt a resolution favorable to the Greek viewpoint. Morrison replied that the British government would ignore such a resolution.[11]

The first Greek mention of the Cyprus problem in the United Nations was made in 1950 at the Assembly's fifth session, when Member of Parliament Gregory Kassimatis, in spite of the contrary advice of Ambassador Alexis A. Kyrou, the Permanent Representative of Greece to the UN, obliquely referred to the issue. It was necessary, he told the Political Committee on October 25, to proclaim the principle of the right of peoples to self-determination, regardless of the national interest of great empires. Foreign domination, whether by enemies or friends, was always an evil! [12] The following year, at the Assembly's sixth session, in Paris, the Greek representative Jean Politis, again without mentioning the island by name, referred to the question in the general debate as an instance of discrimination that was not consonant with the spirit of the UN Charter. It ought to be remedied either by an official interpretation of the Charter or through measures taken by the administering power on its own initiative, he added. The Greek representatives on the Third Committee (Human Rights) and the Fourth Committee (Trusteeship and Non-Self-Governing Territories) likewise referred to the Cyprus question. These hints in the United Nations triggered a meeting in Rome between Foreign Secretary Eden and the Greek Undersecretary of Foreign Affairs, E. Averoff-Tossizza, but the Britisher insisted he could not take up a matter that did not exist.

The United Nations was gradually drawn more and more into the picture the following year as the Third Committee invited the Commission on Human Rights to submit recommendations about the question of implementing the principle of self-determination at the next session of the Assembly.[13] Should this occur, as it very probably would by the beginning of 1953, Ambassador Kyrou, reported to his government, a legal title would doubtlessly be established for the Cypriot people to ask the United Nations to supervise a repetition of the plebiscite on the island on January 15, 1950. Such a resolution, if used carefully and without excesses, would constitute, he believed, a very important psychological weapon for carrying out direct Greek-British negotiations concerning Cyprus—with participation, if possible, of the United States because of common NATO interests in the Mediterranean.

In 1952, the year Greece and Turkey became members of NATO, the Greek government continued its approaches to the British government. In May, 1952, Venizelos, then Foreign Minister, spoke to the British Ambassador in Athens and handed him, for transmission to Lord Halifax, an unofficial note on the issue. In June and July, other *démarches* were made either in London or in Athens, and the standing Greek offer of bases in Greece was reaffirmed. At the same time, although the Greek government firmly rejected the persistent pleas of Makarios for a recourse to the United Nations, its representatives at the seventh session of the Assembly directly or indirectly again referred to the Cyprus question both in the general debate and in the Third and Fourth Committees. That session, by adopting the earlier-mentioned Resolution 637 (VII) which called upon member states to promote the right of self-determination among non-self-governing peoples,[14] inaugurated a new period in the organization's history during which self-determination issues became the subject of considerable debate.[15] The United States voted against resolutions A and B of that triple resolution.

The year 1953, in the world arena, featured Stalin's death (March 5) and the Korean Armistice (July 27). In the Balkan arena, it witnessed, on February 25, the signing of the Ankara Pact—a five-year Treaty of Friendship and Co-operation among Greece, Yugoslavia, and Turkey—and, in the Greek sector, the conclusion of a U.S.-Greek agreement, on October 12, on the use of naval and air bases in Greece.

For the Cyprus question, that same year was one of ominous new developments. Field Marshal Alexander Papagos, his prestige from victory over the Fascist Italian forces in 1940 enhanced by his more recent success in 1949 against the Communist-led guerrilla forces of Markos Vafiadis, had become Premier after a substantial success of his Greek Rally party in the general elections of November 12, 1952. Both before the elections,[16] when he also raised the question of expropriating the British-owned company cultivating the reclaimed basin of Lake Copais in Boeotia, and early the next year, he spoke to Sir Charles Peake, the British Ambassador in Athens, about the Cyprus question. As a solution he proposed the granting of a liberal Constitution to the Cypriots, with a plebiscite to follow within two years, to give the people an opportunity to decide their own future. He also repeated the offer of bases on Greek territory. In somewhat sibylline terms, on the other hand, he informed Ethnarch Makarios that he would seek a solution of the Cyprus problem "within the framework of current realities." [17]

September 21 and 22 were turning points. On September 21, Ambassador Kyrou, as mentioned earlier, raised the question in the general debate at the eighth Assembly, cautiously warning about the possibility of a recourse to the international organization if no bipartite negotiations with the British government were forthcoming. In Athens, the next day, when the Greek Premier met Foreign Secretary Eden, the latter dryly reaffirmed that for the British government there was no Cyprus question at the present nor could there be one in the future. In December, in a conversation with the Greek Ambassador in London, Vassili Mostras, Eden stuck to the same inflexible attitude. The British government, he warned, had the means to repulse a recourse to the United Nations, and, should it become necessary, the British Delegation would walk out of any committee meeting that might discuss the question.[18] At its eighth session, the Assembly, it should be noted, adopted Resolution 742 (VIII) on November 27, 1953. One of its operative clauses provided that the self-government of non-self-governing territories could be primarily attained through independence but could also be achieved by association with another state if done freely and on the basis of absolute equality.[19]

The following year, 1954, while British and American plans to organize the defense of the Middle East were under way and a great importance was being attached to Turkey as a pivotal "northern tier" state, the Greek government, even more pressingly than before, reiterated its threat to resort to the United Nations, if no bipartite negotiations took place on the Cyprus problem. Public statements, first by Kyrou, then by Foreign Minister Stefanos Stefanopoulos, strengthened the commitment to such action. On its side, the British government, in spite of several *démarches* by the Greek Ambassador in London, remained adamant. Selwyn Lloyd, Minister of State, predicted "toil and moil" if the Greek government persisted in its course. In the House of Commons on March 15, Eden publicly committed his government to an inflexible attitude. At the same time, behind the scenes, the British government indicated it was ready to grant self-government to the Cypriots, with the possibility left open for them to decide their own future after a period of ten to fifteen years.

April was a cruel month of decision for the Greek government. At a conference of April 15 attended by Foreign Minister Stefanopoulos; Director-General of the Ministry for Foreign Affairs, Kyrou; the Greek Ambassador in London, Mostras; and another high ranking diplomat, Premier Papagos, decided to go ahead with the recourse to the United Nations unless bipartite negotiations took place. Earlier that same month he had informed Eden of this intention, though stressing that the Greek government was ready to enter into friendly negotiations in order to find a solution to the Cyprus question.[20] At this conference of April 15, the Premier, disregarding the views of the Greek Ambassador in London, seemed convinced that the British feared so much the idea of a public exposure of the Cyprus question in the United Nations that they would in the end agree to enter into bipartite negotiations with the Greek government on the issue. He also expressed optimism about the matter of dealing with the Turkish government on the Cyprus issue. Yet, a few days earlier, the Turkish Ambassador in Athens had quite plainly indicated that his government desired the maintenance of the status quo in

Cyprus; that any negotiations over the status of the island should be tripartite, i.e., include not only Britain and Greece but Turkey as well; and that a debate in the United Nations would undermine Greek-Turkish relations.[21]

May 3: Premier Papagos committed himself publicly to his decision of April 15 to resort to the United Nations if no bipartite negotiations with the British began. On May 14, the British government through the diplomatic channel once again expressed its equally inflexible views [22] and on July 28 quite emphatically committed itself in public to them. The Undersecretary of State for the Colonies, Henry Hopkinson (later Lord Colyton), after announcing proposals of a new constitution for Cyprus, stated in response to Labour Opposition questioning that it was always understood and agreed that there were certain territories in the Commonwealth which, because of their particular circumstances, could "never" expect to be fully independent. While adding he was not going as far as that (with regard to Cyprus), he reiterated that the question of the abrogation of British sovereignty could not arise and that British sovereignty would remain. A day earlier, after long and frequently interrupted negotiations, the British and Egyptian governments had signed the "Heads of Agreement" that was to lead to the conclusion of a final agreement on October 19, 1954, under which the British undertook to withdraw their troops from Egypt within twenty months. As a result, Britain decided to implement its decision, taken in principle since December, 1952,[23] to transfer its Middle East Command to Cyprus.

Certain Greek officials responsible for handling the Cyprus question welcomed Hopkinson's statement—somewhat impolitic, Churchill was to suggest [24]—as new proof of British intransigence and of the need to resort to the United Nations. On August 20, the Greek government sent to the UN Secretary-General its recourse on the Cyprus problem together with its long explanatory memorandum. Another response was the printing of a postage stamp showing a huge inkblot on the page from Hansard that contained Hopkinson's "never" statement to the Commons on July 28.

A statement of August 19 constituted the public response of the British government to the Greek moves. In this statement the British government argued that with the exception of a brief period in the fourth century B.C., Cyprus had never belonged to Greece (an indirect reminder that it had belonged to the Ottoman Empire), and that the Russian danger which had brought Great Britain to Cyprus in 1878 still existed. The strategic considerations that required continued British sovereignty over the island were: first, that British control of Cyprus was essential for the fulfilment of British strategic obligations in the Middle East and to NATO; second, that a Cyprus base leased from Greece could not afford the necessary security of tenure; and, third, that Britain would no more consider relinquishing sovereignty over Cyprus than over Gibraltar, and its experience in Egypt showed that bases without sovereignty could not always be relied upon.

In this statement of August 19, the British government also contended that the internal political development of Cyprus had been retarded by the Greek Cypriot rejection in 1948 of the proposed constitution, and that the Communist party in Cyprus was now a real menace to democratic development in the island. In conclusion it asserted that the Cyprus question was entirely within the domestic jurisdiction of Britain and that UN intervention would therefore be contrary to Article 2, paragraph 7, of the Charter. Debate in the General Assembly, it maintained, would not but exacerbate feelings at a delicate stage, thus indefinitely delaying the political progress of Cyprus which it was the responsibility of Britain to promote. The debate, moreover, would also serve the purpose of the U.S.S.R. to foster differences among the Western allies.

A chorus of hostile items and editorials in the Turkish press presaged the Turkish government's attitude, which paralleled British unwillingness to talk over the Cyprus question with the Greek government. When Premier Adnan Menderes, at the invitation of Papagos, stopped briefly for dinner in Athens on his flight back to Ankara on June 7, the Turkish Ambassador in Athens adjured Ambassador Kyrou against any raising of the Cyprus question by the Greek Premier. Such a conversation, he said, would have extremely undesirable consequences for the Greek-Turkish alliance.[25] Then, at a meeting of the three Balkan Accord members at Bled, in Yugoslavia, where the Balkan Treaty of Alliance, Political Co-operation, and Mutual Assistance was signed on August 9, Foreign Minister Stefanopoulos sought to raise the question with his Turkish colleague but the latter curtly replied: "There is no Cyprus question." After the Greek recourse had been sent to the United Nations, the Greek Premier sent a Turkish-speaking Greek member of Parliament, George Bakalbassis, to Ankara, to probe the Turkish government's attitude. On his return, Bakalbassis reported that Menderes had asked him to convey to the Premier the courteously ambiguous assurance that Greek-Turkish relations and friendship were far more important than the Cyprus question.[26] The Turkish Premier was far more explicit on August 31, when he publicly declared that Cyprus would never be annexed to Greece.

Ten days before the Assembly opened its ninth session on September 21, the Greek Permanent Mission under Ambassador Kyrou, in this first recourse to the United Nations of one NATO member against another, started its *démarches* with other permanent missions to the world organization and heads of arriving delegations, in order to secure the inclusion of the Cyprus item in the Assembly's agenda and, in general, to muster support for the Greek viewpoint on this item. The delegations of the Soviet bloc states were approached only at social occasions.[27] At one of these, Kyrou asked Andrei Y. Vyshinsky, head of the Soviet Delegation, to refrain from speaking on the issue when the General Committee and the Assembly would debate the question of the item's inclusion in the agenda. Vyshinsky got the point, said he would, and kept his promise. With representatives of allied NATO states and of colonial countries, on the other hand, Kyrou argued that a negative stand on their part toward the demand of a people as civilized and as mature as the Cypriots would fully justify the charges of the Cominform states and of the anticolonialists that the West's incessant statements about freedom were mere cant and that their seemingly reasonable arguments about their "sacred mission" of gradually educating immature colonial peoples were nothing but a pretext for keeping them in slavery.[28]

The Greek Delegation also got the UN Secretariat to recommend that the Cyprus question be discussed in the Political not the *ad hoc* Committee, and at the earliest if, of course, this item were included in the agenda. Also, in order to attract the sympathy of the Asian delegations, Greece withdrew its suggested candidacy for one of the seven vice-presidencies of that session of the Assembly, thus leaving the post open for an Asian state. Indeed, Burma was elected to that office.[29]

On September 23, the General Committee examined the Cyprus item. By 9 votes to 3, with 3 abstentions, it recommended its inclusion in the Assembly's agenda. Among the abstainers were the United States, Colombia, which the Greek Delegation had expected to vote affirmatively, and the Netherlands, whose representative had been persuaded to do so by the head of the Greek Delegation.[30] In spite of the British argument that the United Nations was not competent to consider the Cyprus question because it lay essentially within Britain's domestic jurisdiction and thus fell under the provisions of Article 2, paragraph 7, of the UN Charter, the first hurdle had thus been overcome.

In its estimate of the outcome of the voting in the Assembly on the matter of including the Cyprus item in the agenda, the Greek Delegation again turned out to be overoptimistic. Whereas it had expected 39 affirmative votes, 9 negative votes, and 12 abstentions, the Assembly adopted the General Committee's recommendation on September 24 by 30 votes to 19, with 11 abstentions. Among the abstainers was the influential anticolonial but Commonwealth member, India, whose representative, V. Krishna Menon, explained his stand by saying that as raised in the United Nations, the Cyprus question was not one of Cypriot nationhood and independence but a dispute over the island's possession.[31] Kyrou ascribed this great difference between expectations and results to the effectiveness of the arguments that the British Delegate, Lloyd, had presented; to energetic British backstage pressures on other delegations; and, last and not least, to the powerful backstage intervention of the U.S. Delegation with other delegations.[32] On becoming aware of this American opposition, about which more will be said later, the Greek diplomat felt that the inclusion of the Cyprus item in the agenda had been a triumph.[33]

After this initial success, which now made possible a face-to-face public debate on the Cyprus dispute in the UN forum, i.e., within an organized environment of third parties, the Greek representatives in the Assembly committees were instructed to determine their attitude toward the various items under considerations and to vote on the tabled resolutions in ways that would best serve the interests of Greece in the Cyprus question. Such tactics would communicate to the allies the importance that the Greek government attached to that question. They would also influence favorably, it was hoped, the debating and voting attitudes of the delegations of uncommitted Asian, African, and Latin American states when the turn came for the Cyprus item to be considered in the Political Committee. Thus, in the debates on the questions of Morocco and West Irian (Dutch New Guinea) in the Political Committee; or on the status of Indians in the Union of South Africa in the *ad hoc* Political Committee; or on human rights and non-self-governing territories in the Third and Fourth Committees, the Greek representatives appeared as champions of human rights and subject peoples instead of necessarily following the policy lines of the leaders of the West on these matters, even though Greece was aligned with the West.[34] Greek officials, too, directed, as will be seen, a great deal of attention to the most difficult problem of all: trying to get the U.S. Delegation to maintain a neutral attitude as well as secrecy about its political viewpoint regarding the undesirability of any substantive resolution on the Cyprus problem.[35]

The Greek Delegation wanted an early debate of the Cyprus item in the Political Committee, but was unable to prevent that Committee from deciding on October 8 to take up that item last.[36] As a result, the Cyprus item was discussed, if not considered,[37] at the very end of the Assembly's session in four meetings of the Political Committee on December 14 and 15.

Although at these meetings the Greek together with the British and Turkish representatives as well as representatives of twenty other member states spoke on the Cyprus item, the Greek Delegation also failed to reach its supreme goal in the United Nations: the adoption of its draft resolution under which the Assembly would have expressed "the wish" for the application of the principle of self-determination to the population of Cyprus.[38] Neither this draft resolution nor any second-best proposal—one that would urge the conduct of Greek-British negotiations for dealing with the problem [39]—were even put to the vote. Giving precedence to a draft resolution tabled by the representative of New Zealand, the Committee and then the Assembly adopted Resolution 814 (IX), which had incorporated some amendments put forward by the Delegations of Colombia and El Salvador, perhaps backed by the United States,[40] and had been acceptable to the Greek Delegation. In Resolution 814 (IX), adopted by show of hands by fifty votes to none, with eight abstentions, the Assembly decided "for the time being"—a formula borrowed from the same Assembly's Moroccan and Tunisian resolutions—not to consider further the Greek item on the Cyprus question.[41] The representatives not only of Britain, Turkey, and the United States but also of Greece were among those who voted in favor of this resolution. In the roll-call vote that took place in the Political Committee concerning the preamble of the resolution and preceded the vote on the resolution as a whole, there were sixteen not eight abstentions—not only those of the five Soviet bloc states but also of Turkey and ten other states (France, Luxembourg, Burma, Thailand, South Africa, Uruguay, Yugoslavia, Australia, Belgium, and Chile). That same roll-call vote revealed that Greece, Britain, and the United States, together with forty-one other members voted in favor of the preamble.[42]

Both the British and Turkish representatives, when interpreting their vote before the Assembly, made the reservation that their affirmative votes should not be construed as implying the recognition of the Assembly's competence to consider the subject matter of the Cyprus question. And the former (Anthony Nutting) maintained that the Assembly by this resolution had not merely postponed consideration of the Cyprus item but had decided that, under the prevailing circumstances, it would be unwise to bring this "explosive matter" into the arena of "contentious debate." [43]

The Greek representative, on the other hand, commenting on his delegation's vote, chose to interpret the Assembly's decision to include the Cyprus item in its agenda as a recognition of "the international character of the question of Cyprus." And he also committed himself to the interpretation that the resolution adopted signified that the Assembly had merely postponed "for the time being" taking any decision "on a question which remains pending before the United Nations." [44] The words "for the time being" may have had for Kyrou an esoteric meaning—the implication that the Assembly would no longer be justified in setting aside the issue, if the situation in Cyprus deteriorated, as he expected it would. Had he not warned the Assembly in September, when urging it to consider the Cyprus item and take a decision on it, that the apparent calm on the island was "the quiet that precedes the storm"? [45] To those, like Kyrou, who were aware that George Grivas was getting ready to wage unconventional warfare in Cyprus,[46] this venture in the United Nations may have seemed like a last effort to achieve a settlement of the question without covert resort to force.

In publicly evaluating the political results of their first recourse to the United Nations concerning the Cyprus problem and in defending the handling of the question against charges by the Opposition, Greek government officials emphasized the "side effects" [47] of the debate in, and the negotiations with the world organization and tended to present their interpretative commitments [48] as objective gains. Thus, in the Greek Parliament on February 7, 1955, Premier Papagos, after reporting at great length on his government's futile efforts to engage in negotiations

with the British government over Cyprus and saying he was not disposed
to regard the matter as closed and that there had been no other way of
dealing with the problem except to go to the United Nations, observed
that Resolution 814 (IX), though not ideal for the Greeks, was a favorable solution, a good omen on the way toward a solution of the Cyprus
problem. The Assembly, he said, had "affirmed" in this resolution its
competence "to seize itself of the matter," though it had considered it
inappropriate "for the time being" to take a decision on it. The Cyprus
question had now been brought out in the open. It was no longer an
internal affair of Britain. It had become an international question and the
United Nations could deal with it. Besides, the sixty members of the
United Nations had been informed about the Cyprus question. Foreign
Minister Stefanopoulos, in his report to Parliament, emphasized the same
points after stressing that the raising of the question was fully in accord
with the aims of free peoples seeking to organize a world based on justice
and freedom. He added that the recourse to the United Nations had
helped project the Cyprus issue before "international public opinion." [49]
As Kyrou, the chief spokesman about the Cyprus issue in the Assembly,
was to write, the debate in the Political Committee whether to consider
further the Cyprus item had made it abundantly possible for the Greek
government to present its views on the substance of the Cyprus dispute.[50]

Greek foreign policy–makers of 1954 who, as indicated, envisaged the
recourse to the United Nations as leverage toward an extra-UN goal—
bipartite negotiations with the British over the issue—were to a very
limited extent successful in achieving this objective, though they did not
mention this in Parliament, and Eden, on October 25, flatly denied in the
Commons that any conversations with the Greek government had taken
place during the previous three months on the Cyprus question.[51] Thus,
in September two successive ultrasecret efforts were made, not through
normal diplomatic channels, to approach Premier Papagos with proposals that suggested the possibility of some arrangement. The Greek intermediaries were Panayotis Pipinelis, a distinguished former diplomat
turned politician, and Constantine Maniadakis, former Minister of Public
Order in the Metaxas regime of 1936–41. In the approach to the former, it
was suggested that Britain did not reject the possibility of some sort of
enosis. However, because of British strategic interests, the internal security on the island would somehow have to be safeguarded by Anglo-
Greek co-operation. In the approaches made through Maniadakis, which
started on September 25, two days after the Cyprus item had been
included in the Assembly's agenda, a high official of the British Embassy
in Athens explained that these exchanges should be formally unofficial
but in substance were highly official. The conclusion of an agreement
would make possible the withdrawal of the Greek recourse from the
Assembly's agenda. The British were prepared to recognize in principle
the right of self-determination of the Cypriots and to permit the exercise
of this right within eight years, on the basis of an agreement to be

reached between the British and Greek governments. Meanwhile, the
Cypriots would be granted a most liberal and democratic constitution
that would also have to meet with the approval of the Greek government.
These talks, however, which lasted for about two months, until the end
of November, came to nought. Premier Papagos rejected further contacts
for reasons not precisely known—possibly because of the imminent debate of the Cyprus item in the Political Committee and of the feeling that
these negotiatory exchanges, carried through unorthodox, non-diplomatic
channels, were not conducted in good faith but were merely a feint, a
diversionary British maneuver, for achieving the side effect of hindering
Greek "parliamentary diplomacy" in the United Nations, by a show of
willingness to negotiate outside the world organization, or for undermining Kyrou's position in the Foreign Ministry.

In the Greek Parliamentary debates of February 7, 1955, that followed
the first recourse of the Greek government to the United Nations over the
Cyprus problem, some Opposition leaders declared that the outcome had
been a betrayal by the United Nations of its ideals.[52] None attacked the
government's decision to resort to that organization, though one of them
(Spyros Markezinis) cautiously asked why the question should have
been raised at the Assembly's ninth session, and another (George Papandreou) noted that by its action Greece had found itself in dangerous
diplomatic isolation from its allies and had given the opportunity to the
U.S.S.R. to pose as a standard-bearer of freedom.[53] And all Opposition
leaders charged the government with having badly handled the whole
affair. The necessary preconditions for a successful outcome in the
United Nations had not been secured, they said. The preparations for the
recourse had been inadequate. The Premier and the Foreign Minister
had shown a lack of courage by not leading in person the struggle in the
United Nations and by letting diplomatic officials wage the battle. The
delegation should have insisted on a strong draft resolution of its own
and should have refrained from voting in favor of Resolution 814 (IX).[54]
Generally, Greek foreign policy–makers had been overoptimistic about
the outcome.[55] One Opposition critic, in particular, observed that the
Greek policy-makers had not given the recourse a sufficiently anticolonial coloring so as to attract the support of the thirty-five members of the
anticolonial group in the United Nations. Instead of referring to Articles
10 and 14 of the Charter in the recourse, they should have invoked
Article 73 of the Charter concerning non-self-governing territories as well
as Resolution 637 (VII). Had they done so, no problem would have
arisen about the competence of the Assembly to consider the matter.[56]
Instead, they had regarded the recourse as a threat for getting bipartite
negotiations started and had hoped that the United States would finally
intervene to persuade the British to enter into such negotiations. But the
precondition for such a strategy was a favorable U.S. attitude. It was in

this sector, all Opposition leaders agreed, that the government had made its gravest misjudgment.[57]

What had been the attitude and policy of the leader of the West toward this dispute between NATO allies and its airing in the United Nations? The Greek Parliamentary debates were quite revealing. If Greek governments prior to that of Papagos had not resorted to the United Nations over the Cyprus issue, it had been largely because they had learned in 1951, after inquiries through the diplomatic channel, that the United States did not regard as timely the raising of the issue in the United Nations, though generally it viewed with sympathy the Cypriot cause.[58] And when the Greek government in 1954 finally resorted to the United Nations over the issue, in spite of the predominant role Britain was supposed to play in eastern Mediterranean and Middle Eastern affairs under a sort of "gentleman's agreement" with the United States, quite an imbroglio occurred, which seems to have been due partly to a shift in the tactical lines of the U.S. government and partly to a misunderstanding of the U.S. attitude on the part of the Greek officials responsible for handling the issue in the United Nations.

Late in January, 1954, Secretary of State John Foster Dulles, when informed by Kyrou (on his way to Athens from the United Nations, to take over the post of Director-General of the Ministry for Foreign Affairs) that the Greek government was likely to resort to the United Nations if the British government persisted in refusing to enter into bipartite talks on the future of Cyprus, had shown considerable reserve.[59] On July 28, as this Greek move became ever more likely because of continued British adamancy (revealed very starkly that same day by Hopkinson's statement in the House of Commons), the U.S. government communicated its views on the issue to the Greek government in a way that should have dashed the somewhat unfounded Greek optimism about the attitude of America in this colonial question which affected the special U.S.-British relationship in NATO and throughout the world. In this note, the Secretary of State unequivocally expressed the U.S. government's opposition to the proposed recourse to the United Nations and suggested the need for talks between the Cypriots and the British government for the purpose of arriving at a step-by-step solution to the problem.[60] Dulles also referred to Turkey as a party primarily concerned in the future of the island. The policy inaugurated by the Balkan Pact should be continued, Dulles urged. And the unity of the Western alliance should remain intact.

The Greek government, in a long and acrimonious reply of August 3,[61] responded to this note by placing the blame for the tension in and over Cyprus on British intransigence and non-acceptance of bipartite talks. It was under pressure on the part of "public opinion," it asserted, so that it would be unable to alter its course and not resort to the United Nations. With many arguments, the Greek government insisted on the policy line it had firmly set down since mid-April.[62] After referring to the guarantees that Greece would give to the Turkish minority in Cyprus, if the island were to become part of Greece, the Greek government stated in this note that having to choose between a step-by-step solution of the Cyprus problem and the definite worsening of friendly relations with Britain and Turkey, it preferred the latter. It also expressed its conviction that the powerful leader of the West would, in the end, support the Greek cause. Having received no reply to this note, Cyprus decision-makers in Athens may have wishfully believed that U.S. silence somehow meant acceptance of the Greek views and that the U.S. government, because of its anticolonial origins, tradition, image, would maintain at least a neutral attitude during the debate on the Cyprus question and the attendant resolution-making in the Assembly.

As the Greek government was about to send its recourse to the United Nations, Kyrou, on August 16, talked over the matter with the U.S. Ambassador in Athens, Cavendish W. Cannon. He asked for U.S. neutrality during the airing of the Cyprus issue in the United Nations.[63] A month later, the U.S. government defined its stand. In a conversation of September 16, 1954, with Phaidon Anninos-Kavalieratos, the Greek chargé d'affaires in Washington, William Oliver Baxter, Deputy Director of the Office of Greek, Turkish, and Iranian Affairs at the State Department, made it clear that his government regarded the discussion of the Cyprus question in the United Nations as undesirable. Therefore, at the stage of the debate in the General Committee on the matter of including the item in the Assembly's agenda, the U.S. Delegation would abstain from voting (this was consistent with the traditional American support of the principle of freedom of discussion in the United Nations). If the item were included in the agenda, then the U.S. Delegation would take part in the debate on the draft resolutions tabled and would determine its position toward them on the basis of their content. If other governments inquired what the American stand in the matter would be, the U.S. government would limit itself to informing them about it. In other words, it would not try to exercise pressure, to get support and votes for the views and resolution it favored.[64] The Greek chargé observed that such an attitude would cause great disappointment to the Greek government as well as to the Greek and Cypriot people.

During the two-stage decision-making on the inclusion of the Cyprus item in the Assembly's agenda on September 23 and 24, the U.S. Delegation abstained from voting both in the General Committee and the Assembly. In the latter, however, it voted in favor of an Iraqi proposal (not adopted because of a 24–24 tie vote with 12 abstentions) that a decision on the inclusion of the item be postponed for a few days.[65] And, in the view of the Greek Delegation, backstage activities of the U.S. Delegation had been largely responsible for the discrepancy between the Greek estimates of the number of votes that would be gathered in the Assembly and the actual voting results. Before September 22, members of the U.S. Delegation, when asked by other delegations, had not sought to exert any influence and had replied that the case should be judged on its merits. The morning of September 22, however, Secretary of State Dulles had returned from his flying trip to Bonn and London (September 16–17) and had conferred with members of the U.S. Delegation. The decision had been taken to help out the British Delegation through various backstage activities, such as friendly *démarches* with other delegations, with the aim of preventing the Assembly from adopting the General Committee's recommendation that the Cyprus item be included in the Assembly's agenda. What exactly lay behind this new situation, which the Greek Delegation, basing itself on the Baxter-Kavalieratos conversation of September 16 (its third point, especially), had not expected, is difficult to say. Kyrou believes that Dulles had decided to help the British in the Cyprus question in exchange for the assistance that Eden was giving him in the matter of Franco-German relations after the French Parliament had buried EDC (European Defense Community) on August 30, 1954.[66] But perhaps the Secretary of State had been told by the British government of its ultrasecret moves toward talking over the Cyprus question with Premier Papagos without the knowledge of the Greek Foreign Ministry and particularly of its Director-General who was handling the issue in the Assembly.[67] This could explain why Dulles had sought to prevent the inclusion of the Cyprus item in the Assembly's agenda, and after having failed to do so, to postpone as much as possible the debate of the issue in the committee, in the hope that in the meantime an Anglo-Greek agreement would have been reached which would make debate unnecessary.

Whatever the case may be, the results of those intense American backstage lobbying activities together with the British threats in the General Committee of a walkout in case the Assembly considered the Cyprus item [68] were, according to the Greek Delegation, that several states that had been expected to abstain during the vote in the Assembly joined the ranks of negative voters with certain other states that had been expected to vote in favor of the General Committee's recommendation. Likewise, it was in consequence of U.S. backstage activities that the Political Committee, as mentioned earlier, decided to discuss the Cyprus item last.[69]

Because of what the Greek Delegation felt to be a repudiation of the U.S. promise to remain neutral during the UN handling of the Cyprus issue, Kyrou, on October 12, asked his government to carry out certain *démarches* with the U.S. Ambassador in Athens or to study the possibility of not having the Cyprus question discussed at all in the United Nations. Next day, he flew to Paris, to talk over this matter with Premier Papagos and Foreign Minister Stefanopoulos who happened to be there at the time.[70]

In Athens, on October 16, Ambassador Cannon informed the Greek Vice-Premier, Panayotis Canellopoulos,[71] that the U.S. Delegation was likely to vote against any Greek draft resolution that called for self-determination for the Cypriots, indeed against any draft resolution that touched on the substance of the question. Secretary of State Dulles in person conveyed a similar warning to Premier Papagos in Paris, at a lunch on October 23, 1954, at the home of John C. Hughes, U.S. Ambassador to NATO (neither Stefanopoulos nor Kyrou were invited). The Greek Premier, in response, sent a memorandum on the Cyprus question to the Secretary of State as well as a personal message to President Eisenhower, complaining about the U.S. stand.[72]

Back in New York, Kyrou, on October 23, had a long conversation with Ambassador Henry Cabot Lodge, Permanent U.S. Representative to the UN. He entreated him to do all in his power to get his government to revert to the neutral attitude Baxter was believed to have promised on September 16. On his part, he promised to convey to Lodge well in advance a copy of the Greek draft resolution so that the State Department might have ample time to study it and come up with suggestions for changes. Accordingly, on November 15, he sent a copy of this draft resolution, in its first version, to the U.S. Delegation, perhaps still under the erroneous impression that if the "substance" of this draft were extremely moderate, the United States might be swayed into favoring it, though it had already made it clear that it opposed any substantive resolution at all.[73]

In a personal letter of November 16, Secretary of State Dulles, on President Eisenhower's behalf, replied to the Greek Premier's note of October 23 and more or less repeated the two earlier American warnings of opposition to any sort of substantive draft resolution. He expressed the hope that it would be possible to avoid a further public worsening of Greek-British relations, and his regret about any misunderstanding that might have arisen over the attitude of the U.S. Delegation at the United Nations.[74] The United States, he stressed, considered the most important point in the whole question to be the maintenance of good relations among allies. The Cypriots and the British authorities were the parties most directly concerned, and the Greek government should exert its friendly influence on the non-Communist Cypriot leaders to encourage them seriously to negotiate with the British. On its side, the U.S. government would use its influence to encourage the British government actively to pursue such negotiations. In other words,[75] the U.S. government was convinced that the discussion of the question at that time in the United Nations and the adoption of any substantive resolution at all would harm the good relations between certain friends and allies of the United States.

From this point on, the Greek government and Delegation at the United Nations directed their main efforts toward making sure that the U.S. government and Delegation would at least maintain complete secrecy about the intention to vote against any substantive resolution on the Cyprus item, lest the knowledge of this negative attitude should influence the decision-making of other governments and delegations. Such an assurance, it was believed, had been obtained from the U.S. government.[76]

Concurrently, despite a fourth U.S. warning, of December 11, conveyed to the Greek Foreign Minister in Athens about the negative American attitude toward any substantive resolution, and despite the statement that the U.S. government regarded the Greek draft resolution as substantive and had instructed Lodge to vote against it—a warning coupled with a reiteration of the American intention to exert no pressure on other states against the Greek viewpoint [77]—the Greek Delegation, though advised of this warning, watered down for a third time its draft resolution. It deleted from its preamble a reference to the maturity of the Cypriots as an argument for their being recognized the right to determine their own future. Kyrou hoped this might help the U.S. government change its mind.[78]

The evening of December 12 came, and with it a first-page story in the city edition of the *New York Times* of December 13. This story shattered any lingering hopes Ambassador Kyrou and his government may still have entertained that the negative U.S. attitude toward a UN handling of the Cyprus issue could somehow be kept secret. Under great headlines, the newspaper disclosed that the United States was opposed to any consideration of the Cyprus question in the United Nations and would vote against any substantive resolution put forward. The Greek government, it added, had been duly informed of this stand.[79]

Indeed, in Athens, earlier, likewise on December 12, Ambassador Cannon who, as mentioned, had informed the Foreign Minister the day before that the U.S. government was opposed to the Greek draft resolution and would vote against it, had handed Premier Papagos a message from Secretary of State Dulles. In this message, Dulles first reminded the Premier that in his letter of November 16 he had written that the United States, though opposed to any substantive resolution, would exert every effort to find ways of lessening the tension created by the Cyprus problem. He then informed him that, according to information he had received from the U.S. Delegation in New York, the Greek draft resolution, if put to a vote, had no chance of gathering the majority required for its adoption. "We ourselves would be obliged to oppose such a resolution because we do not believe that under present circumstances the mediation of the United States would be useful." The best way out, then, for the unity of the West and the preservation of Greek prestige would be to support a resolution under which the Assembly would not discuss the Cyprus item at all. It was self-evident, Dulles observed, that future Assemblies would not be bound by such a resolution. Dulles added that he had come up with this suggestion because the Premier, at their Paris meeting of October 23, had said that perhaps it would be better not to have the Cyprus item discussed at all in the Assembly, were the United States unable to stay neutral.[80]

At the Assembly next day, Lodge informed Kyrou about the delivery of this note and its contents. He also categorically denied that the report about the U.S. attitude had been leaked to the press by his delegation. Lodge also disclosed to Kyrou that on the morning of December 14, as soon as the Political Committee would meet to start the debate on the Cyprus item, "a friendly delegation" would table a draft resolution proposing that the question not be considered further by the Assembly. Kyrou, who was convinced the Greek draft resolution would be adopted by the Political Committee by the simple majority required there, firmly stated he would fight such a proposal. Lodge, somewhat upset, said that an exception might be made to allow the Greek Delegate to present his government's views on the question. Kyrou retorted he was not asking for charity but would demand that anybody wishing to speak should be allowed to do so.[81]

How the representative of New Zealand, Leslie Munro, invoking a point of order, tabled on December 14 in the Political Committee the draft that became Resolution 814 (IX); the procedural question Kyrou raised; the wrangle that followed—all these are part of the public record.[82] The point to retain is that during the discussion in the Committee, Lodge stated that his government had reached the conclusion, after deliberate thought and lengthy consultation with those "directly concerned," that a prolonged consideration of the question could only increase tensions and embitter national feelings "at a time when the larger interests of all concerned were best served by strengthening existing solidarity among freedom-loving nations." [83]

All in all, as a result of its recourse to the United Nations, the Greek government conjured up from among the ranks of allied third parties not directly concerned with the Cyprus issue a formidable new antagonist over the question of the appropriateness of the procedure of resorting to the United Nations for promoting the Cyprus question in the world arena. At the tenth Assembly in 1955, Secretary of State Dulles vainly asked Foreign Minister Stefanopoulos not to insist on the inclusion of the Cyprus item in the Assembly's agenda.[84] And the U.S. representative in the General Committee adhered to the view that consideration of the Cyprus item in the Assembly was not likely to promote the purposes and principles of the Charter and expressed himself in favor of a peaceful settlement through negotiations "by the countries concerned"—a method recommended in Article 33 of the Charter. Moreover, as a result of Eden's urgent pleas with the U.S. government,[85] he even voted this time against the inclusion of the Cyprus item in the Assembly's agenda. The British representative, he said, had given assurances that his government would actively pursue a practical program that would afford the Cypriots a greater opportunity to attain their legitimate aspirations. The United States, he added, pledged particularly to "its Greek friends" that it would continue an active interest in the Cyprus question. At the eleventh Assembly, on the other hand, the U.S. Delegate did not oppose the item's inclusion. Again, however, he maintained that "the parties" should seek a solution outside the United Nations because they had not yet considered all possible solutions. The United Nations, he added, should make no proposal that would aggravate the situation and render a solution more difficult. The U.S. government, on its part, was prepared to help "the governments and the people concerned" to find a constructive solution.[86] As will be seen, at the twelfth Assembly, while on stage a verbal clash was taking place between the protagonist, Greece, and the two antagonists, Britain and Turkey, a dramatic contest about suitable procedures for dealing with the Cyprus question was going on backstage between one of the least influential non-caucusing micropower members of the United Nations and the indubitably still most influential non-caucusing superpower in the organization.[87]

What has been said about the motivations of Greek foreign policy–makers, their ostensibly desired aims and their evaluations of the results of their first recourse to the United Nations over the Cyprus question, is valid in the main for the four subsequent Greek recourses to that international organization over that same issue. The responses, however, of the antagonists or of third parties to the Greek policy moves as well as to EOKA's activities in Cyprus, which began in spring, 1955, led to the setting up of several secondary and tertiary goals, some of them of a defensive character.

Again going to the United Nations for a "battle" was motivated not by a belief that the United Nations was capable of providing a solution to the Cyprus problem, but by a sense of frustration, of desperation occasionally, by a desire to act, to do something, in the face of continuing, if not rising, pressures emanating from Cyprus, Greek "public opinion," and the Opposition, and in the absence of any prospect of a satisfactory settlement. To a certain extent, then, these moves may be regarded as symptoms of irrational behavior in international conflict, serving to refute the saying that "diplomacy is the art of the possible." Even if the best possible conditions were obtainable—which was never the case—if namely the United States or the British antagonist were to support certain substantive proposals outlining the framework of a solution to the Cyprus problem and even if the Assembly were to adopt these proposals, Greek foreign policy–makers felt that the United Nations, at the most, could only *lead* to a solution.

However, the practical implementation of these moves provided also examples of rational and artful conduct in international politics. Their main aims—and here the above-mentioned saying had validity—were to achieve certain side effects.

The interpretative commitment made by the Greek representative when Resolution 814 (IX) was adopted by the Assembly in December, 1954, provided a new rationale for bringing the Cyprus question once again to the Assembly's attention, as the Greek request of July 25, 1955, addressed to the Secretary-General reveals (see Appendix B). Since December 19 of the previous year, Premier Papagos had committed his government to such a move and Foreign Minister Stefanopoulos had restated this commitment in January, 1955, with Ethnarch Makarios concurring.[88] As Foreign Minister Stefanopoulos argued before the tenth Assembly on September 23, 1955, whereas the initial proposal of New Zealand at the previous Assembly was conceived by its sponsor as an adjournment *sine die*, the Assembly decided otherwise and adopted an amendment changing the adjournment *sine die* into a provisional adjournment, "for the time being." As will be seen, this technique of commitments to a new recourse to the Assembly was used again at the eleventh Assembly and during its aftermath in official statements in the Greek Parliament.[89]

The Greek government's covert endorsement early in 1955 of the unconventional warfare that George Grivas—under the *nom de guerre* of "Dighenis"—was preparing to wage added a new dimension to such commitments. For EOKA's founding Charter, drafted in 1953, proclaimed that the organization's activities aimed at drawing the attention of "international public opinion" to the struggle waged in Cyprus and would be continued "until international diplomacy—*the United Nations*—and the British" were forced to examine the question and find a solution to it (italics added).[90] Thus, from 1955 on, for the Greek government to refrain from supporting the above purpose by not resorting to the United Nations would have been tantamount to abandoning Grivas and his Cyprus struggle.

If the lack of diplomatic negotiations with the British government had led the Greek government to go to the United Nations in the first place, in 1954, and the failure of the tripartite London conference (August 29–September 6, 1955) [91] led it to persist in its recourse to the United Nations in 1955, which, as mentioned, was rejected when the Assembly decided against including the Cyprus item in its agenda, so did the breakdown of the talks between Governor Sir John Harding and Ethnarch Makarios [92] early in March, 1956, together with the deportation of the latter to the Seychelles islands a few days later, trigger the third Greek recourse to the United Nations, of March 13, 1956 (see Appendix C). This move, Premier Constantine Karamanlis told Parliament, was motivated by a desire not only to exert pressure upon the British but also to bolster the morale of the Cypriot people. As such, it was a response to the governmental terrorism which Governor Harding had instituted by introducing emergency regulations in mid-Autumn, 1955,[93] in efforts to counteract EOKA's agitational terrorism, which had started in spring of that same year. As long as Makarios was in exile, the Premier warned, no diplomatic negotiations could take place. The recourse to "parliamentary diplomacy" was the only move available to the Greek government. Or, as the Foreign Minister said, the recourse to the United Nations, though not a solution, was a means for promoting the issue on a world-wide scale and for exerting strong diplomatic pressure for negotiations—which constituted the only means for solving the problem.[94] In justifying before the Greek Parliament the fourth and fifth recourses to the United Nations over the Cyprus question, Greek government spokesmen were to invoke similar arguments.[95]

Both externally and internally, resorting again to the United Nations in spite of increasingly adverse circumstances served as a show of firmness, of determination. Conversely, not resorting to it again would be interpreted as a sign of a decline in the intensity of Greece's interest in the issue, of a certain lack in disputative or agonistic zeal, of weariness, of willingness to come to terms, even to give up the entire struggle. Just as the introduction of a bill in the U.S. Congress is often a counterweight for warding off charges of negativism,[96] so it was, in part, with both the original and the subsequent four recourses of the Greek government to the United Nations in the Cyprus dispute. In varying degrees, the government felt it had to ward off charges of lack of enthusiasm for the "sacred cause" that politicians, friends or foes, newspapers, and, of course, the Cyprus Ethnarchy or Grivas, leveled against it on various occasions.

The commitment to resort to the United Nations, like the commitment to a particular interpretation of an UN resolution, as will be seen, enabled the Greek government to justify its rejection of probes or proposals to enter into negotiating procedures it regarded as undesirable, for instance negotiations within the framework of NATO or of another tripartite conference.[97] As a "battleground," the General Assembly offered a more favorable terrain for verbal battles than either of the above-mentioned alternatives. In the Assembly, the Greek government could find third-party allies. These included potentially not only a respectable number of uncommitted but anticolonialist states but even Greece's own normal foes, the members of the Soviet bloc, who were also foes of the antagonist of Greece and of the entire alliance that bound together antagonists and protagonist. After the massive influx of new members late in 1955, the number of such potential allies had significantly increased.

In another tripartite conference, on the other hand, Greece would find itself isolated and having once again to face its two formidable antagonists, while in NATO Councils it was unlikely to find third-party allies, except Iceland. In that international regional organization, in which decisions are taken informally, unanimously, without a vote, warnings about the dangers of undermining the alliance's cohesion and appeals for interallied harmony were likely to predominate, together with suggestions that the weakest state, which was disturbing the status quo by asking for redistributive negotiations, should toe the line. In that organization of a primarily strategic character, members would tend to be receptive to strategic arguments such as Britain's or Turkey's, even though these and particularly the latter's might not, strictly speaking, be

directly connected with the immediate strategic goals and the formal
geographic scope of the military alliance and might even refer to a
hypothetical post-NATO era.

The atmosphere in the Assembly was far different. It was favorable to
libertarian, non-strategic appeals and was pervaded by the spirit of the
Charter. For the Greek case, this multipartite treaty offered several useful
weapons, such as Article 1, paragraph 2, that mentions self-determination.
And UN "legislation" provided certain valuable Assembly resolutions—
Resolution 637 (VII), for example, which refers not just to the principle
of, but to the right to, self-determination. Also, in the United Nations,
proceedings were public, whereas in NATO or ad hoc conferences, they
took place as a rule behind closed doors, and publicization of the Greek
and Greek Cypriot viewpoints constituted an important intermediate
objective of Greek foreign policy–makers and Makarios. In brief, for the
Greek side, the genius loci of the Assembly was more propitious than
NATO's, even though, as the Greek government had well understood by
the time of its third recourse to the Assembly, many UN members might
be sympathetic to changes in the status quo only to the point that
excluded enosis or, as the antagonists of Greece termed it, the annexation
of Cyprus by Greece. The thought that the UN Security Council, if
resorted to instead of the General Assembly, might refer the question to
NATO under Article 52, paragraph 2, of the Charter, concerning the settlement of disputes by regional organizations, may, indeed, among other
factors, have inhibited the Greek government from making such a move
on the two occasions it examined this possible course of action—in
March, 1956, when Makarios was deported to the Seychelles and then in
summer, 1958, when bloody clashes occurred in Cyprus between Turkish
and Greek Cypriots.[98]

The ostensible goals and desired effects of the subsequent Greek
recourses to the United Nations remained fairly constant, since in the
view of Greek foreign policy–makers the "internationalization" of the
Cyprus issue had already been achieved—through the first recourse of
1954 as well as through political events that followed outside the United
Nations, such as the aforementioned tripartite London conference. First
came the ostensible goal in the United Nations of getting the Assembly to
adopt Greek draft resolutions mentioning self-determination or, in the
case of the last recourse, independence for Cyprus, and, as a corollary
goal, of preventing the adoption of an adverse resolution. Second, came
the goal of exerting, through resort to the United Nations, leverage for
initiating negotiations on the future of Cyprus outside the United Nations. Third came the goal of publicizing the Cyprus question.

The Greek government, as indicated at the outset, never attained its
maximum resolutionary goal. It persisted in its quest for a UN resolution
calling for self-determination or independence, but this persistence
merely led to Resolutions 1013 (XI) and 1287 (XIII), none of which
contained reference either to self-determination or to independence, even

in their preambular paragraphs. The closest the Greek government ever came to this supreme resolutionary goal was getting the text of its own draft resolution—somewhat amended but mentioning the "right" of self-determination in its operative clause—put to the vote at the Assembly's twelfth session and adopted by the Political Committee. This, as will be seen, was correctly to be regarded by the Greeks as a "pioneering success" in the annals of the United Nations. For it was only in 1960, at its fifteenth session, that the Assembly adopted for the first time a resolution referring to the right of self-determination (in both its preambular and operative clauses) in the concrete case of a decolonization dispute. This was Resolution 1573 (XV) of December 19, 1960, on the Algerian question.[99] But by then, the antagonist of the Algerians and of their Afro-Asian sponsors in the United Nations, the French government of General Charles de Gaulle, had recognized this right for the Algerians on September 19, 1959.

The tactical reasons that led the Greek government to assert, despite its failure to attain its maximum resolutionary goals in the United Nations, that these resolutions, in favor of which the Greek Delegation had voted, represented at least a modicum of success will be explained at greater length later.[100] Suffice it to mention here that they were partly connected with the specific problem of dealing with the Turkish factor which had clearly come to the public surface since the Cyprus debate at the ninth Assembly in 1954. At that Assembly, although Ambassador Selim Sarper had refrained from asking to present his government's views on the Cyprus item during the General Committee's debate on the inclusion of this item in the agenda, during the debate in the Political Committee he had unequivocally warned that no settlement of the question would be lasting unless it was agreeable to Turkey.[101] At the London tripartite conference the following year, Foreign Minister Fatin Rustu Zorlu most emphatically had reasserted this view. Then, at the Assembly's eleventh session, in November, 1956, Sarper laid great stress on the view that in the Cyprus question, Britain, Greece and Turkey were "the three countries primarily concerned." [102] Since the draft resolutions finally adopted by the Assembly, unlike other draft resolutions or proposals that had been put forward formally or informally during the consideration of the issue, neither referred to the parties concerned by name nor even used the words "parties concerned," these texts appeared acceptable to the Greek Delegation.

Besides, as will be seen, Greek foreign policy–makers showed considerable ingenuity and resourcefulness in using even these far from wholly satisfactory resolutions to promote their Cyprus policy outside as well as inside the United Nations in various ways. Thus, they exploited Resolution 1013 (XI) within the sphere of covert activities and intra-group relations in order to persuade Grivas at least to suspend his acts of unconventional warfare. And in the international sphere, by their own interpretation of this deliberately ambiguous resolution, they justified not

only their negative attitude to two proposals for entering into negotiations over the Cyprus problem outside the United Nations, but also their
fourth recourse to that international organization.

As for the efforts of Greek foreign policy–makers to obtain negotiations
over the future of Cyprus by resorting to the United Nations, these were
not altogether fruitless. Resolutions 1013 (XI) and 1287 (XIII) called
indeed for negotiations outside the United Nations "for a peaceful,
democratic, and just solution." However, in these extra-UN negotiations,
the Greek government never achieved its goal in terms of the participants
desired. Whereas in 1954 its aim had been to get bipartite negotiations
started with the British government, the Cyprus settlement of 1959 was
based, first, on bipartite Greek-Turkish negotiations, a procedure the
Greek government had strenuously tried to avoid as soon as it became
clearly aware that Turkey insisted on being a party directly concerned in
the settlement of the Cyprus dispute and as long as the Turkish government adhered to the view that partition was the only acceptable solution.
Since the earlier-mentioned ultra-secret talks of September, 1954, the
closest it believed it ever came to bipartite negotiations with the British
government over the island's future was when bipartite talks took place
between Harding and Makarios (October 4, 1955–March 3, 1956), after
the tenth Assembly refused to include the Cyprus item in its agenda in
1955. In these talks, which ended in a deadlock and Makarios' deportation, the Greek government took part through the diplomatic channel,
though not as a principal. Since then, until the end of 1958, the Greek
government, as will be seen, vainly sought to have this partial success of
bipartite negotiations between the British and the Cypriots repeated and
brought to a successful end, in order to prevent Turkish participation in
the negotiations as "a party concerned"—even in the face of Opposition
charges that such a procedure implied recognition by the Greek government of the validity of the original British view that Cyprus was not an
international question [103] but one that concerned exclusively the British
government and the Cypriots and involved issues of self-government, not
of self-determination. The great importance the Greek government attached to this goal is revealed by the fact that until the very eve of the
Cyprus debate in the Political Committee at the twelfth Assembly, the
Greek Delegation was prepared to withdraw its own draft resolution that
referred to self-determination if the British Delegation, during the Committee debate, were willing publicly to commit itself to entering into
such bipartite negotiations and agreed that the relevant statement be
embodied in a draft resolution tabled for adoption by the Assembly.

In the last analysis, the major payoff of the Greek recourses to the
United Nations resided in the publicity side effects of the debates and
negotiations in the Assembly, which these ventures in "parliamentary
diplomacy" triggered. Not only Premier Papagos and his Foreign Minister but their successors, too, emphasized these points in the evaluations
they made in Parliament of these ventures. Thus, Foreign Minister E.

Averoff-Tossizza repeatedly was to recognize that in 1957 the UN process provided useful opportunities both for intergovernmental communications and for communications to constituencies of other states over the head of their governments, i.e., for propaganda about the Cyprus question.[104] At the same time, he acknowledged as a serious disadvantage the fact that the UN debates tended to confirm the view that Turkey was a party directly concerned in the Cyprus issue, regardless of Greek efforts to refute the Turkish arguments,[105] and that in Turkey, where the news of the debates was published, public opinion tended to become excited, with results that affected Turkish policy and led to a deterioration of Greek-Turkish relations. Finally, he does not seem to have been unaware that the consideration of the same item year after year could lead to growing weariness if not boredom among representatives of third party states and that, after the novelty of the first recourse had worn off, diminishing returns from propaganda could be expected from debates on the dispute at successive Assembly sessions unless the question suddenly took—or was given—a novel twist.

In legislative bodies of pluralistic political communities, it has been pointed out, the introduction of a bill often serves as publicity for the bill's introducer or for the pressure group that backs him.[106] As the Greek recourses over Cyprus indicate, the same may hold true of requests to the United Nations for consideration of a particular issue and of the introduction of draft resolutions at various points in the process of "parliamentary diplomacy." Thus, while the major realizable aim of these recourses were the side effects of drawing attention to the dispute and publicizing its substance as seen from the viewpoint of the Greek and Greek Cypriot "pressure groups," one must also take into account that mysterious psychological alchemy by which personalities playing a public role identify with a cause. In other words, the strivings and desires of the main actors, of Premier Papagos, Ethnarch Makarios, Ambassador Kyrou, and the retired Colonel Grivas to play a role in Greek political history were involved as the "third variable" in the launching and waging of this struggle for Cyprus that went on in the United Nations and other international forums as well as through the diplomatic channel and unconventional warfare on the island.

It was Papagos, no Cypriot, who from his first moment as Premier (and even earlier) ardently wished "to link his name with Cyprus" [107] and took the bold decision of making the first recourse to the United Nations, dealing with the Cyprus question without referring it to the Cabinet and signing with his own name the relevant document, though, unlike his successor, Karamanlis, he did not attend in person the opening meetings of the Assembly in order to add the weight of his prestige to the Greek recourse and promote the Cyprus question in the United Nations and through the mass media of the United States. And it was Ethnarch Makarios, a Greek Cypriot, who ceaselessly pressed the Greek government to resort to the United Nations in the first place, and supported, though with certain vacillations, the schemes of Grivas for strong-arm operations on the island. As for Kyrou, a Cypriot Greek rather than a Greek Cypriot, he had been implicated as Consul of Greece in Nicosia in the anti-British disturbances that had broken out in Cyprus in 1931.[108] With his journalist brothers, he showed a tenacious interest in the Cyprus question and, at the initial stages of the Cyprus case, worked with and on both the Ethnarch and the Greek Premier. He believed, after Papagos had won a handsome majority in the elections of November, 1952, together with a huge majority of seats in Parliament, that here, at last, with a strong government at the helm, was an excellent opportunity for raising the issue.[109] Earlier he had been much more circumspect about the advisability of raising this issue.[110] *Suaviter in modo, fortiter in re* was his favorite motto by 1954. He also may have felt that the international setting was propitious for raising this interallied issue, judging from a speech of his, of March 1, 1954, in which he asserted that the "cold war" had come to an end because of the West's vigorous response to the Soviet threat to Europe and Korea.[111] For these personalities as well as for Grivas, another Greek Cypriot, whose role will be analyzed later,[112] the resort to the United Nations served not only to publicize the Cyprus question in world politics but also to project their names in the global arena and especially in the arena of Greek politics and eventually in the annals of modern Greek history.

Enhancing in this way their own image as national leaders, these personalities, by their actions, molded Greek public opinion, the pressure of which they invoked as a rationale for their recourses to the United Nations and of their Cyprus policy as a whole. And in the interactive process between leader and led, they, in turn, were reinforced by public opinion.

However, the UN debates on Cyprus and other such publicization measures helped Greek policy–makers to focus the attention of the Greek people not only on this question and, in the first instance, on the inability of the United Nations to contribute in an unambiguous way to its solution but also to the friendly, hostile, or indifferent attitudes of other governments toward the Greek point of view. Thus they stimulated national feelings of friendship and hostility in ways that did not strengthen the relationship between leaders and led, because the leaders were also attached to the NATO alliance, whose members, except for Iceland, failed to support the Greek viewpoint on the Cyprus question.

Bringing, then, this question to the United Nations was the fulfilment of a rather unpleasant duty. The three-year resistance of several pre-Papagos governments to Makarios' repeated pressures in this matter suggests the degree of official Greek hesitation to engage in such a difficult struggle against a great power and an ally, in the face, too, of the disapproval of the alliance's leader, and at a time of considerable international tension in a still acutely bipolarized world. Greece risked isolating itself by such a move, as certain Opposition leaders observed in 1955.[113] Going to the United Nations involved the public airing of the "most difficult problem" of foreign policy Greece had ever had to face, Premier Karamanlis stated in 1956.[114] It was a heavy responsibility, as his Foreign Minister was to acknowledge the following year.[115] There were risks of acrimonious controversy with allies otherwise considered both valuable and staunch. The attrition rate of some of the foremost proponents of this struggle reveals the personal career risks involved in getting engaged in it. In 1955, Kyrou, after the first recourse to the Assembly, felt compelled to place himself at the disposal of the Foreign Ministry, perhaps because he became aware that the British government—the Intelligence Service, in his view—had tried to bypass the Ministry as being too much under his domination and, as already mentioned, had started talks on Cyprus with the Premier himself through other modalities. And in May of the following year, Foreign Minister Spyros Theotokis who had sought to find some formula of settlement had to resign from the Karamanlis Cabinet because of pressures emanating from the Ethnarchy and the Opposition which, after Makarios' deportation to the Seychelles, charged him with insufficient crusading zeal in the Cyprus cause.[116] Premier Karamanlis himself, as this study will reveal, almost became a Cyprus casualty in the early months of 1958, but for the opposite reason! [117]

All in all, a realistic awareness of the Assembly's political limitations as an instrument of Greek foreign policy in the Cyprus question could not allow any Greek government or Foreign Minister seriously to nourish any hope of a conspicuous and positive victory in that international arena that would really redound to party or personal political advantage in the domestic arena, even though foreign policy–makers invoked Opposition criticism and aroused "public opinion" as a means to exert pressure on the U.S. government, for instance, for obtaining support in the Cyprus dispute. On the contrary, painful political confrontations with the Opposition in Parliament usually followed the deliberations in the United Nations,[118] and these occasionally created difficulties in the conduct of foreign policy in other sectors and served to strengthen the arguments fostered by Greece's external opponents that Greece was an unreliable ally. It sems doubtful to this writer that any politician—unless he were masochistically inclined—would enjoy such difficult, thorny, bitter encounters.

Once the decision had been reached to resort to the United Nations, both government and Foreign Minister would, of course, do their utmost, like athletes entering a contest they know they cannot win yet resolved to do their damnedest and exhilaratedly enjoying any victories they might achieve in the preliminary rounds, perhaps breaking their own records, though not the records of others. Thus, they would always start out by introducing a draft resolution referring to their maximum goal in the United Nations, even though progressively they had serious doubts they would ever succeed in getting it adopted and were aware that even if it were adopted, UN resolutions were not legally binding. The documents on which this case study had been based, replete as they are with terms such as "battle" and "strategy" taken from warfare's world of discourse, suggest the degree to which Greek foreign policy–makers were activated, partly at least, by the non-rational idea of a "struggle for the struggle's sake" in their recourses to the United Nations. The great efforts exerted to obtain certain intermediate goals or purely tactical victories made these seem more valuable than if they had been achieved more easily. And, once the debate was over, the conductors of Greek foreign policy emphasized any slight gain believed to have been obtained from the confrontation with the antagonist in the UN forum.

Besides, the Greek government was aware that a recourse to the United Nations and the debate that might ensue in the Assembly had a harassment or nuisance value with regard to the antagonist.[119] This effect could be judged by the efforts the antagonist made in order to prevent the recourse to the United Nations or to block its results if the Assembly seized itself of the matter—just as jamming of international broadcasts testifies to the political effectiveness of these broadcasts directed to a constituency of another state. As this case study reveals, the antagonist may try to hinder the inclusion of an item he dislikes in the agenda of the Assembly. If unsuccessful in this effort, he may seek to delay, postpone or shorten the Assembly's consideration of the item. Finally, even though resolutions are not legally binding, he surely will exert strenuous efforts to prevent an unfavorable resolutionary outcome by various procedural maneuvers—introducing amendments or resolutions of his own— counterharassing the harasser.[120] A counter-recourse to the Assembly is an extreme form of such a response. At the eleventh Assembly, the British government resorted to such a technique, charging Greece with aiding morally and materially EOKA's agitational terrorism in Cyprus (see Appendix E).

Before closing this introduction it should be noted that the first Greek recourse to the United Nations seems to have served not only as a precedent for resorting again to the Assembly at subsequent sessions of that body but also as an educational experience for Greek foreign policy–makers concerning the potentialities of the Assembly as an instrument for promoting a particular foreign policy interest of a small non-caucusing state such as Greece. As a result, after an initial overestimation of these potentialities in 1954, a more realistic approach prevailed in the subsequent Greek recourses to the Assembly over the Cyprus issue. This more realistic approach affected both the judgment of Greek policy-makers about the value of recourses to the United Nations as one among several techniques for promoting in the world arena the Greek and Greek Cypriot goals and the style of handling the issue in the United Nations.

During its first recourse to the Assembly, the Greek Delegation seems to have misjudged the role of the United States as a potential anticolonial power. It also relied too heavily on the belief that the anticolonialist members of the United Nations would automatically determine their stand on the Cyprus item purely on the basis of anticolonialist principles rather than on their estimate of their own national interests as a whole, in which matters of principle were but one of the factors to be considered. It failed to take into account cross-cutting solidarities of certain anticolonialist states with the colonialist antagonist, in the case of Jordan, for instance, which depended so heavily on British support for its existence. It disregarded the tendency of Asian and African anticolonialists not to be unduly concerned about the fate of a European people subjected to a colonial regime by another European state. And it was not sensitive enough to the fact that Greece's association with European colonial powers, through NATO, compromised, in the eyes of many anticolonialists, its position on Cyprus in terms of a South versus North alignment, in spite of economic solidarities in this respect—Greece being among the least developed of developed countries or the most developed of underdeveloped ones. As will be seen, at the twelfth Assembly, in 1957, on the only occasion that a draft resolution—its operative part being Greek—referring to self-determination was put to the vote, eight anticolonial members (Burma, Cambodia, Ceylon, India, Iraq, Laos, Malaya, and Nepal) abstained from the vote, even though they had sponsored or voted in favor of anticolonial draft resolutions in the questions of Algeria and West Irian at the eleventh and twelfth Assemblies. And one member state—Pakistan, which in Kashmir had an *enosis* problem of its own—went so far as to cast a negative vote on this resolution.[121] It was only at the thirteenth Assembly that a number of anticolonial states got together to sponsor a Cyprus draft resolution that favored the Greek anticolonial viewpoint which, by now, was couched in terms of independence, not of self-determination for the island.[122] The general overoptimism of 1954 is reflected, too, in that the Greek Delegation estimated that its moderate draft resolution, which eventually was not put to the vote, would be adopted by the Political Committee by 37 or 38 votes to 12, with 7 or 11 abstentions,[123] whereas in 1957 an almost identical resolution which also included certain amendments put forward by the antagonists was, when put to the vote in the Political Committee (larger in membership than it was in 1954), adopted only by 33 votes to 20, with 25 abstentions.

With regard to style, a comparison of the Greek presentation of its Cyprus case in 1954 with that presentation at subsequent sessions of the Assembly reveals that on the first occasion the Greek Delegation tended to approach the engagement as though it were a judicial contest with the Assembly's being a sort of court of justice. The style of its chief spokesman was more like that of a plaintiff in a civil suit before a tribunal than that of a contestant in a political debate in a quasi-parliamentary body. Kyrou, who had had a long experience with the United Nations as his country's Permanent Representative to the organization from August,

1947–January, 1954, and had also served as Greek Delegate on the Security Council in 1951–53, originally had been rather skeptical about the political potential of the United Nations. By 1954, however, he seemed to have been "taken in" by the impressive prestigious aspects of the role that delegates play as representatives not only of their government's ethnocentric interests but also—to coin a neologism—of cosmocentric interests, the interests of the world society or community which the United Nations symbolizes.[124] While not unaware of the strong wind of anticolonialism that was blowing over a large part of the world, in presenting to the Assembly the Cyprus issue, he not only invoked "the principle of equal rights and self-determination" of Article 1, paragraph 2, which the U.S.S.R., one of the two superpowers peripheral to Europe, had imbedded into the Charter,[125] but laid great stress on the legalistic-moralistic terms of the Charter, which reflected the spirit of the founding father of the United Nations, Cordell Hull.

The text itself of the first Greek recourse (see Appendix A) reveals these idealistic if not utopian tendencies. It refers, for example, to "the new order established by the Charter"; to "the new international community"; to the Atlantic Charter, to "justice and freedom." And, metaphorically, the United Nations is "a court of law"—"a judge," to whom one resorts after "having exhausted all remedies." And in his speech in the Political Committee on December 14, he referred to the Assembly as "the open conscience of the world" [126] and asserted that the principle of self-determination was "an integral part of the Law of the United Nations." [127] Finally, in his interpretation of vote on December 17, he insisted on the idealist view that "a legal instrument . . . had its own intrinsic and objective meaning which does not vary according to the interpretation which the parties concerned are eager to place upon it." [128] To use an Aristotelian category, the rhetorical style of this diplomat tended toward the forensic or judicial.[129] In a book he published shortly after this recourse, he steadfastly adhered to these notions about the United Nations in response to attacks on the part of certain realists who emphasized the pre-eminently political character of the Assembly.[130]

By 1956–57, on the other hand, the style, as will be seen, was far different. It was much less legalistic, judicial, forensic; more political, realistic, parliamentary. The rhetoric, to refer once again to an Aristotelian category, tended toward the deliberative, being directed toward the future in order to sway the listener toward political action rather than to establish a question of innocence or guilt for past action.[131] The word "colonialism," with its strongly negative connotation, was used to a far greater extent in the later explanatory memorandums than it had been during the first recourse. The issue now was more clearly cast in terms of self-determination rather than of international justice.

Personality and background differences, greater experience, a new situation in Cyprus, a different UN environment, changes in the world setting—these may have contributed to this difference in style and approach. In contrast to 1954, when quite an *engagé* Cypriot Greek professional diplomat struck the dominant note in Greek policy over Cyprus, an experienced parliamentarian politician from the Greek mainland was, since 1956, the usual spokesman.[132] The new political, realistic approach may have been largely the consequence of such personal and professional differences.

But experience, too, teaches realism. Voting forecasts of the Greek Delegation at the twelfth Assembly turned out to be remarkably realistic in contrast to what had happened during the somewhat utopian phase in the handling of the Cyprus question three sessions earlier. To be sure, more adequate diplomatic preparation and more *démarches* with other delegations may have helped in this respect. As a result, expectations of having any Greek draft resolution put to the vote would now be regarded as a success. Having the Political Committee adopt it albeit in an amended form was to be considered a triumph.

Circumstances by 1957 also were to make it easier for the Greek policy-makers to adopt a more realistic approach than the one adopted in 1957. Since April, 1955, violence from below generating violence from above and, in turn, violence between the two ethnic groups on the island had erupted in Cyprus. Tension between Greece and Turkey had risen greatly. Consequently, whereas in 1954 the cause of self-determination for the population of Cyprus had to be argued primarily on rather abstract grounds of morality, justice, and freedom, on grounds of higher rather than positive law, how to find a solution to a dangerous situation developing in the eastern Mediterranean had become by 1957 a matter of practical politics, of peace-keeping. A real situation called for realistic, practical handling.

If greater realism led to less of a disappointment about the outcome of UN deliberations on the Cyprus question in 1957 than it did in 1954, it also permitted a greater appreciation of the relative successes achieved in these deliberations. These successes were somewhat easier to achieve than they had been in 1954. For, since December, 1955, the membership of the United Nations had greatly increased. And, whereas 1950–55 in the organization's life had been a phase of American dominance, the new phase that the United Nations now entered was featured by the growing influence of the anticolonialist Asian-African group [133] at the expense of the colonialist states, with which the United States, albeit with reluctance, often had to align itself, because of the close ties it had with them and its special relationship with Britain—both results of the cold war confrontation. In 1957, then, the Greek task was slightly easier than it had been in 1954. Had the Greek government waited for the 1960's to raise the Cyprus question in the Assembly instead of doing so in 1954, it might have come closer to success in getting that organ of the United Nations to adopt the draft resolutions it had introduced on earlier occasions, although, as this study suggests and others have pointed out, Western—United States—persuasion by 1961 may have led Latin American member states to refrain from backing, as they often had until then, anticolonial initiatives.[134]

But perhaps in the 1960's the U.S. attitude, too, might have changed, not to mention the British attitude.[135] Greater Greek and Greek Cypriot patience in raising the Cyprus issue in the United Nations and outside it might have permitted its consideration in a more favorable international setting. For if the Greek recourse of 1954 and the outbreak of EOKA's operations coincided with the prepublicized transfer of the British Middle East Command from Suez to Cyprus, the consideration of the Cyprus item by the eleventh and twelfth Assemblies in 1957 and 1958 coincided, respectively, with the sudden and unanticipated Soviet firsts in missilery and spacemanship and the quasi-ultimatum of Khrushchev on Berlin, not to mention two post-Suez, Middle Eastern crises focusing around Syria, Lebanon, Jordan, and Iraq. Materials presented in this study suggest that these events, while rendering the three main parties to the dispute particularly receptive to the idea of accommodation and conciliation, also had a certain subtle impact on the U.S. government's attitude toward the Cyprus dispute. While seeking to maintain its aloofness, uncommitted-ness, and neutralism with regard to the substance of a dispute that divided three of its NATO allies and threatened the stability of NATO's southeastern flank, the U.S. government, with Dulles as Secretary of State, may have felt obliged to suggest a speedy and final settlement of this dispute at all costs at a time when it greatly needed a united NATO front and the good will of its three divided allies and especially the co-operation of the British and Turkish governments in order to deal effectively with the sudden political and strategic problems created by a short-lived technological lag—the so-called missile gap—and especially the Berlin crisis. A public symptom of this attitude may have been the U.S. vote for the Iranian draft resolution at the thirteenth Assembly in December, 1958, a matter to be dealt with in the Epilogue.

Of course, a change in the U.S. attitude with regard to the Cyprus problem in 1960's in a direction favorable to the Greek viewpoint might have been accompanied by a corresponding shift, but in the opposite direction, of the attitude of the U.S.S.R. and its satellites. Such are the vagaries of politics.

Part One

Chapter One

February 26, 1957:

The UN Expresses "Its Earnest Desire"

A. *UN Resolution 1013 (XI)*

At its eleventh regular session and its 660th plenary meeting, the General Assembly of the United Nations, on February 26, 1957, adopted Resolution 1013 (XI), which dealt with the Cyprus question. After a debate on, and consideration of, the Cyprus item, which had lasted for ten meetings, from February 18–22, the Political Committee had recommended this resolution for adoption by a show-of-hands vote, with seventy-six members voting in its favor, none opposing it, and only two abstaining—Afghanistan and Panama. Under Resolution 1013 (XI), the General Assembly, having considered the question of Cyprus, believing that the solution of that problem required "an atmosphere of peace and freedom of expression," expressed its earnest desire that "a peaceful, democratic and just solution" would be found "in accordance with the purposes and principles of the Charter of the United Nations, and the hope that negotiations will be resumed and continued to this end." [1]

Introduced in the Political Committee by the Delegation of India, this resolution replaced a draft "that never was," which had been favored by the U.S. Delegation and circulated, but never tabled, by the Delegation of Thailand. It also replaced four other draft resolutions that had been tabled—two by the Greek Delegation, one by the British Delegation, and a fourth one by the Delegation of Panama.

Of the two Greek draft resolutions,[2] the first one, which had been tabled on February 18, 1957, at the outset of the debate in the Committee and was based on the Greek recourse of March 13, 1956 (see Appendix C), asked, in its preambular clauses, the Assembly to recognize: the right of the people of Cyprus to self-determination; the serious deterioration of the situation in Cyprus; the vital importance of freedom and peace on the island—not only to the people of Cyprus but to all peoples in the area; and the contribution that an equitable solution of the question would make to peace and stability throughout the entire area. In its operative clause, this draft resolution asked the Assembly to express the wish that the people of Cyprus be given the opportunity to decide their own future by the application of their right to self-determination. The second Greek draft resolution, tabled in response to Britain's counter-recourse of October 12, 1956, on the Cyprus issue (see Appendix D), requested the Assembly to set up a seven-nation fact-finding committee to investigate British charges of Greek support for the Cyprus terrorists and the Greek countercharges of governmental terrorism—of atrocities or violations of human rights committed by the British authorities in Cyprus against the people of the island.

The British draft resolution,[3] likewise tabled at the outset of the debate in the Committee, after noting in its preambular clauses complaints by the British government of support in the form of arms, ammunition, and money for terrorist organizations in Cyprus by the Greek government, and after observing that Athens, in spite of repeated British representations, had regularly broadcast special programs containing incitements to insurrection and violence, requested the Assembly in its operative clause to call on the Greek government to take effective measures to prevent support or encouragement from Greece of agitational terrorism in Cyprus. As for the Panamanian draft resolution—in no way U.S.-inspired—it urged the Assembly to set up and send to Cyprus a five-state fact-finding commission.[4]

Mainly instrumental in the decision not to put to the vote the above British, Greek, and Panamanian draft resolutions in the Political Committee had been the U.S. Delegation, which, on February 21, advised the Greek Delegation of its decision to oppose all the draft proposals that had been tabled before the Committee, the Panamanian one included. The U.S. Delegation, on the other hand, would support a draft proposal circulated but not tabled by the Delegation of Thailand—the Delegation head of this ally of the United States, through membership in SEATO, was President of the Assembly during that session. This Thai proposal would provide that the Assembly, having considered the Cyprus question, believed that a satisfactory solution could be achieved in an atmosphere of undisturbed peace and tranquility and expressed its hope that through the resumption of further negotiations a solution might be achieved satisfactory to all parties concerned, in accordance with Charter of the United Nations.

To such a draft resolution, however, the Greek Delegation was unalterably opposed, because, if adopted, it would give Turkey a sort of legal title as a "party concerned" in the Cyprus question and a veto right over any solution, and this the Greek government wished to prevent at all costs. The Greek Delegation was informed that the State Department had instructed the U.S. Delegation to prevent a vote from being taken on all the other draft resolutions. The procedural maneuver to be applied would be as follows: A draft resolution that the Thai proposal be voted on first in the Committee would first be tabled. If this proposal was adopted by the required simple majority of the Committee, the content of the Thai draft resolution would be immediately voted on and in all likelihood passed. Then, a third proposal would be made not to put to the vote the four other draft resolutions. If, now, this last proposal, too, was adopted, only the Thai resolution would be left—to be submitted to the Assembly and adopted there by the required two-thirds of members present and voting.

Against such a procedural trap, the Greek Delegation felt helpless, inasmuch as the U.S. Delegation would be backing it. Indeed, the proposed procedural maneuver revealed an American intention to get a vote in favor of the Thai proposal against the will of the Greek Delegation, and this was felt to be a repudiation of the U.S. government's promise to remain neutral in the Cyprus issue. The Greek Foreign Minister, E. Averoff-Tossizza, in a very tense tone, drew the attention of Ambassador James J. Wadsworth, Deputy to the U.S. Representative to the United Nations, to the serious dangers of such an American attitude, and sought to dissuade the U.S. Delegation from following such a course of action, which would have disastrous repercussions in Greece. Wadsworth promised to convey these views to the State Department. Because of the American stand, the Greek Delegation realized its position was extremely difficult. At one point it even considered tabling a motion requesting the Committee to postpone a decision. This was particularly disheartening at a moment when it perceived favorable possibilities shaping up for getting a simple majority at least in the Committee for its draft resolution that called for the recognition of the Cypriot people's right to self-determination. Although the Delegation of Thailand had promised not to submit any draft resolution against the Greek Delegation's wish, the latter feared that such a resolution might be submitted by the Colombian Delegation, which, it believed, was the most faithful organ of the United States in the United Nations at that time.

V. K. Krishna Menon, Minister of Defense and head of the Indian Delegation, to whom the Greek objections to the Thailand proposal had been explained on February 21, took the initiative, however, of proposing a draft resolution of his own, which the Greek Foreign Minister and the principal members of his delegation regarded as very satisfactory (as compared with the Thai proposal). Next day, the State Department agreed that this Indian draft resolution should replace the Thai one. As a result, on the proposal of the representative of Guatemala (duly seconded), the Indian draft resolution was voted on first, was passed by the Committee, and, after the sponsors of the other draft resolutions at the request of the representative of Iran, Nasrollah Entezam (a former President of the Assembly), did not press for a vote on theirs, was adopted by the Assembly as Resolution 1013 (XI). Krishna Menon, it should be added, in referring to his resolution in the Committee, had stated that his delegation approached the Cyprus problem in the belief that it was one of Cypriot nationality, concerning only the people of the island and their right to independence, in conditions that maintained the territorial integrity of the island. That many Cypriots spoke Greek did not mean that they were Greek, any more than English-speaking citizens of the United States were British. He hoped the Greek Cypriots would realize that independence was the only solution. India regarded Cyprus as the homeland of its peoples, entitled to nationhood and independence.[5] This was exactly what Krishna Menon had said when the Greek government first raised the Cyprus question before the United Nations in 1954. He had repeated this view in 1955.[6]

Interpreting this resolution before the Committee, the Greek Foreign Minister warned that his delegation was not withdrawing its own draft resolutions but merely was not pressing their being put to the vote. He hoped they would not have to be revived within six months at the next session of the Assembly because, by then, democratic conditions would have prevailed in Cyprus. He also stressed that he had voted in favor of the Indian resolution because his government had always felt that prior to self-determination a period of democratic self-government could exist.[7] Furthermore, because many delegations had very earnestly stressed that the union of Cyprus with Greece—enosis—was impossible, that it had been a great mistake to pose the Cyprus problem in that way, and had insisted on the creation of an independent state, the Foreign Minister had emphasized particularly that his delegation sought to obtain recognition of the principle of self-determination for the people of Cyprus, not enosis, and had repeatedly let it be understood that the Greek government would accept a solution of the problem by the creation of an independent state of Cyprus. He had underlined, too, that the Turkish Delegation, when challenged by him to adopt the same position on the issue, had, by its silence, indicated that it refused to do so, creating an impression of intransigence before the Committee.[8] However, he added, reporting back to Athens, he had never bound himself to the solution of the problem through the creation of an independent Cyprus.

As a token of good will toward the British Delegation, the Greek Foreign Minister on February 23 called on the Secretary-General of the United Nations, Dag Hammarskjöld, and advised him that he was withdrawing the file on British atrocities which he had sent to the Secretariat as supporting evidence for the second of the two Greek draft resolutions he had tabled.[9] He expressed the hope that the British, inspired by the constructive debate in the Assembly and the moderate resolution which had been passed, would immediately proceed toward the settlement of the Cyprus question. He was also aware that nothing would prevent the Greek government from again raising these charges if it was believed expedient to do so. On his side, Hammarskjöld congratulated the Foreign Minister for having accepted, in spite of his controversy with the British during the debate, the formulation of a resolution that was very satisfactory for the progress of the Cyprus question and that kept the door open

for a friendly settlement. He expressed regret over the British atrocities
and termed the contents of the file on this matter as dangerously explosive.

With regard to the text of the Indian resolution, all foreign delegations,
Averoff-Tossizza reported to Athens, considered it a very great success
for the Greeks. The text was so categorical and clear that any misinterpretation was excluded. He drew attention to the words "freedom of
expression," a "just and democratic solution." "Earnest desire," he said,
was quite strong for UN phraseology. True, the text itself did not define
the parties between whom negotiations should be carried out. However,
except for the Turkish and British interpretations, almost all other interpretative statements had made it clear that there should be negotiations between the Cypriot people and the British government. This was
demonstrated by the word "resumed," which exclusively referred to the
interrupted negotiations between the Ethnarch (Archbishop Makarios)
and the Governor of Cyprus, Field Marshal Sir John Harding (October 4,
1955–March 5, 1956).[10] The Tripartite London Conference of 1955 (August 29–September 7, 1955) had the Middle East and Cyprus as its
subject, but, since it had failed, it had come to an end—i.e., had not been
interrupted.[11]

But even if one assumed for a moment that not only Anglo-Cypriot but
other negotiations were implied by this resolution, this would not mean
tripartite but multipartite negotiations, with the participation in such
talks of all countries that had claimed to be concerned in the issue. Many
countries, Syria and Egypt, for instance, had expressed such a concern
during the debate on the Cyprus question in the United Nations.[12] The
contentions that only tripartite negotiations were implied in this resolution were unfounded. Finally, the word "continued" in the resolution
meant that repeated negotiations should be insistently continued in spite
of any initial disagreements or failure in reaching agreement. These
aspects of the resolution, Averoff-Tossizza recommended, should be explained to the Opposition leaders and expounded at a press conference in
Athens. The Radcliffe draft constitution, he noted in conclusion, had
been derided by most speakers as a solution to the Cyprus problem.[13]
Partition, too, of the island, as another solution, had been condemned.[14]

Diametrically opposed to the Greek interpretation of the resolution
was the British government's. Based on the comments that Commander
Allan H. P. Noble of the British Delegation to the Assembly had made
before the Political Committee [15] as well as on a statement by Governor Sir John Harding over the BBC on February 24 and his interview in
the *Observer*,[16] the British view was, as Greek chargé d'affaires Dimitri
Nikolareïzis reported from London, that the resolution adopted condemned *enosis*, hence terrorism on the island (which advocated *enosis*),
and, by implication, Makarios, as well; that it justified the British policy
of fighting EOKA as the only way for restoring "an atmosphere of peace"
to the island; and that it recommended new tripartite negotiations be-

tween Britain, Greece, and Turkey. As for the British press, it nowhere mentioned the interpretation according to which the resolution called for the resumption of negotiations between the British government and the people of Cyprus.

As soon as the vote in the Assembly was over, the Greek chargé d'affaires in London, on instructions from the Foreign Minister, carried out a verbal *démarche* at the Foreign Office, saying that regardless of the conflicting interpretations of the resolution adopted by the Assembly—a usual United Nations tactic—the obligation was created for all interested parties to contribute to the relaxation of tension in order to promote the possibility of a solution of the Cyprus question. The Greek Foreign Minister, he underlined, as a demonstration of his government's good will, had advised Noble of his decision to withdraw the file on atrocities he had deposited with the Secretariat and had indeed done so already. It was hoped that the British government would appreciate this gesture, especially if it took into account the justified—from the Greek view-point—reaction of the political members of the Greek Delegation, members of the Greek Parliament, who not only were strongly opposed to the withdrawal of this file but also wished to raise the matter before the UN Security Council. Finally, however, the Greek Foreign Minister had imposed his own line on them in his sincere effort to contribute toward a substantive solution to the Cyprus problem and to the restoration of Greek-British ties.

The Greek Foreign Minister would like to hope, the chargé d'affaires continued, that this effort of his would meet with a due response on the British side. The content of the resolution itself was clear. It became even clearer in the light of the debate and the interpretations given. Beyond any propagandistic publicity, positive British actions were now needed for a solution. The Greek government always regarded the freeing of Makarios and the restoration of freedom of expression and other human rights in Cyprus as the indispensable first step in that direction. The Foreign Minister realized, of course, that the expression of existing good British intentions could not take place from one day to another. His government, nevertheless, had been greatly disheartened by Governor Harding's statements concerning the resolution passed. These demonstrated a regrettable mentality of suppression and a refusal to face realities. The Greek government wished to believe that these statements did not represent the intentions of the British government in its further handling of the Cyprus question. If they did, the results would be catastrophic.

In Ankara, meanwhile, acting Foreign Minister, Ethem Menderes, explained to the Grand National Assembly on February 25 that the resolution adopted meant that all terrorist activity should cease, and that the United Nations hoped the question would be solved in a fair fashion by negotiations between the parties concerned. The resolution's importance was, he asserted, that self-determination, which concealed *enosis*, had been rejected. At the same time, the matter should be solved not by the United Nations but between the interested parties—a viewpoint Turkey always maintained. There was this pleasant aspect to the picture, too: both neighboring and remote states had adopted to a great extent the Turkish views. He hoped the Greek government, in compliance with the international consensus, would start out on a new, reasonable, and moderate line. Earlier in his speech, he had observed that Greek-Turkish friendship should have greater importance than Cyprus. Sincere and friendly relations between the two nations were beneficial for Turkey and a matter of necessity for Greece. The restoration of these relations should take place as fast as possible.[17]

B. The Greek Parliament and Resolution 1013 (XI)

Back from New York, Foreign Minister Averoff-Tossizza as well as the entire Greek government had to face one of the fundamental "validators" of policy in a Parliamentary system of government, the Parliament itself, in which three of the Opposition parties—"aspiring decision-makers"—had tabled motions of no confidence in the government, because of its handling of the Cyprus question in the United Nations.[18] The debate on these motions took place from March 11–15, 1957, and was waged in extremely lively fashion.

The Greek Foreign Minister himself bore the brunt of the attack. This was neither the first time, nor would it be the last. As successor to Theotokis, who, after Makarios' exile to the Seychelles, had fallen a victim of Parliamentary and Ethnarchic attacks concerning his handling of the Cyprus problem, Averoff-Tossizza had assumed the post of Foreign Minister late in May, 1956. He was to maintain himself there until eight years later, except for short interim periods during which caretaker governments, prior to elections, took charge of this high office as well as of the government as a whole. As the chief actor in this study, he deserves, therefore, some biographical attention.

Born in 1910, in Thessaly, of a moderately well-to-do family originating from Epirus, in northwestern Greece, he belonged to the generation of Greeks that matured in the decades that followed the "Micrasiatic catastrophe" (the disastrous defeat of the Greek armed forces during their expedition into Anatolia in 1919–22) and the Treaty of Lausanne of 1923, which not only closed as was then felt and realized an entire chapter, if not volume, in Greek-Turkish relations, but irretrievably shattered the Greek equivalent of "Manifest Destiny"—the "Megali Idea" (Great Idea)—which, for the previous post-independence Greek generations had been the lodestar of Greek nationalist aspirations in the Balkans and eastern Mediterranean. For this new, post-Lausanne generation, nationalism had turned inward, as it were. The almost complete disappearance of any irredentist Greek populations outside the realm of the Greek state; the need to resettle on Greek territory almost one and a half million refugees from outside the Greek state's boundaries, from Turkey primarily; perhaps the whole spirit of nationalist weariness that was evident in the wake of World War I—all these had contributed to the replacement of the earlier outward-directed goals of Greek nationalism, symbolized by the basically anti-Ottoman or anti-Turkish "Megali Idea," of which the most extreme form consisted of unrealistic dreams to re-establish a Greek empire centered on Constantinople recaptured, by the basically materialistic, economistic, and realistic ideals of national economic development, of "economic growth," to use a popular post–World War II term.

It was, thus, no accident that Averoff-Tossizza, like others of his generation, turned his attention to the "dismal science," studying it, together with politics and law at Lausanne, and publishing studies (in French or Greek), on the Balkan Customs Union or Greek population problems, for instance. Nor was it an accident that in his earlier political career, from 1946 on, he had on various occasions served as Minister of Supplies, or of National Economy, or that he once jokingly stated in Parliament, when Minister of Foreign Affairs, that he would have much preferred to serve as Minister of Agriculture,[19] a post he had held in the first government of Karamanlis from February to May, 1956, as well as in an earlier government, that of Sophocles Venizelos. If he was a fervent admirer of that great statesman of his father's generation, of Eleftherios Venizelos, it was because he admired him not as the instrument, agent, and promoter of the "Megali Idea" and signer of the Treaty of Sèvres but as the champion of a new deal in Greek-Turkish relations and as the leader of this new national ideal of economic, social, and cultural development of a Greece no longer drawn by territorial claims and quartered by external aspirations. Indeed, during his years of study at Lausanne, where he had had a brief experience as a journalist, Averoff-Tossizza had cultivated the friendship of several Turkish students there, who, later, like him, would achieve positions of eminence in Turkish public life. It was, then, somewhat ironical that he should later become the principal handler of an issue that touched a sore nerve in Greek-Turkish relations and that, on several occasions, Turkish officials should charge that his policy in the Cyprus issue represented a revival of this "Megali Idea," which to them, quite naturally, was so repugnant.

During World War II, arrested by the Italians in 1942 because of his resistance activities, Averoff-Tossizza was deported to a concentration camp in northern Italy, whence after eighteen months he managed to escape, joining the Allies. Setting up an undercover organization entitled "Freedom or Death," he worked with the British in underground activities that led to the saving of a number of Greek and allied hostages. Later he wrote a book "*Chronicle of a Secret Organization*" about this experience. Then, in the first postwar elections in Greece, he was elected a deputy for the department of Thesprotia, in Epirus, and healthily ambitious and well-married, to a London Greek shipowner's daughter, made for himself a successful political career, at first joining the Liberal party, which E. Venizelos had founded, then going over to the National Radical Union (ERE), which Karamanlis had set up early in 1956 by excluding dyed-in-the-wool conservatives and attracting younger elements and liberals.

Averoff-Tossizza's first official involvement in the Cyprus affair had occurred, as mentioned already, before he assumed the post of Foreign Minister in the Karamanlis government in 1956. Toward the end of 1951, when serving as Undersecretary for Foreign Affairs in the Cabinet of Nicholas Plastiras and at a time when the Greek Delegation to the sixth General Assembly had for the first time been instructed publicly to mention the existence of the Cyprus problem, Averoff-Tossizza, after a *démarche* of the British Ambassador in Athens, Sir Charles Peake, had hastened to meet Anthony Eden in Rome, only to be told by the Foreign Secretary on November 15 that no Cyprus issue, in the British government's view, existed, nor could exist in the future.[20] From 1956 to 1964, as Greece's chief foreign policy–maker, directly or indirectly, and more often the former, he would have to handle for his government this complex, delicate, and dangerous problem. It was he who would have to wage the political and diplomatic struggle going on through regular diplomatic channels, in the forum of the United Nations, at NATO Council meetings, or, through other officials, at the Council of Europe. Alternating appeals to sentiment with calls for reason, as one of his chief diplomatic aides in the United Nations commented, he would argue, bargain, and trade, Ulysses-like, in conducting these official, overt, often public activities, with considerable virtuosity. In his adroit and flexible policy and in his intellectual fecundity in putting forward a great variety of proposals for solving the Cyprus problem, he never seemed to lose sight of the final goals of self-determination—or, as he put it in 1958, of full freedom [21]—for the people of Cyprus, until partition of the island seemed to become so imminent that Ethnarch Makarios himself decided to propose—as a lesser evil—the setting up of Cyprus as an independent state which originally was an Indian solution.

A conference that the Greek Foreign Minister had with Secretary of State Dulles on February 13, 1957, before the debate of the Cyprus item in the Political Committee at the eleventh Assembly illustrates his approach and the techniques he used in conversations with U.S. officials concerning the issue. After thanking the Secretary of State for the neutrality promised during the consideration of the Cyprus item in the Assembly,[22] he emphasized that the attitude of the United States was of great importance because the other NATO allies would vote against the Greek viewpoint, therefore making the United States the only remaining link of Greece with NATO. If the United States, too, took a negative stand, he implied, the Greek people would be wholly unable to understand why Greece should remain a member of NATO. And the task that the Greek government was carrying out with confidence would become useless if new elections were to take place soon, which was most likely.

With regard to the debate in the United Nations, he said further, the Greek Delegation had no intention of exacerbating the debate, which could have good results if it were carried out within civilized limits. This would be particularly the case if a reasonable resolution were adopted. Because the Greek people were affected greatly by the Cyprus question and in Turkey public opinion had been excited to a considerable degree, a point of high tension had been reached.[23] It was therefore of importance "for the fever to drop" before a final solution was given. One such solution might be placing the island under NATO, seeking a transitional situation and then, after a period of five to seven years conducting a plebiscite on the island. Purely as a personal opinion and in order fully to disarm Turkey, he suggested later during this talk that if Turkey did not consider the above solutions expedient even a third solution might be examined in order to dissipate Turkish fears about the possibility of the union of Cyprus with Greece. A plebiscite, namely, should take place with regard to two questions only: First, did the people of Cyprus wish to remain within the British Commonwealth, as a Dominion? And, second, did it wish to become independent? In order to make this proposal more credible, he said that he considered that Greece would accept that the independent state of Cyprus should not be able to be united with its motherland Greece. But, the best way above all to achieve progress would be for Britain to enter into negotiations with the Cypriots and not through the interposition of other governments that had no right of active intervention.

With regard to the attitude of Turkey, he sought to show that this was not well founded, because the Greek government was prepared to take measures to allay any anxieties on the Turkish side. Thus, with regard to Turkish security, his government was prepared, regardless of the maintenance of a British or NATO base on Cyprus, to agree to the demilitarization of the island on the part of Greece. With regard to the economic sector, if the Turks considered that Cyprus was economically linked to Turkey, the Greek government would gladly agree to a sort of customs union of Cyprus with Turkey and with Greece. With regard to the Turkish minority, his government was absolutely willing to give to the Turkish Cypriots all the recognized rights of minorities which the Greek government had respected with punctiliousness for many decades with regard to the Turks in northern Greece. Indeed, in this respect, it was willing to go further and allow UN control as well as the right of members of this minority to resort directly to the United Nations if they felt they had reason to complain about their treatment. Finally, the Greek government would allow the Turkish minority to have dual nationality and be exempted from conscription.

In general, the Foreign Minister, in his talk with John Foster Dulles, underlined the moderation and spirit of compromise of the Greek government, the Cypriots, and Ethnarch Makarios, who was wise and whose contribution to finding a solution to the Cyprus problem was most valuable. On the other hand, he observed that it was extremely dangerous to permit the intransigence of the other two parties to aggravate the situation. If, for instance, the United States accepted the validity of Turkey's interest on ground of contiguity, then the question automatically became more complicated. Other states such as Syria or Lebanon or even Egypt—which had experienced an unjust attack on its territory with Cyprus as the launching point of this attack—would have reasonable grounds and the right to interfere in the matter and would do so. The U.S.S.R., too, would seek to take advantage of the situation. Had it not maintained in 1945 that it needed an island in the eastern Mediterranean as a fueling base? Thence, Averoff-Tossizza went on to explain to Dulles the Greek Delegation's intentions during the Assembly's consideration of the Cyprus item, with the Secretary of State stating in reply that he had been impressed by the Foreign Minister's exposition of the Greek views and that he was fully in agreement that it was necessary to lower the temperature in the Cyprus dispute. However, Dulles added that he was not fully persuaded to support the Greek position and seemed to admit that some of the arguments of the opponents of Greece and especially of the Turks had impressed him somewhat.[24]

But the story itself will reveal various facets of Averoff-Tossizza's handling of the Cyprus problem during 1957—how he resorted to certain other warnings about Greece's position in NATO and how, at the same time, he sought to maintain this interallied dispute within certain bounds in the aftermath of the Suez affair, during the year of Soviet firsts in missilery, and at the time of the Syrian war scare. In this delicate task he was not only responsible to the Prime Minister and the Cabinet under the Greek Parliamentary system but had to deal with a superpatriotic Opposition that was particularly vociferous, especially on the extreme left-wing and extreme right-wing registers;[25] with Ethnarch Makarios and his narrow, insular, 400,000-strong Greek Cypriot constituency in mind; and, finally, with what had become an unavowed instrument of Greek foreign policy in Cyprus, George Grivas (today General George Grivas-Dighenis) who was anything but a docile instrument and, quite naturally, viewed the problem from his own hole in the ground on the island. For Averoff-Tossizza, on assuming the post of Foreign Minister three months after Makarios' exile to the Seychelles, regularly communicated with Grivas in Cyprus, thus sometimes combining in his own person the roles of the two Dulles brothers (he had, as mentioned, some experience in underground activities during World War II, having been awarded a British medal for his work). And, even though Grivas' hierarchical superior was the Ethnarch himself at the top of the Greek Cypriot organizational pyramid, it was Averoff-Tossizza who saw to it that arms, other supplies, and especially financial aid were again sent to "Dighenis"[26] in activities certainly smaller in scale than, but analogous in content to, those often attributed to the CIA. In a coexistential world and one of the United Nations and of alliances, international conflict, it would seem, is waged more and more in the nether regions, those of the political id.

During the Parliamentary debate of March 11–15, 1957, the Opposition's attacks were directed against Resolution 1013 (XI) because of its vagueness; against Krishna Menon's sponsorship of it and his comments and interpretations of it; against Averoff-Tossizza's acceptance of this resolution, his interpretation and comments on it both inside the United Nations and in Parliament, and his view that the whole affair was a success for the Greek government's handling of the Cyprus question; against the entire policy of the Greek government in the Cyprus question, since 1955, of which the handling in the United Nations was regarded as but a new dark symptom; and (on the part of EDA, the Communist façade party of the United Democratic Left), against the entire foreign policy of the Karamanlis government with its pro-Western basis.

More specifically, to start with the mildest criticism, this consisted of maintaining that the outcome of the debate in the Assembly on the Cyprus question was no cause for jubilation—no success, no betrayal either. Resolution 1013 (XI) said nothing, said everything, said nothing [27]—had contributed nothing to a step-by-step solution of the problem. There was little real difference between it and the Thai proposal.[28] Sharper charges were that the concept of a Cypriot nation, which Krishna Menon had enunciated, had been allowed to remain uncriticized during the UN debate [29] and that the topic of British atrocities or violations of human rights in Cyprus, like that of the anti-Greek riots in Istanbul of September, 1955, had been shoved under the rug, not exploited.[30] It was also held that in spite of the Greek Foreign Minister's interpretation, the resolution really supported the British viewpoint and that if it called for the resumption of bipartite negotiations between the British government and the Cypriot people, as the Foreign Minister maintained, this meant that the matter had once again been recognized as one of domestic jurisdiction for Britain under Article 2, paragraph 7, of the UN Charter.[31]

The sharpest charge of all was, of course, that the struggle of EOKA as well as the goal of getting the principle of self-determination applied to the people of Cyprus at a reasonable and fixed time had been abandoned.[32] Resolution 1013 (XI) nowhere mentioned self-determination.[33] Krishna Menon's comments on it, which were taken to be an authentic interpretation of this resolution,[34] that independence for Cyprus (a corollary of his concept about the existence of a Cypriot nation) was the best solution, implied exclusion in perpetuity of the possibility of the Cypriots to opt, through the application of the principle of self-determination, for enosis.[35] The Greek Foreign Minister, himself, had appeared to have accepted this idea of an independent Cyprus, when, at one point of the debate, he had affirmed that Greece had no annexationist views on the island and, in a rhetorical question, had dared the Turkish Delegation to issue a similar statement with regard to Turkish aims in Cyprus.[36] The Greek government, in its whole policy toward the Cyprus question, the Opposition held, was motivated by a spirit of abject compromise and concessions. Since 1955, its policy had been to close the Cyprus question. It had never really fought for the goal of self-determination.[37] Instead of accepting a glorious defeat—which did not involve a responsibility—it had come to terms, George Papandreou coleader of the Liberal party, declared. This did involve responsibility.[38]

Where were the leaders of the Free World in the Cyprus case? the extreme left taunted. The Greek Delegation had not exploited the support of the anticolonial states (meaning the Soviet bloc states, primarily). Greece was not really isolated, as the government maintained. It was isolated only from the Western World. It was but a pawn in NATO. The Greek Delegation at the United Nations had withdrawn its own draft resolutions because of U.S. pressures.[39] Self-determination was opposed not only by the United States but by SEATO and the Baghdad Pact states.[40] Whereas leaders of some of the smaller parties called for the setting up of a coalition government to deal with the whole Cyprus question, the Republican party (i.e., a party that favored the setting up of a republic in Greece) suggested a policy of withdrawing from NATO and of "uncommittedness" or neutralism; and EDA, shrewdly, continued not to plug for anything beyond that.[41]

On their side, the Foreign Minister and other Parliamentary spokesmen for the government emphasized the gains believed to have been made through the UN consideration of the Cyprus question. Averoff-Tossizza stressed the length of the Committee debate on it, the number of speakers who had taken part in it, and the dignified presentation of the Greek viewpoint. Several of the opponents' arguments, he said, had been successfully rebutted, as had the British charges that the Greek government had organized a resistance movement on the territory of another state and thus had violated the rules of International Law. Grievous blows had been dealt to the idea of partition, and the prompt rejection by the Greek government of the Radcliffe proposals had been explained with the result that the Greek position did not seem intransigent. All in all, the debate had given him the opportunity to stress that Greece would never abandon its demand for self-determination for the Cypriot population.[42]

Both Averoff-Tossizza and other government spokesmen also gave quite a detailed and accurate account of happenings in the Assembly, not only onstage but backstage. Thus they disclosed that the efforts to find a compromise draft resolution had started twelve days before the debate began.[43] They also revealed that, at one point of the backstage conversations, a proposal had been made (by the Peruvian Chairman of the

Political Committee, Victor Andrés Belaunde) to postpone the debate of
the Cyprus item altogether, and that the Greek Delegation had threatened to stage a walkout from the Assembly if such a proposal was
pushed.[44] However, the government spokesmen studiously avoided mentioning that the U.S. Delegation had supported and sponsored the Thai
plan, which the Greek Delegation had strenuously opposed, and from
which it had been saved by the *deus ex machina* of the Indian draft
resolution.

Along the lines that have been mentioned earlier,[45] Averoff-Tossizza
minutiously analyzed Resolution 1013 (XI), stressing the favorable elements he discerned in it and noting that several other delegations had
given similar interpretations of it, especially in the question of who the
parties to the negotiations should be—the British government and the
people of Cyprus, not Britain, Greece, and Turkey, as the opponents
maintained. After thus publicly committing himself once again to this
interpretation, he emphasized that the term "freedom of expression" in
that resolution meant general freedom—the freeing of Makarios, the
closing of the concentration camps, the end of the emergency regulations. Besides, he observed, in Britain certain elements in the Labour
party had given interpretations similar to those of the Greek government;
and the Bureau of the Ethnarchic Council of Cyprus, the mayors of the
island's main cities (other "validators"), and many individual Cypriots
had not only congratulated him on the handling of the matter in the
United Nations but had also welcomed the resolution adopted. The
liberation of Makarios would greatly contribute to progress toward a
solution of the Cyprus problem, he emphasized. The government was
striving to achieve this and hoped the British government would free
him. Pacification could be achieved only through negotiations with Makarios, Averoff-Tossizza declared.[46]

Concerning the handling of the matter of British violations of human
rights in Cyprus, the Foreign Minister recounted how he had deposited
with the UN Secretary-General a file containing depositions of 237 Cypriots who had charged the British authorities with tortures. This file, he
had informed the Political Committee, would be at the disposal of a
commission of neutrals, were such a body set up. Furthermore, he had
stated that if such a commission were to find that most of these charges
were baseless, he himself would resign as Foreign Minister and withdraw
from public life. If, however, these charges were true, then it would be
up to the British authorities to punish as war criminals those who had
perpetrated such atrocities. The impression created in the committee, he
said, had been far greater than if he had these documents circulated
among the delegations. In general, evaluating the atmosphere in the
United Nations and the usefulness of the documents, he had preferred to
maintain their secrecy instead of seeing their power evaporated, as it
were, by their publication.[47]

As for the goal of self-determination, which the Opposition, not for the first time, accused him of having abandoned, the Foreign Minister pointed out that this concept was subsumed in the resolution's reference to "the principles and purposes of the Charter," which includes a reference to the principle of self-determination (Article 1, paragraph 2). This was more specific than just the reference to a "solution in accordance to the Charter" of the Thai proposal. He also noted that the Assembly had never adopted any resolution calling, in its operative part, for the application of the principle of self-determination in the case of a particular country. Of course, he strongly emphasized that the Indian resolution, unlike the Thai proposal, contained no reference to a solution acceptable "to the parties concerned" or "to the three parties concerned," as some earlier backstage proposals had provided. In other words, thanks to the Indian resolution, Turkey had been prevented from getting a sort of legal title as one of the parties concerned, which would also give it the right to veto any proposed solution of the Cyprus problem.[48] To the assertion that the Thai proposal, if tabled, put to the vote, and passed by the Political Committee, could have been blocked in the Assembly, Averoff-Tossizza replied by pointing out that resolutions passed by that committee were usually adopted by the Assembly, and that even if not adopted by it, they still preserved an element of moral pressure.[49] He also pointed out that in the Political Committee he had stated he was merely not pressing for a vote on the Greek draft resolutions, but was not withdrawing them, reserving, as it were, his right to table them again at the next Assembly.

"The direction toward independence is not a Greek maneuver," he solemnly declared, in answer to charges that he had not only abandoned self-determination but had also espoused Krishna Menon's proposal that the setting up of an independent state in Cyprus would be the best solution to the problem, "But I ask you," he added in words that were to be quoted against him by his Turkish and British opponents,—therefore, by his Greek political opponents, too—"if in order to reach *enosis* one were obliged to make the maneuver of a temporary independence, would he who had done this deserve criticism?"[50]

Another government spokesman, Gregory Kassimatis, Minister without portfolio, who had headed the Greek Delegation for a while at the Assembly and, earlier, had toured various Asian countries in order to get the support of their governments in the Cyprus question, said something similar in his speech when he asked why, if international conditions demanded it, was it more permissible to accept a temporary limitation of self-determination under the guise of self-government than independence?[51] On this occasion, however, he did not reveal to Parliament, as he would two years later during the debate over the Zürich and London agreements on Cyprus, that Krishna Menon (late in 1956 but before the British government put forward Lord Radcliffe's constitutional proposals on December 19) had proposed to introduce into the Political Committee a draft resolution calling for the creation of an independent Cyprus and that the Greek government had not assented to the submission of such a draft resolution, with Ethnarchy representatives, in the absence of Makarios, then in exile in the Seychelles, taking likewise a negative stand.[52] It was left to another government spokesman to hint as much. Andreas Stratos, in his speech in support of Greek policy during the eleventh Assembly, disclosed that in a private conversation after the resolution had been passed Krishna Menon had told him he could not understand the Greeks. They were wise and intelligent, but in some cases were strange and understood nothing. He had insisted on the independence of Cyprus. For him freedom was independence. If Cyprus became independent, who could prevent it from uniting with independent Greece? [53]

In his speech, Kassimatis defended the governmental policy on the Cyprus problem since October, 1955, when Karamanlis succeeded Papagos as Premier upon the latter's death. Before that, five mistakes had been made in handling the question, he maintained. The original recourse had been introduced with a request for *enosis*, not self-determination (see Appendix I). The demand for *enosis* might be "our final wish and desire," but in the United Nations it could not have any impact. Almost all states, especially those of Latin America, had territorial problems with their neighbors. Consequently the idea of *enosis* was rejected on the ground that the United Nations was prohibited from considering the revision of treaties and the annexation of territory by one state at the expense of another. The second mistake had been that Greece itself had moved for the recourse, after a plebiscite had been carried out in Cyprus in 1950. Thus, the demand for self-determination was suspect. Third, Turkey had not been consulted on the Greek recourse. Then, during the debate the number of favorable votes in the United Nations had been overestimated. Finally, Greece, in 1954, had voted together with the majority of other member states for postponing the consideration of the question "for the time being." [54]

Since March, 1956, however, considerable progress had been achieved. Greek foreign policy–makers had striven to persuade everybody, especially the anticolonial states, that Greece was not crypto-colonialist. The eleventh Assembly had not only included the Cyprus question in its agenda, whereas it had excluded it at the previous session, but had also debated the question at great length, although Greece was not a member of any group of nations, like the Anglo-Saxons, Arab-Asians, or Turkey (through the Baghdad Pact of 1955). Kassimatis also underlined that on January 2, 1957, the Colombian representative had failed to get the Political Committee to adopt his proposal that the Korean and disarmament questions be discussed first, with a decision on the order of the discussion of the remaining items—the Cyprus question, included—to be left for later on. In the midst of a ceaseless clash of interests between the two blocs, Kassimatis said, Greece had maintained a dignified and independent stand, without for a moment losing its permanent external orientation or concealing that it was part of the Free World and that it would remain so while fighting for its right.[55]

The Assembly, in the view of two other Greek government spokesmen—Stratos and Constantine Tsatsos, Minister in Charge of the Prime Minister's Office—had adopted a resolution that the former termed one of the best ever adopted [56] and the latter one of the best possible ones under the prevailing circumstances, because it was procedural and, from the viewpoint of substance, suggested only a very general framework that excluded a colonialist solution and called for one based on the wishes of the majority. Analyzing Krishna Menon's statements and comments on the resolution, Tsatsos also drew a subtle distinction between the Indian's statements to the effect that he wished only to define a procedure through his draft resolution that would lead to some solution among those that fitted in its broad framework, and his statements concerning his government's preference of independence among the various possible solutions to the problem. In other words, Krishna Menon in no way had interpreted the resolution as limiting the concept of self-determination to independence only.[57]

C. Tsatsos also charged the Communist façade party with always desiring to keep open the Cyprus question in order to create a split between Greece and its allies, while in Cyprus it turned against "Dighenis" and EOKA who were trying to free Cyprus. Thus, it was allied, in effect, with the British and the Turks who were also fighting "Dighenis" and EOKA.[58]

But the governmental spokesmen also tried to show that since 1954 the American attitude in the Cyprus problem had improved. Whereas in 1954, the U.S. government had advised against the first Greek recourse to the United Nations, and in 1955 had voted against the inclusion of the second Greek recourse in the Assembly's agenda, at the last Assembly, it had maintained a neutrality, "not as benevolent as we deserved but still benevolent," said Kassimatis.[59] Another governmental member of Parliament, Savvas Loizidis, a Cypriot by birth and since 1931 quite involved in the Cyprus struggle,[60] noted that the U.S. Delegation on the eve of the debate on the Cyprus question in the Political Committee had informed the Greek Delegation of its intended neutrality, and during the debate its spokesman had said he believed none of the draft resolutions tabled would contribute to a solution. Yet he had stated that his delegation would offer its good offices for a constructive solution. This strict neutrality, thus, in no way was synonymous with indifference. This U.S. interest, Loizidis said, began as the moment approached for taking a decision on the various draft resolutions and for voting. As a U.S. representative had explained, his government's policy was to see to it that the relations between the disputants should not worsen as a result of the debate so that its own relations with the disputants should not suffer, and to gain time so that the United States might find a constructive solution.[61]

None of the Greek government spokesmen referred to the fact that at an early phase of the backstage exchanges on the Cyprus question, the Italian government had suggested a draft resolution that the Greek government rejected on February 3,[62] or that the U.S. delegation, after repeated efforts by Greek government officials in Washington, Athens, and the United Nations to get the U.S. government to clarify its position on the question, had come forward with a draft proposal that it hoped would be tolerable, even though not satisfactory, to all parties concerned, but which six days later it had preferred to drop. Under this draft, the Assembly, considering that the needs of peace and good relations between nations required a solution of the Cyprus question at the earliest, would have expressed the hope that renewed negotiations might lead to concrete progress in the achieving of a solution, and it would have appealed "to the parties concerned" to abstain from any actions or measures that might increase existing tension and render a solution more difficult. When informed by Ambassador Wadsworth of this proposal on February 6, the Greek Foreign Minister had immediately observed that it lacked absolutely any substantive content. Why would the Assembly adopt such a resolution? Wadsworth responded that it was not through resolutions that pressure could be exerted but mainly through the debate which allowed all delegations to express their views and exert pressure toward a certain direction.

Averoff-Tossizza, although promising to refer this proposal to Athens, made the preliminary remarks that the words "in accordance with the principles of the Charter" should be added at the end of the first operative clause of the proposed text, and that the UN Secretary-General should be entrusted with the task of submitting a report on the course of the question at the next Assembly.[63] He also predicted to Wadsworth that the Greek government would insist that the negotiations in question should be carried out between the British government and the Cypriot people. In transmitting this proposal to Athens, he drew attention to the danger lest the second operative clause of the draft provide a basis for demands that the Greek government denounce the activities of "Dighenis" and lest it be exploited by the British in Cyprus as a condemnation of EOKA on the part of the United Nations. Although the State Department accepted the proposed reference to the principles and purposes of the Charter, the British and Turkish Delegations rejected any reference to negotiations between the British government and the Cypriots.

As for the Greek Delegation, it showed a clear preference for the maintenance of full and sincere American neutrality as a minimum it could seek from its American friends, inasmuch as the United States felt unable to support a fair and just solution because this would displease the British and the Turks. Having received positive evidence that the United States had started exerting pressures on governments friendly to Greece in order to hinder their support of the Greek proposals concerning self-determination for the Cypriot population, Averoff-Tossizza, in a conversation with Wadsworth, had protested about these acts, which he termed unfriendly, and had warned that his government had the duty of report to Parliament and public opinion about events that might jeopardize the political position of the United States in Greece. The over-all result had been that the U.S. Delegation had not gone ahead with its proposal and informed the Greek Delegation accordingly on February 12. The concept of neutrality, explained a high official of the U.S. Delegation, did not mean lack of interest in the matter on the part of the United States; it merely meant a neutral attitude toward the conflicting views of the parties concerned. It was an attitude of "interested neutrality," with the United States reserving its right to intervene if the debate became too acrimonious, as a State Department official told the Counsellor of the Greek Embassy on February 15.

In Parliament, Greek government spokesmen reporting on the Cyprus proceedings at the eleventh Assembly stressed the lessons gained from the first Greek recourse to the Assembly in 1954 about the real nature of the United Nations and about what that international organization could and could not do. The Foreign Minister, for instance, observed in realistic terms that the United Nations was not a court of justice and did not judge on the basis of laws and legal precedents. It was a universal political arena in which all nations of the world gathered and the interests of all nations clashed.[64] In that arena, what occurred mainly was the projection of various issues. What could come out from this arena was moral and political pressure for the solution of problems. That was all the United Nations could achieve. The debate, if of course carried out widely and well, could be useful, because, in addition to enlightening the eighty odd governments, it also enlightened world public opinion on issues, through the proceedings and the radio. Therefore, a broader pressure was exerted upon the nation whose conduct was under scrutiny. If the Assembly's resolution was good, it was useful, too, because, beyond the moral pressure it exerted within the United Nations, it exerted pressure, too, on the government of the responsible country. This pressure was not a small weapon. Exactly for that reason the opposing side sought each time to prevent either the inclusion of items in the agenda of the Assembly, or, should these items be accepted for debate, the adoption of any resolutions at all or of resolutions that were clear and useful to the protagonist. Consequently, both debates and resolutions were important weapons. But even when both these objectives had been achieved, even then one should have no illusions. There had been many good debates and many good resolutions, which the states concerned had never implemented nor even taken into account.

In full awareness of this situation, the Greek government had resorted to the United Nations for the Cyprus question, because it had no other course of action open in order to promote the issue,[65] or because, as C. Tsatsos put it quite succinctly, it was not possible to wage war against Britain, and no negotiations with Britain had ever taken place.[66] Because of the character of the Assembly as a political arena, not as a court of justice, Averoff-Tossizza explained further, efforts were always made, even before the debate began, to find compromise solutions. Most of the countries did not wish to take sides against one of the parties to a dispute, and governments, while taking into account the principles of International Law, in the last analysis defined their attitude on a particular issue on the basis of political interest. One country belonged to a political bloc; another exported 70 per cent of its commodities to one of the parties involved in the dispute; a third one was aware that a solution to one of its own problems depended on that state. Hence, all exerted an effort for the adoption of a resolution which would not be in opposition with the disputants and especially with the most powerful of them.[67]

It was left to Savvas Loizidis to make a lengthy analysis of the course of the Cyprus question at the eleventh Assembly. Starting out with certain remarks about its composition and atmosphere, Loizidis observed that most of the eighty members of the Assembly belonged to groups which, though not as monolithic and disciplined as the Eastern bloc, acted in co-operation or at least maintained among themselves friendly relations of consultation and mutual support. The Asian-African group—twenty-nine states in all—was composed of all the Asian states (the Arab states and Japan included) as well as of all African states, except for the Union of South Africa, which belonged to the Commonwealth. To this group Turkey belonged. And this was important for the Cyprus problem. Then, there was the Latin American group of twenty member states. Third, came the Western group, with the United States and the countries of the British Commonwealth, minus the Asian and African countries. This group also included the European countries, except for the Communist ones and Greece—a total of nineteen states. Then there was the Eastern bloc, with nine member states. The total amounted to seventy-seven member states. Three remained: Greece, Yugoslavia, and Israel—the latter isolated, because of the Suez affair. Yugoslavia, having no problem pending before the United Nations, did not experience the results of isolation. Having no commitments to any group, it enjoyed freedom of movement. Greece (non-caucusing, like the other two) [68] geographically belonged to the European community of nations and was a member of NATO. However, not only had it no position in the United Nations close to the Western states, but it was under "the tragic disadvantage" of having Britain, one of the most powerful states of the West, as an opponent. It opposed France over the Algerian problem, the Netherlands over the question of West Irian, and, finally, Portugal in the Fourth Committee, on Trusteeship and Non-Self-Governing Territories. Turkey, on the other hand, another of the opponents of Greece, Loizidis pointed out, was not only a NATO state but had ties with other states through the Baghdad Pact. As mentioned, it also belonged to the Asian-African group.[69]

With regard to the general colonial-anticolonial dichotomy in the

United Nations, Loizidis observed that, as long as the United States allied itself with the anticolonial powers, in the Algerian question, for instance, or appeared to be neutral, as in the Cyprus and West Irian items, it was able to block the adoption of resolutions, because of the lack of the required two-thirds majority. The Asian-African group, if cohesive and supported by the Soviet bloc, would do the same. As a result, the Assembly, in colonial issues, tended to end in compromise resolutions. Even a simple majority in colonial matters was doubtful, he added, whenever the United States threw its weight behind the colonial powers, on the ground that one should wait for developments. At no other session of the Assembly, he observed, had such tremendous influence of the United States been evident over most of the Latin American member states, over many European ones, as well as over some members of the Asian-African group itself.[70]

With regard to the specific debate on the Cyprus question at the eleventh Assembly, which Loizidis analyzed at length, seventy-eight out of eighty delegations had attended the debate in the Political Committee—Hungary and the Union of South Africa being absent. Out of these seventy-eight delegations present, fifty-one had spoken on the Cyprus problem (in the Political Committee, either during the general debate or the discussion centering around the resolution-making). Fifteen of these had unreservedly and absolutely supported the Greek draft resolutions: Yugoslavia, Romania, Syria, Afghanistan, Egypt, Sudan (indirectly), the U.S.S.R., the Ukrainian S.S.R., Ethiopia, the Byelorussian S.S.R., Jordan, Czechoslovakia, Poland, Tunisia (indirectly), and, of course, Greece. Also favoring the Greek draft resolutions were Guatemala, Ecuador, and El Salvador, which, however, had declared they would vote first for the Indian draft resolution. Absolutely in favor of the British draft resolution and endorsing the Anglo-Turkish views were, on the other hand, six states: Australia, New Zealand, Pakistan, Portugal, Britain, and Turkey. Also for Britain, but moderately and without stating they would support the British draft resolution, were three more delegations (Canada, France, Belgium). Delegations favoring a purely compromise solution and recommending negotiations were twenty-three (Ceylon, Philippines, United States, Spain, Liberia, Iraq, Norway, Bolivia, Panama, Ireland, Austria, Thailand, China, Venezuela, India, Iran, Italy, Argentina, Nepal, Japan, Iceland, Mexico, and Colombia). Thus, out of the fifty-one delegations that had spoken on the Cyprus question in the Political Committee, fifteen had been in favor of Greece, six in favor of Britain, and absolutely in favor of a compromise there had been twenty-three, with six more tending toward that direction.

Among the delegations that had not made speeches, those of Albania, Bulgaria, Yemen, Saudi Arabia, and Morocco could be regarded as absolutely favoring the Greek draft resolutions, while absolutely in favor of the British draft resolution there were perhaps two (Luxembourg and the Netherlands), Loizidis said. The remaining twenty-one delegations should be regarded as favoring a compromise resolution inasmuch as the whole atmosphere favored a moderate resolution in accordance with the Algerian precedent. That these had not asked to speak were indications of moderation and of a preference for a moderate resolution. The conclusion was that fifty-one of the total seventy-eight delegations present at the debate had favored a compromise solution calling for negotiations. This did not necessarily reflect the number of delegations that opposed the principle of self-determination. Another statistic based on conversations with various delegations had revealed that thirty-five out of the fifty-one delegations that had made speeches on the Cyprus question favored self-determination for Cyprus. Most of them, however, on various grounds, had argued that for the Cypriot people to achieve self-determination a compromise resolution calling for negotiations was indicated for the time being.

In such an atmosphere, Loizidis continued, the Greek Delegation had either to conform with the general spirit of compromise that prevailed or intransigently to insist on its own draft resolution. If, however, it did the latter, the Indian draft resolution would have been withdrawn and one based on the Thai proposal would have been tabled, with motions not to put to the vote the other draft resolutions (the Greek ones included). Perhaps such a proposal, passed by the Political Committee, might have been blocked in the Assembly—with the result that no resolution at all would have been adopted. This, however, had not been the view of the other members of the Greek Delegation. Besides, the appearance of the Indian resolution had caused several friendly delegations to incline toward its adoption. If anything, one feared one's own intransigent supporters, such as the Soviet bloc members, lest they decide to abstain. As for the interpretation of the Indian resolution, Loizidis emphasized that out of the twelve delegations (Greece's included) that had interpreted their vote, only those of Britain and Turkey had given interpretations that were opposed to the Greek one. The delegations of Mexico, Bolivia, Egypt, Yugoslavia, and Ecuador had supported the Greek viewpoint, whereas India's had favored the concept of bipartite negotiations between the British government and the Cypriot people as the correct procedure for making progress toward a solution of the problem.[71]

Neither Loizidis nor other Greek government spokesmen dealt in Parliament with the subtle bargaining efforts that the Soviet, Bulgarian, and Albanian delegations to the Assembly indulged in before they declared their intention of supporting the Greek viewpoint during the consideration of the Cyprus item in the United Nations. Here are some relevant facts. On January 28, after a Yugoslav representative at the Assembly told the Permanent Greek Representative to the United Nations that a Bulgarian representative had stressed to him Bulgarian difficulties in the matter of supporting the Greek Delegation in the Cyprus question, because of Turkish pressures, the Greek diplomat met his Bulgarian colleague and did not derive a favorable impression from his talk with him. This, he thought, constituted an important indication of the Soviet attitude in the Cyprus question. When the Permanent Soviet Representative was approached, he expressed the wish to be informed about the point reached in Greek relations with Bulgaria. As for the Albanian, he asked his Greek colleague what had happened to a joint Greek-Albanian statement on boundary markers that was to be signed. He let it be understood that a delay in signing this agreement could be interpreted on the Albanian side as indicating the lack of any desire of Greece to normalize Greek-Albanian diplomatic relations. This, incidentally, had been an objective pursued by the Albanian government since 1955, when, in a note of June 30 addressed to the UN Secretary-General, it had asked him to convey to the Greek government its desire to establish normal diplomatic and good neighborly relations with Greece, while subsequently rejecting the conditions the Greek government had then put forward on August 3 in response to this démarche.[72]

In reporting to Athens about these Soviet bloc attitudes, the Greek diplomat observed that one should not take Soviet bloc support for granted. It was natural that the Soviets, who realized the importance of their votes in the Cyprus question, would make their support dependent on exchanges of lesser importance which, however, the Greek government would be unable to avoid by dilatory tactics and vague promises.

The next day, the Greek Foreign Minister conferred with the head of the Soviet Delegation, V. Kuznetsov. Expressing the desire to see an improvement in Greek-Soviet relations, he stressed the progress that had already been achieved in all sectors but did not fail to emphasize that Greek-Soviet relations were a matter that ought to be faced with realism and prudence so that the common effort should not be impeded by an untimely speeding up of the regular tempo followed in the past. He reminded the Soviet diplomat that he had developed these points concerning the political position of Greece because of its membership in NATO to Foreign Minister Shepilov, who had fully and sympathetically understood them. Kuznetsov agreed. He, too, expressed the desire for improved relations with Greece for the sake of peace. The participation of Greece in NATO, which the Greek Foreign Minister, he noted, had termed as absolutely defensive, allowed margins for co-operation in other sectors. In this connection, he asked Averoff-Tossizza to study carefully the Soviet item—complaint by the U.S.S.R. of intervention of the United States in the domestic affairs of certain states [73]—inscribed in the agenda of the Special Political Committee as well as the relevant Soviet draft resolution that condemned U.S. operations in the "gray" and "black" area of the spectrum of international politics, and to communicate to him later what the Greek Delegation might do on this item and whether, and up to what point it would be able to support it. Averoff-Tossizza promised to study the matter with all due attention but took the opportunity of explaining to Kuznetsov the great difficulty this item presented for the Greek Delegation because of the multiple ties of Greece with the United States.

Drawing the Prime Minister's attention to these Soviet bloc attitudes, Averoff-Tossizza expressed the view that it was not desirable to make any *démarches* with the embassies of Soviet bloc states in Athens because it might give the impression that the Greek government had been intimidated. He also asked the Greek Embassy in Washington to inform the State Department of these attitudes, together with other matters, however, so as not to create the impression that the Greek government was making any threats. On the particular Soviet item mentioned by Kuznetsov, he advised great care. Even a Greek abstention would be extremely difficult because the United States was the accused and Russia the accuser. At any rate, he too felt that the attitude of the Soviet bloc in the Cyprus question had not been fully secured. Albania and Bulgaria, he thought, might abstain—even though with the latter, in contrast to the former, an agreement had been reached on August 16, 1955, by a joint Greek-Bulgarian commission for the avoidance and settlement of frontier disputes. Since it was not possible to give any substantive satisfaction to the Soviets beyond mere verbal expressions, he favored the signing of the Greek-Albanian statement and requested Athens to give him the powers to sign it.

In response to these developments, the Greek government advised the Foreign Minister that in principle it would have no objections to offering substantive evidence of its desire to re-establish normal diplomatic relations with its two Iron Curtain neighbors. The moment, however, was very unsuitable because if the Greek government did so, it would seem to be yielding to blackmail, and the reaction of public opinion would be most lively. Premier Karamanlis requested that it should be explained to the Soviet Delegation that a favorable attitude of the Soviet bloc in the Cyprus debates would create a favorable atmosphere which would lead the government, after the UN consideration of the matter, to agree to measures aiming at the normalization of diplomatic relations with Greece's northern neighbors.

On February 5, during a lunch of the Soviet Delegation, the Greek Foreign Minister developed the reasons that Greece at the present difficult moment in Greek-American relations would be unable to support the Soviet draft resolution or assume any attitude that might be unfavorably interpreted on the U.S. side. At length he explained this position and added that if in the Soviet draft resolution there were certain painless paragraphs, it would be possible for the Greek Delegation to abstain from voting on them as a demonstration of good will toward the U.S.S.R. On the draft resolution as a whole, however, it would be unable to assume a similar attitude. Apparently the frankness with which the Foreign Minister spoke was persuasive and created a favorable atmosphere. On his side, Kuznetsov explained that his request in no way was intended as a means to exert pressure, as certain Athens newspapers had charged. He had merely wished to inform the Greek Delegation about a matter in which the U.S.S.R. was concerned, and this because of the better relations that were developing between their two countries. Averoff-Tossizza gave an appropriate explanation about the Greek press comments and, finally, Kuznetsov told him confidentially that the Soviet Delegation intended to support the Greek Delegation in the Cyprus question.

A week later, the Soviet and Romanian ambassadors in Athens called on C. Tsatsos, Minister in Charge of the Prime Minister's Office, and categorically stated that their delegations at the Assembly would vote in favor of the Greek draft resolution referring to self-determination for the population of Cyprus. In New York that same day, the Acting Foreign Minister of Albania met Averoff-Tossizza and inquired about developments in Greek-Albanian relations and in particular about the delay in signing the agreement about the emplacing of markers on the Greek-Albanian border. The Greek Foreign Minister explained in general terms his government's policy that tended toward the normalization of relations with all states of the Soviet bloc and emphasized the progress that had been achieved in that direction. However, the agreement with Albania could not be signed now lest the impression be created in Greece that this had been done under pressure in connection with the voting on the Cyprus question. He promised, though, to sign this agreement as soon as he returned to Athens.

The public record indicates that it was only on February 8, 1958 (i.e., after the twelfth Assembly, when, as will be seen, the Greek draft resolution referring to self-determination was put to the vote with the Soviet bloc members voting in its favor) that a Greek-Albanian agreement was reached, not over land boundaries, but for the purpose of co-operating in the minesweeping of the Straits of Corfu. Three days later, representatives of the general staffs of Greece and Bulgaria signed in Thessaloniki four protocols settling all issues likely to arise along the 300-mile Greek-Bulgarian border.[74] That year, too, witnessed the conclusion of trade agreements with the U.S.S.R. and Poland, also the relaxation of trade controls with Communist China.

In an overarching speech on March 15, the last day of the debate in Parliament concerning the handling of the Cyprus question at the eleventh Assembly,[75] Premier Karamanlis, who had attended the Assembly's early meetings in November, 1956, for the specific purpose of promoting the Cyprus question in the United Nations as well as in the United States, repeated what he had told Parliament on earlier occasions, namely that Cyprus was the most difficult problem his country had ever had to deal with. Greece had to face powerful adversaries. It belonged to no particular group of nations. Consequently it did not enjoy the solidarity and backing of a bloc of its own. The struggle was being waged in the midst of an international crisis—which meant that Greece had to take care about its own security and that many other countries took a different attitude than they would have in the absence of this crisis. Finally, Greece had to wage this struggle within the framework of an alliance. Thus the problem bristled with dramatic contradictions. There were moments when an action that promoted the Cyprus question could be harmful to free Greece and, conversely, there were moments when an action that was correct for national policy could be harmful for Cyprus. The government, he reiterated, was obliged for reasons of more general national interest to maintain the alliance and within it to wage the struggle for Cyprus.

The Premier continued with a short summary of the history of the Cyprus case to enable his listeners, as he said, to get a more realistic understanding of the question. In 1950, the plebiscite in Cyprus had taken place, in which the Cypriots had sought *enosis* (union) with Greece. The Greek governments of 1951–52 (headed by current Opposition party leaders), he reminded Parliament, had agreed to bring the matter before the United Nations.[76] Then, in 1953, Premier Alexander Papagos had decided not to resort to the United Nations, stating he would like to exhaust the possibilities of a friendly settlement with Britain. By 1954, the latter's position was known. In response to any *démarche* of the Greek government, the British government had replied "never." Under the circumstances, the first Greek recourse to the United Nations had been made in 1954. The Tripartite London Conference between Britain, Greece, and Turkey had followed in 1955, with its known results.[77] That same year, the Greek government had submitted its second recourse to the United Nations (see Appendix B) which had been rejected. Negotiations then had started—on October 4—between Ethnarch Makarios and the Governor of Cyprus, Sir John Harding. These (with one break) had lasted until March, 1956, and had been interrupted by the deportation of the Ethnarch to the Seychelles.[78] Immediately, the Greek government had submitted a new recourse to the United Nations (see Appendix C) and had maintained that no other way of promoting the Cyprus question existed. The aims of the recourse had been a wide debate of the question and a resolution. Both had been achieved. Moreover, outside of the United Nations, his government had rejected the draft Constitution prepared by Lord Radcliffe. It had maintained, all in all, an impeccable and "relentless" attitude in handling the Cyprus question, and it was difficult to substantiate the charge that his government had sought to close the matter or had failed in its policy.

On March 15, the government, in the vote that followed in Parliament on the motions of no confidence, did not lose. As against 135 votes cast by the Opposition, it obtained 161.[79] The day before, it had been learned that Grivas—"Dighenis"—in Cyprus had issued a proclamation offering a truce. One Opposition leader, Papandreou, had deplored this news; another, S. Venizelos, had raised the question of whether this offer had been due to Greek government pressure on EOKA's leader. Foreign Minister and Premier denied having any contacts with him. Besides, the former said, Grivas was not the sort of person who would yield to the pressure of any government, Greek or other. The Opposition regarded these denials as the correct thing to do—regardless of truth.[80]

Chapter Two

Relaxation and
Tension in Point-Counterpoint

A. *Grivas' Truce Offer*

Even before the General Assembly had adopted Resolution 1013 (XI), the Greek government had been trying to restore, to a certain extent at least, "an atmosphere of peace" to Cyprus. Late in November, 1956, after the Cyprus item had been included in the Assembly's agenda, the Greek Consul-General in Nicosia, Angelos Vlachos, had recommended a new truce. "Dighenis," however, had rejected this idea. The British representative in the UN, he argued, might point to the truce as an indication that negotiations were possible—in order to frustrate the debate on the Cyprus question in the United Nations. Besides, from the military viewpoint it was difficult for him to disengage himself at that time. Nor was he sure that the foe would respond in the same way, by suspending his operations against him. Then, in January, the Greek Foreign Minister, through the Greek Consul in Nicosia, again had suggested to "Dighenis" the temporary suspension of operations—a truce. The leader of EOKA, however, once again had rejected this suggestion. The British, he contended, would take the proclamation of a truce as a sign of weakness and would exploit the announcement both internally and externally, especially in the United Nations, by stating that EOKA had been forced into declaring a truce, because of the recent British successes against it. Also a truce would have an undesirable effect both on the EOKA fighters who wanted continuous activity and on the population which waited to see what could be achieved. Governor Harding, finally, was most likely to declare again, as he had when Grivas had offered his first truce (August 16, 1956), that he would be no party to it.[1] As a result, EOKA would suffer blows without returning them. Grivas therefore instructed the continuation of operations in accordance with a tempo defined in a special order, and envisaged the possibility of a truce only during the time of the debate on the Cyprus question in the United

Nations, or after a resolution was adopted, depending on that resolution's nature.[2]

No sooner had the Political Committee passed the Indian resolution on February 22, than Anthimos, the Metropolitan Bishop of Kition, approached Grivas with the suggestion of, if not a truce, at least a temporary and unofficial suspension of operations prior to proclaiming one. Then, on February 24, the Greek Consul in Nicosia proposed to him the immediate proclamation of a truce, in compliance with the resolution of the United Nations. If there was delay in this, he pointed out, the British were likely to take the initiative and seek to involve the Turks in their negotiations with the Greek government.

To these proposals Grivas replied in a letter of February 28 to the Greek Consul. He wrote that his own analysis of the situation indicated that the British government would seek to achieve a dynamic solution and to impose the Radcliffe draft constitution upon the people of Cyprus. At least this would be the British line until the Eisenhower-Macmillan meeting in Bermuda took place. This seemed evident both from the words and deeds of the Governor as well as from the debate in the House of Commons and House of Lords. Harding himself took this line. It was Grivas' observation that whenever an opportunity arose for a new course in the Cyprus question, the Governor immediately carried out spectacular operations and informed his government that the sedition was at its last gasp. Thus, he influenced London's decisions. The same thing had happened again this time. Under such conditions, Grivas wondered whether it would be expedient to proclaim a truce. He was not quite sure of the benefits that could be gained by one. The opponent was likely to continue his operations with the adverse results he had mentioned on the previous occasions when suggestions for a truce had been made to him. Besides, an official proclamation of a truce would render the opponent more inflexible and obstinate, because he would read in such a gesture a sign of weakness. It could be argued, he acknowledged, that regardless of the above shortcomings of a truce, its moral repercussions would be important in the international arena. Sentimentality, however, in his view, ought to be eschewed. About such matters one should think realistically.

The attitude of Sir John Harding seemed to justify Grivas' analysis. On February 24, the Governor of Cyprus had interpreted the resolution passed by the Political Committee in the way mentioned earlier—which would justify the drive against EOKA he was engaged in at the time in an effort to liquidate it and thus restore "an atmosphere of peace" to the island. The next day he had had the island showered with thousands of leaflets predicting that the days of EOKA were numbered. Furthermore, in a statement to a British newspaper (*The Observer*), he had declared that he would go ahead with the application of the Radcliffe draft constitution to Cyprus. Grivas, nevertheless, in spite of his own views, wishing to deny to the foe any propaganda advantages he might derive from EOKA's stand, advised the Greek Consul in his letter of February 28 that he would limit his operations to defensive measures and was willing even to suspend them, without, however, officially proclaiming a truce. He would also go ahead and prepare the ground for a truce, which he would proclaim if the certainty existed that the opponent would respond in a like manner. At the same time, Grivas started preparations for a new struggle and issued orders for the organization of city groups and youth groups, as well as of new groups of guerrillas in various provinces.[3]

Finally, on March 14, Grivas proclaimed that, in compliance with the spirit of the Assembly's resolution and in order to facilitate the resumption of negotiations between the British government and the real representative of the people of Cyprus, Ethnarch Makarios, he was willing to order suspension of the operations as soon as the Ethnarch was freed. Thus, he did not immediately proclaim a truce, but set down certain conditions for one. Such an approach seemed to him preferable not only because it set the start of negotiations as a precondition for the proclamation of the truce but also because it helped prevent creation of the impression that this decision was a sign of EOKA's weakness.[4] And he had good reason to be sensitive to this matter, for, since the beginning of the year, large-scale British operations had taken a mounting toll of his forces. Several of his top guerrillas, such as Markos Drakos, had been killed. His top liaison officer had been captured. His lieutenant, Grigoris Afxendiou, had been destroyed by hand grenades, incendiary bombs, and flaming gasoline in his hideout near the Monastery of Makhaira on March 3, after an eight hour battle, which journalists had been invited to watch. And his own hideout had almost been found.[5]

This other *dramatis persona* of the Cyprus play, whom the British would never capture, had arrived in Cyprus in November, 1954, to start his exercise in unconventional warfare. A military man par excellence, a strict disciplinarian—over himself as well as over others—this staunch believer in the traditional values of Eastern Orthodoxy represented an interesting contrast to the Ulysses-like voluptuary of power and representative of the post-Lausanne generation of secularly-minded Greeks, the Foreign Minister. Gaunt, short, ascetic, with burning black eyes and a black mustache (a British author thought he looked like Groucho Marx),[6] Grivas—born in 1898—was Averoff-Tossizza's senior by twelve years. In many respects he was a representative of an earlier strain of Greek nationalism—that of the irredentist period.[7] This was not inexplicable. Unlike the Foreign Minister, he was no mainlander from territory that was Greek since 1830. He was, by birth, a Cypriot; and among those Greeks who remained outside the territory of Greece, whether in Cyprus or the Dodecanese (ceded to Greece in 1947 under the Italian Peace Treaty) or Northern Epirus (southern Albania), irredentism often held on with greater tenacity than it did among the Greeks living within the boundaries of the Greek state. Thus, Grivas' prototype could be found not among the sophisticated, "Europeanized," secularized Greeks of the interwar period but among those who, at the turn of the nineteenth century, had waged unconventional warfare in the European territories of the Ottoman Empire, while concurrently in conflict with Bulgars and Serbs who were engaged in similar activities.[8] A photograph taken of Grivas on the Troodos range in Cyprus and captured by the British in 1956 [9] shows the leader of EOKA standing, full face to the camera—grave, mustachioed—his weight firmly set on the left leg (no Praxitelean sinuosity, of course), the right foot set somewhat apart and at a higher level, as though bestriding the invisible body of a fallen foe (the classical victor's pose). This stance, iconographically, is reminiscent of the photographs, chromolithographs, or popular paintings—by Theophilos, for instance, the Greek Douanier Rousseau—of Pavlos Melas, the best-known of those Greek officers, who, with no government support, set out on his own to fight in Macedonia against not only the Turks but also the Bulgars, and, after losing his life there in 1904, became a national hero.

Grivas' rhetoric, as his various proclamations indicate, included frequent references to the classic commonplaces of Marathon and Salamis; Sparta, with Leonidas and his three hundred at Thermopylae; the Greek War of Independence of 1821; the "epic of Albania." [10] It contained no reference, on the other hand, to the "Megali Idea" and its Byzantine ambience, though his own *nom de guerre*—"Dighenis"—was that of a legendary Byzantine hero and marchman whose fabulous feats are sung to this day in Cypriot and Greek villages.

But Grivas and his *enosist* activities were no mere throwback to pre-World War I Greek irredentism and nationalism. They had elements of the integral, anti-Communist Greek nationalism of the late interwar period, of the bourgeois paternalist type symbolized by dictator John Metaxas—a military man like Grivas. They were also imitative of postwar anticolonial nationalism of non-European, even anti-European, peoples.

The fundamental aim of EOKA—to draw attention to the Cyprus problem and to get "parliamentary" as well as conventional diplomacy to examine it and find a solution to it [11]—reveals the extent to which Grivas' activities were closely connected with the anticolonialist and essentially anti-European struggles that broke out throughout the world after World War II, fed by lavish promises that served, as witness the Atlantic Charter, the purpose either of marshaling the support of subject peoples for the allied war effort or of stimulating resistance in enemy-occupied territories—promises, which, in many instances, were soon to boomerang against those who gave them.

Since 1948, this colonel, who retired from the Army at his own request, had been discussing with a small circle of non-governmental politicians, former politicians, or private individuals—some of them Cypriots like Achilles Kyrou, brother of Alexis A. Kyrou, the champion of Cyprus in the United Nations, and all with quite extreme right-wing political views—the possibility of resorting to violence in Cyprus for the purpose of promoting the cause of the island's union with Greece.[12] But it was only in May, 1951, that, with this circle's encouragement, Grivas went to Cyprus to study on the spot the feasibility of such activities. Arriving on the island in July, he conferred there with his old acquaintance from wartime Athens, the new Archbishop and Ethnarch of the island, Makarios III, who appeared to listen to his proposals with a great deal of skepticism. Nonetheless, by August, Grivas had concluded that small guerrilla groups could be set up in Cyprus and that the sabotage of military targets could be carried out.

The following year, at another meeting of the same circle, Grivas expounded his findings, and, though Makarios, who chaired this meeting, did not feel sure whether the colonel would find a sufficient number of Cypriots to take part in his venture, Grivas was convinced that he could. Two committees—political and military—were set up at that time. Makarios was formally appointed as president. And in October, 1952, Grivas made another trip to Cyprus. Staying there for five months, he reconnoitered the mountainous regions of the island and coastal locations suitable for secretly unloading the materiel that would be sent in. He also set up small nuclei of individuals for waging unconventional warfare and for receiving and concealing the materiel as it arrived. On his return to Athens, he made known his decision that the struggle would be waged by Cypriots exclusively.[13] At a meeting of the committee on March 7, 1953, presided over by Makarios, the participants took a solemn oath, pledging full secrecy and complete dedication to the struggle. Grivas was officially appointed to lead the operations. At this time, too, he drafted his general plan of action and EOKA's charter.[14]

To the preparation of this plan and its implementation, Grivas brought the knowledge of military strategy and tactics that he had derived from his training as an Army officer at the military academies of Greece and then France, prior to World War II; from his experiences during the occupation of Greece and especially its immediate aftermath, when he had organized anti-Communist groups in Athens—the X-ites—which in a particular quarter of the city near the temple of Hephaistus called Theseion had kept at bay the Communist bands seeking to take over the Greek capital in December, 1944; and, finally, from his own post-retirement studies of the techniques through which the Communists manage to agitate, mobilize, and organize various groups for carrying out effective violent action. In this way, too, Grivas, somewhat of a graphomaniac, like many other revolutionary conspirators, as witness Blanqui or Lenin, and believing as they did, that words were weapons, was quite a modern operator in unconventional warfare.

Late in October, 1954, as the British were transferring their armed forces from Suez to Cyprus, implementing their decision to set up on the island the Middle East Command after the Anglo-Egyptian agreement of October 19, this childless man, inspired by a desire to emulate the achievements of his outstanding brother-in-arms, Field Marshal Papagos, whose star had risen to supreme political heights, left his wife and Athens to dig himself into the land of his birth, literally living in holes dug in the ground of his motherland, and maintaining his physical strength, it is said, by eating 24 oranges a day and little else. Thence, imbued with a profound sense of national mission, and hierarchically subordinated to the Ethnarchy of which he was the military arm, he directed his organization, which consisted mainly of youths who dedicated themselves to committing acts of heroism-terrorism to the extent of killing not only other people—some of them of their own age—but also of being killed themselves. In the process he set up a remarkable intelligence and liaison network the secret of which he refrains from revealing in his writings; a local industry for the production of primitive but useful military hardware, since it became increasingly difficult to get supplies from Greece; and a small political organization for organizing passive resistance, strikes, and public demonstrations. His multifarious activities were to pin down on the island at least 20,000 British troops, though these were not his only foes. There were the Greek Cypriot Communists to deal with; those among the Turkish Cypriots who sided with the British or with the Turkish government; and, finally, the "traitors" among the Greek Cypriots themselves, who either sided with the British or opposed EOKA's operations.

As indicated in a document seized by the British in 1955 shortly before Grivas actually began his operations, the Communists on the island were not to be accepted for membership in his organization and were asked not only to refrain from opposing it but also from getting involved in it, if they were sincerely interested in *enosis*. As for the Turks of Cyprus, they were to be regarded as brothers in the struggle against the alien ruler and were merely asked not to put themselves in the way of the struggle and become agents of the British in opposing it. They could rest assured in the knowledge that after liberation had been achieved, Cypriots, Greeks, and Turks would all live together in peace and friendship.[15]

The co-ordination between EOKA's activities and "parliamentary diplomacy," conceivable only in our era of communications, was to be the subject of friction between the Foreign Minister and the retired, but far from inactive, colonel. But this had been the case from the very outset, when, in the night of March 31–April 1, 1955, Grivas, through acts of sabotage directed mainly against British military targets, began his unconventional warfare, while the Ethnarch, from a balcony of the Archiepiscopal Palace, was anxiously watching to see the spurts of flame from the first explosions in Nicosia and to hear their dull boom. If these initial acts of violence seemed to constitute an escalatory response of the Cypriots to the Assembly's decision in December, 1954, not to consider further the Cyprus question, this was according neither to the Ethnarch's nor to the Foreign Minister's plan. A high Greek diplomatic official had countermanded Makarios' order to Grivas for the operations to begin during the committee debate of the Cyprus item. Indeed, as already mentioned, it was only after the failure of the Greek government's first venture in "parliamentary diplomacy" with regard to the Cyprus question that Premier Papagos, Karamanlis' predecessor, gave his blessing to Grivas and his undercover activities. Before that, he had refused to encourage them.[16]

B. British Moves—Their Immediate Impact

Three days after Grivas had proposed a truce, Governor Harding launched a new antiguerrilla operation in the region of Tylliria based on a report planted by Grivas himself to the effect that his hideout was in that region of the island. And a curfew that was to last fifty-four days was imposed on the village of Milikouri, while newspapers reported that Grivas was about to be captured.[17] The rise in the optimism of the British Security Forces that the campaign would very soon end successfully was reflected in the decision of March 18 to reduce the rewards offered for information leading to the arrest of Grivas and other EOKA leaders from £10,000 and £5,000 to £1,000 and £500, respectively.[18] That same day the Governor of Cyprus flew to London where the British Cabinet, under Eden's successor, Harold Macmillan, had discussed Grivas' truce proposal and other matters connected with the Cyprus question. On his arrival, Sir John underlined that Grivas was not offering a cessation of hostilities but merely their suspension. Newspaper reports suggested the existence at this time of a sharp division of opinion within the British Cabinet, with some members opposed to Sir John's intransigent views.[19] The new British Premier, it should be noted, on taking over his post, had told the House of Commons on January 9 that Britain would never withdraw from Cyprus, and this suggested a slight modification of the attitudes taken by his two conservative predecessors, Churchill and Eden, who on assuming the premiership in 1951 and 1956 respectively, had stated that Cyprus was an integral part of the Commonwealth and a necessary segment of the British defense perimeter in the Mediterranean. The British government's attitude at this conjuncture was defined in the House of Commons a few days later.

On March 20, the Secretary of State for the Colonies, Alan Lennox-Boyd, made it clear that the British government envisaged tripartite talks among Greece, Turkey, and Britain, with NATO participation through the Secretary-General of that regional collective security organization, as the most desirable procedure for trying to reach a settlement of the Cyprus dispute. He announced to the Commons that the British government had accepted in principle an offer the Secretary-General of NATO, Lord Ismay, had made to use his good offices for conciliation in the Cyprus question in search of an acceptable solution of the differences between the governments of Greece, Turkey, and Britain.

Ismay's offer (originally for arbitration by NATO members not concerned in the Cyprus question) had been made in accordance with the resolution on the peaceful settlement of disputes the Council adopted on December 13, 1956, approving a report prepared by a committee of three. This resolution not only empowered the Secretary-General of NATO to offer his good offices informally at any time to the parties in dispute, and, with their consent, to initiate or facilitate procedures of inquiry, mediation, conciliation, or arbitration, but urged that disputes among NATO members be submitted to NATO good offices machinery before recourse to other international agencies.[20] It should be added that the Greek representative had accepted this report with the reservation that matters which came before NATO and were not solved or matters on which a procedure had started in another international organization would not be subject to the NATO preliminary procedure. He also accepted the possibility of concurrent jurisdiction, but without any suspension of procedures under way. In the Cyprus discussion, the British representative had held that NATO should deal with the Cyprus question only if Greece withdrew its recourse from the UN—eliciting a negative Greek response and the charge that Britain and Turkey had accepted NATO competence only after the Greek recourse to the United Nations had advanced.

In his statement of March 20, Lennox-Boyd also took note of EOKA's truce offer if Makarios were released, and revealed that the Ethnarch's attention had been drawn to this truce offer and that he had been asked to make a clear public statement calling for the cessation of violence by EOKA. In the event Makarios issued such a statement, the British government would be ready to bring to an end his detention in the Seychelles islands, though there could be no question at this stage of his return to Cyprus. In the debate that followed on this statement, Lennox-Boyd made it clear that he considered NATO conciliation activities a priority, not discussions over the Radcliffe draft constitution—an internal problem, in his view. In answer to critical questioning, he also stated that the government of Cyprus would not respond to EOKA's truce offer by suspending operations, because this might permit EOKA to regroup and rearm.[21] Neither Lennox-Boyd nor the Opposition (to any serious extent) [22] referred to Resolution 1013 (XI) as a norm of behavior to be followed in seeking for a solution of the Cyprus problem. This was consistent with the British attitude that British-Cypriot relations were matters of essentially domestic jurisdiction and therefore, under Article 2, paragraph 7, were beyond the competence of the United Nations.[23]

Turkey accepted Ismay's good offices offer. The Greek Cabinet, however, after considering it for five hours, did not,[24] perhaps fearing it might lead to arbitration, hence to partition. In a statement of March 20, Premier Karamanlis invoked the Greek interpretation about the proper procedures for implementing Resolution 1013 (XI) and underlined that the Cypriots considered the liberation of Makarios as an indispensable condition for any constructive British-Cypriot negotiations over the future of Cyprus. Two days later, in a letter of March 22 to the UN Secretary-General concerning the Cypriot reaction to this resolution, the Greek Permanent Representative to the UN, Christian X. Palamas, emphasized that the British government, in accepting Lord Ismay's offer of good offices, had totally ignored the United Nations. In the absence of the main interested party, the people of Cyprus, for whom the Greek government was acting merely as an agent, no conclusive discussions could be held, he stressed. The Greek government, he added, was not disposed to bypass the United Nations, since the Cyprus issue was "pending" before that international organization, in the sense that Resolution 1013 (XI) was waiting for adequate implementation, and compliance with this resolution and its adequate implementation were now a direct responsibility of the United Nations.[25]

On March 28, in the House of Commons, Lennox-Boyd made public Archbishop Makarios' response of March 22, to the British government's statement of March 20. In this reply, Makarios asked EOKA "to declare the cessation of all operations, given that the British Government will show a spirit of understanding by abolishing simultaneously the present state of emergency. . . ." The Ethnarch, in this letter, repeated a passage from a letter of February 2, 1956, to the Governor, in which he had made it a condition of agreement that emergency military measures and emergency legislation should be revoked and an amnesty for all political offenses granted.[26] The UN resolution was a starting point toward a final settlement of the issue, Makarios also wrote. It was, he understood, "an expression of the wish of the United Nations for bilateral negotiations between the British government and the people of Cyprus." It was, the Ethnarch said, in the spirit of this UN resolution, and in order to facilitate a resumption of such negotiations that EOKA had declared its readiness to suspend operations if he were released. His personal release, he added in conclusion, would never be the object of bargaining, and he was convinced that his return to Cyprus would create a response from the people which would be a factor that ought not be underestimated. Earlier that year, in January, the Greek government, it should be noted, had learned that the Ethnarch would be prepared to discuss the Radcliffe plan if he were freed but would prefer to be freed after the beginning of the UN debates. A period of self-government was unavoidable, he felt, since the British would not abandon Cyprus before five or ten years. The Turks ought to get a broad autonomy within the constitutional framework, he believed, but the idea of a geographic distribution of the island ought to be excluded. When freed, he would be ready to denounce violence, and he was certain that EOKA would obey him.

The Secretary of State for the Colonies told the House of Commons that while the British government could not regard this statement as the clear appeal to end violence in Cyprus for which it had asked, it nevertheless considered that in the present circumstances it was no longer

necessary to continue the Archbishop's detention. He had therefore instructed the Governor to cancel orders for Makarios' detention and to
arrange a passage from the Seychelles on the first available vessel.
Further, an immediate safe-conduct out of Cyprus would be offered to
the leader of EOKA and to any other foreign nationals who were members
of that organization and were at large in Cyprus. This offer of safe-
conduct would also be extended to members of EOKA who were British
subjects and still at large, provided they gave an undertaking not to enter
any British territory while the legal state of emergency continued to exist
in Cyprus. Lennox-Boyd, however, made it clear that there could be no
question of an immediate abolition of the state of emergency, the timing
of which would be in the hands of the Governor. He also observed that
the British government did not accept the Greek government's interpretation of Resolution 1013 (XI) that the Archbishop had adopted in his
statement. There was no inconsistency in that resolution and conciliation
by NATO, with which it was the British government's intention to press.
Later, when it had been seen how the work of conciliation was going, the
government would be better able to turn, with more hope of success, to
discussing the Radcliffe draft constitution and other internal matters.
Then, of course, Lennox-Boyd continued, "there will be talks and it will
be necessary for Greek and Turkish representatives to be chosen." The
representation should be broadly based and, as head of the Ethnarchy,
the Archbishop would obviously be one of the representatives of the
Greek Cypriots.[27]

Although Macmillan denied shortly afterward that President Eisenhower had raised the matter during their Bermuda meeting (March
21–24, 1957), the President did play a role, behind the scenes, in this
British decision to release the exiled Ethnarch, and informed Premier
Karamanlis of this. Late in 1956, the Greek Foreign Minister had predicted in Parliament that this move was likely, basing his prediction on
the fact that Eisenhower, during his meeting with Karamanlis on November 15, 1956, had shown great understanding when the latter had explained that without Makarios no progress at all could be achieved
toward a solution of the Cyprus problem.[28] Indeed, during this meeting,
Karamanlis had not only developed to the President the Greek views
on the Cyprus question, stressing that the United States ought to exert its
influence with the British and the Turks for an early settlement of the
dispute, lest it become graver, should the Arab states or the U.S.S.R.
interfere, but had also asked Eisenhower personally to intercede in favor
of the immediate liberation of Makarios. The President had approved of
this idea inquiring—and learning—about the Ethnarch's whereabouts.
He had expressed his lively desire to help in a settlement and promised to
do what he could, adding, however, that the role of the United States
was somewhat delicate because the dispute involved friends.

Church bells rang in Cyprus and Greek flags were flown at the news of the forthcoming release of Ethnarch Makarios from his exile in the Seychelles. The Turkish Cypriots, though, were dismayed. Their leader, Dr. Fazil Kuchuk, sent a wire of protest to the Turkish Premier, Adnan Menderes.[29] And in the area of Marathassa-Tylliria, the military operations continued, with a helicopter vainly calling by loudspeaker upon Grivas to surrender and take the opportunity of the safe-conduct offered by the British government to leave the island.[30]

As for Makarios, still in Mahé, he stated at a press conference on March 29 that he intended to go first to Athens and then to London, and expressed the hope that he would later be allowed to return to Cyprus. Otherwise he was not prepared to negotiate. Such negotiations, he maintained, could only be held between the British authorities in Cyprus and him, as the representative of the Greek Cypriots. Although he rejected demands by the Turkish Cypriots that they be represented in such discussions, he was prepared, he said, to see their rights "internationally safeguarded," particularly in matters of education and religion. Any solution involving the partition of the island was "impractical" and definitely rejected, he added. On April 6, Makarios sailed from Mahé for Tamatave, Madagascar, on the Onassis-owned Greek tanker "Olympic Thunder." Five days later, he left Madagascar for Nairobi, where he warned that if any further executions of EOKA fighters by the British authorities occurred, the way to pacification would be barred and terrorism might revive. He would not make any comments on the Radcliffe draft constitution, he also said, until he was allowed to return to Cyprus.[31]

In Athens, Premier Karamanlis, welcoming on March 28 the British government's decision to release the Archbishop, described it as an important step toward a solution. He expressed the hope that Makarios' release was a sign of the British government's desire to seek a peaceful and just solution which would lead to a restoration of the old friendship between Greece and Britain.[32]

The Greek government, furthermore, decided to restore normal diplomatic relations with Britain by sending the Greek Ambassador, Vassili Mostras, back to London, whence he had been recalled when Makarios had been deported to the Seychelles on March 9, 1956. It also indicated its willingness to resume full co-operation with the other NATO allies in the eastern Mediterranean, which would involve the use of Greek air and naval bases by British and Turkish armed forces and co-operation with them in NATO exercises.[33]

The restoration of normal British-Greek diplomatic relations was not altogether smooth, it should be added, punctuated as it was by the resignation of the respective ambassadors. Sir Charles Peake, the British Ambassador in Athens, who had returned to London on April 5, after the announcement two days earlier of his replacement by Sir Roger Allen, Minister at the British Embassy in Bonn, was reported on April 11 as having resigned from the Foreign Office.[34] Likewise on April 11, it was announced that Ambassador Mostras had resigned from the Greek Foreign Service [35]—to be succeeded by Yorghos Seferiadis, who six years later was to become the Nobel Prize winner in poetry.

Did Sir Charles Peake's rather painful confrontation with the Greek Foreign Minister on April 1 have something to do with his recall from Athens? One cannot say for certain. At this meeting, at any rate, which Seferiadis also attended, Averoff-Tossizza informed the British diplomat of the discovery of British wiretapping activities from an annex building of the British Embassy by agents enjoying diplomatic immunity. Sir Charles was so upset he could hardly conceal his confusion. An experienced diplomat, he of course denied very forcefully that his Embassy was involved in such an outrage. The Foreign Minister, in order to convince him, suggested they should both go immediately to the annex of the British Embassy, which enjoyed diplomatic immunity. He could show him there the wiretapping installation in operation. Naturally, the British Ambassador steadfastly refused to do so, claiming he was unable to participate in counterintelligence activities directed against his own Embassy. Under the circumstances, the Foreign Minister told him he would instruct the security services to ascertain the existence of another recorder in the act of intercepting the conversations over another telephone line. This could be done in accordance with international rules.

These British wiretapping activities involved the telephone lines of the following: the Greek Member of Parliament of Cypriot origin, Savvas Loizidis, from about mid-September to November 15, 1956—after which the wiretappee left for the Assembly; of an ordnance officer of the Greek Army, from February 9 to April 1, 1957; and of Premier Karamanlis himself, from February 20 to April 1, 1957. The probable aim of these British intelligence operations was to gather information about the Greek government's activities, particularly with regard to the Cyprus issue, and to get supporting evidence for the British charges aired in the eleventh Assembly that the Greek government was fomenting, assisting, and directing the armed struggle in Cyprus. Thanks, though, to the timely discovery of these wiretapping activities, the Greek government had fed the British intelligence services with items of misleading information (supposed intentions of Premier Karamanlis to accept an invitation to go to Moscow or to conclude some sort of political agreement with Egypt and other Arab countries, as a counterbalance to the Baghdad Pact; possible attempts by outraged extremist Cypriots against the lives of the British and American ambassadors). These items, as the Greek Foreign Minister himself was able to ascertain, had been conveyed either by the British Ambassador himself or by members of his entourage to other members of the diplomatic corps in Athens, such as George V. Allen, the U.S. Ambassador, or had found their way into speeches delivered by the British Delegate at the eleventh Assembly. So at least the Greek government maintained in a pamphlet on these British intelligence activities, which it planned to circulate at the twelfth General Assembly if it thought it expedient to do so but finally never did.[36]

The resignation of Ambassador Mostras was no symmetrical event designed somehow to cloak the resignation of his British opposite number. No sooner had the Greek diplomat arrived in London than a pro-government Athens newspaper attacked him, and, as a result, he felt he did not enjoy his government's confidence in handling in Whitehall the principal issue in Greek-British relations, the Cyprus problem. Internal intrigues—in the Greek Foreign Service—may have also been involved. It should be noted that this diplomat who served in London as Ambassador of Greece since 1953 was vulnerable to such intrigue. For, faithful in the performance of his professional duties, he had never failed to caution his government since 1954 about the lack of adequate political means available to Greece for achieving the desired ends in Cyprus; about the dangers that lurked in a policy both of ignoring the Turkish factor with resultant harm to Greek-Turkish relations and of underestimating the intensity of British reactions; and about the tendency of overestimating U.S. support in this issue as well as of misconstruing the attitude of the British Labour party toward the Cyprus problem.

C. New Tensions in Greek-Turkish Relations

The news of the British government's decision to release Makarios from detention and its offer of a safe-conduct to Grivas and certain other EOKA members was received with surprise and apprehension in Turkish official circles and in the press, which had rejoiced at the news of his exile a year earlier. The Turkish government, however, assumed an outwardly reserved attitude toward this British decision and welcomed the assurances given that Makarios would not be allowed to go back to Cyprus and that the military and emergency measures would be continued in the island for the time being. It also reaffirmed its intention to abide by the terms of Resolution 1013 (XI) which, in its view, recommended tripartite negotiations as the appropriate procedure for dealing with the Cyprus problem.[37] Phenomena, though, similar to those of transference in individual psychology were soon observable both behind the scenes and publicly, with new tension in Greek-Turkish relations.[38]

In a long exchange of views on April 12 between the Greek Foreign Minister and U.S. Ambassador Allen, the latter started out by inquiring about the views of the Cypriot hierarchs—a topic that Averoff-Tossizza felt was not the main purpose of this meeting which Allen had requested. After listening to the Foreign Minister's reply, the Ambassador said that his government was worried about Turkey's attitude in the Cyprus question and asked the Foreign Minister to read a secret three-page cable received from Washington that morning. This cable conveyed to Allen the text of a note of the Turkish to the British government which had been delivered two days earlier. The note was drafted in a stiff tone (Averoff-Tossizza thought he could discern that it was in the style of the Turkish Ambassador in London, Nuri Birgi, strengthened at certain points with the touch of Turkish Foreign Minister Zorlu) and was a follow-through of an earlier note—with the rationale that Premier Adnan Menderes had been obliged to postpone a statement he wished to make before the Grand National Assembly, having received no reply to his first note.

Without any of the customary introductory niceties, the Turkish government, in this note, informed first the British government that the dissatisfaction in Turkey was such that the Turkish authorities had been obliged to take certain military and police measures in order to prevent the occurrence of unpleasant events. It then drew the British government's attention to its concern about recent developments in the Cyprus question, which had taken place without any consultation with the Turkish government. It expressed extreme dissatisfaction because of this and demanded that points of co-operation be explored in future if such points existed. The Turkish government also drew the British government's attention to possibly dangerous developments if the policy of retreating before the terrorist tactics of EOKA and of ignoring Turkish views were continued. In conclusion, it expressed the opinion that the yielding attitude of Britain, the intransigent attitude of Makarios and of other factors, and many other events proved daily that the symbiosis of the two ethnic groups in Cyprus under any form of self-government was impossible (a hint that Turkey, which had approved of the Radcliffe constitutional proposals, was reconsidering its attitude).

In comment, Averoff-Tossizza told Allen that this note, together with press reports and other information from Turkey, indicated that the Turks had been annoyed by the UN resolution and by the stand of the British government, and that they feared future developments, when the Labour party would come to power in Britain. They were playing a last card of blackmail in the hope of getting something now, because they realized they could get nothing later.

This was one possible interpretation, Allen replied. He feared, though, that it might not be a matter of blackmail but a sign of real displeasure, which could lead to very unpleasant developments.

The Foreign Minister observed that if he meant by unpleasant developments the hints the Turkish Ambassador in Athens, Settar Iksel, had dropped to him a few days earlier about the creation of a guerrilla movement among the Turks in Western (Greek) Thrace, he should not be worried. Such a movement would be almost stillborn. It would not have time to create problems.

Allen answered that this was one of his many worries but not the most serious one. His government feared that the Turks would make preparations for occupying certain islands of the Dodecanese, and, should Brit-

ain decide to withdraw from Cyprus, were determined to seize it by
military force. It was his personal opinion, he said, that the idea of a full
withdrawal from Cyprus was ripening in Britain. This process would be
greatly helped by anti-British attacks carried out in Turkey as well as by
a very stiff stand on the part of the Turkish government. The British
might one day, in some sort of face-saving procedure, for example
through the dispatch of an investigation commission to Cyprus, or even
without any pretext at all, cede their bases to NATO and send Cyprus to
the devil, because it had made them lose one friend after another without
any countervailing benefits. Allen insisted that this was a likelihood and
that in such a contingency it was believed that the Turks would hasten to
seize the island by military force.

Averoff-Tossizza replied that a similar thought had been conveyed to
him the previous summer—through Foy D. Kohler, then Counsellor of
the U.S. Embassy in Ankara. On that occasion, he had reacted in a very
lively fashion. But now he felt he could not react in the same way. The
facts that had followed the Anglo-French invasion of Egypt had convinced him that any Turkish attempt of the sort Allen had outlined
would create such an international furor that Turkey would become a
laughing stock, and the results would be extraordinarily grave. Kohler, it
should be explained, coming from Ankara after a fortnight's rest in
Rhodes and on his way to Washington, had continually stressed in a
conversation of August 8, 1956, with Averoff-Tossizza in Athens, that
though the contingency of a Turkish war against Greece was unlikely, it
was a case that should not be excluded. He had mentioned with particular insistence the possibility of the Turks seizing some of the Greek
islands in the Aegean and simultaneously denouncing the Lausanne
Treaty. And he saw no likelihood of an effective Greek reaction to such a
Turkish move. Averoff-Tossizza, however, asserted that if neither NATO,
nor another international organization, nor the United States itself effectively intervened within a few days in order to frustrate such an act of
violence by which one ally would seize territories of an unmixed ethnological composition belonging to another ally, the Greek reaction would
be more than decisive and effective. He was aware, he said (without
Kohler's contradicting him), that the Turkish general staff had studied
such an operation, but the Greek government, too, had studied how to
counteract such an improbable eventuality. In spite of Turkish naval
superiority, none of the Turkish naval vessels that would take part in
such operations would remain afloat. And regardless of the balance or
imbalance of land and air forces, the Greeks would be faithful to their
traditions and would attempt an operation in the direction of eastern
Thrace, with great hopes of success—because they would not be alone.
In this connection he insisted that if the Turkish attack took place and
the allies remained indifferent, the Greeks would not hesitate not just to
accept, but to ask for, aid from any state that offered aid. It should be
added that later, in September, 1956, the Turkish Ambassador in Athens,

Iksel, in talks with the Greek Foreign Minister, had repeatedly mentioned war as a means for solving the Cyprus question.

Allen, on his side, insisted that developments with regard to Turkish military action over Cyprus would not be the same as they had been in the case of the attack on Egypt. In Suez, there had been an invasion of a state, whereas in the case under discussion the invasion would occur at a point where a vacuum had been created,[39] and in a territory which seventy-eight years earlier had belonged to Turkey. The repercussion of public opinion would be different, especially in allied countries. He did not think that Greece could face such a contingency by relying on international public opinion and its weight.

The Greek Foreign Minister responded by saying that, of course, in this odd hypothesis, he did not rely on international public opinion for dealing with such a contingency. Most of all he relied on his certainty from earlier contacts that the Turks were fully aware that the Greek reaction would be swift and warlike. In consequence, they would also have to face risks of material damage, which would not be negligible. And it would be they who would have provoked a war, even though such a war were to remain limited and localized. But, beyond this, he was relying on a substantial percentage of international public opinion, which had the United Nations at its disposal. In that forum, international public opinion could be mobilized. And Greece, in such a case, undoubtedly would enjoy American support, because American public opinion, brimming over with indignation, would demand that the policy that had been followed against other aggressors be followed against Premier Menderes.

During this conversation, Allen sounded out the Foreign Minister about the possibility of Greek military action. Averoff-Tossizza did not remain unresponsive to this probe. He told him that Greek military action was excluded both in Cyprus or elsewhere. Only in the event of Turkish military action either against territory under Greek sovereignty or against Cyprus should it be considered certain.

The American Ambassador, turning to another subject that Kohler had broached in his talk with the Greek Foreign Minister the previous year, said his government had grounds for serious concern over the Patriarchate of Constantinople and the Greeks in Istanbul. The Turkish government was so annoyed that sudden measures against the Patriarchate ought not to be excluded. Averoff-Tossizza replied that he, too, had received disturbing reports on the subject. His government was doing all it could to avoid anything that could be construed as a provocation, but it could not wait for what the government-guided Turkish mobs or even the Turkish government itself would do. Because the Patriarchate and the Greeks of Istanbul lived under a Damoclean sword, he added, the possibility of solving the Cyprus question by an exchange of the Turks in Cyprus for the Greeks in Istanbul might be explored. This, Allen responded, would be an excellent idea. It would help stabilize

Greek-Turkish relations, because the questions of Cyprus and of the Greeks and the Patriarchate in Istanbul constituted a permanent threat to these relations and to Greek-Turkish co-operation. He doubted, however, whether the Greek government would be able to impose internally such a solution, and whether the Turks, in spite of the removal of their community from Cyprus, would be able to cease having an interest in that island which lay so close to Turkey.

Averoff-Tossizza replied that on the Greek side so great was the desire for a solution of the Cyprus question and so vivid the awareness of the dangers that the Greeks in Istanbul faced, that these matters could be dealt with in agreement with the Opposition. On the Turkish side, however, the maintenance of an interest in Cyprus even after the Turkish community was removed from the island would mean naked imperialism and inexcusable intransigence, because care could be taken to cover them in this sector, too—the sector of the military reasons which Turkey invoked when it spoke of the possibility of its encirclement by Greece. Allen agreed that the Foreign Minister was quite right in what he said, but this did not mean that the Turkish view changed—that Turkey, namely, was suffocating, as it were, in the embrace of the Greek islands. Unfortunately, Averoff-Tossizza retorted, it was not possible to alter the region's geographical configuration to please the Turks, toward whom Greece was showing considerable understanding but without any reciprocity. Indeed, he added, they showed so little understanding that they were planning to extend their territorial waters to twelve miles and announce this decision at the next meeting of the Foreign Ministers' Council of NATO, which was to meet at Bonn in May. In such a case surely there would be unpleasant discussions in the Council. Should the Turkish government reach such a decision, his government, too, he warned, would immediately announce the extension of Greek territorial waters to the same number of miles. American experts would then have to be called in to solve the resultant problem, which would be most complex. Allen said he, too, had received similar reports. He had asked the U.S. military attaché to bring him a map on which the twelve-mile territorial waters would be drawn in order to see what this meant.

Ambassador Allen went on to express his concern that the Greek government, by appearing to be too intransigent or by insisting in advance on too many details of a future solution of the Cyprus problem, might push the U.S. government into supporting partition of the island—which, of course, was not a good solution, but, in the absence of any understanding, could become one as a way out of a situation that poisoned the Alliance. Averoff-Tossizza replied that it might be a good idea to compare the news coming from both sides of the Aegean. On the one side, here he was telling Allen that the two Cypriot hierarchs just emerging from detention were speaking the language of conciliation and co-operation. On the other side, the Turks, with an arrogant air, "were doing us the favor of warning us that with difficulty they were protecting us from massacres and war." Allen agreed that the comparison was in favor of the Greeks. But this did not remove the difficulties. He agreed, too, that the Opposition in Greece was very reasonable. Venizelos, whose wisdom he praised, had told him recently, he said, that a solution of the Cyprus question should be sought in the creation of an independent state. When he—Allen—had observed that this would not be possible, because the Turks feared that the establishment of an independent Cyprus would merely be a step toward *enosis*, Venizelos had said that appropriate international guarantees should be given to Turkey that the island would never be united with Greece. This would not bother the Greeks at all, he had added, simply because a second Greece would have been set up in this way. Venizelos also had expressed the view that Makarios, in his recent statements, ought to have spoken with greater sympathy for the Turks. He would have advised him to propose that in any sort of self-government in Cyprus, the Turks, though constituting only 20 per cent of the population, should have 33 per cent of the power in their hands. This would disarm the Turks without in any way harming the Greeks.[40]

Averoff-Tossizza concurred with Allen's esteem for Venizelos' sound judgment and said he would take into account his views on the Cyprus question. It should be added that Allen, at one point during the conversation, when told that the Greek government might under certain circumstances become more intransigent than it was, inquired whether Greece might not resort to NATO in this matter or agree that the discussion in that organization be limited exclusively to the question of bases in Cyprus—so that the Greek government should not appear too intransigent to such an approach and hostile toward NATO. Averoff-Tossizza replied that as long as only the question of bases was involved, it would be possible to examine this matter with favor.

From this conversation, the Foreign Minister derived the impression that the American Ambassador had not tried to frighten the Greek government by his disclosures about the Turkish government's attitude but was merely speaking very frankly. His government really was worried about this development. This seemed evident from the way in which he had insisted on the view that the British might suddenly withdraw from Cyprus, and that Turkey, in such a case, would try to step in and seize it. Allen had wished to probe the intentions of the Greek government in such a contingency, which could be carried out by the British and Turkish governments acting in collusion. Quite possibly the State Department had instructed him to inform the Greek Foreign Minister about the Turkish note and to say what he had said in that exchange of views.

Two days after this conversation of April 12, the Greek Foreign Minister, evidently having reported to Premier Karamanlis the disturbing tenor of this talk, urgently asked the Turkish Ambassador in Athens to call on him at his home. He told him that according to not absolutely confirmed information but from good sources he had learned that disturbances were being planned in Izmir and Istanbul and were imminent. After drawing his attention to the consequences that such events would have on the future course of Greek-Turkish relations, he told him that his government felt that the anger of the Greek people had reached such a point that tactics of "tooth for tooth" and "eye for eye" would become unavoidable. He repeated this phrase twice, adding that his government would take all measures to protect the Turks in Greece as it would also take any other action necessary for protecting the dignity and rights of the country. Iksel replied he had no relevant information but promised to report back to Ankara this conversation. A friendly talk on the subject of Turkish finances followed.

Amid Turkish press charges that the Patriarchate in Istanbul was involved in political support of the Greek claims to Cyprus, and Turkish press demands that the Patriarch be ousted from Turkey,[41] Greek-Turkish tension rose further the following day, April 15, because of a direct *démarche* of the Turkish with the Greek government. It left its mark on the record of a meeting that took place at about 10:00 A.M. between Premier Karamanlis and the U.S. Ambassador, at the Premier's home, in the presence of the Greek Foreign Minister. Before the conversation started, Averoff-Tossizza had received a very urgent and important cable from Ankara. He read it rapidly offhand, and immediately communicated it to the Premier and then to Ambassador Allen. The latter seemed to be ignorant of neither the fact that this note was being sent to the Greek government nor of its contents. The gist of the Turkish note, which had been transmitted through the Greek chargé d'affaires in Ankara, was that if the welcome given by the Greek government to Archbishop Makarios when he arrived in Athens, was to be markedly official in form, the Turkish government would regard this as an unfriendly act and an unnecessary provocation.

In a controlled but rather tense tone, Premier Karamanlis immediately told Ambassador Allen that the Turkish provocations were not new. The dramatic events of Istanbul and Izmir of September, 1955, had been a highpoint of such provocations. The Turks continually interfered in a just Greek cause and regarded the caution shown by the Greek government as a sign of weakness. They believed they could reach the point of humiliating the Greeks and were assuming an ever more threatening attitude. He himself, in spite of his own character, had been extremely patient. He waited in the hope that, after the arrival of Makarios in Athens, it would be possible to proceed toward a reasonable solution of the Cyprus question, which would allow Greece to restore, with the passage of time, its good relations with Turkey. The Turks, however, a few days before Makarios' arrival—probably in order to prevent the establishment of a common and reasonable line of action with the Ethnarch—were now presenting this note with its dire predictions which not only teemed with inaccuracies but was insulting as well. He no longer felt disposed to respond with excessive caution and patience. Because of its contents, this note would be returned to the Turkish government as unacceptable. And the stand of Greece would change decisively. The Turkish threats had repeatedly obliged the Greek government to take certain military measures. The number of such measures would multiply and, without anything being done to arouse anxiety, would be such as to permit Greece to wage war if war eventually broke out. The carrying out of Turkish threats to seize certain Greek islands would mean the immediate outbreak of a war, in which Greece would hurl itself with all the determination it could muster. The repetition of such threats, especially to third parties, obliged the Premier to consider what he should do. The American attitude indicated that the United States was not unable, but did not wish to bring Turkey to its right mind effectively. Because of this and because, too, the Turks had spoken to the Americans about the seizure of Greek islands, the Greek government was obliged, regardless of the alliances of which it remained a member, to start exploring in what way and through what combinations it could face the contingency of a war with Turkey. The Premier stated that he was well aware he was expressing shocking thoughts, but the situation of an ally threatening another ally under the eyes of the other allies was so shocking that it was only with shocking thoughts that he, too, would have to face the situation.

Premier Karamanlis also wished Ambassador Allen to know that, even if these threats were not carried out but others were—which seemed more likely—such threats could not remain unanswered. If events similar to those of Istanbul and Izmir of 1955 were to recur, or if the Patriarchate was driven out and measures were taken against the Greeks of Istanbul, Greece would not react as it had in the past. In the past it had reached the point of having albums published with photos of the atrocities committed during the Istanbul riots, but had finally refrained from circulating them. Today Greece would retaliate in kind, if not in the multiple. It would sever diplomatic relations with Turkey; it would resort to the UN Security Council; it would take measures against the Turks in Thrace (whom, at any rate, the Greek government would protect against individual retaliation and would not be the first to touch). All these measures and others, too, which he had not yet thought about at the moment, he would take forthwith. At any rate, he wished both the Allies and the Turks to know that he was determined not to accept any insult to the dignity of his country and would protect it by war if need be.

The situation, Premier Karamanlis went on to say, was extraordinarily disturbing and also unjustified. The Turks at that moment had no cause for complaint and certainly were not justified in speaking with insolence, because a pan-Hellenic committee in a state as free as Greece was preparing a reception for Archbishop Makarios. Nor would the Turkish stand be justified, even if the Greek government, on Makarios' return, were to draw up an intransigent line. Turkey would have at least a pretext then, but again no substantial justification, because even in case of intransigence, Greece would be saying: this is our thought on the matter, and our struggle will be waged by peaceful and diplomatic means. Turkey, however, even before a new line had been drawn up, declared, on the contrary, that it would resort to lawless and non-peaceful means. The situation, Karamanlis said, was intolerable, outrageous. He requested Ambassador Allen to inform his government of his decision to deal with matters in the ways he had explained.

Evidently worried, Ambassador Allen agreed that the Turkish note was bad and that the gesture was unfortunate. He was aware, too, of the Greek reaction. Without, however, wishing in any way to make suggestions, he hoped that the Greek government would not react in an emotional manner to this situation, but deal with it in the most intelligent way possible so as to put in a difficult position those who had committed this blunder. He himself promised to help as much as he could.

The evening of that same day, April 15, Foreign Minister Averoff-Tossizza, at his own request, called on Ambassador Allen at 8:30 and advised him about the Greek government's response to the Turkish note, which was termed "an unacceptable intervention in Greek domestic affairs." He also informed Allen that his Cabinet colleague, Constantine Tsatsos, Minister in Charge of the Premier's Office, had invited the directors of all Greek newspapers and had told them the government had reasons to believe that incidents might occur in Izmir and Istanbul. He urged them, therefore, to avoid publishing anything that Turkey might regard as a provocation. Allen said he particularly appreciated this action as one that testified to the Greek government's prudence and good will. Averoff-Tossizza further told Allen that what Premier Karamanlis had said that morning faithfully expressed the policy the Greek government would follow—to such an extent, indeed, that also the leaders of the Opposition, Venizelos and Papandreou, had been informed about it. Both Opposition leaders had agreed that Greece could respond only with war to the carrying out of the Turkish threats to seize Greek islands, or, with the other means which Karamanlis had mentioned, in case the other Turkish threats—against the Patriarchate or the Greeks in Istanbul— were fulfilled. The Foreign Minister also drew Allen's attention to the Premier's view that any threat voiced or even a complaint uttered by anyone before he (Karamanlis) had decided what line he would draw up in the Cyprus question after consulting with Makarios was unacceptable—the more so since, with the exception of a few superpatriots, the Greek government perceived that all persons playing a role in the Cypriot case were assuming a reasonable attitude. All showed full understanding of the difficulties inherent in the question and were prepared to discuss, in a spirit of absolute good will, a reasonable step-by-step solution, but in no case would they be willing to pull down their flag of freedom under any conditions. Asked by Allen what the two Opposition leaders had said when told of the Premier's attitude, Averoff-Tossizza replied that Papandreou had voiced no opinion but had limited himself to asking certain questions of minor importance. Venizelos, on the other hand, had said in front of Papandreou that he believed that self-determination for Cyprus was no longer feasible and, as he had told Allen, that the solution would be to set up in Cyprus an independent state, with its independence guaranteed by the United Nations, of which Cyprus would become a member.

The Greek government gained further insights into Turkish motivations, attitudes, and tactics on April 16 from a conversation between Foreign Minister Averoff-Tossizza and the Yugoslav Ambassador in Athens, Miso Pavicevic. A very highly placed Turkish official, whom the Yugoslav diplomat did not wish to name, had told the Yugoslav Ambassador in Ankara that the Cyprus problem had taken an unfavorable turn, and Turkey was very displeased. This high official, whom Averoff-Tossizza, during the course of the conversation, guessed was Premier Menderes himself, had said that the Turkish government refused and would always refuse to recognize any decision that would result from negotiations over Cyprus between the British and Greek governments or between the British government and Ethnarch Makarios. It would acquiesce only in tripartite negotiations. These could be carried out either directly or indirectly, through NATO, or through any other mediators. Nor would Turkey accept any form of self-government for Cyprus. As matters had developed, the Radcliffe draft constitution was already outdated, and Turkey could not accept it. The sole solution was through the island's partition. Without partition the Cyprus question would end very badly. Partition could be carried out *de facto* or *de jure*. The unnamed Turkish high official, in conclusion, had inquired in rather veiled terms whether the Yugoslav government, in view of the seriousness of the problem, might be willing to issue a statement to the effect that the partition of the island would constitute a desirable solution, as long as Greece and Turkey accepted it.

A few words are called for here about the background of the proposal of partition, which was the Cyprus solution the Turkish government was to favor throughout 1957—if not later—in a sort of *basso continuo* played against the Greek variations on the theme of self-determination. At least as early as the beginning of 1956, there had been indications that Turkish politicians and government officials had been thinking of dropping their original stand of insisting either on the maintenance of the status quo in Cyprus or on the island's cession to Turkey, and of demanding instead the territorial dismemberment or partition of the island, by invoking the same principle that the Greek government had invoked, namely that of self-determination. On February 25, in the Grand National Assembly, Hikmet Bayur, former secretary of Atatürk and Ambassador to Pakistan, while asserting that for the destinies of nations strategic and geopolitical reasons had ceased having importance, suggested the partition of Cyprus between Turkey and Greece just as India and Pakistan had partitioned their peninsula. Parts of the island opposite Turkey should go to Turkey. The rest could remain for the Greeks. Propaganda for partition should start immediately, he added. This view should be put forward at international conferences. In April of that same year an American expert in Turkish affairs told the author that a member of the Turkish Information Office in New York had disclosed to him that the Turkish government would propose the partition of Cyprus as a solution to the problem, in order to undermine the ethnological arguments of the Greeks. Then, on July 19, a Conservative Member of Parliament suggested in the House of Commons that partition ought to be seriously considered as a solution.[42]

Later that year, a long and interesting exchange of views between the Greek Foreign Minister and Ambassador Iksel in Athens on October 6 created the clear impression in the former's mind that the Turkish envoy wished on that occasion, among other things, to sound out the Greek government on the subject of partition as a solution to the Cyprus question. Averoff-Tossizza stated he could not even discuss this question, which a "certain English Lord" had proposed. When asked how the Greek people would react to such a solution, he replied he had spoken to no one about it, lest he were regarded as searching for an unlikely solution. Partition, instead of solving the problem, would create another problem. The Cypriots themselves, at any rate, would have to be asked about their views on the matter.

In reply to the Greek Foreign Minister's rather bantering counterquestion: how did he, the Turkish Ambassador, view such a solution, Iksel replied that such a principle had been applied in other parts of the world. In the case of Cyprus, it could either be very good or very bad: very bad, if the Russians wished to exploit it in order to continually create problems, and if Greek-Turkish relations were bad; very good, if these relations were good—in which case there could be protection of minorities on both sides and facilities for people to move voluntarily from one part of the island to the other. In response to another question of the Foreign Minister, he said he did not know how such a solution would be viewed in Turkey, but he thought, at that moment, that if in the case of an eventual solution it proved indispensable that the change-of-regime provisions should be clearer, this could be combined with a solution, according to which, when self-determination was decided, it would exclusively or at least primarily aim at the island's partition. Averoff-Tossizza again laughingly told him that at the most he could whisper with great caution to others about partition, to test their reaction, if this was conducive of getting out of a dead end. However, he could never do even that if partition were to put off indefinitely the matter of self-determination.

Before parting, the Foreign Minister stressed that he had carried out this discussion exclusively on his own account without having consulted either his government or his services. His exclusive purpose had been to exchange views, in order to see what points of contact might exist, upon which one might build. What had been said did not constitute the official position of his government, although, naturally, his capacity as Foreign Minister deprived the talks of the nature of an absolutely unofficial conversation. Finally, the proposal for partition, which, as suggested above, was of Turkish provenance, was put forward in the House of Commons on December 19, 1956, by Lennox-Boyd in the guise of a British commitment to double self-determination (i.e., to the application of the principle of self-determination separately for the Greeks and the Turks on the island) as one of the eventual options that the British government would consider when the international strategic situation permitted and self-government had been working satisfactorily.[43] That same day he had presented the Radcliffe draft constitution for self-government in Cyprus, having made it clear to the Greek government beforehand that the two proposals were linked, part of a whole.[44] Early in February, 1957, it should be added, the Greek government learned from its chargé d'affaires in London that Birgi, the Turkish Ambassador there, had told him that the British government, though it had communicated nothing to himself or to Ankara on the subject of partition, had prepared plans for a voluntary transfer of up to 100,000 Greek and Turkish Cypriots and for the maintenance of British bases in two zones of the island.

That the Turkish government, over a month before Lennox-Boyd made this statement of December 19, 1956, in the Commons, viewed with favor the solution of the Cyprus problem through the island's partition is indicated by the fact that a State Department official, E. R. Williams, on November 9, 1956, discussed what were then considered by Greek officials as "well-known rumors" about a British plan for the island's partition and said that the Turks and other NATO allies favored this plan but that the Hispaniola precedent invoked by the Turks was not at all encouraging in view of the tension in the relations between Haiti and the Dominican Republic.

This rather negative attitude of the U.S. government to such a solution of the Cyprus problem, it might be added, was reiterated by William M. Rountree, Assistant Secretary of State for Middle Eastern, South Asian, and African Affairs, on January 18, 1957 (i.e., after the Lennox-Boyd statement of December 19) in a conversation with the Greek Foreign Minister in Washington. In this conversation, which was attended also by Robert D. Murphy, Deputy Undersecretary of State, Rountree had said that he had studied this solution and believed it enclosed certain dangers even if the parties concerned were to agree to it.

On April 17, Foreign Minister Averoff-Tossizza and other Cabinet ministers, together with Archbishop Dorotheos, the primate of the autocephalous Orthodox Church of Greece, and President of the Pan-Hellenic Committee for Self-Determination for Cyprus (originally for *enosis*), joined in the enthusiastic welcome that was given to Archbishop

Makarios when he arrived by plane in Athens. As head of the ancient autocephalous church of Cyprus, Makarios was accorded the military honors normally given to Prime Ministers. It was commented abroad that the official welcome had been somewhat toned down in response to the Turkish warning of April 15. It was noted that Premier Karamanlis had not gone to the airport to receive the Archbishop but had called on him later that day.

The next day, Premier Menderes declared there could be no clearer proof of the Greek partnership with Archbishop Makarios than these demonstrations, "which had been organized by the Greek Government itself." The most noteworthy aspect of the matter, from the point of view of international norms and rules lay in the fact, he said, that the Greek government had participated officially in full force in the welcoming ceremonies. The Turkish Premier then termed the reception of Makarios in Athens "a deliberately inflated expression of the long-standing Greek aspiration for the annexation of Cyprus."

In response to Menderes' statement, the Greek Foreign Ministry, on April 19, issued a declaration to the effect that the Greek government did not intend to make any hasty judgment on, or draw premature conclusions from the Turkish Premier's words. It was hoped that these utterances had been made in a moment of nervous irritation. In point of fact, Mr. Menderes had made three important errors: First, in insolent terms appropriate to a Sultan, he had arrogated the right to criticize the Greek government's action in purely domestic matters. Second, he had drawn arbitrary conclusions from facts concerning foreign policy and had expressed himself publicly in a manner that lacked objectivity. Thus, he had damaged good-neighborly relations between Greece and Turkey. Third, the Premier had insulted the revered head of an independent Orthodox Church who was held in particular honor in Greece. The Greek government, however, would not follow the example of the Turkish Premier, but confined itself to pointing out that no people, and in particular the Greek people, could be provoked and insulted without making an appropriate retort.[45] A few days later, it was reported that the Greek government had instructed its representative at NATO headquarters to draw the attention of the organization to the high tension in Greek-Turkish relations.[46]

Efforts the Belgian Ambassador in Athens exerted to get the two parties together for a mutual explanation of the situation resulted in a meeting, at his home, between the Greek Foreign Minister and the Turkish Ambassador on April 22. Iksel said that in view of this meeting he had asked Ankara for instructions concerning what he should say both generally as well as in particular after the recent exchange of notes and statements between the Greek government and his own. On the basis of the cable he had received in response to his request, he stated that after a period of tension in the relations between Turkey and Greece, which had lasted for many months, a period of relaxation had followed. During that period, the Greek government and the Foreign Minister, in particular, had repeatedly uttered many courteous words to the Turkish government and had shown friendship and a good disposition. Concurrently, however, every effort was being exerted to promote the Cyprus question in a way that was opposed to the attitude that Turkey had assumed. And certain advantages had been gained. Turkey realized that this constituted a tactic. If the Turkish government left this tactic unanswered and did not act in accordance with its views, the Cyprus question could develop in such a way that a deeper rift would occur in Greek-Turkish relations. It was in that light, Iksel said, that the recent actions of the Turkish government ought to be viewed. The Turkish government had now decided to act in a way diametrically opposed to the Greek government's actions, since the latter insisted on a solution of the Cyprus problem that Turkey would not accept. After this summary of his instructions, Iksel referred to the reception accorded to Archbishop Makarios as indicative of the Greek government's solidarity with him.

To these opening remarks of the Turkish Ambassador Averoff-Tossizza replied by saying that the tactics of friendly manifestations corresponded to his own personal convictions, which for many years were known in Turkey and which Premier Menderes himself, Foreign Minister Zorlu, and Birgi, Ambassador of Turkey in London, had recognized. It was, therefore, odd that they should now say that these friendly manifestations were resorted to for the purpose of promoting more effectively the Cyprus question. He had believed and still believed that Greek-Turkish friendship was most useful for both countries, and it was with great sorrow that he was witnessing the loosening of these ties and the ruination of the structure which, in an altogether incredible manner, Eleftherios Venizelos and Kemal Atatürk had set up seven years after the war which had ended a long period of Greek-Turkish discord. As matters were now developing, however, one had dark forebodings about the future. If exchanges such as those that had most recently occurred were to continue, if Turkey believed it could speak to Greece as it had spoken, if Turkey felt it could behave toward Greece as much greater powers behaved toward weaker states, then from one word to another such an atmosphere might be created that words would inevitably be followed by deeds. The tone of the Turkish communication of April 15 as well as the astonishing public statement of Premier Menderes three days later could not but arouse reactions which, if continued, would make it hard to avoid the severance of diplomatic relations. The Turkish Ambassador agreed that such a danger of rupture of diplomatic relations existed.

At this meeting of April 22 with the Turkish Ambassador, Averoff-Tossizza observed further that his government had given no cause for offense. It had shown forbearance and not only had it refrained from reciprocating in kind, but, in order to maintain diplomatic ties, it had not sought to exploit the events to its advantage, as it could have. Despite all these unpleasant manifestations, the Greek government had not taken the initiative. Whereas the Turkish government spoke most provocatively, the Greek government replied in a restrained tone. Perhaps Turkey, feeling more powerful than Greece, was, for that very reason, tempted to speak as it did. This criterion, however, could lead very far; therefore, it was dangerous. At any rate, the Turkish government should know that on the Greek side this was not acceptable.

Ambassador Iksel replied that his government thought that it was the Greeks who were acting provocatively. Greece, ignoring Turkey, had raised the Cyprus question. Greece had proclaimed its solidarity with Makarios, who was the leader of EOKA and, apparently, was mixed up in EOKA. Although the Greek government was aware of the Turkish government's opposition to Makarios' tactics, it had organized for him a huge reception.

To Averoff-Tossizza's remarks, which were rather lively in tone, that Iksel was interfering in an internal matter by referring to Makarios' reception in Athens, and that this reception had not been organized by the Greek government, which had been merely represented at it, the Turkish Ambassador responded by denying he was interfering in internal Greek affairs. This reception had been important mainly from the viewpoint of foreign policy. Besides, he maintained, the organization of the reception by the Greek government was crystal clear. Iksel then went on to charge that Makarios' speech in Athens had been extremely intransigent. Greek foreign policy, too, and the Greek government's solidarity with Makarios likewise testified to an intransigent stand. Averoff-Tossizza rebutted this argument.

The discussion, thus, arrived at the focal point: the Cyprus question, the sole but gravest cause of the deterioration in Greek-Turkish relations. The Turkish Ambassador repeated the views that his Yugoslav colleague in Athens six days earlier had disclosed to the Greek Foreign Minister as coming from an unnamed high Turkish official in Ankara—Premier Menderes himself, in the Foreign Minister's guess. Iksel, namely, said, that for Turkey it was no longer a question of self-determination or of self-government for Cyprus, nor even of acceptance of the Radcliffe draft constitution for solving the Cyprus problem. Partition of the island was the only possible solution. Insisting on the advantages of partition as a most ethical solution of the problem that would settle matters the soonest, he developed the following points: First, one more frontier between Greece and Turkey would not constitute a disadvantage. Second, partition would not kill Cyprus economically, because a regime of economic communications would be set up between the two parts of the island. And third, the Greeks had wrongly linked this solution with an exchange of populations, because the populations would remain where they were under a system of minority protection on both sides. Merely the voluntary movements of Turks from the Greek part to the Turkish part, and of Greeks from the Turkish part to the Greek part would be facilitated.

Stimulated by a remark on the part of Averoff-Tossizza concerning a solution the Greek Minister had rejected on an earlier occasion, Iksel said further that his government could not envisage a solution either of partition through a plebiscite that would take place after a period of self-government or of independence, because, after the Turks had lived for some years under an essentially Greek administration, how many of them would dare express themselves in favor of partition of the island? The Turkish arguments against self-government or independence, the Greek Foreign Minister had no difficulty in rebutting, he felt. The Turkish Ambassador's response, he observed, merely proved his lack of confidence in the desire of the Turks of Cyprus for partition of the island.

After quite a lengthy and detailed discussion, the Greek Foreign Minister told the Turkish Ambassador that he was faced by an altogether intransigent Turkish policy that accepted nothing else except partition, and immediate partition at that. The Greek government, for many reasons, could not accept this solution. As he had told him in the past, if the Greek government decided to support partition as a solution to the Cyprus problem, it would be unable to act, because it would be immediately overthrown, since the Greeks of Greece and of Cyprus considered such a solution most distasteful. Iksel countered by saying that the Greek government, by an appropriate propaganda, could persuade the people to accept such a solution. He then reverted to the question of Makarios, terming him a very intransigent person, the organizer of EOKA, and manipulator of the Church for political purposes. Since Greek policy depended on what the hierarchs of Cyprus and of Greece would say and Greek policy generally was subordinated to the Church, it was very difficult for the Turkish government to negotiate with the Greek government, he said. Averoff-Tossizza, needless to say, refuted these views as he thought they deserved. During the conversation, which lasted for two hours, Averoff-Tossizza mentioned a few items of a gossipy nature concerning, for example, the explanations Menderes had given to a foreign ambassador about the reasons that Premier Karamanlis had not gone to the airport to welcome Makarios on his arrival in Athens—Iksel seemed annoyed.

The general conclusions the Greek Foreign Minister reached after this conversation were that there was a deepening rift in Greek-Turkish relations and a decision on the part of the Turkish government to achieve whatever was possible in the near future by a determined and unyielding attitude. It was clear that the Turks felt they had lost ground in the Cyprus question and were greatly concerned about this. They also realized that in Britain the Conservative government was shaky and that the likely rise to power of the Labour party would create an unfavorable perspective from their viewpoint, and very shortly, too. At any rate, they had a feeling that time was not working in their favor. This Turkish attitude, Averoff-Tossizza predicted, would not change soon, unless the Turkish government had to face the pressure of far greater and more powerful factors.

Two days later on April 24, at an official dinner in honor of Ambassador Iksel who was leaving his Athens post, both he and the Greek Foreign Minister exchanged their familiar views on the Cyprus question, together with profuse assurances that both governments attached great importance to the state of their mutual relations. Iksel was even more categorical on this chapter than he had been in the past. The creation of the Common Market, he added, was an additional reason for close co-operation between Greece and Turkey, because it created a serious threat to the economies of both countries. Concerning the Cyprus question, he again insisted, courteously this time, that partition was the only solution to the problem. He placed special emphasis on its advantages. At one point he mentioned that if the Greek government insisted so much on the application of the principle of self-determination in the case of the people of Cyprus, the Turkish government would conclude that it would also raise the issue of self-determination in the case of the islands of Imroz (Imbros) and Boczaada (Tenedos), two small Turkish islands at the southwest mouth of the Dardanelles. There, too, he said, the Greek population was in a majority: indeed, in one of these islands, to a greater ratio than in Cyprus. Because he insisted so much, Averoff-Tossizza replied that, though he had told him on another occasion that both those islands had been dealt with in the Treaty of Lausanne, he would venture as a personal view, upon which, moreover, he was prepared to undertake a personal commitment, that if it were possible to solve the Cyprus question on the basis of the known Greek approaches to the matter, he would agree to support the view that this solution be accompanied by Greek agreement to receive the Greeks of Imroz and Boczaada in Greece without requesting anything in exchange, either from the viewpoint of a population of equal size or of any other nature. This statement, Averoff-Tossizza thought, had impressed Iksel somewhat. He did not believe, however, that Iksel would try to exert any influence in Ankara in favor of such a *quid pro quo,* because his mind was so much fixed on the idea of partition. Toward the end of their talk, Iksel warned the Greek Foreign Minister against seeking a solution which would be based on the concept of setting up Cyprus as an independent state, under any form whatsoever. He did not believe it was possible to build upon such an idea. Averoff-Tossizza responded smilingly that this was another sign of intransigence.

Earlier that same day, the Greek Foreign Minister had met the U.S. Ambassador at his home. The latter had communicated to him the contents of a State Department cable instructing him to convey to Ethnarch Makarios the opinion of the U.S. government that he should go to London as soon as possible with the request to try to find a solution there of the Cyprus problem in a co-operative spirit. Allen was also instructed to emphasize that the United States would not understand the Greek government's adamancy in refusing to have the Cyprus question brought up in NATO for examination there in the way Lord Ismay had proposed. With regard to the latter, Averoff-Tossizza remarked that his government well understood why it did not wish to resort to NATO. It would go there only if the framework within which a solution would be given had been defined. Without committing his government, but expressing his personal view, the minimum required for accepting NATO's good offices would be some guarantee that the recommendations made there would exclude partition as a solution to the Cyprus problem. Allen seemed specially attentive to this suggestion.

During the discussion that followed, the U.S. Ambassador turned to the partition issue without expressing himself about it unfavorably, as he had done in the past. When the tension in Greek-Turkish relations was mentioned, he asked Averoff-Tossizza whether it was true that he intended to request the arrest of seven Turks of Thrace and their trial—a report he had received from his services that morning. The Foreign Minister replied that an important Greek personality had been arrested among other Greeks in Istanbul, and he intended to order that the files be searched for the names of any Turks in Greece who were engaged in anti-Greek acts. His government's tactics were to retaliate in kind to Turkish provocations. Ambassador Allen reacted courteously but firmly. He advised greater *sang-froid*. One action could lead to another. The Greek government should preserve for itself the advantage of a wise policy.

At this point, the American Ambassador started the exposition of a viewpoint that astonished the Greek Foreign Minister and, together with reports from the Greek Embassy in Washington, led him to think that perhaps the attitude of the U.S. government toward Greece was changing. Allen said that the remark Averoff-Tossizza had so often made that the Greek government had been conciliatory whereas the Turks were intransigent [47] was not quite correct. The Turks, at the outset, had favored the maintenance of the status quo in Cyprus. With great persistence they had supported this view, stating that if the status quo were to be done away with, then Cyprus should revert to where it had belonged before its seizure by the British. Although, then, they had strongly fought on that basis, they were now making an important concession. They would be satisfied, they said, with only part of the island. This approach, they contended, should constitute the basis for a definitive solution of the Cyprus problem. The issue would no longer be left in suspense, with all the undesirable consequences of this suspense for more general policy, they pointed out further. Thus, the Greek government should accept that the Turks, too, on their side, considered they had been conciliatory and maintained in good faith that it was the Greek government that was intransigent, because it had brought about changes in its policy without ever renouncing the final goal of its Cyprus policy.

In a rather friendly tone, the Greek Foreign Minister rebutted these arguments and explained how the matter had started and how, from concession to concession and with full recognition of the need to cover the legitimate interests of Turkey in Cyprus, the Greek government had arrived at proposals which were internally dangerous to itself while externally facilitating a solution. He also stressed the provocative attitude of the Turkish government in words and deeds and observed that until recently his government had not exploited this attitude nor had even reacted to it.

On his side, the U.S. Ambassador, though agreeing that the Greek government had behaved very well toward the Turks in Thrace in spite of Turkish provocations, whereas the Turks had behaved very badly, insisted that in the matter of the intransigence of the Greek and Turkish governments it was not easy to maintain that only one of the parties had shown a spirit of compromise. The Turkish nervousness of recent weeks was rather justified, he added, because from the start of the UN debates the Turkish government felt it had lost several rounds in the Cyprus case and, indeed, some of them because of the intervention of Britain and the United States. Consequently, the Greek government, which found itself in a somewhat victorious position in the Cyprus question, should not respond to this nervousness, so as to maintain its advantageous position.

D. Greek-Soviet Confrontation over Nuclear Bases

The attitude of the Greek government earlier, in April, 1957, toward the leading state of the other great power bloc is revealed in a conversation that took place on April 3 at the Greek Foreign Ministry between the Greek Foreign Minister and the Soviet Ambassador in Athens, Mikhail Sergeev, at the latter's request. After speaking about many minor matters concerning especially the cultural and tourist relations between Greece and the U.S.S.R., in which the Foreign Minister gave satisfaction, and after making many inquiries about the Cyprus question, Sergeev asked for information about reports to the effect that Greece intended to cede nuclear bases on its territory.

Averoff-Tossizza replied he knew nothing about this matter, which had never been raised with his government. He supposed, he said, that such reports had been published because of analogous matters raised in other countries. However, in view of Sergeev's particular persistence, the Foreign Minister told him it was not unlikely that the problem would be posed, because Greece did have allied obligations, which it did not ignore, even though concurrently it was conducting a friendly policy toward the U.S.S.R., many tangible examples of which he had given that morning. Sergeev hastened to observe that it would be good if such a subject were not posed, because the Americans, fearing nuclear war, sought to set up nuclear bases in other countries so that retaliation, which these bases would provoke, could not touch their own country, but other countries. After replying two or three times, avoiding the substance of the matter and insisting that the question had not come up, Averoff-Tossizza felt obliged to touch on the matter's substance, since the Soviet Ambassador stressed with such particular insistence that, in case of a nuclear war, retaliation against countries which had nuclear bases on their territory would be catastrophic, and responsible politicians should be aware of this and take measures to avoid it.

Very calmly, the Greek Foreign Minister told the Soviet Ambassador that the factor of danger could not be used on Greece, because Greece had never taken that factor into account. This was one of the rare times, he said, that he felt he was not speaking merely in the name of the present Greek government but also in the name of succeeding Greek governments which would continue a NATO policy and a policy of concurrent friendship toward the Soviet bloc. He was fully aware that the dangers of a nuclear war were not the usual ones of war as known before the atomic era. However, either one was a member of an alliance and fulfilled the obligations that flowed from it, or one was not a member of it at all. It was likely that NATO would ask Greece for other bases, and if it did, this request would be examined from the viewpoint of the defense needs of the country and of its allies. If the Greek government concluded that it had to accept them, it would do so regardless of the concomitant dangers.

After the Soviet diplomat again insisted on the magnitude of the danger involved—it was clear from his calm tone that on the instruction of his government he was issuing this warning—the Greek Foreign Minister observed that in October, 1940, the situation for Greece was suicidal, because the U.S.S.R. was, more or less, an ally of the Axis, and the Axis, at any rate, had nothing to fear on the part of the U.S.S.R. because of the Moscow agreements, as it also had nothing to fear on the part of the United States, which in no way desired to enter the war and probably would not have entered it, had it not suffered the terrible provocation of Pearl Harbor fourteen months later. At the time the whole of Europe was occupied by the Axis and was working for it, and Britain was on her knees, suffering daily bombings, Greece, which had a dictator at its head whom it did not love, had decided without any hesitation not to reckon with the dangers that, though not of the same quality, were more or less the same in extent as those of an atomic war. A people with such precedents clearly could not react to future eventualities but on the basis of its obligations and of its broader conception about its own history, not on the basis of the magnitude of the material danger.

Leaving the Ministry of Foreign Affairs together, the Greek Minister and the Soviet Ambassador found themselves before a great crowd of reporters who asked whether the latter had delivered a note concerning the question of nuclear bases. Averoff-Tossizza categorically denied that he had. He also denied that the question had been discussed. When two reporters remarked that the news about the delivery of such a note had come from the Soviet Embassy, Sergeev did not react. When questioned, he replied that he did not understand Greek, but it was well known he spoke Greek very well indeed.

Later that same day, meeting the U.S. Ambassador in connection with another matter, the Greek Foreign Minister told him about his conversation with Sergeev, which, in the light of the Soviet announcement a few months later about the successful test of an ICBM, and the launching of the first Sputnik on October 4, might have been an effort to forestall the contingency of the Greek government's granting the U.S. government the permission to set up in Greece Intermediate Range Ballistic Missiles (IRBM's) to counteract the temporary Soviet advantage in rocketry. Allen expressed his deepest satisfaction. Averoff-Tossizza told him he would continue a policy of friendship toward the U.S.S.R. in economic and cultural matters, but on basic subjects, such as the common defense, he would maintain the same determined attitude in accordance with the basic line of the Greek government. Later that month, at a press conference on April 12, General Lauris Norstad, Supreme Commander of NATO, stated in reply to questions concerning rockets that there were not many IRBM's in NATO Europe and that he did not believe that Soviet IRBM's constituted an immediate threat to any NATO member.[48]

The question the Soviet Ambassador had raised on April 3, together with certain other foreign policy items, became the subject of debate in the Greek Parliament between May 20–24. Summing up the views he had expressed to Sergeev, the Foreign Minister recounted that he had told him that Greece had no nuclear bases on its territory and none had been requested of the Greek government. In response to the Soviet Ambassador's insistence to learn what the Greek government intended to do if faced with such a request, he had said that his government, having in mind national interests, would decide as a sovereign state on whether it should accede to such a request. He had also observed, he said, that the Soviet *démarche* constituted an intervention in Greek internal affairs.[49]

In this debate the leaders of two center Opposition parties, unlike the left wing, did not disapprove of the Foreign Minister's stand in this matter, though Papandreou, of the Liberal party, stated that if nuclear bases were to be the general rule for all states of the Free World, Greece, too, should share in the danger involved.[50] In other words, should there be greater dispersal it should be to a maximum—not on a selective allied basis.

Apotropaically, on the other hand, the leaders of EDA, the United Democratic Left, who, in effect, were acting as spokesmen of the outlawed Communist party of Greece (KKE) and as intermediaries of Soviet foreign policy, charged the government with wanting to grant nuclear bases to "the foreigners," and to have Greece join in the "dance of death" and become victim of a nuclear holocaust. One of them incidentally observed that nuclear bombs made no distinction between leftists and rightists. At great length, in comparison with the pro-Western political leaders in the Greek Parliament, EDA spokesmen dwelt on the grave dangers of nuclear bases on the territory of small states. They referred to recent statements by Nikolai A. Bulganin, Chairman of the Council of Ministers of the U.S.S.R., that small states ran the risk of obliteration in a nuclear encounter. In their support of Soviet nuclear diplomacy at the dawn of the ICBM age but prior to the Polaris epoch, EDA leaders contended that the Great Powers, by asking for bases on the territory of small states, were seeking to divert from their own territory the opponent's nuclear strikes. Agreeing to the establishment of such bases on Greek territory, they maintained, would run counter to the argument that NATO was merely an alliance for defense. In case of a nuclear war, the shift from defensive to offensive action was instantaneous. The purpose of Ambassador Sergeev's *démarche* of April 3, they explained, had been merely to inform the Greeks that whether or not they were members of NATO was their business, but they should not grant nuclear bases to other states that would enable the latter to carry out nuclear strikes against the U.S.S.R. Small states risked becoming like a chunk of meat thrown to the wild beasts, which was always devoured but allowed the thrower to escape. Nuclear bases on the territory of other states should not be permitted or, if they existed already, should be abolished. Did nuclear bases exist in Greece already? Even if they did not, how about the U.S. Sixth Fleet which was in Greece "all the time"? Was that not a nuclear base? With such arguments and rhetoric, the left-wing leaders in the Greek Parliament sought further to jolt Greek morale and confidence in the West, which was already undermined because of the Allied stand in the Cyprus question.[51]

On this occasion, Opposition leaders also criticized the Greek government's adherence, on May 2, to the "Eisenhower Doctrine." They stressed the dangers of involvement in Middle East hostilities and in matters that divided the Arab world. By acceding to this "Doctrine," Greece had dropped its opposition to the Baghdad Pact, of which the new U.S. policy statement was but a continuation. Thus, the antagonists in the Cyprus controversy, Britain and Turkey, had been strengthened, while Egypt and Syria, which opposed the "Doctrine," had been antagonized. At least, in adhering to this statement of U.S. policy, the Greek government should have obtained in exchange assurances of American support in the Cyprus question.[52]

President Eisenhower, it will be recalled, had enunciated this doctrine on January 5, 1957. This statement represented a response to the collapse of British influence in the Middle East after the Suez fiasco of late autumn, 1956. It reflected the great concern of the U.S. government, lest the U.S.S.R. be tempted to fill the vacuum there by launching direct action. Although it included proposals for economic as well as military aid to states occupying this vital area in world politics, the "Eisenhower Doctrine," duly blessed by Congress, succinctly suggested that the

United States was now consciously extending its security commitments to the Near and Middle East and was ready to fight, if necessary, to keep that area from going Communist as a result of military aggression. This meant that the U.S. government, more than ever before, was vitally interested in maintaining and strengthening the cohesion of NATO's southeastern flank, which the Cyprus dispute threatened to disrupt.

Chapter Three

Deadlock:

Greece Opts for a UN Battle

A. *A Complete Cessation of EOKA Operations?*

During their conversation of April 24, the U.S. Ambassador asked the Greek Foreign Minister about the possibilities both of a complete cessation of EOKA's activities and of Grivas' departure from Cyprus. Such developments, he believed, would help make progress in the Cyprus question. Averoff-Tossizza replied that, aside from the usual information he had from Cyprus, he could not know much more. EOKA's activities had stopped, at any rate, and Greek propaganda favored continuation of this lull. As long as the matter of possible solutions through negotiations remained in suspense, he saw no reason for EOKA's activities to start again. Concerning the matter of Grivas' departure from Cyprus, he knew nothing. However, he did not consider it likely, unless a solution seemed to emerge—even if that solution were only of a relatively satisfactory character—and, especially, unless an amnesty was granted to all those who had worked with Grivas, and Makarios was allowed to return to Cyprus. Allen inquired then about the state of Grivas' health because of reports he had that the Colonel was suffering from a heart ailment. The Foreign Minister replied that he, too, had received similar reports, but these had been denied. Apparently, Grivas himself spread such reports on purpose, in order to get British forces to search for many days in regions where he was supposed to be lying sick.[1] According to his information, Grivas was not only in excellent health but had at his disposal abundant means. With difficulty he was restrained from starting action again.

The covert, unavowed, "black" aspects of the Cyprus question—the relations between the Greek government, Makarios, and Grivas, which Ambassador Allen had lightly touched upon in his inquiry—had been developing meanwhile somewhat along the following lines. Lennox-Boyd's refusal on March 20 to accept Grivas' truce offer of March 14, and his efforts to obtain assurances that EOKA violence would altogether cease and to get rid of its leader and its cadres still at large by promising a safe-conduct for them if they wished to leave the island, quite naturally constituted a proper subject for Grivas himself to consider. In a letter of April 3, which the Greek Consul-General in Nicosia conveyed to Athens, Grivas suggested that if it was felt expedient to give the British government a way out for negotiations on the substance of the Cyprus question, the complete cessation of the struggle might be advisable, provided the negotiations were based on the recognition of the principle of self-determination for the people of Cyprus. Without such an explicit condition, on the other hand, the definitive windup of the struggle would render the British government more intransigent than before.

To Grivas' great indignation, however, a letter he received on April 5 though the Greek Consul in Nicosia (dated, it appears, April 2, the day before Grivas sent his own letter) indicated that if Grivas regarded it expedient, the Greek Foreign Ministry had no objection to the ending of his activities. This could be publicly announced the day of Makarios' arrival in Athens. Perhaps a proclamation on Grivas' part announcing such a decision could be prepared. Makarios, of course, would be consulted on this matter. Replying that same day, the leader of EOKA denied he had ever written that he would halt the struggle and leave Cyprus. In his letter of April 3 he had merely stressed, he wrote, that the decision to cease the struggle was not his but the political leadership's business. "My dropping the struggle," he added, "as long as the necessary guarantees for a successful solution of the Cyprus question were not assured, would constitute desertion, and I am not capable of such a shameful act." The letter he received in reply, on April 8, infuriated him still more. The Greek Consul wrote that he supposed his government, in drafting its reply, had been under the impression created by newspaper reports that Grivas was about to be captured. Its attitude had been dictated by a sincere desire to prevent this from happening. "My personal security," Grivas replied stiffly to this note, "cannot be the price for ending the struggle. It is preferable for me to fall honorably [on the field of battle] than to surrender, as the British government demands." Summing up the thoughts he had expressed in previous communications, he reiterated that the complete cessation of his activities "would be justified only as long as the indispensable conditions for a favorable solution of the Cyprus problem were assured through the diplomatic channel." Otherwise it would be preferable to continue the struggle until the next session of the Assembly. He had the means to do so, but his capabilties would be enhanced if he were strengthened in matériel. He also warned the Greek government that if the foe did not halt his operations, he would shortly resume his activities. The armed struggle would be combined with passive resistance.

Complaining to Ethnarch Makarios, in a letter of April 9, about the Greek government's attitude, Grivas charged it with lack of frankness and honesty in its conduct toward the people of Cyprus. The Greek government should make up its own mind and say one of two things: that it was interested in the Cyprus question or that it did not believe that this cause should dictate its foreign policy. If it took the latter course, "we would know that the Cypriot question would never be solved by diplomatic means, and then we would take our own stand." Instead of making such an honest and frank admission, however, the government was trying by various devices "to make it impossible for us to continue our struggle, and to bring about its cessation—all this without letting us know what is the purpose of such cessation." In conclusion, Grivas, admitting he was quite upset, informed the Ethnarch of the Consul's suggestion that he issue a proclamation on the eve of the original date of Makarios' arrival in Athens, and expressed the fear lest the purpose of this suggestion had been to place Makarios before a *fait accompli*.[2]

Three days later, April 12, Grivas received a letter from "Isaakios"—the Greek Foreign Minister's pseudonym in this correspondence, as Grivas has revealed in his memoirs [3]—who acknowledged receipt of his note and said he had not yet reached any conclusions and could say nothing until he had conferred with the Ethnarch. With regard to Grivas' fate, "Isaakios" expressed deep anxiety. This was not a matter merely of sentiment, but of importance for the cause itself. "Your loss would be a mortal blow from many angles. Today, a Marshal of the British Empire was unable to vanquish you, and you and the Cypriot people have been victorious. This allows various ways of handling the question—which would be impossible without your legendary feats. . . . You have glorified the name of the Greek soldier." This fulsome praise, however, did not soothe the irritation Grivas felt at these expressions of solicitude and anxiety for his own safety.[4]

While Governor Harding was insisting that Grivas should get out of the island, the Foreign Office felt that since EOKA had become inactive and its liquidation was regarded to be a matter of a few weeks or at the most a few months, to release Makarios had been a great mistake, because it created the impression of a Greek victory and of British inability to deal with Grivas. As for the Greek government, it had still not decided, much to Grivas' continued annoyance, whether a complete cessation of EOKA's struggle should be announced. On April 18, the day after Makarios' triumphant arrival in Athens, Grivas received a note from the Greek Consul in Nicosia to the effect that if such complete cessation of activities was decided upon, the Ethnarch himself would announce it. The British, Grivas was told in this note, were preparing to suspend their own operations.[5]

On April 22, however, EOKA's leader received two letters dated April 17 and 18 from the Greek Consul-General in Nicosia, Vlachos. In the first of these, the Greek Foreign Minister was reported as agreeing with Grivas' views. As matters stood, he believed it was to the national interest that he should stay on in Cyprus. In spite of that, it could not be ignored that the loss of Grivas through a heroic death would be a terrible blow for the cause. In the second of these notes, Grivas was told that Makarios had been informed about the situation and that he agreed that the truce should be strictly maintained in spite of any possible provocations. To these two notes Grivas replied by pointing out that the unilateral truce was being maintained at the expense of the cause, because the foe could concentrate all his operations on one spot, without being harassed, and was carrying out extensive operations.[6]

Some days later, Grivas received a letter dated April 24 from his normal superior, the Ethnarch himself, in reply to his own letter to him of April 9. After expressing his pride and satisfaction in the Colonel's superb struggle and saying that the gratitude of Cyprus to him would always be immense—"you have become," he wrote, "a legend and a symbol"—Makarios wrote he thought the truce was an excellent idea. The question now arose, however, of whether the truce should be definitive. After the UN resolution had been adopted, he believed that a peaceful atmosphere should be created for bipartite talks. "We never entertained the belief that you would militarily defeat the British, but we believed that by your armed action you would make an international issue out of our cause, so as to force, if possible, a political solution in accordance with our demand for self-determination. The first objective has been achieved; the second, not yet. And in this we face many difficulties, which we shall try to overcome. The question, though, arises: in view of the present situation (from the Cypriot and international viewpoint) is the further continuation of the armed struggle to our interest or not? I am not absolutely well informed," Makarios continued, "about the situation in Cyprus. From what I understand, though, I sincerely believe that some way must be found to end operations without any detriment to your own prestige." In conclusion, the Ethnarch sought to get Grivas' views on this issue. When conveying this message to Grivas, the Greek Consul advised him that the Foreign Minister was in agreement with the Ethnarch's views.[7]

At this moment of difficult decision in Athens, Grivas replied to Makarios' letter on April 27, taking a "hard" line. In this long missive, EOKA's leader blamed the Greek political leadership for not having achieved a political solution, and alleged it had not sufficiently exploited EOKA's successes. The political leadership in Greece was more interested in alliances with those who always begged in times of danger but kicked aside the ally as soon as the danger passed and the moment arrived for sharing the fruits of victory, he asserted. What particularly disturbed him was the myopia of the politicians when confronted by the dangers of their tactics of going against the will of the people and of keeping the people tightly bound to various alliances, which they detested because they detested those who were their comrades in arms in these alliances. Who the Ethnarch's informants were about the situation in Cyprus, he did not know. But, he believed, they were the least suited persons to serve as such. The Ethnarch, Grivas wrote, had been surrounded by the decay of the cities and by those who remained opportunist observers, whereas the decent worker, the peasant, and generally the toiler were not being heard. He had been surrounded by the press, which, in order not to be closed down, was carrying huge headlines about the successes of the security forces, while putting into a corner in small type the successes of EOKA. He had been surrounded by the so-called elite who not only took no part in the struggle but were angered whenever curfews interrupted their easy life. He had been surrounded by those who, because of their position in society, should have protested about the atrocious crimes being committed against the life and property of the struggling people, but preferred to remain silent in order not to be shut up in concentration camps. One recommendation he wished to make to the Archbishop: that he should take no decision until he contacted the really struggling people of the island.

Coming now to the issue involved, Grivas maintained in this letter of April 27 to Makarios that unless all the necessary preconditions for a favorable solution of the Cyprus question had been assured, the definitive cessation of the struggle was unthinkable. If such preconditions were not assured, it would be a tremendous mistake to cease the struggle, merely in order to appear nice or moderate. "The people who had been incited into this armed struggle would curse us," he wrote, "for giving it up without any positive results, and would wonder why this struggle had ever been started." The people, Grivas maintained, were still ready to suffer any sacrifice as long as the purpose for which they were struggling was being served. Furthermore, British policy would become more inflexible if all activities were ended, and it was doubtful whether it would go beyond any concessions of the Radcliffe "pseudo-constitution" type. Britain, because it had to maintain in Cyprus such large forces, was in a difficult position, for economic reasons, and because of its decision to reduce the number of its armed forces. Thirdly, both AKEL, the Communist-controlled Cypriot party for Raising up the Working People, and international communism would exploit the cessation of the struggle. "Our struggle," he asserted, had greatly weakened AKEL, in the ranks of which only the fanatic Communists remained. AKEL was following the nationalist line not out of conviction but by necessity, because it could not go against the will of its own members, the majority of whom approved of EOKA's struggle. Nevertheless, the AKEL leaders were lying in wait to exploit any mistake. They proclaimed that they were opposed to the way in which the struggle was being waged, and if this struggle were to end, they would appear on the stage and declare how right they had been in urging massive and democratic claims by demonstrations, protests, etc., in which case they would not only strengthen their hold on their own party members but would also attract to AKEL ranks many of those nationalists who would be disgusted by the failure of their own approach. Moreover, "it should not be excluded that they would finally take over the leadership of the armed struggle on a basis different than our own—in which case . . . they would no longer obey the Ethnarchy but follow their own line."

Finally, in deciding whether to end definitively the armed struggle, the Turkish factor should be taken into consideration, Grivas wrote. The Turks, in case this struggle ceased, might, incited by the British, undertake one of their own, supposedly to safeguard their rights but really to terrorize the Greek Cypriots and to prevent them from protesting or appealing for self-determination. In conclusion, Grivas suggested that Makarios should reach no decision on the matter until he was fully informed about the situation in Cyprus by getting information from people who really represented the opinion of the struggling people. The best way to do so, of course, would be by coming to Cyprus. At the same time he assured him that even if the Ethnarch's decisions in the end were opposed to his own views, he would abide by these decisions, because the responsibilities of the struggle were such that harmonious co-operation was of primary importance.[8]

On April 30, Grivas received a note from Consul-General Vlachos who sought to present for his consideration a full picture of the situation from the technical aspect. There were good indications that the British were likely to consider the departure from Cyprus of EOKA members sentenced to death and of those who were being tried. Those who were wanted might be facilitated to leave or, if they preferred, allowed to remain on the island, provided they appeared before the police authorities once a week. If this was not achieved, then all those who were wanted would depart. The Consul-General and the Consul would mediate in such arrangements, and they were at Grivas' disposal for the technical handling of the matter in accordance with his suggestions. On the question of the principle itself, Vlachos submitted the thoughts that the cessation would be voluntary—in which case the opponent would not be able to gloat in triumph; that the moral superiority of the Greek side would be enhanced from the viewpoint of international public opinion because of compliance with the UN resolution; that the departure of Governor Harding would be justified; that the Archbishop's position would be fortified in circles of British public opinion because he would appear as a peace-maker; that his return to Cyprus would be facilitated; and that the position of the Labourites would be strengthened.[9]

To this note Grivas replied on April 27, acknowledging the correctness of the above thoughts but observing that the expected results were possibilities only, not certainties. The armed struggle together with passive resistance was a strong weapon in support of diplomacy. Full cessation of the struggle should be bought by the opponent at a price: certain safeguards or guarantees that would insure a favorable solution of the Cyprus question.[10]

Indicative of the soul-searching and vacillation going on in Athens concerning the question of deciding whether EOKA's activities on Cyprus should cease altogether was that it was only on May 17 that Grivas got a reply to his letter of April 27 to Makarios. In the meantime, behind the scenes or in public several small political collisions in time and space had occurred in Athens, Bonn, Bursa, Strasbourg, Nicosia, London, and New York, with regard to the Cyprus problem.

In Athens, on May 2, backstage, a leading member of the majority National Radical Union (ERE) party in the Greek Parliament, Constantine Rendis, had emphasized to Makarios that Greece was internationally committed to respect Resolution 1013 (XI), as were the Cypriots, too, who had addressed themselves to the United Nations (through the Greek government), and had urged the Ethnarch to take the initiative of starting negotiations with the British government. Thus, possibly, a NATO debate of the question might be forestalled. Rendis suggested further that the Ethnarch should not set the question of his return to Cyprus as a precondition for starting negotiations but as a measure that would contribute to the restoration of peace and calm on the island. The Greek government, he added, also felt an obligation to save the fighters in Cyprus who constituted a national capital, and to settle the question of persons convicted, condemned, or under trial. Makarios, however, had been hesitant to follow these suggestions and had indicated he preferred to rely on certain undisclosed talks, which, he said, were taking place with Governor Sir John Harding on the matter of pacification, and to await the results of the discussion of the Cyprus problem, which was expected to take place at the imminent session of the NATO Foreign Ministers' Council at Bonn. On the other hand, as Grivas was to learn after he returned to Athens in 1959, the Ethnarch, at this time, had ordered the cessation of arms-sending to Cyprus.[11]

At the Foreign Ministers' NATO Council at Bonn, also on May 2, while Foreign Secretary Lloyd supported Lord Ismay's suggestion for using NATO conciliation facilities and said he preferred such a method of settling disputes to the public forum of the United Nations, Averoff-Tossizza sought to avoid throwing open for discussion the Cyprus question, though he did not altogether close the door to discussion of the issue in that forum. The Belgian Paul-Henri Spaak, whose appointment to the post of Secretary-General of NATO was announced shortly after, agreed with him that it would be better for preliminary talks to precede any such discussion in NATO. In a very long conversation of May 2 with the Minister of Foreign Affairs of the German Federal Republic, Heinrich von Brentano, Averoff-Tossizza emphasized Turkish inflexibility in insisting that partition was the only possible solution to the Cyprus problem and underlined the Greek government's willingness to acquiesce in various other solutions, including the setting up of an independent state of Cyprus.

According to press reports at this time, on the other hand, agreement in principle supposedly had been reached to solve the matter within the framework of NATO on the basis of a plan attributed to Secretary of State

Dulles. The island would be placed under the aegis of NATO and governed by three commissioners with a regime of self-government based on an improved version of the Radcliffe draft constitution.

Probably in response to such reports, Ethnarch Makarios, after Averoff-Tossizza's return to Athens on May 6, categorically stated in public that he rejected any NATO intervention in the Cyprus issue and insisted on a UN handling of the matter. United Nations trusteeship, in contrast to NATO trusteeship, was a matter that could be discussed. Moreover, in an interview with the *Manchester Guardian,* he not only re-emphasized the need for resorting to the United Nations on the basis of the principle of self-determination but also stated that the restoration of peace in Cyprus did not depend on the departure of Grivas from the island, but on other matters mentioned in his letter of March 22 to the British government, namely the raising of the emergency measures. Nor could his return to the island be related to the future of Grivas.[12] Then, on May 15, in a televised interview, the Ethnarch stated that the first step toward the solution of the Cyprus problem should be self-government as a transitional stage to self-determination. At the latter stage, the Cypriots would be able to choose between *enosis,* the creation of an independent state, and independence within the Commonwealth.[13] As against the older formula of "self-determination within a fixed and reasonable period of time," Makarios was now reiterating the concession he had made at the time of his first conversation with Harding on October 4, 1955, though to the Opposition he appeared to be groping toward a new formula: "self-determination safeguarded as far as time was concerned." [14]

In Turkey, Premier Menderes, in a speech delivered at Bursa on May 3, explained that his government had made a sacrifice by accepting partition as a solution to the Cyprus problem, instead of insisting on its original thesis that in the event of a change in the island's status, Cyprus should not go to Greece but revert to Turkey. The two basic aims of Turkey were being safeguarded, however, he explained, because if Cyprus were partitioned, it would not be in danger of passing into foreign hands and thus becoming a threat to Anatolia, and the Cypriots of Turkish origin would attain the honor and happiness of living under the Turkish flag.[15] And in Cyprus, Dr. Kuchuk, back from Ankara, echoed these views in a speech made ten days later. Partition, he said, was the only solution to the Cyprus problem.[16] And at Strasbourg, Turkish representatives to the Council of Europe were telling their Greek colleagues that whether Greece liked it or not, no solution could be given to the Cyprus problem to which Turkey would not agree.[17]

In Britain, Colonial Secretary Lennox-Boyd, in reply to questions by Labour Members of Parliament on May 1 and 8 had made it clear that Governor Harding would not suspend operations as long as armed men were still at large in Cyprus, and that the British government was always ready "to receive views" on the Radcliffe constitutional proposals. On the international level, he once again insisted that the best way of meeting Resolution 1013 (XI) was through a NATO handling of the issue. Moreover, he indirectly rejected Makarios' proposal that there be a UN trusteeship in Cyprus prior to self-determination.[18]

In New York, finally, Sir Pierson Dixon, Permanent Representative of Britain to the UN, advised Hammarskjöld in a note of May 11, that his government considered the Greek government had arbitrarily sought to establish its own interpretation of Resolution 1013 (XI)—an interpretation that apparently would preclude the Greek government from regarding itself as an interested party—and complained about that government's negative attitude toward Lord Ismay's good offices proposal.[19] The reply of Makarios to Grivas' long and anxiously inquiring letter of April 27, finally arrived on May 17. In it, the Ethnarch now expressed full agreement with the view of EOKA's leader that it would not be expedient to wind up operations at present. After the failure of Makarios' initiative (to be mentioned later) to get negotiations with the British started again, the Greek Foreign Minister himself, in a letter of June 6 to Grivas, confirmed fully the Ethnarch's instructions. It was expedient for the leader of EOKA to stay in Cyprus, "Isaakios" wrote. It was inexpedient, however, for him to resume action before the UN General Assembly had adopted a new resolution on the Cyprus issue. There would be problems, though, he was aware, if inertia risked dissolving the organization. At any rate, only if a relatively acceptable solution was assured would it be worthwhile for Grivas to leave the island. As long as he had not been captured, whether he was active or not, he remained the elusive victor. He had yielded somewhat but had not submitted. This was of help to the government's handling of the affair. Were he to be captured or killed, his services and heroic acts would surely be recognized in history. Today, however, he would be defeated. And this would be a great blow to the government.[20]

B. Deadlock

Whitehall's outlook on the Cyprus tangle at this point, as described in a Belgian diplomat's report to Brussels, during the second week of May, was conveyed at this time (perhaps by Spaak) to the Greek Foreign Minister for his information. The British government, according to this report, felt that it had gone as far as it could in the way of concessions—in other words, that a deadlock had been reached. It had proposed the Radcliffe draft constitution which included a promise of self-determination when circumstances would permit it to be applied. It had even suggested immediate self-determination, with partition of the island. It had managed to get Ankara to accept these concessions. The

British government had also accepted the good offices offered by NATO's Secretary-General. Finally, in order to leave no shadow of doubt about its good faith, it had freed Makarios.

All these concessions had been disdainfully rejected by Athens, the Foreign Office felt. It did not conceal its displeasure at the Greek government's attitude. It maintained that for several months the Greek Foreign Minister, with evident bad faith, was seeking to persuade all foreign diplomats of his conciliatory spirit and of the efforts he was making to find a moderate solution. In reality, he and his colleagues, the Foreign Office maintained, were doing everything to envenom the situation in Cyprus. At the same time he had subtly dropped threatening hints of a possible Greek neutralism, even of the Communist danger. Whitehall was convinced that this blackmail was without foundation in fact and that the Greek General Staff was too well aware of the military situation of the country to allow a break with NATO.

The Foreign Office affirmed further that the Greek government had never been prepared to make the slightest concession and had never had any other goal than the attachment of Cyprus to Greece. Certainly, its statements had varied according to circumstances. At the beginning of the crisis, the Greek government had clamored for immediate *enosis*. Since that thesis was too reminiscent of an immediate *Anschluss* to be popular in the United Nations,[21] Athens had changed its refrain and started talking about self-determination. As soon as London and Ankara had declared that the Turks in Cyprus as well as the Greeks there had the right to self-determination, and that this solution would lead to the partition of the island, the Greek Foreign Minister had again changed tactics and had started a propaganda campaign for the full independence of Cyprus which, in his mind, would go far beyond the Radcliffe draft constitution. The local government would, indeed, control the police, the customs, and justice. He had affirmed that he was ready to give guarantees against the demands which the Cypriot irredentists would surely formulate in order to achieve union with Greece. The Foreign Office did not hesitate to brand these assurances as hypocritical. To prove this charge, it cited various statements by Greek politicians, for instance Averoff-Tossizza's statement of March 11, 1957, in the Greek Parliament that anyone, who, in order to arrive at *enosis*, refused to accept independence as a transitional measure, deserved to be criticized. Was not the thesis of independence a progress of the Cypriot question as a whole? he had asked.[22]

Whitehall's mistrust of Athens, however, did not mean that Britain wished to maintain the status quo in Cyprus. On the contrary, it considered that the situation could last no longer. It had no desire at all to keep 20,000 men indefinitely on Cyprus to serve as targets of EOKA. Thus, if the offer of mediation made by the Secretary-General of NATO continued to be rejected by Athens, or, if accepted, yielded no results, the British government had decided to act on its own authority. The policy it would follow in that case was not officially fixed, but it was hinted that the only possible solution would be the partition of the island between Greece and Turkey. Britain would keep its sovereignty over the bases it considered necessary to keep on the island. While the above reflected the official position of the Foreign Office, this position, the writer of this report commented, was one of battle at the moment that it was hoped that negotiations would be resumed. It was difficult to see how the solution envisaged would facilitate the situation in Cyprus. But, it was quite evident that Whitehall wished to get out of this hornets' nest and very probably would be prepared to make more important concessions.

Likewise conveyed to the Greek Foreign Minister, and presenting Ankara's outlook at this conjuncture of mid-May, 1957, was another Belgian diplomat's report, in comment on his London colleague's analysis of the British viewpoint. The Turkish, like the British government believed it was up to Athens now to propose a solution to the Cyprus problem. Like London, Ankara considered it had gone as far as it could in the way of concessions. The undulating policy of Mr. Averoff-Tossizza, which presented one façade externally and another façade internally, had wearied the Turks as much as it had the British. The Greek blackmail (neutralism, Communist danger) was appreciated in Ankara at its real value. Turkish government circles underlined that if Greek public opinion weighed so much in the policy of the Greek government, the fault lay entirely with the government, which by its statements before Parliament, its radio appeals, its undisguised support of agitators of all kinds, from Makarios to Grivas, had served to excite minds and create a climate of hostility against Britain and Turkey and to revive the ancient hate against Turkey.

In the Turkish Foreign Ministry, as in the Foreign Office, people, according to this Belgian diplomat's report, were persuaded that the sole aim of Greece was the annexation of Cyprus pure and simple. Because of all the fluctuations of Greek policy, its denials, and its insinuations, Turkish statesmen were convinced that the guarantees that Mr. Averoff-Tossizza offered were entirely bereft of any value. Where, however, Ankara differed with London was over the methods to be adopted. The British, weary as they were of the situation, had really decided to abandon the island in a more or less proximate future. If, in order to do so, they had to make further concessions, it was beyond doubt that they would. Ankara, on the other hand, was goaded by a public opinion that had become more and more alerted to the issue and could not acquiesce and allow Cyprus to be attached to Greece. A break of relations with Greece would follow and then, in the opinion of the Belgian diplomat, war.

The Turkish government, which had demonstrated patience and moderation during the past years, intended to defend the Turkish minority at all costs. All efforts has been made to prevent the press from exciting public opinion, and if the Turkish newspapers had become more violent in writing about the Cyprus question, it was only when they had replied to innumerable attacks against Turkey, which Greek newspapers of all shades of opinion had published. The Greek, commented the Belgian diplomat, was intelligent, subtle, and volatile; the Turk, slow, terribly obstinate, and brutal in his reactions. If the Greek felt he was in a bad position, he would get out of it with a pirouette. The Turk, on the contrary, would exert force, and one should pay homage to the wisdom and moderation of Premier Menderes,[23] who, after the painful experience of September, 1955, had been able to act as a brake on the extremists in his country and had done everything in his power to prevent the Cyprus question from acquiring a religious character. The Turks felt that the British were ready to drop everything. Hence their great anxiety.

The Turkish and British charges against Greek foreign policy–makers at this juncture, it should be added, had not been conveyed to the Greek government merely in this indirect, non-public way—through the diplomatic channel of a third, non-involved but allied state, a national of which had been appointed Secretary-General of NATO. They had been the subject of a note of April 25 from Ambassador Sarper to the UN Secretary-General. In this letter, the Turkish Ambassador charged that hopes for a peaceful, just, and democratic settlement of the Cyprus question in accordance with Resolution 1013 (XI) had been "seriously imperilled" by statements of Greek government members made during the Greek Parliamentary debates of March 11–15. The declarations they had made before the Assembly "did not reflect the true aspirations of the Greek Government . . . their attitude had not been sincere but had been assumed, to quote the exact words of the Foreign Minister of Greece, as a 'deviation' aiming at the ultimate goal which is the annexation of Cyprus." Averoff-Tossizza's proposal before the Political Committee to sign an agreement for the independence of Cyprus guaranteed against annexation had not been made by him seriously. Had it been accepted, he would have retracted it under the pretext of consulting his government.

In this letter to Hammarskjöld, Sarper also referred to the statement by Kassimatis to the effect that these maneuvers had been necessary, because "the United Nations does not permit the union of Cyprus with Greece." [24] With regard to this matter, the Turkish Ambassador charged that "the contradictions and disparity between the declarations made by the Greek government at the United Nations and the official statements made by the same government at the Greek Chamber of Deputies cannot be considered as compatible with international good faith" and could only serve to increase international tension and aggravate the situation regarding Cyprus, "in the hope of frustrating a solution in harmony" with Resolution 1013 (XI). The letter of March 22 sent to the UN Secretary-General by the Permanent Mission of Greece constituted a further example of the same sort of tactics.[25] It was an attempt "to misrepresent" to UN members the reasons for the Greek government's refusal to find a satisfactory solution through mediation between Turkey, Greece, and

Britain, as the Secretary-General of NATO had suggested to the three governments. An arbitrary interpretation of Resolution 1013 (XI) had also been involved in that letter. Negotiations between Archbishop Makarios and the Governor of Cyprus had been a cover for negotiations by the Greek government "with the Archbishop acting in the foreground for reasons of expediency." The *White Book* published by the Greek government on the conversations demonstrated this.[26]

Ambassador Palamas responded to these charges in a long letter to Hammarskjöld on May 17. In it, he also made remarks about the latest developments in the Cyprus problem. The hopes, he wrote, that rose when Makarios was released that negotiations between the people of Cyprus and Britain would be resumed, were fading away, and the situation was now drifting again. The British forces were continuing their anti-Cypriot operations in full swing, the emergency regulations were still in effect, and the peaceful conditions called for by Resolution 1013 (XI) "were restored unilaterally by the Cypriots alone." As time was passing by, action for effectively implementing this resolution could not be reasonably delayed any further. This resolution constituted a responsibility for all UN members who had voted for it. And compliance became a more distinct obligation for the parties mainly interested— Britain and the people of Cyprus.

The policies and actions of the Turkish government constituted the most disturbing element in the picture, Palamas continued in this letter. That government had strongly opposed Makarios' release, reacting in a most violent manner. A vicious press campaign had been launched against the Patriarchate and the Greek minority in Istanbul, and partition was presented as the only solution of the Cyprus problem. The Permanent Representative of Turkey to the UN was then taken to task for having sought in his letter of April 25 to cast doubts on the substance of the Cypriot claim, by producing "allegedly contradictory statements by Mr. Averoff-Tossizza in the Greek Parliament," and by distorting "the true meaning of the debate in the Greek Parliament" by the use of excerpts from speeches arbitrarily taken out of context. Ambassador Sarper had contended that the Greek Foreign Minister had declared in Parliament that the "ultimate goal" of Greece was the annexation of Cyprus while denying it in the United Nations. This was completely untrue. During the entire debate in the Parliament, Mr. Averoff-Tossizza had never spoken of the union of Cyprus with Greece, still less of its annexation by Greece. He had merely declared, in answer to questions from the Opposition, that the Greek government's ultimate aim was that the population of Cyprus, being a highly civilized and mature people, should freely determine its own future. The Greek government would abide by whatever decision the Cypriot people would take.

In the course of the debate in the Political Committee, the Turkish Delegate, on the other hand, had never replied whether his government would be ready to sign an agreement for the independence of Cyprus, excluding annexation. A question had been asked: no proposal had been made. To ask someone whether he is selling his house was quite different from proposing to buy it at a given price and under specific terms and conditions. The absence of a reply, the Greek diplomat went on to say in this letter, rendered more evident that Turkey's opposition to self-determination for Cyprus, on the ground that this would lead to *enosis*, merely masked the desire to realize Turkish territorial ambitions on the island, when circumstances appeared propitious. The last section of this long note to the UN Secretary-General sought to rebut Turkish arguments that Greece desired the perpetuation of the Cyprus question, and that it was arbitrarily interpreting Resolution 1013 (XI). This note reiterated the Greek view that the United Nations enjoyed a sort of primary jurisdiction in dealing with the Cyprus question, and concluded by defending Makarios against "vilifying attacks" and attacking the moral stature on the leader of the Turkish Cypriots, Dr. Kuchuk.[27] This Greek-Turkish exchange through letters to the UN Secretary-General served as a focus of powerful Opposition attacks against the Greek Foreign Minister and demands for his resignation in the Parliament debates of May 20–25.[28]

C. *The Precedent for Bipartite Talks*

In this letter to Hammarskjöld, the Greek government once again had revealed its eagerness for a bipartite approach as a procedure most suitable for solving the Cyprus problem. The reasons for this have already been suggested. A review, however, of the Harding-Makarios talks of late 1955–early 1956 that ended with the Ethnarch's deportation to the Seychelles will not only help clarify further this matter but also shed light on the background of this aspect of the story, as well as on another of its main actors, the youngest of the three but perhaps the most renowned on the world scene.

After the failure of the London Tripartite Conference,[29] the anti-Greek riots and demonstrations in Istanbul and Izmir, both in early September, 1955,[30] and the UN refusal of September 23 to include the Cyprus question in its agenda,[31] Ethnarch Makarios, on September 30, publicly stated he was willing to meet the newly appointed but not yet arrived Governor of Cyprus, Field Marshal Sir John Harding. Harding chose to respond to this initiative. Under his instructions, it seems, even though his main task had been defined as the suppression of the rebellion, as his statement to the *Times* of September 27, indicated, he was free to decide whether or not to talk with Makarios. For he was also supposed to make new political efforts aiming at the introduction of a constitution, without entering, however, into detailed discussions on this constitution, for the British feared a diversion and also wished to consult the Turks in this matter.

The two men met on October 4, the day after Harding's arrival in Nicosia, and two days before Karamanlis, in Athens, took over the premiership of Greece, after Papagos' death. At this meeting, the Ethnarch handed the Governor a note in which he dropped his demand for self-determination within a fixed and reasonable time and expressed willingness to discuss self-government, which he had earlier denounced as "the grave of self-determination." [32] He expressed, namely, willingness to cooperate with the British in framing a constitution for self-government, provided the British government recognized the right of the people of Cyprus to self-determination and agreed that the time of the implementation of this principle be discussed between the British government and representatives of the Cypriot people who would have been elected according to the constitution that would be established and applied.[33] The Governor, however, after consulting with London, came up with a counterproposal on October 7 that was identical to the one which Foreign Secretary Macmillan had made at the London Tripartite Conference on September 6 and which both the Greek government and Makarios had rejected.[34]

The Governor urged the Ethnarch to put off for the time being the question of British recognition of self-determination in principle but said that the British government would be ready to discuss that issue with Cypriot representatives at a reconvened conference, once self-government had come into existence. When Harding and Makarios met for a third time on October 11, there was a deadlock. The Ethnarch remained unwilling to accept the British proposals and insisted on his own terms. It became clear he wished to exclude the Turkish government, perhaps even the Greek Government, from future constitutional discussions. As for the Governor, he was unwilling to agree to these conditions.[35] Meanwhile, he was bringing in military reinforcements and starting anti-EOKA operations, imposing curfews, and carrying out searches, while Grivas, on his side, was preparing to renew his own activities, which, it will be recalled, had started on April 1, 1955.[36]

Then, on October 14 and 15, in Athens, Averoff-Tossizza's predecessor, Foreign Minister Theotokis, had separate exchanges of views on this deadlock with British Ambassador Sir Charles Peake and U.S. Ambassador Cannon. At the first of these meetings, Sir Charles underlined Makarios' rejection of Harding's counterproposals, whereas at the second meeting, Cannon indicated by his attitude that the U.S. government, in spite of earlier assurances that it would help in finding a solution outside of the United Nations through quiet diplomacy, was not prepared yet to do so.[37]

At the Foreign Ministry conference of October 15, which followed these two meetings, Theotokis made it clear to a group of top Greek diplomatic officials that efforts should be exerted to get the Harding-Makarios talks going again. Such a bipartite procedure, he maintained, would exclude the Turkish government from the negotiations and would be less distasteful to the British government, which preferred to negotiate with the Ethnarch rather than with Greek government. Britain, it should be recalled, had always refused talks with Greece on the grounds that the questions of Cyprus and of the island's internal regime were matters of British domestic jurisdiction, not an international question. In the Foreign Minister's view, such bipartite talks would be preferable because of the forthcoming elections in Greece, in which the two extremist parties of left and right should be prevented from exploiting the Cyprus issue. Makarios, therefore, would be the principal in these negotiations, while the Greek government would stand by, giving him its support and co-operation. The purpose of such talks? To find a solution to the Cyprus problem that would preserve the demand of the Cypriots for self-determination, obtain for them genuine self-government, and, thus, bring an end to their sufferings. Such talks would prove that the Greek government was not intransigent and permit it to resort again to the United Nations with some justification, were these talks to fail. It was a matter of finding the appropriate formula, Theotokis stressed at this meeting. A real rapprochement of views was occurring, he said. The negotiations should go on. The U.S. factor was not yet ripe.[38]

Three days later there was another meeting of fundamental importance between Theotokis and Sir Charles Peake to prepare the ground for a meeting between the Greek and British foreign ministers at the forthcoming NATO Ministerial Council in Paris. Hopes were expressed that an acceptable formula for solving the Cyprus problem would be found. From Washington, on October 21, came a cable from Ambassador George V. Melas, who asserted that only a small gap now remained between the proposals of Harding and Makarios, with the implication that this gap might easily be bridged.[39]

The Macmillan-Theotokis meeting took place on October 25. But before that, the latter, having in mind Dulles' advice that the Greeks and the Turks should get together and talk over the Cyprus question, and believing that Greece might enjoy a temporary advantage over Turkey, which found itself in a bad position after the anti-Greek demonstrations and riots in Istanbul and İzmir, had met with Fuat Köprülü, Zorlu's predecessor as Foreign Minister, at the Turkish Embassy. At one point of the conversation, however, Ambassador Birgi intervened, suggesting it might be better to let things cool off, instead of operating à chaud, i.e., when the situation was inflamed. As a result, the conversation came to nought.

More successful seems to have been Theotokis' meeting with Macmillan. The two foreign ministers agreed that the resumption of the Makarios-Harding negotiations was advisable; also that the two governments "would keep in close touch and co-operate, through their respective ambassadors, in seeking an appropriate basis and, more precisely, a suitable formula, to that effect." At this meeting Theotokis asked Macmillan to make a proposal that would permit the Ethnarch to resume the talks. If the formula put forward was similar to the one presented by Governor Harding, obviously there could be no ground for resuming these negotiations.[40]

Toward the end of this meeting, Theotokis inquired whether the British government would commit itself to compelling the Turkish government to accept any agreement reached between Harding and Makarios. Macmillan hesitated, but Sir Harold Caccia, who was present, intervened, saying that the Turks could have no word in the matter since the agreement would be one between the Governor and the Ethnarch. When the Greek Foreign Minister repeated his question, Macmillan undertook the commitment proposed. Theotokis felt great satisfaction. However, he may not have taken into account the possibility of the British government consulting the Turkish government about its attitude toward a particular formula, prior to any reaching of agreement between Harding and Makarios.

Next day, the Greek Foreign Minister made the first of ten *démarches* with the British on the question of granting an amnesty to EOKA fighters. Minister of State Lloyd maintained that it was necessary to impose order by force before going ahead with further (unspecified) developments. On his side, Theotokis argued that the restoration of order—pacification —would be achieved only by a political solution. If the causes of violence were removed, then there was a way of solving the problem in Greek-British relations. If, on the other hand, efforts were made to impose order by force, not only the Cypriots but the Greeks, too, would be alienated. Elaborating the latter theme in instructions of October 31 to the Greek embassies in London and Washington, the Foreign Minister warned of the danger lest Moscow exploit the Cyprus question in the upcoming Greek electoral campaign unless some satisfaction were given to the Greek government on this issue.[41]

On November 21, the British formula—its first version, as matters turned out—was conveyed to the Greek government in Athens, and, an hour later, to Ethnarch Makarios in Nicosia. Prepared since October 20 and stiffly and unwillingly accepted by the Turkish government,[42] it consisted of a draft statement that Prime Minister Eden would make before the House of Commons on the Cyprus question. It contained references both to self-determination and to the long-standing offer of "a wide measure of self-government now." [43]

The Ethnarch, acting first, without hesitation rejected this formula as unsatisfactory.[44] He declared he could not agree that treaties or any other obligations of the sovereign power derived from any source—a condition mentioned in the British draft proposal—could in any way affect the application "of the inalienable right of self-determination of the Cypriot people." [45] Yet he recognized that some progress had been achieved. Indeed, under this formula, the British government was willing to state that in accordance with the principle embodied in the UN Charter, the Potomac Charter, and the Pacific Charter,[46] it was not its position "that the principle of self-determination can never be applicable to Cyprus." It was its position "that it is not now a practical proposition, both on account of the present strategic situation and on account of the consequences on the relations between the NATO powers in the Eastern Mediterranean." It would, therefore, have to satisfy itself that "any final solution safeguards the strategic interests of the United Kingdom and her allies." [47] The British double-negative formula concerning self-determination, which Secretary of State Dulles was to term "awkward," appeared to be a response to the dropping of the Greek and Cypriot demand for self-determination "within a fixed and reasonable period."

The Greek Foreign Minister, when informed by the British Ambassador of the Ethnarch's rejection of this formula, appeared "very shaken." He had not expected Makarios to break off negotiations so abruptly. The Greek government had found the British formula an advance. He did not feel, however, that his government was in a strong enough position to take a constructive action or to exert pressure on Makarios.[48] In its formal rejection of the British draft formula of November 21, the Greek government made long comments on its substance and explained in rather tortuous prose that since it had been asked to assist in the reaching of an understanding, it had been under the impression that the British government would consult it beforehand about any new formula it intended to put forward so as to get its appraisal about the acceptability of this formula to the Ethnarch and the majority of Cypriots. Besides, the memorandum that accompanied the British draft formula had indicated that no margin was left for discussion. Under those circumstances, the Greek government felt unable to recommend to Makarios a formula that it hardly had any time to examine.[49] United States pressure seems to have been behind this British proposal of November 21 because, two days earlier, the Greek Ambassador in Washington had cabled to Athens that a high State Department official had told him: "We must continue exerting pressure on the British; you, on Makarios, for a resumption of the negotiations." The Ambassador had observed in response that Makarios had dropped his central demand for setting a fixed and reasonable time limit for the application of self-determination, whereas the British had insisted on the Macmillan proposals." [50]

Eden, it seems, was greatly angered by Makarios' rejection of the British formula. He ordered the cessation of any further efforts to negotiate with him.[51] On the island itself, because of EOKA's intensified activities, Governor Harding, on November 27, declared a state of emergency and introduced very stringent security regulations. Next day, he placed the 10,000 British troops in Cyprus on a war footing for a period of three months.[52] Nevertheless, after the Greek government explained at length the reasons for its negative stand in a memorandum of December 5, prepared in close co-operation with the Ethnarch in response to repeated British notes—including a personal message of Eden to Karamanlis [53]—asking Athens to press Makarios into accepting the British formula, negotiations continued with the Greek and British governments, this time, as principals.[54]

The U.S. government backed these British initiatives, and the U.S. Consul in Nicosia met Makarios twice and informed him that his government viewed favorably the British formula of November 21. Indeed, in the second of these visits he warned the Ethnarch that if he rejected this formula, he would get even less support than in the past for the Cyprus case in the United Nations. Makarios, however, would not be swayed. He replied that the recourse to the United Nations had made Cyprus a world problem and that the organization would continue to be a useful platform for his purpose.[55]

On December 4, the British government learned that, in the view of the U.S. Ambassador in Athens, the Ethnarch was a prisoner of the extremists and should be extracted from this position by offering to him a modification of the British formula of November 21. Accordingly, on December 9, a second, modestly revised draft of this formula was handed to the Greek Foreign Minister together with an *aide-mémoire,* which elucidated certain points the Greek government had raised in its memorandum of December 5.[56] Six days later, Premier Karamanlis himself, in a conversation with Sir Charles Peake, expressed willingness to advise Makarios to agree to a resumption of the exchanges of views, as long as the British formula were to constitute not a take-it-or-leave-it affair but a basis for negotiations, together with the Greek memorandum of December 5.[57] In answer to a question about the matter of self-determination, Karamanlis told Sir Charles that, in his opinion, the Cypriots would be able to accept a proposal bereft of the condition contained in the British formula referring to "allied obligations" and including, instead, a reference to 5–10 years as a period after which self-determination would be applied. On his side, the British Ambassador inquired whether a fixed time might be mentioned, but under the condition of the estimate of the international situation prevailing at that time. Karamanlis, however, rejected such a formulation. The Ambassador, at any rate, explained he had no authority to negotiate.[58]

Likewise on December 15, the Greek government presented two alternative drafts of the statement that it suggested the British Premier might make in the House of Commons on the Cyprus situation.[59] The text of the first alternative read as follows:

Her Majesty's Government adhere to the principles embodied in the Charter of the United Nations, the Potomac Charter and the Pacific Charter to which they have subscribed Their position is therefore that the principle of self-determination is applicable also to Cyprus.

Her Majesty's Government have offered a wide measure of self-government now. If the people of Cyprus will participate in constitutional development and self-government has proved itself, during a test period of four years or sooner, a workable proposition, Her Majesty's Government are prepared to discuss the future of the island with the elected representatives of the people of Cyprus for a final solution which will satisfy the wishes of the people of

Cyprus and guarantee the rights of all sections of the community while being consistent with the strategic obligations of Her Majesty's Government in the Eastern Mediterranean.

The text of the second alternative, was identical, in its first paragraph, to the above text's first paragraph. Its second paragraph however, read as follows:

Her Majesty's Government have offered a wide measure of self-government now. They will, as soon as practicable, work with the elected representatives of the people of Cyprus for a final solution which will satisfy the wishes of the people of the island and guarantee the rights of all sections of the community while safeguarding the strategic interests of Her Majesty's Government in the Eastern Mediterranean.

Both of these versions, handed to Caccia in Paris, put the British recognition of the principle of self-determination in a simple positive, not double-negative form, and the first, longer one, introduced a fixed time element for discussing the future of the island with representatives of the people of Cyprus.

Evidently commenting on these alternatives, Eden doubted that the U.S. government would be tempted to study them and thought that they would be completely unacceptable to the Turkish government. "It is not," he noted, "our strategic interests only which have to be safeguarded but the joint working of NATO in the eastern Mediterranean." Two days later, the British Ambassador in Ankara warned that any further modification of the formula was likely to produce an explosion in Turkey.[60]

On December 16, in Paris, the British Foreign Secretary handed the Greek Foreign Minister a note mentioning that the U.S. government regarded as constructive and progressive the revised British formula of December 9. The British government therefore hoped, ignoring the two alternative Greek proposals of the day before, that the Greek government would decide to ask the Ethnarch immediately to reopen discussions with Governor Harding or to express its own view to the Archbishop that he might express the opinion that constitutional advance would be fairly based upon the revised formula and the British government's explanations of it. In conclusion, the British government expressed hope "for a firm and courageous stand" by the Greek government, which might be decisive in inducing the Ethnarch to co-operate. Failing this, the British government would be obliged to put an end to the present state of indecision and announce its position publicly.[61]

In a long and detailed memorandum of December 21, the Greek government responded to the British note by saying that, in spite of its misgivings, it did see a possibility for a resumption of the Harding-Makarios talks if these were based on both the revised British formula and the Greek memorandum of December 5, as had been suggested in the conversation between Premier Karamanlis and Sir Charles Peake of

December 15.[62] Then, shortly before Christmas, the Greek government
sent to Nicosia Alexis Liatis, Director of the Diplomatic Office of the
Foreign Minister, to become informed about the situation there, to advise
the Ethnarch what the Greek government could do to help him further,
and to suggest to him that he should resume his talks with Governor
Harding, evidently on the basis of the revised formula offered by the
British on December 9 [63] and of the December 5 memorandum of the
Greek government.

Finally, on January 9, 1956, after these negotiations between the British and the Greek governments, the Harding-Makarios talks were resumed. During these, the Governor, on January 13 and 27, came up with
a third and fourth version of the British formula first put forward on
November 21.[64] Both versions continued to refer to self-determination in
a double negative wording. The last one read as follows:

> Her Majesty's Government adhere to the principles embodied in the Char-
> ter of the United Nations, the Potomac Charter and the Pacific Charter, to
> which they have subscribed. It is not therefore their position that the principle
> of self-determination can never be applicable to Cyprus. It is their position
> that it is not now a practical proposition on account of the present situation in
> the Eastern Mediterranean.
> Her Majesty's Government have offered a wide measure of self-government
> now. If the people of Cyprus will participate in the constitutional develop-
> ment, it is the intention of Her Majesty's Government to work for a final
> solution which will satisfy the wishes of the people of Cyprus, be consistent
> with the strategic interests of Her Majesty's Government and their allies and
> have regard to the existing treaties to which Her Majesty's Government are a
> party.
> Her Majesty's Government will be prepared to discuss the future of the
> island with representatives of the people of Cyprus when self-government has
> proved itself capable of safeguarding the interests of all sections of the
> community.

Together with this fourth version of the original British formula, Harding
also sent to the Ethnarch a draft statement according to which the latter,
"having taken note of the statement of policy . . . made by Her Majesty's Government on the future of Cyprus," would tell the Governor that
he found this statement acceptable as a basis on which to co-operate with
the Government of Cyprus in the introduction of a Constitution and in
the development of self-government, and that he would advise his fellow-countrymen to do the same. Under this proposed statement, the
Ethnarch would inform the Governor that he agreed that the framing of
a constitution and the development of self-government could not proceed
in an atmosphere of violence and disorder. Therefore, he would assure
the Governor that he would use all his influence to bring an end to acts
of violence and lawlessness so that constitutional government might be
introduced in an orderly manner.[65]

In a covering letter of January 28, Governor Harding explained that
with regard to the questions Makarios had raised about the form of the

constitution that the British government had in mind, he could not add to the statements already made at different times by the British government. The details should be a matter for discussion with all sections of the community at the appropriate time. The Ethnarch, at any rate, could reserve his position on that point. After warning him about "the grave consequences of a failure to reach agreement on the basis proposed," and stating he would be ready for another meeting with the Ethnarch, if, within the terms of this covering letter and the enclosures, he considered there was any matter that required further explanations, Harding made it clear this was the last offer. As far as the substance of the statement was concerned, he wrote, he was not in a position to make any further changes.[66]

Meanwhile, on January 25, Köprülü issued a four-point statement on the Cyprus problem. His government, he said, was actively concerned with the progress of the issue and was maintaining close contact with the British government on the subject. Although Turkey accepted the principle of self-determination as an international principle, it did not believe this principle could be applicable in all parts of the world and especially in Cyprus. For the adoption of self-government in that island, terrorism ought first to be eliminated, law and order restored, and animosities between the different communities removed. Even when these were achieved, the Turkish community in Cyprus ought to take part in the island's administration and government and enjoy equal rights with the other communities. The Turkish government had conveyed these views to the British government. Ethnarch Makarios, the Foreign Minister observed, could not have the right to assume the position of representing the people of Cyprus. Governor Harding, he noted, had talks also with representatives of the Turkish community in Cyprus.[67]

In reply to the above British proposals and Sir John's covering letter, Ethnarch Makarios, after a series of meetings with representatives of Cypriot nationalist organizations,[68] in a long letter of February 2, reiterated that the proposed statement on self-determination was not satisfactory to the Greek people of Cyprus, because it recognized this principle as applicable to Cyprus only in an indirect manner and stated merely that its application was not permanently ruled out. That application was made dependent "on conditions so general and vague, subject to so many interpretations, and whose fulfilment would present so many difficulties to ascertain objectively, as to create reasonable doubt about the positive nature of the promise which is given regarding the final solution of the question in accordance with the wish of the people of Cyprus." For that reason he could never affix his signature under the British draft if this were to take the form of a bilateral agreement. On the other hand, the Ethnarch accepted Governor Harding's invitation to co-operate with him and representatives of the (Turkish) minority in the framing of the constitutional regime, after the British statement had been made as put forward in the draft statement. However, since there had been no elucidation of the meaning of the term "wide measure of self-government" promised in the British statement, the Ethnarch went on to outline five fundamental principles he regarded as prerequisites for agreeing that the proposed constitution would set up "a regime of genuine self-government." [69] These fundamental principles should be defined in advance. Agreement on them would create "the prerequisites for the appeasement of the present tension and will permit the soonest possible elaboration and operation of the constitution of self-government in an atmosphere of calm." And, in the phrase he was to repeat in his statement of March 22, 1957, to the British government, after affirming that he would contribute to pacification, naturally, in the full measure of his powers by making the appropriate statements, he wrote: "However, such pacification will be brought about more quickly than by anything else, by the policy to be followed simultaneously by Your Excellency. This should be a policy of appeasement capable of inspiring the citizens with a feeling of freedom and safety. Thus emergency military measures and emergency legislation would have to be revoked and an amnesty should be granted for all political offenses." [70]

This last question of pacification, amnesty, and public security—transitional measures toward drafting a constitution, introducing self-government, and applying it—together with continued doubts about the genuinely liberal character of the constitution the British government proposed to offer, seem to have been the stumbling blocks to any agreement, insofar as the Cypriot factor was concerned. In reply to the Ethnarch's above-mentioned letter of February 2, Sir John Harding, on February 14, emphasized mainly the matter of the island's pacification, expressing his government's satisfaction about the Archbishop's assurances of "his readiness to exert every effort to find a way of reducing the present tension." Welcoming also the Ethnarch's acceptance of his invitation to co-operate with him and all sections of the community in the framing of a constitution, Harding reiterated, concerning the Ethnarch's request for a clarification of certain points about the British views about a constitution for Cyprus, that he had to make it clear "that the form of any Constitution must arise out of full discussions with representatives of all communities."

Then, Harding went on to repeat that his government was offering "a wide measure of democratic self-government" and outlined six points to be taken as a basis of discussion of the proposed constitution itself. The British government, he added, could enter into no commitments about the position of the separate communities under the constitution before discussions had taken place at which representatives of those communities had expressed their views. In three of the remaining four paragraphs of his letter, the Governor reverted to the question of "persistent violence and disorder" and noted that these had increased the difficulties of introducing constitutional government. Fear and intimidation had stifled free expression of opinion, he observed. The minorities were more concerned than before about the possible consequences for them of the advent of self-government. He trusted that as soon as his government made its statement of policy on Cyprus, the Ethnarch would issue the appropriate statement and "take active steps to use all his influence to bring an end to violence and disorder." Then he—the Governor—would more easily be able to relax the emergency provisions without endangering public security. As an earnest of his desire to see peace and normality restored, he intended to repeal certain of the emergency regulations as soon as there was positive evidence of a genuine response to the Ethnarch's appeal against violence. As conditions on the island reverted to normal, he would be prepared to repeal other parts of these emergency regulations.[71]

At this juncture, three days before the general elections of February 17 in Greece, the Greek government cabled to the Ethnarch that he should feel free to unreservedly reject the British proposals and rely on Greek government support if he felt the British elucidations were not acceptable.[72] Thus, at a turning point in the Cyprus dispute the final decision fell on the shoulders of the Ethnarch.[73]

The status of these talks at this point is indicated by two documents, of February 24 and 25: a note summarizing the explanations which John Reddaway, Assistant Administrative Secretary to Governor Harding's Office had handed to Nikos Kranidiotis, Secretary-General of the Ethnarchy, concerning the constitutional proposals; and a letter from Makarios to Harding.

In the first of these documents, Reddaway explained that the Governor, in his letter to the Ethnarch of February 14, had not asked Makarios to commit himself on the form of the constitution. He had asked him to co-operate in constitutional discussions and, as part of this co-operation, to denounce violence. It would be open to the Ethnarch to reserve his position about the form the constitution should take.[74]

In his letter to the Governor, the Ethnarch emphasized that in his desire that the island would spend in peace the period up to the application of the principle of self-determination, he had made every possible concession beyond which "our national conscience and natural dignity do not permit us to go." He had made it clear in his letter of February 2 that his co-operation in the framing and operating of a constitution of self-government would be possible for him only insofar as the fundamental democratic principles described in that letter [75] were clearly established "now" as a basis of the Constitution that was being offered. Harding's letter of February 14, however, Makarios continued, had not clarified certain basic points in the substance of the general principles of the constitution the Ethnarch regarded as desirable. Nor had it contained any adequate assurance concerning the early repeal of all the emergency laws, or any mention at all about granting an amnesty for all political offenses. Both of these points, Makarios asserted, constituted an indispensable precondition for the normalization of the island's political life.

Yet neither side wished to appear responsible for the breakdown of the talks. At this point, Eden felt he could no longer delay making public the series of offers his government had made to Makarios for settling the Cypriot problem. Besides, it seemed to him that his government has gone as far in concessions to Makarios as it was reasonable to expect the Turkish government to accept at this stage.[76] Nevertheless, at Governor Harding's suggestion,[77] Colonial Secretary Lennox-Boyd flew to Nicosia. At a meeting with Makarios, which had been preceded by no fewer than nineteen explosions in the capital of Cyprus within a few minutes of each other, he stated on February 29 that when law and order had been re-established on the island there would be "an amnesty for all those convicted of offenses under the Emergency Regulations (or of comparable offenses, prior to their enactment) which were committed before (date to be settled) except those involving violence against the person or the illegal possession of arms, ammunition, or explosives which would come up for review in accordance with normal rules." The Governor was prepared to repeal all emergency regulations at a pace "commensurate with that of the re-establishment of law and order." He would be prepared, he explained, to give these undertakings on the understanding that the Ethnarch would co-operate in the framing of a constitution and encourage his fellow-countrymen to do the same; and that he would appeal for the cessation of violence and hereafter would use all his influence for the restoration of peace and order.

In connection with the problem of framing a constitution, Lennox-Boyd referred the Ethnarch to the British objectives outlined in the Governor's letter of February 14. Under these, he noted, summarizing them, it was proposed to send a Constitutional Commissioner to Cyprus who would draw up a liberal and democratic constitution in consultation with representatives of all sections of opinion in the island. This constitution would reserve to the Governor all powers in the fields of foreign affairs and defense. Public security, likewise, would be reserved to the Governor as long as he thought it necessary. As quickly as consistent with an orderly transfer, control of all other departments would be handed to Cypriot ministers responsible to a legislative Assembly representing the people of Cyprus. The Constitution would provide for an elected majority in the Legislative Assembly and would safeguard the interests of all sections of the community. It would be for the Constitutional Commissioner to recommend what arrangements should be made for this purpose, including the precise composition of the elected majority, which he would define in accordance with normal liberal constitutional doctrine.[78]

At one point of these negotiations, Makarios, advised, as mentioned, by the Greek government that he should feel free to reject the British clarifications if they seemed to him unsatisfactory,[79] was inclined, it seems, to accept the British proposals in spite of his grave misgivings. That same day, however, he changed his mind. Whose advice did he take in this instance? Did Grivas' cautioning counsel contribute to this *volte-face?* It is difficult to say. The fact is, though, that Grivas was convinced the British authorities, during the transitional period of indefinite length in which the Governor would keep in his hands full control over public security, would do everything to liquidate EOKA and its supporters. Accordingly, he had advised the Ethnarch that he would in no way put down his arms, unless the British government gave clear guarantees to apply what had been agreed upon; withdrew the troops and police brought in to combat his activities; granted a general political amnesty; and did not keep control over internal security.[80]

On March 5, while Lennox-Boyd, in the Commons, was giving his account of the talks [81] and of their breakdown, Ethnarch Makarios, in a defiant press conference on the same subject, charged outright that the British side had displayed no good will for finding a basis for a reasonable agreement. The Cypriot people, he maintained, had been invited to accept a regime of self-government "under which it would be doubtful whether they would be in control of their own Assembly, and on the basis of which it was certain that the sovereign colonial power would be able to intervene indefinitely in all fields under the pretense of 'protecting public security.' Such a regime . . . would be unacceptable even to a people just emerging from savagery. Its offer, even as a transitional stage," he continued, "would be a mockery to us who have clearly demonstrated the high liberal principles in which we believe by having first proposed every possible constitutional guarantee and protection for the Turkish minority, with whom we wish always to live in peace."

British "insistence and stubbornness clothed in vague phraseology," Makarios went on to charge, "was based on the pretense that they could not tie in advance the hands of the Constitutional Commissioner who was to be sent here and who, in their opinion, should have an absolutely free hand in drawing up the island's constitution, the islanders' own contribution thereto being restricted to mere consultation." But, he said further, it could escape no one's attention that the Constitutional Commissioner would be British and, consequently, an instrument of the British state. In the face of such intransigence, he declared, the wish for pacification of the country would in no way lead him to betray the elementary rights of the Cypriot people, or "to withdraw from positions essential to secure the possibility of a democratic administration which had never for one moment ceased to be our sole and final aim."

Finally, after expressing his regret at the British attitude, the Ethnarch declared: "In no way shall we lower the standard of self-determination. We shall fight to the end, by passively resisting the illegal sovereignty of our despot on the island, by vindicating our rights internationally from the United Nations forum where the Greek government will shortly bring the issue, and in general by omitting nothing that would lead to the satisfaction of our sacred national claims." [82]

Likewise on March 5, the British authorities in Cyprus started jamming, on an "experimental" basis, the broadcasts of Athens Radio to

Cyprus, which had been the object of repeated protests on the part of the British Ambassador in the Greek capital since March, 1955. In retaliation, the Greek authorities discontinued relaying the daily BBC programs to Greece in Greek.[83]

Then, four days after Makarios' impassioned press conference, the British abruptly deported its spokesman to the Seychelles, as he was about to fly to Athens. A long release of that same day by Governor Harding revealed British awareness of the extent to which the Ethnarch was implicated in EOKA's establishment and activities. In the British view, the specific grounds of disagreement between the Governor and the Ethnarch were symptoms rather than the cause of the breakdown of negotiations. The Ethnarch's attitude in the final phase of the discussions had convinced the British government that his purpose in putting forward his demands concerning the form of the constitution was to concentrate immediate power in his own hands in order to facilitate the early annexation of Cyprus by Greece.[84]

The Greek government, in response to this British measure, recalled its ambassador from London, and on March 13 formally asked the UN Secretary-General to place the Cyprus question on the provisional agenda of the Assembly's eleventh session. Moreover it raised the matter before the Council of NATO and in May resorted to the Commission of Human Rights of the Council of Europe. As for Grivas, who in mid-February had ordered the temporary abatement of sabotage and other operations in spite of his suspicions about British good faith in the Harding-Makarios talks, he braced himself for an all-out struggle. The first British civilian was killed shortly thereafter and on March 20, a time bomb was found under Governor Harding's mattress.[85] At this time, too, Reddaway made a trip to Ankara, after which Turkish Cypriot activities flared up, with attacks against Greek Cypriot properties taking place likewise on March 20.

The first official reaction of the U.S. government to the news of Makarios' deportation was not satisfactory to the British government but was modified after a *démarche* of the British Ambassador in Washington, Sir Roger Makins, with the State Department on March 13.[86] The evidence for this is found in two successive statements, of March 12 and 13, issued by Lincoln White, the official spokesman of the State Department. These, incidentally, also suggest the true paternity of the Thai proposal made in the course of the resolutionary struggle that led to the adoption of Resolution 1013 (XI) by the Assembly in February of the following year.[87]

Points made in the first White statement but omitted from the second were that the United States was not a party "to the negotiations which had been in progress" and "had no advance information on the British moves of the last few days affecting Cyprus." And unlike the first statement, the second one did not underline that the United States had been encouraged by the steady progress made during the last four months and that "it had *earnestly* hoped that basic agreements might be reached which would enable the people of Cyprus to achieve their *legitimate desire* of co-operation in the establishment of a government truly representative of the people of the island." Nor did the second statement repeat the words contained in the first that "we are confident that a solution may be reached which will take into account and safeguard the legitimate interests of all parties concerned," or that "we *earnestly* hope that despite *the present reverses* no one will lose sight of the overriding objective which is the re-establishment of an atmosphere in which negotiations can be resumed and carried to a successful conclusion" (italics added).

The second White statement was far less substantive and "colorless" than the first one. It said merely that the United States had not itself been "a party to the Cyprus issue" and that its sole effort had been to encourage "those directly concerned" to find a fair and just solution. Although expressing great disappointment that the substantial progress made toward such a solution "through private discussion" had not resulted in final agreement, the United States, according to this release, was convinced that further progress could be made once an atmosphere conducive to negotiations could be re-established. The United States was ready to assist its friends in the achievement of a just solution to the Cyprus problem and viewed present problems with sympathetic concern. It was, however, confident that a solution could be found that "would strengthen over-all Western interests"—a sentence not contained in the first statement. President Eisenhower, at his press conference of March 14, emphasized the NATO aspect of the problem. This was a point that Eden, as mentioned earlier, was eager to emphasize.

The U.S. government, at this time, was, it should be recalled, very anxious about the general situation in the Middle East. After the Geneva summit conference of July 18–23, 1955, and the "spirit" of relaxed tension it had generated, the East-West conflict had suddenly revived. It focused primarily on the Middle East as a result of the Czech-Egyptian arms deal announced on September 27, which appeared to be a Soviet reaction to the conclusion of the Baghdad Pact earlier that year. On February 24, 1956, indeed, Secretary of State Dulles had told the Senate Foreign Relations Committee that he saw some danger of war in that area.

Although not a member of the Baghdad Pact and resisting British efforts to get it to join, the United States was squarely behind that pact and hoped it might be extended to other Middle Eastern States. Jordan, however, had refused to become a party to it. Indeed, while the Harding-Makarios talks had reached a deadlock, King Hussein on March 1, 1956, had abruptly dismissed the commander of the Arab Legion, Lieutenant General John Bagot Glubb, together with two senior British officers, and had ordered their expulsion from the country forthwith. In Jordan, now, only certain British military detachments remained, whereas in Iraq, the British had turned over to the Iraqi government two lesser bases, under the Baghdad Pact. The contraction of British influence in the Middle East was going on as Soviet interest in the region was becoming more intense. Cyprus remained as the most obvious assembly point for small, highly trained, units in the area should the need arise. Later that year, during the Suez invasion, its strategic usefulness was tested.

It had not been the first time that the British authorities had deported a high prelate of the Eastern Orthodox Church of Cyprus because of his political activities. After the "disturbances" of October, 1931, two of the island's bishops, those of Kition and Kyrenia, had been banished for their role in the seditious acts that had led to the burning down of the Governor's House in Nicosia.[88] Of course, to exile the Archbishop himself was an even more serious step. For the head of the Church of Cyprus— autocephalous since 431 A.D., a status reconfirmed in 478, when Emperor Zeno conferred upon the Archbishop the patriarchal privilege of carrying a scepter and of signing his name in cinnabar red—could correctly be called the elected representative of the Greek Cypriots, who were of the Eastern Orthodox faith. He was not only *not* appointed by the Patriarch of Constantinople, with whom he was linked with no administrative ties, but, in a modernized version of the apostolic tradition, was elected to his office in two-stage, indirect elections, the lowest stage of which included the mass of the faithful gathered in their churches and choosing local representatives, who then nominated official delegates to sit with the bishops and abbots on the electoral college, which, in turn, elected the archbishop.[89]

But the Archbishop of Cyprus was even more than the elected religious leader of his Eastern Orthodox flock and head of the Church. He was also their Ethnarch—the leader of the *ethnos*, the nation of the Greek Cypriots. Thus he had *imperium* as well as *sacerdotium*. The ethnarchic role, of a secular rather than of a religious character, went back not to early Christian and Byzantine times but to the Ottoman period, when the Ottoman administration, applying the *millet* system to the various non-Muslim peoples in the Ottoman Empire, vested their religious leaders with certain civilian or political powers over their flock and with certain responsibilities vis-à-vis the government.

Furthermore, perhaps part of the whole secularization going on all over the world, these ethnarchic functions of the Church of Cyprus were becoming, in some respects, institutionalized, and their importance had increased. When the British Labour government in 1946 repealed a law of 1937 that provided that the choice of the Archbishop should be approved by the Governor of the island, and a new Archbishop was, in consequence, elected the following year, the Council of the Ethnarchy was established, in 1948, with a smaller executive organ, the Ethnarchic Bureau, being set up a little later.[90] This, in 1956, was composed of eleven members, a number of them prominent laymen. Moreover, as the advocates of the *enosis* movement again grew more vociferous, certain other ancillary organizations made their appearance in the early 1950's, when Makarios had become Archbishop. The Christian Orthodox Union of Youth (OHEN) was organized, directly under the control of the Archbishop and the bishops; also the Pan-Cyprian Youth Organization (PEON)—with Grivas' assistance. When, in 1953, the British authorities refused to renew the registration of the latter organization, more than half were absorbed in the former, while a number of them joined EOKA—the unavowed instrument of "external" and "internal" coercion of the Ethnarch, the civilian leader, as it were.[91]

As a whole then, here was an institution—the Ethnarchy—which was consubstantial with the Church of Cyprus and suffused with its prestigious religious radiance—sometimes to its disadvantage, especially in external relations, in an epoch as secular and materialistic as the twentieth century. At its disposal were the quite considerable financial resources of the Church, the properties of which have been conservatively estimated at about $18 million.[92] For the particular struggle in which it was involved since the early 1950's, it was helped, too, by certain groups of Greeks; by the autocephalous sister Church of Greece; and from early 1955 on, except for a brief interlude from October, 1955, to July, 1956, by the Greek government, especially insofar as Grivas and EOKA were concerned.[93] Greatly influential among the Cypriot peasantry, which farmed its extensive landholdings, this ethnic-religious organization exerted pressures not only against the British authorities in Cyprus but even upon the Greek government, affecting, as already evident, the foreign policy conducted by both states and, consequently, their relations with other countries as well—with Turkey in particular.

The goal, the ideal of this ethnic pressure group? The union of Cyprus with Greece or *enosis*. This, since 1878, when Britain took over the island's administration from the Ottoman Empire, meant first getting rid of British rule—formally colonial since 1925.[94] Hence, in the first instance, the character of the Cyprus question as a dispute between the Ethnarchy of Cyprus and of Greece, on the one hand, and Britain, on the other. Frequently expressed by petitions on the part of the Archbishop-Ethnarch,[95] this goal of union with Greece, while potentially leading to the cession of the island to Greece on the part of the sovereign state that ruled it—on the basis of a perfectly good legal title—and, as a result, to the annexation of Cyprus to Greece, involved for those Greek Cypriots who believed in this goal, not a distasteful act of selfish acquisition or coercion, or the change from one master to another one, which the term "annexation" (used by the opponents to denigrate *enosis*) implied, but an act of voluntary and pleasurable surrender, feelings of an aspiration fulfilled.

But the matter of Greek irredentism and irredentist aspirations that underlies the ideal of *enosis* had already been touched upon when dealing with Grivas and his brand of nationalism.[96] Suffice it to re-emphasize here that in mid-twentieth century it was not surprising that this ultimate goal should be expressed in anticolonialist terms—with the British government, too, compelled to acknowledge that, in part at least, here was a colonial problem. Nor was it astonishing that this goal should have been formulated in that anticolonial phraseology embedded by the two extra-European superpowers in the UN Charter as a demand for the application of equal rights and the "principle" of self-determination of peoples, or of the "right" of self-determination, to the people of Cyprus.[97]

Given, then, the institution he headed—and still heads; given its goal; given, too, our times; it was not unnatural that Makarios III, Archbishop and Ethnarch of Cyprus, should seem to be a secular personage in religious robes and the paradoxical opposite of the monk in uniform that was Grivas. In terms of post-iconoclastic Byzantine political theory, he was a shepherd of bodies rather than of souls. Or, if one may apply to this prelate of the Eastern Orthodox Church the Gelasian distinction, Makarios, whether he chose so or not, wielded—and wields—far more often the temporal rather than the religious sword. And, of his two roles (a third one was added since he became President of the Republic of Cyprus) he concentrated primarily on that of the Ethnarch, shaping the institution itself to his own image, in the process, and, in the main, handling the Cyprus question in person and on his own responsibility.

In this temporal role, the nationalism of this "idealist who has the shape of a fish and moves like a serpent," as Makarios' Turkish Cypriot arch-foe, Rauf R. Denktash, is said to have called him, tends to revert to an earlier archetype than does Grivas' nationalism. Because of historical and geographic reasons it seems closer to the pre-1830 strain of modern Greek nationalism. It is, namely, bereft of Slavophobia and of its later avatar, communistophobia, and features a pronounced anti-Turkish thrust, which, as the Turkish Cypriot and Turkish factors gradually emerged as the main obstacles to the goal of *enosis* through self-determination, came more and more to the fore—creating a major threat to Greek-Turkish and Cypriot-Turkish relations.

Born Michael C. Mouskos, on August 13, 1913, at Ano Panagia, a village at the western end of Cyprus, in the province of Paphos, Makarios was of peasant stock.[98] In his early youth he tended his father's flocks on the mountainside. At the age of thirteen, however, after his mother's death, he was attracted to the monastic form of life and entered the monastery of Kykko for the novitiate. This did not prevent him from getting his secondary education at the Pan-Cyprian Gymnasium in Nicosia, the oldest and largest Greek secondary school in the island. At an early stage of his career, the stubbornness of his character was revealed when in spite of the orders of his spiritual father, the Abbot of Kykko, he refused to grow a beard and reached the brink of being expelled from the monastery for this act of insubordination. The year before World War II broke out, he went to Athens, to study theology on a fellowship of the monastery. The Axis occupation of Greece pinned him there. In 1942 he graduated from the Theological School of Athens University, where he also took courses in law. For a while he served as a deacon of the church of St. Irene in Athens—dark, sullen, taciturn, in the memory of one who met him at that time. Early in 1945, after the Communist rebellion in December of the previous year, he got acquainted with Grivas, then head of the anti-Communist X-ites. Ordained a presbyter and priest in 1946, he came to the United States on a scholarship from the World Council of Churches for further theological studies at Boston University.

What, if any, were the political forces that propelled this tenacious yet mercurial young priest to his rapid rise in the Cypriot hierarchy—his election as Bishop of Kition at the age of thirty-five—would be interesting to find out? Unlike Grivas, however, the Ethnarch is rather cautious in putting down things on paper, much less in publishing memoirs. "Wingéd words" are his strength. As any rate, his activities in favor of *enosis* soon became evident. The plebiscite in Cyprus of January, 1950, the results of which showed 97 per cent of Greek Cypriots in favor of union with Greece, has been credited to him. When the Archbishop of Cyprus died later that same year, the Bishop of Kition, at the age of thirty-seven, succeeded him as Makarios III. In his enthronement speech on October 20, 1950, the new Archbishop and Ethnarch declared he would neither sleep nor rest until union was achieved with "the Greek mother." [99] Did he then—does he today—envisage the consummation of this union, which would be a death blow to the ancient Church of Cyprus, as possibly leading to his own rule over the new Helladic motherland that would emerge from full and unconditional *enosis*? No one can tell. Some of his left-wing supporters, however, seek to cast him in such a role, hoping that such a happening, which has some sort of historical precedent in the rise of another irredentist Greek, the Cretan Eleftherios Venizelos, to power in Athens of 1910, might not only fulfil aspirations for *enosis* but also bring the monarchy to an end in Greece and tear away that country from its NATO allies.

While still Bishop, Makarios, late in 1949, had publicly stated that he did not believe "as some traitors and friends of England do, that *enosis* will be realized within the framework of Anglo-Greek amity. *Enosis* is not granted; it can only be won by a continuous struggle." For him, self-government without self-determination within a reasonable and fixed time limit was "the grave of self-determination," and he who declared himself in favor of self-government was "a traitor to *enosis*." The Ethnarch feared the potentially de-Hellenizing effects of various measures the British authorities had been introducing in the educational field. [100] Imbued with a strong sense of justice and a powerful desire to be remembered in history, this prelate stubbornly waged his struggle in various ways, both overtly and covertly—with shifting strategies and flexible tactics, and in various arenas with a marked predilection, however, for the United Nations. His setting up of two youth organizations had already been mentioned. Then, among overt activities, there were propaganda; agitation; speeches; sermons; proclamations; demonstrations; Pancyprian Assemblies; petitions to the British Governor or the Colonial Secretary or other high British officials; resolutions addressed to the British, Greek, or other governments, to various international organizations, including NATO, and above all, to the United Nations. Covertly, on the other hand, there was the close, often competitive co-operation with Grivas, who, as mentioned, had started out his own planning and preparations independently of the Ethnarch, but had ended up by being his subordinate, formally as well as actually, at least until Makarios was deported to the Seychelles.

Outside of Cyprus, Ethnarch Makarios, an indefatigable traveler, sought to draw the attention of the world to the fate and future of his island. Publicist of the Cyprus cause, he traveled to several Arab countries (Egypt, Syria, and Lebanon in 1952), and to the United States, where several "Justice for Cyprus" committees had been set up. Moreover, at the United Nations he met representatives of various states and in 1955 attended, as an observer, the Bandung Conference of uncommitted Afro-Asian nations. Concurrently, he sought to get allies in his struggle and, first and foremost, the support of the Greek islanders' natural ally, Greece.

Makarios' constant and shrewd pressure in that direction was specifically aimed at getting the Greek government to resort to the United Nations over the Cyprus problem. "International public opinion" in a shrunken world would, he hoped, be mobilized in favor of his island's cause—with deeds of heroism in unconventional warfare explosively drawing public attention and contributing to the same end. The Ethnarch sent his first appeal to the United Nations early in 1951. The year before, however, a Cypriot deputation had gone to the United Nations to publicize the results of the plebiscite of 1950.

In the pressures he exerted on the Greek government since 1951 to resort to the United Nations over the Cyprus problem, Makarios at first met with rebuffs. Premiers S. Venizelos, Nicholas Plastiras, and even Papagos (at the beginning of his premiership at least) had refused to go along with this idea of a recourse to the United Nations.[101] For instance, in 1952, when the pertinacious Ethnarch threatened to raise the question directly with the Greek people—and eventually did, over Athens Radio—Venizelos (then Foreign Minister) plainly told him: "It is not you who will conduct Greek foreign policy." Nor would he be swayed by Makarios' other threat: that he would ask another state, Syria, to sponsor the Cypriot cause in the United Nations.[102] From 1951 until 1954, generally, Greek governments, as mentioned already, preferred to raise the Cyprus question quietly with the British government, through the diplomatic channel, and were averse to resorting to "parliamentary diplomacy," except through hint-dropping at the sixth, seventh, and eighth sessions of the UN General Assembly.[103] It was only after the repeated failure to get any bipartite negotiations started with the British government that Makarios and those in the Greek Ministry of Foreign Affairs, like Ambassador Kyrou, of Cypriot origin, who seems to have shared the strategic views of the Ethnarch, saw their desires fulfilled: the Greek government's recourse to the United Nations in August, 1954. And, it was only when that procedure had proved fruitless, that the specialists in violence had their way—with the Greek government feeling justified in transforming them into proxies of its foreign policy by giving its blessing to the unconventional warfare that Grivas and Makarios had planned and prepared, without governmental support.[104]

D. Makarios Proposes Bipartite Talks

Late in May, after deciding against full cessation of Grivas' operations, Makarios, "as spiritual and elected national leader of the Greek people in Cyprus," wrote to Prime Minister Macmillan, expressing his eagerness and readiness to take part in the name of the people of Cyprus in bipartite conversations, on the basis of the application of self-determination in accordance with the UN Charter. The Turkish Cypriots could be represented in these talks when the safeguarding of their minority rights was under discussion. In this letter of May 28, Makarios quoted Resolution 1013 (XI) and asserted that the Cypriot people had signally contributed to a considerable extent to the restoration of peace on the island, as that resolution had urged. The resistance movement had declared a truce on March 14, and since then had maintained it. The British authorities in Cyprus, on the other hand, had not taken any corresponding measures for bringing about peace in the island and for restoring to the Cypriots their freedom of expression. On the contrary, they had kept the emergency measures in force, and had continued large-scale military operations, arrests, and imprisonments without trial, while methods of incredible tortures were being applied to a greater extent than they had been before. The British authorities, the Ethnarch wrote in this letter, should, in compliance with the UN resolution, put an end to all emergency measures that, aside from their oppressive character and the concomitant trials they imposed upon the people, prevented freedom of expression and, because of the prohibition of his own presence on the island, prevented, too, his indispensable personal contact with the people of Cyprus, whom he represented.

The British government's reply to Makarios' letter came four days later, conveyed through the new British Ambassador in Athens, Sir Roger Allen. In this letter, the British government declared that under the prevailing circumstances it would be incompatible both with the responsibilities of the Cyprus government and with the requirements of an atmosphere of peace and freedom of expression, specified in Resolution 1013 (XI), to allow the Archbishop's return to Cyprus. Nor could it accept the proposal that the future of Cyprus be decided through bipartite talks between the Ethnarch and the British government. Other and wider interests had a right to be consulted. However, as the British government had declared earlier, it would be happy to study the views of any persons or communities in Cyprus, the Archbishop included, on the proposals for self-government made in the Radcliffe draft constitution. With regard to self-determination, the British government's views had been stated by the Colonial Secretary on December 19, 1956.

In this letter, which was not addressed to Makarios himself but to a member of the Ethnarchy, Zenon Rossides (later Permanent Representative of Cyprus to the UN), the British government referred to various offers and measures it had made or taken to reach a settlement of the issue or to comply with the Assembly's resolution—to the Radcliffe draft constitution, to Makarios' release, to the relaxation or raising of some of the emergency regulations in Cyprus, and to the British government's acceptance of the offer of good offices made by NATO's Secretary-General. It also expressed its regret that there had been no corresponding contribution of the Archbishop toward an improvement of the atmosphere. The Archbishop, it pointed out, had, since his release, made public statements rejecting the Radcliffe proposals. Moreover, he had denied the right of the Turks of Cyprus to any effective participation in the discussion of the future of Cyprus, and had set his own return to the island as a condition of his own participation in talks, without being clearly disposed to dissociate himself from the terrorism taking place in Cyprus. These statements certainly had not improved the prospects of an agreed settlement. As long as the threat of the resumption of terrorism remained, the government of Cyprus would not be carrying out its duty if it interrupted its efforts to discover and arrest well-known evil-doers, who still remained at large and who had chosen not to avail themselves of the offer of a safe-conduct to leave the island. Were terrorism on the island to be resumed, the Archbishop, by his refusal to denounce the use of violence for political ends, would bear a heavy responsibility before world opinion for any subsequent loss of life.[105]

After the above reply, the Ethnarch declared there was no ground for reaching an understanding on the basis of the above note. Concurrently, the British authorities in Cyprus continued their operations against an inactive EOKA, once again coming very close to discovering Grivas in his hideout the night of June 6.[106]

Moreover, on June 25, in an oral answer to questions by Labour members of Parliament, the Undersecretary of State for the Colonies, John Profumo, reiterated that the British government was not prepared to enter into bipartite negotiations with Makarios because the latter had laid down unacceptable conditions for discussions. If he withdrew them, it would be a different matter.[107] On July 16, Rossides, on behalf of the Ethnarchy, observed that the Ethnarch's concern was that the Turkish Cypriots should not be implicitly given a voice equal to that of the majority in deciding the future of the island but that they should have a voice proportionate to their ratio in the total population.[108]

Meanwhile, early in June, Premier Menderes from Karachi where he was attending a session of the Council of the Baghdad Pact, attacked Makarios' proposal for talks with the British. "There was not the slightest doubt," the Turkish Premier asserted, that the Archbishop knew in advance that there was no possibility of his proposal, which was "totally contrary" to the UN resolution, being accepted. His letter had been "merely a political maneuver or, rather, an artifice." The prelate's pretense to represent himself as a spokesman for the people of Cyprus had "no connection with reality." There would have been no need to dwell upon his action, were it not that he was acting in concert with the Greek government. The truth of the matter was that Makarios "belongs to the category of a mere prelate, of the type encountered during the last phases of Ottoman history, that engaged in agitation and provocation to set different elements and factions against each other, while finding it possible to escape retribution by hiding their guilt under clerical robes." What made the matter deplorable was that from one point of view Makarios was acting as a vanguard and spokesman for the Greek government. It was necessary, however, for that government to realize the need to put a definitive end to "the scandalous terrorism in Cyprus" and to agree that the sole constructive path to be followed lay in the matter being discussed "seriously and level-headedly among themselves by the three interested parties." The Greek government, Menderes went on to say, would do well to censure the proposal Makarios had made to the British Prime Minister for the purpose of inventing "a pretext to reactivate terrorism." The British reply, Menderes maintained further, had revealed that the British government did not recognize Makarios as a representative of the people of Cyprus. In conclusion, he pointedly praised the British reference to Lennox-Boyd's commitment of December 19, 1956, to eventual double self-determination, in other words, to eventual partition.[109]

E. Spaak's First Probes Blocked—New Greek Recourse to the UN

Two conversations of June 14 and 26, respectively, between the Greek Foreign Minister and the American Ambassador in Athens indicated, among other things, that after the British government had rejected Makarios' offer of bipartite negotiations and the Turkish government had subsequently rebuffed an effort by the newly appointed Secretary-General of NATO, Spaak, to prepare the ground for a solution to the Cyprus problem, the Greek government felt that no other course was left open for it than to raise the issue again at the next UN General Assembly, as Makarios desired. Earlier in June, the press had reported that the

Greek government might make a new recourse to the United Nations, unless Britain acted on the matter of Cyprus' future.[110] And on May 20, Averoff-Tossizza had solemnly stated before Parliament that the Greek draft resolution on self-determination, introduced at the eleventh Assembly, would be revived before the next Assembly if no solution to the Cyprus problem had been reached in the meantime.[111]

In the first of these conversations—of June 14—which took place at Allen's request, the U.S. envoy inquired whether the Greek government had received a note from Spaak in which NATO's new Secretary-General suggested some sort of independence for Cyprus for a fixed period of years as a tentative solution to the problem.[112] Allen expressed particular satisfaction about this note, especially because the indications had multiplied that the British had decided to leave the island, and it became ever more likely that upon doing so they would invite the Greeks and the Turks to occupy parts of it. He said he did not know the extent to which the Greek government realized this was a serious contingency, and wondered whether, in view of that danger, it should not make haste to do something to forestall such a British operation.

In Allen's opinion, Makarios' insistence on self-determination for the island was leading faster and more surely to partition, whereas, by the application of "some kind" of self-determination, the danger of partition could be averted and one could wait for better days to come. The American Ambassador thence proceeded to suggest that it might be a good idea to study the possibility of securing the departure of Grivas from Cyprus but on condition Makarios was allowed to return there immediately. The Ethnarch, then, in agreement with local elements, could start negotiations and perhaps even apply some satisfactory sort of self-government.

The Greek Foreign Minister replied that many Greek officials as well as Makarios did not regard as likely the danger of partition and that he could not believe that such a criminal plan could be applied without the immediate and effective appearance of an intense reaction. Personally, though, he thought that the danger of partition being imposed by the British through their withdrawal from the island would be serious. In several other cases the British had done the same thing. And, because he believed the danger was grave, he was extremely worried, perhaps more than any other Greek. With an almost mathematical accuracy he could predict developments if such a withdrawal took place. If neither the Sixth Fleet nor someone else did not hasten to prevent the installation of the Turks on the island, in order to permit a further settlement of the island's fate, he regarded it as certain that the following events would occur:

Cyprus would find itself in a ceaseless bloodbath under the glint of constant flames of fires set by the Greeks and the Turks of Cyprus. It would be futile to think whether "Dighenis" or EOKA existed, because as long as one was certain that the population was fanatically opposed to such a solution, and as long as youths between fifteen and twenty had become used to fighting, the battle would be fierce and bloody, regardless of the existence of an organization. If Grivas did not exist, another "Dighenis" would arise, perhaps a greater fanatic than he.

Second, in Greece there would be political chaos. The government, because of much smaller events concerning the Cyprus question, already had been shaken, Averoff-Tossizza asserted. If one part of the island were to be occupied and were it to become clear that such an event could not be reversed, the government would be able to stay in power for only a few days. In such tense circumstances, it would be impossible to hold elections, both because the situation would have to be dealt with immediately and because elections could not be allowed at a time when a very sharp anti-Western atmosphere would be prevailing. The political result, then, would be the establishment either of a dictatorship, with all its disastrous secondary results, or of a coalition government. But in the atmosphere prevailing between government and Opposition, and with the policy lines to which the latter had committed itself, a coalition government fatally would turn out to be a government driven by the most fanatical slogans; it would have neither cohesion nor *sang-froid* for dealing with the grave internal and external problems or with the Cyprus question. Consequently, there would be a leap into political chaos.

Third, no matter how bizarre and shocking this might sound, Averoff-Tossizza was obliged to predict the outbreak of a Greek-Turkish war, within a few weeks or a few months. The Cretan problem had led to the war of 1897—a war between a Greece of two million people and the then all-powerful Ottoman Empire. The Cyprus question, in the event the contingency mentioned by the American Ambassador took place and at a moment when blood would be shed daily and threats would be exchanged between Athens and Ankara, would, in a similar way, lead to a war between Greece of nine million people and Turkey of twenty-five million. As categorically as he could, Averoff-Tossizza affirmed to Allen that these were his real thoughts, and the latter agreed that the danger of such a development indeed existed.

In continuation, the Greek Foreign Minister told the American Ambassador that in order to deal with this real and terrible danger, real and practical solutions were required, not the formulation of hopes without any results. For instance, concerning the suggestion about the return of Makarios to Cyprus in exchange for Grivas' departure from it, how could one be sure that Grivas would leave? His own information from Cyprus was that Grivas was not at all weak and that he was in the process of developing a powerful political and anti-Communist action.[113] If he did not act at this time, this was only because he believed a satisfactory solution would be found. Under these circumstances, how could he be persuaded to leave the island? But assuming that Grivas was persuaded to leave Cyprus and that he left the island, he—Averoff-Tossizza—did not see how Makarios, by going to Cyprus, had any probabilities of retreating in the direction that Allen had suggested ("some kind of self-determination"). Of course, if Makarios went to Cyprus, he would be much stronger than he was now, staying in Athens. But this would not mean that he would be able to drop the demand for self-determination, which was the demand of all Greeks in Cyprus. The only thing he would be able to do would be to work more effectively for a solution that would lead step by step to self-determination. But this matter, as facts cried out loud, was not being dealt with at all. Therefore, Makarios would not be able to reach that point even if he were to find himself in Cyprus—with Grivas having left the island.

As a practical confrontation of the whole matter, Averoff-Tossizza proposed that Spaak should try, if possible, to lead to a desirable solution within two or three months. Should he fail, one should resort to the United Nations and agree beforehand to make sure that the Assembly would adopt a clear resolution concerning the solution that should be applied in the Cyprus question. Such a solution, the Greek Foreign Minister believed, would be the creation of a state with a guaranteed independence of not over ten years and the setting up of a regime of trusteeship. After appropriate preparation and with a great deal of political courage, the Cypriots might be persuaded to accept such a solution, he thought. If the U.S. government were to agree on such tactics, then the Assembly surely would adopt a resolution that would be clear and unambiguous, not open to misinterpretation, and which, therefore, could be implemented.

If, indeed, Britain wished to get rid of the problem, it would agree to this implementation under the pressure not only of a large segment of British public opinion but also of international public opinion. Moreover, Britain could tell Turkey that it was obliged to comply with the UN resolution. Thus, its position vis-à-vis the Turks, whom it was anxious not to displease, would be facilitated. Turkey, on the other hand, would not have to yield in face of opposition on the part of Greece or of another state, but in the face of UN resolution. To facilitate the Turkish government's acceptance of such a solution, one could offer it, beyond this, various other concessions, especially of an economic nature. Allen, clearly disturbed, said he fully agreed with what Averoff-Tossizza had told him and inquired whether he should convey the contents of this conversation to the State Department. The Foreign Minister assented, and the conversation then turned to Middle Eastern problems.

In the second exchange of views between the Greek Foreign Minister and the U.S. Ambassador in Athens, which took place on June 26, it became quite clear that the Greek government by now had definitely decided to resort again to the Assembly on the Cyprus question. Averoff-Tossizza asked Allen to define more clearly the U.S. government's attitude in the Cyprus question, inasmuch as he had reached the conclusion that the only procedure which could bear some results was through the United Nations, along the lines he had delineated in their previous conversation. The American envoy, faced with insistent questioning in this matter, replied that it was not possible for his government to inform another government about the attitude it would assume, and this with all the details about which Averoff-Tossizza was asking him. To do otherwise would be committing one's self very much in advance. This, he thought, the U.S. government would never do in a matter that concerned more than one of its friends. His own personal impression was, though, that the State Department did not sympathetically view partition as a solution to the Cyprus problem, and that it regarded the creation of an independent state of Cyprus with a guaranteed independence for a fixed period of time as very reasonable and expedient. Finally, he, personally, believed that if such a solution were proposed in the United Nations, the United States would support it. Averoff-Tossizza then asked him again to convey to the State Department the profound concern that the Greek government felt about the consequences of the non-solution of the Cyprus problem for Greek foreign policy in its entirety, and its insistence on getting a concrete and most detailed possible reply concerning the attitude that the U.S. Delegation would assume in the Assembly with regard to the various solutions to the Cyprus problem. Allen promised to transmit this request to the State Department and inquired whether the Greek government would resort to the United Nations in any case, instead of accepting the mediation proposed by Spaak.

Averoff-Tossizza replied that his government would accept with pleasure a satisfactory solution achieved by mediation. Such an effort should be made. However, he did not believe that Spaak would achieve any results by intervening. Allen agreed. According to his information, the Turkish government, in reply to Spaak's note, had said that the solution of the Cyprus problem through the island's partition represented a great concession on the part of Turkey, and that the solution that Spaak had suggested—the creation of an independent state for a fixed number of years—constituted no solution at all (evidently meaning that this solution was fully consonant with the Greek aims). The postponement of Spaak's trip to Ankara, which had been due to this Turkish reply, Allen agreed, indicated that the chances were slim of any successful exploration of the problem by Spaak. Indeed, as Averoff-Tossizza learned a few days later, Premier Menderes, on reading Spaak's note, had been seized with a "*colére bleue*" ("blue anger") and had ordered that the Secretary-General of NATO be informed that he could not be received in Ankara before five or six weeks. At this point, Spaak, while believing that the Turks were intransigent, vacillated between two positions: Should he actively intervene but with very slim chances of success and great probabilities of "burning his wings" and running the risk of damaging NATO? Or should he refrain from intervening and still have to face the danger of the deeper repercussions of the Cyprus problem on NATO's cohesion?

The Greek preoccupation at this time with the matter of resorting once again to the United Nations over the Cyprus problem is also revealed in an undated paper prepared by the appropriate services of the Foreign Ministry concerning the possibility of such a new recourse. An indispensable condition for any further successful handling of the Cyprus question both generally and specifically in the United Nations was a better, if not completely favorable, attitude of the United States toward the Cyprus question, this paper acknowledged. Unfortunately, all indications both from the periphery and the center were ominous. The U.S. diplomatic machinery not only did not function in favor of the Greek view, not only did it not remain neutral, not only did it systematically incline toward the British view, but it also offered itself as a channel through which the British aims (aims of prestige, in the last analysis) were conveyed to the Greek government; and attempts were made, by the creation of some sort of feeling of hard necessity, to impose them on Greece.

As supporting evidence of the above analysis, three cases were mentioned. In the first, the First Secretary of the U.S. Embassy in Athens, in a dinner conversation of May 17, had suggested to a member of the Greek Foreign Ministry that, in view of the possibility of a sudden withdrawal of the British from Cyprus, it might be a good idea to suggest their maintenance in Cyprus through a mandate or a trusteeship. Two days later, a Washington dispatch reported that such a proposal was a British one. In the second case, a Secretary of the British Embassy in Athens had suggested to another Greek diplomatic official, in connection with the Spaak plan (involving as mentioned earlier guaranteed independence for Cyprus for a fixed period), that Commonwealth membership of the new state might be maintained. The third case was the conversation between the Greek Foreign Minister and the U.S. Ambassador of June 14. In the course of it, as will be recalled,[114] Allen, expressing anxiety about the possibility of a British withdrawal from Cyprus, had wondered whether the Greek government should not make haste to do something to forestall such a British operation.

Under such circumstances, the potentialities of a Greek recourse to the United Nations were limited. It was, of course, true that the Assembly was no blind instrument of U.S. foreign policy. Nonetheless, the attitude of the United States carried such weight there that the success of any effort in that forum depended to a great extent on the Americans. At any rate, a new recourse to the United Nations should not be regarded as a self-contained, autonomous move but as part of a larger whole: the more general efforts to solve the Cyprus problem. Therefore, it was a function of other efforts aiming at a settlement that were being carried on outside the United Nations. Without knowledge of these, the Foreign Ministry service hesitated to put forward any more general recommendations.

Limiting itself, however, to the purely tactical aspect, the appropriate

Foreign Ministry service described the Greek aims through the United Nations in the following terms: At the stage of the debate on the inclusion of the Cyprus problem in the agenda of the Assembly, any reference to the substance of the question should be avoided, because it could turn out against the Greek viewpoint. The Greek recourse, accordingly, should be presented as a follow-up of Resolution 1013 (XI). Second, the British item inscribed in the previous Assembly's agenda should not be considered as automatically re-included in the agenda. Third, an effort should be made to secure the permanent and continuing interest of the United Nations in the Cyprus question by calling for the establishment of an investigation commission or a conciliation group, for instance, or for the appointment of a mediator. Fourth, efforts should be made to prevent unilateral British moves in Cyprus and to secure UN co-operation or consultation in the event of a British decision to change the island's status. These were the four maximal objectives that could be pursued in the United Nations.

As for the recourse itself, it could be presented in one of three forms: First, there could be a recourse on an altogether different basis from the previous one. Such a possibility ought to be studied only in the event a basis for such a recourse appeared to exist because of intergovernmental activities carried on outside of the United Nations. A second possibility would be to repeat the recourse made at the previous Assembly. The advantage of such an alternative was that the previous Assembly had accepted this recourse for discussion. But there were also some disadvantages too; for instance, the acceptance of this recourse together with the British counter-recourse. The third possibility—already mentioned— would be to present the recourse as a follow-up of Resolution 1013 (XI). If such a recourse were preferred, it would be possible to invoke the truce which EOKA had maintained in spite of the systematic campaign of liquidation undertaken by the British authorities in Cyprus, and to say that the Cypriot element had complied with that resolution. It could also be stated that the British government had not implemented that resolution by committing atrocities of various kinds against the population of Cyprus and by carrying out various other oppressive measures, and that it had taken no initiative nor accepted any proposals to resume negotiations as recommended in the UN resolution. It was, of course, self-evident that the British with the aid of the Turks would seek to prove that the Greeks insisted on their desire to annex the island, that the Cypriot leadership insisted on the union of Cyprus with Greece, and, consequently, that it was they who were violating the spirit of the UN resolution. It could, therefore, be predicted that the debate would follow the "Menon theory," under which the question of the island's independence was primarily involved. Accordingly, the Greek Delegation would have to declare whether it stood firm on its assurances concerning the independence of Cyprus, which it had given at the previous Assembly. On this basic point that lay outside its competence, the appropriate service of the Ministry for Foreign Affairs could make no recommendations. The subject of atrocities, it was suggested further in this planning paper, could be used in a separate recourse to be discussed in the Third, not the First Committee. The advantage of such an approach would be that the debate would thus be bereft of political acerbity, and the issue would be argued on humanitarian grounds with greater probabilities of support even on the part of delegations which were friendly to the British but were unable to close their eyes to British atrocities. In this context, it was noted that until then the Third Committee had never taken any decision concerning a concrete case—except in the matter of forced labor, which had political overtones.[115] That Committee usually showed great reserve whenever the debate was transferred from the sphere of abstract principles to that of concrete political responsibilities. At any rate, the subject of atrocities in all likelihood would seriously poison the atmosphere. Hence, it ought to be studied together with parallel intergovernmental activities concerning the Cyprus question.

On July 2, the preparatory work for the fourth Greek recourse on the Cyprus question to the Assembly's twelfth regular session started at the Greek Ministry for Foreign Affairs, with both Permanent Representative to the UN Palamas as well as G. V. Melas, Ambassador to the United States, present. Both had been called to Athens for that purpose. Premier Karamanlis presided over the first meeting. Ten days later—July 12—the recourse was sent to the UN Secretary-General with the request that it be included in the Assembly's provisional agenda, and with the promise that an explanatory memorandum would be sent in due course in conformity with rule 20 of the rules of procedure [116] (see Appendix D). That same day, a Greek government spokesman was reported as stating that there would always be time to suspend action before the United Nations, should a proposal satisfactory to the people of Cyprus be put forward by the British or any other quarter.[117] About a month later it was announced that the explanatory memorandum would be submitted by mid-September.[118]

The recourse—Greece's fourth over Cyprus—represented a partial synthesis of the two Greek draft resolutions submitted at the previous Assembly. It consisted, accordingly, of two subitems: subitem (a) referred to the "application, under the auspices of the United Nations, of the principle of equal rights and self-determination of peoples in the case of the population of the island of Cyprus," i.e., to the very heart of the problem, as the Greek government had formulated it since the first Greek recourse in 1954, at the ninth Assembly; subitem (b) referred to "violations of human rights and atrocities by the British Colonial Administration against the Cypriots."

Mentioned in subitem (b) of this recourse, the question of the ill-treatment of arrested and detained Cypriots by members of the British security forces had been raised, it will be recalled,[119] by the Greek

Delegation at the previous Assembly but, after the adoption of the resolution sponsored by India, the Greek Foreign Minister, as a gesture of good will toward Britain, had withdrawn the relevant file, which his delegation had deposited with the Secretary-General. This issue of governmental terrorism was not new. Two years earlier, on May 9, 1955, the Permanent Greek Mission to the UN had sent a letter to the Secretary-General, for circulation among member states, charging the British authorities in Cyprus with "a policy of brutal suppression in order to stifle any expression of the will of the people," and drawing attention to the activities started by "Dighenis" in April in response to this policy.[120]

The following year, after the exile of Makarios and the intensification of Harding's campaign against EOKA, the Greek government, on May 7, 1956, resorted to another international forum, the European Commission of Human Rights, and called for the implementation of the Convention for the Protection of Human Rights and Fundamental Freedoms in Cyprus. The target of this application under Article 24 of the above convention [121] was certain legislative and administrative emergency regulations—the deportation of Makarios included—which the British authorities had introduced in the island. On June 2, at its fifth session (May 28–June 2, 1956), the Commission declared admissible this application despite the British invocation of Article 15 of the Convention,[122] and referred the matter to a seven-member subcommission set up under Article 29 of the Convention and consisting of the Commission's Greek and British members and of five more members of the Commission chosen by lot, with instructions that it ascertain the facts and at the same time explore the possibilities of a friendly settlement based on respect for human rights, as required under Article 28 of the Convention. To present the Greek case, the Greek government engaged the services of the distinguished Belgian international jurist, Henri A. Rolin. On September 28 the subcommission met in Strasbourg to determine the procedure to be followed. Taking into account the time limit given to Britain to reply to the charges presented by the Greek government, it provisionally decided to begin the examination of the Greek application on November 12. Between November 14–18, the subcommission also decided to pursue its efforts to achieve a friendly settlement. Meeting again from December 18–20, it observed, on December 18, that certain measures (arrests, detentions, and deportations) continued in Cyprus. The British government, it proposed, should draw the attention of the Cyprus authorities to the measures of detention at home, and, as required under Article 15, paragraph 3, of the Convention, should keep the Secretary-General of the Council of Europe informed about the emergency measures applied in Cyprus. The Greek government, on its side, should recommend to Athens Radio the avoidance of any incitements to violence. The subcommission also set up a three-man group which was expected to recommend the liberation of Makarios to the subcommission and through it to the British government. The British representative, however, informed the subcommission that a British statement had been made public in Nicosia on December 18 to the effect that the laws about whipping juveniles and collective punishments had been revoked and that certain administrative and legislative measures in force would be modified. As a result, the subcommission merely took cognizance of this British statement. This did not satisfy the Greek government. In instructions of December 21 to Stamatis Merkouris, the Greek representative in Strasbourg, Averoff-Tossizza insisted that the subcommission should go to Cyprus to study the situation on the spot and that, regardless of the British concessions, it should issue a condemnatory decision.

Then, between January 18–20, 1957, several members of the European Commission of Human Rights had sought to get the two parties together, and these had stated their readiness to seek a basis for such a settlement.[123] On February 2, the subcommission met again, to discuss the findings of the three-man group that no effective measures had been taken for the freeing of Makarios. It requested that assurances be given that the revoked measures should not be reintroduced; that curfews should not be imposed without clear security reasons; and that information should be provided about the relaxation of emergency press measures. The British government was asked to reply by March 1. In the three-man group, it should be noted, the British representative argued that the question of Makarios' liberation was being used for purposes of political exploitation. The Turkish representative supported this view. On March 2, the British accepted the above proposals but opposed the liberation of Makarios. On March 29, finally, while the subcommission favored this step as well as the relaxation of the emergency measures, reserving its right under Article 28 (a), to carry out an investigation on the spot, the United Kingdom's Solicitor-General reported on the good news (announced in the Commons the day before) that his government had decided to release the Ethnarch from his detention in the Seychelles.

Charges about tortures and the ill-treatment of individual Cypriots then became an issue and led to a new Greek application to the European Commission of Human Rights. In his earlier-mentioned letter of May 28 to Macmillan, Ethnarch Makarios had referred to this matter.[124] So had Athens Radio on June 11—in lurid detail—with the Greek government reported a few days later as having made charges of use of brutal methods by the British authorities in Cyprus in order to extract confessions.[125] As for the governing body of the International Labor Office (ILO), it had decided, at the end of May, to draw the attention of the British government to the inherent danger of abuse that was involved in holding persons indefinitely in custody without trial, because of the difficulty of obtaining evidence by normal legal procedure, and to the importance of the right of all persons detained to receive a fair trial at the earliest possible moment.[126] That same month came a British riposte to all these charges: the Cyprus government published a *White Paper* entitled *Allegations of Brutality in Cyprus*. Governor Harding himself prefaced this paper, which sought to refute the charges of atrocities made by Cypriot or Greek spokesmen.[127] Then, on June 19, the Cypriot counterthrust. Makarios, in a press interview, released a long announcement to the press, claiming he had in his possession 317 signed statements by Greek Cypriots who had suffered various degrees of torture at the hands of the British security forces. He requested an investigation of these charges by an impartial international commission.[128] And on June 20, the Permanent Greek Representative to the UN, commenting on the UN report on Hungary, mentioned the issue.[129] On July 5, the European Commission of Human Rights reportedly decided to invite the British government to suspend all executions of Cypriots since they had been imposed on the basis of emergency regulations, and to request an on-the-spot investigation. The British government was asked to give its consent to such an investigation by July 20.[130]

The Greek government lodged its application with the European Commission of Human Rights against the British government on July 17, 1957, five days after submitting its new recourse to the United Nations.[131] It alleged forty-nine cases of "torture or ill-treatment amounting to torture" in Cyprus, again invoking Article 24 of the European Convention for the protection of Human Rights and Fundamental Freedoms. This application was communicated to the British government to enable it to submit its observations on the admissibility of the Greek application. These observations, in writing, were sent in on August 19. The British government opposed the admissibility of the Greek application, arguing that this would bring not even the beginning of proof about an action or an omission that would constitute on the part of the British government a violation of the aforementioned Convention; that admissibility would not be in accord with the provisions of the rules of procedure concerning the introduction of a complaint before the Commission; and that the domestic legal remedies available had not been exhausted in the cases brought forward by the Greek government (as required under Article 26 of the Convention). On August 28, the Commission, under Article 45, paragraph 1, of its rules of procedure, invited agents and counsellors of the parties to appear before it on August 30 to give, to the exclusion of all substantive means, their oral explanations on the admissibility of the Greek application. These oral explanations were made on August 20, and September 2, 3, and 4. On the latter date, the Commission invited the Greek agent to present his evidence for the forty-nine cases and asked certain questions from the British agent. On September 16, the Greek agent provided certain clarifications—*précisions*—while eleven days later the British agent replied to the questions the Commission had posed, and on October 2 and 4, made observations on the Greek note of September 16. Finally, on October 14, the Commission declared the Greek government's application of July 17 admissible in twenty-nine cases and inadmissible with respect to the remaining twenty, the latter on the ground that domestic remedies had not been exhausted.[132]

Meanwhile, with regard to the first Greek application to the European Commission of Human Rights—of May 7, 1956—concerning certain legislative and administrative emergency measures introduced in Cyprus by the British authorities, the subcommission set up in June, 1956, had decided to carry out an on-the-spot investigation to ascertain the existence and extent of a public emergency "threatening the life of a nation" (in the terminology of Article 15 of the convention), and the circumstances under which the curfew regulations had been applied in Cyprus.

The fourth Greek recourse to the United Nations on the Cyprus question had been transmitted amid a welter of press reports about differing views between the Greek government and Makarios on this matter, about solutions proposed by Spaak, about the supposed forthcoming transfer of the British Middle East Command Headquarters from Cyprus to Kenya together with a reduction of the number of British troops on the island, about British intentions to propose a new tripartite conference to deal with the Cyprus problem. Governor Harding had flown to London on July 6, and then, after conferring with Lennox-Boyd on July 7 and 8, had taken sick and had gone to the hospital. The *Tribune*, a Labour party organ, reported that differences of view had arisen between Macmillan and Lennox-Boyd over the Governor's further usefulness on the island.[133]

Reporting from London on July 14, the new Greek Ambassador, Seferiadis, who had presented his credentials to Queen Elizabeth II on June 26, wrote to the Foreign Minister that the British-Turkish team, which seemed indissoluble, constituted the most formidable difficulty in handling the Cyprus problem. A high British official had told him that the British government would accept any solution to the problem on which the Greek and Turkish governments would agree.[134] As for U.S. foreign policy, it seemed to be vying with British foreign policy in flattering the Turks as much as possible, in order to secure their co-operation in the Middle East after the Suez fiasco. The Americans did not have an experience in international affairs commensurate with their colossal material strength, and felt an ill-concealed inferiority complex in such matters vis-à-vis the British—hence their desire to outdo the British in currying Turkey's favor. As a result, the Greek government, at the forthcoming Assembly, would have to face the same difficulties it had faced at the previous Assembly, the Ambassador predicted.

One relatively bright spot was, though, that the British government seemed to have given up the idea of dismemberment for Cyprus—for the time being at least. Of course, it could revert to such a threat in order to exert pressure on Greece and make it accept the new proposals that it was preparing. About these one could be certain of one thing: the British government would seek to exclude the contingency of *enosis*—which it regarded as a necessary corollary to the abandonment of the idea of partition. In its demand for the application of self-determination, the Greek government would face great difficulties. These would have to be faced when the British proposals were conveyed to the Greek government. The Cyprus problem ought to be settled. This was in the interest of all. But up to what point could Greece retreat? Perhaps it would be desirable to prepare one's self for a long war of attrition, for trench warfare, bearing in mind Turkey's insistence on having the question closed now. The new British views about the diminishing strategic value of the island [135] could serve as an argument in favor of such temporizing tactics. With the lapse of time, such a policy might yield results. With the British, nothing was done immediately. After referring to his own efforts to create an atmosphere as favorable as possible with regard to the new British proposals which were expected—he had observed earlier that London for his good Turkish colleague was a real paradise for such activities on the Turkish side—he wondered whether a solution, which would entail the granting of Dominion status to Cyprus, coupled with a prohibition of withdrawal from the Commonwealth for a certain fixed period of time, should be proposed on the Greek side. Such a proposal would flatter the Conservatives. In conclusion, he wrote that the illness of the Governor of Cyprus had caused a delay in the consultations within the British government on matters pertaining to Cyprus and new possible moves. Perhaps this slowness was due to disagreements within the Cabinet, Seferiadis added.

F. *The House of Commons Debate on Cyprus*

During the long debate on Cyprus in the House of Commons on July 15, the seventh major one on that subject since May, 1955,[136] Colonial Secretary Lennox-Boyd refused a public inquiry into the Cypriot and Greek allegations of ill-treatment of Cypriots. "It would be out of the question," he said, "for there to be an inquiry of any kind involving the summoning of witnesses whose lives would be in danger if they were brought and gave evidence." [137] As for the British "Aspiring Decision-Makers," they accused the British government of not acting appropriately not only in this particular issue but also in the whole matter of reaching a settlement of the Cyprus problem. In a cat's cradle of political interaction, of interplay between foreign and domestic politics of two states in conflict, the internal foe—Her Majesty's Loyal Opposition— often seemed to echo the external foe's polemics, supplying him in the process with new and eminently quotable arguments if not making common cause with him, superficially at least, against the common foe.

The speech of the Labour party's Shadow Colonial Secretary, James Callaghan, during this long and lively debate [138] not only is a counterpart of the Greek Opposition attacks on the Greek government but similarly illustrates the complexities that the parliamentary debate of foreign policy may create for external decision-makers operating within the framework of a parliamentary system. It also reveals certain substantial

changes in British policy with regard to Cyprus, which were coming to
the surface in the aftermath of the Suez fiasco, especially in the sphere of
strategic considerations.

Callaghan started out by charging that the government had taken no
positive or constructive action to lower the tension in the island or to
bring together the elements of the population that had to live together
there if Cyprus was to pursue its future peaceably. No conversations with
the Greeks or the Turks had taken place. Makarios had not been brought
into the discussions. Since the end of March, the Colonial Secretary had
answered the Opposition's questions in a series of elegant evasions. He
had not carried the Cyprus matter forward one iota since the end of
March, though since the middle of that month there had been a truce in
Cyprus and not a single political murder had occurred. There was
nothing but indecision and drift from the government, which had failed
to take advantage of the opportunity presented by the cessation of
violence. It had given time to EOKA to regroup as well as propaganda
material for Makarios, who had been released, though he had deliberately refrained from responding to the appeal to cease violence.

"The Colonial Secretary discovered, as other gaolers before him had
discovered, that it is far easier to lock up a man than to find a good
reason for releasing him if he will not recant." What was the point of the
release, Callaghan asked, if it was not followed up? Why had the government left the situation in a suspended state? Why was it not possible now
to talk with Makarios? Why had the British government rejected the
Ethnarch's proposal for bipartite talks on the subject of what Callaghan
assumed Makarios meant—the internal future and self-government of
Cyprus? If the government had been in earnest about trying to secure a
settlement in Cyprus, why had it not taken the trouble to find out what
the Ethnarch meant, "instead of indulging in a long-range shouting
match with him?" No one had found out, or, if the government had, it
had not told the Commons. After quoting a Makarios interview with
Lord Lambton,[139] Callaghan asked Lennox-Boyd very directly: Was he
ready to enter into negotiations with representatives of the Greek Cypriots—of whom, he had no doubt, Makarios would be one—and representatives of the Turkish Cypriots in London or at any other convenient
place, to settle or, at any rate, to start negotiations about, the constitutional future of Cyprus?" Unless the Colonial Secretary gave a clear and
categorical affirmative answer that he was ready to discuss the future of
the island with Greek and Turkish Cypriots, he was guilty of the grossest
bad faith, because for months he had led the Commons to believe that he
need only a cessation of violence in the island to enable constitutional
progress to be made.

After this charge of governmental indecision and drift and this call for
action, Callaghan requested the Colonial Secretary and the government
"to disabuse themselves or, at any rate, some of their supporters, of the
ridiculous notion that partition would be any solution to the problems of

Cyprus." The Colonial Secretary should rule out partition from all discussions.

Turning next to the question of the future of Cyprus as a strategic base, Callaghan observed that for three years the Commons had been told that Britain held Cyprus, because the island was essential to British oil supplies and to British lines of communication in the Middle East. When the Greek Cypriots said they were willing to allow the British a base on the island, the government's reply had been: "A base on the island is not enough; what we need is Cyprus as a base, not a base in Cyprus." No less than £12½ million had already been spent or committed in the last three years to transform Cyprus into a base, and now the Minister of Defense—Duncan Sandys—had returned from Cyprus and the Middle East to say that what was really needed was not an island as a base after all, but a couple of airstrips "so that atomic bombers may fly off in pursuance of our defense against the USSR." [140] In three years, Callaghan went on to say, the government had brought Greece and Turkey to the edge of war, had strained British relations with NATO and the Baghdad Pact. For three years the government had repressed the island, "which is under a military dictatorship," and now it stated that "it was all for nothing; what we need is a couple of airstrips." The government, he charged, had been guilty not only of a great waste of public money, [141] not only of straining Britain's relations with its allies unnecessarily, but also, as far as the people of Cyprus were concerned, of sacrificing their hopes as free men to choose their own government for the sake of an apparently non-vital British strategic base.

For two years, Callaghan continued, the island had been living in a state of emergency. In the jails there were men sentenced to death, but the sentence had not been carried out. There were still 1,000 men and women under detention in Cyprus. [142] No charges had been brought against them, and a prosecution had not been heard. Coming now to "the constantly repeated allegations of brutality on the part of certain of the British security forces," he dealt at some length with a particular case that strongly suggested the use of brutal methods. He then declared that, in view of these allegations, the government owed it to the good name of the British people to have them investigated. He also argued that the time had arrived when it would be more advantageous for Cyprus to replace Governor Harding by a civilian, who would have some knowledge of political matters, if the shooting part of the operation was now over.

In conclusion, the member of Her Majesty's Loyal Opposition asked the government not to be obsessed by the attitude of the Turks to the extent that they applied a veto to any forward moves the government itself might wish to take. Of course, there was no one in the Commons who did not wish to see a close and confident relationship with Turkey, which was linked to Britain both by treaty and many friendships. However, the Turks could not be allowed to blackmail Britain—or anyone else for that matter. One simply could not afford to put the Turks in a position in which, by using 20 per cent of the population of Cyprus, they were able to stop any forward move for the remaining 80 per cent. If one did have a duty, this major duty should lie with the overwhelming numbers of the population on the island. The government should tell the Turks it desired to see the Turkish minority in Cyprus properly safe-guarded, whether the Radcliffe constitution was finally adopted or not. He could not believe that the Turkish government valued its relationship with Britain, its membership in the Baghdad Pact and NATO so lightly that it would be willing to throw all this overboard in the face of the most solemn guarantees from the British government about the treatment of the Turkish minority. If it did throw them overboard, it would be shown that Britain had been clinging to a very fickle ally by mistake. The government's policy, insofar as it was based on a desire to please the Turks and not to offend them, was not only doing itself an injustice but was doing the people of Cyprus a great injustice. Britain was saying to them: "Our interests are such, our relationships with Turkey are of such character, that we must not give you your freedom. Because we wish to please Turkey . . . (and) to avoid any strain on our alliances, you must not have the elementary right of free men to choose your own govern-ment . . . to build your own institutions and to choose your own associ-ates. All these things are to be subordinated to the interest of Britain in her relationship with Turkey." [143]

In answer to charges that the Labour party was making it more difficult to get a settlement of the Cyprus question by creating the impression that if it came into power it would grant immediate self-determination—with the result that negotiations with Makarios or other parties to the problem were "bound to be bedevilled" by a "let us wait and see" attitude—Callaghan made it clear that the Labour party view was that quite a long period of self-government should precede the exer-cise of self-determination by the people of Cyprus. [144]

In response to these and other charges of the Opposition, the spokes-men for the British government referred to Makarios' release and to the offer of a safe-conduct to Grivas, mentioning this time in this connection the spirit of Resolution 1013 (XI). "With the lifting of one little finger," Makarios could bring to the island the atmosphere of peace and freedom of expression mentioned in that resolution, said Undersecretary of State for the Colonies Profumo. [145] And the Secretary himself, Lennox-Boyd, explained that the word "resume" mentioned in that resolution, "certainly did not mean precisely the same form of negotiation as has taken place before." It meant, he said, the resumption of talks "with those people most likely to bring a solution." And, in the government's view, the most likely solution would come through the good offices of NATO. Finally, the Colonial Secretary said that while it would be unfortunate if the island were divided, if self-determination were to be applied there, it would have to be, as he had made clear in his statement of December 19, 1957, in the Commons, on the basis of self-determination for both the Greeks and for the Turks.[146]

Shortly after, in a speech delivered at Bedford on July 20, Premier Macmillan reminded his audience that Cyprus was not just a colonial problem. If it had been, it would have been fairly easy to solve, along the familiar lines. It was a strategic and international problem, and thus involved "ourselves, as well as the people of Cyprus—who are divided into two groups—and also the Governments of Greece and Turkey." It involved also NATO and the Baghdad Pact, and anyone who tried to find a solution without taking all these into account was beating the air.[147]

By July 31, Sir John Harding was back in Nicosia. Though a new British statement on Cyprus was expected in the House of Commons on August 1, none was made. Secretary of State Dulles, in London on July 29, reportedly had discussed the problem with Lloyd, his British colleague, and Turkish Ambassador Birgi. After a meeting of August 2, the latter was reported to be displeased with his conversation with Dulles. Turkey, he had warned, might reorient its policy toward the neutralist bloc, if its views on Cyprus were not supported.[148]

That Ethnarch Makarios, toward the end of July, had been influenced by the Spaak proposals as well as by the Greek government views and British charges of intransigence is indicated in an interview published on July 21 in the Cypriot newspaper *Eleftheria* in which he released a sort of trial balloon. He was ready, he said, to discuss plans for the real independence of Cyprus if these did not exclude eventual self-determination. Grivas learned more about this attitude (it went against the decision of the Pan-Cyprian National Assembly, he noted) from a letter he received four days later from Vlachos, the Greek Consul-General in Nicosia, who confirmed the above mentioned view of the Ethnarch. The Turks, Vlachos explained, opposed such a development, because they were aware that the slogan of independence was gaining ground. Were it realized, no international guarantee nor international formula would be capable of preventing the natural course of independence toward *enosis*. Selling, of course, this idea to the Greek public would raise difficulties. In his reply of July 29 to this note, the leader of EOKA observed that for the British there were many forms of independence that were granted to colonies in order to perpetuate subjugation to, and dependence on, Britain. Consequently, no talks should start before the form of independence was put forward. In his opinion, the British would give nothing that would be satisfactory. "We were yielding to force and threats, whereas we have more trumps in our hand then they." Greek policy, he added, was "a policy of dollars." [149]

While reorganizing his sorely tried forces, Grivas had resisted the temptation of breaking the unilateral truce offered in mid-March, in spite of the operations, provocations, and propaganda on the part of Governor Harding's forces, the purpose of which was, he thought, to draw him out

into the open at a moment of weakness. This, however, had not prevented him from issuing various leaflets—which led to friction with the
Greek government. For, as the Greek Consul in Nicosia had informed
him, these leaflets were quoted in British government complaints to the
Greek government as indications that, in spite of the truce, it was EOKA's
intention to resume its activities. Nevertheless, by mid-August, Grivas
felt fully ready to start again his operations.[150]

Chapter Four

Greece Avoids a
New Tripartite Conference

A. *British Probes for a Tripartite Conference*

Barely three weeks after the Permanent Mission of Greece to the UN had asked the Secretary-General to place the question of Cyprus on the provisional agenda of the twelfth Assembly[1] (seven weeks, namely, before the opening of the Assembly), Sir Roger Allen, the new British Ambassador in Athens,[2] was received on August 3, at about noon, at his own urgent request, by Foreign Minister Averoff-Tossizza at the Ministry for Foreign Affairs. Consulting two notes, he told the Foreign Minister that his government was concerned about the disturbing effects of the Cyprus question on NATO and had therefore decided to make a new effort to find a solution to this question. The real difficulty resided in deciding the matter of the island's final regime. If agreement could be reached on this matter, the rest could be easily settled. Experience had shown that it was not possible to achieve agreement through bipartite contacts between the governments concerned. Perhaps the British government would examine the possibility of inviting representatives of Greece and Turkey to London toward the beginning of September. The United States would be prepared to take a close interest in such a conference, and Spaak, the Secretary-General of NATO, had been invited to attend as an observer. The British government would come to such a conference with an entirely open mind. There would be no agenda. All solutions from *enosis* to the status quo would be discussed. The only factors the British government wished to cover were:

a. Essential military facilities under British sovereignty.
b. Protection of the island from Communist infiltration.
c. Ensuring peace and tranquility on the whole island.

The purpose of such a conference—which would take place behind closed doors—would be to find a solution acceptable to all from the international viewpoint so that the way would then be open for settling internal problems through direct talks with Cypriot representatives. Such talks, the British government believed, were indispensable, but could only follow an agreement on the principles for reaching a settlement on the international level.

Sir Roger then said he had received instructions to point out to the Greek government that a critical point had been reached in the Cyprus question. The continuation of the crisis would harm everyone as well as make the eventual solution more difficult. Recent conversations in London and Athens had allowed the British government to believe that the Greek government shared this view. Likewise sharing this view were the U.S. government and Spaak. Both favored a new effort by the British government. This, together with their participation, meant that the talks would be on an altogether different basis than the tripartite conference of 1955 had been. The British government he reiterated, would arrive at the conference table open-mindedly. It would discuss all solutions. Success would depend on an analogous response on the part of the other participants in the conference.

The British government, Sir Roger went on to say, was aware of the importance the Greek government attached to British talks with the Cypriots;[3] and it agreed with this. The British government's thoughts on the need for a tripartite conference were no substitutes for such an approach, but aimed at achieving the indispensable international agreement, without which such talks with the Cypriots would have no likelihood of success. In the view of the British government, talks on the international and the national levels were complementary parts of a whole procedure. The British government did not underestimate the internal difficulties of the Greek government, but the other governments, too, had internal difficulties. The Turkish government had publicly advocated partition. Were it to accept the British invitation—and the British government believed it would—it would be charged with weakness and inconsistency. Likewise, in Britain, there were many political currents. Consequently, all governments concerned should show strength and candor.

Such a complex problem, Sir Roger re-emphasized, could not be advanced toward solution through bipartite talks. Were the Greek government to accept the thoughts of the British government, the latter would be prepared prior to the envisaged conference to discuss any matter through the diplomatic channel. The only point that the British government wished to emphasize was that it could undertake no commitments, because to do so would be contrary to the entire spirit and aim of the conference.

The British envoy also underlined that his government through this *démarche* was in no way formulating an invitation to a conference. It did not wish to create any difficulties for the Greek government and was ready to answer any of its questions. Time, though, was pressing, if such contacts were to take place in September and preparations were to be made for this conference. Sir Roger also underlined that the present contact was secret and that his government hoped the Greek government, too, would maintain secrecy on what was a preliminary sounding. To this, the Greek Foreign Minister immediately agreed.

Asked by the British Ambassador about his first reaction to this sounding, the Greek Foreign Minister replied he was unable to tell him anything before consulting the Prime Minister and discussing this matter with him in detail. Here was a very grave decision to take.

The five points the British Ambassador emphasized that had impressed the Greek Foreign Minister as he listened to this *démarche* were: (1) if, finally, Greece were to attend a conference in London, it would not have to face an Anglo-Turkish front; (2) if in the eventual discussions, solutions were reached, such as those the Greek government had already envisaged, Greece would not find itself in a minority; (3) if the Greek government believed that the problem was how to hammer into the heads of the Turks a solution other than theirs—partition of Cyprus between Greece and Turkey—the only way to do so would be to bring them around a table for talks such as those envisaged by the British government; (4) circumstances had changed and the Greek government should not think it would find itself participating in a conference such as the tripartite one of 1955; and (5) if all parties insisted, the Americans, too, would consent to sit down at the conference table.

That same day, the Foreign Minister, after informing Premier Karamanlis of this British *démarche*—the Premier recommended extreme reserve because of the dangers an affirmative reply would entail—received the U.S. Ambassador, at his request (Sir Roger had foretold this call to Averoff-Tossizza, who already knew about it). The American Allen informed the Foreign Minister that his government had sent identic notes to the Greek and Turkish governments, expressing the belief that the British would come to the talks with good will and an open mind; that the United States desired such talks; that it hoped the two governments would examine the matter favorably, without putting conditions in advance of their acceptance; and, finally, that it believed the best hopes for finding a solution resided in quiet diplomacy and, for that reason, it earnestly urged the maintenance of the strictest secrecy—including secrecy of the fact that the talks would take place in London.

To this last remark, Averoff-Tossizza replied that such secrecy was wholly outside reality, because it was impossible to keep secret the calling of such a conference. But, regardless of secrecy—which would be strictly kept for a certain period on the Greek side—he wished to avoid misleading the U.S. Ambassador with false impressions, and informed him that it was most unlikely that the Greek government would accept an eventual invitation to the envisaged conference. While not denying that the British motives behind the idea of convoking a tripartite conference might possibly be different from those which had led to the conference of September, 1955, and that perhaps there was a likelihood of its achieving some results, two basic matters were involved: First, the Greek government believed and held that the question of Cyprus was one that primarily concerned the British government and the Cypriot people, though other countries, including Greece and Turkey, had indirect interests. Hence, in accepting an invitation such as the one outlined, Greece would be abandoning its basic position and espousing the view that its own indirect interests had priority not only over those of other countries but also over the interests of the Cypriot people, who had the right to have the first and basic say in this matter. Such an acceptance would be even more distasteful to the Greek government, since, in its opinion, the United Nations, too, in Resolution 1013 (XI), had endorsed this viewpoint. Resorting again now, as it was, to the United Nations, Greece would appear to be repudiating this basic position. Second, as long as it was known that Turkey insisted on partition of Cyprus as the sole solution, the results of the suggested conference would be negative and much evil would flow from it. If it were really desired to persuade Turkey to drop the idea of partition, this could be done through the diplomatic channel without calling a rather dangerous conference.

In London, likewise on August 3, Permanent Undersecretary Sir Frederick Hoyer-Millar (later Lord Inchyra) had invited Greek Ambassador Seferiadis to the Foreign Office and had informed him of the British *démarche,* again stressing the harm done to the Allied front and NATO by the continuation of the Cyprus dispute, and enjoining the maintenance of secrecy vis-à-vis Archbishop Makarios too. The Turkish Ambassador in London, Birgi, had been advised of this proposal the previous day. Seferiadis, expressing his personal view, was pessimistic about the outcome of such a proposal for a conference, which coincided with the opening of the General Assembly. All concessions were being requested from the Greek government, he said, inasmuch as Turkey was always asking for tripartite negotiations. Besides, what could one expect from such a conference, since the Turks continually insisted on the island's dismemberment? "The center of gravity is on Athens now," said Hoyer-Millar. "No," the Greek diplomat replied, "you have cast the whole weight upon Athens."

When the British official suggested that Greece now should show real statesmanship, the Greek envoy could not refrain from replying that statesmanship did not mean that a government should sign an act of suicide. The poet-diplomat felt that the fragile confidence between British and Greek government officials had again been dealt a most grievous blow. Whereas Foreign Secretary Lloyd, late in July, had intimated to him that a new proposal, of a substantive character, was about to be made, here now was Britain reverting to procedures that reminded him of the dearly-paid experience of September, 1955. And, as he had told Sir Charles Peake the day before—after his recall as Ambassador in Athens and his resignation from the Foreign Office, Sir Charles was working with Colonial Secretary Lennox-Boyd—doubts could be entertained concerning the earnestness of the British approach. Lennox-Boyd was about to take off for a ten-day yacht cruise. The Foreign Secretary was leaving for a three-week holiday. For explaining the British behavior, the Greek Ambassador commented to Athens, there were only two hypotheses: either an intrigue was afoot to create difficulties for the Greek government, or something had happened since July—a strong Turkish reaction?—which had brought about the change. At any rate, the British proposal betrayed signs of improvisation and a characteristic lack of imagination. It was a reversion to the attitude taken during the previous General Assembly on the eve of Krishna Menon's proposals, which had brought to nought the Thai proposal calling for negotiations between the parties concerned. A tripartite conference would be tantamount to a recognition of Turkey's ability to play its well-known game. At the same time he feared lest a Greek refusal result in a new deterioration of Greek-British relations. Yet it was better that this should happen now than later. As a matter of tactics, he would prefer no hasty refusal, to avoid charges of thoughtlessness. Before giving the negative answer, a period of cold silence might be allowed to elapse.

B. The Precedent for a Tripartite Conference

The "dearly-paid experience of September, 1955"—the London Tripartite Conference on the Eastern Mediterranean and Cyprus (August 29–September 7) together with the anti-Greek riots in Istanbul and Izmir, which had punctuated it on September 6 [4]—had contributed to grave tension in Greek-Turkish relations as well as to non-participation of Greek forces in NATO exercises in October of that year. Like the new proposals, those which had led to the tripartite conference of 1955 had been authored by Britain, with Prime Minister Eden in the Commons announcing the invitation to it on June 30, and explaining that there would be no fixed agenda to the conference and that discussions should range widely over all the questions involved without prior commitment by any party.[5] On that occasion, too, the Greek government had been reluctant to accept this invitation. It realized that Turkish participation in it involved recognition of Turkey as a party concerned in the Cyprus question. Besides, participation in the conference (especially when its opening date was postponed to the end of August, giving a Machiavellian appearance to the British invitation, regardless of the real motives for this postponement) would make it more difficult to have the Cyprus item included in the General Assembly's agenda for discussion. If the Greek government had finally accepted this invitation, it had been largely due to the belief that it involved British recognition that Cyprus was an international question, not one of domestic jurisdiction, as the British government had inflexibly maintained until then. Some Opposition party leaders, but for certain conditions, had favored Greek acceptance of the invitation and/or participation in this conference. They had also urged upon the government a common goal: self-determination for Cyprus within a fixed and reasonable time limit.[6] Besides, on that occasion, too, just as in August, 1957, the U.S. government favored such talks. Thus, in a conversation with Ambassador G. V. Melas in the State Department, Secretary of State Dulles had strongly urged Greek acceptance of the British invitation. Although the Ambassador forcefully told him he believed this conference was "a trap," he was convinced, he said, the British were acting in good faith. "Good luck," he exclaimed, to the departing diplomat.

Makarios, on the other hand, in a press statement of July 16 in Athens, had criticized the Greek government's decision. He would have preferred a new recourse to the United Nations and a refusal to attend the tripartite conference unless the British government committed itself to granting self-determination to the Cypriots. In his view, too, convocation of the conference was a trap designed to undermine Greece's recourse to the United Nations. The Cyprus question was not a political issue between Britain, on the one hand, and Greece and Turkey, on the other. It was purely one of the self-determination and concerned only the British government and the Cypriot people—and the Greek government only insofar as it acted as the Cypriot people's mandatory for safeguarding their right of self-determination.[7]

The Turkish government had fewer reasons to hesitate than the Greek government in accepting the British invitation to the London Tripartite Conference. In contrast to the Turkish press, which declared that the alliance with Britain and Greece would become valueless if the Greek Cypriots obtained enough self-government to enable them to achieve *enosis*, it had behaved until then with restraint. Eden, however, urged it to become more outspoken and to make it clear that Turkey would "never let the Greeks have Cyprus."[8] The London Conference gave it the opportunity to do so.

At the London Tripartite Conference, Macmillan, then Foreign Secretary, after presenting his government's viewpoint and listening to the statements of the Greek and Turkish foreign ministers, came up with a proposal for self-government for Cyprus, not for self-determination. In reply to two questions put to him by Foreign Minister Zorlu, he clearly committed his government to the position that it did not "accept the principle of self-determination as one of universal application," that "exceptions should be made [to that principle] in view of geographical, traditional, historical, strategical and other considerations," and that Britain intended to maintain its sovereignty over the island.[9]

The Greek Foreign Minister, Stefanopoulos, insisted, on the other hand, on asking for self-determination on behalf of the population of Cyprus. The Greek government would accept and respect "any decision that may duly be taken by the population of Cyprus, no matter what that decision may be." His government, he also made clear, did not ask that the right of self-determination be immediately granted. It realized that a transition period of "free government" would have to intervene during which the Cypriots of Greek and Turkish origin would, "proportionately to their numerical strength and on a footing of equity, administer their territory through their duly elected representatives." The duration of this period would be "fixed in a reasonable and objective manner." Although denying that his government was seeking to bring about the union of Cyprus with Greece, he detailed the guarantees the Greek government would grant the Turkish minority, thus implicitly not excluding union as a result of the exercise of the right of self-determination.[10]

Turkey's views, as expressed by Foreign Minister Zorlu, were that the status quo should be maintained. If this were to be upset, the island should revert to Turkey. The principle of self-determination could not be applied in Cyprus. Turkey's interest in Cyprus was based on history, proximity, economy, military strategy and "on the sacred right of all countries to existence and security." Zorlu thought that, under existing conditions, not even self-government in Cyprus was possible as long as the Greek government had not given up its claim for self-determination. He also hinted that a change in the status of Cyprus would amount to a revision of the Treaty of Lausanne and open the way to Turkish counter-claims against Greece in Thrace and the Dodecanese.[11]

Both the Turkish and the Greek governments rejected the British proposals for self-government in Cyprus—the first Macmillan plan. This plan provided for: (1) An assembly with an elected majority and an appointed minority, with a proportionate quota of seats reserved for the Turkish minority. (2) A council of ministers that would be responsible to the Assembly, except for foreign affairs, defense, and public security, which would be reserved for the Governor. A Cypriot chief minister to head the new administration would be chosen by the Assembly with the Governor's approval. (3) A special British-Greek-Turkish commission that would be set up in London—by the conference—to put the plan into effect and to act as a center for discussing differences arising out of self-government, which it had not been possible to solve locally in Cyprus.[12]

In brief, the conference had served to highlight the divergence of views on the Cyprus question at that time, with Britain wishing to maintain its sovereignty over the whole island; Turkey agreeing, provided that, in the event of a change in its status, the island would be ceded to Turkey; and Greece insisting that the right of deciding their own future after a fixed and reasonable period be granted to the Cypriots. Politically, the conference underlined the potential Greek-Turkish antagonism over the issue—a side effect that Eden had deliberately sought to achieve when calling the conference in an effort to counteract the thesis that the Cyprus troubles were due to old-fashioned British colonialism.[13] Britain, the sovereign over the island, was thus placed in the position of mediator in a dispute between Greece and Turkey over the future status of an island that belonged to neither of these states.

From the Greek viewpoint, the London Tripartite Conference of 1955 had indeed been a painful experience, which should not be gone through again if possible. Eden had exploited the Greek-Turkish tension engendered by this conference, the last day of which had been punctuated by the anti-Greek riots in Istanbul and Izmir, in order to persuade the U.S. government to oppose this time even the inclusion of the Cyprus item in the agenda of the tenth General Assembly. The Greeks were to blame, he argued, for having ever raised the Cyprus question. If they were now encouraged to appeal to the United Nations, this would make both them and the Turks more rigid in their attitude and inflame the situation on the island.[14] Greek Opposition leaders, too, exploiting the General Assembly's refusal to include the Cyprus item in its agenda mainly because of the negative votes of Greece's ten NATO allies and the fourteen votes of friends of these allies, had squarely raised the question of whether the alignment of Greece with NATO damaged rather than served the interests of Greece, had urged a reappraisal of Greek foreign policy, and had called upon the government to resign forthwith, threatening to resign from their own seats in Parliament together with all their followers. Thirdly, the Turkish riots in Istanbul and the attacks on the homes of Greek NATO officers at Izmir together with the burning down of the Greek Consulate in that city also had unfavorably affected Greek public opinion toward American foreign policy. For the relevant message of Secretary of State Dulles which the U.S. Ambassador in Athens handed to Premier Papagos ten days after these riots, appeared to Greek newspapers of all shades of political opinion as placing on the same footing the victims of these riots and their perpetrators, because a virtually identic note had also been sent to the Turkish government.[15]

In response to these events, the Greek government recalled the Greek unit sent to fight in Korea with the UN forces, as well as the Greek officers serving under NATO command at Izmir. It also informed its allies that the Greek position in NATO might become problematic if these allies did not show a better understanding of Greece and if Turkey failed to give full moral and material satisfaction for the September "vandalisms." As a result of this latter *démarche*, the Turkish government organized a ceremony in Izmir, during which Turkish troops saluted the Greek flag. It also passed a law granting reparation to the Greeks whose property had been damaged or destroyed during the September riots. Finally, the Greek government obtained the abolition of a measure adopted in 1948 under which U.S. nationals serving in American non-diplomatic missions in Greece were exempted from the jurisdiction of Greek courts.

C. The Impact of the British Probes and Their Continuation

Two days after Sir Roger Allen's *démarche* of August 3, the Greek Foreign Minister, accompanied by two top officials of the Ministry for Foreign Affairs, called on Ethnarch Makarios and informed him that difficulties had arisen in London concerning the formulation of new British proposals on the Cyprus question and especially in the matter of the future exercise of the right of self-determination by the Cypriot people. These difficulties were due to the fact that any formula on this matter acceptable to the Greek side met with a Turkish refusal, and *vice versa*. As a result, the British government seemed to be orienting itself toward a decision to call a new tripartite conference without a fixed agenda. Averoff-Tossizza expressed his anxiety at the prospect of such a British proposal. Were Greece to accept the invitation, it was possible—aside from other drawbacks—that the recourse to the United Nations would be harmed, with the British and Turks putting forward the argument that the Cyprus question was already under discussion tripartitely. If, on the other hand, Greece rejected the invitation, its opponents at the Assembly might accuse it of recalcitrance and of non-compliance with Resolution 1013 (XI). At any rate, for reasons that did not require explanation, rejection of this proposal was preferable to its acceptance.

Concerning the fate of the new recourse to the United Nations, Averoff-Tossizza made the following predictions: First, probabilities were very few for the adoption of a resolution that would favor independence for a fixed period of years. Second, there were more, but not many, probabilities for a resolution to emerge that would be unfavorable to the Greek viewpoint. Third, there were a great many probabilities for a resolution to be adopted that would be vaguer than the one the previous Assembly had adopted. This latter outcome—or the adoption of no resolution at all—would not be at all satisfactory. In such a case, it would be inevitably necessary to face the contingency of a resumption of EOKA activities. Since it had been learned that the Turkish minority in Cyprus was being armed, the struggle on the island would assume the character of more widespread bloodshed and continuous reprisals by both sides, with unpredictable consequences. It was, thus, inescapable that if matters took such a course, both the Cypriot people would suffer terribly, and Greece, in trying to promote the issue, would find itself at a new dead end.

Faced with such contingencies, the Greek government believed it would be expedient to propose concrete solutions acceptable on the Greek side and get the United States to espouse one of these solutions and put it forward. He, Averoff-Tossizza, could perceive three such solutions: First, independence for the island for some short time, after which the right of self-determination might be exercised only when the Cypriot government requested this from the United Nations and the latter acceded to this request. Second, independence for a longer time, e.g. twenty years, after which the Cypriot people would be entitled automatically to exercise their right of self-determination. Third, self-government for ten years at the most, after which the right of self-determination might be exercised without any limitations. The Greek government now wished to know whether Makarios agreed to the accept-ability of any of the above three solutions.

With regard to the possibility of a tripartite conference, the Ethnarch observed that the Greek refusal to participate in it should not necessarily be regarded as a sign of an intransigent mood. For instance, the Greek government could explain that it saw no benefits accruing from a new and "agendaless" conference and that only harm could result from its certain failure.

Concerning the three solutions which the Greek Foreign Minister had outlined, Makarios replied that if it were possible for one of the three solutions to be proposed by a third state, then he believed agreement could be reached and the Cypriot people would accept this solution. When Averoff-Tossizza told him about a fourth solution, suggested by the Greek Ambassador in London, that would salvage British prestige, namely, that Cyprus remain for a while within the Commonwealth and also enjoy Dominion status for a period as short as possible under twenty years—after which an unlimited right of self-determination might be exercised—the Ethnarch replied that this solution, too, placed, in order of value, between the second and the third one, could be acceptable after the discussion of details.

While the Greek Foreign Minister and the Ethnarch were agreed on the need to rebuff the British government in its efforts to make arrange-ments for a tripartite conference in London, NATO pressure, too, was being exerted upon the Greek government to accept such a procedure for dealing with the Cyprus question. Spaak, the Greek Foreign Minister learned from the Greek Permanent Representative to NATO, Ambassador Michel Melas, recommended acceptance of the British proposal for talks, with an American official and the Secretary-General of NATO present as observers, though he himself would have preferred diplomatic exchanges until a common ground was found. Dulles, Spaak said, at first had refused to allow U.S. participation, even through an observer, in a matter in which the United States was not directly involved. However, if the Greek government requested it, he would accede to sending an observer. As for the first reaction of the Turks, this had been unfavorable. They regarded the Americans as favorably inclined toward the Greeks and considered Spaak himself as a Philhellene—which he was, he said, if supporting the rights of people was called Philhellenism. In Spaak's view, the British, naturally, had put forward their proposal in order to solve the Cyprus problem before the General Assembly met. For, in this way, they would avoid unpleasant debates in front of the Soviets or, at least, improve their position during the debate. At any rate, it seemed that the British government had dropped the idea of dismemberment of the island. Greek rejection of the British sounding for a conference, Spaak believed, would dangerously strengthen the impression of international public opinion that it was the Greeks who were unyielding. This would redound to Turkey's benefit. Such a rejection would also be exploited against the Greek government in the United Nations. Turkey's refusal, on the other hand, or its offer of unacceptable terms during the proposed conference, would strengthen Greece.

On August 6, in a new British effort to prod the Greek government to take a more positive attitude toward the sounding made about the calling of a tripartite conference, Sir Roger Allen once again urgently asked to see the Greek Foreign Minister. Because of their previous conversation and the slowness in his getting a reply, he felt, he told him, that the Greek government had hesitations on the matter. Therefore, he had asked his own government to give assurances against partition, in the hope that this would facilitate Greek participation in the proposed conference. He realized his government could not speak very clearly on the matter but he had received a cable from London that went far beyond the point he himself had expected his government to go. Accordingly, the British government could not undertake any commitment but could provide the assurance that the preparation for partition was not—Sir Roger said this twice—among the aims of these soundings for calling a tripartite conference. The British government insisted on its sincerity. Its soundings were due to efforts made in good faith to find a solution acceptable to all in a spirit of friendship. If the Greek government did not take part in such a conference, it would bear the responsibility if the final solution was not to its satisfaction. The Greek government should take advantage of the opportunity offered to develop its arguments against partition and persuade others about the practical value of its own compromise views. The British government categorically stated that no secret understanding existed at the expense of the Greek views. It also categorically denied that it was responsible for the leak to the press concerning secret soundings.[16] It promised to investigate how this leak had occurred. Indeed, the Foreign Office soon issued a *démenti* of Athens press reports concerning preparations for a tripartite conference.

In reply, Averoff-Tossizza said these statements brought about little change to the facts of the matter. His government, in any case, was studying the question in detail, and no great delay would occur in delivering a reply. He let it be understood that, in spite of Greek good will, he did not think it was possible to accept the suggestion, and he briefly explained the reasons for this attitude.

Next day, August 7, the Foreign Minister handed to Sir Roger Allen the Greek reply to the British verbal *démarche* of August 3. In this note, the Greek government expressed particular appreciation of the need for solving the issue of Cyprus in order to eradicate a serious cause of disturbance of the indispensable concord between NATO members. For this reason, the Greek government, though supporting a cause, the justice of which no one could dispute, had always been willing to discuss and support a solution that would be just but would also take into account the objective interests of any party concerned. However, the settlement of the Cyprus question could be achieved only on a realistic and just basis. Otherwise, the problem would not be solved. It would simply be covered up. Namely, in the body of the Western World an open wound would be left, which every so often would weaken it.

Once again desirous of contributing to the finding of a solution in the above spirit, the Greek government did not regard it imperative at this moment to draw attention to various points in the British Ambassador's communication of August 3, upon which it had views of its own. On this subject, the Greek government had a clearly defined position. It considered that the issue concerned basically the British government and the Cypriot people. This the United Nations had accepted through Resolution 1013 (XI). However, if the essential preconditions for the achievement of a just and reasonable solution acceptable to all Cypriots were created beforehand, the Greek government would not refuse to accept any kind of procedure that would lead to such a result. But the envisaged procedure was wholly inappropriate. It placed the full burden of difficulties and disadvantages upon the shoulders of the Greek government. It could lead to no results. And it enclosed serious dangers. It could lead to no results, because the preparation required had not been made, and it was known that at least one of the invited parties insisted upon one and only one solution, which was a very evil one from all points of view. Second, according to firm information, Turkey was about to have elections. Third, the proposal had been made practically on the eve of the Assembly's session. As for the dangers, these consisted of the fact that a failure of the proposed talks would officially confirm existing disagreements. From this confirmation, greater tension would follow with all its evil consequences for quite some time. Then, such a failure would deprive public opinion of the hope that a compromise solution could be found by negotiations. For these reasons, the Greek government believed that the issue could be examined through any sort of procedure only as long as conditions had been created beforehand which allowed, if not a certainty, at least a well-based hope that a solution would be found. Although these preconditions were known from various past conversations, the Greek government was willing fully to clarify them through the diplomatic channel in contacts that would prepare the way for calling together a really constructive conference. The Greek government especially appreciated the spirit in which the British Ambassador in Athens had presented the subject as well as the eagerness of such a distinguished personality as Mr. Spaak to contribute to this new effort, which, unfortunately, the Greek government did not regard as practical and constructive.

During this meeting of August 7 with Sir Roger Allen, Averoff-Tossizza added verbally that the Greek position concerning the British soundings would not have been far different, had no leaks occurred, though it had become more difficult after such leaks to the press. Prime Minister Karamanlis, he said, wished to stress the need for close relations with

Britain, and would like to negotiate with the British. However, whenever efforts were made for secret conversations, leaks to the press had occurred, and this had alarmed him. Finally, Averoff-Tossizza emphasized that the Greek government had not fully shut the door and was prepared to negotiate, if the ground were prepared in advance.

On this occasion, the Foreign Minister also communicated to Sir Roger the three suggested solutions involving an independent or self-governing Cyprus—eventual self-determination never excluded—he had outlined to Makarios two days earlier. The Greek government, he explained, would accept one of these, without, however, proposing it itself. He also believed, he said, that his government would not meet with difficulties on the part of the Greek Cypriots if it asked them to guarantee the minority rights of the Turkish Cypriots as well as their participation in the administration of the island proportionately with their numbers in the entire population of Cyprus. If the first two solutions were also to include the condition that Cyprus should remain within the Commonwealth, he added, the Greek government believed it could not easily accept them. Nevertheless, because it earnestly desired to exhaust all efforts in order to achieve a solution tolerable to the Cypriots; to facilitate the British government in the acceptance of such a solution; and to avert a deeper damage to the already disturbed harmony within NATO ranks, it would agree to study these solutions as well, even with the aforementioned variation, as long as Cyprus was assured full independence with the preconditions mentioned—of a UN decision for ending this independence, or of a twenty-year period of guaranteed independence.

In response, the British Ambassador maintained that conversations were the best way for facilitating Britain in preparing a good plan, but expressed doubts about the acceptability to his government of the Greek ideas of independence—with eventual self-determination—for Cyprus. He also read to Averoff-Tossizza the telegram assuring him that the purpose of the proposed conference was not to prepare the ground for partition.

In spite of the preliminary Greek rebuff, which was publicly disclosed two days later,[17] the British government continued its efforts in a fashion that suggested to the Greek Ambassador in London that this was a tactical maneuver designed to strengthen Britain's bargaining position. A new British démarche was to be made on August 12. Meanwhile, both the Secretary-General of NATO and the U.S. government spokesmen expressed their regrets at the Greek position. The United States, it was believed, hoped that neither the Cyprus nor the Algerian question would be discussed in the General Assembly. The State Department also wished there existed some way of preventing a visit to Washington by Makarios, who, in contrast to the Greek government, was believed to be intransigent. Needless to say, when the Ethnarch learned this, he was not exactly pleased.

Meeting President Eisenhower on August 8—on the occasion of the symbolic presentation of a gift for the Farm School of Thessaloniki, which operates under American auspices—the Greek Ambassador in Washington, George V. Melas, turned the conversation to the Cyprus question and referred to the British tripartite conference soundings, explaining the reasons why his government refused to take part in such a conference. In spite of Greek eagerness to contribute toward finding a constructive solution, the intransigent stand of Turkey, which insisted on partition, rendered nugatory any conference and could only cause further harm to allied relations. The President expressed some surprise. He said he was informed, and thought, that the situation had improved. He regretted now to hear that the signs of improvement were superficial only—as the Greek envoy had explained to him.

This American regret was expressed next day in clearer terms by William M. Rountree, Assistant Secretary of State for Middle Eastern, South Asian, and African Affairs, in a talk with the Greek Ambassador. The U.S. government, Rountree said, expected some sort of solution to emerge from a tripartite conference, or at least some benefit to be gained from the search in common for a solution and through contacts between representatives of the three countries. Ambassador G. V. Melas repeated the Greek arguments against such a conference (Turkish insistence on partition, the precedent of 1955, etc.). There was also Resolution 1013 (XI) which had been authentically interpreted, he said, without anyone, except for the British and Turkish Delegations, regarding it as referring to tripartite negotiations. It was dangerous to ignore decisions of this universal organization, he added.

Rountree countered by saying that the American interpretation of this resolution was that it implied either bipartite or tripartite talks—to which Melas replied by reminding him that the U.S. representative had made no reservation nor explanation of his vote when the opposite interpretation had been made in the Assembly. As the conversation went on, it emerged that the British government had given no assurance to the United States against dismemberment as a solution to the Cyprus question. Such an assurance, Rountree said, had been given only to the Greek government—in very vague terms was Melas' response. When Rountree observed that just as the Greeks refused to attend the proposed tripartite conference, because of Turkish insistence on partition, so could the British and the Turks refuse to do so because of Greek insistence on *enosis*, the Greek Ambassador pointed out that his government was willing to discuss independence of the island as a solution, as were the British. To this Rountree replied: "You will not get independence now." The Ambassador concluded that British intentions probably did not differ much from those formulated under the Radcliffe draft constitution which, as mentioned, had been published on December 19, 1956, and, according to Sir Charles Peake, Sir Roger Allen's predecessor in Athens, would not be considered again by the British this year.

Out of these complex and subtle diplomatic exchanges that began with the British initiative of August 3, one important new fact had emerged: For the first time, the British government had indicated verbally to the Greek government that it was no longer interested in maintaining sovereignty over the entire island of Cyprus, but only over its bases there.[18] In this connection, it should be recalled that since 1951, when the Greek government, for the first time in the postwar period, raised in an official manner the Cyprus question with the British government, not only had it never objected to the maintenance of British bases on the island, should it be ceded to Greece, but it had also stated it would be glad to grant bases to Britain in other parts of Greece.[19] The Greek position on British bases in Cyprus had been reiterated at the London Tripartite Conference in September, 1955, as well as during the Harding-Makarios talks that followed.[20]

The new British attitude concerning a base in Cyprus rather than Cyprus as a base was also communicated to the Greek government for the first time in writing in an *aide-mémoire* at their meeting of August 12, which had been arranged again at the British Ambassador's urgent request. In this document,[21] the British government expressed regret over the contents of the Greek government's reply to the informal suggestions conveyed to it on August 3, and recapitulated the tentative proposals that had been made lest the Greek government should be under any misapprehension about their nature or purpose. This note, furthermore, contained additional considerations to which the British government wished to draw the Greek government's attention. To the latter's reply concerning the risks involved in the conference's failure, the British government considered that more serious dangers would arise if no talks took place, since the conclusion would be drawn that in the view of one of the parties concerned the problem was indeed insoluble. Concerning the Greek government's reference to Resolution 1013 (XI), there was, it seemed, a difference between the two governments in the interpretation of its precise meaning.[22] However, since the British government did agree that talks with the Cypriots were necessary for any settlement, it did not feel this difference was insuperable. Concerning, finally, the Greek government's objection to the timing of the proposed meeting, the British government wished to state categorically that its proposals were not motivated by tactical considerations so far as the United Nations was concerned, but by a genuine desire to reach a settlement. September had been proposed solely in order to allow a reasonable time for preparation before the talks began.

In a final section to this note, the British government welcomed the Greek government's offer to engage in talks through the diplomatic channel, to prepare a constructive conference. And it wished to assure the Greek government that it had been its intention throughout that the proposed conference should be preceded by a period of careful preparation. Indeed, with this in mind it had suggested that it would be ready to discuss matters further, prior to the actual conference and through the diplomatic channel. The British government would, of course, do the same with the Turkish government. Its only reservation was that it could not enter into commitments before the conference, since to do so would be contrary to the purpose and spirit of the proposed meeting. Accordingly, it was glad that in his explanatory observations on the Greek government's communication, Mr. Averoff-Tossizza had assured the British Ambassador that the Greek government was not insisting that agreement in substance about the ultimate solution of the Cyprus problem should be reached in advance. For these reasons, the note concluded, the British government sincerely hoped that the Greek government, whose desire for good relations the British government warmly reciprocated, would give further consideration to the proposals that had been made and had been recapitulated.

After skimming the above-mentioned document, the Greek Foreign Minister observed, first, that it included a section that regarded him personally, to the effect that he had told Sir Roger in previous talks that the Greek government would not insist that agreement in substance about the ultimate solution of the Cyprus problem should be reached in advance, and that the British government welcomed this attitude. He wished, he told the British Ambassador, to be very precise on such delicate matters and drew his attention to the fact—asking him to transmit these points to London—that he had said that prior to any participation of Greece, it was not indispensable to define a solution in detail, but to define the preconditions that would insure the success of the conference. In this sense, the broad framework, in which a solution would be found should be set down. Sir Roger agreed that the discussion had been along the lines mentioned by the Greek Minister and said he had conveyed them thus to the Foreign Office. He promised to draw anew to this point the attention of the appropriate official in London.

To Sir Roger's inquiry about the impression created by this *aide-mémoire,* Averoff-Tossizza replied he did not think this new document presented any appreciable differences if compared with the content of the conversations he had had during previous meetings with the British Ambassador. This was particularly the case in the area of the reservations that the Greek government had made in its reply. Sir Roger did not altogether disagree but observed there were some elements that might make the Greek government change its mind—for instance, the telegram (mentioned earlier) concerning British assurances that the purpose of the proposed conference was not to prepare the ground for partition. This was indeed gratifying, rejoined the Greek Foreign Minister, but insufficiently so, because of the vagueness of the assurance. The British Ambassador went on to emphasize that the participation of the United States was now certain [23] and that Spaak, too, regarded such a conference most useful and had said so to the British representative to NATO. Thus, it was almost impossible, Sir Roger argued, for the Greek government not to accept an invitation for a conference, were it sent. He finally observed that the raising of many emergency measures in Cyprus (announced on August 8),[24] though deprecated by Athens newspapers,[25] was an important event and again testified to the good intentions of the British government. All in all, he reverted to the need for Greek acceptance of the invitation, if this were eventually sent. He insisted that this would be the best way for burying partition, and perhaps, too, for finding an immediate solution. At any rate, he reiterated, the suggested conference would be altogether different from the tripartite one of 1955 and would be imbued by an altogether new spirit.

Because of the British Ambassador's special insistence, his efforts to stress his government's sincere intentions, and his possible misunderstanding of the grounds for the negative Greek attitude, Averoff-Tossizza expounded once again his government's view. The conference, he acknowledged, was likely, indeed, to meet in a different spirit. It appeared, however, similar to the tripartite conference of 1955. Neither did the participation of Spaak and of a U.S. observer alter the form, since in essence the concept of solving the Cyprus question through talks between the British government and the Cypriot people would be dropped, and the solution through tripartite conversations would be accepted. The latter would be understandable only if there were serious hopes of achieving a solution. But, because of Turkish intransigence, achieving a solution appeared unlikely. He did not wish to conceal the fact that many countries in the eastern Mediterranean that had friendly relations with Greece had observed, both during the debates in the Assembly as well as later, that if the Cyprus problem was not solved by direct talks between the British government and the Cypriot people, they, too, had a claim to being asked, because they, too, had a direct concern in the matter.[26] Hence, were Greece to accept tripartite talks, it would seem as though it was denying the existence of these interests and was dropping the view it had supported in the United Nations and which the United Nations had adopted.

To the British Ambassador's remark that Greece could accept the invitation to a conference, while publicly stating it persisted in its views but was taking part in talks preparatory to a solution, the Greek Foreign Minister replied this could be done, and many reservations of various kinds could be included. The fact, though, would remain that such a course would represent the abandonment of a clearly defined line. To adopt the view that this tripartite conference would be altogether different from that of 1955, he would have to be in a position to demonstrate it. To do so, did he have the right to use publicly what the British Ambassador had told him in the recent conversations? Sir Roger anxiously asked which particular points Averoff-Tossizza had in mind. For instance, the Foreign Minister said, could he state publicly that the British Ambassador had told him that this conference would be a method for hammering into the heads of the Turks a good solution (as he had said during the conversation of August 3)? [27] Such a public statement would enable him to argue persuasively that the spirit of the envisaged conference was indeed different. Sir Roger, clearly worried now, stated that the Foreign Minister could quote such phrases neither publicly nor even among wider official circles. He had told the Foreign Minister personally these things, to help him realize the difference in atmosphere that existed. Exactly for that reason, the Foreign Minister assured him, he had not mentioned those phrases even to colleagues, not wishing to expose him. But this only proved that, in form and substance, the conference would differ very slightly from the one of 1955. Only very few would be able to hope secretly that its aims were different.

The British Ambassador then asked the Foreign Minister whether the Greek government would be facilitated by a public British statement to the effect that if Greece were to accept the invitation to the suggested conference, even with the aforementioned reservations, the British government would not oppose the inclusion of the Greek recourse in the agenda of the Assembly. Averoff-Tossizza replied he believed this would not help. On the one hand, he saw no danger of the Cyprus question's being excluded from the Assembly's agenda. On the other, even if the inclusion of this item were thus made secure, the debate in the United Nations would be more difficult, because of Greek participation in the suggested conference. Consequently, the only way for Greece to discuss participation in that conference would be to create the preconditions for the conference's success.

Undaunted, the British diplomat persisted in his efforts. With much argumentation, presented sincerely and in good faith, he urged Greek participation as being in the interest of the whole case. Referring to British willingness to discuss any point in advance, he observed that the Greek government would be free to develop in such prior discussions certain compromise solutions it believed the Cypriots could accept. He himself thought these solutions would be listened to with much sympathy.The Greek Foreign Minister stated in response that if the British government made a statement that these solutions would be the subject of the conference, he, personally believed the Greek government could participate—without his being able to guarantee this.

Sir Roger, now, stressing categorically that he spoke for himself only because he so eagerly wished to help Greek participation—though he was fully aware of its difficulties for the Greek government—inquired whether a statement of the British government, to the effect that the Greek government could present these solutions at the conference, would facilitate participation. Most categorically, Averoff-Tossizza replied in the negative. Sir Roger then tried out another suggestion. He inquired about a British statement, which he regarded unlikely, conveyed through the same confidential channels, to the effect that, while taking all precautions that no commitment would be involved, in the judgment of the British government, these Greek solutions constituted a reasonable basis for discussions. Averoff-Tossizza replied that the reservations about non-commitment did not destroy the meaning of this phrase as Sir Roger had said it—in which case, he believed, the Greek government would at least discuss participation in a tripartite conference.

After renewed efforts by the British diplomat to dissuade the Greek official from rejecting the British informal suggestion for a tripartite conference, the meeting ended. The Foreign Minister had not concealed his lack of optimism and had said a reply could not be expected before two or three days, because of the heavy burden of work. What had impressed him, though, in this conversation were certain points that differed somewhat from what had been said in the earlier talks. For instance there was, now, the British government's written statement that Britain was no longer interested in preserving its sovereignty over the entire island but only over its military facilities there. Then, there was the British emphasis on the need for talks with the Cypriot people, whereas earlier the British government had stressed that such talks would deal with internal affairs only. Third, U.S. participation was clearly envisaged, provided the parties concerned desired it. Fourth, there was the paragraph, to which the British Ambassador had particularly drawn his attention, under which British government would be disposed to discuss with the Greek government points of interest to it, before the conference convened.

A day later, the Foreign Minister was informed by the Greek envoy in London, who had had a talk with Assistant Undersecretary at the Foreign Office A. D. M. Ross concerning the Athens conversations between the Minister and the British Ambassador, that the British government desired that a definitive, not a transitional, settlement be reached at the envisaged conference. And from Washington he learned that Undersecretary of State, Christian A. Herter (replacing Dulles who was absent on leave), had expressed hopes that tripartite talks would be carried out—in which case the United States would be disposed to attend through an observer. It was clear, commented the Greek Ambassador there, that the U.S. government had complete confidence in the British and had no desire to intervene nor any thought concerning the further course of the Cyprus question either outside or inside the United Nations.

August 14, at about noon, a new meeting of the Foreign Minister with the British Ambassador, at the latter's urgent request, took place. Sir Roger handed Averoff-Tossizza another *aide-mémoire* in which it was said that the British government had already explained to the Greek government its own requirements regarding any eventual solution (sovereign bases, peace and tranquillity, security from Communist infiltration). Subject to this, it reiterated its intention that the proposed conference should consider with an open mind any suggestions that the participants cared to put forward. While for the reasons already given to the Greek government, the British government could not enter into any advance commitments, it considered that the three proposals mentioned by the Greek Minister for Foreign Affairs to the British Ambassador on

August 7 and 12 [28] were among those which could reasonably be discussed at the proposed conference.

After reading this *aide-mémoire*, Foreign Minister Averoff-Tossizza observed it did not cover the condition he had made that the three compromise solutions constitute the basis of the London talks, because it mentioned that these solutions could be reasonably discussed *"among others"*—which meant that partition, too, could be discussed. Sir Roger replied it was impossible to do what the Foreign Minister had asked, because this would constitute a preconference commitment on the part of Britain. This would be contrary to the purpose of the convocation and would not be correct vis-à-vis third parties. He added that in any case this document represented a success for Greece, because regardless of whether it included the qualifying words "among others," it accepted the view that the Greek compromise solutions would be reasonably discussed at the proposed conference. Averoff-Tossizza answered appropriately while Sir Roger again eagerly supported his own arguments in favor of Greek participation.

The Greek Foreign Minister then went on to tell the British Ambassador that he personally had been put in a very difficult position, because what Sir Roger had told him at their various recent meetings suggested that Greece ought to attend the conference in order to isolate Turkey. This led him to believe that Greece should agree to participate. On the other hand, in order not to expose him, he realized he could use neither publicly nor confidentially the various phrases the British Ambassador had uttered in the course of their repeated conversations. As a result his argumentation for going to London was very weak. Might he, at least, report to the Cabinet that this was the impression the British Ambassador was continually giving him with his words? Sir Roger, as Averoff-Tossizza expected, replied in the negative. It was not possible, he said, to create problems internationally, and he could not agree that in his talks he had reached the point the Foreign Minister had mentioned.

Sensing that the British diplomat fully understood the difficulties the Greek government faced in the matter of the proposed conference, the Foreign Minister explained that his refusal was in no way inspired by a feeling of bitterness but by a sense of realism. He added that even if it were supposed that general reasons and the solution of the question called for acceptance of the invitation, a very serious domestic problem would arise which would have grave consequences on the evolution of the question. If the Greek government decided to attend the suggested tripartite conference, and not only the Opposition but also the Cypriots themselves and the Greek press disapproved, it would then be going to the conference table without the slightest prestige and without any real ability to contribute to the achievement of a solution.

The British Ambassador concurred in the correctness of this observation, but remarked he did not believe that such a domestic reaction would occur. The director of a big progovernment newspaper, whom he had sounded out, said that in her judgment the Greek government should take part in the proposed new London conference.[29] Averoff-Tossizza countered by saying that, on his side, his own soundings with the press had led him to the opposite conclusion. The editorials in the entire Athens press proved it. He insisted that the Greek government, in considering a negative reply to the British proposal, was in no way influenced by the opinion of others but by objective arguments. The latter, as Sir Roger knew, were stacked against acceptance of the invitation. He assured Sir Roger, nevertheless, that his government was studying with great care the suggestions of the British government. Therefore, no answer was likely before August 16, since there were thoughts of discussing the matter at length among a larger circle of ministers.

During this conversation, the Greek Foreign Minister noticed, the British Ambassador had said he had the impression Prime Minister Macmillan was dealing personally with this matter, to the extent that, if he himself did not compose the texts, at any rate he saw them before they were sent. Moreover, Sir Roger, in presenting his own views, had mentioned at one point that these were the views of the Prime Minister— correcting himself afterward, saying he had mentioned him by mistake. Averoff-Tossizza, wondering whether Sir Roger had intentionally done so or whether these words had accidentally escaped him, concluded that the British Ambassador was personally transmitting the views of the Prime Minister on the following matters: Macmillan did not expect an immediate result from the proposed conference but was determined not to let the Cyprus issue remain deadlocked and to achieve some really positive progress, to the detriment of none of the participants.

Another note of the Foreign Minister about this conversation of August 14: the British Ambassador at some point had mentioned that all the usual machinery used in conferences would be resorted to in order to achieve an agreement. In reply to Averoff-Tossizza's question of what he meant by this machinery, Sir Roger replied he meant the behind-the-scenes possibilities of intervention by the U.S. government and by Spaak, in order to persuade the Turks. Averoff-Tossizza smilingly observed such machinery could also be used in order to persuade the Greeks too. Sir Roger, also smiling, replied it had been agreed that it was not the Greeks who were intransigent.

Somewhat later that same day, U.S. chargé d'affaires James K. Penfield, in the absence of the Ambassador, called on the Greek Foreign Minister and informed him of a brief State Department cable conveying the view that the proposed talks constituted the desirable tactics for obtaining a good compromise solution. The department was gratified to learn that the Greek government was studying the matter without closing the door altogether. It had been favorably influenced, because of the good will and spirit of understanding that, in its opinion, the British government was showing, and it hoped the Greek government would reverse its initial negative stand.

The Secretary-General of NATO, who was kept posted through British channels of Sir Roger's new *démarche*, continued to plead for Greek acceptance. As Spaak saw it, the proposed conference would be of a preparatory character, with the fate of Cyprus to be finally settled at a new conference, in which the Cypriots would take part. Though he expressed understanding of the Greek caution and reserve, because of precedents, and agreed that the Radcliffe constitutional plan and Lord Ismay's initiative in March, 1957, had been unfortunate, he held that the situation had changed since then. The British no longer ascribed military significance to the island as a whole and were ready to abdicate their sovereignty over it. The Turks were the main obstacle. Until quite recently the British had used them as a pretext but now they were sorry they had done so. Turkey, which, of course, had substantial interests in Cyprus, because of the Turkish minority, had overstepped the proper bounds. Indeed, Spaak added in this talk of August 15 with a member of the Greek Delegation to NATO,[30] the British position had now changed to such an extent that for Greece the danger lay not in the further stay of British troops on the island but in the contingency of their sudden withdrawal—in which case Greece would find itself face to face with Turkey. Five days later, in a conversation with Ambassador M. Melas, Spaak again stressed that possible Greek suspicions of British intentions, though understandable if one took into account the past, were in his view unjustified, first, because he believed the British now were sincere in their desire to arrive at a final solution, and, second, because both the Americans and he, as NATO's Secretary-General, would be present at the talks. From the Turks, he added, he had received no news yet. He only knew that the British and the Americans were persistently exerting pressure upon Ankara, for Turkey to take part in the proposed conference. He feared that the commitments the Turkish government would make to voters during the expected elections [31] would render a compromise more difficult both for the government as well as for the Opposition.

It was only on August 27 that the Greek government delivered its final answer to the British soundings, which had started on August 3.[32] Meanwhile, in spite of certain gains it felt it had made during these exchanges, it still believed that no result could be achieved by a tripartite conference at this time. Turkey, according to firm information, was sharply reacting against the alternative compromise solutions which the Greek government had put forward to the British. The Turkish government maintained that any of these solutions would surely lead to the union of Cyprus with Greece and to the disappearance of the Turkish minority from the island. And the Greek Ambassador in London, after a meeting with Assistant Undersecretary Ross at the Foreign Office on August 15, saw no indication of British intentions beyond those which the Anglo-Greek exchanges in Athens had revealed. If the tripartite conference was not just a tactic and honestly was not aimed against Greece, the objectives could be none other than to persuade Turkey to abandon its excessive demands, through the participation of Spaak and the Americans as observers. But it was difficult for him to believe this. If this was so, it would be much easier for Spaak and the Americans to exert their persuasive powers through secret and dispassionate bipartite contacts with Turkey rather than at a tripartite conference such as the previous one, which had served as a stage for spectacular speeches by Turkish Foreign Minister Zorlu. At a tripartite conference the Turkish government would be far too exposed before public opinion to be able to retreat.

Consequently, the Ambassador Seferiadis saw no other purpose in the proposed conference than the following one: Turkey had already prepared, well concealing its own game, a second line of retreat in the nature of a proposal, which, of course, served Turkish interests and which Turkey wished Greece to accept. Such a proposal would be unacceptable to the Greek government. In other words, Turkey would retreat from its position in favor of partition and, proclaiming its conciliatory spirit, would take up this new line by proposing, for example, an Anglo-Turkish-Greek condominium (or something similar) over Cyprus. (There were press reports, at the time, about such a solution which had been faintly outlined at the London Tripartite Conference of 1955 and presaged the Macmillan partnership plan, which the British government was to present the following year, on June 19, 1958.) In such a case, what would the Greek government do? It would either have to yield to pressure or refuse. In the latter case the British would be strengthened in maintaining that only one solution remained: dismemberment. Since he nowhere saw any sincere desire of persuading Turkey to come to its senses, he could find no argument to convince him that Turkey would not succeed in attempts such as the one he had above outlined. Nonspectacular exchanges of views at the eve of or during the work of the General Assembly, where the three states would be represented, would perhaps be the best procedure to follow.

Such considerations were not mentioned in the Greek *aide-mémoire* of August 27 to the British government, but they shed light on some of the unavowed factors that led the Greek government to reject the British overtures for a tripartite conference as a fresh approach to the Cyprus question. In this note, the Greek government, underlined it had very carefully considered the *aides-mémoire* that the British Ambassador had left with the Greek Minister for Foreign Affairs on August 12 and 14 after the informal suggestions from London concerning the calling of a conference on the Cyprus question, and observed, first, that beyond its reply to the initial soundings, it had maintained strict secrecy vis-à-vis the press and continued intending to do so. Reports in certain daily papers attributed to official sources had been entirely inaccurate. The Greek government then went on to affirm that it shared the views of the British government about the need of maintaining the unity of the Western Alliance and about the untoward consequences the Cyprus question could have on this unity. For that very reason, in handling on behalf of the people of Cyprus and by its mandate a cause, the justice of which no one could deny, it had always shown a spirit of moderation, had avoided provocations or reactions similar to the provocations of others, and had taken, in the not remote past, initiatives which could have facilitated a reasonable solution to the Cyprus problem. In accordance with the above spirit, the Greek government had approached the recent overtures from the British government. Its reply was prompted by a spirit of realism and objectivity. And it should be understood that Greece, though viewing the United Nations as an outstanding instrumental factor in international life, would not have resorted to it—much less denounced friends before it—had it been possible to reach a solution through other adequate procedures.

After this exordium, the Greek government, in this note, expressed its regret at its inability to perceive how the procedure the British government proposed could lead to a solution of the Cyprus question. It was actually true that what the British Ambassador had said to the Minister of Foreign Affairs, and, more particularly what had been stated in the *aides-mémoire* of August 12 and 14 marked certain fundamental developments in the attitude of the British government concerning the Cyprus issue—developments which the Greek government duly appreciated. It was also true that the presence at the proposed negotiations of a personality of universal prestige, such as Mr. Spaak, and of a representative of the United States would constitute useful assets in such negotiations. It remained, nevertheless, a fact that not all parties mainly concerned would take part in these talks. It was also a fact that no preparatory work had been done, so some assurance might exist that the conference would have a positive result. On the contrary, the failure of these talks appeared unavoidable. In fact, according to the Greek government's information, the Turkish government had asked for the postponement of the conference until the end of October, namely after the elections to the Grand National Assembly had taken place. Thus, the proposed talks would be conducted against the background of the aftermath of an electoral campaign that would accentuate already existing intransigence, and this while the problem would be up for discussion before the United Nations.

But even if the above considerations were put aside, this Greek note of August 27 went on to say, the lack of any agenda or of certain prerequisites for the discussion rendered improbable the achievement of any useful results from the talks and constituted negative factors that could generate new tension in Greek-Turkish relations. The Greek government could not disregard the events which had originated from the tension that was created after the tripartite conference of 1955. Nor could it disregard the consequences that arose out of the release of Archbishop Makarios—a situation for which Greece bore no responsibility.[33] Likewise it could not ignore various other crises that had recently marked Greek-Turkish relations. These crises engendered great risks, the gravity of which was perhaps less apparent to those who were not directly involved. On its own account and for the benefit of the Allies, the Greek government wished to avert the renewal of such crises and was gravely concerned lest the proposed conference, without having any foreseeable possibility of success for the aforementioned reasons, lead on the contrary to another Greek-Turkish crisis with all its attendant grave results.

Denying that it was its intention to enlarge at the present moment upon its basic position in the Cyprus question, the Greek government observed in this note that it was well known that it believed:

A. The issue lay between the British government and the people of Cyprus, as also set down in Resolution 1013 (XI).
B. Other states had indirect interests of greater or lesser importance which should undoubtedly be considered and taken care of in any agreed solution.
C. In no case should one of the aforementioned states have the power of a quasi-veto upon any agreed solution. No such power of veto should lead to a solution that would disregard the fundamental principles of the UN Charter.

The Greek government was convinced that the solution concerning the future of a very civilized people should be based on the aforementioned principles when sought by democratic governments. At the same time, it did not underestimate the complexities resulting from other aspects of the problem. Therefore, though it espoused and advocated the just claim of the Cypriots to exercise their right of self-determination within a short period, it had shown a spirit of great understanding and had formulated suggestions that it believed would be acceptable to the Cypriots. These suggestions would also provide for the interests and susceptibilities of all countries indirectly concerned.

These suggestions, the Greek government was aware, according to this note, were now considered as reasonable by many countries, including certain great powers. However, for the multipartite talks to lead to useful results, the various parties should be sounded out, not on the extreme position they had adopted, but on their intention to revert to a reasonable position. Such a procedure would permit establishing in advance whether any common ground existed between the various points of view. In the absence of such a common ground, the multipartite talks were bound to fail and create another crisis in the relations of the countries concerned. In such circumstances there was no other alternative than to wait and concentrate one's efforts on a solution of the problem through the United Nations.

At any rate, wishing to approach the question of the proposed talks in the same spirit of good will, objectivity, and realism, the Greek government was willing to further clarify through the diplomatic channel its attitude on the Cyprus issue, as well as the conditions that, in its opinion, would render possible the convocation of a really constructive conference. Insofar as these conditions were concerned, it felt it was necessary here only to draw the attention of the British government to the *aide-mémoire* of August 12, according to which the British government was glad to note that Mr. Averoff-Tossizza, in his explanatory observations on the British government's communication, had assured the British Ambassador that the Greek government was not insisting that agreement in substance about the ultimate solution of the Cyprus problem should be reached in advance. In order to avoid any misunderstanding, it was necessary to make it clear that, as the Greek Foreign Minister had pointed out after reading the above *aide-mémoire,* and as the British Ambassador had agreed, the statement of Mr. Averoff-Tossizza did not terminate at that point, but went further—to say that the conditions necessary to insure the success of the conference ought to be laid down in advance so that a just solution might be reached.

In conclusion, the Greek government, in this note of August 27, assured the British government that, though it was unable to deprive the Cypriot people's claim to self-determination of its support—no country could have done otherwise—it earnestly desired to see Greek-Turkish relations restored and Anglo-Greek friendship resume its former cordiality.

This Greek *aide-mémoire* of August 27, evoked a rather acid British reply on September 4. However, before coming to this, it is noteworthy that "Isaakios," in a long letter dated the day before the Greek *aide-mémoire* was handed to the British Ambassador, explained the situation to the leader of EOKA in his Cyprus hideout. The Turkish factor, he stressed, remained dominant "in our sacred cause," and had been strengthened by the recent events in Syria,[34] even though the attitude of the Turkish government itself had become more decorous—with a more moderate tone and the granting of damages to the Greeks of Istanbul whose property had been destroyed in the riots of September 6, 1955—as compared with its previous intolerable and provocative attitude at the time of the release of Makarios from his detention in the Seychelles. Nonetheless, Turkey put forward an unyielding demand for the partition of Cyprus as the only possible solution. On the other hand, there had been changes elsewhere.

Most of the allies were now persuaded that the solution should be sought in the creation of an independent Cyprus without a guarantee of independence in perpetuity. The British seemed to be accepting such a solution, as long as they could keep a base on the island and Turkey agreed. The latter, however, vehemently rejected such a solution on the grounds that, sooner or later, the independent state would unite with Greece; that no guarantee of independence could resist the change of international conditions; that, during the period of independence, fanatic Greek Cypriots would dominate the new state and, no matter what guarantees were granted, the Turkish minority would eventually disappear; and, finally, that during this period of independence, the new state of Cyprus would in essence constitute a self-governing province of Greece through military, political, and other accords, and Greece would have two votes in international organizations. In spite of the correctness of these arguments, third parties insisted on their views and, if they did not go ahead, this was only for reasons of more general policy, namely not to stir up violent reaction in Turkey—which, it seemed, was threatening to denounce the Baghdad Pact.

After referring to the insistent British soundings and to the impression they had created that the purpose of the proposed conference was to make the Turks realize within an allied framework that they were isolated, and after reporting that the Greek government had, nonetheless, rejected these proposals, "Isaakios" explained the dilemma that Greece faced in dealing with these British soundings. A positive reply would be to the disadvantage of Greece, because it would weaken, especially in the United Nations, its argument that the issue was one that affected directly only Britain and the Cypriot people. Moreover, a positive reply would also have such domestic repercussions that the Greek representative at the proposed conference would be bereft of any prestige, and the Turks would play the card of Greek intransigence. A negative reply, on the other hand, had its own shortcomings too. An opportunity would be lost to exert pressure on Turkey. Greece would seem to be unyielding and unwilling to take into account not only great objective difficulties but also great international problems. "Isaakios" then went on to analyze, as he had to Makarios, the various possible outcomes of the debate in the United Nations,[35] and ended by stressing the difficulties caused by domestic factors. The internal situation, he wrote, did not help. The relations between government and Opposition were worse than ever before. The economic situation was progressing very well. There was great progress and a feeling of confidence and stability. But this, together with Premier Karamanlis' age as compared with his opponents', had aroused attacks of such a nature that any possibility of co-operation, even of contact, was excluded. Relations of the government with Makarios, on the other hand, were very good. He himself was aware only of a certain dissatisfaction and irritation caused by a number of demagogic partisans in Athens, who criticized quite irresponsibly. He did not exclude the possibility that such manifestations would lead Karamanlis to elections.[36] Feeling very strong, the Prime Minister would probably wish to clean up the situation, which had become both provocative and annoying. However, there was nothing positive about this. Unfortunately, because of the anger of the people over the Cyprus issue, the Communists were fluttering their wings again.

Grivas replied to this letter of "Isaakios," urging a strong diplomatic counteroffensive not just diplomatic defense, at a time when he himself, during his second unilateral truce, was greatly concerned about insuring his capability to handle not only the British and Turks on the island, who were acting either together or separately, but also the Communists, who often betrayed EOKA men to the British authorities.[37] "We should create," he wrote, "such an international situation for the Anglo-Americans that they will have to reckon with Greece, which they had kicked aside in favor of Turkey, ascribing greater importance to the latter's geographical location and material power than to the faith and steadfastness of the Greeks."

EOKA's leader then expounded his own views about the strategic value of Greece and of the countries of the Middle East. But these views will be analyzed elsewhere and in connection with those of the Greek Foreign Minister, which were different. Suffice it to note here that, in Grivas' opinion, the conditions were very favorable for Greek diplomacy to exploit most effectively its relations with Yugoslavia and the Arab countries. The Baghdad Pact, in his view, was but a house of cards. Because of the non-participation of the Arab countries, it had no defense in depth. While he maintained he was not up-to-date concerning diplomatic activities taking place backstage, he urged, at any rate, continued insistence in the demand for self-determination. No other solution would be fully satisfactory (the indications of late July that Makarios was orienting himself toward a solution that envisaged independence had greatly disturbed him).[38] The realization of this demand was the exclusive task of diplomacy. The purpose of the armed struggle was to support the diplomatic struggle—which alone could not solve the problem. From the United Nations, too, he did not expect much. The struggle would be waged outside the international organization. Although UN resolutions would provide no solution, they would perhaps help in finding one. In the United Nations the right of self-determination should be consistently supported. No solution that excluded this right should be accepted.[39]

D. Final Greek Rebuff to the British Probes

In its reply of September 4 to the Greek aide-mémoire of August 27, the British government noted with regret that the Greek government had not been able to accept the suggestions embodied in the aide-mémoire delivered to it by the British Ambassador in Athens on August 12. The British government did not find convincing the arguments the Greek government advanced in support of its attitude. It had already declared its readiness to enter into preparatory discussions with the Greek government prior to the proposed conference itself. Taking into account the possibility of general elections in Turkey in the near future, it would be prepared to consider any alternative date that the Greek government cared to suggest and that would be convenient to the other parties concerned. The British government believed that the absence of a fixed agenda would contribute to the flexibility of the discussions and thus obviate the risk of increased tension, which the Greek government feared. It had made it abundantly clear that the purpose of the governmental talks it had proposed could be to prepare the way for subsequent discussions with the representatives of Cyprus and not in any way to exclude the latter from participation in the settlement. In any case, it was difficult to reconcile the Greek government's objection to the proposed conference, on the grounds that not all the parties mainly interested would take part, with its claim, which the British government could not, of course, accept, to be acting on behalf and by the mandate of the people of Cyprus. The latter claim also appeared to conflict with the further assertion in the Greek government's *aide-mémoire* that the issue lay between the British government and the people of Cyprus. However, the British government did not wish to enter into controversy with the Greek government. It adhered to the view that the procedure it had suggested was the most likely to lead to a settlement satisfactory to all concerned, and it sincerely hoped the Greek government would reconsider its position in the matter. In particular it trusted that the Greek government would avoid action at the United Nations which would embitter the atmosphere and render a solution correspondingly more difficult. It was with that consideration in mind, as the Greek government would be aware, that the British government had refrained from tabling an item of its own at the forthcoming session of the Assembly. Its forbearance in this respect should not, however, be misinterpreted as indicating indifference to the course of events there, and the British government wished formally to record that the responsibility for any difficulties which might result from an acrimonious dispute at the United Nations would not rest with it.

In spite of this new note, the Greek government did not reconsider its position. In an *aide-mémoire* of September 6, handed by the Foreign Minister to Sir Roger Allen, it expressed its regret that its views, though motivated by good will and put forward in a practical spirit, had so far failed to influence the British government's approach to the problem. It still believed that the procedure envisaged by the British government could not lead to positive results but to risks of a dangerous and, therefore, of an undesirable situation. Animated by the best of intentions, the Greek government could not but persist in the constructive views it had expressed in its previous *aide-mémoire* about the necessity of arriving through the diplomatic channel at a pre-agreed basis of discussions. These views could in no way be altered by the argument that the Greek government was contradicting itself when it said that the Cypriots would not be represented in the proposed talks. In fact, the British government, by refusing to recognize in its *aide-mémoire* the quasi-mandatory role of the Greek government with regard to the Cypriots, was defeating the very basis of its own argument. Had the British government adopted the Greek position (i.e., had it resumed talks with the Cypriots) and had these talks made real progress, it would surely have seen the Greek government acting as a trustee whose mission had come to an end, and assuming a quite different role. Nor could the views of the Greek government be altered by the concluding paragraph of the British *aide-mémoire* of September 4—which it earnestly wished had not been included in the *aide-mémoire*. From various official contacts, the British government was well aware that it was not among the intentions of the Greek government to bring about a deterioration of Anglo-Greek relations or to create tension in the United Nations. It undoubtedly also had in mind certain cases (intelligence cases mentioned earlier) [40] in which some British diplomatic officials in Athens had resorted to improper and inadmissible methods against the Greek government, on which, nevertheless, the latter had kept the strictest secrecy. The Greek government had kept secrecy in all other instances in which it was felt necessary to do so. Therefore, the insinuation about who would bear the responsibility for the eventual deterioration of the situation was unjustifiable. On the other hand, nothing would be more inaccurate than to interpret as a sign of weakness the well-intentioned attitude of the Greek government and its earnest desire to see Anglo-Greek relations resume their previous cordiality. The Greek government had on its record many instances when it had tried with courage, discretion, and good will to seek a satisfactory solution to the Cyprus problem, which was so close to the heart of the Greek people. The responsibility, therefore, for any deterioration of the situation would rest with those who did not act effectively in reaching a solution. It was not the intention of the Greek government—unless it were driven to do so—to cause an acrimonious discussion in the United Nations. Once more, the Greek government wished to assure the British government that, in the belief that the Cyprus problem would one day find its just solution, it was handling the issue in such a way as not to irreparably impair the possibility of resuming Anglo-Greek friendship, and hoped that this constructive approach would be reciprocated by the British government.

After the British Ambassador read the Greek government's above reply, he expressed lively annoyance at the reference to improper methods the British Embassy in Athens had used against the Greek government, and asked the Foreign Minister to delete the offending paragraph from the *aide-mémoire*. In London it would be regarded as a threat, he argued. Averoff-Tossizza assured him this was no threat, that it could not constitute a threat unless he were forced by the British to use it as such—by false accusations such as those they had made in the past to the effect that the Greek government was using such or similar methods. [41] The proof of this was that, whereas he could have seriously embarrassed the British government by revealing these methods, he had not done so but had maintained an exemplary secrecy, because almost no one in Greece knew anything about them. When, however, the Greek government was giving so many examples of good will in spite of an extremely difficult internal situation with regard to the Cyprus question, and the British government, on the eve of the Assembly's session, felt the need of coming up with an *aide-mémoire* in which, in essence, the Greek Govern-

ment was told: "Be careful, little Greeks, because if the situation worsens
you shall bear the responsibility," the Foreign Minister was obliged to
reply that his government had always behaved in good faith, to invoke
certain proofs of its good faith, and to retort: "I, too, am not afraid of
you, and, because I am right, you will bear the responsibility, if the
situation becomes worse." The *aide-mémoire* the British Ambassador had
handed him on September 4 had been a stiff one and called for a stiff
reply. Although agreeing absolutely with the Foreign Minister, Sir Roger
merely asked him again to delete the aforementioned paragraph. Averoff-Tossizza, however, refused to do so and, adding that perhaps Sir
Roger was not aware of the full extent of the affair (which had occurred
earlier, during the service in Athens of his predecessor), revealed it to
him in a few words, observing that in this fashion inaccurate information
had been channeled to the British, which had then been publicly repeated by British Delegate Noble at the previous session of the Assembly.[42]

A little later that same day, September 6, the Foreign Minister met
U.S. Ambassador Allen and cursorily read to him the Greek reply to the
British *aide-mémoire*. The American found it dignified and reasonable.
Averoff-Tossizza then told Allen that the British document together with
a complaint that the new Turkish Ambassador in Athens, Nuredin Vergin, had lodged earlier that day concerning certain alleged anti-Muslim
incidents in Greek Thrace [43] had led him to suppose that preparations
were under way for the debate in the Assembly, and that a new stiffening
of British-Turkish policy toward Greece loomed on the horizon. On its
side, the Greek government was eager for an improvement of relations,
but it had decided to deal with any stiffening of position on the other
side with a corresponding stiffening in its own policy. It was unacceptable that the British should place responsibilities upon the Greeks, as
though they were in the right, and that the Turks should stage incidents
and then complain—they who had so greatly provoked the Greeks,
whereas the Greek government had provoked no one. He asked Allen to
inform the State Department that it was the policy of the Greek government to improve matters steadily but not to give in to ridiculous threats
and even more ridiculous provocations such as those of the Turks.[44] The
American Ambassador took notes, especially about the incidents in
northern Greece, in Thrace, which had been the object of the Turkish
Ambassador's *démarche* that same day. He told Averoff-Tossizza it was
his personal opinion—which he would convey to the State Department—that these incidents had, indeed, been staged by the Turks, with
the forthcoming General Assembly in mind. In his view, the Turkish
government was trying to prove that Greeks and Turks could not live
together peacefully so that it could better support the concept of partition or, perhaps, of a new exchange of populations. The Foreign Minister
then inquired whether newspaper reports of a change in U.S. policy had
foundation in fact. Allen categorically denied this was so. The press

reports were probably derived from the fact that Loy W. Henderson, Deputy Secretary of State, had returned from the Middle East greatly disturbed, because of developments in Syria. Henderson himself (on his way back to Washington he had stopped in Athens briefly) had assured him he had not broached the Cyprus subject during his trip. Allen's reply elicited expressions of gratification on the part of Averoff-Tossizza, who observed that if an unfavorable American stand on the Cyprus question were added to the American government's rather insulting attitude toward Makarios (referred to above),[45] unpleasant repercussions would have to be expected in Greece. The conversation ended with an exchange of views on the Syrian crisis which had caused the United States to send to the area not only Henderson but also weapons to Iraq, Jordan, and Lebanon, and had raised doubts in the mind of the Greek Foreign Minister of whether these latter measures could be justified on the basis of the "Eisenhower Doctrine." This "Doctrine," it will be recalled, had been enunciated earlier that year [46] and Greece had adhered to it on May 2.

While the above diplomatic conversations were going on backstage and were barely audible to the public, three official Greek voices, those of the Foreign Minister, Ethnarch Makarios, and Premier Karamanlis, were heard in the open. At a press conference of August 28, Averoff-Tossizza presented at length the Greek views on the way in which Turkish anxieties about security, minority, and economic matters might be taken care of [47]—views he was to repeat before the General Assembly. Likewise at the end of August, Makarios, as he was about to embark for the United States, to inform American public opinion about the Cyprus question and to follow the debates on the question in the United Nations, stated he would accept self-government as a stepping stone to self-determination and that he was willing to take part in a conference in which each aide would be represented in accordance with its numerical strength—having in mind, of course, the population of Cyprus. Makarios also expressed the hope that the United States would abandon its policy of non-involvement in the Cyprus question. His object before the United Nations was, he said, to obtain the right of self-determination for Cyprus, as "the only solution consistent with democratic principles." [48] (The Ethnarchic Council, under his chairmanship, had decided to insist on this line on August 28.) Makarios also charged that Britain was trying to present the Cyprus problem as though it were a Greek-Turkish dispute in order to play the role of a mediator in the matter,[49] and expressed approval of the Greek government's reserved attitude toward the proposed tripartite conference. Premier Karamanlis, on the other hand, at a press conference, of September 5, stated that he would not reject a solution providing for an independent Cyprus if this was acceptable to the Cypriot people. His government, he added, would take no part in any conference on the future of Cyprus unless there were preliminary assurances that self-determination would be granted to the people of the island within a fixed period. Karamanlis also pledged Greece's continued adherence to the Western bloc, in spite of bitter feelings toward Britain and Turkey over the Cyprus issue. He suggested, too, that Greece, not being a colonial power, might play a pacifying role between the West and the Arab states.[50]

Meanwhile, the Turkish government was reported as pressing the United States to join the Baghdad Pact in response to Syria's drift toward the Soviet bloc, and the Turkish propaganda campaign for partition of Cyprus was in high gear, with the state-controlled radio and Istanbul and Ankara newspapers publishing many articles daily urging such a solution for the Cyprus question.[51]

On his way to New York for the opening of the General Assembly, the Greek Foreign Minister stopped in Rome and Paris. In the French capital he conferred with a number of Greek diplomats, the Ambassador to Britain included. On September 12, at Orly airport, he also had a meeting with Spaak, which engendered new efforts on the part of NATO's Secretary-General to play a sort of good offices role in the search for a Cyprus solution, even though Premier Menderes had, as will be recalled, discouraged him from visiting Ankara in June.[52] Congratulating Averoff-Tossizza for his handling of the British soundings concerning a tripartite conference in London, Spaak noted that, though the Greek government had rejected this suggestion, certain tactics and arguments resorted to had led the British government to make statements on the Cyprus question that were useful for its further progress toward a solution. In this connection, Spaak laid special emphasis on the reasonableness of the alternative proposals the Greek government had put forward and on the value of carrying out talks with the Cypriots themselves. The proposed conference would not be the best procedure for dealing with the problem, he believed, but it would have an advantage: It would help bring pressure to bear on the Turkish government which, in his opinion, was now the sole obstacle to a solution.

During this meeting with the Greek Foreign Minister, NATO's Secretary General expressed the belief that a solution envisaging dominion status for Cyprus for a period of fifteen to twenty years at the utmost had great chances of success. Ways, of course, would have to be found to persuade Turkey to accept such a solution. It would be necessary to formulate this proposal in such a way that would enable the Turkish government to accept it. Somewhat less optimistic was Spaak, on the other hand, about a solution that would grant full and guaranteed independence to Cyprus for a fixed number of years. Averoff-Tossizza, at this point, made it clear that after such a period either of Dominion status or of independence, only a plebiscite would be acceptable to his government for deciding the island's future.

The lively interest of NATO's Secretary-General in favor of the inclusion

of the Greek recourse in the General Assembly's agenda was also revealed in this lengthy conversation with Averoff-Tossizza at Orly. In
Spaak's view, non-inclusion of the Cyprus item in the agenda would be a
grave mistake. He would, he said, exert every possible effort to persuade
the British not to oppose the item's inclusion so as not, among other
things, to put the other NATO countries, too, in a difficult position during
the vote at that stage of the Greek recourse. The Greek Foreign Minister,
on his side, underlined that a rejection of this recourse could spark the
outbreak of renewed violence on Cyprus because of the despair such a
decision would arouse among the Greek Cypriots and because of the
tactics of arming the Turkish minority. Both locally and regionally the
results of such an outbreak would be incalculable. Although not believing that the rejection of the recourse was probable, he drew Spaak's
attention to the fact that the British government was opposed to it mainly
because of the references to British atrocities it contained. With regard to
the tripartite conference, which the British government had sought to
convene, Averoff-Tossizza explained in detail why his government had
not accepted this proposed procedure. He stressed the extremely dangerous effects the certain failure of such a conference would have had.
Finally, he argued that since almost all parties except the Turkish government considered that solutions which would provide for the independence of Cyprus without excluding self-determination were reasonable, the best way for applying such solutions would be for the Assembly
to adopt a resolution recommending such a solution, with the Western
Allies and the Secretary-General of NATO, in particular, settling afterward
the details and proceeding to the implementation of the Assembly's
recommendation. In response, Spaak said such a possibility of utilizing
the United Nations in a substantive manner in order to promote a
solution of the Cyprus problem had not occurred to him before. He
promised to study the matter further.

Part Two

Chapter Five

Greece Gets Item 58
Included in the UN Agenda

A. *Preliminary Diplomacy on Item 58 in the UN—*
The Explanatory Memorandum

Unaffected by its awareness that the United States did not favor a new UN debate on the Cyprus issue, but preferred quiet diplomacy outside the world organization on a tripartite basis,[1] the Greek government went ahead with its recourse to the United Nations. Accordingly, while dealing with the various problems these British diplomatic soundings and their NATO aftermath had created, it sought to make sure that its Cyprus item would not be excluded from the agenda of the Assembly, as it had been in 1955, because of the opposition of the majority of its NATO allies and their friends in the United Nations, the United States included.

During the second week of September, the Greek Permanent Mission to the UN was approached by a member of the Permanent U.S. Mission to the United Nations, Norman Armour, Jr., and was asked to refrain from referring to the Cyprus question in the forthcoming debate of the Hungarian question in the Assembly, on the ground that such references would lessen the political impression that the United States wished to create during the debate on the Hungarian item. The Greek response to this request was that there was no intention of speaking about the Cyprus question during that particular debate but that it was absolutely impossible to avoid mentioning incidentally the case of Cyprus which, in substance, it was maintained, did not differ greatly from that of Hungary. Greek public opinion was sensitive to linking the Hungarian to the Cyprus question, especially when it noticed the American interest in the former in contrast to the American indifference toward the latter.[2] The statements of President Eisenhower and Secretary of State Dulles that they did not intend to receive Ethnarch Makarios, because he represented only certain *enosist* circles, had had very unpleasant repercussions in Greece. The Greek Delegation would gladly be of assistance to the U.S. Delegation on all possible occasions, but when the policy of the

United States did not assist Greece, it was most difficult to do very much.

That the United States, though viewing the Greek recourse with little favor, would experience some difficulty in reaching the point of opposing the inclusion of the Cyprus item in the Assembly's agenda was disclosed by Rountree to Ambassador G. V. Melas at the State Department on September 9. Because the United States had taken no decision yet with regard to the problem of finding the needed solution to the Cyprus problem that would be acceptable to all, it continued to believe, said Rountree, that the United Nations was unable to provide a solution. The Greek envoy, although fully agreeing with this last remark, maintained that it was an uncontrovertible fact that the United Nations could *lead* to the finding of a solution—with Rountree not disagreeing. In the exchange of views concerning the calling of a tripartite conference in London, Melas added, the Greek government had shown great moderation, and it was only the extreme intransigence of Turkey that had compelled it to resort to the United Nations and to avoid a tripartite conference, the certain breakdown of which would have led to new tensions in Greek-Turkish relations. Everything depended on Turkey, he argued, and on occasions when pressure had been exerted, the results had been excellent. Rountree, however, remained silent.

The American official's words and silences aroused the anxiety of the Greek Foreign Minister about American intentions. The previous year, at the same stage of the recourse, some Greek policy-makers thought that the United States had favored the Cyprus item's inclusion in the agenda of the Assembly only because the British government had sent in to the United Nations a recourse of its own on the same question. Did the United States perhaps intend to intervene backstage this year in order to block the inclusion of item 58 in the Assembly's agenda? It could argue that the period of implementation of Resolution 1013 (XI) had not yet been exhausted and, therefore, a new UN debate on the matter should be postponed. A *démarche* with the U.S. Ambassador in Athens might be desirable, Averoff-Tossizza—on his way to New York—advised his government. A request might be made for an explicit promise of American support at the stage of the debate on the inclusion of the item in the Assembly's agenda. In such a *démarche* it could be stressed that aside from the undesirable political effects both in Greece and in Cyprus of a decision to exclude this item from the Assembly's agenda, a debate of the Cyprus question in the United Nations could this time be of considerable value, because a resolution that referred to a reasonable status of independence for Cyprus would constitute progress toward a solution of the problem. Moreover, a debate held on a high level would help more than anything else in persuading the Turkish government to abandon its absolute intransigence. On its side, the Greek government could promise to accept that the debate on the question take place toward the end of the Assembly's session, as the penultimate item.

This Greek anxiety about the intentions of the U.S. government was allayed by an Athens cable of September 12, which brought the news that Ambassador Allen had said that his government had no arguments for opposing the inclusion of the Cyprus item in the Assembly's agenda and that he, personally, did not share the feelings of Greek pessimism about the American attitude in this matter.

As for the British views on the inclusion of the Cyprus item in the Assembly's agenda, they had been clearly disclosed on September 11. In a conversation with Ambassador Palamas, Commander Noble, of the British Delegation to the Assembly, had said he did not believe it would be necessary to enter into a broad debate on this question, because his delegation did not intend to oppose the item's inclusion. The main difficulty, however, resided in the second part—subitem (b)—of the Greek recourse, which referred to violations of human rights in Cyprus and to British atrocities.[3] His delegation could in no way accept this subitem and would, therefore, oppose the inclusion of the Cyprus question that contained a reference to such matters. The Greek diplomat replied vaguely, saying that Commander Noble could discuss that problem with the Greek Foreign Minister when he arrived in New York. At the same time, he intimated that the British government bore some responsibility for the violations of human rights mentioned in subitem (b) of the Greek recourse since it had refused the dispatch of a British Parliamentary mission of inquiry to Cyprus to study whether these charges were well founded.[4] Noble took this opportunity to express regret at the Greek refusal to consider participation in the London tripartite conference his government had suggested in August. He would be happy, he added, to meet the Greek Foreign Minister to talk over matters with him.

Doubts concerning the possibility of including the Cyprus item in the Assembly's agenda, because of the references to British atrocities contained in subitem (b) of the Greek recourse, had already been expressed by Italian Premier A. Zoli in a talk with the Greek Foreign Minister in Rome, on September 10. To these doubts, the latter had responded that in case the item was excluded from the agenda it was likely that, against the will of all national-minded Greek political parties, the Greek people would decide to withdraw Greece from NATO.

From Oslo, the Greek Delegation learned a day or so later that the five Scandinavian states—Denmark, Finland, Norway, Sweden, and Iceland—favored the inclusion of the Cyprus item in the agenda of the Assembly, though during the debate they would refrain from any denunciation of Britain with regard to the charges of atrocities submitted by the Greek government.

The reference to British atrocities in the Greek recourse was creating daily, however, more and more difficulties. The British and their friends, the Greek Delegation learned, intended to react very sharply to these allegations. They would charge that the evidence on which these accusations were based was fabricated and, in the hope of preventing the inclusion of the Greek recourse, as formulated, in the Assembly's agenda, would invoke Article 2, paragraph 7, of the UN Charter, which provides that the United Nations should not intervene in matters that lie essentially within the domestic jurisdiction of a state. Representatives of Latin American states that were friendly to Greece indicated, too, they would have difficulties in voting for subitem (b) of the Greek recourse. Some started fearing lest a precedent be created for upsetting completely Article 2, paragraph 7, of the Charter, with the result that the door would then be wide open for recourses to the United Nations on the part of Soviet bloc states charging tortures and atrocities against Negroes in various countries, the United States included. Legally, their position was sound but not unshakable, the Greek Delegation felt. As for Article 60 of the European Convention on Human Rights and Fundamental Freedoms, this did not bind the United Nations, but only Greece and the other European signatories of this convention.[5]

Because of such reactions and Noble's firm opposition, the Greek Delegation, already since September 12, had reached the conclusion that the best thing to do would be to negotiate a graceful retreat on the matter of the inscription of subitem (b) of the Greek recourse in favor of a better agreement on the substance. Ethnarch Makarios was in accord.

In taking, however, a final decision on such a serious matter, the Foreign Minister sought counsel from Athens. If the Greek recourse as formulated were put to a vote in the General Committee paragraph by paragraph, he explained by cable to the Prime Minister, only the first subitem, which called for self-determination for the Cypriots, was likely to be adopted; the second one would be rejected. How would it be possible then to arrive at a vote without waging a battle on the inclusion of the item in the Assembly's agenda, especially since it had become clear that some delegations were sure to invoke Article 2, paragraph 7 of the Charter? And how would it be possible, in supporting the inclusion of the item in its present form, to speak with moderation and not cause any harm? Before him he saw three alternative courses of possible action. The first one would consist of waging the battle with the use of all means (no holds barred), resulting in a probable defeat over subitem (b) in the voting and with a small danger of even losing on subitem (a). The second course of action would consist of not using the depositions of the victims of the atrocities during the debate in the General Committee, and of waging combat in the most dignified way possible, with the resultant loss of only subitem (b) during the vote. The third course of action would consist of yielding, after a brief discussion, to the expected appeals, which would be numerous as well as persuasive, and of declaring before the General Committee that the Greek Delegation did not insist on the inclusion in the Assembly's agenda of subitem (b) of its recourse, and would accept the correctness of the juridical arguments, if such were raised, concerning the concurrent Greek recourse to the European Commission of Human Rights at Strasbourg, which was already dealing with such charges of violations of human rights in Cyprus.[6] In the view of the Foreign Minister, this last course of action was preferable. However, it was also the course that lent itself most easily to exploitation by demagogues in the Greek domestic arena. The government would be charged, for instance, with lacking courage, he predicted, or with abandoning the sole weapon it had for exerting pressure and persuasion on Britain.[7] Makarios favored taking the second of the above-mentioned alternative courses. The Greek Ambassador in Washington, on the other hand, stressing the dangers of such a course, disagreed. Indeed, in his opinion, the Greek explanatory memorandum of September 13 was far too sharp in tone. Averoff-Tossizza himself did not agree with this latter view. Personally, as he had already said, he favored the third, most moderate line of approach. But he would like Athens to advise him on this matter.

In this explanatory memorandum of September 13 sent by Ambassador Palamas to the Secretary-General as promised in the original Greek recourse of July 12 (see Appendix D), the Greek government stressed that since 1954 it had acted on behalf of the people of Cyprus and had consistently and repeatedly requested the United Nations to take action in order to help apply the principle of self-determination to the Cypriots, who were striving for freedom from the "ruling colonial power." The last two years this struggle had gained in momentum, with heavy losses in human life and property. This dangerously drifting situation endangered peace in a most vital area of the Middle East. During the six months that had passed since the Assembly had adopted Resolution 1013 (XI), the situation had eased for the British authorities. The people, however, were still being oppressed. Only minor changes had been brought to the emergency regulations. While the Cypriots had complied with this resolution, the British forces unilaterally were using violence against them. And no progress had been achieved in solving the main problem: freeing the Cypriots from colonial rule. The ruling power had taken no initiative in that direction. It had flatly turned down a proposal to this end by Ethnarch Makarios. Instead, the British government had proposed tripartite negotiations within NATO for dealing with this problem. In such procedures, however, the Greek government could not get involved, because the Cyprus question would thus have been partly or wholly withdrawn from UN jurisdiction. Besides, these procedures were not in accord with Resolution 1013 (XI). To accept them would not have been in accord with the mandate the Cypriot people had entrusted to Greece and could have led to solutions running against the will of the Cypriot people. An issue of freedom and of fundamental principles should be settled according to the Charter, the Greek government maintained. Greece was willing to continue contributing toward a peaceful solution to the problem, not seeking to secure any benefits for itself, having no claim to formulate, and disposed to make every reasonable concession and sacrifice in the cause of peace. It could not, however, disregard the rights of the Cypriot people, and, in discharging its responsibility, it was bound to oppose action by other quarters that would be detrimental to the Cypriot cause.

The Greek government, according to this explanatory memorandum, would have preferred not to refer another aspect of the Cyprus question to the Assembly. But in its files it had some five hundred signed charges of inhuman practices, brutalities, and atrocities committed by the colonial authorities against prisoners or persons arrested for interrogation. The matter was thus too serious to be passed over in silence. The methods and techniques used suggested practices of special personnel, with the toleration, if not approval, of at least some of the British authorities. These practices of bodily and mental torture, defined by International Law as "crimes against humanity," [8] were a challenge not only to the British people but also to the international community. The "noble British people" had had such close ties with the Greeks that whenever they fought great struggles for freedom, the Greeks had never been neutral or foes of the British but always their companions in arms. Because such methods were unknown to the British people, and the British government could not condone them even though bearing the ultimate responsiblity for them, the whole issue should be thoroughly investigated and dealt with. The Assembly perhaps could find an answer to the plight of the victims and the indignation of the civilized world. In the light of the situation, the Greek government called upon the Assembly to examine anew the Cyprus issue and take the proper steps for dealing with it.

A day later, the requested instructions arrived from Athens. In handling the matter of the inclusion of the Cyprus item in the Assembly's agenda, the General Committee's adoption of the first subitem of the recourse should be secured. Anything that might endanger the inclusion of the Cyprus item in the agenda should be avoided. Considering it unlikely that the Greek recourse would be passed as a whole and again stressing that the passage of subitem (a) of the recourse should be achieved, Athens expressed preference that the second subitem be withdrawn rather than rejected by a vote. It expressed hope that Makarios would agree in this procedure. The concurrent recourse to the European Commission of Human Rights and Article 60 of the European Convention on Human Rights could be invoked as grounds for withdrawing subitem (b).

Also transmitted from Athens were certain comments of Premier Karamanlis on the Greek explanatory memorandum of September 13. It should be remembered, the Premier suggested, that the British government had let months pass by before resorting to the diplomatic channel. Generally, it carried out its peace offensives at the eve of Assembly sessions. In 1955, it had called the London Tripartite Conference. In 1956, it had offered the Radcliffe draft constitution. And in 1957 it had suggested a new London tripartite conference. Thus, the British proposals did not aim at achieving progress in the solution of the Cyprus problem but at preventing debate of the issue in the United Nations. For four years, in other words, Britain had refused to discuss the matter and since 1954 had come up with proposals that demonstrated both its unwillingness to achieve a solution and its lack of good faith. After seven years of efforts there remained nothing else for Greece to do than to go again to the United Nations and ask for a new debate of the Cyprus issue. Although, it was recognized, the United Nations did not promote as much as it should the issue, this year it should go ahead toward a substantive solution, because if no measures were taken peace might be endangered. The disputed question of self-determination, the Premier observed, was now recognized indirectly even by the Turks, who sought the partition of the island in the name of self-determination, and also by the British, who acknowledged it should be applied to Cyprus at an appropriate time.

The Cyprus question as well as the subordinate theme of British atrocities were discussed at some length at a meeting of September 17 between Secretary of State Dulles and Foreign Minister Averoff-Tossizza, with Ambassador G. V. Melas, Rountree, and other State Department officials present. After a brief remark on his visit to Egypt,[9] Averoff-Tossizza gave a lengthy exposé of the Cyprus question, stressing the likelihood of new bloodshed on the island. Such bloodshed would be of a worse nature than before, he warned. It would involve a local clash between Greeks and Turks which could have dangerous consequences of a broader, regional character. The best procedure for making progress toward a solution of the problem, he maintained, would be for the Assembly to adopt a resolution recommending one of the alternative compromise solutions that the Greek government had put forward the previous month.[10] Dulles, on his side, appeared to attach great importance to the Cyprus question and to desire its speedy solution. The British, he was convinced, wished now to get rid of the question and were prepared to accept almost any solution. The only remaining difficulty was Turkey. On the whole, the Secretary of State appeared sympathetic with the Greek views. Firmly but politely, however, he strongly objected to any references to British atrocities at the stage of the debate over the inclusion of the Cyprus question in the Assembly's agenda. In a problem as difficult and as complex as the Cyprus issue, for the solution of which all were working, he said, if hate were injected from the very outset, new difficulties would be created. The Greek Foreign Minister animatedly explained in detail that it was impossible not to mention atrocities when they were being perpetrated. It would be immoral and explosive for his government to conceal them, he said. But he was prepared to deal with the matter in a dignified way and without demagogy. It would be harmful for the United States, which played a leading role in the Hungarian question, to seek to cover up the question of tortures in Cyprus, he added. Neither Dulles nor Rountree agreed with these arguments. Both insisted that the matter should not be raised in sharp discussion during the General Committee's debate on the Greek recourse. Rountree said that the British probably would accuse the Greeks of atrocities. Averoff-Tossizza retorted that he would be glad to accept such a debate. On the basis of this discussion, Ambassador Palamas concluded that it was likely that a third party would propose to the General Committee a change in the title of the Greek recourse. His conclusion turned out to be correct.

B. The General Committee Recommends Inclusion of Item 58 in the Agenda

Next day, September 18, the sixteen-member General Committee of the Assembly, fulfilling one of its main functions,[12] discussed item 58 of the provisional agenda to decide whether it should be included in the General Assembly's agenda. Sir Leslie Munro, of New Zealand, who, on the occasion of the first Greek recourse over Cyprus in 1954, had moved that the question be not considered further by the Assembly,[13] presided. His chairing of the proceedings led to certain tense moments, for when viewed against his earlier role in the Cyprus question as a British proxy, his methods could be easily construed by the Greek representative as being peppered with parliamentary "gamesmanship."

Sir Leslie Munro (President): Now item 58 relates to Cyprus. Does any member wish to make an observation?

Mr. Selwyn Lloyd (United Kingdom): I object to the inclusion of this item.

Sir Leslie Munro (President): Well, under those circumstances, having heard the representative of the United Kingdom, I have received a letter from the permanent representative of Greece in which he asks to be invited to participate in the debate on this matter under rule 43 of the rules of procedure. I take it the Committee has no objection to the representative of Greece, I ask him therefore to take place at the table of the Committee. Is there any member of the Committee who would first wish to be heard before I call upon the representative of Greece? I call upon the representative of Greece.

Mr. Averoff-Tossizza (Greece): Greece was led once again to ask that the question of Cyprus be included in the agenda of the twelfth session of the General Assembly. We did not take this initiative with a light heart. As a member of this great family of nations, Greece would have been happy had the question of Cyprus been resolved, or had the question of Cyprus developed in such a way that one might anticipate a solution to it. We are fully conscious of the difficulties encountered by this international community in its march towards the future. We all hope that the future will be full of hope, but we know that it is greatly imperilled. We have before us an atomic . . . (interruption)

Sir Leslie Munro (President): The representative of Turkey wishes to be called to the table and, subject to the consent of the Committee, I think that it would be proper to invite him to take his place. . . . There appears to be no objection and I ask the representative of Turkey to take his place at the table. I apologize to the representative of Greece for interrupting him. I ask him to proceed.

Thereupon, the Greek Foreign Minister continued his speech, first briefly referring to the dangers of nuclear accidents of the atomic age. He would have been very glad, he said, to spare the Assembly from turning once again to a serious problem, which seven months earlier it had directed toward a peaceful, democratic, and fair solution, in accordance with the principles and purposes of the UN Charter. He was the first to regret that the substantive aspects of the Cyprus problem were virtually at the same spot as they had been during the last session of the Assembly. The resolution adopted had not been implemented. No substantial progress had been attained toward a solution to this problem. The people of Cyprus today were facing the same problems they had faced when the Greek Delegation, for the first time, had put before the Assembly its request for freedom from the colonial yoke pursuant to the Charter's provisions on the right of self-determination of all peoples. But for a few minor changes in the island, the situation was serious and precarious, he maintained. In spite of having met the request of the Assembly, of having suspended armed conflict, of having expressed their acquiescence in support of the Assembly resolution, of having expressed their desire to co-operate by means of negotiations in finding a peaceful solution to this problem, the people of Cyprus had found that their lot was unchanged and that the situation in the island was still fraught with great danger.

From the political angle, the British government had rejected any suggestion to negotiate with the people at all, Averoff-Tossizza went on to say. "A great prelate, Archbishop Makarios, according to age-old tradition, according to his popular election, and according to his moral stature, as unquestioned spiritual and political head and leader of the overwhelming majority of the people of Cyprus," was, it was true, no longer a prisoner. He was, however, still an exile who was refused the right to return to his fatherland. The Assembly had recommended that negotiations be resumed with the occupying power, but the London government has rebuffed any such effort.

With regard to the island's administration, Governor Harding was met with a vacuum. Recognizing that his main opponent was the people of Cyprus, he had launched reprisals against the civilian population. Military operations had proceeded with great intensity, as in the past, in the mountains, cities, and villages. One of these villages, to cite but a single instance, had been under a curfew for fifty-four days, and this had taken place since Resolution 1013 (XI).[14] During these fifty-four days of agony, the peaceful villagers had seen their houses destroyed, their cattle decimated by hunger and thirst. In spite of this resolution, the gallows played their role and summary courts passed sentences, and those in police stations worked overtime.

If the island had become pacified by its own resolve and the head of the resistance was still there and had not yet been captured by "the Marshal of the Empire with his 30,000 troops," it was because the idea that this leader of the insurgents represented was an idea that could never be chained or shackled, the Greek Foreign Minister declared. The fact was that Cyprus, an island that enjoyed a civilization equal to that of any other Mediterranean country, continued, even after Resolution 1013 (XI), to be a colony administered in a shameless fashion by some petty provincial dictators who in no way respected the wishes of the population and who created a situation that was fraught with peril and was untenable and intolerable. This, objectively, with no exaggeration whatsoever, was the factual situation in Cyprus, said Averoff-Tossizza.

It was greatly regrettable that Britain, which in other cases had acted with foresight, wisdom, and generosity, refused to grant to the people of Cyprus what it so gladly conferred upon other peoples. Britain, the Greek Foreign Minister contended, was wrong to impede the application of the Assembly resolution on this subject. These errors did not serve Britain's interests. Britain might well be heading straight into an impasse by seeking to deal with the future of the Cypriot people in their absence. Britain was trying to introduce extraneous elements which could not have a greater weight in the matter than the Cypriots themselves. It wished to revive the tripartite negotiations [15] and not give a hearing to the party principally concerned. To frustrate the people of Cyprus, to prevent them from determining their own destiny would be tantamount to relinquishing the only sound basis for a solution. "We would be working on a foundation of sand and would be leading directly into political bargaining." This would be to commit not only an injustice but an error fraught with serious consequences.

Any solution that was not imbued with the spirit of justice and peace would be no solution at all, said Averoff-Tossizza. "We cannot, therefore, follow a course proved by events to be false and erroneous and shown by the recent tragic past to be dangerous for the life and human dignity of our peoples and for the friendship which Greece would wish to extend to certain countries." The people of Cyprus had asked the Greek government to entrust its destiny to the United Nations. The United Nations had already taken up this question and, in a first resolution, had taken direct responsibility for this question. The United Nations should decide how to implement this resolution. Cyprus was a question; it would remain so. Any subsequent developments should take place within the framework and, at the very least, under the vigilant supervision of the United Nations.

But there was another aspect of the Cyprus problem that, unfortunately, the Greek Delegation was compelled to bring up again, Averoff-Tossizza went on to say. During the Cyprus debate in the First Committee in February, he had informed the United Nations of the atrocities committed by administration officials in Cyprus, and had mentioned 237 instances of torture. He had stated, too, that if an objective inquiry proved that these charges were unfounded, he would resign from his government and retire from public life, for he would have felt that he would in this way have been guilty of impeaching the honor and integrity of Britain.[16] Unfortunately, Britain had not grasped the opportunity for clearing the colonial administration in Cyprus of these very serious charges. The proposal he had advanced at the last session was still valid. Perhaps this year it would meet with greater success. If, however, his proposal once again was rejected, then the case should be discussed by the United Nations, for there were two important aspects in this area.

One was a general aspect. For not only Cyprus was involved. There were political, legal, and moral factors which, *per se*, were of concern to the United Nations and which should therefore be taken up by the Assembly. This question involved the survival of torture methods, tortures perpetrated against human beings and the interest of the international community. Under the influence of World War II and the political problems it had created, international law has formulated certain new principles regarding the respect for freedom and human rights. These principles could not be ignored either by governments or by petty provincial dictators, who at times felt superior to their government. Here was a case in which these principles, for which all mankind fought and suffered, should be applied. This issue should be taken up by the United Nations.

But what particularly had led the Greek Delegation to raise this issue again was that torture had been widely used even after the passing of Resolution 1013 (XI). As was well known, it had been the Cypriots who had been responsible for the restoration of quiet and order. Nevertheless, atrocities had taken place in substantial number, the Foreign Minister asserted. The Greek government had evidence of such atrocities and felt that the proofs it had would withstand any scrutiny.

He repeated what he had stated frequently: his government did not consider the British people responsible for these atrocities; it felt sure that as a civilized people, they disapproved of such atrocities and in fact probably did not suspect that such atrocities had taken place. Nor did his government contend that the British government supported such atrocities. Quite to the contrary, the British government would disown them. But in the final analysis, the British government was responsible for its acts and did not wish to believe that some of its colonial organs had acted as torturers. That was why the British government was reluctant to have any satisfactory investigation carried out. It was not possible to have the person indicted asked to carry out an investigation of the indictment. This would be to go too far, and would not satisfy even the most naïve and credulous person. Without touching on the substance of the matter, his delegation had evidence that local authorities had used torture in Cyprus against a few hundred human beings at the very least. It asked that this evidence be debated, or that an investigation be carried out, if the latter procedure were preferred. That was why the Greek

Delegation had suggested the inclusion of subitem (b) in item 58. The United Nations had been set up to protect life, to protect human rights and human freedoms, and no one here could reject this proposal.

The question of tortures and atrocities was only one aspect of the Cyprus question, Averoff-Tossizza said further. It existed because of the Cyprus issue. If Cyprus were free from the colonial yoke, then torture would be done away with as would also the other atrocities. It was necessary, therefore, to tackle the problem primarily from the angle of the liberation of the people of Cyprus. The United Nations, at its previous session, had worked in that direction and had brought substantial assistance to the people of Cyprus. Unfortunately, the work and the suggestions of the United Nations had not been carried out or further developed. The Greek Delegation, the Greek Foreign Minister concluded, appealed to the protection and to the spirit of justice of the United Nations, and that was why it was confident in requesting inclusion of this item in the agenda of the twelfth General Assembly.

Lloyd, the British representative, now spoke. Once again he emphasized that his government objected to the inclusion of item 58, as proposed by the Greek government. His objections to subitem (a) on legal grounds were well known. They had been explained both in the United Nations and elsewhere. The application of the principle of self-determination in Cyprus, or in any other non-self-governing territory under British administration and sovereignty, was a matter exclusively for the British government to decide, he declared. When Malaya's admission was being approved the day before, many tributes had been paid to Britain's record in these matters. Britain, of all countries, had no reason to be on the defensive when it came to issues of self-determination. But that did not affect its legal position. He would not go today into another aspect of the matter—the *enosis* aspect. This item was really designed to promote the union of Cyprus with Greece. But that was another issue.

At the eleventh session of the Assembly, Britain had put down an item on support from Greece for terrorism in Cyprus (see Appendix E). That was an international issue with which the Assembly was clearly competent to deal. And the British Delegation had not pressed its objection to inscription of the Greek item at that session of the Assembly, on the understanding that its item would also be discussed with it. Thus, the discussion of the Cyprus item at the eleventh session had not been without value. Some of the facts of this complicated situation had become better known.

Although he had some doubt whether now, so soon after the last debate, another discussion would also prove very useful, he would not raise objections to the discussion of the Cyprus question on a proper basis some time during the current session. However, he could not accept the terms in which the Greek item was formulated as set out in subitem (a), for the reasons he had already given. He would therefore vote against it as it stood.

Now, said Lloyd, he wished very much that that was all that he needed to say about item 58. Unfortunately, he had to turn to subitem (b) of the Greek item, against the inscription of which he would also vote. He wanted to make the British position very clear. He would not be voting against this subitem because Britain would have difficulty with the charges that the Greek government might bring under this subitem. His reason for voting against it was that a fundamental principle of the Charter was here at stake. At the time the Charter had been drawn up, it had been clearly understood that the United Nations was not competent to consider complaints or allegations against the internal administration of member states. It was on this understanding, which was embodied in Article 2, of the Charter,[17] that the governments concerned had signed the Charter. He had no doubt that if that principle had not been accepted many governments would not have signed the Charter. And that really was a principle that could not lightly be set aside, because a decision to do so would have incalculable consequences. Any disgruntled faction in any country that could procure the services of another power to aid and abet it would be enabled to bring to the United Nations complaints against its own government. And there were, he thought, few governments that would really approve the use of the United Nations for that purpose. It would be most dangerous for the future of the United Nations itself. And yet that, in fact, was what was involved in subitem (b) of the Greek item.

Now, it was not the occasion to attempt to deal with the substance of these charges of atrocities, Lloyd went on to say. A large number of these allegations had been published both inside and outside of Cyprus by those who wished to increase the difficulties of solving this complicated question. Many would think that Britain's known reputation in the conduct of colonial affairs would be in itself sufficient refutation of charges against the administration in Cyprus of responsibility for atrocities. Nevertheless, the British government had thought it right to examine these charges, and every one of them had been investigated. It had its own standard of conduct in these matters and had tried to be scrupulous in maintaining that standard. In the one or two cases where people had overstepped the mark, disciplinary action had been openly taken without any regard to the political consequences. But so far as the charges of "atrocities" were concerned, his delegation would not have the slightest difficulty in showing how ridiculous they were. And, he repeated, the reason that his delegation was voting against the inscription of this item was not because of any difficulty.

The distinguished Foreign Minister of Greece had given one example of "atrocities." He, Lloyd, now would give one example of the kind of calumny which was being put forth. Archbishop Makarios had said on June 19, in Athens: "Miss Loulla Kokkinou lost her front teeth after a rough blow by a sadist tormentor. This cowardice at least cannot be denied by the Government of Cyprus, as its marks are still there. Such unspeakable and abominable atrocities against all sense of morality were perpetrated under the eyes of the Government of Cyprus." The facts were that a medical certificate dated June 20, 1957, stated that Miss Kokkinou had all her natural front teeth in place except one which is false. Her dental records showed that she had lost this tooth at some date prior to June 24, 1955. And she had been arrested for the first time on May 23, 1956.[18] And that showed the type of allegation that was being made against Britain.

But he would not go further into these charges, Lloyd said. If subitem (b) was inscribed, one would not only be dealing with a series of unfounded allegations, many of them based upon statements obtained by terrorists under threat of murder. One would also have to attack many of the actions of the Greek government. But his delegation did not want to do so because it did not believe it would contribute to a settlement of this matter.

He had said earlier that if it were the view that discussion of the Cyprus question at this session was likely to prove constructive, the British Delegation would not object. Since the Assembly had passed its resolution last February, his government had done everything possible to procure a solution to the Cyprus question. It had released Archbishop Makarios from detention, though the assurances received from him on the subject of terrorism were admittedly not very satisfactory. It had relaxed many of the security precautions and regulations on the island. It had welcomed the attempt to find a solution within the NATO framework. Since progress in this way proved impossible because the Greek government was not prepared at this stage to co-operate in finding a solution in this way, the British government had been making determined efforts to find other methods of discussion, acceptable to the Greek and Turkish governments. It had stated its willingness to discuss a new and liberal constitution for the island with the representatives of the Cypriots. He did not need to go further at this stage into those efforts.

Lloyd, at any rate, thought that discussion of subitem (b) would not only be entirely wrong in terms of the fundamental principles of the Charter, but it could not fail to increase the tension surrounding the problem of Cyprus, when it was the duty of "the three governments concerned" to work for a relaxation of tension.

The last time he had spoken about the inscription of an item on Cyprus, three years earlier, in September, 1954, he had predicted, Lloyd reminded the Committee, that

a debate in New York could do nothing but exacerbate feelings, set Christians against Moslems and produce internal strife which the Cypriots had hitherto been spared. The resulting tension might extend far beyond the island of Cyprus itself. A public disputation between the representatives of Greece, on the one hand, and the representatives of some of Greece's allies, on the other, might jeopardize friendly relations in that part of the world. From such a situation only those elements which sought to profit by international discord would derive satisfaction.[19]

Every one of those things in fact had happened. And he believed again today if this item were inscribed in these terms, and followed by the necessary debate, it would make infinitely more difficult the task of reaching a settlement. During the last three or four months, there had been a slight relaxation of tension. The tone of Britain's exchanges with the Greek government had improved, and he gladly gave credit for that where it was due.

It was because inscription of the item in its present form would make much more difficult a settlement of this vexing problem, and because of the legal grounds that he had indicated, that he asked the General Committee not to inscribe this item. Three years earlier little attention had been paid to his forecast. Lloyd, in conclusion, asked with respect to what he had said today to be considered most seriously by those who had the responsibility of voting upon this matter.

Seyfullah Esin, of Turkey, after thanking the President and the members of the General Committee for having given him the opportunity of presenting the views of his delegation on the inclusion of item 58 in the agenda, stated that the item concerned Cyprus, "an island which lies off the shores of Turkey and of which part of the population is Turkish; an island, the present status of which was decided upon in the form of transfer of sovereignty from Turkey to the United Kingdom in the Treaty of Lausanne, signed between Turkey, the United Kingdom, Greece and other governments." For these reasons, among others, which were all well known to the members of the General Committee, the people and the government of Turkey had a direct interest and were concerned in any discussion that dealt with the international status of Cyprus. In this procedural debate, however, he would refrain from dealing with the substance of the question and confine his remarks exclusively to the subject under discussion, namely, the demand of the Greek government to include the Cyprus question in the agenda.

The Cyprus question had first been brought to the United Nations by the Greek government in 1954.[20] That year, Esin reminded the committee members, having heard the parties concerned, the Assembly had considered that it was inappropriate for the time being to pass a resolution on Cyprus and decided not to discuss further this question. In 1955, the Greek government had demanded again the inscription of the Cyprus question on the agenda, but both the General Committee and the Assembly had rejected this demand.[21] In 1956, the British government and the Greek government each had proposed a subitem to be included under the general heading of the Cyprus Question. The position of the Turkish Delegation at that time stood on the records of the General Committee and the plenary meeting of the Assembly.[22] Turkey maintained its views on the limits of the competence of the Assembly but was not opposed to the inclusion of the item in the agenda. In so doing, it placed its faith in the wisdom, the common sense, and the deep sense of justice and practical realities existing in the Assembly for acting as a general guide within the limits of its legal possibilities to show the way toward a peaceful, democratic, and just solution. The Turkish government took this attitude as a further contribution in its efforts to arrive eventually at a peaceful and just solution of the Cyprus question, which had already caused such grave and needless damage to the relations between Turkey, Britain, and Greece. This conciliatory attitude was in line with the resolution adopted by the Assembly on February 26, 1957.

It was only natural, Esin continued, that perhaps none of the three governments mainly concerned in the Cyprus question should find every part of the existing resolution on Cyprus entirely to its own liking. But he was deeply convinced that if good will and sincere desire for a just solution existed among every one of the three governments, the resolution did include all the necessary elements for working together toward such a solution. Indeed, during the brief period that had elapsed since February 26, the Assembly's resolution had already been successful to some extent to paving the way toward an eventual settlement. If this progress had been only casual because of the refusal of one of the parties to resume negotiations, except under its own terms, it was still the Turkish view that reason, common sense, and justice would eventually triumph in the just direction by the United Nations.

This being the situation after the debate that had taken place in the first months of 1957, the Turkish government found puzzling, to say the least, the attitude of the Greek government in demanding again the inscription of this item on the agenda on July 12, hardly over four months after the adoption of Resolution 1013 (XI). It was difficult to see how the Greek government could sincerely desire to follow the path indicated by the United Nations and yet demand the reopening of the debate only four months after this resolution had been adopted, especially bearing in mind that during the brief period pacification had made important steps forward, and efforts were being made for resuming the negotiations. In spite of the provisions of rule 20 of the rules of procedure, which required that all items proposed for inclusion in the agenda should be "accompanied" by an explanatory memorandum, it had taken the Greek government two entire months after its request to present such a document. This peculiar interpretation of rule 20 naturally brought to mind the possibility that the desire to lure the debate on Cyprus might have preceded the exact establishment of the legal grounds upon which such a request was to be based. Furthermore, the wording in which the Greek request had been presented indicated no desire to seek compliance with the spirit manifested by the Assembly only some months earlier, but rather an attempt to rekindle bitter discussion and division in the hope of confusing the United Nations as a means of propaganda concerning the well-known ambitions of Greece on Cyprus.

Subitem (a) was a reiteration of the wording that had been used by Greece during the last four years. It included the lofty principle of equal rights and self-determination, which the Turkish government considered as one of the main pillars of international relations. As the distinguished members of the Steering Committee were informed, among "the three governments mainly concerned" in the Cyprus question, both Turkey and Britain had accepted the principle of self-determination. But the Turkish government opposed the use of this principle as a means of furthering annexationist ambitions. Therefore, the reiteration of the previous wording in subitem (a) would not only be misleading, but also might bring about a repetition of the debate that had taken place previously in the Assembly.

As for subitem (b), apart from its contradiction to the provisions of Article 2, paragraph 7, of the Charter, it was worded in a language reminiscent of the worst phases of the cold war, which had been happily left behind in the work of the United Nations, as a period to which everybody hoped it would not be necessary to revert. In conclusion, the Turkish Delegation took account of the discussions which had taken place only some months earlier in the United Nations on the Cyprus question. The title of the new Greek demand, the way it had been presented, and its wording all led to the belief that "we may be faced not with the sincere effort to arrive at a peaceful, just and democratic solution; not with the desire to pave the way for a settlement satisfactory to all concerned; but rather with an attempt to use the august Assembly as a means of spreading propaganda and confusion and thus increasing tension and bitterness over this question." He wished, Esin said in conclusion, to draw the attention of the members of the General Committee to these views and anxieties of his delegation. He reserved his right to intervene again as might be deemed appropriate in the General Committee and in the Assembly.

Sir Leslie Munro (President): I call upon the representative of Norway.

Mrs. Aase Lionaes (Norway): The Delegation of Norway will vote in favor of the inscription of the question of Cyprus on the agenda. We would, however, prefer to have the item inscribed in a completely neutral way, so as not to prejudice in any way the problems involved. We may assume that there will be no opposition to inscription of the item under a neutral heading and likewise no opposition to discussing all the international aspects of the Cyprus question during this session.

In order to avoid the prolongation of an unfortunate procedural debate which also may involve questions of substance at this stage of our deliberations, my delegation, therefore, proposes that item 58 be included on the agenda under the following heading: "The Cyprus Question." Thank you.

The representative of Iran, Djalal Abdoh, spoke next. His delegation, he said, was not opposed to the inclusion of this item in the agenda of the Assembly. However, he thought that this question, as submitted by the Delegation of Greece, was such as to prejudice the very substance of the question. Therefore, it would be more appropriate to adopt a wording that would not prejudge the substance of the matter. It was in this spirit that his delegation wholeheartedly supported the proposal made by the representative of Norway. The representatives of Venezuela, Thailand, the Netherlands, and Ceylon likewise supported the Norwegian proposal.

V. V. Kuznetsov, of the Soviet Union, spoke next. Although the question of Cyprus had been repeatedly discussed in the United Nations, the problem of a peaceful settlement of this question in the spirit of the UN Charter remained unsolved, he declared. At its eleventh session, the Assembly had adopted a resolution in which the wish had been expressed for a peaceful, democratic, and just solution to be found to this question. One might have thought that appropriate negotiations would have been held with the representatives of the people of the island of Cyprus and that the unconditional right of the population of Cyprus to its inalienable right of self-determination would have been recognized. However, the island was still under the yoke of colonialism. Emergency laws continued to operate, which transformed the island into an enormous concentration camp. The British government, in the Soviet view, was taking no effective measures to come to an agreement with the representatives of the population of Cyprus, bearing in mind the unfaltering aspiration of the Cypriots to realize their inherent right to self-determination. In certain circles, plans were being concocted for the partition of Cyprus, for the turning of the island into one of the atomic bases of NATO and into a military strong point of "the colonizers in the Eastern Mediterranean." But it was perfectly obvious that a further militarization of the island would harm the cause of reducing international tension and that all these military and colonial plans did not correspond to the hopes and longings of the population of the island of Cyprus. Therefore, the Soviet Delegation considered that the question of Cyprus should be discussed at the twelfth session of the Assembly and supported the proposal of the Greek Delegation for the inclusion in the agenda of this session of the question of Cyprus.

The representative of Guatemala, E. Arenales Catalan, said his delegation would like to explain its position on this question. But he had noted that the representative of Greece had asked for the floor. Perhaps it might be better to call upon him first, and then he could speak later.

Sir Leslie Munro (President): It would be customary for a member of the Committee to speak first if he so desires. As I understand, the representative of Greece wishes to speak in reply. So the normal course would be first to hear the representative of Guatemala. That is so. That suits your convenience? The representative of Guatemala.

Mr. E. Arenales Catalan (Guatemala): Mr. President, I understood you to say that it is the practice for members of the General Committee to speak first if they wish to do so. . . . Personally, I would prefer to hear from the representative of Greece before speaking. Unless, of course, the views which he is about to express are not specifically relevant to this vote.

Sir Leslie Munro, accordingly called on the representative of Greece. Averoff-Tossizza said that in his statement he had avoided going into the matter of substance. He regretted that the British representative, and especially the Turkish representative, had gone into the substance of the question. He would avoid doing so in the brief analysis he intended to make. However, he was compelled to note two or three basic points that had been raised. One on which both of the distinguished representatives had dwelt in particular were the rights of the parties concerned. He was happy to note that the representative of Turkey had made some progress, because he had referred to the governments mainly concerned. However, it was the position of the Greek government and, he thought, the position of logic and morality that this question was a question between the people of the island and the British government. There were other governments indirectly concerned; they were not the only ones. Those whom the problem concerned could be no other than the people who were a civilized people, and the government that was the dominating government or the dominant government. The others were only indirectly concerned. He also did not wish to dwell on what he could almost call the charge of the *enosis* movement. This had been cleared up and he hoped it would be further clarified in the Political Committee and the Assembly. He denied that Greece claimed the union of the island with itself. Greece claimed that a people enjoying a three-thousand-year-old civilization should have the right to self-determination. Greece stated that when this had been achieved, it would applaud the result of a plebiscite and it would accept whatever the people wanted, applauding if they wished to be an independent state, a member of the Commonwealth, or anything else. He preferred to leave the other points of substance that had been raised, because he would not wish to prolong this discussion or make the discussion more controversial, and he would like to maintain it on the high level on which it had begun.

There was, however, a question of law, Averoff-Tossizza argued. The British Foreign Minister had raised that point, and the representative of Turkey had supported him in that. He thought that he was in a position to maintain that Article 2, paragraph 7, had nothing to do with this case, and had never concerned Cyprus. Article 73 of the Charter concerned Cyprus.[23] The colonial administration of a territory could not fall within the provisions affecting domestic affairs of a dominant power. If it were not so, why should Cyprus, contrary, for example, to the county of Manchester, come under the Colonial Office in London? Why was a whole set of laws applicable to Cyprus and to other British Crown Colonies, and not applicable to Great Britain itself? Why under the Charter had the United Kingdom submitted reports, however incomplete these might be, to the United Nations under Article 73, concerning non-self-governing territories? Why had it not submitted reports on Manchester county? If Cyprus was, under Article 2, paragraph 7, "within the domestic jurisdiction of the United Kingdom," what British colony were the United Nations discussing here for several years? "Gentlemen, British, you were the ones who fired first—you have done that several times since Louis XV [24]—and you were the first to describe Cyprus as a colony."

But if Cyprus was not a colony, the Greek Foreign Minister argued further, if it was not a non-self-governing territory, and if it fell not under Article 73, but under Article 2, paragraph 7, there were no non-self-governing territories in the world. The case of Cyprus was a case of a people different from its dominant people by its religion, language, and origin, Averoff-Tossizza continued. It was a case of an island fighting for its freedom. If it was to be considered that this was a metropolitan territory, then there were only metropolitan territories left in the world. This would be logically absurd, and he was sure that the Committee could not follow that point of view.

However, there was another legal argument

in our favor, and a very strong one . . . Article 55 of the Charter says that the United Nations shall promote the universal and effective respect of human rights and fundamental freedoms for all. Can one promote that respect if one refuses even to discuss charges concerning the violations of human rights in Cyprus? That can be done, but only in flagrant violation of Article 55. But we would also have to violate another article, Article 10. Article 10 says that the General Assembly may discuss any question or any matters within the scope of the present Charter. Now, the violation of the human rights of the Cypriots falls clearly under the provisions of Article 55.

And, for the time being, he added, his government was not asking for any measures. It was merely asking for a discussion of the matter, in all its aspects, which was clearly authorized by Article 10. Those who refused to discuss the Greek complaint concerning violation of the human rights on Cyprus, would do well to move for the abolition of Articles 10 and 55. It was unnecessary to have articles in the Charter which had beautiful phrases but which were not applied.

As for the substance of the charges concerning atrocities, which his British colleague had refuted by citing an example, he would tell him that if all the Greek cases were like that, then it was in his interest to have not only a discussion, but a committee of inquiry. He thought he could tell him that such cases of teeth removed by dentists would not be presented to an investigation. And, as his colleague had spoken some words in which it had appeared that he would be the accuser and he, the Greek Foreign Minister, the defendant, he would tell him as far as he was concerned, he was happy to accept that reversal of roles, because he would be a defendant who asked for the charges to be considered, whereas the British representative would be the innocent party asking that his innocence not even be discussed.

Averoff-Tossizza said he did not want to go into greater detail on the other aspects of the argumentation, but he wished to answer now to the proposal the representative of Norway had made. First of all, according to one of the rules of procedure, one could not change the title of an item. Rule 22 said: "Items on the agenda may be amended or deleted by the General Assembly by a majority of members present and voting." The Norwegian proposal was not an amendment. It would amount to a complete change or a complete reversal[25] of the item which his delegation had proposed. He therefore thought that the rules of procedure ruled out the adoption of that proposal. Moreover, it seemed to him really difficult for such an important question, one with so many implications, to be included under such a succinct heading, a heading that gave no explanation of its contents. If a new wording were to be proposed, it should at least have some indication, some reference to the aspects of the questions that should be discussed. He could hardly imagine that such an important question, a question with such great implications, could be proposed by the mere name of the question, without any aspects, without any points for discussion. As regarded his delegation, it was not a member of the Committee, but it reserved its right to combat that proposal for the reasons he had just mentioned, and to press for a vote on the wording as proposed by his delegation.

He recognized the good will that inspired the representative of Norway in making her proposal and the good will of the other members who supported her proposal, and he paid tribute to that good will. The purpose was not to hide questions but to discuss them in broad daylight, provided that there was good will and frankness. The Committee had seen that even last year's discussion and the brief discussion which had just taken place had been carried out by the Greek Delegation with sincerity and consideration for its friends.

Sir Leslie Munro (President): I trust that this debate will not become one of substance. The question before the General Committee now is a proposal by the representative of Norway that the item be called the Cyprus Question. Without myself expressing any opinion on the merits of that proposal, it is within the competence of this Committee to make such an alteration; it has done so in the past. The matter is not yet on the agenda, and I think it can be altered if that is the will of the Committee. I call upon the representative of Guatemala.

Arenales Catalan said he was sure that the President would understand that he wished to hear first from the representative of Greece so that he might be fully acquainted with his reaction to the Norwegian proposal. Speaking only as a member of the General Committee, he proposed to vote for the inclusion of item 58 and for the inclusion of the other items in the agenda; and he would vote in this way because of the following principles, which he developed at great length. First of all, in the view of Guatemala, the Charter was an instrument for international coexistence. In principle, therefore, he would vote for the inclusion of all items, though he could quite understand that other delegations might for political reasons object to the inclusion of a particular item. Second, under Articles 34 and 35 of the Charter,[26] the Assembly was supposed to take up those questions or situations that were likely to give rise to international disturbances or international friction. The Cyprus case had already given rise to international friction. Third, questions coming under the above two articles were not matters that could be considered as falling strictly within the domestic jurisdiction of states, under Article 2, paragraph 7, of the Charter. Moreover, he viewed with great sympathy the thesis that international jurisdiction existed in the field of human rights, so that here, too, certain limitations were imposed upon the scope of Article 2, paragraph 7, of the Charter.

As to the wording proposed by Greece, in connection with subitem (a), the representative of Guatemala continued, he would like to say that he had no reservation whatsoever to submit. For the record, however, he had to differ with the views expressed by the British representative. Implementing self-determination in a non-self-governing territory was a matter that also came under the competence of the United Nations. As to subitem (b), the Delegation of Guatemala considered that from the viewpoint of international jurisdiction in the field of human rights, it could support the inclusion of this subitem without any reservations. However, the wording used in that subitem tended to prejudge the substance of the issue, even if this was not the intention of the "accusing party." He did not know what procedure the President proposed to follow with regard to the suggestions made by Mrs. Lionaes of Norway. He did not know whether it would be considered a separate motion or an amendment, or how this proposal would be put to the vote. Personally, he would prefer the wording suggested by the delegate of Norway. If this wording were not adopted by the Committee, then he would vote for the proposal in the wording suggested by Greece.

Sir Leslie Munro (President): The representative of Guatemala would be reminded we are formulating at the moment questions as to the form of the item. . . . We don't as a rule put formal amendments in this Committee. It just is a question of what is the sense of this Committee on the matter, and I would like to know whether there are any other representatives who wish to speak on this matter. The representative of France.

G. Georges-Picot stated that the French Delegation would vote against item 58 as worded for the same reasons which had already been explained by the British Delegation. Jiri Nosek, of Czechoslovakia, on the other hand, after observing that his delegation had supported at the ninth, tenth, and eleventh session the Greek request for inclusion of the item of Cyprus in the agenda of the Assembly, declared it strongly supported the inclusion of item 58, as proposed by the Greek Delegation, in the agenda.

The representative of Tunisia, Mongi Slim, stated he would not go into the substance of the matter, because a question of procedure was being dealt with. The Tunisian Delegation would support the inclusion in the agenda of the question of Cyprus for a certain number of reasons which had been set forth by his colleagues who were in favor of the inclusion. In particular, he would like to emphasize another point that has not yet been emphasized. The committee was dealing with a question which has already been the subject of a lengthy debate at the Assembly's previous session. That was a question of which the Assembly has already been seized, and which concerned three members of the United Nations. This did not mean, of course, that it concerned only those three members. It also concerned all of the other littoral Mediterranean states that were interested in having concord, peace, and international co-operation reign in that area. It also concerned all of the members of the United Nations because of the very principles involved in the question: The principle of self-determination of peoples, the principle of putting an end to a dispute between a people that was trying to free itself and a situation that still kept it removed from its liberation and independence. In the hope of seeing the Assembly contribute, by a discussion, to a *rapprochement* of points of view to find or to suggest or recommend a solution that might be in keeping with the principles of the Charter, the Tunisian Delegation would vote in favor of the inclusion of this question.

Lloyd, at this point, said he did not propose to attempt to deal with many of the arguments which had been raised, but only with legal aspects. These arguments had been deployed many times before, and he simply reiterated the British view that, under Article 2, paragraph 7, and on the position of non-self-governing territories, the terms of Article 73 quite clearly showed by inference that the British construction was correct, because political development had been expressly excluded from the information to be transmitted to the Secretary-General. However, he did not propose to develop these legal matters further on this occasion. He really asked only to speak again so that he might make his comment on the proposal the Norwegian representative had put forward. He expressed doubts about the value of further discussions so soon. However, he did recognize, and had always recognized, that there were certain international aspects of the Cyprus question. A certain number of governments were fairly directly concerned and others perhaps more indirectly. Therefore, in order to try and approach this matter in a constructive manner, he was prepared to say that he would not oppose the inscription of an item in the terms put forward by the Norwegian representative. He only hoped that if an item were inscribed in those terms, the tone and the substance of the subsequent discussion would contribute to the settlement of an extremely complicated problem, as his government most earnestly desired.

The representative of China, T. F. Tsiang, said his delegation had, during the last three years, held the opinion that the question of Cyprus was within the competence of the United Nations. At times it had entertained doubts concerning the practical utility of a debate in the sense that a debate might not contribute to a settlement of the problem. Now, as the debate had developed, it appeared that a large majority of the Committee members favored the inscription. The last statement of the British representative showed that he was not entirely opposed to the inscription, but the debate so far had been more on the form of wording. Now, he did not think that wording was worth all the time spent. He hoped that the representative of Greece might find his way to accept the suggestion of the Norwegian representative. If, however, for some reason, he was determined to object to that form, he, the representative of China, suggested, not as an amendment, that to subitem (a) the phrase be added "Question of" and not "Application of the Principle." In subitem (b), he would suggest addition of the words "Complaint of." He thought that if "Question of" were added to subitem (a) and "Complaint of" to subitem (b), then the subitem would be neutral.

Sir Leslie Munro (President): Now, just before I call upon the representative of Greece, we have spent some time naturally on this problem of importance, but all that we are dealing with now is the question of the inclusion of this item. But, first of all, of course, it has to be formulated. Now, as I understand the position, the representative of the United Kingdom opposes the inscription of the item in its present form. There is, however, before us a proposal by the representative of Norway that the item be called alone the "Cyprus Question." Now . . . the representative of the United Kingdom accepts that formulation and will then not oppose the inscription of the item. Now the representative of Greece, of course, is entitled to be heard at any time, but the question of voting on this is for the members of the Committee. Now, we do appear to be getting fairly near to the stage when we are—when most of the members of the Committee are prepared to agree to the inscription of the item under the heading "The Cyprus Question." I hope we can expedite our procedure. I know that all the members of the Committee will agree with me there. And I now call upon the representative of Greece.

Averoff-Tossizza stated he would say only two words: the proposal of the representative of China had demonstrated the difference between an amendment and a new title. And he would like to refer to what he had said regarding rule 22 of the rules of procedure. The Chinese proposal was an amendment. The Norwegian proposal was equal to the abolition of a formula and the creation of another, entirely different and much narrower one. He was ready, he said, to accept the amendment proposed by the representative of China. He was not ready, however, for reasons that he had already explained, to accept the proposal of Norway.

Sir Leslie Munro (President): I should point out, before I call upon the representative of Turkey, what I have already pointed out: that items on the agenda might be amended or deleted by the General Assembly, but this item is not on the agenda. The representative of Turkey.

Ambassador Esin declared that, of course, his delegation was not on the General Committee, but if the Cyprus Question were included in the agenda in the form the Delegate of Norway had proposed, his delegation would not oppose inscription when the matter came to the Assembly.

Sir Leslie Munro (President): Well, now, I think that we can proceed to find out what is the sense of the Committee on this matter. The proposal—I prefer not to call it an amendment, because we hear formulated the title of an item—the proposal of the representative of Norway is that the item be inscribed on the agenda under the title "The Cyprus Question." May I take it that the members of the Committee are agreeable to the item being inscribed in that way? The representative of the Soviet Union.

Mr. V. V. Kuznetsov (Soviet Union): Mr. President, I listened carefully to the last statement of the representative of Greece, and the Soviet Delegation will support the wording of the item in the form proposed by the Greek Delegation.

Sir Leslie Munro (President): I will put the matter to the vote. That the item be described—that item 58 be described simply as "The Cyprus Question." All those in favor raise their right hand. The representative of the Soviet Union.

Mr. V. V. Kuznetsov (Soviet Union): It seems to me that, under the rules of procedure, since the Greek Delegation maintains its proposal and is only accepting an amendment thereto, it has the right to be voted on first and, therefore, I would ask you to adhere to the rules of procedure in the present case.

Sir Leslie Munro (President): I think what seemed that we—a little order please—it would seem that the proposal of the representative of Norway is in the nature of an amendment and it has been put first, and I propose to put it first to the vote.

The voting on the proposal of the representative of Norway is as follows: 11 in favor, none against, 4 abstentions. The proposal is therefore adopted. The representative of the Soviet Union.

Mr. V. V. Kuznetsov (Soviet Union): Mr. President, I would like to say that the Soviet Delegation abstained on the proposal made by the representative of Norway. The Soviet Delegation considers that this item would have been more correctly inscribed under the wording proposed by the Greek Delegation. Thank you.

Sir Leslie Munro (President): The representative of China.

Dr. T. F. Tsiang (China): Mr. President, I did not insist upon my wording. In fact, I voted for the Norwegian wording in the interest of harmony and the early conclusion of this debate.

Sir Leslie Munro (President): Guatemala.

Mr. E. Arenales Catalan (Guatemala): In explanation of my vote, I would like to say that I voted in favor of the proposal moved by Mrs. Lionaes of Norway because, in any case, there will be a full opportunity to debate this matter in the General Assembly and because the vote in the General Committee, as the ballots would show, would lead us at all times to support the inclusion of this item.

Sir Leslie Munro (President): The representative of Tunisia.

Mr. M. Slim (Tunisia): I would only like to explain my vote, Mr. President. I would have preferred to vote for the proposal of the Delegation of

China, but, with a view to getting the largest majority possible and the best co-operation in the General Committee, I voted for the Norwegian proposal, because I consider that, since it is not restrictive and not being defined precisely, the contents of the wording "Cyprus Question" would allow a general debate on the question.

Sir Leslie Munro (President): The representative of Czechoslovakia.

Mr. J. Nosek (Czechoslovakia): Mr. President, in my previous speech, I stated explicitly my delegation was supporting item 58 in the form as proposed by the Delegation of Greece. For this reason, I abstained to vote for the proposal made by the representative of Norway. Thank you.

Sir Leslie Munro (President): I understand that the representative of Greece wishes to be heard, but it might be best if I did assume from the Committee now that this item is included in the items inscribed in the Agenda under its new title. The representative of Greece.

Mr. E. Averoff-Tossizza (Greece): I would like, in the first place, to express my astonishment that the proposal of Norway has been considered as an amendment, while it is, I think, the first instance in the United Nations when a title is altogether changed. I have already said, a few minutes ago, that the proposals of the representative of China are amendments; the other is not an amendment. Secondly, I would like to state that I have noted with pleasure that the proposer, i.e. Norway, was careful to say at the beginning of her statement that under this title, all aspects of the problem could be discussed. This interpretation was also given by the distinguished representative of Tunisia, and I think that it is the right interpretation, should the Assembly accept this title.

Sir Leslie Munro (President): I understand then that the Committee agrees to the item as it is now described included in the agenda. It is so.

As the above record indicates, during the entire debate on the inclusion of item 58 in the Assembly's agenda, the U.S. representative on the General Committee, Ambassador Lodge, remained silent. In a sense, however, he was speaking through the mouth of the Norwegian representative, who had proposed that the title of the item be changed prior to its inclusion in the agenda. This *mise en scène*, which NATO's Secretary-General had apparently suggested, had been prepared backstage by the United States.

This U.S.-backed Norwegian proposal not only facilitated the inclusion of the Cyprus issue in the Assembly's agenda but also did not preclude the eventual discussion of the themes of self-determination and of British atrocities contained in the Greek recourse as submitted initially. Thus, as the Greek Delegation reported to Athens, nothing of substance had been lost by this change of title. This compromise solution also had forestalled a vote in the General Committee on subitem (b)—a procedure which the British Delegation apparently desired but which the Greek as well as the U.S. Delegation wished to avoid. Such a vote, the Greek Delegation had concluded, would have resulted in the sure rejection of subitem (b). And, had the U.S. representative contributed to this rejection by a negative vote or even by an abstention, a furor would have been stirred in Greece, and the United States would risk having its image tarnished at a moment when it was playing a stellar role in the Hungarian question.

Ethnarch Makarios, it should be added, expressed full satisfaction with the outcome of the General Committee's debate. And, as Lodge acknowledged, the Greek interventions in this debate had created an excellent impression.

As this debate in the General Committee clearly revealed, the novel feature of the debates of the Cyprus item at the Assembly's twelfth session, in contrast to those of the previous one, was that this time the Greek government and the British and Turkish antagonists had at their disposal Resolution 1013 (XI), so their statements were to constitute, to a certain extent, reports about their own compliance with this resolution, while containing charges of non-compliance against the opponent.

C. Non-UN Diplomacy over Cyprus at the UN and Outside

On September 20, the day the Assembly debated the General Committee's recommendation that the Cyprus issue be included in the Assembly's agenda, the Greek Foreign Minister met, at his own request, Foreign Secretary Lloyd in the UN building and discussed not only the handling of the Cyprus item in the Assembly and the Political Committee but also the substance of the question. On his side, Lloyd pressed for a tripartite conference.

Averoff-Tossizza said he would have to make a general observation about accepting the item as "The Cyprus Question," indicating that it had been possible for his delegation to do so only on the basis that any points could be raised in the substantive debate. Asked if he intended to use the word "atrocities" in his speech before the Assembly, he said he did not mean to do so. Lloyd responded by saying that if he spoke on those lines, he would follow him, indicating that the British Delegation reserved its position under Article 2, paragraph 7, of the Charter that what individual representatives said was their own responsibility and that it hoped the debate would improve and not hinder the chances of a settlement.

After discussing the substance of the Cyprus question, along lines to be mentioned below, the Greek Foreign Minister turned to the handling of the Cyprus item in the Political Committee. Greece, he said, hoped that the matter would not come up for discussion there before December. That would be one month after the Turkish elections. The Greek Delegation would strive for the adoption of a resolution about independence, he said, with no change in this regime for twenty years, in case it felt sure that such a resolution would be adopted by the Assembly. Otherwise, he warned, it would be forced to fight for a resolution calling for the application of the principle of self-determination to Cyprus.

In his remarks on the substance of the Cyprus question, Averoff-Tossizza emphasized that his government sincerely desired a settlement of the question. It was not doing too badly in internal affairs. If it could get a settlement, it would fight an election on it. And he was certain of the government's victory at the polls, he told Lloyd. The Greek government, he went on to say, proposed three alternative solutions for the Cyprus question. Under the first of these, Cyprus would be granted Dominion status, subject to the condition that it should not change that status for twenty years at the maximum. A second solution would be again the granting of Dominion status to the island, but on condition that after three Parliaments of four years each the question of changing that status should be placed before the United Nations for its decision. If Britain wished to block a change in the island's status, it might be able to command the necessary one-third (plus one) of the Assembly's votes. A third solution would consist of introducing self-government for a decade with a colonial constitution. (In this connection it would be wiser not to refer to the Radcliffe proposals but such a constitution might be along the lines proposed by Lord Radcliffe.) At the end of that decade, a plebiscite should be held to decide the island's future.[27]

The Foreign Secretary replied he was not going to voice any opinion about any particular solution to the Cyprus problem. His government had been working for a tripartite conference. In its view, any solution would have to be acceptable to both the Greek and the Turkish governments. The British government had believed that its suggestion that Spaak and a U.S. official should attend as observers the proposed tripartite conference would make it easier for the Greek government to take part in it. It wanted a meeting to which the parties concerned, forgetting the past and concentrating upon the pros and cons of each possible solution, would come with genuinely open minds. His government was anxious that Greece, Turkey, and Britain should meet around a table with that attitude in mind. The Greek Foreign Minister, on the other hand, said it was a political impossibility for his government to attend such a conference. In any case, he did not think it would do any good and would simply end in banging the table. There could not be the kind of open-minded approach that Lloyd had indicated.

The Greek Foreign Minister then reiterated the sincerity of his government's desire for a settlement. He had genuinely tried to improve the atmosphere over the past few months and had detected signs that the Turks were not so intransigent as before. Both Premier Karamanlis and he would be quite prepared to go to Ankara to talk to the Turks after the elections if they thought it would do any good—it being understood that basic agreement was reached previously.[28] It was really vital for the free world that the division between Greece and Turkey be ended, and that the path to Slav expansionism be blocked by the re-creation of the Greek-Turkish alliance.

The British Foreign Secretary said he would consider what the Greek

Foreign Minister had said. He asked him about his future movements. Averoff-Tossizza answered he intended to go back to Athens in about ten days' time, but would come back to New York at short notice if it were thought that it would be of any value. Lloyd then asked him about a report he had received that he—the Greek official—had indicated willingness that the question of self-determination be left undecided for a period of years, or, in other words, that there should be some agreement on some constitution for Cyprus, followed by a discussion of the international status of the island in X years' time. The Greek Foreign Minister said that such an idea did not represent the views of the Greek government. His government could not possibly entertain it. In the course of the conversation, he said that Ethnarch Makarios was a co-operative and very reasonable man. Also he did not think there was any chance of the island's going Communist. Furthermore, although saying that he felt hopeful because of recent developments, he remarked that he felt extremely anxious lest the struggle in Cyprus be reactivated after an unfavorable turn in the situation. As a result, Greek-Turkish communal strife on the island would have to be faced for the first time. As was well-known, the Turkish minority had been armed. Such developments would drive the Cypriots to despair and have fatal repercussions on Greek-Turkish relations. In such an eventuality, a break of diplomatic relations between the two countries would be virtually inevitable.

At this juncture, the news from Ankara was that Foreign Minister Zorlu, in a sort of monologue on the occasion of the protocol visit of the new Greek Ambassador to Turkey, George Pesmazoglou [29] (he had presented his credentials to President Celal Bayar on July 3), had stated that the partition of Cyprus was the only solution acceptable to the Turkish government. Any delay in reaching such a solution was in favor of Turkey, which had territorial rights over Cyprus. At the same time, he maintained that the co-operation between Turkey and Greece was necessary for the maintenance of Turkish friendship, the price of which was partition. Turkey did not claim Cyprus but would not acquiesce in letting one more Turk come under Greek rule. The bitterness between the two countries, he contended, was due to the Greek press, which continually created problems, insulted political personalities, and tried to depict the Turkish people as belonging to an inferior civilization. The Greek government rejected a calm discussion of the problem. Its insistence on raising the issue before the United Nations poisoned the atmosphere. To these remarks the Greek Ambassador replied that Greece did not recognize any Turkish territorial rights to Cyprus; that Greek friendship also had its price; that in Greece the press was free, in contrast to the Turkish press, in which Turkish members of Parliament were publishing incendiary articles. In spite of Zorlu's attitude, the Ambassador reported to Athens, he felt that after the Turkish elections and the end of the debate on the Cyprus issue in the United Nations, the Turkish government would be disposed to discuss some solution other than partition, since it constantly inquired what sort of guarantees would be given to protect the Turkish minority on the island from discrimination on the part of the Greek majority.

D. The General Assembly Adopts the General Committee's Recommendation to Place Item 58 on Its Agenda

On September 20, the Assembly discussed placing item 58, together with other items, on its agenda. Here is what the record reveals: [30]

Sir Leslie Munro (President): With regard to item 58, the representatives will notice that, in paragraph 4 of the report of the General Committee, document A/3670, the General Committee decided to recommend the inclusion of this item under the title "The Cyprus Question." Before I call upon the first speaker, the representative of Greece, I would draw the attention of the General Assembly to rule 23 of our Rules of Procedure, which limits the number of speakers to three in favor of and three against inclusion.

Averoff-Tossizza observed that in the General Committee, the Greek Delegation had wholeheartedly urged that the question of Cyprus should be inscribed on the Assembly's agenda under the detailed wording which it had proposed. However, it had noted an urgent wish by a large number of representatives in the General Committee that the item should be given a briefer, more general heading that would authorize the discussion of any points related to the question. Therefore, in order to meet the position of the other delegations and taking into account that the title proposed by the General Committee covered all the aspects of the Cyprus question, his delegation was not opposed to the proposed wording. Because of the brevity of his statement, he would like, he said, to reserve his right to speak again if other delegations raised points which required a reply on his part.

Esin, of Turkey, on his side, noting that the General Committee had decided to recommend the inclusion of item 58 in the agenda under the title "The Cyprus Question," emphasized that the debate in the General Committee had started with a division. The position of the Turkish Delegation in this matter was well known to the members of the United Nations and had been placed on the record. He did not intend to take up the precious time of the Assembly by reiterating the details of its intervention in the procedural debate that had taken place in the General Committee. His delegation had objected to the way in which the Greek demand had been presented to the United Nations. The British representative had previously raised other objections from the point of view of his own government. However, there was a tendency within the General Committee to try to find a basis for harmonizing, so far as possible, the views of the parties concerned on the question of the inclusion of the item dealing with Cyprus. It had thus been suggested that the item should be included on condition that it was redrafted to its present form. In line with this conciliatory attitude, which had asserted itself in the General Committee, the Turkish Delegation had declared that it would not oppose the inscription of the item in the form recommended by the Committee. His delegation continued to hold that position.

In this connection, Esin indicated that, in view of the partial improvement in the situation which had taken place during the brief period that had elapsed since February 26—the date on which Resolution 1013 (XI) had been adopted—his delegation continued to have doubts on the wisdom of reopening a debate that might increase tension. It believed, on the contrary, that the high interests of the Cyprus peoples and the cause of friendly and peaceful relations in the Middle East could best be served by sincere efforts to arrive at a peaceful, democratic, and just solution of the Cyprus question along the path indicated by the Assembly just over six months earlier. In spite of these views, his delegation had decided not to oppose the inscription of the item in its present form in the agenda of the Assembly, placing faith in the wisdom, the deep sense of justice, and the feeling of practical reality which existed in the Assembly, acting as a general guide within the limits of its legal possibilities to contribute to a solution satisfactory to all concerned.

Lloyd, speaking next, reminded the Assembly that when the question had been discussed in the General Committee, he had said, in effect, that Britain would not object to a discussion of the Cyprus question if it appeared likely that such a discussion would prove constructive. Once again he reserved the position of the British government with regard to Article 2, paragraph 7, of the Charter. He would not repeat again what he had said the day before in the General Committee about that matter and about other aspects of the problem. He did not deny that there were international aspects to the Cyprus problem, and, therefore, he would not oppose the inscription of the item. What would be said during the debate would be, according to the rules, the responsibility of the representative making the statement, but it was the hope of the British government that when the debate came, it would promote and not hinder the chances of a settlement.

Sir Leslie Munro (President): Under those circumstances, I think that the Assembly would agree to the fact that this item is inscribed on the agenda.

[Item 58 was placed on the agenda.]

Mr. Averoff-Tossizza (Greece) (from the floor): I want to. . . .

Sir Leslie Munro (President): No, you may not speak. The item is inscribed on the agenda.

Mr. Averoff-Tossizza (Greece) (from the floor): On a point of order.

Sir Leslie Munro (President): No, you may not speak. The speakers are limited to three, and there is no question of a point of order. The item is inscribed.

Mr. Averoff-Tossizza (Greece) (from the floor): There is a point of order.

Sir Leslie Munro (President): No, there is no point of order involved at all. . . .

In spite of this rebuff, Averoff-Tossizza, on a point of order, spoke again while the inclusion of item 61—the treatment of Indians in South Africa—was being discussed at the same meeting of the Assembly. Referring to the rules of procedure, he criticized the President for his attitude, getting applause from many representatives. The verbatim record reveals this incident as follows: [31]

Sir Leslie Munro (President): I recognize the representative of Greece on a point of order.

Mr. Averoff-Tossizza (Greece): At the end of the very brief discussion on the inclusion of the Cyprus question, I asked for the floor, Mr. President, on a point of order. You told me: "There is no point of order." I am sorry to have to tell you that it is not for you to decide that there is no point of order. The rules of procedure do not give you that right. On the contrary, the rules of procedure give us the right, give to representatives the right, to raise any point of order, and it is for you to pass on it. If your ruling is challenged, it is for the General Assembly to pass on the matter. But you, Mr. President, did not even know to what point of order I was raising—and, before knowing it, you said that it did not exist.

Every point of order might be raised in the Assembly, the Greek Foreign Minister maintained—even the way in which the President conducted business was a point of order. Therefore, according to the most elementary logic and according to rule 73 of the rules of procedure, which was perfectly clear, it was not for the President to state whether there was a point of order.[32] If the President arrogated to himself the right to state whether there was a point of order, Averoff-Tossizza asserted, a precedent would have been created which would be very dangerous to free discussion in this world Assembly. "Fellow representatives," the Greek Delegate declared,

if, when you raise a point of order, our President has the right to tell you that there is no point of order, then I prefer that we ourselves declare that we cannot pass on procedural points. That, at least, would be more elegant and less dangerous. . . . It is a question of our rights on the basis of the rules of procedure. As regards our rights and our dignity, we are all equal, regardless of the difference which may exist as far as physical force is concerned. . . .

Sir Leslie Munro (President): The representative of Greece will always find me the careful custodian of the rules of procedure of this Assembly. The rule with which we were dealing is a rule which says there are three speakers on either side, and the representative of Greece had spoken. It was perfectly clear to me that it was agreed that the item should be inscribed. It was agreed by the countries concerned; it was agreed by the representative of Greece himself. I was utterly unable to see how a point of order could be raised. And I am satisfied indeed that no point of order has been raised. I want to assure the Assembly that every member here will have the right to raise a point of order where a point of order can be raised. I can assure them of that fact. But if—I say this with great respect, and I have the greatest respect for the representative of Greece, and who here has not?—raising a point of order is merely a device for making a further speech, then I think that is wrong.

Apparently, the Foreign Office in London felt satisfied with the course of affairs in the matter of the inclusion of the Cyprus item in the Assembly's agenda, Ambassador Seferiadis reported. It, too, desired that the debate on the substance of the question take place toward the end of the Assembly's session. Foreseeing a victory for the Democratic party led by Celal Bayar in Turkey (in the general elections set for October 27), it hoped that it would then be possible to find a solution acceptable to the three parties concerned. The British government, on the other hand, objected to a solution reached through the United Nations but was not opposed to the "blessing" by the Assembly of any solution agreed upon in advance.

As for the attitude of the United States, in spite of its pro-British bias, it had not harmed the Greek cause at this stage, the Greek Delegation felt. There were, however, renewed indications that the American stand concerning the substance of the question was not encouraging from the Greek viewpoint. Averoff-Tossizza, at a meeting of September 23 at the State Department with Undersecretary of State Christian A. Herter, Deputy Undersecretary of State, Robert D. Murphy, and Rountree, was told by the latter, who summed up the State Department's view, that the Cyprus question was showing great progress. No one would have imagined such progress a year ago. The British were sincere in their desire to reach a settlement. The wishes of the Cypriots would be satisfied, but no one could say when. Consequently, the Greek government should not be in a hurry and create interallied difficulties through debates in the United Nations. In that international forum, the United States could not help on the basis of the alternative solutions of the Cyprus problem that the Greek government had proposed [33] unless the British and the Turkish governments agreed. Rountree foresaw support for a "colorless" resolution, hinting that the previous Assembly's Thai one, recommending negotiations between the parties concerned, was harmless since it was procedural in character and did not touch upon the substance. [34] He also insisted on resort to the tripartite conference, which the British had pursued since early in August.

Four days later, in a conversation of September 27 with Ambassador Lodge and James W. Barco, Counselor of the U.S. Delegation to the General Assembly, the Permanent Greek Representative to the UN warned that it was his government's position that if it were not possible to find a reasonable solution acceptable to the Cypriots before the debate in the Political Committee started, the Greek Delegation would be obliged to insist on a draft resolution calling for self-determination in Cyprus, and would press for a vote on it in all possible ways. He therefore stressed that the United States should exert its influence to achieve a satisfactory solution before the debate began in the United Nations. The improvement of the situation in Cyprus, he said, was fragile. It concealed an increasing threat of most serious complications caused, on the one hand, by provocations planned in Ankara, for instance, on the part of armed Turkish minority, and, on the other, by the desperation of the Cypriot people, should Greek efforts in the United Nations fail. The United States, he urged, should clearly define its position, since the Greek Foreign Minister had exhausted all possible limits for an elastic handling of the question. If in the absence of a supervening solution, he was obliged to place before the United Nations the demand for self-determination and the matter came to a vote, each delegation would have to take a position vis-à-vis the Greek and Cypriot people. The Greek Delegation, the Greek diplomat warned, would also have to expose any procedural devices designed at getting around the difficutly of more positive decisions by the United States. Barco agreed on the need for a solution so that a debate in the United Nations might be avoided. He stressed that his delegation would underline to the State Department the dangers of a debate but added that it was Washington that had the exclusive decision-making powers on political matters. He also observed that Turkey was the main obstacle but had the impression that Ankara's attitude appeared somewhat improved.

E. The World Ambience and Item 58 in the General Debate

While the various items were being placed on the Assembly's agenda, the general debate was going on. It not only allowed the parties concerned in the Cyprus question and their respective supporters to present once again in public their respective views on the question, if they so wished, but also revealed the world political atmosphere in which the Cyprus question was evolving. This atmosphere appeared quite highly charged though less so than it had been at the previous General Assembly, which had taken place in the midst of the Hungarian uprising and the Suez affair.

Neither Dulles nor Gromyko nor Lloyd in their speeches referred to the Cyprus problem. The tense situation in the Middle East, however, took up quite a large part of their respective statements. As far as space was concerned, it was theme number two in the statements of both the American and Soviet Delegates—theme number one being that of disarmament and armaments regulation and control. Although neither the Soviet nor the American spokesman referred to the Soviet achievements in missilery, it can be safely assumed that this was a matter that was uppermost in everyone's mind, when reviewing the world political situation.

Dulles, on September 19, reminded the Assembly that the rulers of Russia had long sought domination in the Middle East. In 1940, when

Soviet leaders were seeking a division of the world with Hitler, they had stipulated "that the area south of Batum and Baku in the general direction of the Persian Gulf is recognized as the center of the aspirations of the Soviet Union." Then, between 1945 and 1949, Central Europe had become the principal theater of Soviet activities, and these, after the adoption of the Marshall Plan and the establishment of NATO, had shifted to the Far East in support of the Communist revolution in China and the wars in Korea and Indochina. In 1955, after the successful defense of Korea and the conclusion of SEATO and other defensive pacts, the Soviet rulers again had made the Middle East the center of their external efforts. They had begun intensive propaganda designed to incite the Arab nations to believe that with Soviet arms, Soviet technicians, and Soviet political backing they could accomplish "extreme nationalist ambitions." This Soviet Communist effort had made progress in Syria. One consequence of this was that Turkey now faced growing military danger from the major buildup of Soviet arms in Syria on its southern border, a buildup concerted with Soviet military power on Turkey's northern border. The week before, the U.S.S.R. had sought by intimidation to prevent Turkey from making internal dispositions of its own security forces. The Soviet Communists, Dulles charged, after referring to the "Essentials of Peace" Resolution 290 (IV) of 1949, appeared to be engaged in "acts, direct or indirect, aimed at impairing the freedom, independence or integrity" of certain nations of the Middle East in violation of this resolution. The United States believed that these Soviet acts could lead the recipients of Soviet arms, perhaps unwittingly, into acts of direct aggression.[35]

In his speech, of September 20, Gromyko started out with a long attack against the United States, NATO, and SEATO, and played up the theme of peaceful coexistence. After going into an extensive exposition of the Soviet views on disarmament, he dwelt at some length on the situation in the Middle East. After Egypt, Syria now had been selected as "the victim of imperialist intrigues." Crude political and economic pressure, he charged, was being applied to that country; plots were being hatched against its government; and it was threatened more and more frequently with direct military intervention. This had occurred, he maintained, because the people and government of Syria were not willing to submit to foreign dictation and refused to allow their country to be drawn into aggressive blocs. That the Eisenhower Doctrine was completely at variance with the interests of the peoples of the Middle East was proved by the activities of the United States in relation to Syria. Syria was not threatening its neighbors, nor was the U.S.S.R. threatening in some way the Near and Middle East. The organizers of the provocation with regard to Syria were alleging ever more noisily that the U.S.S.R. had dangerous plans concerning that area. Dulles had referred to "extreme nationalist ambitions." The Soviet government, Gromyko declared, saw nothing extreme in this. It was the indisputable and inalienable right of every people to desire to maintain its national independence. This desire was in full conformity with the principles of the United Nations. The strengthening of the independence of the countries in the Middle East and their complete liberation from the consequences of colonialism were essential for the maintenance and the strengthening of peace in that area. The U.S.S.R. could not remain indifferent and observe from afar the attempts that were being made to turn the Near and Middle East "into a permanent hotbed of armed conflict. The organizers of these conflicts understand that the Soviet Union cannot view such a state of affairs impassively, since its own security is affected." [36]

In his address of September 24, Lloyd devoted several paragraphs to efforts to refute some of the points Gromyko had made in his speech, underlining omissions or understatements in the Soviet representative's exposition. The major part of his statement, like those of his Soviet and American colleagues, dealt with the problem of disarmament and arms control. After charging the U.S.S.R. with conducting a policy of opportunism in the Middle East, he referred to Soviet propaganda in the area as an indication of the extent to which the Soviet government was not living up to the draft declaration it had submitted to the Assembly, calling upon all states to base their relations on the principle of non-interference in one another's internal affairs for any motives of economic, political, or ideological character. He then underlined as a grave new factor: the introduction of Soviet-bloc arms into the Middle East. Some believed, he said, that the purpose behind all this was to prestock forward bases for the U.S.S.R. itself. The deliveries were on such a scale as to give some color to this suggestion. After briefly referring to the situation in Syria, Lloyd, like Dulles before him, called for respect of the "Essentials of Peace" resolution of 1949. [37]

Lloyd's opening remarks about the state of the United Nations—"its achievements, its failures, its strength, its weaknesses, its standing in the world, the hopes for its development in the future"—were germane not only to the Suez issue in which Britain was so greatly involved but also to the Cyprus problem in the sense that they suggested the awareness of some of the inconvenient aspects of the organization for its members at one time or other. Summing up Hammarskjöld's views—published in the introduction to the Secretary-General's annual report—Lloyd observed that the United Nations was not a superstate, nor an authority enforcing its laws upon the nations. Nor was it a parliament of individually elected members legislating for the world or an instrument of negotiation between governments. It could, however, blunt the edges of conflict between nations and serve a diplomacy of reconciliation. Its tendency was to wear away or break down differences and thus help toward solutions. The real limitations upon the actions of the United Nations did not derive from the provisions of the Charter or from the system of one vote for one nation regardless of strength or size, but resulted from the facts of international life. The balance of forces in the world set the limits within which the power of the United Nations could develop. The British government, Lloyd thought, could broadly accept these views. Any blame of the institution should be attributed to the member states that collectively constituted the strength or weakness of the United Nations. The Assembly had a most useful function to fulfil as a forum for international debate. That annual meeting afforded an occasion for colleagues with similar responsibilities to meet together. The United Nations should also be a place for mediation and conciliation, for reducing sharpness in controversy, and for promoting settlement.[38]

Coming now to some weaknesses or defects in the practical operation of the United Nations, Lloyd said he had to admit that in fact some controversies were sharpened by discussion in the Assembly; that some countries, bitterly resentful of any criticism of their own internal affairs, were only too ready to use the procedures of the United Nations to interfere in those of other nations; that certain processes of evolution in human relations, political or otherwise, were complicated and not facilitated by bitter argument in the Assembly.[39]

Although to the uninitiated, the speech of the Greek Foreign Minister in the general debate on September 26 may have seemed fairly innocuous because, unlike the address of Premier Karamanlis in the general debate at the previous Assembly, it did not dwell at any great length on the Cyprus question, it did carry, nevertheless, certain messages to other parties to the Cyprus dispute, to groups of UN members as well as to the organization as a corporate entity. A representative of a friendly country—unnamed—had asked him that morning whether he would deal with the question of Cyprus in his speech, Averoff-Tossizza started out by saying. This had pained him, he said, because although it was true that the Greek people felt much concern and anguish over that question, it was equally true that Greece took a deep interest in the broader questions of international politics. He would, indeed, venture to say that his government's interest in the Cyprus question stemmed in large part from its great interest in international issues. For the Cyprus question raised a number of questions that reached far beyond that island's shores, such as "the right" of peoples to self-determination. Disregard for this right had an unfortunate effect on the relations of Greece with nations it respected and wished to have as friends. It involved, too, the question of the continuation of colonialism and colonialist methods in the mid-twentieth century. All this constituted a serious international problem.

However, he would speak on broader issues, the Greek Foreign Minister said, and first, on the organization of the United Nations. Churchill, he observed, had recently criticized the principle of equality of all states in the Assembly's voting system. This opinion, which was not new, could be very harmful to the United Nations if it were widely held and adopted, Averoff-Tossizza maintained. Great powers, he acknowledged, had responsibilities far greater than those of small or medium-sized countries. Therefore he could not maintain that they should have *de facto* equality with the latter. In almost all fields, he observed further, the great powers held a predominant position in the United Nations, either by virtue of their statutory rights (in the Security Council, for example) or because of the influence they exerted in the Assembly. What proposal, he asked, could command two-thirds of the votes in the Assembly if two or three great powers opposed it? It was very well known that it was not with their own two or three votes that these great powers would obtain that result. In truth, there was no cause for commiseration with the great powers over their lot in the United Nations. Nor was there any cause to regret the more than justified juridical equality established among member states. Just as in every human society the weak or incapable man occupied, by force of circumstances, a position different from that of the strong and capable, though both had the same claims to life and the fundamental principles on which social order was founded, so countries small and large should enjoy complete equality in certain areas of international life, and more particularly in the Assembly. This equality, he emphasized, was guaranteed in the United Nations by the uniform application of the rules, by freedom of speech, and by equality of vote in the Assembly. Equality of vote and equality in relation to certain fundamental rights made it possible for the small and medium-sized states, through the United Nations, to take a stand and to exert a certain influence upon great international issues. This was one of the chief and most useful functions of the United Nations.

He did not wish, Averoff-Tossizza said further, to go into an evaluation of the work of the United Nations. He drew, however, attention to the manifold activities of the organization and the specialized agencies in the economic and social field and to the fact that grave international crises could not have been settled without the moral force and effective action of the United Nations. Here was a world platform which representatives of nations great or small were immensely privileged to ascend in order to proclaim their ideas and argue their cases. While no one, of course, could deny that UN resolutions were not binding and "are sometimes too colorless," they exerted great political and moral influence. They were receiving increasing attention even from those who refused to comply with their recommendations. This proved that the Assembly had become the primary instrument by which "world public opinion can express itself and exert pressures—strong or weak, according to circumstances—upon international policies." That was no mean achievement, though obviously much remained to be done.

After expatiating upon the theme of the effects of technology on the development of a new sense of universality—a new reality that called for new political methods and concepts—the Greek Foreign Minister observed that, even problems of an apparently regional nature tended to assume a universal aspect. All this was highly encouraging, but "we are in the midst of an evolving situation, and we ourselves must develop and constantly adapt ourselves in order to be able to meet the circumstances."

Averoff-Tossizza then went on to pay tribute to Dag Hammarskjöld for the establishment of the United Nations Emergency Force (UNEF) for dealing with the Suez crisis. This peacekeeping force had no precedent in history. He was convinced that one should consider adopting in a permanent form this procedure, which had already proved its merit. This would be to the interest not only of the small states but also of the great powers. The danger of an atomic war lay less in the possibility of a premeditated nuclear aggression than in the outbreak of more or less limited conflict that might spread and set the world ablaze. The precedent of UNEF would constitute one of the most effective weapons in the arsenal of the United Nations, he said, qualifying this statement with the juridical concept that such forces should not be used except with the consent of the countries concerned. The existence of a permanent fire-brigade force of the United Nations, he said further, would have a preventive effect. "Situations are sometimes created for the sole purpose of turning them to advantage," he added—a statement which people "in-the-know" could construe as a message in the direction of Turkey, whose threats of action against the Aegean islands had been conveyed, in August, 1956, and April, 1957, to the Greek government through the U.S. diplomatic channel.[40] "Sometimes adventures are embarked upon in the hope that there will be time for the successful pursuit of some unavowed political objective." Sometimes, undemocratic calculations connected with domestic politics led to dangerous trends, to provocation and even to ill-considered action. Remarks of welcome addressed to Ghana and Malaya, as new states and new members of the United Nations, gave Averoff-Tossizza the opportunity to note that his country for the past four years had been upholding "the cause of a civilized people seeking to free themselves from the yoke of colonialism." In this connection, he also paid tribute to Britain for having satisfied the aspirations of the peoples of Ghana and Malaya but expressed bitterness and astonishment that Britain should pursue a completely different policy in its dealings with Cyprus.

In a long concluding section of his speech, the Greek Foreign Minister spoke about the Middle East and emphasized the important role of the Arab world in that "meeting place of the most diverse religions and ideologies, as well as a junction of three continents and world shipping lanes . . . one of the nerve centers of the world." In the past, the great powers, since the times of the Great King of Persia and Alexander the Great, had tried to occupy the Middle East or at least to impose themselves in that region by winning the friendship of the local potentates. At the root of the current uneasiness in that crucial area were relics of this mentality, which provoked local as well as more widespread reactions.

The Arab world—the geographic and human core of the area—was no longer what it was some decades earlier, he said, along lines parallel to those expressed by Arab states, and Syria especially, in response both to the "Eisenhower Doctrine" formulated earlier that year, and to the subse-

quent discovery of a plot to overthrow the Syrian government, which the
United States supposedly had masterminded. The basic characteristic of
the area was nationalism. With a single flame, pan-Arab nationalism
burned from Casablanca to the Persian Gulf. A radical change had
occurred among these young nations, which knew that at one time or
another in history their ancestors had occupied a place that other great
nations held in the moral and material leadership of the world. The elite
of these young Arab nations sprang from the people and for this reason
would not suffer their brothers to live in worse conditions than did the
peoples of other countries. These countries, too, aspired to economic
development, and their national susceptibilities were more acute than
those of peoples who had a long established tradition of independence
and sovereignty that was respected by all. If one failed to take account of
these changes and of the actual situation, one could not deal with the
problems of the Middle East realistically." To propose or to apply a
policy materially useful and just, but to do so in a manner offensive to the
pride of these fine peoples, would be tantamount to adopting a policy
that was doomed to failure." And he then referred to the case of
Egypt—not of Syria—as an example.

Greece, Averoff-Tossizza emphasized further in his speech, was located
close to the Arab world. For the last 3,000 years, the Mediterranean had
united the Greeks and the Arabs.[41] Some of the characteristics of the
Greek people, that of the seafarer, the merchant, the emigrant who
fraternized with those among whom he lived, had further strengthened
the bonds of Greece with the Arab peoples. Experience had taught the
Greeks that nothing of any lasting or beneficial effect could be done in
the Middle East as long as the two basic aspects of the problem were not
taken into consideration: First, co-operation to raise the low level of
living, even if this entailed certain sacrifices for the more developed
countries; and, second, full respect for the independence and national
dignity of the Arab peoples. These conditions were in conformity with
the UN Charter's principles, among which that of the self-determination
of peoples was the master principle.

In the peroration of this speech, which underplayed the Cyprus question and contained no reference at all to the charges of British atrocities
against the Cypriots, Averoff-Tossizza returned to the matter of technical
progress and to the two alternative paths to which humanity could be led
by it: that of destruction and that of prosperity and material progress.

Following the example of the British and Greek representatives in a
sort of tacit truce in polemics, the Turkish representative, Ambassador
Esin, referred very briefly to the Cyprus question in his general debate
speech of September 27.[42] That question, he observed, was one of particular interest to his country because of the island's proximity to Turkish
shores and because part of its population was Turkish. Since his government's views were known to the Assembly and since a debate would take

place in the Political Committee, he would not make any further comments on that political question.

Unlike the Greek representative, who had emphasized the importance of the United Nation's novel venture in peace-keeping, Esin, in his speech, devoted several paragraphs to the problem of disarmament, as had Dulles, Gromyko, and Lloyd before him. Turkey's policy, he said, was based on the conviction that enduring peace could be attained only through a universal, general disarmament in the field of both conventional and nuclear weapons, together with effective international control measures. Practical proposals for attaining this goal should be based, first, on the preservation of security, and, second, on the gradual buildup of mutual confidence. Turkey, a profoundly peace-loving nation, had no other aspiration but that of devoting its work and economic resources to the attainment of a higher level of economic welfare. If a heavy burden of armaments had been assumed by his countrymen, this had not been a matter of choice but the result of dire necessity due to the conditions that unfortunately prevailed in the world.

Turning to the situation in the Middle East, the Turkish diplomat declared that his government considered as a happy development the attainment of full independence and sovereignty by the Arab countries of the region. This Turkish attitude was not new. During some of the darkest days in his country's history, when the very existence of Turkey as an independent sovereign state was in danger (hint, here, to the Greek expedition to Anatolia of 1918–22), the Turkish Chamber of Deputies had voted the National Pact, of which the first article proclaimed and demanded self-determination for territories inhabited by Arabs.[43] Later on, Turkey, at Lausanne (in 1923), had refused to accept any provision that might directly or indirectly imply its approval of the system of mandates over Arab countries. And in 1932, when Turkey became a member of the League of Nations, its acceptance had been conditioned not to imply recognition of the mandates over Arab countries.

Turkey considered the full independence and sovereignty of the Arab countries as one of the essential prerequisites for the establishment of peace and security and the progressive development of the Middle East. It was for these reasons that his government had shown concern and anxiety "over the recent increase of efforts made by the Soviet Union in regard to the Middle East in general, and Syria in particular," Esin declared. Turkey had affection and respect for the people of Syria and valued that country's independence, sovereignty, and territorial integrity. It considered a strong, prosperous, and independent Syria on its southern border as an additional guarantee to Turkish security. That was why the Turkish government was following recent events in Syria with attention and concern from the security viewpoint. Caution and vigilance were even more necessary, since recent events in Syria had taken place concurrently with a campaign of propaganda and false rumors aimed at discrediting Turkey and spoiling its relations with its southern neighbors. Allegations of this nature had been made by a powerful country with which Turkey had a long common border to the north. If that same country constituted a reserve of arms and ammunition on Turkey's southern flank, the Turkish government would naturally be obliged to appraise, in calm and dignity, the significance of such an event from the viewpoint of Turkish security and to take such internal measures within its frontiers as were customary in all independent countries desiring to live in peace and security.

Coming now to the United Nations, the Turkish Ambassador underlined, as Lloyd had, the remarks made by the Secretary-General in the introduction to his annual report, namely that the United Nations was not a superstate or a parliament of elected individual members, but that, in spite of its limitations, it was a valuable instrument for negotiation and diplomacy which were conducive to reconciliation. On the question of the revision of the Charter, Esin said his government favored an appropriate increase in the membership of the Security Council and the Economic and Social Council. After briefly referring to some of the political, social, and economic questions that were on the Assembly's agenda, he emphasized his country's role in regional arrangements—Turkey's membership in NATO and the Baghdad Pact, "defensive organizations created for the purpose of maintaining international peace and collective security." He then paid homage to NATO for having played an outstanding role in preserving peace, and observed that the Baghdad Pact was not only aimed at bolstering collective security but also had opened new possibilities for economic and cultural co-operation among its members.[44]

Representatives of fourteen member states mentioned the Cyprus question in their speeches in the general debate and all but one supported the Greek and Greek Cypriot view. The Irish representative did so on September 20, observing that the principle of self-determination was the key to the solution of the Cyprus and Algerian questions and to Germany's reunification. The Malayan, Hungarian, and Yugoslav representatives mentioned it on September 25, with the first referring to the Irish representative's statement, and the second remarking that in spite of Resolution 1013 (XI), the problem still remained unsolved, with the British authorities continuing their terror and keeping more than 1,000 Cypriots in prison, "whom they are torturing in the most barbaric manner." The Ecuadorian and Yemeni representatives, on September 27, likewise referred to the Cyprus item. The former, though not mentioning Cyprus by name, attacked the perpetration of alien authority over territories whose people were fully capable of self-government and asserted that his country would always give resolute support to people that claimed the exercise of their right to self-determination. The latter declared that the Cyprus question was a living example of the colonial powers' disregard of the human and political rights of other peoples.[45]

The Pakistani representative, on the other hand, on September 30, noted the absence of a settlement and underlined Turkey's security and minority interests in Cyprus.[46] On October 2, the representatives of Ceylon and Saudi Arabia touched on the matter. The Ceylonese was encouraged by the improvement in the situation on the island and, welcoming EOKA's cease-fire, expressed his opinion that conditions appeared favorable for a settlement, and his faith in the principle of self-determination. The Saudi Arabian noted that the Cyprus question together with that of West Irian were among the outstanding problems that disturbed the mind of freedom-loving peoples.[47] As for the Egyptian representative, he expressed the ardent hope on October 3, that the question of Cyprus and the people of Cyprus would soon be blessed with better luck and a better fate than they had had so far, again underlining that it had been from Cyprus that "last year's murderous attack" had been launched upon his country.[48] Finally, the representatives of Syria, Tunisia, Lebanon, and India, the first two on October 7, the last two on October 8, mentioned the Cyprus question. The Syrian expressed his country's concern with the matter because of the island's closeness to, and historical links with Syria. Only the application of the right of self-determination, he said, could solve the problem. The Tunisian stated that his government's attitude toward Cyprus was inspired by the same principles it followed in the Algerian and Hungarian questions. The Lebanese expressed the earnest hope that statesmanship and common sense would triumph in the case of Cyprus, a problem that had marred the relations among three close friends and allies. Like his Ceylonese colleague, he, too, thought that the outlook had improved. In his view, the position of the parties concerned had become much closer than when the question had first been placed on the Assembly's agenda. It was his government's hope, he added, that nothing would be said or done that would nullify the gains already made, and that no effort would be spared in surmounting the obstacles that remain in the path of a happy, contented and prosperous Cyprus. The Indian representative, finally, merely included the Cyprus question among other "great colonial problems," and turned his attention mainly to the Algerian problem.[49]

F. The Foreign Minister Reports on Phase I of the UN Struggle

Reporting on September 30 to Premier Karamanlis on the first phase of the Cyprus question in the Assembly, for the purpose of enlightening him on the outlook and of getting guide lines for the difficult task ahead, the Foreign Minister noted that the outcome of this phase had been successful. Everybody in the United Nations, both friends and others, were agreed that the Greek Delegation had appeared both dignified in general while imbued with a fighting spirit. The issue had been included in the agenda and in a way that permitted its discussion from all angles. Hence, the rabble-rousing statements of the Opposition about a supposed set-back of the Greek Delegation at this phase of the struggle were nothing but nonsense. These statements could not stand up to any criticism and were unworthy of attention in this report, the purpose of which was different. It was enough to observe in this connection that the Opposition, trying to trade on the national cause to its own advantage and for picayune party purposes, would criticize whatever the Greek government did, and would distort intentions, facts, results.

The purpose of his report, the Foreign Minister explained, was to develop some of his thoughts on the second phase of the struggle in the United Nations which lay ahead. This phase was far more critical, because the evolution of the question depended so much on its outcome. And he referred not only to the debate on the substance of the question but also to the resolution that would be adopted by the UN Assembly.

The debate in the Assembly would serve to enlighten the representatives of the eighty-two member states about the various facets of the Cyprus question. This, in turn, would be projected to a certain degree before world public opinion. He underlined the words "to a certain degree," he wrote, because the projection of the question depended on the extent to which, and the objectivity with which, the world press would report on the Cyprus debate. With the exception of the Greek press and the Greek-language newspapers outside Greece, he could not say he was satisfied with either the scope or the objectivity of the reportage about Cyprus in the world press.[50] On the contrary. And this, indeed, in spite of all the information efforts the government had made since 1956.

The debate itself he did not fear. He could predict with some confidence that, on the whole, it would be in Greece's favor, because of the assistance of the Permanent Mission and especially of the Permanent Greek Representative to the United Nations. More specifically, however, he would like to make the following observations on the subject of the debate: First, this debate would again confirm the impression that Turkey was a party seriously concerned in the Cyprus question. It mattered little whether the Greek Delegation managed to refute the Turkish arguments on this matter. In the international political arena, arguments, no matter how worthy, unfortunately were not of primary importance. Of primary importance was the power of each country in all factors and the decision of a particular state to assume attitude A or B. This created a real fact, a real international situation. This affected the political judgment of third countries. Whether the real situation that was created was just or moral, was, unfortunately, of only a secondary importance in the international arena. If, then, Turkey, as was likely, were to insist on its intransigent stand during the debate in the Assembly, its role as a directly concerned party would again be highlighted.

Second, an acrimonious debate could have effects both on the course of the Cyprus question and more generally on the relations of Greece with the West. Whether the debate would be acrimonious, however, did not exclusively depend on the Greek Delegation's handling of the issue. Others could exacerbate it, and then reasons of national dignity would make it imperative for the Greek Delegation to reply in kind, thus embittering the discussion further.

But one ran the risk of exacerbating the debate merely by vehemently denouncing the British atrocities and violations of human rights in Cyprus. This was really a very delicate point that had to be taken into account in the debate. In Greece it was believed that such denunciations constituted a powerful weapon in trying to solve the Cyprus question.[51] This view was erroneous. Only the threat of denouncing these atrocities constituted a weapon, and a small one at that. For the British, of course, would prefer no airing of such charges. This weapon was lost, however, the moment the denunciation was delivered. The argument that Britain would be humiliated or obliged to retreat because of such charges was worthy only of the bad faith of the Opposition or of those who were totally ignorant of the international climate. Few governments were likely to be indignant about the atrocities committed in Cyprus when very many governments were not angered by atrocities that both quantitatively and qualitatively were incomparably greater than these. And even fewer would dare express their indignation. The Premier was already aware that foreign ministers of important states—not only of the west—had expressed their distaste because the Greek government was resorting to these charges of British atrocities. Such acts, they said, always happened during struggles. Besides, these governments, because of their relations with Britain, could not publicly accept that such acts had been committed. The world press, too, as facts had shown, tended to ignore the subject or at the most devoted a few lines only to this issue. As for the British, they would gloss over these acts while nourishing a feeling of bitterness toward Greece, as they had most explicitly and earnestly stated. The Labourites, too, would share this feeling. In a peculiar way, they were the allies of Greece in the Cyprus question. Consequently, there should be no delusions. Denouncing atrocities was no effective political weapon. Airing such charges before the United Nations could be justified on other grounds: the victims demanded it: public opinion in Greece and Cyprus demanded it in the belief that the cause of Cyprus would be promoted in this way. Both these arguments deserved attention. The first of these created a sense of moral obligation. As long, though, as the promotion of a very difficult national cause was of primary importance, it was the task of the Greek government and of responsible Cypriots—and by this, of course, he meant Makarios—to weigh the pros and cons of using these atrocity charges and to decide in what way and to what point it would benefit the cause to resort to these charges. It was his task, at the present phase of the Cyprus issue in the United Nations, Averoff-Tossizza wrote, to draw the Prime Minister's attention to the above problem and to add the following: A rather stiff stand of the Greek Delegation in the matter of atrocities in Cyprus would undoubtedly create an unsympathetic atmosphere for the debate. All but about fifteen delegations would be embarrassed during the debates—including those favorably disposed to the cause—obliged as they would be, because of their bonds of interest with Britain and the Common-wealth, to avoid touching the matter or even to raise doubts about the veracity of these charges.

But, far more serious than the question of the debate in the Assembly, the Foreign Minister continued in his report to Premier Karamanlis, was the subject of the resolution that might emerge from these debates. This time the international atmosphere generally was not favorable. Britain was no longer the gravely accused party it had been the previous year because of the Suez affair. On the contrary, in many matters it seemed conciliatory. And it was exploiting to its own advantage the independence it had granted to many of its former colonies. As a result, its liberalism had received a great deal of praise on the part of the Assembly, and Britain all in all had appeared in a sympathetic light. The fires of Suez had died down. The memory of governments was short. The situation in the Middle East and especially the crisis over Syria had frightened many, even some of Greece's good Latin American friends. This tended to create a climate of compromise and tepidness. When one had more serious causes for anxiety, it was easier to say with regard to the Cyprus question "remove this cup."

The Foreign Minister explained further that India, which had helped the Greek Delegation at the previous Assembly, had explicitly stated this time that, unless Britain was in agreement, it could not intervene. And India's example influenced the stand of many Asian countries. As matters stood at the moment, the most one could expect from India was neutrality in case of controversy.

Also known was the attitude of the United States, which guided or at any rate influenced many votes in the Assembly. The United States desired and worked for a solution of the Cyprus question that was closer to the Greek viewpoint than it was to the Turkish one, Averoff-Tossizza affirmed. However, in no case would it reach the point of creating coolness in its relations with Britain and Turkey because of the Cyprus question. Thus, with regard to the UN handling of the Cyprus question, the United States had made it clear that if Greece, Britain, and Turkey did not agree on any particular draft resolution, it would work for the adoption of a "colorless" one. He had invoked all possible arguments to buttress the Greek viewpoint—sometimes, indeed, with some sharpness. But the U.S. officials concerned would not yield.

The Arab countries were divided. They would take into account primarily their own interests. Averoff-Tossizza observed in this connection that it was very revealing that the delegations of Egypt and Syria, which doubtlessly would help the Greek Delegation in matters of substance, had rejected Greek proposals that they ask to appear before the General

Committee as parties concerned, when the matter of the inclusion of the
Cyprus question in the Assembly's agenda was being considered. Their
delicate relations with Britain and Turkey, as their replies to the Greek
Delegation had clearly suggested, had led them to take this negative
stand.

It was characteristic, too, of the general outlook that such close friends
of Greece as Carlos Romulo of the Philippines and José Vicente Trujillo
of Ecuador had failed to mention the Cyprus question in the addresses
they had delivered during the general debate, even though they had had
the opportunity of doing so because of the topics they had touched upon
in their speeches.

All these facts did not mean that Greece had lost its supporters in the
Assembly. On the contrary, to the ranks of Greece's supporters could
now be added the Federation of Malaya and, very probably, Ghana.
India was the only exception.

The fact remained, however, that, although the Greek Delegation
would wage its battle with faith and pride, the outcome would depend
on the number of votes each side could muster; and the number of
supporters of the Greek views on Cyprus was not sufficient, and many
delegations viewed with favor the trend toward the adoption by the
Assembly of a "colorless" resolution.

Under the circumstances, the Foreign Minister believed that a Greek
draft resolution calling for the application of the principle of self-
determination to Cyprus would very probably be rejected by both the
Political Committee, where a simple majority was required, as well as by
the full Assembly, in which a two-thirds majority was needed. In spite of
all the demagogic pressure for waging a lively battle and suffering a
proud defeat,[52] such an eventuality should be avoided.

The issue of self-determination would not, of course, be closed in case
of defeat, he observed. It could be raised again. But it would already
have suffered a grievous blow while Turkey, both inside and outside the
United Nations, would brandish the argument that, since the Assembly
had voted against the Greek draft resolution, it had rejected the application of the principle of self-determination to Cyprus. Any retreat, and
even postponement of a UN decision on the issue of self-determination
would be preferable to such a rejection, regardless of whether for reasons
of principle and of tactics it was necessary to wage the Cyprus battle by
invoking self-determination.

A draft resolution that recommended independence for Cyprus and
did not at the same time exclude self-determination for the Cypriots
might be submitted by some delegation among those that were favorably
disposed toward the Greek viewpoint. However, as long as the United
States opposed such a proposal, the Assembly would not be able to adopt
it. Indeed, because of India's attitude of abstention, even the Political
Committee would reject such a proposal. Since the Greek Delegation
should acquiesce in the tabling of such a draft resolution only if it was

certain that two-thirds of the members voting would favor it, this course could not be followed. For tactical reasons, nevertheless, the Greek Delegation should welcome such a motion, if it were made by another delegation, as a constructive proposal that was consistent with the principles of the UN Charter.

Any other useful resolution—one, for instance, that would entrust the UN Secretary-General with the task of implementing Resolution 1013 (XI) or a resolution calling for negotiations between the Cypriots and the British government—appeared likewise incapable of gathering the required two-thirds vote or even an absolute majority of members voting, if the United States opposed it.

The Foreign Minister, on the other hand, felt that the Greek Delegation would be able to block the adoption of a draft resolution that was unfavorable to the Greek viewpoint, for instance, a proposal that would recommend tripartite negotiations, for it would be able to preserve the one-third (plus one) of the full Assembly's negative votes which were needed for doing so. But even this could not be regarded as absolutely certain. The Greek Delegation's blocking ability would depend to a great extent on the way in which the draft resolution would be formulated and on the limits that the United States would wish to reach in order to gather enough votes in favor of such a resolution. For example, at the previous Assembly strong Anglo-American pressure had been exerted among various delegations in favor of a proposal such as Thailand's that referred to a solution acceptable to the parties concerned. Similar pressure this time could lead to the adoption of such an unfavorable resolution. From his own experience, Averoff-Tossizza knew that friends, even when lightly pressed by third parties, said: "It is unreasonable for you to ask us to vote against a draft proposal that says that the solution must be acceptable to all the parties concerned."

Then, the Foreign Minister pointed out that, as seen at the previous Assembly, there were procedural ways for preventing a draft resolution from being put to the vote. For instance, another draft resolution could be tabled and put to the vote before the Greek proposal. Thus, Greece, in the end, could be denied even that so-called proud defeat (regardless of whether this defeat was harmful or not) for which the Opposition clamored.

In his report to the Premier, the Foreign Minister concluded that the most likely thing to emerge from the Assembly and the controversy with Britain and Turkey in that forum would be an entirely "colorless" resolution. This did not mean, of course, he hastened to add, that this year, too, the Greek Delegation would not do battle with faith and determination. But it was indispensable to be fully aware of the resources the delegation had at its disposal. To overestimate these resources was a sign either of the crass ignorance of those who thought that Athens was the center of the world, or of low demagogy, or of the vulgar fear of being charged with defeatism. From the overestimation of the resources available to

Greece, only harm could result. He, personally, as a responsible member in the Premier's government, was obliged to give his opinion, even at the risk of being termed a defeatist by the superpatriots of the day. The latter could offer nothing to the struggle. On certain occasions, they had even dared to criticize the fabulous feats of EOKA or to disapprove the raising of the Cyprus question in the first place. He felt obliged to state his own views, moreover, because these were based upon strictly objective criteria, and an unfavorable outcome for the Greek recourse to the United Nations would have unfavorable effects on the sacred cause.

Such an unfavorable outcome, the Foreign Minister wrote further, in all probability could provoke the resumption of hostilities in Cyprus. These would develop differently than before because the Turkish minority had now been armed and desired to stir up trouble. The Turkish Cypriots could not act against the Greek population except through reprisals directed as much as possible against EOKA. These reprisals in their turn would lead to counter-reprisals, and Cyprus, thus, would be rent by chaotic strife, drenched in blood, and set ablaze. Besides, EOKA, in spite of the heroism of its members and its excellent leadership, would be unable to withstand for long such a two-pronged struggle. Developments, thus, would lead to EOKA's weakening, to the greater exhaustion of the Cypriot population, and to the conviction among third parties that the Cyprus problem was more complex than it appeared to be at first glance. Facts would show that the two communities could not live together peacefully. This, in turn, would strengthen those who favored partition of the island as a solution and would lead to a grave deterioration in Greek-Turkish relations. No one would be able to say how far this deterioration could go. Regardless of the more general consequences of such developments, this would render even harder than before the real promotion of the Cyprus question.

For anyone who handled the Cyprus question, Averoff-Tossizza remarked in his report, the above thoughts created a sense of very grave responsibilities. The tactics that, in his opinion, should be applied were the following:

With full use of the most effective weapons Greece had in its diplomatic armory, all possible efforts should be exerted to reach a satisfactory solution of the Cyprus question before the actual debate on the Cyprus question began in the Political Committee. Under the prevailing circumstances, any solution that granted real and full self-government to the Cypriots and did not exclude self-determination should be regarded as acceptable.

At the same time, the Foreign Minister advised that all persons whom the Premier deemed competent and appropriate should explore the Greek potential in the United Nations. If they reached the same conclusions that he had reached, they would, first, realize that it was desirable to handle the matter of atrocities (to be discussed also at Strasbourg, by the European Commission of Human Rights) more or less in the same way as it had been handled at the previous Assembly. Second, they would discover that the crucial question in the United Nations would be defining the objective, in case it became clear that the Greek draft resolution would be rejected. Should postponement, a "colorless" resolution, or something else be sought? Third, they would realize that public opinion in Greece and Cyprus would have to be gradually prepared so that the abrupt dashing of hopes did not cause keen disappointment and undesirable reactions. He, at any rate, believed that the Greek Delegation should wage the battle for the application of the principle of self-determination to Cyprus, while also acting backstage for getting the most constructive resolution possible. Among such resolutions there could be a cautious and rather vague draft that simply recommended independence (not self-determination) for Cyprus. This, in spite of the opposition of the United States, would have a few chances of adoption, because many delegations would find it difficult to vote against it, and others would abstain from the vote. If, however, at the last moment the possibility of any useful resolution's being adopted was precluded, and if it seemed certain that the Assembly would adopt a "colorless" resolution, then the Greek Delegation should strive to get the Assembly to postpone any decision on the issue, not indefinitely but until its next session. For obvious reasons, he would prefer such a postponement to the adoption of a resolution that said nothing. In such a case the struggle should be based on the rationale for postponement, which would either have to be constructive or completely "colorless."

In conclusion, the Greek Foreign Minister informed the Premier that he was sending Makarios a copy of this report and suggested that it was now up to the Premier to communicate its contents to those among his collaborators whom he regarded as competent, in order to canvass their views. He should listen, of course, also to the views of worthy representatives of the Cypriot people, and thus reach a conclusion on setting down the general guidelines that he should follow in the United Nations. In a sort of postscript, Averoff-Tossizza added that the recent statements of the British Labour party facilitated the debate in the United Nations but did not affect what he had said concerning a resolution. On the contrary, under the pressure of the Labour party, it was likely that the Turkish government would pursue with greater insistence than the British or the American government the adoption of a resolution that would somehow buttress its interests as well as its position as a party concerned. A resolution that recognized Turkey as a party concerned would always have unpleasant consequences for the future, and a "colorless" resolution would not be exactly pleasant either.

Grivas, it should be added, was kept posted by Averoff-Tossizza about the results of the first phase of the struggle in the United Nations. Both the Greek government and Makarios were pleased with the results, "Isaakios" informed the leader of EOKA. The second phase, however, would be much harder, not so much in the debate as at the stage of adopting a resolution. Here, the combination of numbers, not justice, was decisive, and the number of votes depended on national interests. At the first phase of the debate over the inclusion of the Cyprus question in the Assembly's agenda, even close friends and neighbors, who were also very anti-British, had refused to be of help. All experts predicted that it would be impossible to get the Assembly to adopt a resolution calling for immediate self-determination for Cyprus. Even anticolonialist states favored the adoption of an altogether "colorless" resolution. Turkey was pressing for a resolution that would call for a solution "acceptable to the three parties concerned." The West was considering various ideas of a semi-independence or full independence for Cyprus that would not exclude self-determination at some point, but it was unwilling to exert pressure on the Turkish government to accept them. The attitude of the Labour party was invaluable. However, one should not imagine that any specific date for a solution was imminent. Evidently, because Grivas was regarded as a sort of military instrument and not a participant in policy-shaping and policy-making, the various alternatives for possible action in the United Nations were not conveyed to him by the Greek Foreign Minister.[53]

Chapter Six

Vain Greek Initiatives
through the Diplomatic Channel

A. Greek Probes with the U.S. and Britain for a Solution Outside of the United Nations

SG of NATO   Spaak, in contrast to Lloyd, who had been unwilling to voice any opinion about the alternative Greek compromise proposals put forward by Averoff-Tossizza in their conversation of September 19, or any other solution to the Cyprus problem, seems to have been stimulated by the thought of the various alternative solutions the Greek Foreign Minister had outlined to him on September 12 at Orly. In a long conversation, on September 21, with Ambassador M. Melas, after hinting that it had been due to his initiative that the "Anglo-Norwegian" *mise en scène* had been achieved in the General Committee, which ended in the adoption of the Norwegian formula for including item 58 in the Assembly's agenda, he reiterated the belief he had expressed to the Greek Foreign Minister at Orly that, because of the threat of a Soviet presence in Syria, it was more than ever necessary to settle disputes between allies, so that all, starting with the Turks and the Greeks, should not be destroyed by the U.S.S.R. The solution that had the greatest probability of success, in his opinion, was the following: first, the independence of the island should be guaranteed by some or all NATO allies for a long period (twenty years at least); second, guarantees should be granted to the minority; third, either the British should maintain sovereignty over their bases on the island or these should be ceded to NATO; fourth, after twenty years a conference should be called, to decide, together with the inhabitants of Cyprus, the question of the final status of Cyprus without any commitment concerning the solutions that would be accepted (this last provision for satisfying the Turks who would be able then to develop their own views on partition). In fact, it would be understood that after twenty years of independence, the choice would be between continued independence or *enosis*. In brief, the Cypriots would get their independence immediately and formally, while the final solution would be left to the next generation, which, at any rate, would take decisions without over-concerning itself with the desires of the present generation, even if written treaties existed.

In order to make this solution more palatable to the parties concerned, Spaak thought of presenting this plan in the form of an appeal to the three governments on behalf of the other twelve NATO states. He wished to know the views of the Greek government and of Makarios about this proposal. He would also sound out the Turkish government. As for the proposed appeal, Spaak contemplated issuing it after the Turkish elections of October 27 in the hope that the Cyprus debate in the United Nations, which inevitably would intensify passions, could be put off until the end of the session. All these, of course, were mere plans.

On October 2, the Secretary-General of NATO had another long exchange of views with the Greek Foreign Minister who was on his way back to Athens. Spaak, on this occasion, not only discussed various plans for solving the Cyprus problem but also emphasized the tripartite conference, which the British government had tried in vain to convoke. Spaak started out by inquiring about the possibilities of Greek participation in the proposed London conference and insisted on the known arguments that this conference would provide the best means for averting partition and for promoting the Cyprus question. Averoff-Tossizza, on his side, repeated the familiar arguments against participation in such a conference, unless the general framework of the solutions to be discussed there was defined. Spaak then spoke about the Turkish attitude toward the proposed conference. From a conversation with Ambassador Sarper, the Turkish representative to NATO, he had gathered that the Turkish government, shortly after the Turkish elections, would declare its acceptance of the British proposal—because it was sure the Greeks would refuse to attend. He—Spaak—at any rate had remained under the impression, without having any concrete evidence, that Sarper was less intransigent than he had been in the past. Then Spaak inquired what the Greek government's attitude would be toward a conference to which the Cypriots, too, would be invited—a procedure which he regarded as immeasurably more appropriate. Averoff-Tossizza replied this was a new thought that he had discussed with no one, but if four Cypriot Greeks and one Turk were invited, the nature of the conference would have changed, and it was his absolutely personal opinion that there were some probabilities of the Greek government's changing its mind.

Concerning his own initiative and plan, Spaak now was somewhat reserved. He said that on many sides it might be welcomed. He was sure, though, that the Turks would accept his proposals only if, after the end of the proposed twenty-year period of independence, the matter of Cyprus' status remained open for re-examination. Naturally, this re-examination would in no way automatically abolish the island's independence, the extension of which would be secured, but would deal only with the question of the regime that would follow, were independence abolished. Averoff-Tossizza replied it was exactly this point that made it difficult for his government to accept such a solution. Acting on behalf of the Cypriots, his government, he knew, would accept a period of twenty-years' independence only on condition that after the end of that twenty-year period they would be absolutely free to determine their future as they wished. Averoff-Tossizza also suggested that if the same proposal was made for a much shorter period, namely for ten years, then the Cypriots themselves should be asked whether they would accept. Generally, he did not rule out the plan Spaak had proposed but clearly indicated that this solution was not among those which his government would easily accept. Spaak, on the other hand, again stressed he did not see how the Turkish government could accept something like this plan without at least some way out that would allow it to save face. Until then, the Turkish government had strongly opposed any idea of independence for Cyprus. This, it said, was a sure way toward *enosis,* which they could never accept.

Spaak then posed many questions to the Greek Foreign Minister about possibilities, for instance, of Cypriot independence outside the Commonwealth, but with the right of Cyprus to participate in NATO, or of an independence burdened by servitudes exclusively related to matters of change of regime and of minority safeguards. The stumbling block in the whole discussion, however, was the matter of the most appropriate procedure for deciding the island's future after the period of independence within the Commonwealth had ended. Averoff-Tossizza insisted that the Cypriots should then be free to determine their own future. Spaak explained why the Turks would accept no such provision. Defining his position in greater detail, the Greek Foreign Minister referred not merely to Greek domestic reasons but also to the sure refusal of the Cypriots themselves to accept anything less. Indeed, among them was a large segment of extremists who were unwilling to accept even the other compromise solutions put forward by the Greek government. Consequently, below that level no other solution was possible for the Greek government.

The Greek Foreign Minister, in this exchange of views with NATO's Secretary-General, once again expressed his anxiety about what might happen on the island after the debate on the Cyprus question in the United Nations was concluded. If the Cypriots now were peaceful, this was because they believed they would shortly get a tolerable solution to their problem. If, however, their hopes were shattered because the United Nations adopted some sort of "colorless" resolution, then it was certain that the struggle would be resumed. Because the Turkish minority had been armed, the struggle would turn into a series of reprisals and counter-reprisals between the two communities, into an orgy of fire and blood. With hostilities starting again in Cyprus—Grivas had proclaimed he would resume the struggle in a fiercer way if he was convinced that no solution was being reached [1]—the situation would become extremely grave. The island would suffer terribly. The problem would become even more complex and its solution even more difficult than it was now. With Greeks and Turks fighting on a neighboring island, passions would be inflamed both in Greece and Turkey, and relations between the two countries would become extremely tense, with the severance of diplomatic relations becoming unavoidable in a matter of weeks.

Spaak agreed that such a development was extremely undesirable. Greece, he said, could expect nothing but a non-substantive resolution from the United Nations and, during the debate, the Greek representatives would find themselves in great difficulties if Turkey had, in the meantime, agreed to participate in the proposed tripartite London conference and Greece was the only party that had refused to do so. He did not see how the Greek Delegation could persuade others of Greece's good will if others exploited this refusal. Besides, regardless of efforts to maintain the debate on a high level, it would be impossible for it to be gentle. And this bitterness would foment fanaticism both among the Cypriot people as well as among Greeks and Turks. Furthermore, there were many countries, Spaak said, that would like to help Greece but could not do so in the United Nations in front of their enemies and in matters concerning interallied differences.

The Secretary-General of NATO finally stated he would tell the British that, after this meeting of his with the Greek Foreign Minister, he was convinced that the London conference could not take place but that, if the Cypriots were invited, there might be some possibility of calling this conference. If, however, no possibility at all existed for convoking such a conference because of the Greek refusal, he would consider getting in touch with the twelve other NATO members so that either they or he, empowered by them, might issue an appeal to the governments of Britain, Greece, and Turkey, asking them to accept a solution of the Cyprus question based on the creation of a state member of the Commonwealth which would be a member of NATO, would fully safeguard the rights of the minority, and would be unable to withdraw from the Commonwealth before a period of twenty years. He would make no mention about any obligation to rediscuss the matter after the lapse of this twenty-year period, but, he observed, it should not be excluded that the British government would make counterproposals on this chapter.

About three weeks later, on October 22, the Secretary-General of NATO, appearing somewhat discouraged, informed the Greek representative to NATO, Ambassador M. Melas, that four days earlier, on October 18, he had conferred with the British representative and his experts on Cyprus, and had derived the impression that the British had not yet decided but were still hesitating and examining all possible solutions. They were not very happy about his idea of transforming Cyprus into a Dominion for a period of twenty years, because they preferred a definitive solution. When Spaak was reminded by the Greek diplomat that the solution envisaging a Dominion status for Cyprus should presuppose full freedom of decision for the Cypriots after those twenty years had passed, he again said that, in his opinion, the Turkish government would never accept this solution. At the most, it would agree to the calling of a new conference after the lapse of that twenty-year period, in order to take a decision.

With regard to another idea of his, Spaak also said that the British experts, without excluding the participation of Cypriot representatives in a conference of British, Turks, Greeks, Americans, and himself, had remarked that it was difficult from the legal standpoint to organize such a conference, since the Cypriots were British subjects, and it was not easy to find a formula that would permit British representatives, Cypriot leaders, and foreign envoys to sit together at a joint international diplomatic conference.

But, said Spaak, what mainly had disappointed him was the impression the British had derived that, because of Greek unwillingness, the calling of a conference was impossible during the brief interval between the setting up of a post-election Turkish government and the debate on the Cyprus item in the United Nations. He was particularly worried about the repercussions of this debate, especially under the critical conditions created by the Syrian crisis.

On his side, Ambassador M. Melas drew Spaak's attention to his government's anxiety over the attitude of the Greek press during the Turko-Syrian dispute. Moreover, he ventured the suggestion that Spaak, during his stay in the United States,[2] personally meet Makarios. Such a meeting might serve to dissipate many prejudices and dispel misunderstandings on both sides. Spaak replied that this was a good idea. He would see whether such a meeting—which was extremely difficult— could be arranged without danger of indiscretions.

After this meeting with Spaak, a conversation between the Greek diplomat and his British NATO colleague, Sir Frank Roberts, confirmed several of the points the Secretary-General had made concerning the British attitude. The British diplomat gave the impression that his government saw in the proposed conference a way of persuading the Turks to accept some solution other than partition—an inhuman measure, as Sir Frank termed it. As for the Americans, they continued not wanting actively to interfere but favored the line followed by Spaak, said the British diplomat. In discussing possible solutions, Sir Frank disclosed his personal view that he had been interested by another solution Spaak had proposed—of temporary independence for Cyprus under a non-British High Commissioner who would be empowered to prevent *enosis* and protect minorities, with a diplomatic conference to take place after twenty years, to decide on a final solution. Sir Frank also said that the British government, too, had studied the possibility of a three-state condominium.

After his return to Athens from New York, the Greek Foreign Minister, resorting to some of the weapons Greece kept in its diplomatic armory, tried hard to get American and British support for the alternative Greek proposals for a solution of the Cyprus question or, at least, for Greek efforts in the United Nations concerning that question. He had, accordingly, two meetings with U.S. Ambassador Allen, on October 7 and 11; one with the U.S. chargé d'affaires, on October 17; and two meetings with Sir Roger Allen, on October 10 and 25.

At the first of these meetings, Ambassador Allen told Averoff-Tossizza he had received State Department reports about the excellent impression the Greek Delegation had made in the United Nations. He then inquired whether the Foreign Minister had been satisfied with his New York visit, and, more generally, what impressions had he derived from it. Averoff-Tossizza replied that in certain matters he was satisfied, in others not. He was happy, because the Cyprus item had been included in the agenda of the Assembly without any harm done and in a way that permitted debate on it from all angles. He was, however, unhappy and disturbed because of various slight indications that made him believe that there was a greater stiffness in U.S. policy on the Cyprus problem than there had been before. This had surprised him, on the one hand, because of what Allen had told him in the past, and, on the other, because the information he had of the State Department's conviction that the proposed Greek compromise solutions were reasonable had led him to believe that the United States would warmly support his government. He had, however, discovered that the United States, while believing in the reasonableness of the alternative compromise solutions put forward by Greece, was not willing to help beyond a certain point, because it attached greater significance than it had in the past to the factor of Turkey and to possible Turkish displeasure.

The Foreign Minister then recounted in characteristic detail the conversations he had had in Washington and remarked that in the substance of the Cyprus question the United States would aid with advice only, but without being able to exert pressure upon Turkey, and that in the Assembly it intended to support only a "colorless" draft resolution. Averoff-Tossizza went on to say that he had insistently maintained that if no solution of the Cyprus problem emerged until the debate on the Cyprus question in the United Nations began, and as long as the British government regarded as reasonable the three alternative solutions Greece had proposed, support should be given in the United Nations to a draft resolution that would define the framework of a settlement in such a way that Turkey would be persuaded to give in. He had further explained that this was even more necessary in view of the danger lest an unfavorable or just a "colorless" UN resolution cause acute disappointment in Cyprus and the struggle on the island start again. This time, because the Turkish minority had been armed, a Greek-Turkish clash in Cyprus would inevitably ensue, with grave consequences not only for Cyprus but also for Greek-Turkish relations. Nevertheless, he related, he had met with persistent refusal in Washington, on the ground that Turkey ought not be displeased—and this at a moment when both the Americans and the British agreed that the creation of an independent state, free to do what it pleased after X number of years of independence, was a very moderate and reasonable solution. Under the circumstances, after his stay in the United States and even more now, after having conferred with his cabinet colleagues in Athens, he had reached the conclusion that Greek policy in the Cyprus question would become more unyielding, because of the U.S. attitude in this question.

Ambassador Allen, upset by the Foreign Minister's words, tried to defend his government's policy and persuade Averoff-Tossizza that the Greek government had no right to be displeased. The response he elicited was that the United States had always shown sympathy toward Greece and its government but that in the Cyprus question it was ignoring a just cause. Turkey, with 18 per cent of the Cypriot population Turkish, had the right to regulate the fate of the 80 per cent of the population. Under the circumstances, Greece could not but be displeased, and Greeks such as he, faithful and grateful friends of the United States, could not but react in every way in their power. From the American viewpoint, he stressed further, the unpleasant aspect of the situation was that the United States now appeared as more kingly than the king (*"plus royaliste que le roi"*) in this matter of democratic principle, because, since the Labour party's conference in Britain had adopted at Brighton its well-known policy views on the Cyprus question which referred to the principle of self-determination in connection with Cyprus, this meant that the majority of the British people agreed to apply to Cyprus solutions which the United States did not wish actively to support.

The Labour views mentioned by the Greek Foreign Minister in this conversation with the U.S. Ambassador had been expressed in a statement of October 4 by Mrs. Barbara Castle, who, speaking on behalf of the National Executive Committee of the Labour party holding at Brighton its annual conference, had reaffirmed the clear statement of policy made by the National Executive Committee on September 28, 1955, and had repeated the relevant sentence on Cyprus contained in that statement, according to which the Labour party called upon the British government to give a firm guarantee of democratic self-determination within an agreed period within safeguards for minority rights. The specific number of years of this agreed period, Mrs. Castle had explained further, had not been set down because this was a matter for negotiation between the British government and the Cypriot people. "We are not, like the Tories, talking of a vague and misty future when we talk about self-determination coming to Cyprus," she had added. "We shall endeavor to complete this freedom operation for the people of Cyprus during the lifetime of the next Labour Government." She had also stated that partition was not included in the Labour party's definition of "democratic self-determination." There was no intention of dragging Cyprus through the tragedy of partitioned Ireland. This statement had greatly cheered the Greeks, though it seems to have embarrassed the representatives of the Labour party in Parliament.[3]

Discussion followed on the significance of this policy statement of the Labour party—with Allen not attaching to it as much importance as Averoff-Tossizza did, because, he observed, first, parties behaved differently when in opposition and differently when in power,[4] and, second, from what he had read until then, the Labour commitment was not very concrete. He also remarked that, from one angle, this statement rendered much more difficult the Greek position, because the Greek government would be now under greater pressure on the part of public opinion quickly to achieve a satisfactory solution. Averoff-Tossizza, on his side, argued that the statement was fully binding and that it included quite a few details, especially since it unreservedly recognized the right of self-determination for Cyprus. Thirdly, from the domestic point of view, this statement was of considerable help, because it allowed the Greek government to wait, even though the Greek people rightly did not understand the problem. The Greek government would well be able to say: "We are waiting for the day when Labour comes to power." Finally, he maintained, his government, having accepted many compromise solutions, but never accepting one that did not eventually provide for self-determination, had no reason to change its policy. Nevertheless, that a new, important element had entered the picture for improving it doubtlessly rendered more inflexible the Greek position in other details of the solution that would arise in eventual negotiations. In all this atmosphere, he added, Allen's statement to the newspaper *Kathimerini* had not helped.[5]

With great earnestness, even bitterness, Allen protested. He loved Greece sincerely and warmly, he said, and did not expect such criticism for statements that, if read calmly and in good faith, would seem to say that as long as common sense would determine the conditions in which self-determination would be applied, this would evidently be applied in Cyprus, not in Greece.

Averoff-Tossizza responded by saying that he was aware of Allen's philhellenic feelings and was prepared to read his statement in the same light as he had. Furthermore, there had been no bad intentions on his part in this statement, only an unfortunate formulation. In view, however, of the many signs he had mentioned already, he had wondered whether this statement had been made on State Department instructions in order to arouse certain fears in Greece and render the Greek government more cautious in dealing with the Cyprus question.

Allen categorically denied this. Twenty-seven years he had been in the Foreign Service, he said, and for many of these in highly responsible posts, so he well knew what he could say and what he could not say from the viewpoint of the State Department.

Averoff-Tossizza observed that what Allen had said constituted an unpleasant indication, for which he could not be held accountable. He was well aware of his feelings for Greece, as well as of his convictions about colonialism and other similar subjects. The conversation then turned to other matters, such as the Voice of America's broadcasting ship "Courier," which was stationed off Rhodes, and Athens press attitudes toward the Romanian government's invitation for a Balkan conference which the Greek government had rejected,[6] regarding it as an effort to break up NATO and the Balkan Pact.

The Greek Foreign Minister thought he could discern a similar stiffening in the British attitude, at least in the first of his two conversations with the British Ambassador. On October 10, after a short exchange of views on events connected with the inclusion of the Cyprus item in the agenda of the Assembly, he discussed at some length with Sir Roger Allen the Labour party conference's statement on Cyprus. In one respect, Averoff-Tossizza said, Sir Roger was right in believing that the state of the Cyprus question had remained unchanged after this statement by the Labour party. This statement merely granted something that the Greek government and the Cypriots had decided to accept in a spirit of compromise. Sir Roger, however, was wrong in believing that it did not constitute a capital event in the evolution of the Cyprus question. After this statement, it was now certain that the basic Greek demand would be satisfied by a British government, because the commitment was clear, categorical, and solemn. This allowed the Greeks and Cypriots to wait without anxiety about the island's future. From the viewpoint of domestic policy this statement also eased the position of the Greek government and even of its successors.

Somewhat upset, the British diplomat observed, first, that elections would not take place in Britain before 1959; second, that it was not at all certain that Labour would win; third, that the Labour party in government inevitably was not the same as the Labour party in Opposition; and, fourth, that the Brighton statement was a great misfortune, because it created illusory impressions, risked rendering Greek policy intractable, and frustrated achievable solutions through the establishment of a new regime on the island, while the future of the island would be discussed at another phase later.

The Foreign Minister expressed astonishment at this view, which he termed as wholly unfounded. While acknowledging that the Labour party, once in power, was likely to modify the details, which it had not defined and upon which the Greek government would find a way of reaching an agreement, he could not believe that it could abandon the basis of so solemn a commitment, which had been clearly and unanimously taken. Besides, Averoff-Tossizza said, the Brighton statement had not changed the policy of the Greek government, which maintained its views about the acceptable alternative solutions that it had put forward earlier. Of course, this could go on only for a short while. Time favored the Greeks; events in Cyprus might complicate the situation; and even the most level-headed members of the Greek government were beginning to get annoyed about the blank check Britain had given to Turkey.

Evidently concerned now, the British Ambassador reacted very firmly, though moderately in tone. The proposed alternative Greek compromise solutions to the Cyprus problem were not to the liking of his government, he said. There should be no mistake about this. It was not to be excluded that such solutions would eventually be reached. However, they would not be to British liking. In his estimation, the Labour party's policy statement on Cyprus could have an opposite result on the British government, which might not wish to appear as yielding to pressure exerted by the Opposition. Also, if the British government perceived that Greece was becoming inflexible, waiting for the Labour government to come to power, it was likely that under the pressure of these two factors it would say: "Let anything happen. I am indifferent. Let the Greeks and the Labour party wait for me to lose power." What the Greek Foreign Minister had said, namely that current Greek views still held good but that this would not go on forever, seemed to constitute additional pressure that would not help. From what he knew, Macmillan was not disposed to call for elections before the quinquennial expired, and to remain in power he needed the back-benchers, the intransigents, who were numerous and surely would not forgive him if he yielded in the Cyprus question. Finally, the United States would not exert pressure upon Britain. Indeed, Sir Roger believed, the Greek government had perceived some change in the American stand toward the Cyprus question during the last one or two months. In view of the above, he feared (stressing he was expressing his personal views) it would not be possible to find a solution unless the Greek government became more flexible and more willing to accept solutions achievable under current conditions.

The Foreign Minister countered these arguments by asking whether, as long as it was certain that the Cyprus question would be solved in accordance with the Greek views on self-determination, albeit later, it would not be politically more sensible for the British government not to allow the Labour party to apply this solution, but to apply it itself. This was even more reasonable since, in this way, many very likely complications would be avoided: the Labour party's Cyprus policy statement at Brighton provided the British government with one more argument for persuading the Turkish government to give in. That the Greek views concerning possible solutions would not remain the same forever was not a form of pressure, but a reasonable assertion of facts. The Greek government had eased the situation by proposing a solution that would lead to independence for Cyprus for quite a long period of time, would let the United Nations play a role in the future of the island, and would implicitly recognize the freedom of the Cypriot state to do what it wished after a certain period of time. If the British government were to propose this at the end of 1958 or the beginning of 1959, what Greek government would be able to accept such a proposal if after a few months the probability existed that self-determination could be achieved within a shorter period of time? It was, therefore, consistency with elementary logic, and in no way a tactic of pressure, that led him to say that, if the British government became more difficult, international conditions would too.

As for the changes in American policy, Averoff-Tossizza told Sir Roger, these would not influence Greek policy. In this context, he recounted what he had spoken to the U.S. Ambassador about the possible adverse effects of Greek public opinion on the situation in the eastern Mediterranean. This continuous opposition to a just cause, this non-support of solutions recognized by all as reasonable, this continuous projection of Turkey to the foreground, as though it were everything and had fought with the Allies (during World War II), did not just hurt the Greeks but annoyed them. And this annoyance did not affect only the people, but also members of his government. A favorable decision in the United Nations, it was hoped, would help soothe this annoyance. At any rate, British inflexibility and a possible U.S. change in attitude would not make the Greek government agree to accept less than what it had already proposed.

When the British Ambassador inquired whether Secretary of State Dulles had expressed approval of the alternative Greek proposals, the Foreign Minister replied he had not clearly done so but had let it be understood. Indirectly, the U.S. government had done so in writing. Many Americans, and many Foreign Ministers of NATO countries had expressed themselves favorably on these proposals, and Spaak had told him [7] that an arrangement based on a twenty-year dominion status for Cyprus, with guarantees granted to the Turkish minority, together with NATO membership for Cyprus or a NATO presence on that island, constituted a solution that it would be madness not to accept. But nothing had been done because Turkey insisted on injustice. Greece perhaps ought to realize that neutrality in time of war and arrogant intransigence after the war were politically much more productive than the opposite.

After underlining the dangerous results which the arming of the Turkish Cypriots would have—they had recently set off two bombs in Nicosia—Averoff-Tossizza argued that, in the absence of a solution, no other course remained but for the United Nations to adopt a resolution that would open the way to a solution and to the return of Ethnarch Makarios to Cyprus. Sir Roger, in reply, explained in a few words that no such thing could be done. From this conversation the Foreign Minister concluded that his government was now faced by a new intransigent turn in British policy with regard to the Cyprus question, perhaps because of tactical considerations after the Labour party Conference's policy statement on Cyprus at Brighton; perhaps, too, because of strongly negative Turkish reactions to soundings concerning the alternative solutions that the Greek government had put forward, with a resultant full British and partial American retreat.

The afternoon of October 11, the day Ambassador Allen was about to leave Athens for Washington, the Foreign Minister invited him to his office to share with him some of his most recent thoughts. First, he told him about his conversation with the British Ambassador the day before. On his side, Allen disclosed that his British colleague had explained to him that the British government had abandoned its intention of maintaining sovereignty over the whole of Cyprus, only in the event the other preconditions (prevention of Communist infiltration, peace and quiet, as mentioned elsewhere) [8] were fulfilled. Otherwise, it would revert to the view that British sovereignty was indispensable over the whole island, not just over the military bases.

Then, the Greek Foreign Minister, taking the opportunity of the British Ambassador's remark the day before that U.S. policy in the Cyprus question had changed, told the American Ambassador that it had required no effort on his part to realize this, but that he had to exert effort in order to perceive some logic behind this change. He was not arguing with him in person, he stressed, because he knew his feelings and thoughts. But he was arguing with him as a State Department representative. The change in policy of the United States and, generally the U.S. attitude toward the Cyprus question, was in accord neither with justice nor with more general political expediency. It was not in accord with justice, for reasons he had often mentioned. As he had told a gathering of senators and representatives in Washington, D.C., the Greek government was eager to cover all the legitimate interests of Turkey in Cyprus— security, minority protection, economic contiguity—or any other legitimate interest they could think of. But the attitude of the United States was not in accord with political expediency either, because suspense over the Cyprus question generally added tension to the already highly charged atmosphere in the Middle East. The coolness in relations between Greece and Turkey created many problems, whereas co-operation between the two countries, especially if it was sincere as it had been in the past, exerted a powerful and beneficial influence in the Middle East. Thirdly, continued American support of the Turkish view and opposition to the Greek one generally weakened the image of the United States in the Middle East and cooled the friendly sentiments of the Greek people toward America to such an extent that this coolness had crept up even into the government itself and irked it. Prime Minister Karamanlis, Averoff-Tossizza underlined, was very upset about this irritation which was taking hold of government members. After the policy statement of the Labour party at Brighton, the reserved attitude of the United States concerning Cyprus, indeed the increased emphasis in this reserve, had become even more repugnant. It showed that America refused to support a cause in which the British themselves would certainly yield some day, a cause which the majority of the British people and NATO countries regarded as just. Such an attitude could not serve well the interests of the United States.

Allen, as best he could, defended his government's policy. However, during the conversation, the Greek Foreign Minister noted, he expressed various views, which he would convey to the State Department—which showed he would defend the Greek views, too, in the Cyprus question, and with regard to the roles of Greece and Turkey in the Middle East. On the other hand, Allen persistently rejected charges of U.S. partiality in this issue, and insisted that the issue was not America's business. To the extent that the United States intervened, it wished nothing unpleasant to happen either to Greece or Turkey. Thus, he said, while Turkey supported partition as a solution to the Cyprus problem, the United States did not.

The Greek Foreign Minister acknowledged this. He also acknowledged that the United States would never let the Turks displease the Greeks too much. Yet, he insisted, Allen had to agree that the Greek government did have reasons to be displeased. There had been, for example, the case of the draft resolution proposed by Thailand at the last Assembly. The United States had prepared an entire procedure to force the Greek Delegation to accept this proposal. If, at the eve of the voting, India had not become so displeased with Britain, and Krishna Menon had not intervened, a resolution against which the Greeks had been fighting would have been imposed upon it. Allen asked the Foreign Minister to refresh his memory about the details of the Thai proposal and observed—as Rountree had done—that it involved a matter of procedure, not of substance. He himself who was a champion of the Cyprus question did not see how a proposal mentioning "a solution satisfactory to all parties concerned" could be opposed. Everyone knew that there were three parties concerned in this question, and it was natural that the three parties should be satisfied, because otherwise there could be no real solution. Averoff-Tossizza replied that if the U.S. Delegation to the United Nations found itself before such a proposal and supported it so naïvely, no complaint could be raised. But both the U.S. Delegation and the State Department were fully aware that beneath this naïve cover lay the possibility of Turkey's acquiring through the United Nations a veto on the Cyprus question. Greek dissatisfaction was very profound. Allen countered by saying that Greece, too, would have obtained a veto through such a resolution. But, Averoff-Tossizza responded, Greece did not wish to have such a veto. It had simplified matters by leaving the issue to be settled between the Cypriots and the British government. Besides, a veto in the name of 18 per cent of the population was unfounded, whereas one in the name of 80 per cent, which was enslaved, was justified. At any rate, the Greek Delegation had been opposed to this resolution and the United States had persisted in its efforts to get it adopted.

During the animated discussion that followed, the Foreign Minister told the American Ambassador that matters were being pushed too far. The day before, he remarked, the United States (through a State Department spokesman), in response to Khrushchev's rocket-rattling threats against Turkey (in an interview published by the *New York Times* on October 10, the Soviet dictator had said among other things, that "if war broke out in the Middle East, rockets could begin flying, when guns began firing"), had declared in effect that it would defend Turkey if anyone attacked it.[9] But, if anyone did attack that country and the contribution to Turkey's defense would have to be of a more general nature, said the Greek official, then he did not see how the Greek people would consent to be mobilized to fight in Turkey's defense.

Greatly agitated, Allen brought up the matters of NATO and of the allied obligations of Greece. Averoff-Tossizza replied he was aware of all these and could guarantee to him that his government, indeed any Greek government composed of national-minded members of the Opposition, would also wish to fulfil all the country's allied obligations. But in this particular case, he went on, he would be lacking in candor if he did not say that in case of an attack on Turkey, it was very likely that no government would be able to mobilize the Greek people to fight in defense of its neighbor. Allen knew the atmosphere; he knew the reactions of public opinion to incomparably less important matters, for instance to his own press statement of a fortnight earlier. How could he think that war in defense of Turkey would be acceptable to the Greek people who would be called upon to fight. There was no need to mention, he added ironically, that Turkey had taught Greece to take such a stand on occasions when Greece had been attacked (during World War II). The Ambassador left the Minister's office in a cordial but clearly worried mood. As for Averoff-Tossizza, he, too, was concerned about Allen's reference to the draft resolution presented at the previous Assembly. Would the "colorless" resolution Rountree had mentioned in Washington be of the Thai type? Had the United States already committed itself to such a resolution? Was it preparing the Greek government for such an eventuality?

On October 17, the Foreign Minister received the chargé d'affaires of the U.S. Embassy, Counsellor Penfield, at the latter's request. The American diplomat began on a non-Cyprus subject: the Dulles-Gromyko conversation of October 5, in which the former had told the latter that the United States desired the independence and happiness of the peoples of the Middle East, invoking his stand during the Suez crisis of 1956, and Gromyko had reacted in a mirror-like way. Each was said to have accused the other of intervention in the internal affairs of the countries of the Middle East, and nothing new, nothing constructive had emerged from this conversation.

The chargé d'affaires then went on to say that the Embassy had been quite upset by comments published in the Athens press that morning about the recall of Ambassador Allen.[10] The reports about the connection between the U.S. attitude about the Cyprus question and the recall were absolutely groundless, he declared. He believed there was no change at all in the attitude of his government concerning the Cyprus question.

The Foreign Minister replied that he himself was telling reporters and other persons who influenced public opinion exactly the same that Penfield had told him about Allen's recall. Yet no one believed him. Indeed, regardless of what he told others, he did not believe that no change had occurred in the U.S. stand on the Cyprus issue. He thence proceeded to explain the reasons for this conviction, repeating approximately the same observations he had made in his two earlier-mentioned conversations with Ambassador Allen. Because of these reasons, Averoff-Tossizza said, he considered that the recall of Allen, who was a known friend of the Greeks and had espoused the Greek views on the Cyprus question and in a very earnest way indeed, was an indication of the change in attitude of the United States as well as of its desire that the Greeks should be aware of this change. Besides, the British Ambassador had drawn his attention to such a change in their conversation of October 10. He knew, of course, that this recall was no sign of disapproval of Allen, who was a very able man and had already "arrived." Allen's appointment at a much higher position—as Director of the United States Information Agency—proved that. However, he could not regard as convincing Penfield's argument that Allen was the only suitable person for filling this high position. It was difficult to believe that no one else had been found for that position and to understand how a very able ambassador should be invited to take it over, after serving only one year,[11] an abnormally short term of service, in Athens, a post which he had requested and in which he had wished to remain for several years. This recall, then, together with the new and rather stiff phase in the British attitude, the Brighton policy statement on Cyprus by the Labour party Conference, and the Turkish views, could not but lead to the conclusion that the attitude of the United States in the Cyprus question had become less flexible.

Penfield countered with several arguments that did not appear persuasive to the Foreign Minister, who finally told him that the matter was important on several accounts, especially since the Labour party's statement of policy on Cyprus had given the Greek government the possibility of waiting. Increased U.S. inflexibility would inevitably engender greater Greek inflexibility. This, in general, was not agreeable. Moreover, whereas until then the situation had seemed to be improving and hopeful, the perspective now was worse and full of dangers. At the first bad turn in the situation said Averoff-Tossizza he feared new bloodshed. The results of this would be extremely unpleasant both locally and more widely. The change to the worse of the American attitude made bad developments more likely. Again, Penfield did not concur in the Foreign Minister's many arguments. The United States, he insisted, was neutral between Greece and Turkey. In a rather lively fashion, Averoff-Tossizza referred, as he had done on earlier occasions, to the U.S. tactics during the Thai proposal at the previous UN General Assembly and to hints that the

United States intended to favor a similar proposal at the current session of the Assembly. He also drew the American diplomat's attention to the dangers of such a stand. Similar policies, he told him, had led many people into opposing camps. Without realizing it, the United States with its policy, was doing the same with regard to Greece.

The general uproar in the Athens newspapers over the report that an unnamed Greek personality in the United States had declared that if Turkey were threatened, Greece would fulfil its allied obligations, was revealing.[12] Greece, the Foreign Minister affirmed, would indeed fulfil its obligations, and the Greek people, too, would be eager to fulfil them, in the case of an attack against West Germany or France. If, however, the attack were launched against Turkey, then, even though the Greek government would wish to fulfil its obligations, the people unfortunately had been led, not by the government but by unacceptable events, to such a state of mind that they would refuse to fight in order to defend Turkey. This was a real situation. It would be blindness not to see this, and it would be a lack of political acumen if one was not seized by anxiety, because of the psychological erosion that was occurring.

When Penfield, although agreeing that matters were thus (very unpleasant), again tried to convince the Foreign Minister that the United States was neutral and wished and worked for a solution to the Cyprus question in a spirit of friendship for all concerned, the Greek official remarked that for him to be convinced had no particular usefulness. It was useful for the people to be convinced, and, even more, for a solution to be found to the Cyprus problem. The conversation then turned to the Syrian crisis, and the Foreign Minister expressed certain anxiety about it, especially because of the arrogant mentality of the Turks. In general he gathered from this conversation that Penfield was greatly concerned about this situation and that he did not entirely rule out a Turkish-Syrian clash.

The familiar negative attitude of the United States toward a UN airing of the Cyprus question, which augured none too well for the Greek efforts in the General Assembly, was once again revealed at a meeting of October 26 between the U.S. Secretary of State and the Greek Ambassador in Washington, G. V. Melas. On this occasion, Dulles not only expressed the view that the United Nations was not the proper forum for dealing with the Cyprus question but also insisted on the need for a direct agreement between the Greek and Turkish governments over Cyprus. The previous year, Murphy, at a conference between top Greek and American officials that took place at the State Department on November 15, 1956, had given Premier Karamanlis somewhat similar advice. "We believe," he had said, "that an effort to reach an understanding with Turkey would have good results." [13] Indeed, even earlier, after the breakdown of the London tripartite conference of 1955 and the anti-Greek riots in Istanbul and Izmir, both of which had underlined the point Eden wished to impress upon the U.S. government, namely that Turkey was greatly concerned in the future of Cyprus and that the question also involved a Greek-Turkish conflict of interests, the U.S. government had suggested Greek approaches to Turkey as a possibly useful procedure for dealing with the question. Now, in late October, 1957, this was a line the British government, too, was to take pains to emphasize through the diplomatic channel.

At a private dinner of October 25, in Athens, Sir Roger Allen transmitted to Averoff-Tossizza a statement to the effect that his government would examine very sympathetically the application of any of the solutions to the Cyprus question the Greek government considered acceptable, as long as Turkey also agreed to this solution. Sir Roger stressed this was a significant development. Averoff-Tossizza, however, differed. He said he regarded this message as having no particular significance, because it in no way removed the main difficulty of the Cyprus question but, on the contrary, merely highlighted its most important aspect—meaning Turkey's attitude.

The British Ambassador, nevertheless, strongly insisted that this new communication was, indeed, a significant step forward, because never before had he told the Greek government that the solutions it had proposed were acceptable, to the liking of the British government. In his most recent talk with the Foreign Minister, had he not stressed the contrary? Capital, he urged, should be made of this development. Had the Turkish government ever been clearly and officially informed by the Greek government of these proposed solutions? Sir Roger inquired. When the Foreign Minister answered in the negative, the Ambassador suggested that the Greek government place these proposals before the Turkish government. It was free to make use of the British note delivered that day in order to find out where matters stood. He particularly insisted on this point. In spite of Sir Roger's insistence, however, the Greek Foreign Minister stated that in no case would he refer to the Turkish government any solution in the form of a proposal. At any rate, he believed that, from all indirect talks that had taken place, the Turkish government was well aware of his own government's views.

Sir Roger, nevertheless, continued to insist. It was one thing to be aware of certain proposals, he maintained, and an entirely different matter to find one's self facing the responsibility of rejecting, if not proposals, at least certain specific thoughts.

The Foreign Minister responded by saying that probably it would be useful to approach the Turkish government, but he did not think it appropriate for either the Greek government to assume this task, or for a third party, such as the British or American government, to do so, if it were merely to state at the same time that the proposed solutions were to its liking. For, as he had stressed to Lloyd on an earlier occasion, it was quite useless for the British government to say that solutions A or B were acceptable to it if, at the same time, it told the Turkish government that it would do nothing to displease it. This was tantamount to a statement that Turkey, in effect, had a veto right on any solution, and it would be stupid for the Turkish government to yield as long as it knew that it depended upon itself for the British government not to yield. The British Ambassador, for the first time, as the Greek Minister noted, denied that his government had allowed the Turkish government to understand that it possessed a sort of veto. At any rate, Averoff-Tossizza promised to think the matter over and give a reply in a few days. Shortly after, he was reminded by the Greek Ambassador in London that there was really nothing new in the British move. On July 4, 1957, Sir William Hayter, of the Foreign Office, had told Seferiadis he believed his government would accept any solution on which Greece and Turkey would agree.[14]

In this conversation of October 25 with Sir Roger, Averoff-Tossizza emphasized at some length, as he had in earlier talks with him as well as with the U.S. Ambassador and the chargé d'affaires, the dangerous effects the Cyprus question was having on the cohesion of the West. Many Greek government officials, he said, were disturbed about the growing anti-NATO sentiments among the Greek people. It was not just a matter of pro-communism or pro-Russianism—though there was some sort of feeling of gratitude for the Eastern bloc, because of its support in the Cyprus question. At any rate, a clear anti-NATO current existed which was such that he was obliged to say that this flank of the Alliance had somewhat weakened. Even though the Germans had been Greece's enemies, he did not think his government would have a great deal of difficulty in mobilizing the Greek people, were a Soviet attack against Germany to occur. If, on the other hand, Turkey was attacked and the war was localized for a few weeks on the Turkish front, he was unfortunately obliged to say and emphasize that—this was the true situation in spite of the Greek government's will—the Greeks would not consent to face death in order to defend the Turkish nation. He said this in spite of his faith in NATO and in its usefulness, and it was for these reasons that he hoped a solution of the Cyprus question would be reached very soon, and to the advantage of Cyprus, in order to halt this downward trend. Sir Roger agreed that matters were thus: the situation was extremely dangerous, and the Greek government would find itself in an extremely dangerous position, because of the considerations that the Foreign Minister had outlined. Hence the need for a speedy solution.

To the above British effort to persuade the Greek government to approach the Turkish government on the Greek alternative compromise solutions to the Cyprus question was there ever any counterpart in the nature of a similar *démarche* of the British Ambassador in Ankara with Foreign Minister Zorlu, for instance? And, regardless of such a British—and/or American—*démarche*, why did not the Turkish government raise with the Greek government the matter of discussing possible solutions to the Cyprus question at this time, aware, as it must have been, of these Greek proposals? Was insistence on partition the only reason for such Turkish restraint? Was it the imminence of the elections? The absence of available relevant archival material precludes a definite answer to these questions. At any rate, after this exchange of views with Sir Roger Allen on October 25, the Greek Foreign Minister had to modify his earlier conclusions about the stiffening of the British position in the Cyprus question, taking also into account the "input" of other new data, such as the news of Sir John Harding's recall from Cyprus (publicly announced on October 15 but with press reports going back to October 1) [15] and of his impending replacement by a member of a well-known Labour family, Sir Hugh Foot (later Lord Caradon); and a letter of October 19 from the Greek Ambassador in London who cautiously indicated that signs were appearing that Turkey was starting to lose ground vis-à-vis Greece.

A slight insight into the attitude of Turkish leaders at this particular time may be obtained from a conversation which the Greek Foreign Minister had on October 11 with the Yugoslav Ambassador in Athens, Pavicevic. This conversation, incidentally, also reveals the strong elements of national pride that colored—and still color—the stuff of Greek-Turkish relations in the Cyprus and other issues. An unnamed high Turkish official (not the Turkish Ambassador in Athens) had told him with great pride, the Yugoslav diplomat recounted in this conversation of October 11 with Averoff-Tossizza, that it was not up to the Turkish government to approach Greece with regard to the Cyprus or any other question but vice versa, because Turkey was such a rich country with twenty-four million inhabitants, while Greece had only seven million (eight million in 1956).[16] Furthermore, within twenty to thirty years, Turkey would have more than eighty million for whom it had enough space, whereas Greece would have twelve million for whom it would not have enough space. Consequently, Turkey was a great power in creation, while Greece was a small country that should understand the imbalance that existed between two countries.

Unwilling to let such views pass unchallenged, the Greek Foreign Minister observed to Ambassador Pavicevic that this Turkish official, as well as his compatriots, seemed to behave like certain young children who wanted to look grown-up in front of their elders, and that an "inferiority complex" which the Turks felt vis-à-vis the Greeks made this unnamed official speak as he did. When the Turks went abroad, they looked around with a telescope to find a countryman, although they saw a great number of Greeks, some of them in important positions, in the United States, Canada, Australia, and many other countries. They went to the theater and saw Greek stars performing, but they saw no Turks. They visited harbors and saw the largest ships in the world flying the Greek flag or bearing Greek names. They would open any European newspaper and read about Onassis, Niarchos, Mitropoulos, Callas, and others. And this was not just a transitory situation. It was permanent and would continue. Therefore, the Turks should learn sometime that they were bigger than the Greeks in one respect, but the Greeks would always be bigger in all other respects that were taken into consideration in international society. Besides, both the size of Turkey and its wealth had led the Turks into the worst financial situation of any country in Europe, and into an unprecedented crisis. Greece, on the other hand, which was so small, had one of the healthiest economies in Europe. Indeed, Averoff-Tossizza asserted, he would never exchange the present or future of Greece for the present or future of Turkey.

B. The Greek Parliament Debates Phase I on Item 58 in the United Nations

Before going back to New York to lead the Greek Delegation in the Committee debate in the United Nations, the Foreign Minister had to run the gantlet of his political opponents in Parliament on October 24. George Papandreou, coleader of the main Opposition, Liberal party, once again charged that the government's policy in the Cyprus question was not one of a "ruthless struggle" for self-determination within a fixed and reasonable period of time. As proof of this he reverted to certain statements that the Foreign Minister had made at the eleventh General Assembly and referred to his attitude and statements during the debate in the General Committee on the inclusion of item 58 in the twelfth Assembly's agenda. Why had he yielded without a fight to the change of title with regard to subitem (b) of the Greek recourse? Why had he not replied to Lloyd's deriding of Makarios' allegations of British atrocities in Cyprus? While correct in opposing tripartite negotiations and preferring Anglo-Cypriot talks under Resolution 1013 (XI), why had he not prevented or protested against the invitation of the Turkish representative to the General Committee's table? And why had he left unanswered the Turkish representative's ironic remarks about the fact that the explanatory Greek memorandum had been submitted two full months after the submission of the recourse? Papandreou also took Averoff-Tossizza to task for having been nice to the British government and for not having blamed it, but the British authorities in Cyprus instead, for the atrocities that had been committed against Cypriots. And why that praise for the British government for having granted independence to Malaya and Ghana? Did that mean that Greece was now asking for independence for Cyprus within the Commonwealth? Generally, Papandreou charged the Greek government with lacking an "agonistic mood." After mentioning with pride the usefulness of the Opposition's "unyielding struggle" and the fact that the Armour Report had noted that this attitude obliged the Greek government to assume an intransigent attitude in the Cyprus issue,[17] he dwelt at great length on the Brighton statement of policy on Cyprus and expressed immense admiration for, and profound gratitude to, the Labour party, which had adopted it, as well as for the majority of the British people. This statement, he declared, constituted a great argument for the Greek government. "We cannot ask for less than what the Labour Party offers," he said. Finally, Papandreou urged Parliament to adopt a unanimous resolution to the effect that it approved only a policy that called for self-determination for the Cypriot people within a fixed and reasonable period of time—a motion the government had rejected in the past and was to reject again on this occasion.[18]

In defense of his government's Cyprus policy, the Foreign Minister observed, in regard to his own handling of the inclusion of item 58 in the Assembly's agenda, that he had warned Papandreou against basing any charges on the records of the meeting in the General Committee. These records, unlike those of the General Assembly or the verbatim but unofficial records of the Political Committee, were summaries only.[19] Quoting remarks he had made on that occasion, he showed that in the exchanges on the subject of British atrocities and subitem (b) of the Greek recourse he had been quite sharp and that he had replied to Lloyd's relevant remarks, though the summary record did not show this.[20] If he had yielded finally to the Norwegian proposal for a neutral title for item 58, this had been because he was aware that if subitem (b) had been put to the vote, the Committee would have rejected it, and this would have caused difficulties in discussing the matter later. Besides, some of the friendliest delegations had asked him not to insist on the mention of atrocities in the title of item 58.[21] As for the Turkish presence in the General Committee, there had been the precedents of 1955 and 1956 (on the latter occasion, Turkey was a member of the General Committee). For this presence, there were analogies from other cases, too—an Australian representative, for instance, had attended the meeting when the General Committee had discussed the inclusion of the question of West Irian in the Assembly's agenda. Concerning the Opposition charges about the over-all Cyprus policy of the government, how about the rejection without discussion of the Radcliffe draft constitutional proposals or of Lord Ismay's good offices offer, Averoff-Tossizza asked. And how about the recourses to the United Nations with the request for the application of self-determination to the people of Cyprus? Were these not indications of governmental combativity? There were, of course, tremendous difficulties in this unequal struggle. Yet, step by step, progress was being achieved—small successes, it was true, but these promoted the issue toward the end that all desired. The United Nations had adopted Resolution 1013 (XI). Ethnarch Makarios had been released. "Dighenis" and the struggling Cypriots supported the solutions provided under that resolution. Progress had been made at Strasbourg. A commission of investigation was going to Cyprus in November, to examine whether the measures taken there were justified or whether they violated human rights in the island.[22] With Papandreou he could agree that the Opposition provided arguments which the government exploited. He could not agree with him, though, that the Opposition was in favor of self-determination, while the government wanted a compromise. It was the government's policy, he categorically declared, to seek a solution based on self-determination—as soon as possible. The difficulties and dangers were great. It was not possible to say that one wanted self-determination within two or three years.[23]

While another Opposition leader charged Averoff-Tossizza (as the latter had predicted in his report of September 30 to the Premier) with not having exploited to the hilt the theme of British atrocities in Cyprus—"a first-rate weapon"—or blamed the government for delays or blunders in the work of the Human Rights Commission of the Council of Europe,[4] extreme left-wing spokesmen again sought on this occasion to undermine Greek confidence in the West by drawing attention to the new balance of strategic power, which seemed to have occurred at this conjuncture of world history, because of the Soviet achievements in missilery that became evident in autumn, 1957. Greece, said the spokesman for EDA, should quit NATO and join its natural friends, the Arabs, in the "camp of peace," which now could boast of sputnik. The leader of the U.S.S.R., he reminded Parliament, had stated that, after the development of ICBM's, bombers belonged to museums.[25] Another left-wing Opposition leader, after analyzing at considerable length the apparent new vulnerability of SAC (Strategic Air Command) bases in the United States, tauntingly asked why the Greek government, which "believed it could expose the country . . . to the danger of total destruction in case of total [nuclear] war," did not have the courage to demand "from those, for the sake of whom we would become a holocaust," that the Cypriots be freed and that "the vandalisms against, and the extermination of," Greeks living in the country "of our other friends and allies," the Turks, should cease?[26]

C. Controlling an Unavowed Instrument of Foreign Policy

In his efforts to impress upon American and British diplomats in Athens, or Spaak in Paris, the urgent need for positive action in order to make progress toward a settlement of the Cyprus question, Averoff-Tossizza had pointed to anti-Western and neutralist public opinion trends in Greece as one of the most important objective political factors that should sway the United States and Britain into taking action with regard to the Greek proposals for the solution of the question and exerting pressure on Turkey for a speedy settlement, if it was desired to avert harmful consequences for the Western Alliance in the region of the eastern Mediterranean and the Middle East. In the Cyprus arena, on the other hand, his problem was not so much to prod as to restrain—by invoking the same factor of public opinion trends. For, on the island itself, Grivas, like Makarios in the United States, or the Opposition in Greece for that matter, although usually agreeing with the Greek government about ends, occasionally disagreed on the means the Foreign Minister used in pursuing these ends, or rather, on the limits he set himself in using these means, as the official who was chiefly responsible for the conduct of Greek foreign policy as a whole.

On the eve of the opening of the General Assembly, Grivas, it will be recalled, had urged, just as EDA was doing, a strong Greek counteroffensive in the diplomatic and political sphere and a policy that could ultimately lead Greece out of NATO and into a sort of axis consisting of Yugoslavia, Greece, and the Arab states, Egypt especially. This uncommitted bloc would, in his view, counterbalance, if not neutralize, the Baghdad Pact, the value of which he deprecated.[27] Moreover, in the Cyprus arena, he favored action, and chafed under the relative inactivity—the second truce of EOKA—to which he had somewhat reluctantly agreed at the behest of both the Greek government and Makarios after Resolution 1013 (XI) had been adopted. Even more, he resented public Greek government criticism of certain statements contained in proclamations he had circulated in the island at that time. Since the Greek government, he argued, was not committed by his actions and moves, he would let no one gag him.[28]

While the period from September 27, when a Greek Cypriot villager was fatally beaten in the first act of EOKA violence since the truce of March 14, to November 9, was marked by the assassination of four more Greek Cypriots in what were widely regarded as warnings against would-be defectors from EOKA's ranks, and of one Turkish Cypriot— a policeman [29]—the Greek Foreign Minister was very anxious that armed violence should not break out again in Cyprus during the Assembly's session, at least not before all hopes were lost, as he wrote to Grivas under his "Isaakios" pseudonym, in an undated letter of, probably, early November, at the latest. The explosion of time-bombs on October 17 at the headquarters of the Cyprus Broadcasting Service and the RAF airfield at Nicosia (Grivas writes he had carried this out, as well as certain other acts of sabotage, in reprisal for the ill-treatment of detainees at the concentration camp of Pyla) [30] had incensed many who feared lest violence start again on the island, "Isaakios" wrote. This atmosphere hindered developments in the Cyprus case. In spite of the dark clouds created by the shocking and evident rise of Turkish influence and of the prospect that any tolerable solution was remote, certain good signs appeared, nevertheless, on the horizon.

The British Ambassador in Athens seemed to be making certain soundings that somewhat encouraged the Greek government. George V. Allen's speech,[31] no matter how much this was due to his own feelings, would not have been such, had the American diplomat not perceived in Washington some intention to help. Both Allen and his Counselor had encouraged Ambassador Pesmazoglou, who was leaving for Ankara, by saying that this time U.S. advice to Turkey would contain certain elements of suasion. If, however, warfare began again on the island, everything would go for a walk. Inevitably, local Greek-Turkish strife would break out in Cyprus, with reprisals against the top people of the island. Nobody, then, would be able to predict the future. The picture would be different; the facts would change; the reactions in Greece, Turkey, and among the great powers would be unknown. Consequently no rational prediction would be possible. In such a chaotic development, an even greater tension in Greek-Turkish relations was likely with all kinds of unforeseeable results for the relations of Greece with its Allies. If this last phase were to arrive, "Isaakios" could not say what the Greek reaction would be. He stressed this, having especially in mind the reaction in Athens to news about the speech of Greek representative Stratos on the Syrian question in the Assembly (on October 28).[32] In all political circles, except those of the left, the adverse reaction had been quite lively—and this, even though the Allies had expressed no displeasure about this speech, publicly at least (for, privately, Allen Dulles had expressed annoyance at the Greek stand in this matter, while Spaak was to do so later).[33] Both the Greek government and he himself, Averoff-Tossizza wrote, had been severely criticized. Many who until yesterday had been superpatriots in the Cyprus question were now saying: "The alliances are being shaken; the powers that might help in a solution are being annoyed; the people are being driven against the West; an acrobatic policy is being conducted."[34] What would happen in case of a great outbreak of public discontent? Might not the people reverse their views? The Foreign Minister, he wrote, had, in the meantime, been authorized to follow the bold policy of the independent line, which could yield results—though, of this, he could not be absolutely certain—if it were conducted with care, measure, and without excesses. In conclusion, again after advising Grivas against the resumption of violence, "Isaakios" expressed the view that the NATO Council summit meeting of December 16-19 would be a turning point. Only there would it become clear whether this policy of the independent line would bear fruit.[35]

In two other letters, of November 3 and 11, "Isaakios" again sought to exert a moderating influence on Grivas. In the first of these he more or less repeated his aforementioned analysis of the political situation and outlook. It seemed clear, he wrote, that it was not the British now who were in the way of a satisfactory solution. Thanks, however, to the Syrian complication, and to the West's belief that a positive Soviet threat existed against the Middle East, the strength of Turkey's position had greatly grown, and the Turks, as a result, had become more intransigent than ever. Again he urged maintenance of the truce until the results of the NATO summit meeting in Paris were known. He also informed Grivas that nothing much could be expected from the United Nations. The Labour party statement had been of capital importance, he remarked, because it condemned partition and committed the party to self-determination for Cyprus—not, however, after a fixed or reasonable time.

He also noted that Turkey was so combative, so unyielding, that it rejected even a solution of independence for Cyprus that would contain guarantees for the maintenance of this independence in perpetuity—a solution that the Greeks, too, rejected. Matters might be moving, but the situation was fluid. It could take a turn for the better or the worse. As he saw things at that moment, the best that could be achieved was a very liberal regime under one form or another, without excluding self-determination and perhaps some machinery that could lead to it. Of course, the agreement of the Greek government and of Cypriot representatives would be required for such a solution. When he would get to New York, he would consult Makarios. After asking Grivas for his views, "Isaakios" outlined his own position. Greece was waging a political and diplomatic struggle in the best and most dynamic way in its power. It had no other possibilities for maneuver. Already what it had done had internally broken the ice vis-à-vis the KKE (Communist Party of Greece) and had aroused a dangerous feeling of gratitude toward the U.S.S.R. Greece could do no more. It was not a matter of ability or courage. Of course, it had to persist. Greece, consequently, had to accept a step-by-step solution, as long as these steps did not exclude self-determination and assured freedom." [36]

The second letter of "Isaakios," of November 11, evidently was a response to an EOKA proclamation of November 9, which had emphasized that the responsibility for any dissolution of NATO unity and for any eventual Greek-Turkish war would rest with the British government. This proclamation had elicited a public statement by the Greek government that, although EOKA had the absolute right to decide upon its action and the extent of the sacrifices it was ready to bear, it had no right to speak about a possible Greek-Turkish war or a split in NATO unity in the eastern Mediterranean. The foreign policy of Greece was decided not by any particular region of Greece nor by any organization but by the government elected by the Greek people.[37] Replying to views Grivas had reiterated concerning the importance of the Balkans in a future conflict, with a Belgrade-Athens-Cairo axis completely neutralizing both Turkey as a bulwark in the Middle East and the Baghdad Pact,[38] "Isaakios" again stressed the need for "measure" so that Greece should not be considered as a completely unreliable ally—because the Cyprus problem, then, would become insoluble since it could be solved only within the Western Alliance.[39] To embark on a full course of neutralism was impossible. For such a neutralist policy, Greece had nothing to lean upon. Nations that conducted such a policy were, at the slightest breath of wind, continually on edge. And for Greece more specifically there lurked in such a policy many other dangers, which he did not enumerate (probably, they seemed to him so obvious, as, for instance, the fact that in an axis such as the one proposed by Grivas, Greece deprived of NATO membership, would be isolated and thus might fall under the domination of Yugoslavia or Bulgaria, against which it would have no counterbalance). "Isaakios" observed further that, at this very time, the matter of the further strengthening of the armed forces of Greece (and of its very weak Navy) was being decided.[40] Any open hostility toward Turkey would only lessen the possibilities of building up these forces. As for the uncommitted nations, to which Greece had granted political favors, these were intent on their own affairs, and far too weak. And they would not unsheath their swords for the sake of Greece. Generally, the attitude the Greek government had assumed until then (co-operation with Nasser; the visit of Premier Karamanlis in August to Cairo; the reception of Yugoslav Vice-President Edvard Kardelj on October 21; the posture toward the Arabs, especially in the Syrian crisis) had already created the impression of a proneutralist policy. This had had several undesirable consequences, while causing useful anxieties among the Allies. Turkey, on the other hand, sought to capitalize on this impression and persuade the Allies of Greece's unreliability. The situation, thus, was on a razor's edge. Great caution was required. After again emphasizing that, because of the Cyprus question, public opinion was now showing signs of sympathy toward the U.S.S.R., "Isaakios" concluded that the only policy possible under the circumstances was persistence in the alliances but with an independent spirit. While combativity in the Cyprus question was necessary for reasons of both a moral and national order, and opposition to certain allies might be called for, great care should be exerted so as not to cause basic harm.

D. Continued Deadlock in British and NATO Diplomacy on Cyprus

It is tantalizing and not entirely purposeless to trace the further fate of the vain British effort to convoke a tripartite conference on the Cyprus question late in 1957. This effort foreshadowed several procedures and measures that were resorted to, and agreed upon, at the London Conference of 1959 on Cyprus, which was tripartite in character with the inclusion, however, of representatives of the Greek and Turkish Cypriots—a suggestion Spaak had put forward in October a year and a half earlier, to be rebuffed at that time by the British government on legal grounds.

With regard to Spaak's plan of late 1957, the British government never rejected it outright. It appreciated the efforts of the Secretary-General of NATO and expressed willingness to include his plan in a conference on Cyprus, provided it were possible to discuss there other plans as well.

For the Greeks, however, certain aspects of the plan aroused new anxieties. According to a conversation of November 12 between the Greek Ambassador in London and Assistant Undersecretary of the Foreign Office Ross, Spaak's proposal that the British bases in Cyprus be ceded to NATO or that Cyprus become a member of NATO, together with the Greek government's assurances of willingness to see to it that the legitimate security needs of Turkey would be covered in a Cyprus settlement, elicited expressions of British satisfaction that Greeks, too, had taken into account the "Turkish preoccupation," as Spaak had informed the Foreign Office. What exactly was this "Turkish preoccupation," Seferiadis inquired. For instance, Ross replied, the establishment of a NATO base with British, Turkish, and Greek military contingents present. But, the Greek diplomat countered, his government had never requested the presence of Greek troops in a base on Cyprus. He could not understand at all why the matter should be complicated by this idea of introducing Turkish troops into the island. How was it possible for the Turks to imagine that they could be threatened by a weaponless island, in which a completely modern British base would be set up? There was the matter of minorities, Ross replied. Astonished, the Greek Ambassador asked: Did this mean, for instance, that a Turkish colonel attached to the NATO base would be able to intervene in order to protect the Turkish minority? If this were so, a catastrophic confusion would ensue. The minority, if Turkey was really interested in it, could be absolutely safeguarded by international guarantees and even by some sort of court composed of international personalities of unassailable reputation. To such a court everyone would be able to go for the slightest matter. Ambassador Seferiadis went on to remind the Foreign Office official that on an earlier occasion, about mid-August, he had told him that his government was prepared to cover all Turkish legitimate interests but was unable to accept either the dismemberment of Cyprus or some substitute for it. Unfortunately, he added bitterly, the Turks were doing everything to remind other people that they were pursuing the same profitable policy they had followed in the case of the Sanjak of Alexandretta (in 1938), when, in the name of a Turkish minority living in that part of northern Syria, they had managed to annex the entire region. In Cyprus now they seemed to wish in one way or another to get a piece of the island, in the name of their small minority there.

In a conversation with Spaak on November 14, the Greek Foreign Minister, on his way back to New York again for the debate of item 58 in the United Nations, having in mind the above exchange (which indicated a slight Turkish shift from insistence on partition), made it clear he could be committed neither more generally nor personally to the Spaak plan. The thought of a base on Cyprus, manned by British, Greek, and Turkish troops, was dangerous, especially if it implied that Turkish troops would constitute a sort of guarantee for the Turkish minority. Spaak's ideas could serve as a foundation for discussions, provided, first, the bases to be maintained on the island were purely British or NATO's, without the participation, in the latter case, of Greek and Turkish forces; and, second, that those states that would decide on the question of a change of regime after a period of Cypriot independence was agreed upon (Spaak, it will be recalled, favored a twenty-year period) would not be Greece, Britain, Turkey, and Cyprus only but also the United Nations or, if this were impossible, the Council of NATO, taking a decision by a majority vote.

In this conversation with the Greek Foreign Minister, Spaak expressed the belief that the British sincerely wanted a solution but avoided displeasing Turkey. He stressed the need for another tactic and said he intended to ask for an active intervention of the United States, which had encouraged him to work in a mediatory fashion in an effort to reach a settlement. When he expressed bitterness about the Greek stand in the UN debate over the Syrian complaint, Averoff-Tossizza explained to him Greek policy toward NATO and the Arabs, also the mentality of the Greek people and the very grave dangers of the situation in Cyprus if the armed struggle were resumed on the island.

The United States continued throughout to maintain an attitude of non-involvement in the substance of the Cyprus question while at the same time encouraging the initiatives taken by the British government for dealing with this problem on a tripartite basis, favoring Spaak's efforts to find a solution, recommending Greek-Turkish talks, and, as usual, preferring quiet diplomacy to open debate of the issue in the United Nations.[41] However, according to well-informed sources, certain State Department officials were now engaged in the study of the various possible solutions of the Cyprus problem, even as one of the major preoccupations of the U.S. government at this juncture seems to have been the vital problem of countering the temporary advantage the U.S.S.R. was believed to be enjoying in ICBM's by setting up U.S. bases for IRBM's on the territory of NATO allies, and was already negotiating with Turkey, among other countries, on this particular matter. One of the solutions studied in the State Department was guaranteed independence for Cyprus. Under it, any change in this independent status would be prohibited without the consent of the guarantors who would consist of an international organization acting through states appointed for this purpose, with Turkey and perhaps Greece included in this body. Another approach—for implementing Resolution 1013 (XI)—would consist of entrusting the UN Secretary-General with the task of trying to find a solution through contacts with the interested parties in Ankara, Athens, and Nicosia.

Toward the end of November, Spaak learned that the British government had agreed to inform the Turkish government of his plan without exerting any pressure upon it, but saying it deserved to be discussed. As a result, he apparently asked the U.S. government to press the Turks in the same direction. The Greek representative to NATO again reminded him that his government could study this plan as a possible basis for negotiations only if mention of a Turkish military presence on the island were deleted. Spaak replied this was the case. The British, while expressing regret at Greek intransigence on this matter, intended to communicate to the Turkish government a plan that provided for the maintenance of only British bases on the island.

In spite of certain reports at the end of November that the Turkish government was showing signs of less rigidity, the Greek government, by the beginning of December, felt it had indications—certain articles of an anti-Greek character in the Turkish press and threatening measures against Greek citizens in Istanbul [42]—that the Turkish government had rejected the Spaak proposals, which had been conveyed to it by the British government, and that it again insisted on partition of the island as a solution of the Cyprus problem.

Chapter Seven

The Greek Delegation
Prepares for the Main UN Battle

A. The Attitude of Various UN Members toward Item 58

Sounding out, urging, bargaining and negotiating with, and persuading or dissuading other governments and their delegations at the United Nations in efforts to muster support for the Greek viewpoint in the Cyprus question had already started well before the battle for the inclusion of item 58 in the Assembly's agenda had been won. In a sense these activities had started in 1954, when the Greek government had first raised the Cyprus question in the United Nations. These efforts continued on the part of Greek diplomatic officials and the Foreign Minister himself not only in New York but in Athens, Washington, and other capitals until the very last moment, as the debate on that item and on the Greek draft resolution was about to begin in the Political Committee. Quite a number of diplomatic *démarches*, for instance, were made at the Foreign Minister's instructions on the very eve of the debate on the Cyprus question in the Political Committee in December, after the Greek draft resolution had been tabled. Others, as will be seen, took place while that debate was going on—and even after. This time, however, no special diplomatic missions were sent out to various countries in which Greece had no embassies or legations in order to enlighten other governments about the Cyprus problem, as had been done on the occasion of the previous General Assembly, when, for instance, Ambassador G. V. Melas went to Mexico, Minister Kassimatis and Ambassador Liatis toured Asian capitals, and Member of Parliament Petros Garoufalias visited Moscow.

As Averoff-Tossizza had reported to Athens on September 30, India, whose attitude affected many of the fifteen Asian and even African delegations, did not intend this time to intervene actively in the Cyprus question, in contrast to its important activities at the previous Assembly. The British, Krishna Menon had told the Foreign Minister on September 27, had been quite annoyed at the initiatives he had taken then, when at

first, backstage, he had proposed, as will be recalled, independence for
Cyprus and then had come up with a draft resolution which the Assembly had adopted. India, as a member of the Commonwealth, could not
continually create problems for Britain, especially with regard to a
country that, like Greece, was an ally of Britain in NATO. It would
intervene only at the request of the British. Krishna Menon was to tell
Makarios more or less the same thing later, adding that the Cyprus
problem should evolve on the basis of the UN Charter's Article 73 on
Non-Self-Governing Territories, not on the basis of the principle of
self-determination. Late in November, on the other hand, when the
Greek Ambassador in New Delhi, in conversations with two undersecretaries of the Indian Ministry for Foreign Affairs, sought to find out
whether the Indian government would support at least a draft resolution
recommending peaceful settlement of the Cyprus dispute through bipartite negotiations, he was told that India always regarded that the principle of self-determination should be applied in colonial territories, in spite
of the reservations and limitations to this principle made by Krishna
Menon because of the Kashmir problem; that it believed in the democratic principle of majority decisions; and that it was absolutely opposed
to partition. The Indian Delegation to the United Nations had been
instructed accordingly, and also told to keep in touch with the Greek
Delegation. This, as will be seen, led to some interesting initiatives on the
part of Krishna Menon and at critical moments proved quite valuable,
even decisive in the view of the Greek Delegation.

Many other Asian and African states (Thailand, the Philippines,
Burma, Ceylon, Cambodia, Nepal, Liberia, for example) also showed
considerable restraint. The delegations of these states were inclined
toward abstention, with the exception of Ethiopia's, which promised a
positive vote this time in exchange for Greek support of the Ethiopian
frontier claims against Somaliland. Iran and Pakistan, on the other hand,
had the impression that the Greek position on the Cyprus question was
most inflexible. These two allies of Turkey through the Baghdad Pact
were inclined to believe that Greece aimed only at achieving *enosis*. The
government of the former sent instructions to its delegation that it
support only a solution that would be acceptable to the three parties
concerned, while the government of the latter authorized its representative at the United Nations to decide for himself on the spot what attitude
should be maintained.

From the eleven Arab states then members of the United Nations,
there were favorable indications—Iraq, Libya, and Jordan excepted.
Since September 2, the Arab League had resolved to continue supporting
the Cypriot claim for self-determination.[1] Although the Delegations of
Egypt and Syria, as mentioned earlier, had not been helpful at the stage
of the inclusion of item 58 in the Assembly's agenda, by refusing to
request, as parties concerned, an appearance before the General Committee, they intended to help in the substance of the case. To the close

co-operation of the Greek Delegation with the Arab states for some years and especially during the Suez crisis of 1956,[2] would now be added new moral obligations of the Arabs to Greece. The Greek Foreign Minister, it will be recalled, had made favorable references about the Arabs in the general debate on September 26,[3] and, during the discussion of the Syrian crisis in October and of the Algerian question in late November and early December, the Greek representative supported Arab attitudes and viewpoints by speeches or vote. In the later question, on December 5, the Greek Delegation voted in favor of the Arab-Asian draft resolution on Algeria. (Besides, Greece had no official diplomatic relations with Israel.) As a result of these political attitudes, both Tunisia and Morocco, countries that had close ties with Turkey, were to take the Greek side in the Cyprus question. Of the greatest political importance was to be the vote of Iraq. The new Iraqi government in Baghdad and the Iraqi Delegation at the twelfth Assembly, because of its composition, was far less favorably disposed toward Britain than had been the case previously, under the government of Nuri es Said, with Fadil Jamali as Foreign Minister. The latter, it will be recalled, had proposed at the ninth Assembly in 1954 postponement for a few days of a vote by the Assembly on the matter of including the Cyprus item in the agenda.[4] Iraq, nevertheless, remained a member of the Baghdad Pact. Its position therefore was difficult. A favorable factor, however, was that the leader of the Iraqi Delegation, Dr. Mousa Al-Shabandar, was a close friend of the Greek Foreign Minister. This would contribute greatly to the friendly stand of Iraq during the debate in the Political Committee and in the voting—as well as to the recall of Iraq's Permanent Representative to the United Nations, Dr. Hashim Jawad, following strong Turkish governmental representations after the voting had taken place.[5] As for Libya and Jordan, faced by pressure and pulls from Turkey, on the one hand, and from the Arab League, and, in particular from its Secretary-General, Abdel Khalig Hassouna, on the other, they were to opt for political absence.

With fewer efforts to bargain over their votes than at the previous Assembly, the nine member states of the Soviet bloc promised to support the Greek views in the Cyprus question, in spite of certain complaints about the negative attitude of the Greek government toward certain demands or desires concerning, for instance, the establishment of a Soviet airline communication through Athens, the improvement ("normalization") of Greek relations with Bulgaria and Albania, or the proposal of the Romanian Foreign Minister, Chivu Stoica, for a Balkan conference. In spite of the Greek rejection of Stoica's proposal, the Romanian Undersecretary for Foreign Affairs said his government would wholeheartedly support the Greek draft resolution. Moreover, as will be seen, the Soviet Delegation proved to be of procedural help in the matter of the order of the debate of the Cyprus item in the Political Committee and even during the debate itself.

Yugoslavia, a member of the Balkan accord and pact of 1953 and 1954, also intended to support the Greek viewpoint. The undersecretary of the Foreign Ministry in Belgrade sent instructions to the Yugoslav Delegation at the United Nations to extend this backing to backstage activities too. The Yugoslav government was reported as having fully realized the necessity for Turkey not to be recognized as a party concerned in the Cyprus question.

Western European countries, members of NATO, especially those that still had colonies of their own, were hardly expected to endorse the Greek viewpoint, as precedents in the United Nations indicated. Iceland, the "old faithful," was the only exception. At the Quai d'Orsay the Greek envoy was told, as the debate on the Cyprus question was about to start late in the Assembly's session, that if the Algerian question did not exist, the expression of French sentiments toward the claims of the Greek Cypriots would be different. Not even an abstention could be expected on the part of the French Delegation. As for the Portuguese government, it sent instructions to its delegation at the United Nations to reiterate the hope that the Cyprus question would be settled between the parties concerned, Turkey included. During his *démarche* at Lisbon, the Greek Ambassador had been reminded of the unfriendly attitude of his government on the question of non-self-governing territories. The Italian government? Until the last moment it was reported as not having yet defined its position. Finally, it voted against the Greek draft resolution. The Netherlands, too, reached the same decision with Foreign Minister Joseph M. A. H. Luns telling the Greek Ambassador at The Hague that, during the debate on the question of West Irian (Dutch New Guinea), he had twice invoked the solidarity of NATO countries, asking the Greek Delegation to abstain—in vain. Since the Greek government had no accredited representatives in Oslo or Copenhagen, the Ambassador in Bonn made some efforts with the Norwegian as well as with the Danish government. And at the United Nations, Ambassador Palamas tried to persuade Ambassador Hans Engen, in order to get Norway at least to abstain on the Greek draft resolution. He argued without success that at one point in the debate on the Algerian question, the Norwegian Delegation had decided to abstain, even though an ally, France, was involved. The Norwegian diplomat, during this conversation, however, mentioned references the Greek Foreign Minister had made to British atrocities in Cyprus, and this remark had made the atmosphere very unpleasant.

European states, non-members of NATO, also were difficult to persuade. In Stockholm, Foreign Minister Osten Unden, when approached by Ambassador Kyrou, showed great reserve. At the Oslo Conference of the Nordic Council, he said, it had been agreed to avoid supporting any plan that involved even indirectly a change in sovereignty, and Sweden would vote only in favor of a draft resolution calling for peaceful settlement—with the result that it voted against the Greek draft resolution. As for Spain, it voted in the same way, in spite of assurances on the part of the Spanish government to the Greek Ambassador in Madrid that its delegate would be instructed not to reject the concept of self-determination (the matter of Gibraltar may have weighed in this unfulfilled Spanish intention). Austria, on the other hand, reminded of its desire for self-determination in South Tyrol but also having in mind the attitude of most Western European states, was to abstain.

With regard to the twenty states of Latin America, members of the OAS (Organization of American States), soundings of the head of the Permanent Mission of Greece to the UN, Ambassador Palamas, indicated that a favorable attitude could be expected from Guatemala, Ecuador, Uruguay, El Salvador (somewhat restrained), Costa Rica, Panama, and Mexico. The remaining Latin American delegations tended rather toward abstention or a negative vote, as long as the United States would ask them to do so. Argentina and Chile were exceptions. Because of British pressures and connected economic considerations in Buenos Aires, Argentina (in spite of its claim to the British-held Falkland or Malvinas Islands) was inclined toward an abstention that tended to turn into a negative vote. It was the same with Chile, where, according to information available to the Greek Delegation, the Turkish Ambassador in Santiago had labored successfully in favor of his government's views. A pleasant surprise, though, was the attitude of the Brazilian Delegation under Oswaldo Aranha, who some years earlier had served as President of the Assembly. In contrast to the Permanent Representative of Brazil, Dr. Cyro de Freitas-Valle, whose "reactionary" personality at the previous Assembly had prevented a favorable stand by Brazil, Aranha from the outset showed sympathy and understanding and promised to help the Greek Delegation when the time of voting arrived. Though, it was not easy to alter the Brazilian stand from one day to another and change over from a negative to an affirmative vote, he promised abstention. As events would show, he kept his promise.

The "older Commonwealth" member states—Australia, Canada, and New Zealand—were not altogether neglected, even though their negative attitude was well known from the past, with the latter having played a prominent role in 1954 in trying to prevent the Assembly from considering further the Cyprus question. Thus, in response to a Greek diplomatic démarche in Canberra, the Australian Undersecretary for External Affairs said that the Australian Delegation at the Assembly would be unable to vote for the Greek draft resolution unless it were amended.

But the main obstacle in the way of the adoption of a draft resolution referring to self-determination for Cyprus in the United Nations was, in the Greek estimate, the stand of the United States. When the time for the debate and voting came up, the attitude of the leader of NATO, the OAS, and SEATO, could decisively affect the attitude of other member states of the United Nations, even if the U.S. government would not seek to exert influence on various governments through the diplomatic channel in order to bend them to its view. As the Foreign Minister had observed in the general debate, what proposal could get two-thirds of the Assembly's votes if two or more great powers opposed it? In the Greek Delegation's estimate, about twenty-five positive votes could be expected, regardless of the U.S. stand and the opposing pressures of Britain and Turkey. In case, however, the United States maintained an attitude of neutrality, there were positive hopes of obtaining a simple majority in the Political Committee—the above estimates being based on the tabling of a draft resolution mentioning self-determination. The experience, however, of the U.S.-supported Thai proposal at the eleventh session of the Assembly, not to mention the difficulties stemming from the U.S. attitude at the time of the first Greek recourse to the United Nations in 1954, had left quite a deep impression in the minds of Greek foreign policy–makers. Hence, there was continuous apprehension about what the U.S. Delegation might or might not do in connection with the draft resolution to be introduced.

B. The Greek Pro-Arab Stand in the Debate on the Syrian Crisis

While the Greek Foreign Minister was absent from New York from the beginning of October until mid-November, trying to exert pressure outside the United Nations for achieving some progress toward a solution of the Cyprus question, the Greek Delegation in New York went on with its regular work in the various committees of the General Assembly. The debate on the Syrian complaint that took place in the full Assembly between October 22–30 provided it with an opportunity for indirectly promoting Greek policies in the United Nations in the matter of the Cyprus issue, in a way that annoyed CIA head Allen Dulles. Ethnarch Makarios, meanwhile, was active in presenting the Cyprus question before the American public in press interviews, speeches, private contacts with prominent political and diplomatic figures (Spaak included), and through radio and television appearances, including network programs, such as "Meet the Press" (NBC) and "College News Conference" (ABC).[6]

At the request of the Syrian Delegation on October 15, the Assembly had taken up the complaint about threats to the security of Syria and to international peace. The Syrian Delegation claimed that its country was facing a military threat as a result of heavy, unprecedented, and unwarranted concentrations of Turkish troops near the Syrian-Turkish border, as well as from certain provocative acts, such as the violation of Syrian air space by foreign military planes and armed raids from Turkey, into Syrian territory. The Syrian Delegation also charged that Turkey, in co-operation with the United States and certain Western colonial powers, had sought to overthrow the Syrian government. It requested the dispatch to the Syrian-Turkish border of a fact-finding commission to invesigate the situation and report to the Assembly and the Security Council within two weeks after the adoption of this resolution.

During the debate on this complaint, the Greek representative and Member of Parliament, Stratos, stated that his delegation was prepared to vote in favor of the Syrian request.[7] In his speech of October 28, which was based on the sharper of two drafts, to be delivered in the event the Greek representative were to speak before his Soviet colleague—which was the case—Stratos argued that the Arab world should be left alone and that "persistent efforts . . . made" to rescue the Middle East should be abandoned—a shaft clearly directed against Western and U.S. policies at the time, as symbolized by the "Eisenhower Doctrine," to which, as mentioned, Greece had nevertheless adhered. Deploring the virulent resumption of the "cold war," which the Syrian war scare had precipitated, it was high time, he said, to put an end to the dangerous game being played in the Middle East. Reiterating the main theme that the Foreign Minister had developed in his general debate speech of September 26, but with emphasis on Syria rather than Egypt, Stratos stated that the Arab world "should be allowed to develop its economy, and, in particular, its integrity and national pride should be protected for it is understandably sensitive to anything that savors of an obsolete but stubborn and unrepentant colonialism." Furthermore, the Greek representative also took issue with the Turkish contention that the government of any sovereign state had the right to take whatever military measures it believed necessary for its security and that this matter lay within the sphere of a state's domestic jurisdiction. Abnormal military preparations and their concentration along the entire length of a frontier was of equal concern to the country on the other side of the frontier, even if the preparations were for defense. If the latter country believed its security was threatened, the peace of the entire world was involved to a certain extent, he maintained in this speech, which created quite a stir in Greek and allied circles, though the Greek Delegation felt it to have been of value in Greek relations with the Arab countries.[8]

It should be understood, Stratos also said, that it was in no one's interest to divide the Arab world and shatter its unity. Unity did not mean uniformity, but rather a political cohesion of a variety of systems, local ideas, and interests. The unity of the Arab world, he asserted, was a safeguard both for the Arabs and for world peace. "Let there be an end to the attempts to divide or protect them." When the Arab states or Arab peoples really needed protection, they could always apply to the United Nations. "Then we shall all be there, great and small, to show an active and genuinely disinterested solidarity on their behalf." Greece was vitally interested not only in the maintenance of peace in the eastern Mediterranean but also in the development of good-neighborly relations and mutual confidence among all the peoples living in that area. The Greek people had a deep sense of international solidarity, he declared. They understood and were convinced that their own freedom was threatened whenever the freedom of others was threatened.[9]

In a conversation with Lodge next day, Ambassador Palamas saw fit to explain the content of Stratos' speech and drew attention to the critical state of Greek public opinion, especially after the extreme pro-Turkish manifestations of the United States in the General Assembly. The United States, he stressed, should revise its attitude on the Cyprus question in order to avoid any more unpleasant consequences. Lodge fully understood these points, but saw no possibility of a more positive attitude of the State Department on this question.

C. The First Committee Decides When to Consider Item 58

On November 11, the Political Committee, at its 898th meeting, decided the order in which the Cyprus and other items would be considered. Item 58 would be debated after the debate on the two other "colonial" questions, of West Irian and of Algeria. The U.S.S.R.'s item on peaceful coexistence would be discussed last. At this meeting, Stratos, the Greek representative, underlined that, in accordance with rule 100 of the rules of procedure, the Committee should examine all questions that the Assembly had allocated to it and devote the necessary amount of time to each question. The order in which the Committee took up items on its agenda, he added, was important only if a delegation had weighty reasons for requesting priority for a specific item. The Greek Delegation, he declared, did not feel it was in a position to withstand the friendly pressure placed on it to the effect that the Committee should consider the questions of West Irian and Algeria before the Cyprus question. However, in order to insure the observance of the above-mentioned rule, the Greek Delegation requested that not more than a week should be spent in considering each of the remaining agenda items.[10]

Backstage the Indonesians had expressed a desire for the early discussion of the West Irian question, and the Asians and Arabs, pressured by the Algerians, persistently had asked the Greek Delegation's help in getting priority for the Algerian question. What the Greek Delegation wished primarily to avoid was having the Cyprus question discussed last, lest the relevant debate be too much compressed by the terms of the closing date of the twelfth Assembly's session. Deputy Minister Kuznetsov, of the Soviet Delegation, was of help in this. After a *démarche* of the Greek Delegation, he agreed that the Cyprus question be considered before the Soviet item on peaceful coexistence, though, as he stressed, he attached special importance to his government's item and did not wish it to remain last for discussion. At any rate, he acknowledged that since the Cyprus question concerned more directly the fate of a specific people struggling for freedom, it was reasonable for it to have priority over a matter of a more general political nature.

This time, in contrast to its impatient attitude in 1954 when the Cyprus question was first included in the agenda of the Assembly,[11] the Greek government, in its desire to see all margins for political settlement exhausted, was not unhappy about this delay. It still hoped that, after the Turkish elections (October 27), the new government would have time to give signs of reasonable, conciliatory intentions, instead of continuing to insist on the partition of Cyprus—even though, in certain political circles there was some skepticism about this likelihood.

D. Backstage Talks with the U.S., British, Indian, and Turkish Delegations

Meanwhile, until the day arrived for the Political Committee to take up the Cyprus item for discussion, the Greek Delegation did not set aside this matter. It explored ways of handling the delicate issue of violations of human rights in Cyprus by the colonial authorities, and means by which perhaps it might derive certain advantages by refraining in general from too harsh a logomachy in the debate. After the Foreign Minister's return to New York on November 11 a new round of Greek contacts with other delegations was noted.[12]

It will be recalled that the handling of charges of British atrocities, brutalities, or tortures committed against, or inflicted upon, Cypriots by the British security forces in Cyprus had troubled the mind of the Greek Foreign Minister at the stage of the inclusion of the Cyprus item in the Assembly's agenda. Such charges, the Greek Delegation realized, could generate an unfavorable climate during the debate and jeopardize the possibilities of adoption by the Political Committee of a draft resolution that would include the mention of self-determination. This question of human rights violations had constituted a controversial issue, which since 1956 had been drawn to the attention of the delegations. After the eleventh Assembly, the issue had been publicized further, as mentioned earlier,[13] especially through Makarios' press conference in Athens on June 19, a response to Governor Harding's *White Paper* of June 11, refuting Greek allegations of acts of brutality by the British forces. Finally, the issue had been crystallized in subitem (b) of the Greek recourse to the United Nations, only to be dissolved, as it were, in the process of passing through the acid voting test of the General Committee, and to be included in the agenda under the whole item's neutral title.[14]

Nevertheless, the Greek Delegation still felt that the threat of further development of this theme—like that of British intelligence activities mentioned earlier about which the Greek government had printed a booklet, which it never circulated[15]—could serve as leverage against the British. It held that, if this theme were to be the object of some particular Greek purpose after the debate in the Political Committee had started, the logical thing to do would be to submit a special draft resolution on the subject. Although such a course of action would cause displeasure among many friendly delegations—because of the possible moral humiliation and exposure of Britain, which belonged to the Free World—such matters constituted for all delegations quite a fearful political difficulty. This difficulty would now be piled on to those that already inhered in the substance of the Cyprus question and were considerable. Only the Communist delegations would exploit this opportunity to intensify their attacks against the West. Thus, debating the question of atrocities and submitting, furthermore, a draft resolution on this matter would tend to be counterproductive and lead to the risk of losing some friendly votes.

A conversation of November 20 between Ethnarch Makarios and the Greek Foreign Minister reveals several of the political and moral dilemmas the Greek government faced in dealing with this matter. The Foreign Minister, referring to the reasons mentioned above, explained to Makarios that intensive use of the subject of British atrocities could harm the handling of the Cyprus question. He expressed the view that during the debate he could perhaps refer in a vivid fashion to the past but stated he would not exploit the issue to the hilt inasmuch as, since the recourse to the United Nations had been submitted, the Labour party had committed itself to self-determination and the Greek Delegation did not wish to offend it. Besides, the person mainly responsible for those atrocities, Governor Sir John Harding, had been recalled—defeated—and the Greek government was now waiting to see what the policies of the new Governor would be. Sir Hugh Foot was regarded as a Liberal. Finally, the Council of Europe—its Commission of Human Rights—had seized itself of the Greek recourse on this matter, and the Greek government hoped this question would be investigated by that international body. The Foreign Minister further explained that such a presentation would lessen the Eastern bloc's possibilities of exploiting the question of atrocities, would create a favorable atmosphere in the United Nations and facilitate the handling of the Cyprus question.

Makarios, however, disagreed with the Foreign Minister's arguments. He considered that the Labour party promises regarded the future. One could not drop valuable arguments in exchange for an uncertain future. Second, Harding's departure still left intact many illiberal emergency measures, and only through a denunciation of these measures was it possible to protect the population. Third, should the Greek Delegation fail to denounce the British atrocities, it would give the impression that it had no solid facts in its possession to substantiate its charges. Besides, the concern of the Allies about the annoyance created in Greece by the Cyprus question would be lessened. Makarios also maintained that there was no positive hope of getting a favorable resolution from the United Nations or of achieving some progress in the matter, in exchange for not being a nuisance. Finally, public opinion in Greece and primarily in Cyprus would not forgive the non-use of the subject of tortures, and intolerable and dangerous criticism would ensue.

On his side, the Foreign Minister told Makarios he had been authorized by the Greek government to handle this issue of atrocities in the best way possible; that he had not yet reached a decision on the matter; that he would give more thought to it, and would refer it to Athens, after receiving the views of other Ambassadors—in London, Washington, and at NATO.

The aforementioned London, Washington, and NATO diplomatic missions supported the moderate views of the Foreign Minister. Ambassador Seferiadis, for instance, cabling from London on November 23, observed that the issue of atrocities should be be dealt with according to its usefulness in the Cyprus question but stressed that taking up this issue at the Assembly would unavoidably be exploited by Iron Curtain countries, with certain advantages accruing to the Turks. And the Turks were the main difficulty in the entire question. Also, in an atmosphere that included reports that Makarios might be allowed to return to Cyprus (though these reports turned out to be premature), and Labour party hopefulness concerning the new Governor, it would be undesirable to provide the opponent with arguments to the effect that, because of the Greek attitude, good intentions had been prevented from materializing. In his view then, from his vantage point and under the circumstances, the United Nations was not the suitable forum for raising the issue. Besides, the representative of the Ethnarch in London believed that presenting a case of British atrocities before the United Nations would damage the Cypriot and Greek position with British public opinion, regardless of political colorations.

Because, however, Ethnarch Makarios insisted, and, because, according to reports of the Greek Consul in Nicosia, the dropping of the atrocities issue would cause bitter disappointment in Cyprus and create the impression that the Greek Delegation was abandoning the defense of a question in which Cypriot public opinion was extremely sensitive, the Foreign Minister finally decided to use the theme more widely in the debate than he had originally intended. It is worthy of note that Makarios had held that it would be preferable to lose five to eight votes in the Political Committee rather than refrain from presenting this theme of atrocities before the United Nations. The Greek Permanent Mission, at any rate, which had been systematically gathering data, through the Greek Consulate in Nicosia, about what it regarded as violations of Resolution 1013 (XI) by the British authorities, had, since August, arranged for the printing of a Black Book. Published by the Ethnarchy, copies of it were sent to all delegations a few days before the debate started.

The possibility of introducing a draft resolution on atrocities was not neglected either. It was judged more expedient, though, not to table it from the outset but to keep it in reserve, depending on developments during the debate and as a response to expected denials of charges by the British Delegation. It was at the same time realized that introducing such a resolution would pose new problems for the various delegations in the matter of deciding whether the proposed censure of Britain did not pertain to matters that lay essentially within the domestic jurisdiction of Britain. Also, since the Commission of Human Rights of the Council of Europe, in mid-October, had decided to deal with the same issue, questions of conflicting jurisdictions could arise.

In view of the difficulties and dangers that inhered in the debates on the Cyprus question (not only because of the atrocities theme, which would be included in them with some moderation), the Greek Foreign Minister more generally regarded it his duty to explore other means, too, for avoiding an acrimonious debate. The Greek government, under Premier Karamanlis, politically persisting in its alliances and in the steadfast orientation of its policy toward the West, was, naturally, interested in avoiding a crisis that could create insuperable difficulties and harm the Cypriot cause as well as weaken more vitally the ties of Greece with its allies. Of course, the Greek Delegation would struggle with all the determination it could summon in order to succeed in its objective. But Greece did not control the affairs of the United Nations. Nor were the dangers limited to the failure of the Greek Delegation's efforts. The greatest and most serious danger was the recognition of Turkey as a party concerned in the Cyprus question and the adoption by the United Nations of a relevant resolution that would confer upon Turkey such a title. Another most undesirable outcome would be the rejection of a draft proposal referring to the need of applying to Cyprus the principle of self-determination. This would enable the British and Turkish governments to justify their arguments to the effect that Britain was not obligated to make any concessions to the Cypriot people because the United Nations had rejected self-determination. Such an argument could delay even more the evolution of the question. Moreover, it could justify the policy of the Conservative government vis-à-vis the Labour party.

Both the Permanent Mission and the Foreign Minister himself studied carefully all these consequences of an unfavorable outcome of the debate in the Assembly. The head of the Permanent Mission of Greece to the UN, having in mind the consequences of failure, had suggested that the Greek Delegation keep open the possibility of a retreat to a second line of defense, if at some point it seemed clear that there was danger lest Turkey be recognized as a party concerned or self-determination be outvoted. In general, it was realized that the conditions in which the battle for self-determination would be waged were so difficult that it was indispensable to be prepared for any contingency. Possible failure could have adverse effects for the persons handling the case, but should in no way affect adversely the Cypriot case.

Ethnarch Makarios, it should be stressed, was kept posted of all these various deliberations of the Greek Delegation on the eve of the debate of the Cyprus question in the Political Committee of the General Assembly, and he, like Grivas, expressed the view that the battle for self-determination had to be waged regardless of the danger of not getting a simple majority even in that Committee. What mattered, in his view, was not so much the result as the way in which the battle would be fought.

In exploring means for deriving certain advantages by offering to refrain from generally bitter polemics, the Greek Foreign Minister, after careful study, formulated, for presentation to the American and British Delegations, two alternative proposals. Although these could be regarded as dangerous for the opponents, they would, if rejected, at least testify to the good will and desire of the Greek Delegation to avoid, out of consideration for the more general Allied interest, a debate that risked poisoning even more the relations of Greece with its allies.

Accordingly, on November 26, the Foreign Minister, in a conversation with Ambassador Lodge, in the presence of Ambassador Palamas and Counsellor William R. Tyler, Director of the Office of Western European Affairs, after drawing attention to the acrimony that the debate would inevitably have, and to his own determination to insist at all costs that a Greek draft resolution referring to self-determination be put to the vote, made the following proposals: Bitterness in the debate would be avoided either if the antagonists accepted a draft resolution that included an explicit mention of self-determination, without, however, any reference to when self-determination should be implemented, or if the British Delegate made an official statement that talks would start between the British government and the Cypriot people, in order to search for a solution in accordance with the principles of the UN Charter. After such a British statement, the Greek Delegation (in what it regarded its last line of retreat) would limit the debate and propose the adoption of a draft resolution that would include the text of the aforementioned statement. In urging such an approach, the Foreign Minister stressed earlier arguments used in talks with U.S. officials to the effect that neither Greece nor the United States nor other states could deny something that the British, through the Labour party, had promised to apply some day.[16] Lodge promised to study this suggestion and recommend it to the State Department. He showed sympathetic understanding of the issue, which deeply disturbed him. Makarios, it should be added, had approved of both these alternative proposals. Indeed, he regarded the second one, which defined the parties concerned, of such outstanding value, were it accepted, that he now would be willing to forego any mention of the issue of atrocities.

A day later, Lodge, who had not only shown a lively interest in the two Greek proposals but had submitted a favorable report on them to the State Department, and had followed up the matter in talks with the British Delegation, emphasized, at a dinner, the frankness, moderation, and alliance-mindedness of the Greek Foreign Minister. A copy of Lodge's report was received shortly afterward by G. V. Melas, the Greek Ambassador in Washington. The latter, on the same day Averoff-Tossizza

met with Lodge, had conferred with the Greek Desk Officer at the State
Department on the matter of the U.S. attitude on the Cyprus question
during the forthcoming debate in the Political Committee. The United
States, the Greek envoy had been informed, desired the most moderate
debate possible but recognized that aspects of substance inevitably
would be dealt with in it. Therefore, it could not oppose a detailed
exposition of views on both sides. As for the resolution itself, the State
Department would like it to be drafted along lines as close as possible to
those of the previous Assembly's Resolution 1013 (XI). At the same time,
the United States was aware of the need for certain improvements in
wording, which would not touch on the substance of the resolution, but
would make it more palatable to Greek and Cypriot public opinion.
Eight days earlier, it may be added, Murphy and Rountree had told the
representative of the Cypriot Ethnarchy, Rossides, that the United States
would be happy with far less: the adoption of no resolution at all by the
Assembly.

Advised by the U.S. Delegation about the Greek proposals of November 26, the British Delegation got in touch with the Greek Delegation for
a mutual exploration of intentions in view of the imminent debate on the
Cyprus question. On November 27 a meeting took place attended not
only by the Greek Foreign Minister and British Undersecretary
of State, Noble, but also by the chiefs of the respective permanent
missions to the UN, Sir Pierson Dixon, and Palamas, and the First
Secretary to the British Delegation to the UN, A. R. Moore. The Britishers stated they wished to be informed about the Greek views concerning
possibilities of reaching an understanding about the debate, in order not
to harm the course of the Cyprus question, and said they had had a
similar conversation with the Turkish Delegation. In reply, Averoff-
Tossizza proceeded first to a general and lengthy review of the Cyprus
problem. He explained that both the current and succeeding Greek
governments would persist in their effort to reach a solution of it by
self-determination and that there was a strong desire to revive friendly
relations with all allies and especially with Britain (in this connection, he
recounted the efforts made on the Greek side in order not to damage the
preconditions for such a revival). His government, he added, was inspired by a like desire with regard to relations with Turkey—which,
however, was not reciprocating but was assuming an unreasonable stand.
At this point, the Foreign Minister reiterated the ways in which his government proposed to cover Turkey's objective interests, and observed
that neither Secretary of State Dulles nor any one else had mentioned
any other such objective interests of Turkey. But Turkey, he continued,
was asking for either a part or the whole of Cyprus, or its maintenance
under the colonial regime. Such claims the Greek government could never
accept, because it considered them unjust and imperialistic. Averoff-
Tossizza then turned to the subject of the internal difficulties that his
government faced in the Cyprus question. Neither the British nor the

Turks faced such difficulties with regard to their own domestic audiences, he maintained. He also dwelt on the grave dangers that hung over the island, if, because of the disappointment of the Cypriots with the United Nations or NATO, the struggle began again—as he was certain it would. After the arming of the Turkish minority, this struggle would develop into a Greek-Turkish conflict on Cyprus.

More specifically, with regard to the debate in the United Nations, the Greek Foreign Minister explained the reasons he could not forego references to British atrocities. He could, however, recommend to his government a moderate and very brief debate, first if agreement could be reached for the adoption by the United Nations of a resolution calling for the application of the principle of self-determination in the case of Cyprus. When asked for more precise details, he said that the wording of such a resolution might be very cautious so that this document would not call for the immediate application of that principle, but at least would include an explicit mention of self-determination. He expressed surprise that the British and especially the allies were unwilling to make such a gesture, which would facilitate agreement during the transitional period, inasmuch as the Labour party, by its statement of policy on Cyprus, had committed itself to the idea that Britain, some day, should apply the principle of self-determination to the people of that island. Second, and as an alternative to the first proposal, matters in the Assembly debate would be facilitated, he said, if, at the beginning of the debate, the British were willing to announce that the order prohibiting the return of Makarios and of his companions to Cyprus would be rescinded and that the new Governor of Cyprus would start talks with representatives of the Cypriot people in order to find a solution in accordance with the principles of the UN Charter. In response to such a statement, he, the Greek Foreign Minister, believed he could get his government's authorization to declare in the United Nations that, if it was possible for such a statement of the British Delegation to constitute the text of a draft resolution, he could see no reason for prolonging the debate, in the hope of favorable developments. Without a resolution that would in substance express one of the alternative proposals he had outlined, he would be obliged, much to his regret, to wage a very lively debate in which he would sincerely try to avoid envenoming the atmosphere, though he could not be sure of the extent to which he would succeed in this.

The British officials asked for certain clarifications of a secondary importance, thanked the Greek Foreign Minister for having spoken as he had, and promised to study the proposals. They neither committed themselves nor assumed a negative attitude, nor took refuge behind arguments of Turkish intransigence. This, together with a remark by Turkish Delegate Sarper at a reception later that afternoon to the effect that another talk with the British should be expected, and that afterward a talk with the Turks ought to take place, made the Greek officials wonder whether a change in attitude toward Turkey was taking place. A slight new development in the Spaak plan—mentioned elsewhere [17]—added strength to this conjecture.

But these wishful thoughts were dispelled next day when First Secretary of the British Delegation Moore telephoned Ambassador Palamas and inquired whether his impression was correct that the Greek Foreign Minister had spoken about a possible agreement between Britain, Greece, and Turkey for avoiding an acrimonious debate. He was preparing his report to the Foreign Office and wished to have the above confirmation. With scarcely concealed anger, the Greek diplomat replied that the Foreign Minister had never mentioned such a thing, and, if Moore reported nonexistent matters, there was a grave danger lest the atmosphere, instead of becoming calmer, grow tenser. He then repeated the main points of the two Greek proposals and drew Moore's attention to the need of avoiding absolutely any misunderstanding on such delicate matters.

On December 2, when Secretary of State Dulles, in Washington, received the Greek Foreign Minister, with Ambassador G. V. Melas, Rountree, Francis O. Wilcox, Assistant Secretary of State for International Organization Affairs, and two aides present, both sides supported the same arguments and no new element emerged. Dulles, though smiling and in a good mood, at the outset at least, was careful to avoid giving any promises when the Greek Foreign Minister asked for U.S. help both in the substance of the Cyprus question and in the United Nations resolution. The Secretary of State mentioned the gravity of the consequences of the subject, and the American interest in the matter. He considered the British government sincere in its efforts to find a solution but could say nothing about the stand of the American government in the United Nations, because he had not dealt with this matter—except that it would try to accomplish something constructive and, if this proved impossible, see to it that no harm be done. The special discussion with Rountree extended to economic matters. The American official praised the achievements of the Greek government in the economic sector and said that the U.S. government had occupied itself with aid a great deal and would somehow respond to the Greek requests. With regard to the Cyprus question, he did mention the expediency of tripartite negotiations because through them, he maintained, the British would exert pressure on the Turks. In his talk with Dulles, the Greek Foreign Minister had also put forward his government's position and views on the Middle East and had explained its stand in the Syrian affair. Greece, he said, had not been overly upset by the Soviet sputnik (of October 4), but feared far more the Middle Eastern situation, because this was not being faced, and if it deteriorated and the Middle East were fully infiltrated, then Europe would be enslaved because of its dependence on Middle Eastern oil, Asia would be cut off, and Africa would become the next area of infiltration.

At the United Nations next day, December 3, Noble and Sir Pierson Dixon advised the Greek Delegation of the British reply to the two Greek alternative proposals of November 27. This was altogether negative. The British government could not accept the proposals, the British officials said. And they had not yet made up their minds what sort of draft resolution on the Cyprus question they would support. The Greek Foreign Minister, on his side, said he would persist in a resolution that referred to the principle of self-determination. Should this receive an absolute majority in the Political Committee, as he expected it would, this would help the British with the Turks, if the latter really wished to become reasonable, he observed. The British let it be understood they could not promise negotiations with the Cypriots if violence broke out again. The Foreign Minister replied he was not responsible for what was happening on the island, and some acts of violence could be ascribed to the Turks of Cyprus. The British officials also inquired whether negotiations between the three parties and with the Cypriots might be mentioned. Averoff-Tossizza responded by saying he could commit no one on such a delicate issue but was of the opinion that this was a matter of intention and formulation. If it clearly followed from the formulation that the Cypriots constituted the main factor in the negotiations, and that the other matters would be discussed with the other parties concerned, the idea could be considered. To the British inquiry of whether sharpness in debate on the Greek side would be due to disagreements over the issue or to internal, domestic reasons (for domestic consumption), the Foreign Minister replied that such a tone would be due to disagreements, since the Greek government was unable to accept the basis of tripartite discussions and a solution that did not include the principle of self-determination and they—the British—took a negative stand. Domestic factors were matters not of demagogy but of political realism. No one in Cyprus would be able to understand why the Greek Delegation did not exploit in the United Nations the issue of British atrocities, which were facts. Generally, as the Greek Delegation saw it, the essence of the British view was that the debate in the United Nations should not be harmful to the course of the Cyprus question. For this purpose, the British Delegation hoped to be able to speak first in the Political Committee—having submitted such a request a fortnight earlier. The Greek Foreign Minister replied that he agreed that all efforts possible should be made not to exacerbate the debate but that he would try to speak first, not giving significance to what the British would say, as long as he considered they did nothing to promote the political substance of the question.

After the British Delegation had rejected the alternative Greek proposals that were designed to lessen the likelihood of acrimonious discussion in the United Nations, at a price, the Greek Foreign Minister, that same day, recommended to Premier Karamanlis in Athens that the draft resolution urging self-determination for the people of Cyprus be supported to the end, and that any attempt to block a vote on this should be opposed, as well as any other resolution. He predicted in the Political Committee

30–35 votes in favor of such a resolution; 27–30 against it, with 17–25 abstentions. The toughest problem, however, would arise when this recommendation of the Political Committee came up for a vote in the Assembly. The result of the voting in the Political Committee would have a bearing on this matter. If no great reduction in the number of favorable votes appeared likely in the Assembly, he would not attach much importance to the rejection by that body of a draft resolution that referred to self-determination. As for the debate itself, it should, in principle, be quite sharp with a reasonable use of the topic of British atrocities but not to such an extent as to cause harm to allied circles. Whether, of course, further debate could be kept within these limits would depend on the acerbity of the British and Turkish speeches. For tactical reasons, only after the beginning of the debate and in response to expected denials of these charges on the part of the British Delegation, did he intend to propose the setting up of a committee to investigate the charges of atrocities. According to his information, the delegations of the Soviet bloc member states would seek to exploit the subject of atrocities. However, the nature of these would not allow too great an exploitation. The Greek Delegation could set aside its own draft resolution only if another proposal was presented that would constitute a positive step forward and would be adopted by the great majority of member states. The members of the Soviet bloc, he noted, did not seem inclined to vote this time in favor of a compromise draft proposal, even though this might be of a constructive nature, but wished to bring to a vote a draft resolution that referred to self-determination. After asking for instructions on the course of action he had outlined above—on such delicate matters, Averoff-Tossizza believed, his cabinet colleagues, too, should express their views—he informed the Prime Minister that he intended to deposit next day (December 4) with the Secretariat the Greek draft resolution as a precaution against the contingency of another draft resolution being deposited first, which then would enjoy priority rights in being put to the vote (under rule 132 of the rules of procedure of the General Assembly).[18]

At a meeting of the whole Greek Delegation and the staff members of the Permanent Greek Mission to the United Nations on December 4, Averoff-Tossizza issued his final instructions on the course of action to be followed. Since there was no other way out to achieve progress in the Cyprus question through a United Nations resolution, it was necessary, he said, to support a draft resolution that aimed at self-determination, even though the final rejection of this resolution by the Assembly would have undesirable results. In essence, it was a matter of choosing between two evils: A majority in favor of the resolution was likely in the Political Committee, though a change for the worse would not be excluded, or even a rejection, in case the United States assumed an unfavorable or very hostile attitude. Should a small majority be achieved in the Political Committee the postponement of a decision by the Assembly would be

preferable. One could not, however, be sure of obtaining this postponement, he said. The decision would depend on the number of votes
obtained in the Committee and the atmosphere that prevailed at the
time. Except for the Greek Ambassador to Washington, who believed it
unlikely that a majority would be obtained for the Greek draft resolution
in the Political Committee and regarded the rejection by the full Assembly of a resolution recommending self-determination as basically undesirable for the entire Cyprus question, all present at this meeting concurred in this plan of action.

Quite consistently with the tactics of trying to prevent Turkey from
being brought into the Cyprus question as a party concerned, the Greek
Delegation did not seek out the Turkish Delegation at the Assembly for
soundings and exchanges of views, much less for bargaining purposes.
Nor did such soundings occur outside the forum of the United Nations.
Yet this did not mean that no contacts at all with the Turkish Delegation
took place at the United Nations. One such contact, at a reception of
November 26, has been already mentioned. But there were others too.
Thus, on November 19 and 25, two talks occurred between Greek and
Turkish officials, Ambassadors Palamas and Sarper. Moreover, on De-
cember 4, at the request of the Turkish Delegation, a meeting took place
between the heads of the two delegations attended by their aids.

At both the first and the second of these Greek-Turkish meetings, the
Turkish Ambassador urged postponing the debate on the Cyprus question in the United Nations, to create the relaxation that was indispensable for finding a solution. To buttress his argument, he invoked the
extremely critical international situation (the Syrian crisis, no doubt;
perhaps, too, the achievements of the U.S.S.R. in military technology as
revealed by the successful test-firing of an intercontinental ballistic
missile announced on August 26, and the launching of the sputnik on
October 4). At the second of the above meetings, the Turkish Ambassador also stated that the Cyprus question would be discussed at the
upcoming summit meeting of the NATO Council but did not wish to say
under what guise it would be raised. In the United Nations, he said, the
question could be debated the following year, and Britain and Turkey
would be glad to back a Greek proposal for postponement. Ambassador
Palamas, on both occasions, excluded any such possibility of postponement
under existing conditions. At the first of the above two encounters, it
should be added, Sarper launched a long tirade against Makarios. After
discussion, though, he had to admit that the Ethnarch's actions had been
very moderate, especially within the framework of the United Nations,
where he had avoided creating difficulties and maintained a very dignified
attitude. When the Greek diplomat stressed that Makarios constituted a
political capital without which no solution would be possible, the Turkish diplomat acknowledged that this perhaps was true. What irked him,
though, was that Makarios proclaimed everywhere that Turkey had no

right to interfere in Cyprus and that Britain caused the interference. This was a dangerous mistake, he said. It provoked a fierce reaction in Turkey. The Cyprus question could not be solved without agreement with Turkey. The Turkish diplomat with some signs of anxiety also inquired about the Greek government's impressions of Sir Hugh Foot, the newly appointed Governor of the island. The Greek official replied that since Sir Hugh had not got down to work, no particular impression could be formed. The information about him, however, was rather good. Clearly annoyed, Sarper said that even good can do evil. Matters were not so simple as his Greek colleague thought.

At the meeting between the Greek Foreign Minister and Ambassador Sarper on December 4, with Ambassador Palamas and a number of Turkish diplomats also present, the Turkish Delegate observed that the Cyprus question would not be solved by the United Nations. The purpose of meeting, though, was to exchange views so that the debate and the resolution that ensued should not render a solution more difficult. In this conversation, which lasted for over an hour, the most substantial points were Turkish assertions that regardless of internal policy or of the recourse to the UN nobody could solve the Cyprus question unless the three governments of Britain, Greece, and Turkey reached an agreement. Hence, as long as this was certain, it would be better to accept a unanimous resolution of the United Nations recommending negotiations between the three parties to be mentioned by name so that the question could actually be promoted and the situation not be rendered more intractable because of the debate.

The Greek Foreign Minister, in a lively fashion, countered by saying he was convinced of exactly the contrary. The course of History would impose the application of self-determination in Cyprus in spite of Turkey's reaction and in spite of the fact that Turkey was an important factor in the Middle East and had certain interests in Cyprus that had to be taken into account. From the very outset, Greece had believed this. It did even more so now, after the Labour party, through its Brighton policy statement on Cyprus, had clearly committed itself to the principle of self-determination. Averoff-Tossizza also stressed that his government sincerely believed that the question concerned first of all the Cypriots themselves. For by their refusal, they could render useless any solution upon which Greece, Britain, and Turkey had reached agreement beforehand. Finally, he emphasized the common interest in good Greek-Turkish relations and the exclusively conciliatory character of the Greek draft resolution that recommended negotiations between the British government and the Cypriots.

The Turkish officials, on their side, maintained they were not worried by the Labour party's views on Cyprus expressed at Brighton.[19] On the other hand, forecasting that the Greek draft resolution urging self-determination for Cyprus would not get more than twenty affirmative votes, they expressed concern lest the Greek Delegation expose itself thus to a defeat, with the Soviet bloc countries as its main allies. Purposely, the Greek Foreign Minister (his forecasts about the outcome of the voting differed, as mentioned above) said perhaps the Greek draft resolution would not get more votes than those predicted by the Turkish officials. For domestic reasons, however, he preferred such a defeat—in which case, in the absence of another resolution, the previous one, 1013 (XI), would remain valid. The Turkish diplomats countered by saying that such an event would make matters more difficult for the Turkish government internally because if the United Nations were to reject self-determination, the Opposition and the more extreme elements in the government would become more uncompromising. Averoff-Tossizza responded by saying that History would correct this drawback too.

Concerning the forthcoming debate on the Cyprus item in the United Nations, the Turkish officials said they had instructions from their government not to exacerbate it, unless the Greek representatives did. Personal attacks would be avoided, except in retaliation. The Greek Foreign Minister assured them he would follow the same tactics, but, he warned, insults against Ethnarch Makarios would provoke a sharp reaction. The Turks responded by saying they would comment only on some of the Archbishop's statements, and asked the Greeks not to be too categorical in formulating their position. Averoff-Tossizza answered he would neither insult nor hurt their dignity but would be unable not to be categorical as long as the Greek position was clear. In conclusion, the Counsellor of the Permanent Turkish Mission, Turgut Menemencioglou, outlined the main points of the speech which Ambassador Sarper intended to deliver at the opening of the debate. The tenor of the outline was, indeed, moderate.

Several matters incidental to the substance of the Cyprus question which Ambassador Sarper and his colleagues had mentioned during this meeting struck the Greek Foreign Minister as noteworthy. First, Premier Menderes was said to have been criticized as having abandoned his old position of favoring the maintenance of the status quo and having accepted partition instead as a solution to the Cyprus problem. The supposed evils of independence for Cyprus were mentioned—to which Averoff-Tossizza had replied it was unnecessary for him to reject this assertion, because for the Cypriots the question would be, if independence were achieved, when and how could it come to an end, so that they might finally be able to express their own will about their future. (Independence was still considered by the Greek government at this point as merely a transitory stage prior to the free exercise of the right of self-determination.) Thirdly, Sarper had stressed the danger of Soviet intervention in Cyprus—a possibility that the Foreign Minister denied. It was also interesting that when Averoff-Tossizza had explained the measures that the Greek government proposed to take in order to safeguard the legitimate interests of Turkey in Cyprus, the Turkish Ambassador had not replied, as the Turks had always done, that these measures were inadequate. He had merely stated that, as an Ambassador who did not find himself on the same level as the Foreign Minister, he could not discuss these points, though these could be discussed in Paris, at the summit meeting of the NATO Council. In this connection, Sarper had pointed out that until the NATO Council session started on December 14 two days were available during which it might be possible to discuss the Cyprus question behind the scenes since Premier Menderes was arriving in Paris the evening of December 12. Finally, the Turkish Permanent Representative to the UN, Ambassador Esin, in reply to the Greek Foreign Minister's remarks about the indispensability of prior recognition of the principle of self-determination, had repeatedly spoken in what seemed to the Greek an odd way, in a manner that did not exclude a tacit or some other sort of covert recognition of this principle. In reporting this conversation to Athens, however, Averoff-Tossizza hesitated, wondering whether he should ascribe any particular significance to such vague statements. Was a diversionary maneuver involved? He could not say. The matter was worth reporting, though, because of the source. Generally, the impression he had derived from this conversation was that the Turks had not abandoned their intransigent attitude, though they had dropped their arrogant tone. No one could say whether this was a good omen or just the result of allied pressures.

The above Greek-Turkish meeting of December 4 at the United Nations, during which Ambassador Sarper gave the impression that his government was angling for talks between Averoff-Tossizza and Zorlu in Paris, took place at a not very propitious moment in Greek-Turkish relations, but in an atmosphere bristling with signs of acute Turkish discontent and of insistence on partition. The Greek government interpreted these signs as a negative reaction to Spaak's proposals on the Cyprus question, which the British government had communicated to the Turkish government at about this time.[20] Because of the concrete effects of this Turkish reaction, Averoff-Tossizza, on November 30, had instructed the Greek Embassy in Washington to draw the State Department's attention to incendiary editorials, published in both governmental and Opposition Turkish newspapers, which incited the Turks against the Greek element in Istanbul and against the Patriarchate of Constantinople; to the deportation of a number of Greek traders and journalists established in that city for several decades; and to the fact that the newly-formed Menderes government had restored to positions of authority almost all those officials who had been politically and administratively responsible for the anti-Greek riots of September 6, 1955, in Istanbul. The Greek government emphasized that on its side it was seeking to the best of its ability to restrain the anger of the Greek press—which was really free—and that it continued taking solicitous care of the welfare of the Turkish minority in Thrace. The State Department was asked to make appropriate recommendations to the Turkish government. A similar démarche was made with NATO's Secretary-General.

As for Turkish Foreign Minister Zorlu, he maintained, in response to a protest of December 6 by the Greek Ambassador, Pesmazoglou, in Ankara, that the deportees had committed acts dangerous to the state. And he promised to provide evidence for this. Orders had been issued, Zorlu added, that the deportees be given a forty-eight hours' advance notice. These instructions, he said, did not indicate any intention of continued deportations but were of a preventive character against any contingency. The Turkish Foreign Minister asked the Greek Ambassador to reassure his government that no prescribed plan existed for deporting Greek citizens from Turkey. With regard to the press attacks against the Greek minority in Istanbul, he ascribed these to contraband in foreign exchange carried out and to provocative profits made by the Greek element established there (under the Treaty of Establishment of 1930).[21] He would be justified, he said further, in complaining about attacks against the President of Turkey and the Premier that had appeared in the Greek press.

A few days later the Turkish Foreign Minister was informed that the Greek government and public opinion were not satisfied with the explanations given for the deportations. The recurrence of new, similar arbitrary measures, the Greek government warned, would inevitably cause a serious regression of efforts to restore tranquil relations between the two countries.

On December 6, Averoff-Tossizza, accompanied by Ambassador Palamas, met with Krishna Menon and Ambassador Arthur S. Lall. The Indian Defense Minister said he would abstain from voting on a Greek draft resolution referring to self-determination. He again insisted that the Greek Delegation should use Article 73 of the Charter, to push Cyprus forward to independence. The Greek Foreign Minister, however, replied that Article 73 recognized a situation, the abolition of which was being sought by the Cypriots, and that only the Cypriot people could decide on independence or any other solution.

The evening of that same day, after reports emanating from British and American circles in the United Nations to the effect that a text acceptable to the Greek Delegation would be drafted, the Greek Foreign Minister was invited to see Ambassador Lodge late in the afternoon. With four advisers present on his side, Lodge announced he was happy to say that the American efforts with the British had been fruitful. He had obtained from the British Delegation a statement which, he was sure, the Greek Delegation would regard as satisfactory, and which would be included in the speech to be delivered by the British representative before the Political Committee. Containing in essence a promise of negotations with the Cypriots for self-government, not self-determination, and tripartite talks for finding a solution acceptable to the three parties, the draft of this proposed British statement was as follows:

Her Majesty's Government have long been trying to move toward self-government in the island. Over the years we have had discussions with Cypriot leaders on this and the offers of discussion which we have made remain open and can be taken up at any time.

But the Cyprus problem is not a straightforward colonial problem of the kind we are dealing with—not without success—in other parts of the world. For reasons which we all know well and which I need not repeat, it has also become an international question affecting the relations between Greece and Turkey, and the United Kingdom. The solution which we seek is one acceptable to the three governments and to the peoples of Cyprus and to achieve this end we are ready to enter into discussions at the appropriate time with all concerned.

Although this statement seemed to contain certain constructive proposals, it was in essence unacceptable to the Greek Delegation. The Greek Foreign Minister said so immediately, adding that, at any rate, he would refer it to Athens. He explained that the proposed text added nothing really, because, though it mentioned negotiations with the Cypriots, it also mentioned solutions acceptable to the three governments concerned. Lodge seemed very disappointed. He did not seem quite to understand the Greek attitude. As for Averoff-Tossizza, he was disturbed lest rejecting such a proposal which had a reasonable and attractive appearance create the impression that the Greek Delegation was intractable—with, possibly, a resultant loss of votes in the Political Committee. Could it have been that Lodge had not well understood the content of the two alternative Greek proposals made to him on November 26? His good faith could in no way be impugned. These were some of the questions that puzzled members of the Greek Delegation. Lodge, at any rate, asked the Greek Delegation to propose an amended text that it would regard as acceptable, and Averoff-Tossizza promised to do so, though, he warned, he saw no hope that the British would accept his amended text.

In order to dispel any possible further misunderstanding, the Greek Delegation also decided to accompany the text of its proposed amendment with a covering letter that unequivocally set down the content of the two alternative Greek proposals presented to the American and British Delegations, respectively, on November 26 and 27. In this letter it was pointed out that the first paragraph of the proposed British statement mentioned self-government, not self-determination, even though it was well known that the negotiations held in Cyprus in 1955–56 between Ethnarch Makarios and Governor Harding dealt mainly with the issue of self-determination.[22] Then, by recognizing Turkey as one of the principal factors in the problem, the proposed British statement granted Turkey a veto power over any solution. The Greek government adhered to the view that the people of Cyprus had an unrestricted right to determine its own future, and the Greek government was not entitled to alienate this right. This, of course, did not mean that the legitimate interests of any other country that might be affected by any prospective solution should not be duly and fully covered. Thirdly, while the proposed statement made no mention at all of self-determination—the main issue—it indirectly endorsed the Turkish thesis by referring to the "peoples" (in the plural) of Cyprus—in an attempt to give to the Turkish minority an equal status to that of the majority. As all knew, in Cyprus there was only one people, the Cypriot people, consisting of a Greek majority of 80 per cent and of a Turkish minority of 18 per cent.

The Greek Delegation's version of the statement which the British representative might make before the Political Committee read as follows:

Her Majesty's Government have long been trying to find a solution of this issue in conformity with the principles of the Charter. Over the years we have had discussions with Cypriot leaders on this and the offers of discussion which we have made remain open and can be taken up at any time.

In case a solution acceptable to the British Government and to the people of Cyprus, when found, affects the legitimate interest of other countries, its relative international implications will be met through international negotiations.

It was not, of course, astonishing that the British Delegation rejected this version. The very essence of the Greek and Cypriot aims at the United Nations was expressed in the two paragraphs of the above text.

The whole matter could be summed up as follows: through the debate the Greek Delegation wished to obtain either the recognition of the principle of self-determination or the acceptance of bipartite talks between the British government and the Cypriots to implement the principles of the UN Charter. The Greek proposal aimed at getting the British to give the Greeks what they wanted without a debate that could be very unpleasant for the British. That the British should reject the Greek proposals was natural, as long as they believed that, through the debate, Greece, at any rate, would be unable to achieve what it wished to achieve. In this bargaining process, the avoidance of a debate, no matter how painful that debate might be, because of the theme of atrocities, did not constitute a sufficient price for the recognition of the substantive Greek claims. For the Greeks, however, who were aware that the Greek proposal would be unacceptable, the above action had the advantage of giving the impression of conciliatory intentions, and justified the development of the theme of atrocities—since these intentions were not reciprocated by the opponent.

E. Preparing the Greek Draft Resolution

The draft resolution itself was prepared by the Greek Delegation after much study and discussion. It was communicated to Makarios, who fully approved of it in its final form. Its declarative or preambular clauses referred to Resolution 1013 (XI) by expressing the Assembly's concern that "no progress had been made toward the solution of this problem in compliance with the operative paragraph of Resolution 1013 (XI)"—which, as will be recalled, included the expression of hope that negotiations would be resumed in order to find "a peaceful, democratic, and just solution" to the Cyprus problem. The second preambular clause of the draft resolution in a warning against further procrastination, asserted that the situation in Cyprus was "still fraught with danger," and that a speedy solution of the Cyprus question was required in accordance with the principles of the UN Charter in order to secure peace and stability in the area. As for the single operative clause, this literally revived the wording of the Greek draft resolution introduced at the previous Assembly and finally not pressed to a vote. In this clause, the Assembly would express its wish that the people of Cyprus would be given the opportunity to determine its own future by the application of its "right to self-determination." [23] At the very core of the Greek draft resolution lay the concept of self-determination. As long as Greece insisted on this, all other points in the draft were bereft of political significance. They served merely as a framework for self-determination. Reference to that principle or right had been purposely omitted from the draft resolution's preamble. It was estimated that if that concept were mentioned in the preamble, too, it would be easier for the opponents, during the struggle over its adoption, to delete this reference from the operative part and limit it in the preamble through the sort of phrasal framework that is customary in the United Nations. A formal concession would thus be made to the Greek Delegation at the substantial sacrifice of self-determination. The French and U.S. delegations had pressed upon the Asian-Arab states such a device during the debate on the Algerian question, with the result that only the preambular, not the operative part of the relevant resolution contained a reference to self-determination.

Precautions were taken, as mentioned above, to submit this draft resolution to the Secretary of the Political Committee, Dragoslav Protitch, five days before the day scheduled for the debate, in order to insure priority against any other draft resolution that might be submitted by the British or the Turks. It was circulated to the Committee on December 9, the day the debate opened.

When the Greek Cabinet under the chairmanship of Premier Karamanlis cabled from Athens on December 6 its approval of the plan of action that the Foreign Minister had outlined three days earlier, the die was cast. The Greek Delegation was told to insist on its draft resolution that called for the application of the principle of self-determination to the people of Cyprus. No compromise draft resolution should be discussed unless it represented substantial progress and was acceptable to a substantial majority. In case even a small favorable majority was achieved in the Political Committee, the debate and vote on the resolution should, in principle, be pursued in the Assembly, because in such a case it would be

extremely hard to justify any direct or indirect effort to get a postponement of the decision. If, however, the rejection of the Greek draft
resolution by the Assembly was foreseen, then, either a compromise
resolution should be accepted before the Assembly if this was judged
satisfactory, or if this was not satisfactory, a postponement should be
sought. In deciding whether to seek a postponement or to go ahead to a
vote with a danger of rejection, Makarios should be invited to take a
position. Postponement at all costs should be sought if in either the
Political Committee or in the Assembly there seemed to be a chance of a
draft resolution favoring the Turkish views being adopted. With regard
to the theme of atrocities, it was the Greek government's opinion that, in
view of the categorical suggestions of Labour leaders (conveyed through
the Greek Ambassador in London) and reports from Strasbourg, where
the Commission of Human Rights of the Council of Europe was studying
the question, this theme should be handled in a mild and moderate way,
regardless of the demands of domestic consumption and only with the
real interest of the Cyprus question in mind.

On Sunday, December 8, on the eve of the debate, the Foreign Minister sent instructions to all Greek diplomatic authorities abroad asking
them to exert every possible effort to get the government to which they
were accredited to support the demand for Cypriot self-determination.
To diplomatic missions accredited to NATO member states—Britain and
Turkey excepted—he urged emphasis on the argument about the undesirable impression that would be created among the Greek people if all
NATO countries were to vote against the Greek draft resolution. Greek
diplomats in countries in which the political atmosphere appeared more
favorable, were advised to present arguments to the effect that a vote in
favor of the Greek draft resolution would help Britain persuade Turkey
to adopt a less intransigent attitude. In cases of countries in which an
unfavorable political climate prevailed, a request for abstention at least
should be made. In certain cases, Averoff-Tossizza himself sent personal
cables to colleagues of his in NATO countries in an effort to get their
governments' support.

No illusions should be entertained that the debate would not be
extremely tough, the Foreign Minister informed the various Greek diplomatic representatives abroad. Seventeen states had supported the Algerian cause but by procedural devices they had been defeated. In the
Cyprus question, he would try to keep the tone of the debate on a high
level, avoiding gratuitous acerbities. But he would insist that the Greek
draft resolution be put to the vote. Very probably, attempts would be
made to transform this draft into a "colorless" one through the introduction of amendments. Because voting on amendments had a priority over
the voting on the text itself of a draft resolution (under the rules of
procedure of the Assembly), a very dangerous situation could be created.
Through clever formulas, the minds of doubtful delegations could be
swayed, and pressures could be exerted. A still greater danger—the

Greek Delegation had faced it at the previous Assembly—and one which had already raised, as it were, its ugly head backstage, was the effort Turkey was making to obtain the title of a party concerned. This was difficult to deal with. It cunningly appeared in formulas in which the hope was expressed "for a solution acceptable to the three parties concerned" or for "a solution acceptable to the peoples of Cyprus and the three parties concerned." To those who were not aware of the complexities of the Cyprus question, such formulas sounded reasonable. Nevertheless, the struggle to get a sufficient number of votes in favor of the Greek draft resolution, the Foreign Minister estimated would result in a victory in the Political Committee. In the Assembly, however, to obtain the required two thirds of the votes or even an absolute majority of members present and voting was impossible. Yet the Greek Delegation would not retreat unless a draft resolution was presented that was assured of a two-thirds vote in the Assembly and constituted a satisfactory step toward a fair solution of the Cyprus question. Such an outcome, however, did not seem likely, because of Turkey's very bitter opposition to any satisfactory solution.

Part Three

Chapter Eight

December 9:
The Battle in the Committee Begins

A. The 927th Meeting of the First Committee [1]

Uttering words that might nurture an anti-Western spirit would be inevitable, should the United States not maintain a sincere and earnest neutrality both in the matter of amendments to the Greek draft resolution and other procedural devices during the debate of the Cyprus question in the United Nations. So did Averoff-Tossizza cable to Premier Karamanlis on Monday morning, December 9, before going to the United Nations. He was determined to wage a fierce and fair battle, although no one expected a favorable verdict. U.S. chargé d'affaires Penfield, in Athens, should be advised of the Greek attitude. He himself would give instructions for similar *démarches* with the U.S. government to be made through the Greek Embassy in Washington. If such devices were resorted to in order to block the Greek draft resolution from being put to the vote and especially if such devices were aimed at a direct or indirect mention in the draft resolution of Turkey as a party concerned, he would walk out of the Assembly, consulting Makarios prior to taking such a critical step, even though, perhaps, such consultation might be difficult, if events moved too fast in the Political Committee.

Shortly before the session of the First or Political Committee began at 10:30 A.M., the Permanent Greek Mission to the United Nations arranged to have the Secretariat circulate a document containing, under a covering letter of December 8, "a factual account of the situation prevailing in the island both before and after the General Assembly adopted Resolution 1013 (XI) during its eleventh session," and suggesting the degree to which the Cypriots had conformed to the hopes expressed in that resolution.[2] In this document the situation in Cyprus before and after that resolution was presented with brief facts under various headings— emergency regulations, concentration camps, executions (by hanging), prisoners' tortures, military and police repressive action, mistreatment of the clergy, curfews, and peaceful reactions of the people to British violence. With regard to the British announcement of August 9 that thirty-three of the eighty-nine emergency regulations had been repealed,[3] it was asserted in this document that a closer study revealed that this was true of nine regulations only, mainly because the majority of the cases covered by the regulations repealed were still fully covered by other provisions of regulations that still remained in force. Thus, eighty still remained in effect.

Something more than verbal action was taking place that same day in Cyprus where the new Governor, Sir Hugh Foot, had arrived a week earlier. An island-wide strike took place on December 9, and widespread disturbances occurred in a local counterpart of the conflict going on in New York. Over 100 people were injured during these disturbances, twenty members of the security forces included, and 150 arrests were made. Next day, after rumors that a Turkish policeman had been injured in riots in the Pan-Cyprian Gymnasium, several hundred Turkish Cypriot demonstrators marched into the Greek Cypriot quarter in Nicosia and caused considerable damage before the security forces drove them off. In this second clash, about eighty people were injured, forty-one members of the security forces included. Sixty-eight arrests were made. The authorities imposed a curfew in the capital of Cyprus for the first time in nine months.[4]

At the United Nations, meanwhile, Chairman Djalal Abdoh of Iran started out by formally announcing that the First Committee, at its 927th meeting, would now take up the Cyprus question. He asked the members of the Committee who wished to speak to combine their general debate on the question with the debate on the draft resolution submitted by the Greek Delegation. Then, after announcing the time for a number of next meetings and indicating that the British, Greek, and Turkish representatives would start out the debate with their statements, he reminded the Committee that the deadline for the end of the Assembly's session had been set for December 14 and, therefore, the items on the Committee's agenda should be concluded on December 13 at the latest.[5] Because of the deadline, one or perhaps more night meetings would be necessary.

The British representative, Commander Noble, opened the debate on item 58. It will be recalled that the Greek Foreign Minister, at his meeting with Noble and members of the British Delegation on December 3, had objected to such a procedure, saying he would like to speak first, since it was Greece that was raising this question before the United Nations.[6] Eventually, however, Averoff-Tossizza had not pressed this point. Not only had the British asked for priority two weeks earlier, but Noble had argued he had statements to make that could influence the course of the debate. The Greek Delegation, therefore, had not thought it worthwhile to insist further on this formal point. In the debate on the Algerian question both at the eleventh and the twelfth sessions of the Assembly, the French Delegate had spoken first. Moreover, that the

Greek Foreign Minister would speak immediately after the British representative had certain advantages. It would give him the opportunity to reply off the cuff to the main points of the British argument, before he delivered his set speech.

Noble started out his speech, which turned out to be relatively brief as well as subdued, by stating that he was sensible to the responsibility that fell on him to place "this grave matter in the proper perspective of history and practical politics." Stressing then "the special ties of friendship and alliance" of Britain with Greece and Turkey, and the understanding and sympathy which had grown up between the peoples of the three states over a long period, he stated that Britain valued highly this friendship and greatly regretted that "a problem which appeared to divide us should, year after year, be a matter of contention in the forum of the United Nations." At this particular juncture in world affairs, the three governments, whose heads were shortly to meet in Paris (at the summit NATO Council meeting),[7] should remember and reassert their links of friendship. Much that seemed difficult, even impossible, could be done if it were undertaken in a spirit of amity and co-operation. Accordingly, it was his hope that the debate in the Committee would avoid acrimony and would lead to a better atmosphere for solving this difficult problem. "It would be tragic if anything said here were to damage the prospects of fruitful negotiations and eventual compromise," he declared.

Some had called the Cyprus dispute a colonial matter, Noble went on to say. It was, though, ironical for Britain to be attacked for repressive colonialism in Cyprus the year when Ghana and Malaya had become full members of the Commonwealth as well as of the United Nations. The problem, in fact, was not a straightforward colonial one. If it were, there would have been steady progress on the lines so successfully followed elsewhere in British colonies. Although it was not his government's seeking, the core of the problem was now international disagreement. Its main dangers were to international relations. As well known, the Greek and Turkish governments held widely differing views on the problem. It was the aim of the British government to find a solution acceptable to all concerned.

Although the Cyprus problem had become an international question, continued the British representative, it also had its difficulties and dangers inside Cyprus. His government's position on Article 2, paragraph 7, of the Charter was well known. It had been again explained in the General Committee when the Cyprus item had been discussed there.[8] The internal aspects of the problem, he reasserted, came within the British government's sovereign jurisdiction and were not a matter for international discussion.

Noble then went on to develop the proposition that "the right way for friends to resolve a dispute is to discuss it among themselves." If there was friendship, if there was a will, then surely a way could be found. Friends should constantly bear in mind that their friendship was greater

than their dispute, and this demanded from each of them some contribution to a compromise solution that would be satisfactory to each. That
was the spirit with which his government approached the problem, he
assured the Committee. Britain, after all, had had long and wide experience in resolving international problems through discussions. It had
indeed been said that Britain had a genius for compromise. His government would like some opportunity to prove it in this matter, but it took
two, and in this case more than two, to make a compromise.

These thoughts he had tried to express about the need for a peaceful
and friendly atmosphere "and for quiet discussion among the parties
concerned with the object of reaching a compromise solution" were
precisely the thoughts that had inspired Resolution 1013 (XI), Noble
maintained. It had been—and still was—the whole object of his government to make progress in the spirit of that resolution, he added in this
obeisance to the United Nations. After that resolution, some progress had
been made. Further progress along the same lines was now required. The
essence of any solution was that it be acceptable to the "peoples" of
Cyprus, to his government and to the Greek and Turkish governments.
The British government, he said, had made great efforts to reach such a
solution, and he would not burden the Committee with all the background to this dispute, which had been fully explored in previous debates. Looking, however, to the future, it was often helpful to see what
methods had been tried in the past and with what results. He would,
therefore, proceed to summarize events before the passage of Resolution
1013 (XI), anxious not to reopen past wounds and hoping that the
summary would be accepted as "strictly objective."

In his recapitulation of the background of the Cyprus question, Noble
started out by observing that the policy of successive British governments
had been to promote "self-government" in Cyprus. All sections of the
British people desired this, and there was a very widespread feeling of
dissatisfaction and distress in Britain that the path that so many nations
in the Commonwealth had trod should seem blocked by so many obstacles and difficulties in this particular case. After World War II (in 1947),
the government had made proposals for a liberal constitution. However,
not only the Communists but also the nationalist movement headed by
the Orthodox Church had rejected them. The latter's declared aim had
long been the union of the island with Greece: what was known as
enosis.[9] Although the offer remained open, there was no change in the
position until 1954, when the British government of that day made a new
proposal for discussions about self-government. This, too, had been rejected.[10]

By 1954, a new factor had come to complicate the situation, Noble
continued. In spite of the feelings of sympathy which the campaign for
enosis had aroused in Greece—and Noble acknowledged here the
strength of these feelings—successive Greek governments over a long
period had followed a policy of non-intervention in the Cyprus question.

By 1954, however, this long-standing policy had been reversed.[11] The Greek government was openly conducting a campaign for *enosis*, producing, he stressed, sharp protests from Turkey and leading, among other things, to a deterioration in Greek-Turkish relations.[12] That year, the Greek government had brought the Cyprus question to the Assembly's ninth session. After a debate "which unfortunately did nothing to improve international relations," the Assembly had decided not to consider the Cyprus question further at that session.[13]

The outbreak of the "terrorist movement" in Cyprus, on April 1, 1955, had been the next development,[14] Noble observed. In special broadcasts beamed to the island Athens Radio had started inciting the Greek Cypriots to violence. The Greek government had admitted that the Athens Radio was under its control, but in spite of more than twenty official protests had done nothing to prevent continued encouragement to violence. The terrorist leaders had arrived in Cyprus secretly from Greece during 1954 and had spent the first months of 1955 in building up their organization with arms, ammunition and money, sent from Greece by leading Greek officials. But, Noble said, he had gone into some detail about these matters at the Assembly's eleventh session.[15] The point he wanted to make now was that the active support from Greece for the *enosis* movement and for terrorism in Cyprus had created an international question, which was at the very core of the problem—whatever regrets one might have about this. The union of Cyprus with Greece was an international aim.

Recognizing the international character and dangers of the problem, the British government, continued Noble in his recapitulation of the background of the question since the end of World War II, decided in 1955 to see whether some arrangement might be worked out with the Greek and Turkish governments for mutual co-operation in promoting the welfare of the "peoples" of Cyprus. At the London Tripartite Conference (August 29–September 7, 1955), his government had put forward new proposals, suggesting that the problem be tackled in two stages. The three governments should immediately form a permanent committee which would, in the first place, consider a constitution for Cyprus and thereafter try to smooth out any difficulties that might arise in the working of self-government. Since it was clear that the three governments did not agree on the ultimate future of Cyprus, the British government had suggested that their co-operation should be without prejudice to the eventual status of the island. It hoped that the experience of the three governments working together to promote the welfare of the "peoples" of Cyprus would gradually bring their viewpoints closer together and thus resolve the problem. It suggested this might be helped if the conference reconvened, when self-government was working, with representatives of the Cypriot communities present to consider the future of the island.[16]

Unfortunately, that imaginative proposal for sharing responsibility in

Cyprus had been rejected, said Noble. It had been a real attempt to get to the heart of the problem and bring together all the interested parties, the Greek and Turkish communities in Cyprus and the Greek and Turkish governments, as well as the British government. The latter had urged moderation on all sides and had stressed that if there was to be a solution, there must be a compromise. When the Assembly, at its tenth session in 1955, voted not to include in its agenda the Cyprus question, which the Greek government had brought forward, it had recognized the importance of avoiding public acrimony.[17]

Noble then recounted that three weeks after "the breakdown" of the tripartite conference in London, the Governor of Cyprus had begun conversations with Archbishop Makarios, on the one hand, and with Turkish Cypriot leaders, on the other. These had lasted for five months, coming to an end in February, 1956, when the Archbishop had refused to take a stand against violence, had insisted that an over-all Greek Cypriot majority in the proposed legislative assembly should be conceded before safeguards for the Turkish community were discussed, and had demanded that Britain should swiftly hand over control of the police to the Greek Cypriots.[18] This last claim had been particularly difficult to accept since it had become clear that the "terrorists" took their orders from the Archbishop. "The chief terrorist" had recorded in his diary on March 1, 1956, that he was ready and awaiting orders from "Gen"—the code word for the Archbishop—to begin. Unfortunately, the orders had come.[19] That was why the Archbishop had been deported and why he could not be allowed to return to Cyprus at this stage. The British government had, however, made it plain that it was prepared to discuss self-government with a representative group of Cypriots, which could, of course, include the Archbishop.[20]

Members of the Political Committee were, of course, aware, Noble observed at this point, that in the United Nations the campaign for *enosis* had been conducted in the name of self-determination.[21] His government, he maintained, had always supported the principle of self-determination, as the development of the Commonwealth proved. In December, 1956, therefore, it had thought it right to reaffirm in an unmistakable way its support for the principle of self-determination, "which must, of course, apply equally to the Greek and Turkish communities in Cyprus."[22] But in applying the principle of self-determination, it was necessary to make sure that this did not create greater problems than it solved. Therefore, the British government at the same time had proposed that the first step should be to set up self-government. Self-determination should not be applied until a greater measure of confidence had been established, and the delicate situation in the eastern Mediterranean had become more stable. Accordingly, his government had accepted, likewise in December, 1956, the findings of Lord Radcliffe, who had made an independent study of a Constitution for Cyprus.[23] This scheme provided for a democratically elected Assembly with a Greek Cypriot majority and a government, which would have the confidence of the Assembly. This government would control all the affairs of Cyprus except those that properly belonged to the Turkish Cypriots, and police, defense, and foreign affairs, which Britain would retain, to keep the balance between the communities and to help in maintaining peace and stability in the area. The government had made clear that it intended to discuss the proposed constitution with representative Cypriots of both communities. Before doing so, it had attempted to enlist the sympathy of the Greek and Turkish governments, which had asked for advance notice of Britain's intentions. Unfortunately, before the British government could speak to the Cypriots, Athens Radio had announced Greek opposition to the proposals and had declared that any Greek Cypriot who showed interest in them was a traitor. As a result, these constructive proposals had been rejected without having received the consideration they merited.[24]

This, then, had been the position when the Committee had considered the Cyprus question at the previous Assembly. Resolution 1013 (XI) declared that the solution of the problem required "an atmosphere of peace and freedom of expression." His government, said Noble, had sincerely tried to take constructive initiatives in the spirit of this resolution, the operative clause of which he quoted. Within a few weeks of the debate, it had released Archbishop Makarios, offered a safe-conduct out of Cyprus to all terrorists,[25] and begun a comprehensive relaxation of the emergency regulations, although it was conscious that intimidation continued and that, in spite of the truce (in Noble's somewhat mordant quotation marks), the terrorists were rebuilding their "shattered organization." Even before that, the British government had unconditionally accepted the offer of the then Secretary-General of NATO to each of the three governments concerned to use his good offices for conciliation.[26] In spite of the Greek government's negative attitude, his government hoped that he might be able to make progress and was therefore careful to do nothing that might damage this prospect. Eventually, however, it had become clear that it was unlikely that any significant progress could quickly be made by this method alone.[27] "Thus in the middle of this summer, my government was faced with the breakdown of yet another initiative," Noble said at this point, evidently making a roundup of his own recapitulation of events from 1945 on.[28]

In spite, however, of the numerous rebuffs received, which hardly suggested any great desire to reach a compromise, the British government, Noble said, had been unwilling to allow the problem to drift on.[29] It decided another effort to solve the problem should be made. Previous attempts at international agreement had shown that the positions of the parties were so far apart that there was no prospect of settling a detailed agenda for discussion. If discussions were ever to begin, each of the parties should be assured that it would not be barred from bringing up any consideration that it deemed relevant. Experience had also shown that agreement was likely only if all the parties concerned would consider wider interests and not insist on the complete fulfilment of their aims. In short, each of the parties concerned had to realize that equally strong views were held by others and that a settlement required a willingness to compromise on all sides. His government had therefore concluded that the best and possibly the only hope of making progress was by private discussions between the British, Greek, and Turkish governments. Accordingly, it had informally suggested to the Greek and Turkish governments that "we should get around a table and discuss the whole problem with open minds and without insisting in advance on any particular solution."

Going further into this public disclosure of these British soundings for a tripartite conference, which, it will be recalled, had been launched early in August,[30] Noble explained that no fixed agenda had been envisaged for that conference, which should be free to discuss without prejudice every solution so far mooted—enosis, self-determination within a fixed time limit, self-government leading to self-determination at an unspecified time, guaranteed independence, condominium with plural nationality, partition, the maintenance of full British sovereignty, and any other suggestions that might be put forward. A discussion on these lines should be without prejudice to the position of any of the parties. The purpose of the conference, the proceedings of which should be in private, would be to find a solution of the international aspects of the problem acceptable to all concerned. It would thus pave the way for a subsequent settlement of the internal problems in direct discussions with the Cypriot representatives. The British government had indicated that if the idea of a conference were accepted, it would be prepared to hold preliminary discussions with the other governments concerned to clear the ground for the meeting. This of course would not have involved any prior commitments, for that would be contrary to the purpose and spirit of the proposed conference.

There had been an extensive exchange of communications about the possibility of some such tripartite meeting, Noble told the Committee, without revealing the conditions his own government had put forward for calling a tripartite conference.[31] The Greek government, however, though not rejecting the idea of a conference, had insisted that the basic outlines of a solution should first be agreed upon between the governments concerned through diplomatic channels. As a result, it had not been possible to reach agreement that the conference should be free to discuss any solution that had been or might be put forward.

In addition to the above difficulty, it also had emerged after a great deal of discussion with the Greek and Turkish governments that there had been a problem about timing as well. In order to make progress as quickly as possible, his government, Noble said, had suggested that the

conference meet in early September but had offered to consider any
other date. Others had thought that discussions could not usefully be
held before the Turkish elections and perhaps before the Committee had
again debated the question. Although the British government understood
these reasons, it did not agree with them. It thought the matter too
urgent for delay.

Turning now to a "regrettable development" he had to mention, Noble
went on to say that during the last two months, while the Assembly had
been meeting, there had been some recrudescence of lawlessness in
Cyprus. There had been at least six murders, two attempted murders,
four cases of sabotage, and many attempts to intimidate the moderate
elements of the population. It was difficult not to associate this renewal
of terrorist activity with the fact that a further discussion of the Cyprus
question was about to take place in the Assembly. It certainly looked like
a form of pressure upon the Assembly.[32]

This underlying tension in the affairs of the island could not be
ignored. Cyprus once again was at the crossroads and what was said in
the Committee could well affect the course of events on the island, Noble
warned. In February, the Committee had unanimously recognized that
the problem's solution required an atmosphere of peace and freedom of
expression. This was still true. The Committee would be doing less than
its duty if it did not impress upon those who had dedicated themselves to
violence that there was no more certain way of wrecking the prospects of
a settlement than by reverting to terrorism. The British government had
recently appointed a new Governor, Sir Hugh Foot. He had a reputation
for wise, liberal, and progressive administration, and he had been asked
to report when he had had time to reassess the situation in Cyprus. It
would be tragic if a resumption of widespread violence was to occur at a
time when the British government believed there was a real prospect of
making progress toward a solution.

In spite of the difficulties he had mentioned, and, Noble added, he did
not want to dwell upon them unduly, exchanges of views between his
government and those of Greece and Turkey continued. That was a
hopeful sign. It constituted some progress. These exchanges had been of
a confidential and exploratory character. The Committee, of course,
would not expect to be given any indication of their nature. The Turkish
elections were now over and soon the Committee would have completed
reconsideration of the Cyprus question. His government hoped that, in
these circumstances, it would be possible to make progress toward a
solution. It still believed that a meeting to discuss all relevant questions
would be helpful. It was sure in any case that the Committee would
encourage the governments concerned to persevere in efforts to find a
compromise solution. Noble could tell the Committee that his government was willing to discuss with its Greek and Turkish friends any
solution for the Cyprus question, and that it would give the most sympa-

thetic consideration to any proposal that commended itself to both the Greek and Turkish governments.[33] Re-emphasizing the British desire for talks with "the parties concerned," Noble said,

> we want to enter into discussions with them to see whether, with equal goodwill on all sides, an agreement cannot be found. We have the welfare of the peoples of Cyprus at heart. We are most anxious to settle the dispute so as to restore the long friendship which is the natural state of relations between our three countries. We are also anxious lest the continuance of this dispute should impair the stability of the area.

The British government bore the responsibility for the government of Cyprus, Noble underlined. "We must see that any future arrangement provides for order, internal security and good government, and for the protection of the rights of all the people. We have strategic responsibilities in Cyprus which must be safeguarded effectively in any future arrangement." He did not need to specify what these were, since everyone knew that Britain had traditional friendships, alliances and interests in the area and was a member of two organizations of collective self-defense in accordance with Article 51 of the UN Charter.[34] "But these duties and interests leave us a margin for compromise."

Summing up his government's position on the matter in terms identical to those that his delegation had communicated backstage, through the U.S. Delegation, to the Greek Delegation on December 6,[35] Noble proclaimed his government's intention of seeking for a solution acceptable to the British, Greek, and Turkish governments, and to the "peoples" of Cyprus, and its readiness "to enter into discussions at the appropriate time with all concerned." He then rounded out his careful and blandly moderate rhetoric by reverting to his opening theme. His government, he reiterated, bearing in mind its own responsibilities, the welfare of "the peoples" of Cyprus, the legitimate interest of Greece and Turkey in the future of the island, and the friendship between "our three countries," was convinced that there was room for compromise. It thought that this was the idea that underlay Resolution 1013 (XI). It was sure that this would also be the most constructive message that could emerge from the debate in the Committee.

Before ending his speech, Noble briefly referred to the document the Greek Delegation had circulated as the Committee opened its debate. He had seen it for the first time when he arrived in his place at the meeting that morning, he said. He had not had time to study it and might well wish to exercise his right of reply to it in due course. Noble, it will be noted, chose not to comment at this point on the Greek draft resolution. All in all, he had argued against UN interference in efforts to find a solution of the Cyprus problem and had expressed himself in favor of a new tripartite conference between Britain, Greece, and Turkey in order to arrive at a settlement acceptable to the three parties concerned and to "the peoples" of Cyprus. And he had emphasized the alliance as well as the strategic aspects of the issue, denying that the question was of a purely colonial character.

As the Greek Delegation had expected, there was nothing constructive in the British representative's speech—from the Greek viewpoint. On the contrary, the intention of the British government to create new complications in the Cyprus question seemed quite evident. The aim? To impose the view that the solution should indispensably satisfy the three parties concerned. Generally, when the gravity of the problem and the dangers it enclosed were reckoned with, the British Delegate's speech had made a poor impression, it was felt.

The Greek Foreign Minister, before reading his prepared statement, first spent some time rebutting off the cuff certain points Noble had made in his address. In general, he sought to promote the familiar Greek policy view that Britain and/or the United Nations should unambiguously express themselves in favor of self-determination for the people of Cyprus as a whole, and that bipartite talks between the British government and the Cypriot people provided the best approach for implementing Resolution 1013 (XI) as a step toward abolishing colonialism in Cyprus.

"When my colleague from the United Kingdom pressed for speaking first today," Averoff-Tossizza said, "I hoped he would convey to us some good news. This has not been the case, and the disappointment in Greece, and especially in Cyprus, will be all the greater. Disappointment leads to despair, while despair leads to excesses and is the harbinger of worse things to come." Before responding to a number of fundamental points his British colleague had raised, the Foreign Minister had to answer a number of specific questions to which Noble had seen fit to revert—questions fully discussed at the previous session of the Assembly that, he thought, had been disposed of. The British representative had repeated the accusations he had made against the Greek government about the sending of supplies from Greece to EOKA in Cyprus. At that time, the Foreign Minister said, he had replied and had circulated documents proving that there had been at least four attempts by British authorities to send arms to Cyprus in the form of shipments from Greece.[36] Why had these attempts to stage fake shipments been made if there had been true shipments from Greece? he had asked on that occasion. The veracity of these documents had been questioned. He had requested that a suitable committee examine them to determine their authenticity and had suggested that, if that committee found that these documents were false, he would be the first to accept that conclusion.[37]

Continuing the counterattack, Averoff-Tossizza proceeded to cast doubt about the credibility of Noble's statement that Archbishop Makarios was "the leader of those described as terrorists." If that was true, why had the prelate not been brought before a court martial and given a chance to prove his innocence instead of being swiftly exiled? Why had the man accused of being the head of a revolutionary movement been exiled without being granted the right to prove that he had nothing to do with the uprising, which, the Greek representative added, was "a popular spontaneous uprising?" He reserved the right to answer, if necessary, other points raised in Noble's speech after he had had an opportunity to study it. However, he felt duty-bound to reply immediately to two or three specific points.

The British representative had spoken about the Radcliffe draft constitution, which he had termed a constructive solution. Averoff-Tossizza regretted to say that, if the British government continued to consider that document as constructive, no solution to the Cyprus problem would emerge through the will of the British government. As he had pointed out at the previous session of the Assembly, the Radcliffe Constitution reserved for the Governor a veto right in all fields. Whereas, on its face, the Constitution suggested that there would be a Parliament, the Governor would have the right to decide what questions would lie within the competence of the Parliament, and his decision would not be subject to any challenge.[38] Having this provision in mind, who could seriously speak in terms of a Constitution? "Was this not rather an act designed to cover up the continuation and perpetuation of unadulterated colonialism?"

A sentence in Noble's speech to the effect that the British government had tried to make progress with self-government coupled with a clear statement on the principle of self-determination, might be considered as constructive, the Greek Foreign Minister declared. If that was so, the people of Cyprus and the Greek government, which represented that people, since the Cypriots themselves could not have a free voice, would make their contribution on one condition: "a clear statement on the principle of self-determination." This principle had been clearly enunciated by "Sir" Anthony Eden until July, 1956,[39] but had been fundamentally challenged in December, 1956, when the British government had made it clear that what it had in mind when it spoke of self-determination was the partition of the island.[40]

With regard to the exchanges of views that Noble had mentioned toward the end of his speech, Averoff-Tossizza said he could say just one thing: In those exchanges of views, the Greek government, clearly and unambiguously, had explained "to our British friends" the Greek position that the problem was one between the British government and the people of Cyprus, and that no other conversations could be entered into unless that particular basis was recognized and unless an approach was accepted that was in keeping with that premise.[41] He would deal, however, at length, with this matter in the body of his speech, on which he would now embark.

He had come before the Committee, Averoff-Tossizza said, with a feeling of both profound respect, because it was his honor to address the representatives of almost all the countries of the world assembled to labor for the greater well-being of mankind, and of responsibility, too, because he was dealing with a question that concerned the freedom, the well-being, and the dignity of a half million human beings. This meant that he would speak about the reassertion "of our most noble principles." He was, he added, fully aware of the grave task that rested upon him. The problem, however, was not an abstract one. It involved a people who were suffering, fighting, hoping. Its immediate interests and its future interests, its will, and its psychology were so many factors that had to be taken into consideration.

The problem was not just an insular one. It was, he emphasized, a colonial problem with which it would be unrealistic to deal while disregarding its broader political implications. These broader implications could not alter the problem's form or its substance, though they had to be taken into account, especially since these political influences and implications concerned countries with which Greece, as a spokesman for the Cypriot people, and the Cypriot people themselves, were anxious to maintain close and friendly relations in the future.

After these preliminary remarks concerning the universal, anticolonialist, and human-appeal features of the Cyprus question, the Greek Foreign Minister assured the Committee that throughout the discussion he would be as dispassionate and constructive as possible. At its past session, the Assembly had adopted Resolution 1013 (XI), and more than fifty representatives had taken part in the Committee debate, which had been sometimes rather animated but always profound and meticulous. There was no need therefore to deliver a long speech on the problem's history. It would, nevertheless, be useful to recall the fundamental facts of the problem, because it was necessary to clarify some of its aspects that other quarters had persistently represented erroneously or perhaps tendentiously.

Starting out with the ethnic factor, as he had done at the eleventh session of the Assembly,[42] Averoff-Tossizza referred to British population statistics (80 per cent Greeks; 18 per cent Turks, 2 per cent other ethnic groups) and denied that the majority of the Cypriots was Levantine, not Greek, and devoid of the characteristics of an ethnic personality. A plebiscite under the auspices of the United Nations, he said, could not fail to show that the overwhelming majority of the population was Hellenic in race, language, religion, mores, culture, and feelings.[43]

The second argument that had been advanced to impress those who had not had sufficient time profoundly to study the problem was based on the Treaty of Lausanne.[44] In order to suggest respect for treaties, it had been argued that the Treaty of Lausanne forbade a change in the status of Cyprus, because it granted certain rights to Turkey. However, Resolution 1013 (XI) had rendered a decision on that point. As a result, a detailed reference to the documentation was not necessary. Just as any other treaty concerning Turkey, the Treaty of Lausanne in no way precluded self-determination for the people of Cyprus. None of its clauses, either explicitly or by interpretation, could be viewed as constituting an obstacle to that. He would revert to this argument only if it

were absolutely necessary to do so, but he desired to make one observation because he had just studied some of the records of the Lausanne
Conference. The Treaty had been meticulously drafted. It had ended one
era and opened another. The statesmen who had presided at the time
over Greece and Turkey, Eleftherios Venizelos and Kemal Atatürk, respectively, were fully aware that this treaty was of special importance
and that matters should not be left in a penumbra of ambiguity. Everything should be clear, they felt. And everything had been made clear,
thus facilitating the application of a principle that Greece had always
meticulously observed: the principle of respect for treaties.

Concerning the argument that Cyprus was of strategic importance
and, therefore, questions of national security for other countries were
involved, Averoff-Tossizza declared, "we would be very happy if those
who championed that argument sincerely believed in it, because that
argument could be answered easily and well." He observed, to begin
with, that quite a few countries could invoke reasons of strategy or
security to demand the occupation of Cyprus or to dictate its form of
government. It was not possible to consider the strategic interests of one
party and ignore similar and equally valid interests of others.

To recognize, on the other hand, "that the use of brute force can
deprive thousands of human beings of their freedom and dignity for
strategic reasons would lead us to the worst excesses of the eighteenth
and nineteenth centuries," Averoff-Tossizza declared further. After so
much suffering and so much bloodshed for the cause of freedom, it could
not be argued, he contended, that a people should live in subjugation, as
the slave of another people, because strategic reasons called for this. To
adopt such a thesis would create a sinister precedent. Everyone would
invoke his own strategic interests. Everyone, especially the great powers,
whose interests were far more extended and whose responsibilities were
heavy and covered the whole world, could, under this theory, have the
right to occupy certain areas that they felt had strategic importance for
them. Such pretensions had always miscarried and had never been recognized. Security problems sometimes merited attention. Certain areas,
from the strategic point of view, might well justify the interest of neighboring countries. No effective machinery yet existed for the defense of
peace, and it was therefore understandable that protection against possible springboards of attack should be sought. However, in the case of
Cyprus, it had been recognized that, for a number of reasons, the island
was so defective as a military base that it could never seriously be used as
such. For instance, during World War I, Britain and its allies had pressed
upon Turkey on a number of fronts, including the front in the Palestine
area, but Turkey's southern shore had never been attacked from the
British base on Cyprus, and this at a time when British naval power was
supreme in the Mediterranean. This proved, if proof was necessary, that
Cyprus could not seriously endanger anyone.[45]

But to deal with this question more generally and more seriously, the

Greek Foreign Minister offered certain suggestions having in mind the Turkish interest. International practice had frequently recognized that certain regions in the world should not become hotbeds of alarm and anxiety. To neutralize such situations various means had been used, such as bilateral or multilateral treaties that imposed international servitudes, which occasionally went as far as complete demilitarization of certain areas. If Cyprus was of such strategic importance that a country might feel endangered by it, what would be more reasonable than to ask for a military status for the island that would make such a danger impossible? International treaties had established the complete demilitarization of several Greek islands close to Turkey's shores,[46] but in the case of Cyprus nobody had asked for this or for anything like it. What had been asked was that Cyprus should continue as a colony that should be occupied by a certain power for the strategic needs or convenience of some. This made one recognize that the argument about the strategic importance of Cyprus was advanced only to support the imperialistic and colonialist thesis. Cyprus threatened no one. Others might threaten Cyprus.

Cyprus, the Greek Foreign Minister continued, was inhabited by a civilized people, who for many years had been demanding and striving to obtain its liberty and, through the Greek government, was asking for UN support. Could the United Nations tell the Cypriots that they were not the real owners of the island, that they were the property of another people?[47] Were the United Nations to do that, it would not be "the supreme temple of liberty." It would be a mere slave market. This the United Nations surely could not do. On the contrary, the United Nations had settled the legal question by declaring itself competent to deal with the problem,[48] and it had tried, if not to give an immediate solution, at least to support an equitable one. Thus it had adopted Resolution 1013 (XI).

If from the juridical viewpoint, Resolution 1013 (XI) was perhaps the most important development in the Cyprus question, from the political viewpoint, too, it constituted an important act, the proper value of which, however, depended on the attitude of the parties concerned. Alas, it was too well known that the Assembly was no tribunal;[49] that it was vested with no executive powers, and that it possessed no means of implementing its desires and recommendations. Their implementation depended on the degree to which the parties concerned proved ready and willing to abide by them. In the case of Cyprus, the United Nations had done its duty. It had given a first opinion. It was necessary now to see how those to whom the United Nations had addressed itself had responded.

After quoting Resolution 1013 (XI) in full, the Greek Foreign Minister observed that, "according to the usual procedural ritual," the resolution had two parts: a preamble and an operative part. In this particular case, he could perceive a distinction in substance. In adopting this resolution, he found that the Assembly sought first to pacify the island, namely, to restore a normal situation there by re-establishing conditions of freedom of expression and suspending recourse to violence. This recommendation was addressed to the Cypriots and the British authorities alike, because a return to conditions of non-violence could only be effective if the active resistance of the Cypriot patriots ceased simultaneously with the arbitrary acts of repression by the British.[50] Under this resolution, however, the Greek representative went on to say, pacification was not the objective; it was the preliminary condition. The objective was the resumption of negotiations between Cypriots and British with a view to finding an equitable and democratic solution in keeping with the principles of the Charter.

The Greek Foreign Minister, like the British representative in the preceding speech, sought thence to present the effects on the Cyprus question of this resolution, but he painted a picture that differed from the British one and limited himself primarily to the events of 1957. How had the Cypriots responded to the Assembly's appeal for pacification and resumption of negotiations? The British government's attitude on these two points would also be seen. Thus, he said, it would be possible to draw a parallel between the compliance of the two parties and assess responsibilities. He would cite facts. The conclusions would emerge by themselves.

After the adoption of Resolution 1013 (XI), the ethnarchy of Cyprus had officially expressed its satisfaction at the action taken by the United Nations. And, on March 4, the mayors of Cyprus, the elected representatives of the people, had published a similar communiqué. Then, on March 14, EOKA had issued its truce offer, the entire text of which Averoff-Tossizza read to the Committee, emphasizing the reference it contained that this organization was "complying with the spirit of the resolution of the United Nations. . . ."[51] Since that day, EOKA's action had completely ceased, he said, questioning the contrary assertion of Noble, who had "cited eight incidents said to have occurred during the past two months."[52] But could these incidents in fact be imputed to EOKA? One of these surely could not, Averoff-Tossizza thought. In fact it could not be attributed to Greeks at all. A bomb had exploded in front of the offices of the British *Times of Cyprus*.[53] Everything had been done to attribute the incident to EOKA. It so happened, however, that this newspaper had always defended the cause of the Greeks of Cyprus, the application, namely, of the principle of self-determination without partition. And, by coincidence, the building occupied by the *Times of Cyprus* belonged to the Orthodox Archdiocese. Under these circumstances, it was rather difficult to attribute this bombing attempt to EOKA. "Permit me, my British colleague," he added, "to cast doubt on the suggestion that EOKA broke the unilaterally declared and unilaterally respected armistice."

Averoff-Tossizza then recounted the statements of March 22 and 29 by Makarios, then still in the Seychelles, which contained "an appeal to the Cypriot combatants and to the British government . . . for the re-establishment of peaceful conditions on the island" or in which he had reiterated (at his press conference of March 29) his hope that EOKA would suspend its activities and the British authorities would abolish their emergency measures in order to restore an atmosphere of peace and confidence that would permit the resumption of negotiations.[54] "What more could the people of Cyprus and their banished chief do to create the atmosphere of peace for which the Assembly had called?"

"With regard to pacification what was the action of the British government?" Averoff-Tossizza now exclaimed. After citing a statement of February 27 by Lord Home, Secretary of State for the Commonwealth, who had greeted the UN resolution as a "welcome breath of realism" and one that would leave the British government and the people of Cyprus to settle between themselves the future of the island, the Greek representative called this a clear recognition of, and unique basis for, negotiations between the British government and the people of Cyprus. It had been a clear indication to the Cypriots to respond to those intentions.[55] Indeed, on March 13, Colonial Secretary Lennox-Boyd, had told the House of Commons that "it would be quite wrong to assume that the British Government would do nothing in pursuance of the UN resolution." [56]

"But, alas, those hopes soon wilted." On March 14, Governor Harding had honored these declarations by having Evagoras Pallicaridis hanged, solely because this young Cypriot possessed a weapon which, in fact, was not in a fit state to be used.[57] "This abominable crime of hanging a man because he possessed a useless weapon stirred the indignation of the civilized world." Senator James J. Fulton, for example, had made a number of representations, in efforts to save the young man from the hangman's noose, phoning even to Governor Harding himself. But the Marshal had been implacable.

This tragic episode, Averoff-Tossizza explained, illustrated the state of mind in which the Governor of Cyprus and his administration had responded to Resolution 1013 (XI). It was, therefore, small wonder that the British authorities had failed in their duty to pacify the island by restoring normal order and freedom of expression as provided for in this resolution. The only reason for the improved situation in Cyprus had been that EOKA had ceased hostilities and had complied with it. This should be known, especially by the United Nations.

"Colonial oppression," on the other hand, had weighed even more heavily on the shoulders of the people than it had before, the Greek representative maintained. "One might be tempted to believe that the victor over the Mau-Mau—the Governor and his assistants—had received the message of pacification from the United Nations with fury in their hearts." Once again, "the so-called forces of order bore down on the people so that none who resisted might go unpunished," even as "the intrepid warrior, Dighenis," was on the point of escaping the army of police and the thousands of specialists who were doing everything possible to defeat him and punish the people for having resisted.

This led the Greek Foreign Minister to "the most poignant aspect of the Cyprus drama, the one dealing with certain practices resorted to by the organs of colonial repression." The subject was painful for some, if not for all. It was equally painful to him, and he would not tackle it out of sheer malice.[58] For the sake of justice and objectivity he had to declare, as he had done on other occasions both in the United Nations and outside, that the British people could surely not be considered responsible for the dreadful deeds he had referred to. Britain was the dearest friend of his country. Greece had been friends with Britain in good and in bad days. "Better than all others, we know the nobility and liberalism of its great people." He therefore felt entitled to say that the policy in Cyprus was "not worthy of the soul of the British people, and, by the same token, the atrocities perpetrated in Cyprus were not willed or consented to by the bulk of the British people." Alas, it was, nevertheless, true that these deeds had occurred and had been perpetrated by men wearing British uniforms, "which so many thousands of Britishers were still wearing with honor." The distinction he was drawing between the British people and the British torturers might have induced him not to speak about these "sinister activities of the colonialist monsters" in Cyprus if these activities had been all in the past. No one would have been happier than he himself if these atrocities and tortures had stopped the day after the Assembly had adopted Resolution 1013 (XI). But this had not been the case. The same methods had been used thereafter. He would be remiss in his duty were he to pass them over in silence. For, as long as colonialism remained in Cyprus, these practices which continued to be resorted to, could well become a permanent line of action and policy in order to prolong the present situation.

It could be argued that since the adoption of Resolution 1013 (XI), a number of emergency measures had been revoked—Noble had made that point—and that the man considered as the principal culprit, Field-Marshal Harding, was no longer in Cyprus but had been replaced by a man who enjoyed an excellent reputation both in Britain and abroad. With pleasure the Greek Foreign Minister recognized that all of this was true, but he did so with some apprehension that all this was not sufficient to allow anxiety and alarm to subside. While some emergency measures had been revoked, others remained, and enabled the colonial authorities in Cyprus even at that moment to arrest anyone they thought fit and let such persons rot in prison and concentration camps, or to hand them over to the tender cares of the torturers without a judgment or judicial inquiry.

His government, the Greek Foreign Minister said, did not question the liberal personality and attitude of the new Governor. It was aware that he had a good reputation, which had not been created without deeds to bolster it. What was required, however, was not a mere change of personality but a change of policy. If colonialism persisted, and if the struggle for liberation which had been unilaterally suspended was resumed, and if repression was resorted to by the same methods, what would the new Governor be able to do? In the last analysis he would either have to submit or resign. It was more than doubtful that he alone would have the power to change the situation, if all the conditions that determined the situation remained the same and if colonialism continued to dominate it.

In asking the United Nations to act for the abolition of colonialism in Cyprus, Averoff-Tossizza stated he was at the same time obliged to ask the United Nations to take interim measures to preserve the lives, the well-being, and the elementary human dignity of the population. It was not for purposes of phrase-mongering that he was using the words "life, well-being, elementary human dignity," because they were precisely the things that were at stake.

Averoff-Tossizza acknowledged that since the Pallicaridis case the hangman's noose had been idle. A number of victims had been spared [59]—not all, because some had been killed on the pretext of having tried to escape, but there had been fewer casualties. This was surely due to the unilateral cease-fire EOKA had proclaimed. In candor, though he had to say that nothing had changed with regard to everything else, the number of specific cases was smaller, but the cases were there. This was inadmissible in an atmosphere of calm and peace. What were these cases? At some length, the Greek representative went on to describe one example: the tribulations of the inhabitants of the village of Milikouri upon whom a curfew had been imposed for fifty-four days, because it was thought that "Dighenis" and his lieutenants were hiding there.[60] There had been several cases of similar inhuman treatment—long detentions without judgment; searches in villages, endangering crops and causing loss of cattle; collective punishments; doing harm to innocent peasants or peaceful artisans; tortures during inquiries. And these had occurred after Resolution 1013 (XI) had been adopted and the ceasefire proclaimed by EOKA. He had used the terms "tortures during investigations." This was a bold assertion—bold, because one could well question it and because it was difficult to prove. The Greek government had questioned it until it had received irrefutable proof. But the men who had suffered those tortures had written and signed detailed depositions. By affixing their signatures to these depositions and by giving their civil status and addresses, these men had accepted the risk of being punished again, perhaps even more severely, for having openly accused their torturers. This was no fiction. These were facts. Subsequently these people had found means of getting these documents into the hands of the Greek government. Some of these cases consisted of tortures which a hardened police might describe as "light"; others were embarrassing even for a professional; still others were monstrous and of horrible cruelty.[61]

The Permanent Mission of Greece to the UN had in its possession detailed documentation on this score, and this would be used according to the decision that the United Nations might take, Averoff-Tossizza said. He would avoid reading the testimony of the tortured persons. The document circulated by his delegation at the beginning of the Committee's meeting mentioned the number of these depositions and contained only statements of facts. He could, in addition, refer to the *Black Book* which the Ethnarchy of Cyprus had published and which had been made available to all delegations. The dates covered in the latter book did not include the list of the latest cases of torture.

The Greek Foreign Minister then referred to news about the two most recent cases.[62] In view of the documents that had been circulated, he thought it unnecessary, however, to read out these testimonies and to take advantage, at the close of the Assembly, of the precious time that remained. Also he did not wish to risk creating the impression that his government was attempting to use them for anti-British propaganda. Nothing could be further from his mind. "We do not engage in anti-British propaganda since it is we ourselves who announce that these atrocities are certainly contrary to the will of the British people. Where was the propaganda, when eminent British people have themselves strongly protested the practice of torture?" He could quote texts, if necessary, to show how thoroughly the British had been moved by this aspect of the drama. But this was not his intention. He reminded the Committee that during the debate on the inclusion of item 58 in the Assembly's agenda,[63] he had gone so far as to say that not only the people, but also the British government even while bearing responsibility for these acts, surely could not have authorized them. He said, however, that the British government indirectly fostered their perpetration by refusing to recognize the validity of these accusations. In addition, therefore, to its responsibility of law, it assumed the responsibility and onus of fact. But he did not intend to exploit this painful question for political purposes or use it for purposes of propaganda, he reiterated. "Our only purpose for the time being is to stop the colonial torturer in his atrocious business by casting light on this and on his acts." There was no other way at his disposal except to ask the United Nations to act against Cyprus colonialism and deal with this painful aspect of the problem and remedy it. Everybody knew that just by doing this, the United Nations, might, by its moral weight, relieve the plight of the Cypriot people.

If one looked at the substance of the question, this was the abolition of colonialism on Cyprus. The evil had to be rooted out. It affected the life of the entire people. It represented a great danger and a constant threat to the peace of the world. In that field, it was sad to note, he said, that, in spite of the appeal of the United Nations, the British government had undertaken no serious move to advance by negotiations toward a political solution of the problem. It was true that it had "discontinued the deportation" of Makarios, "the great prelate, who is the spiritual and political elected chief of the Greeks on Cyprus." But even though the Archbishop had been freed, he was still in exile, condemned to live far from his people. This considerably reduced the political scope of the British government's gesture. In addition to the question of fairness, there was also the question of usefulness. "By his moral prestige, his firmness and wisdom, the Archbishop would not only be a factor of stability but also one or normalization if he were in Cyprus, because by the will of the people, he is the only one who would make contacts possible and would make understandings valid," Averoff-Tossizza asserted.

Comparing now the respective attitudes "of the two parties," the British and Cypriots, toward the recommendation concerning the immediate resumption negotiations, Averoff-Tossizza noted that, on the side of the Cypriot people, Makarios, on May 28, 1957,[64] had sent a letter to the British Premier asking for the abolition of the emergency measures and for the resumption of negotiations on the application of the right of self-determination. Another letter, of July 16, to the British Ambassador in Athens, had further clarified the Archbishop's position. It had indicated that Makarios did not reject the right of the Turkish Cypriots to have a voice in talks over the future of Cyprus as a minority, in proportion to their ratio in the population, but was concerned lest that minority, in taking part in such talks, should impliedly be given a voice equal to that of the majority, whose will would thus be frustrated. Moreover, the free trade unions of Cyprus as well as the Greek mayors of the island had asked the government to resume negotiations with the representative of Archbishop Makarios, as had, for that matter, EOKA itself, in its truce offer. Thus, the Cypriot side had exhausted all initiatives for resuming the negotiations undertaken in autumn of 1955 between the Governor of Cyprus and the Archbishop, which had been severed and had led to the deportation of the latter,[65] and for implementing Resolution 1013 (XI). Incidentally, Averoff-Tossizza observed, these negotiations had focused not merely on self-government for Cyprus, as Commander Noble had said in his speech. In other words, their purpose was to "make progress with self-government, coupled with a statement on the principle of self-determination." [66]

Averoff-Tossizza thought that in all good faith one should pay tribute to the Cypriot people's attachment to the cause of a peaceful settlement and to their confidence in the United Nations. "A people in revolt, a people who had fallen victim to the worst exactions and tortures, declares itself prepared to negotiate with those who dominate it in order to seek a friendly solution.

At this point, the Greek Foreign Minister again drew the Committee's attention to the unilaterally proclaimed armistice of EOKA. The Greek government, he asserted, had always refused the least contact with that liberation army, because it could not be in contact with an organization acting with armed might against the authorities of a friendly and allied country "from which we are only separated by the Cyprus question." However, even while it never had had such contacts, the Greek government always had frankly voiced its admiration for this liberation struggle, which was as heroic as it was unequaled. This admiration also applied to the fact that EOKA had proved capable of proclaiming an armistice. From his own experience in undercover activities together with his British friends during World War II, he knew how great the peril was for a secret organization once it stopped acting.

Loss of prestige, even discredit of the chief; discouragement, even defection by the members; weakening or even disruption of the secret machinery—these were the mortal dangers of idleness for an undercover army. Nonetheless, "Dighenis" had twice proclaimed truce tests—the first in August, 1956. It had lasted for only ten days, because "the Marshal of the Empire" had refused to accept it. His answer, "worthy of an empire, worthy of the most beautiful days of colonialism," was, for ten days, "terms of unconditional surrender"—an answer that proud men would nowhere accept.[67] The second "armistice" had been that which had been proclaimed nine months earlier "in response to you, gentlemen, because you had implicitly asked for it in your decision of General Assembly Resolution 1013 (XI)." He could not but emphasize the strength, the beauty of these two "armistices." "Isolated on a remote island, besieged under forcible occupation, EOKA calmly offered twice to the British the very cease-fire that the French are asking the Algerians to grant, but in vain; and this in order to be useful to peace, and at . . . great peril."

Unfortunately, after the second truce, after Resolution 1013 (XI), the attitude of the British government had changed only superficially, not substantively, Averoff-Tossizza reiterated. To all Cypriot overtures, the British government had replied negatively. It had refused all offers of negotiations. The British Ambassador in Athens, in a letter of May 30 addressed to Makarios, had rejected the Archbishop's proposals for the revocation of the emergency measures in Cyprus and the opening of negotiations. He had even threatened, at the end of this letter, that Britain might proceed to the island's partition. The Colonial Secretary and his Undersecretary had repeated this threat in the House of Commons on July 6, 1957.[68]

"To sum up, we are, to our great regret, obliged to note that the British Government has replied 'No' both to the Cypriots and to the United Nations. It is a 'No' which is not far removed from a 'Never'—a 'Never' which was pitted against all the peaceful demands of the Cypriots and of the Greek Government alike," [69] Averoff-Tossizza declared.

Coming now to the tripartite formula of negotiation, about which the British Delegate had spoken "brilliantly," the Greek Foreign Minister asserted that the British government, "according to a method which is dear to and almost traditional in British policy," had "once again had recourse to tactics designed to create confusion and to shift its own responsibilities on the shoulders of others." [70] This tripartite formula, he maintained, aimed at eliminating the people of Cyprus as the principal and essential factor in the problem and at showing that there could be no solution except through negotiations between the parties concerned—which would be Britain, Greece, and Turkey. He had to point out to the Committee that, besides setting aside the people of Cyprus as a factor, the tripartite formula—"invented in London, adopted in Ankara, and naïvely given the blessing by certain foreign ministries—seemed intended to isolate Greece so as to compel it either to betray the Cypriots, whose spokesman Greece was, or else to take upon oneself the responsibility of breaking off relations."

In 1955 the tripartite formula, Averoff-Tossizza recounted, had given rise to the London conference, to which Greece had gone in all good faith, only to discover immediately the atmosphere of isolation that had been prepared for it. That dismal conference had ended in a complete stalemate and had been followed by the anti-Greek outbreaks in Istanbul on September 5–6—events which had profoundly affected Greek-Turkish relations and on which the Greek government had never wished to publish the copious and frightful documentary information it had.[71] One might have thought that in this tragic experience London would have found sufficient reason for abandoning thenceforth the unfortunate tripartite formula. Unfortunately, this had not been the case. The British government had not proved sensitive to such considerations. What it was still demanding was the prolongation of its colonial presence in Cyprus and the avoidance of recognition of the right of self-determination for the Cypriots. Incomprehensible as this might seem to those who knew the liberal policy of Britain in other colonies, it was, nevertheless quite true in the case of Cyprus. Furthermore, the British government had not hesitated to use the tripartite formula again, this time with certain variations, which Mr. Noble had listed—if one could call variations, offers of mediation or conferences whose two principle features were, first, that they constantly disregarded or relegated to second place the chief interested party, the people of Cyprus; and, second, that they placed emphasis on factors whose interests should certainly be taken into consideration, but in no case could be regarded as more important than, or prior to the interests of, the people of Cyprus.

At this point, Averoff-Tossizza felt it his duty to dwell—"in all sincerity, without any hidden motives, and without any desire to envenom the atmosphere"—on the position of Greece. The attitude of Greece, he said, was clear. No person of good faith could cast doubt upon it. In connection with the Cyprus question, Greece had received the mandate to present and defend the cause of the liberation of the people of Cyprus by means of the application of the principle of self-determination. Greece had accepted that mandate, not only because four-fifths of the population of Cyprus were Greek by origin, language, religion, and culture—which alone would justify its action—but also because, over and above all, the cause was a just cause.

It should be noted, he added, that Greece spoke in the name of the Cypriots, "because that subject people is unable to plead its own cause here." That it did so did not mean at all that their rights could be ignored and that "we, having our mandate, can fail to pay heed to those who have rights." The right of the people of Cyprus to self-determination and equality, and its right to live in freedom and dignity were recognized in the relevant articles of the Charter. "It was our duty to defend those rights. It is not our right to set them aside. The Cypriots may set aside anything they like for themselves, but we may not."

British and Turkish propaganda, the Greek Foreign Minister continued, "accuses us of nourishing expansionist ambitions and of desiring to enlarge our own country by wresting away a territory that belongs to a friendly power. We shall never know," he added, courteously sarcastic, "to what extent the Turkish arguments are English or the English arguments Turkish. But, whatever their origin, it is not difficult to recognize that they are false." Cyprus, in the first place, belonged to no one but its own people. Britain did not risk losing anything that belonged to it. The people of Cyprus, in spite of their colonial dependence, he definitely said, did not belong to Britain.

He wished to point out to the Committee, Averoff-Tossizza went on to say, that Greece was the only party that proclaimed it had no claim on Cyprus, and that it was invoking no rights on that island. Britain, on the other hand, was trying to press its own colonial rights, while Turkey, on the basis of the Turkish minority and strategic arguments, was trying to insist on rights much greater than any justified by the existence of such a minority of by such strategic arguments. "Against invalid and outdated colonial rights, and against unjustified covetousness, we oppose," he declared, "the total and exclusive rights of the Cypriots." In the Cyprus question, he re-emphasized, Greece was not seeking profit for itself, booty or recompense. It was demanding everything for Cyprus, nothing for itself.

"But, we are asked, alas very often, what will happen if, on the day the people of Cyprus becomes free, it decides to unite with Greece? We know that *enosis* is displeasing both to the British and to the Turks. But allow me, in the first place, to say that we are here to do what is just and reasonable, even if what is just and reasonable is displeasing to some among us." However, he added, with another tinge of sarcasm, even if one were to accept the desire of the Anglo-Turkish holy alliance as representing international law, it would be monstrous to say that, simply to prevent *enosis* in the future, the people of Cyprus should be condemned to perpetual servitude. One saw there the evil pretext of colonialism, which clung to its prey.

The people of Cyprus were and should be the main factor in the problem before the Committee, the Greek representative reiterated. The entire people of Cyprus might decide in favor of independence. It might decide in favor of partition of the island. It might decide to remain in the Commonwealth. It might decide to establish links of close co-operation with Turkey, its Arab neighbors, and with Greece. It might serve as a rallying point instead of being the apple of discord, if it were allowed to base its future upon its great civilization and its great wisdom. Greece was willing in advance to accept any decision that the Cypriot people took freely. This was an official declaration the Greek government had often made.

Among the solutions he had just mentioned was that of partition of the island. "We know very well," he said, "that partition is not a solution." Wherever it had been utilized, it had created greater problems than those that had given rise to partition. Furthermore, in Cyprus, the intermingling of the Turkish minority with the mass of the population excluded the application of such a formula. There was not one town, not one district, no matter how small, where the Turks were in a majority, he pointed out. In the history of the application of the right of self-determination and of international plebiscites, there was no precedent for a partition on the basis of the decision of the majority and the decision of the minority.[72] Wherever it was decided upon, it was done so on the basis of the will of the majority.

In an appeal to the self-interest of all member states (the Greek counterweapon to the British and Turkish arguments about the need for respect for the principle *pacta sunt servanda*), Averoff-Tossizza observed that each of the representatives present represented a state, and each of them knew full well that there was not in the world an entirely homogeneous state without any minorities. One could therefore imagine what might occur with regard to world peace "if we decided to set up a precedent of this nature, if we agreed to discuss a solution that recognizes to a minority the right to shatter national unity and carry with it the territorial substratum to which it laid claim." In spite of all the arguments "our main objection to partition is that it is contrary to the will of the people, who must be recognized as sole masters of their future." It was this capital argument, Averoff-Tossizza said, that forced his government, above all, not to accept tripartite negotiations.

In point of fact, the Greek representative asserted, there was only one party concerned: the people of Cyprus. Britain was not so much a party concerned as a party responsible, since it was "the holder of the liberties of the Cypriots." All the rest was marginal to the problem of the liberation of Cyprus and the abolition of the colonial regime in the island. At the very center of that problem there were only the British and the Cypriots. Perhaps on one point or another certain states might have certain specific considerations to make known. Turkey might be concerned with the fate of the Turkish minority. This was perfectly understandable. Perhaps Turkey, Greece, Syria, Lebanon, and even the great powers might be concerned about certain aspects of the problem concerning national security in the geographical region of the island. This also seemed legitimate. It should also be recognized that the people of Cyprus should be given the possibility of exercising their right of self-determination and that they should make known their views. It was then and only then that one could truly and fully consider the possible incidences on the international level and seek a way of satisfying the legitimate concerns of the other parties. "But there, too, we must be frank and objective, and we must declare quite clearly that, as we see it, this concern, no matter from what quarter, if well-founded, must be fully satisfied. But these concerns on the part of others cannot and should not in any way be turned into a veto upon which the fate of an entire people may rest." Furthermore, the idea of "the parties concerned," in the absence of the truly interested group—the people of Cyprus—could not for one minute stand a careful analysis. It would be naïve, he added, to believe that the number of parties concerned could be limited to two or three; namely, that it could be narrowed down "to the partners that you want to include in this group," if the only basis of the problem—Cyprus and its people—were abandoned.

On the international level, Averoff-Tossizza argued further, although the Turks, the Greeks, and the British had their word to say, they were not the only ones. To deal with a subject on an international level was to submit for international consideration a problem upon which all parties concerned made known their views. Otherwise the impression might be created of a plot or conspiracy designed to act for the benefit of some and to the detriment of others. In this connection, the Greek Foreign Minister referred to a speech by Krishna Menon in the Indian Parliament on March 27, 1957, in which the Indian had said that his delegation had initiated in the United Nations the conception that the people mainly concerned were the Cypriot people, and that Cyprus was not to be bargained off between Turkey, Greece and Britain. The Syrians, Krishna Menon had noted on that occasion, had said that while Turkey was only forty-five miles from Cyprus, Syria, was only thirty-seven miles away. The issue of Cyprus, he had added, was not a matter of a country being sliced up between various people. This had represented a degree of success in the process of conciliation, and the basis of it had been that the parties involved were Britain, as a metropolitan power, and the Cyprus people as the people who were not free, and therefore if they wanted to remain as part of the sisterhood of nations of the Commonwealth, it was up to them. The Indian government, Krishna Menon had stated further, both publicly and privately, had always taken the view that the remedy lay in recognizing before it was too late, and by not giving too little, the demand of the Cypriot people for independence.

Nothing could be clearer, Averoff-Tossizza averred. It was not necessary to remind the Committee that Krishna Menon had been the father of Resolution 1013 (XI) or that he, as well as a number of other representatives, had spoken in the same way, equally categorically and equally explicitly.[73]

Assuming, however, that one accepted the theory of the "interested parties" as the framework for negotiations, and, that, for some reason or another, Greece were forced to betray its mandate and accept a compromise based upon giving up the rights of the people of Cyprus, how could anyone impose on the Cypriots a solution contrary to their will? "Should we use force and violence again?" He saw no other way. The British administration and the colonial torturers would then be supported by Turkish and Greek gendarmes. "This alliance of jailers that is proposed to us here, on the basis of a tripartite agreement, is offered us in the United Nations as a way of bringing peace and liberty to the people of Cyprus. This argument *ad absurdum* illuminates clearly the underlying problem and should sweep away all doubts."

"So we come to the intransigent attitude of the British Government," the Greek Foreign Minister told the Committee. "This is the official policy of the United Kingdom, and there can be no doubt about that." It was true, though, he went on to acknowledge that in a democratic country such as Britain, public opinion, the state of mind of the people, was a determining factor. Even as the policy of the British government was such as he had described, the British people, in their great majority, recognized the rights of the Cypriots and, judging from the press, had rallied to them regardless of political affiliations. The great majority of the publications in England, many of them with conservative leanings, had stated their understanding of, and at times their sympathy for, the Cypriot cause. But this cause had found its deepest echo, had been adopted in all its just and reasonable scope, in the Labour party itself. In this connection Averoff-Tossizza quoted at length the relevant resolution adopted on November 27, 1957, by the Labour party's National Executive Committee. This recognized the right of the people of Cyprus to determine their own future after an agreed interim period of self-government.[74] The Greek Foreign Minister on this occasion expressed his feelings of admiration and appreciation for the Labour party, whose resolution had produced great rejoicing in both Cyprus and Greece. Such gestures were in keeping with the liberal tradition of the British people as a whole. Britain's liberalism was a decisive factor in the evolution of the world toward an international society in which arbitrariness would disappear and justice would reign. The prestige of the Labour party on the international level had been maintained.

"We are told," he went on to say, "that the Labour party was the Opposition and that it was therefore easy for it to make promises today that may not be kept tomorrow . . . when the Labour party becomes the government.[75] But," he added, "we know what part of this statement is true and what part is exaggeration." What was important, in his view, was that the resolution of the Labour party respected principles, because the British people as a whole were attached to principles. Thence, after observing that the Assembly, too, discussed principles recognized by the Charter but not their ways of implementation, he posed the question:

Can we do less for the people of Cyprus than that which half of the British people has solemnly committed itself to on a level of principle? Can we do anything else but recognize the right of self-determination which the Labour Party has recognized as applying to Cyprus? What logic, what political consid-erations could be invoked on our part to justify a negative vote on the principle which lies at the very basis of that policy which will be applied in Cyprus some day on behalf of the British Government? What would our refusal today mean today, since ultimately the government concerned will not refuse that principle?

After this appeal to the Committee, an appeal he had also made in his talks with Ambassador Allen in trying to get U.S. support in the Cyprus issue,[76] Averoff-Tossizza began his peroration by invoking the picture of the people of Cyprus painfully following its *via dolorosa* since 1954. The Cypriots, whose suffering and rights were great, were asking "us"—the United Nations—to recognize these rights which were cardinal points in "our Charter." The people of Cyprus were an overburdened colonial people. Had they or had they not the right to live like any other people, free and equal "to the rest of us?" Was there in this hall, or was there not, a place for Cyprus? That was the question that the Greek Delegation's draft resolution had the honor to submit to the Assembly.

At the eleventh session, the Greek Foreign Minister once again re-minded the Committee in his rhetoric of identification, "we accepted" a resolution proposed by India and "we expressed the hope" that this unanimously adopted resolution, "which sprang from the great political and spiritual and moral power inherent in the Indian nation," would lead to a true change in the situation and would open the road to the liberation of the people of Cyprus. That was why he had not pressed to a vote the resolution the Greek Delegation had submitted then. He had declared, however, that he would not withdraw this draft, that it would still stand, and that it would be revived if the solution provided for in Resolution 1013 (XI) was not implemented by the time of the Assembly's next regular session.[77]

The statement he had just made proved that the hopes and aspirations of the Cypriot people had been ignored. Tyranny still reigned in Cyprus. He was forced to revive the Greek Delegation's draft resolution, "which had been held over from the last session." In doing so he was fulfilling the mandate of the Cypriot people. But this was a mandate of the Greek people as a whole—with no exceptions whatever, because the people of Greece, through its sacrifices for freedom and liberty, had the right on its own behalf, to demand freedom for the Cypriots. Greece had not hesi-tated a moment "when the whirlwind of the Nazi and communist forces had swept practically all over Europe." When "heroic Britain" was all alone and on its knees, Greece went into the unequal fight because liberty was at stake. After almost eight years of war, the United Nations had invited Greece to fight for the freedom and liberty of Korea. In proportion to its population, Greece had played a part that was no less than that played by others.[78] Therefore, the Greek people had the right to ask the United Nations no longer to permit the people of Cyprus to live

under a colonialist regime. The dead as well as the living had the same
right to demand this.

But, Averoff-Tossizza concluded, reverting to his role as an international actor,[79] he was also speaking on behalf of principles. Did any one
dare to give him one case where "the fundamental principles of our
democratic age" had been more clearly betrayed than in Cyprus? Could
anyone for a minute think that these people had not suffered enough to
be permitted their liberty? Could anyone doubt that it was their will to
be free? Could anyone question their degree of civilization and their
ability to be free? "What then would be left of our faith in those
principles whose value, importance, and beauty we have never ceased to
proclaim if we did nothing to help these martyred people to recover their
freedom?"

Something specific must at least be done, the Greek Foreign Minister
declared. It was with a feeling both of overwhelming responsibility to
the quick and the dead, on whose behalf he spoke, and of anxiety for his
suffering brethren who believed in the United Nations, that he appealed
to all members to vote in favor of the draft resolution his delegation had
had the honor to submit to the Committee—

The meeting rose at 1:05 P.M.

B. The 928th Meeting of the First Committee

In the afternoon of December 9, the Turkish views were heard before
the Political Committee at its 928th meeting. Ambassador Sarper underlined that the Assembly, once again at the Greek government's request,
was discussing the question of Cyprus—"an island which lies off the
shores of Turkey and on which part of the population is Turkish—an
island the present international status of which was decided upon in the
form of a transfer of sovereignty from Turkey to the United Kingdom in
the Treaty of Lausanne, signed between Turkey, the United Kingdom,
Greece and other governments." After thus summarizing the four basic
reasons for the "direct interest and concern" of the people and government of Turkey in the discussion, the Turkish representative, like his
British and Greek colleagues who had preceded him, sought to set the
tone of the debate on a high level by underlining "the sincere regret" and
"sorrow" that his government felt at "the division and bitterness" between Greece, Turkey, and Britain which had been caused by the
Cyprus question during the last years. As several speakers had stated at
the previous debate over this question, the three countries had nothing to
gain from the deterioration of their mutual relations. About the relations
of his country with Greece in particular, he observed,

we in Turkey believe that the two countries, geographically placed as they
are, have a common destiny, so that anything which might harm the real

interests of the one will constitute an equal danger for the real interests of the other.

The vigorous propaganda that had been going on for several years, Sarper went on to say, had inflamed passions, agitated and aroused public opinion in Cyprus and elsewhere, creating confusion and obscuring the essential points of agreement in the real issues as well as the remaining points of discord, in a "deluge of slogans, passionate appeals, recriminations and counter-recriminations, accusations and counteraccusations." As a result the time had arrived for stripping down the Cyprus question to its bare essentials "so that it may be discussed in calm and serenity for the purpose of discerning the issues involved . . . and of preparing a more appropriate atmosphere for exploring the possibilities which exist to achieve progress toward a solution satisfactory to all concerned."

He wanted, he said, to stress the words "satisfactory to all concerned," because, in the first place, Cyprus lay forty miles off the shores of Turkey and nearly 700 miles away from Greece,[80] and in all history, even before the rise of the Ottoman Empire, it had been a part of Asia Minor, never a part of Greece.

From this point, which he had developed far more extensively at the previous Assembly's session,[81] the Turkish representative moved on to the background of Britain's legal title to Cyprus, referring to the agreement of 1878 which put the island under British administration under the terms of a Turkish-British alliance for the defense requirements of Turkey; to the Lausanne treaty, under which sovereignty over Cyprus was transferred from Turkey to Britain in 1923; and to the continued validity of that treaty to which Greece among other governments, was a party.

Thirdly, Sarper stressed the ethnic factor—the existence in Cyprus of "two distinct communities with completely different cultural, ethnic, religious, linguistic, and national backgrounds and aspirations." Although the ratio had varied in the past, he acknowledged that "at present" the Greek-speaking community on the island itself was larger than the Turkish community. Nevertheless, he did not go much into the background of ethnic developments in Cyprus, as he had at previous Assembly sessions.[82]

The Turkish representative then went on to plead that to base one's self upon this third factor alone, to the exclusion of all the others, and to hope for a solution of the Cyprus problem "in the form of a *Diktat*[83] of one of the three interested governments" could only be termed as a proposition that "besides being against all the rules of justice and equity, is also completely lacking in realism." One only had to remember some of the basic facts and realities to see why any unilateral solution was inconceivable.

In order "to bring the Cyprus question from the domain of ambiguous fantasy down to the constructive path of facing the realities," Ambassador Sarper continued, the first constructive step forward would be to eliminate as far as possible "such epithets, slogans, accusations and counteraccusations as are irrelevant to the problem under consideration and to its final solution." Accordingly, he went on to assert that terms such as "colonialists," or "colonial oppression" which were used in Greece to characterize the British regime in Cyprus were "smears," and he sought to defend his own government against charges that it had been supporting colonialism by its policies.[84] The real issues involved in the Cyprus question, he contended, "have nothing to do with colonialism." That Cyprus was currently under a colonial status, he acknowledged. This fact, however, "does not and cannot make of this island a candidate for annexation by another distant country which has no right to put forward such a claim." Turkey prided itself in being one of the first nations in Asia to have effectively risen against all forms of colonialism, he said.

"The Cypriot Orthodox Church and the extremist elements in Greece," the Turkish representative went on to charge, were responsible for constantly frustrating "all efforts to reach a satisfactory settlement," because they considered such solutions as hindering the ultimate annexation of Cyprus to Greece. Classifying the issue as one of "colonialism *versus* anticolonialism," he reiterated, could not give the necessary clue for finding an answer to the problem. Instead then of repeating "irrelevant slogans," his government would prefer to eliminate stale recriminations and concentrate as far as possible on the present and the future.

To a lesser extent than during the previous Assembly,[85] Sarper then touched upon the matter of the Turkish attitude toward the principle of self-determination. His government, he wished to reiterate, considered "the lofty principle of equal rights and self-determination, as one of the main pillars of international relations." What his delegation opposed, however, was the "use of this lofty principle as a means for furthering annexationist ambitions or for incorporating under Greek rule over 100,000 Turkish Cypriots against their will." The original Greek claim on Cyprus, he reminded the Committee members, had been first declared openly and officially as "*enosis*," whereas during the recent years a change in tactics had been adopted by the partisans of *enosis* who presented this claim as stemming from the principle of equal rights and self-determination of peoples.

But his delegation had dealt with this matter during the debates at the previous Assembly.[86] An abstract discussion on the merits of the principle of self-determination was not sufficient, Sarper asserted, to solve the real problems involved in the Cyprus question. At this point, he reminded "the distinguished Foreign Minister of Greece" of certain declarations that "the great Greek statesman," Eleftherios Venizelos, had made during the Lausanne Conference (Venizelos, it will be recalled, had been not only the architect of the famous but abortive Treaty of Sèvres but also, in co-operation with Kemal Atatürk, of the new era of Greek-Turkish

friendship inaugurated in 1930). In these declarations, which referred to
Western Thrace, where the Turkish population, Sarper said, outnum-
bered the Greeks in a ratio of four to one, the Greek statesman had
argued in response to a Turkish request for a plebiscite there, to be
carried out under international control, that it was true that democratic
principles inclined him to accept the right of peoples to self-
determination but that this right did not constitute the only relevant
factor in the solution of questions about the disposal of territories inhabited by mixed populations.[87] Sarper assured the Committee his purpose
for bringing up this question was not to rekindle old fires. He merely
wished to ask the "distinguished Foreign Minister of Greece" if he did
not feel that the time had come for certain circles in Greece to give
serious thought to the words of "this great Greek patriot and statesman"
and to study their relevance to the Cyprus question. Such an approach
could bear fruitful results.

After drawing the Assembly's attention to the manner in which the
Greek government made use of only certain parts of the UN Charter,
"giving its own interpretation of these parts and carefully evading mentions of other articles and principles which are also included in the
Charter," the Turkish representative proceeded to a lengthy juridical
analysis of certain points in Article 73 of the Charter. This, together with
Article 74, deals with non-self-governing territories. In his analysis, Sarper dwelt particularly on the second paragraph of that article which
provides that one of the duties of the administering states should be:

to develop self-government, to take due account of the political aspirations of
the peoples, and to assist them in the progressive development of their free
political institutions, according to the *particular circumstances of each territory
and its peoples* and their varying stages of advancement.

Emphasizing the above italicized words ("particular circumstances of
each territory and its peoples"), he maintained that in Cyprus there
existed both particular circumstances and two different peoples, with
entirely different cultural, linguistic, religious and national aspirations.
As a result, Article 73, paragraph (b), of the Charter left no alternative to
the administering power in Cyprus but to take account of this particular
circumstance, and the British government's statement of December 19,
1956, repeated subsequently in the House of Commons, on the conditions
in which the principle of self-determination might eventually be applied
in the special circumstances of Cyprus on a basis of equality to the Greek
and Turkish communities, was in line with the spirit and the letter of this
article of the Charter.

After dwelling in some detail on the *travaux préparatoires* that took
place in 1945 at the San Francisco Conference with regard to the drafting of this article of the Charter and showing that it had not been by
accident that Articles 73 and 76 of the Charter were the only ones in
which the word "peoples" in the plural was used in conjunction with the

words "each territory" in the singular, which proved that the Charter's drafters had deliberately taken into account that in some non-self-governing territories that had not assumed the characteristics of a nation or a state, it was possible to have more than one people,[88] the Turkish representative re-emphasized that there were two completely different peoples living in Cyprus and that there was no Cypriot nationhood—a statement evidently aimed at the Indian contention that such a nation existed.[89]

Continuing along this line, the Turkish representative stressed the strained, even hostile, relations unfortunately prevailing between the Turkish and Greek communities, and the fact that the Turks and Greeks lived in different sections of towns or in separate villages, had separate religious institutions and schools, separate professional, social, and even athletic organizations. "Ever since the time when the Turkish Cypriots ceased to be a majority because of emigration to Turkey and other factors, the new Greek-speaking majority in Cyprus" had exerted pressure upon the Turkish Cypriots in economic matters, in municipal affairs, and in their professional and private contacts, Sarper asserted. "Since the arrival from Greece of extremists who organized terrorism in an attempt to intimidate the Cypriots who are opposed to *enosis,* co-operation and coexistence between the two communities had become totally impossible," he maintained. EOKA had not only been responsible for the loss of innocent lives among the Turkish Cypriots but had also issued proclamations to the "Greek-speaking Cypriots" demanding that they cease all contacts with the Turks and threatening with most severe punishments those who acted against these orders. As a result, collaboration between the two communities had become impossible so that these had been split as separate Greek and Turkish organizations. This regrettable situation was not the fault of the Turkish community. But the fact remained that the Turkish Cypriots refused to be placed under the rule of the Greek government or of the Greek Cypriot community. This was undeniable, he declared.

In spite of these facts, all the actions, proposals, statements, and policies of the Greek government as well as of the Cypriot Orthodox Church are aimed at bringing about through the annexation of the entire territory of Cyprus against the will of the Turkish Cypriots and in contradiction to stipulations of treaties signed by Greece.

That was the issue under discussion—not the question of freedom, liberty, and political progress for the Greek and Turkish elements of the population. There was no disagreement about the latter question.

Reverting to the choice of words—"the particular circumstances of each territory"—in the above-quoted paragraph of Article 73 of the Charter, the Turkish representative said it was a self-evident truism, an axiom, that the particular circumstances of each non-self-governing territory had to be taken into account. The Charter on this point had merely reaffirmed one of the main bases for seeking political and juridical solutions within a framework of equity, justice, and the existing realities. He then referred to two examples of the application of this principle in settlements concerning the incorporation of territories in already existing states: First, to the case of the Aland islands between Sweden and Finland, which the League of Nations decided should go to Finland because of historic, geographic and strategic reasons, although their inhabitants had overwhelmingly voted in a plebiscite to join Sweden,[90] and, second, to the case of the Trieste region, inhabited by a mixed Italian and Yugoslav population—this case being finally solved by having one part of the territory placed under Italian administration and the other part under Yugoslav administration.

Referring to the Cyprus problem, Sarper observed that even the Greek draft resolutions presented to the Assembly spoke of the "population of the island of Cyprus," not to Cypriots, and that Greek statesmen spoke of "Greek Cypriots" and "Turkish Cypriots." Just as there was no Triestan nationhood, so there was no Cypriot nationhood. In these circumstances, he submitted, it was not the independence of a nation that was being discussed but the change of sovereignty of a territory with a mixed population from one country to another. The word "independence" in connection with Cyprus, he asserted, had never been used seriously but was only meant to serve as a stepping stone for "the annexation of the island by Greece." The formula of independence, even an independence guaranteed by the United Nations, had also had its supporters in connection with the so-called Free Territory of Trieste provided for in the Italian Peace Treaty of February 10, 1947. However, it had proved impossible to implement such a formula in a territory that lay between Italy and Yugoslavia and was inhabited by Italians and Yugoslavs.

Thence, for a third time, and more extensively than he had done earlier, the Turkish representative referred to the propinquity of Cyprus to Turkey to justify his country's interest in the island's status. Here was an offshore island of the Turkish mainland that commanded "over its vital routes of communication, defense, and trade," and was of no importance to Greece from the point of view of its defense or communications requirements. Could these circumstances be ignored? However, he did not develop this important strategic point to the same extent that he had at the Assembly's eleventh session.[91]

Then there was the matter of balance, of equilibrium, which the Treaty of Lausanne had brought about in 1923 by mutual consent of the countries concerned. This treaty, Sarper observed, had provided for the revision and re-establishment of the existing frontiers between Turkey and Greece. In that general settlement, "the Turkish province of Western Thrace, with a population that was overwhelmingly Turkish" had been ceded to Greece "as a conciliatory sacrifice on the part of Turkey." That there had been no question of including Cyprus among the Greek domains at that time had helped reach a balance "even if this was in favor of Greece." This treaty was still valid. Was it proposed not to disregard these particular circumstances? Could the Assembly ignore all the elements that went together to establish an international agreement and take only one article of this agreement out of context—the one by which Turkey had yielded its sovereignty over Cyprus to Britain—and modify it through a resolution? Was it suggested that the existence of this general treaty, which also included two articles on Cyprus, was not one of the circumstances to which due account should be given? Should the circumstance that the Turkish Cypriots refused to accept the solution of being incorporated into Greece be ignored, in deciding about the future of a territory with a mixed population?

After reiterating that Article 73, paragraph (b), had nothing to do with any situation that might exist in independent and sovereign countries whose political status had already been formed but dealt only with non-self-governing territories, the Turkish Ambassador stressed that the case of Cyprus offered no similarity with any other problems that faced the United Nations, even though the Greek Delegation had often sought to establish the contrary. "We are confident," he said, "that, in its wisdom and profound sense of responsibility, the General Assembly will continue to recognize the necessity of studying each case presented to it as a particular question requiring a particular attention and judgment on its own merits."

Coming now to Resolution 1013 (XI), the Turkish diplomat compared the situation before that resolution had been adopted with the situation that had developed afterward. His government, he noted first, had accepted as a reasonable basis for negotiations, whereas Greece had not, the statement of December 19, 1956, by Colonial Secretary Lennox-Boyd that the British government was prepared to consider the exercise of the right of self-determination by both the Greek and the Turkish community separately [92] (raising for the Greeks, as will be recalled, the specter of possible partition of the island). Second, Sarper deplored the violence and terrorism occurring prior to Resolution 1013 (XI) that "was taking a tragic toll of the Cypriot population, the greatest number of victims being among the Greek Cypriots who were opposed to the annexation of Cyprus by Greece." [93] Turkish Cypriots, too, were falling victims "of the Greek terrorist organization headed by Colonel Grivas of the Greek Army," and "the official radio stations of Greece were encouraging violence, and a press campaign was being conducted . . . with the aim of creating bitterness among the Greek people against the United Kingdom and Turkey."

Under such circumstance, the Turkish representative continued, the Assembly, at its previous session, had heard the views of the Greek government and finally had adopted Resolution 1013 (XI), which he quoted in full. "It was only natural," he observed, "that perhaps none of the three governments directly concerned in the Cyprus question" should find every part of that resolution wholly to its own liking. Yet, he stated, this resolution did include all necessary elements for co-operation in working toward a solution if a sincere desire for a peaceful, democratic, and just solution existed among every one "of these three governments." If, on the other hand, one government assumed an intransigent attitude in the hope of imposing its own *Diktat* upon the others, then the Assembly's conciliatory efforts would have been wasted, and, regardless of the wording of any resolution, progress toward a settlement would be further delayed.

Since Resolution 1013 (XI) had been passed, the general trend of developments in the Cyprus question, in spite of obstacles that still remained, had, nevertheless, been hopeful. Terrorism on the island, Sarper acknowledged, had decreased to a considerable extent, even though Grivas remained there and, immediately before the debate in the Assembly, there had been signs of increased underground activity. The support furnished from Greece to terrorist activities in Cyprus, the increase or decrease of such activities for tactical purposes, and the threat of further violence "unless unjustifiable extremist demands are accepted," were matters that had all been denounced in the previous Assembly,[94] Sarper said.

Since the previous debate, the Turkish representative observed further, the British government had relaxed some of the emergency measures it had imposed. It had released Makarios from the Seychelles, even though he had not denounced terrorism and violence. This had created an atmosphere more conducive to agreement and settlement.

In this atmosphere, Sarper noted, there had been proposals for the resumption of negotiations between the British, Turkish, and Greek governments. One of these proposals (Lord Ismay's) had been in the form of an offer to mediate between Turkey, Britain, and Greece, for the purpose of a resumption of negotiations. Turkey and Britain had accepted this proposal. Greece had not. Then, the British government had made further efforts to have a resumption of negotiations. Turkey had accepted these offers. Greece had refused them.[95]

The Greek government, Ambassador Sarper went on to say, had not accepted negotiations except under its own terms and on condition that its own aspirations for Cyprus were recognized in advance. In all appearance, its interpretation of Resolution 1013 (XI) had coincided with that of Archbishop Makarios, who, in his letter of May 28, 1957, to the British government had expressed willingness to engage in bipartite talks on behalf of the people of Cyprus on the basis of the application of self-determination in accordance with the UN Charter "in a spirit of good will and mutual understanding and on the conditions provided by the resolution." [96]

He did not know what experts had advised the Cypriot Ethnarchy on this interpretation, but, if extremist politicians had devised such an interpretation of Resolution 1013 (XI) for reasons of internal politics, he regretted to have to say that in the international field, to his knowledge, there had never been such a misrepresentation of the text of an international document.

Invoking, first, International Law to support this charge, the Turkish representative drew the Committee's attention to established international practice and to a number of specific rulings in the International Court of Justice that there could be no interpretation of an international agreement through the addition of words not provided in the original text. He also argued that prior to the Assembly's resolution, Britain, Turkey, and Greece had carried out negotiations on the Cyprus question at the Tripartite London Conference of 1955. "To interpret the General Assembly resolution in the sense that it urges a change in these procedures, that it recommends dropping all tripartite negotiations and hopes for the opening of bilateral talks in which the United Kingdom will have to accept in advance all aspirations of the Greek government, and the Turkish government will be excluded, is a most fantastic manner of approach to this question," he declared. Argumentation of this kind could only obstruct and frustrate the hopes and desires of the Assembly.

Ambassador Sarper proceeded then to attack the premises that underlay the Greek interpretation of Resolution 1013 (XI)—the viewpoint that the parties primarily concerned were the British government, on the one hand, and the people of Cyprus, on the other. These premises, in the Turkish representative's view, were, first, that the Turkish and Greek governments were not interested parties in the Cyprus question. Therefore, negotiations for a solution could take place only between the population of Cyprus and the British government. Second, that of the two ethnic communities in Cyprus, the Greek-speaking community was larger. Therefore, only the Greek-speaking population had a right to negotiate on the future of the island. Third, that the leader of the Greek Orthodox Church in Cyprus was this community's leader. Therefore, only he could negotiate with the British government.[97]

On the first of the above premises, he had already expounded the reasons the Turkish government regarded itself as an interested party in any discussion affecting the status of Cyprus. As for the Greek government, it had disproved by its own actions the assertion that it was not interested in the question. On the second of the above premises, Sarper observed that Cyprus was not an independent, sovereign state or a national entity. Its status had been decided by the Treaty of Lausanne which had also settled the fate of territories inhabited by Turks and Greeks. If a change in the status of Cyprus was to be discussed, on what grounds could it be claimed that one ethnic community would decide not only on its own future but also that of another ethnic community? How could it be argued that "the balance established by the Treaty of Lausanne between Turkey and Greece which had a total population of 33 million, could be completely upset by the sole decision of a handful of majority—a majority of 300 thousand—in one relatively small territory?"[98] Article 73 of the Charter did affirm, among other things, that due account should be given to the aspirations of the peoples of each non-self-governing territory, but to say that the Greek community would decide about the fate of the Turkish Cypriots and that they would negotiate both on their behalf and on behalf of the Turks was a proposition that it was impossible to understand.

As for the third premise of the Greek interpretation of Resolution 1013 (XI), namely that bipartite negotiations should take place between the Greek community in Cyprus and the British government, Ambassador Sarper saw fit to refer to previous negotiations on the Cyprus question. He not only once again underlined that tripartite negotiations between Turkey, Greece, and Britain had taken place in 1955[99] but also that after the London Tripartite Conference, Harding had conducted a series of consultations separately with the representatives of the Turkish and the "Greek-speaking" community and that the latter consultations—between Harding and Makarios[100]—had been in essence "carried out by the Greek government itself—with the Archbishop acting in the foreground for reasons of expediency." To buttress this argument he referred to a statement contained in the Greek *White Book* of 1956 that these consultations between the Ethnarch and the Governor—the Turkish Delegate avoided using the term "negotiations" which the Greeks did—had the "active support and co-operation of the Greek Government."[101] Furthermore, he noted, that when Makarios had arrived in New York, he had stated that he was going to collaborate with the Greek Delegation to the Assembly. While not questioning the Greek government's right to collaborate or act in concert with any person of its choice, Sarper went on to state, the meaning of the Greek viewpoint that bipartite "consultations" were the sole appropriate procedure for dealing with the Cyprus problem was that the Greek government had devised a formula for entering itself into negotiations while excluding Turkey. This was an attempt to impose a unilateral solution, to monopolize negotiations and to make believe that such was the feeling of the Assembly. For this formula also included the acceptance of the Greek point of view in advance.

In the peroration to the first part of his prepared address, Sarper reiterated the points he had made at the outset—the need to discuss in frankness and sincerity the question of Cyprus without resort to propaganda or counterpropaganda. The vital interests of countries and of peoples could never be decided upon with a play of words or a twisting of the facts. The experts who had advised the interpretation of Resolution 1013 (XI) in the manner he had described had, in reality, rendered service to no one. They were responsible for the unnecessary prolongation of the existing situation and the needless continuation of tension when progress could have been achieved long ago toward a solution satisfactory to all concerned. His own government's desire for a peaceful, just and democratic solution, he said, using the terms of Resolution 1013 (XI) "had not been shared by all elements involved in the Cyprus issue." The Greek government had hastened to submit a new recourse to the United Nations on July 12, in spite of "some progress . . . already. . . . achieved." And it had submitted its explanatory memorandum two months later, in spite of the provisions of rule 20 of the rules of procedure which requires that "all items proposed for inclusion on the agenda should be accompanied by an explanatory memorandum." This suggested, he said, that the Greek government wished to use the rostrum of the United Nations as a means for propaganda. Such tactics, he continued, could not be in the true interest of the "Greek-speaking" Cypriots or the Turkish Cypriots. Nor could they benefit the Greek, Turkish, or British governments.

In conclusion, Sarper expressed the view that Resolution 1013 (XI) included all the necessary elements for co-operation between the "three governments directly concerned," if a desire for a peaceful, democratic, and just solution of the Cyprus question was shared by these three governments. Since that resolution had been adopted considerable progress had been achieved for the creation of a more suitable atmosphere for the resumption of the negotiations "between the three governments concerned." The only cause for the delay in achieving progress toward "a reasonable and satisfactory solution of the Cyprus question" was that the Greek government "had rejected all efforts for such negotiations." Endeavors, however, to impose a unilateral solution with the aid of such tactics as violence, terrorism, propaganda, and misrepresentation of facts could have no possibility of success. Such methods had damaged not only the interests of the two communities in Cyprus but also the co-operation between Turkey, Greece, and Britain "which had hitherto maintained excellent relations."

It was his delegation's hope, Sarper declared, that the debate might contribute toward the achievement of further progress in the Cyprus question by eliminating all attempts to conceal the real issues involved. He expressed confidence that the Assembly would not fail in discharging this important duty so that a solution might be achieved in accordance with the letter and the spirit of the resolution it had adopted.

This, Sarper explained, was the end of the statement he had prepared in his first comments in the debate. However, having heard "the amazing statement made by Mr. Averoff-Tossizza this morning, I feel compelled now to answer a few points which were raised by him." For other points he would have answers in the course of the debate. He begged the Committee to bear with him for a few more minutes.

He was extremely sorry that Averoff-Tossizza had seen fit to bring into the debate the propaganda of the fanatic extremists of the Greek-Cypriot organizations, accusing British forces of atrocities, tortures and other acts that would exist only "in the mediaeval imaginations of the mediaeval-minded organizations." His delegation had no doubt that the answers of the British Delegation would prove to the Assembly the unfounded and unfair character of these charges. Turkey today was an ally and a friend of Britain, but this had not been the case in all history. Indeed, Sarper noted, there had been unfortunate periods in which "we have met the British not around a friendly conference table, but on a bitterly fought battlefield." Basing himself on the testimony furnished by Turkish soldiers and officers who had fought the British in one of the bitterest battles of the world, at Gallipoli (during World War I), he wished to state that the British soldier had accomplished his duty in an honorable way. To accuse him of atrocities and tortures was a cynical attempt to slander. He was sorry that such elements had been introduced into the debate.

In his first statement in the debate, Sarper went on to say, he had tried to evade any detailed reference to certain aspects of the Cyprus question that had been exposed to UN members and to world opinion during the debate at the previous session. Among the aspects he had not chosen to elaborate again had been the instigation, organization, and support from Greece of terrorist activities in Cyprus. But when "the terrorist organizations, which have perpetrated hideous crimes, now attempt to launch a campaign against those whose duty it is to maintain order and justice, and when the representative of Greece to the General Assembly introduces this campaign into our debate, I feel compelled to mention briefly a few undeniable facts . . . a minimum of facts which have been established by all neutral observers and which either cannot be denied or have already been accepted by the Greek Government itself."

In the first place, Sarper said, it was an undeniable fact that the field commander of the "terrorists" in Cyprus, Colonel Grivas, was a regular officer of the Greek Army who had been smuggled into Cyprus from Greece, "having been especially detached from the Greek Army by the previous government of Greece. The names of other specialists of terrorism who had come to Cyprus from Greece were also known."

In the second place, Sarper went on to say, "terrorist action in Cyprus has been responsible of the most hideous crimes against the Turkish population of the island." Only the previous week the names of four more innocent Turks had been added to the tragic list of victims.

In the third place, "Greek terrorism" in Cyprus had also been used as a tool of intimidation against Greek Cypriots who were opposed to the annexation of the island by Greece. Greek "terrorists," he reiterated had killed a greater number of Greek Cypriots than the total number of their victims among the Turkish and the British communities. This was a matter of facts and figures, which could not be denied. It was also irrefutable proof that the aim of the Greek "terrorists" was not so much to harm the alleged oppressor as to terrorize the Cypriots themselves in order forcefully to obtain their co-operation for the ultimate annexation of Cyprus to Greece.

In the fourth place, Sarper said, Greek ships had been caught in the act of smuggling arms and ammunition into Cyprus; the official government radio stations of Greece were continuously instigating, encouraging, and glorifying acts of "terrorism"; and Greek statesmen and government officials had made and continued to make statements in praise of violence and terrorism in Cyprus—all these had been cited with ample documentation during the debate that had taken place ten months before.[102]

"The terrorist organizations, which have committed the most hideous crimes and are now trying to appear as martyrs of an injustice," Sarper continued, "must be acting under the false impression that the General Assembly is short of memory. If we have not taken up this subject in more detail during the present debate," he added, "this was because the facts are already known to world opinion and because we thought it appropriate to make our contribution in the effort to bring calm, serenity, and a reasonable approach to our discussions." But when those who were guilty of the present tragic situation tried to present themselves as innocent victims of an injustice, when propaganda booklets to this end were distributed to the delegations in the United Nations by organizations that had up to now glorified terrorism,[103] and when the representative of Greece saw fit to introduce these elements into the debate, "we cannot," said the head of the Turkish Delegation, "help making note of certain facts which are known all over the world."

The Foreign Minister of Greece, Sarper continued, had said in his opening statement that Greece did not demand the annexation of Cyprus to Greece, but that it desired the application of the principle of self-determination so that the population of Cyprus might decide for itself upon the island's future status, and so on. Of course, even as far as that went, this statement did not deny the desire of the Greek government to annex Cyprus. But, even in the manner in which it had been presented, the statement did not reflect the true course of events that had led to the present situation in Cyprus. As a matter of fact, the only aim of those who had first created this "artificial issue" and had thrust it upon public opinion in Greece had been to agitate in favor of the territorial aggrandizement of Greece through the annexation of this distant island.

It was true that in the past years there had been individuals among the "Greek-speaking" Cypriots who had expressed the desire to see Greece annex Cyprus. The Turkish Cypriots had always expressed the desire to see Cyprus returned to Turkey. But these ambitions and desires were in the realm of platonic wishes. Peace and calm reigned over Cyprus. The greatest majority of the Cypriots had not been seized by the propaganda and agitation organized from outside. They had not been intimidated by "the organizers of terrorism" who came to Cyprus from other countries.

The turning point had come between 1948 and 1951, said the Turkish representative, repeating more or less his exposé at the Assembly's previous session.[104] This period coincided with the defeat of the Communist insurrection in Greece and with the adherence of Greece to NATO. A maneuver designed as a counteroffensive in face of these events had come promptly. The extreme left had espoused for the first time the cause of enosis,[105] and thus the co-operation between extreme left and extreme right had come about. During this period an unprecedented campaign of agitation had been started both by the extreme right and the extreme left, the former representing the Church, in favor of enosis, "which means union or annexation of Cyprus to Greece"—or Anschluss.[106] All attempts at constitutional reform on the island had been turned down by the two extremist political forces. For different reasons, neither the extreme right nor the extreme left had found any advantage for themselves in constitutional reforms in the advance of democracy. Their own political interest could profit only from the continuance of agitation for the annexation of Cyprus to Greece. Accordingly, pamphlets had been distributed, speeches delivered, a press campaign started, in which no other word was used for the Greek claim on Cyprus except enosis "or 'annexation.'" Most of these societies and organizations, although not all of them, had only recently replaced in their titles the word enosis, or "annexation" by the word "self-determination." In this way, for reasons that should be clear to anyone, the name of the "Pan-Hellenic Committee for the Enosis of Cyprus" had been changed to the "Pan-Hellenic Committee for Self-Determination in Cyprus." This Commission's President was the Archbishop of Athens.

The idea of linking up the demand for the annexation of Cyprus to Greece with the principle of self-determination, Sarper continued, had been a recent one. It had been adopted for reasons of expediency in the United Nations, and only after a minority in Cyprus had been so organized as to convince the extreme annexationists that they could now swing a part of the Cypriots to co-operate with them.

A second turning point had occurred in 1951, in Sarper's view, when the Greek government for the first time officially took upon itself the claim for the annexation of Cyprus. On February 15, 1951, in the Greek Parliament, Premier S. Venizelos had first brought forward this claim by declaring that he desired officially to "proclaim the Greek Government's demand for the union of Cyprus with Greece, the Motherland." [107] After that date and up to the decision of the Greek government to get the support of members of the United Nations, the official position continued to be openly based on a claim for "annexation." The formula of self-determination had been introduced, Sarper reiterated, as a tactical expedient in the United Nations. After quoting a press report to the effect that Makarios, in an interview published on September 13, 1955, had acknowledged that a change in tactics, not in ultimate aims, was involved in this shift from the demand for enosis to the battlecry for self-determination,[108] Sarper went on to refer to an interview of the Bishop of Kyrenia published on February 4, 1956, in which that prelate was reported as saying that "the real danger in accepting Britain's self-government offer was that this would dampen Cypriot ardor for union with Greece. We should stick to self-determination at once," the Bishop had added, "and without any intermediate stage. Self-government takes us further away from that goal." In other words, commented the Turkish diplomat, who had cited these same passages at the Assembly's eleventh session,[109] any kind of application of the principle of self-determination that might allow the Cypriots to express their opinion freely in opposition to annexation was discarded as dangerous. For, in the eyes of the bishop of Kyrenia, it was only good as a tactical weapon in the agitation and propaganda for the annexation of Cyprus.

When the Greek government in 1954 had first asked the United Nations to intervene in the Cyprus question, Sarper went on to say, it had presented its claim under the title: "Application under the auspices of the United Nations of the Principle of Equal Rights and of Self-determination of Peoples in the Case of the Population of the Island of Cyprus." But, in the explanatory memorandum of August 16 that accompanied the request for inclusion of this item in the Assembly's agenda, the words "union with Greece" and "self-determination" had been used interchangeably (see Appendix A). On December 14, 1954, he had drawn the Assembly's attention to the fact that in this explanatory memorandum the apparent interest in self-determination was inextricably mixed up with statements and allegations claiming that Cyprus belonged to Greece—in fact, that "Cyprus is Greece itself." [110]

This had been the manner in which the Cyprus question had been first introduced to the United Nations. This was still the manner in which it was being handled by the Greek government, Sarper declared. During the debate at the previous session, the Foreign Minister of Greece had made the assertion that Greece did not aim to annex Cyprus but desired only to end the colonial rule of the island. However, faced with vehement criticism on the part of Opposition parties, the Greek government had been obliged to admit in Parliament that these words were a "maneuver." In fact, the statements of such eminent Greek statesmen as Mssrs. Papandreou, Venizelos, and the late Kartalis, as well as the questions asked by them of the Greek government in Parliament, had all helped to clarify any ambiguity as to the position of the Greek government in favor of *enosis*. Among the speakers who had taken the floor on that occasion on the side of the Greek government was Mr. Stratos, a member of the Greek Delegation at the current session of the Assembly, and he had illustrated the maxim that brevity was the soul of wit by summarizing with great precision the aims of the Greek Delegation to the Assembly. On March 14, 1957, he had said that "our representatives to the United Nations had three aims: First, to inscribe the question on the agenda. Second, to obtain that it be discussed. And, third, to make an effort for obtaining the solution of the question of *enosis*." That statement had been made in the Greek Parliament and the gentleman who had made it was now in the Greek Delegation.[111]

Enosis, Sarper hammered on, meant the annexation of Cyprus to Greece. He could find no more convincing words than those Mr. Stratos

had used to explain the real meaning of the language used by the
Foreign Minister of Greece during the debate on the Cyprus question
both at the previous and at the current session of the Assembly.

Sarper then referred to another statement the Greek Foreign Minister
himself had made in Parliament—a statement, which Opposition leaders
had vainly sought to exploit to force him to resign from his post. During
the debate on Cyprus at the eleventh Assembly, Sarper recounted, Averoff-Tossizza had also stated that Greece did not demand the annexation
of Cyprus to Greece. Faced with the criticism of Greek policies in regard
to Cyprus formulated by a great number of speakers in the Political
Committee, he had gone so far as to ask him—Sarper—whether Turkey
would be ready to sign an agreement for the independence of Cyprus,
guaranteed against annexation—a question asked in order to impress the
members of the Committee. That this question had been asked could be
verified from the verbatim records of the debate in the Committee, at the
Assembly's previous session. However, a few weeks after the UN debate,
Averoff-Tossizza, speaking in Parliament, had declared that this statement he had made in formal debate in the United Nations had been a
"maneuver" designed to embarrass the Turkish Delegation.[112] "I fail to
understand," Sarper declared, "how the Turkish Delegation can be embarrassed by such self-confessed maneuvers." However, he added, he
could see that others might be embarrassed when the Assembly was
informed that a statement made by a representative at this table was
lacking in sincerity according to the confession made by the same representative only a few weeks after the debate.

The Turkish representative then recounted how his delegation, on
April 25, 1957, had addressed a letter to the Secretary-General of the UN
in which were mentioned certain public statements by Greek government
members in Parliament, statements which denoted that the aim of the
Greek government in the whole campaign organized around the Cyprus
issue was the island's annexation. The Greek Delegation, in reply to this
letter, he added, had objected on the ground that the Turkish representative had attempted to interfere in the internal politics of Greece.[113] In
reality, he had been very careful to cite only statements by Greek
government members, avoiding any statements of the Greek Opposition.
Clearly the quotation of public statements made by members of a government could not be termed an attempt to intervene in internal affairs.
The Greek Foreign Minister, on the other hand, had made ample reference to statements and resolutions of the British Opposition. He had also
given the Committee his own interpretation of the ideas of the British
Labour party concerning Cyprus.[114] That party was not represented in
the Assembly and had no possibility of accepting or rejecting the interpretations Mr. Averoff-Tossizza gave of its policies. It was, therefore,
the opinion of the Turkish Delegate that any interpretations made by Mr.
Averoff-Tossizza of such statements were interesting only from the point
of view of informing the Committee about his own ideas concerning this

matter. In any case, Ambassador Sarper had his own interpretation, which was different from the Greek Foreign Minister's—and he, Sarper, had just as much right to his interpretation as Averoff-Tossizza had to his.

Turning now to another statement by the Greek Foreign Minister that the Greek people had heroically fought to defend their country when it had been invaded by the Nazi Army during World War II, Ambassador Sarper stated that "we in Turkey have great admiration for the gallant manner in which the Greek people defended their country." He added, however, that Mr. Averoff-Tossizza had tried to link this question with the demands of Greece on Cyprus and "at this point, our points of view differ." His delegation could not conceive that the fact of having defended itself conferred upon a country the right to turn and ask for the annexation of a territory that was under the sovereignty of one of its allies who had helped in its liberation. The Greek Foreign Minister had referred, Sarper added, to the tragedy and devastation that had befallen Greece during World War II. This was a subject on which Turkey had the greatest sympathy for the Greek people. The devastation of their country had caused profound sorrow in Turkey, as elsewhere. But he could not see the point of linking that tragedy with the Cyprus question, which had nothing to do with it. He thought it would be more helpful to discuss the Cyprus question on its own merits.

In another passage of his statement, said Sarper, continuing his rhetorical offensive, Averoff-Tossizza had made certain insinuations about the demonstrations that had taken place in Istanbul two years earlier. Unfortunately, there had been some damage to property—though there had been no loss of life—during these demonstrations, which Averoff-Tossizza had called "anti-Greek riots." [115] When such unfair and unjustifiable insinuations in one part of the Greek representative's statement were made, and when one also noticed in another part of the same statement his reference to the devastation caused by foreign armies, Ambassador Sarper added, "we are naturally reminded of the complete and hideous devastation to which a great part of Turkey was subjected by the Greek Army of invasion only a few decades ago. And in a manner that will be relevant to the item presently under discussion, we wish to ask the following question: What was the Greek Army of invasion seeking at the gates of Eskisehir, Ankara, and the heart of Turkey? Was it to prove the sanctity of the right of self-determination that some adventurers tried to colonize the Turkish people at that time?"

After merely adding that if he had refrained from bringing up these matters in the debate, any initiative taken by the Greek Foreign Minister would certainly not remain unanswered, the Turkish representative came to an abrupt stop.

To the ears of the members of the Greek Delegation, Ambassador Sarper's address sounded unexpectedly sharp in tone, acrimonious, if not vituperative. Particularly provocative, especially when compared with the lengthy first part of the speech, which was quite moderate in tone and in the main followed the lines which the Turkish Delegation had disclosed to the Greek Delegation at their meeting of December 2, was the second part—the remarks the Turkish representative had made after he had read his set speech, on the pretext of replying to concrete points contained in the Greek Foreign Minister's address in the morning. These remarks included not only a reiteration of the familiar charges of expansionism and of an exclusive pursuit of *enosis* on the part of Greece but also personal attacks against the Foreign Minister himself, even though, at the aforementioned Greek-Turkish interdelegation meeting, the Turkish diplomats had said that they would avoid personal attacks except in retaliation.[116] In tone, these remarks reminded the Greek Delegation of the harsh, bitter, diatribes Foreign Minister Zorlu had indulged in at the Tripartite Conference in London, of September, 1955.[117] These outwardly extemporaneous remarks, it was observed, had been read from a long text, which had been prepared obviously well in advance. This device had fooled no one. As Ambassador Sarper was to confide to the Greek Permanent Representative to the UN after the debate was over, this part of the speech had been drafted on instructions from Zorlu himself, who had insisted on its inclusion in the Turkish Delegate's address.

The points of substance in Sarper's speech that impressed the Greek Delegation were the novel Turkish efforts to establish a legal foundation for partition by reference to Article 73 of the UN Charter; the harsh reference to the Greek expedition to Asia Minor during the aftermath of World War I; the allegations of support to EOKA in Cyprus; and the quotations from statements and speeches of various Greek politicians, the Foreign Minister included, as well as of Ethnarch Makarios and the Bishop of Kyrenia concerning self-determination as a cover for *enosis*.

Not taken aback, however, by the asperity of the remarks contained in the second part of the Turkish diplomat's address, and in order to neutralize their effect, Averoff-Tossizza advised the Committee Chairman of his desire to make a brief statement in exercise of his right of reply. The next speaker on the Chairman's list was the Soviet representative. Nonetheless, he consented, as the Chairman announced, that the Greek representative be given the floor.

The Greek Foreign Minister started out by making clear that his speech would not be a reply to Ambassador Sarper's statement. Before a reply could be made, careful consideration to his statement ought to be given. He would say, however, that Mr. Sarper, as the defender of a lost cause, was brilliant. He had tortured arguments and put them on the rack in order to make certain nonexistent points. But he—the Greek Foreign Minister—would like to raise a number of questions, on which, he felt, required comment.

Mr. Sarper, arguing as he had at the previous session of the Assembly, had said that Cyprus lay forty miles from Turkey and 700 miles from the Greek coast. Any atlas would show that the respective distances were forty and 135 miles. And there was a great difference between that and the distances Ambassador Sarper had given.

Mr. Sarper, Averoff-Tossizza continued, had also mentioned the example of the Aland islands which, in spite of their Swedish population, had been awarded to Finland. The Greek Delegate was sorry to have to tell him that this was not an island, but 300 islands, eighty of which were inhabited by 21,000 people. Mr. Sarper would surely recognize that 300 islands inhabited by 21,000 people were a very different matter from a single island inhabited by more than 500,000 people.

Mr. Sarper had also raised another argument, which had nothing to do with the Greek position, as he would later show. He had said that Cyprus had never belonged to Greece. But had New York ever belonged to the Americans?

He would also mention another point, fleetingly, however, because his colleague, Mr. Loizidis, would dwell upon it at greater length. The question was that of coexistence between the Turkish minority and Greek majority, which Mr. Sarper had termed totally impossible. That totally impossible coexistence, Averoff-Tossizza asserted, had lasted for more than five centuries without there having been any incidents between the Turks and the Greeks, not even during the course of Greek-Turkish wars. That this coexistence had continued even during these wars proved there was a brotherhood between those peoples which could continue. He would mention facts to prove the point. He wished to take the opportunity to say that it was a mistake to refer to the differences between the Greeks and the Turks and to say that they were separated by five centuries of animosity. During those five centuries, there were certain wars between Greece and Turkey, but they had not lasted for more than twenty to thirty years. During the rest of those five centuries there had been peaceful, friendly, and fraternal coexistence, which had left good memories to Greeks and Turks and had proved that, in spite of the wars which had separated them on certain issues, they could still live in a friendly and orderly way.

The Greek Foreign Minister also took the opportunity of referring to the war which, he thought, Mr. Sarper had been wrong in mentioning—the war which had brought the Greek armies to Asia Minor. That war had occurred because Greece had been invited to take part in it by Britain, France, and Italy who, under the Treaty of Sèvres had invaded Asia Minor and asked Greece to occupy the coast that it did occupy.[118] That example was ill-chosen, because that had not been a war carried on by Greece, but a war carried on by the Allies of the period. He would recognize that Turkey had responded with a pride and a courage that gave it its national independence, but care, he thought, should be exercised before mentioning that war as a war of Greek conquest. It had been a war of Allied conquest, an Allied conquest in which Greece had been invited to take part, but certainly it was not a Greek war.

Averoff-Tossizza then proceeded to say that he would not comment on the Turkish Ambassador's remarks concerning Colonel Grivas. He remarked, nevertheless, that, if the head of EOKA was a colonel of the Greek Army, he was a colonel who had been born in Cyprus, received his education in Cyprus, and attended military academies in Greece and in France. After World War II, he had withdrawn from the Army. Therefore, it was not correct, as Mr. Sarper had said, that he had been demobilized in order to carry out special tasks and, backed by the Reserve, sent to Cyprus. Grivas, hearing that his people claimed freedom and liberty, had felt it was his duty to go to that island to fight for that freedom, because he had found that peaceful methods had given no results. Therefore, the fact that he was a Cypriot serving in the Greek Army in no way proved that the Greek government was involved in this affair. It was not involved, and no proof could be produced that it was involved. The only proof that had been offered had been given to the Committee by Mr. Sarper, and to this he, the Foreign Minister, had replied.

The Greek Foreign Minister also felt called upon to make another remark. Mr. Sarper, he said, had tortured many texts but had not tortured the text of the declaration of Archbishop Makarios in which the latter had said he was ready to undertake negotiations on behalf of the Cypriots. However, he had passed over in silence the fact that only that morning he, Averoff-Tossizza, had read to the Committee a letter from the Archbishop which completed his first declaration and which revealed Makarios' concern that "the minority should not, in taking part in talks on the future of Cyprus, be impliedly given a voice equal to that of the majority whose will would be thus frustrated," but that this did not mean that, he, the Archbishop, refused the Turkish Cypriots "the right to have a voice as a minority proportionately to their ratio of population."

"This is the difference. That is where the difference of view is which has created this debate and caused this problem," Averoff-Tossizza exclaimed. On behalf of his country, Ambassador Sarper, "very brilliantly submitted to you, as he knows, the argument that 18 per cent of the people have the right to cast a veto over the will of 80 per cent. That is the essence of the matter. I accept that this was submitted to you in such a way that those who are unaware of the true situation may be impressed. But I leave it now to you to decide whether 18 per cent can make rules for 80 per cent."

Concluding his intervention, the Greek Foreign Minister reiterated that there were many points upon which Sarper's remarks called for an answer. He reserved his right to reply to these points the next day. He trusted he would be able to convince the Committee.

The Chairman of the Committee declared at this point that he was prepared to call on the representative of Turkey provided the next speaker, the representative of the U.S.S.R., had no objection. Did the

Soviet representative object to allowing the representative of Turkey to speak first?

Y. V. Peive, no full Soviet delegate, but President of the Academy of Sciences of the Latvian S.S.R., had, it will be recalled, permitted the Greek Delegate to speak when the latter had asked for permission to exercise immediately his right of reply. This time, however, he replied he preferred to speak in accordance with his place on the speaker's list.

The Cyprus question, Peive said, had been repeatedly discussed in the United Nations. It had been raised there as early as 1954. At that time, the United Nations, because of the negative attitude assumed by a number of delegations, especially those of Britain and the United States, had decided not to adopt a resolution on this question. But the Cyprus problem had become so acute and events on the island so stormy that it had been proposed for discussion again at the tenth session of the Assembly in 1955. At that session again, the efforts of the states interested in maintaining a colonial regime in Cyprus had succeeded in frustrating consideration of the question, and it even had failed to be included on that session's agenda.

Nevertheless, Peive continued, events had irrefutably proved that no efforts of individual delegations to divert attention from the Cyprus question in their own egoistic interest could be crowned with success, because the reasons that had given rise to the posing of the question in the United Nations had not been removed. It sufficed to recall the indignation that had overtaken the Cypriots when they had learned of the UN decision. All over the island there had been demonstrations, meetings, and strikes of protest in which the overwhelming majority of the adult population had taken part.[119] Moreover, this decision not to include the Cyprus question in the Assembly agenda had given rise to indignation in the most diverse strata of the population of Greece and in countries other than Greece.

Also without useful results had been the talks that had taken place toward the end of 1955 and the beginning of 1956 between Governor Harding of Cyprus and the leader of the Cyprus Orthodox Church, Archbishop Makarios. "As well known," the negotiations on the British side had proposed nothing more substantial than "the notorious concept of self-government," leaving in the hands of the British authorities the right of control over the foreign policy of Cyprus, its defense and its security.[120]

In March, 1956, the Latvian Soviet representative continued, Archbishop Makarios and a group of his aides had been arrested and exiled to the Seychelles.[121] Such actions best revealed not only the true intention of the British concerning Cyprus and their determination to maintain a colonial regime on the island at all costs, but also the methods that they were prepared to revert to in order "to solve" controversial problems. Instead of contributing to the island's pacification, the ruling circles of

Britain obdurately had transformed Cyprus into their marshaling base assigned to securing the interests of British monopolies in the Near and Middle East.

"You must recall," Peive said, "the unedifying role foisted on Cyprus during the Anglo-French-Israeli aggression against Egypt in the autumn of 1956. Not only was the island a troop concentration center; it was also an airbase from which military aircraft carried out incursions over Egypt."

The record, therefore, Peive relentlessly continued, had demonstrated the "unwillingness of those responsible for the destiny of Cyprus to solve the Cyprus question in the interests of the population of the island. Small wonder, then, that the eleventh session of the General Assembly had had to deal again with the Cyprus question." As a result, Resolution 1013 (XI) had been adopted. In it, the Assembly noted that the solution of the Cyprus question required an atmosphere of peace and freedom of expression. The earnest desire was expressed that a peaceful, democratic, and just solution would be found in accordance with the purposes and principles of the UN Charter. The Assembly had also expressed the hope that negotiations would be resumed and continued to this end.

During the consideration of the Cyprus question at the last session of the Assembly, many kind words and kind wishes had been addressed to the Cypriots. But in what ways had things changed since then? Peive asked. "Why is it that we are again faced with the necessity of considering the question?" It should be recognized, he said in reply to his own question, that Resolution 1013 (XI) had remained merely as a kind of wish that the British government had flouted. What had the British colonial administration on Cyprus done to create on the island an atmosphere of peace and tranquility? Nothing. The situation on the island continued to be tense. The people were still deprived of the most elementary political rights. So-called emergency legislation remained in force. British troops on the island were being systematically used for mass dragnets, searches, and other repressive measures against the population. Curfews were regularly imposed in towns and villages, utterly paralyzing the life of the population. In June, Archbishop Makarios had declared that he had accurate evidence of the cruel treatment of detained Cypriots by the Cyprus authorities. The Greek Ministry for Foreign Affairs had published at the time a similar statement, which announced that it had in its possession the depositions and complaints of the victims. The actions of the Cyprus colonial authorities had given rise to proper and legitimate indignation in Britain, where public opinion demanded an investigation and punishment of the culprits. Both in the British press and in Parliament, the question of lawlessness and brutalities in Cyprus had been repeatedly raised. The British authorities on the island, however, had refused to engage in public investigations or inquiries into the activities of police organs on the pretext that that would weaken their effectiveness in the struggle against the terrorists.[122]

The attempts to represent the activities of the national liberation movement as the activities of a handful of terrorists, Peive continued, merely to justify a policy of repression and violence against the island's population had been repudiated by life itself long since. "Even the British conservative journal," *The Spectator,* had criticized the policy of the government in Cyprus and had emphasized that "the national liberation struggle of the Cypriots is a movement which enjoys the unanimous support of the population."

What did all these facts suggest? Peive wondered. They made it clear that the part of Resolution 1013 (XI) that appealed for the creation of an "atmosphere of peace and freedom of expression" in Cyprus had not been complied with. It was necessary to put an end to this abnormal situation which had been created in Cyprus by the colonial administration. World public opinion insistently demanded that arbitrariness in Cyprus be halted; that emergency legislation be revoked; that political prisoners be released; that democratic rights be restored; and that Cypriots be given an opportunity to enjoy their freedom again. These were so many preconditions for the creation of a situation that would contribute to a swift solution of the Cyprus question in the interests of the island's people and world peace.

One could not fail to note that that part of Resolution 1013 (XI) which dealt with "a peaceful, democratic and just solution" of the question had so far remained a scrap of paper. The British government, which continued to retain the island as a colony, had so far failed to take any measures that would contribute to a peaceful solution of the Cyprus question on the basis of recognition of the Cypriots' inalienable right to self-determination. At the end of 1956, the draft "of the so-called Radcliffe Constitution" had been worked out, under which the British government was to grant the semblance of self-government to the population, and which was unanimously rejected by the people of Cyprus.

Since then, the Soviet representative observed, Britain had put forward no new constructive proposals for removing the Cyprus question from its present deadlock. Moreover, Britain had refused the proposal of Makarios in 1957 that bipartite conversations on Cyprus take place on the basis of the application of the principle of self-determination, in conformity with the UN Charter.[123] In fact, the British government continued, he asserted, to evade a solution of this problem on all sorts of pretexts, edifying and otherwise.

At the same time, the press of Western countries was repeatedly publishing information on the preparation of plans for the so-called settlement of the Cyprus question through the mediation of NATO. There were reports about the possibility of partitioning Cyprus into a Greek and a Turkish section while retaining British bases on the island. There were reports, too, about granting independence to the island under the aegis of NATO, and so on.[124] All this, Peive asserted, was surely linked with plans for the further militarization of the island and its transformation not just into a *place d'armes*, but into a nuclear base whose existence would not only increase tension in that region of the world but would seriously prejudice the future of the population of Cyprus itself. It was well known that the British authorities had officially declared that British forces in the Middle East would in the future include bomber squadrons based on Cyprus and capable of delivering nuclear weapons.[125]

The United States, the Soviet representative asserted, was also interested in setting up air bases and guided missile bases on Cyprus with a view to using the island for aggressive American designs in the Near and Middle East, in accordance with the Eisenhower-Dulles doctrine. The population of Cyprus was unwilling to permit the maintenance of military bases on its territory. "The truly peace-loving feelings of the Cypriots have been repeatedly expressed in the statements of their representatives. In particular, at the session of the World Peace Council in Colombo, in June, 1957, the representative of the people of Cyprus indicated that plans for the utilization of the island as an atomic base were plans for the preparation of aggression." He emphasized that "the people of Cyprus was not a party to those plans."

In the concluding part of his speech, the Soviet spokesman observed that numerous suggestions had been heard for the future disposition of the Cyprus question, but, in spite of their variety, "they are all remarkably unanimous in one respect, namely, they are designed at all costs to divert attention of public opinion from the only genuine method which is capable of solving the Cyprus question in the interest of the population and in the interest of the strengthening of world peace. That method is the method of unreserved recognition of the right of the Cypriots to self-determination. That is why," he added, "we are able to declare with conviction that all proposals which ignore the desires and aspirations of the population of the island are capable only of complicating the problem of Cyprus and doing harm to the cause of peace. One cannot really expect the peace-loving and freedom-loving Cypriot people to agree to solutions which would be adopted behind its back and counter to its vital interests. The colonialists should understand this simple truth which has been proved by the general course of history. It was time," he said, "that they drew the appropriate conclusions from these lessons. The Cyprus question should and must be solved in the spirit of the UN Charter," he declared, "and in the spirit of the decision taken by the eleventh session of the General Assembly. This means that a genuinely democratic and just solution of the Cyprus question would have to provide not only for an atmosphere of tranquility in Cyprus, the restoration of democratic freedoms, the withdrawal of all foreign troops from the island and the liquidation of all foreign military bases on Cypriot territory, but also for the immediate recognition of the Cypriot's inalienable right to self-determination."

After this speech of the Soviet representative, the Chairman of the

Committee, since no other representative wished to speak that afternoon, adjourned the meeting after announcing that because the full Assembly was gathering next morning on the Algerian question, it was likely that discussion on the Cyprus item in the Committee would be resumed in the afternoon at 3:00 P.M.

C. Backstage Diplomacy in the UN and in Washington

When the meeting rose, at 5:50 P.M., the Greek Foreign Minister spoke to Ambassador Lodge in the presence of some of his advisers and drew his attention to the asperity of the tone and content of the Turkish representative's speech. This boded ill for the debate. In the handling of the atrocities theme he himself had been careful not to be provocative but, since he had now been uncouthly provoked, he would have to reply in kind.

Lodge inquired whether the Greek Delegation would persist in its draft resolution calling for self-determination to be applied in Cyprus. In answer to the Foreign Minister's affirmative reply, he said that the stand of the U.S. Delegation would be unfavorable. When asked whether his delegation would vote against it, he said he did not yet know. If, however, the U.S. Delegation were asked by third states about its attitude, it would say it did not favor an affirmative vote for the Greek draft resolution. Averoff-Tossizza adjured him to maintain a strict neutrality. Tension in Athens had reached such a point that it had been necessary to place the embassies of the United States, Britain, and Turkey under guard. Premier Karamanlis, he said further, had fought quite a fight to keep Greece in the Western camp after the terrible events in Istanbul of September, 1955. He had argued that the United States, to which Greece owed such a debt of gratitude, understood the rights of the Cypriots but remained neutral simply in order not to displease other friends. If new facts confirmed the belief of the Greek people that the United States was opposed to the rights of the Cypriots, the Greek government might very well be unable to maintain its hold and would not be in a position to guarantee what might happen because of popular fury. Lodge assured him he understood the gravity of the matter and wished to do everything in his power to aid the Greek government.

What were the Greek predictions about the outcome of the voting in the Political Committee, Ambassador Lodge inquired. Averoff-Tossizza replied that, with American neutrality, 37–40 favorable votes were expected, 30 negative, and about 10 abstentions. With American opposition, however, the forecast changed. Lodge thought this forecast reasonable, with his advisers concurring. He then inquired what the Greek Delegation would do after the vote was taken in the Political Committee, also whether it would accept a draft resolution calling for negotiations with the Cypriots. The Greek Foreign Minister replied that, without being able to commit himself, it might be possible to decide not to insist on a vote in the Assembly, and examine a proposal of postponing the matter of a vote there in order to seek a solution in the meantime. As an alternative, it might be possible to examine a proposal for negotiations between the British and the Cypriots for a solution in accordance with the principles of the UN Charter. He explained, however, at length, why such negotiations could not be combined with tripartite negotiations on the substance of the issue. In conclusion, again he entreated him to maintain neutrality. Lodge promised to try.

In Washington, meanwhile, in the afternoon at the State Department, the First Secretary of the Greek Embassy, Themistocles Chryssantho-poulos, acting on the Foreign Minister's instructions of December 8,[126] had developed to E. R. Williams, in the presence of Bruce Lowell Laingen, the Greek viewpoints (the Greek Delegation's determination to press for a vote on its draft resolution, in spite of all opposition tactics; the probable reaction in Greece to a unanimous negative note of NATO Delegations; the Greek efforts to avoid gratuitous acrimony during the debate; the advantages of the most favorable possible reception of the Greek draft resolution, in order to help Britain exert pressure on Turkey). On his side, Williams, who had not yet been fully informed about the debate carried out that day in the United Nations, but had only seen the summary press wires about it, said that, of course, instructions had been given to Ambassador Lodge concerning the U.S. attitude during the debate, but these were in the guise of general directives, which left Lodge with considerable discretionary authority. This would enable him to decide on the final stand, depending on the course of the debate and the spirit that prevailed at the moment among the other delegations. On the other hand, Williams avoided commenting on the text of the Greek draft resolution, though he had it in mind. He only said it was along the lines which the Greek Foreign Minister had explained to Secretary of State Dulles. The latter, he added, had not yet taken cognizance of it, however. After the Greek diplomat expounded his government's attitude with regard to Turkey's efforts to acquire the title of a party concerned, Williams said that in this matter the attitude of the United States was very delicate, because, in its view, Turkey was a party concerned. The Greek official responded by briefly developing the legal arguments against such a view and added that the Greek government repeatedly had offered guarantees on matters in which Turkey had a legitimate interest (Muslim minority, defense). It was unthinkable, he maintained, for Turkey to be regarded as interested in sovereignty, because by treaty—that of Lausanne of 1923—Turkey had explicitly ceded this sovereignty to Britain, which held it today.

When Williams noted with pleasure the Foreign Minister's decision to keep the debate on a high level but Laingen intervened, saying that the word "butchery" in the Greek Foreign Minister's speech had been unfortunate,[127] the Greek official replied it was unfair to judge a whole speech from one word taken out of a press summary, and expressed the hope that the Greek decision to refrain from submitting a draft resolution concerning British atrocities would be duly appreciated, in spite of the extreme pressure of public opinion in Greece. To this Williams replied that the United States appreciated this practical manifestation of moderation.

In New York, later that same day, the Greek Delegation was informed by the State Department that the American Delegation while avoiding taking any overt initiative would try to prevent a vote from being taken on the Greek draft resolution. As a result, while the debates went on in New York at the United Nations, determined Greek efforts were made through the diplomatic channel in Washington to get the U.S. government to alter its stand.

Chapter Nine

December 10:
The Voice of
the United States
Is Heard above Other Voices

A. *Backstage Diplomacy in Washington*

Because the Assembly met in the morning at UN headquarters to deal with the Algerian question, there was only an afternoon meeting of the Political Committee on December 10. Backstage though, and in Washington, First Secretary Chryssanthopoulos had another long conversation at the State Department, with Joseph J. Sisco, of the Office of UN Political and Security Affairs, in the presence of Laingen, and Henry F. Irwin, of the United Kingdom desk. Lodge, the Greek diplomat was told, had been instructed to make a brief speech which, in content, would be similar to the one he had made at the previous Assembly.[1] He would advise against doing anything within the framework of the United Nations that would prejudice a solution or would render more difficult the conduct of quiet diplomacy—the only procedure through which the United States believed the Cyprus question could be solved. But, the Greek official observed, the repetition of the earlier American stand would make matters more difficult for the Greek Delegation this time. Whereas at the previous Assembly both the Greek and British delegations had submitted draft resolutions of their own, and under those circumstances the attitude of the United States could be looked upon as impartial between the two, this time, such an attitude would be clearly directed against the only draft resolution submitted, the Greek one. Sisco agreed. Exactly for that reason, he added, the Greek government had been urged not to submit such a resolution. Chryssanthopoulos countered by saying that the Greek Delegation had submitted its draft resolution only after its efforts had failed to find a compromise solution that would somewhat promote the issue.

The State Department official, nevertheless, reiterated that the U.S. government believed no solution could emerge from the recourse to the United Nations, but only from diplomatic negotiations. It therefore wished to leave this channel open. His own government, too, the Greek diplomat retorted, had demonstrated its desire to resolve the issue through negotiations. It had taken part in the tripartite conference of London in 1955 with the well-known results. The British government, on the other hand, remembered this diplomatic course of action only once a year, at the eve of the Assembly's session. The last Assembly had adopted an anodyne resolution, but no diplomatic negotiations had ensued. How could the United States be sure that the same thing would not happen again this year? The Greek government had lost its patience and its confidence in diplomatic negotiations, after waiting five years.

Could the Greek Delegation at the United Nations rely on complete United States neutrality? the Secretary of the Greek Embassy asked Sisco at this meeting. The U.S. Delegation, he pointed out, had maintained neutrality in the case of West Irian (Dutch New Guinea). The Greek people would have difficulty in understanding how it was possible for more votes to be gathered in favor of self-determination for the semi-savage people of New Guinea than for the Cypriot people. The State Department official replied that the State Department had tried the previous year to prepare a blueprint for general policy on all colonial questions so that the United States might be able to present a consistent and unified position on such matters on the level of practical policy. However, it had discovered that this was not feasible. Hence, whereas the United States had adhered to a neutral position in the question of Dutch New Guinea, it had not done so, for other reasons, with regard to the Algerian question. From the viewpoint of the United States, the Cyprus question presented another problem. This was a matter of political necessity, even though the United States appeared to behave inconsistently as a result.

When asked by the Greek diplomat what would be the position of the U.S. Delegation, in case other delegations inquired about its views on the Greek draft resolution, Sisco replied that the State Department believed that if the Greek draft resolution were adopted, this result would be to render more inflexible the Greek government. Negotiations, thus, which his government regarded as the only course that could lead to a solution, would become more difficult. He agreed, moreover, with the Greek official's remark that such an attitude of the U.S. Delegation would affect the vote very adversely for the Greek resolution. The desire of the United States, Sisco said, was to maintain the balance that existed between the interested parties so that further negotiations might be facilitated.

At this point, the Secretary of the Greek Embassy observed that it was well known in advance that the Greek resolution could not gather a two-thirds majority in the Assembly, and only such a majority could render the Greek position more inflexible. The Greek Delegation simply wished to get a sufficient number of votes to be able to exert effective pressure for starting negotiations that aimed at a real solution. It did not expect American support—no matter how much it desired it. It did, however, expect real neutrality on the part of the United States. This would be expressed by the U.S. Delegation's abstention not only from voting on the draft resolution but also from exerting any influence upon states that were friendly to it, allowing them thus to vote according to the dictates of their conscience. This would allow the Greek draft resolution to gather a sufficient number of votes, not in order to achieve final adoption, he reiterated, but in order to exert pressure for starting effective negotiations. Thus, the final American aim, i.e., starting negotiations, would be promoted. The current American policy, on the other hand, which would lead to a reduction in the number of votes favorable to the Greek draft resolution, risked increasing the current inflexibility of the Turks and the British, and this would render difficult the start of negotiations.

Although the State Department official agreed with the above observations, he repeated that the State Department insisted on the need for finding a compromise solution by the adoption of a resolution acceptable to the three governments. And he gave no answer to the question of what the United States position would be if no such solution were found. With regard to the speeches in the Political Committee the previous day, Sisco said he thought those of Commander Noble and the Greek Foreign Minister had been moderate in tone, but he had not yet read the Turkish Delegate's speech.

B. The Debate in the First Committee

In the First Committee, at its 929th meeting, on December 10, the debate on item 58 was resumed at 3:00 P.M. The Permanent Representative of Ceylon was the first speaker.

In a lengthy and serenely detached speech that contrasted with the acidulous tone of the statements of the main contestants and with the "cold war" speech of the representative of the Soviet Union the day before, R. S. S. Gunewardene expressed the hope that Cyprus might follow the same political course as his own island, which had been a British colony until 1948. The Cypriots, whether Greek Cypriots or Turkish Cypriots, should be given the right to determine their own future and then to associate themselves with any state or group of states they chose, he maintained, in a mild version of the views that Krishna Menon espoused.[1] Deploring both terroristic and repressive measures—agitational and governmental terrorism—he observed that while he understood the need for firm measures when violence stalked the country, police action and harsh legislation "could not effectively stifle movements that sprang from the soul of the people." Accordingly, he urged the British to withdraw the repressive measures that were still in effect and to declare an amnesty. The two parties to the problem, in his view, were the British government and the people of Cyprus. By the latter he meant both the Greek and the Turkish Cypriots, together.

Neither reasons of history, nor logic, nor even expediency could justifiably complicate the problem in introducing, or seeking to introduce, the views of parties other than the people of Cyprus itself.

Sir Hugh Foot, the new governor, should recommend the appointment of a Royal Commission such as the one which had prepared the way for Ceylon's independence. If the solution of the question were based on the recognition of the existence of two separate ethnic units in Cyprus, the inevitable and logical conclusion would be that Cyprus, small as it was, would have to be partitioned. This would harm not only the Greek Cypriots and the Turkish Cypriots but also the neighbors of Cyprus who had a legitimate interest in the area, and to whom a prosperous, united, and satisfied Cyprus was of supreme importance. The United Nations should in no way contribute to the creation of a fourth artificially divided country. The world was struggling with three artificially divided countries already. Ceylon, in 1948, had about one million citizens of Indian origin out of a total population of 8.5 million. India, fortunately, had not taken a position similar to Turkey's with regard to Cyprus, and Britain had not sought the Indian government's views on the question of the Indian minority in Ceylon. Neither the arguments of propinquity nor those of strategy which Turkey had raised appeared convincing to the representative of Ceylon. The former argument nullified the concept of common frontiers. In this connection, too, Gunewardene pointed out that some islands governed by Greece were very much closer geographically to the Turkish mainland than to Cyprus.

With regard to the strategic argument for maintaining the status quo, he was unable to see how Turkey could be regarded as an interested party so as to prevent the execution of an otherwise reasonable and logical process of constitutional development, which would be similar to the one which had led India, Pakistan, Ghana, Malaya, and his own country to full independence. Neither Greece nor Turkey should perceive any danger to their territorial integrity if the people of Cyprus, recognized as Cypriots, were permitted to determine their own future as they wished. It was common sense that if the inhabitants of a territory were discontented and therefore became indifferent or even disloyal, the strategic asset of such a territory would be greatly restricted. The British government, he urged in conclusion, should without delay co-operate with the people of the Crown Colony to achieve a basis of understanding which would commend itself to the two parties and to the United Nations. In Asia, with very few exceptions, most of the one-time subject peoples were now self-governing and sovereign. The theater of nationalism had now moved to west Asia and Africa. It was therefore not difficult to understand the feelings of the people of Cyprus.

After this speech, which the Greek Delegation, quite understandably, regarded as warm support of its own viewpoint (in spite of its espousal of what the Parliamentary Opposition termed the "Menon theory" of a special Cypriot nation),[2] Foreign Minister Averoff-Tossizza proceeded to reply to Ambassador Sarper's statement of the day before, rather more thoroughly than he had until then, as he put it. At the previous meeting he had brought out only some points that had not required careful refutation. He could easily prove, he asserted, that the Turkish argument was fallacious, but he would find it difficult to imitate Mr. Sarper's tone and attitude, and would not engage in personal attacks such as those in which Mr. Sarper had engaged. He knew not whether this was the taste of the Turkish government and public. It was certainly not his own. It was the usage neither of the Assembly nor of official Greek persons or of his country. Nor was it certainly one of his personal habits to engage in matters like that. He left this manner of discussion to Mr. Sarper and would confine himself to arguments.

But before taking up this matter, he wished to dispose of certain points that Ambassador Sarper had raised the day before. To begin with, the Greek Foreign Minister continued, the substance and form of Mr. Sarper's speech reminded him of the substance and form of some speeches of foreign ministers and other Turkish statesmen. It was perfectly obvious that threats were meant and intimidation wished. "But we are not scared," he stated.[3] Force had been mentioned twice. Political consequences had been mentioned. "Greece, however, was prepared to face them . . . because we are championing a just cause, which will be just regardless of any adversity, and we are in duty bound not to betray it. We are prepared to face the consequences of our policy, because not only is it a fair and just and ethical policy, but also because we have always applied it by peaceful means."

Could the Turkish government cite one case in which Greece had uttered threats? Could it cite one case in which a Thracian or Dodecanesian Turk, whom Greeks regarded as their brethren, had been attacked in his person or in his goods even when all Greeks in "Constantinople" were suffering outrages? Could Mr. Sarper cite one case of frontier or territorial water incidents in which the Turks might have lost their lives or suffered grave losses or damage? He could continue, Averoff-Tossizza said, the questions with regard to acts "we do not commit against others, but which were committed against our people." But he would not. It was enough to say that his country had done damage or harm to no one. He wished to make it clear that "we sincerely and profoundly desire good relations with both the United Kingdom and Turkey." The past linked Greece closely to those two countries. If Mr. Sarper had seen fit to "kindle the fires from old ashes, we would like to say that we want to forget these ashes. We are looking at towns and villages where Greeks and Turks lived together in brotherhood for centuries in spite of these ashes."

As for Britain, the Greek Foreign Minister went on to say, there was no need for him to state that his government and people were thinking back with nostalgia to the lengthy and beautiful days of British-Greek friendship and co-operation. And, parenthetically, he wished to add, he did not need the testimony of others about the honor of British soldiers. Greece knew this better than anyone else. He himself, even while making accusations against some torturers in Cyprus, had always paid tribute and continued to pay tribute to the British people and British soldiers. Greece wanted their friendship and always wanted their friendship. For this it had paid a high price and continued to pay it.

Calm and patience in spite of everything was the present price Greece was paying for this friendship. But other prices were being asked of it: to betray its brethren in Cyprus; to accept that 18 per cent should determine the destiny of eighty per cent; to accept the notion that the people in Cyprus should forever live under some sort of colonialism. This was a price Greece would never pay—never, for the sake of no one's friendship, Averoff-Tossizza said, repeating more or less what the Greek Ambassador had told Foreign Minister Zorlu in a conversation of late September.[4] If this was the price of friendship with Britain and Turkey, then the die was cast. The choice was made and Greece would not pay this price. It was no use trying to intimidate Greece. Greece was not afraid. He had outlined at great length the causes and reasons for this policy. Mr. Sarper, however, had flagrantly misunderstood the matter of the heavy Greek sacrifices from 1940 to 1949. Mr. Sarper had attributed to him words and intentions that had never been his. He had charged that he, the Greek Foreign Minister, had said that Greece, because of these heavy sacrifices, asked the United Nations to sanction the annexation of Cyprus. Let Mr. Sarper look at the record. He had said, and he repeated, that the sacrifices were not worth more than those of others, but that after having sacrificed almost a tenth of its population in the name of freedom, the Greek people felt that it had the right to ask in its own name that freedom should also, and at last, be granted to the Cypriots.

In a rather inelegant attack, Mr. Sarper had surely presented his case with sincerity. He did not question his sincerity, Averoff-Tossizza continued. But perhaps the Turkish Ambassador did not have before him the text of his speech and may not have grasped exactly what he meant to say. "I wish to repeat it in the name of our sacrifices, which surely have been heavy. We ask nothing for Greece. We did not make our sacrifices as mercenaries. We offered them with gladness for our country and for liberty, and this fact gives us no right to claim a recompense. It gives us the right, however, to demand liberty for our brethren in Cyprus." No one could deny this right to Greece; no one, large or small, belligerent or non-belligerent in the last war, respected and dear friend or threatening friend. Whether freedom meant annexation, that was a point to which he would revert later, and, he believed, the ineluctable conclusion was bound to be negative. Liberty did not necessarily mean annexation.

But, continued the Greek Foreign Minister, before dealing with this important question, he would like to say a few words on a point that had astonished him: the odd accusation that his delegation co-operated with Archbishop Makarios and that the Greek government utilized the Archbishop or was utilized by him.[5] The Greek government dealt with this colonial problem in the name of the 80 per cent of the people of Cyprus, and it was understood that it co-operated with the "great representative" of those 80 per cent of the people of Cyprus. Certainly, he, the Foreign Minister, would elicit his advice and his opinions without asking anybody's permission. His government had sought to get his advice; it had requested his advice, even when it had been officially threatened and insulted before his return from the Seychelles.[6] He would not refer to the arguments. This sort of argument, he thought, was not at the proper level of the debate. That was why, ignoring certain other details, he would address himself to another set of Turkish arguments.

The first of the Turkish arguments was original, strange, unprecedented: the thesis of the total suppression of the notion of the majority and the minority. This notion, Averoff-Tossizza maintained, was established, recognized, and consecrated by international law in international practice. Yet, Ambassador Sarper had told the Committee that this notion was of no importance. It displeased Turkey, and the Turkish representative swept it away in a rather cavalier fashion. On Cyprus, the majority of four-fifths of the population was really a majority. It was, supposedly, one community among others, a Greek community. By the same token, the minority was a Turkish community. Between these two communities, under the Turkish version of international law, there would be full equality of rights and fact.

Those members of the United Nations that had minorities in their countries, the Greek Foreign Minister emphasized, should ponder well the prospects of the new Turkish version of law. From now on their unity was no longer composed of a great majority of the population plus some minorities, but henceforward their nations should consist of a number of communities, of different races and religions, all of them equal in law. Each of these minorities would have not only the right to secede at will from the national body, but also to subject the destiny of other minorities and communities to its caprice. The *Diktat* that Mr. Sarper had "the poor inspiration" of citing was not the will of the majority, which, under generally recognized democratic conceptions, has the right of decision, but the arbitrary will of an acting minority—for, as he would prove later, it was the Anglo-Turkish intention to transform the Turkish minority in Cyprus into an acting minority.

The Turkish representative, it was true, Averoff-Tossizza continued, had drawn a certain distinction. He had spared already independent states and at least had allowed those to exist and function on the basis of the concepts of majority and minority. The Turkish community theory did not affect them—at least for the moment.[7] It was applicable, however, to non-self-governing territories. The peoples of those territories, from now on, would have to deal with this calamity reserved for them by the "new Turkish discovery." Not only must they endure the yoke of colonial administration, but also they would have to face another obstacle arising on the path to their emancipation. Within the populations of the non-self-governing territories, the ethnic, religious, and other minorities were said to constitute distinct communities—peoples that, under this new theory, would have the right of self-determination. Under these circumstances, needless to say, the liberation or independence of colonial peoples would become more than problematic, if not impossible. The members of the United Nations should ponder these theories.

Averoff-Tossizza, proceeding further with his deliberative rhetoric, what were, he asked, these non-self-governing territories? Who were the peoples that the Turkish representative wished to force to pay so high a price for Turkish designs on Cyprus? These colonial peoples were those the United Nations hoped to see seated in its midst some day. The Turkish representative had vigorously insisted on his country's liberalism and anticolonialism. Verbal professions of faith were easy, but, in fact, Mr. Sarper had done nothing other than give legal expression to the colonial maxim of "divide and rule." The Turkish representative, wishing to recognize the right of self-determination of a minority and not finding in the Charter's articles referring to self-determination anything that supported his thesis, certainly had to fall back on Article 73 of the Charter.

Article 73 of the Charter, Averoff-Tossizza argued, did not deal with the right of self-determination. On the contrary, it was a declaration regarding non-self-governing territories. Necessarily one had to refer to this charter of non-self-governing Territories, since one was dealing with the functioning of a colonial regime. This had nothing to do with the problem posed by the abolition of that regime in implementing the right of self-determination as applied under Article 1, paragraph 2, of the Charter. Under Article 73, the obligations of colonial administrations were one thing and the right of enslaved peoples to liberty and independence was another. These two questions ought not be confused. Mr. Sarper, who had had long experience in the United Nations and who surely was not naïve, knew full well that all colonial questions under Article 73 were referred to the Fourth Committee, whereas problems about the application of the right of self-determination—political problems primarily—were usually referred to the Political Committee. All these problems came under Article 1, paragraph 2, of the Charter. Cases in point were the appeals to the Assembly concerning Tunisia and Morocco some years earlier, and those of West Irian, Algeria, and Cyprus at the present time.[8]

Why had not Greece referred to Article 73 in the Cyprus question, Mr. Sarper had asked. Very simply, said the Greek Foreign Minister, the people of Cyprus considered themselves ripe for independence and did not address themselves to the United Nations to insure that Article 73 should be implemented in that island in one way or another. What the people of Cyprus wanted was that Article 73 should cease to be applied, and there was nothing in the Charter or elsewhere that could be construed as justifying the thesis that minorities were endowed with the right of self-determination. During the debate on Algeria, had anyone ever suggested that the European minority in Algeria enjoyed as a minority the right of self-determination and that, because of this fact, it also had the right not only to secede from the remainder of the indigenous population, but to carry away half of the national territory with it? Even France had not gone so far as to formulate so preposterous a thesis. On the contrary, through the *loi cadre* and the single electoral roll, it had embraced the notion of the complete fusion of minority and majority. What would the Algerians, their Arab friends, and those who supported that cause say here of the gift Mr. Sarper was offering to them: that they had not thought of Article 73 of the Charter and that they should heed this new theory

Although as he said, he thought the examination of this matter was a waste of time, Averoff-Tossizza, out of sheer curiosity, as he put it, was eager to find out how the Turkish argument was supported even within the scope of Article 73. This article—73 (b), which he cited textually— said that in certain non-self-governing territories there could be one or more peoples whom the administering authority should take into consideration according to their varying stages of advancement. The obligations of the administering power were mentioned here. But what did this have to do with the application of the right of self-determination and the right of these populations?

Mr. Sarper had also suggested that the Charter, in this paragraph, eliminated the notion of majority and minority in non-self-governing territories. In this connection, the Greek Foreign Minister noted the attitude of Britain in another UN forum two years earlier when, through its representative, Undersecretary of State for the Colonies Hopkinson, it had officially declared that "in such a small territory as Togoland under British administration it might have been assumed that the peoples of the territory should follow the normal procedure when their wishes were being consulted that the views of the majority should prevail over the views of the minority. That was what was understood by normal democratic processes. It was also the usual conception of the plebiscite." [9] But he would not read a great deal of what Mr. Hopkinson had said. Hopkinson had stated further that the royal commission that went to Togoland had opted for a plebiscite according to the will of the majority. That plebiscite had taken place. It had been heeded and observed, although the southern section of that country had not voted with the majority. There was a distinct section of the country that had voted against the majority. However, it had been the totality of the votes of all the provinces that was taken into consideration in order to solve the question of Togoland. And this had been done according to the will of the British government and the principles it had seen fit to follow. At that time, the Greek Delegation had taken the occasion of expressing its pleasure because the British Delegation had again so solemnly affirmed these principles. It had expressed the hopes that Britain would observe them in all other questions in the future and on all other occasions. The Assembly, he had to say, deserved somewhat greater solicitude and respect when arguments were presented to it.

The Turkish-Greek hostility, which had been invoked by some in the Assembly and was of some importance, should be analyzed, albeit briefly. Greek-Turkish hostility in Cyprus, he asserted, was a figment of the imagination. It was fabricated and produced for a specific purpose by colonialist policy. For more than three hundred years, the most complete concord, harmony, co-operation, friendship, and amity prevailed. The British colonial administration, however, had sown a seed that would yield a bitter harvest of hatred and bloodshed. The Committee could be sure that he was not exaggerating the facts. More eloquent than words was the record.

The day Greece gave in to the insistence of the Cypriots and agreed to place their case before the United Nations, the British government decided to forge the instrument of discord between Greeks and Turks, he charged.[10] More than ever before in Cyprus it egged on the Turks against the Greeks in accordance with the best practices of the Colonial Office and especially of the local colonial authorities. The instrument of police repression in Cyprus was formed by the mass utilization and enlistment of Turks in the so-called auxiliary police, which was composed almost exclusively of Turks. Elements of the Turkish minority were recruited for that force.[11] Thus the administration of the island had been chosen from among the least desirable elements of the Turkish population. Most Turks in Cyprus, of course, were good, honorable, and decent people. They would never have accepted to serve in this sort of body. But the level of recruitment of the auxiliary police among the Turks was a blot of shame on the records of colonial history. He had a sad collection of detailed reports on this question which he would hold at the disposal of those who wished to study it. The fact remained that the auxiliary police was used against the Cypriot population. A large number of torturers were Turks from this minority. The Greek government believed that the colonial administration, in so doing, had been guilty of a genuine crime. The transformation of a small minority into an instrument of oppression against the overwhelming bulk of the population was tantamount to making an attack against the unity, dignity, and life of the majority of the population of Cyprus.

Continuing on this theme, Averoff-Tossizza stated that the colonial administration had gone further. "Before the half-closed eyes of the authorities," strange acts had taken place and continued taking place. Although the Cyprus fighters had engaged in a campaign against the British forces for more than two years—which proved they had the facilities to act if they had wished to do so—only Greek houses and stores in Cyprus had been set afire—not a single Turkish shop or residential building. This was quite significant.

What was revealed every day and what reached even the international
press was more dangerous yet and concerned the immediate future, the
Greek Foreign Minister declared. It was obvious that the struggle of the
population against the British forces was to be transformed into an
armed internecine struggle between the Turks and the Greeks on Cyprus.
As a result, the British, as "indispensable spectators on Cyprus," would
speak of a fratricidal struggle and say: "We have to be here in order to
keep these people apart." A few days earlier, the world press had
published a dispatch to the effect that a new Turkish organization had
issued a proclamation promising to assassinate Archbishop Makarios if he
returned to Cyprus. This was something that was fraught with grave
consequences. Reuters (a British news agency) had distributed and
broadcast this information. What could be the consequences of these
dangerous games? Greek-Turkish enmity in Cyprus would have the most
dangerous consequences. It was a danger to the peace of the world. It
was his duty to draw this to the Committee's attention. Colonialism in
Cyprus was busily preparing another attempt against the security of this
region and against peace at large. He trusted that the British government
would take all necessary measures against these dangerous activities. He
hoped also that those who had assumed the heavy responsibility for the
defense of peace and security throughout the world would take all
necessary measures to prevent the worst from happening. For its part
the United Nations should do its duty before it was too late.

What were the other points in Mr. Sarper's speech? Well, there was the
refrain of *enosis*, which the Assembly had been hearing since 1954.[12] This
tedious repetition sounded a note that became more and more false. Why
all these attempts to gather evidence—phrases out of context, snatches of
conversations, and so on? And to prove what? To prove that in Cyprus
and in Greece there were those who wanted *enosis?* Well, nobody denied
that. Were there not those in Turkey who proclaimed that Cyprus was
Turkish even though 80 per cent of the population of the island was
Greek? Was there not in Turkey an organization called "Cyprus is
Turkish"? And were not the horrible events in Constantinople in September, 1955, due to that organization and its activities? But he did not wish
to bore the Committee with these idle findings.

"Whether or not there are supporters of *enosis* in Greece," the Greek
Foreign Minister stated, "we have repeatedly declared here on behalf of
the Greek Government—and we declare this anew in the form of a
solemn undertaking—that we will respect the decision of the people of
Cyprus, whatever it might be." As far as Greece was concerned, he
added, that would settle the question for good. And, he asked: "Why will
the Turkish representative not make a like statement here? That would
be the only statement, which would be in conformity with democratic
principles and in keeping with the Charter. Instead, Mr. Sarper came
here and stated that the 18 per cent Turkish minority would not accept a
decision of 80 per cent of the population; that the Turkish minority of 1

per cent was not a minority; that the Greek majority of 80 per cent was
not a majority; that the Turkish minority was a community, and so on
and so on." If sophistry had been invented in Greece, surely it was
practiced in Turkey with much more consummate skill than anywhere
else, he observed.

The representative of Turkey had invoked the case of Trieste in
stating that partition would be an applicable solution for the Cyprus
problem since it was a formula that had been successfully applied in
resolving a dispute that involved two of Greece's good friends, Yugoslavia and Italy. Another example he had invoked—that of the Aland
islands—he, Averoff-Tossizza, had shown the previous day, had been
poorly chosen indeed, because it was utterly dissimilar to the problem of
Cyprus.[13] But, as far as Trieste was concerned, he would say this: In
Trieste, partition had, in fact, been practicable because the two populations resided in distinct portions of the territory. The bulk of the inhabitants of the city itself were Italians, whereas the hinterland, as it were,
was inhabited by persons of Yugoslav origin. In these circumstances, the
partition of the territory corresponded to a physical separation of the
population that existed already and was established by the status quo,
and it was that fact that made the Trieste formula possible. But to claim
that the same formula could give the same results in the case of Cyprus,
where the Turkish minority was completely mixed up with the overwhelming Greek majority, and where there was not a single district,
however small, with a Turkish majority, "would be to display a lack of
realism and a political disingenuousness with which . . . Turkish statesmen are not endowed."

Coming now to a specific incident in Greek-Turkish relations on Cyprus that the Turkish representative had mentioned in his speech—the
reported murder of three Turkish Cypriots near Paphos,[14] allegedly by
EOKA—Averoff-Tossizza observed that, responding to similar allegations
made by the British representative, he had no information on that score.
Nevertheless, he doubted that those acts had been committed by EOKA.
He had even mentioned one case, presented by the British representative,
in which a Greek almost certainly was not the author of a certain
incident.[15] In the case of the three Turkish Cypriots assassinated near
Paphos, the British-controlled Cyprus radio had announced that two
Turkish Cypriots had been arrested and were under investigation or
indictment on charges of having perpetrated the triple murder. In this
case, as in others, an attempt had been made to create false impressions
for propaganda purposes by the unscrupulous distortion of facts. What
was clear was, he reiterated, that for the past two and a half years there
had been an organization that had been fighting the dominant colonial
force. Not one Turkish shop or house had been burned down. There had
been many Greek ones.

With regard to the status quo set up by the Treaty of Lausanne, the
Turkish representative had maintained that the authors of that treaty had

created a balance that any subsequent change would break. The exercise of the right of self-determination by the people of Cyprus, he had suggested, would destroy that balance. Turkey, therefore, could not accept it. In connection with this argument, the Greek Foreign Minister wished to remind Sarper that the Turkish government's response had not always been the same whenever the upsetting of a balance or equilibrium was involved. The case of the sanjak of Alexandretta (Hatay) strikingly revealed how the Turks were wont to respond to such matters. In this case, Turkey (in 1938) had annexed a district which, under the Treaty of Lausanne, did not fall within Turkey's frontiers—frontiers which that Treaty purported to draw definitively. At the time of the annexation—carried out over the vigorous protests of Syria—the Turkish government had displayed no scruples about upsetting the balance—for the good reason that this balance happened to be in its own favor. A territory inhabited by a number of distinct populations—nine, to be precise—of which those of Turkish origin made up hardly 39 per cent, had thus been annexed. With the votes of a part of the other populations, Turkey had obtained a majority of 53 per cent in the election. Turkey, thus, used two yardsticks, two sets of weights, two measures in determining its position toward the maintenance of the balance established by the Treaty of Lausanne.

Averoff-Tossizza then proceeded to deal with the remarks Ambassador Sarper had made about Resolution 1013 (XI). Said the Foreign Minister: in seeking to attribute to the Assembly intentions which it certainly never had when it adopted that resolution—namely the intention of considering the Turkish government as party to the negotiations—"Mr. Sarper had spoken ironically about my experts on whose opinions my government and I based ourselves in declaring our view that the negotiations should take place between the British government, on the one hand, and the people of Cyprus, on the other. Mr. Sarper had professed to wonder who those experts were. To satisfy his curiosity, I propose to name them and challenge him to question their authority." At the head of this list of experts was the resolution's author—Krishna Menon, head of the Indian Delegation. The other experts were the heads of the delegations of Bolivia, Ceylon, Ecuador, and Yugoslavia, who, in interpreting their own votes on Resolution 1013 (XI), had been at one in stating their opinions. The record was there, and the Turkish representative would find what these experts believed. He would also find, Averoff-Tossizza added ironically, what his lone expert thinks—his lone expert being Mr. Noble, the representative of Britain. The Foreign Minister then, once again, quoted verbatim a passage from a speech of Lord Home in the House of Lords on February 27, 1957, which he had previously cited in support of the Greek interpretation of Resolution 1013 (XI).[16] All members of the Committee, he said, would think the same thing as his experts.

"But enough of discussion and controversies." He would conclude on a note that might help to shed some brightness on this dangerous gloom. If he had addressed himself the day before to the British representative, it had been because he had wished to bring out certain observations that could not possibly remain unanswered. Noble's sober speech bespoke "our difference of views." He, the Foreign Minister, did not think it necessary to burden the record with the already outlined arguments. However, he wished to re-emphasize the one particularly constructive section he had noted in Commander Noble's speech:

Once again we tried to make progress with self-government coupled with a clear statement on the principle of self-determination. We gave the Greek and Turkish Government advance warning of this and invited discussions with the Cypriots.[17]

If in this statement, "principle of self-determination" meant what that term usually meant, Averoff-Tossizza declared, his government was prepared to co-operate, and he was convinced that the Cypriots themselves would be prepared to co-operate. Almost nobody in Greece or Cyprus—least of all the Greek government—had rejected the idea of a period of self-government prior to the exercise of self-determination, he stressed. What the form of such self-government should be; what its duration; what the guarantees, which should fully cover any legitimate interest— these were surely the proper object for negotiations. To envisage negotiations in that light for purposes of self-government, after which true and democratic self-determination would be applied—these proposals were good, democratic, constructive. Under this aspect, the Greek government declared its readiness to support them and do its best to insure their success.

In this sense—a reasonable and conciliatory and constructive sense—the Greek draft resolution facilitated matters, Averoff-Tossizza underlined. It disposed of the question of principle, which was "the kingpin of our difficulties." This draft resolution left the elaboration of the solution and of its details to sound, sober, and democratic negotiations, "which we all hope to further."

This was, he added, the frame of mind in which the Greek government contemplated this matter. That was why the Greek government was firmly convinced that, if this dangerous problem was solved, "you will be helping effectively if you vote in favor of our draft resolution." And, if he could deduce from the passage from Mr. Noble's speech that it was likewise the frame of mind of the British government, then, he believed, "we are on the eve of a good sound, and proper solution of the Cyprus problem."

The Foreign Minister's speech, the Greek Delegation felt, created a very deep and favorable impression among the various delegations as well as an atmosphere of diffuse sympathy for Greece and the Cypriot struggle. And Averoff-Tossizza had not replied to the personal attacks that Ambassador Sarper had launched against him.

The representatives of Egypt, Yugoslavia, and the Ukrainian S.S.R.

spoke next, in that order, generating with their statements a real psychological current in favor of the Greeks. Egypt's Foreign Minister Mahmoud Fawzi observed that his country had favored self-determination for the Cypriots since 1954. As both a UN member and an eastern Mediterranean country, it had been more recently concerned by the island's use, in 1956, as "a springboard for aggression against Egypt." Resolution 1013 (XI) had not been complied with. Violence and repression continued, as his distinguished colleague and friend, the Greek Foreign Minister, had made clear in his speeches. The Greek draft resolution offered an appropriate and constructive step toward a solution of the problem. "We trust it will meet with the enthusiastic approval of the Assembly," he concluded in this very brief speech that avoided any direct attacks on the British or the Turkish positions.

In an almost equally brief speech, the Yugoslav representative, Srja Prica, likewise expressed his country's concern in the Cyprus question, justifying this on the ground of the close geographical, political, and historical ties Yugoslavia had to the area and the friendly relations it maintained with "the three governments directly concerned." Guided by the principles of the Charter, he hoped for a peaceful solution to the question that would respect the right of the Cypriots to self-determination. The Greek draft resolution provided a constructive, realistic, and positive approach. It also refuted all charges that Greece was making territorial claims or that the Cypriots were prejudging the outcome of the negotiations that should take place between their representatives and the British government and should determine the scope and the methods for reaching a solution. The Cypriot people, in spite of their high economic, cultural, and political development, had never been given the opportunity of deciding their own fate. This development could not be kept within the confines of a colonial system which had resulted from transitory political and strategic considerations and institutions inherited from the past.

F. Y. Makivchuk, the Ukrainian representative, listed as a journalist, who spoke next, did not touch on the strategic aspects of the Cyprus problem for Britain, NATO, and the United States which had so greatly exercised his U.S.S.R. colleague the day before. He emphasized the theme that Britain was still practicing colonialism of the worst kind in Cyprus, having "unleashed a full-fledged colonial war" in that region, and had not complied with Resolution 1013 (XI), while EOKA had declared a truce. Taking strong exception to the British appellation of the EOKA fighters as "terrorists," he reminded his listeners of the similar struggle of the American colonists against British rule and of the fighters in Kenya, Algeria, and Oman. He also introduced the legal argument, which others, too, were to put forward, to the effect that the relevant provisions of the Treaty of Lausanne were no longer valid. Not only the Cypriots themselves had never been consulted about that treaty, but Article 103 of the UN Charter provided that this Charter was to prevail in the event of a conflict between the members' obligation under the Charter and their obligations under any other international agreement. A free decision by the people of Cyprus, he concluded, was the only reasonable solution of the question in the interests of peace and security.

Then, the American Delegate, Ambassador Lodge, spoke. For more than three years, the Cyprus question had been before the Assembly, he observed. On each occasion, the United States had made clear its conviction that those "directly concerned" must themselves work out the eventual settlement. It did not think that Cyprus was the sort of problem that UN debate could solve in the absence of an agreement between the parties. This, though, did not mean that discussion in the Assembly might not be useful.

On completion of the debate on the Cyprus problem at the previous Assembly, the United States entertained high hopes that those "most directly concerned" would be able to enter into fruitful negotiations. It had been generally recognized that no settlement was possible unless it took full account of all pertinent interests. These interests, Lodge noted, involved three of the closest allies of the United States as well as the people of the troubled island. Because of the very character and divergency of the interests of those involved, the United States had constantly maintained—and still believed—that "quiet diplomacy" held the greatest promise for the development of a solution. Referring then to Article 33 of the UN Charter, which provides that parties to any dispute "shall, first of all, seek a solution by negotiations, inquiry, mediation, conciliation, arbitration, judicial settlement, resort to regional agencies or arrangements, or other peaceful means of their own choice," Lodge declared further that the United States did not believe that all these avenues for peaceful settlement had been exhausted. While acknowledging that some progress had been achieved toward improving the circumstances in which any one or more of these avenues might be followed, Lodge stated that in these circumstances it would be a mistake for the Assembly at this time to endorse any specific solution. All in the Assembly should be moderate and avoid actions and statements that could make a solution harder, he urged. Expressing hope that those directly concerned would seek to create an atmosphere more conducive to further negotiations—the people in the island of Cyprus included, who should have an opportunity to make their views known at an appropriate point—and that stability and tranquility would prevail on the island, because "violence or any external interference would only heighten tension and lead to more violence," he stated that his delegation intended to apply one standard to any proposals made during the debate: would they help to create conditions that would facilitate an eventual solution? The United States stood ready to assist the governments and peoples concerned in getting together for further discussions when circumstances would make this useful.[18]

The American representative's speech, which altogether ignored the

Soviet charges that the United States wished to transform Cyprus into a
NATO base, slowed down, the Greek Delegation felt, if it did not altogether reverse, the psychological current of warm sympathy for the
Greek viewpoint which the previous addresses had generated. As learned
later, the State Department had instructed Lodge to speak among the
first that day, in order to influence by his views other representatives
before they had expressed their own. Although Lodge had mentioned
that any solution proposed should be acceptable to the people of Cyprus,
the rest of his speech represented the complete espousal of the British
and Turkish viewpoints. Moreover, that he had finally maintained that it
would be a mistake for the Assembly to recommend any specific solution
to the Cyprus problem struck a grievous body blow to the Greek draft
resolution, the Greek Delegation felt, and would seriously impede the
struggle which had been proceeding so favorably until then. It was
decided, therefore, to lodge strong protests with the U.S. Delegation over
this speech.

Meanwhile, in spite of the negative American attitude, which Lodge's
speech had clearly disclosed, other speeches were heard by the Committee supporting the Greek views, which warmed the chilly atmosphere
that had prevailed immediately following the American's speech. Two of
the speeches that followed—of the Romanian and Colombian representatives—were excellent from the Greek viewpoint. Sandwiched between
was another somewhat bitter morsel—an intervention by Commander
Noble.

The speech of the Romanian representative, Edouard Mezincescu, was
not just a judicious mix of the anti-British, anticolonialist arguments presented to the Committee by the Soviet and Ukrainian representatives but
had a regional character of its own, with the faintest of irredentist overtones suggestive of Romanian territorial discontent. After charging, like
the Soviet speakers, the British government with non-compliance with the
previous Assembly's resolution in Cyprus, the Romanian declared that
Greece had been entirely justified in raising the Cyprus question before
the United Nations, bound as she was to Cyprus by "indisputable national affinities of community, of language, and culture." Though the
Romanian government, he immediately added, was guided, in its relations
with other states, by the principle of respect for obligations assumed under treaties, nevertheless the Constantinople Agreement of June 4, 1878 [19]
between Britain and Turkey, the Order in Council of 1914,[20] and the
Treaty of Lausanne had been negotiated without the consent of the people
of Cyprus. Therefore, these international instruments could furnish no
basis for preventing the Cypriots from exercising their right of self-determination. Nor could the strategic interests of Britain or the existence
of minority groups in the island justify any denial of the exercise of this
right. The interests of peace and security, the Romanian representative
concluded, were paramount, and the United Nations should use all its
influence to eliminate colonial domination over Cyprus, thereby creating

favorable conditions for the solution of all the other aspects of the problem and strengthening peace and international co-operation in the Mediterranean.

The British representative then spoke, directing his remarks to certain statements the Greek Foreign Minister had made the day before, and reserving his right to reply to some other remarks Averoff-Tossizza had made that same day. The Greek representative's speeches so far had disappointed him, he said. He—Noble—had hoped the debate would be uncontentious and that it would promote rather than hinder progress toward agreement between all the parties concerned. He still thought that was the right way to approach the question. The riots of the Greek Cypriots followed by the riots in retaliation of the Turkish Cypriots which had just taken place in Cyprus [21] showed only too clearly how delicate and dangerous that situation was and how important it was to discuss quietly the problem without acrimony and with the intention of promoting a solution.

Although, Noble continued, he would have no difficulty in disposing in detail of the stream of charges and assertions made by the Greek Foreign Minister, he did not think it would be conducive to an atmosphere of calm and statesmanship if he joined issue on points that were far removed from the objective in view. He would therefore limit himself to one or two statements of fact.

The first related to the situation in Cyprus since Resolution 1013 (XI). The Greek Foreign Minister contended that EOKA had responded satisfactorily to the hopes of the Assembly for a peaceful atmosphere on the island. Unfortunately, the facts did not bear this out. True, the terrorist organization, seriously disrupted at the time, had declared a truce and refrained for a period from actual murders. During the last two months, however, the number of murders carried out by the terrorists each week was the same as that for many periods before Resolution 1013 (XI). In addition to murders and attempted murders, there had been a good deal of violence against moderate Cypriots, and the population had been threatened by broadcasts, by letters, and, physically, by masked men carrying arms. In order to substantiate these charges, Noble went on to cite two EOKA resolutions, the one of November 19 which called upon the people of Cyprus for new struggles, in all fields—with the gun, passive resistance, "all-out struggle;" the other, of the previous week, in which it was declared that "the only slogan which the Cypriot people had adopted is: 'Either now or never.' It will continue its struggle with Dighenis until it achieves what it is fighting for." [22]

Turning now reluctantly, as he said, to the allegation the Greek Foreign Minister had made about the conduct of the authorities in Cyprus toward suspected terrorists, Noble stated that at the outset of the debate his government had hoped that nothing would be said that would in any way impede the efforts it was making to procure a just and lasting settlement of this complex problem. He did not wish to strike a new or contentious note, but he hoped it would be understood that he simply could not allow the allegations made by the Greek Foreign Minister to pass uncorrected. Mr. Averoff-Tossizza had alleged that British troops and authorities in Cyprus had been guilty of atrocities. That was a grave charge, one which he had in no way substantiated. It was very easy for anybody to reel off a list of charges of that kind against an administration responsible for maintaining law and order in the face of terrorist activities. The Greek Foreign Minister might have mentioned that his own government had been brought before the Assembly on similar charges during the civil war in Greece, and Britain had been among those which had defended Greece against these charges at that time. Many might suppose that Britain's reputation was a sufficient rebuttal of the charges which Mr. Averoff-Tossizza had seen fit to air. Many also thought that it was neither right nor helpful to discuss such allegations in this Committee. However, he did not wish to give the Committee the impression that he was unwilling to answer the Greek charges. It would have been more helpful if the Greek government had brought these charges to his government's attention before giving them wide publicity. On those charges which were new, he reserved his right to reply. Many, however, were very old. For the most part they had been fabricated long after the time the incident was alleged to have occurred, solely for the purposes of the political and propaganda campaigns for *enosis* and also in order to divert the security forces from their task of eliminating political violence and fear from the life of the island. The great majority of the accusations which the Greek Foreign Minister had made before the Committee were the same as those that the Greek government had frequently publicized before. The Cyprus authorities had investigated every allegation precise enough to make investigation possible. They would continue to investigate any new allegations as they arose. In his speech before the General Committee, Mr. Lloyd had showed that many of the charges were plainly ridiculous.[23] He—Noble—would not again quote the examples Mr. Lloyd had given. The Committee, Noble went on to say, had then decided not to inscribe the Greek item on atrocities on the agenda.

In one or two cases, Noble acknowledged, in which there had been some irregularity, the authorities had not hesitated to prosecute. Investigations had shown, however, that in the majority of instances, the allegations had been deliberately trumped up for political ends. He did not wish to describe at length the methods of intimidation and terrorism that had been used to produce these fabricated charges, but would refer to one case among those mentioned in the document circulated by the Greek Delegation on December 9.[24] It was claimed, in this case, that the Abbot of Makhaira had been cruelly tortured in February, 1957. Complaints had been made three weeks later by a Greek Cypriot lawyer. As soon as these had been received, a senior officer discussed the question with the Abbot himself who stated he had not asked the lawyer to visit him and that he had had no intention before the visit to make a complaint. Because, however, it had become known in Nicosia that he had been interviewed by the security forces, the Church, which was very powerful, had sent the lawyer to see him and he had had to find some excuse for the admission he had made to the police regarding his association with the terrorists. The Abbot was a very frightened man and told the official that he could not forget what had happened to a brother abbot who was murdered by EOKA terrorists in his own monastery in front of the monks. Having explained his predicament, he withdrew the allegation, which he knew to be false and which he had made only under severe pressure.

Proceeding to another issue and emphasizing the importance of maintaining a sense of objectivity and balance, the British representative went on to refer to the citations made by the Greek Foreign Minister from the correspondence exchanged between Rossides, the representative of Ethnarch Makarios, and the British Ambassador in Athens, Sir Roger Allen.[25] The Foreign Minister, Noble said, had not quoted the last letter in that correspondence—a letter from the British Ambassador to which there had been no reply. Part of this letter referred to the Archbishop's view, expressed in a letter of July 6, 1957, that Turkish representatives should only be permitted to take part in talks concerning their minority rights and safeguards, and that he would regard as unacceptable their participation in talks on the future status of the territory in which they lived. The British government, however, considered that the Turkish Cypriots were entitled to a proper say in the future of the island. If that was now Archbishop Makarios' view, continued this letter, "Her Majesty's Government will welcome it as a step forward." There had been no reply to this letter (the date of which was not given), Commander Noble observed.

He had tried to give some of the realities of the situation, the British representative said. Although the Greek Foreign Minister had not said much about what his government would be prepared to do to promote an improvement in international relations and in the situation in Cyprus, he had spoken at some length about the British position. The British position, in fact, was somewhat different from the description the Foreign Minister of Greece had given of it. He would, therefore, like to correct any misconception there might be about his government's position.

The Cyprus situation, Noble reiterated,

is a complex one. We may regret this complexity, but there is nothing to be gained by ignoring the difficulties and realities of the present situation. The Greek Cypriot leaders want to join Greece, and the Turkish Cypriot leaders oppose this. The Greek and Turkish governments have, in various ways, played and are continuing to play a considerable part in the Cyprus question. The United Kingdom has been and is trying to maintain peace and stability in the island, between allies in dispute and in the area as a whole. In our view, there must be a solution agreeable to all concerned—that is, to both communities in Cyprus and to all three governments.

Noble concluded by saying that he had described at some length the great variety of procedures his government had initiated over a number of years.[26] Talks had been held with both governments, sometimes in conjunction with talks with leaders of both communities, and sometimes separately. "We have also had separate talks with leaders of the Greek and Turkish communities without the governments. We neither exclude any of the parties nor give any of them a favored position. Our offers of discussion with the Cypriot leaders of both communities remain open. As I say, for some months now, we have been negotiating with both the Greek and Turkish governments. We believe that some progress has been made in the spirit of the February resolution. What is now required is further talks, and more progress along the same lines."

The last speaker in the Committee on December 10 was Ambassador Roberto Zuleta Angel, Permanent Representative of Colombia to the UN. There were four basic considerations which should be kept in mind in seeking a settlement of the Cyprus problem, he maintained. First, the aspirations of the Cypriot people to decide their own future in no way ran counter to the rule of *pacta sunt servanda,* of the sanctity of treaties, one of the essential bases of international law. By virtue of treaties, Cyprus was a British Crown Colony, and the UN Charter had termed that type of territory a "non-self-governing territory." Britain, by ratifying the Charter, had committed itself to respect the principle of self-determination set forth in Articles 1, paragraph 2, and 55, of the Charter. It had likewise committed itself to the provisions of Article 73 on non-self-governing territories, under which members agreed to develop self-government, to take due account of the political aspirations of the peoples, to assist them in the progressive development of their free political institutions, according to the particular circumstances of each territory and its peoples and their varying stages of development. Thus, it was crystal clear that there was no question of setting aside international treaties. It was a matter of fulfilment by Britain of commitments contained in the Charter—which, too, was an international treaty.

Second, the principle of self-determination appeared very clearly in the Charter. Indeed, it was a right, though not an absolute right, but was subject to certain regulations. For the abuse of this right would lead to extremes that obviously would be contrary to the unity and security of states. It was also subject to certain specific conditions to be fulfilled by the people concerned who should have reached a sufficiently high level of economic, social, political and cultural development to enable them to set up a viable entity. Since the people of Cyprus had fulfilled those conditions and were capable of deciding their own future, the principle of self-determination was applicable to it. It was gratifying to listen to the British representative confirming that his government was still in favor of the policy that was inherent in the principle of self-determination. As the representative of Ceylon had observed, Britain had

not only been one of the champions of that principle but, in numerous
cases, had given it practical application.

Third, the principle of self-determination could not validly be invoked
to justify territorial claims or the annexation of territory. Under the
Charter, its aim was to permit peoples to become independent of foreign
domination, not to achieve a change in domination. He had therefore
noted with great pleasure the statement of the Greek representative,
who, as a spokesman of a people that was unable to make its views
known directly to the United Nations, had said "he had not come to us
with claims other than those which were entrusted to us to voice."

Fourth, Zuleta Angel acknowledged that "account should be taken of
the legitimate interests, the sacred rights, of the Turkish minority" in
Cyprus but declared that

it would be extremely dangerous to recognize to a national minority within a
state the claim that, because it is a national minority, it had a right to set up a
state within a state.

A distinction ought to be made between the protection of minority rights
and self-determination. There was only one method of applying that
principle to non-self-governing territories in which there were persons of
different nationalities. That was the traditional democratic method
whereby the will of a people was found out: to find out the will of the
majority. With regard to appropriate procedure for progressing toward a
solution, the Colombian representative agreed with his U.S. colleague
that a solution of the Cyprus question should be sought through negotiations between the parties concerned, i.e., outside the United Nations. He
disagreed, however, that these should be tripartite in character, i.e.
between Britain, Greece, and Turkey. Only the people of Cyprus should
decide their own future. The negotiations should be between them and
Britain, namely should be bipartite, in accordance with Resolution 1013
(XI). Colombia would support any proposal aimed at implementing the
principle of self-determination.

To the members of the Greek Delegation this closing speech sounded
quite magnificent. Its monumentality in structure and substance was
admired. And it seemed to demolish the Anglo-Turkish arguments and
recognized the absolute justice of the Cypriot people's cause. Moreover,
this speech aroused Greek hopes that it would counteract the effects of
the U.S. representative's speech among Latin American delegations or at
least among a number of them. Colombia, it was felt, was inspired purely
by principles—having no particular ax to grind, no special bonds of
interest with the parties to the dispute, and taking no account of the U.S.
attitude.

As soon as the meeting of the Committee rose, at 6:00 P.M., the entire
Greek Delegation, from Foreign Minister to secretaries, strongly pro-

tested to all levels of the American Delegation against what was considered to be an unprovoked unfairness toward Greece—Lodge's speech in the Committee. The Foreign Minister, aware by now of the results of that same day's *démarche* by the Greek Embassy official at the State Department, had a talk that evening with Lodge, which led him to draw unpleasant conclusions. All this meant that the United States intended to intervene backstage. It was clear that it did not wish to displease the Turks who had started getting worried. Without interference of the United States, it was possible to get as many as 37 votes, he believed. But, with U.S. interference, the results would depend on the degree of pressure exerted. An unfavorable vote on the Greek draft resolution could not be excluded. It was necessary, therefore, to press as much as possible, even to arrive at threats of not having Greece represented at the NATO summit Council meeting by its Prime Minister or of staging a walkout from the United Nations.

The assurances that the deputy to the U.S. representative to the United Nations, Ambassador Wadsworth, gave to Ambassador Palamas as soon as the afternoon meeting was over, to the effect if the Greek draft resolution was put to the vote that the U.S. Delegation would abstain were greeted with expressions of wry skepticism on the part of the Greek diplomat. He knew enough, he said, about the machinery of the United Nations so as not to be deluded by this assurance. If the resolution referring to self-determination came up for a vote, he told Wadsworth, the U.S. Delegation would not vote against it, not certainly because it did not wish to do so, but because it was not in a position to do so. In spite of all its power, the U.S. Delegation, he continued, found itself incapable of proceeding to the public execution, as it were, of the principle of self-determination. Abstention was not the case. The case was whether the U.S. Delegation would allow the Greek Delegation to put to the vote its draft resolution and whether it would not try to frustrate this by other, indirect, devious means. Wadsworth, with his ingrained American frankness, acknowledged that his delegation indeed aimed at preventing the Greek draft resolution from reaching the voting stage.

Chapter Ten

The Battle Continues:
Third Parties Take Sides

A. *Backstage Diplomacy in the UN and Washington*

Reaching agreement over a compromise draft resolution became the objective of many delegations friendly to the Greek Delegation—those of Mexico, Lebanon, Peru, for example—in soundings with the Greek representatives, as soon as the opposition of the United States to the Greek draft resolution became clear. Friendly counsel was given in that direction, because, given American opposition, nothing else but a compromise solution appeared possible. The Greek Delegation categorically rejected all such proposals and emphasized its determination to insist on its draft resolution.

When the Mexican Delegate said his delegation had received instructions to abstain from voting on the Greek draft resolution, Averoff-Tossizza immediately instructed the Washington Embassy to lodge a protest about this with the State Department. Since 1954, Mexico had always supported Greece; so its intention to abstain this time, together with many other indications, suggested to the Greek Delegation that the United States was exerting powerful pressure backstage on other governments against the Greek draft resolution.

In this note, delivered to Rountree by Secretary Chryssanthopoulos, the Greek Foreign Minister pointed out that the delegations of several Latin American countries which had always voted favorably for Greece in the Cyprus issue had received instructions from their governments to abstain from voting on the Greek resolution. He attributed their change of position to Ambassador Lodge's statement in the United Nations, as well as to strong pressures exerted by the U.S. government upon the governments of these states. He wished to protest against such action. He had asked only for American neutrality on this issue and had not expected such strong action. The ultimate vote on the Greek draft resolution by the Political Committee, he added in conclusion, regardless of results, represented a question of survival for the Greek government, and the Foreign Minister considered the present attitude of the U.S. government in this matter as unfriendly to his own.

Commenting on this protest note, Rountree observed it was a very strong statement. Laingen, who was present at its delivery, escorted the Greek diplomat as he was leaving, and inquired what particular delegations had received instructions to abstain. The Mexican was one, replied Chryssanthopoulos. The State Department official then went on to stress the following two points: First, he personally did not know whether any pressure had indeed been exerted on any Latin American countries. Second, the United States certainly would prefer to see a draft resolution acceptable to all interested parties. However, because of the contingency that the Greek draft resolution would be put to the vote, those in charge in the State Department were ceaselessly conferring in order to decide which would be the final American attitude, and no decision had yet been taken on the matter.

On his side, the Secretary of the Greek Embassy reiterated the points he had made to Sisco the day before. He observed, furthermore, that his government regarded Lodge's statement, when compared with the one he had made at the previous Assembly, as a retreat at the expense of Greece. Finally, he expressed hope that the U.S. government, even at this late moment, might be able to revert to a policy of strict neutrality, allowing other delegations to vote according to their conscience. By doing so, it would certainly open the way to fruitful negotiations.

In New York, the morning of December 11, before the 930th meeting of the Political Committee began, Krishna Menon, accompanied by the Permanent Indian Representative to the UN, Ambassador Lall, called on the Greek Foreign Minister at his hotel and proposed a compromise resolution which was blessed, he said, by the Americans but had not yet been shown, he maintained, to the British and the Turks. As a compromise resolution, this draft did not seem bad to the Greeks. In brief, it provided that the Cypriots should be given the possibility of realizing and maintaining their freedom. Once again it revealed Krishna Menon's strong inclination toward independence for Cyprus as a solution to the problem and betrayed his aversion to self-determination—because of the Kashmir question. The Greek Foreign Minister gave most earnest consideration to this Indian proposal. He consulted the members of his delegation, all of whom, with the exception of Cyprus-born Savvas Loizidis, expressed the opinion that it should be accepted.

However, neither Averoff-Tossizza nor Krishna Menon, who the evening of that same day called on Ethnarch Makarios, was able to persuade him of the desirability of such a course of action. Perhaps in fear of Grivas' adverse reaction, Makarios stubbornly insisted that the battle for the adoption of the Greek draft resolution that referred to self-determination should be waged to the end. The outcome was that the

Greek Foreign Minister, thanking Krishna Menon for his initiative, explained to him that the Greek Delegation rejected any idea of compromise. He also asked the Indian to refrain from any further mediatory efforts and assume the most favorable attitude possible toward the Greek draft resolution. Krishna Menon agreed to this, promising, too, not to take part in the debate in order not to influence other delegations at the expense of Greece. He would make his explanation of vote after, not before, the voting had taken place. He kept his promise, and this attitude, as well as another timely contact with the Greek Delegation, proved to be very helpful to the Greek position at a critical moment.

B. The 930th Meeting of the First Committee

In the Committee on December 11 the debate went on in the morning, afternoon, and evening. The Greek Foreign Minister thought it would be useful for the Greek Delegate and Member of Parliament, Savvas Loizidis, to intervene in the debate. Because of his Cypriot origin, Loizidis would be able to interpret more directly the Cypriot views on certain points about the situation on the island and emphasize the theme of how good the relations between the Greeks and the Turks in Cyprus had been until British intrigue and the policy of the colonial administration had caused hostilities to break out between the two communities. He would also speak on the matter of British atrocities and, without tabling any concrete draft resolution, propose the dispatch of an investigatory commission to Cyprus for checking on these charges.

In the debate that took place in the morning, Loizidis spoke last. Speakers from ten other countries—Czechoslovakia, Bolivia, Afghanistan, Belgium, France, Turkey, the Federation of Malaya, Syria, Nepal and Byelorussia—preceded him. Six of these speakers were inclined toward the Greek viewpoint.

In a rather lengthy address, Josef Ullrich, Czechoslovak Ambassador and Permanent Representative to the UN, proved to be far more of a conformist than his Romanian colleague had been the day before. He hewed close to the themes the representatives of the U.S.S.R. and of the Ukraine had previously presented. He, too, charged the British with non-compliance with Resolution 1013 (XI), and attacked partition and the Radcliffe draft constitution,[1] the latter on the ground that it would have indefinitely prolonged the colonial status of Cyprus. Self-determination, he observed, was being denied to the people of the island on military and strategic grounds—which was impermissible. But he also asserted that the United States was seeking to convert Cyprus into a military base against the "socialist" and Arab countries—to buttress the "notorious Eisenhower-Dulles Doctrine"—and therefore now favored the creation of an independent Cyprus, whose sovereignty would be guaranteed by NATO. The people of Cyprus, he declared, were firmly rejecting proposals of this type as well as "any forced NATO mediation," because they did not wish to have their territory turned into a NATO atomic base or to be associated with "the aggressive forces" of the Baghdad Pact against its neighbors. Negotiations should be immediately resumed with the representatives of the Cypriot people who requested compliance with Resolution 1013 (XI). The recognition of the right to self-determination should be the starting point of such negotiations.

The Ambassador and Permanent Representative of Bolivia to the UN, German Quiroga Galdo, spoke after the Czechoslovak representative. Like his Colombian colleague the previous day, or the Guatemalan and Panamanian representatives at later meetings of the Committee, he did not follow the example of the representative of the leading power of the O.A.S., the United States, by limiting himself mainly to procedural advice, but boldly ventured into the substance of the question in a manner that must surely have delighted the members of the Greek Delegation. In his very lengthy speech, which was a baroque variation of Zuleta Angel's coolly classical quadripartite address and was festooned with garlands of historical examples, the Bolivian first emphasized that his country had no material interest in the Cyprus question and was inspired by very friendly sentiments toward Britain, Greece, and Turkey. Hence, he would speak "with complete impartiality and serene justice and in accordance with the principles of the Charter."

With regard to the first point, which concerned Britain, Cyprus was a colonial problem, even though Britain's legal claim over the island was indisputable, based as it was on the Treaty of Lausanne which, in the Bolivian's view, with regard to Cyprus had been merely a bilateral agreement between Britain and Turkey, of which the other signatories had merely taken note. The Cypriot people had been consulted neither about this treaty nor the earlier one, of 1878, "when they were given a new master." Coming now to the matter of the conflict between this legal right and the duties of Britain under the Charter and introducing a sort of organismic version of the *clausula rebus sic stantibus* of international law, he argued that "treaties, like human beings, grew old and died" and at a given moment had to be revised or replaced by others in keeping with a new situation "created by the evolution of the international community." That Britain transmitted information on Cyprus to the United Nations clearly showed that the legal ties binding the metropolitan country to the colony had been changed or weakened "just as if the Treaty of Lausanne had lapsed, and a return had been made to the Convention of 1878, under which Britain was merely the island's administrator." Since the Lausanne Treaty, "a great deal of water had flowed under the bridges of the Thames." The British Empire had become a Commonwealth of sovereign and independent states. The age of colonialism was past. Nationalism was rampant. "What was the worth of the Treaty of Lausanne in face of the events that were shaping human destiny?" At present, the only wholly valid multilateral treaty was the

UN Charter. Britain's colonial problem in Cyprus therefore could be settled only by applying the principles of the Charter and that of the rights of peoples to self-determination.

The second problem concerned the part played by the Greek government and people in the Cyprus question. Rightly or wrongly, Greece had been accused of actively intervening in the Cypriot rebellion and of reviving old claims over certain territories "cut off from the mother country by force of circumstances." Greece, since it acquired independence in 1830, had gradually rounded its geographical and political frontiers by the unification of territories inhabited by inhabitants who spoke "the noble tongue of Homer," which, modified in the course of centuries "by the vocabulary of barbarians," was "the intangible receptacle of the nation's soul." Accordingly, it was not strange that the Greek state, after heroically resisting the Nazi and Fascist invaders, should have sought to bring back into the national territories the Greek-speaking communities at a time when the political map of the world was being redrawn. Thus, although Greek statesmen, and the Foreign Minister in particular, had explicitly stated their country did not wish to annex Cyprus, could one doubt that the Greek nation still hoped for the achievement of the ideal of *enosis?* Certain events which had occurred in the previous seven years implicitly if not explicitly raised a question of reunification, for instance, the participation of Greece in the debate as the natural spokesman for the Cypriots or the plebiscite of 1950 in Cyprus.[2] The latter, in spite of the allegations of the colonial authorities, had been accompanied by no fraud. This was proved by the fact that Britain since then had refused to allow any consultations of the same type under UN auspices. The third question arose from Turkey's interest in the future of the Turkish Cypriots. Ankara's concern was fully understandable but, in the Bolivian view, the proposal to partition the island was unacceptable. The demographic facts of the situation were no ground for a kind of judgment of Solomon, which would deprive the island of centuries-old advantages it had drawn from its political and geographical unity." Partition, as recent history had demonstrated, brought no good results. The Turkish minority should be guaranteed its free development, with respect for its national characteristics, its language, and its religion.

Coming now to the fourth problem—that of the Cypriot people themselves—the Bolivian representative asserted that when a people took up arms against foreign oppression, the purpose of the rebellion always was to achieve freedom and political independence. "The appearance of guerrillas, generally called bandits or wrongdoers, was a most favorable sign that the time for cowardice and scorn had ceased." Nothing could oppose that movement: neither regular armies nor military leaders from the best army schools. The history of Latin American rebellions was full of episodes that had become legends in which "the humble priest places improvised weapons under his priest's garb and puts himself at the head of a group of peasants in order to attack the colonial representatives in the cities and countryside of his native land." In Cyprus, the internment and exile of Makarios who, spiritually speaking, was the foremost guerrilla fighter in the Cypriots rebellion had merely stimulated the passion and courage of the insurgents. That the Ethnarch had been able to persuade the rebels to observe the truce for an indefinite period proved that he was the acceptable party to take part in negotiations which, taking into account the economic and strategic interests of Britain in Cyprus, would enable the Cypriots freely to decide their own political destiny.

In conclusion, Quiroga Galdo noted that, in spite of Resolution 1013 (XI) and certain beneficial results that had followed, the will to impose rather than to negotiate a settlement persisted. Accordingly, the time had come for the United Nations to express strongly the general wish that the parties to the dispute resume negotiations. These parties should provide for a plebiscite under UN auspices. By this method, the people of Cyprus, regardless of origin, would be able to announce their decision on the points raised simultaneously by Britain, Greece, Turkey, and the Cypriot people themselves. These points were: Did the people of Cyprus wish to become part of the British Commonwealth? Did they wish to be united with Greece? Did they wish to be united with Turkey? Did they wish to become a sovereign and independent state? Only then would it be possible to say that half a million people had been able to find their destiny under the auspices of the United Nations.

This speech was followed by others which, in contrast, clearly espoused the British and Turkish viewpoints.

Ambassador to the United States Dr. Najib-Ullah, representative of Afghanistan, an uncommitted Asian and Muslim state, emphasized that in spite of the genuineness of the Cypriots' "desire for independence," the people of Cyprus did not form a homogeneous entity, but consisted of a large majority of Greeks and "a very distinct" minority of Turks. Although not considering that co-operation between the two "communities" was impossible, he was convinced that a satisfactory solution could not be reached unless that difference were taken into account. He favored, therefore, double self-determination for the Cypriots. The Afghan Delegation did not intend to go into the troubles and tragedies of Cyprus during that year but had heard with satisfaction Noble's statement that Britain was ready to consider possible solutions on the basis of the right of self-determination through unconditional negotiations conducted in a spirit of broadmindedness. The interested parties should negotiate in a spirit of good will and objectivity and take into account the legitimate aspirations of the people of Cyprus and their right to self-determination. A solution could not be reached by UN discussions alone.

The representatives of two colonial states and NATO members, of Belgium, first, then of France, spoke next. Both backed the British view that Cyprus involved an internal matter which fell under British domestic jurisdiction and that for that reason UN intervention was impermissible under Article 2, paragraph 7, of the Charter, which forbids any UN interference in realms essentially within the domestic jurisdiction of member states. However, whereas the Permanent Representative of Belgium to the UN, Ambassador Joseph Nisot, also said that the principle *pacta sunt servanda*, which the Colombian representative had invoked at the previous meeting, imposed respect for this particular provision of the Charter, and stated he would continue to refrain from taking part in the debate on the question, his French colleague, Ambassador Guillaume Georges-Picot, Permanent Representative of his country to the UN, dwelt at somewhat greater length with the item, along lines somewhat similar to those suggested by the United States. In view of the problem's complexity, he said, a solution should be sought in an atmosphere of tranquility and calm reflection. For the peaceful settlement of the question more suitable procedures existed and, legal considerations apart, UN intervention would not necessarily promote the solution desired. His delegation would take a stand toward any draft resolution in the light of these considerations. Moreover, without abandoning the fundamental position of principle dictated by the Charter, he proceeded to an examination of the facts of the case, since the British government had not opposed a debate on the question. In his opinion, the situation in Cyprus had developed favorably since Resolution 1013 (XI) had been adopted. Especially encouraging signs of this were the liberation of Makarios, the attenuation of the emergency measures, the considerable decrease of armed encounters on the island, the appointment of a civilian governor, and, more particularly, the continuation of talks between the governments concerned. His delegation had also noted with satisfaction the statements of the representatives of the three states chiefly concerned. Britain had reaffirmed its intention to set up self-government in Cyprus. Greece had repeatedly stated it had no territorial claim to Cyprus. And Turkey was not considering an extreme formula calling for partition of the island. These facts formed an excellent basis for a compromise solution. Confidence should be placed in the British government, and the United Nations should refrain from complicating its task by its actions. With regard to the Greek draft resolution, his delegation had explained at length at the Assembly's previous session what attitude should be taken toward the proclamation, on the part of the Assembly, of a right "to which some seemed to attribute magical effects." Britain, as the British representative had explained at that same session, was the sole judge of the conditions under which the people of Cyprus could attain self-determination. The draft resolution was, therefore, useless, at least in its existing form. But it was also dangerous because it could encourage further incidents which might ultimately boomerang against those directly responsible and run counter to the goal they professed to seek. For these reasons, the French Delegation would be unable to vote for the Greek draft resolution.

The Turkish Delegate, using his right of reply with the Chairman's permission, spoke after his French colleague. In response to Averoff-Tossizza's complaint about the tone of the second part of his opening statement of December 9, Ambassador Sarper underlined a passage in the first part of his statement in which he had said that it was his delegation's opinion that the time had long since arrived for the Cyprus question to be stripped down to its bare essentials so that it might be discussed in calm and serenity for the purpose of discerning the real issues involved, preparing a more appropriate atmosphere, and exploring the possibilities that existed to achieve progress toward a solution satisfactory to all concerned. This continued to be his delegation's opinion, Sarper said. If, in the second part of his statement, which was in the form of a reply, he reluctantly had been obliged to mention certain facts, that had been an unpleasant task. However, he did not think that its initiation could be attributed to the Turkish Delegation. But he preferred to leave aside any recriminations and to answer a few points.

The Greek Foreign Minister had said that the Turkish point of view was that 18 per cent of the population—that proportion was not correct, Sarper added parenthetically—should decide the fate of 80 per cent of the population of Cyprus. As a matter of fact his delegation had never said that the Turkish Cypriots should decide upon the fate of the Greek Cypriots. It had said that if self-determination were applied to Cyprus, then, in the special circumstances of that territory, it should be applied equally to the Turkish and the "Greek-speaking" Cypriots so that each of those peoples could decide upon its own fate. Therefore, it was not Turkey that demanded that the Turkish Cypriots should decide upon the fate of the "Greek-speaking" Cypriots. The situation was exactly the reverse. It was the Greek Delegation that insisted that the Greek community should decide upon the future of the Turkish Cypriots, even to the extent of incorporating more than 100,000 Turks under Greek rule against their will. The Turkish Delegation's attitude was conciliatory, because it recognized certain rights for each community in certain eventualities. The Greek attitude, on the other hand, was intransigent, and, in the special circumstances on Cyprus, was clearly against all rules of equity and justice, as well as unrealistic.

In his first statement, Sarper continued, he had mentioned that unfortunately the Greek Delegation had often sought to establish similarities between the situation in Cyprus and other situations having nothing in common with that issue. Mr. Averoff-Tossizza had, for instance, spoken about sovereign and independent states and said that it would be a calamity to recognize the right of secession to minorities. The Turkish government fully agreed with that point of view. Far from implying such a state of affairs in regard to independent countries or to national entities in non-self-governing territories, he had said exactly the opposite in his first statement. However, Cyprus was not an independent state, nor did a distinct Cypriot nationhood exist. Furthermore, it had not been Turkey which had asked for a change of sovereignty in Cyprus but the Greek

government which had placed this question in the political arena. Therefore, even if Mr. Averoff-Tossizza's argument were relevant to the question, it would apply to the Greek position in this matter, and not to the
Turkish one.

In another part of his statement, the Foreign Minister of Greece had
claimed that if the Turkish Cypriots refused to be incorporated with
Greece, this would be a new calamity to non-self-governing territories
since it would create a precedent that would hinder the prospects of
independence for many lands which all hoped to see as new members of
the United Nations. Sarper really admired the great ability with which
Mr. Averoff-Tossizza had tried to link the Cyprus question with a problem that all had very much at heart, Sarper went on to say. However,
even the most superficial examination of this argument would show that
it was based on a fallacy. The Cyprus question was not one that arose
from the prospects of independence of a national entity. Cyprus was a
land in which there was a Turkish community and a "Greek-speaking"
community. Immediately north of Cyprus there was an independent
Turkish nation, and 700 miles away there was an independent Greek
nation. If the question of a change of sovereignty for Cyprus was to be
considered in the form of the annexation of the land to one or the other
of those two countries—if, he emphasized, such an eventuality were to be
considered, and according to the Greek viewpoint such an eventuality
should exist—then the retracing of the frontiers between the two countries, not independence for a national entity, would be the question
under discussion.

In international law, questions relating to accession to existing states
were in a class by themselves. In such questions a great number of
circumstances had to be taken into account, Sarper observed. These
questions had nothing to do with the independence of non-self-governing
territories. The Cyprus question, therefore, could never constitute a
precedent for these. In any case, even if the disposal of territories having
a mixed Turkish and Greek population were to create a precedent for
other cases, with which, he maintained, the Cyprus question had nothing
in common, Greece would have created the worst precedent, because, as
he had already stated, it had annexed the Turkish province of Western
Thrace which had an overwhelming majority of Turks. That annexation
had been made through the denial of the right of self-determination.

The Greek Foreign Minister's position about the relations between the
Turkish and "Greek-speaking" Cypriots, Sarper continued, had not been
easy for him clearly to understand during the last two years of his
pleading the cause of Greece in the Assembly. Sometimes the Foreign
Minister had said that these relations were good. At other times, as in the
letters he had circulated the previous year, he had said the opposite. The
day before he had expressed concern about the possibility of tragic strife
between the two communities and had warned the Assembly that Britain
was to be blamed for such an unfortunate eventuality. Sarper hoped this

eventuality would never take place. There could be no greater calamity than an increase in the tension that had already caused such a strain both in Cyprus and in the area. He wished, however, to point out that his delegation had explained in detail during the last debate the main reasons for the tension between the two communities in Cyprus. The regrettable tension had been heightened by the press campaign in Greece against the Turks in general and the Cypriot Turks in particular, of which he had given many examples at the previous session of the Assembly.[3] Furthermore, the hideous acts of Greek terrorists against innocent Turkish Cypriots had made the situation more dangerous. The propaganda and agitation for *enosis* had placed the Turkish Cypriots in a state of self-defense, in a state in which they felt they must do all that was in their power if they were not to find themselves under the rule of a government that had taken a position so tragically against them.

These were the real reasons for the tension between the two communities, said Sarper. These were the sources of danger that responsible statesmen in all the three governments concerned should try to eliminate. The leaflets the Greek terrorist organization was continually distributing promised the Turks of Cyprus a dire future if they fell under Greek rule and insinuated that their day would come. During the rioting that the Greek terrorists were now instigating to impress the Assembly,[4] they had issued grave warnings to the Turkish Cypriots. According to information of December 8 from the Turkish Consulate in Nicosia, the Turks in the village of Mitsada had been warned over loudspeakers to leave their homeland immediately. The Turks had asked for the protection of the Governor.[5] In such circumstances, how could it be expected that the Turkish Cypriots would place themselves under the custody of the Turkish community on another island ceded to Greece. In the two years following 1898, when Prince George of Greece was appointed, by international agreement, High Commissioner to the then Turkish island of Crete, the Muslim population of that island had diminished by more than 40,000. The Turkish Cypriots pointed to other examples that caused their anxiety about their own future if they were placed under Greek rule. A lack of understanding of these anxieties would not be conducive to a satisfactory solution of the Cyprus question.

The Foreign Minister of Greece, Sarper observed, had also blamed the Turkish Cypriots for being more numerous than the Greeks in the island's auxiliary police force.[6] The reason for that was that the Greek terrorists either killed or intimidated Greek policemen who co-operated with the Cyprus authorities. The terrorists aimed at enforcing their own law, the law of terror, in Cyprus. Since the Turkish people of Cyprus were the first target of such a disorder, how could they be blamed for co-operating on the side of law and order? Mr. Averoff-Tossizza had also insinuated that Turkish policemen had been responsible for cruelties. Such assertions based on the evidence adduced by criminal terrorists were hardly worth an answer. However, he—Sarper—had to point out that Greek

government organs had made other unpleasant and unjustifiable accusations against the Turkish Cypriots. The outstanding result of such unjustifiable accusations was to increase the ardor and determination of the
Turkish Cypriots not to be ruled by those who showed such a denial of
justice toward them.

Concerning the Greek Foreign Minister's statement that six representatives in the United Nations had agreed with him on the interpretation of
Resolution 1013 (XI), Sarper asserted he had not had the opportunity to
study all of these statements again. At any rate, whatever their contents
might be, he had the deepest respect for them as every delegation was
entitled to its own understanding of a text, provided no additional words
were necessary in order to arrive at a certain meaning. However, he
could not see Mr. Averoff-Tossizza's point in citing the names of these six
delegations, since nine other delegations during the course of the debate
had taken an explicitly different point of view, and seven others had
expressed themselves implicitly in the same direction as those nine delegations. He did not wish to make a point about this fact, because the
resolution's text and the conditions under which the "interested parties"
had accepted it were clear and required no explanation.

As he had said in his first statement, Sarper concluded, if a sincere
desire for a peaceful democratic and just solution existed among all the
parties directly concerned, Resolution 1013 (XI) included all the necessary elements for co-operation to this end. On the other hand, if one
government were to assume an intransigent attitude in the hope of
imposing its own point of view upon others, then the conciliatory efforts
of the Assembly would have been wasted, no matter what the wording of
a resolution might be. In the afternoon or evening, Sarper added, he
would intervene again to disclose the views of his delegation on the draft
resolution which the Greek Delegation had tabled.

The Political Committee then listened to the Permanent Representative to the UN of a new member state, the Federation of Malaya. Dr.
Ismail bin Dato Abdul Rahman, like Gunewardene of Ceylon, favored
independence for Cyprus and referred to his own country's march from
colonial status toward independence as a useful analogy. Malaya had
resolved problems similar to those currently met with in Cyprus: that of
the relationship between a colony and a colonial power; that of a racial
minority; and that of parties concerned whose interests would be altered
by a change of status of the country. The question of racial minorities
had delayed or even hindered many a dependent territory from becoming independent, because people in the dependent territory thought in
terms of majority and minority in their fight for freedom, due to the past
policy of the colonial power to divide and rule. Thinking in such terms,
though, was wrong. It was the duty of leaders wanting to liberate their
country from the colonial yoke to determine majority opinion on the
question of independence in each racial group and to weld the racial
majority opinions into a national unity fighting for the independence of

the country. Accordingly, he would suggest that the Greek Cypriots try to get a majority of opinion among the Turkish Cypriots on the question of independence, by peaceful and democratic means. To harp on the point that because 82 per cent of the population was Greek Cypriot and only 18 per cent Turkish Cypriot—the latter being a minority must abide by the decision of the majority—was to frighten further those Turkish Cypriots who would otherwise favor independence.

Fully supporting the Greek viewpoint was the extremely long, arabesque-like speech by the Vice-Chairman of the Delegation of Syria, Farid Zeineddine, who, while lending support to some of the arguments of his Egyptian and Soviet bloc colleagues, put forward certain specific historical[7] and geographic points of his own, to justify his country's concern over the Cyprus question, and to explain why he believed Syria was entitled to participate in any international negotiations that might take place over the future of Cyprus. In his view, based mainly on his own summary of his statement, first, the Cyprus question, being an issue of national liberation, should be solved by the application of the principle of self-determination, either by a plebiscite under UN supervision or by any other means. Second, in order to facilitate the liberation of the island, negotiations between the two parties concerned, namely, the people of Cyprus and the British government, should be entered into. The United Nations was in duty bound to insist that such negotiations be started and concluded in a manner insuring an agreed solution on the basis of freedom for Cyprus. Britain should not seek to frustrate or forestall UN action by invoking domestic jurisdiction. It should comply with Resolution 1013 (XI). Thirdly, the Turkish minority should be given all those constitutional and international safeguards that would insure the continued enjoyment of its life as a minority. On the international level, the Syrian government believed that the countries neighboring Cyprus would be legitimately concerned to the extent of seeing that Cyprus was not used by any power as a base to stage attacks against any other power in the region.[8] Therefore, Syria, Greece, and Turkey were entitled to take part in negotiations that might aim at demilitarizing or neutralizing Cyprus—an objective favored by Syria and proposed by Greece.[9]

Likewise seeming to lean toward the Greek viewpoint was the representative of Nepal, who, in his brief address, unlike the previous speaker, could hardly invoke arguments of propinquity for showing concern in the island's fate. Rishikesh Shaha, Ambassador and Permanent Representative to the UN, expressed sympathy for the people of Cyprus who were engaged in a life-and-death struggle for the right of self-determination. He also understood the Greek government's interest in the struggle of the Cypriots of Greek origin, though their methods might not be approved by all. Britain, however, had already conceded in principle the right of self-determination to the people of Cyprus. It was merely a question of how and when that right was to be implemented. Although the interest of the Greek and Turkish governments in the question was understandable, it was for Britain and the people of Cyprus to solve the problem without any pressure from outside. The right of self-determination should be exercised in accordance with democratic procedure. Partition would provide no solution.

A national minority in the ratio of one to eight could scarcely benefit from a partition of the country when that minority population was interspersed with the majority population and scattered all over the territory.

It was encouraging that the Greek Foreign Minister had welcomed the British representative's reference to progress toward self-government, and this seemed to show that negotiations might lead to a solution that would be satisfactory to all. As the U.S. representative had urged, he felt (somewhat inconsistently) that, in view of the British government's efforts after the adoption of Resolution 1013 (XI), the question could be solved through quiet diplomacy and negotiations. Nepal was confident that Britain would act in the spirit of fairness and understanding, which had been its tradition in colonial questions.

G. K. Novitsky, Adviser and Assistant to the Minister of Foreign Affairs of the Byelorussian S.S.R., spoke next, emphasizing, like his colleague Peive, both the strategic and anticolonialist aspects of the Cyprus question. In connection with the former, he attacked Britain's intention, mentioned in the British *White Paper* on Defense, to use the island as a base for nuclear squadrons.[10] In connection with the latter, he sharply dissented with the assertion of the British and Turkish representatives that Cyprus was not a (purely) colonial question. Like his U.S.S.R. and Ukrainian colleagues, he charged the British with non-compliance with Resolution 1013 (XI). But, unlike them, he denied Sarper's statement that EOKA's struggle was losing its intensity.[11] The struggle—a just one like that of other colonial peoples—was growing, he asserted. The United Nations should see to it, he maintained, that all colonial peoples secured the right to "self-determination and independence." The people of Cyprus, too, should have the right to exercise self-determination. Neither he nor the other Soviet spokesmen, it should be noted, ever attacked the Turkish proposal for the island's partition. Nor did they refer to the aspirations for *enosis*.

The Committee then listened to Savvas Loizidis, of the Greek Delegation. While the Greek Foreign Minister had stated his delegation's position on item 58, Loizidis said that he would speak as a member of the delegation but, being a Cypriot, would give some first-hand facts on this problem and make an appeal to his fellow representatives in the Committee. In doing so, he felt obliged to stress, first, that the question was one that primarily concerned the Cypriots themselves. On their own initiative, long before the Greek government had decided to sponsor their item, the Cypriots had knocked at the door of the United Nations. In

1950 a Cypriot mission had been seen for the first time in the United
Nations, enlightening representatives on the Cyprus question and asking
for moral support. As a member of the Cyprus mission of 1950, he could
not forget the kindness of Mr. Entezam, of Iran, who, after his election as
President of the fifth Assembly, had received the Cypriot mission and
had listened to it in a very courteous manner. The same courteous
attention had been extended to the Cypriot mission of 1950 by Prince
Wan Wathayakon of Thailand, Mssrs. Belaunde of Peru, Romulo of the
Philippines, and Thor Thors of Iceland.

In 1950, Greece, believing in a friendly solution outside the United
Nations, had not wished to sponsor the Cyprus item. The following year,
at the sixth Assembly in Paris, a Cypriot mission again had given a
reminder of the existence of the Cyprus question. At the seventh session,
in 1952, Archbishop Makarios himself had appeared in UN circles and
had got in touch with many delegations. Again, Greece decided not to
sponsor the demand of the Cypriot people for self-determination, trying
once more to find a solution outside the United Nations.[12] During that
session, on December 16, 1952, the Assembly passed Resolution 637
(VII).[13] This resolution recommended to the administering powers the
application of the principle of self-determination in the non-
self-governing territories. Since Cyprus was a non-self-governing territory, the Cypriots naturally requested the administering power to respect
this resolution,[14] but in vain. The following year, on August 10, 1953,
therefore, Archbishop Makarios, on behalf of the Greek Cypriots, who
constituted 81 per cent of the whole population of the island, submitted a
petition to the UN Secretary-General asking for the realization of the
right to self-determination so far as the Cypriot people were concerned.[15]
The petition had to be sponsored by a member state in order to have the
possibility of being included in the agenda. Once again Greece had not
wished to sponsor it, continuing its efforts to find a solution outside the
United Nations.

Loizidis went on to recount how the Cypriots had then decided to find
another member state that would be willing to sponsor their petition. He
himself had been authorized to come to the United Nations and appeal to
delegations of several member states for their sponsorship, and had got in
touch with some delegations and discussed the matter with them. In a
letter to the Asian-African group, which, at that time, was the champion
of self-determination, he had asked for permission to appear before them
and to speak to them. Prince Wathayakon, who, in September, 1953, was
chairman of this group, had kindly replied that this request would be put
before the group for consideration. At that moment, however, the Greek
Delegation had declared in the Assembly that the Cyprus petition concerned Greece, but that Greece was looking forward to having bipartite
negotiations with Britain and that, if that effort proved of no avail, then
it would ask for inclusion of the Cyprus question in the agenda of the

next session.[16] Greece had tried to have bipartite discussions but had met with an obstinate refusal on the part of the British government. That had been "a further mistake" of the British government, which later had been repeatedly the subject of reproach in the House of Commons. After that refusal, Greece had been obliged to sponsor the Cyprus demand before the United Nations at the ninth Assembly in 1954.

As a result of the Greek recourse in 1954, the Cyprus item had been included in the agenda, but the Assembly had decided not to pass a resolution recommending a solution of the question. That had been a "mistake" on the part of the United Nations, Loizidis asserted. This hesitation to assist a people demanding respect for the principles and purposes of the United Nations amounted, he thought, to responsibility for the developments which followed on the island. The Cypriots, receiving no response either from Britain or from the United Nations, had been driven to active resistance against their colonial status. After the Assembly in 1957 had passed Resolution 1013 (XI), which expressed the desire that a peaceful, democratic, and just solution would be found in accordance with the purposes and principles of the UN Charter, this resistance had stopped. Unfortunately, however, the desired result had not been achieved. The Assembly therefore once again faced the Cyprus question and, he believed, was fully conscious of the consequences of its current responsibility.

The day before, Loizidis continued, the U.S. representative had advised patience and the solution of the problem through quiet diplomacy.[17]

You have heard about the evolution of the Cyprus problem. I have heard about quiet diplomacy for solving our problem, since I was a schoolboy in Cyprus. We waited and we waited. Our patience, the patience of my generation—my patience—was already exhausted in 1931, when we had the first uprising and when I was exiled from Cyprus, because I took part in that uprising.[18] Again the Cypriot people showed patience. A second world war came. But now again their patience is exhausted. That is why the Cypriot people are driven to what is called violence. We do not like violence, but we are driven to it after so many years in which we have tried to find a solution through peaceful means.

Perhaps the British representative would remind the Committee that both he and his brother were connected with the present "terrorism" in Cyprus or that his brother was in prison because of that "terrorism" in Cyprus.[19] He was obliged to say that he considered it an honor to be a fighter for the freedom of his country. "In 1931, I was called a ringleader; now we are called terrorists. If you knew the Cypriot students, their intellectual and moral level you would understand for what ideology these people are fighting. Our Foreign Minister," Loizidis continued, had mentioned the case of Pallicaridis, who had been executed in Cyprus. This young man's last letter reminded him of a certain American "terrorist," Nathan Hale, who, about to be executed by British soldiers, had said he regretted to have but one life to give for his country. Such were the "terrorists" of today in Cyprus. Poems in the British press, he added, had praised Pallicaridis as a hero and a patriot.

At this point, Loizidis asked the Chairman of the Committee whether he wished him to continue or to wait until the afternoon meeting. The Chairman thought it might be preferable for him to continue his statement in the afternoon. In a hint directed at Loizidis, he also reminded the Committee that representatives who participated in the debate were supposed to represent the delegations of which they were members. The meeting rose at 1 P.M.

C. The 931st Meeting of the First Committee

After the chairman announced that the list of speakers on item 58 had been closed at noon of that day, and the Secretary of the Committee, Dragoslav Protitch, read the list—"Greece, New Zealand, Hungary, Australia, Sudan, Netherlands, Ethiopia, Ireland, Guatemala, Portugal, Uruguay, Pakistan, Turkey, Panama, India, United Kingdom, and Greece"—Loizidis continued his statement at the afternoon meeting of the Committee, its 931st, after assuring the Chairman he would try to comply with his advice to speak as a member of the Greek Delegation, not as a Cypriot.

Reviewing at some length the matter of the relations between the Greek and Turkish communities in Cyprus, Loizidis observed that when the Ottoman Sultan (Selim II) had conquered Cyprus in 1571, no Turks had been living there and, when Turkey had given up the island to Britain in 1878, the Greek character of the island had not changed at all. Some Turks, consisting at the beginning of soldiers and officials, had taken up residence in Cyprus, constituting always a small minority in comparison with the large Greek majority. Moreover, while the Greeks, from the very first day of the British occupation, had greeted the coming of the British as a step leading to freedom, the Turkish minority, on the other hand, had regarded Greek aspirations for freedom to be quite natural and quite reasonable, and never raised any serious objections.[20] On the contrary, the Turkish minority in Cyprus—and the Turks in Turkey, as well as the whole world—knew very well that with the cession of the island to the British, Turkey had given up Cyprus forever. Turkey, furthermore, by entering the war in 1914 against the Entente, had given Britain the opportunity to abrogate every obligation derived from the treaty of 1878 and to annex the island on November 5, 1914. By Article 20 of the Treaty of Lausanne in 1923,[21] Turkey did nothing but recognize this annexation. Legally this article had been a mere declaration of the territorial status in Cyprus, which had existed *de jure* since 1914, and *de facto* since 1878. Turkey had made no reservation whatsoever. What was more: the Turkish minority in Cyprus not only had agreed to the annexation in 1914, but, at a mass meeting, had condemned Turkey's entry into the war and had remained loyal to Britain.

The Turkish minority had always lived on very friendly terms—in brotherhood, and in the closest social and professional co-operation—with the Greek majority, even through the years of war between Greece and Turkey,[22] Loizidis asserted. In municipal councils as well as in commercial or athletic associations, the Turkish Cypriots co-operated in harmony with the Greek Cypriots. Here in the Committee, a Cypriot lawyer present, Zenon Rossides, had reminded him that for eighteen years he had been among Turkish colleagues in athletic associations and in the municipal council of Kyrenia. He himself had personal experience of such relations. He had been born and brought up in Cyprus. With other Greek schoolboys he had shared games with Turkish schoolboys. In social and professional relations in everyday life, there was no difference between Greeks and Turks. Many of his best friends in Cyprus were Turks. When practicing law in Cyprus, he had many Turkish clients, though he had never failed to struggle for the liberation of his island. Indeed, at the time of the national uprising of 1931 against the British, the Turks had sympathized with the uprising, and the last day before his arrest and his deportation, he had been given refuge in a Turkish home.

It was only in the last years, after the Greek Cypriots started their international campaign for the application of the principle of self-determination on the island, and after the British-Turkish co-operation for opposing the Cypriot aspiration had been established, that attempts were made to excite and inspire fanaticism among the Turkish minority. In spite of some riots instigated the previous year by an extremist Turkish leader,[23] the large majority of the Turkish community continued to have good relations with the Greek community. On August 30, 1957, the Governor of Cyprus had stated that, with only the exception of the old incident of the village of Vassilia, in the villages and districts he had visited, he had ascertained that Greek and Turkish Cypriots were living in harmony and that their relations were friendly.

After citing a letter of a Turkish newspaperman published in a Greek-language newspaper of Istanbul as another confirmation of the good relations prevailing between Greek and Turkish Cypriots,[24] Loizidis proclaimed that the Greek Cypriots were chivalrous, generous, humane, and hospitable. They were determined to continue living in friendly brotherhood with the Turkish minority. The application of the principle of self-determination to Cyprus would only be to the benefit of the Turkish minority. The Greek majority had always stressed its will to safeguard the rights of the Turkish minority and to guarantee their protection through the United Nations. In a free island, he declared, both Greeks and Turks would have equal political and social rights. Moreover, the Turks would have their special rights safeguarded and guaranteed in matters concerning their religion, education, family laws, and religious and welfare institutions. To the charges of Ambassador Sarper about the

Cretan precedent, Loizidis responded by quoting from a statement by a British Labour party Member of Parliament, P. Noel-Baker, in the House of Commons in 1956. This indicated that at the time of the Greek-Turkish exchange of populations in 1923, the Turks in Crete had stated that throughout the ten years of war between Greece and Turkey (1912–22) "no Greek had ever raised a hand against us." [25]

Coming now to the Cypriot complaints of ill-treatment and tortures, Loizidis said that Committee members had heard the leader of the Greek Delegation on this matter and had received the *Black Book* of the Ethnarchy of Cyprus. He, himself, had also had the opportunity of hearing trustworthy evidence and reading statements. It was very difficult for him to speak of these instances, however. He had personally known a great number of persons who had been tortured, and that was why he would be carried away by emotion, were he to describe in detail the hideous atrocities inflicted upon them. Therefore, he asked the Committee to read the Ethnarchy's book on violations of human rights on the island, instead of hearing him recite them.

Nevertheless, with regard to Mr. Noble's allegation the day before that one could not speak in the Committee about the ill-treatment of Cypriots because this item had not been included in the agenda, he was obliged to say that this was an error. The truth was that in the General Committee a proposal had been submitted by the other members that, in order not to prejudge the matter, a generally neutral heading ought to be chosen. However, all representatives had declared that the door was open to discussion of all matters connected with Cyprus.[26]

Nor could he leave unanswered and accept the assertion of the British representative that all these questions about ill-treatment and atrocities were propaganda, Loizidis said. He then quoted at great length a story published in a British newspaper by a British journalist [27] in order to support his view. Before the Commission of Human Rights at Strasbourg, Loizidis added, he had appeared for questioning in connection with cases of ill-treatment and torture. Of course, the procedure there was secret, and he could say nothing about it. However, the Commission, according to the published resolution, had decided that twenty-nine of the forty-nine cases presented by the Greek government were prima facie admissible and should be investigated.[28] With this type of problem, however, Loizidis went on to say, there would be, on the one hand, complaints, and, on the other, accusations that the complaints were slander. In such circumstances, he thought the best thing would be to appoint an investigation committee.

In a peroration that turned out to be quite long, Loizidis, "as a Cypriot and as a member of the Greek Delegation," appealed to all members of the Committee to do their duty toward the United Nations and the principles of the Charter; and to respect Resolution 545 (VI) of the Assembly, which provided that "all peoples shall have the right of self-determination;" and Resolution 637 (VII), which provided that member states "shall uphold the principle of self-determination of all peoples and nations, and shall recognize and promote the realization of the right of self-determination of the peoples of non-self-governing territories." Loizidis furthermore observed that a few days earlier the Third Committee had adopted by fifty votes to none, with thirteen abstentions, a resolution that would shortly be adopted by the Assembly. Under this resolution, the Assembly was to express the hope that member states would, in their mutual relations, give due respect to the right of self-determination, and that those states that were responsible for the administration of non-self-governing territories should promote the realization and facilitate the exercise of this right by the peoples of such territories.[29] It would be inconsistent and illogical, Loizidis maintained, "if one day we decide to recommend the exercise of the right of self-determination by peoples of a non-self-governing territory, and the next day we refuse to the people of a non-self-governing territory, such as Cyprus, the exercise of this right." Loizidis appealed to the British government to respect the principles of the UN Charter, and to treat the people of Cyprus at least as it had treated the inhabitants of British Togoland the previous year, when it had allowed this people to express their will on their future through a plebiscite under the supervision of the United Nations. In this plebiscite, the expressed will of the majority had been taken into consideration in a most praiseworthy democratic way. Although the southern provinces of that territory had shown a majority in favor of separation, the principle of self-determination had been applied in the right way. The overall result had been taken into account and the will of the Majority had been respected.

"We appeal," he declared,

to the European countries to be mindful of our spiritual and cultural links, and our common responsibilities toward the principles and purposes of the United Nations. We appeal also to the countries of the Asian-African group to be mindful of their history, of their perpetual campaign for the self-determination of peoples, and of the Bandung resolution regarding freedom and the termination of colonialism. We appeal to our friends of the Latin American countries to remember the struggles of their own countries for freedom and self-determination, and to follow the liberal spirit of their fathers and grandfathers.[30]

The previous year, Loizidis revealed, he had appealed privately to Ambassador Sarper, "our very distinguished representative of Turkey," and to other members of the Turkish Delegation, to join in efforts to preserve Greek-Turkish friendship. He had tried to persuade Mr. Sarper and "our friends of the Turkish Delegation" that he himself and all Greek Cypriots desired to live in brotherhood with the Turkish minority and were interested in the Turkish minority, if not more, at least in the same way as they themselves in Turkey were interested. Now, once again he appealed to them to face the question of Cyprus in a democratic, liberal, and humane way and, especially, in a modern spirit. He appealed to the conscience of all Committee members to stand on the principles of humanity. The people of Cyprus were fighting for their freedom. They were doing only "what every one of you would do in their position." The population of Cyprus—450,000 people—had made its decision for freedom or death. It was asking the United Nations for no more than moral support. "In expressing the wish that the people of Cyprus be given the opportunity to decide their own future, you will merely render moral support. You will merely be accelerating the solution of the problem."

Any hesitation, on the other hand, would mean more bloodshed, more pain and horror in prisons and concentration camps and interrogation rooms.

Who of you would have upon his conscience such consequences? Although your decision is one of life or death, we do not think it should be difficult for you to decide. You will be complying with the principles of justice and freedom if you express the wish for self-determination for the people of Cyprus. You will furthermore be complying with the principles of morality and humanity. You will help the Government of the United Kingdom to bring about more speedily something which they know they will do, some day, and you give them an opportunity to merit praise here, next year, for their enlightened colonial policies. You will be acting in accordance with the majority of British public opinion and with the tenets of the Labour Party.

Regarding Turkey and the Turkish minority, Loizidis said that his delegation had already stressed the wish of the Greek majority to have all rights of the Turkish minority safeguarded and guaranteed under the auspices of the United Nations. "The objections . . ."

The Chairman: I call upon the representative of Turkey on a point of order.

Mr. Sarper (Turkey): The Greek representative has used the pronoun 'we.' In what connection does he use this word? 'We want to live in peace with the Turkish minority,' and so on and so forth. Is he speaking in the capacity of the Greek Cypriots or is he speaking in the capacity of a representative of Greece? I would like to know because I shall have to interpret his statement according to his answer to this question.

Mr. Loizidis (Greece): It is clear that in speaking about the Greek majority and the Turkish minority living together in Cyprus, I spoke as a Cypriot, and I must beg your pardon again. You see, my two capacities are indivisible. That is all I can say. I am an exiled Cypriot; I now live in Greece. I am now a Greek subject, elected to membership in the Greek Parliament, and also of the Greek Delegation and in the latter capacity I am here but, unfortunately, I cannot forget that I am a Cypriot.

Mr. Sarper (Turkey): In order to be in a position to speak on behalf of the people of a non-self-governing territory, this representative, or would-be representative, has to obtain the permission of the Committee. Will you please call the gentleman to order, or put it to the Committee as to whether his presence as representative of Cyprus is acceptable or not?

The Chairman: I believe that I have already drawn the attention of the representative of Greece to the fact that he can only speak and participate in the debate in the Committee in his capacity as representative of Greece.

Mr. Loizidis (Greece): I have only a few more words to say, as I am at the end of my statement. I do not think it useful to discuss this point.

After this exchange, Loizidis went on to say that the objections which had been made—by Syria for example—in connection with the security of the eastern Mediterranean area were, in his view, outmoded. The conception of neighborhood and of neighbors had changed in meaning. With atomic weapons and ballistic missiles, Europe and America were neighbors, and, considering the tremendous scientific progress that had been made and would be made in the future, the conception of a neighborhood would, in a few years, apply also to the earth in relation to the moon and the planets. Having in mind this tremendous scientific and technical progress, "we face the future with horror if we do not develop a parallel moral progress, especially in our international relations." Quoting a passage from the Republic, in which Plato wrote that kings should be inspired with a love of true philosophy, a wise prince, he said, who followed in Plato's spirit was sitting "among us." Many wise statesmen and diplomats who took care of the affairs of, or played an influential role in, the governments of their countries were sitting around this table and sharing the responsibilities of this Committee. He appealed to them to approach the problem with the high and noble principles which, he was sure, governed their thinking.

In all respects, the Cyprus question was crystal clear and the application of the principle of self-determination, in its true meaning, to the people of Cyprus, was a test case for the United Nations, Loizidis concluded. It was up to the Assembly to decide in favor or against self-determination. The Greek Cypriot people had already decided—as might be seen in the press.[31] They were determined to obtain their freedom and, in any case, to live in brotherhood with the Turkish minority in Cyprus.

The supporters of protagonist and antagonists were evenly divided that afternoon. Of the twelve speakers heard, two from the Antipodes, old Commonwealth members, and allies of the United States through SEATO and the ANZUS Pact, supported the British viewpoint. So did two NATO members. Two Baghdad Pact members—one of them also a SEATO member—supported the Turkish viewpoint. On the other hand, two Latin American states, members of OAS, supported the Greek viewpoint, as did a Soviet bloc member and three unaligned states. Neither the Panamanian nor the Indian representative, though on the list of speakers announced by the Committee secretary, spoke at that meeting, nor, as a matter of fact, the representatives of the parties to the dispute.

New Zealand's representative, T. C. Larkin, of the Department of External Affairs, referred to his country's ties with Britain, Greece, and Turkey to justify its concern with the Cyprus question. He regretted the divisive effect of this question between those countries which were linked in a partnership on which, to a certain extent, international peace and security depended. His delegation had always doubted the wisdom of a UN debate on the question.[32] It hoped the Assembly would resist the impulse of endorsing, directly or indirectly, what was, in spite of the Greek government's disavowal, a demand that Britain cede part of its territory. The Greek request that the Assembly consider the issue merely and simply as a colonial one was dangerously deceptive. Besides, the Greek draft resolution disregarded British sovereignty over the island which the Greek government itself acknowledged. And there was no reason to believe the Greek assertion that Britain had failed to fulfil—or indeed had sought to evade—the Charter provisions on non-self-governing territories. "The solemn declaration by which Britain had affirmed that it would apply the principle of self-determination in Cyprus in conditions which would enable all of the population freely to express their views not only rang true but made sound political sense." The best way for Greece to advance the cause of self-determination for the Cypriots would have been to support the development of institutions of self-government. Lawlessness and terrorism did not produce an atmosphere propitious to such a development. Nor was Britain obstructing progress toward a settlement on the international plane, as the Radcliffe constitutional proposals, the release of Makarios, the various attempts to start discussions indicated. These positive British efforts deserved more than a summary rejection by the Greek government, which also sought to dissuade the people of Cyprus from considering these proposals. The Cyprus question could not be solved by forcing Britain to yield to pressure for the "premature exercise" of self-determination by the Cypriots. A solution did not involve just Britain and the people of Cyprus, as several speakers had maintained. It involved the reconciliation of many interests: those of the Greek and Turkish inhabitants of the island who were to make the final choice, and those of the Greek, Turkish, and British governments. The Assembly should help create a favorable atmosphere for such a reconciliation. New Zealand would support any proposal to that end.

Ambassador Peter Mod, Permanent Representative of Hungary to the UN, in his speech, followed the general Soviet bloc line. He blamed "one member" of the Assembly for having refused to solve the Cyprus problem in accordance with the provisions of the Charter, although world public opinion and UN organs had dealt with the problem for four years. The British position on the issue, he asserted, since Hopkinson's famous "never" statement in the Commons on July 28, 1954,[33] had remained essentially the same, except that it was now disguised so as not to appear diametrically opposed to the provisions of the Charter. In spite of Resolution 1013 (XI), Britain continued to use all types of colonial oppression against the Cypriot people. The Greek government, consequently, was perfectly justified in raising the question in conformity with the interests of the Cypriots and the spirit of the Charter, and in focusing on two points: self-determination and the atrocities of the British authorities

against the Cypriot people. The whole problem should be solved in
accordance with the spirit of the Charter. In spite of Britain's strategic
considerations, and of objections dealing with history, constitutional law,
international law, geography, and ethnography, which certain delegations had raised, the right of self-determination should be exercised by
the Cypriot people. The Committee, therefore, should help the people of
Cyprus to exercise this right. It could choose a number of constructive
methods, keeping in mind two fundamental points in order to avoid
failure. First of all, the fate of Cyprus could be decided upon only by the
people of Cyprus themselves. Therefore, any measure that was to solve
this problem without the consent of the Cypriots or against their will
would obviously be unacceptable. Second, a solution ought to be peaceful. Hence, as a first step toward a solution, the current colonial oppression and the state of emergency and all the different types of oppression carried out against the Cypriots should be abolished. The Hungarian
Delegation would support any efforts to find a solution to this question of
Cyprus, taking fully into account the fundamental points just mentioned.

A careful critique of the Greek approach and draft resolution by
Australia's Permanent Representative to the UN followed the Hungarian's speech. E. Ronald Walker, like his New Zealand colleague, noted
first his country's particularly close relations with all three of the countries most directly involved in the Cyprus question. With regard to
Greece, he not only mentioned the Australian troops which had fought
there during World War II but also the great number of Australians of
Greek descent (through post-World War II immigration). His government was also concerned over the problems of the people of Cyprus. The
more restrained and conciliatory tone of the debate on the Cyprus
question indicated that since the Assembly's previous session the situation there had not deteriorated but, on the contrary, showed beginnings
of improvement. His delegation and, he believed, the vast majority of the
other delegations, shared the desire expressed by Noble that acrimony be
avoided in debate and that this debate might lead to a better atmosphere.
"All recognized the truth in Commander Noble's words that much that
seemed difficult, even impossible, could be done if it was undertaken in a
spirit of amity and co-operation." [34]

Since the last Assembly, this spirit of amity and co-operation was basic
to Britain's approach in this matter, as evidenced by the release of
Makarios, the offer of safe-conduct out of Cyprus to terrorists, the relaxation of emergency measures which had begun, and the British attempts
to arrange private discussions among the British, Greek, and Turkish
governments. These attempts had not succeeded—through no fault of
Britain. But they offered what was perhaps the best prospect of a solution. While all would watch developments in Cyprus with close interest
and deep concern, and would desire to encourage the new Governor and
wish him success in his difficult and supremely important task in Cyprus,
he doubted whether the Assembly could do more than that. "But we have

before us . . . a draft resolution proposed by the Greek Delegation, which does ask us to do rather more." This draft resolution invited the Assembly to express its concern that no progress had been made toward a solution of the problem in compliance with Resolution 1013 (XI). To adopt this would imply that the Assembly had examined and evaluated developments in the past nine months and had concluded that no progress had been made. However, although the statements of representatives had been heard, there had been no investigation, and the impression gained from the statements was that there had been some progress toward a solution, not as much as one would have liked; not as much as the Cypriot people would have liked; not as much as Britain would have wished. But one should be patient. British efforts were in compliance with Resolution 1013 (XI).

The Greek draft resolution's third preambular paragraph, particularly following the second one,[35] was rather alarmist in tone, the Australian said. It suggested that the situation was fraught with danger. Did that mean that more violence was likely? This paragraph also suggested that a solution in conformity with the Charter was required at the earliest possible time. But this was true of all problems. One desired, namely, a solution in conformity with the Charter at the earliest possible moment. That paragraph went on to day: "To preserve peace and stability in that area." Did this mean that there was no need for the careful development of solutions which took account both of conditions inside Cyprus and of the need for good relations between Britain, Greece, and Turkey? The history of the problem undoubtedly emphasized its extreme delicacy. Any precipitate attempt at a solution that did not meet the complexities of the situation would not, he feared, preserve peace and stability in the area. Some little time and much patience might be entailed in working out a solution, exactly because the solution should conform to the principles of the Charter and be such as to preserve peace and stability.

Coming now to the operative paragraph of the Greek draft resolution, which expressed the wish that the people of Cyprus would be given the opportunity to determine their own future by the application of their right to self-determination, the Australian warned the Assembly to exercise great care before adopting resolutions on self-determination and always to have regard for the provisions of the Charter. Article 1, paragraph 2, of the Charter, which stated that one of the purposes of the United Nations was

To develop friendly relations among nations based on respect for the principle of equal rights and self-determination of peoples, and take other appropriate measures to strengthen universal peace,

indicated that respect for that principle was advanced as a basis for friendly relations among nations, and that the development of friendly relations based on respect for this principle was one of the appropriate measures for strengthening universal peace. Then, in Article 55 there was the second important reference to self-determination. This was set forth in Chapter IX dealing with international co-operation—the promotion of higher standards of living, etc., and the promotion of universal respect for human rights and fundamental freedoms. The relevant passage read:

With a view to the creation of conditions of stability and well-being which are necessary for peaceful and friendly relations among nations, based on respect for the principle of equal rights and self-determination of peoples.

As this passage indicated, again the emphasis was on peaceful and friendly relations, the principle of self-determination being only one of the bases of such relations. The Greek draft resolution, on the other hand, used words vaguely reminiscent of the Charter but not Charter language. It referred not to the "principle" but to a "right" of self-determination. If one wished to use Charter language applicable to the domestic problem of the system of government in Cyprus, one should turn to Chapter XI on non-self-governing territories. Here, Article 73 (b) seemed most relevant:

To develop self-government, to take due account of the political aspirations of the peoples . . .

This, he asserted, was the avowed purpose of Britain in Cyprus. The claims of Greece and Turkey to speak for the inhabitants of Cyprus had not rendered more easy the execution of this policy. But one should also take into account the paragraph that came right after the previous provision in that same chapter of the Charter:

To further international peace and security.

Since the whole of Chapter XI had been written within the system of international peace and security set up by the Charter, he could not accept the Greek argument that Britain was wrong in wishing to discuss the Cyprus question with both Greece and Turkey. In his first statement before the Committee, the Greek Foreign Minister had said that "this tripartite formula is aimed at eliminating the people of Cyprus as the principal and essential factor in the problem," whereas later he had stated: "Greece had received the mandate to present and defend the cause of the liberation of the people of Cyprus by means of the application of the principle of self-determination." [36]

As far as the Charter was concerned, the Australian representative maintained that it was the responsibility of Britain to develop self-government in Cyprus. In that connection, the United Nations had no right to intervene under Article 2, paragraph 7, of the Charter. Nor did Greece have such a right under the Charter, or a mandate recognizable by the United Nations. Britain, on the other hand, was well within its rights under the Charter if it considered desirable to have tripartite negotiations in the interests of the people of Cyprus, and with a view toward promoting peaceful and friendly relations with Greece and Turkey. Indeed, it should be commended rather than criticized for approaching the matter in that way. After reiterating his delegation's constant opposition to any attempt to have the Assembly intervene in matters that were essentially within the domestic jurisdiction of any state, Walker concluded by restating the view that the Greek draft resolution was inappropriate as a practical method for advancing a solution to the complex Cyprus problem. For that reason, his delegation would vote against that draft resolution if it were brought to a vote in its existing form. He hoped the Committee would reject it.

The address of this old Commonwealth member was followed by another one which clearly favored the Greek Cypriot viewpoint, as this had been put forward by the Greek Delegation at the ninth Assembly, in 1954. Yacoub Osman, Ambassador and Permanent Representative of the Sudan to the UN, stated that the desire of the Cypriots for self-determination and possible union with Greece was understandable, since four-fifths of the island were of Greek culture. Even before World War I they had been led to believe that the day of freedom and union with Greece was approaching, he said, quoting statements by William E. Gladstone, Winston S. Churchill, and David Lloyd George, which the Greek Delegation had presented in 1954 to buttress its position.[37] Yet in the space of fifty years, there had been no progress toward this ideal, and it was only comparatively recently that the Cypriots had used other than peaceful means to achieve their aims, by waging a struggle against heavy odds. After referring to the (ostensibly bipartite) Harding-Makarios talks of 1955–56,[38] the representative of Sudan appealed to the British government to find a solution acceptable to all parties and particularly the people of Cyprus. While attacking partition as not practicable, he favored the introduction of safeguards for the Turkish minority in any future Constitution of the island. His delegation firmly stood by the right of the Cypriot people to self-determination, already accepted by the British government.[39] The effective exercise of this right, he concluded, would ease world tension and create an atmosphere conducive to friendly relations among the parties directly concerned.

C. W. A. Schurmann, Ambassador and UN Permanent Representative from the Netherlands, a NATO member which had faced decolonization problems in Indonesia similar to those of Britain and other colonial powers, took, on the other hand, the British side in the argument. Britain's task, now that terrorism was abating, was no longer so much to make right prevail over wrong as to reconcile certain opposing aspirations—the treaty rights invoked by Turkey, the principle of self-determination supported by Greece and the Greek Cypriots, the rights and wishes of the Turkish Cypriots, and, finally, Britain's own obligations and responsibilities under the Charter. Britain had expressed willingness to continue consultations with all the parties to the dispute—the Greek

Cypriots, the Turkish Cypriots, Greece, and Turkey—and to consider any solution acceptable to all, instead of imposing a one-sided solution. This was a fair proposal that deserved the wholehearted co-operation of all parties concerned and provided the best possible basis for a fair and lasting settlement. It could certainly not be the task of the Assembly to express preference for one kind of solution or another. The wisest course was to take care not to harm, restrict, or prejudice the chances for an ultimate meeting of minds of all those whose rights and aspirations had to be considered, and to leave full scope to Britain to devise a solution and thereby serve the best interests of all the parties.

The Committee then listened to Ato Yawand-Wossen Mangasha, alternate representative of Ethiopia, an African country which had never been a colony, though for a brief time during the interwar period, Fascist Italy had annexed it. He reiterated his government's earlier support of the Greek viewpoint. The people of Cyprus, he observed, desired to emancipate themselves from their colonial status and had resorted to political agitation and even force to compel Britain to accede to their desire. Quite justly on grounds of geography, and cultural and racial affinity, the Greek government had espoused this cause. Finally, the British government, even though in a negative way, had conceded that the people of Cyprus were entitled to determine their future status by the application of the principle of self-determination. The issue separating the parties had thus narrowed down to considerations of devising appropriate machinery for applying that principle. For, in spite of the little material change in the situation on the island since the previous Assembly, it was evident that the parties directly concerned had not only recognized the importance of the question but wished to settle it as amicably as possible. The Ethiopian Delegation, he stated in conclusion, would support the Greek draft resolution.

Ireland's representative likewise supported the Greek viewpoint, not unexpectedly directing his main fire against partition as a solution of the Cyprus question. Conor Cruise O'Brien, Counsellor of the Department of External Affairs, noted first that since the Assembly's previous session some progress had been made in creating an atmosphere of peace and freedom of expression mentioned in Resolution 1013 (XI), but none had been achieved toward a peaceful, democratic, and just solution likewise referred to in that resolution. And, although there were some hopeful signs for the future because Sir Hugh Foot was replacing Sir John Harding as Governor of the island, nevertheless, certain statements made by the British and Turkish representatives suggested that instead of a democratic and just solution, what was being prepared for Cyprus was partition, "that expedient of tired statesmen." In spite of Commander Noble's assertions that Britain always supported the principle of self-determination, it was hard to see how the partition of northern Ireland could be reconciled with the ordinary and accepted interpretation of the principle of self-determination. He, at any rate, would give full support to the Greek draft resolution. He could not understand the term "self-determination" to mean that, because there were different ethnic groups in Cyprus, the island should be divided between them. The integrity of Cyprus as a geographic and historical unit should be preserved, and the future of that unit should be decided democratically by the majority of its inhabitants. Turkey had, of course, the right to inquire what guarantees the majority of the island's population was prepared to give to the minority in respect of religious, educational and other human rights, and could also call on the Assembly for a reinforcement of those guarantees. But the Irish Delegation could not regard the existence of a Turkish minority in Cyprus or the proximity of Cyprus to Turkey or the fact that Turkey once ruled Cyprus as giving Turkey any right to have a say in whether, how, or in what form Cyprus should be allowed to exercise self-determination. If self-determination was to be achieved, the parties to that achievement could only be the people of the island itself and Britain. Certainly, Turkey had no claim to exercise a veto on the right of the Cypriots to self-determination, and Britain, were it to concede such a right of veto, would be wrecking all hope of the peaceful and just solution for which the Assembly had called.

A similar pro-Greek viewpoint was voiced by the next representative, Emilio Arenales Catalan, Ambassador and Permanent Representative of Guatemala to the UN, who praised his Irish colleague's "brilliant" speech. After reading part of the statement on Cyprus he had made at the previous Assembly,[40] reminding the Committee that his delegation then had been prepared to support the Greek draft resolution that recognized the principle of self-determination for the people of Cyprus, and explaining why, nevertheless, it had voted in favor of Resolution 1013 (XI), he observed that since the adoption of that resolution negotiations unfortunately had not been resumed for finding a solution to the Cyprus problem. Hence the time had now come for the United Nations this time to make known its unambiguous views about the right of the people of Cyprus to self-determination. He agreed with the Greek Delegation that there were only two parties to the problem: the people of Cyprus and the British government. He also observed that the Radcliffe draft Constitution provided no basis for a solution of the problem because, among other things, it failed to mention self-determination. Neither arguments about the revision of treaties or about strategic matters should stand in the way of a declaration on the part of the United Nations of the right of self-determination which should be granted to the people of Cyprus. Regardless of what the problems of international security might be, the Delegation of Guatemala felt that the West did not want its security in exchange for the slavery of any people. Implicitly, the Guatemalan attacked the concept of double self-determination and partition, while expressing sympathy for Turkey's concern with the protection of the Turkish Cypriot minority on the island. If the United Nations, he reiterated, did not now make a clear pronouncement on the question of self-determination, it would be very difficult for negotiations to solve "how" and "when" self-determination was to be implemented. For these reasons, Guatemala would vote in favor of the Greek draft resolution. It also appealed to Committee members and particularly to Latin American nations, "whose independence had cost so much blood and life," to do likewise.

In a briefer speech, G. Ahmed, the Ambassador and Permanent Representative of Pakistan to the UN, unlike the previous three speakers, supported the British and Turkish viewpoints on the issue. This was not altogether surprising. His country was not only a member of the Baghdad Pact and of SEATO but, because of the Kashmir dispute, was at loggerheads with India, whose views, known since previous Assemblies, had been echoed with varying degrees of accuracy by the representatives of Ceylon, the Federation of Malaya, and Nepal. Pakistan, he said, was disturbed by this dispute with concerned some of its direct or indirect allies. Cyprus was not a simple colonial problem. The legitimate strategic interest of Britain in the island's future could be reconciled with the political aspirations of the Cypriots, but the real difficulty was that Greece and Turkey were at odds over the island's future. Since there was no Cypriot nation nor Cypriot nationalism, there was the problem of applying in Cyprus the principle of self-determination to two distinct national groups. The use of the terms "majority" and "minority" was misleading. Besides the points made by the Turkish representative to justify his country's interest in Cyprus and, in particular, the importance of the island to the security of Turkey's communications with the outside world could not be ignored. These factors presented a genuine impediment to UN attempts to lay down a basis of a solution to the problem. Pakistan welcomed the reaffirmation by the British and Turkish representatives of their acceptance of Resolution 1013 (XI), which represented the correct approach. It hoped that Greece would show moderation and patience in the interests of the Free World and its friendship with Britain, and that the parties concerned, and the Greek Cypriots, especially, would create the necessary climate of compromise for the success of any negotiations that might be undertaken.

Favoring, on the other hand, the application of the principle of self-determination to the people of Cyprus was Ambassador and Permanent Representative of Uruguay to the UN, Enrique Rodriguez Fabregat. Deploring that, in spite of Resolution 1013 (XI), the "painful" features of the Cyprus question had not changed, he expressed hope that a renewed effort would be made to solve the problem in accordance with the Charter. Like his Bolivian colleague, he praised Britain, Greece, and Turkey, the three countries directly concerned, for their contributions to culture, civilization, and human progress. But, he said, after having developed that theme at some length, there was a fourth party, "the main actor, the true star of the drama—the people of Cyprus." It was only these people that could, by their will, decide their own future. The

Uruguayan Delegation had maintained that same viewpoint in both the Algerian and Hungarian questions. In speaking about the latter, he himself had observed that the violation of the principle of self-determination "would in every case be a retrograde step in time as well as in institutions, and, also, in the way of thinking of men." Implicitly attacking the concept of the island's partition, he remarked, as his Irish colleague had done, that one should speak of self-determination without any sophistries and without adding anything that would turn this principle into a "confused way of dispersing and shattering nationalities" as Hitler did. The principle of self-determination, which had led the Bolivians to independence, "had its taproot in the condition of man as a political and social unit." The people of Cyprus had all the qualifications for exercising the right of self-determination, for it was neither backward nor underdeveloped. Any draft resolution introduced in the Committee should include a clear and categorical affirmation of that right.

The representative of Portugal, a colonial country and NATO member, quite expectedly supported the British view. Vasco Vieira Garin, that country's Ambassador and Permanent Representative to the UN, regretting the divergence of views between three countries with which Portugal had strong ties of friendship, believed the Cyprus question could be settled only through the tripartite negotiations advocated by Britain. All three parties wanted to reach a solution which would be in the interests of the people of Cyprus, but opinion was sharply divided on the sort of negotiations to be undertaken. Under Resolution 1013 (XI), the Assembly had expressed its conviction that the prerequisite of any useful negotiations was the cessation of terrorism. The release of Makarios, the safe-conduct offered to EOKA members, and the truce proclaimed and observed by the leading terrorist organization in Cyprus had led to some improvement in the local situation. The recent revival of violence, coincidental with the UN debate, was a further argument against UN intervention. If terrorism by extremist elements prevailed, it was obvious that "freedom of expression," referred to in Resolution 1013 (XI), could not be achieved for a minority, or the moderate elements in a majority, who would be unable properly to participate in the framing of constitutional machinery. That resolution, thus, implied a clear condemnation of terrorism. If now all parties co-operated, the measures of the British government for progressively relaxing the emergency measures would soon create the conditions of freedom of expression required under Resolution 1013 (XI). Turkey had declared its willingness to consider suggestions for a satisfactory solution. It was to be hoped that Greece would not press for a restricted (bipartite) sort of negotiation which might cause the disregard of the responsibilities and legitimate interests of other parties. It was not wise to discuss in the Committee a question so obviously meant to form the subject of negotiations among the three parties concerned. Besides, the Cyprus question was a matter essentially within the domestic jurisdiction of a member state and therefore unsuitable for discussion in the United Nations. Resolution 1013 (XI) still offered the best prospect for the resumption of tripartite negotiations now that a more favorable atmosphere in the island had been achieved. He therefore hoped the Committee would facilitate progress by adopting a text on the lines of that same resolution, possibly coupled with an appeal to the population of Cyprus to observe calm and restraint.

Although not on the list of speakers, the representative of Iran, a country member of the Baghdad Pact, made a relatively brief statement, with none of the Committee members objecting. Former President of the Assembly Entezam took a line that did not favor the Greek draft resolution. Coming to the Committee with no preconceived idea or prepared speech, he had delayed, he said, his statement in order honestly to form an opinion concerning a solution, and had taken a few notes related to the arguments presented by both sides. The more he listened to the speakers, the more thorny and unique he found the problem. Cyprus reminded him of the Palestine case. In both, majority and minority were so divided by their nature and aspirations that it was difficult—perhaps impossible—to find a solution that would guarantee satisfaction to the two communities involved. Of course, there were many differences. Britain had a League of Nations mandate over Palestine, whereas with Cyprus its relations were those of a metropolitan country toward a colony. Then, in the case of Palestine, Britain itself had come to the United Nations for aid and counsel, whereas in the Cyprus case Britain was far from ready to drop its rights over the island, and two other member states had come there claiming the right to speak on behalf of the Cypriot people, and basing this right on what they considered ethnic and linguistic community interests. The United Nations, above all else, should respect the right of the people of Cyprus to self-determination, and means should be found for insuring the application of this right while excluding the possibility that one part of the population might abuse this right for the purpose of victimizing the other part. The United Nations, Entezam continued, could either urge all parties [41] to resume their interrupted negotiations, in other words adopt a resolution like the previous one; or it could itself take over. In the latter case, it would have to be allowed complete freedom to act in accordance with the means and methods at its disposal. The Assembly would then appoint a commission to make a thorough on-the-spot study, consult with the people involved, and present a plan to the Assembly. But it was inconceivable to ask the Committee to adopt such a decision, since an Assembly of eighty-two states could not be expected to resolve a problem of this kind and find a satisfactory solution within three days by simply waving a magic wand. Hence, only the first alternative remained open.

In the Iranian's view, the Greek draft resolution was too little, if the United Nations was expected to solve the problem by itself. But it was also too much, if—as hoped—one were to limit one's self to recommending to the parties that they resume negotiations. In conclusion, he would prefer to forget those parts of speeches in which the speakers had let themselves be carried away by their emotions, however justified, and remember the solemn statements of the three parties principally concerned, who had stated they were anxious to preserve the profound friendship that bound them.

The meeting rose at 6:10 P.M.

D. The 932d Meeting of the First Committee

After the antiphonal chorus of various UN members was heard in the morning and afternoon meetings of the Political Committee on December 11, it was mainly the three monodists who took over the stage at the evening meeting of that Committee—its 932d.

Ambassador Sarper started out by stating the Turkish Delegation's position on the Greek draft resolution. Like last year, he said, the Greek Delegation had come forward with a "drastic" draft resolution, the adoption of which was calculated to bring about the ultimate annexation of Cyprus to Greece and the subjugation of the Turkish Cypriots under Greek rule against their will. He was therefore compelled to point out certain features of the draft resolution before the Committee.

The implication of the second preambular paragraph of this draft, demanding that the Assembly should express its concern "that no progress had been made toward the solution of this problem in compliance with the operative paragraph of resolution 1013 (XI)," would be that Britain and Turkey had been responsible for the delay in the implementation of that resolution. In reality the situation was just the opposite. The operative paragraph of Resolution 1013 (XI) mentioned not only the desire for "a peaceful, democratic, and just solution" in accordance with the purposes and principles of the Charter but also "the hope that negotiations will be resumed and continued to this end." This paragraph of the resolution, in other words, excluded any unilateral solution. It asked for a negotiated solution among the parties concerned, and now the party that refused negotiations on several occasions, when well-intentioned offers had been made, had presented a text which might give the impression of reversing the charges. This would be unfair, unjust, and detrimental to the eventual satisfactory solution of the Cyprus problem. If then, the idea of referring to Resolution 1013 (XI) was to be retained, that paragraph of the preamble of the Greek draft resolution would have to be entirely rewritten so as to reflect the true situation, which was the opposite of what was implied in the Greek draft. The Assembly might take note of the statements of the Turkish and British representatives to the effect that they were willing to take part in negotiations, as hoped for in Resolution 1013 (XI), while at the same time noting that the Greek government, up to the present at least, had refused to take part in the negotiations.

In the next paragraph of the Greek draft resolution, Sarper continued, the Greek Delegation stated "that the situation in Cyprus is still fraught with danger and that a solution in conformity with the principles of the Charter and at the earliest possible time is required to preserve peace and stability in the area." It was difficult to understand the meaning of that paragraph, Sarper maintained. During the debate at the previous session, on February 18, 1957, he had drawn the attention of the members of the Assembly to certain passages in the Greek explanatory memorandum circulated on June 13, 1956, in which it was stated in one part that Greece was against the use of violence, while in another it was argued that violence was justified under certain conditions.[42] This question required clarification. In the light of these considerations, he was extremely sorry that the Greek government had seen fit to include the contents of that paragraph in the draft resolution. That paragraph stated that the situation in Cyprus was "still"—and he stressed the word "still"—fraught with danger unless a solution was reached at the earliest possible time.

The next paragraph implied that this solution should be "the extremist Greek solution." Taken together, the two paragraphs could be interpreted by extremists to mean that war and the terrorist movement should continue until the one-sided Greek draft resolution was adopted. He thought the Assembly would not be inclined to give grounds for any such false interpretation, not only by the perpetrators of these acts but also by the Assembly.

Now, said the Turkish Ambassador, he wished to comment briefly on the operative paragraph of the Greek draft resolution. This paragraph aimed at completely reversing the Assembly's decision contained in the operative paragraph of Resolution 1013 (XI). After quoting in full the text of that operative paragraph, Sarper went on to say that, in conformity with the UN Charter as well as with the principles of equity and justice, the Assembly had thereby recommended unanimously that a peaceful, democratic, and just solution should be found through negotiations. Now, however, the Greek Delegation proposed that the Assembly should reverse this decision in order to show its preference for a unilateral and extremist point of view in the form of a solution to be imposed on the other two interested parties. Furthermore, the wording of the operative paragraph of the Greek draft resolution contained two parallel formulas with the same meaning, so that if one were deleted in a gesture which might be taken as a compromise, the other would still suffice for the extremists to maintain that if a vote of the majority of the "Greek-speaking" Cypriots expressed a desire for the annexation of Cyprus to Greece, then the frontiers of the area should be retraced accordingly, so that "over a hundred thousand" Turkish Cypriots would be placed under Greek rule against their will.

The Turkish Delegation had repeatedly stated that the Turkish government considered the principle of self-determination as one of the pillars of its foreign policy. But it had also stated that it did not accept the Greek interpretation of the principle with regard to Cyprus. It had cited articles of the Charter, general rules of international law, specific stipulations of existing treaties, and examples of well-known precedents, to prove that the Greek interpretation of this principle, as far as its eventual form of application in Cyprus was concerned, was unjust, and not only unjust but also impracticable.

The words "self-determination" or "to decide their own future," however, in the course of the bitter debates which had, unfortunately, taken place around the Cyprus question, had assumed, as interpreted by extremists, other meanings than those accepted by general rules of equity and justice, as well as by the Charter, Sarper maintained. If the Greek draft resolution were to be adopted, those who gave an extremist interpretation to these words as far as the Cyprus question was concerned, might feel encouraged to persist in their demands so that the solution of this tragic question would be rendered even more difficult than it was today.

At the end of the previous debate on the Cyprus question, at the eleventh Assembly, when all the parties directly interested had voted in favor of Resolution 1013 (XI), the Turkish Delegation, said Sarper, cherished great hopes for an early solution of that tragic issue which might be satisfactory to all concerned. Its hopes were greatly increased when, in the first months that followed the debate, considerable progress had been achieved in the direction of creating a more suitable atmosphere for an eventual solution. Although, later on, a series of efforts toward reaching a solution had been frustrated, it still maintained the view that, given time and patient effort, the spirit embodied in Resolution 1013 (XI) might eventually overcome all obstacles.

The Greek draft resolution, however, and the position the Greek Delegation had assumed during the current debate had confronted the Assembly with the situation of having to do away with all the progress that had been achieved in spite of great difficulties and thanks to important concessions on the part of some interested parties, Sarper contended. The fact of putting forward this draft resolution presented the danger of placing the Cyprus question back where it had first started in the Assembly three years earlier.

The Turkish Delegation, if the Greek draft resolution were put to the vote, would vote against it. It hoped, Sarper said, the Assembly would give a new example of its deep wisdom and of its sense of justice and equity by solidly opposing the adoption of such a draft resolution. He had to respectfully point out to the members of the Committee, Sarper warned, that if this draft resolution were adopted, the solution of the Cyprus question might be indefinitely delayed, and he was sure that was not the desire of the Assembly. He reserved finally his right of reply in accordance with rule 116 of the rules of procedure.[43]

Before the British and Greek representatives delivered their statements, the Ambassador and Permanent Representative of Panama to the UN, Jorge H. Illueca, presented his government's view on the Cyprus question. Although he did not come out in favor of the Greek draft resolution, he tended to support the Greek viewpoint particularly in certain matters of interpreting Resolution 1013 (XI). After reminding the Committee that Panama, at the previous Assembly, had introduced a draft resolution but had withdrawn it to permit the adoption of a text acceptable to all the parties concerned,[44] he expressed regret that, in spite of Resolution 1013 (XI), no peaceful, just, and democratic solution had yet been found, so that the situation had become more serious. It would serve no purpose to try to apportion the blame for this, but one had to acknowledge that the non-application of that resolution "had placed the United Nations in an invidious position not only vis-à-vis the heroic Cypriots, but also world public opinion." The question now was whether a resolution drafted in more categorical terms than the previous one should be adopted. Although some delegations at the eleventh Assembly had refused to accept the Greek draft resolution referring to the exercise of the right of self-determination by the people of Cyprus, because they feared such a resolution set a precedent that might endanger the interests of the colonial powers, nevertheless, in Resolution 1013 (XI), the Assembly had recommended a solution in accordance with the purposes and principles of the Charter. This meant in fact that the parties concerned should be guided in particular by Article 1, paragraph 2, of the Charter which calls for the development of friendly relations among nations "based on respect for the principle of equal rights and self-determination of peoples."

It was true (as the Australian representative had pointed out) that this Article referred only to the "principle" not to the "right" itself. However, that Article had provided the basis for several resolutions in which the Assembly had affirmed the "right" as well as the "principle"—for instance, resolutions 421 (V)[45] and 545 (VI).[46] Therefore it could be said that Resolution 1013 (XI) implicitly recognized the "right" of the people of Cyprus to self-determination. The people's ability to exercise that right was unquestioned, and there could be no doubt that the great majority of the people desired independence, as the Cypriots of Greek origin who were fighting for independence formed 80 per cent of the island's population. The Greek Foreign Minister had stated at the Committee's 927th meeting that Greece asserted no claims on Cyprus but had supported the people of Cyprus because four-fifths of the Cypriot population were Greek in origin, by language, religion, and culture, and because it was depending on a just cause. The Delegation of Panama did not doubt the sincerity of this statement, which opened the way to a solution that would guarantee the interests of the minority groups on the island. It could not approve of the use of violence, for it believed that right invariably triumphed over oppression. The debate, all in all, had made a number of facts clear. The people of Cyprus were fully qualified to exercise the right of self-determination. Greece asserted no rights to the island. Turkey did not dispute the right of the people of Cyprus to self-determination, provided the exercise of that right did not result in annexation or bringing the Turkish minority under Greek rule against its will. Britain was ready to grant self-government to Cyprus. Lastly, Greece, Britain, and Turkey had reaffirmed their desire and their will to reach an agreement. Under those circumstances, an appeal by the Assembly this time would not go unheeded. He hoped the Assembly would find a compromise solution which would be acceptable to the three states and would take into account the interests of the party principally concerned, the people of Cyprus. His delegation would vote for any draft resolution that would guarantee the "inalienable and sacrosanct" rights of the people of Cyprus.

Commander Noble spoke next. A good deal of discussion about who should play what part in the solution of the Cyprus question had been heard, he wryly commented. One thing, however, he said, was certain: of all the governments represented in the Committee, none was as closely and essentially concerned than his government, which bore responsibility for Cyprus. He had to repeat therefore the British view on the question. After re-emphasizing that his government had long been trying to move toward self-government on the island, he repeated the two-paragraph statement that he had made in his opening address, which had been conveyed to the Greek Delegation by the U.S. Delegation on December 6; i.e., before item 58 came up for Committee discussion.[47] His delegation believed that Resolution 1013 (XI) was useful. It did not attempt to state what the problem's solution should be. As the U.S. representative and others had said, he stressed, it would be wrong for the Committee to establish guidelines by which a solution should be sought. Resolution 1013 (XI) suggested procedures. First of all, it said that a solution required an atmosphere of peace and freedom of expression. Noble was sure that all agreed on this. All, too, surely agreed that, at least until the week that immediately preceded the new Cyprus debate, conditions on the island had noticeably improved. But now the situation had again become serious, and the balance between order and disorder was delicate. He thought that the events of the past few days had proved this, and it was something he was sure members of the Committee would bear in mind. He asked the Committee to remember that relaxation all around had followed Resolution 1013 (XI). He sincerely believed that much depended on the message that would go forth from the Assembly as a result of the new debate. If this message were partial and took into account only some of the factors involved, this might make conditions much worse, he asserted. There was, thus, every reason to observe moderation in Committee proceedings and resolutions.

The second thing that Resolution 1013 (XI) had done, Noble continued, was to suggest that the way toward a peaceful, democratic, and just solution would be through the resumption and continuance of negotia-

tions. In the years and months before that resolution, Britain had initiated a wide variety of procedures, of which he had already informed
the Committee. For reasons over which his government had no control,
none of these procedures had yet worked. After Resolution 1013 (XI),
his government hoped a new start had been made and accepted a new
procedure—the good offices for conciliation of the then Secretary-
General of NATO. But, by the middle of summer, it had become clear,
largely because of the Greek reaction, that by itself it was not sufficient.
Then his government had begun exchanges with the Greek and Turkish
governments with a view to reaching broad agreement on the central
problem, namely, on the future international status of Cyprus. This had
been in the spirit of Resolution 1013 (XI). If agreement could be
reached on this question, the other problems would fall into line more
easily. These talks did not exclude conversations with the Cypriot leaders. On the contrary, the discussions with the two governments were
intended to facilitate talks with the Cypriot leaders. These exchanges
with the Greek and Turkish governments had gone on for some time and
had not ended.[48]

Therefore, the main point Noble wished to emphasize was that the
Committee should reaffirm Resolution 1013 (XI) and encourage the
continuance of talks that would neither favor nor exclude any of those
concerned. That, he thought, was common ground as well as common
sense. The Greek government, he imagined, would agree with these
sentiments. But their absence from the Greek draft resolution was one of
the main reasons why it was not acceptable to Britain.

The second main reason why the Greek draft resolution was unacceptable was that it attempted to go beyond the question of procedures.
It did exactly what many delegations had said the Assembly should not
try to do. It sought to lay the basis on which the solution of the Cyprus
question should be attempted, and it did so by invoking the principle of
self-determination. His government supported this principle and had
applied it in many parts of the world when it had had the responsibility.
It wanted to apply it to Cyprus too. But principles had to be applied in a
way suitable to each particular case. In the special case of Cyprus, the
campaign in Cyprus and in Greece for *enosis* had immensely complicated
the problem of the application of the principle. It had turned the issue
into an international one of a very difficult kind.

The British representative thought the Greek Foreign Minister overlooked this whole side of the picture and ignored the tension that would
ensue not only on the island itself if the Committee followed him on the
path he proposed. The British government could not ignore the consequences. It was necessary to see the picture as a whole. That was really
the answer to the question which Mr. Averoff-Tossizza had put to him
the day before in connection with a passage in his—Noble's—opening
speech.[49] This statement, which Noble quoted, related, he said, quite
clearly to the proposals that Britain had made in December, 1956. These

proposals—the Radcliffe draft constitution—had been accepted by the Turkish government and rejected by the Greek government. They were still open. And he was glad to note the readiness of the Greek Foreign Minister to discuss self-government, which, he had agreed, should precede self-determination. The British government was anxious that such discussions should be held in private among those concerned. In such discussions, an effort should be made to concentrate on points of agreement and leave aside for the time being matters on which there was at present no agreement.

The Greek draft resolution, finally, Noble declared, raised points on which there was no agreement. It should not be assumed that there would always be disagreement. He felt that, if talks continued, a new spirit of co-operation might grow which might facilitate the solution of these problems. Accordingly, he asked the Committee to reject the "partial proposals contained in the Greek draft resolution" and to encourage the continuance of talks between all those concerned, in a spirit of co-operation.

The turn now came for the Greek Foreign Minister to make what in effect was his last speech in the Political Committee on the substance of the Cyprus question as a whole, on the debate which had taken place on the question and on the draft resolution his delegation had tabled. In this long address, he replied to several points made not only by the representatives of Britain and Turkey, but also by the representative of the United States. And he not only hinted, as Loizidis had done earlier that day, that he was not unprepared to accept the dispatch of a UN commission to Cyprus for checking on the authenticity of the charges of tortures and violations of human rights on the part of the British authorities on the island (having at hand an appropriate draft resolution, should Noble consent to such a proposal), but he also repeated the offer he had made in his opening statement concerning a possible demilitarization of Cyprus, in order to allay the security anxieties of the Turkish government. Moreover, he put forward proposals for setting up international safeguards for the Turkish minority on the island and for securing Turkish economic interests there as well as any other legitimate Turkish interest connected with the island. Finally, he not only expressed his willingness to modify the text of the Greek draft resolution to meet some of the objections the representatives of Australia and Turkey had raised but also dangled before the Committee certain further possibilities of amendments to this draft resolution.

First of all, feeling compelled to counteract the impression that Lodge's speech had created the day before, the Greek Foreign Minister ventured to criticize it in what he felt to be a friendly fashion, without hurting the United States and the American position on the issue. No matter how mild that criticism was, the Americans seemed, nevertheless, to have been taken aback by it. Indeed, as will be seen, this criticism triggered a diplomatic protest backstage. Perhaps, the Greek Delegation felt, the Americans were not used to criticism expressed in public—at least when this was voiced by allies.

In his desire to reply succinctly to those who had spoken, Averoff-Tossizza started out by saying that he had not prepared a written text. He had, therefore, to beg the Committee's indulgence. At the end of this debate on "the last vestige of colonialism in the eastern Mediterranean," he thanked the Committee, which had taken so much trouble, and the representatives who had spoken. The speeches had been of a high quality. Many of them had contained an unsurpassed logic. It was now to be seen how far this logic would help in arriving at a solution to the problem. He did not think that now, at the end of the meeting, he would take up the various statements and reply to them individually. There was one statement, however, which he would like very briefly to mention, because a person for whom he felt particular admiration had made it. This person represented a country very close and very dear to his own, a country to which Greece owed deep gratitude for very important reasons. He referred to the U.S. representative, Mr. Lodge, and to his statement.[50]

Mr. Lodge, the Greek Foreign Minister continued, had made a very wise statement. He had advised negotiations, mediation, arbitration, and other means, and he had also mentioned the Charter as providing those means. These were very wise counsels. They had, however, only one defect. They were about twenty years too late, because, during the past twenty years, there had been negotiations, attempts at mediation, talks and unbelievable efforts to reach a solution. All that Mr. Lodge had mentioned had been tried. He himself remembered having had, in November, 1951, a special meeting with Mr. Eden. He had tried to obtain a simple, vague promise, but the only answer he could elicit was: "I cannot take up a question that does not exist."[51] During World War II, a promise had been given. "Fight for Greece and Freedom" was a slogan prevalent in Cyprus. That slogan alone had led to the enlistment of all the Cypriots in the British Army; yet no result had been achieved. Thus, while he acknowledged the wisdom of the counsels of the U.S. representative, they were, he repeated, some twenty years too late.

He would like to make another brief remark on this point, Averoff-Tossizza went on to say. Some tens of thousands of American citizens of Greek origin lived in Massachusetts, and he knew from them that Mr. Lodge was not only a former Senator and a distinguished diplomat but was also a leading personality in the United States. He knew that in other countries he was considered as such, and he had to say that he, too, shared that view. However, Mr. Lodge might permit him to say that his speech of the day before represented an exception to the rule that made a person a leading personality. Averoff-Tossizza knew, of course, that the exception confirmed the rule, but he had to raise a point. Mr. Lodge, at the end of his speech, had advised the Assembly not to vote for any resolution. He felt that this advice represented a slight flaw in Mr. Lodge's role as a leading personality. It was not possible for the Assembly to say that it wanted no decision. Some decision was required. What decision? He would outline this briefly to the Committee.[52]

He did not wish to deal with all the points the Cyprus question raised—points of law, of UN competence, and of the Lausanne Treaty. It was his impression that everyone had been able to form a very clear opinion upon those points. He would, therefore, analyze the "crystallization reached by the various points of view," because he believed that the debate had been very useful and had indeed made possible a clear crystallization of positions, from the analysis of which conclusions could be drawn.

But before proceeding to this analysis, Averoff-Tossizza declared, he would briefly deal with the "most distressing of all the questions which had been raised in the course of this debate—the question of tortures." The day before he had drawn a very clear distinction when he had said he did not accuse the British people of the British nation, but certain colonialist officials.[53] In raising this question, his purpose had not been propaganda or polemics or the idea of obtaining additional votes in the Committee, but to shield the people of Cyprus from these atrocious methods and also to table a draft resolution calling for the setting up of a committee of inquiry. Had he tabled such a draft resolution, which would be in order, his purpose would have been to achieve a desired result. Several representatives, however, even among those with whom he had the closest ties, had advised him not to place them in a delicate position and not to request the establishment of such a committee. The setting up of such a committee would, nevertheless, be based on unshakable logic. Mr. Noble had been right in saying he—the Greek Foreign Minister—was making very serious charges.[54] But Noble had made an even more serious charge, when he had said that the Foreign Minister had used and developed an argument that was fabricated and not strictly true. "What would be more simple, then, than to make an objective study of these charges in order to see whether we have been put in the wrong as the result of having been given false documents?" As he had stated at the previous Assembly, if a UN committee were to find that the majority of the documents were forgeries and that his arguments were false, he would consider himself so greatly exposed before the nation which was very dear to him, and he would withdraw from politics and retire to private life.[55] However, if this idea of a test was not accepted and certain delegations were placed in a delicate position—which meant that the committee in question would not be established—then he would consider that he should, at the request of the majority, refrain from making this proposal.

Cyprus had recently witnessed a recrudescence of events which were distressing to everyone, the Greek Foreign Minister went on to say. He drew the Committee's attention to a cable from the Consul-General in Nicosia about a proclamation the Mayor of that city had issued—an appeal to all inhabitants of the capital "to lock deep within their soul all feelings of indignation with regard to the shameful events of recent hours" and avoid "any exaggerated reaction" likely to "damage our sacred cause irreparably." [56] Although this was the spirit of the leaders of the Greek people of Cyprus, it was not within their power to contain the feelings of a people in revolt for their freedom, the Greek Foreign Minister said. "And there lies the basic cause of all the events that have taken place, the cause of the disturbances, the cause of the repression." He would even go so far as not to reproach the British and Turkish members of the auxiliary police who committed these acts in Cyprus because that was their mission. To put an end to those acts, it was necessary to abolish that mission. In this connection, he cited an editorial from the *Times of Cyprus*, of December 10, which not only raised the question of whether the forceful methods some units of the security forces used did not do more to provoke trouble than to prevent it, but also asked officialdom in the island to treat more seriously the disturbing mass of evidence that the punishment to Turkish trouble-makers was considerably more lenient than that meted out to Greeks. These were not charges against the Turkish minority, Averoff-Tossizza emphasized. The Turkish minority on Cyprus, he asserted, like the Turkish minority in Thrace, consisted for the most part of fine people. But, the day before, Mr. Sarper himself had acknowledged that it was necessary to have Turks in the regular and auxiliary police because colonialism existed, and whether or not one wished it, the revolt against colonialism turned against the auxiliary police, made up of Turks, with the result that both nationalities, which had lived like brothers for centuries, were now set against each other.

But, coming now to his analysis which had to do with the very substance of the Cyprus question, the Greek Foreign Minister observed that, as a result of the debate, two points of view had crystallized: Some representatives maintained that this question should be settled by applying the principle—and he stressed the word "principle"—of self-determination without setting forth in the United Nations the time and place of its application, but leaving these matters for the British government and representatives of the people to decide by means of negotiations among themselves.[57] Other representatives maintained that negotiations should take place between the three parties concerned and the representatives of the people of Cyprus.[58] He would not repeat his delegation's arguments in support of the position that the first view was by far the most correct but would proceed immediately to another question:

Why this difference in view? There was only one cause for this difference, Averoff-Tossizza asserted. It was that Turkey believed that, if the principle of self-determination were applied by means of negotiations between the British government and the people of Cyprus, its interests would be impaired.

What were the Turkish interests with respect to Cyprus? The first

legitimate interest had to do with the existence of a minority, the Greek
Foreign Minister noted. He would not reply by saying that Greece had
had experience with minorities; that Greece had had a large Jewish
minority, which had fought on the Greek side and had shed its blood
with the Greeks; that Greece also had Turkish minorities with which
brotherly relations prevailed, with no one suffering in spite of the tension. He would even go further to meet that argument. He had proposed
that a neutral committee, set up by the United Nations or by agreement
with Turkey, should determine the status of the Turkish minority on
Cyprus. His government would have no right of veto. That committee
might decide what it wished with regard to participation, cultural or
religious freedom, and so forth—anything that it wished. And the United
Nations would safeguard that status, possibly through a commissioner to
follow up the implementation of that status. Could there be any doubt
that a status so determined would meet the interest of the Turks?

To Turkey's strategic arguments and interest with regard to Cyprus, he
had also given certain replies, the Greek Foreign Minister continued. He
had said that Turkey had never been attacked from Cyprus. He admitted
that perhaps that was not adequate. He could add further that if Greece
had once gone into Asia Minor, as Mr. Sarper had recalled,[59] it had been
on the invitation of four great powers, because there were Greeks in Asia
Minor who were there no longer, and that Greece was a country that
would never be able to attack Turkey. However, he would set aside all
these arguments to go on to another one that met them all. Since Turkey
felt threatened from Cyprus, he would propose that the United Nations
determine for the island a perpetual military status that would safeguard
Turkey against any attack from Cyprus.

The representative of Turkey and sometimes the Turkish government,
Averoff-Tossizza went on to note, had also stated that they had an
economic interest in Cyprus and that Cyprus was part of Asia Minor. The
representative of Syria, on the other hand, had asserted that Cyprus had
always been a part of Syria. He—the Foreign Minister—would say that
Cyprus was not part of anything but belonged to its people. He recognized, nevertheless, that, although Turkey had an agricultural economy
that was parallel (not complementary) to that of Cyprus, it was seeking
to carry out a program of large-scale industrial development, which, he
hoped, would succeed. Consequently its economy might allow it to
develop economic relations with Cyprus. To secure this interest, too, an
internationally guaranteed customs union or status might be in order, so
that both Turkey and Greece might have access to the Cypriot market on
an equal footing. A free port system—customs relations with both countries—would be set up. Although he did not consider this Turkish argument as being very objective, he would like to meet it, too, because he
knew that in order to defend a cause well, every argument of the
opposing side had to be fully met.

One of the most responsible men in the world,[60] to whom he had

presented these proposals, had told him: "You have removed the island."
He, Averoff-Tossizza, had asked him whether he could see any other
legitimate interest of Turkey in Cyprus. If there were one, he had assured
him, the Greek government would meet that one, too, with the same
good will and it would meet it fully. Now, before the Committee, he
repeated that statement. He was absolutely convinced that, with the
friendship Greece had for Turkey, with the need which Greece and
Turkey had for relations between themselves, and with the good will of
the people of Cyprus, any other objective argument that might be advanced would be met in the same way.

One argument, however, Averoff-Tossizza declared, could not be met:
that by which the 18 per cent of the population should have the right of
veto over the future of the island.[61] This argument was contrary to
political morality and to political stability. That was the tragedy. Turkey,
for reasons into which he would not delve, maintained that this was what
should happen. There had been only one case in the entire world in
which the minority had settled the fate of the majority, and that was the
case of Palestine. That case deserved his government's sympathy. But one
could see the results.

Several representatives had been rather impressed by the argument
according to which there would be self-determination for everyone, of
course, but also self-determination for minorities,[62] Averoff-Tossizza observed further. He had already explained that self-determination for
minorities *should* not be applied. In the particular case of Cyprus, there
was a further and stronger reason why that *could* not be applied. The
population on the island was so intermixed that not even the smallest
district existed in which the Turks were in a majority. If necessary, and if
such a district existed, that approach might be considered. But the
population was intermixed. But even if there were such a district, the
rule of the single electoral college should prevail. Would the seventeen
sponsoring states of the resolution on Algeria have supported that resolution, had it contained the idea that self-determination meant self-
determination for the French minority?

He did not wish to engage in polemics, Averoff-Tossizza asserted. He
had set forth his case as objectively as possible, and he had a very strong
feeling of responsibility. This responsibility, which weighed upon him,
was a very unusual one. He was speaking of an island that was in a state
of unrest, where blood was being shed, and which stood between three
friends. Mr. Noble in his statement had recalled that Britain had helped
Greece. Greece knew that and was very grateful for it. Britain had not
only helped on the occasion Mr. Noble had mentioned, but on other
occasions too. It was also true that Greece had done its utmost to help
Britain, especially when it had fought on its own against almost the
whole of occupied Europe. The Greeks, he reiterated, recognized they
owed very much to Britain. But, when it was a question of a civilized
island, an island where blood was being shed, an island which set at

dangerous odds three friends, an island which caused such strong feeling in the Greek people; when it was a question in which everything depended on Cyprus, then there was no question except that of Cyprus. That island spoke through him, and everyone would understand the heavy responsibility that weighed upon him now.

But it was not only the island that spoke through him, the Greek Foreign Minister continued. A matter of principle was at stake. If he was pressing for a vote on his delegation's resolution, it was because he believed that it would be the first time that the United Nations would be voting on such a principle. "It cannot be that twelve years after the establishment of the United Nations, the question of self-determination cannot be put to the vote. Do we dare . . . face up to this responsibility at least once every twelve years?" It was for this reason that he was pressing for a vote on the Greek draft resolution—to his regret and in spite of his contacts with some men whom he respected very much.

But he had to make a clarification, Averoff-Tossizza added. Some representatives had raised the question of the preamble to this Greek draft resolution. The representative of Australia, whom he thanked for his mention of the ties between Australia and Greece, had given an interpretation of the preamble that certainly was not the one the Greek Delegation intended.[63] Other men, for whom he had great respect, had said they had doubts about the wording of the preamble. He was not here to make charges by means of words, he assured the Committee. When his delegation had stated in the preamble of its draft resolution that there had been no progress in the Cyprus question, it did not mean that someone was responsible for that. When it had said that the situation was fraught with danger, that this situation was fraught with danger, and that EOKA was going to renew its activities, his delegation did not mean that this was the Greek government's intention. He, therefore, proposed, if this were acceptable to the Committee, to delete that phrase from the preamble, or, as an alternative, the vote could be taken paragraph by paragraph so that a draft resolution could be adopted that would merely say that, having examined the question of Cyprus, the Assembly expressed the wish that the people of Cyprus would be given the opportunity to determine their own future by the application of their right to self-determination.

Averoff-Tossizza then expressed his regret that the proposal he had made the day before to Mr. Noble, because of the interpretation the latter had just given to it, could no longer be considered as valid. Mr. Noble had explained, in reply to his question whether he meant self-determination as the Greek Delegation understood it, that this was self-determination for all.[64] This was a more elegant formula for describing partition, the Foreign Minister remarked. He noted with pleasure that, in the Committee, representatives had not wished to use the word "division" or "partition," but had found a more elegant formula, which, however, amounted to the same thing. Once again he declared that if Noble's

statement dealt with self-determination as the Greek Delegation understood that concept, his government would be prepared to help bring
about negotiations for self-government, covered by a clear statement for
self-determination.[65] If the Committee really desired to be helpful, it
could say that, in principle, self-determination was applicable to Cyprus.
Only the principle, Averoff-Tossizza emphasized, was involved. It was
not necessary to say how and when that principle would be implemented. As to the "how," of course, it would be said that the democratic
way of implementation was meant (i.e., by its application to the whole
population as a single entity, regardless of ethnic origin). But the means
of implementation would not be voted upon—only the principle itself.
Was there anyone who could reject the application of this principle of
self-determination? "By what logic, gentlemen, can you say No to us, No
to the enslaved people who speak through me?" All that interested the
people of Cyprus was that one day, by some means, it might be assured
of exercising its right of self-determination. That was the only question.
Everything else could be settled easily.

Exercising his right to reply, Ambassador Sarper spoke next. He had
listened, he said, very carefully to "the very interesting statement" made
by the Foreign Minister of Greece. Objectively examined and analyzed it
proved two points: First, that the Cyprus question was extremely complex. And, second, that only negotiations between the governments concerned and consultations and discussions with the representatives of the
peoples of Cyprus could solve this complex question. Mr. Averoff-
Tossizza very efficiently had proved these two points. As a matter of fact,
he had pleaded and proved the Turkish case more eloquently than
he—Sarper—could have done. In passing, the Greek Foreign Minister
had also mentioned the question of partition. For reasons known to many
representatives and very well-known to Mr. Averoff-Tossizza, he was not
going to dwell on this question at the present stage of the debate. If he
wished it and the Committee desired it, though, he could do so at a later
stage.

Now, there was one question that he could ask Mr. Averoff-Tossizza:
Why was he negotiating with the Turkish government across the Committee table—sitting so far away as he did? Better, much easier, more
normal ways existed for negotiating than across a table in the presence of
eighty-two delegations, Sarper underlined. By that he did not mean that
the eighty-two delegations should not be concerned and interested in this
matter, but, since the Greek Foreign Minister had proved the complexity
of the Cyprus question, since he had proved that his question could be
solved only by negotiations, by reasonable negotiations, with good will
and good intentions, why should one not do that? That was the case his
delegation wanted to prove. It had not, perhaps, been efficient enough in
furnishing the proofs. But the Greek Foreign Minister had been, and he
thanked him very much.

Insisting on his right of reply, the Greek Foreign Minister declared he could answer with great pleasure the question asked by Mr. Sarper. He agreed that these questions were more profitably discussed around a smaller table. But there was one difficulty which had caused the debate, namely, the non-recognition of the "principle"—and he insisted, the "principle"—of the right to self-determination. If that were recognized as applicable to Cyprus, then, obviously, the other questions regarding Cyprus could well be solved between the British government and the representatives of the Cypriots. If the "principle" were recognized, he repeated, the negotiations would be fruitful. Regarding the other questions, certainly there could be negotiations—these questions, of course, being marginal to the main question, which was self-determination.

After this bargaining effort that seems also to have included the suggestion that he was even prepared to replace in his draft resolution the term "right" to self-determination with the term "principle" of self-determination, should another delegation wish to propose such an amendment, Averoff-Tossizza concluded his intervention with a few remarks of ironic courtesy for Ambassador Sarper's previous comments.

"I should like to point out to the Committee that the general discussion on the question of Cyprus is closed," the Chairman then said. As decided, this debate had dealt also with the draft resolution before the Committee, he observed. Nevertheless, the representatives of China had asked to speak on the draft resolution, and he—the chairman—would call on him. After that the voting would take place. "I call on the representative of the United States on a point of order," he suddenly said. "We have had a very long hard day. The hour is getting late," said Ambassador Lodge. "I think that we would all make better decisions if we had a night's sleep. Therefore, under rule 119, I move the meeting be adjourned until tomorrow morning." [66]

The Chairman stated that, under rule 119 of the rules of procedure, this motion of the U.S. representative had to be put to the vote immediately. If there were no objections to this motion for adjournment, he would consider it adopted.

"As does Mr. Lodge, I recognize that a good night's sleep is helpful," said the Greek Foreign Minister. "But I think that if we sat here until 10:10 this evening, to stay a few minutes more to vote on the question and to finish, it would, I think, be more constructive and permit us to sleep more calmly and longer tomorrow morning. Naturally if the Committee feels tired . . ."

"I must say, I was not in order," the Chairman intervened, "when I allowed the representative of Greece to speak. Under rule 119 of the rules of procedure, a motion for adjournment must be put to the vote immediately without discussion."

"Had I known that, I would not have asked to speak," said Averoff-Tossizza.

"If you do not have any objections to the motion for adjournment made by the representative of the United States," said the Chairman, "I shall consider that the motion is adopted."

"I would like the Committee to vote," said the Soviet representative.

"There is a motion for adjournment and there cannot be any debate," said Lodge.

"I shall ask the Committee to express its views on the motion for adjournment submitted by the representative of the United States," said the Chairman. "We shall now vote on that motion."

The motion to adjourn was adopted by a show of hands—49–7, with 21 abstentions.

Before adjourning, the Chairman told the Committe that after hearing the representative of China at the next meeting, a vote would be taken on the draft resolution the Committee had before it. The Committee would then proceed without interruption to the consideration of the last item on its agenda.

Among the abstainers on the vote over the American Delegation's motion for an adjournment was the Greek Delegation. The general impression was that the motion for adjournment had been a blow against the Greek Delegation. The atmosphere had seemed most propitious because of the many speeches that had been favorable to the Greek draft resolution and the repeated interventions of the Greek Foreign Minister. The criticism he had ventured of the American stand had awakened among delegations of the smaller states a sense of solidarity with the Greek Delegation. In this way, it had contributed to a betterment of the Greek position. A positive impression prevailed that, had the Greek draft resolution been put to the vote that evening, it would have gathered in its favor the simple majority of members present and voting required for it to be adopted by the Committee as a recommendation to the Assembly. But Ambassador Lodge had, once again, intervened. The purpose? To prevent the Committee's adoption of the Greek draft resolution and to gain time for proposing amendments and for exerting political pressure on various delegations, especially those of Latin America.

E. Backstage

No sooner had the Political Committee's evening meeting ended at 10:15 P.M. than the representatives of Canada, Denmark, Norway, and Chile (none of them had taken part in the Committee debate) were mobilized by the U.S. Delegation and met with the British in a conference that lasted well into the night, for the purpose of drafting amendments to the Greek draft resolution. The Greek Delegation was kept away from these activities, which were carried out in absolute secrecy, for it was natural not to betray aggressive designs to the foe, who, in this instance was the Greek Delegation. It was learned (after the Assembly had taken its decision on the Cyprus item) that the British Delegation had drafted the amendments and that the U.S. Delegation had then approved them—after which the representatives of the four above-mentioned smaller states were invited to sponsor these amendments. Apparently, the representative of Ireland, Ambassador Frederick H. Boland, had been prodded to join the other representatives as a cosponsor, on the ground that his participation would inspire with confidence the Greek Delegation and the delegations that supported the Greek viewpoint. Members of the U.S. Delegation, in particular, had exerted great pressure on the Irish Ambassador, arguing that they were asking him to do what he had done in the case of the amendments that had been proposed to Arab-Asian draft resolution on the Algerian question—amendments that Ireland had cosponsored. The Irish representative, however, had categorically refused to go along with these proposals, saying that the content of the proposed amendments was unacceptable to his delegation.

On their side, the members of the Greek Delegation did not remain with their arms folded. By all means in their power they set themselves down to the hard task of trying to find out what was being devised against their own draft resolution. At any rate, because it appeared clear that the procedural attack would assume the guise of proposals for amendments to the Greek draft resolution, the Greek Foreign Minister, with the General Assembly's rules of procedure in hand, planned out the Greek counterattack. Evidently the aim of the opponents would be to introduce amendments that would delete from the Greek draft resolution any reference to the right of self-determination of the Cypriot people; and, because under the rules of procedure, amendments are always voted on first, it would be easy for the Committee to vote in their favor, not in favor of the Greek draft resolution, which called for the application of the right of self-determination to the people of Cyprus. The result would be the transformation of the Greek draft resolution into an Anglo-Turkish one, which would then be adopted by the Committee.

To deal with this clear danger there was only one way to react: by submitting a subamendment, i.e., an amendment to an amendment. Under this procedure, the reference to the principle of self-determination would be restored into the draft resolution and would have to be voted on first. At that crucial juncture, it should be added, the Greek Delegation felt that the whole matter of self-determination, the vital question of the freedom of a people to decide their own future, had been transformed into a matter of procedure, the outcome of which depended on the recognition or non-recognition of this right of the Cypriot people. The Committee, the Delegation was, nevertheless, convinced, would vote for a text that referred to self-determination in spite of the opposition of the United States, the reaction of which would not go beyond abstention from voting. The question, however, was: Would it be possible for the issue of self-determination to be put to the vote?

Chapter Eleven

December 12:
The Greek Side Wins in
the Committee Battle and India Comments

A. Backstage

Averoff-Tossizza returned to the United Nations that morning with his plan for a counterattack ready and with the determination to overcome all hurdles, regardless of consequences. Because of the expected amendments, the opening of the meeting of the Political Committee was delayed. It was 11:00 A.M., but these had not yet been circulated. The whole tactic, the Greek Delegation felt, was not to allow it enough time to study these amendments and react appropriately. Of course, under the rules of procedure, the delegation had the right to request a twenty-four-hour postponement in order to study these amendments before they were put to the vote.[1] Practically, however, this was undesirable not only because the Assembly's session was reaching its end but also because it was not in the interest of the delegation to give time to its opponents to exert pressure upon the governments of other member states for their acceptance of the amendments to the Greek draft resolution.

Half an hour before the text of these amendments was mimeographed and circulated by the Secretariat, the Canadian representative gave a copy of these amendments, which were cosponsored by the Delegations of Canada, Chile, Denmark, and Norway, to Ambassador Lall of the Indian Delegation. Naturally, he asked for the support of the Indian Delegation in getting these amendments adopted by the Committee. The Indian representative, however, conveyed the text of these amendments to the Greek Delegation. The result was that, as soon as the meeting began, the Greek Foreign Minister had his subamendment ready.

The amendments—four in all—cosponsored by the above four states, three of which were NATO members and one a member of the OAS, regarded three points in the preambular clauses of the Greek draft resolution, and wholly replaced its operative clause. This latter change, of a radical character, deleted any reference to self-determination and contained a recommendation for negotiations between those concerned in the Cyprus question. Under this particular amendment, the Assembly was asked to express "its earnest hope that further negotiations and discussions between those concerned will be promptly undertaken in a spirit of cooperation with a view to finding a peaceful, democratic and just solution, in conformity with the purposes and principles of the Charter of the United Nations." In other words, as the first amendment to the preambular clauses of the Greek draft resolution provided, the Assembly, in effect, would merely reaffirm Resolution 1013 (XI), while adding a reference to "those concerned" that was unpalatable to the Greek Delegation. Under the other two amendments to the preambular clauses of the Greek draft resolution, the Assembly would express "its concern that more progress had not been made toward the solution" of the Cyprus problem, and would consider further "that the situation in Cyprus is still fraught with danger and that a solution at the earliest possible time is required to preserve peace and stability in that area." [2]

B. *The 933d Meeting of the First Committee*

The 933d meeting of the First Committee started out with a statement of the representative of China, Yun-wu Wang, a member of parliament. After praising the moderation and constructive approach the "three states principally concerned" had shown in the debate, he expressed his conviction that an acceptable solution was not impossible to find, as soon as the psychological and emotional factors had yielded to a spirit of compromise and co-operation. The British government was experienced in the application of the principle of self-determination to dependent peoples. The British representative had told the Committee that his government was prepared to enter into negotiations with the Cypriots for the determination of their political future. What was needed was the "atmosphere of peace and freedom of expression" called for by Resolution 1013 (XI). There was no reason to doubt the sincerity of Britain's pledge to satisfy the legitimate aspirations of the Cypriot people. Account, of course, should be taken of the interests of the Cypriots of Turkish origin who were apprehensive for their future, once the political status of the island had changed. China, always a staunch supporter of self-determination, believed, however, that at the current juncture the Assembly should merely exert moral pressure on the parties for an early resumption of negotiations in the search for "a peaceful, democratic, and just solution in accordance with the purposes and principle of the Charter." The dispute should not be allowed to get out of hand and to undermine an alliance on which the peace of so vital a part of the world depended. These considerations would determine his delegation's view.

A short Greek-Turkish exchange followed. Ambassador Sarper said that new information he had received justified the fear he had expressed at the previous meeting that the Greek draft resolution, far from promoting a solution, might lead to an increase in violence and bloodshed. The very fact of the presentation of the "extremist" draft had actually encouraged the members of EOKA to perpetrate acts of violence and to cause unprecedented disorders. Pressures, intimidation, threats, and assassinations had created an intolerable situation for the Turkish Cypriots. In spite of the Greek representative's affirmations, the murder of three Turkish villagers, to which he had referred previously,[3] had been the work of the EOKA. In view of that situation, the Turkish government had asked the British government to insure the protection of Turkish Cypriots, who went in fear of their lives. The riots, threats, and violence organized by the "Greek terrorists," Sarper contended, were causing unrest, instability, and danger of disaster in the island. Dr. Kuchuk, the leader of the Turkish community in Cyprus, had sent cables to the secretaries-general of the UN and of NATO, and the Prime Ministers of Turkey and Britain, informing them of the dangers in which the Turkish community in Cyprus found itself and expressing his fear that the "Greek terrorists" were preparing a civil war. In these cables, he had also explained that the Turkish Cypriots, who were unarmed, had to defend themselves against well-armed terrorists, and urgently requested the above-mentioned persons to do all in their power to protect the Turkish Cypriots.

The adoption of the Greek draft resolution, Sarper maintained, would not only delay a solution of the Cyprus question by encouraging Greek extremists to persist in their actions, which were "designed to bring about a unilateral *Diktat*, but would be interpreted as a justification of their acts by those who were preparing a civil war and disaster in Cyprus." For those reasons, he earnestly appealed to the sense of justice, equity, and responsibility of the members of the Committee not to encourage extremist tendencies and, therefore, to vote against the Greek draft resolution.

Averoff-Tossizza responded to the Turkish representative's statement by saying first that he would refrain from entering into the substance anew. He was obliged, however, to point out to the Committee that according to the latest reports "published even in the press of this city," the property destroyed by arson had belonged to Greek Cypriots, not to Turkish Cypriots. With regard to the Greek Cypriot leaders' attitude, he pointed out that the new Governor of Cyprus, Sir Hugh Foot, had visited the Mayor of Nicosia, Themistocles Dervis, who was, of course, a leader of the Greek community in Cyprus, to thank him for the way in which he had dealt with the situation and for his appeal to the population to maintain calm in spite of provocations and the burning of property.

Sarper countered by saying that the destruction of property to which the Greek Foreign Minister had referred had been a reaction to the destruction of life which he—Sarper—had mentioned. According to the Turkish Delegation's information, the Governor had visited the Mayor of Nicosia in order to ask him to use his influence with the Greek population of Cyprus, particularly the EOKA "terrorists," and to induce them to show greater moderation.

The Chairman intervened at this point. Before calling upon the representative of Greece, he said he wished to appeal both to him and the representative of Turkey not to go into details too much on the aspects of the question which, though important, might nevertheless give rise to a very detailed debate, and this, at the late hour, might further delay the Committee's work.

Averoff-Tossizza stated it had been Mr. Sarper who had opened the discussion. He himself merely had wished to point out that the Governor had visited the Mayor of Nicosia after the latter's appeal to the people for calm. With regard to the three murdered Turks, he said the authorities had arrested two other Turks and were questioning them to ascertain whether they were involved in the affair.

The representative of Canada, Wallace Nesbitt, Vice-Chairman of his delegation, spoke next, to introduce the expected four-state amendments and explain the reasons why his delegation cosponsored them. In view of the moderation of the debate, he said, he hoped that the parties would be able to reach a satisfactory settlement in the near future. He was glad to note that the Greek representative had expressed his government's willingness to accept certain parts of the statement made on behalf of the British government.[4] In the circumstances, he felt that it was especially important that the Assembly should do nothing that might impede direct negotiations between the parties most concerned. Whatever views might be held concerning the competence of the Assembly to discuss the item, it would surely be agreed that any resolution adopted should be one which would further opportunities for agreement between the parties. His delegation had therefore joined with Chile, Denmark, and Norway in submitting a number of amendments which were, in its view, necessary to make the Greek draft resolution conform to that criterion.

The Canadian representative then proceeded to explain these amendments. The first amendment reaffirmed Resolution 1013 (XI) because, as representatives of all points of view had recognized, that resolution indicated the proper direction for progress in the dispute. The second amendment expressed the Assembly's concern that more progress had not been made toward the solution of the problem. It was not true to say, as stated in the Greek draft resolution, there had been no progress. The Greek representative himself had called attention to certain recent developments, including the appointment of a civilian governor and the relaxation of some of the emergency measures in Cyprus. Those were certainly hopeful developments, though the situation clearly remained disquieting. Accordingly, he hoped that the Committee would unanimously adopt the second amendment to the preamble. As for the essence of the third and fourth amendments, this was intended to express the Committee's earnest hope for a solution in accordance with the principles of the Charter. That wish had been expressed only in the preamble to the Greek draft resolution. The operative paragraph would thus refer to the purposes and principles of the Charter rather than specifically and uniquely to one of these principles (namely, the right of self-determination), as the Greek draft resolution had done. The debate had proved that in spite of the general agreement on the value of self-determination in principle, there was no agreement on the precise manner in which it should be interpreted in the problem under consideration. As the Malayan representative had shown, the right of self-determination should in the case in point be related to the position of minorities as well as to the majority.[5] In any case, self-determination was only one of the principles raised by the tragic problem. Canada was deeply aware of the rights of minorities but considered that the issue might be prejudiced by overemphasis on one right only. The right of self-determination was, of course, one of the important principles in the issue before the Committee. The Committee, however, was confronted with a problem as complex as the Charter itself. Only by viewing all the principles of the Charter in their organic and interrelated context would it be able to find a truly equitable and, in the best sense, democratic solution. The Assembly should confine itself to stressing the principles involved without prejudging the many aspects of this difficult problem. It should express its heartfelt wish that the parties most concerned would give those principles a lasting and meaningful application.

The Greek Foreign Minister responded immediately. Although expressing astonishment at the amendments, he was ready, he said, to accept with pleasure the amendments to the preamble of the Greek draft resolution. However, he was firmly opposed to the amendment of its operative paragraph since it was no longer an amendment but completely altered the content of the original. In order to avoid a lengthy discussion, he would not raise the question of whether, under rule 131 of the rules of procedure,[6] one had the right to submit amendments which completely changed the meaning of a draft resolution. Nevertheless, he wanted to say that such a proposal was absolutely unacceptable to his delegation. Its mission in coming here had been to seek, for the first time in the United Nations, a vote on the question of self-determination. "We shall not leave that mission by the wayside," he affirmed.

He noted with regret, Averoff-Tossizza continued, that in the case of Cyprus as in many others, members resorted to amendments as a maneuver designed to block the adoption of draft resolutions by altering their meaning. His delegation had the right to reply to this maneuver by a countermaneuver, because it absolutely had to press for a vote on the word "self-determination." This countermaneuver was perfectly simple and entirely in keeping with the rules of procedure. To that end, he submitted a subamendment to be voted on before the joint amendments of the four states. This subamendment would not deal with the preambular part of the draft resolution, but only with its operative part. It would replace the four-state amendment and would read as follows:

Expresses the earnest hope that further negotiations and discussions will be undertaken promptly in a spirit of cooperation with a view to applying the right of self-determination in the case of the people of Cyprus.

Although his amendment was a countermaneuver, it was a subamendment to the amendment of the four states because it preserved the new ideas introduced in this four-state amendment. It kept the words "negotiations and discussion," "promptly," and "spirit of co-operation." However—and this the Greek Foreign Minister did not see fit to mention—it included no reference to "those concerned," an expression abhorred by the Greek but used in the last of the four-state amendments.

He did not wish to betray the mandate of insisting on the word "self-determination," which had been entrusted to him, Averoff-Tossizza continued. In this regard, he would like to appeal to the great powers, which were great in their power, and to the small powers which had the right and should rally around the principle—for principles were their strength—and tell them:

Do not adopt such a tactic as has been suggested here. I represent a country that is alone and is fighting alone for a people suffering under a colonial regime. We are fighting for a principle. I am not lucky enough to belong to a national family. The Algerian question was defended by eleven brothers of the same young and vigorous family. If a Latin American question were to be discussed here, it would be defended by the countries of the new world that Stefan Zweig called "the world of tomorrow," and which I would call . . ." the world of today,"

But Greece did not belong to such a family. He had come here alone, with the strength of his right, the right of this people, which had lived through anguished hours under a colonial regime. He fought here with the strength given him by principles. That was why he insisted on this point. This was a question that was very close to him. He spoke to the Committee with profound emotion, because he felt all alone here.

Where are we going? . . . After so many beautiful hopes, after all the blood that has been shed during the last war, will this very important committee become an organ which manufactures resolutions that each can interpret at his pleasure? Is this going to be our role? Are we going to follow this dangerous path? Are we going to be the body that produces amendments and counter-amendments which block decisions upon which we have to vote? And are we then only going to vote on decisions that either say nothing or say what each one wants to say?

He had asked these questions. It was up to the members of the Assembly to question themselves, because this was a very serious moment. It was the hour in which, for the first time, "we are called upon to vote and to take a position on a principle."

The virtuosity of the Greek Foreign Minister in alternating procedural arguments with appeals to the sentiments of freedom and justice, the

Greek Delegation felt, created an atmosphere of disfavor toward the amendments to the Greek draft resolution the four states had proposed.

The Greek viewpoint received support from the Egyptian Delegation. Ambassador Omar Loutfi, Permanent Representative to the UN, was convinced, he said, that the delegations of Canada, Chile, Denmark, and Norway had submitted their amendments in a desire for compromise, but he was unfortunately unable to share their views on the question. In his opinion, their amendments completely altered the Greek draft resolution and were therefore contrary to the provisions of rule 131 of the rules of procedure, which reads in part:

A motion is considered an amendment to a proposal if it merely adds to, deletes from, or revises part of that proposal.[7]

Comparing the proposed fourth amendment with the operative paragraph of the Greek draft resolution, he remarked that it could hardly be claimed that the new text was a real amendment, since it neither deleted from nor revised any part of the original text. Thus, the operative paragraph of the Greek draft resolution read:

Expresses the wish that the people of Cyprus will be given the opportunity to determine their own future by the application of their right to self-determination.

The fourth of the four-state amendments, on the other hand, by which it was proposed to replace the above Greek operative paragraph, read:

Expresses its earnest hope that further negotiations and discussions between those concerned will be promptly undertaken in a spirit of co-operation with a view to finding a peaceful, democratic and just solution, in conformity with the purposes and principles of the Charter of the United Nations.

It was difficult to contend that the new paragraph was really an amendment. It was a new proposal, entirely different from that tabled by the Greek Delegation. On grounds of principle, he requested the sponsors of the amendments to reconsider their proposals, in particular their fourth amendment, in the light of rule 131 of the rules of procedure.

Syria's representative, Zeineddine, also attacked the four-state amendments. He greatly regretted, he said, that these had been submitted. No matter the intentions of the cosponsoring delegations, these amendments were designed to make the text not clear but vague because it was considered that in the circumstances it was better not to be too precise. Moreover, they represented an attempt to introduce a repetition of Resolution 1013 (XI), which had solved practically nothing. If the United Nations proceeded along these lines of trying to suit its actions to convenience, it would find it increasingly difficult to assist parties in settling their disputes in the spirit of the Charter. The fourth amendment mentioned negotiations and discussions, but the Assembly, in Resolution 1013 (XI), had suggested the same thing, and the negotiations that had taken place since then had put the attainment of a peaceful, democratic, and just solution further away than ever. Two issues were involved in the Cyprus question, Zeineddine went on to stress: the liberation of a people living under a colonial domination and the possibility of using the island as a military base. The question of liberation would not be solved unless the people of Cyprus and the British government found, through negotiations, a way of applying the principle of self-determination. Such negotiations had not as yet been carried out. To solve the international problem raised by the use of the island for military purposes, the island would have to be declared neutral and demilitarized. All the neighboring countries, including Syria, which was also an heir of the Ottoman Empire, would have to participate in the necessary negotiations. That second question, however, had not yet been brought before the United Nations. The joint amendments applied indiscriminately to both problems and would only delay their solution. They did not amend the draft resolution but steered the question in a different direction. His delegation was therefore compelled to vote against them. The subamendment introduced by the Greek Delegation restored the proper perspective. It helped return to the path of liberation. Although efforts to find a compromise solution were laudable, it was nonetheless true that the time had come to act in conformity with the UN Charter and not to complicate further the problem for reasons of expediency, instead of solving it. He did not want to make any reflections upon the good intentions of the delegations that had submitted the amendments, but in his view such a trend would render the solution of the Cyprus problem almost impossible.

The Permanent Representative of Haiti to the UN, Emile Saint-Lot, likewise supported the Greek viewpoint. His delegation, he noted, deliberately had not taken part in the debate, which, in its opinion, had cast full light on the delicate problem of Cyprus. It seemed to him that the parties concerned were more or less agreed on the existence of the right of self-determination for the people of Cyprus. His delegation, therefore, proposed to support the Greek draft resolution, which, in its operative part, recognized the right of self-determination for the people of Cyprus. The operative part was in keeping with the formally expressed will of the parties concerned and was likewise in keeping with the principles of the Charter. Recognition of this right would be one accomplishment of the debate and, even if the negotiations were to continue as this draft resolution urged, these would proceed from a specific basis, which would be recognition by all the parties concerned of the right of self-determination.

For the amendments submitted that morning he would not vote, the Haitian said, because, in their operative part, the only achievement from the debate would be nullified, namely, the consensus of the Assembly and the agreement of the parties concerning the existence of the right of self-determination. The amendments deleted, brushed aside that right. But, the representative of Haiti added, those with legal training knew full well that the existence of a right was one thing, but its exercise was another. The Assembly might well recognize a right as set forth in the Charter and may say that a people was entitled to benefit from that right. It could not judge the situation. All it could affirm was the existence of a right. It did not wish to demand the exercise of a certain right. The exercise of a right might be prevented by natural or legal obstacles.

The Declaration of Human Rights stated that every human being was entitled to take part in the formation of the government of his country. But the exercise of that right was conditional on a host of natural and juridical factors. There were certain requirements and conditions for the exercise of a right. With the Greek subamendment, one could still affirm the existence of the right of self-determination for the people of Cyprus or "the peoples of Cyprus," but the modalities of implementation had to be determined in the course and as a result of negotiations. The Assembly could not refuse to admit this unless it was prepared to lacerate the Charter and say that the right of self-determination was a mere figment of the imagination, a soap bubble, because, when it was actually invoked, it was argued away by subtleties and procedural stratagems. If this went on, the people would simply lose faith in the United Nations. The Assembly should affirm the existence of the right and leave its exercise to the parties concerned. That was the least it could decently do. Therefore, his delegation would vote for the Greek subamendment. The operative part would then be not only in conformity with the statements of the parties concerned and the formal provisions of the Charter, but also in harmony with the aspirations of the martyred people of Cyprus.

Ambassador Sarper then spoke. He would try, he said, to be as brief as he could. After citing the fourth of the four-state amendments, he contended that this was no repetition of Resolution 1013 (XI), but that it went further than that one. However, even if one were to admit for the sake of argument that it was a repetition of that resolution, he saw nothing wrong with that. Resolution 1013 (XI) contained all the elements necessary for an agreed solution. He could even say it contained all the elements included in the Greek draft resolution. If the resolution adopted at the previous Assembly had not been implemented in all its aspects, it was neither the resolution's nor the Assembly's fault. The responsibility for its limited success lay squarely on the shoulders of the intransigent opponent. The Assembly, he believed, should leave sufficient latitude for all concerned to achieve an agreed and constructive solution. If this session were to adopt a resolution merely for the sake of adopting a resolution, he doubted very much if that would have an effect on the solution desired by all. There were at least half a dozen UN resolutions, even Security Council resolutions, which could not be implemented simply because some of them had been adopted just for the sake of adopting a resolution without examining all the aspects of its relation to the international situation. As far as his delegation was concerned, it did not want to assist in the adoption of a resolution whose implementation would be made impossible. To do so would not be in conformity with realism and with the possibilities of the very complex situation in Cyprus.

The Greek Foreign Minister, Sarper continued, had made a very eloquent appeal. His appeal, however, was directed primarily to emotions rather than to reason. His delegation, on the other hand, wanted to act reasonably, and in a way that would be conducive to the solution of the Cyprus question in a manner that would give satisfaction to the Assembly and to all concerned, including the Greek Delegation. One could not afford to ignore the international implications of this extremely complex problem. One had to be politically-minded, practically-minded, realistic in dealing with it.

With all due respect to the Foreign Minister of Greece, his amendment to the four-state amendments was, as he had admitted, a tactic. On the other hand, in the Turkish Delegation's opinion, the amendments presented by Canada, Chile, Denmark, and Norway were no tactic. These were the sort of amendments that would leave, as he had said, sufficient latitude to the parties concerned, and particularly to the administering power, to make contact with other interested parties and with the peoples of Cyprus in order to achieve an agreed settlement.

No one would be happier than he, Sarper assured the Committee, if one could reach an agreed solution of the question of Cyprus. However, as Mr. Averoff-Tossizza had admitted, through the tactics of the Greek Delegation and by appeals to the emotions of the members of the Assembly, this could not be achieved. "We are a political committee. We must . . . deal with realism, and we must be politically-minded. I appeal to your reason, gentlemen. Leave us the necessary latitude which will be conducive to the solution of the Cyprus question."

The Chairman, at this point, reminded the Committee that the draft resolution and the amendments thereto were being discussed. Therefore, he entreated the representatives to limit themselves to those two matters without a discussion that would give rise to a repetition of the general debate. He then called on the representative of Norway.

Ambassador Engen said he would address himself very briefly to the draft resolution and the amendments submitted thereto. He had listened with some surprise to the Greek Foreign Minister's contention that the motive that underlay the submission of these amendments, which his delegation had the honor to cosponsor, should be considered to be in the nature of a tactical maneuver. With all sincere respect for the Greek representative, he did not think that his delegation could accept that contention. As he had said when discussing the Algerian question, the overriding consideration for his delegation when making up its mind with respect to a proposal that was before the Committee was the following: A delegation had submitted an issue to discussion by the United Nations. He assumed that the purpose of submitting that issue was to have it discussed and dealt with in accordance with the rules of procedure and with the purposes and principles of the Charter. The main function of the United Nations was, of course, to be not only a forum for debate, but also one in which various views could be harmonized. It did not appear to him to be the most natural thing in the world to contend that it was the duty of UN members to take a draft resolution submitted by the delegation of a country that was a party to a dispute, regard it as being the last word in the discussion, and vote Yes or No on the outcome which that particular delegation felt would be the proper outcome in the United Nations.

His delegation, the Norwegian representative continued, had listened very carefully to the views the parties "most directly concerned" had expressed, and it was his sincere opinion that the text the Greek Delegation had submitted, though, of course altogether understandable from the Greek government's viewpoint, did not appear to be necessarily the best solution to emerge from this debate. He said this with all respect, and did not think it was the view of the Greek Delegation that other delegations did not have the privilege to submit for the Committee's consideration language that differed from the language submitted, in this instance, by the Greek Delegation, without running the risk of their motives' being doubted in any sense of the word.

The Norwegian Delegation, Engen continued, had joined in proposing these amendments because it felt very honestly and very sincerely that they expressed in a better way the feeling or the opinion of the members of the committee. If that was not the case, it was for the Committee to decide otherwise. If the majority of the Committee felt that this was the better way of expressing itself, then it would, in accordance with its rules of procedure, vote accordingly. If it was in disagreement with the sponsors of the amendments, it would show that by its vote.

He had noted with great pleasure, the Norwegian representative went on to say, that the Greek Foreign Minister had accepted the first of the three amendments. That left the fourth amendment, which dealt with the operative part of the Greek draft resolution and represented, of course, the crux of the matter. In that regard, he would say this: Statements had been made—very eloquently and, he thought, correctly—concerning the value and importance of self-determination. His government did not for one second, of course, deny anybody this right and did not for one second dispute that the right of self-determination of peoples was one of the basic points in the Charter. But there were other basic points of the Charter that should not be pushed aside when dealing with a question of such complexity as the Cyprus problem. In order to solve this problem, all the basic rights embodied in the Charter should be brought into play, not only the right of self-determination. His government believed that this idea that reference should be made to the broader rights included in the Charter, and that these rights, all of them, should be applicable to the whole population of Cyprus—its majority and its minority—was better expressed in the wording of the operative paragraph it had taken the liberty of submitting to the Committee. That had been the whole idea behind the reference to the rights of the peoples of Cyprus in the fourth of the amendments. In these amendments, the cosponsoring states were asking that, through negotiations and co-operation between all the interested parties, an effort be made to find a solution in conformity with the purposes and principles of the Charter. And the Charter entailed more rights than simply the right of self-determination.

He would like to say a few more words about the amendment the Greek Delegation had submitted. He had to confess that this proposal put the Committee in a rather strange situation as far as the parliamentary rules were concerned because it was presented as an amendment to an amendment, whereas, of course, it was in substance a reintroduction of the operative paragraph of the Greek draft resolution, which the four states were seeking to amend. If the Committee permitted this to be considered as an amendment to the four-state amendments, then he did not know where matters would end. If it was the privilege of the Greek Delegation to reintroduce its operative paragraph in the way it had done, namely, in the form of a subamendment, then it was, of course, also the privilege of the cosponsoring four powers to reintroduce their amendment as a new subamendment, and one could go on that way for a very long time. Ambassador Engen therefore respectfully requested the Chairman of the Committee to take under very serious consideration whether, under normal parliamentary rules, the amendment the Greek Delegation had submitted was actually in order.

The representative of Guatemala, David Vela, on the other hand, expressed views in support of the Greek thesis. Guatemala, he said, recognized that the prestige and power of the United Nations resided in principles. As a small power, it was also aware that all its own moral force resided in defending such principles and in adhering very closely to the rules of procedure of the United Nations. Therefore, although his delegation wished to pay tribute to the good intentions of the powers that had submitted amendments to the Greek draft resolution, he had to refer to the procedural aspect of the question and also to the substance of the amendments themselves.

Regarding the procedural aspect, Vela was of the opinion that only the preambular parts of the four-state amendments could be considered as amendments. This, he thought, was the reason why the Greek representative had not objected to having the preambular paragraphs of his draft resolution amended. However, although no one could deny the usefulness of a preamble, the resolution itself lay in its operative part. In the case of the Greek draft resolution, the operative part was the fourth paragraph, and the amendments the four states had submitted would wholly change the tenor of this draft resolution. The text of that draft resolution was crystal clear and required no explanation. If it did require an explanation and lend itself to different interpretations, the Greek

Foreign Minister had emphatically stated that what the Committee was being asked to vote on was a principle set forth in the Charter to which no one had objected during the twelve years of the existence of the United Nations, and which had never been put to the acid test of a vote in the Assembly. The Guatemalan representative respected principles so highly that during the debate he had stated that he saw no objection to voting in favor of the Greek draft resolution, and he had also appealed to the Committee unanimously to adopt that draft resolution.

The substitution of the operative paragraph of the Greek draft resolution along the lines the four states had proposed would not be an amendment, the Guatemalan representative maintained. In that four-state proposal, the operative paragraph of Resolution 1013 (XI) was repeated in practically the same way, and, although a reaffirmation of Resolution 1013 (XI) would be included, that would add nothing, because the suggested new operative paragraph was almost an exact repetition of that resolution. In the fourth "amendment" proposed by the four states, the Assembly would express the earnest "hope," whereas, under Resolution 1013 (XI) the Assembly had expressed the earnest "desire." He did not think that the United Nations could be asked to be satisfied with the few results achieved by that resolution.

On the specific case of Cyprus, Vela argued there was a definite reason for applying the principle of self-determination. None of the parties that had spoken had stated their sovereignty over the island, and more than one of the parties had expressed their desire to recognize the right of self-determination for the people of Cyprus. Perhaps, as the representative of Haiti had said, the question was "how" and "when," and that question would be solved by negotiations. It might also be true that the problem was complex. The essence, however, of this problem was the fate of a people, and, in considering it, the Committee and the Assembly should recognize that it could only be solved on the basis of the moral and human values of liberty and justice. Although he agreed that the question might be surrounded by interests and by responsibilities which he fully appreciated, he nevertheless believed that, once the outline of the negotiations had been set, those interests and modalities could be negotiated. That outline was the right of the people of Cyprus to self-determination. That was the question that confronted the Committee, and all the interests, which seemed to be so opposed because of the complexity of the problem, might better be understood if the Committee and the Assembly were this year to take a step forward in the field of law and of right so as to make effective the affirmation of a principle contained in the UN Charter.

The problem, Vela continued, could be solved by good will on the part of the parties concerned. And, no matter how much one respected and understood the interests and the responsibilities of certain parties in a region which politically and strategically was important, one should remember that the only party that could speak concerning the justice of its cause was the people of Cyprus. The proposed deletion of the operative paragraph of the Greek draft resolution and its substitution by another one would not satisfy the aspirations of this people. Nor would it favor a solution of the problem, since Resolution 1013 (XI) certainly had not obtained the degree of understanding that it was supposed to have done. Although one might refer again to this resolution, and although good will would still exist on the part of the parties concerned, negotiations would not be possible until the Assembly had pronounced itself as it should, clearly, on the crux of the problem; namely, the right of the people of Cyprus to self-determination.

For these reasons, Guatemala would be unable to vote in favor of the four-state amendment. First, it did not wish to create a precedent that would be contrary to the rules of procedure. This would be done, if the Committee voted in favor of an amendment that was not really an amendment but rather a completely new proposal submitted out of order. Second, the amendment was unacceptable to his delegation because the principles of the Charter were not respected and followed.

We have to prove that the principles contained in the Charter are not merely words wielded in the field of debate. We have to maintain peace, we have to promote freedom, and we have to encourage justice all over the world. Although in this Committee, we are told that we are a political committee, we are a senate of the highest and most noble politics and, as such, we cannot be divorced from the principles of the Charter.

The representative of another Latin American state, Peru's Ambassador Belaunde, took a different view from that of his Guatemalan colleague. He wished first of all to assure the Greek representative that Greece was not alone and without support in the United Nations. Was his "noble country not a member of the UN family, of the Greco-Latin family, of all the countries that are proud of having received the immortal message of Greece, the [Anglo-]Saxon countries which, perhaps more than the Latin countries, have cultivated Greek literature?" All had gone along with Greece not only in the cult of the glory that was Greece, but also in enthusiasm for the heroism of Greece in the last wars. His delegation had argued with considerable fire with Mr. Manuilsky (of the Ukrainian S.S.R.) when Greece, Albania, and Yugoslavia were being discussed in the United Nations. And it had supported the efforts made to secure the return of Greek prisoners and children.[8]

The Cyprus problem, Belaunde went on to say, could not be simplified, however. One could not use the mathematical means of isolating an unknown, or the physical method of isolating an element. Nor could one use the method of certain philosophical theories. In diplomacy, there was no isolation of facts, no division of international complexities, no placing of any matter between brackets. The United Nations was faced with an integral reality with its essential nucleus and its surrounding circumstances, with its adherent elements which were inseparable. It would be a grave error if, when faced by a problem, one followed the parenthetical or process-of-elimination method of discussing situations.

The first and paramount interest should be that of the people of Cyprus, comprising the Greek and Turkish Cypriots. The second interest was that of the country that at present was exercising sovereignty over Cyprus and had responsibilities and obligations regarding the Western World and peace in the whole world. If one set aside or overlooked this interest, one would be less than a statesman. Then, there were other aspects: the most admirable hope of Greece that Cyprus might wish to join Greece; the sacred interests of Turkey; and the peace of the world itself.

Although there were visible, tangible factors, there were invisible and intangible factors too, Belaunde continued. After all, were not the ambitions of other powers also directed toward the Mediterranean? If the Cyprus question was a complex one, he had to say, in all friendship, that one could not give it a unilateral solution. One could not say: take one principle of the Charter, apply it to Cyprus, and that is that. Suppose that tomorrow Cyprus were to express its will publicly. How would that principle be applied? How would one implement such a desire expressed by the people if there was no agreement between Greece, Turkey, and Britain with regard to the interests of Cyprus? Obviously, this would give rise to a new situation in Cyprus. Therefore, as far as the Peruvian Delegation was concerned, the main defect in the original Greek draft resolution was the absence of any mention of negotiations. Although he respected the concern of Greece, which the Greek draft resolution reflected, he could not agree to the methods outlined in the draft. That was why he had studied the amendments most carefully. He was not worried about procedural questions. The representatives of Greece, "in his great intelligence," had said he would accept three of the amendments. He was worthy of congratulations, for showing a wide understanding of facts. The language of the amendments was more friendly, more conciliatory than that of the Greek draft resolution. It was the kind of language that should be used in the United Nations.

We are united: these words surely mean something. We must not be disunited. We may be separated at times, but our tendency is toward unity, toward unanimity, because unanimity or overwhelming majority is the only guarantee of the moral influence of a resolution. That is why we put every effort into reaching unanimous decisions. Sometimes we prefer eloquent speeches, but at others we prefer quiet, subtle negotiations in the corridors in order to find what may appear to be a vague formula, but one that is filled with a deep meaning which reflects the entire mandate of world public opinion in favor of conciliation, peace, and understanding.

The amendments were not maneuvers nor tactics, Belaunde asserted. "Tactics are used for predominance, but when some powers are trying to bring together differing points of view, they renounce predominance." They desired conciliation. That was what the United Nations was for. Its duty, after discussing problems at great length, after discussing them in the three levels he had mentioned—first, the interests of the people; second, the interests of the United Nations; and, third, the finding of a solution—was to exert efforts tending toward a solution. Words might be imperfect, but behind their imperfection lay the spirit of the United Nations. Declarations made in the debate at times might not be exactly right. The words used by the Delegations of Canada, Chile, Denmark, and Norway did not include self-determination. However, the British and other representatives had used these words. They, as well as the Norwegian representative, had said: if we do not use the word "self-determination," it is because it is not the only principle in the Charter and because this principle, when dealing with a complex population, can give rise to different interpretations. However, the principle was there, accepted by all, and when one spoke of the principles of the Charter, one said not only "in conformity with the principles and purposes of the Charter," but also in fulfilment of these principles and purposes. Naturally all members of the United Nations were extremely pleased to have the principle of self-determination. All would like this principle to be applied universally without immediately having different implications come up, without having reservations, without having doubts as to implementation.

In a somewhat rambling and incoherent peroration, which referred to the purposes and principles of the Charter and contained expressions of hope according to a Spanish subamendment,[9] that the parties concerned—not only Britain, Greece, and Turkey, but also the Greek and Turkish Cypriots—should proceed to negotiations, Belaunde concluded that for the moment his delegation favored the four-state amendments.

The Chairman, then, pointed out that the deadline of the Assembly made it necessary to speed up the debate. There was still another item on the Committee's agenda to be discussed. On the speakers' list were Greece, El Salvador, Uruguay, Britain, Tunisia, Canada, Bolivia, Iceland, and Iran. He proposed that after hearing the representatives of Greece and Turkey, the Committee should adjourn, to meet in the afternoon at 3:00 P.M. Then, after the other representatives had spoken, he would close the debate on the draft resolution and the amendments and go on to the vote.

Since there was no objection, the proposed procedure was adopted.

Foreign Minister Averoff-Tossizza: As I was not aware that there were so many speakers on the list and since I may wish to exercise my right of reply, I would prefer not to speak now but later, at the end.

The Chairman: In view of the statement that has just been made by the representative of Greece, I propose to adjourn the meeting and to continue the debate on the draft resolution and the amendments . . .

Mr. Noble (United Kingdom): I will be very brief, but I think it would be convenient that I should explain to the Committee how my delegation will cast its vote on the amendments introduced this morning by the Delegations of Canada, Chile, Denmark, and Norway, and the sub-amendment introduced by the Foreign Minister of Greece.

In his previous interventions in the debate, Noble explained, he had tried to set out the Cyprus problem as his government saw it. It was not a straightforward colonial problem. Because of the campaign for *enosis,* it had become an international problem. His government was not responsible for that. The responsibility lay with those who had promoted the campaign. But Britain was faced with the responsibility for the international problem created in this way. It was not an insoluble problem, given the will on all sides to work for a solution. His government believed there was ground for a compromise, but it was a difficult and complex problem. If it was handled wrongly, however, grievous consequences could follow both in the island and elsewhere, he emphasized. It was not, in his delegation's view, for the Committee to endorse any particular solution or indeed—and this he thought was very important—even to point the way to such a solution. This should be worked out between the three governments concerned and the two communities in Cyprus. What the Committee should do, since the problem had become so acute, was to point to the procedures that should be followed in the search for a solution. In doing this, the United Nations should bear in mind the full complexity of the problem. It should not single out one aspect of it. Least of all should it endorse the campaign for *enosis* which, as all knew by then, was being waged in the United Nations under the banner of self-determination to the detriment of the principle itself. As he had said before, it was not that he did not support the principle of self-determination, but, as many representatives, in addition to himself, had pointed out, it was the application of that principle that was always difficult, and it was especially so in the particular case of Cyprus with its international complications.

The British Delegation would, therefore, vote against the Greek sub-amendment. If it was rejected, it would support the four-state amendments. And if they were carried, it would support the draft resolution as a whole.

The meeting rose at 1 P.M.

C. Interlude Backstage

During the debate, as a favorable atmosphere seemed to develop for the Greek viewpoint, the Canadians offered to the Greeks a minor modification of the four-state amendments, but the Greeks rejected the offer, with Makarios in agreement. Thus by the end of the Committee's meeting an atmosphere of obstinacy had arisen during the debate over a matter in which "the powers that be" seemed, in the Greek Delegation's view, to be striving to smother the voice of justice and right. Particularly among certain Latin American delegations, which attached considerable importance to procedural honesty, a sentiment of clear dissatisfaction had arisen.

The Chairman of the Political Committee, Abdoh, of Iran, found himself facing the following dilemma: Were the four-state amendments real amendments in the sense of the rules of procedure of the Assembly or did they constitute a new proposal? Was the Greek subamendment a true amendment or merely a redrafting of the original Greek draft resolution?

The outcome of the struggle would depend on the answer given to those questions. But who would provide the answer? If the Chairman himself made a ruling, the Committee would have to challenge it in order to overrule him. This was difficult to achieve, the Greek Delegation well realized. Overruling the Chairman occurred seldom, because of the delicate position of all delegations vis-à-vis the chief officer of the Committee. If, on the other hand, the Committee itself were to decide without the Chairman's intervention, the outcome would be different. Under the existing indications it was felt that the decision of the Committee would be in favor of the Greek viewpoint, namely that the Greek subamendment was a true amendment and therefore should be put to the vote before the four-state amendments.

During the two and a half hours that elapsed between the time the morning meeting of the committee ended and 3:30 P.M., when the afternoon meeting began, the fate of the Greek subamendment was literally in the balance.

The first action of the British and Americans in support of the Norwegians and Canadians (the representatives of Chile and Denmark, in this case, played the role of silent bystanders) consisted of efforts to persuade Chairman Abdoh to issue a ruling in accordance with their views. In spite of his absolute integrity, the Iranian found himself under tremendous pressure. Realizing the difficulties of the problem and faced with dubious opinions expressed by the appropriate services of the UN Secretariat, he started to yield.

On its side, the Greek Delegation took several measures designed to promote its own cause in the Committee. While the Foreign Minister in New York, assisted by members of his delegation, sought to devise new plans of action, he instructed the Greek Embassy in Washington to make a démarche with the State Department. In the démarche, Counselor of the Greek Embassy Kavalieratos called on Rountree and, in the presence of four of the latter's aides, told him that the attitude of the U.S. Delegation could cause catastrophic developments in Greece since the United States was the only remaining active link between Greece and the West. At a moment when the heads of government were about to meet in Paris to take measures for strengthening NATO, this was a matter of concern not only to Greece but to the entire Western Alliance. The Greek government therefore believed that the U.S. Delegation should place no procedural or other impediments in the way of the Greek draft resolution and should assume an absolutely impartial attitude. At a moment when the British representative, two days earlier, had maintained that his government, too, recognized the right of the Cypriot people to self-determination, it was difficult for the Greek government to understand why the U.S. government should object to the Assembly's recognition of that principle.

In reply to the above points which the Greek diplomat emphasized, Rountree categorically denied that the United States had indulged in any backstage activities with Latin American or other delegations, and expressed displeasure at the tone of the Greek Foreign Minister's protest with the Department the day before. He also maintained that the attitude of the U.S. Delegation at the United Nations had been fully in accordance with what the Greek government had been informed in advance about this stand. The Greek diplomat responded by saying that neutrality and impartiality had been promised, but deeds did not seem to confirm this promise.

With the pessimistic views that Kavalieratos had expressed concerning the possible catastrophic results in Greece, in the event of an unfavorable UN action, Rountree dissented. The history of Greece, he stressed, excluded such eventualities.[10] The Greek diplomat retorted that the history of Greece consisted of devotion to principles and ideals— which its friends seemed to be abandoning.

In this conversation, Rountree (like Dulles, earlier) expressed his conviction that the principle of self-determination would eventually be applied in the case of Cyprus. The problem remained of finding a way to implement this principle. Quiet diplomacy, he reiterated, would accomplish what neither debates nor UN resolutions could achieve. He also expressed regret at the first part of the Greek Foreign Minister's speech the previous day at the Political Committee's evening meeting, terming it a personal attack on Ambassador Lodge. Kavalieratos explained that the Foreign Minister's intention had been simply to rebut arguments the U.S. Delegation had presented before the Committee.

In New York, meanwhile, the Greek Delegation was studying ways and means for dealing with the threat of a ruling by the Committee's Chairman, by virtue of which the Greek subamendment would be put aside and the four-state amendments put to the vote first. The delegation also studied what steps it should take, should its efforts in that direction fail. The Greek representative could challenge the Chairman's ruling and ask the Committee to proceed to a vote on this challenge. But then there was the danger lest the motion be defeated, because many delegations, not wishing to participate in what would in essence constitute a motion of censure against the Chairman, were likely to abstain. If the challenge were lost, then self-determination, too, would be lost, because the four-state amendments would have priority in the vote. Indicative of the extent to which the vote of the various delegations depended on the order in which amendments and subamendment were put to the vote was the fact that the Yugoslav representative, in spite of categorical instructions from his government to vote in favor of the draft referring to self-determination, told the Greek Foreign Minister he found himself in a very difficult position, because if the four-state amendments were first put to a vote he would be unable to vote against them. At the most, he could abstain. Of course, he added, if proposals referring to self-determination were put to the vote, then he would vote in their favor.

At this critical point, the Greek Foreign Minister decided that if the procedural devices of the opponents succeeded in strangulating, as it were, any reference to self-determination for the people of Cyprus, he and the entire Greek Delegation would walk out from the Assembly. This decision—a step he had suggested earlier in a cable to the Prime Minister—was an extremely grave one, because of its possible repercussions and political consequences. It was, however, he felt, the only way left open to the delegation for reacting against those who were planning to silence the Greek plea for self-determination in Cyprus. And, from the viewpoint of the course of the Cyprus question in the United Nations, a Greek withdrawal was, he believed, preferable to the defeat that would be inflicted were the Committee to adopt the four-state amendments.

In this contingency planning, the details of how and at what point the Greek Delegation should walk out of the Political Committee were studied. It was decided to stage this walkout if the Chairman of the Committee issued an unfavorable ruling. The Foreign Minister would immediately express his complete opposition to such a ruling, emphasizing that it imposed an unfair and unacceptable position upon Greece, and would declare that the trampling of the rules of procedure of the Assembly had been so flagrant that he preferred not to place the Committee in the difficult position of overruling its Chairman. As a symbol of his protest against the intervention of the powerful member states of the United Nations, the Greek Delegation, he would announce, was withdrawing in its entirety from the twelfth Assembly.

As soon as this grave decision was taken, the U.S. Delegation was informed of it. This news burst like a bombshell among its members, who immediately got in touch with the State Department. From that moment on, the Greek Delegation had reasons to believe, a change occurred in the U.S. attitude, and the U.S. Delegation decided to refrain from supporting the adoption of the amendments cosponsored by Canada, Chile, Denmark, and Norway, whereas originally, as the Greek Delegation learned afterward, it had assured the Norwegian Delegate, Ambassador Engen, that it would unreservedly support the imposition of the four-state amendments in the Committee.

But the Greek Delegation proceeded to activities in another direction too. In order to avert a possibly unfavorable ruling by the Chairman of the Committee, it appealed to Ambassador Lall, of the Indian Delegation, as well as to Ambassador Loutfi, of the Egyptian Delegation, and to the acting permanent delegate of Lebanon, Karim Azkoul, for their assistance. These representatives of some of the most important members of the Afro-Asian group in the United Nations called on Chairman Abdoh and earnestly urged him against issuing any ruling on the amendments and subamendment, and on their respective priority when put to the vote. Otherwise, they warned, they would be obliged to vote against his ruling. It was also noteworthy that the head of the Iranian Delegation, Ambassador Entezam, though instructed by his government to support Turkey in case of a vote, sent a note to his Iranian compatriot and Committee Chairman and counseled him against giving in to pressures and issuing a ruling on such controversial matters. He advised Abdoh to avoid any personal intervention and to present the question of the amendments and the subamendment to the Committee with the request that it take the appropriate decision.

The result of these activities was that a few minutes before the afternoon meeting of the Committee began, its Chairman, having listened, as it were, to the voice of prudence, informed the Permanent Greek Representative to the UN, Palamas, that he would refrain from issuing a ruling on the controversial question of the four-state amendments and the Greek subamendment. He would let the Committee decide freely this matter, he said. This news, of course, caused a sense of great relief among the members of the Greek Delegation.

But before the procedural battle was resumed at the afternoon meeting of the Committee and regardless of the attitude of the Committee's Chairman, the Greek Delegation mobilized allies for its plan of action. The Foreign Minister met with Loutfi of Egypt and Zeineddine of Syria, who undertook to insist on the view that the four-state amendments were not genuine amendments to the Greek draft resolution. Therefore, as entirely new proposals, they should be put to the vote after, not before, the original Greek draft resolution. If the Committee were to reject this view, it would be maintained in a second, stronger line of defense, that the Greek subamendment was, at any rate, far more in accord with the rules of procedure than the four-state amendments. Consequently this subamendment should be put to the vote first, before the four-state amendments. Friendly Latin American delegations were kept posted about the above plan of action and promised to support these views during the debate. It was under such circumstances that the last meeting of the Committee on item 58 of the Assembly's agenda opened. The debate took place more or less along the lines foreseen by the Greek Delegation, with opposition to the Greek viewpoint manifested particularly through the interventions of Ambassadors Engen and Sarper, the respective heads of the Norwegian and Turkish Delegations.

D. The 934th Meeting of the Political Committee

The afternoon session of the Committee began with its Chairman announcing the following countries having speakers on his list: El Salvador, Uruguay, Tunisia, Canada, Bolivia, Spain, Iran, Turkey, and Greece.

Rodriguez Fabregat of Uruguay, however, started the ball rolling. His delegation, he reminded the Committee, had stated in the general debate its belief in the principle of self-determination of peoples.[11] However, it would in no way be offended or shocked by the acceptance of the first paragraph of the four-state draft amendments. This paragraph and some of the subsequent ones dealt with the preamble of the resolution. He wished to see fulfilled what he had expressed the day before on behalf of his delegation: that the draft resolution should carry no words of acrimony, nor words of recrimination or rancor, nor any words that might stimulate or cause such feelings; that the draft resolution should rather maintain, on a positive and affirmative basis, without ambiguities, certain essential principles contained in the Charter, and at the same time encourage any and all types of discussion, any and all efforts to bring together the parties directly concerned with the problem so that those principles could be entirely and completely applied and fulfilled.

But, the Uruguayan continued, the problem was different when one came to the operative part of the four-state amendments. Consistent with what he had said at different times, his delegation would vote in favor of the amendment the representative of Greece had submitted, in the same way, namely, as it would have on the operative part of the Greek draft resolution itself.

Once, twice, even ten times, whenever this question had come up in the Assembly, in the Commission on Human Rights or in the Economic and Social Council—in connection with Hungary, Algeria, and so on—the Delegation of Uruguay had stressed and maintained, Rodriguez Fabregat observed, that the principle of self-determination of peoples came "to us direct from history," from the annals of Uruguay, which, thanks to this principle, had become an independent state and "a member of this vast family of American and world nations." It had been that principle which had determined the independence of the Latin American countries. This principle should, now, be included in a resolution of the Assembly, "when we have to adopt a resolution not to increase dissension but, rather, to take into account one of the fundamental aspects of the dispute, namely, the fact that the interests of the inhabitants of Cyprus ought to be considered as paramount."

As he had said the day before, the people of Cyprus were one of the most developed in their progress and their culture, and most able and qualified to decide their own future. Frankly, he did not see why any one should ask the Committee to amputate from the draft resolution the words "self-determination," which definitely implied a principle of a high and noble nature that was contained in the Charter, particularly when so many representatives came from countries that had applied that principle because of their faith, their determination, and their decision to take part in the history of the world. At the very time the Assembly could and should include a word of this kind, the representatives in question did not wish to use the term "self-determination." Once again, the Assembly was offering the parties to this drama every chance to find a peaceful solution to the problem in accordance with the purposes and principles of the Charter, and if in a resolution one could say that this was in conformity with those purposes and principles—if one could wrap up in the general, vague definition all the purposes, all the principles, and all the spirit of the Charter—why, then, should the mention of one of these principles by name be avoided? The principle of self-determination was presently at stake, and it could well be mentioned in an Assembly resolution. Nothing had even been said there to deny it; rather everything had been said to reaffirm it. If it was affirmed every minute in the spoken word, why should it not be affirmed in the written word also? It was, after all, part and parcel of "our own creed, and the very root of our democratic belief." His delegation would support the affirmation of this principle.

The Delegate of Uruguay also expressed the wish that further negotiations and discussions between the parties concerned be promptly undertaken so that, by peaceful means and along the lines of affirmation of the principle of the right of these peoples, a solution might be found, leaving to one side for the time being the discussion of the bloody conflict because that conflict had achieved nothing and because that draft resolution itself stressed that this conflict had been nothing but a cause for concern and worry to the world.

It was necessary for the Assembly to adopt a resolution, Rodriguez Fabregat maintained. The world was watching the United Nations study this problem. It required not a closing of the debate in a sterile fashion and with a resolution that contained no decision whatever. By voting on behalf of his delegation as he had voted in previous cases,[12] he would be following the view expressed by his delegation when the questions of Algeria and Hungary were being discussed. The question of Hungary might be different from that of Cyprus in many aspects, but basically what underlay the two questions was the same idea: respect for what was contained in the Charter. Thus, he would vote, he reiterated, in favor of the subamendment proposed by the Greek Delegation, as he would also vote in favor of the words of peace to be included in the preamble and the first part of the draft resolution.

The representative of Tunisia, Mongi Slim, spoke next. The main differences between the Greek draft resolution and the four-state amendments and the Greek subamendment related to the operative part of the original draft resolution, he observed. What was involved? In his opinion, a resolution adopted by the Committee should reflect, as faithfully as possible, the consensus expressed in the Committee. None of the interested parties—Britain, Greece, Turkey—had spoken against self-determination for Cyprus. A number of delegations had expressed legitimate apprehensions concerning the substantial number of Cypriots of Turkish origin. The Tunisian Delegation was unable to share these apprehensions, though it was aware that every country, when becoming liberated, had one imperative duty, and that was to assure to all minorities every guarantee and safeguard required by fairness, justice, and international law. The Greek draft resolution expressed the wish that the Cypriot people be given the opportunity to apply their right to self-determination. This was proper and necessary. The Cypriot people surely should be able to exercise a right clearly recognized by the Charter, and it was only proper for the Assembly to recognize this legitimate right. Otherwise, the Assembly would be involved in a moral denial of justice.

The day before, Slim noted, the Committee had heard clear and unambiguous statements by the representative of Greece concerning the comprehensive safeguards that would be granted. He was speaking on behalf of his own country, and he was surely speaking in an authoritative manner as regarded the intentions of the Greek Cypriots. In view of these assurances of the Greek representative, Slim said, surely no one should oppose the operative paragraph of the Greek draft resolution, which was flexible enough for all necessary conversations and negotiations for an amicable and friendly settlement of the dispute.

The Delegation of Tunisia therefore would vote in favor of this paragraph as formulated in the original Greek draft resolution. It preferred that text to the Greek subamendment of the four-state amendments. The original Greek draft resolution left enough room for the principle of negotiations between the parties and for all necessary safeguards to dispel any apprehensions that might legitimately be voiced. When a people struggled for freedom and dignity, the United Nations was in duty bound to recognize its legitimate right to free self-determination. In his delegation's opinion, this recognition could not be construed as encouraging or fostering rebellion. On the contrary, when a people's sacred rights to dignity and liberty were not recognized, disorders, disturbances, and trouble were likely to arise, in spite of the best intentions of the world. That was why he would vote against the four-state amendment to the operative paragraph of the Greek draft resolution, said Slim. And, although he preferred the operative paragraph of the original Greek draft resolution, that was why he would vote in favor of the Greek subamendment.

Bolivia's Quiroga Galdo was another supporter of the Greek subamendment. His delegation considered that the four-state amendment to the operative paragraph of the Greek draft resolution was intended only to offer a parliamentary way out for the Committee and to leave the situation exactly the same as it was in February when the Assembly had adopted Resolution 1013 (XI), which so far had not been applied. His delegation noted with sorrow that every time the Committee faced the urgent need to apply the principle of self-determination, impressive procedural acrobatics were indulged in, which obviously made the principle inapplicable, since the resolutions themselves were inapplicable. Words and phrases, no matter how subtle, could not disguise or dissimulate the dramatic events that had taken place in Cyprus. The reiterated

and constant application of certain types of subterfuges for the postponement of discussion sowed only fear in the public opinion of smaller
countries which considered that two of the principles of the Charter that
were of great importance were those of self-determination and non-
interference in the domestic affairs of states.

It would be very sad, Quiroga Galdo continued, if the way in which
the Committee was now discussing the Greek draft resolution, and especially the efforts to eliminate from it the mention of the principle of
self-determination, led world opinion to consider that the United Nations
was carrying out a ventriloquist diplomacy. Therefore he had to draw the
Committee's attention to the dangers of assuming an attitude it had no
right to assume. It was the Committee's duty to analyze these problems
with strict objectivity and impartiality. For the reasons he had just given,
with a clear conscience he would vote in favor of the Greek subamendment because it included a clear mention of the right of self-
determination, since the overwhelming majority of the members of the
Committee recognized that in the case of Cyprus, the application of this
principle was imperative.

The Committee then listened to the views of the Permanent Representative of Spain to the UN, Ambassador José Felix de Lequerica, who
formally introduced a subamendment which Belaunde of Peru had
mentioned and endorsed. Lequerica proposed that in the operative paragraph of the four-state amendments the Assembly should express "the
wish" instead of "the earnest hope" that further negotiations should be
promptly undertaken. He thought this would be closer to the truth and
might offer greater satisfaction to the Greek Delegation.

His delegation, the Spanish Ambassador continued, would vote for all
the four-state amendments, because it found them more efficient and
more constructive than the Greek draft resolution, which contained the
well-known words about "self-determination." The ancients used to say
numina nomine—names become gods. This had happened with the word
"self-determination." Self-determination had become a noble concept. All
accepted it because it was merely the application of history, and history
was an example of constant self-determination. However, perhaps this
concept could not be applied hastily and nervously to all problems at all
times. Perhaps in the scope suggested it could not be applied to all
countries where a legality existed that did not depend on the will of any
organ outside the country, not even of the United Nations itself. Perhaps
this was the case with Cyprus, which was linked to Britain by a treaty,
though Britain itself had recognized the international character of the
problem. He would like to quote the representative of Argentina, who,
during the debate on the Algerian question, had observed that the words
"self-determination of peoples" of Article 1, paragraph 2, of the Charter,
referred only to the freedom of sovereign peoples to choose a government. Neither this article nor any other provision in the Charter incited
non-self-governing peoples to rebellion, i.e., peoples who, under Article

73 of the Charter, "have not yet attained a full measure of self-government." [13] While he was not in a position to accept this "doctrine," of his Argentine colleague, he certainly gave it all due importance, and he thought that the Greek Delegation should take it into account when taking practical decisions. Those nations that generically might be called the Asian-African nations had taken this into account when discussing the Algerian question. Why, then, should the Committee not follow the same road in discussing Cyprus? Cyprus might be a somewhat different case than Algeria, but it was identical in regard to the application of self-determination. Without prior self-determination, Cyprus had covered much of the road toward the fulfilment of its own claims. The Committee did not have to decide. History and the recognition of reality, the sacrifices of its heroes, had taught exactly what Cyprus stood for. There were more principles than self-determination in the world, as Mr. Belaunde of Peru had pointed out. And, after all, the Committee was not sitting here as the International Court of Justice. There were other historical realities to which resolutions had to bow, and without having applied a plebiscite, which obviously would be the end of this tragic and arduous process, many of the nations had already voted in favor of Cyprus itself.

At the same time, De Lequerica continued, the United Nations was an organization with laws that should be respected. There was the juridical title of Britain to Cyprus, and the British representative had been extremely liberal regarding the interpretation of this title. There were the titles of Turkey—the Turkish population required guarantees, because of its proximity to the Turkish coast and also because of the strategic value of Cyprus. The Committee had heard a "very wise and moderate statement from the representative of Greece." Why, then, should one quibble stubbornly over one word? The representative of Argentina had defined this word. Why, then, should this word not be replaced by some wording that would prove that the Assembly respected the historical process that was taking place in Cyprus? One knew that the will killed and the spirit revived. "Let us not be killed by the will dividing the Committee into two camps on a question in which, spiritually, the Committee has never been more united. Let us try to find a unanimous solution based on the highest of principles." The Greek representative, he was sure, would accept these views, and he hoped that Canada and the delegations associated with it would accept the Spanish amendment. Mr. Belaunde had reminded the Committee that the history of Cyprus had made its people the greatest of philosophers and the greatest of thinkers.[14] He would like to beg the Foreign Minister of Greece, whose understanding and wisdom he admired, not to close the door to a solution because of the verbal specter. "Let him accept a reality which we all support in good faith. Let him not force us to participate on a vote. We are not superstitious in our belief because we believe in the United Nations and must follow the spirit and the letter of the Charter." He would dare rhetorically to invoke Minerva, the patron goddess of Athens, to communicate her wisdom to the Greek Delegation and make them servants of her great purposes, which so often imparted wisdom to Athens and helped the world to solve the problems which faced Greece.

Iceland's Ambassador and Permanent Representative to the UN, Thor Thors, on the other hand, expressed himself in favor of the Greek suba-mendment. Although there were several aspects of the Cyprus question on which his delegation would have liked to have expressed itself in order to avoid any misunderstanding about its attitude, at the last moment in the work and procedure of the Committee he would be very brief. He first emphasized his great satisfaction that in the Committee debate the statements of the British representative, who repeatedly referred favorably to the principle of self-determination, and the open attitude toward friendly negotiations expressed in the speech of the Greek Foreign Minister, showed that a mutual understanding and an eventual agreement were closer now than they had been when the matter had been discussed at the previous Assembly. This indicated movement in the right direction.

The Icelandic Delegation was greatly and mainly concerned about the future and the welfare of the people of Cyprus as a whole, both the Greek population and the people of Turkish descent. Cyprus should be regarded as one country and one political and geographical unit. However, as the Greek Delegation had promised in the debate, all guarantees should be given to the Turkish minority in Cyprus, and all the people of the island, of both Greek and Turkish descent, should find, in the course of time, ways to live together in peace and friendship. All the people of Cyprus should be allowed to exercise their right of self-determination, and thus they themselves, and they alone, should decide on whatever form of government and whatever alliance or alignment that they might wish to establish with any other country. The unfortunate present situation in Cyprus could not be allowed to endure.

The Greek draft resolution now before the Committee, the representative of Iceland acknowledged, needed improvements and amendments. It was not, for example, correct to say that no progress had been made toward settling the problem. The debate and various events since February in the Committee had clearly revealed that considerable progress had been achieved. One should therefore be thankful to the Canadian Delegation for having taken the lead toward improving the Greek draft resolution. The Chilean, Danish, and Norwegian delegations were also to be congratulated for having joined Canada in this endeavor. Had these four-state amendments been accepted as a compromise and gained unanimous approval, the Delegation of Iceland could have joined in that approach. Greece, however, had presented a subamendment emphasizing the principle of self-determination. In this circumstance, his delegation felt bound by conviction and the history of its people to support that amendment, and would vote in favor of it. Should the Greek amendment be defeated, he would vote in favor of the four-state amendment.

The Icelandic Delegation did not wish any shadow of doubt to exist about its true and faithful adherence to the principle of self-determination and stood with firmness and conviction behind the just and democratic claim of the advanced and intelligent people of Cyprus that they be given the right to decide their own fate and future. The Greek Foreign Minister had remarked in the morning that he was standing all alone. This, happily, was not the case. But even if it were, he could seek consolation and encouragement in what the great Norwegian writer and philosopher, Henrik Ibsen, once said that the strongest man is he who stands most alone. "Let us also remember that the fairest cause often seems far away, but in the course of time and development, it will win."

Entezam, of Iran, came next, saying his statement would be a brief explanation of vote. It would be meaningful only if the Committee decided to vote on the Greek subamendment. If that subamendment were put to the vote, his delegation would be obliged to vote against it. But he would like to make it clear that this negative vote would in no way be construed as a denial of the legitimate right of self-determination to the people of Cyprus. This recognition was indirectly involved in the phrase about the "purposes and principles of the Charter of the United Nations." Spelling out, however, this affirmation at the present juncture would, in his opinion, only render the negotiations more difficult. That was why he would vote in favor of the four-state amendments.

Canada's Nesbitt intervened very briefly at this point to inform the Committee that the Spanish subamendment was acceptable to the four states sponsoring the amendments to the Greek draft resolutions.

Ambassador Sarper followed. When he had spoken that morning, he said, he did not have the text of the "subamendment, so-called" presented by the Greek Delegation. Now, with this text before him and with the Chairman's permission, he would like to comment briefly on it. This subamendment, besides being an admitted tactical move—he stressed "admitted," because the Greek Foreign Minister had said that it was a tactical move—had three major defects. One of them was that the subamendment deleted from the original amendment presented by the four states the words co-operation "with . . . those concerned" in the fourth paragraph. This deletion was important because it closed all the doors to negotiation. The motive that inspired this deletion was dangerous and should rightly worry the Committee. The second defect was in the third line of "this so-called subamendment." Whereas in the Charter the words "self-determination" were always preceded by the words "equal rights and," to read as a whole "equal rights and self-determination," the third line of the Greek subamendment said merely "the right of self-determination." This was not only a misinterpretation of the Charter, but, if he might use the expression, it was a distortion of the spirit of the Charter. The third defect was to be found in that same third line of "the so-called subamendment." Everywhere in the Charter the word "people" appeared not in the singular but in the plural form as "peoples," because there were many peoples in the world. More especially, Article 73 (b) of the Charter, which was relevant to the case of Cyprus, referred to "territory" in the singular and to "peoples" in the plural. Hence the use of the word "people" in the singular, in the Greek subamendment was another distortion of the spirit and the letter of the Charter. The danger lay therein that with mere slogans like "self-determination" and the use of a word like "people," in both cases evading the spirit and the letter of the Charter, the Greek subamendment might catch the imagination of those who were not careful enough, every time they had an amendment or a text in front of them, to read the relevant Charter article. The subamendment caught the imagination but imagination alone would not do the trick.

A solution was desired, Sarper went on to declare. That was why he was trying to fight this subamendment with all the conviction at his command. This subamendment was contrary to the wording and to the spirit of the Charter, and especially of the relevant article in the particular case under discussion. Consequently it was unacceptable to his delegation. He would even go a step further. Because of the spirit and motive that inspired this subamendment, it could not even be improved. The motives were questionable, because the very word "negotiations" had been deleted. The subamendment was contrary to Article 33 of the Charter.[15] It was contrary to the principle of the First Committee itself. It avoided negotiations. The subamendment was nothing. It was a play of words. It was designed to catch the imagination and to hook, if he might use that expression, votes. That was all. This brief intervention, he was sure, would draw some answers from perhaps several quarters. Consequently, he reserved his right of reply.

Averoff-Tossizza followed the Turkish representative. He thanked, first of all, Belaunde of Peru, "the great orator of the Committee," for having said that the Greeks and Latins were relatives. This relationship existed for 3,000 years but unfortunately it was a bit remote, he said. "We are distant cousins, but not exactly of the same family." If that were not so, Latin America would have risen for Cyprus as the Arab world had done in support of Algeria.

Turning now to the remarks of the Norwegian representative, the Greek Foreign Minister said he was sorry that what he had said that morning had been misconstrued. He certainly had not wanted to say that the four-state amendments had been submitted for tactical purposes or as a stratagem. The intention surely was to help in the solution of a thorny problem. He would never have dared to have spoken otherwise about four countries that he honored and held dear or about the "worthy representative of Norway, whose Minister is my friend and, in fact, one of the most eminent statesmen in Europe." Intentions, however, frequently were good but the results were otherwise. He did not find it difficult to say that these good intentions had in fact paved the road of what he had characterized that morning.[16] It was not a deliberate tactic. It was designed to bring about a new resolution through an amendment to the resolution, and this amendment did not say anything his delegation wanted it to say. After all, it was his government that had presented this item for discussion in the United Nations.

He had been very gently accused by the Turkish representative, Averoff-Tossizza continued, of having tried to "hook" the emotions of the Committee. He would not deny that he had spoken with emotion and had addressed himself to the emotions of the Committee's members. Therefore he pleaded guilty to the charge. But was it not from emotion that the most beautiful things of the human soul stemmed—everything that was spontaneous, true, beautiful, humane? On the other hand, to the charge that, having addressed himself to emotion, he had failed to recognize realities, he pleaded innocent. He had looked at this question in a spirit of complete realism, he maintained. As the Committee had seen throughout the debate, the people of Cyprus, on whose behalf he was speaking, wanted to know first of all whether in principle they would be able to determine their own future. That was the basis of the question. If that issue were not resolved, ancillary issues could not be resolved either. This was the true shape of realism. First of all, the Committee should decide the issue that the people coming before it demanded. Then, ancillary problems would be dealt with. Surely, he had not disregarded these ancillary problems. He, himself, the day before had spoken about Turkey's interests, and had tried to prove that these interests could and should be safeguarded and that "we are all prepared to work in order to safeguard them." How should this be done? It should be done through negotiations, of course. However, such negotiations could take place only once the fundamental issue of self-determination of the people was disposed of. "That is why you would be responding not only to your emotions but also to your sense of logic and realism if you vote for self-determination."

"How can you vote for self-determination?" asked the Greek Foreign Minister. "Have I asked you to vote that the self-determination of the people of Cyprus shall be applied within a year or two or in this form or that?" He had not specified any modalities or procedures. He had asked for nothing under that heading. He had merely asked the Committee to recognize the fundamental right that would surely prevail in Cyprus, because this was the current of history and the will of the majority of the English people.[17] He had asked the Committee to proclaim what history and the British people wanted to see applied in principle in Cyprus. Therefore, while pleading guilty to the charge of emotion, he pleaded innocent to the charge of lack of realism.

He knew full well that the United Nations was not a court of law,

Averoff-Tossizza continued. He knew that the United Nations was a political body that worked with certain difficulties because of the multiplicity of interests that came together in it. But he did not accept the notion that the United Nations was an organism that merely bred resolutions which were interpreted in each country at that country's discretion, or meant nothing at all. That was a point he would not accept. "We are a world parliament, and we should face the issues brought before us as a parliament. We should do so with a sense of morality and a sense of realism." This could be done only by voting for the right of self-determination for Cyprus, which was the foundation stone and the prior condition for any other negotiations for all peoples.

Returning now to the amendments, Averoff-Tossizza contended, first of all, that these were not amendments at all. According to the spirit of the rules of procedure and the letter of rule 131 in particular, an amendment could not be a proposal that completely altered what the original mover had proposed. Yet this was precisely what the proposed amendments would bring about. He wondered whether any jurist, as a jurist, or a group of professors of International Law, if asked whether these were amendments, would in fact legally rule they were amendments rather than a resolution in a new form. On this basis he rejected the four-state amendments as being at variance with the rules of procedure of the Assembly. If these proposals, however, were accepted as amendments, then he would contend that his amendment to the amendments was the genuine article, a real amendment to the four-state proposals. Why was it the genuine article? It was so because he had accepted three of the paragraphs of the preamble. He had also accepted a part of the operative part that was not found in his original draft resolution. As entitled to under rule 131 of the rules of procedure, he had deleted some words and had added others. The Committee was therefore faced with a manifest instance of a four-power amendment designed to reverse the meaning of the Greek draft resolution and bring forward another proposal, whereas his delegation proposed a genuine amendment to the four-state proposal.

Having now made the Greek Delegation's position clear with regard to the rules of procedure, he would now define its position with regard to the voting. It would vote in favor of its "counteramendment." If its "counteramendment" were adopted, it would vote in favor of the whole draft resolution thus amended. If, on the other hand, its "counter-amendment" were rejected, it would vote against the amendment sponsored by the four states. In this way, if the Greek draft resolution were thus unfortunately amended, his delegation would vote against its own draft resolution.

Concluding his statement, Averoff-Tossizza appealed to all nations on the Committee, large and small alike.

We cannot leave these people under a colonial regime forever. In order not to leave them in that predicament, we must give them the fundamental assurance that some day they may be able to exercise the right of self-determination. . . . We cannot escape from, or sidestep our principles. We must demonstrate to the world that we respect our principles, to the point of declaring that they are applicable, without interfering with the relations between states or stating the modalities of implementation of these principles, the applicability of which we proclaim.

Lacking that, he felt strongly that the member states would be diminishing the "significance and prestige of this great Areopagus of the world." And, he added: "Let it not be said, as Mr. Sarper has said, that the principle of self-determination is contrary to the Charter. This principle, as we recognize it, does not entail the creation or abolition of minorities or the creation of nations. The principle, as we recognize it, is not a principle which we should escape but one which we should proclaim and respect." That was the minimum, and if the members of the United Nations did not accept this minimum, they would be sapping "this beautiful edifice which was built with so much blood and which harbors so much hope."

To this last remark of the Greek Foreign Minister, Ambassador Sarper retorted that, perhaps because of their distance from each other at the Committee table, the Foreign Minister had not heard him well. He, Sarper, had not said he was against the principle of self-determination. This was a misquotation. He had said, and he repeated, that nowhere in the Charter was the word "self-determination" used without being preceded by the words "equal rights and." Mr. Averoff-Tossizza, he charged, also handled a little lightly the difference between the singular and the plural form of the word "people." Therein lay all the difference. He dared anyone to show him one single place in the Charter where the word "people" was used in the singular form. Especially in Article 73 (b), the article relevant to the Cyprus question, the word "territory" was used in the singular, and the word "people" was in the plural. As he had tried to explain in the article's original draft, "people" had been in the singular but after long debates and deliberation, it had been changed to the final, plural form that appeared in the Charter. This could not be ignored by the Committee and should not be ignored by the Greek Delegation, which pretended to base its contention on the Charter and at the same time distorted the Charter's spirit and the wording.

The Chairman: I call on the representative of Peru who wishes to speak on a point of order.

Mr. Belaunde (Peru): Would it be too much to ask the Chairman of the Committee to allow us half an hour for meditation and intellectual repose before we get to the vote? I would ask for a half-hour's recess of the meeting.

The Chairman: The representative of Peru knows full well that we are on the eve of the ending of the session and we still have an entire item on the agenda of this Committee. Even if we had night meetings tonight and tomorrow night, which I intend to propose, we shall not have the necessary time to take care of the items on the agenda if we do not make an effort to dispose of the present item as swiftly as possible.

The Chairman added he felt in duty bound to press the representative of Peru, for whom he had great respect, not to insist on his proposal for a recess but to allow the Committee to go on to the vote. "We have had a comprehensive debate in this Committee, and I think the time has come to pass on to the vote. I therefore appeal to the representative of Peru and urge him not to press his motion."

Mr. Belaunde (Peru): I shall not insist on it, but if some representatives had a desire for meditation at this moment, I would appreciate it if they would support me in my view.

He was willing, however, to bow to the Chairman's decision. "I feel very close to you, because I, too, have shouldered the same responsibilities, and I only wish that I had been able to do so as efficiently as you."

"I am grateful to the representative of Peru," said the Chairman, who then outlined the situation. Before the Committee was the Greek draft resolution, to which the Delegations of Canada, Chile, Denmark, and Norway had proposed amendments. According to the Greek representative's statement, his delegation accepted the first three paragraphs of the four-state amendments. Lastly, the Greek Delegation had presented an amendment to paragraph 4 of the four-state amendments. There was also an amendment to the four-state amendments, submitted by Spain. This Spanish amendment had been accepted by the cosponsors of the four-state amendments and would therefore be regarded as having been incorporated in those amendments.

"In accordance with general practice," continued the Chairman, "we should proceed to vote as follows: first, on the Greek amendment to the four-state amendments, and then on paragraph 4 of the four-state amendments." There was, however, one point to which he felt duty bound to draw the Committee's attention, though he did not feel that the Chairman could take a position on the matter. The point was the following: If there were no objections, he would be obliged, as he had stated, to put to the vote first the Greek amendment to the four-state amendments. Nevertheless, that raised certain misgivings in his mind. He had had conversations with some members of the Committee and with jurists who were well versed in the subject. He had been advised that this subamendment, even though presented in the form of an amendment to an amendment, was actually an attempt to revive the original Greek text. He had been advised also that "if we are to abide by the spirit as well as by the letter of our rules of procedure, we will have to think in terms of two amendments to the original text, one being the more remote." [18]

The Chairman added that he was simply presenting the different aspects of the question to the Committee, without, however, feeling that he could take any position whatever. His feeling as to procedure to be followed was this: In conformity with established practice, he would have to put to the vote first the Greek subamendment unless there were objections. If there were objections, he would have to ask the Committee to pronounce itself on this matter of procedure.

"May I thank the Chairman for the objective spirit in which he is visualizing the situation and the able manner in which he has placed it before the Committee," said Zeineddine, the representative of Syria. He felt obliged, however, to refer to a point of order which the representative of Egypt had raised in the morning. This point of order related to the application of rules 131 and 132 of the rules of procedure. Citing the last sentence in rule 131—"a motion is considered an amendment to a proposal if it merely adds to, deletes from or revises part of that proposal"—he stressed the word "merely" and observed that an amendment might come under the outward appearance of an amendment though in fact it completely denatured the original proposal. Paragraph 4 of the four-state amendments, in his opinion, changed the nature of the original Greek proposal and was no mere revision of it or an addition to it.

When the rules of procedure were being discussed in the early days of the United Nations, Zeineddine continued, the question had been raised as to what a proposal put forward as an amendment should be in order to be considered an amendment. There had been a current of opinion to the effect that the general rule applied in many bodies should also be applied in the rules of procedure of the Committee, namely, that an amendment should be accepted by the party which had moved the initial proposal in order for it to be considered an amendment, since otherwise an amendment could substantially change a proposal. This idea, however, had not been completely acceptable, and, therefore, this particular part of rule 131 had been added so as to place a limitation upon the consideration of an amendment as an amendment. It was clear that the amendment contained in paragraph 4 of the four-state amendments completely changed the operative part of the original Greek proposal. In fact, it neither added to that proposal nor deleted from it. It simply called for the deletion of the operative paragraph and for its replacement by something else, which was the text proposed as an amendment.

The discussion which had taken place since the Egyptian Delegation had first raised the point of order had revealed that the objectives of the four-state amendments and of the Greek proposal were so much at variance and their contents so different that they could not be held together, the Syrian asserted. This was of some importance, because if these "so-called" amendments were considered to be amendments, whereas in reality they constituted a new proposal, the Committee would be going along with the intention of the movers of these amendments to try to avoid rule 132 of the rules of procedure, which said:

If two or more proposals relate to the same question, a committee shall, unless it decides otherwise, vote on the proposals in the order in which they have been submitted. A committee may, after each vote on a proposal, decide whether to vote on the next proposal.

That was something the Committee should not do. This was a tactical move in his delegation's view. It was a move to attempt to obtain priority by other means over the initial draft resolution introduced by Greece. He did not think that the Committee would relish this kind of action, no matter what the reasons behind it might be, because this would amount to frustrating the Committee in its attempt to apply rule 132.

Under these circumstances, the Syrian Delegation's point of order, which he would first put as a formal motion, was that the original Greek proposal should be voted on first, and that, afterward, the fourth "so-called amendment" proposed by the four states should be voted on, because it was in fact a new proposal and agreed neither with the terms of rule 131 nor with the meaning of rule 132.

The Chairman, before calling on the next speaker, announced that the Delegations of Peru, Liberia, Australia, Norway, Egypt, and Lebanon, had asked to speak in the procedural debate on the point of order the Syrian representative had raised. He proposed to close the discussion after the Committee had heard the Lebanese representative. It was so decided.

Ambassador Henry Ford Cooper, Chairman of the Delegation of Liberia to the UN, requested a separate vote on each of the four-state amendments. The Chairman, however, explained that since the sponsor of the original draft resolution had already accepted three of the four amendments introduced by the four states only the fourth amendment remained to be voted upon, and the question of a division of the vote would not apply in this case.

The Senior Adviser of the Australian Delegation, J. D. L. Hood, addressing himself strictly to the procedural point which had arisen in the Committee, stated he certainly did not desire to add confusion but merely to find clarification of the position in which the Committee found itself. His understanding of the Chairman's remarks a few minutes earlier had been that he had given a ruling that the amendments submitted by the four states were in fact amendments, within the terms of rule 131 of the rules of procedure, to the text of the original Greek draft resolution. With all respect to the observations of his colleague from Syria, he found himself entirely in agreement with what he had taken to be the Chairman's ruling. To him it appeared that here was plainly a case of revision of a proposal. He therefore had no doubt that the Chairman's ruling would be substantiated.

Coming now to what had been called the subamendment of the Greek Delegation, Hood observed that the Chairman had made no ruling. Therefore, it was for the Committee to decide how to deal with this new proposal. He wished merely to submit at this stage that, in the Australian Delegation's view, the Greek subamendment was tantamount to a revision of the original Greek draft resolution and should be dealt with in that light by the Greek representative. With deference he would suggest that the Greek representation submit to th Committee, if he so desired, a new resolution incorporating the proposition put forward as a subamendment. He did not think it proper that the Committee should be asked to vote first on "this so-called subamendment," which, in reality, was a revised proposal by the Greek Delegation and should be dealt with accordingly. Hood added that he had not at the time supported the suggestion of the representative of Peru for a short adjournment, but it could turn out that this would be the wisest course for the Committee to follow if the Delegation of Greece would look at the matter in this light. He would intervene again to attempt to obtain further clarification in this matter.

One of the sponsors of the four-state amendments, Engen, of Norway, intervened next in this procedural problem which had arisen in the Committee. He fully appreciated the misgivings the Syrian representative had with respect to the amendments cosponsored by the Norwegian Delegation, since all were entitled to have misgivings about things. However, he did not wish to go into any detailed analysis and proof of why the four-state amendments, in the Norwegian Delegation's view, were real amendments. He simply wanted to say that a vast amount of experience in the work of the United Nations was assembled in the Committee, and if one went through the records one would find an ample number of precedents in which amendments of this kind had been introduced to draft resolutions and had never been challenged on the ground of not being amendments. He could, of course, ask the Secretariat to find out, but that would be superfluous, even impossible at this late stage of the Committee's proceedings. Nor did he think this necessary, because he was sure that all the representatives present could recall many examples of amendments of this kind that had never been challenged. There was nothing extraordinary about these amendments.

With regard to the Greek subamendment, said the Norwegian representative, he maintained the remark he had made at the morning meeting, namely, that in substance and to a large degree also in form it was a reintroduction of the original proposal to which the four-state amendment had been submitted, and he very respectfully submitted that if this was accepted as a subamendment, he did not see how such a course could be in conformity with ordinary procedure. The cosponsoring states could avail themselves of the same privilege accorded to the Greek Delegation and reintroduce their amendment as a subamendment to the Greek subamendment, and one could go on like that for a very long time. However, to show respect for the Committee and for orderly procedure, he did not propose to press this point, which would create an intolerable procedural situation. As far as his delegation was concerned, therefore, it would accept that the question of priority be decided by the Committee, whose duty it was to decide. While he would oppose the proposal made by the representative of Syria with respect to priority, he fully granted him the right to introduce that proposal.

In the light of the statement made by the representative of Norway, said the Chairman at this point, he wondered whether the representative of Syria and the other speakers on his list now wished to speak on the matter. It appeared to him that it might be better if the Committee immediately voted on the Syrian proposal, which [he mistakenly thought] was to the effect that the subamendment submitted by the Greek Delegation should be voted on first. This was a question that naturally had to be decided by the Committee itself, which was a master of its own procedure.

Loutfi, of Egypt, though not insisting on speaking, asked for a clarification. He thought (correcting the Chairman's mistaken impression) that the proposal the representative of Syria had made was rather to the effect that the sense of the Committee should be taken as to whether the four-state amendments were to be regarded by the Committee as amendments.[19] As far as he was concerned, he respectfully suggested that the Chairman first take the sense of the Committee whether the four-state amendments were to be regarded as amendments, and then take the sense of the Committee in the same way as to whether the Greek subamendment was to be regarded as an amendment.

The Permanent Representative of El Salvador to the UN, Ambassador Miguel Rafael Urquia, declared that under different circumstances he would have added the voice of his delegation in support of the views expressed by other delegations, especially that of Syria, to the effect that the four-state amendments were really not amendments but a separate draft resolution, because if one studied them carefully, one saw that, apart from keeping the first paragraph of the preamble of the Greek draft, everything else, including the operative part, was considerably modified. At this stage of the Committee's work, however, he did not think it worthwhile to become embroiled in such a procedural issue, especially since the Chairman himself had just stated that there should be no recess of the meeting even for a few minutes, as the representative of Peru had suggested. Since the session of the Assembly was drawing to a close and the Greek Delegation, the sponsor of the original draft resolution and one of the three parties mainly concerned, had accepted as amendments the proposals of the four states, he thought the Committee should go ahead and vote as soon as possible. The Greek Delegation had submitted a subamendment to the four-state amendments—which proved that it considered the latter to be amendments. He therefore asked the representative of Syria not to press his proposal but to allow the Committee to go on to vote.

Lebanon's alternate represenative, Edward A. Rizk, said he, too, had misgivings about the four-state amendments and to a certain extent shared the views expressed by the Syrian representative (namely, that these really were a new draft resolution). He hoped, however, that in the interest of harmony and orderly procedure the Syrian representative would not press his proposal that the original Greek draft resolution be voted on first. Rizk entirely agreed that the procedure set out by the Chairman for the voting order was correct and was certainly in conformity with the rules of procedure. The Chairman had said that some eminent jurists had expressed the opinion that the Greek subamendment was an effort to revive the original Greek draft resolution. If this kind of reasoning were followed, then he was sure that those eminent jurists, whoever they might be, would also have to be consulted on the four-state amendments, and he thought the Chairman would agree with him that their verdict would be that the four-state amendments were themselves a new resolution and not amendments at all, and that therefore the Committee would have to vote first on the original Greek draft resolution and go back to the proposal made by the representative of Syria. He therefore repeated that the order of voting proposed by the Chairman should be followed in order to avoid confusion and perhaps even an exacerbation of the debate, which, he was sure, no one wanted.

The Syrian representative at this point stated that in view of the late hour and of the observations just made, his delegation, while continuing to hold that the "so-called amendments" presented by the four states amounted to a new resolution, could also see that if these were amendments, then there was also an amendment to those amendments, as the representative of Lebanon had just said. If the Committee could proceed to vote first on the amendment to the amendments, then on those "so-called amendments" of the four states, and then on the original draft, he thought that would be a way of saving time.

After this statement, the Chairman described the situation as follows: "The representative of Syria submitted a motion that the Greek subamendment be voted on first. Since the Committee is master of its own procedure, it is for the Committee to decide on this procedural question." He would, therefore, invite the members of the Committee to pronounce themselves on the Syrian representative's motion that the Greek subamendment be put to the vote before the fourth paragraph of the four-state amendment.

"I believe there has been a misunderstanding," Arenales Catalan of Guatemala intervened. The representative of Syria, he explained, had withdrawn his motion, since he was willing to agree to the procedure that the Chairman himself had originally suggested. "You did not actually decide on the method of voting," he told the Chairman, "but you suggested that first of all the Committee should vote on the so-called subamendment or counteramendment of Greece, then on the so-called four-state amendment, and, thirdly, on the Greek draft resolution." The representative of Syria was not pressing his motion that the Greek subamendment be voted on first. He had simply withdrawn his motion and had said he was willing to abide by the Chairman's suggestion. Therefore, it was not necessary to ask the Committee to pronounce itself on what was a non-existent motion. Rather, the very wise original suggestion made by the Chairman should be followed.

"I thought," said the Chairman, "that the sense of the Syrian motion was that which I explained. However, I will ask the representative of Syria to clarify the position."

Zeineddine, the Syrian representative, said he had put his motion as clearly as he could. It did not deal with the Greek subamendment or counteramendment but with the fact that the "so-called four-state amendment" was a proposal that should be voted upon after the original Greek draft resolution had been voted upon. That would be in accordance with rule 132 of the rules of procedure. However, when he had understood, but perhaps mistakenly so, that it was the Chairman's intention to begin by voting on the Greek counteramendment, then on the four-state amendment, and finally on the Greek draft resolution, then he had agreed on that procedure, so that the discussion might not be prolonged. If he had understood correctly the procedure the Chairman had suggested, then he would withdraw his motion. If that was not the case, then his motion stood.

Norway's representative said he had understood his Syrian colleague's intervention to mean that, by his proposal, he wanted the Committee to decide on the priority of the voting. Now he understood that he had made the maintenance of his proposal contingent upon whether the Chairman would put the proposals before the Committee in the following order: first, the Greek subamendment; then, the four-state amendment; and then the Greek draft resolution. If the Chairman maintained this order of voting, the Syrian representative would not press his proposal. Speaking as one of the sponsors of the four-state amendment, he himself had made the point for the record. He would not challenge the order of voting, but, as he had said, if the Syrian representative's motion were put to the vote, he would have to oppose it.

"If there is no objection," said the Chairman, "to putting to the vote first the counteramendment of Greece, then I shall do so. Then I shall put the four-state amendments to the vote, but that, of course, would depend upon the result of the voting on the Greek subamendment. The Committee will now vote upon the Greek subamendment."

In the vote that was taken by roll call [20] on the Greek subamendment to the amendments cosponsored by Canada, Chile, Denmark, and Norway, 33 member states voted in favor; 18 voted against it; while 27 abstained from the vote. Thus, the Greek subamendment was adopted by the Committee.

This victory for the Greek Delegation had been due, in the personal view of the Permanent Greek representative to the United Nations, to the combination of three factors: the vigorous Greek diplomatic *démarches* in Washington; the threat of a walkout by the Greek Delegation from the Assembly; and, primarily, the favorable turn in the procedural battle in the Political Committee.

As though by magic, the Greek Delegation noted, the entire procedural attack against self-determination which had been mounted in the morning had melted away. As the atmosphere of the debate had turned in favor of the Greek procedural viewpoint (especially after the Chairman's refusal to issue a ruling of his own on whether the Greek subamendment was a genuine one or whether the four-state proposals were genuine amendments, now new proposals), Ambassador Lodge, who had not taken part in this intricately fierce procedural debate just as he had refrained from speaking during the debate in the General Committee on the matter of including the Cyprus item in the Assembly's agenda, had been observed whispering something in the ear of his deputy, Ambassador Wadsworth, who was seated behind him. Wadsworth, then rising from his chair, had walked up to the Norwegian representative and, in his turn, had whispered something in Engen's ear. From that moment the opposition to the Greek procedural viewpoint subsided. And the point Engen had made that the Political Committee might have to decide the question of the respective voting priorities of the Greek subamendment and the four-state amendments to the original Greek draft resolution was not put to the vote, while the Syrian representative, on his side, had not insisted on his own point of order, provided the voting order proposed by the Chairman was followed.

The detailed results of the roll-call vote on the Greek subamendment were as follows:

In favor: Albania, Bolivia, Bulgaria, Byelorussia, Costa Rica, Czechoslovakia, Ecuador, Egypt, El Salvador, Ethiopia, Ghana, Greece, Guatemala, Haiti, Hungary, Iceland, Indonesia, Iraq, Ireland, Lebanon, Morocco, Panama, Poland, Romania, Saudi Arabia, Sudan, Syria, Tunisia, Ukraine, U.S.S.R., Uruguay, Yemen, Yugoslavia.

Against: Australia, Canada, Belgium, Chile, Colombia, Denmark, France, Iran, Italy, Luxembourg, Netherlands, New Zealand, Norway, Portugal, Spain, Sweden, Turkey, United Kingdom.

Abstaining: Afghanistan, Argentina, Austria, Brazil, Burma, Cambodia, Ceylon, China, Dominican Republic, Finland, Honduras, India, Israel, Japan, Laos, Liberia, Federation of Malaya, Mexico, Nepal, Nicaragua, Pakistan, Paraguay, Peru, Philippines, Thailand, United States, Venezuela.

Cuba, Jordan, Libya, and the Union of South Africa had absented themselves.

The roll-call vote revealed that the Soviet bloc voted *en bloc* for the Greek subamendment; that the Arab League states did likewise, with the exception of Jordan and Libya, both absent; that eight out of the twenty members of the Latin American group voted for that subamendment, while two voted against it, nine abstained, and Cuba was absent; that the Asian-African group (excluding the Arab League states) was divided, with most of them following India's example and abstaining. Voting against the Greek subamendment, on the other hand, were the "old Commonwealth" states and all NATO states, with the exception of Iceland, which voted for the subamendment, and the United States, which abstained. In contrast to Ireland and Yugoslavia, which voted in favor of the subamendment, Spain and Sweden voted against it.

After the Greek subamendment had been adopted, the Chairman observed that since the Greek Delegation had accepted the first three paragraphs of the four-state amendments, he would ask the Committee to vote on the original draft resolution submitted by Greece as amended, first of all, by the three paragraphs, which the sponsor of the draft resolution had accepted and, second, by the adoption of the Greek subamendment.

The representative of Turkey, however, raised a point of order. The amendment proposed by the four states, Sarper said, remained. Either it was included in the original Greek draft resolution and the first three paragraphs of the amendments were contained in the original draft resolution, or the amendment presented by the four states still stood as an amendment. In either case, whatever the Chairman's decision might be, he begged him to put to the vote separately the first three paragraphs together first, and the last paragraph separately from the rest. He requested division.

Taking note of this request, the Chairman observed, however, that the Greek draft resolution contained a first paragraph—"Having examined the question of Cyprus"—which had not been amended in any way, if he understood correctly. Then came three paragraphs submitted as amendments by the four states, which the sponsor of the original draft resolution had accepted, followed by the Greek subamendment as adopted by the Committee. Therefore, he would put to the vote, first of all, the first paragraph, which was maintained as it was; then the next three paragraphs, which were acceptable to the draft resolution's sponsor; finally, he would put to the vote the draft resolution as a whole.

The first paragraph of the preamble was adopted by 72 votes to none, with three abstentions. And the rest of the preamble, as amended, was adopted by 75 votes to none, with 4 abstentions. In both the cases the vote was taken by a show of hands.

Finally, the Chairman put to the vote the draft resolution as a whole. A roll call vote had been requested. The draft resolution, as amended, was adopted by 33 votes to 20, with 25 abstentions. The detailed results of this roll-call vote were as follows:

In favor: Albania, Bolivia, Bulgaria, Byelorussia, Costa Rica, Czechoslovakia, Ecuador, Egypt, El Salvador, Ethiopia, Ghana, Greece, Guatemala, Haiti, Hungary, Iceland, Indonesia, Iraq, Ireland, Lebanon, Morocco, Panama, Poland, Romania, Saudi Arabia, Sudan, Syria, Tunisia, Ukraine, U.S.S.R., Uruguay, Yemen, Yugoslavia.

Against: Australia, Belgium, Canada, Chile, Colombia, Dominican Republic, France, Iran, Italy, Luxembourg, Netherlands, New Zealand, Nicaragua, Norway, Pakistan, Portugal, Sweden, Turkey, United Kingdom.

Abstaining: Afghanistan, Argentina, Austria, Brazil, Burma, Cambodia, Ceylon, China, Finland, Honduras, India, Israel, Japan, Laos, Liberia, Federation of Malaya, Mexico, Nepal, Paraguay, Peru, Philippines, Spain, Thailand, United States, Venezuela.

A comparison of the two roll-call votes carried out, first, on the Greek subamendment, and, second, on the draft resolution as a whole, reveals that three member states—the Dominican Republic, Nicaragua, and Pakistan—changed their abstention on the subamendment into a negative vote on the resolution as a whole. Spain, on the other hand, which had voted against the Greek subamendment, abstained from the vote on the draft resolution as a whole.

The resolution adopted by the Committee read as follows:

The General Assembly
Having examined the question of Cyprus,
Reaffirming its resolution 1013 (XI) of 26 February, 1957,
Expressing its concern that more progress has not been made toward the solution of this problem,
Expresses its earnest hope that further negotiations and discussions will be undertaken in a spirit of co-operation with a view to have the right of self-determination applied in the case of the people of Cyprus.

After the vote, several delegations explained why they had voted as they had. Rafael de la Colina, the representative of Mexico, whose delegation had supported the Greek viewpoint on the Cyprus question on earlier occasions, explained his abstentions. He felt, he said, that from the point of view of timeliness and political expediency, and because of the extreme complexity of the question, the text as approved could be slightly amended in a way that would make it acceptable to the great majority of members. At any rate, he wished once again to express the sympathy of his delegation toward the legitimate aspirations of the people of Cyprus and to reaffirm its unshakable adherence to the principle of self-determination of peoples, which his country had vigorously defended in its historical development. His delegation hoped that, before the matter was brought to the Assembly, it would be possible to agree on a text that a great majority of the entire Assembly could accept. If this could be the case, the laudable purposes of re-establishing peace and tranquility on the island, which had suffered so much, would be encouraged, with full guarantees being given to all elements of the population and with the consequent acceleration of the process of liberation and progress of the suffering Cypriot people. However, if a single compromise text were not arrived at, his delegation reserved its right to change its vote at the plenary meeting of the Assembly.

But in the Greek Delegation's view, the most important of all the explanations of vote given was that of the head of the Indian Delegation. His delegation, Krishna Menon said, had abstained from taking part in the debate and in the voting on the Cyprus question, because, after laborious efforts made by itself and by various other delegations, it had become clear that any decision taken at present that did not command the overwhelming majority support of the United Nations, not necessarily unanimity, was not likely to fulfil the purposes of the Charter. In the attempts his delegation had made, it had had the co-operation of both the Greek and the British Delegations, and it was not as though there was an attitude of absolute intolerance but rather an attempt to reach some point at which it would be possible to come before the Assembly and obtain agreement, as had been the case at the previous session. But that has been still prevented by the existing gaps.

Any question that was brought before the Assembly in the context that this question was brought forward, Krishna Menon continued, could be effectively decided only if there was co-operation in the sense he had mentioned. The government of India was neither unconcerned nor insensitive to this matter, India's position was the same as stated at the previous session: that Cyprus was a colonial question. "We stand four-square by the independence of the Cypriot people and their right to be a sovereign state entitled to membership in the United Nations." [21] Cyprus had a checkered history that went back two or three thousand years. Yet it had remained an entity, being ruled by the Egyptians, Persians, Romans, Byzantines, captured by the Arabs, conquered by Richard Coeur de Lion, King of England, sold by him to the Knights Templars because he could not administer it, and then it had been passed on to the Republics of Genoa and Venice, and finally had come under Ottoman Turkish rule for 300 years. Turkish interests had been such that in 1878 Turkey had passed on that administration to Britain. Then World War I had come, in which Turkey had been on the side of the Central Powers, and Britain had annexed Cyprus.

At a later stage he would come to the Indian view with regard to the interest of other countries in Cyprus. It had been argued, Krishna Menon noted, that this was not a straightforward colonial question.[22] He would not like to be cynical and say that colonial questions were never straightforward because colonialism was not straightforward. There were no colonial questions that did not have complications. Cyprus was part, under the British Constitution and the Proclamation of 1951, of Her Britannic Majesty's other realms, the realms beyond the Seas. It was a Crown Colony, just as Ceylon was before it became independent. The legal sovereignty of Cyprus rested with the United Kingdom. The political sovereignty of Cyprus, however, rested with the Cypriot people. And when the legal sovereignty, which had been obtained by annexation, would be removed, then the Cypriot people—regardless of their nationality, whether they were of Greek, Byzantine, Armenian, or Turkish ancestry—would be members of what would be the Cypriot state, when they became an independent nation. There was one thing further, however, which probably was somewhat esoteric to other people. It was not possible even for a parliament or a government easily to change the status of the island just by a speech, because the status of Cyprus had been conferred by letters patent in 1925.[23] Letters patent were beyond the jurisdiction of Parliament. It was possible for Parliament to reduce the salary of judges, but it could not reduce their status, because the latter was covered by letters patent.

The Indian government's view about non-self-governing territories or colonies was that they were entitled to and should have independence so that they might take their place in the comity of nations, Krishna Menon declared further. This was not a denial of whatever right to self-will or self-election there might be. But there ought to be a "self" first. A subject people could not choose, and therefore its independence had to be established.

His delegation, Krishna Menon continued, had stated at the previous Assembly that it did not consider that this land and its people should be the subject of a controversy to determine who—the British, the Greeks, or the Turks—should have them. It was time that the Cyprus people, after all the years of subjection, came into their own nationhood. Therefore he fully stood by their independence. He hoped that the British government, in the pursuit of its liberal policy in government that had become part of the general thinking of the British people, would find its way in the speediest possible time to resolve the question in a manner which was not now before the Assembly; namely, by enabling the people of Cyprus through peaceful means to attain and to maintain their independence, and for their country "to take its place around this table as an independent nation." His neighbor came from Iceland. The population of Iceland was 166,000. Cyprus had a population of half a million. If Iceland could be a member of the United Nations and make effective contributions, there was no reason why any other country should not.

Cyprus, as an independent country located in the Mediterranean with all the considerations which had been spoken about, in which "we are not particularly interested," would be safer, Krishna Menon contended, because it would be in the interests of the great powers not to interfere with it. His government, therefore, looked to the day when the Cypriot people, evoking their great sense of nationalism, their industry, and their particular position in the world, would be able by their efforts to attain their independence, aided by the sympathy of the Greeks and, he had no doubt, of the Turks and of the rest of the world, as the debate in the Committee and the liberal attitude existing in the metropolitan country toward former colonial territories had shown.

"It was necessary for us, however," said Krishna Menon, "to deal with what is called the tripartite claim." He hoped that neither his Greek nor his Turkish colleague would take exception to this, because it was his duty to state his delegation's position. Reference had been made to the Treaty of Lausanne. The argument was that an equilibrium established by that treaty had conferred upon Turkey certain rights. He had looked through the Treaty and had found that Article 16 stated:

Turkey hereby renounces all rights and title whatsoever over or respecting the territories situated outside the frontiers laid down in the present Treaty.

That was not only with regard to Cyprus, but to everything else. When it came more specifically to Cyprus, Article 20 stated:

Turkey hereby recognizes the annexation of Cyprus proclaimed by the British Government on 5 November 1914.

It was not even as though Turkey had ceded the island. The act had already taken place, and Turkey, by the solemn treaty of which it was one of the high contracting parties, had agreed to the annexation and had recognized the sovereignty of His Britannic Majesty over the island, and that Cyprus had become part of the British Empire. Then, there was Article 21 which stated:

Turkish nationals ordinarily resident in Cyprus on 5 November 1914 will acquire British nationality.

So it was not only as though the territory had been taken. Nobody had been interested in keeping these Turkish nationals Turkish. They acquired British nationality. The above article went on to say that if any Turkish national still remained a Turk, he had to go back to Turkey. But he would not go into the matter of how many did go back to Turkey. That was a different question. But they could not remain in Cyprus. If they did, under law they became British subjects. They became Cypriots.

In order to maintain his objective position, it was necessary to state, Krishna Menon maintained, that the parties to the Lausanne Treaty were the British Empire, France, Italy, Japan, Greece, and Romania. Consequently, Greece also, by these texts, had become a party to the annexation and the establishment of this separate entity. He therefore thought that, although there might be many considerations, these, too, might be taken into account.

The Indian Delegation's position was that the main parties in this matter were the peoples of Cyprus who were entitled to their freedom, and the British government, which at present held possession and authority over the island. Krishna Menon also stated that his government had asked him to say that, although India had been a sizable part of the British Empire, the mightiest known in modern times, it had, in establishing its independence, denounced acts of violence on either side. "We therefore subscribe neither to methods that go beyond the necessities of the ordinary maintenance of law and order or which exercise force in any way over subject peoples, nor to methods of terrorism that will never establish the independence of a people." For fifty years in his own country there had been groups of people who had thought there was a short cut to freedom. There was no short cut except in the organization of the masses behind the idea of national independence.

The Indian Delegation's abstention had not been due to any support of colonial rule or any desire to see a state of subjection, Krishna Menon explained. It was, first of all, due to the consideration that in the whole debate one had heard so much about the interests of Britain, Greece, and Turkey. So far as his delegation was concerned, the Greeks had come to the United Nations, as they had said, more or less representing the rights of the people of Cyprus in the same way as his government had brought before the United Nations the question of the people of Indian and Pakistani origin in South Africa. The Indian government at no time had said that these people were Indian nationals. They were not Indian nationals, and India would not accept them. It wanted them to remain in South Africa. They were South Africans. But India had come to the United Nations on this matter partly because of cultural, racial, or other affinities; partly because of its allegiance to the Charter; partly because of the violation of human rights; and because it thought this was a problem that might lead to very serious international complications in the future, and to racial conflicts. It regarded the fact that Greece had inscribed the item merely in that aspect and not as a territorial claim by Greece to Cyprus.

"What the Cypriot people will do when they are independent is not for us or for the United Nations to decide," Krishna Menon asserted further in an important passage not summed up in the official records.[24] "It is the essence of independence that people must make even their mistakes. If they do not make mistakes, often they do not make anything at all. So what happens in the future is not for us to decide. But any decision that has the odor, the color or anything of that kind of conditioning their alignment in a future way would be inconsistent with the whole conception of national independence."

It had not been easy for his delegation to refrain from taking part in the debate on a colonial question, Krishna Menon declared. But the greater part of the Cyprus question had been wrenched out of this context on account of past history. At the previous session, the question had been rehabilitated to its position of a colonial liberation. This liberation, apart from all these theories, could be established successfully and speedily only in modern conditions by the peaceful process of negotiation. Krishna Menon shared the hopes of the Mexican Delegation that it might be possible in the next day or two to find some method by which the United Nations would be able to speed up the process of peaceful negotiation, not for the purpose of putting off the day of Cypriot independence, but so that Cypriot national independence might become reality. Cyprus then would be able to take its place, even as other countries had done in recent times, "round these tables as a free and equal member of the comity of Nations."

What struck the Greek Delegation as particularly significant in the Indian representative's speech was the clarity and categorical character of his position concerning independence as an approach to the Cyprus problem. This time, Krishna Menon had made it abundantly clear that independence could not mean a limitation of the right of self-determination but, on the contrary, presupposed this right. A people should first become free, and afterward it would be free to choose the regime it preferred. The United Nations could be concerned only with the first aspect of the matter. The second—self-determination—was an affair of the people themselves. It was, at the same time, an inalienable right, as long as freedom had already been achieved. In the Greek Delegation's view, it should be added, the Indian attitude toward the Cyprus question had consisted throughout of two main features: First, was India's desire not to remain aloof from any anticolonial struggle; second, was its fear lest any UN resolutions on the Cyprus case, adopted on the basis of the principle of self-determination, establish a precedent that might have dangerous repercussions on the Kashmir question. As a way out, Krishna Menon had put forward the idea of independence for Cyprus.

After this explanation of vote which, to the ears of the Greek representatives, also sounded like the best possible argument against the Turkish proposal of partition for Cyprus, the Turkish allegation of a Greek territorial claim to Cyprus, and the Turkish arguments about the dangers of treaty revision, Ambassador Lodge spoke very laconically. The U.S. Delegation, he said, had abstained, having particularly in mind that the Cyprus problem involved the interests of three of its closest allies— Greece, Turkey, and Britain—and the people of Cyprus. Its abstention reflected the approach to the problem he had outlined in his speech on the item. He had pointed out then that Cyprus was not the kind of problem that could be solved by UN deliberations in the absence of agreement among the parties.

The explanations of vote of the representatives of Spain, Ceylon, and Iraq followed. De Lequerica said he had voted against the Greek sub-amendment, because he had favored the four-state amendments, as amended by his delegation. In the final vote, he had abstained in the hope that to do so might increase the chances of finding a solution and because he had doubted the wisdom of diminishing the chances of success by the deletion of a part of the text proposed in the four-state amendments. The result had been a division of the Committee. Only thirty-three countries had expressed themselves in favor of the Cypriot desires, whereas forty-five others had either voted against them or had abstained. From the UN point of view, to divide the Committee had been a tactical error. An atmosphere of concord and understanding should be created that might permit the Assembly to take a more unified point of view, satisfy the desires of the people of Cyprus, and express the respect owed to the Charter as well as to the states concerned in this question.

Gunewardene, of Ceylon, explained that this delegation's attitude had been an expression of confidence that the British government would rise to its responsibilities in the same spirit and with the same understanding it had displayed in the case of other countries having a colonial status. He upheld the principle of self-determination and was confident that in due course that principle could be applied to Cyprus. Since Cyprus was a Crown Colony, the only parties to the dispute were Britain and the people of Cyprus as a whole. Ceylon strenuously opposed the partition of Cyprus and hoped that the appointment of Sir Hugh Foot as Governor would mark a new and auspicious chapter in the history of Cyprus. As he had done in his speech during the debate, Gunewardene urged the British government to consider sending a royal commission to Cyprus, to carry out on-the-spot investigations with a view to hearing evidence from all Cypriots and to recommend a constitution insuring full self-government for Cyprus with adequate constitutional guarantees and safeguards for the protection of the Turkish minority. He was certain that Britain would take a definite step forward in the very near future to insure the independence of Cyprus. Gunewardene, the Greek delegation felt, seemed embarrassed because British pressure had compelled him to abstain from the vote.

Iraq's Permanent Representative to the UN, Ambassador Hashim Jawad, said his delegation had not taken part in the general discussion of the Cyprus question, the purpose of which had been to reassess the progress made. It had been anxious to hear the views of the parties concerned in order to reach a decision about future action to expedite the settlement of the dispute. In the light of the discussion, his delegation had examined the Greek draft resolution and had concluded that the draft as a whole did not completely reflect the real and objective facts of the situation. It had been satisfied that the four-state amendments improved the preamble but the text proposed for the operative part was further removed from the principle, which it considered to be an integral part of the case. Accordingly, it had supported the Greek subamendment. Iraq had the highest respect for the principle of self-determination, one of the pillars of the Charter and of the peace of the world. It recognized the legitimate right of people to exercise the right of self-determination and believed that the Cypriots as a whole, both of Greek and of Turkish origin, were entitled to a politically independent status in accordance with the principles of the Charter. It also believed that the United Nations should take action to facilitate the solution of the existing conflict and create conditions conducive to a final settlement, which should guarantee the freedom of the people of Cyprus and provide for a state constituted on democratic bases. In promoting the independent future of Cyprus in a free and democratic way, it was, however, essential for the parties concerned to provide all the constitutional and international guarantees to safeguard the rights and liberties of the Turkish minority. His delegation's vote (which had greatly angered the Turks and was to cost him his position as Permant Representative of Iraq to the UN) had been cast in the spirit of the Charter without forgetting Iraq's close and friendly relations with Britain, Turkey, and Greece, and, above all, in support of the peoples struggling for independence and freedom, as the Algerians were.

Noble, in explaining his vote, said that the British government bore the responsibility for the maintenance of law and order in Cyprus and was also vitally interested in the preservation of good relations "between our friends, Greece and Turkey." His delegation had voted against the Greek subamendment because it thought it would not only create a serious situation in Cyprus and elsewhere but also increase the difficulty of finding a solution to the problem that would be acceptable to all concerned. Because his delegation had been obliged to vote against the operative paragraph of the draft resolution as amended, it had been unable to support the paragraphs of the preamble. Although the British government supported the principle of self-determination, it thought that, in applying that principle, the special circumstances of each individual case ought to be taken fully into account. The principle should not create greater problems than it solved. In the case of Cyprus there were a large number of special circumstances and considerations of a particularly grave nature. He did not believe that the draft resolution which had just been adopted by a very small majority and which would be recommended to the Assembly for adoption disposed of those difficulties.

The Chairman: The representative of Greece has indicated a desire to speak. I must draw his attention to the fact that as the sponsor of the draft resolution, he cannot explain his vote.[25] However, if it was for a point of order, I can call on him.

Averoff-Tossizza assured him it was concerning a point of order that he wished to speak. He addressed to him his thanks, which, he was sure, were shared by the entire Committee. "You have guided these difficult and thorny discussions in a remarkably able manner." These thanks were the more valuable, he held, since they were addressed to a Chairman who belonged to a country that, unfortunately, had voted against the Greek draft resolution. This was additional evidence of his lack of bias and of his objectivity, which were superimposed on very great ability. The Greek representative also thanked the members of the Committee who, in taking part in the debate, had kept it at such a high level that it had been a real pleasure to follow it.

"We have now concluded the examination of the Cyprus question," the Chairman declared. "The Rapporteur will submit a report to the General Assembly upon the debate." He then went on to suggest the time schedule for the next meetings which were to be devoted to the discussion of the last item on the Committee's agenda—the Soviet item on "peaceful coexistence."

Generally, while the Greek Delegation was fully aware of the impossibility of getting the Assembly to pass the resolution recommended by the Committee, it immediately concentrated on the problem of what to do next. And it enjoyed a sense of elation, of victory. The Turks regarded the result of the voting in the Committee as a disaster for the further course of the Cyprus problem, Athens was informed. The British considered that the intransigence of both Greeks and Cypriots would increase because of this success. With their mere twenty votes, they had been humiliated.

This jubilation was publicly echoed in Nicosia and Athens. The *Times of Cyprus,* for instance, carried a headline GREECE WINS IN UN. In Athens, *To Vima,* a moderate Opposition paper, called the voting results a "moral victory," and termed the Committee's decision most encouraging for Cyprus and honorable for Greece. *Kathimerini,* a conservative, pro-government newspaper, underlined that this success had been achieved in the face of the opposition of countries that had often proclaimed their devotion to the principles of freedom, democracy, and justice. Tribute also was paid in the Greek press to the Foreign Minister for the ability with which he had handled the case and for his skill in defeating the procedural maneuvers of the British Delegation and its supporters.[26] The King and Queen conveyed to him their congratulations.

The results of the voting on the draft resolution on item 58, interestingly enough, had come quite close to those the Greek Delegation had forecast in a cable to Athens nine days before the vote was taken in the Committee. Then, 30–35 votes in favor had been predicted, with the actual number turning out to be 33; 27–30 negative votes had been expected, with the actual number falling below that estimate, at 20; and 17–27 abstentions had been predicted, with the actual number— 27—reaching the maximum foreseen.

The abstentions, the Greek Delegation realized, required more particular analysis. Five of the explanations of vote had, as seen above, referred to abstentions. It was natural, too, the Delegation acknowledged, that each of the interested parties should seek to present these abstentions as indications of a fundamentally favorable attitude toward its own viewpoint. Thus, the British and the Turks tended to regard the abstentions as given in favor of their views. The Greek Delegation, on its side, believed it useful to adopt the contrary interpretation. However, for its own guidance, it believed it necessary to have an objective picture of the situation.

Among the twenty-seven abstainers, two main political trends could be discerned. First, there were states sympathetically inclined to the idea of the liberation of peoples under colonial rule. Particular reasons, however, had prevented them from casting a favorable vote. Second, there were other states that would have preferred to vote against the principle of self-determination in the Cyprus issue but, for special reasons again, had found themselves incapable of doing so. India and most of the Asian states (Burma, Cambodia, Ceylon, Laos, the Federation of Malaya) belonged to the first category of abstaining states. To the second belonged the United States, which the Latin American states (Brazil, the Dominican Republic, Honduras, Nicaragua, Paraguay, Peru, Venezuela) would have imitated, had it decided to cast a negative vote. This was a matter that should not be ignored, the delegation noted, in making future estimates of the potentialities of the United Nations in dealing with the Cyprus question.

Chapter Twelve

December 14:
Anticlimax in the General Assembly

A. *Backstage at the UN*

On December 13, the Greek Foreign Minister called a meeting of all members of the delegation. The purpose: to take a decision about the further handling of the Cyprus question in the General Assembly. There were three alternative methods, it was ascertained during this conference, for dealing with the situation. The first could consist of finding a satisfactory compromise resolution acceptable to the Assembly. But no matter how favorable such a resolution might be from the Greek viewpoint, it would inevitably constitute a retreat when compared with the Committee's resolution, because, in order to widen the majority required in the Assembly (to two-thirds), it would be necessary to arrive at a compromise formula. Basically, the whole matter was whether it was better to be left without any Assembly resolution at all by having Committee's recommendation rejected in the Assembly through the lack of the required two-thirds majority than to get at least some resolution adopted.

Although during this conference neither the Foreign Minister nor other members of the delegation viewed sympathetically the prospect of abandoning the Committee's recommendation, nevertheless, because any decision on this matter inevitably would have to take into account a possible concrete compromise proposal that could be achieved, it was decided to listen to compromise proposals if they were offered, without making any commitments, and, more specifically to listen to the thoughts of de la Colina, the Mexican representative, who had informed not only the Committee but also the Permanent Greek Representative to the UN the day before that he intended to propose to the Greek Delegation certain satisfactory compromise solutions.

The second possible method for dealing with the issue when it came before the Assembly would be to seek a postponement of the Assembly's decision. Such a postponement was possible. There were precedents for such a tactic. At the previous Assembly, the Greek Delegation had given thought to such a move if its draft resolution were put to the vote and adopted by the Committee. Of course, the fierce opposition of the Turks and the British to a postponement of the Assembly's decision should be expected. Such a tactic, if successful, would result in the adoption of no resolution at all. Meanwhile, however, the recommendation of the Committee would remain in suspense—an unpleasant situation for the opponents. And, though remaining a mere recommendation, its legal survival would, in the Greek view, be assured. Both the Foreign Minister and other participants in the conference agreed that such a course was infinitely preferable to the others. In this way the expected rejection of this recommendation by the Assembly would be avoided, with several gains being made from the political and UN viewpoint. It was, nonetheless, decided to let Ethnarch Makarios have a decisive opinion in this matter as Athens, too, had so instructed. He would judge the whole question from the vital vantage point of Cyprus. If the Ethnarch agreed, then the Foreign Minister would undertake to wage one more hard battle in an effort to obtain a postponement of the Assembly's decision on the Committee's recommendation, with serious hopes of winning in spite of all the difficulties reckoned with.

The third possible method for dealing with the issue of the Committee's recommendation when it came before the Assembly would be to exert all efforts to preserve in the Assembly all the positive votes the draft proposal had gathered in the Committee. If, however, this course of action were taken, the Greek Delegation felt that there was a serious danger of seeing the number of these favorable votes reduced because of the political pressures the opponents were expected to exert in order to reverse partly or wholly the Committee's favorable verdict.

As soon as the Greek Delegation's conference was over, the Foreign Minister, accompanied by Permanent Representative to the UN, Palamas, met with Ethnarch Makarios and discussed the various courses of possible action. Averoff-Tossizza explained to Makarios his own views and those of his delegation as follows: If it was regarded that a good simple majority margin could be maintained in the Assembly, then one should go ahead. If, however, there was a risk of falling below a majority by more than three or four votes—in which case full defeat was not excluded—then one of the three possible courses outlined above should be followed. With regard to the first of these, he noted that the compromise proposal could be made through another delegation, for instance, with an amendment adding to the Committee's draft certain phrases that would give satisfaction to the Turkish minority in order to try to get the required two-thirds vote of the Assembly. Such an amendment could say many things as long as it did not impinge on the application of self-determination to Cyprus and left this principle absolutely clear of conditions and obligations.

With regard to the second possible course of action—trying to get a postponement of the Assembly's decision—Averoff-Tossizza noted that it would be difficult to achieve because the British and Turkish Delegations were unlikely to consent to such a proposal. In case of success, however, the capital gained in the Political Committee would remain intact.

Makarios categorically rejected the first and second solutions. He regarded it as impossible for the Greeks to gather fewer votes in the Assembly than the British and the Turks and expressed the desire that the Greek Delegation insist on a vote being taken on the Committee's recommendation. He himself assumed the responsibility for the consequences as long as the Greek government acted as a trustee or mandatory for Cyprus. The Ethnarch's objections to the first of the three possible courses of action were well taken and politically most persuasive, the Permanent Representative believed. He was less convinced, however, by Makarios' arguments against seeking a postponement of the Assembly's decision. One of these arguments was that the Delegation would be charged with not daring to do battle in the Assembly. The Permanent Representative believed that an effort to get a postponement should be made because this would assure for the Greek Delegation a better legal and political position in the United Nations than a course leading to rejection of the Committee's recommendation, which was a certainty. If this battle for a postponement failed, inevitably the point would be reached of having the Committee's proposal rejected by the Assembly. But, by trying first to get a postponement of the Assembly's decision, there was a hope of gaining something, and there was nothing to lose. The Greek Foreign Minister, at any rate, after having presented to Makarios his arguments in favor of such a course of action, insisted no longer. The Greek government, he felt, could not but take into account the opinion of Makarios and regard it as decisive.

When the members of the Greek Delegation, after these conferences, arrived at the United Nations, they noticed that an Anglo-Turkish attack in all directions was in full swing, with the Americans remaining strictly neutral. Even the traditional British efforts to preserve appearances and good manners seemed to have vanished in this offensive. The British Delegation had mobilized its entire personnel, its friends, its servants. In the corridor that led to the conference hall of the Political Committee which was now considering the Soviet item on "peaceful coexistence," and at a point that commanded the hall's entrance and exit, Commander Noble was stationed. Buttonholing the representatives of other member states who were passing by, he whispered to them, full of smiles, compliments, and promises, his government's messages concerning Cyprus. At some distance from Noble stood Sir Pierson Dixon who catechized those representatives who had escaped the Commander's cordon. As for another member of the British Delegation, P. M. Crosthwaite, he was observed running around giving instructions to auxiliary and lower ranking personnel to carry out this sort of lobbying among their opposite numbers in other delegations. The spectacle presented by the British Delegation apparently caused general mirth. Even friends and faithful commented on this all-out British vote-getting drive in scarcely concealed sarcastic tones.

Of course, the Greek Delegation officials were not insensitive to the serious dangers this British vote-getting campaign entailed for the course of the debate in the Assembly. They learned that the British government had expressed to its delegation its earnest regret at the defeat inflicted in the Committee the day before. This was not reassuring. If the entire British Delegation showed such activity in the United Nations, it was clear that the entire diplomatic armory of the United Kingdom and possibly of Australia and New Zealand, too, had been set in movement in order to alter in the Assembly the results of the vote in the Committee.

For these reasons, the Greek Foreign Minister undertook an immediate campaign in order to neutralize the frenetic activities of the British by all means available to Greece. On the one hand, all members of the Greek Delegation approached all their friends in the Assembly and asked them for their assistance. On the other, the Foreign Minister sent out a whole series of telegrams and cables to all Greek embassies and diplomatic and consular officials abroad, even to a certain number of honorary consuls who enjoyed some measure of influence, in order to contain those governments whose favorable attitude, he feared, might possibly change in the Assembly, and, if possible, to persuade certain others, whose representatives on the Committee had abstained, to change their attitude into an affirmative one.

To the corridor efforts of the Greek Delegation, the representatives of Guatemala (Arenales Catalan), of Bolivia (Quiroga Galdo), and Panama (Illueca) gave invaluable assistance. They worked with, and on, Latin American representatives in an effort to neutralize the unbearable British pressures. Friends of Greece among the Arab delegations made similar efforts. In this sector representative Stratos capitalized on the services he had rendered to them at various times in many matters of concern to the Arab states. His speech on the Syrian issue, it will be recalled, had stirred up some controversy.

All efforts exerted by the Greek Foreign Minister and members of the Delegation inside and outside the United Nations in order to counteract the massive British pressures on various delegations and governments cannot, of course, be enumerated. As examples of these efforts, though, it is worthwhile noting that the Foreign Minister, in talks with representatives of Latin American countries providing flags of convenience to Greek and other merchant shipping, invoked the prestige of the Greek shipowners. Also, he instructed the Greek diplomatic representative in Vienna to exert special efforts with the Ministry for Foreign Affairs to persuade Austria to change its abstention into a positive vote. Likewise, he cabled Kyrou in Stockholm to try to persuade the Swedish government to change its negative vote at least into an abstention. And, since the representative of Jordan had absented himself from voting in the Committee, the Foreign Minister cabled His All-Holiness Benedict, Patriarch of Jerusalem, to intercede with the King of Jordan in order to assure both Jordanian presence and a favorable vote in the Assembly.

Much less spectacular than the British efforts were those of the Turkish Delegation. Ambassador Sarper fell sick and remained in bed for a day. As learned later, he limited himself to requesting his government's intercession in order to achieve a change of vote on the part of certain countries and of Iraq, in particular (a Baghdad Pact ally), and to get two of the absentees, Jordan and Libya, to attend the Assembly and vote against the Committee's resolution.

In the afternoon of December 13, Mexico's Permanent Representative, de la Colina, the bearer of a compromise resolution said to have been approved by the U.S. Delegation, met his Greek colleague, Ambassador Palamas, and disclosed to him his proposal. This consisted of deleting the word "self-determination" from the Committee's resolution and replacing it with the words "of the provisions of the Charter," with indirect reference to negotiations "between the interested parties and the Cypriot people." Aware of the views of the Greek Foreign Minister and of Makarios on this matter, the Greek diplomat rejected this proposed amendment outright. His delegation, he emphasized, could make no substantive concession on the draft adopted by the Committee, he said. Asked whether the Greek Delegation might hope for a positive vote of Mexico in the Assembly, de la Colina replied he had requested his government's approval for such a vote but had received no answer yet. Confidentially he expressed surprise at his government's attitude, which was not in accord with the ideological line consistently followed by Mexico in questions involving the principle of self-determination. (The Greek representative wondered whether the ambition of the Mexican Foreign Minister, Padilla Nervo, to play some role in the matter of disarmament—he had proposed himself indirectly for the position of High Commissioner on Disarmament—had something to do with Mexico's unusual stand on the Cyprus question.)

Later that same afternoon, Ambassador Lodge, at his own request, met with the Greek Foreign Minister. He inquired about the Greek views concerning the course of the Cyprus question in the Assembly and about the various efforts made by several delegations to propose compromise draft resolutions. Averoff-Tossizza replied that a compromise resolution was impossible because his government considered indispensable the inclusion of the principle of self-determination in any proposal and the exclusion of any reference to three interested parties. The Turks, on the other hand, wanted exactly the opposite. It would be best to proceed to a vote without acrimonious debate, he stated. The Greek Delegation, he added, was gratified with the victory achieved in the Committee, whereas the Turkish Delegation would be relatively satisfied because the resolution passed by the Committee would not gather the required two-thirds vote in the Assembly. Thirdly, since the Committee's proposal was expected to gather approximately the same number of positive votes in the Assembly, the entire Cyprus cause would be well advanced. In this connection, Averoff-Tossizza expressed the hope that American neutrality would continue at this stage of the debate as well. From this conversation he derived the impression, though Lodge avoided expressing an opinion on the Greek attitude, that the State Department at least would prefer the unanimous adoption of a compromise resolution by the Assembly.

Informing Premier Karamanlis of these decisions and developments—the Premier was in Paris then for the upcoming summit NATO Council meeting—the Foreign Minister asked him for his views as soon as possible. The Turkish Delegation, he observed, which had requested the earliest possible debate on the Cyprus question in the Assembly, had now changed its mind and had asked that the debate be carried out in its normal order. This meant that the debate would probably take place on Saturday, at the Assembly's afternoon meeting. Evidently the Turks were waiting for the effects of backstage activities. If Sarper's sickness continued the next day, too, this would be useful for the Greek cause, because he was an able debater.

It should be added that next morning, at Lodge's instructions, Counsellor of the UN Delegation Norman Armour, Jr., met Permanent Greek Representative Palamas and told him that because there had been reports about a Greek intention to seek a postponement of the Assembly's decision on the Committee's proposal his delegation was profoundly disturbed. He wished to be assured that these reports were not true. The Turks, he added, on no account would accept such a measure, and the pursuit of a postponement on the part of the Greek Delegation would raise tension dangerously. Both Turkey and Britain, after their failure in the Committee, were anxiously awaiting the moment when its recommendation would be snuffed out by its expected failure to gather the required two-thirds vote in the Assembly. The Greek diplomat assured Armour it was not the Greek Delegation's intention at all to seek a postponement of the vote. In the Assembly the question would take its regular course.

That the U.S. Delegation would be instructed to abstain when the Committee's resolution came up for a vote in the Assembly was learned from Athens, where on December 13, U.S. chargé d'affaires Penfield assured the Greek government of this. It should not be concluded, he had added, however, that this abstention meant any change in American policy in the Cyprus question. The U.S. government continued to be firmly convinced that a solution to this problem could be found only through direct negotiations. In any eventual tripartite conference in which Britain would participate together with Spaak and an American official as observers, the Greek government could feel certain that, if the Turkish government insisted on partition of the island, it would find itself isolated.

Outside the forum of the United Nations certain violent happenings in Athens on December 13 added a new discordant note to Greek-American relations. At 1:05 and 1:25 A.M. at one of the barracks of the American airbase at Elliniko, three explosions, triggered by a clock mechanism, took place. They caused light damage to two generators of electric power. And at 1:45 A.M. other explosions occurred at the USIA Library on Stadium Street in Athens, causing significant damage to furniture and to books. The first reaction of the Greek police was that these almost simultaneous explosions together with the news of the last few days and reports concerning the supposed acceptance by Greece of certain NATO bases were indications of possible Communist activity, without excluding, however, other motives.

George V. Allen, now Director of the USIA in Washington, conveyed this news to the Greek Foreign Minister by phone, reading to him the relevant cable. The Foreign Minister immediately instructed the Washington Embassy to express the regrets of both his government and himself to the State Department. He requested that it be emphasized that such activities were not in accordance with the customs of the Greek people and that these incidents should be attributed to subversive elements that desired to stir up passions and create problems.

In Athens, the following day, U.S. chargé d'affaires Penfield called on the Premier's deputy and handed him a note of protest in which the U.S. government expressed its anxiety about these explosions, which, he stated, had created a deep impression in the United States. His government expected the Greek government to make every effort to apprehend and punish the persons responsible for these criminal acts and believed that for the sake of the common interests and the close friendship that existed between Greece and the United States, the Greek government would take all possible measures to prevent any further regrettable incidents of this sort.

The U.S. chargé d'affaires added that his government could not view such incidents without relating them to statements made before the Assembly by the Greek representative, who had spoken unfavorably about the American representative.[1] The latter, he observed, had been acting on the instructions of the U.S. government, which aimed at promoting understanding on matters that were of concern both to the people of Cyprus and to some of America's closest allies. The American shock at the unfortunate incidents that had occurred was all the greater, because the U.S. attitude of abstention on the Greek proposal was the very attitude that the Greek Prime Minister himself had requested from the United States. Penfield, in conclusion, expressed his government's regret that the Greek government had deemed it necessary to proceed on December 11 to a verbal protest to the United States on the groundless charge about a supposed "hostile" American attitude in the Assembly.[2]

On Monday, December 16, Counsellor Kavalieratos of the Greek Embassy in Washington called on Rountree at the State Department and conveyed the message of the Greek Foreign Minister, which also dealt with Penfield's *démarche* in Athens. In reply, Rountree explained that the chargé d'affaires in Athens had not intended to mean that the statements of the Foreign Minister in the Assembly had provoked the explosive incidents in Athens. Penfield had only been instructed to proceed with both topics at the same meeting. Rountree also emphasized that the U.S. position, presented by Ambassador Lodge in the Assembly, had not been a new one. On the contrary, it had been repeatedly made known to the Greek government. The Greek diplomat, on his side, repeated the argument that the reason for the Greek protest of December 11 had been the public presentation of the American attitude before the Committee, which would lead many other delegations to assume an attitude unfavorable to the Greek viewpoint. Rountree countered by expressing appreciation for this explanation but insisted that Lodge had been speaking as a representative of his government. Exactly for that reason, Kavalieratos replied, the Foreign Minister had regarded it as bad to address himself directly to Lodge in his criticism. The American official, at any rate, expressed the hope that in spite of these frictions, these were matters that belonged to the past. In future everything possible would be done to avoid any further friction in American-Greek relations. The outcome of the debate in the United Nations, he said further, could not prevent a practical effort from being made toward achieving a solution of the Cyprus problem. The Greek diplomat responded by expressing the view that the moral victory achieved would contribute to Britain's taking wiser counsels and coming up with a proposal for a constructive solution.

It was not the first time, it should be noted, that anti-United States demonstrations had taken place in Greece in connection with the UN decision-making in the Cyprus question. At the time of the first debate of this question, on December 14, 1954, demonstrations had occurred in both Athens and Thessaloniki because of the U.S. attitude toward the first Greek appeal to the United Nations over Cyprus. In Thessaloniki, demonstrators had publicly burned British and American flags and had destroyed equipment, books, and display cases of the USIA. As a result, the Greek government, on December 16, 1954, had banned all pro-Cyprus demonstrations.[3]

B. The General Assembly Rejects the Committee's Recommendation

Meanwhile, the debate in the Assembly had taken place in the afternoon of Saturday, December 14. Shortly before it began, a member of the British Delegation was observed triumphantly pushing forward to his seat the representative of the Union of South Africa, who usually absented himself from Assembly meetings on political matters because of the question of apartheid, and, accordingly, had taken no part at all in the voting on the Cyprus issue in the Political Committee. At the very last moment, however, this member of the British Delegation had managed to fish him out and had brought him into the Assembly hall in order to have him vote against the Committee's recommendation. "I brought in the South African," he cried triumphantly to Ambassador Sarper, who gratefully waved his hand.

At about the same time, Noble had managed to isolate the representative of Ghana in a supreme effort to get him to abstain from voting. The Greek Foreign Minister, however, was already aware of the British pressures on the Delegation of Ghana. Patiently he waited until the Ghanaian's freedom of movement was restored, and then, for a few moments, he managed to speak to him before the meeting began. To the African's question of whether Greece would accept a solution of independence for Cyprus, after which the Cypriot people could decide in sovereignty about its further fate, Averoff-Tossizza answered in the affirmative. He promised to make such an assurance from the rostrum of the Assembly. Thus, at the last moment the greatly endangered vote of Ghana was assured for the Greek side.[4]

In the Assembly no debate occurred.[5] Only explanations of vote were given before or after the vote was taken. Before the voting started the Greek Foreign Minister asked to be the last speaker.

The *rapporteur* of the Political Committee, Ambassador Franz Matsch, Permanent Representative of Austria to the UN, before stating that the First Committee recommended its draft resolution to the Assembly for adoption, reported that the debate in the Committee again had shown the complexity of the Cyprus problem because of the special circumstances involved. The overwhelming majority of the representatives, he said, had expressed concern that more progress had not been made toward a solution of the problem since the adoption of Resolution 1013 (XI). They had felt that in view of the serious situation on the island of Cyprus, a solution should be found as soon as possible. However, different opinions had been expressed concerning the manner in which the Assembly might contribute to the achievement of a solution. A large number of representatives had contended that it would not suffice merely to repeat the ideals embodied in Resolution 1013 (XI). They had emphasized the need for the Assembly to set up an outline for negotiations between Britain and the representatives of the people of Cyprus with a view to having the right of self-determination of peoples applied in the case of the people of Cyprus. Other delegations, on the other hand, had maintained that the Assembly, in view of the special circumstances existing in the case of Cyprus, should not in any way prejudice further negotiations between Britain, Greece, Turkey, and the representatives of the people of Cyprus. They had therefore suggested that the Assembly should express the wish that by such negotiations a solution would be found in conformity with the principles of the Charter, which include the principle of self-determination.

The Permanent Representative of Ghana to the UN, Daniel A. Chapman, spoke next. Throughout the discussions in the Committee on the Cyprus question, the sympathies of his country, he said, were with the point of view advocating the application of the principle of self-determination for the people of Cyprus. His delegation's understanding of the principle, as applied to Cyprus, was that the island's people would have the right to independence, to be followed by whatever decision they might choose to take regarding their future association with other states. He had had the opportunity of reading the record of the final statements, particularly in the explanations of votes made by various delegations, and he had sought clarification of various points made in those statements.

Now a doubt had arisen in the mind of the Ghana Delegation, which he would like the representative of Greece to clear up. Was it correct that self-determination meant, for the Greek Delegation, *enosis* or the annexation of Cyprus by Greece, without Cyprus' first being afforded the opportunity to attain independence, so that it would be free to take a decision, as a sovereign state, with regard to annexation by Greece or the entering of any other type of association with other countries? In voting in the Committee in favor of the draft resolution now before the Assembly, the understanding of the Ghana Delegation had been that the application of the right of self-determination to the people of Cyprus would lead to negotiations between the representatives of the people of Cyprus and the British government on steps to be taken toward granting independence to Cyprus. An independent Cyprus, eligible for membership in the United Nations, would then be, in his view, sufficiently free and sovereign to carry a step further the exercise of its right to self-determination, if it so wished, and enter into whatever association it desired with other states. If this view of the Delegation of Ghana was shared by the Greek Delegation, it would vote for the draft resolution. Otherwise it would abstain.

Dr. Al-Shabandar, of Iraq, stated that, as explained in the Political Committee, his delegation, consistent in its stand of upholding the principle of self-determination in all questions discussed and voted upon by the Assembly, had voted for the draft resolution on Cyprus that supported this principle, one of the most important aims of the Charter. It realized, however, that self-determination was not by itself a solution to as complex and as difficult a problem as that of Cyprus. There was an important Turkish minority that had to be taken into account in any final solution. The views and circumstances of the Turks on Cyprus had to be given due weight, and their rights and welfare had to be respected in accordance with the principles of the Charter and international law and also in the interest of good international relations, without which no solution to this question could be attained. The problem was of greatest importance to Greece, Britain, and Turkey, as well as to the entire world. His delegation believed that, given time, patience, and the good will of the parties concerned, this question would be solved according to the principles of the Charter and to the satisfaction of all. Such a solution would not only relieve the world of one of its difficulties but would also contribute very much to the welfare of the population of Cyprus and restore the friendliest relations between nations.

Iraq, Al-Shabandar continued, took special interest in seeking and hoping for a friendly and just solution, because it had very friendly feelings for the people of Cyprus, whose welfare and prosperity should be the most important consideration in the problem. It also entertained the friendliest of relations with Turkey, Britain, and Greece, and certainly would not wish to do anything against its allies nor would it want to harm friends. His delegation did not see how a radical solution could be found and implemented if the present difficulties were not overcome. It believed that unless and until all parties concerned reached agreement, the Cyprus question would remain one of the most important problems of the United Nations and threaten the safety and security of the Middle East as well as that of the whole world. For these reasons, his delegation did not believe that the draft resolution before the Assembly could really contribute to a solution of the problem. Mindful of the difficulties and complexities of the problem and aware of the number of the parties concerned, it believed that "direct, quiet, and friendly negotiations" could lead to a practical and acceptable solution. His delegation therefore at this stage would be unable to support the draft resolution. This, of course, would in no way change its stand concerning its belief in self-determination.

Speaking for the Pakistani Delegation, Minister Plenipotentiary Agha Shahi intervened to make his position clear on the draft resolution on the Cyprus question the Committee had recommended. This draft resolution favored applying the right of self-determination to the people of Cyprus but, he feared, did not take all due account of the legitimate rights and interests of all national groups in Cyprus and especially of the Turkish population whose right to exercise self-determination had not been adequately safeguarded. The wording, he contended (repeating one of the Turkish arguments), was not in full conformity with Article 1, paragraph 2, of the Charter, which enjoined respect for the principle "of equal rights and self-determination of peoples." Had the draft resolution been faithful to the Charter's wording, his delegation would have voted in its favor because it was a strong supporter of the principle of self-determination. When, however, it looked at the resolution as a whole, it felt, in this particular case, that it would not be conducive to a just and peaceful solution of the problem. His delegation could not, in good conscience, become a party to a resolution that gravely prejudiced the interests of the Cypriot Turks in the negotiations between the parties concerned on the future international status of the island. By declaring, in effect, that the right of self-determination was for the benefit of the Cypriot Greeks alone, the draft resolution imperiled the human rights and legitimate aspirations of the second most important national group in Cyprus. He did not impugn in the slightest the motives and intentions of those who had supported the draft resolution in the Committee, but he feared that the consequences flowing from the draft resolution adopted by the Committee might well be different from those intended.

Some representatives, the Pakistani continued, had emphasized that minority rights could be protected through constitutional safeguards. He would, however, like to point out that a constitution does not exist in a vacuum. In the last analysis, sovereignty, under any democratic Constitution, had to reside with the majority. No constitutional guarantees could ever alter this inescapable truth. In this context, it should not be forgotten that the Turko-Greek estrangement in Cyprus was unhappily rooted in the past, and it was not possible to remedy such a situation by applying safeguards which were more properly applicable to fully constituted states of a different variety. In the view of the Pakistani Delegation, the Committee's resolution oversimplified the solution of the problem. It was weighted against the legitimate rights and aspirations of the Cypriot Turks. Unless the balance were redressed, his delegation would be compelled to vote against it, as it had in the Committee.

José Serrano, Ambassador and Permanent Representative of Chile to the UN, now stated why his delegation had voted against the draft resolution approved by the Committee and would do so again. His delegation, he recounted, had sponsored, together with the Delegations of Canada, Denmark, and Norway, amendments to the Greek draft resolution which, it considered, provided a more realistic approach to the question. These were also more likely to gain unanimous approval, in that both the preambular and the operative parts strictly adhered to the general principles of the Charter. His delegation had no objection whatsoever to the principle of self-determination or its liberal application, and the other sponsors of the amendments had been quite clear on this point too. However, it did consider that the Cyprus problem could not be solved by the application of this principle alone with disregard to the other provisions of the Charter or the treaties in force.

Belaunde, speaking for Peru, declared that it had been his delegation's consistent policy in dealing with political problems to bring about conciliation, create conditions favorable to a solution satisfactory to all parties, and, as much as possible, avoid technical terms that might lend themselves to varying applications or interpretations or, worse still, to dangerous partiality. It therefore had tried to find a formula that would go a step further than Resolution 1013 (XI) and thus lead to a solution of the complex problem that might reconcile the interests of the inhabitants, both Greek and Turkish, of Cyprus with the important interests and responsibilities of Britain on the island and with the interests and rights of the Turkish minority. Unfortunately, these attempts at conciliation had failed, and that failure had shown once again that the best policy for the Assembly in problems of this kind was to seek a solution acceptable to the parties concerned. After the failure of this attempt, "we have arrived, by means of an interesting debate and the intelligent application of parliamentary procedures, at the proposal now submitted by the Committee for the General Assembly's approval." The Peruvian Delegation, he said, had serious objections to this draft resolution. It commended the Greek Delegation for having accepted the first three amendments "generously submitted" by Canada, Chile, Denmark, and Norway. In the fourth amendment, however, as adopted by the Committee, there was no mention of the need for all parties concerned to take part in the negotiations and discussions. Moreover, the principle of self-determination was overemphasized and applied without any reservations or reference to the principles of the Charter. In all conscience, therefore, the Peruvian Delegation, Belaunde concluded, could not vote in favor of the draft resolution submitted. Since, however, it felt that every possible effort should be made to find a conciliatory solution, it would abstain, as it had done when the resolution had been discussed in the Committee.

The representative of another Latin American country spoke next. Alfonso Araujo, Ambassador and Permanent Representative of Colombia to the UN, affirmed his country's unswerving adherence to the principle of respect for, and the inviolability of, public treaties, and its policy of supporting the rights of peoples to determine their own form of government and their future status. In taking political decisions, the Assembly, in his view, should give impartial consideration to all the factors involved in each problem, neither excluding nor emphasizing any particular one so that none of the parties directly concerned might feel discriminated against and thereby prevented from negotiating or settling the differences at issue. Since the conciliatory four-state amendments had been prompted by these same considerations, the Colombian Delegation had been prepared to vote in favor of them. Because, however, the draft resolution now before the Assembly departed from that conciliatory spirit, it would vote against it. In conclusion, he expressed the earnest hope that the Cyprus question would meet with a speedy and peaceful solution acceptable to all parties concerned and would promote the happiness and welfare of the entire population of that island.

Ambassador Sarper stated his delegation would vote against the draft resolution presented by the Committee. He would not tax the Assembly's patience by repeating what he had several times said about that draft resolution's real meaning during the Committee debate. In voting against it, the Turkish Delegation was conscious that the draft resolution, if adopted, would not only be unjust but would add further and serious complications to the existing complexity of the Cyprus question. He therefore hoped that the Assembly would not support the draft resolution, bearing primarily in mind the interest "we all have, in our hearts and minds, in a solution; we must leave the door open to efforts made in good will and in a spirit of cooperation conducive to a settlement acceptable to all concerned and in the best interests of the United Nations as a whole."

Argentina's Permanent Representative to the UN, Mariano J. Drago, explained that his delegation had abstained in the vote on the draft resolution adopted by the Committee in the hope that the states concerned in the Cyprus question would arrive at a conciliatory resolution. Since unfortunately this had not been the case, he felt that the absolute terms of the draft resolution approved in the Committee would not help to insure the continuation of negotiations in an atmosphere of calm. This vote, however, in no way altered Argentina's cordial and friendly feelings toward the government and people of Greece.

Averoff-Tossizza came next. He would first say a few words about the significance of the vote as it affected the Cyprus question. Then he would briefly deal with the vote in general. He did not want to go into the details of the long debate on Cyprus in the Political Committee. Nevertheless, he felt it necessary to emphasize, and at the outset, what his delegation had made clear during that debate, namely that the Assembly was making a decision of principle. "We are not deciding how or when it should be applied." That was a fundamental element of this vote, he contended.

What we must ask ourselves is whether, in voting for the application of the principle to Cyprus, we are helping to achieve a practical solution. I firmly believe we are . . . because . . . the great majority of the people of Cyprus is willing to negotiate and discuss all aspects of the problem in an atmosphere of good will but only on one fundamental prior condition, namely that it is decided that the principle of self-determination will one day be applied. How can it be said, therefore, that we are making it impossible to reach a solution when we vote so that the prior condition, stipulated by the people, is established and the negotiations can be carried on?

It had been said in the building, he continued, not by delegations—he did not know by whom—that the decision taken by the Committee would cost a thousand lives in Cyprus. On the contrary, that the Committee had taken the decision it had, had already restored calm in Cyprus. According to the *New York Times* of that same day, Greek Cypriots had hailed as a victory the vote in the United Nations on the Cyprus issue,[6] and the island had had its quietest day since the previous Saturday. After the United Nations had taken its decision, the island's new Governor had been able to visit the narrower streets in Nicosia, and had been acclaimed and embraced by the people "who await your decision." That was how that decision—a decision of principle—promoted cooperativeness and a peaceful and agreed solution of the question.

The debate in the Committee—held at a high level that merited congratulations—had sufficiently clarified the situation. Although he did not want to keep on talking about the Cyprus question, the Greek Foreign Minister declared, he wished, nevertheless, to say a word or two about the meaning "of our vote." It was his heartfelt conviction that this was a historic moment for the United Nations. This would be the first time in twelve years that the United Nations had taken a definite stand on the application of the principle of self-determination. It was really a historic moment, for, though the United Nations over the previous twelve years had achieved great things in the field of economic co-operation in the technical and in other fields, and though it had already solved some very serious international crises, it had, nevertheless, avoided taking a stand on certain questions of principle and was now doing so today, for the first time.

On the basis of the explanations made before the Assembly, he did not know what the result of the vote in the plenary meeting would be. But he did know that the vote in the Committee had been a victory in itself and a proof that the United Nations was reaching maturity and that blood shed at its founding and the hopes placed in it were not in vain.

At this point, the Greek Foreign Minister digressed to answer "yes" without the slightest doubt to the question asked earlier by the representative of Ghana whether the Greek government agreed that Cyprus, before deciding on its fate, might become an independent state.[7]

About the meaning of his delegation's vote, Averoff-Tossizza then said he would like to say a few words more. The other day, he had had the bad idea—and he apologized for it—of appealing to the members, saying he was the advocate of this question, the advocate of principle, and that he was alone and had no racial family.[8] Now he had to admit that he did belong to a family and that this family was stronger than all others—the family of right and justice. It had given him the support of the thirty-three states that had voted for the Greek draft resolution in the Committee. And both the favorable votes and the abstentions on that draft resolution revealed the odd spectacle of former colonies of European countries now helping the last European people under colonial domination to achieve their freedom. But the decisive hour had come; the time for polemics past. "The time had come for us to shoulder our responsibilities: we shall discharge them by the way we vote."

Noble then said a few words in view of the Greek Foreign Minister's statement. His delegation had tried to approach the discussion of the Cyprus question in a constructive spirit. Britain was responsible for the administration of the island. Problems connected with it fell mainly on Britain's shoulders. His government most earnestly wanted to find a solution acceptable to all concerned for the dispute about the future of Cyprus. Its record elsewhere showed that it could do this if it received the co-operation of the others concerned. His government believed there was room for compromise. It had tried and would continue to try to find one. It was in that spirit that at the outset of the proceedings in the Committee his delegation had given a progress report on developments in the ten months since the Resolution 1013 (XI) had been passed. He had done his utmost to make this report objective and uncontentious. He had showed that there had been some progress, that tension had eased on the island, and that in spite of setbacks, diplomatic contacts on the subject were continuing with the Greek and Turkish governments. This progress, he believed should be consolidated. With further efforts and good will all around a solution could be found.

The representative of the United States, Noble stressed, had spoken for many when he had said that "we here should not try to impose a solution to this problem in the absence of agreement between those directly concerned." His delegation agreed that quiet diplomacy was required and that the United Nations should encourage procedures that would lead to this. He believed that many delegations did in fact share this view. It was evident, however, that the Greek Delegation did not. It had rejected all suggestions for a quiet debate and a moderate solution. It had sought to gain support for an extremist solution to the problem. In the debate, a vote had been avoided on the constructive middle-of-the-road amendments put forward by Canada, Chile, Denmark, and Norway. The Assembly had also heard the high principle of self-determination invoked in order to achieve *enosis*. That was the answer he would give to the question the representative of Ghana had put, and members would note that it differed from the answer given by the Greek Foreign Minister. He knew that many delegations had felt that UN procedures were being used rather cynically to promote a cause that was not openly avowed and would not be supported if it were.

The British Delegation, Noble emphasized, was strongly opposed to the draft resolution accepted in the Committee. He had given the reasons for this in the Committee and would now do no more than allude to them very briefly. In his delegation's view, the United Nations should not try to lay down the lines on which the Cyprus question should be solved. Still less should it do so in a one-sided manner and ignore the other aspects of a complex and difficult issue. Which side of the problem did the draft resolution approved in the Committee bring out? It brought out the distortion of the principle of equal rights and self-determination of peoples—a distortion under which a campaign had for so long been waged on behalf of *enosis*. The draft resolution—which, incidentally, employed language that did not figure in the Charter—was therefore totally unacceptable to his government. Its adoption by the United Nations could only serve to inflame an already dangerous dispute.

In this important matter, said the President of the Assembly, Sir Leslie Munro, if the Turkish representative wished to reply, he was prepared, with the Assembly's assent, to let him do so. Ambassador Sarper, however, withdrew his question on a point of order.

"We can now proceed to vote on the draft resolution recommended by the First Committee in its report," said the President. "The representative of the United Kingdom has asked for a vote by roll-call." Australia, having been drawn by lot by the President, was called upon to vote first.

The result of the vote was 31 in favor, 23 against, with 24 abstentions. The draft resolution was not adopted, since it had failed to obtain the required two-thirds majority.

The detailed results of the roll-call vote were as follows:

For: Albania, Bolivia, Bulgaria, Byelorussia, Costa Rica, Czechoslovakia, Ecuador, Egypt, El Salvador, Ethiopia, Ghana, Greece, Guatemala, Haiti, Hungary, Iceland, Indonesia, Ireland, Lebanon, Panama, Poland, Romania, Saudi Arabia, Sudan, Syria, Tunisia, Ukraine, U.S.S.R., Uruguay, Yemen, Yugoslavia.

Against: Argentina, Australia, Belgium, Canada, Chile, Colombia, Denmark, Dominican Republic, France, Iran, Italy, Luxembourg, Netherlands, New Zealand, Nicaragua, Norway, Pakistan, Portugal, Spain, Sweden, Turkey, Union of South Africa, United Kingdom.

Abstaining: Afghanistan, Austria, Brazil, Burma, Cambodia, Ceylon, China, Federation of Malaya, Finland, Honduras, India, Iraq, Israel, Japan, Laos, Liberia, Mexico, Nepal, Paraguay, Peru, Philippines, Thailand, United States, Venezuela.

Cuba, Jordan, Libya, and Morocco had absented themselves. The Greek delegation had no explanation for these absences, which, as far as the Muslim states were concerned, may have been due to a desire to avoid the embarrassment of a public decision that deviated from the voting behavior of the Arab bloc, because of economic dependence on the West.[9]

A comparison between this vote and the vote in the Political Committee reveals that in the Assembly, Argentina and Spain changed their attitudes from abstentions to negative votes; that Iraq changed its affirmative vote to an abstention; that Morocco, which had voted affirmatively in the Committee, absented itself; and, finally, that the Union of South Africa, absent during the Committee vote, had cast a negative vote.

Before the Assembly turned its attention to the next item, Noble asked to bear with him again just for a moment. As the representative of the government responsible for the administration of Cyprus, he naturally welcomed the failure of the draft resolution which, as he had already said, was a one-sided and misleading proposal. Its endorsement would, in his view, have led to increased tension in Cyprus and elsewhere and would have made even more difficult the solution of what was already a complex problem. He thought that the Assembly's decision was a wise one.

"But where do we stand now? I think this is something we must all be clear about," the British representative continued. "Ten months ago a resolution was adopted unanimously at the eleventh session [1013 (XI)] calling for an atmosphere of peace and freedom of expression, and the resumption and continuance of negotiations for a peaceful, democratic and just solution, in accordance with the Purposes and Principles of the Charter." That resolution stood. The British government had sought to give effect to it. It believed that since its passage there had been some progress—though not enough. This could only be done—and he would emphasize this—with the co-operation of all concerned. To this task, he could pledge the most sincere and earnest efforts of Her Majesty's government. Few disputes had been so painful to his government as this one over Cyprus. It involved the happiness and welfare of the inhabitants of the island and Britain's relations with two valued friends and allies. "We in the United Kingdom want to see the question solved and the United Kingdom Government will do everything in its power to work toward a solution."

The Greek Foreign Minister: "I wish to repeat a phrase just uttered by the United Kingdom representative. 'Few disputes,' he said, 'have been so painful to us'." This dispute was also very painful to the whole Greek nation, Averoff-Tossizza declared. However, there could be no question of betraying the mandate of the people of Cyprus. That was why his government had dealt with this painful question and was unshakably determined to pursue it. He wished to assure the Assembly that its vote, though not a conclusive decision, constituted a step toward the solution all desired. That thirty-three representatives in the Political Committee and thirty-one in the Assembly had voted for the application of the principle of self-determination, while twenty-five had refused to vote against it, indicated the existence of a moral force which would be appreciated by all and would certainly contribute to a solution of the problem. He thought that even with this vote, "whether you voted in favor or whether you abstained, you have made a very important contribution, for which I consider it my duty to thank you most sincerely on behalf of the people of Cyprus."

In these final remarks, it should be noted, the Greek Foreign Minister did not commit himself to a new recourse to the Assembly's next session, as he had done at the previous session of the Assembly,[10] if no solution had been meanwhile achieved.

Outside the Assembly hall, Ethnarch Makarios, who had taken upon himself the responsibility of having the Greek draft resolution put to the test of a vote in the Assembly, declared that the majority of the United Nations both in the Political Committee and the Assembly had recognized the right of the Cypriot people to self-determination. This event, in his view, constituted a moral victory and a tremendous step forward toward a favorable outcome of the Cyprus question. Because of the powerful reaction of the colonial powers and the strong pressure they had exerted on various delegations, the majority required in the Assembly had not been obtained. This, however, in no way lessened the significance of the victory achieved, which was a blow against colonialism. He did not doubt that the colonial regime of Cyprus would soon be ended, because that was the will and determination of the Cypriot people which would not cease struggling until they achieved the application of the right of self-determination on their island. He wished to emphasize the clever handling of the Cyprus question on the part of the Greek Delegation and, more particularly, of Foreign Minister Averoff-Tossizza, who had defended the rights of the Cypriot people with courage and ability.

In Cyprus itself, on the other hand, another general strike was called on December 16, as a mark of dissatisfaction with the Assembly's rejection of the Greek draft resolution. It passed, however, without serious incidents [11]—which had not been the case with previous protests about UN resolutions on the Cyprus question. A "Cyprus Airways" car was set on fire in Nicosia and some British military cars were stoned at Morfou.[12]

C. The Greek Mission to the UN Evaluates the UN Struggle

It could not be doubted in good faith that the Greek Delegation and the Foreign Minister personally had scored a first rate political success in this struggle on the Cyprus issue at the twelfth General Assembly, the Permanent Mission of Greece to the UN reported to Athens several days later. This success had been even more astonishing both because it had been achieved within an unfavorable political climate and because it was disproportionate to the capabilities and political potential of Greece. Of course, it was acknowledged, the justice of the Cypriot cause had been a factor in this success. But it had been but one among many others, for justice in the United Nations constituted always a very relative and limited factor.

The political climate prevailing at the twelfth Assembly had been vastly different from that of the previous session. At the eleventh Assembly, the attack of Britain and France on Egypt and Israel's aggression had excited anticolonial passions and hardened the position of the anticolonialists against the two above-mentioned colonial powers. At the same time, the relations of those two powers with the United States had been tense. At the twelfth Assembly, on the other hand, this favorable atmosphere for the promotion of anticolonial causes had changed, even though the Algerian question had helped maintain the cohesion of the Arab states and of certain Asian and African states. U.S.-British relations had radically improved and the co-operation between the U.S. and British delegations to the United Nations had been restored, again becoming as close as it had been in the past, before the Suez affair. The United States had helped Britain in the Oman question, and in the Assembly the two delegations had been in constant consultation for the purpose of harmonizing their respective stands. Because of the Syrian crisis and the Soviet Delegation's attitude, a cold war atmosphere had been created. This had affected many delegations, especially Latin American ones. Therefore there was some restraint on their part in supporting, on anticolonial items, for example, views the U.S.S.R. also supported. Because, too, of the Syrian crisis, the Turkish factor had been strengthened. The United States had waged a battle in the defense of Turkey even though this might not have been to the liking of some delegations, especially of certain Asian-African ones. However, as all acknowledged, this American attitude had constituted a positive gain for Turkey. Indeed, in the corridors of the United Nations, the twelfth Assembly had been called the "Turkish session."

As a result of such an international political climate, Greece, in the Cyprus question, had to face two strengthened opponents. In this very unfavorable situation, the only Greek reaction had been the position taken by the Greek Delegation in the debate on the Syrian crisis. The Greek representative's speech on that occasion had forced American officials to realize that their policy vis-à-vis Greece, which was closely linked to their support of Turkey in the Cyprus question, could not be ignored without danger of damage for the Western bloc.

Other unfavorable factors, in the Greek Mission's view were: the failure of the disarmament debates (the withdrawal of the Soviet Delegation from the disarmament committee and its refusal to return to it even after the West had broadened that committee's composition). This attitude certainly was not unrelated to the launching of the sputnik, on October 4, which testified to the uncontrovertible technological progress of the U.S.S.R. and to the U.S. lag in this particular field. The result had been a greater tension in the cold war. All in all, an atmosphere of vague anxiety had pervaded the halls of the United Nations at the twelfth Assembly, and this had generated a sense of great restraint which, in turn, meant difficulties in the way of bold decisions.

A strictly objective judgment, in the Greek Mission's estimate, would attribute the success achieved in the Cyprus question, in spite of the unfavorable political climate that prevailed, to three factors mainly: First, to the good preparation of the case on the Greek side and to the personality of the Foreign Minister himself who had won general sympathy and had demonstrated great courage at critical moments, as well as a remarkable tenacity and maneuvering capacity. Second, to the tactical mistakes of the adversaries who complacently had relied on their superiority and on American support beyond any permissible bounds. Third, to the indubitable fact that Greece, though a very small state, had been able to generate considerable influence because of its historical and moral tradition. When Greece was expressed as a faith, as an idea, as a human condition, and as an eternal value, the Greek Mission felt, it constituted a capital of unlimited potential.

In the purely political sphere, the following points were noteworthy, in the Mission's view. The factor of the United States presented two interesting aspects. With regard to the Greek attitude toward the United States, while the overwhelming majority of Greeks were agreed that maintaining friendship with America was imperative, the current crisis over the Cyprus question had proved that preventing the United States from making mistakes at the expense of Greece depended to a great extent on the handling of Greek-American relations on the part of the Greek government. The second fundamental aspect in the U.S. factor was that the American attitude toward the Cyprus question had not fundamentally changed. Had the abstention of the U.S. Delegation from the voting constituted a manifestation of a positive turn toward neutrality, then the entire position of the Cyprus problem would have been altered in a very favorable fashion. This has not been the case, however, even though for more general reasons both the Foreign Minister and the Greek press had created the impression that the Americans, by their abstention, had aided the Greek Delegation in getting the majorities obtained. The fact had been that the U.S. Delegation had unwillingly abstained, having been forced to do so (no matter how incredible this might appear) by the tactics of the Greek Delegation and by the psychological situation created in the Assembly. Lodge, in the interpretation of his delegation's vote, had left no room for doubt that his government's policy in the Cyprus question remained the same as it had been before, and that it continued to be aligned with the Anglo-Turkish views. The American abstention had thus been clearly an incidental event.

The above analysis, the Greek Mission believed, was of basic importance in preparing plans for the further handling of the Cyprus question. Incidental and accidental factors were not likely to be repeated. Only the permanent factors remained. It was up to the Greek government to face this matter in the way it considered most expedient. Without a change in the attitude of the United States toward the Cyprus question, the course of this issue within the framework of the Western Alliance remained more than problematic.

Another factor of major political importance, in the Greek Mission's evaluation of the handling and outcome of the Cyprus issue in the Assembly, had been the attitude of the main European states, most of them NATO allies. This attitude, too, presented two interesting aspects: First, these states had voted against the draft resolution that referred to self-determination for Cyprus. This was a much graver matter than seemed at first glance. Such a negative vote on the part of these states had been registered in the United Nations for the first time. On previous occasions, the colonial powers and their satellites in this particular issue had expressed their political opposition to Greek initiatives that aimed at bringing the Cyprus question before the United Nations with the argument that "one should not wash one's dirty linen in public," or by references to Article 2, paragraph 7, of the Charter. For instance, in 1954, the NATO states had voted against the inclusion of the Cyprus question in the Assembly's agenda and then had frustrated the adoption of a substantive resolution on the issue. The following year, they had again voted against the inclusion of the Cyprus item in the Assembly's agenda and had managed to have it excluded from the agenda. Then, at the next Assembly, after joining the Anglo-Turkish front in calling for the adoption of a resolution that would recommend negotiations "between the three parties concerned," they had yielded somewhat by voting unanimously Resolution 1013 (XI), which had been based on Krishna Menon's draft resolution. This time, however, the vote of Greece's NATO allies against the resolution calling for the application of the principle of self-determination to the case of Cyrpus acquired a very special political significance. It could mean nothing else than the denial to the people of Cyprus of the right to live in freedom and to decide its own future. This was particularly the case of delegations that had not proceeded in any way to explain the sense of their negative vote. In this context, the Greek Mission submitted that it would be advisable for the Greek government to address to each of the governments concerned a signed note of protest with the objective of receiving, if possible, replies that would confirm that the negative votes cast—justified on other grounds—in no way implied a denial to the Cypriot people the right to self-determination and freedom. Gathering such favorable replies could strengthen the Greek position and, at the appropriate time, these could turn out to be useful within the framework of the United Nations.

The second aspect in the conduct of the European allies of Greece through NATO that merited particular attention was that some of these states, Canada and Norway, for instance, and Denmark to a lesser extent, had acquiesced in being used as instruments of attack against the Greek draft resolution before the Political Committee. In a dispute involving NATO allies—Greece, on the one side, and Britain and Turkey, on the other—the least that one might have expected from the other members of the alliance was for them to maintain an attitude of neutrality and to abstain, when the draft resolution came to the vote. That these allies had, on the contrary, cast votes against the Greek proposal and that some of them had transformed themselves into instruments of the British and the Turks in order to combat the Greek and Cypriot position were matters of special political importance and called for a protest, as the Greek Foreign Minister had done in a *démarche* with his Norwegian colleague, Halvard Lange, and Permanent Representative to the UN Ambassador Engen.

The obverse of protests, the Greek Delegation recommended to Athens, should also be attended to. The Greek government should express its thanks to all governments without exception that had voted in favor of the Greek viewpoint through personal letters of the Foreign Minister to his colleagues in such governments. The Soviet bloc countries could be thanked through the diplomatic channel, and the required contact with Albania, a country with which Greece had no diplomatic relations, might be made for this purpose through the Albanian Permanent Mission to the UN.

The Greek UN Mission refrained from making any predictions or judgments about the further course of the Cyprus question. It observed, at any rate, that if one of the contingencies the Greek government envisaged was to resort again to the Assembly at its next session, it was indispensable that all margins of political action with regard to states that had voted against the proposal should be exhausted, and all efforts should be made to consolidate the advantages gained from certain other states that had voted in favor of the Greek point of view. Concurrently, diplomatic efforts should be directed toward swaying in a favorable way the governments that had abstained from voting in the Cyprus question. Turkey and Britain, as soon as the debate was over, had drawn their own political conclusions from it and had started working hard to promote their own interests. The Greek government should do at least the same in order to preserve and widen the ground from which it might launch future initiatives.

All in all, the evolution of the Cyprus question in the United Nations had been at the outset difficult and slow. But this evolution had revealed a consistent and continuous progress. The question had first knocked at the door of the United Nations in 1954. The door then had opened. The item had entered the United Nations, but, after a summary discussion, a decision on the question had been postponed for the time being. Then, in 1955, the door had not opened at all. The inclusion of the Cyprus question in the Assembly's agenda had been rejected. Yet these first two recourses, of 1954 and 1955, had struck blows at the procedural obstacles. They had brought the Cyprus question to the attention of the United Nations. Without these two recourses, no substantial progress could have been achieved. They had constituted a political preparation and a procedural conquest. In 1956, the Cyprus question had not only been included in the Assembly's agenda but, for the first time, had been debated at great length, and the Assembly had adopted Resolution 1013 (XI). Then, the debate at the twelfth Assembly had witnessed substantial progress toward acceptance of the idea that the principle of self-determination ought to be applied in the case of Cyprus. In other words, for the first time, some progress in the substance of the case had been achieved. Without Resolution 1013 (XI) that major political success in the Political Committee could never have been achieved. For the first time the Committee had adopted a resolution that expressed the hope that the principle of self-determination would be applied in the concrete case of a people under a colonial regime. This resolution was a milestone for the Cypriot people on the road to freedom. And for the United Nations it constituted a starting point for a more radical solution in the freeing of non-self-governing territories. Of course, that resolution had not obtained the required two-thirds vote to be adopted by the Assembly. Legally it had been voided. Politically, however, it remained a victory and a positive conquest. And the United Nations, rebelling against itself and against the conformity of ambiguous formulas and a policy of political surrender, had stepped forward toward a horizon of real action. Of course, too, neither the Cyprus problem had been solved nor had the United Nations suddenly ceased being what it had been. And the same obstacles to the freeing of Cyprus still remained. And a great deal would have to be done until the recent success in the Political Committee was translated into the language of reality and facts. Moreover, it was not unusual to witness in the UN process retreats from progress and escapes from success. But all these were temporary and passing phenomena. The seed sown today would ripen into grain tomorrow. One could look forward with good heart and confidence to harvest time.

From the viewpoint of the United Nations, the Greek Mission noted in conclusion, Resolution 1013 (XI) constituted the only existing concrete title in the Cyprus question. After the recent debates, this title had been clarified, as it were, in a very favorable fashion. Formally, however, that resolution still stood. No other UN resolution existed on the Cyprus issue. Consequently, every possible care should be taken on the Greek side to avoid anything that could undermine or tarnish it. Ethnarch Makarios, it should be added, clinging to the Greek interpretation of Resolution 1013 (XI), publicly reiterated on December 24, after he returned to Athens, that the Cypriots were opposed to tripartite negotiations but were ready to resume talks with the British on the basis of self-determination.[13]

D. The Greek Parliament Debates the Handling of the Cyprus Question in the UN

Reporting to Parliament on January 20, 1958, about the handling of the Cyprus question in the United Nations, Foreign Minister Averoff-Tossizza soberly stressed that the recourse did not in itself constitute a political purpose through which the government believed that the Cyprus question would be surely promoted. It was a policy chosen by Greek governments because of the evolution of the problem. The government had sought to promote the matter by all means that could lead to useful results, without creating difficulties. Unfortunately all efforts exerted either by the Cypriots themselves or by the Greek government had remained without results. At one point it had been hoped that there would be a way of promoting the issue without resorting anew to the United Nations—because of the adoption of Resolution 1013 (XI). Although this resolution might not have been to the liking of many who were not familiar with UN resolutions, this one had been regarded as hopeful, calling, as it did, for a just and peaceful solution and opening the way for a final settlement. Nevertheless, in spite of EOKA's truce, of Makarios' release, of Harding's recall, and of the relative relaxation of certain emergency measures on the part of the British authorities on the island, no substantial progress had been achieved on the basic issue of ending colonialism in Cyprus. Efforts to convoke a tripartite conference had been made but the Greek government had rejected these overtures.

For all these reasons, it had been necessary to resort once again to the United Nations, since there were no other means for supporting the just cause of the Cypriots. In this recourse, the Greek government had not been inspired by any spirit of hostility or of intransigence but by a constructive spirit in order to promote the cause of justice and liberty. The Greek Delegation, it was true, had refused to discuss any of the compromise proposals submitted to it either before the debate or in the course of the debate.[14] It had done so, however, because these proposals in no way contributed to the promotion of the issue; on the contrary, they complicated it. Nevertheless, the spirit of the Greek Delegation had been constructive. Its aim was to achieve progress in the struggle. Thus, the delegation had indicated that it was ready to drop the battle if it were possible to achieve a resolution that would surely lead to negotiations between the British government and the Cypriots for a solution based on the principle of self-determination.[15] These conciliatory views, however, had not been endorsed. As a result the battle had been waged. No understanding could be reached because the other side had considered that no mention of self-determination should be made and that tripartite negotiations should be referred to. The battle had thus been waged over the issue of whether the resolution should or should not include a reference to "the parties concerned." Thus, at the Committee's eighth meeting on the Cyprus question (on December 12), the quintessence of the amendments proposed was the reference to negotiations "between those concerned." [16]

Averoff-Tossizza then emphasized the difficulties created by the four-state amendments. These, he explained, might well have been adopted, because most of the delegations generally disliked having to vote on texts that created problems between their own country and other countries, and preferred, if they had to vote, to do so on a text that expressed harmless wishes and avoided friction, especially with powerful states. Thence, without mentioning at all the backstage struggle with the United States, he described the "hard procedural struggle" which had taken place, explaining its complexities at some length. Fortunately, with the support of many friends and after a long struggle, a victory had been achieved.

With regard to the results of the voting in both the Committee and the Assembly, he did not wish either to overestimate or to underestimate them. Even if the resolution had received the two-thirds vote required for adoption, it would have had only an indirect effect of moral pressure, since it was not enforceable. At the same time, he could not belittle the value of the voting on the Cyprus question. This time, the Committee, which constituted a sort of kiln in which resolutions were fired and was a preparatory organ for UN resolutions, had prepared and had voted for a resolution under which the United Nations would recommend the application of self-determination as a solution of the Cyprus problem. Indubitably, this had been a gain and a means for moral pressure. In the Assembly, this resolution had not gathered the required two-thirds vote but at least had obtained a simple majority. Here, too, then, was a possibility for exerting moral pressure.

Averoff-Tossizza further stressed that the Greek draft had been the only one mentioning self-determination ever to be put to the vote. Thus it represented a pioneering event in the history of the United Nations. The

Algerian draft resolution had mentioned self-determination merely in its preamble. Besides, it had never been put to the vote.[17] But the extent of the success could be judged by the strong opposition the Greek draft resolution had aroused. This had become manifest on the diplomatic plane and in the backstage diplomatic pressures exerted on several delegations to get them to abstain or to vote against the draft resolution. All in all, a very difficult battle had been fought, and its result had been a pioneering success. Both the members of the delegation and of the Permanent Mission, as well as Makarios, had contributed to this success and deserved congratulations.

With regard to the future, Averoff-Tossizza continued, the government of Premier Karamanlis had proved that it was handling the Cyprus question with faith, determination, and pugnacity. In this very difficult problem, it was not following a policy of blind intransigence nor one of ignoring the difficulties involved. It was pursuing a dignified and realistic policy and had never yielded in its support of the cause. To ignore the difficulties inherent in the question meant simple demagogy. While it did not consider that Turkey should have a veto power over the fate of the island, the Greek government, nevertheless, took into account the Turkish concerns for the Turkish minority in Cyprus, for the strategic outlook, and for other matters. Hence, it felt particularly bitter at Turkey's negative response, its refusal to co-operate for the purpose of doing away with colonialism in Cyprus. The Greek government desired very much to co-operate with Turkey. It believed that Greek-Turkish friendship was of crucial importance for both countries. However, Greece would never abandon the cause of Cypriot freedom for the sake of friendship with Turkey.[18]

Time, at any rate, was working in favor of Cypriot freedom, said the Foreign Minister. It was working in favor of twentieth century realism which in the last analysis meant the victory of the ideas of freedom and justice. This did not mean that the Greek government would shut itself up in a tower of blind intransigence. It would do so, if necessary, but it preferred to help in the process of History. It was well aware that before Cyprus became a paradise of Greek-Turkish symbiosis and a new link in Greek-Turkish co-operation, it could become a hell that smashed existing links of friendship. Hence, as long as the other side showed understanding and good will, the Greek government was always desirous of doing all it could to help in a healthy development of the situation. The basis for this, however, could not but be the satisfaction of the demands of the Cypriots, who in the mid-twentieth century were still living under a colonial regime. Otherwise, if no good will and understanding were shown, the Greek government, Averoff-Tossizza stated, would, on the one hand, wait for time to work matters out, and, on the other, continue its struggle for freeing Cyprus. How would it continue this struggle? Greece had proved it could fight very effectively and without fear of the consequences. And it would continue waging its political struggle in whatever way possible—in any international forum and in any country. He hoped, however, it would not be necessary to wage these battles, and with aroused expectations was waiting to hear about the measures the British government would soon announce. Both the Greek government and the great majority of the Greek people were looking forward to the day when the traditional, close, and sincere friendship with Britain would be revived.

The Foreign Minister, in conclusion, stressed that a subcommission of the European Human Rights Commission was investigating on the spot whether certain emergency regulations introduced in Cyprus contravened the provisions of the European Convention on Human Rights.[19] Then he turned to the question of nuclear bases, which had been discussed at the NATO summit Council in December of the previous year.[20]

Venizelos, speaking for the main Opposition on January 21, charged that the Foreign Minister, in his efforts to get the United Nations to adopt a resolution mentioning the principle of self-determination for Cyprus, had been, as it were, trying to push open an already open door. Had not Britain and even Turkey recognized this principle since 1955 in various ways and with various qualifications and in various forms, double self-determination included? If they had opposed the Greek draft resolution, this had simply been because the more convenient proposal of the four states had been at hand, which put off self-determination to the Greek kalends. But, what was much worse, the Foreign Minister had made certain important concessions in a fashion that altered the entire situation and caused harm to the Cyprus cause. First of all, Venizelos charged, the Foreign Minister had weakened his original proposal by accepting the replacement of the word "wish" by the word "hope." [21] Moreover, as a result of his reference to "a spirit of co-operation" in his subamendment, he had introduced the idea that self-determination would be applied only after a procedure of negotiations and discussions. What would happen, though, Venizelos asked, if no agreement were reached in this "spirit of co-operation?" Simply, the principle of self-determination would not be applied. Averoff-Tossizza himself, he said, had provided this interpretation when, on December 11, at the evening meeting, he had explained his resolution and had repeatedly stated that Greece was prepared to take into account all the legitimate interests of Turkey (minority, strategic, economic) and—even worse—any other Turkish interest.[22] The Foreign Minister, Venizelos observed, had not asked for the automatic and immediate exercise of the right of self-determination. Moreover, not only had he not at least left open or vague the terms of this right's implementation, but he had explicitly committed Greece to the position that self-determination should not take place before the Turks had been fully satisfied. In other words, in order to facilitate the acceptance of the "principle of self-determination," which the British and Turks for a long time had accepted, Averoff-Tossizza had agreed to condition the exercise of self-determination on the satisfaction of the Turkish demands—all this in order to get the satisfaction of having the word "self-determination" included in the record of the debate. Thus he had subordinated the application of self-determination to the interest of Turkey; i.e., to the interest of a state to which the Greek government had continuously denied the right of having any opinion at all about the future of Cyprus.

In this connection, Venizelos quoted in translation Sarper's remarks at the 932d meeting of the Political Committee on December 11 that the Greek Foreign Minister had recognized the need for negotiations between the governments concerned and through contacts and talks with representatives of the two communities in Cyprus.[23] He furthermore cited a statement the Greek Ambassador in Ankara had made to the Turkish newspaper *Milliet* to the effect that the main thing was not the settlement of the matter because this, one day, would surely be reached, but the finding of a solution that satisfied the inhabitants of Cyprus as a whole and would be acceptable both to Turkey and to Greece.

In conclusion, Venizelos attacked Averoff-Tossizza for having suggested, when trying to prove the possibility of peaceful symbiosis of Greeks and Turks in Cyprus, that the Greek expedition to Asia Minor after World War I had been an "imperialist war." Before going to the next item—the matter of nuclear bases—Venizelos expressed amazement that the Greek government had ever dared propose before an international gathering an agreement with Turkey, whereby the union of Cyprus with Greece would be prohibited forever—an allusion to the Foreign Minister's question at the eleventh Assembly.[24]

When Venizelos finished his speech, Averoff-Tossizza replied to the various charges made—pointing out, for instance, that the British recognition of self-determination for Cyprus led the way to partition. He observed in this connection that, during the debate, Noble, in response to a question of his, had reaffirmed the British commitment to double self-determination.[25] Averoff-Tossizza also declared that it was the permanent policy of Greece to seek a settlement that would safeguard Turkey's legitimate needs.[26]

The leaders of other Opposition parties—S. Allamanis, I. Iliou, and S. Papapolitis—followed lines of argument similar to those of Venizelos, producing also arguments of their own. For example, Allamanis, of the Republican party, not only clung to the old charge that the policy of demanding the application to Cyprus of the principle of self-determination within a fixed and reasonable time limit had been abandoned but observed that the majority of thirty-one of the UN membership which had favored self-determination for the Cypriots constituted quite a miserable result as compared with the fifty-one members that had voted for Resolution 1013 (XI), which, supposedly, had endorsed the principle of self-determination, as the government had contended during Parliamentary debates in March.[27] The leader of EDA, on the other hand, stressed that many of the favorable votes had not resulted from any successful efforts on the part of the Greek Delegation, but had been cast by members of the Eastern bloc, in spite of the Greek government's opposition to these states. Moreover, he harped on the charge that the Greek government had never sufficiently exploited the subject of the Turkish riots of Istanbul of September 6, 1955, nor of the British atrocities in Cyprus. Finally, he underlined that, according to a French journalist's report, the U.S. government was displeased with Greek policy with regard to Cyprus and wished to see the question put away in the freezer.[28] As for the leader of EPEK, Papapolitis, he observed that the fact remained that the Greek government had been unable to persuade the Allies and the United States, in particular, that only a just solution of the Cyprus question could strengthen the ties among the members of the alliance. Progress called for more than mere procedural victories. The only correct policy in the Cyprus question, in his view, was continuous and persistent efforts to persuade the United States to throw all its weight in favor of the just struggle of the Cypriots.[29]

E. Coda

Likewise on January 21, Lennox-Boyd appeared before the House of Commons. He declared that the British government was not prepared to make a statement on the Cyprus question, in spite of expectations it would do so after the Cabinet conferences with Governor Sir Hugh Foot in London between January 2–6 and a report on the Cyprus radio that, though no startling developments were to be expected, a British plan would be announced in the Commons on January 21.[30] Under this plan, as this was conveyed to the Greek government through Callaghan, the shadow Cabinet Colonial Secretary of the Labour party, self-government would again be offered to Cyprus as well as self-determination within a fixed date. If the Greek Cypriot population were then to ask for *enosis*, the Turkish Cypriots would enjoy a similar right to ask for union with Turkey. The British government, in general, and Sir Hugh Foot, in particular, Callaghan had affirmed, strongly condemned dismemberment of the island as a final solution. If the Greeks co-operated in such a plan—which reminded them of the Lennox-Boyd proposal of December 19, 1956[31]—the emergency measures would be immediately raised, and this would make possible the return of Ethnarch Makarios to the island. The Governor would then start negotiations with representatives of the Cypriot people for the purpose of drafting the constitution that would be applied during the period of self-government.

The postponement of any Cyprus announcement in the Commons on January 21, the Greek government learned, had been because Foreign Secretary Lloyd was leaving for Ankara on January 24 to attend a meeting of the Council of the Baghdad Pact and wished to discuss the Cyprus issue with the Turkish government before proceeding to a public statement. Indeed, Foreign Minister Zorlu, in a statement of January 10, had not only declared that no decision on the future of Cyprus should be taken before the Turkish views had been requested but once again had insisted on partition as the only solution acceptable to his government.[32] Earlier that month, on the other hand, the Greek government had been advised through the diplomatic channel that the Turkish government now tended to limit itself to a demand for a military base on Cyprus. The Turkish Foreign Minister, regretting he had not had the opportunity of meeting his Greek opposite number during the summit session of the NATO Council (December 12–19, 1957), had indicated he was ready to meet him anywhere to confer on the Cyprus issue. At that session of the Council, incidentally, because Spaak intended to devote a long paragraph to the Cyprus issue in his statement, the Turks had decided to raise the issue. Finally, however, they did not do so. Premier Karamanlis had warned Spaak that if the Cyprus issue were raised, then he would consider it a major item and definitely would request its full discussion in all its aspects. He would underline before the NATO Council the UN Political Committee's decision and would put forward self-determination as a demand in NATO, since that body included only allied countries. Informed by Spaak of Karamanlis' views, Premier Menderes refrained from touching on the Cyprus issue in his speech before the NATO Council.[33]

It is, however, beyond the scope of this study to relate the negative attitude the Turkish government assumed toward the Foot plan[34] put forward by Lloyd during his stay in Ankara or to deal with the conference the British Foreign Secretary had with Foreign Minister Averoff-Tossizza and other high Greek government officials in Athens between February 10–12, 1958. Suffice it to add that on his return from Athens Lloyd told the Commons on February 18, in response to a question, that in case of diplomatic failure the British government would go ahead and make its own policy on Cyprus and stand by it.[35]

On the island itself, meanwhile, Grivas, on January 11, had issued an order for the contingency of a decision to resume operations. Other orders followed, on January 16 and 19—the former concerning defensive measures against the Turkish Cypriots whose movements had become ever more threatening; the latter dealing with the problem of keeping up the morale of the Greek Cypriots. Shortly after, in a long letter to Makarios, he reiterated his strictures of Greek government policy along lines mentioned earlier.[36] Time, he felt, was working against the Greek cause, and he doubted whether it would be possible at the next session of the Assembly to secure the same number of votes in favor of the Greek viewpoint in the Cyprus question if that question were once again raised in the United Nations. He doubted, too, whether the policy of trying to solve the question within the framework of the Western Alliance was approved of by the majority of the Greek people, and in view of this he urged resort to elections. He would wait, however, he wrote, until the end of February to see what sort of policy the Greek government was following. After that he would act "in accordance with his conscience, his obligations toward the struggle, and his responsibilities toward Cyprus and Hellenism, because Cyprus had become a pan-national question." [37] In response to this letter, which contained the advice that the Greek government should revise its foreign policy, the Greek Foreign Minister explained that the margins for such a revision were limited. Turkey, "Isaakios" wrote, enjoyed an outstanding position in the Western world. The United States would never want to lose Greece but even more it would not wish to lose Turkey. If it ever found itself in the need of choosing between the two countries, it would prefer Turkey. From the current British government he expected no solution of the question. Therefore, it would be necessary to keep the matter open until the Labour party came into power. [38]

In Athens, in mid-February, there was a government crisis, [39] and then, on March 4, two days after Premier Karamanlis handed in to the King his Cabinet's resignation and recommended resort to elections, the leader of EOKA ordered the resumption of operations, with emphasis on selective sabotage and passive resistance, not on attacks on human targets. On March 7 four bombs exploded in the RAF airfield near Nicosia. [40] Other bombs exploded in government workshops and warehouses or pumping installations serving military camps during the month that followed. [41]

Epilogue and Conclusions

The Last Battle
over Cyprus in the United Nations

There was one more Greek recourse to the United Nations on the Cyprus question, one more battle, at the Assembly's thirteenth session, before the diplomatic two-stage negotiations between Greece, Turkey, Britain, and the Cypriots (both Greek and Turkish) led to what appeared at the time to be a definitive settlement of the Cyprus question in February, 1959. The Greek government, which, at the twelfth Assembly had not committed itself to a new recourse, was not very much in favor of such a move. But Ethnarch Makarios was. As in 1952, at one point he had warned that he might ask another state to sponsor the islanders' cause if Greece did not do so. Once again the desire to do something, the unthinkability of war, and the lack of negotiations left no alternative other than a recourse to the Assembly.[1] But this time the success of 1957 in getting a draft resolution tabled by the Greek Delegation put to the vote and passed at least by the Political Committee was not repeated.

The whole "last battle" over Cyprus in the United Nations took place at a time when the situation on the island had greatly worsened, as the Greek Foreign Minister in 1957 had repeatedly predicted it would. Bloody clashes between Greek and Turkish Cypriots had occurred in 1958, with the cost in lives amounting to forty-six Greek Cypriots and fifty-six Turkish Cypriots by the end of the year, not to mention other casualties and a great deal of material damage. The Turkish Cypriots now had their own armed Turkish Defence Organization, TMT (*Türk Mukavemet Teskilati*), Volkan's successor late in 1957, which had become the Turkish counterpart of EOKA, except that its aim was *taksim* (partition) or, politically speaking, separate self-determination for the Turkish Cypriots. Early in 1958, Dr. Kuchuk, Makarios' Turkish counterpart, who, unlike the Ethnarch, was allowed freely to move both inside and outside Cyprus, sought to emphasize the point Ambassador Sarper had made in the Assembly, namely that the symbiosis between the Turkish and Greek Cypriots was impossible, so that partition of the island was the only solution. He, and other Turkish Cypriots, deplored Sir John Harding's recall and the initially softer approach of the new Governor, implying that the latter was pro-Greek.[2] The Greek Cypriots, on their side, complained that the British administration treated Turkish Cypriot demonstrators and agitational terrorists more leniently than it did their own. All in all, by early summer, 1958, Greek-Turkish warfare by proxies was being waged on the island, with the President of the UN Security Council informed of the Greek and Turkish government views on developments, in communications of June 13 and 19, and June 13 and 16. There were, too, well-founded reports about the concentration of Turkish irregulars on the Turkish mainland north of Cyprus, in Cilicia, and these greatly disturbed the Greek government, because it feared lest these irregulars infiltrate the island. Besides, the expectations of Greek foreign policy–makers that British Labour party support would somehow be helpful for achieving terms of settlement favorable to the Greek and Greek Cypriot viewpoint were now dwindling. Because of the casualties inflicted on British civilians and military personnel on the island, even left-wing Labourites such as Aneurin Bevan now favored a speedy settlement and were reluctant to speak out in support of the Greek Cypriot cause as they had done before. They informed the Greek government that if the situation continued and no agreement were reached with Turkey, the British government would be obliged to withdraw from its bases on the island and invite the Turks to occupy its northern part and the Greeks its southern part,[3] so that the island would be *de facto* partitioned.

If the Syrian "war scare" had constituted a regional source of acute anxiety in the again quite sharply bipolarized world of 1957, with Soviet firsts in missilery and spacemanship aggravating the situation from the Western viewpoint on a worldwide scale, the summer of 1958 had witnessed a grave new Middle Eastern crisis. The pro-Western monarchy of Iraq, a Baghdad Pact member, had been violently overthrown on July 14. As a precautionary move and as a stabilizing operation, U.S. Marines had landed in Lebanon, and British troops were flown to Jordan. Both these small Middle Eastern states had complained to the United Nations about intervention in their internal affairs on the part of the newly established United Arab Republic—the former, in May, before the Iraqi revolution; the latter on July 17. In response to the Lebanese appeal the UN Security Council had sent UNOGIL (United Nations Observation Group in Lebanon) to Beirut early in July. Then, in the Far East, where Mao Tse-tung had the impression, because of Soviet ballistic achievements, that the east wind was prevailing over the west wind, a grave crisis broke out in the Taiwan Straits.

In the most permeable and sensitive Greek arena itself, even though Karamanlis and his party, ERE, had won in the general elections of May

11, 1958, EDA, the Communist façade party, had gathered a record of 24 per cent of the votes in these elections, largely as a result of the anti-allied sentiments that the West's attitude in the Cyprus question had engendered among the Greek people. Since these elections had been conducted under an electoral law that was partly based on proportional representation, and Premier Karamanlis had tailored this law to suit the wishes of Papandreou, the Opposition leader, who, overestimating his party's strength, had insisted on high percentages in the distribution of Parliamentary seats, EDA had emerged in Parliament, for the first time, as the leading Opposition party.

Indeed, the political crisis that triggered these elections—the sudden resignation from Karamanlis' party of fifteen of its Parliamentary members on February 27, 1958—had not only been precipitated by the Premier's announced decision to alter the electoral law in conformity with Papandreou's wishes but, to a certain extent, was not unconnected with the Cyprus question. For the non-EDA Opposition leaders, it seems, in spite of their outward intransigence, so manifest in parliamentary debates, kept on assuring the allies that the Greek national interest imposed the closing of the Cyprus question and that this could be achieved only through the setting up of a coalition government which would undertake such a responsibility. This view, according to Karamanlis, had been so assiduously cultivated that the Americans and British believed that if his government were overthrown, he would be obliged to co-operate with Papandreou and S. Venizelos—in which case the Cyprus question would have been dealt with in the above spirit. In this plan, the first signs of which appeared late in 1957, the leading elements had been not only the owner of an influential newspaper of Athens and a member of the King's entourage, but also the U.S. chargé d'affaires, who was thinking in terms of U.S. policy.

In the text of its recourse, dated August 15, 1958, the Greek government, instead of using its customary formula of "self-determination under the auspices of the United Nations," merely asked for the inclusion of the "Question of Cyprus" in the General Assembly's agenda (see Appendix F). In its explanatory memorandum, dated September 12, it emphasized that the issue was one of freedom and self-determination (note the order of the words). The British government, it charged, continued to deny to the Cypriots their right to freedom and self-determination. In spite of Resolution 1013 (XI), it had avoided entering into direct negotiations with the Cypriots. Also it had not taken into account that the Political Committee at the Assembly's previous session had adopted a resolution calling for the application of the right of self-determination for the Cypriot people and that by a simple majority, the Assembly had likewise favored it. Since the end of the twelfth Assembly, the British government had sought for a provisional solution. The Greek government, with Makarios in agreement, had said that the only provisional solution it would accept was the establishment of a genuine and democratic self-government in Cyprus. The British government, however, had come up with the Macmillan plan on June 19, 1958.[4] In the view of the Greek government, this plan was not only undemocratic "because it totally ignored the right and the will of the 80 per cent majority of the population" but "because it called three foreign governments to share in the continued alien domination over a non-self-governing territory and its population" and thus was contrary to the Charter. The plan also prejudged the future by preparing the ground for the island's partition.

Meanwhile the Turkish minority had taken violent action against the Greek population. The purpose of these attacks was to demonstrate the need of partition as a final solution. The Turkish government was also threatening direct intervention. A chaotic situation prevailed on the island. Thousands of Greeks were held in concentration camps. The situation had entered a critical phase. The British attempts to impose a solution could lead to very serious developments that could endanger peace and security in the whole area. The Greek government hoped that the Assembly would take whatever action it deemed appropriate "to alleviate the plight of the population of Cyprus, to remove all foreign threats of interference . . . and to assist the Cypriots to realize their legitimate claims in accordance with the relative provisions of the Charter."

During the two-stage decision-making on including the Cyprus item in the Assembly's agenda, no difficulties were experienced this time. On September 22, the Assembly, at its 752d meeting, decided to include the Cyprus question in its agenda.

In Athens that same day, Barbara Castle, Vice-Chairman of the Labour party, revealed that Ethnarch Makarios, in his now famous interview with her, had come out for setting up, after a fixed period of self-government, an independent Cyprus, not as a provisional or interim solution, but in perpetuity, unless United Nations were to approve of a change in status.[5] The Greek foreign policy–makers, whom the Ethnarch had not consulted before making this particular public announcement, were annoyed. They were keeping in reserve this proposal, which Makarios had endorsed backstage a few days before the Greek government transmitted its explanatory memorandum to the United Nations, with the intention of springing it upon the Assembly at an appropriate moment. And, anxious to prevent the implementation of the Macmillan plan[6] which, they feared, ultimately would lead to the island's partition, they had also decided to propose to the British that the whole Cyprus question be put "in the freeze" for at least three years with EOKA ceasing completely its operations.

In accordance with this intention, the Greek Foreign Minister, at his request, met his British colleague at the latter's apartment, with other officials present on both sides. Averoff-Tossizza proposed suspension of the plan's application. In exchange, he was prepared to recommend to

Athens the withdrawal of the Cyprus item from the Assembly's agenda.
Lloyd, however, was obdurate. His government had officially committed
itself to the Macmillan plan. If it dropped this commitment, perhaps
EOKA would cease its operations, but a Turkish EOKA would start similar
activities. Since Cyprus was so close to Turkey, reinforcing the Turkish
EOKA would be very easy. "Until now we have been unable to persuade
you. Today I am convinced we cannot persuade Turkey. As a result, in
one case, our alliance with Greece is endangered, and the bloodshed is
the fault of the Greeks; in the other case, we have the same consequences
for our alliance with Turkey, the bloodshed being the fault of the Turks.
Since you did not listen to us and were in a hurry, since you chose to
ignore the Turks altogether, since we put forward many solutions and
now have exposed and committed ourselves to the Macmillan plan, we
have no other alternative but to apply it. Do you wish to accept it? We
shall be happy. If you do not, we shall apply it with the Turks as best we
can. Sooner or later a part of the population will help us. . . . With
regard to the withdrawal of your recourse, this would have some importance in order to avoid acrimonious debates. However, it does not bother
us very much. You will accuse us; others, by whom we have stood, will
praise us. And you will get no resolution. I would prefer that the recourse
were avoided so that your relations with Turkey do not become even
cooler than they are now. Otherwise, the recourse has no great significance. Withdrawing it cannot constitute for us the basis of a bargain in
which we, in exchange, would revise the policy to which we are committed." [7]

Matters in the Assembly thus took their course. On November 3, the
British government transmitted to the UN Secretary-General a *White
Paper* which contained a highly selective account of the discussion on
Cyprus that had taken place in NATO in September–October, 1958.[8] On
November 26, the Greek government transmitted likewise to the Secretary-General two legal opinions by non-Greek international jurists of
world repute on the Cyprus question. These contained, among others,
rebuttals of the Turkish contentions at the previous Assembly about the
interpretation of Article 73 (b) of the Charter.[9]

For the antagonists, the experience of 1957 seems to have served as a
lesson and a warning. Britain was first to introduce a draft resolution on
the Cyprus item with the procedural advantages that might accrue from
this initiative. Greece immediately followed. Turkey came next submitting for the first time a draft resolution of its own.

Other delegations, too, introduced draft resolutions on the question,
that of Iran for instance, whose proposals were unpalatable to the
Greeks. To the Greeks' rescue came India and nine other states with
another draft resolution. Another one, introduced by Colombia, would
not be opposed by the Greek Delegation, in contrast to a resolution
tabled by Belgium.

The British Delegation, by its proposal, introduced on November 25 in the Political Committee, sought in effect to get the Assembly to endorse the British government's efforts to implement or impose the Cyprus "partnership plan" for self-government which Prime Minister Macmillan had announced on June 19. These efforts had already begun since the "appointed day"—October 1, 1958—over strenuous Greek government objections.[10] The British draft resolution, like all others except the Colombian one, recalled Resolution 1013 (XI) and proposed in its operative paragraphs that the Assembly invite the British government to continue its efforts to arrive at "a peaceful, democratic and just solution," and the other parties to co-operate to that end. It also asked the Assembly to call upon "all concerned to put an end to terrorism and violence in Cyprus." [11]

For its part, the Greek Delegation, this time, sought to get the Assembly to approve in principle the establishment of an independent Cyprus instead of urging it to call for the application of the principle or right of self-determination to the population of Cyprus, as it had done at previous sessions of the Assembly since 1954. Introduced like the British draft resolution on November 25, the Greek draft resolution, in its operative paragraphs, proposed that the Assembly invite the British government to help the Cypriots toward instituting "the status of independence" following a period of "genuine and democratic self-government," in which adequate guarantees would be provided for the protection of the Turkish minority and for its participation in the island's administration. This draft resolution proposed the setting up of a five-state good offices committee for implementing the above points.[12] Not even in its preambular paragraphs did the Greek draft resolution refer to the principle or right of self-determination.

It was Turkey, now, that was calling for self-determination, but for the Greeks and the Turks of the island separately, in a way that could lead to the partition of Cyprus. During the debates at the Assembly's twelfth session, it will be recalled, the Turkish Delegation had favored this line,[13] which Lennox-Boyd had put forward on December 19, 1956, when he had presented to the House of Commons the now forgotten Radcliffe draft constitution.[14] Third in order of submission on November 25, the Turkish draft resolution, in its operative paragraphs, proposed that "the three governments directly concerned" should resume and continue their efforts in a spirit of co-operation in order to reach a friendly solution "in application of the principle of equal rights and self-determination" in accordance "with the particular circumstances of Cyprus and its peoples," in conformity with the purposes and principles of the Charter. It also provided that the Assembly should call upon all concerned to refrain from supporting or encouraging violence in Cyprus and from resorting to radio broadcasts and other media of diffusion in a way that harmed relations between the two peoples of the island.[15]

After the experience of the previous session of the Assembly, the Turkish government had launched quite a diplomatic campaign for winning friends and influencing people in support of its viewpoint on the

Cyprus question. For instance, within three months, it had set up eight new embassies in countries where it had had no regular diplomatic representation in the past. It had also sent special missions to several countries in efforts to enlist their government's support. This time, too, in the debate in the United Nations, Turkey was represented by Foreign Minister Zorlu himself, who was assisted by a specially large mission, totaling twenty-one officials as compared with fifteen the previous year. And the Turkish Delegation, which on previous occasions had refrained from supporting the cause of the Algerians, now cosponsored with the Arab states a draft resolution on the Algerian problem. All in all, to muster support among the Arab countries, the Turkish government sought to exploit the common Muslim heritage.[16]

The Colombian draft resolution, introduced in the Political Committee on November 28, called upon the Assembly to set up an observation group which would assist "all the parties concerned" in resuming and continuing their negotiations for the purpose of finding a peaceful, just, and democratic solution of the Cyprus problem. At the request of the parties concerned, this observation group could assume the functions of a good-offices committee.[17]

As for the Iranian draft resolution, introduced on December 1,[18] and eventually adopted by the Political Committee with amendments, it urged something more than the tripartite conference that the British government had suggested to the Greek and Turkish governments in August, 1957. It hewed close to the procedure Spaak had first mentioned in mid-September, 1957, during his exploratory talks with the Greek Foreign Minister. On that occasion, it will be recalled, he had suggested Cypriot participation in the tripartite conference the British were trying to convene.[19]

Likewise on December 1, a draft resolution prepared by Krishna Menon and cosponsored by nine other states had been circulated. The names of the sponsors—Ceylon, Ethiopia,[20] Haiti, Iceland, India, Ireland, Nepal, Panama, Sudan, and the United Arab Republic—when compared with the attitudes of these states on the Cyprus question at previous sessions of the Assembly, suggest that their joint proposal was closer to the Greek than to the British or Turkish viewpoint. Indeed, it was definitely "antipartition" in character. Under the operative paragraphs of this ten-state draft resolution, in its once-revised form, the Assembly would urge "all concerned, particularly the Government and the people of Cyprus" to endeavor to establish conditions for the cessation of violence in Cyprus helpful to peaceful negotiations. It would also request the British government to continue negotiations with a view to promoting self-government in Cyprus, in accordance with the provisions of the Charter, and "the preservation of its integrity." The Assembly would also state that for a peaceful, equitable, and stable settlement, effective provisions for the protection of all legitimate minority interests were essential. Finally, it would call upon all member states to co-operate to this end, "undertaking to respect the integrity of Cyprus" as well as its self-government, when the latter was fully attained.[21]

The draft resolution Belgium tabled on December 2 proposed that the Assembly call upon "all concerned" to use every possible means for putting an end to terrorism, and recommend that they resume and continue their efforts in a spirit of co-operation with a view to reaching a friendly solution in accordance with the purposes and principles of the UN Charter.[22]

One can imagine the labyrinthine complexity of backstage consultations, negotiations, and exchanges that went on with the introduction of all these seven draft resolutions in the Political Committee. The public debate itself, which lasted for ten days, through fifteen meetings, testifies to this complexity. In addition to the representatives of Greece, Britain, and Turkey, representatives of forty-six other countries in the eighty-two member United Nations of 1958 took part in it. Eight explicitly condemned partition as a solution.[23] All agreed that negotiations between the parties concerned were desirable in order to find a solution to the Cyprus problem. Around the issue, two different positions crystallized. A large number of representatives expressed the view that any resolution adopted should contain fundamental elements or guidelines for the future negotiations. Others urged the Assembly not to point the way to any particular final settlement, so as not to prejudge the future.[24]

Commander Noble, in particular, maintained that none of the parties should at present be asked to drop their long-term aspirations with regard to Cyprus because of the strong communal feelings being expressed at the time on the island. His government, he said, continued to be ready for negotiations with the Greek and Turkish governments, and also with representatives of both Greek and Turkish Cypriots. He denied that his government favored the partition of Cyprus.

Foreign Minister Averoff-Tossizza, reasserting that the Cyprus question was a colonial issue, again called for negotiations between the British government and the Cypriot people. As a solution he put forward guaranteed independence for Cyprus, following a period of self-government, and adequate guarantees for the protection of the Turkish minority and for its participation in the island's administration. He also maintained that partition of the island should be excluded.

Foreign Minister Zorlu denied the existence of any Cypriot nation or political entity. The island's inhabitants, he insisted, constituted two distinct communities with different national aspirations. The Turkish minority wished to be treated not as a minority but as an entity that was entitled to the same rights as the Greek community.[25]

The resolutionary struggle, as Averoff-Tossizza explained in his report to the Greek Parliament on December 11,[26] centered around the ten-state and Iranian draft resolutions. The Greek Delegation estimated that the first of these, which included many aspects favorable to the Greek viewpoint though not calling for Cypriot independence, had excellent chances of gathering the required two-thirds vote in its favor. Suddenly, however, even before it had been formally introduced, Noble, at the 1003d meeting of the Political Committee on December 1, warned that adoption of this draft resolution might provoke not only civil war in Cyprus but even "a wider conflict." [27] This "threat of war," designed to prevent the Assembly from freely deciding on the issue, as the Greek Foreign Minister termed this warning, inevitably created a deep impression among members of the organization whose primary function is to maintain international peace. And this impression was assiduously cultivated backstage where a lively campaign was waged with all governments in order to prevent them from voting in favor of the ten-state resolution. As a result, two of the draft resolution's sponsors said they would withdraw and abstain if that resolution were put to the vote. [28]

Concurrently, the opponents of this draft resolution proceeded twice to revise the Iranian draft resolution in order to attract votes in its favor. The third version of the Iranian draft became thus more "colorless" than the two preceding ones, hence less offensive and more acceptable to many delegations. From the original text, phrases that would cause the friends of Greece to vote against it, for example, passages indicating a preference for partition [29] or others that might be construed as condemning EOKA's activities or as casting blame on the Greek government for the failure of diplomatic negotiations, were deleted. Yet even this third "watered-down" version was not to the taste of the Greek Delegation because of its reference to "the three parties directly concerned." Besides, the Greek Delegation continued to believe it was futile to recommend negotiations without defining in advance the general framework of the solution. [30]

When the U.S. Delegation made it clear backstage that it would vote in favor of the Iranian draft resolution as finally revised, it became evident that any motion to request a voting priority for the ten-state draft resolution was bound to fail. [31] As a result, on December 4, during the debate on resolution-making at the 1009th meeting of the Political Committee, the Greek Delegate proposed three amendments to the Iranian draft resolution. [32] The Turkish Delegation countered with three subamendments to the Greek amendments (imitating the tactics of the Greek Delegation at the previous Assembly). [33] And the Committee decided to give voting priority to the Iranian draft resolution and to the Greek amendments and Turkish subamendments. Voted on first, two of the latter were adopted by the Committee, and the Turkish Delegation withdrew its third subamendment. Although the second Greek amendment, as subamended by Turkey, was adopted by the Committee, the third Greek amendment, likewise subamended by Turkey, was not. As for the first Greek amendment, this the Committee adopted. The Iranian draft resolution, as amended, was then put to the vote. In a roll-call vote requested by the representative of Greece, the Committee adopted it by 31 to 22, with 28 abstentions (i.e., by a majority that did not insure its adoption by the Assembly). Greece voted against this resolution as did Guatemala, Iceland, India, Ireland, Nepal, Panama, the United Arab Republic, Yemen, Yugoslavia, Bolivia, Ceylon, and Ethiopia, together with the U.S.S.R. and eight other Soviet bloc states. Four Arab states— Lebanon, Saudi Arabia, Sudan, and Tunisia—which at the previous Assembly had voted in favor of the Greek viewpoint, abstained from the vote, while Jordan, which at the previous Assembly had absented itself, voted this time against the Greek viewpoint, i.e., in favor of the Iranian resolution. These changed attitudes, which the Opposition in the Greek Parliament underlined,[34] were ascribed to the change of Turkish diplomacy mentioned earlier.[35]

After this defeat, which it regarded as a Turkish victory because the Iranian resolution referred to a conference "between the three governments directly concerned," in accordance with the first Turkish sub-amendment to the second Greek amendment adopted by the Committee, the Greek Delegation withdrew its own draft resolution. The British and Turkish Delegations did likewise. At the request of the sponsors, the ten-state draft resolution was not put to the vote. The Political Committee then voted on the Colombian draft resolution. Because of a 17–17 tie vote, it was not adopted. The Greek Delegation voted in its favor. Britain, however, together with Turkey and several other states, including the U.S.S.R. and its eight cohorts, voted against it. Likewise rejected was the Belgian draft resolution.[36]

The Iranian draft resolution adopted by the Political Committee recalled Resolution 1013 (XI). It urged that a conference be convened between "the three governments directly concerned and representatives of the Cypriots" at which there would be a discussion not only of the interim arrangements of the administration of Cyprus but also of a final solution, with the assistance, if desired, of governments and personalities acceptable to the interested parties. Such a conference, according to this resolution, offered the best hope of peaceful progress toward an agreed solution of the Cyprus problem. To meet the legitimate aspirations of the Cypriots, self-government and free institutions should be developed in accordance with the Charter.[37]

On this occasion, the United States, as already noted, did not abstain from the vote on the Iranian draft resolution as it had done at the twelfth Assembly when the Greek draft resolution had been put to the vote. It voted in favor of the resolution the Greek Delegation opposed—as the left-wing Opposition in the Greek Parliament duly underlined.[38] In the Committee debate on the substance of the Cyprus question, the U.S. representative, Barco, on November 28, had limited his government's concern in the question to matters of procedure once again, expressing his delegation's gratification that "the three governments directly concerned"—a phrase anathema to the Greeks—had recognized that only negotiation and conciliation could provide a solution to the Cyprus problem. Moreover, this time he had gone as far as to state that the

United Nations "was not the proper place" to seek a solution to that problem. The greatest contribution the world organization could make toward the settlement of the question would be to insure the resumption of negotiations in a manner consistent with Article 33 of the Charter. His delegation's attitude toward the draft resolutions tabled would be determined, he said, by the extent to which they enhanced or impaired the chance of fruitful negotiations.[39]

In publicly committing the U.S. Delegation in favor of the Iranian draft resolution on December 4, Lodge maintained that this resolution would help encourage the resumption of negotiations everyone agreed were necessary. He could not understand, he added, why several delegations thought that, because a draft resolution did not contain certain provisions which they desired, it must be against their interests.[40] The U.S. government's attitude on this occasion, Averoff-Tossizza suggested to Parliament, might have been a *quid pro quo* for the British support of the U.S. position with regard to Communist China.[41] Needless to say, backstage it led to vehement Greek diplomatic protests in Washington, where Greek Ambassador Liatis charged that the U.S. government had failed to keep its promise to remain neutral, with State Department officials saying that Ambassador Lodge had exceeded his instructions.

Under these circumstances, many of the most faithful supporters of the Greek position had felt unable to vote against the Iranian draft resolution, and this had led them to abstain. The opponents, nevertheless, the Greek Foreign Minister observed in Parliament, had suffered a political defeat in the Committee in spite of their victory. For, he argued, in a battle that involved Greece, on the one side, and Britain and Turkey, supported by the United States, on the other side, the latter had managed to get in their favor only thirty-one votes out of a total UN membership of eighty-two. Of the twenty Latin American delegations that usually followed the policy line of the Free World, three had voted against the Iranian draft resolution and eleven had abstained.[42]

The evening of December 4, after the Political Committee had adopted the Iranian draft resolution, Averoff-Tossizza, somewhat dejected and quite exhausted, was talking with some Greek journalists at the entrance of the Committee hall, when the Turkish Foreign Minister came up and congratulated him for the splendid fight he had put up in the debate. The Greek Foreign Minister reciprocated, adding that both were using their talents in a *petite politique* not a *grande politique* (they were conversing in French), while their countries were threatened by terrible common dangers. Zorlu agreed. He, too, regretted that the Cyprus question had played such a disproportionate role in the foreign policy of both countries. "Your insistence, however," he added, "that Cyprus is inhabited by a people that includes a small minority and that the island plays no role in our security does not allow even the start of a discussion." When his Greek colleague countered by saying that his government had proposed the island's demilitarization, Zorlu, interrupting, observed that demilitarization meant that when the British left the island, as they surely would one day, then Cyprus would fall an easy prey to any enemy of Turkey. To this Averoff-Tossizza responded by emphasizing that his government took into account those Turkish worries that were well founded. Although he could not recognize the Turkish minority as a people, he could recognize it as a community which, however, was close to another, much larger one. "If you do not recognize," he added, "that in no case can 80 per cent be equal or even close to 20 per cent, any discussion is impossible." The Turkish Foreign Minister replied that if the subjects of security and of a Turkish community were accepted, one might have disagreements but at least it would be possible to talk over the question and seek a solution. "Should we meet?" he asked. The Greek Foreign Minister answered in the affirmative, while saying that he was not optimistic and, at any rate, one should wait first to see what would happen in the Assembly next day.[43]

Whether the Iranian draft resolution would have gathered the required two-thirds vote in the Assembly of members present and voting, as a result of British and Turkish backstage efforts to muster this sort of majority, is a moot point, though Sir Pierson Dixon, of the British Delegation, was reportedly confident that, because of the pledges given by numerous delegations, such a majority would be forthcoming.[44] At any rate, backstage, de la Colina, the Mexican representative who had voted for the Iranian resolution, called on the heads of the U.S., British, Turkish, and Iranian Delegations and explained that, while all who had voted in favor of it recognized that Greece was wrong in opposing a reference to "the three governments directly concerned," they felt, nevertheless, that Greece was right in opposing that resolution since one of the parties concerned favored partition of the island—an unacceptable and unnatural solution. Thus, he warned, those who had voted for the resolution might not do so again in the Assembly, since they were unwilling to inflict a defeat upon Greece. Other delegations, too, it seems, made similar démarches.[45] Their aim was to find a resolution that would be acceptable to all. As for the Greek Delegation, it saw no reason for opposing such initiatives. Because of the means of pressure available to the antagonists, it felt that an increase in the number of votes in favor of the Iranian resolution was likely in the Assembly, even if the required two-thirds vote were not forthcoming. Besides, it thought it desirable not to displease friends belonging to the Latin American group which as a whole represented a force of twenty votes.[46]

Ambassador Lodge, by his attitude, contributed to this atmosphere of conciliation. Already during the resolution-making phase of the debate in the Committee, he had favored a suggestion for a short recess made by the representative of Mexico for the purpose of seeing whether some sort of compromise might not be achieved between the sponsors of the Iranian and the Indian (ten-state) resolutions. The British, however, eager at that point to score a victory over the Greeks in the Committee, had opposed such a suggestion. After the Committee vote, Lodge conferred with the Greek Foreign Minister who pleaded for full U.S. neutrality in the Assembly. The American, on his side, urged conciliation and the avoidance of acrimony. He confided to Averoff-Tossizza that he, together with certain other U.S. officials, had often registered their strong disagreement with the State Department about the handling of the Cyprus question but had been unable to convince the person responsible for conducting policy (Dulles?) of that policy's wrongness. Later, Lodge urged conciliation and avoidance of acrimony upon the British and the Turks, as well.

A meeting followed, at 10:30 the morning of December 5, which was attended by the heads of the Delegations of Britain, Greece, Iran, Mexico, Turkey, and the United States. Lodge suggested that the Iranian resolution be dropped. Another resolution should be adopted, he thought. Agreement on a new one was not easy to reach. The British and Turkish Delegates yielded inch by inch, as the Greek Delegate put forward his proposals. At one point, Averoff-Tossizza felt that no progress was being made and proposed an adjournment of the talks. He preferred, he said, to be defeated in a matter for which he was fighting rather than to compromise with something he did not like. Finally, agreement was reached on the text of a new draft resolution.[47]

As a result, the Iranian draft resolution adopted by the Political Committe was never put to the vote in the Assembly. In the afternoon of December 5, after the Austrian Chairman of the Committee, Matsch, submitted his report on the Cyprus item to the Assembly, de la Colina, the Mexican representative, recommended to it the text of another draft resolution "negotiated with all the parties directly concerned" and expressed the hope that the Assembly would adopt it unanimously and that there would be no need for any further debate or explanations of vote. He asked the President of the Assembly to take up this draft resolution first. After inquiring whether there were any objections to the Mexican proposal and ascertaining that there were none, the President asked the Assembly to vote on the new draft resolution. The Assembly adopted it without objection—namely, without even the procedure of a formal vote. Only the Soviet representative made a statement in connection with the vote that had been taken. He directed his charges mainly against the Iranian resolution which had not been put to the vote, saying that it made no mention of the principle of self-determination and that the tripartite conference it recommended was a cover for referring the Cyprus question to NATO. With regard to the Mexican resolution, he expressed regret that it represented a return to Resolution 1013 (XI) instead of taking a step forward and insuring a settlement in accordance with the interests of the people of the island and with their aspirations toward free and independent development. The outcome, he maintained, was "a direct consequence of the antipopular attitude of the principal colonial powers," including Britain and the United States, which gave no thought to the national interests of peoples but were concerned only with their own military-strategic interests.[48]

In this outwardly innocuous and colorless document that was adopted as Resolution 1287 (XIII), the Assembly, having considered the question of Cyprus and recalling Resolution 1013 (XI), "expressed its confidence" that continued efforts would be made "by the parties" to reach a peaceful, democratic and just solution in accordance with the UN Charter.[49] Since the text of this resolution sponsored by Mexico, had, in the last analysis, really been the outcome of an agreement reached primarily between the Greek and Turkish Foreign Ministers, for both outranked the other negotiating officials, the words "expressed confidence" indicated an implicit commitment of the two "External Decision-makers" of Greece and Turkey to start negotiations.

Resolution 1287 (XIII), moreover, somewhat assuaged Greek feelings of frustration and pride, for it seemed merely to reiterate Resolution 1013 (XI), albeit against a new situation in Cyprus and a different international backdrop than that of early 1957. In his report to the Greek Parliament on December 11, Averoff-Tossizza observed that as compared with the original draft resolutions tabled by Greece, Britain, and Turkey, Resolution 1287 (XIII) was negatively equal for all three governments. It favored no one's desires. It could even be maintained that there had been a slight gain for the Cyprus question because the United Nations, by this resolution, though not entering into the substance of the question, had confirmed its active interest in it. This would exert a slight moral pressure. At the Assembly's previous session, he reminded Parliament, certain delegations had favored the adoption of no resolution at all. A second small gain had been that the United Nations, by this resolution, had indirectly adopted the view that the bloody drama of Cyprus had not been settled. The debate had been useful. Toward the end of it there had been a relaxation in the tone of the Turkish statements; for what reasons he could not say, even though he had had private talks with the Turkish Foreign Minister.[50]

Sir Pierson Dixon, too, after the Political Committee had adopted the Iranian draft resolution, had been seeking a success, not a victory.[51] Were all these more conciliatory attitudes that eventually led to the settlement—temporarily at least—of the Cyprus dispute in Zürich and London in February, 1959, due to apprehension over the possibility of new and greater violence in the island? Were they to be attributed to grave new developments outside the Cyprus arena such as the new Berlin crisis Khrushchev had triggered with his quasi-ultimative letter of November 27 that came as a climax after the missile gap shock of 1957, the high tension in the Taiwan Straits, and the jolting series of crises of 1957-58 in the Middle East? It is difficult to say for sure, though the Berlin crisis was on everyone's mind at the time and had aroused fears of war.

The fact is, at any rate, that prior to the negotiations that took place for replacing the Iranian resolution with the "Mexican" one, the Greek

Foreign Minister had committed himself to meeting the Turkish Foreign Minister after the Assembly had taken a decision on the Cyprus question. Thus new perspectives opened for negotiating a settlement of the question.

This conversation not only seems to have influenced the Turkish Foreign Minister in favor of dropping the Iranian draft resolution next day. It also led to a two-hour meeting with Averoff-Tossizza in the Delegates' Lounge of the UN building, the morning of December 6—the day after the Assembly adopted Resolution 1287 (XIII). In their exchange of views, they prepared, for reference to their governments,[52] the ground for further negotiations. These talks continued in Paris, on December 18, when after informal discussions that included Foreign Secretary Lloyd, the Greek and Turkish foreign ministers sketched the outlines of the basic structure of the independent state of Cyprus.

In Cyprus, following a last-minute reprieve granted by Governor Sir Hugh Foot to two convicted EOKA members about to be hanged (in Paris the foreign ministers of Greece and Turkey had jointly asked Foreign Secretary Lloyd to stay the executions),[53] Grivas, on Christmas Eve 1958, issued a proclamation for a new truce, the fourth of its kind, which was to be his final one. The UN resolution, according to this proclamation (its text had been drafted in co-operation with the Greek government), constituted a clear condemnation of the abortive Macmillan plan. Even before the UN debate had begun, he noted, he had relaxed his activities and had declared his intention to create an atmosphere of peace. EOKA, he declared, would continue to respect the UN decision as long as the other side likewise ceased its activities. Awaiting to see how the British government would implement the UN resolution, EOKA was ready either for a long-range armed struggle, if the British were to continue their intransigence, or for the cessation of the struggle, as long as a just solution were given to the Cyprus problem, a solution that would satisfy the demands of the Cypriot people.[54] Between this Christmas truce proclamation and February 13, 1959, when the settlement of the Cyprus question was achieved in London, no further agitational incidents occurred.[55]

After the British ambassadors in Ankara and Athens called on the foreign ministers of Turkey and Greece on December 25 and 28, respectively, Greek-Turkish negotiations continued through the diplomatic channel and especially through the Greek Ambassador in Ankara. The two foreign ministers met again in Paris (January 18–20, 1959) and sought to iron out some of the major points of difference that remained unresolved. Makarios was kept informed and approved. The stage was now set for the summit meeting between Premiers Karamanlis and Menderes, which took place in Zürich, February 5–11, 1959. Greece, which at the outset had been seeking bipartite negotiations between itself and Britain and then, since 1956, between the Cypriots (represented by Makarios) and Britain, and had resorted to the United Nations to achieve these side effects, among others, thus had to enter first into negotiations with Turkey—a bipartite procedure it relished the least, though the U.S. government had urged it upon the Greek government at least as early as November, 1956,[56] and the British government, in late October, 1957, had sought with particular insistence to emphasize it as acceptable to itself.[57]

After the Greek and Turkish premiers, meeting in Zürich, reached agreement on the basic structure of the new state of Cyprus and had outlined the terms of two other international instruments concerning Cyprus—the Treaty of Alliance between Greece, Turkey, and Cyprus, and the Treaty of Guarantee between Britain, Greece, and Turkey—the British government, together with representatives of the Greek and Turkish Cypriots, came into the picture. The negotiations that took place in Lancaster House—after a dramatic suspense created by Makarios' sudden refusal (due to pressure on the part of certain other Greek Cypriot representatives and to misgivings about the Treaty of Alliance and certain provisions of the Treaty of Guarantee) to support what he had acquiesced in before going to London—led to an agreement for settling the dispute [58] which had come into the open five years earlier.

On March 1, 1959, after an absence from Cyprus of almost exactly three years, Archbishop and Ethnarch Makarios returned to Nicosia where great crowds of Greek Cypriots gave them an overwhelming welcome. As for Colonel Grivas "Dighenis," he finally issued a message on March 9 fully endorsing the London agreement, calling on all Cypriots to rally around the Ethnarch, and proclaiming the need for "harmony, unity, and love" instead of the "paean of war." Eight days later, the leader of EOKA, in a Dakota of the Greek Air Force, returned to Greece which he had left more than four years earlier and was greeted in Athens by the Archbishop of Athens and Foreign Minister Averoff-Tossizza in a state reception during which vast crowds welcomed him back as a national hero.

Evidently aware of the extra-United Nations talks that were going on between Greece, Turkey, and Britain that followed in the wake of the thirteenth Assembly, the Permanent Greek Representative to the world organization did not consider it fit to devote a long special report on the handling of the Cyprus item at that session as he had done at the previous one. In a somewhat disenchanted report on the thirteenth session as a whole, he observed that an atmosphere of weariness had pervaded the proceedings. The way in which the various items had been dealt with revealed a routinization of the work and a lack of cohesion and solidarity among UN members. Yet, he asked: "Do we feel concern for the Indonesians with regard to the question of West Irian?" Could other nations, he implied, likewise feel much concern about the Cyprus question? The United Nations, he observed, had managed to transform drama into a routine. Bureaucratization was prevailing. And great personalities were distinguished by their absence. A notable exception:

Pablo Casals and his cello recital. He, momentarily, had brought harmony to the United Nations.

Yet, in an extraordinarily devious way, the United Nations, it might be said, had contributed to the settlement of the Cyprus question, for in the Zürich and London agreements the collective will of the General Assembly for "a peaceful, democratic and just solution," as expressed in Resolutions 1013 (XI) and 1287 (XIII), had been fulfilled—or so it seemed at the time. Beneath the corporate veil of the United Nations, two of the most influential third-party member states of the organization at the time, the United States and India, had exerted their political will and weight. The United States, wishing to avoid any public commitments on the substance of the dispute between three of its close friends and allies, had since 1954 helped steer the United Nations away from the adoption of any substantive resolution on the Cyprus question and, favoring only procedural or colorless resolutions, had pressed the three parties concerned into reaching a settlement outside the United Nations. At Zürich and London, it had seen this procedure followed and a settlement achieved. Only in a very roundabout way was the substance of this settlement American: through the Indian movement for *swaraj*.

India, on the other hand, had exerted its will in the realm of substance, in favor of a solution based on independence, the highest form of self-government. And the Zürich and London agreements had been based on this concept. Ever since Krishna Menon, at the ninth Assembly in 1954 had maintained that Cyprus was really a question of freedom and independence of the Cypriot people, this concept had germinated and had started to grow in the atmosphere of the United Nations. In 1955, in the Assembly debate over the inclusion of the Cyprus item in the agenda, Krishna Menon had re-emphasized this idea.[59] He had done so again at the eleventh and twelfth Assemblies.[60] Indeed, as revealed in this study, at the eleventh Assembly, backstage, he had even proposed the tabling of a resolution that could call for independence for the Cypriot people.[61] Although the Greek government had rejected this proposal, it had taken up this concept, at first as a device to show up its conciliatory spirit and the possibly expansionist aspirations and intransigence of the Turkish government, then as the basis for an interim solution leading to self-determination, after a period. NATO's Secretary-General, too, had meanwhile adopted a similar view.[62] So had Makarios, who regarded such a solution acceptable if it were proposed not by Greece but by another party.[63] At the twelfth Assembly, however, when the Indian Defense Minister again reverted to a proposal similar to the one he had made to the Greek Delegation at the Assembly's previous session, the Ethnarch rejected this approach, even though the Greek government, by this time, was prepared to favor it.[64] It was only at the thirteenth Assembly that both Makarios and the Greek policy-makers adopted fully Krishna Menon's approach to the Cyprus problem, when they themselves publicly proposed the setting up of an independent Cyprus not merely as an interim stage toward self-determination but in perpetuity.[65] As a result of this formal abandonment of self-determination and of *enosis,* the antagonists desisted from demands for partition or from the implementation of measures that could lead to partition and agreed to work out a settlement of the Cyprus question based, in the last analysis, on the concept of independence the Indian had favored at the outset. In terms of world alignments, the settlement of this intra-NATO dispute was thus a victory of the South over the North. By yielding first to this sort of solution, Greece had sided with the victor.

CONCLUSIONS

This case history of the handling of the Cyprus issue by the Greek "External Decision-maker" inside and outside the United Nations in 1957 especially, as well as his reports on this handling to the "Aspiring Decision-makers" and the "Validators" of Greek government policy, provides certain answers to some of the questions raised in the Introduction. Greece, during the period 1954–1958, resorted so persistently to the United Nations over Cyprus simply because its governments found themselves in a situation in which they preferred to act rather than to refrain from acting and believed that they had no appropriate alternative technique of statecraft available for promoting a cause to which they attached considerable importance for ethnocentric reasons. Recourses to the UN General Assembly were, in brief, responses to situations in which diplomacy was believed fruitless and war unthinkable. The Greek decision-makers acted no differently from decision-makers of great powers, even of superpowers, whenever these found themselves in a similar situation, as witness the United States with its recourses to the Assembly over the Korean and Hungarian questions in 1947 and 1956, respectively, the latter together with Britain and France; or the U.S.S.R. with its complaints about U.S. aggression against China addressed to that same UN organ in 1950 and 1954,[1] or quite recently with its recourse to the Assembly in the Middle East crisis of 1967.

These Greek recourses were also a complement to a technique of force below the level of war. In this respect, too, they were not unique, as witness the Soviet and Ukrainian recourses to the Security Council in 1946 over the "Greek Question" or the most recent recourse of the United States to that same UN organ over the question of Vietnam, not to mention the recourses to the General Assembly of groups of Arab or Asian and African states concerning the questions of Morocco, Tunisia, or Algeria, or Britain's complaint to that same body in 1956 concerning the moral and material aid the Greek government was providing overtly and covertly to EOKA and the Greek Cypriots.

If at certain times the Greek decision-makers gave thought to resorting to the Security Council but preferred instead to go to the Assembly over the Cyprus question, this was partly because the antagonist was a veto-wielding member in that UN organ or because the particular composition of the Security Council at the time did not seem favorable; partly because they wished to avoid having their recourse referred to NATO, in which the atmosphere might not have been too favorable and the advantages of publicity were lacking; and partly because they did not desire to deepen the rift with their allies in that regional organization, upon which Greek security was felt so greatly to depend.

In this particular technique of statecraft, the human instruments used on the overt level are not merely the "External Decision-maker," certain political personalities, and the diplomatic personnel of the protagonist state [2] but also the UN Secretariat with its staff of international civil servants and especially its conference organization and public information services. As for the non-human instruments, these include not only the national apparatus of communication but also that of the United Nations as well as its founding document, the Charter, which makes possible the reiteration of normative ideas to which all its signatories have solemnly subscribed though often flouting them in practice. To an extent that depends on the specific influence that the protagonist may exert on other member states, the representatives of these states may be momentarily transformed into human instruments of the protagonist's policy.

Recourses have as their targets [3] the decision-makers of the antagonist state as well as its "Aspiring Decision-makers," if such exist, and groups that are believed capable of shaping the foreign policy of the target state; the decision-makers of third states; the UN Secretary-General who under Article 99 of the Charter has certain possibilities of autonomous political action, with regard to the Security Council at least, that do not depend of express *ad hoc* authorizations envisaged in Article 98; and, finally, the constituencies of all these states and of the host state in particular.

To deal with these recourses, the antagonist, assisted by his friends likewise seeks to use the United Nations as an instrument of his own policy, his own national interest, in order to defend himself or to counterattack. The full transformation of the United Nations into an instrument of national policy is, of course, never fully achievable, though world powers regard the United Nations not only as an arena and a center for harmonization but also as a stake in world politics. Under certain circumstances, however, superpowers wielding considerable influence over a large number of states or a large group of states may on occasion come closer than small non-caucusing states to achieving this transformation. It is in this sense only that it is correct to say that when the United

Nations serves the national interest of the superpowers the organization is allowed to go forward, and that when it does not, its evolution is hindered.[4]

The methods and tactics small states use to insure the best possible outcome of their recourses to the United Nations in no way differ, judging from this Cyprus study, from those used by great powers or superpowers in promoting their ethnocentric interests in the ostensibly cosmocentric institution called the United Nations nor from those used by any political group that is seeking to promote its goals in a legislature, for instance, of a pluralistic political community. Words, however, will differ in weight. Thus, it may suffice for a member of a delegation that is influential in the United Nations merely to inform representatives of other member states of his government's attitude toward a particular question the Assembly is considering in order to get support for this attitude. The representative of a small and non-influential state, on the other hand, may have to plead, importune, insist, predict, warn, even threaten, in order to exert pressure on the representative of another state, and all this possibly in vain.

Consequently, the representative of a small state, like the representative of the U.S.S.R., a non-influential superpower in the United Nations, especially during the period covered by this study (as contrasted to its indubitable influence and potential outside the United Nations) is aware—or becomes so through hard experience—that the effects he may achieve by his recourse to the United Nations are likely to be limited. He realizes that there will be a considerable gap between the ostensibly desired effects of his recourse to the United Nations (as these effects are expressed in the draft resolution he introduces) and the effects that are finally achieved. He is aware that he cannot really expect the Assembly to back with its moral authority his viewpoint and proposals by adopting them in the form of his own resolution. What he realistically hopes to achieve—or learns to hope to achieve—are side effects: drawing the attention of the society of statesmen to the dispute and its evolving aspects; explaining his side of the story to representatives of third states; publicly unmasking the antagonist government before the eyes of representatives of third states; conducting propaganda among constituencies of other states or political groups in other states; demonstrating firmness of purpose in the pursuit of an objective not only to other governments but also to the home constituency; harassing the antagonist; exerting pressures, directly or indirectly, for negotiations with a view toward a settlement.

The recourse and the proceedings that ensue engender a host of secondary and tertiary objectives in dealing with the reactions of the antagonist and of representatives of third states and with the machinery of the United Nations. Government spokesmen, on the domestic stage, for instance in Parliamentary debates, tend quite naturally to emphasize the favorable side effects achieved and the victories gained in secondary and tertiary objectives, perhaps revealing in the process some aspects of the backstage struggle in the Assembly that suggest that the outcome might have been worse than the one finally obtained. Intragovernmentally, on the other hand, for non-public use, government and high diplomatic officials prepare for the Cabinet and the Foreign Ministry soberer evaluations of the proceedings and the outcome of the UN deliberations on the item.

But even if a state or group of states that is influential in the United Nations is far more likely than a small non-caucusing state to get the Assembly to adopt a resolution that is to its liking, as this and other studies reveal,[5] Assembly resolutions resemble "pseudo-agreements."[6] Since they are not only not enforceable, as rules of International Law are not enforceable, but are not even considered as legally binding under international law, Assembly resolutions concerning government policies are not international pacts and record no settlement, just as is the case with "pseudo-agreements." Nonetheless, like "pseudo-agreements," they may not be altogether devoid of political value if the parties concerned read in them certain implications and regard them as a symbol of some sort of tacit bargain. And, if the relations between the parties to a dispute are strained, the Assembly resolution that registers a consensus among these parties might be considered, like a "pseudo-agreement," "a promise to become more accommodating to each other in the future,"[7] as was the case with the Indian, and, to an even greater extent, of the Mexican resolution on the Cyprus question at the eleventh and thirteenth Assemblies, respectively. Thus, they may be something better than second-level agreements—agreements to disagree. For they may represent commitments to try to agree.

By showing in detail how the machinery of the General Assembly works when a state feeds into it a dispute between itself and another state and how resolutions may be the output of this machinery, this study has highlighted the character of the Assembly as an arena for conflict which statesmen use for purposes of political probing and as a ground for maneuver, as an instrument for mobilizing collective concern, as a forum for intergovernmental communications, as a platform for propaganda, and as a lever for negotiations outside the United Nations. But it has also shown how the world organization may, especially through the actions of third-party states, function as a center for "harmonization."[8] The subtle process by which verbal discord may turn into verbal concord, so that the organization is transformed from an arena of conflict into a center for "harmonization," will be traced below.

Einstein once defined an event in the physical world as a collision in time and space. The commitment to resort to the United Nations over a dispute is a political event, a political collision in time and space. It may set off a chain of other events, of other political collisions. Some of these may take place within the United Nations—others outside it. Article 33, paragraph 1, of the UN Charter may be partly responsible for the generation of the second type of collision. It counsels parties to an international dispute that endangers international peace and security to resort first to various extra-UN methods of peaceful settlement before they go to the United Nations for its assistance.

As a result, if a dispute is brought to successive sessions of the Assembly, a counterpoint pattern of "parliamentary diplomacy" interweaving with conventional diplomacy may be observed.

Such a pattern at least, is observable in connection with the five successive recourses of the Greek government to the United Nations between 1954–58. Thus, Greek government probes through the diplomatic channel of the British government's attitude preceded the Greek decision to resort to the United Nations in 1954 while the inclusion of the Cyprus item in the Assembly's agenda that year triggered British informal negotiations with the Greek government, outside the normal diplomatic channel.[9]

The failure of these negotiations and the lack of any substantive resolution on the part of the UN Assembly in 1954 was then followed by a new recourse to the United Nations and by the London Tripartite Conference of 1955[10] which led to no agreement as did the recourse to the Assembly, which, at its ninth session, decided against including the Cyprus question in its agenda. The Harding-Makarios talks started shortly thereafter, against a background of secret Anglo-Greek and Anglo-Turkish diplomacy.[11] The failure of these talks, in March, 1956, triggered a new round of "parliamentary diplomacy," initiated by the third Greek recourse to the United Nations. Out of this move and out of the British counter-recourse to the United Nations, and of the Assembly deliberations that followed, Resolution 1013 (XI) emerged. This recommended resort to non-parliamentary diplomacy for reaching a settlement of the Cyprus dispute. Ostensibly for the purpose of complying with this resolution, both Britain and Greece came forward with various proposals for resuming negotiations.[12] However, none were resumed. And there was a renewed deadlock. The fourth Greek recourse to the United Nations was then made, to be followed shortly after by British probes for calling a new London tripartite conference.[13] At the twelfth Assembly, "parliamentary diplomacy" was once again tried but resulted in the adoption of no resolution—which left Resolution 1013 (XI) still valid. New diplomatic exchanges, new proposals for settlement followed. New failure. New recourse to the Assembly, which adopted Resolution 1287 (XIII). Although overtly a virtual repetition of the previous one,[14] covertly this resolution constituted an implicit promise of Greece and Turkey to enter into extra-UN negotiations through the diplomatic channel over the Cyprus question. When the diplomatic negotiations that ensued led to a settlement, this interweaving pattern of "parliamentary" with conventional diplomacy naturally came to an end.

This interweaving of conventional with "parliamentary" diplomacy in the Cyprus question during a half decade, it should be added, may not have always been closely connected with the desire of the parties to the dispute to conform with Article 33 of the Charter mentioned above. Some of the earlier diplomatic probings and negotiations of the antagonist may have aimed not at reaching a settlement of the dispute outside the United Nations but at achieving merely certain side effects, at demonstrating that the dispute was not of a purely colonial character, or at neutralizing the recourse to the Assembly and the UN process—in both cases for purposes of "maintenance," [15] for preserving the status quo and avoiding any negotiations aiming at redistribution. So at least, did the Greek government suspect with regard to several British diplomatic moves.[16]

Within the United Nations itself, the recourse to the Assembly, a body which, to a certain extent and within certain limits, can be regarded as a gathering of small groups, the delegations, generates other political events or collisions. Some of these take place necessarily in public—up-stage [17]—in an orderly way. Others occur backstage according to the demands of the moment in exchanges which the UN proceedings do not record but which may leave traces in the diplomatic record and occasionally, as this study has shown, come to the public surface in Parliamentary debates. "Parliamentary diplomacy" in the United Nations takes place, in other words, on two levels. The one is formal, public, and up-stage; the other is informal, secret, and backstage. On the public level, the members of the delegations tend to take legalistic-moralistic poses; on the secret one, they get down to naked politics. In this respect, "parliamentary diplomacy" is very much like the legislative struggle in the U.S. Congress and in similar multiparty legislative bodies which has been described as "a drama played behind closed curtains." [18] The secret exchanges—quiet diplomacy, to use a euphemism—may take place between permanent missions to the United Nations and/or delegations to the Assembly and may also involve Assembly officials, the Secretary-General and Secretariat members in what has been termed "corridor" or "office" diplomacy.[19] But they may also be conducted, sometimes simultaneously, through the diplomatic channel in the form of démarches with Foreign Ministries of other states or the diplomatic representatives of other states stationed in the national capital. Of course, intragroup activities also occur backstage among members of the same delegation as this study indicates. So do communications with the group at home, in the national capital—the Cabinet or a smaller group of Cabinet officials—if time permits.

Most of these backstage exchanges focus on the various public events or collisions the recourse to the United Nations leads to, and especially on the matter of bringing the UN process to a formal conclusion through the adoption of an appropriate resolution by the Assembly. However, not all of these exchanges refer to UN modalities for dealing with the issue, as witness the exchanges of views between the Greek Foreign Minister and his British and American colleagues at the twelfth Assembly or the

Foreign Minister's crucial meeting with his Turkish colleague toward the close of the thirteenth Assembly which opened the way for a settlement of the Cyprus question outside the framework of the United Nations.[20] Indeed, as this case study has shown, even the drawbacks of the publicization of an interallied dispute in the United Nations may become the object of backstage negotiations if the contestants have an unequal interest in having their dispute aired in the United Nations and if a third-party ally, while not formally opposing a public debate of the dispute, hopes this will not be too acrimonious. The protagonist who believes he has something to gain from having the dispute considered in the United Nations—publicization constituting for him a slightly higher rung on the escalation ladder of politico-diplomatic action—may be willing to forego the expected gain if the antagonist is willing to grant an equivalent, feeling he has something to lose from the debates in the United Nations. Even if the antagonist rejects this offer, the protagonist may still feel he has gained something by having made it, because to third party members of the alliance he will have appeared willing to spare the alliance the strain of publicization of the dispute in the United Nations.[21]

In the process that takes place in the Assembly, eight events or collisions may be distinguished. Three of these depend on sovereign decisions of the protagonist. The other five bring into play non-sovereign, community, UN decisions in which the parties to the dispute and their supporters as well as third parties use the rules of procedure of the Assembly to promote their political ends, constructively or obstructively, depending on the viewpoint. As a whole, these eight events, together with the private and informal exchanges that accompany them, constitute the full span of "parliamentary diplomacy" practiced in the Assembly. The entire process resembles, as noted earlier, the legislative struggle in domestic politics of a multiparty system,[22] though it is far more loosely knit, less organized, and, as already mentioned, Assembly resolutions— its output—are even less effective than are the rules of international law.

In the first of these eight collisions, the protagonist in a sovereign decision, declares his intent to get the Assembly debate and consider its dispute with the antagonist. In other words, he expresses the desire that the annual world conference deal with its dispute. Accordingly, he requests the Secretary-General to place the issue on the Assembly's provisional agenda as a supplementary or as an additional item, depending on whether he sends in this request at least thirty days before the date fixed for the opening of a regular session or less than that.[23] Under rule 20 of the rules of procedure, at this stage he is supposed to transmit an explanatory memorandum which, in varying degrees of brevity, sets forth the basic arguments for the recourse as well as his viewpoint about the dispute. Basic documents or a draft resolution should accompany, if possible, the memorandum, under this part of rule 20 that was adopted in 1949.[24] As this case study shows, it is not imperative to send in this memorandum simultaneously with the request for the item's inclusion in the provisional agenda. Nor is it necessary at this point to come forward with any basic documents or any specific proposal in the guise of a draft resolution—a bill in the terminology of domestic politics. Thus, the recourse itself may offer two separate opportunities for making news.

After this preliminary publicization of the protagonist's intentions and views, comes his first engagement with the antagonist: in the Assembly's General Committee, which consists of the President and vice-presidents of the Assembly and of the chairman of its seven committees. Under rule 43 of the rules of procedure, a member requesting the inclusion of an item in the agenda, if he is not represented on the General Committee, is entitled to attend any meeting of that committee at which his request is discussed, and may take part, without vote, in the discussion of that item. Under a liberal interpretation of the rules of procedure by the General Committee,[25] the antagonist or another interested state may be allowed to take part in the discussion. If the antagonist or another member of the committee opposes the item's inclusion in the agenda and resorts to obstructive maneuvers, a contest takes place at this point between those who favor the item's consideration by the General Assembly and those who do not. The debate ends in a decision to recommend to the Assembly the item's inclusion in the agenda or its non-inclusion or its inclusion in the provisional agenda of a future session of the Assembly.[26] Although the contestants at this point are supposed merely to put forward their reasons and arguments for or against such a recommendation of the General Committee and not to start a debate on the substance and merits of the case "except insofar as this bears upon the question whether the General Committee should recommend the inclusion of the item in the agenda,"[27] this is rarely feasible.[28] Yet the Chairman of the General Committee seeks to insure compliance with this rule, and the contestants, aware of the business ahead, restrain themselves to a certain extent in their word duel. Since this collision is resolved by resort to a vote, it generates not only publicity but also secret communications and negotiations of protagonist and antagonist with other members of the General Committee as well as among themselves sometimes. As this study reveals,[29] conflict and negotiations may occur, too, over the form in which the item will be recommended for inclusion in the agenda. And a compromise may be achieved that somewhat blunts the protagonist's publicity objectives by replacing connotational with denotational words in the item's title.[30]

The debate in the Assembly over the General Committee's recommendation comes next. This third collision or event in the UN process, like the previous one, may involve backstage exchanges, but these are more complex, since all members of the United Nations take part in the decision-making. It results in a community decision by a majority of votes of members present and voting. Under rule 23 of the Assembly's rules of procedure, the debate must be limited to three speakers for and three speakers against the General Committee's recommendation for inclusion of the item in the agenda. The President of the Assembly may limit the time allowed to speakers under this rule. A majority of members present and voting may amend or delete an item on the agenda, under rule 22.

Regardless of whether this decision is construed as a decision on the competence of the Assembly to consider the item, or on the merits of the case, this third collision is of critical importance. On its outcome obviously depends whether the remaining five will take place at that session of the Assembly. Although the Greek Delegation encountered no difficulties at this stage at the twelfth or thirteenth Assembly's session with regard to the General Committee's recommendation on the Cyprus item, this had not been the case in 1954 with regard to the same question. On that occasion, the representative of Iraq, speaking on a point of order, had proposed that a decision on the matter of including the Cyprus item on the agenda be postponed for a few days. In the Greek Delegation's view, this was a maneuver of the antagonist and his supporters who sought to gain time for vote-getting purposes that would lead the Assembly to reject the General Committee's recommendation for inclusion of the item in the agenda. The relevant proposal, however, was put to the vote and failed of adoption because of a tie vote.[31]

If the antagonist has shown a desire to avoid having to wage a debate of the dispute in the United Nations and has exerted direct or indirect efforts to block any discussion or consideration of the issue in the Assembly, perhaps arguing that the issue is not internationally negotiable and invoking for this purpose Article 2, paragraph 7, of the UN Charter,[32] both the General Committee's favorable recommendation for including an item in the agenda and the Assembly's approbatory decision represent for the protagonist two preliminary political victories. The opposite is true if the General Committee and the Assembly decide against the item's inclusion in the agenda. At the tenth Assembly in 1955 the Greek government suffered such a defeat; at the ninth, eleventh, twelfth, and thirteenth, on the other hand, it emerged victorious from these collisions.

The fourth opportunity for publicizing one's viewpoint and for engaging in verbal warfare is provided by the general debate with which each annual regular session of the Assembly opens. In this collision, however, no voting takes place, no test that involves possibilities of victory or defeat. On this occasion, although each representative usually makes a broad *tour d' horizon* of the international scene, basing himself on the Secretary-General's annual report to the United Nations and emphasizing certain points of major importance in world affairs, he may refer in various ways to the particular dispute to which his government is a party and present his viewpoint on it. The antagonist as well as representatives of third-party states may take part in this general skirmish. Even before the Greek government ever resorted to the Assembly over the Cyprus issue, it used, as mentioned, the general debate as a platform to draw the attention of the world organization to the existence of that problem.[33] At the Assembly's twelfth session, on the other hand, it did not much exploit this opportunity for intergovernmental communications and propaganda, although it cautiously conveyed certain messages to the parties concerned and to those among the third parties that might be "in the know." [34] Backstage, a sort of verbal cease-fire had been tacitly reached.[35]

Providing an opportunity for maneuvering for position prior to the main engagement, the fifth collision occurs when the Committee to which the particular item has been assigned decides, possibly by vote, the relative order in which it will consider it. This decision again means that backstage communications and negotiations are likely in order to influence the outcome of the voting. If the protagonist wants an early consideration of his item while the antagonist wants the opposite, another struggle occurs. The outcome may spell victory or defeat, albeit of a minor character. Such a conflict took place at the time of the first Greek recourse over the Cyprus question in 1954, when the antagonist, in spite of the Greek Delegation's preference, managed to get the item placed at the end of the Committee's list, perhaps in the hope either that the debate might be briefer if it took place toward the end rather than at the beginning of the Assembly's session [36] or that the ultrasecret British-Greek negotiations concurrently going on outside the United Nations might meanwhile result in some agreement.[37] There was conflict, too, at this point, during the eleventh Assembly, when the Committee Chairman, backstage, suggested that the consideration of the Cyprus item be postponed for the next session of the Assembly. When the Greek Delegation responded to this proposal by threatening to stage a walk-out, he had to yield, however.[38] At the next Assembly, matters were different. The Greek government was testing the possibility of extra-United Nations developments in the Cyprus question and was not unwilling to have the Cyprus item discussed in the Political Committee toward the end of the Assembly's session.[39]

When the item comes up for consideration in the Political Committee, the sixth and seventh collisions take place in the UN process, often in a telescoped way, for reasons of logic and economy of time. Two are the subjects of the verbal engagement: first, the dispute and its substance; and, second, the proposals about the terms of agreement—the draft resolutions protagonist, antagonist, or third parties have tabled in the Committee for its adoption. If the merits of the case are commented on, then certain remedies embodied in draft resolutions may commend themselves. During these two collisions, to be dealt with at greater length below, the results of the negotiations that have taken place backstage on the subject of terms of agreement come to the public surface as commitments. The public, "parliamentary" (in the strict sense of the word) aspects of the whole process are very much in evidence. Backstage exchanges may affect not only the resolutionary outcome but even the whole tone of the public debate. And a new, semifinal round of backstage talks is likely to occur, centering around the matter of the final terms of agreement the member states in the Committee will recommend to the Assembly for its adoption.

The eighth and last collision in the UN process occurs when the Assembly, in full session, examines the report of the Committee's *rapporteur* and the resolution the Committee may have recommended for adoption. Although distinct in time, this collision is closely related to the previous one. During both, each party tries by various methods to achieve the adoption of the draft resolution it favors and to obstruct the one it opposes either by preventing it from being put to the vote or, if it is put to the vote, from being adopted—at least in the form in which it was introduced. A final round of backstage consultations, negotiations, and bargaining may thus take place at this final collision, for the Assembly does not necessarily adopt the resolution the Committee has recommended because, as is well known, on important matters a two-thirds majority of Assembly members present and voting is required,[40] and the Assembly may not only reject the Committee's recommendation but may adopt an altogether new resolution. In the Cyprus question the former occurred at the Assembly's twelfth session, the latter at its thirteenth.

The eighth collision in the UN process is the most important one. It represents the climax in the Assembly's resolutionary process and may spell final victory or final defeat or simply a draw. However, the general debate on the substance of the dispute in the sixth collision, and the struggle to get the Committee to adopt a favorable recommendation to the Assembly in the seventh, may represent for the protagonist the high point of his endeavors, especially if he has no hope of achieving victory in the Assembly by getting it to adopt a resolution he favors but attaches value to the UN mainly as a forum in which he can publicly present his viewpoint to the world.

Since the debate on the substance of the dispute and on the draft resolutions tabled in the Political Committee may last more than one day, the sixth and seventh collisions often provide more than once fare for the daily mass media that cover the work of the United Nations. Consequently they have great propaganda value. While giving the antagonist the opportunity to air his viewpoint, this debate also makes possible public expressions of support on the part of third states not directly concerned in the dispute. Among groups not hostile to such third-state supporters, their favorable arguments may sound more objective, hence, more persuasive, than those presented by the contestants themselves.

In the sixth collision—on the substance of the dispute—protagonist and antagonist, not necessarily in that order, first present to the Committee set statements that contain their arguments and the points of view to which they are committed at that particular point of their dispute, thus, insuring that these will be placed on the UN record. In these statements they develop at great length and with much detail viewpoints and arguments of a political, legal, or factual nature that they had presented with greater brevity and in a procedural guise at the earlier collisions in the UN process. They may also refer to relevant new events in the situation which occurred since these earlier collisions.

If the two collisions take place more or less at the same time, the polemical features of the debate mingle with the negotiatory aspects of "parliamentary diplomacy," the purpose of which is resolution-making. The Assembly thus becomes an arena of conflict-harmonization or a center of harmonization-conflict. Protagonist and antagonist, in their verbal confrontation over the substance of the question, not only present once again the reasons why, in their view, the particular dispute should or should not be raised in, and considered by, the United Nations. They also hurl charges against each other, making use of connotational terms.[41] They shield themselves against these by denials. They hurl back countercharges, using their right of reply,[42] often improvising their lines. They utter predictions, warnings, even veiled threats.[43] They also appeal to third parties, even to each other, or to the United Nations as a corporate body.[44] In their arguments they seek to show off their rectitude and to enhance their prestige. Or they aim at impressing each other and third parties with the firmness of their position and the steadfastness of their adherence to their commitments and proposals, or with their friendly and peaceful intentions. They also try to win small victories in a debating point.[45] In order to test each other and demonstrate their flexibility and desire for accommodation, they may publicly commit themselves to certain proposals that are distinct from those embodied in the draft resolutions tabled.[46] Whether unintentionally or intentionally (for purposes of "gamesmanship"), representatives speaking without prepared statements may misunderstand what another representative has said or may resort to altogether erroneous arguments which they afterward strike off the official records.[47] They may also become quite vague, rambling, and incoherent, perhaps to gain time while formulating their thoughts.[48]

Although verbal restraint tends toward the minimum in the Committee when the major debate on the substance of the dispute takes place, nonetheless, if protagonist and antagonist seek to attract third parties to their cause in order to get support for their respective viewpoints and draft resolutions (this is not always the case), they are likely to carry on their polemics within certain limits which affect the tone and even the substance of the debate. They thus may resist the temptation to indulge in too angry speeches. The process of harmonization sets in. This is even more so in the case of an interallied dispute when cross-cutting solidarity narrows the extreme of polarity.[49] Indeed, implicit or explicit understanding to refrain from the public use of verbal weapons too heavy in caliber and too poisonous in fall-out may be reached backstage beforehand in order to prevent a worsening in relations and an aggravation of the divisive effects of the dispute on the alliance as a whole.

As this case study has revealed, at the twelfth Assembly, the Greek

Foreign Minister not only showed relative restraint in dealing with the
Cyprus issue in the general debate but, in the Committee debate he did
not emphasize, as much as Makarios and the Greek political opposition
would have liked, the theme of British atrocities in Cyprus. He also
refrained from drawing any parallel between EOKA's struggle and that of
the Hungarian freedom fighters. Indeed, at one point prior to the
Committee debate, there seems to have been an informal understanding
between the Greek and Turkish Delegations to refrain from personal
attacks except in retaliation. This understanding was not kept on the
Turkish side for reasons beyond the will of the Turkish Delegation
itself—or so, at least, the Greek Delegation was led to believe.[50] Besides,
both protagonist and antagonist, in contrast to their conduct at the
Assembly's previous session, refrained this time from washing a good
deal of their "dirty linen" in public. Neither the British nor the Greek
Delegation exploited the information they had about each other's "black"
operations.[51] And, although it was the Turkish Delegation which underlined these aspects of the Cyprus struggle on the Greek side,[52] the
Greek Delegation never referred publicly to the threats of war the
Turkish government had made backstage on several occasions since
August, 1956;[53] and it limited itself to mentioning only in very vague and
general terms a situation "fraught with danger" to the peace and security
of the area. Like interallied intelligence activities or support of subversion, interallied war threats are unwelcome evidence of serious cracks
in the cement of allied cohesion. Their official disclosure does not make
matters better. Hence, partly at least, the Greek reticence.

During the seventh collision in the UN process, which centers on the
draft resolution or resolutions tabled, bipartite and multipartite negotiations and bargaining take place in public. These moderate still further
the polemical aspects of the debate on the substance of the dispute in the
previous collision. Thus, although neither Britain nor Turkey was willing
to negotiate with Greece within the framework of the United Nations on
the basis of the Greek draft resolution and, together with the United
States, did not believe that the United Nations could be helpful in
leading to a solution, the Greek Foreign Minister assumed toward both a
negotiating stance during the Committee debate of the Cyprus item at
the twelfth Assembly, though he was fully aware of the British and
Turkish attitudes, through prior backstage exchanges. To the British
representative he once again made it clear that the Greek government
and Makarios were willing to accept a period of self-government for
Cyprus if a satisfactory British statement about the application of self-
determination was forthcoming[54]—obtaining in response another confirmation of the British government's commitment to its position of not
excluding the possibility of double self-determination for the Cypriots in
an eventual settlement.[55] And to the Turkish representative he
unequivocally proposed to see to it that any legitimate Turkish interest in
the island (security, minority rights, economic, even other) would be

safeguarded in an eventual settlement of the Cyprus question.[56] When this statement elicited the Turkish representative's response that a more suitable procedure for discussing such proposals would be to negotiate quietly outside the United Nations, the Greek Foreign Minister replied he was prepared to do so, provided the antagonists and/or the United Nations were to recognize in principle the right of self-determination of the Cypriot population as an indivisible whole.[57]

During this public bipartite or multipartite bargaining which aims also at gathering support and votes of third parties, intrapersonal role conflicts [58] may come to the fore, as the set speech and the interventions of the Greek Foreign Minister during the debate on the draft resolution tabled at the twelfth Assembly suggest. In these, he emphasized his role as spokesman for the Cypriots and de-emphasized his role as a representative of Greece as a whole. He also underplayed his country's position as a member of NATO, though he moderated the tone of his statements and proclaimed his government's desire for good relations with its NATO allies, Britain and Turkey, and his regret about the existence of this interallied dispute. Taking up an unequivocal position among the ranks of anticolonial states, he discreetly presented himself as a champion of the small states against the great powers, especially the Western ones. He also referred to the activities of Greece as an ally during World War II. Finally, he highlighted his country's role as a signatory of the Charter and laid great stress on the need to uphold the liberal principles and humanitarian values of the founding instrument of the United Nations.

The contestants tend to emphasize this latter role—of members of the society of nations rather than of representatives of sovereign states coexisting not always in harmony—when the Committee considers their particular draft resolutions, just as they do earlier when the General Committee and the Assembly consider the inclusion of the item in the Assembly's agenda. As a result, the organization's character as a center for "harmonization" comes again strongly to the fore. The contestants tend to present their interests as UN interests, just as in domestic politics pressure groups and their spokesmen emphasize that the bill they back are "for the public good." Invoking the "community spirit," they mask their ethnocentric viewpoints in cosmocentric terminology. As the debate over the Greek draft resolution at the twelfth Assembly reveals, "we," referring to the United Nations, often displaces the words "my government" or "my delegation." In the Political Committee, for instance, the supporters of the Greek draft subamendment underlined that both sides had expressed their faith in the principle of self-determination. Why then, they asked, should there be opposition to this draft which mentioned a principle all UN members recognized? Not to vote for the draft subamendment would harm the organization's prestige and influence. The United Nations should affirm its principles in a positive way. By adopting this draft, it should demonstrate that it respected its principles.[59] The antagonist and his supporters, on their side, likewise invoked the Charter in registering their objections to this draft resolution. Thus, the Turkish representative attacked the substance of the subamendment as "unconstitutional.[60] Others played up the theme of the need for unity, for consensus, for unanimity, for conciliation, for harmonization, invoking the rationale that the United Nations should be united, not merely a forum for debating questions and for jousting over proposals, which were then put to the vote merely in order to find out how many and who favored those proposals and how many and who opposed them.[61] Furthermore, unlike the protagonist and his supporters, who, in their desire for change invoked a rationalist or idealist view of the UN interest,[62] they tended to emphasize the psychological realist view of this concept since their aim was to prevent the United Nations from endorsing any specific change in Cyprus.[63] Under this approach "the public interest becomes . . . a symbol for the attempt to recognize and consult interests that might be forgotten or overlooked in the pressure of political combat." [64] The various provisions of the Charter, they argued, were interrelated. Hence it was inadvisable to refer to only one of its principles. They warned against the danger of distorting the Charter by placing too great an emphasis on the specific principle of self-determination at the expense of other principles and of the totality of the Charter's purposes and principles. They appealed for a sense of realism in the matter of insuring compliance (i.e., to the desirability of avoiding the adoption of any resolution with which one of the contestants would not comply—with resultant harm to the prestige and influence of the United Nations). The opponents of the Greek draft argued further that the United Nations should do nothing that would impede direct negotiations between the parties concerned for the purpose of reaching a settlement of the dispute.[65] In response to such veiled threats of noncompliance in case the Greek draft were adopted, its supporters asserted that the Assembly, by adopting a resolution mentioning self-determination for the Cypriots, would be merely affirming the existence of the Cypriot people's right to self-determination. The modalities for implementing this principle or right would be dealt with by the parties concerned.[66]

While protagonist and antagonist indulge in their moderately fierce verbal jousting over the substance and merits of the case and over their respective proposals and draft resolutions, a gathering of third parties surrounds them that hardly fulfils the presupposition of rhetoric: a public that can be swayed.[67] For these bystanders of the verbal quarrel, the representatives of other member states, assume various attitudes that are usually based on instructions received from their government in advance of the debate. Thus the drama has somewhat the character of the theater of the absurd.

Some members take part in the debate and consideration of the issue. Others remain silent. The third-party speech-makers present their governments' views on the dispute, perhaps, too, on the draft resolutions tabled. Some, unwilling to take sides in public, may declare themselves in favor of a speedy termination of the debate and propose resort to other, non-public procedures for dealing with the dispute and settling it.[68] Others, on the contrary, may provide verbal support to protagonist or antagonist. Thus, the conflicting voices of two groups of representatives are heard in a drama that has no single playwright, no single director (because the chairman's role is very limited), no strict limits of time that would permit a continuous high level of attention—hence, in the long run, resultant weariness and boredom.

In this play, the silence of some of the bystanding representatives does not necessarily mean non-interest, non-alignment, neutrality, and eventual abstention from the voting. It might merely signify a desire to avoid statements that might gratuitously offend one of the contestants, or favorable words for one with whom one may otherwise not be on speaking terms. The cases of Denmark and Albania during the consideration of the Cyprus question at the twelfth Assembly illustrate such meanings of silence.

Verbal alignment does not necessarily mean voting alignment. It precludes neither abstention from eventual voting nor even a negative vote on a draft resolution the verbally supported party favors, as witness the attitudes of Ceylon and Colombia, when the essentially Greek draft resolution was put to a roll-call vote in the Committee and the Assembly at its twelfth session.[69] Hence, the Greek Foreign Minister's wry remark before the Greek Parliament that in the United Nations the best debate may change opinions but not votes.[70]

Nor does silence during the debate preclude, of course, voting in support of one or the other parties to the dispute either by an affirmative or a negative vote, as witness the examples of Albania and Denmark likewise at the twelfth Assembly.[71] Finally, the publicly expressed distaste for a draft resolution one of the parties to the dispute favors is incompatible neither with an abstention when voting takes place on that distasteful draft resolution nor with backstage efforts to prevent the adoption of this draft resolution, as the example of the United States reveals during decision-making on the Cyprus item at the same Assembly.[72]

Whenever voting is resorted to at any of the five collisions that involve community decision-making, the party that favors a particular motion or draft resolution seeks to get those members of the organization who are opposed to it at least to abstain from voting; those who are inclined to abstain, to take part in the voting and cast a favorable vote; and, finally, those who are in favor, not to change their mind and their vote either by abstaining or by casting a negative vote. The antagonist naturally exerts strenuous efforts in the opposite direction.

As against the glory of public speech-making, there is, then, backstage, the shame of vote-getting, log-rolling, vote-swapping, horse-trading, arm-twisting, buttonholing, of making sure that your friends are "present and voting" in your favor or at least abstaining. When the moment for voting arrives, asking the Chairman of the Committee or the President of the Assembly for a roll-call vote is one way of checking whether your friends are indeed present and voting and faithful to the commitment they had assumed backstage to vote in a certain way. In contrast to the show-of-hands vote that tends to be the rule whenever a consensus has been achieved beforehand, a roll-call vote is a symptom of an unresolved conflict in UN decision-making.

Such vote-getting campaigns which are familiar in domestic legislatures of two-party or multiparty political systems are resorted to by states great and small.[73] Success in these campaigns depends on influence. This case study reveals how the United States, in the last analysis, managed to get Assembly resolutions 814 (IX), 1013 (XI), and 1287 (XIII) adopted, even though it, too, in the last two cases, yielded by accepting draft resolutions different from those it had favored or supported in the Committee or backstage.

What does a small state have to offer in exchange for favorable votes or at least abstentions in matters that are of particular concern to it? Precious little: its own verbal support and vote in other issues in which it is not directly concerned but other states are. Of course, as in a legislature, in the case of an issue in which an acute bipolarization has occurred so that votes are expected to be quite evenly distributed on both sides, a single vote for one side or the other may be of critical importance. Thus, in the Political Committee at the twelfth Assembly, Greece's vote against a seventeen-state resolution on the Algerian question supported by the United States and Britain led to a tie vote—i.e., to the resolution's non-adoption.[74]

Otherwise, in the diplomatic arsenal of a small state international political or economic incentives and disincentives for backing vote-getting diplomacy—attitudes of *do ut des*, promises of *quid pro quo*, or threats of tit for tat—are far from abundant, especially if that state, as was the case with Greece, does not belong to any particular caucusing group in the United Nations. Its arm-twisting capability is very limited. If this small state is involved in an interallied dispute with a more influential ally, it is not likely to get voting aid from its other allies. In the Cyprus case, Greece's only NATO supporter was Iceland. The most this small third party can expect from allies is some sort of neutral stand in the debate and, in voting, an abstention. Neutrality, however, on the part of an influential allied state in the case of a dispute in which the contestants are quite unequal in potential and influence means that the most influential of the parties to the dispute is favored by such a stand. If, on the other hand, a counteralliance exists, the small state protagonist may feel reasonably sure of getting voting support from its members, the foes of its own alliance, without having to concede much in return[75]— except for remaining adamant in its contentious attitude.[76] The mere fact of having raised the interallied issue may be enough to warrant this support. The same holds true if other member states individually happen to be foes of the antagonist state.

Voting support for a small state may be forthcoming, too, from states that have grievances similar to the one that is being aired in the United Nations. Ireland, for instance, could hardly do anything else but "identify" with the Greek views about the integrity of Cyprus and oppose the Turkish proposals for the island's partition if it wished to be consistent with the position it assumes with regard to a national claim of its own.

When a normally dominant power refrains from exerting countervailing pressures, the lack of any direct political concern in the dispute because of a sense of sheer physical and political remoteness from the epicenter of the dispute may be conducive to a modicum of political detachment with regard to the merits of the case itself as measured against certain norms, certain principles enunciated in the Charter, and to an independent attitude in voting. This might lead a member state to vote in favor of the cause of the small state protagonist as a demonstration of its rectitude, of its commitment to basic principles of international conduct, perhaps, too, of its independence from the normally dominant power. Yet such lofty attitudes may not be unmixed with psychological feelings of identification with the viewpoint of one of the contestants. The Delegation of Bolivia, for instance, at both the twelfth and thirteenth Assemblies, voted on the same side as the Greek Delegation did. Was this out of pure detachment or out of a desire to assert its independence vis-à-vis the United States whose delegation had abstained during the vote on the Greek draft resolution at the twelfth Assembly and, at the next one, had voted in favor of the Iranian draft resolution which Greece opposed? Or was this Bolivian attitude—a "deviancy" with regard to the attitude of the United States—related to the fact that Bolivia nourished irredentist views in the matter of the maritime provinces lost to Chile in 1897? Or was this "deviancy" an expression in foreign policy of the Bolivian government's Leftism? That among several Latin American states, which Soviet and Communist propaganda often calls "lackeys of imperialism," a desire existed to assume an independent stand in the Cyprus issue vis-à-vis the dominant power in the Western Hemisphere is suggested by the fact that when the United States abstained from voting on the Greek draft resolution at the twelfth Assembly, Costa Rica, Ecuador, El Salvador, Haiti, and Uruguay voted for this draft resolution. The following year, on the other hand, when the United States voted in favor of the Iranian draft resolution, these states did not vote against it as Greece did but merely abstained from voting. Perhaps this attitude represents the equivalent in international voting behavior of protest voting in the domestic arena. This hypothesis would not conflict with the finding that a poor, imperfectly Westernized Latin American state, even though it is most closely bound economically with the United States, may vote less with the West than the advanced and thoroughly Europeanized ones.[77] In such instances, the emerging solidarity of the developing nations in opposition to the developed ones—the alignment of South *versus* North—seems to have exerted a cross-pressure on the alignment of East *versus* West. Perhaps, too, such voting behavior constitutes the expression of a diffuse dissatisfaction with world conditions and of the loose solidarity existing between small states against the "powers that be." Such symptoms of small-state solidarity against the great powers are not unprecedented, as witness the alignments at the United Nations Conference on International Organization at San Francisco in 1945 over the question of the voting procedure in the Security Council under Article 27, paragraph 2, of the Charter. The foregoing does not mean that personal friendships between representatives of member states in the United Nations also may not influence voting behavior, as witness the Iraqi representative's stand on the Cyprus question at the twelfth Assembly, which led to his recall.[78]

Although, as has been pointed out,[79] states often bring disputes to the United Nations in order to exert pressure on another state to enter into negotiations with it, for the most part the state submitting the dispute or situation would also like to get the United Nations to support its position, pass a sort of judgment on the rightness of its claims, and call for appropriate measures by the antagonist. The same may be said of the Greek government's ideal purposes when Greece resorted to the Assembly five times between 1954–58. In three of its five recourses, the Greek government set in motion a political process that stimulated the Assembly into adopting three resolutions in which the Greek representative positively acquiesced by his vote. However, these achieved effects fell far short of the ostensibly desired effects revealed in the draft resolutions the Greek Delegation had tabled on those occasions as contrasted to the unavowed but *ex post facto* publicly acknowledged side effects achieved. For, whereas these Greek draft resolutions referred to self-determination or, in the case of the last recourse, to independence, the resolutions that the Assembly finally adopted contained no such references. How did it happen, then, that the Greek Delegation started out by supporting one proposal and finally voted for an altogether different one?

The rather complete picture of how a particular government and its delegation to the Assembly experience the process of UN resolution-making, starting from the search for a suitable draft resolution, continuing with the problems created by the reactions of the antagonist as well as of third parties, and ending with the acceptance of a resolution, provides an answer to the above question. It reveals that a most complex process of shifting objectives, a feature of bargaining, takes place, which eventually may lead to "harmonization" in the United Nations, i.e., to resolutions that fall short of the ostensibly desired effects pursued by the protagonist yet, nevertheless, become acceptable to him as well as to the antagonist and to a great number of third-party states. This picture illustrates, in other words, the well-known political phenomenon of draft resolutions, like bills in legislatures of multiparty political systems, being seldom adopted in the exact form and content in which they were introduced, even if their sponsor is a state or a group of states as influential as the United States or the Afro-Asian caucusing group were at the particular phase in the life of the United Nations under study.

The preparations for resolution-making start well before the public debate takes place in the United Nations, even before the recourse is sent to the Secretary-General. They begin when the protagonist, seeking ways of promoting a particular national interest in international society, decides that a recourse to the United Nations may be a suitable technique for doing so and studies means for insuring the best possible outcome for his contemplated resort to the resolution-making machinery of the Assembly. Through bipartite diplomatic probes, he seeks first to discover the attitudes and reactions of the most influential governments toward such a move and toward the proposals that he might table for the Assembly's consideration.[80] Through *démarches* and appeals, he attempts to influence favorably each member of the United Nations as he prepares his campaign in the Assembly. He may seek suggestions for draft resolutions and sponsors for his proposals. And he continues these diplomatic activities and negotiations at the various stages through which his recourse has to pass before he finally formulates the text of his draft resolution and tables it in the Committee.

At the twelfth Assembly, for example, although the Greek draft resolution was not tabled until December 7 when the Political Committee was about to take up the Cyprus item, the Greek Foreign Minister, even before the Greek recourse to that Assembly had been prepared, sounded out the U.S. Ambassador in Athens on June 14, namely, over six months earlier, in efforts to get the United States to support or at least not to oppose a substantive proposal that would call for the setting up of a state of Cyprus, the independence of which would be guaranteed for not less than ten years. Then, after the recourse had been sent to the Secretary-General, he urged Secretary of State Dulles in September to give support to a substantive proposal that would recommend as a solution of the Cyprus problem one of the alternative proposals the Greek government had put forward in August. He also conferred with Krishna Menon, the head of another influential delegation, who at that moment was reluctant to take any initiative as he had done at the previous Assembly. Two days later, the Greek Foreign Minister put forward to the British Foreign Secretary a proposal similar to the one he had made to Dulles. Otherwise, he warned, the Greek Delegation would table a draft resolution that would be similar to those tabled in 1954 and 1957, at the ninth and eleventh Assemblies. A similar warning was conveyed to the U.S. government on September 23.[81]

Two months later, after failing in his efforts to get things moving outside of the United Nations along lines preferred by his government, the Greek Foreign Minister started another round of resolutionary efforts. He sounded out Lodge with a new proposal as an alternative to the draft resolution which he had tentatively decided to table and which mentioned self-determination. If during the Committee debate the British Delegate was willing to state that his government intended to start negotiations with the Cypriots in order to seek a solution in accordance with the principles of the United Nations, he, the Foreign Minister, would not insist on his own draft resolution and would support the adoption of a resolution that would embody the text of the British statement.[82] At this point, then, the Foreign Minister was ready to shift from one goal to another, from a resolution of a substantive character to one that would be largely procedural, though it would mention who the parties to the negotiations should be. It was only after the British Delegation rejected this proposal and, in turn, came up with a counterproposal which the Greek Delegation found unacceptable, that the latter tabled its own draft resolution that mentioned self-determination for the Cypriots and was quite similar to the draft resolutions introduced at the Assembly's ninth and eleventh sessions.[83]

As this study of the genesis of the draft resolution of 1954 has revealed, in drafting this particular proposal for the Assembly's consideration, the Greek Delegation "watered down" in advance the text of its draft resolution so as to make it moderate in tone, hence attractive to third-party members of the United Nations who were waiting to see what sort of draft resolution would be tabled, before making up their minds whether to vote in its favor.[84] Extremist draft resolutions appear repugnant to third parties who have not yet quite taken sides, just as extreme polemics during the debate of the question may likewise affect their attitude in a negative way. The result is, as has been pointed out, that resolutions concerning governmental policies are generally framed in a language calculated to avoid giving offense even to those governments that are not expected to comply.[85]

If then the protagonist really desires to attract the maximum possible number of third-party votes to his draft resolution and not issue just a ringing manifesto,[86] the less influential he is and the more powerful the expected opposition is, the greater is the likelihood that his draft resolution will be moderate in tone. Thus, in 1954, though the title of the first Greek recourse and explanatory memorandum together with their diplomatic and UN background clearly suggested that the Greek government wished to propose the conduct of a plebiscite in Cyprus under UN auspices with the goal of achieving *enosis*, the Greek Delegation formulated its draft proposal in the form of a wish—a *voeu*—on the part of the Assembly that the principle of self-determination be applied to the people of Cyprus. Moreover, it diluted its original text three times in vain efforts to make it acceptable to the United States, whose attitude, it realized, would be of crucial importance in determining the outcome if the draft resolution were put to the vote [87]—which it never was.

Once the delegation has committed itself to a specific draft resolution and has tabled it, it may engage in a new round of efforts through the diplomatic channel and contacts in the United Nations with representatives of other states to persuade the members of the organization to assume a favorable attitude toward this proposal and support it if it is put to the vote. Although it is hard to change voting intentions of other governments at this late stage of the game,[88] it seems that in the UN resolutionary struggle, as in domestic political campaigns, "every cartridge must be fired because among the multitude of blanks one may be a bullet." [89]

The multipartite negotiating for support and for votes that takes place in public over a draft resolution that has been tabled, may lead to further revisions in its text, as its sponsor presents arguments designed to make his proposals appear even more attractive to third parties, if not even to the opponent. Invoking the community spirit, he may resort to arguments about rules of accommodation.[90] In response to informal suggestions or criticism leveled against his draft resolution during the debate or backstage, he may proclaim his willingness to modify its text in order to take into account these observations. Indeed, in quite a sophisticated move, by the way in which he has drafted his resolution, he may purposely leave it open to proposals for amendments, and during the debate he may suggest his willingness to accept such amendments, should the antagonist or third parties wish to propose them.[91] Finally, if the opponent or his proxies react by proposing amendments to the draft resolution, the sponsor may respond by accepting at least those amendments which he believes do not radically alter the character of his draft resolution.[92] Thus, as contrasted to what might be called "pre-emptive dilution," a process of dilution by conflict and compromise may take place in public.

Instructions sent to those handling a question in the United Nations illustrate this process of shifting goals in a way that somewhat approximates the model distinction made between a so-called "sham bargaining range," an "estimated bargaining range," and an "ordering of preferences in political negotiation." [93] Thus, during the eleventh Assembly, six days before the debate on the Cyprus item began in the Political Committee on February 18, 1957, the Greek Premier and Cabinet instructed the Foreign Minister in New York to insist basically on a resolution referring to the right of self-determination and requesting the British government to apply it in Cyprus. Such insistence, however, they added, should continue only to the point where this draft resolution seemed to be in danger of being rejected in the Assembly. If rejection was certain, then the proposals of other delegations, which were better than a rejection or a simple postponement and which did not create dangerous future commitments and complications, ought to be examined. Among such proposals, the one that was closest to the Greek one and best advanced the question should be proposed and supported. Proposals referring to the need for tripartite negotiations ought not to be accepted. Within these general guidelines, the Foreign Minister was given full authority to maneuver comfortably, while the Premier and the Cabinet were ready to respond immediately to concrete questions.

If at one point or another, the protagonist, too, or a third party had taken measures designed to counteract or neutralize the protagonist's draft resolution no matter how diluted this has become, "harmonization," "conciliation," accommodation, or adjustment with regard to a draft resolution may take place, if the protagonist prefers agreement to no-agreement. As a result, both protagonist and antagonist may find themselves voting in favor of the same draft resolution. One method for achieving this result is to incorporate in a third draft resolution certain features of the draft resolutions the parties to the dispute have introduced, so as to create a sort of synthesis. At the eleventh Assembly, Averoff-Tossizza proposed such a synthesis of draft resolutions, without success, however.[94] Another method for achieving accommodation is to introduce amendments that will make the amended resolution palatable to both parties to the dispute. At the ninth Assembly, by this method, the draft resolution of the antagonist's proxy became acceptable to the protagonist.[95] A third method for achieving accommodation is to introduce a third draft resolution, as a result of which the contestants, disarming themselves, as it were, withdraw their own draft resolutions and then vote for the new one the third party has tabled.[96]

Resolutions 1013 (XI) and 1287 (XIII) are examples of this type of accommodation, of adjustment by substitution. The first of these, as compared with Resolution 814 (IX), which is a fine example of a purely procedural resolution,[97] was graced with a shadow of substance, no matter how "colorless," how deliberately ambiguous that substance was.[98] The last of these resolutions, though likewise introduced by a third party and reiterating more or less the previous one, had been the outcome of direct negotiations between protagonist and antagonist, so that there could hardly be any doubt that both would vote for it, since the sponsoring state was acting as a proxy for both.[99] Because neither protagonist nor antagonist could see a sure victory if his own draft resolution were put to the vote, and because the substitute draft resolutions were such that both could regard their adoption as a partial victory or, at the least, not as a defeat, the contestants found both resolutions acceptable and voted in their favor.

Of course, if the protagonist prefers no-agreement to agreement, then accommodation is unlikely, in the sense of having both parties to the dispute eventually voting for the same draft resolution. The Assembly may adopt the protagonist's draft resolution and a resolution will be the outcome, but not accommodation. The Assembly, too, may reject this draft resolution, as it did the essentially Greek draft resolution on the

Cyprus issue at its twelfth session. On that occasion, the Greek Delegation rejected compromise proposals that representatives of Mexico, Lebanon, Peru, and India made backstage; fought back with a subamendment the amendment introduced by the antagonist's proxies; and, after considering the possibility of getting the Assembly vote for a postponement of a decision on the draft resolution the Committee had adopted, pressed ahead for a vote on its own somewhat amended draft resolution, even though it knew that the Assembly would reject it. Especially in the mind of Makarios, the withdrawal of the draft resolution in favor of one proposed by a third party or the acceptance of amendments that would be the equivalent of a withdrawal, would have borne the shameful stigmata of a one-sided retreat from the field of battle.[100] Had the antagonist put forward a draft resolution of his own instead of amendments through proxies, would retreat have been easier, provided it were joint? This is a moot point. This case study suggests at any rate that during a particular phase in the life of the United Nations and with regard to a particular type of issue, it was harder for third parties to formulate a draft resolution acceptable to both parties to a dispute, when only the protagonist had tabled a draft resolution than when the antagonist, too, had done so.

Even before one or both parties to the dispute table their draft resolutions, a middle group of third-party members may initiate mediatory activities, sometimes with the parties to the dispute seeking them out. A desire to exercise diplomatic skill or to get the satisfaction of exerting some political influence on the destinies of others without damage to one's self, or, it should be added, perhaps to some advantage to one's country or even one's self in another sphere,[101] may motivate some of these middlemen—the "fire brigade," as certain writers have called them, having in mind the role of these third parties during the Suez crisis.[102] A genuine sense of international responsibility, a disinterested need to play the role of a member of international society, and the wish not to see the United Nations fail to take a decision, may inspire others. In the former group may be found the proxies or cryptoproxies of the disputants. In the latter are those who seek to play a genuine intermediary role by trying to discover a common ground on which to base a proposal for somehow conciliating the parties to the dispute, even though this might be by purely verbal or formal means, in order to allow the Assembly to adopt some sort of recommendation with a degree of consensus that will include the votes of both protagonist and antagonist. The dividing line between the two basic types of middlemen—the proxies and cryptoproxies, on the one side, and the genuine mediators, on the other—may be quite blurred. For a proxy or cryptoproxy to be successful, he must, as much as possible, assume the guise of an honest broker. And the genuine mediator must not only be honest but, like Caesar's wife, appear so.

Because the line between genuine mediators and cryptoproxies is very thin, and because each of the contestants has its own preferred middle solution, the intervention of the middlemen in the resolutionary process does not necessarily mean the immediate end of conflictual decision-making, a symptom of which is the roll-call vote, or the immediate emergence of consensual decision-making, which is usually conducted by a show-of-hands vote. An intermediate contest between mediating states that replaces the struggle between the parties to the dispute and their respective draft resolutions, may occur over the third-party proposals and/or draft resolutions, before a consensus is reached. Thus, at the thirteenth Assembly, the resolutionary struggle in the Committee really centered around two third-party resolutions: that of Iran, which Britain and Turkey favored but Greece opposed; and that of the ten states led by India, which Greece favored and Britain and Turkey opposed.[103] During the eleventh Assembly, after backstage proposals by Italy, the United States, and Thailand, all of which were unpalatable to the Greek Delegation, India came forth with a proposal of its own. This became acceptable to protagonist and antagonist, and the Assembly eventually adopted it.[104] The final vote on the Indian draft resolution at the eleventh Assembly like the vote on the Mexican draft resolution at the thirteenth, no longer constituted a symbolic battle between two groups in conflict. Carried by a show of hands, or even without a formal vote, both formally affirmed a consensus reached beforehand, represented a success for the Assembly as a corporate body, and allowed the contestants to withdraw honorably from the UN arena neither defeated nor victorious.

The deliberate ambiguity [105] of both these resolutions, whose texts were almost though not quite identical, made possible their acceptance by the parties to the dispute, hence their adoption by the Assembly. The results, however, of these resolutions were altogether different as was their genesis—which suggests two different functions of ambiguity. Although Grivas' truce and Makarios' release followed the adoption of Resolution 1013 (XI), and this suggested a measure of compliance with it, this Assembly recommendation failed to stimulate any resumption of negotiations for finding "a peaceful, democratic and just solution" to the Cyprus problem. By its ambiguity it merely served to wrap up the debate and consideration of the Cyprus item in the United Nations, and the contestants, by the interpretations they gave to it, used it as a shield or as a sword during the debate of the Cyprus item at the next Assembly, as is often the case with statutes in a legislature which are the result of a struggle, a compromise, an armed truce, and a prelude to the next conflict.[106] Both internally and externally the protagonist exploited the resolution's deliberate ambiguity for his own political purposes, resorting to various quasi-legal techniques of interpretation—referring, for instance, to the backstage negotiations that went into this resolution's shaping as though these were a sort of *travaux préparatoires* or invoking the number of "favorable" interpretations of the resolution that other delegations had given to it, the sponsor included, in violation of rule 129 of the Assembly's rules of procedure.[107]

Needless to say none of these interpretations are legally authoritative. Nor does any special organ exist to determine the correct interpretation of these somewhat sibylline resolutions which, in any case, are not legally binding. To set up a procedure for clarifying deliberately ambiguous resolutions would be to defeat their very purpose which is, precisely, accommodation, or a semblance thereof, by ambiguity. As for the antagonist, he probably felt that the deliberately ambiguous Resolution 1013 (XI) changed essentially nothing in the existing balance. Since the opponent was an ally, perhaps he saw no reason for objecting to the papering up of the dispute with such a document. Third-party states, members of the same alliance, certainly must have welcomed this "colorless" resolution which the United States directly or indirectly favored. It spared them the pain of having to choose sides in public between allied contestants and friends.

If in the case of Resolution 1013 (XI) ambiguity had been the price paid for reaching a semblance of consensus in the Assembly and for getting the contestants to reaffirm their adherence to norms of international behavior to which all UN members had subscribed, ambiguity in the case of Resolution 1287 (XIII) served to cover a specific implicit commitment of the contestants to transform their backstage exchanges in the United Nations that had led to the formulation of a mutually acceptable resolution into at least the first step toward further exchanges, in order to achieve "a peaceful, democratic and just solution" of the Cyprus problem outside the forum of the United Nations, through the diplomatic channel. Built into it was already something more than the mere verbal compliance, with mental reservations, usually symbolized in the Assembly by the affirmative votes of the contestants and the interpretations of their votes. As a result, Resolution 1287 (XIII), though recalling the earlier resolution and equally ambiguous in form, served as a prelude not to the next conflict, as had occurred with Resolution 1013 (XI), but to accommodation—to further "efforts" by "the parties" to achieve a settlement, to a new cease-fire in Cyprus, to the agreements of Zürich and London, to Makarios' return to Cyprus and to Grivas' departure from the island.

In conclusion, here are ten comments on this case study in the light of various politico-socio-psychological hypotheses and findings of students of conflict and conflict resolution.

1. This case study has indicated not only that resort to "parliamentary diplomacy" serves as a substitute for conventional diplomacy, with lack of the latter serving as grounds for resorting to the former, but that commitment to "parliamentary diplomacy" may also serve as grounds for not agreeing to negotiations through diplomatic channels or *ad hoc* conferences.

2. This case study also seems to confirm the views of certain sociologists and psychologists that conflict in the General Assembly is a "substi-

tute for violence." [108] On more than one occasion, Greek politicians themselves acknowledged as much.[109] However, the covert support Greek
governments gave to the application of force through unconventional
warfare or agitational terrorism in Cyprus indicates that the above hypothesis must be somewhat qualified. It is not possible to answer in the
affirmative without reservations the question whether "battles in parliamentary diplomacy are substitutes for more violent battles elsewhere," [110]
just as one cannot answer with a categorical affirmative the question of
whether ballots in domestic politics are substitutes for bullets. "Parliamentary diplomacy," namely, does not necessarily exclude some forms of
force. Without too great an effort, it can be imagined that simultaneously
with the outbreak of war between two states, the two belligerents would
resort to the UN Security Council. Indeed, under Article 51 of the
Charter, states are obliged to do so.

In this possible relationship between "parliamentary diplomacy" and
resort to force of a liminal character, decision-makers may view the latter
either as a presupposition, a complement, a support of the former, or as a
measure to be applied only after this type of diplomacy or diplomacy of
the conventional type has been attempted but has failed. In the first
approach, which was that of Grivas, resort to force is viewed as a
technique complementary to "parliamentary" or other diplomacy. In the
second, which was that of Kyrou, it served as a higher rung in a series of
moves arranged in the form of an escalation ladder. And it is only in the
latter case that one can say that "parliamentary diplomacy" is a substitute
for "more violent battles elsewhere." The same of course, may be said of
support to agitational terrorism, of war by proxies, or of limited war.
They, too, serve as "substitutes for more violent battles elsewhere."

But whatever the approach used, resort to liminal force, or crossing the
threshold of violence, may spell the difference between the mere debate
of the conflict in the United Nations and its consideration by the United
Nations. For regardless of when force is first resorted to, regardless, too,
of the question of where "Justice" lies in the conflict, the United Nations
is an international instrument that deals with peace-keeping and thus,
ironically enough, provides an incentive for the use of force, to a certain
degree at least, if a party to a conflict is seeking to draw the organization's attention to this conflict. If blood isn't spilled, the society of nations
isn't interested. In a broader context, if conflict breaks out, its exacerbation or escalation may be a prerequisite for UN or other mediation (in
the broadest sense of the word), thence to de-escalation and perhaps to
the resolution of the conflict.

3. This study suggests that a recourse to the United Nations and the
conflict that ensues in the Assembly makes possible a displacement of the
goal of the protagonist who no longer aims at reaching a solution of the
unsatisfactory situation that led him to resort to the United Nations but
merely at releasing tensions that arise from this situation,[111] even though
the protagonist had a rational political goal in resorting to the United

Nations and desires to achieve at least certain side effects from this action. As is often the case of the legislative struggle in a domestic political institution such as the U.S. Congress, the way in which the battle has been fought and the intellectual and vital stimulus which the debate in the United Nations has generated, are in themselves things that matter.[112]

4. It has been pointed out that when a third party intervenes in a conflict between two, the possibility arises of an alliance between one of the parties to the conflict and this third party.[113] This is exactly the objective of the protagonist when he resorts to the United Nations. He seeks to get the Assembly—the maximum possible number of its members—as an ally. The antagonist, on his side, tries to prevent this from happening and even to transform this "third party" into an ally of himself. In pursuing this goal, the parties seek to get the Assembly to justify their own position, to condemn the opponent's or at least to avoid the condemnation of their respective positions. In other words, they seek to get the Assembly to fulfil a function of "legitimization" or "delegitimization," [114] or, more correctly, of "moral justification" or "moral condemnation," since the resolutions of the Assembly that pertain to the conduct of governments are not, as well known, legally binding—which means that the Assembly had no authority to "legitimize" or "delegitimize."

5. This case study has confirmed the proposition that conflict may bring persons and groups together which otherwise have nothing to do with each other.[115] It has shown how the resolutionary struggle Greek representatives waged in the United Nations engendered temporary voting alignments that corresponded neither to actual political alignments in the world arena nor to the caucusing groups that have evolved in the United Nations for purposes of elections to various UN organs or for filling the various official posts at the annual sessions of the Assembly.[116] The Greek support for, courting of, and co-operation with, representatives of several Latin American or Arab League states, not to mention the exchanges with members of the Soviet bloc, illustrate this socio-political process in the arena of the Assembly. They represented efforts to extend influence through combinations,[117] in this instance of an *ad hoc* character.

6. The United Nations General Assembly is not only an arena of conflict but also a center for harmonization of conflicting interests. Thus, a recourse to the United Nations is not only a challenge for a verbal conflict, a debate, but also a move toward conflict resolution through implicit mediation, in the broadest, not in the international juridical, sense of that word. The basic interaction changes from a dyad into a triad, as though the conflict had turned into a law suit and litigation, as the "third person" interposes himself between the parties to the conflict.[118] In the Cyprus case this was particularly evident with the first recourse to the United Nations when the Greek government approached the Assembly as though it was an international tribunal.[119] However, since the United Nations is neither a tribunal nor has at its disposal a

police force to enforce its decisions, the process of implicit mediation resembles conflict resolution not in a developed institutionalized body politic but in a primitive society which, like the United Nations, has neither courts nor police.[120] The shift in the style of Greek foreign policy-makers from the idealist to the realist approach to the General Assembly and from "forensic" or "judicial" rhetoric to "deliberative" rhetoric noted in the introduction [121] was an adaptation to the fact that the United Nations is no legal system of a "vertical" kind but is "horizontal" in structure.[122]

7. In primitive societies the transformation of conflict interaction from a dyadic to a triadic form that leads to implicit mediation may sometimes occur, it has been pointed out, without the actual physical presence of third persons, with the system itself becoming the third person.[123] This is obviously not the case with recourses to the Assembly even though speeches there often refer to the "society" or "community" of nations and to the UN spirit. The Assembly is composed of a gathering of third parties, the representatives of member states; and, as this study has shown, their actions and interactions interweave with the political maneuvers of the parties to the conflict in ways that may lead to verbal moderation, verbal conciliation, and eventual accommodation. Quite correctly, then, it has been said that the United Nations is primarily a collection of third parties, a setting in which states not involved in disputes may exercise whatever conciliatory influence they may possess or be capable of generating.[124]

8. The UN process has certain socio-political by-products—somewhat awkwardly called "non-resolution consequences" in a recent article [125]—which are illustrated in this study and should not be confused with the side effects pursued when resorting to the United Nations. The search for allies in a conflict situation may have socio-political consequences of a wider temporal range and may extend beyond the Assembly arena. To achieve success in this search, a state may decide to strengthen its diplomatic relations with other states by sending roving missions of political and/or diplomatic representatives to the capitals of countries in which no permanent diplomatic missions are established. Both the Greek and the Turkish government resorted to such methods at various times in order to promote their respective viewpoints on the Cyprus question. States in conflict may proceed further and set up permanent diplomatic missions in states in which they had none prior to the conflict. Greece, for example, before raising the Cyprus question in the United Nations in 1954, had no embassy in New Delhi but shortly thereafter established one for reasons clearly connected with the Cyprus case. And Turkey, after the Cyprus debate at the twelfth Assembly in 1957, opened permanent diplomatic missions in eight countries, to gain support of its viewpoint in the Cyprus question—or so at least the Greek government believed. Finally, because of the exigencies of the conflict, representatives of states that have no normal diplomatic relations and perhaps no

diplomatic ties at all with each other may get in touch during sessions of the Assembly, perhaps at social gatherings, and may even reach understandings that have effects on the relations outside the United Nations. The Greek-Albanian and Greek-Bulgarian backstage bargaining at the eleventh Assembly illustrate this type of by-product of the UN process.[126]

9. Certain sociologists of conflict between small groups have maintained that between-group relations are largely the result of within-group relations. If there are within-group conflicts and there is a desire to maintain cohesion, between-group conflicts may be consciously cultivated, they maintain, in order to guarantee existing conditions, because in outside conflicts internal cohesion is likely to increase.[127] Other sociologists of conflict between small groups, however, believe that intergroup attitudes and behavior are determined primarily by the nature of relations between groups and not primarily by the pattern of relations and attitudes within the groups themselves. When friendliness already characterizes between-group relations, they believe, harmonious in-group relations probably contribute to solutions of mutual problems between groups.[128]

Finally, according to a study based not on the research about small-group behavior but on an effort to deal with international and national political phenomena of conflict according to certain measures that permit quantification, the finding has been put forward that the relationship between external and internal conflict is small but increases with a time lag.[129] This finding supports the conclusion of another sociologist that the presence or absence of general war and internal disturbances are fairly independent of one another.[130]

Does the present study of the Cyprus conflict confirm or deny any of the above views? Was this external conflict in any way related to phenomena of internal conflict? Did the Greek government raise the issue in 1954 deliberately in order to maintain and/or increase internal cohesion in the Greek body politic? Regardless of the government's political intentions, did this conflict over Cyprus with Britain and Turkey lead to an increase or a decrease in internal cohesion? Without having attempted to gather all the relevant materials that might help in providing answers to these and similar questions, the writer ventures to make certain tentative observations, basing himself mainly but not exclusively on the materials presented in this case study.

Although it has been said that in 1955, at least, there had been a deterioration of the Greek economic situation, "from which some distraction was desirable," [131] with Cyprus providing that distraction, if, nevertheless, certain phenomena listed by the author of the aforementioned finding that the relationship between external and internal conflict is small are taken as measures of domestic conflict, the decade 1950–60, during which the Cyprus conflict germinated, broke out, reached its climax, and then was resolved (temporarily at least), can be characterized as a period of relative domestic quiet, political stability, and economic growth in Greece as compared with the period 1940–49. It was distinguished by the absence of guerrilla warfare, an outstanding feature of 1945–49, and there were no revolutions or coups d'état, purges, political assassinations, or domestic violence. Ballots replaced bullets at three general elections during this period. The elections of November 6, 1952, ushered in a decade of rule which, to a degree unusual for Greece, featured no serious government crises nor internal political turmoil. This suggests that it is possible to have external conflict without phenomena of internal conflict and that the relationship between external and internal conflict may be less than small.

On the other hand, one might say that there was a relationship between an internal conflict—that between the doves and the hawks examining the Cyprus question—and the external conflict with the British and the Turks over Cyprus and that the internal conflict—and its resolution—led to the external conflict. Thus, the Greek government, when raising for the first time the Cyprus question in the United Nations, did refer to the pressure of "public opinion" as a motive for doing so, and "pressure" suggests an internal conflict, between the government itself and certain influential persons or influential groups or the "public" as a whole. But one might also say that there was another sort of relationship between external and internal conflict, in which the former "caused" the latter. For on various occasions, there were "antiforeign" demonstrations of an anti-British, anti-Turkish, anti-American, anti-NATO, anti-UN character, as well as heated and noisy debates in Parliament between members of the government and leaders of the Opposition over the Cyprus conflict. During this period, namely, if anything led to internal disturbances it was the external Cyprus conflict or foreign policy problems connected with NATO, for instance.[132]

The above remarks point to the difficult methodological problems involved in studying relationships or non-relationships between political and sociological phenomena. One type of analysis might confirm the views of that sociological school of thought which maintains that between-group relations are largely the result of within-group relations; another might indicate the possibility of a reverse interaction. And with regard to measures of conflict, it is possible that "antiforeign demonstrations," placed in the class of measures of external conflict, might, in spite of their outward character, constitute antigovernment or domestic demonstrations under an antiforeign guise. Indeed, several of these demonstrations, such as the one of May 9, 1956, in Athens during which four or five persons were killed and about 300 injured with USIA window panes smashed,[133] seemed to be of an antigovernment character and expressions of domestic discontent. If viewed in this light, the raising of the Cyprus question in 1954 could be regarded as a measure designed to prevent domestic conflict, i.e., to forestall the erosion of national cohesion, of cohesion between the government and its pro-Western policies and the Greek people. It is noteworthy that Premier Papagos resorted in effect to such an argument when he told the British Ambassador in Athens that if Cyprus were annexed to Greece, one would be able to say that Greece in its entirety had been annexed by Britain, in other words that the cohesion of the Greek people in terms of pro-British sentiments would be greatly increased. Later on Foreign Minister Averoff-Tossizza used this argument in a different way when pleading for a favorable settlement of the Cyprus conflict that would prevent an erosion of Greek cohesion in terms of pro-Western sentiments.

But regardless of political intentions, did the cohesion of the Greek body politic increase or decrease during the 1950's? The answer would be "Yes" if the trend toward neutralism among pro-Western political groups because of discontent over the attitude of the West toward the Greek viewpoint on the Cyprus question were considered as an indicator. If, on the other hand, the question were to be examined in terms of pro-Eastern *versus* pro-Western orientation, the answer would be "No." A glance at the results of three out of the total of four general elections between 1952–61, those of 1952, 1958, and 1961,[134] suggests that after the Cyprus conflict flared up in 1954, there was a decline in pro-Western sentiments among the Greek people but that these rose again after the resolution of the conflict in 1959–60. In the first of these elections, 82.26 per cent of the popular votes went to pro-Western political parties and only 9.55 per cent went to the Communist façade party. In 1958, however, the latter received 24.42 per cent of the popular vote while the former obtained only 79.39 per cent of this vote. Finally, in 1961, after the Cyprus conflict had been resolved, the pro-Western parties received 83.9 per cent of the popular vote as against 15.1 per cent for the pro-Eastern party. Although the Cyprus conflict was not the sole factor that accounts for the psephological variations, it is likely to have weighed quite heavily in the balance. Here again then is an indication that, in certain circumstances at least, intergroup relations affect within-group relations rather than the reverse.

If the question is approached in more limited terms of Parliamentary cohesion, it may be observed that it was a government with a huge majority in Parliament that raised the Cyprus question in the United Nations, whereas it was a government with a decreased majority acting under continuous Opposition fire that contributed to the resolution of the Cyprus conflict. This would confirm that school of sociological thought whose proponents maintain that in small group relations at least "intergroup relations and behavior are determined primarily by the nature of the relations between groups and not primarily by the pattern of relations and attitudes within the groups themselves." In the elections of November 16, 1952, the Rally party of Papagos received 49.22 per cent of the popular votes and a huge majority in the Parliament—247 out of 300 seats. As mentioned in the Introduction, it was this feeling of great political strength that to a considerable extent motivated the Director-General of the Greek Foreign Ministry in pressing forward the Cyprus question. This, incidentally, suggests that a sense of domestic political cohesion rather than of domestic conflict between rulers and ruled and an overwhelming Parliamentary cohesion may be conducive to the outbreak of intergroup conflict. In the elections of May 11, 1958, on the other hand, the ERE party (National Radical Union), under the leadership of Karamanlis, Papagos' successor received 41.16 per cent of the popular vote, obtaining 171 seats out of a total of 300 in Parliament. Yet it was this government, stronger by only six seats as compared with the previous one that emerged from the elections of 1956,[135] which managed to reach a solution of the Cyprus problem—after which its domestic support at the polls rose to 49.6 per cent and its Parliamentary majority rose to 174 seats out of 300. This solution, it should be added, was facilitated by the adoption by both the Greek and Turkish leaders of a superordinate goal: the re-establishment of close Greek-Turkish relations, with Cyprus regarded not as an apple of discord but as a factor of harmony.

10. In spite of the earlier-mentioned finding that the relationship between external and internal conflict is small, its author suggests that while "there may be no 'simple' relationship between domestic and foreign conflict behavior . . . there may be a causal relationship which is being obscured by other phenomena—i.e., the relationship may be mediated by a third variable such as the personality characteristics of the national decision-makers." He cautions, however, against the "third variable" interpretation for aggregate data but proposes that the "third variable" interpretation may be valid for individual level characteristics as distinct from aggregate data.[136]

This case study, by dwelling in some detail on three of the top personalities involved in this conflict on the Greek side at least, does touch on this question of the "third variable," the personality characteristics of certain decision-makers. It would be necessary to proceed further along these lines, and also examine the top British and Turkish personalities involved in this conflict and then their interaction as opponents and as partners in the conflict, trying also to discover how these individuals viewed each other in the course of this conflict, which might include also respective stereotypes about each other. For the emergence of this conflict a study of the interaction of the clusters of Greek, Cypriot-Greek, and Greek Cypriot personalities, such as Papagos, Kyrou, Grivas, and Makarios, with the cluster of British personalities, such as Eden, Hopkinson, Lennox-Boyd, and Lloyd, would have to be carried out, with an analysis of how they played their various roles at various times as ethnocentric foreign policy–makers, partycentric leaders in the domestic arena, cosmocentric actors in the United Nations, perhaps, too, simply as egocentric individuals in terms not only of behavioral but also of other schools of psychology.

Here are some indications of how some of the actors viewed each other. Of Foreign Minister Averoff-Tossizza, Sir Hugh Foot (now Lord

Caradon) wrote that he "was equally and brilliantly articulate in English, French, and Greek. He was well groomed, dark, elegant, eloquent, with a mind like quick-silver and a generous enthusiasm. When I think of the qualities we have always admired in the Greeks, including the gift of political courage, I think of him." [137] Of Premier Karamanlis, he wrote that he was "good-looking with an easy dignity of carriage and manner. . . . In his presence one always had a sense of his fairness and steadiness." [138] As for Grivas, he was, according to Sir Hugh, a fanatical master of hit-and-run guerrilla warfare, with a great vanity and a sense of melodrama, but with a soldier's honor. To many British officials, he adds, Grivas was a maniac.[139]

On the other hand, Grivas had no esteem for Sir Hugh Foot, in spite of the good opinion members of the Greek government (unnamed) and Ethnarch Makarios had formed about him. He considered him as being too full of himself and as believing that he could fool everyone and that he considered everyone his intellectual inferior. In Grivas' eyes, Sir Hugh was a mixture of double-facedness and underhandedness, an intriguer.[140] In contrast, Grivas esteemed Sir Hugh's predecessor as Governor of Cyprus for his military virtues. He regarded Sir John Harding as the most powerful and dangerous adversary he had ever had to face in Cyprus. He liked his frankness and outspokenness, but he also considered him arrogant, too hasty in action, obstinate. Sir John, he thought, lacked any knowledge of mass psychology and had managed to antagonize with his "ridiculous" propaganda even the neutrals among the Greek Cypriots. Harding, in Grivas' eyes, had no political acumen. In this sector, therefore, the influence of his entourage was paramount.[141] Incidentally, Grivas' respect for Sir John was reciprocated by the British Governor and Field Marshal, who acknowledged that "Dighenis" was "a highly skilful organizer and an expert guerrilla leader" and "a man of great personal courage and endurance, a stern disciplinarian . . . unsparing with his subordinates as with himself." [142]

The clash of wills that occurred in the British Embassy in Athens on September 22, 1953, when the convalescent Etonian, Oxonian, and freeman of Athens, Foreign Secretary Robert Anthony Eden (today 1st Earl of Avon) stiffly told Premier and Field Marshal Alexander Papagos who, like De Gaulle, had been at Saint Cyr, that there was no Cyprus question at all,[143] seems to have been the moment when the leaders of the two initial clusters of "third variables" started tying up Cyprus into a knot which their respective successors, Prime Ministers Macmillan and Karamanlis, joined by Menderes, had so great a difficulty in trying to untie. Incidents such as this one, which starkly personalized the clash between the forces of Greek irredentism on the wane and of British imperialism couchant, triggered an immensely complicated chain of events, of incidents and accidents, while Grivas and Makarios were planning to resort to violence in Cyprus. Hopkinson's off-the-cuff answer to a Labour M.P. on July 28, 1954, which created the impression that Cyprus would never become free; [144] Kyrou's misjudgment of American attitudes, based perhaps on wishful thinking, on stereotypes about Americans and their anticolonialism, and abetted by some sort of communications failure on the part of the State Department or Dulles himself; [145] Makarios' rejection of Harding's final proposals; [146] the British decision to deport the Ethnarch to the Seychelles—a few days after the King of Jordan had abruptly dismissed John Glubb Pasha as head of the Arab Legion; the bomb that did not go off under Harding's mattress; [147] Averoff-Tossizza's rhetorical question at the 855th meeting of the Political Committee on February 19, 1957; [148] the "intolerably insulting behavior" of Zorlu, who,[149] however, in the eyes of his Greek colleague, had qualities of a statesman—all these contributed to the Gordian complexity of the Cyprus knot just as did, perhaps, the facts that Eden had a very authoritarian father; that Lennox-Boyd, when President of the Oxford Union, wore a large red carnation in his button-hole and appeared to Hugh Foot, an undergraduate then, "superior, trivial, supercilious": [150] that Colonel Grivas envied the glory of Field Marshal Papagos; or that Krishna Menon, with his walking stick, was a rule unto himself and, when speaking about Cyprus, was thinking about Kashmir.

All these phenomena of human personality and of human action and interaction, with the present unfolding from the past and into the future, suggest why it may be difficult, if not impossible, to find a simple causal relationship between external and internal conflict in world politics. Incidentally, they also illustrate once again why it is easier to start a conflict than to resolve it. Conflict leads to intense action and interaction between personalities and brings to the fore traits connected with the many personae, the multitude of masks,[151] many of which are incongruous and may, in the last analysis, conceal the irrational components of the self.

Appendixes

Application, under the Auspices of the United Nations, of the Principle of Equal Rights and Self-determination of Peoples in the Case of the Population of the Island of Cyprus

Letter dated 16 August 1954 to the Secretary-General from the President of the Council of Ministers of Greece

On behalf of the Royal Hellenic Government and of the Greek nation as a whole I have the honour to request you, under rule 14 of the rules of procedure, to include in the agenda of the next regular session of the General Assembly of the United Nations the item entitled:

"Application, under the auspices of the United Nations, of the principle of equal rights and self-determination of peoples in the case of the population of the island of Cyprus."

I. In view of the repeatedly and solemnly expressed will of the overwhelming majority of the people of Cyprus for union with Greece, which they regard as their mother-country, my Government, fully aware of its responsibilities to the past, present and future of the Hellenic nation and in application of Article 1, paragraph 2, of the Charter, which establishes the right of self-determination of peoples, requests that the people of the island of Cyprus be allowed to express themselves on their future in complete freedom and under the auspices of the United Nations. My Government is taking this step in the belief that it will provide a satisfactory solution to a question which is likely to impair "the friendly relations" that have so far prevailed between Greece and the United Kingdom and "the general welfare" of the international community.

Availing itself of the new order established by the Charter of the United Nations, at the price of the great sacrifices made in the course of the Second World War, the Hellenic Government bases its request to the General Assembly on the relevant provisions of the Charter, and specifically on Articles 10 and 14 and on Article 1, paragraph 2. It also reserves the right to refer to Article 35, paragraph 1, if it considers such a course to be justified by subsequent developments.

My Government's action, taken both on its own behalf and at the request of the entire Greek nation, in addressing to the United Nations an appeal for justice and freedom for the Cypriots, is proof of Greece's complete confidence in the Organization.

II. Cyprus is a Greek island which has been inhabited by Greeks for thousands of years. When the name of Cyprus appears in history for the first time, the island is mentioned as being Greek because of its gods and of its population. There has been no change since. The periods of foreign rule which have succeeded each other in the course of three thousand years of history have always represented only a passing, temporary and transitory element. Greece alone has been the lasting element, the unalterable factor, the only permanent reality in the island of Cyprus. It would not be enough to repeat that Cyprus belongs to the Greek world; Cyprus is Greece itself.

Today according to statistical data supplied by the British colonial authorities, of a total of 511,000 inhabitants, 80.2 per cent are Greeks (this does not include approximately 120,000 Greeks who have emigrated from Cyprus to Greece, to Egypt and other parts of Africa, to the United States or to London). Of the remaining 19.8 per cent, 17.9 per cent are Turks, and 1.9 per cent are of various other nationalities.

In 1878, the British administration, under the nominal sovereignty of the Sultan, succeeded the Ottoman domination. In November 1914, Cyprus was annexed to the British Empire, and in 1925 the Government of the United Kingdom made the island a crown colony. Today, in Cyprus, one of the most ancient cradles of Western civilization, the colonial status still survives, imposed on a people whose destiny has been linked with the cause of freedom.

It is true that on 17 October 1915, following the declaration of war between Great Britain and the Ottoman Empire, the British Government implicitly recognized the Greek character of Cyprus by offering the island to Greece on condition that Greece entered the war on the side of the Allies. Greece fulfilled this condition two years later, but the British Government had by that time forgotten its promise. On many occasions, however, British statesmen and other eminent persons (Gladstone, Winston Churchill, David Lloyd George, Ramsay Macdonald, Ronald Burrows, W. Pember Reeves, H. G. Wells, Arnold Toynbee, etc.) have recognized the right of the people of Cyprus to seek union with Greece. But the United Kingdom authorities have invariably refused to take into consideration this unanimous wish of the great Hellenic national majority of the island's inhabitants.

On the morrow of the last world war, the people of Cyprus, having actively and effectively participated in the common struggle, and trusting in the principles of justice and freedom proclaimed in the Atlantic Charter and subsequently established by the Charter of the United Nations, reaffirmed their will to be united with Greece. A plebiscite was organized by the Greek Orthodox Church in January 1950. Ninety-five point seven per cent of the voters voted for the union of Cyprus with Greece. The results of this plebiscite were duly communicated to London. A delegation from Cyprus deposited a copy of the voting returns with the United Nations.

The British Government turned a deaf ear to these expressions of opinion and appeals. In May 1953 the Governor of Cyprus replied once again to the Archbishop of the Orthodox Church of Cyprus that no change in the status of the island of Cyprus was envisaged by Her Majesty's Government.

More categorical by far was the statement on Cyprus made by Mr. Hopkinson, Minister of State for Colonial Affairs, in the House of Commons on 28 July 1954. Mr. Hopkinson went so far as to say:

"It has always been understood and agreed that there are certain territories in the Commonwealth which, owing to their particular circumstances, can never expect to be fully independent."

Under these circumstances, it is not difficult to understand why the semblance of a constitution, like that discussed at that same meeting of the House of Commons, has no chance of being accepted by the Cypriot people, especially since the competent members of the British Government did not decline to recognize that this pseudo-constitution was far less liberal than the Constitution of 1948, which had already been rejected by the Cypriots.

Furthermore, five days had hardly elapsed since the above-mentioned meeting of the House of Commons when the British authorities enforced "anti-revolutionary" legislative measures in the island, prohibiting under penalty of excessively severe punishment every manifestation of the will of the people.

This negative policy pursued by the British authorities has brought about a situation which presages no good. Despair and exasperation are not good counsellors . . .

III. As was to be expected, however, developments in the island of Cyprus and the refusal of the Government of the United Kingdom to take into consideration the will of the Cypriot population have had tremendous repercussions throughout Greece.

The Greek people, who had paid a heavy toll that freedom and respect for the will of peoples might triumph, found it hard to understand that these principles, designed to be the foundations of the new international community, should not be equally valid for all. They were disappointed to find that, in absolutely identical circumstances, foreign domination was abolished in the Dodecanese Islands, apparently on the grounds that it had been the domination of a vanquished country, while it was maintained in Cyprus, where the ruling country was among the victors.

The natural solidarity binding together a single people—the inhabitants of free Greece and of Cyprus—and the indignation caused by the unjustifiable attitude of the British Government have resulted in the creation in Greece of a violent current of opinion, the power of which it would be dangerous to underestimate and which the Greek Government was unable any longer to overlook.

Greece has always maintained bonds of traditional friendship with Great Britain. The relations between the two countries have never in the past been seriously disturbed, and during the great crises of recent history the two peoples have invariably fought side by side. During the last war, the comradeship-in-arms by which the two nations were united at the most critical moments of the struggle for the freedom and equality of peoples helped to make these bonds still stronger.

Close and friendly co-operation between Great Britain and Greece have constituted both in the past and in our own days an element of political stability in this region of the Eastern Mediterranean. And this stability was necessary and in the interests both of the international community as a whole and of the cause of peace.

The Greek Government could not, therefore, remain indifferent to the emergence of a new factor in Greek public opinion tending to jeopardize this stability and to bring about a most delicate situation in the field of Greco-British relations.

Since 1949, therefore, every Greek Government has endeavoured to approach the British Government with a view to finding a solution to the question of respect for the will of the Cypriot people.

To all these overtures, which have been made at intervals over a period of four years, the British Government has returned a refusal varying only in the degree of discourtesy of the form in which it has been presented.

By refusing to enter into any discussion or contact on so serious a problem, which could not be solved either by ignoring it or declaring it closed, the British Government lightheartedly assumed a heavy responsibility. To the Greek people's resentment at seeing the will of the people of Cyprus disregarded was added the bitterness caused by the offensive attitude adopted towards the Greek Government's overtures.

Aware of both the present and future dangers inherent in this situation, my Government has resolved to appeal to the United Nations. Nevertheless, in order to exercise to the full the good will and moderation by which Greek policy in this matter has been inspired, it instructed the Chairman of the Greek Delegation at the eighth session of the General Assembly of the United Nations to make the following statement (plenary meeting of 21 September 1953):

". . . The Cyprus question is not to be found among the agenda items of the present session. It is true that, on 10 August 1953, the spiritual and national chief of four-fifths of the Cypriot population addressed to the Secretary-General of the United Nations a memorandum requesting the inclusion of that question in the agenda and the adoption of a resolution recommending that the United Kingdom should accept the right of the people of Cyprus to self-determination, in compliance with the provisions of the General Assembly resolution [637 (VII)] of 16 December 1952. "One may therefore ask why my Government, although under very heavy pressure from Greek public opinion, has not sponsored this request or taken a direct initiative in respect thereof. . . .

"To be willing to go before a judge or an arbiter is, of course, a commendable attitude of mind, especially when one despairs of achieving agreement through direct conversations or negotiations. But normally, no one appeals to a court of law or to an international forum such as this before giving a fair chance to the possibility of direct conversations.

"My Government, therefore, does not at this moment contemplate bringing this matter before this Organization, since it is convinced that the close relations that, so happily, exist between Greece and the United Kingdom make it incumbent upon us not to underestimate either the resources of diplomacy or the political foresight of our British friends. My Government definitely prefers the method of friendly bilateral discussion, since that is warranted by the very nature of our long-standing cordial relations with the United Kingdom and by the felicitous identity of purpose which has always animated the peoples of the two countries. It is our ardent hope that these views are shared by our friends in the United Kingdom and that they, also, consider the task that lies ahead as a worthy object on which to exert their statesmanship. The door will always be open for us to go before a judge, if the ordinary processes of friendly conversations prove to be of no avail. . . ."

Since September 1953 my Government has on many occasions asked Great Britain directly to put an end to the anomalous situation of the island of Cyprus, which was not justified by any legitimate reason. It has taken diplomatic steps both tactful and pressing; it has made approaches to the British Government in the course of private talks; it has exhausted all remedies and employed every known and practicable diplomatic method, but all this, unfortunately, without achieving the least result.

The Government of the United Kingdom has met every Cypriot or Greek request with cold indifference. Moreover, statements made from time to time in the British Parliament added fuel to the fire. This has brought about a situation which, it should be stressed, is likely to "impair friendly relations" between Greece and the United Kingdom as well as "the general welfare" of the international community.

Having exhausted every means of achieving an agreement directly, and having allowed all the time limits provided for under the rules of procedure of the General Assembly to elapse, the Greek Government feels compelled to ask the United Nations to redress this situation by securing acceptance of the solution required by justice, dignity and the sacred principles set forth in the Charter. It appeals to the General Assembly in the conviction that the Assembly will achieve a constructive solution conducive to peace and freedom.

The Greek Government reserves the right to furnish, if necessary, additional arguments and supporting documents or any other information, orally or in writing, which may enlighten the Assembly on the substance of its appeal.

Alexander Papagos

Field Marshal of Greece
President of the Council
of Ministers

Letter Dated 23 July 1955 from the Permanent Representative of Greece to the Secretary-General

On behalf of the Royal Hellenic Government I have the honor to request, under Article 14 of the rules of procedure, the inscription in the supplementary provisional agenda of the forthcoming tenth regular session of the General Assembly of the item:

"Application, under the auspices of the United Nations, of the principle of equal rights and self-determination of peoples in the case of the population of the island of Cyprus."

This item having been inscribed in the agenda of the ninth session of the General Assembly remains pending in the United Nations as a result of resolutions 814 (IX) which on 17 December 1954 postpones for the time being consideration of this subject.

Christian X. Palamas

Permanent Representative of Greece
to the United Nations

Greece: Request for the Inclusion of an Item in the Provisional Agenda of the Eleventh Session

Letter dated 13 March 1956 from the Permanent Representative of Greece to the United Nations addressed to the Secretary-General

On behalf of the Royal Hellenic Government, I have the honour to request, under rule 13 of the rules of procedure, the inscription in the provisional agenda of the forthcoming eleventh session of the General Assembly of the item:

"Application, under the auspices of the United Nations, of the principle of equal rights and self-determination of peoples in the case of the population of the Island of Cyprus."

An explanatory memorandum relating to the above item will follow in accordance with rule 20 of the rules of procedure.

Christian X. Palamas

Permanent Representative of Greece
to the United Nations

Letter dated 12 June 1956 from the Permanent Representative of Greece to the United Nations addressed to the Secretary-General

With reference to my letter dated 13 March 1956, I have the honour to transmit to you the explanatory memorandum relating to the item "Application, under the auspices of the United Nations, of the principle of equal rights and self-determination of peoples in the case of the population of the Island of Cyprus," which has already been inscribed in the provisional agenda of the forthcoming eleventh session of the General Assembly.

Following the circulation by the Secretariat of the explanatory memorandum, the Permanent Mission of Greece will send to all delegations of the Member States the "Blue Book" mentioned in the memorandum.

Christian X. Palamas

Permanent Representative of Greece
to the United Nations

Explanatory Memorandum

1. The question entitled "Application, under the auspices of the United Nations, of the principle of equal rights and self-determination of peoples in the case of the population of the Island of Cyprus" has been taken up for the first time by the United Nations since the General Assembly decided at its ninth session [477th plenary meeting] to include the item in its agenda, following a request submitted by the Royal Hellenic Government [A/2703]. A procedural resolution, unanimously adopted, which postponed provisionally further consideration of the item concluded a debate on the substance of the issue [resolution 814 (IX)]. Since then, the Royal Hellenic Government, considering that the situation in the island was deteriorating and that the international implications of this situation were of immediate concern to the United Nations, requested the General Assembly, at its tenth session, to take appropriate action [A/2920].

2. The General Assembly, by 28 votes to 22, with 10 abstentions, decided not to include the item in its agenda [521st plenary meeting]. However, from explanations offered by several delegations as to the true significance of their votes, it was made clear that the decision of the General Assembly had the following, twofold meaning:

(a) The United Kingdom Government pledged itself to seek through peaceful negotiations a just and equitable solution of the problem;

(b) In the face of such a British pledge, many delegations cast a negative vote, having serious misgivings as to the advisability of a public debate at that time and wishing to ensure for all existing factors of good will and understanding the possibility of operating in favour of a peaceful settlement.

3. The Greek Delegation contested the wisdom and efficacy of such an action by the General Assembly since it relieved the United Kingdom Government of the pressure of immediate international responsibility and risked releasing more violence and further colonial excesses. This view was shared by many other delegations.

When, shortly after the decision of the Assembly not to discuss the Cyprus question during its tenth session, Field-Marshal Sir John Harding was appointed Governor of Cyprus, the Greek delegation deemed it its duty to draw the attention of the United Nations to this new British action which, in its opinion, indicated the beginning of a policy of increasingly violent and indiscriminate repression. Britain, said the Greek representative, was now waging war against the people of Cyprus. In spite of British denials, the Greek fears came true.

4. The decision of the General Assembly offered the interested parties some directives for future action. Abiding by its faith in the United Nations, Greece saw itself bound to comply with such directives. It is in this spirit that the Royal Hellenic Government promised its full support and co-operation to Archbishop Makarios, spiritual and political leader of the Greek Cypriots, who accordingly entered into negotiations with the British Governor, Sir John Harding, aimed at reaching an amicable understanding on the fulfilment of the legitimate aspirations of the people of the island.

5. The documents contained in the Greek "Blue Book" give a factual account of the course of these negotiations.

It is only natural for differing parties to try to interpret facts according to their respective views and interests. But in the present instance the cause of the Cypriots is so clear and their rights so well established according to commonly accepted legal and moral rules, that Greece asks only for impartial objectivity in the consideration of the relevant facts.

Conclusions emanating from such an impartial and objective consideration of existing factual evidence may be summarized as follows:

(a) The right of self-determination of peoples, though unconditionally established by the Charter of the United Nations, has not been so recognized by the United Kingdom Government in the case of Cyprus, while self-determination—meaning national independence from foreign rule—is the main purpose and goal of the Cypriots.

(b) The United Kingdom Government refused even to concede real self-government to the Cypriots for what would have been a transitional period. Besides reserving for itself full control of foreign affairs and military defence, that Government sought to retain extensive powers even in the more restricted area of domestic matters. This would have been tantamount to a survival of the colonial administration, and this time, with the consent of the Cypriots.

(c) In spite of a few niceties in words and phraseology, the United Kingdom Government refused to make any substantial concession, while Archbishop Makarios, showing a high sense of moderation, made decisive steps towards compromise and understanding. British colonialism long entrenched in Cyprus stood firmly on its initial position.

Now everyone will realize what the British mean when they talk of negotiations as a means of peaceful settlement.

(d) The breakdown of the negotiations resulted mainly from the unwillingness of the British to disclose what they meant by "elected majority" while retaining the right to nominate an undetermined number of ex officio appointed members of the future Parliament of Cyprus. This undemocratic and wholly inadmissible thesis made apparent the British intention to frustrate the will of the people and to continue to rule against it, as had been the case during nearly fifty years of previous colonial self-government of which the Cypriots had bitter experience.

(e) The negotiations showed clearly what was in the mind of the United Kingdom Government when it talked of self-determination and self-government. Because Archbishop Makarios could not be induced to see things in the same colonial light, he has been punished by arrest and deportation.

The General Assembly will undoubtedly draw its conclusions from this sad but enlightening experience.

6. While the negotiations were carried on, as far as the Cypriots were concerned, in conformity with the views and wishes of the General Assembly, the situation in Cyprus was deteriorating further. New factors emerged from the plight created by the policies of harsh repression allegedly destined to

quell a local resistance movement, but aiming, in fact, at terrorizing the whole population and breaking the people's morale.

A powerful military machine of about 20,000 crack troops, naval forces, special police units and experts in intelligence and manhunting tactics was set up in the island under the command of the Field-Marshal. This has been followed by the complete suppression of all human rights and liberties. In implementing his Government's colonial policies, the Governor has actually transformed the island into a huge concentration camp.

7. According to official British assertions, this is done with the purpose of establishing "law and order" against terrorism.

As this appears to be the crux of the problem, the United Nations is bound to consider it most attentively.

In all national communities, freedom and human rights—that is to say, civic, economic and political rights—constitute the foundation of "law and order." Under the Charter of the United Nations, this democratic conception becomes an international rule and an international obligation. Wherever law and order do not emanate from the free will of the people, but are the expression of forcibly imposed domination, the case becomes one of oppression.

Through the ages, history has given many names to oppression. "Colonialism" is one of these names. "Law and order" expressing oppression is just the negation of law and order in terms of democracy, human decency and civilized standards. It is in vain that the British are trying to create confusion in the present instance. The case is only too clear. Law and order in Cyprus now mean nothing else but British domination and colonial rule arbitrarily imposed and maintained upon a reluctant and subjected population. Actually, material force—that is to say, violence—is the main source of British law and order, as well as the main foundation of British government and administration in Cyprus.

Free men and free peoples have always considered that the only possible answer to violence is violence. The movement of active resistance started in Cyprus is like all movements of liberation. It serves no purpose to try to camouflage the truth by calling it by different names.

8. During the Second World War, the forces of the Axis imposed their rule upon many peoples in Europe and elsewhere. These peoples actively resisted this rule, not because they disliked the Italians or the Germans, but primarily because they were averse to foreign domination in any form.

In fighting the various liberation movements and the underground resistance forces, the Axis Powers contended that their repressive policies aimed at restoring law and order. To this end they abolished all freedoms and human rights; they enacted regulations under which arrest, imprisonment and deportation without trial were permitted; they isolated areas through censorship and by jamming foreign broadcasts; they used deplorable practices of physical punishment and torture; they contrived measures of collective responsibility, which made the innocent pay for the guilty; they violated the most elementary privacy of families; they evicted people from their homes without any other justification than that they were not co-operative when asked to betray their fighting compatriots; they fined villages and towns as a reprisal for any material damage done by the patriots—the Nazis called them "terrorists" and "criminals"; they set up concentration camps, etc.

All the measures listed above are being applied in Cyprus today by British colonial rule trying to breathe life into obsolete and unworkable imperialistic devices.

The British people, who shared sacrifices with all other free peoples of the United Nations fighting for freedom and whose determination in critical times turned the tide of history, should be primarily concerned in this matter. If Governments often fail in their policies, peoples never fail in making history.

9. On the British side there is violence used against freedom. On the Cypriot side there is violence used in favour of freedom. But in neither case is violence to be praised. Greece is against the use of violence. As long as lawful action is left open to the contesting parties, Greece is in favour of such a peaceful approach. And this way of lawful action is the United Nations.

The Greek Government in taking the Cyprus issue to the United Nations in 1954 tried to prevent violence. If it failed in its efforts it was because the United Kingdom Government and other political forces, unmindful of the change of times, frustrated proper action by the General Assembly, thus closing all roads leading to peaceful adjustment. Had the General Assembly from the outset carried out its responsibilities according to the letter and the spirit of the Charter, the world would not have to be faced with a critical situation as the one which has now developed in Cyprus.

It is high time for the United Nations to show wisdom and determination in playing its part properly and in using its political and moral strength to bring about reasonable and constructive solutions.

10. The fact is that war is actually being waged by the British forces against the Greek population in Cyprus, which is now undergoing the tragic process of a most inhuman repression. This has had an immediate and understandable repercussion in Greece. Greek-British relations are being put under heavy strain. British violence and injustice in Cyprus are exasperating Greek feelings.

A politically critical situation has been created the impact of which is particularly heavy on the general conditions of peace and security of the world.

11. Furthermore, recent developments in British policies in the Middle East and in Cyprus are bringing new and so far undisclosed aspects of the present issue into the picture.

It should be pointed out that these new aspects are the direct concern and responsibility of the United Nations.

According to an official statement made by the Prime Minister of the United Kingdom in the House of Commons, which has been followed by similar declarations by the British Secretary of State for Foreign Affairs, Mr. Selwyn Lloyd, the United Kingdom intends to keep the island of Cyprus under colonial rule because of specific strategic and political considerations, in order to be able to discharge its alleged responsibilities in the Middle East. In particular, Cyprus is to be used for the defence of British oil interests.

This latter revelation, which is likely to come as a shock to the United Nations, is most edifying. It calls for close consideration by the world Organization, to which it poses new problems of vital character:

(a) The United Kingdom Government insists on keeping the people of Cyprus in perpetual colonial subjection in spite of the fact that this constitutes a flagrant violation of the relevant provisions of the United Nations Charter. Legitimate British defence interests evidently do not suffice to justify such a stand, neither on the political nor on the military level. In this connexion, it must be recalled that in the opinion of most qualified military authorities in Britain as well as elsewhere, the value of the island as a military base is rather limited.

(b) Therefore, the justification of the British insistence for prolonging colonial rule in Cyprus lies in other hardly commendable policies in the Middle East. These policies as defined by high ranking governmental officials are connected with the display of political influence and prestige in the whole area of the Middle East. This involves the right of carrying out police supervision in the life and political developments of this region, in particular for the defence of British oil interests. Cyprus is understood to serve as the springboard for such action.

(c) The problem considered in the light of this new aspect not only concerns the Cypriots, but the peoples living in that area as well. It also constitutes a challenge to the United Nations.

12. The Royal Hellenic Government, considering:

(a) That the British Government, in refusing the application of the right of self-determination in the case of the people of Cyprus, is violating Article 1, paragraph 2, of the Charter,

(b) That the suppression of all freedoms and elementary human rights is in disregard not only of the letter and the spirit of the Charter, but also of all legal and moral standards of the civilized world, and foments violence in the island,

(c) That the arrest, deportation and exile of Archbishop Makarios, head of one of the most ancient Christian churches and spiritual as well as political leader of the Greek Cypriots, with whom the United Kingdom Government was officially negotiating until the very last moment, constitute a heavy blow and damaging offence to the religious heritage of the world,

(d) That the political implications of forcibly and ruthlessly implemented British colonial rule engender conditions falling under Articles 10 and 14 of the Charter,

(e) That recent developments relating to the constantly deteriorating situation in Cyprus and to conditions of peace and security now prevailing in the eastern Mediterranean fall under Article 35, paragraph 1, of the Charter,

Decided to request the General Assembly to take up the Cyprus problem in conformity with the relative provisions of the Charter of the United Nations and in order to preserve freedom, peace and security.

United Kingdom of Great Britain and Northern Ireland: Request for the Inclusion of a Supplementary Item in the Agenda of the Eleventh Session

Letter dated 12 October 1956 from the Permanent Representative of the United Kingdom of Great Britain and Northern Ireland to the United Nations addressed to the Secretary-General

On instructions from Her Majesty's Government in the United Kingdom I have the honour to request that the following item be included in the supplementary list of items for the agenda of the eleventh session of the General Assembly of the United Nations:

"Support from Greece for terrorism in Cyprus."

An explanatory memorandum relating to this item will follow in due course.

Pierson Dixon
Permanent Representative of the United Kingdom
of Great Britain and Northern Ireland
to the United Nations

Letter dated 12 November 1956 from the Permanent Representative of the United Kingdom of Great Britain and Northern Ireland to the United Nations addressed to the Secretary-General

I have the honour, on instructions from Her Majesty's Government in the United Kingdom of Great Britain and Northern Ireland, to refer to my letter dated 12 October 1956, and to transmit to Your Excellency an explanatory memorandum relating to the item "Support from Greece for terrorism in Cyprus" included as item 5 on the supplementary list of items for the agenda of the eleventh session of the General Assembly (A/3205).

Pierson Dixon

Permanent Representative of the United Kingdom
of Great Britain and Northern Ireland
to the United Nations

Explanatory Memorandum

1. Respect for the sovereignty of individual States, and non-intervention in the internal affairs of any States, are basic concepts inherent in the Charter of

the United Nations. They have been upheld on numerous occasions in United Nations resolutions. A breach of these principles is clearly a breach of the spirit of the Charter and in particular of the declared aim of the peoples of the United Nations to live together as good neighbours; it is likely to lead to a serious international situation and is a matter of concern to the United Nations.

2. The Greek Government does not dispute that Cyprus is British territory. Nevertheless support from Greece for terrorism in Cyprus has continued over a considerable period. In the hope that the several diplomatic initiatives taken by Her Majesty's Government with all concerned would lead to a settlement, Her Majesty's Government have not hitherto brought the matter before the United Nations. Unfortunately this restraint has been misinterpreted, and Greek interference in the affairs of Cyprus has persisted.

3. Despite representations on more than twenty occasions by Her Majesty's Embassy at Athens to the Greek Government, Athens Radio has continued to support the terrorist organization EOKA [National Organization of Cypriot Fighters]. This radio station, which is under the direct control of the Greek Government, has regularly broadcast special programmes to Cyprus containing incitements to insurrection and violence.

4. In addition, the terrorists in Cyprus have received a considerable quantity of material aid from Greece. This has included the supply of arms and ammunition.

5. Members of the terrorist organization in Cyprus have, up to 6 November 1956, murdered 196 persons, of whom 114 were Cypriots. One of the principal purposes of these murders has been to suppress freedom of speech and opinion. This objective has not been disguised by Athens Radio, which has described as "traitors" those Cypriots who exercise their right to oppose the aims of EOKA and the union of Cyprus with Greece and has praised their murderers. It has become increasingly evident, despite their attempts to use the language of democracy, that the object of the terrorists and of those who support them is to secure by forcible means the annexation of Cyprus to Greece.

6. Her Majesty's Government have requested the inscription of this item on the agenda of the eleventh session of the General Assembly as they believe that the time has come for the United Nations to consider this external attempt to change the status of Cyprus by force and subversion, and the methods used by those in Greece who support terrorism in Cyprus.

Greece: Request for the Inclusion of an Item in the Provisional Agenda of the Twelfth Session

Letter dated 12 July 1957 from the Permanent Representative of Greece to the Secretary-General

Upon instructions from my Government, I have the honour to request, under rule 13 of the rules of procedure, the inscription in the provisional agenda of the forthcoming twelfth regular session of the General Assembly of the following item:
"Cyprus:
"(a) Application under the auspices of the United Nations, of the principle of equal rights and self-determination of peoples in the case of the population of the island of Cyprus;
"(b) Violations of human rights and atrocities by the British Colonial Administation against the Cyprians."
An explanatory memorandum relating to this item submitted subsequent to the non-compliance by the United Kingdom with General Assembly resolution 1013 (XI) will follow in due course in conformity with rule 20 of the rules of procedure.

Christian X. Palamas

Permanent Representative of Greece
to the United Nations

Letter Dated 13 September 1957 from the Permanent Representative of Greece to the Secretary-General

Following my letter of 12 July 1957 (A/3616), I have the honour to send you attached hereto the explanatory memorandum of the item "Cyprus" of the provisional agenda of the twelfth regular session of the General Assembly.

Christian X. Palamas

Permanent Representative of Greece
to the United Nations

Explanatory Memorandum

1. Since 1954 Greece, acting on behalf of the people of Cyprus, has repeatedly and consistently requested the General Assembly of the United Nations to take action in order to ensure the application of the right of self-determination in the case of the Cypriots. Such action, being in line with the principles of the Charter, could contribute to the peaceful settlement of the conflict opposing the Cypriot people, striving for freedom, to the United Kingdom, the ruling colonial Power in the island.

2. The delegations of the Member States are well aware of and fully acquainted with the historical background of the problem, as well as with the tragic events which have taken place in the island within the last two years. During this period the struggle between the oppressed people and the British authorities gained in momentum, costing heavy losses in human lives and property. The situation was dangerously drifting, thus imperilling the peace in this most vital area of the Middle East. It is in the light of these developments that the General Assembly, at its eleventh session, assuming its responsibilities under the Charter, adopted resolution 1013 (XI) on 26 February 1957.

3. Since the adoption of this resolution more than six months have elapsed. Considering the developments that have occurred during that time it becomes evident that while the situation, as it now stands, has turned out to be easier for the British Administration and forces, the people still live under harsh oppression. Some changes of a minor importance in the Emergency Regulations have brought no substantial relief to the people. It is sad to notice that compliance by the Cypriots with the General Assembly resolution has resulted in violence now being used against them unilaterally by the British authorities. Such a course of action was certainly not intended by the General Assembly when it adopted the resolution. Furthermore, no progress whatsoever has been made on the road to a solution of the main problem, which was, and still remains, the liberation of the people of Cyprus from colonial rule and the application of their right of self-determination. Obviously, it was up to the ruling Power to take the initiative to start negotiations with the people concerned. No such action has been taken in conformity with the relative resolution of the General Assembly. Instead, a proposal to this end, made by Archbishop Makarios, was flatly turned down by the United Kingdom Government.

4. As referred to in a letter of the Permanent Representative of the United Kingdom, Sir Pierson Dixon, dated 11 May 1957, to the Secretary-General of the United Nations, there has been an offer to deal with this problem on a tripartite basis, within the framework of or in connexion with the North Atlantic Treaty Organization. The Greek Government felt that it did not have the right to get involved in proceedings which were not in line with the resolution of the General Assembly and which would result in the total, or partial, withdrawal of the question of Cyprus from the authority and the responsibility of the United Nations. This would not have been in accordance with the mandate entrusted to Greece by the people of Cyprus. An issue of freedom and fundamental principles enshrined in the Charter should be

settled in accordance with these principles. It must be understood that no solution of the Cyprus question can be agreed upon without the consent of the people of Cyprus. Solutions which run against the will of the people are no solutions at all. In the light of these considerations Greece is willing to continue contributing towards a peaceful settlement of the problem.

5. In the present instance, Greece is not looking to secure any benefit for herself. She has no claim to formulate. She is disposed and willing to make every reasonable concession and sacrifice in the interest of peace. She has no egotistical ambitions. But she cannot disregard the rights of the Cypriot people. In discharging this sacred responsibility, Greece is bound to stand in the way of any action meant to serve designs and ambitions coming from any other quarters to the detriment of the Cypriot cause.

6. The Greek Government has already in its files some 500 signed testimonies substantiating accusations that the colonial authorities in Cyprus in the course of their repressive drive have indulged in inhuman practices, brutalities and atrocities in the handling of prisoners or persons arrested for interrogation. On the very sad picture of the sufferings endured by the Cyprian people this stands out as a black spot of particular gravity. Those accusations are not sporadic and isolated. The number of the victims and the similarity of the tortures, as well as the techniques in atrocity used by the local authorities, can be explained only if such methods were applied by specially trained personnel—in a large number of testimonies the members of a special branch of police are mentioned—and covered by the tolerance, if not by the express approval, at least of some of those discharging British responsibilities in Cyprus. Such an opinion is also shared in some British quarters. This is placing the United Nations before a problem which, though initially linked to the political and other contingencies prevailing in the island, is of a specific character and bears broader consequences. Methods and practices of bodily and mental torture perpetrated against the human being and defined by international law as "crimes against humanity," constitute a challenge to the British people as well as to the international community. The Greek Government would have wished not to have to refer this case to the General Assembly as it has so far avoided disclosing factual evidence in its possession about unacceptable British activities and practices. But, in spite of the fact that the Greek Government is always inspired by the same sense of restraint, this is too serious a case to be silenced. In relation to it, British public opinion has already reacted strongly. The noble British people had entertained with the Greek people such close ties that, whenever the former fought great struggles for liberty, the latter was never its foe or a neutral, but always its companion in arms. Such methods are unknown to the British people and this is why efforts were made in order to have the whole issue thoroughly investigated and dealt with. Such efforts were frustrated by those in the island who had reasons to fear the truth and the punishing anger of the British people. Any impartial public inquiry has been opposed under futile arguments and excuses. The United Kingdom Government, which certainly does not condone the use of such inhuman methods, but which, undoubtedly, bears the final responsibility for it, is bound by the actions of its colonial administration, actions which do not belong to the era of the United Nations. The General Assembly, in considering the case in its particulars and in its wider implica-

tions, could find the answer to the sad plight of the victims and to the indignation of the civilized world. At a later stage full data and detailed particulars will be placed at the disposal of all delegations.

7. It is in the light of the present situation, as stressed by facts, and in pursuance of peace, freedom and justice as defined by the Charter, that the General Assembly is called upon to examine anew the Cyprus issue and take whatever proper and efficient steps it deems necessary to adopt.

Greece: Request for the Inclusion of a Supplementary Item in the Agenda of the Thirteenth Session

Letter dated 15 August 1958 from the Permanent Representative of Greece to the Secretary-General

Upon instructions from my Government, I have the honour to request, under rule 14 of the rules of procedure of the General Assembly, the inscription in the agenda of the forthcoming thirteenth regular session of the General Assembly of the following supplementary item:
"Question of Cyprus"
An explanatory memorandum relating to this item will be submitted in due course, in conformity with rule 20 of the rules of procedure.

Christian X. Palamas

Permanent Representative of Greece
to the United Nations

Explanatory Memorandum

I

1. The question of Cyprus has been included in the agenda of the United Nations General Assembly since 1954 and it is well known to the delegations of all Member States. Its political, legal and moral background, as expounded during the debates at the ninth, tenth, eleventh and twelfth sessions of the General Assembly, remains unchanged.

2. The Cyprus question is an issue of freedom and self-determination claimed by a population living in colonial bondage. This is a crystal-clear issue which could not be confused by anyone acting in good faith. Yet, the quest of the Cypriots for the liberation of their island has, so far, been frustrated by the United Kingdom. In spite of the considerable loss in life and property, in spite of the growing dangers to the peace and tranquillity of this most sensitive area of the world, the British Government continues to deny to the Cypriots the exercise of their right to freedom and self-determination.

II

3. The General Assembly adopted, during its eleventh session, resolution 1013 (XI) expressing its earnest desire that

"a peaceful, democratic and just solution will be found in accord with the purposes and principles of the Charter of the United Nations, and the hope that negotiations will be resumed and continued to this end."

4. The British have systematically avoided entering into direct negotiations with the Cypriots in compliance with that resolution. It, therefore, remains, so far, unimplemented.

5. A draft resolution for the application of the right of self-determination in the case of the population of Cyprus, adopted by the First Committee (by 33 votes to 20, with 25 abstentions), and submitted to the General Assembly at its twelfth session [A/3794, para. 12] fell short of the required two-thirds majority by only five votes.

6. However, this proposal obtained in the General Assembly a relative majority and in any case a large majority of fifty-four of the United Nations Members. Those who voted in favour and those who abstained refused to side with those voting against self-determination.

7. In any case, there was a clear indication of the considered opinion of the great majority of the Member States which should have been taken into consideration by the British Government. It is not a matter of detail that the United Kingdom is responsible to the United Nations for the future and fate of a people living in this dependent territory.

8. It is regrettable that the British Government, pursuing its own political ends and purposes, totally disregarded the rights of the Cypriots to self-determination, deriving from Article 1, paragraph 2, of the Charter of the United Nations, as well as the specific responsibilities of the United Kingdom under Article 73 of the Charter and the legitimate concern shown in this respect by the United Nations.

III

9. During the months that elapsed from the end of the twelfth session of the General Assembly to date, the British Government has engaged in a series of diplomatic consultations with the Greek and Turkish Governments with a view to postponing the final issue and to providing a provisory solution. The Greek Government, with the full consent of His Beatitude Archbishop Makarios, representing 80 per cent of the population of Cyprus, stated that, pending the application of the right of self-determination, the only provisory solution it could accept was that provided in Article 73 b of the Charter, that is to say the establishment and development of a genuine and democratic self-government.

10. The British answer to this moderate and cooperative attitude of the Cypriots was the publication on 19 June 1958 of a new plan. This plan, in its essentials, introduces a system of administrative and governmental separation between 80 per cent of the population and the Turkish minority of 17 per cent with the participation of representatives of the Greek and the Turkish Governments. The plan was rejected by the Cypriots as undemocratic because it totally ignored the rights and the will of the 80-per-cent majority of the population and as unjust and contrary to the principles of the Charter of the

United Nations, because it called three foreign Governments to share in the continued alien domination over a non-self-governing territory and its population.

11. Furthermore, this plan could not be considered as a provisory solution inasmuch as it was prejudging the future by shaping in the present a "pre-partition" scheme.

12. It thus became evident that the British Government had no other concern than to prolong its rule over the island by advancing the idea of condominium with the alternative that the territorial claim of the Turkish Government upon part of the island would have to be complied with. The Turkish minority was called upon to serve as a pretext for and a tool in the perpetration of this "operation."

13. Following a visit of the British Prime Minister, Mr. Macmillan, to Athens, Ankara and Cyprus, the British Government announced its intention to proceed, without delay, with the application of this plan which, though slightly amended, remained basically unaltered. Thus the people of Cyprus, instead of being liberated from the colonial yoke, are now promised two masters, the British and the Turks, instead of one. It is very well known that Greece could never participate in such an enterprise.

14. Mr. Macmillan described his plan as an "adventure in partnership." It would be more appropriate to call it a "partnership in adventurous colonialism."

IV

15. While the British Government was indulging in these sad initiatives on the diplomatic level, the situation in Cyprus, which had been comparatively calm since the adoption in 1957 of resolution 1013 (XI), gravely deteriorated.

16. The Turkish minority, which in the past had lived in good understanding with the Greek population, initiated a violent action against Cypriot life and property. The Greek population was taken by surprise. Having passively suffered heavy losses during the initial stage, it reacted later in self-defence.

17. It is evident that the launching of these Turkish attacks against the Greeks was premeditated, organized and timed with the announcement of the British plan. The aim was to erase the past with a stroke of blood in order to prove that henceforth it would be impossible for the Turkish minority to live in common with the majority of the population. This was intended to constitute a factual platform on which partition could eventually stand.

18. These Turkish moves in Cyprus were coupled with threats of direct military intervention, threats emanating both from responsible Turkish quarters and from the Turkish press.

19. The situation created by this action resulted in tremendous losses in human life and property. It also constituted a serious menace to peace and security. The Greek Government, therefore, was compelled to draw the attention of the Security Council to this situation [letter dated 13 June 1958 from the representative of Greece to the President of the Security Council

(S/4025)]. Today, a chaotic situation prevails in the island, where thousands of Greek Cypriots are held in concentration camps, without specific charge and with no indication that trial will follow.

V

20. In bringing the question of Cyprus once again before the General Assembly, the Greek Government has been prompted by the fact that the situation in Cyprus is now entering a most critical phase. Any attempt by the British Government to impose its plan forcefully against the determined will of the overwhelming majority of the people could lead to very sad developments on the island. The repercussions of such an attempt could imperil peace and security in the whole area.

VI

21. The Greek Government earnestly hopes that the General Assembly, in assuming its full responsibilities, will take whatever action it may deem appropriate in order to alleviate the plight of the population of Cyprus, to remove all foreign threats and interferences in the lawful development of the situation and to assist the Cypriots to realize their legitimate claims in accordance with the relative provisions of the Charter of the United Nations.

Notes

NOTES

PREFACE

1. D. Krech, R. S. Crutchfield, and E. L. Ballachey, *Individual in Society* (New York: McGraw-Hill, 1962), pp. 273, 278.

2. According to the *Scotsman*, June 11, 1958, TMT was born on November 29, 1957, when it took over from the proscribed Volkan underground organization. One of its slogans was "Partition or Death."

3. The terms "protagonist" and "antagonist" taken from the world of discourse of drama criticism will be used throughout to denote what other authors term "the offensive side" and the "defensive side" in negotiations aiming at redistribution or innovation, F. C. Iklé, *How Nations Negotiate* (New York: Harper & Row, 1964), pp. 33, 35.

4. These terms are borrowed from R. C. Noel, "Inter-Nation Simulation Participants' Manual," *Simulation in International Relations* (Englewood Cliffs, N.J.: Prentice Hall, 1963), p. 43.

5. R. E. Riggs, *Politics in the United Nations: A Study of U.S. Influence in the General Assembly* (Urbana, Illinois: Illinois University Press, 1958). The author studies U.S. political methods and influence in the entire spectrum of UN politics during nine successive Assembly sessions from 1946–54. In certain respects it provides an interesting contrast to the present study because it describes the influence during those years of the only non-caucusing superpower in the Assembly.

6. S. Kalogeropoulos-Stratis, *La Grèce et les Nations Unies* (New York: Manhattan Publishing Co., 1957).

7. J. G. Hadwen and J. Kaufman, *How U.N. Decisions are Made* (Leiden: A. W. Sythoff, 1960). Both authors were members of the missions of Canada and the Netherlands, respectively, to the UN, and, as they write in their preface, p. 11, they concentrate on the informal procedures that take place in the organization but do not attempt a systematic description of their own governments' position on the issues discussed.

8. H. R. Alker, Jr., and B. M. Russett, *World Politics in the General Assembly* (New Haven: Yale University Press, 1965). T. Hovet, Jr., *Africa in the United Nations* (Evanston, Illinois: Northwestern University Press, 1963).

INTRODUCTION

1. H. G. Nicholas, *The United Nations as a Political Institution* (London: Oxford University Press, 1959), p. 106.

2. H. F. Haviland, Jr., *The Political Role of the General Assembly* (New York: Carnegie Endowment for International Peace, 1951), p. 104.

3. Iklé, *How Nations Negotiate*, pp. 3–4, defines negotiation as a process in which explicit proposals are put forward ostensibly for the purpose of reaching agreement on an exchange or on the realization of a common interest when conflicting interests are present.

4. *GAOR, Seventh Session*, Annexes, Agenda Item 30, pp. 15–16. Under Resolution 637A (VII), the Assembly recommended that UN members should uphold the principle of self-determination of all peoples and nations and recognize and promote the realization of "the right of self-determination" of peoples of non-self-governing and trust territories, with the wishes of the people being ascertained through plebiscites or other recognized democratic means, preferably "under the auspices of the United Nations." It also recommended that, pending the realization of the right of self-determination and in preparation thereof, member States take practical steps to insure the direct participation of the indigenous populations in the legislative and executive organs of government of those territories, and to prepare them for complete self-government or independence. This resolution consisted of three parts—A, B, and C. Roll-call votes took place in the Committee, indicating conflictual decision-making. Greece voted in favor of all three parts; Britain against. The United States, too, opposed parts A and B, but voted in favor of Part C, thus finding itself on the losing side of this anticolonial resolution. The roll-call votes were, for A, 34 to 13, with 6 abstentions; B, 38 to 10, with 4 abstentions; C, 38 to 7, with 8 abstentions. Turkey abstained on A and B, and was absent from the voting on C. The Egyptian representative on the Third Committee, on November 12, 1952, mentioned six arguments which had been presented against the right of self-determination. (1) There was as yet no clear legal definition of the word "people." (2) The right of peoples to self-determination had not yet been defined. (3) The right was not a human right. (4) A plebiscite was not necessarily the best means of ascertaining the popular wish. (5) Even if it were, it was not necessary for it to be conducted under UN auspices. (6) There were no reference books dealing with the right of peoples to self-determination from which relevant information could be drawn. (*Ibid.*, Third Committee, 443d meeting, November 12, 1952, p. 150.)

5. As analyzed to the author by Spyros Theotokis, Greek Foreign Minister from October 6, 1955, to the end of May, 1956, left-wing newspapers had started harping on the Cyprus question. Right-wing newspapers had seen their sales dwindling, so they, too, had decided to play up the question. In consequence, the government felt it had to do something about it. Thus, in his view, the Cyprus question, in the last analysis, had been a masterpiece of Soviet policy.

6. *GAOR, Eighth Session*, 439th plenary meeting, September 21, 1953, p. 66.

7. Iklé, *op. cit.*, pp. 26–27, describes this type of negotiation to which the negotiations requested by the Greek government on Cyprus belonged—at least until 1958, when the Greek proposal for setting up an independent Cyprus placed the negotiations in the category of those that aim at innovation.

8. This summary is based on S. G. Xydis, "Toward 'Toil and Moil' in Cyprus," the *Middle East Journal*, XX (Winter, 1966), 1–19. In the main only new material is footnoted here.

9. Early in 1946, Foreign Minister John Sofianopoulos, a left-winger, mentioned the Cyprus question in a conversation with Foreign Secretary Ernest Bevin, S. G. Xydis, *Greece and the Great Powers 1944–1947* (Institute for Balkan Studies: Thessaloniki, 1963), p. 198. The previous year, in September, at the time of the meeting of the Council of Foreign Ministers in London, Regent Damaskinos, too, had raised that same question, with Bevin again. The latter explained the difficulties involved in arranging for *enosis* but expressed willingness to refer to the Cyprus question in a joint British-Greek communiqué. The Regent, however, wanted to go back to Athens with Cyprus in his pocket, as it were. Bevin was angered. No joint communiqué was issued. (Ambassador Thanassis Aghnides to author.) Late in 1946, Premier Constantine Tsaldaris likewise referred to the Cyprus question in a conversation with Bevin.

10. *Journal of the Debates in the Greek Parliament* (in Greek) May 23, 1956, p. 429 (Venizelos) (hereafter cited as *GPD*). The leaders envisaged proposing to the British government either the immediate union of Cyprus with Greece but with British bases maintained on the island and others granted on Greek territory, or the granting to the Cypriots of a reasonable period to allow them to decide their own future. Lennox-Boyd, speaking in Parliament on May 14, 1956, confirmed that the Greek government in 1951 had made such a proposal concerning the cession of Cyprus to Greece with the cession of bases on Greek soil as a *quid pro quo*. He added that the Greek government had said that if Britain could not agree to the cession of Cyprus because of the international situation, it should announce its willingness to ascertain the wishes of the inhabitants of Cyprus within a reasonable period. (552 H.C. Deb. [5th Ser.], p. 1737.)

11. The Labour government's reaction to the Greek approaches was even more forcefully expressed and at the highest possible level, when, at an official reception of the diplomatic corps in Buckingham Palace, King George VI stepped out of the line he normally followed at such formal ceremonies and, walking up to the Greek Ambassador, told him he had heard that the Greek government had raised the question of Cyprus. This was a matter of imperial defense, he observed, with the clear implication that it could not be even discussed.

12. *GAOR, Fifth Session*, First Committee, 374th meeting, p. 184.

13. Already at its fifth session, the General Assembly, in Resolution 421 (V) of December 4, 1950, had called on the Economic and Social Council to ask the Commission on Human Rights to study ways and means to insure the right of peoples and nations to self-determination and to prepare recommendations for the Assembly's consideration at its sixth session. Because of lack of time, the Commission, in April and May, 1951, deferred consideration of the question, and the Assembly, by Resolution 545 (VI), which was proposed by the Greek representative on the Third Committee, L. Critas, of Cypriot origin, decided that an article on the right of all peoples and nations to self-determination should be included in the covenant or covenants on human rights and asked the Commission on Human Rights to prepare recommendations on this matter and to submit them to the Assembly. In a separate resolution, 549 (VI), the Assembly asked the Economic and Social Council to instruct the Commission to give priority to the question of self-determination. (*GAOR, Seventh Session*, Annexes, Agenda Item 30 [Memorandum of the Secretary-General, p. 2.)

14. See above, n. 4.

15. Alker and Russett, *op. cit.*, p. 72.

16. As early as August, 1952, before the November elections, Papagos had asked Stamatis Mercouris to inform Peake about his intentions. Peake, however, laughed this message off, saying all Greek governments raised the Cyprus question. Papagos, annoyed, asked Spyros Markezinis to arrange a dinner with Peake, and on this occasion he personally sought to impress the British Ambassador about his earnestness. (Mercouris to author.)

17. *GPD*, February 7, 1955, p. 671 (Papagos).

18. *Ibid.*, pp. 671–72.

19. *GAOR, Seventh Session*, Supplement 17, p. 22 (paragraph 6).

20. *GPD*, February 7, 1955, p. 672 (Papagos).

21. At this meeting of April 15, 1954, Ambassador Mostras observed Britain was not afraid of losing the friendship of Greece since it could very well do its business with Turkey in pursuing its interests in the eastern Mediterranean. Caution ought to be exercised, he added, because it was likely that the British would involve the Turks in the matter. Since January, 1954, he had drawn the Foreign Ministry's attention to the Turkish factor and had predicted the likelihood of tripartite rather than bipartite negotiations. Three days before this conference of April 15, he had spoken to Foreign Minister Stefanopoulos about his anxiety concerning the Turkish attitude and had mentioned the problems of the Patriarchate and of the Greeks in Istanbul, as well as of the Aegean islands. A Turkish statement of February 19, 1954, had indicated that Turkey saw no need for a change in the status of Cyprus, hence of any talks with Greece, over an island that belonged to Britain. On April 2, in reply to a question of a member of the Grand National Assembly, the Turkish Foreign Minister repeated this view. However, if the island's future were to be discussed, the existence of a Turkish minority on Cyprus would give Turkey the right to have a say on the matter. (P. Pipinelis, *Kathimerini*, February 28, 1959.) In 1958, on the other hand, Stefanopoulos told the Greek Parliament that in 1954 and 1955 he had received cables from his Turkish colleague, Fuat Köprülü, as well as from Premier Adnan Menderes assuring him that the Cyprus question would never affect Greek-Turkish relations and that Greek-Turkish friendship was above the small dispute over Cyprus. (*GPD*, December 12, 1958, p. 299.) In 1951, when S. Venizelos went to Ankara as an official guest of the Turkish government and in a private conversation inquired from Menderes what would the Turkish attitude be on the question of Cyprus, the Turkish Premier answered: "Don't worry. This will be solved within the framework of Greek-Turkish friendship." (*GPD*, December 12, 1958, pp. 281–82 [Venizelos].)

22. *Ibid.*, February 7, 1955, p. 672 (Papagos).

23. A. Eden, *Full Circle* (Boston: Houghton Mifflin, 1960), p. 270. The year 1952 is taken from the context.

24. Churchill's statement was made on October 19, 1954, but not in the House of Commons. Kyrou referred to it in his statement of December 14, 1954, in the Political Committee's 750th meeting. (*GAOR, Ninth Session*, First Committee, p. 548.)

25. A. A. Kyrou, *Greek Foreign Policy* (in Greek) (Athens, 1955) p. 279. *GPD*, February 7, 1955, p. 687 (Markezinis).

26. *GPD*, December 12, 1958, pp. 298–99 (Panayotis Canellopoulos).

27. Hadwen and Kaufman, *op. cit.*, p. 31, refer to the social activities that take place during the sessions of the Assembly and note that exchanges of various kinds may take place during such activities. Very seldom, they note, do delegates refuse invitations to such parties. The above example illustrates this process and highlights how even among governments that are definitely not on the same side of the fence, exchanges of importance may take place on such "frivolous" occasions.

28. Kyrou, *op. cit.*, pp. 282–85. Diplomatic *démarches* had been made earlier with

various embassies in Athens and instructions sent to the Greek embassies in other countries to make *démarches* on the matter with the governments to which they were accredited. *Démarches* of the latter kind apparently were not made with the governments of Soviet bloc states. However, the Director-General of the Greek Foreign Ministry handed the text of the recourse, at the time of its transmission to the United Nations, to the representatives of these countries in Athens, with the request that they convey it to their governments. (*Ibid.*, pp. 276–77.)

29. *Ibid.*, pp. 283–84.

30. *Ibid.*, pp. 285–86. Kyrou ascribed the change in the Colombian vote to U.S. backstage pressures, see below, p. 19.

31. *GAOR, Ninth Session,* 477th plenary meeting, September 24, 1954, p. 59. To Foreign Minister Stefanopoulos, in private, Krishna Menon stressed his view that the United Nations was a suitable instrument for decolonization, not for the transfer of territory from one state to another. For that reason, he could only support a proposal for setting up an independent Cyprus.

32. Kyrou, *op. cit.*, pp. 287–90. See below, pp. 19.

33. *Ibid.*, p. 294. Iklé, *op. cit.*, p. 170, notes the psychological phenomenon that if a great effort is made to obtain certain terms, these terms may seem more valuable than if they had been obtained without difficulty.

34. Kyrou, *op. cit.*, pp. 295–96. Whereas at the eighth Assembly Greece had merely abstained from voting on the resolutions on Tunisia and Morocco which the United States opposed, at the ninth Assembly it voted in favor of several resolutions or parts of resolutions which the United States opposed. (*GAOR, Eighth Session,* Annexes, Agenda Items 65 and 57, pp. 5–6, and p. 6 respectively.) At the ninth session, Greece voted in favor of proposals which the United States opposed in the following cases: the Moroccan Question; a paragraph of the Draft International Covenant on Human Rights; an Uruguayan amendment and a Yugoslav amendment concerning the matter of the cessation of transmission of information in Non-Self-Governing Territories under Article 73e of the Charter; a draft resolution concerning the voluntary transmission of information on political developments in Non-Self-Governing Territories. (*GAOR, Ninth Session,* Annexes, Agenda Item 56, p. 3; Agenda Item 58, p. 14; Agenda Item 32, pp. 3–4; Agenda Item 31, p. 5.) Greece also voted in favor of proposals with regard to which the United States abstained in the case of a resolution on the Status of Women in Private Law, the question of West Irian. (*Ibid.*, Agenda Item 59, p. 2; Agenda Item 61, p. 5.) On the other hand, Greece sided with the United States in a U.S. amendment to a Czechoslovak item concerning the prohibition of propaganda in favor of a new war and in the U.S. complaint of detention and imprisonment of UN military personnel in violation of the Korean armistice. (*Ibid.*, Agenda Item 69, p. 2; Agenda Item 72, p. 3.) In the latter case it cosponsored with fifteen other countries draft Resolution 906 (IX) adopted by the Assembly. The scores of agreement with the United States for eighty-six roll-call votes during the first nine sessions of the Assembly reveals that of the fifty-nine UN members Greece came twenty-ninth in rank with 62 votes on the same side as the United States as compared with Turkey which came eighteenth, with 66 votes, and Britain which came thirtieth, with 61 votes. The scores of agreement with the United States on fifty-six non-colonial roll-call votes reveal that Greece came eighteenth, with 49 votes; Turkey, fourteenth, with 50; and Britain twenty-fifth, with 47. (Riggs, *op. cit.*, pp. 167–68.) These tabulations reveal that Greece was more often in agreement with the United States on non-colonial than on colonial questions. The explanation of this largely resides in the Cyprus question.

35. See below, pp. 20–21 for details.

36. Kyrou, *op. cit.*, p. 298. He explains he made no effort to prevent this move

because he had learned from backstage talks that the U.S. Delegation was behind this proposal which the Brazilian representative had introduced.

37. Henry Cabot Lodge, the U.S. Delegate, underlined that the New Zealand resolution did not say that the question should not be discussed; it merely said that it should not be considered. Whereas the word "consider" involved passing judgment, the word "discuss" did not, he explained. (*GAOR, Ninth Session,* Political Committee, 749th meeting, December 14, 1954, pp. 544–45.)

38. The full text of the Greek draft resolution was as follows: "The General Assembly, having examined the item concerning the application, under the auspices of the United Nations, of the principle of equal rights and self-determination of peoples in the case of the population of the island of Cyprus; mindful that one of the purposes of the United Nations, as set forth in Article 1 of the Charter, is 'to develop friendly relations among nations based on respect for the principle of equal rights and self-determination of peoples'; recalling Resolution 637 A (VII), of December 16, 1952, expresses the wish that the principle of self-determination be applied in the case of the population of Cyprus." (*Ibid.,* Supplement 21, p. 5.) The extent of the "watering down" process this draft had undergone is suggested by comparing it with the proposal suggested in the text of the Greek recourse (see Appendix I). Originally, the Greek government had requested "that the people of the island of Cyprus be allowed to express themselves on their future in complete freedom and under the auspices of the United Nations." And in diplomatic *démarches* with the British government outside the UN it had proposed *enosis,* the cession of the island to Greece. (See above, pp. 6–7.)

39. On August 21, 1954, Kyrou told journalists that if the United Nations were to urge immediate negotiations between Greece and Britain on the Cyprus question, the Greek government would not oppose such a procedure, "Hellenic News" (Washington: Royal Greek Embassy Information Service), Bulletin No. 23, August 30, 1954, p. 3.

40. *GPD,* February 7, 1955, p. 678 (Stefanopoulos).

41. The full text of Resolution 814 (IX) reads as follows: "The General Assembly, considering that, for the time being, it does not appear appropriate to adopt a resolution on the question of Cyprus, decides not to consider further the item entitled 'Application under the Auspices of the United Nations, of the Principle of Equal Rights and Self-Determination of Peoples in the Case of the Population of the Island of Cyprus.'" *GAOR, Ninth Session,* Supplement 21, p. 5.

42. *Ibid.,* First Committee, 752d meeting, December 15, 1954, p. 567.

43. *Ibid.,* 514th plenary meeting, December 17, 1954, pp. 538–39.

44. *Ibid.,* pp. 539–40.

45. *Ibid.,* 477th plenary meeting, September 24, 1954, p. 52.

46. See below, Chapter II, pp. 70–71.

47. Iklé, *op. cit.,* p. 27, introduces this term "side effects" and proposes that these, too, are one sort of objectives of negotiations, one of the reasons that governments engage in diplomatic talks. Among specific side effects that are also relevant to negotiations are propaganda or the modification of the political attitude of non-participants.

48. *Ibid.,* pp. 64–65, defines a commitment as a move to convince one's opponent that one will maintain one's current position or implement one's prediction by making it more difficult for one's self not to do so. Explanations of votes in the United Nations often fall, thus, in this category of commitments.

49. *GPD,* February 7, 1955, pp. 673, 677. The goal of "internationalizing" the

issue was not an *ex post facto* rationalization. Kyrou had mentioned it to the press on August 21, 1954, "Hellenic News," Bulletin, No. 23, August 30.

50. Kyrou, *op. cit.*, p. 307. He also notes that thanks to the procedural tangle that occurred during the Committee's discussion, time was secured that enabled the introduction of amendments to the draft resolution tabled by New Zealand.

51. 531 H.C. Deb. (5th Ser.), p. 226 (written answer).

52. *GPD*, February 7, 1955, pp. 681–82 (Venizelos); p. 695 (George Papandreou).

53. *Ibid.*, pp. 684, 697.

54. *Ibid.*, p. 687 (Markezinis); p. 683 (Venizelos); p. 697 (Papandreou).

55. *Ibid.*, pp. 692–93 (Venizelos); pp. 684–85 (Markezinis); p. 696 (Papandreou).

56. *Ibid.*, p. 701 (J. Zigdis). Kyrou maintains that the recourse deliberately was not given a strong negative character, of an anticolonial or other nature, in order to demonstrate moderation. He also argues that reference to Article 73 of the Charter, which mentions only self-government, not self-determination, would have been catastrophic because it would have been sufficient for the British representative to state that his government intended to grant a Constitution to the Cypriots for the General Committee to recommend non-inclusion of the item in the agenda. And, he adds, even were the item included in the agenda, it would have been considered by the Fourth Committee (Trusteeship and Non-Self-Governing Territories) and would have bogged down there. The Arab and Asian states likewise had avoided reference to Article 73 of the Charter in their recourses over Morocco or Tunisia. For the non-reference to Resolution 637 (VII), he explains that this was, first, superfluous, because Article 1, paragraph 2, was invoked; and, second, counterproductive, because it might have irritated the Americans who had voted against that resolution. (Kyrou, *op. cit.*, 281–82.)

57. *GPD*, February 7, 1955, p. 682 (Venizelos); p. 685 (Markezinis); p. 696 (Papandreou).

58. *GPD*, December 12, 1958, p. 290 (Venizelos). According to Stefanopoulos, the United States regarded as untimely the raising of the issue. (*Ibid.*, p. 295.)

59. *GPD*, February 7, 1955, p. 694 (Markezinis: Kyrou, *op. cit.*, pp. 273–74. Kyrou adds that Dulles did not raise any objections of substance to his statement about the continued intransigence of Britain and the need to resort to the UN perhaps misinterpreting this Protestant reserve.

60. Pipinelis, *Kathimerini*, March 4, 1959. *GPD*, February 7, 1955, p. 682 (Venizelos); p. 685 (Markezinis). Venizelos summarized this note as saying that in the U.S. view it was untimely to raise the Cyprus question which would be better promoted outside the United Nations. Markezinis said the letter clearly indicated U.S. disagreement about posing the question and, in addition, U.S. sympathy with views definitely of Greek provenance.

61. *GPD*, February 7, 1955, p. 685 (Markezinis). The speaker, a critic of the government, did not see why any reply should have been expected to this note. *Ibid.*, (Pipinelis).

62. See above, p. 9. Premier Papagos, as mentioned, seemed convinced the British would finally prefer bipartite negotiations to a confrontation in the United Nations.

63. *GPD*, February 7, 1955 (Markezinis). Kyrou, *op. cit.*, p. 336.

64. *GPD*, February 7, 1955, p. 685 (Markezinis). Kyrou, *op. cit.*, pp. 278, 336. The former said that this confirmed almost completely what Cannon had told Kyrou on August 16. The latter, in his book, gives a different version of Baxter's second point

about the attitude the U.S. would assume toward draft resolutions that might be tabled—that the U.S. would determine its position toward them in accordance with their "content." He writes that a favorable U.S. vote would depend on the degree of "moderation" of the "substance" of any draft resolution tabled. The result was that he sought to water down the substance of the Greek draft resolution and was astonished to learn that the United States would oppose any substantive resolution at all. But the "content" of a resolution could be not only substantive but procedural.

65. *GAOR, Ninth Session,* General Committee, 93d meeting, September 23, 1965, p. 11; 477th plenary meeting, September 24, 1954, pp. 59, 22. Had the British Delegate not abstained from voting on the Iraqi proposal as he announced he would, the tie would not have occurred and the motion would have been adopted.

66. Kyrou, *op. cit.,* pp. 286–87; 298–99. *GPD,* February 7, 1955, p. 686 (Markezinis). Eden had proposed the revival and extension of the Brussels Treaty of March 17, 1948, between Britain, France, and the Benelux States, and German participation. Dulles had agreed with him that it would be useful to hold a preparatory conference to consider how best to associate the German Federal Republic with the Western nations on a basis of full equality. As a result, the United States left the initiative with the Europeans, and Eden chaired the London Conference, September 28—October 3, 1954, which studied the problem and agreed, among other things, that Germany should become a member of NATO. In explanation of the Cyprus stand of the United States, it was reported then and later that in exchange for American support in the Cyprus issue, Britain helped the British position with regard to the question of the representation of China in the United Nations and U.S. policy in the Far East. Cedric Foster commentary, Mutual Broadcasting System (WOR), December 16, 1954, "Hellenic News," *Bulletin No. 33,* December 23, 1954, pp. 8–9. C. L. Sulzberger, *New York Times,* July 4, 1955.

67. See above, pp. 15–16.

68. *GAOR, Ninth Session,* 477th plenary meeting, September 24, 1954, p. 53. "We shall not regard discussion—of course, apart from that which takes place today in connection with the matter of inscription—as having any validity, and we shall take no part in it," said Lloyd on this occasion.

69. Kyrou, *op. cit.,* p. 298.

70. *Ibid.,* pp. 298–99.

71. *GPD,* February 7, 1955, p. 682 (Venizelos); Kyrou, *op. cit.,* p. 299.

72. *GPD,* February 7, 1955, p. 675 (Stefanopoulos); 682 (Venizelos); 686 (Markezinis). Venizelos stressed that Dulles had never promised neutrality. Markezinis emphasized that during this conversation, Papagos inquired whether it might not be advisable to postpone for the next Assembly the discussion of the Cyprus issue, while Dulles, as will be seen, reminded him of this in his letter of December 12, 1954, to the Premier. Markezinis noted that *Kathimerini* (regarded as an organ that reflected the government views) had reported from Paris on October 31 that, according to a good source, the Greek government was now disposed to accept the postponement of the UN debate if U.S. mediation would lead Britain to promise immediately the granting of a liberal constitution to Cyprus. Kyrou, said Markezinis, had protested. However, in his book, *op. cit.,* p. 298, Kyrou writes that he raised this possibility in mid-October because of what he regarded as a change, away from neutrality, of the U.S. attitude. At this time, as mentioned earlier, Greek-British conversations had been going on ultra-secretly and outside of the diplomatic channel.

73. Kyrou, *op. cit.,* p. 299. Kyrou mentions that Lodge replied he considered the Greek request very reasonable and agreed to convey to Washington his views to that effect. For Kyrou's construction of Baxter's second point, see above, n. 64.

74. *Ibid.*, p. 299. Kyrou writes that the note was handed to the Greek Ambassador in Washington that day. Evidently this was the same note which Ambassador Cannon delivered to Premier Papagos in Athens that same day. (*GPD*, February 7, 1955, p. 675.) Stefanopoulos read a translation of parts of this note, which, retranslated into English from the Greek, was as follows: "I sincerely regret that there was a misunderstanding about my attitude in the Cyprus question. We were obliged not to oppose the inscription of the item on the agenda because of our friendship toward Greece and because by conviction we support the principle of freedom of discussion in the General Assembly. Nevertheless, we are convinced that consideration of the matter at the present time and the adoption of any resolution would harm good relations between some of our friends and allies. This for us constitutes the most important aspect of the question. Thus, although we do not oppose the desire of the Greek government to bring the Cyprus question before the General Assembly, we shall be obliged to oppose the adoption of any substantive resolution. Nonetheless, we would be happy to seek a way of responding to the problem raised." The climate for efforts to seek such an agreement, this note added rather cryptically, seemed improved. Venizelos, in brief reference to this note, added that the U.S. government promised to keep secret its decision to vote against any substantive resolution and not to carry out any backstage activities against the Greek draft resolution. Such a promise, seems subsequently to have been sought by the Greek government.

75. *GPD*, February 7, 1955, p. 676 (Stefanopoulos).

76. *Ibid.*, pp. 675, 678 (Stefanopoulos); p. 682 (Venizelos), p. 686 (Markezinis). Venizelos asked how was it possible for the government to believe that U.S. diplomacy would be able to conceal its attitude during the entire procedure. Markezinis observed that the British government had ample means to know what the U.S. attitude was, even if Dulles had not advised it of the U.S. intention to vote against any substantive draft resolution on the Cyprus item—which, to this author, appears highly unlikely, since consultations and bargaining with Britain should have preceded the adoption of this attitude by the U.S. government.

77. *Ibid.*, p. 675 (Stefanopoulos).

78. Kyrou, *op. cit.*, pp. 299–300. In his view, this new U.S. *démarche* was no more categorical than the two previous ones. It seems odd that this new watering down of the Greek draft resolution should have been made with the U.S. Delegation in mind, since it was clearly known that the latter would vote against any substantive draft resolution at all. The changes made seem directed rather toward attracting non-European and anticolonial members of the UN to whom the reference to European civilization of the Cypriots would have been irksome and, therefore, from the Greek viewpoint, counterproductive.

79. *Ibid.*, pp. 300–301. *GPD*, February 7, 1955, p. 676 (Stefanopoulos); p. 682 (Venizelos); p. 686 (Markezinis). Kyrou relates that in response to the inquiries of journalists, he replied that he had not yet received any official announcement about such a decision of the U.S. and viewed with reserve the news published in the *New York Times*. The morning of December 13, he gave similar replies to representatives of Athens newspapers in New York. Stefanopoulos told Parliament that Ambassador G. V. Melas (just appointed) had phoned to him about the story in the *New York Times* and had suggested to him that perhaps the Greek Delegation should not press for a vote on its draft resolution because, after the news about the U.S. stand, most of the friendly delegations would surely vote against it. Kyrou, on his side, recommended to the Foreign Minister that the Delegation press for a vote on its draft resolution regardless of the published news. The Foreign Minister concurred with the latter and instructed Kyrou to press for a vote in the Political Committee and then to find a way out when the matter came before the Assembly. He hoped that a simple majority in favor of the very moderate Greek draft resolution could be mustered, but not the two-thirds vote required for final adoption. The Greek Delegation expected that if this

draft resolution were put to the vote, it might gather 37–38 affirmative votes, 12–15 negative ones, and 7–11 abstentions. (Kyrou, *op. cit.*, p. 297.)

80. *GPD*, February 7, 1955, p. 676 (Stefanopoulos).

81. Kyrou, *op. cit.*, pp. 301–2. *GPD*, February 7, 1955, 676 (Stefanopoulos). In reply to Kyrou's protests about the publication of the *New York Times* story, Lodge expressed his personal, friendly feelings for Greece as well as his regret at having "to get the chestnuts out of the fire." Stefanopoulos told the Greek Parliament on February 7, 1955, that the leaking of the news about the U.S. attitude had been the object of a protest lodged with the State Department; that this disclosure could not be ascribed to top echelons in the Department; and that it was certain that some of the lower ones had disclosed the news only a few hours after Cannon had conveyed the message to the Greek Premier. (*GPD, ibid.*, p. 679.)

82. *GAOR, Ninth Session,* First Committee, 749th Meeting, pp. 543–44.

83. *GAOR, Ninth Session,* First Committee, 749th Meeting, pp. 543–44.

84. *Kathimerini*, September 22, 1955. *Times* (London), September 22, 1955.

85. Eden, *op. cit.*, p. 448.

86. *GAOR, Tenth Session,* General Committee, 102d meeting, September 23, 1955, p. 5; *Eleventh Session,* First Committee, 851st meeting, February 23, 1957. The setback of the Greek recourse at the tenth session, coming as it did shortly after the anti-Greek riots in Istanbul and Izmir (see below, Chapter IV, p. 159), caused great bitterness in Greece. Even the government organ, *Kathimerini,* urged on September 25 a purely Greek policy, complained that Greece had been deserted by its allies, and proclaimed that it "must have the courage to stand alone." The government's attitude was to stress the closeness of the Assembly's vote while the Chiefs of Staff pointed out that heavier defense expenditures would be required if Greece were to withdraw from NAO, as some Opposition leaders maintained it should. Likewise on September 25, 1955, *Avghi,* the organ of the Communist façade party EDA, presented to its readers in box form the results of the voting in the Assembly as follows:

For Greece	Against Greece	Abstentions
"The Enemies"	*"The NATO Allies"*	
USSR	USA, Britain, France	"Chiang Kai-shek,"
Byelorussian SSR	Turkey, Belgium,	Burma, Ethiopia,
Czechoslovakia	Holland, Luxembourg,	Haiti, India,
Ukrainian SSR	Denmark, Norway,	Indonesia, Iran,
Poland	Canada	Israel, Philippines,
		Dominican Republic
Colonies or Dependent States	*The Vassals of Our "Allies"*	
Arab: Egypt, Syria, Lebanon, Saudi Arabia Yemen	Panama, Brazil, Venezuela, Honduras	
The Only Allies	*The Friends of Our "Friends"*	
Iceland, Yugoslavia	Pakistan, Iraq, Australia, Chile, Colombia, Cuba, Liberia, New Zealand, Nicaragua Paraguay, Peru, Thailand, Sweden, South Africa.	

The abstention of the Bandung countries (India, Burma, and Indonesia), *Avghi* maintained, underlined the deliberately poor handling of the matter on the part of the government.

87. Both Greece and the United States are non-caucusing member states, T. Hovet, Jr., *Bloc Politics in the United Nations* (Cambridge, Mass.: Harvard University Press, 1960), p. 32. For the influence of the United States in the Assembly, Riggs, *op. cit.*, pp. 35 ff., on U.S. pressure.

88. "Hellenic News," Bulletin No. 33, December 23, 1954, p. 3. No. 35, January 1–10, 1955, p. 2; No. 28 n.d., p. 4 (Makarios speech of January 15, 1955, in Nicosia).

89. See below, Chapter I, p. 42. *GAOR, Tenth Assembly*, 521d meeting, p. 54. Hadwen and Kaufman, *op. cit.*, p. 60, note that if at times it is difficult to get a debate begun in the United Nations, it is often hard to get it stopped.

90. C. Grivas-Dighenis, *Memoirs of the EOKA Struggle, 1955–1959*, (in Greek) (Athens, 1961), Appendix, p. 3 (hereafter cited as *Grivas Memoirs*).

91. See below, Chapter IV, p. 161.

92. See below, Chapter III, p. 127.

93. *Ibid.*, p. 127.

94. *GPD*, April 25, 1956, p. 287; November 30, 1956, pp. 111–12; November 29, 1956, p. 87. On this occasion, the Greek government raised the matter in the NATO Council as well.

95. See below, Chapter XII, p. 500, and Epilogue, p. 511.

96. B. Gross, *The Legislative Process* (New York: McGraw-Hill, 1953), p. 167.

97. See below, Chapters II and IV, pp. 73, 157, 165, 178.

98. In response to questions by the Opposition concerning why the Greek government had not raised the issue of Makarios' deportation to the Seychelles before the Security Council (*GPD*, April 5, 1956, p. 14 [Venizelos]; p. 18 [Papandreou]; pp. 24–25 [Kartalis]; p. 25 [Passalidis]; p. 32 [Tsaldaris].), Foreign Minister Theotokis explained it had not done so because the Security Council's composition at the time made him doubt that it would take a decision to seize itself of the question and invite a representative of Greece to present his views and take part in the debate. Besides, even if the Security Council seized itself of the question, the right of the veto together with the Security Council's composition made it unlikely that a favorable resolution would be adopted (*ibid.*, April 6, 1956, pp. 50–51). At that time the non-permanent members of the Security Council were Australia, Belgium, Cuba, Iran, Peru, and Yugoslavia. Article 52, paragraph 2, of the Charter provides that UN members entering in regional arrangements or agencies should make every possible effort to achieve pacific settlement of local disputes through these regional arrangements or agencies before referring them to the Security Council. In summer, 1958, the Opposition once again raised the question of resorting to the Security Council over the Cyprus question. On that occasion, the Greek government, on June 13 and 19, 1958, informed the Council's President of its views on the question. (For parliamentary debates, see *GPD*, June 10–13, 1958.) In these debates, Opposition leaders urged a recourse to the Council with a complaint against Turkey. (*Ibid.*, June 11, 1958, p. 17 [Passalidis] and p. 24 [Papandreou].) Foreign Minister Averoff-Tossizza reiterated the arguments mentioned above and this time referred to an undesirable outcome based on Article 52. (*Ibid.*, June 11, 1958, pp. 24–25.)

99 *GAOR, Fifteenth Session*, Annexes, Item 71, p. 6. This resolution was passed at the Assembly's 956th plenary meeting.

100. See below, Chapters I, XII, pp. 43, 497, 501.

101. *GAOR, Ninth Session,* 514th plenary meeting, December 17, 1954, p. 538. On this occasion, Sarper stated that his government considered that the status of Cyprus had been fixed by solemn treaty to which Greece was a signatory, and "should any party ever raise in any form whatever the so-called question of Cyprus no settlement can be considered to be based on justice and equity unless the cooperation and consent of Turkey is unequivocally obtained; for otherwise no decision will be lasting."

102. *Ibid., Eleventh Session,* General Committee, 107th meeting, November 14, 1956.

103. See below, Chapter I, p. 50.

104. *Ibid.,* p. 57.

105. See below, Chapter V, p. 234.

106. Gross, *op. cit.,* p. 167.

107. *GPD,* February 7, 1955, p. 686 (Markezinis). See also above, n. 15.

108. *Disturbances in Cyprus in October 1931,* Cmd. 4045 (London: H.M. Stationery Office, 1932), p. 5. His attitude, according to this document, created the impression that with sufficient clamor, diplomatic intervention might be invoked in the cause of the union of Cyprus with Greece. Grivas' operations on the island between 1955–59 were motivated, as mentioned above, by similar considerations.

109. Kyrou, *op. cit.,* p. 272.

110. Since mid-March 1945, for instance, he opposed any raising of the Cyprus issue on the grounds that this might cause harm to the question. (Xydis, *Greece and the Great Powers, 1944–1947,* p. 582 n. 80.)

111. "Hellenic News," Bulletin No. 4 (covering February 21—March 2, 1954), p. 6. Since the death of Stalin, he said in this radio speech in Athens, the West was passing through a period of "cold peace" while the Kremlin leaders were displaying an outward spirit of conciliation.

112. See below, Chapter II, pp. 68–72.

113. *GPD,* February 7, 1955, p. 697 (Papandreou).

114. *Ibid.,* November 30, 1956, pp. 110–11.

115. *GPD,* March 15, 1957, p. 37. Earlier, for instance in Parliament on November 29, 1956, he emphasized the great complexity of the subject which led Greece to confront powerful allies. (*GPD,* November 29, 1956, p. 84.)

116. For relevant debates in the Greek Parliament, *GPD,* April 25, 1956, 273 ff.

117. See below, Epilogue, p. 513.

118. See below, Chapter I, pp. 50–51.

119. *Ibid.,* p. 57.

120. Hadwen and Kaufman, *op. cit.,* pp. 36–37, correctly observe that the great efforts representatives make to block, amend, or defeat certain resolutions that might be directed against their government's policies, even when the proposals are drafted in ambiguous language, indicates the importance they attach to these texts.

121. See below, Chapter XI, p. 467.

122. See below, Epilogue, p. 516.

123. Kyrou, *op. cit.,* p. 297.

124. Hadwen and Kaufman, *op. cit.,* p. 29, note that the attitude of a representa-

tive may be altered by too long a period of service with the United Nations. He might either get an unbalanced view of the organization's importance or become a cynic.

125. R. B. Russell, *A History of the U.N. Charter* (Washington, D.C.; The Brookings Institution, 1958), p. 811.

126. Hadwen and Kaufman, *op. cit.*, pp. 67–68, write "it is necessary to avoid the delusion that the United Nations represents the moral conscience of the world."

127. Permanent Delegation of Greece to the United Nations, "Speech . . . by Ambassador Alexis A. Kyrou . . . 14 December, 1954," pp. 14–15 (mimeographed), in the author's files.

128. *GAOR, Ninth Session,* 514th plenary meeting, December 17, 1954, p. 539. Such an approach illustrates what has been termed "the fallacy of the 'unambiguous meaning,'" M. S. McDougal and R. N. Gardner, "The Veto and the Charter: An Interpretation for Survival," *Yale Law Review,* LX (January, 1951), 262–92, cited in J. Larus (ed.), *From Collective Security to Preventive Diplomacy* (New York: Wiley & Sons, 1965), p. 266.

129. K. Burke, *A Rhetoric of Motives* (New York: Prentice Hall, 1950), p. 70.

130. Kyrou, *op. cit.*, pp. 321–22. He could have explained that this approach had been followed in order to attract the sympathy of American legalist-moralists, since positive support was not to be expected, but he did not do so.

131. Burke, *op. cit.*, p. 70.

132. See below Chapter I, pp. 46–47.

133. Alker and Russett, *op. cit.*, pp. 20–21.

134. *Ibid.*, p. 183. See also below, Epilogue, p. 521.

135. On November 8, 1956, Lloyd told Dimitri Nikolareïzis, Chargé d'Affaires of the Greek Embassy in London, that it was unfortunate the Greek government had raised the Cyprus question in the United Nations two years earlier when there had been still a possibility to find a solution if the question were kept in suspense for a few years in view of other Middle Eastern difficulties.

CHAPTER I

1. *GAOR, Eleventh Session,* Supplement No. 17, p. 4. The Assembly, by a show-of-hands vote, passed this resolution by fifty-seven votes to none, with one abstention.

2. *Ibid.*, Annexes, Agenda item 55, p. 16.

3. *Ibid.*, p. 16.

4. *Ibid.*, p. 17.

5. General Assembly, Eleventh Session, First Committee, 856th meeting, February 22, *Verbatim Record*, pp. 54–56. (Cited hereafter as *Verbatim Record.*) The summary records only, not the verbatim records, are considered as the official record. At one point of his statement of February 22, 1957, Krishna Menon said that because the Cyprus question had come to the Assembly, the existence of Cypriot nationality had been brought to the front of the political scene. At another point, he asserted that Cyprus was a nation whose sovereignty was latent within the people and, "with the dawn of political generosity and conciliation," that latent sovereignty would become an established fact and Cyprus would take its place in the United Nations. At the

Assembly's twelfth session, Krishna Menon was to revert with greater insistence to these views. (See below, Chapter XII, pp. 470 ff.)

6. *GAOR, Ninth Session,* 477th plenary meeting, September 24, 1954, p. 59. See also above, Introduction, p. 12. *Ibid., Tenth Session,* 521st plenary meeting, p. 62.

7. *Verbatim Record,* pp. 47–50.

8. *Ibid.,* February 19, 855th meeting, p. 22. With regard to the contention of the Turkish representative that Greece was aiming only at the annexation of Cyprus, Averoff-Tossizza reminded the Committee on several occasions "that Greece is not aiming at the annexation of Cyprus." He had made formal statements to that effect and did not believe that the Turkish representative had the right to question the value of those statements—the more so since he challenged the Turkish Delegation to reply to a question he had put to it. He had asked the representative of Turkey "if he would be ready to sign an agreement on a solution which would rule out annexation. He had received no reply." He maintained the statement he had made to the effect that Greece was not asking for the annexation of Cyprus. (For the repercussions of this challenge in the Greek Parliament and of the Foreign Minister's handling of the Opposition's charges on the matter, see below, pp. 50–51, also Chapters III and VIII, pp. 110, 112, 344, respectively.)

In his set speech at the Committee's 847th meeting, February 18, 1957, the Greek Foreign Minister said that Greece, through its representatives, had repeatedly declared it was not asking for the union of Cyprus but for the freedom of the Cypriots. It demanded for the Cypriots the application of a fundamental human right, the right to self-determination. Greece would respect the result, whatever it might be, of a plebiscite, even if, for example, the people should decide to continue as a British colony or to form a totally independent state, "which is not out of the question." (*Ibid.,* p. 21.)

Then, at the Committee's 849th meeting, he stated on February 19 that Greece was asking only for the abolition of the colonial regime in Cyprus and the application of the right of self-determination. If the prospect of union between Cyprus and Greece did not exist, would the British government be prepared to liberate the island? If that was so, "let them tell us—and then we, the General Assembly, would certainly be able to find appropriate ways and means to set at rest the misgivings and fears of the British government and fulfil the obligations of the Charter and of the Lausanne Treaty and restore liberty to the Cypriot people." (*Ibid.,* pp. 18–21.) Then, at the 854th meeting, February 21, he stated that Greece was not requesting the transfer of the sovereignty over Cyprus in its favor. Greece did not ask for the island. (*Ibid.,* pp. 91, 98–100.) Late in November 1956, in the Greek Parliament, Averoff-Tossizza had stated that Greece sought the application of self-determination in Cyprus and would respect any decision the Cypriots might take with regard to their future. (*GPD,* November 29, 1956, p. 87.)

9. *Ibid.,* February 20, 849th meeting, pp. 16–17. He did not wish to circulate these documents, he had told the Committee, for the purpose of envenoming the atmosphere still further, but he would deposit them with the Secretary-General so that eventually the Chairman of the Committee and the Assembly's President might study them, "pending the careful study of them and the circumstances surrounding them by a commission of inquiry such as he had called for." He had, he added, considerable misgivings about utilizing these "horrifying and dreadful documents even in this confidential manner." In the event the proposed committee of inquiry were to conclude that the charges made in these documents were not valid, he would leave his post and retire from political life. In the contrary case, it would be incumbent on the British nation to draw the consequences.

10. See below, Chapter III, pp. 114–26.

11. See below, Chapter IV, pp. 158–61.

12. *Verbatim Record*, February 20, 852d meeting, p. 3. The Syrian representative, to justify his country's interest in Cyprus, invoked (like Turkey) proximity and historical arguments, declaring, however, that Syria had no actual claim to Cyprus. (For Egypt, *ibid.*, see 853d meeting, pp. 17–18.) The Egyptian representative asserted that his country had considerable interest in Cyprus, because of that island's strategic position. He underlined that the attack on Egypt in 1956 had been launched from Cyprus.

13. For instance, the representatives of Ceylon, *ibid.*, February 19, 849th meeting, pp. 63–66; the Ukrainian S.S.R., *ibid.*, February 21, 854th meeting, pp. 43–45; the Byelorussian S.S.R., *ibid.*, 854th meeting, p. 62; Poland, *ibid.*, 854th meeting, p. 74. Presented to the House of Commons by Colonial Secretary Lennox-Boyd on December 19, 1956, this plan, in brief, laid down a system of dyarchy, under which external affairs, defense, and internal security were reserved for the Governor, while the local legislature and the ministers responsible to it would be masters in their own non-reserved field. The Governor was to be the final judge of whether any action he felt he should take was within the sphere of his reserved powers and also whether any bill of the legislature did or did not impinge upon his reserved powers. To safeguard the interests of the Turkish Cypriots, the Constitution allotted six seats in the legislature to members elected on a special roll of Turkish Cypriot voters. A "Tribunal of Guarantees" was also envisaged. Its function would be to investigate any complaints of discrimination or other violations of fundamental rights guaranteed by the Constitution. Individuals, associations, or corporations would be able to resort to it. (Lord Radcliffe, *Constitutional Proposals for Cyprus* [London: H.M. Stationery Office, 1956], Cmd. 42.) The Greek government, on December 19, 1956, rejected this plan which had been communicated to it on December 13 by Lennox-Boyd, who visited Athens. It observed that it did not provide for the exercise of the right of self-determination by the Cypriot people and maintained that it was neither democratic nor liberal because, although formally it established the majoritarian principle, in essence it strangulated it by vesting the Governor with almost unlimited powers. In a separate statement, the Greek Foreign Minister observed that the people of Cyprus themselves should have the last word on their Constitution. However, the exile of the Ethnarch and of most members of the Ethnarchy deprived the people of the possibility to freely express their will. He also charged that through the Radcliffe draft Constitution, the British government was seeking to perpetuate the regime of colonialism in Cyprus. In greater detail, he pointed out that under this plan the Governor would have the right to issue decrees subject to no control and could define his powers without control. He attacked six other aspects of this plan and complained that the question of releasing Makarios and of an amnesty had been ignored. (*Kathimerini*, December 20, 1956.) When Lincoln White, the State Department spokesman, said on December 27, 1956, that the Radcliffe draft Constitution might be "a possible first step" toward a solution of the Cyprus problem, although in its present form it seemed "unacceptable in certain respects to some who are concerned with the matter," (*State Department Bulletin*, XXXVI [January 14, 1957], 54) the Greek government issued a further statement, on December 29, explaining the reasons for its rejection of these proposals. It reasserted the points it had previously made and explained that it had not obtained satisfactory answers from Lennox-Boyd about Makarios' release, about the British attitude toward self-determination, and about the possibility of using the Radcliffe plan as a basis for further discussions. Lennox-Boyd had said that his government was willing to listen to any suggestions but was unwilling to start fresh negotiations with the Cypriots and Makarios. Under such conditions, the proposals were unworthy of further study. (*Keesing's Contemporary Archives 1957–1958*, XI, 15473 [cited hereafter as *Keesing's*].) Another reason for the plan's rejection was that it was tied up with the idea of double self-determination for the Greek and Turkish Cypriots—which could lead to the island's partition (*GPD*, February 27, 1959, p. 368 [Karamanlis].) For further reference to this plan and to

the proposal for partition, see below, Chapters III, VIII, pp. 87–89, 306, 312. Eden recounts that the United States declined to support the Radcliffe proposals on the ground that they were not favorable enough to the Greeks. In reply to British explanations, a State Department official observed that there was no Turkish lobby in the United States. (A. Eden, *op. cit.*, pp. 462–63.)

14. See below, Chapter III, pp. 87–89, about the background of the proposal for the partition of Cyprus.

15. *Verbatim Record*, February 22, 856th meeting, pp. 41–43. Noble maintained that the resolution recognized: (1) that the solution of the problem required a calm atmosphere, in which incitements to violence, support for terrorism, intimidation, and other such impediments to freedom of expression were eliminated. A first necessity, in short, was that terrorism and support for terrorism should cease; (2) that the problem was most complex. The resolution permitted the three governments concerned to resume negotiations by such means as they thought fit; (3) that the problem was essentially one that should be settled between all the parties concerned.

16. Also *New York Times*, February 23, 1957.

17. *Proceedings of the Grand National Assembly*, XVII, 800.

18. *GPD*, March 6, 1957, p. 25. The Opposition parties in question were the Liberal party, the Republican party, and the United Democratic Left (EDA).

19. *GPD*, March 11, 1957, p. 35.

20. *Ibid.*, February 28, 1959, pp. 426–27. Also below, Chapter X, p. 417. P. Pipinelis, in his article on the Cyprus question, *Kathimerini*, February 28, 1959, adds that Eden changed the conversation by inquiring about the health of the Greek King, Paul I. In a press statement of June, 1952, Averoff-Tossizza referred again to the Cyprus question.

21. *GPD*, December 13, 1958, p. 342.

22. See below, p. 57.

23. See below, Chapter II, p. 78 n. 38.

24. In the Assembly, the Foreign Minister also told Dulles, the Greek Delegation would table a draft resolution calling for the application of the right of self-determination for the Cypriots in accordance with the Charter because that was the mandate of the people of Cyprus, whom the Greek government represented. Realizing, however, the difficulty of applying self-determination immediately and given the limited possibilities of the United Nations, it would agree to discuss an intermediate proposal put forward by a third party if this proposal recommended negotiations between the British government and the Cypriot people; if it aimed at a solution in accordance with the principles of the United Nations; and if it entrusted the UN Secretary-General with the task of following the course of the negotiations and of reporting on them at the next Assembly. Such a mandate given to Dag Hammarskjöld, he maintained, would be constructive and capable of bringing about very good results so that in the meantime, at the next Assembly, the interval would not elapse without any action, while the concern of the Secretary-General would favorably affect the negotiations. He also said that the Greek Delegation intended to request the establishment of an investigation committee by the United Nations because the second paragraph of the item on Cyprus as adopted on the Assembly's agenda referred to British charges that were unproved. During the conversation, Averoff-Tossizza in general emphasized that a closer and deeper analysis of the Cyprus problem would convince Dulles on which side justice lay but expressed understanding of the political difficulties which the Cyprus question created for the United States. "I give you my word of honor," he added, "that if we did not have this faith [in the justice of the Cypriots' cause], we would not have sponsored the demands of the Cypriots." To this

Dulles responded by saying that he believed this statement but expected the Foreign Minister, too, to believe that the United States had not determined to its own satisfaction who was right because as a neutral party perceived matters, it found that each party concerned considered it was in the right.

Another interesting point Averoff-Tossizza made during this conversation was that Nasser was not opposed to a NATO base in Cyprus and that the Ambassador of Saudi Arabia a few days earlier had told him that the base in Cyprus ought to be entrusted to NATO. From this whole conversation, the Greek Foreign Minister and the Greek Ambassador in Washington who had attended it derived the impression that Dulles had been really convinced about the moderate and constructive attitude of the Greek government; that without having reached a final decision about its definitive attitude, the U.S. government official's thoughts were taking shape in not an unpleasant way. Nonetheless, it remained somewhat disturbing, they felt, that Dulles sincerely seemed to be hesitating as to who really was right in the case. (For the Soviet desire for a base in the eastern Mediterranean, see Xydis, *Greece and the Great Powers 1944–1947*, pp. 182–183.) In 1945, at the San Francisco Conference and then at the Potsdam Conference, the Soviet Government had expressed a desire for a trusteeship over one of the former Italian colonies, preferably Tripolitania.

25. The extreme right-wing afternoon paper *Estia* was particularly intemperate in this respect. It was run by Kyros Kyrou, a brother of Alexis A. Kyrou, who, as mentioned in the Introduction, was foremost among Greek diplomats in promoting the Cyprus question in the United Nations. Another brother, Achilles Kyrou, had been, until his death in 1950, a supporter of Grivas, as the latter was studying the possibility of action in Cyprus. (*Grivas Memoirs*, pp. 14–15.)

26. The memorandum No. 2, addressed to the UN Secretary-General on February 18, 1957, by the Permanent Representative of Britain to the United Nations, *GAOR, Eleventh Session*, Annexes, Agenda Item 55, pp. 6–7, contains information on the supply of arms to Grivas and EOKA and the methods used to get them through—by ship at first, then, by post, by the use of travellers' luggage, by the import of toys (model cats containing half a pound of TNT), even, it was said, of rockets supplied to Greece by NATO. From July, 1956, Grivas received financial aid from Athens. Fearing that supplies, if captured, would implicate the Greek government, he had preferred getting funds. By summer, 1958, all the above methods of smuggling in arms had been discovered, and Grivas was very annoyed. At his insistence, a two-man midget submarine was purchased in the United States which could operate submerged nine feet below the surface of the sea. It was planned to transport it by caïque close to the Cyprus coast but outside territorial waters and launch it from there, with a supply of arms. However, it arrived in Athens after the conclusion of the Zürich agreement in February, 1959. Radar, it should be explained, had rendered unfeasible the dispatch of supplies by caïques or airplane drops. Reaching Cyprus the day Karamanlis and Averoff-Tossizza arrived in Zürich were two hundred dummy oxygen cylinders stuffed with 100 revolvers, 60 Tommy guns, and 17,000 bullets. These dummies had been secretly substituted to the genuine oxygen cylinders when the Scandinavian ship that carried them had stopped off Piraeus. With their lethal load, they weighed the same as the genuine article.

27. *GPD*, March 11 and 13, 1957, pp. 28, 72 (George Papandreou and Panayotis Canellopoulos, respectively).

28. *Ibid.*, March 14 and 21, 1957, pp. 94–95, 121 (Themistocles Tsatsos and Sophocles Venizelos, respectively).

29. *Ibid.*, March 11 and 14, 1957, pp. 30, 97 (Papandreou and Th. Tsatsos, respectively).

30. *Ibid.*, March 12 and 14, 1957, pp. 56, 115 (George Kartalis and Elias Iliou, respectively).

31. *Ibid.*, March 11 and 12, 1957, pp. 31, 49 (Papandreou and Kartalis, respectively).

32. *Ibid.*, March 11, 12, 14 and 15, 1957, pp. 32–33, 47, 62, 111, 120 (Papandreou, Kartalis, Savvas Papapolitis, Iliou, and Venizelos, respectively). "Self-determination within a fixed and reasonable time" was the formula the Opposition regularly used to strike out at the government.

33. *Ibid.*, March 11, 1957, p. 29 (Papandreou).

34. In violation of rule 90 of the rules of procedure of the General Assembly, Krishna Menon had explained his vote. Rule 90 provides that "the President shall not permit the proposer of a proposal or of an amendment to explain his vote on his own proposal or amendment."

35. *Ibid.*, March 11, 12, and 15, 1957, pp. 11, 31, 63 (Papandreou, Papapolitis, and Iliou).

36. *Ibid.*, March 11, 12, and 15, 1957, pp. 31, 63, and 111 (Papandreou, Papapolitis, and Iliou, respectively). For Averoff-Tossizza's relevant statements in the Political Committee, see above, note 6.

37. *Ibid.*, March 12, 1957, p. 47 (Kartalis).

38. *Ibid.*, March 11, 1957, p. 33.

39. *Ibid.*, March 11, 1957, pp. 45–46 (Passalidis).

40. *Ibid.*, March 14, 1957, p. 113 (Iliou).

41. *Ibid.*, March 12, 13, and 14, 1957, pp. 56–57, 78, 117 (Kartalis, Baltadzis, and Iliou, respectively). Baltadzis charged that behind the Indian proposal were the same forces that were behind the Iranian and Thai proposals. He meant the United States. In his statement, Baltadzis expressed the view that, because of the important geographic and strategic location of Greece, such an "independent and national" policy would be effective as leverage for the Greek handling of the Cyprus question. In this connection he referred to a study by former Ambassador Norman Armour entitled *Greece, Turkey, and Iran,* prepared at the request of the U.S. Senate's Special Committee to Study the Foreign Aid Program. (85th Cong., 1st sess. [Washington: Government Printing Office, February, 1957].) According to this study, the defense of Greece, the maintenance of Greek independence, and its alignment with the free world were all vital to the security interests of the United States and were important to western defenses throughout the Mediterranean. The defense of Greece was important to the military and naval forces of the United States and Great Britain in that area and also important to the defense of Turkey and the Straits. Greece, in Communist hands, would threaten the entire Middle East and would also endanger the security of Western Europe. This report also stated that "the life of the present pro-Western Greek government depends largely on the settlement of the Cyprus issue, and if this government should fall, the coalition with pro-Communist representation would probably take place." It also asserted that the Cyprus issue had seriously affected the efficacy of Greek co-operation with Turkey and Great Britain. Until some solution to this crucial problem was found, U.S. security interests and political stability in Greece would remain uncertain, and the Balkan Pact between Greece, Turkey, and Yugoslavia would remain a virtual dead letter. (*Ibid.*, p. 1.) The cautious line which EDA had first presented publicly on April 5, 1956, was once again propounded. Iliou also attacked the Greek Foreign Minister for having stated in a televised interview in the U.S. that he was not opposed to a NATO presence in Cyprus, as long as the British did not remain sovereign over the island. EDA, here, hewed closely to the Soviet view, as expressed in the speeches of the Soviet, Ukrainian, and Byelorussian members of the UN, during the Committee discussion of the Cyprus question at the Assembly's twelfth session. (See below, Chapters VIII, IX,

X, pp. 351, 370, 391.) The EDA position, as propounded on April 5, 1956, by J. Pas-salidis was as follows: "It is not we," he said, "who will support getting out of the Western Alliance and joining the Eastern one. We hold that the position of the country, its interests, place it outside both the Western and Eastern blocs; that they impose upon Greece a policy of independence and especially of friendly relations with all, and an active contribution in the effort to safeguard international peace." Greece would be doing nothing novel, nor would it be experimenting with such a policy. Yugoslavia, Egypt, Austria, Sweden, Finland, India, Burma, etc., followed such a policy. Similarly, other states, members of NATO, were seeking to get rid of heavy obligations to NATO. Their commitments to it were much lighter than those of Greece. "Why then should we hesitate to pursue an independent policy and not start out at least from the example of Norway, Iceland, and France?" (*GPD*, April 5, 1956, p. 27.) In Soviet terms of "peaceful coexistence," this was an invitation to Greece to join the "zone of peace," in which, according to the then prevailing Soviet world-view, the above-mentioned uncommitted states were placed.

42. *Ibid.*, pp. 34–35 (Averoff-Tossizza).

43. *Ibid.*, March 11, 1957, p. 36 (Averoff-Tossizza).

44. *Ibid.*, March 11, 12 and 13, 1957, pp. 36–37, 85, 108 (Averoff-Tossizza, Savvas Loizidis, and Constantine Tsatsos, respectively). Belaunde, on February 11, 1957, approached Andreas Stratos, a Greek Delegate, and asked him whether the Greek Delegation would accept a postponement of the Cyprus debate until the next Assembly in order to avoid the threatened unpleasant results of the debate. He suggested he might issue a statement that he had ascertained the existence of possibilities of negotiations between the parties concerned so as to justify the postponement. Stratos expressed his own negative reaction and informed the Delegation's leader about this proposal. Averoff-Tossizza, next day, called on Belaunde and categorically stated that the Greek government's decision to proceed to a debate was irrevocable. It stemmed from the political and psychological realities in Greece. "If it were supposed for a moment that in spite of our opposition the debate were postponed," he said, "I would immediately resign and before going back to Greece. The Greek Mission to the United Nations would simultaneously be closed down. I would take that decision myself as the competent Minister." The Greek Delegation suspected that the Italians, who had come up with a draft proposal earlier, were behind Belaunde's move and had been incited by the British. Belaunde had suggested Rome as a place for carrying out possible negotiations.

45. See above, pp. 43.

46. *GPD*, March 11 and 15, 1957, pp. 38, 126 (Averoff-Tossizza).

47. *Ibid.*, March 11, 1957, pp. 40–41. The Foreign Minister did not reveal that after the adoption of the Indian resolution he had withdrawn this file from the Secretariat (see above, p. o.). For the handling of this matter in the Political Committee, *Verbatim Record*, 849th, 859th, and 853d meetings, February 19 and 21, pp. 16–17, 27, and 7, respectively.

48. *GPD*, March 11 and 15, 1957, pp. 37–39, 125.

49. *Ibid.*, March 13, 1957, p. 73.

50. *Ibid.*, March 11, 1957, p. 40. It was true he had not mentioned *enosis* anywhere in the debate, said Averoff-Tossizza. He had done so, he explained, because Greece did not ask for *enosis*; it asked for self-determination. And, he declared, Greece would respect any decision which the Cypriot people would reach, even if they decided to remain a colony. In connection with his challenge to the Turkish representative, the Foreign Minister explained he was sure he would not get from him any positive reply to his question of whether Turkey was prepared to accept for Cyprus an independence that would preclude *enosis*, because the Turkish Delegation

had been sounded out by third parties beforehand with regard to such a solution and had opposed it. Thus, his question had not been a formal proposal. It had served merely to show up Turkey's intransigence. (*GPD*, March 12, 1957, pp. 65–66.) For British and Turkish criticism of this statement as well as for the Greek response, see below, Chapter III, pp. 110, 112.

51. *Ibid.*, March 12, 1957, p. 62.

52. *GPD*, February 27, 1959, pp. 386–87. On that occasion, Kassimatis, no longer a member of the government, disclosed without being contradicted by the Foreign Minister, that he himself had elicited the Indian proposal at a meeting with the Prime Minister of India (Jawaharlal Nehru) and that he had even gone as far as to draft a Constitution for the proposed state that would be under a UN guarantee. Greece, not Cyprus, would abdicate from the idea of *enosis,* and any change of the new state's status would depend on a UN decision. In retrospect he regarded the negative Greek stand as a mistake. He felt that in the highly liberal and anticolonial atmosphere that prevailed in the wake of the Suez crisis a draft resolution calling for the independence of Cyprus had great chances of adoption by the Assembly. The Greek government, he asserted, had not had the courage to agree to throw into the ring its consent to Krishna Menon's proposal. Although the government in which he then participated was to blame, so was the Opposition, which at the time had vehemently attacked any idea of independence. In 1957, Loizidis, defending the Greek government and referring to UN backstage activities at the eleventh Assembly, suggested that the Greek Delegation had achieved a success by preventing the tabling of a draft resolution for the setting up of an independent Cyprus. Hence, he argued, Resolution 1013 (XI) did not include Krishna Menon's theory of independence as a solution to the Cyprus question. (*Ibid.*, May 22, 1957, p. 94.) Kassimatis, Acting Head of the Greek Delegation during the early weeks of the eleventh Assembly, together with Ambassadors G. V. Melas and Palamas, but not Savvas Loizidis, favored the Indian's proposal and informed Premier Karamanlis about this, expecting his answer the next day. When no answer was forthcoming, he again called up the Premier, whose reaction was diffidently negative. (Kassimatis to the author.) Grivas provides excerpts from a letter he received from the Greek Foreign Minister either in the last days of December, 1956, or early in January, 1957, in which "Isaakios" referred to reports about an Indian plan for the independence of Cyprus and wrote that it would be difficult to reject such a draft resolution, which should be regarded as satisfactory if no other solution were achievable in the Assembly. (*Grivas Memoirs,* p. 157.) No such formal proposal, however, was forthcoming. Toward the end of January, 1957, Krishna Menon, regardless of his earlier attitude at the eleventh Assembly, told Averoff-Tossizza that he could not agree to support a solution of full independence, with which he sympathized, and counseled a spirit of conciliation. His government, he said, would determine its stand in accordance with the development of the debate and the draft resolutions submitted. It would thus seem that he was now getting closer to the American position. Late in 1956, the U.S. attitude toward the idea of an independent Cyprus was not very sympathetic because of fears lest the small and economically weak state fall an easy prey to communism and Soviet policy.

53. *Ibid.*, March 14, 1957, 105. At the time of the first Greek recourse to the United Nations, when Krishna Menon abstained in the voting on the inclusion of the Cyprus item in the Assembly's agenda, he stated that the real issue was the nationhood and independence of Cyprus and their establishment, not who would have sovereignty over the island. See also above, p. 42, and Introduction, 12.

54. *GPD*, March 12, 1957, p. 58. See also Introduction, pp. 13–14.

55. *GPD*, March 12, 1957, p. 59. The UN discussion about the order in which the Political Committee would debate items on its agenda was as follows: On January 2, 1957, at the 813th meeting of the Political Committee, Colombia had proposed that

Korea and disarmament be discussed first and that discussion on the order of the other items—Algeria, Cyprus, West Irian—be postponed. Greece, on the other hand, insisted that as a matter of principle, the Committee should decide on the order of all items and suggested the following order: (1) disarmament; (2) Algeria; (3) Cyprus; (4) Korea; (5) West Irian. Various other views were expressed, and Jordan proposed that since the Greek proposal was more comprehensive, it should be voted on first. Jordan's proposal, however, when put to the vote was not adopted—with 29 in favor, 29 against, and 4 abstentions. Lebanon, then, came forward with an amendment to the Colombian proposal—the order suggested being: (1) Korea; (2) disarmament; (3) Algeria; (4) Cyprus; (5) West Irian. Colombia stated it was ready to accept the Lebanese amendment and then the Colombian proposal, as amended, was adopted by 58 to 8, with four abstentions. Greece commented that the Committee's vote had made it certain that all items on the Committee's agenda would be discussed. (*GAOR, Eleventh Session,* First Committee, 813th meeting, January 2, 1957, pp. 3–6.)

56. *Ibid.,* March 14, 1957, p. 103.

57. *Ibid.,* pp. 108–9.

58. *Ibid.,* p. 106.

59. *Ibid.,* March 12, 1957, p. 60.

60. He had been exiled from Cyprus since the disturbances there of 1931. (*Disturbances in Cyprus in October 1931* [London: H.M. Stationery Office, March, 1932].) Cmd. 4045. Loizidis is mentioned as an agitator on p. 22. See below, Chapter X, p. 393, for his own account. Moreover, he co-operated closely witth Grivas when the latter was preparing his Cyprus operations. As for his brother Socrates, he was captured in January, 1955, when the ship *Hagios Georgios* was seized with a load of weapons and materiel destined for EOKA, *Grivas Memoirs,* pp. 19, 21, 25, 31.

61. *GPD,* March 13, 1957, pp. 83–84. In his set speech at the 851st meeting of the Committee on February 23, Wadsworth, after expressing regret about the little progress made toward a solution, said that during the previous year the U.S. had tried on every possible occasion to facilitate negotiations, without success. The Charter prescribed the settlement of disputes by direct negotiations. The U.S. believed that in the Cyprus case the parties should continue to seek a solution outside the UN because they had not yet considered all possible solutions. In the circumstances, it would be hardly useful to recommend one solution rather than another. Since the problem was complex and its solution not simple, the primary objective was to encourage a spirit of co-operation on both sides. The U.S. hoped the parties would show the restraint and patience that the situation required. If anything was to be accomplished, it was essential to avoid violence and foreign intervention. As Eisenhower and Churchill had said in 1954, any solution would have to win the support of the island's entire population. In making any proposal, the UN should take care not to aggravate the situation, thereby making a solution more difficult. The U.S. was prepared to help the governments and the peoples concerned, to whom it was bound by ties of friendship, to find a constructive solution. The three draft resolutions presented by Greece and Britain could not contribute to a solution. Those proposals, if accepted, could only aggravate the situation. The U.S. Delegation therefore hoped that their sponsors would not insist on their being put to the vote. (*GAOR, Eleventh Session,* First Committee, 851st meeting, p. 243.) In a joint statement of June 28, 1954, Eisenhower and Churchill had reaffirmed the principles of the Atlantic Charter. "We uphold," they said generally, "the principle of self-government and will earnestly strive by every peaceful means to secure the independence of all countries whose people desire and are capable of sustaining an independent existence." (*Documents on American Foreign Relations, 1954* [New York: Harper & Bros., 1955], p. 64.)

62. *Times* (London), February 10, 1957, reported that the Greeks considered the

Italian proposal an "inimical act" because it regarded Turkey as a "party concerned" and like the U.S. proposal favored tripartite negotiations outside the United Nations.

63. On January 23, 1957, Averoff-Tossizza had spoken to Hammarskjöld about the Cyprus question, but the Secretary-General, probably concentrating on the setting up of UNEF and the aftermath of the Suez fiasco, appeared reserved and said he would express his views on the question after more complete study of it. Whether he did so at a later meeting is not clear from the record available to the writer. At any rate, when Averoff-Tossizza expressed the grave concern of his government about the development of the situation in Cyprus and analyzed the unacceptability of the Anglo-Turkish plan for the island's partition, Hammarskjöld appeared to share the Greek view about partition. The Greek Foreign Minister took this opportunity to observe that the Arab countries regarded the regime of Cyprus as a factor of disturbance throughout the entire Middle East. The idea of bringing the Secretary-General into the picture was reflected in the texts of three draft resolutions communicated by Athens on February 8, 1957, to the Greek Delegation, which had been proposed by three unnamed friendly governments. Under the operative clauses of the first of these, the Assembly would set up a seven-member Committee composed of representatives of neutral states who had no relation at all with the Cyprus question and would study all aspects of the question. Utilizing all appropriate means for finding a solution, it would submit its findings to the Secretary-General. Under the operative clauses of the second of these draft resolutions, the British government, since it exercised sovereignty over the area, would be requested to enter into negotiations as soon as possible with the Greek and Turkish Cypriots in order to find a just and satisfactory solution for all that would be inspired by the principles of the Charter. The Assembly furthermore would entrust the Secretary-General with the tasks of following the course of these negotiations; of offering, if he were asked, his good offices, in order to promote negotiations; and, finally, of reporting about the course and the results of these negotiations at the next session of the General Assembly. Under the operative clauses of the third draft resolution, the Assembly would recommend the speedy and immediate entering into negotiations between Britain, Turkey, and Greece for the purpose of finding a stable and just solution inspired by the principles of the Charter or leading finally to the application of these principles. The Secretary-General would be called upon to follow these negotiations, offering, if necessary, his good offices in order to promote a solution and reporting to the next session of the Assembly about the results of the negotiations. All three draft resolutions had the same preambular clause.

64. The notion that the UN was no tribunal taking decisions on the bases of norms of justice was accepted by the Opposition, e.g., by S. Venizelos. (GPD, November 29, 1956, p. 89.) Its public formulation emerged in 1955, after the failure of the first Greek recourse to the UN, and its foremost exponent was the diplomat, politician and writer on international affairs, P. Pipinelis, "The Cyprus Question and Its Future," Kathimerini, February 5, 1955.

65. Ibid., March 11, 1957, p. 34. The political motive and reason for the first recourse was the British government's refusal to negotiate through the diplomatic channel over the future of Cyprus, see above, Introduction, p. 5.

66. Ibid., March 14, 1957, p. 106.

67. Ibid., March 11, 1957, p. 35.

68. Hovet, op. cit., p. 32.

69. GPD, March 13, 1957, p. 82.

70. Ibid., p. 83.

71. Ibid., pp. 85–86 (also for preceding two paragraphs).

72. Press reports indicated that the Greek conditions had been, first, negotiations between the Greek and Albanian general staffs to end the state of war, which in the Greek view existed between the two countries since 1940, and to conclude a frontier agreement for the prevention of border incidents; and, second, the cessation of Albanian aid to, and abetting of, Greek Communist agents infiltrating Greece from Albania and the return of all Greek military and civilian hostages taken into Albania by Greek Communists during the civil war. It was also believed that the relevant Greek reply to the Albanian proposal upheld the Greek claim to Northern Epirus, a part of southern Albania, but offered to seek a settlement through normal channels. An Albanian statement of August 14, 1955, rejected these conditions. (*Keesing's 1955–1956*, pp. 14302, 14405.)

73. On December 14, 1956, the U.S.S.R. complaint of intervention by the United States in the domestic affairs of certain states had been included in the agenda of the eleventh Assembly. During the discussion in the Special Political Committee, not only the Soviet Union but also Czechoslovakia, Bulgaria, Albania, the Ukrainian S.S.R., Romania, the Byelorussian S.S.R., and Poland emphasized various aspects of U.S. "gray" and "black" activities in their countries by means of broadcasts, the dropping of subversive literature from aircraft or balloons, and the training and introduction of saboteurs and political agitators. The United States rejected these allegations and complained that the U.S.S.R. had merely tried to divert world attention from its own activities to undermine governments of free countries all over the world, and particularly from its intervention in the domestic affairs of Hungary. On February 25, 1957, the U.S.S.R. introduced a draft resolution condemning the subversive activities of the United States against other states as contrary to the Charter. However, the Committee, on February 27, rejected this draft resolution by fifty-three votes to eight, with eleven abstentions.

74. *Keesing's*, 1957–1958, pp. 16340, 16092.

75. *GPD*, March 15, 1957, pp. 130–32.

76. Karamanlis meant that the Greek Delegation to the sixth and seventh Assemblies in 1951 and 1952 had alluded to the Cyprus question both in the Assembly and in the Third and Fourth Committees, in the discussion of human rights and non-self-governing territories. (*GAOR, Sixth Session*, 340th plenary meeting, November 12, 1951, p. 66; Third Committee, December 18, 1951, p. 134; Fourth Committee, November 22, 1951, p. 35, and January 9, 1952, p. 272. *Seventh Session*, 393d plenary meeting, November 11, 1952, p. 213; Third Committee, November 24, 1952, pp. 220–21; Fourth Committee, October 28, 1952, p. 58.) See above, Introduction, pp. 7–8.

77. See below, Chapter IV, pp. 158–61.

78. See below, Chapter III, pp. 114–27.

79. *GPD*, March 15, 1957, p. 141.

80. *Ibid.*, pp. 128–29, p. 134.

CHAPTER II

1. *Grivas Memoirs*, p. 120. Harding's response, which was unsuccessful, was to offer terms of surrender.

2. *Ibid.*, pp. 140, 158.

3. *Ibid.*, pp. 158–59 (also for preceding two paragraphs).

4. *Ibid.*, p. 165.

5. *Ibid.*, pp. 152–55, 161–65. For British accounts of the situation at this time, Dudley Barker, *Grivas: Portrait of a Terrorist* (New York: Harcourt, Brace, 1959), pp. 150–21; Charles Foley, *Island in Revolt* (London: Longmans, 1962), pp. 140–41. Grivas admits that British intelligence had improved and explains what countermeasures he took to deal with this development.

6. Barker, *op. cit.*, p. 10. Sources for this biographical sketch are, in addition, the *Grivas Memoirs*, their English edition by C. Foley (New York: F. A. Praeger, 1964), and Alastos, *op. cit.*

7. S. G. Xydis, "Modern Greek Nationalism," in *Eastern European Nationalism,* ed., I. J. Lederer and P. Sugar (Seattle: University of Washington Press, to be published soon).

8. D. Dakin, *The Greek Struggle in Macedonia 1897–1914* (Thessaloniki: Institute for Balkan Studies, 1966).

9. Barker, *op. cit.* facing page 64.

10. *Archive of Illegal Documents of the Cypriot Struggle 1955–1959* (in Greek), ed. S. Papageorgiou, (Athens: Olympic Publications, 1961). For English translation of Grivas' first revolutionary leaflet, Foley (ed.), *Grivas Memoirs*, p. 208.

11. See above, Introduction, p. 24.

12. The most prominent members of this group or persons closely connected with it were George Stratos, who briefly served as Minister of the Army late in 1946; the earlier-mentioned two Loizidis brothers (Savvas and Socrates); Admiral Sakellariou, who held high posts during the Metaxas regime (1936–41), and Professor D. Vezanis. The journalist brother of Kyrou, Achilles Kyrou, showed an early interest in this project but died in 1950, *Grivas Memoirs*, pp. 14 ff.

13. *Ibid.*, pp. 14–17, 19–20.

14. *Ibid.*, Appendix, pp. 3–5. Foley (ed.), *Grivas Memoirs*, pp. 204–7.

15. Kranidiotis, *op. cit.*, pp. 95–98.

16. C. P. Kalligas, *Agon*, November 17, 25, and 29, 1964. Statement issued from the Colonial Office on August 26, 1956, British Information Services, New York, release T40, August 28, 1956. The latter source suggests that the unnamed diplomat referred to in the previous source, may have been Kyrou, whom Makarios met in Paris (according to the Grivas diaries) probably in the second half of October, 1954, when the head of the Greek Delegation, as mentioned in the Introduction, had flown to the French capital for a few days to consult with Premier Papagos. (See above, Introduction, p. 19.) According to the Grivas diaries, there had been between the two, full agreement on the action to take. "Later, however," to cite the text as published, "the position had changed—they were hoping to get America's support, which would have meant a majority in the United Nations. Kyrou then sent a telegram to the Consul here [in Nicosia] without the Archbishop's knowledge. After America turned against us immediate action was necessary, but it was too late by then since they did not have the means of communicating with us quickly." Grivas himself does not mention these items in his memoirs but acknowledges that these diaries were genuine. (*Grivas Memoirs*, p. 127.) In Foley's edition of Grivas' memoirs, written in co-operation with him, material from the captured diaries is integrated into the narrative, Foley (ed.), *op. cit.*, p. 29. Grivas writes that he received orders from Makarios, who was in the United States, not to start operations until further notice, *Grivas Memoirs*, p. 28.

17. *Grivas Memoirs*, pp. 166–68, 180–82.

18. *Keesing's*, XI (1958), p. 15479.

19. *Grivas Memoirs*, p. 166.

20. NATO Information Service, *Non-Military Co-operation in NATO, Text of the Report of the Committee of Three*, pp. 7–8 (peaceful settlement of intermember disputes). The Greek and Turkish representatives at the December, 1956, NATO Council session had been reported as very moderate in their views on Cyprus—with the former emphasizing that a satisfactory solution could be reached only through the United Nations, and the latter, together with the British representative, reminding the Council of the recommendations of the Committee of Three that such intermember disputes be resolved in NATO, if possible. [*International Organization*, XI (1957), 197.] Since February 7, 1957, Lord Ismay had advised the Greek government that he intended to invite representatives of the three NATO members concerned and that he was willing to offer his good offices for conciliation, on the basis of the above decision.

21. 567 H.C. Deb. (5th ser.), pp. 392–95, 397.

22. J. Griffiths, Labour M.P., mentioned the UN resolution urging the parties to resume negotiations and the context in which he made this statement suggested he meant negotiations primarily between Greece, Turkey, and Britain, though he went on to inquire about talks with Makarios on the Radcliffe draft constitution. (567 H.C. Deb. [5th ser.], pp. 394–95.)

23. As the records of the General Committee of the UN General Assembly reveal, on the five occasions on which the Cyprus question was brought before the UN such a position was consistently adhered to by the British government.

24. S. Mayes, *Cyprus and Makarios* (London: Putnam, 1960), p. 147.

25. Royal Greek Embassy Information Service, *Cyprus before the United Nations*, discussion of the Cyprus question before the Twelfth General Assembly of the United Nations 1957–1958 (*sic*), pp. 280–86. This mimeographed publication is a reproduction of the verbatim records of the debates on the Cyprus question at the twelfth Assembly and will be cited hereafter as *Cyprus before the UN*. Its appendixes also contain texts of certain documents sent to the UN after the eleventh Assembly.

26. See below, Chapter III, p. 124.

27. 567 H.C. Deb. (5th ser.), pp. 1355–57. Makarios' letter was made available in the Vote Office for the Members of Parliament. Its text is quoted from Royal Institute of International Affairs, *Documents on International Affairs*, 1957, p. 412 (cited hereafter as *RIIA Docs., 1957*).

28. *GPD*, November 29, 1956, p. 85.

29. *Keesing's 1957–1958*, p. 15475.

30. *Grivas Memoirs*, p. 168.

31. *Keesing's 1957–1958*, p. 15475.

32. *Ibid.*

33. Royal Institute of International Affairs, *Chatham House Memoranda, Cyprus, Background to Enosis*, London, 1958, p. 30 (cited hereafter as *RIIA Memo, 1958*).

34. *Times* (London), April 6, 1957.

35. *Keesing's 1957–1958*, p. 15660.

36. At the eleventh Assembly, in response to British charges that the Greek government was supporting EOKA with money and arms, the Greek government had countercharged, in a letter of February 19, 1957, addressed to the UN Secretary-General, that British official agencies had endeavored to establish false proof in support of the British allegation of "support from Greece for terrorism in Cyprus." *GAOR, Eleventh Session*, Agenda Item 55, Annexes, 1956–57, pp. 10–16. The

pamphlets prepared on the basis of the discovery of the new British intelligence activities were kept in store, should the British government, at the twelfth Assembly, introduce new charges against the Greek government along the lines of the previous British recourse to the United Nations. One can only speculate about the effects that the discovery of British intelligence activities may have had on the British government's decision neither to raise formally at the twelfth Assembly the matter of Greek support to EOKA in Cyprus, nor to dwell on it at any length during the debate there. *To Vima*, January 19, 1965, mentioned briefly this incident, and so did the *Daily Express* of London, January 18, 1965, which referred to such a story in the Athens *Akropolis*.

37. *Keesing's 1957–1958*, p. 15475. *RIIA Memo, 1958*, p. 30.

38. Late in 1956 and early in 1957 tension had risen between the two countries as a result of Turkish treatment of Greek or Greek Orthodox elements in Istanbul or because of various threats. Thus, in November, 1956, Turkish authorities arrested members of the Executive Council of the "Greek Union of Constantinople" perhaps because the word for union is *enosis*. The Greek Embassy in Ankara tried to get them freed through *démarches* with the Turkish government. Then, in mid-January, 1957, the Turkish Director-General of the Press complained to an official of the Greek Consulate in Istanbul about Greek press editorials and comments published on the occasion of the delivery of new naval units to Turkey. Premier Menderes, he said, was annoyed. He would wait two or three days and if the press campaign continued, he would let the Turkish press freely respond—in which case there would be new tension. Such a situation could lead to unpleasant consequences such as the Patriarch's deportation and the exchange of populations. Britain and the United States, he added, would support Turkey in such an eventuality. Similar Turkish threats were voiced through other channels. Averoff-Tossizza, on January 18, 1957, spoke to Robert D. Murphy of the State Department about a conversation of the Turkish Ambassador in London, Nuri Birgi, with the Greek Chargé d'Affaires there, Nikolareïzis, during which the Turkish envoy mentioned the possibility of massacres in Istanbul, with the participation of army and security forces, and threats of war, as well as a communication from Menderes to Lloyd (content not revealed). Murphy was impressed. He could not conceive, he said, what gain could Turkey expect from such a senseless act. A few days later, Turkish Cypriots set fire to many Greek Cypriot stores and clashes took place in Nicosia, and the activities of the Turkish Cypriot organization called Volkan were much in evidence. Greek Parliamentary debates on January 25, 1957, indicate that leaders of EOKA requested the dispatch of UN troops to Cyprus following these Turkish Cypriot acts, and one of the Greek Opposition leaders urged the Greek government to make such a request. [*GPD*, January 25, 1957, p. 87 (Papandreou); 88 (Kartalis).] On the basis of the watermark on paper which Volkan had used for its proclamations, the Greek government suspected that this organization was in touch with, or dependent on, the British authorities in Cyprus. On February 2, C. Tsatsos, Minister in Charge of the Prime Minister's Office, informed U.S. Ambassador Allen about these reports and expressed lively anxiety about the Turkish stand. Any violent action on the part of the Turks, he warned, would trigger an immediate and lively reaction on the Greek side so that the rift between Greece and Turkey would widen. The threatening attitude of the Turks, he said, was ascribed to U.S. support. The Turks should be warned about the consequences of such manifestations. The U.S. government he suggested, should make an appropriate *démarche* with the Turkish government on the matter. Allen agreed that such a *démarche* was desirable and said he would recommend it to his government. On February 7, Ambassador Michel Melas, Greek representative to NATO, spoke to Lord Ismay, NATO's Secretary-General, about Greek anxieties. The latter promised to draw the attention of the Turkish government to this concern through the Turkish representative to NATO. He also expressed the hope that in the United Nations both sides would refrain from verbal extremism. Likewise on February 7, the State Department informed the Greek

Embassy in Washington confidentially that the U.S. government had communicated with the Turkish government about the Greek denunciations and had advised it to be quiet. In Ankara, finally, on February 8, Premier Menderes, just back from Istanbul, in a conversation with Greek Ambassador John D. Kallergis, ascribed the reports about possible disturbances of an anti-Greek character to irresponsible elements that had an interest in the deterioration of Greek-Turkish relations. He assured the Greek diplomat that all necessary measures had been taken to prevent a repetition of the anti-Greek riots of September 6, 1955. In a friendly tone, Menderes complained that while the Greek government often talked about reviving Greek-Turkish friendship, it took no advantage of opportunities presented to bridge the gap. The revival of this friendship, he added, was also the desire of the Turkish government.

39. It should be recalled that the term "vacuum" was frequently used in the postwar period to describe political areas of the world whence a declining great power—Britain, primarily—was withdrawing as a factor of political influence, with the possible results of the replacement of this influence by that of another great power. The "Eisenhower Doctrine" of early 1957, like the "Truman Doctrine," ten years earlier, had constituted the response of the United States to such a situation—a sort of pre-emptive move. The Arabs resented this term and the whole concept.

40. The matter came up in the Greek Parliament in 1958. [*GPD*, December 12, 1958, p. 281 (Venizelos); December 13, 1958, p. 342 (Averoff-Tossizza); p. 359 (Venizelos).] On the latter occasion, Venizelos explained that his response had been to Allen's question about partition as a solution. When Allen asked whether, in case an independent Cyprus asked for *enosis*, Turkey would have the right to ask for partition, Venizelos said he replied that in that case one should not speak about independence.

41. *New York Times*, April 15 and 17, 1957.

42. *Proceedings of the Grand National Assembly*, X, 720. In the Commons, it was Walter Elliot, a Conservative M.P., who first suggested partition publicly as a solution to the Cyprus problem, 556 H.C. Deb. (5th ser.), p. 1422. On at least two occasions, there were reports that partition had been a Greek proposal which the Turkish Government had accepted as a compromise, in a spirit of conciliation. The Greek government denied these reports. First, on May 2, 1958, in reply to a question concerning a passage in an editorial of the London *Times* of May 1, 1958, which said that the first suggestion for partition of Cyprus had been made on the Greek side, though this had been officially and steadily denied, Michael Pesmazoglou, Foreign Minister in the caretaker Greek government, declared the statement as wholly unfounded. He drew attention to the fact that this idea had been put forward by Elliot in a letter to the *Times* of July 17, 1956 (Greek Embassy, Washington, press release, May 2, 1958). On June 2, 1958, when Averoff-Tossizza again took over the Ministry of Foreign Affairs after the general elections of May 11, the Greek government officially asked the Turkish government to publish its evidence. Instead of a Turkish reply, the Turkish newspaper *Milliet* published a story to the effect that Averoff-Tossizza had made this proposal at a meeting that supposedly took place in Athens on December 13, 1956, with Lloyd, Lord Radcliffe, Sir John Harding, and the British Ambassadors in Athens and Ankara. However, the Greeks pointed out that no such meeting had ever taken place. When Lloyd had passed through Athens on that date, Averoff-Tossizza was away in Paris at a NATO Council meeting. Finally, on June 12, 1958, the Turkish Foreign Ministry issued a release to the effect that this proposal had first been put forward by Lennox-Boyd in the Commons on December 19, 1956, G. Zotiadis, *The Idea of the Partition of Cyprus* (in Greek) (Athens, 1959), pp. 4–5. On the second occasion, Iksel, Ambassador in Bonn, was reported to have told the correspondent of the Greek newspaper *Eleftheria* in August, 1961, that the father of the idea of partition was Averoff-Tossizza himself. Iksel's above-mentioned conversation with the Foreign Minister on October 6, 1956, hardly confirms this view,

which the Turkish government subsequently denied again. Before Parliament, Aver-off-Tossizza denied a charge by Stefanopoulos that the Foreign Ministers of Britain and Turkey had officially stated that the paternity of the idea of partition was Greek, *GPD*, June 11, 1958, p. 32. Outside government circles, it might be added, the idea of partition was circulating earlier than 1956, as indicated by a note this author made of a conversation he had on September 12, 1955, with Alexander C. Sedgwick, correspondent of the *New York Times* in Athens.

43. 562 H.C. Deb. (5th ser.), p. 1272.

44. *GPD*, February 27, 1959, p. 368 (Karamanlis).

45. *New York Times*, April 21, 1957.

46. *Keesing's 1957–1958*, pp. 15649–50 (for the previous two paragraphs as well).

47. See above, p. 82.

48. *International Organization*, XI (1957), 562.

49. *GPD*, May 20, 1957, p. 13.

50. *Ibid.*, pp. 7, 22. This was to be the Greek position at the summit NATO Council of December 12–19, 1957.

51. *Ibid.*, May 21, 1957, pp. 31–32 (Passalidis); May 22, 1957, pp. 104–5 (Iliou).

52. *Ibid.*, May 20, 1957, p. 8 (Papandreou); p. 17 (Allamanis); May 21, 1957, p. 32 (Passalidis); p. 39 (Papapolitis); p. 97 (Iliou); p. 150 (Venizelos).

CHAPTER III

1. *Grivas Memoirs*, p. 181. The obverse of the medal was the fifty-four–day curfew of Milikouri. See below, p. 199.

2. *Ibid.*, pp. 168–70 (for preceding two paragraphs as well).

3. *Ibid.*, pp. 228, 348.

4. *Ibid.*, p. 170.

5. *Ibid.*, p. 172.

6. *Ibid.*, p. 173.

7. *Ibid.*, p. 170.

8. *Ibid.*, pp. 170–72.

9. *Ibid.*, p. 173.

10. *Ibid.*, p. 173.

11. *Ibid.*, p. 174.

12. *Ibid.*, p. 177.

13. *Ibid.*, p. 179. Makarios was also reported as having publicly suggested that the U.S. offer its good offices to solve the Cyprus issue. (*New York Times*, May 16, 1957.)

14. *GPD*, May 20, 1957 (Papandreou), p. 7. See below, p. 115.

15. *RIIA, Docs. 1957*, 414–15.

16. *Grivas Memoirs*, p. 178. Kuchuk was reported as having said, after meeting Governor Harding, that the British government had aligned itself with the Turkish views in favor of partition and against self-determination at a fixed date, with self-government as a transitional stage.

17. *GPD*, May 20, 1947 (S. Allamanis), p. 21.

18. 569 H.C. Deb. (5th ser.), pp. 190–91, 955–56.

19. Photostat in author's file, from the British Information Services, N.Y. In the House of Lords, on March 28, 1957, the Earl of Perth had said that the Greek government had twisted the UN resolution. (202 H.C. Deb. [5th ser.], p. 948.)

20. *Grivas Memoirs*, pp. 173, 174 (the date provided by the author).

21. The Turkish government, in particular, had emphasized the *Anschluss* theme. For example, in his statement of December 14, 1954, before the Political Committee, Sarper, during the discussion of the first Greek recourse to the UN over Cyprus, asserted that the "full and true meaning" of *enosis* "was that expressed by the German word *Anschluss.*" It inspired, he held, an anxiety in a measure equal to that created by that unfortunate thing, "*Anschluss.*" While he had to admit to failure in trying to fathom which one of the two, driving ambition or the lust for excitement, was the greater source of inspiration for such experiments, there was no difficulty in recalling the bitter memories they evoked. "*Anschluss,*" "*Sudeten Germans,*" and their like, had also allegedly been based on the premise of the self-determination of nations. Turkish Information Office, *Turkish Views on Cyprus* (New York, n.d.), p. 7.

22. See above, Chapter I, p. 53, for the Foreign Minister's statement in the Greek Parliament on March 11, 1957. The Belgian account of British views on the Cyprus question at this point also noted that the British referred with distrust to a statement by Savvas Loizidis on April 25, 1956, in the Parliament. (*GPD*, April 25, 1956, p. 307.) Loizidis had said that if during the Harding-Makarios talks, the British had agreed to a five-year period after which the right of self-determination would be exercised, the Cypriots would have accepted any sort of interim government. If, on the other hand, the British did not agree to setting a fixed date for the exercise of self-determination, the Cypriots would not mind that either, provided they got full and complete self-government. For then, with all powers in their hands, the police power included, they would be able to seize self-determination with their own hands within two or three years. On April 10, 1956 (*ibid.*, pp. 116–17), he had sought to show that Makarios, in negotiating with Harding, had never dropped the goal of self-determination for the sake of self-government. Various maneuvers had been carried out to discover what the British exactly meant by self-government. If all powers, internal security included, were in the people's hands, self-determination could be acquired very easily.

23. This same stereotype about Greek as compared with Turkish political reactions was mentioned to the author by Ambassador von Walther, of the German Federal Republic, in Istanbul, in summer, 1964. It would be interesting to discover the source of it. It suggests, to this writer at least, a sort of bargaining stance, with Greek politicians' being expected to exercise their diplomatic agility in the face of the supposed slowness in reaction but forcefulness, if not brutality, of the Turks, once they decide to act. As Menderes was in 1957, so was Inönü, in 1964, praised for restraining the extremists—the implications being that the latter would take over if the Premier fell from power.

24. See above, Chapter I, p. 53, for the statements of Averoff-Tossizza and Kassimatis. The latter, at one point of his speech, had said: "We may strive for *enosis* but not in the U.N." (*GPD*, March 12, 1957, p. 58.)

25. See above, Chapter II, p. 74.

26. Xerox of the Turkish representative's letter, in author's files.

27. *Cyprus before the United Nations,* pp. 287–93.

28. *GPD,* May 20–24, 1957, pp. 9, 10, 15 (Papandreou); pp. 13–16, 54–55, 153–54 (Averoff-Tossizza); pp. 19–20 (Allamanis); pp. 27–28 (Kanellopoulos); pp. 53–54 (Th. Tsatsos); pp. 93–97 (Loizidis); pp. 151–53 (S. Venizelos). Averoff-Tossizza's rhetorical question to Sarper was also briefly mentioned in the Greek Parliament on February 28, 1959. (*GPD,* p. 434 [E. Arvanitakis].)

29. *The Tripartite Conference on the Eastern Mediterranean and Cyprus* (London: H.M. Stationery Office, October, 1955), Cmd. 9594 (cited hereafter *The Tripartite Conference*). For details, see below, Chapter IV, pp. 158–61.

30. On September 6, Turkish mobs sacked hundreds of Greek-owned shops and other premises and destroyed over twenty Greek Orthodox Churches in Istanbul, where there were about 80,000 Greek Orthodox Turkish nationals and 12,000 Greek nationals. At Izmir, headquarters of NATO's South-East European Command, mobs attacked Greek officers' houses and wrecked a Greek pavilion at a trade fair. In Ankara several thousand demonstrators attempted a march on the Greek Embassy. These riots were sparked by a dynamite attack against the Turkish Consulate in Thessaloniki and of the nearby house in which Kemal Atatürk was born. (*Keesing's 1955–1956,* X, 14424.) This dynamite attempt, it was discovered later, had been a result of a Turk's act. Acting Foreign Minister of Greece P. Canellopoulos lodged a strong verbal protest with the Turkish government on September 7. Because no reply was received, a written protest followed on September 9. On September 12, the Turkish government expressed its regrets and gave assurances that the victims would be compensated and measures taken to avert similar outbreaks in the future. On September 8, the permanent representatives on NATO's Council met to consider the situation. No communiqué was issued. (*Ibid.*) Because of strong anti-Turkish feeling generated in Greece, the Greek government took no part in scheduled NATO exercises. By early 1956, the Turkish government decided to award, as an initial indemnity, the sum of 40 million Turkish pounds. On September 18, 1955, Secretary of State Dulles had sent identic notes to the Prime Ministers of Greece and Turkey expressing deep concern at the developments that had adversely affected Greek-Turkish friendship "at a time when these two allies are in great need of mutual understanding." He urged the two countries not to let these "unhappy events" (the Turkish riots in Istanbul and Izmir) destroy their partnership in the free world. Regardless of the causes of the disagreement, the unity of NATO, which was the basis of the common security, ought to be restored without delay.

31. *GAOR, Tenth Session,* 521st plenary meeting, p. 65. The vote was 28 to 22, with 10 abstentions. The General Committee, on September 21, 1955, had recommended non-inclusion. (*Ibid.,* General Committee, 102d meeting, p. 5.) The vote there had been 4 to 7, with 4 abstentions.

32. Cited by Kartalis, *GPD,* April 25, 1956, p. 293.

33. Royal Ministry for Foreign Affairs, *The Cyprus Question. Negotiations 4 October 1955 to 5 March 1956.* Athens, 1956 (cited hereafter as *White Book*), p. 5. This is the "Blue Book" mentioned in the letter and explanatory memorandum of June 12, 1956, of the Permanent Representative of Greece to the UN (see Appendix C). Its cover is white.

34. For this plan, see below, Chapter IV, p. 160. The basic lines of the story are reconstructed from the *White Book* and debates in the Greek Parliament, *GPD,* April 6, 1956, pp. 45–46 (Spyros Theotokis, Foreign Minister); April 25, 1956, p. 285 (Karamanlis); pp. 293 ff. (Kartalis); May 22, 1956, pp. 407 ff. (Theotokis). The substance of the talks themselves appear to have been foreshadowed by the secret extradiplomatic Anglo-Greek talks of September-November, 1954, with Maniadakis as an intermediary. (See above, Introduction, p. 15.) Some of the Opposition leaders,

during these debates, it should be added, had been granted access to the various diplomatic documents mentioned in the debate. Hence, by their remarks, they contributed to the clarification of these talks.

35. Eden, *op. cit.,* p. 456.

36. *Grivas Memoirs,* p. 66. Other measures taken by Harding were: (1) The redistribution of the military forces, after the arrival of reinforcements. (2) The manning of certain police stations with military forces. (3) The taking of extraordinary measures for guarding government buildings and military installations.

37. *GPD,* April 25, 1956, pp. 293–94 (Kartalis).

38. *Ibid.,* pp. 294–95; also May 24, 1956, p. 463 (Kartalis).

39. *Ibid.,* pp. 295–96.

40. *Ibid.,* April 25, 1956, p. 285 (Karamanlis); April 11, 1956, p. 184 (Kartalis); *White Book,* p. 7 (memorandum from the Greek Foreign Minister to the British Ambassador, December 5, 1955).

41. *GPD,* May 24, 1956, pp. 470–71 (Theotokis); 474 (Kartalis). April 25, 1956, p. 296. The Opposition charged that the government was not primarily interested in promoting the Cyprus case by its appeals for concessions but was asking for concessions, in order to fortify itself internally before the elections. This interplay of foreign with domestic policy has several precedents elsewhere. At Tehran, it should be recalled, Roosevelt asked Stalin to go slow on the Polish question, because of the forthcoming Presidential elections in the U.S. Was the President doing this (having in mind the votes of Americans of Polish stock) for domestic reasons? Or was he using this argument simultaneously for foreign policy purposes as well?

42. Eden, *op. cit.,* pp. 450–52.

43. *White Book,* p. 6.

44. *GPD,* April 25, 1956, p. 296 (Kartalis). The Greek government rejected this proposal on November 28, 1955. (*Ibid.,* p. 280 [Karamanlis].)

45. *Grivas Memoirs,* pp. 70–71.

46. *Documents on American Foreign Relations,* 1954 (New York: Harper & Bros., 1955), p. 62, Joint Statement Issued by the President of the U.S. and the Prime Minister of the U.K., Washington, June 28 and 29, 1954. *Ibid.,* pp. 318–19, Pacific Charter, signed at Manila, September 8, 1954. For the former, see above, Chapter I, n. 61. In the Pacific Charter, on the other hand, it was proclaimed, among other things, that "upheld the principle of equal rights and self-determination of peoples and would earnestly strive by every peaceful means to promote self-government and to secure the independence of all countries whose peoples desired it and were able to undertake its responsibilities."

47. *White Book,* p. 6.

48. Eden, *op. cit.,* p. 453.

49. *White Book,* pp. 7–11. In spite of this rejection, the Greek government stated that it considered the British recognition that the principle of self-determination was applicable to Cyprus was most encouraging, even though this declaration was made in a negative way. It believed, however, that the principle of self-determination should be stated in a direct and explicit manner. It had been taken aback by the fact that in the list of treaties that Harding had presented to Makarios, the Anglo-Turkish Treaty of 1878 and the Lausanne Treaty of 1923 had been included. The former had been abrogated in fact (1914) and in law (1925); the latter, though constituting the legal title to the "present British occupation" of Cyprus, included no provisions that precluded the application of the principle of self-determination to Cyprus. The Greek government, accordingly, recognizing the importance of Britain's defense commit-

ments in the eastern Mediterranean and "ready to assist in their fulfilment with all the means at their disposal," suggested that reference to strategic and defense considerations in the British statement be made in general terms—to show that the road to self-determination would be open as soon as other suitable arrangements safeguarding strategic interests had been made. Greece, as a NATO member and an old and steadfast ally of Britain, pledged full support and co-operation toward reaching the best possible arrangements to this effect. However, the value and efficiency of any military establishments on the island would be enhanced by ensuring the good will and co-operation of the people of Cyprus. With regard to the question of self-government, clarification was suggested that the Constitution to be granted would be a liberal one. The Greek government also drew the British government's attention to the advantages of "fixing a reasonable term of time at the expiration of which" the British government would "discuss the implementation of self-determination with representatives of the people of Cyprus." For this last point—a concession from the earlier demand for the immediate agreement on the matter of when self-determination would be applied—the Greek government was severely attacked by the Opposition, Papandreou especially, during the debate in Parliament on the Cyprus problem on April 11, 1956, *GPD*, p. 176.

50. *GPD*, November 29, 1956, p. 92 (Papandreou).

51. *Ibid.*, April 25, 1956, p. 296 (Kartalis).

52. Under these regulations, the unlawful use or possession of firearms, bombs, and ammunition became an offense punishable by death; acts of sabotage became punishable by life imprisonment; the unlawful wearing of military or police uniforms also made the offender liable to life imprisonment; and looting, unlawful drilling, the wearing of disguises, and the harboring of terrorists became punishable by imprisonment from five to seven years. In addition, communities whose inhabitants engaged in unlawful activities became liable to collective punishment such as the imposition of fines, the closing of shops, and confiscation of property; youths under the age of 18 who engaged in such activities became liable to whipping; the Governor was given powers to deport or detain terrorists, impose a censorship, requisition property, and ban the display of flags, slogans, etc.; all public assemblies were banned with the exception of cinema and theatrical performances and religious services; and strikes unconnected with trade disputes were declared illegal. (*Keesing's 1955–56*, X, 14694.)

53. Eden, *op. cit.*, p. 453.

54. *White Book*, pp. 7–11. *GPD*, April 6, 1956, pp. 45–46 (Theotokis); p. 49 (Karamanlis); April 25, 1956, p. 287 (Karamanlis).

55. Eden, *op. cit.*, pp. 453–55.

56. *White Book*, pp. 12–13. The British government, in this note, drew attention to Macmillan's statement in the Commons concerning the timing and conditions in which the principle of self-determination could be applied to Cyprus. That principle, he had said, was a good one. Britain had accepted it in the UN Charter and had honestly and honorably pursued it over a wide area. The question in Cyprus, however, was not whether this principle should be recognized, but whether it should be applied without regard to other considerations of geography, tradition, history, or strategy. Summarizing the attitude of the three governments at the London Tripartite Conference, Macmillan said that for Greece it was "this year, or at any rate in a year or two"; for Turkey, it was "never"; for Britain, it was "for some time." 547 H.C. Deb. (5th ser.) pp. 35–37, 39–40.

57. *White Book*, p. 18.

58. *GPD*, April 11, 1956, p. 177 (Papandreou); pp. 180–81 (Theotokis); April 25,

1956, p. 275 (Papandreou). Both say this conversation took place on December 14, not December 15, the date given in the *White Book*, p. 18.

59. *White Book*, p. 14.

60. Eden, *op. cit.*, p. 457.

61. *White Book*, p. 15.

62. *Ibid.*, pp. 16–18. In the Greek government view, the new British formula still lacked clarity and simplicity and, consequently, was still inadequate for the purpose for which it was intended, namely to be understood and accepted by the people of Cyprus. This formula was even more likely to be misinterpreted in Cyprus because of the proposed reference to Macmillan's remarks of December 5, 1956, in the Commons. In these circumstances, the Greek government felt unable to recommend the new British formula to Makarios or ask him to reopen discussions with the Governor on the basis of that formula (only). The Greek government affirmed in this note that it could not undertake an action that would not only fail to bring about results sought but might cause further deterioration of conditions on the island as well as immeasurable damage to Greece itself and do additional harm to its allies and to the interests of NATO in southeastern Europe.

63. *GPD*, November 30, 1956, p. 111 (Karamanlis). The Premier denied the Opposition charges that the mission of the Greek diplomat was to exert pressure on Makarios to resume negotiations. Pressure could not be exerted, he argued, first because Makarios was not receptive to pressure, and, second, because any government that sought to exert pressure on the Ethnarch would be blown up by Makarios himself. Papandreou, on the other hand (*ibid.*, p. 114), said he had read Liatis' report, and insisted that the purpose of this mission had, indeed, been to exert pressure on Makarios. For other Opposition statements to this effect, see *ibid.*, April 10, 1956, p. 125 (Varvoutis); April 25, 1956, p. 275 (Papandreou); March 12, 1957, p. 56 (Kartalis).

64. *White Book*, pp. 19–20. Final version also in *Cyprus. Correspondence Exchanged between the Governor and Makarios* (London: H.M. Stationery Office, March, 1956) Cmd. 9708, p. 3 (cited hereafter as Cmd. 9708). This text was given by Colonial Secretary Lennox-Boyd in the House of Commons on March 5, 1956.

65. Cmd. 9708, p. 5. *White Book*, p. 21.

66. Cmd. 9708, pp. 4–5. *White Book*, pp. 22–23.

67. *Keesing's 1956–1957*, XI, 14696.

68. Eden, *op. cit.*, p. 457.

69. Cmd. 9708, pp. 6–7. *White Book*, pp. 24–26. These five general principles of the constitution were:

"1. All legislative, executive, and judicial powers, apart from those expressly excepted, would originate from the people of Her Majesty's Government.

"2. Responsibility for the defence and external political relations of the island would be excepted from the above principle and would be vested in the Governor in his capacity as representative of Her Majesty's Government.

"3. The Governor, beyond the powers mentioned in the previous paragraph (2), would exercise the normal duties of a constitutional Head of State; thus he would sign, without having the right to veto, the laws which were enacted by the Assembly within the framework of the constitution, including the budget, and would also sign the decrees which were lawfully issued by the Government. He would entrust the duty of forming the Government to the person enjoying the confidence of the Assembly and would dissolve the Assembly on his advice. Ministers would be chosen freely by the Prime Minister and would, like him, be responsible only to the Assembly.

"4. Representation in the Assembly would be proportional to the composition of the population. Otherwise there would be absolute equality of all citizens and everyone would be eligible to any public office. Exceptions to this rule might be provided for only in the case of special offices which were exclusively connected with the religious and educational rights of the island's communities. Such rights would be fully safeguarded and protected by the Constitution.

"5. A procedure would be defined for the impartial settlement of any difference arising out of the interpretation of constitutional provisions, in particular on questions of disputed authority between the Governor on the one hand and the Assembly or the Government on the other."

70. See above, Chapter II, p. 74. *White book*, pp. 25–26. Cmd. 9708, p. 7.

71. Cmd. 9708, pp. 8–9. *White Book*, pp. 27–28. The six points were:
"1. Her Majesty's Government offers a wide measure of democratic self-government now. To this end a new and liberal constitution would be drawn up in consultation with all sections of the community. Cyprus would be exercised by them through their elected representatives and other organs.

2. The constitution would enable the people of Cyprus through responsible Cypriot Ministers to assume control by a suitably phased process over the departments of Government except those relating to foreign affairs and defence which would be reserved to the Governor and to public security which would also be reserved to the Governor for as long as he deems necessary.

"3. The constitution would provide for an Assembly with an elected majority.

"4. A Cypriot Premier to head the new administration would be chosen by the Assembly with the approval of the Governor. Ministerial portfolios would be allocated by the Premier [subject to (6) below].

"5. The constitution would provide for Turkish membership in the Council of Ministers.

"6. There would be proper safeguards for the rights of individual citizens, the interests of all sections of the Community, and the integrity and independence of the public service.

72. *GPD*, April 25, 1956, p. 297 (Kartalis).

73. *Ibid.*, April 11, 1956, p. 178 (Papandreou).

74. Cmd. 9708, pp. 10–12. *White Book*, pp. 29–32.

75. See above, p. 123.

76. Eden, *op. cit.*, pp. 458–59.

77. *Ibid.*, p. 458.

78. Cmd. 9708, p. 12. *White Book*, p. 33.

79. *GPD*, April 25, 1956, p. 286 (Karamanlis).

80. *Grivas Memoirs*, p. 92. In giving advice, Grivas disclaimed any intention of intervening in the substance of the negotiations.

81. 549 H.C. Deb. (5th ser.), pp. 1715–18. In his statement, the Secretary of the Colonies gave his account of the discussions between Governor and Ethnarch, and emphasized that the outstanding points of disagreement were the amnesty, the reservation of public security to the Governor for as long as he thought necessary, and the question of the Greek elected majority. "As to the future," he said, "the first and most important duty is to restore law and order. We have the resolution and the forces, and it will be done." In the constitutional field, he added, the objective was to reach agreement with the communities in Cyprus in accordance with the principles he had indicated.

82. *White Book*, pp. 34–36.

83. *Keesing's 1955–1956*, X, 14696, 14967, 14221–22. The jamming was stopped on August 11, 1958, and resumed on October 6, 1958. (*Ibid.*, XII, 16482, 16484.)

84. L. Dischler, *Die Zypernfrage* (Frankfurt-am-Main, Berlin: Alfred Metzner Verlag, 1960), pp. 107–9. There was strong circumstantial evidence, it was said, that the timing and intensity of EOKA activities had been adjusted to strengthen the bargaining position of the Archbishop during his negotiations with the Governor. (Colonial Office, *Cyprus. Report for the Year 1956*. [London: H. M. Stationery Office, 1957], p. 4.) In his statement to the Commons on March 14, Eden, after explaining the situation which had led to the British government's decision to exile Makarios, stated: "We do not withdraw. Our immediate purpose must be to defeat terrorism so that the individual citizen in Cyprus—and there are plenty who want a quiet life—can enjoy personal security, and to go on trying to resolve the conflicting interests in this intractable problem. We must safeguard the strategic needs of our country and of our allies. Neither NATO obligations, nor the Tripartite Declaration, nor the Baghdad Pact, can be effectively carried out unless we have the sure and unfettered use of Cyprus. But there is more in it even than this. The Government must be concerned to protect the vital interests of its citizens. The welfare and, indeed, the lives of our people depend on Cyprus as a protective guard and staging base to take care of those interests, above all oil. That is not imperialism. It should be the plain duty of any government and we intend to discharge it." 550 H.C. Deb. (5th ser.), pp. 418–19.

85. *Grivas Memoirs*, pp. 91, 94, 96.

86. *Ibid.*, X, 14761. For texts of the two White and Eisenhower statements, "Embassy Press Releases, March 13 and 14, 1956. Also, for two White statements, *State Department Bulletin*, XXXIV (March 26, 1956), 505–6.

87. See above, Chapter I, p. 40, especially for the U.S. support of the Thai proposal.

88. *Disturbances in Cyprus in October 1931* (London: H.M. Stationery Office, March, 1932), Cmd. 4045, p. 12.

89. Mayes, *op. cit.*, p. 22.

90. N. Kranidiotis, *Cyprus in the Struggle for Freedom* (in Greek) (Athens: 1958), pp. 62–63. Makarios, then Bishop of Kition, was made chairman of the Ethnarchic Council, while the Bishop of Kyrenia, Kyprianos, became vice-chairman. Among the first activities of the Council was to publish a periodical, "Greek Cyprus," and to organize, on October 3, 1948, a pan-Cypriot demonstration to protest against Britain's policy of refusing to cede Cyprus to Greece. Archbishop Makarios II expressed hope that he would live to see the realization of *enosis*.

91. Harding statement of March 9, 1956. *Keesing's 1956–1957*, XI, 14759.

92. Mayes, *op. cit.*, p. 24.

93. Letter of February 18, 1957, from the Permanent Representative of the United Kingdom . . . addressed to the Secretary General, Doc. A/C.1/788, UN General Assembly, Agenda Item 55, *Annexes* Eleventh Session, pp. 7–9. An excellent Greek source confirmed these points in a conversation with the author in summer, 1964, providing the additional information.

94. *State Papers 1925*, CXXI (1929), 74–88.

95. In an address to the first British High Commissioner of Cyprus, after Britain assumed the island's administration in 1878, a high member of the Cypriot hierarchy, the Archbishop himself or the Bishop of Kition, expressed hope that Britain would help Cyprus to be united with Greece. Mayes, *op. cit.*, p. 13. Kranidiotis, *op. cit.*, pp. 25–26. The former, p. 13, notes the connection between education and Greek nationalism. According to a Greek government memorandum of 1919, in 1881, 1895,

1902, 1907, 1911, 1917, and 1919, representatives of the Greek Cypriots, through memorials or resolutions, had reminded the British government of their aspiration for union with Greece. For post–World War II appeals for *enosis,* Kranidiotis, *op. cit.,* pp. 63 ff. From 1953 on, the theme of self-determination appears side by side with that of *enosis,* after the UN General Assembly adopted on December 16, 1952, Resolution 637 (VII) on the right of peoples and nations to self-determination. *GAOR, Seventh Session,* Supplement 20, pp. 26–27. For a 1951 mention of self-determination, Kranidiotis, *op. cit.,* p. 76–77 (Makarios press conference in Athens, April 6, 1951). As late as mid-1954, the clamor was for *enosis,* as witness the resolution of the second pan-Cypriot Assembly, of July 23, 1954, *ibid.,* p. 8.

96. See above, Chapter II, 68–69.

97. During the debates on the meaning of the UN Charter's references to self-determination in the General Assembly various subtle distinctions were made between the "principle" of self-determination and the "right" to self-determination. Powers supporting the status quo often tended to support the former, while foes of the status quo emphasized the latter.

98. This biographical sketch is based on Mayes, *op. cit.,* Alastos, *op. cit.,* official biographies, and a series of articles by C. P. Kalligas in the Cyprus newspaper *Agon,* November 17–December 13, 1964, on the author's interviews with various persons who met the President of Cyprus, and on his impressions from an interview with him on September 10, 1964, in Nicosia.

99. Already in April, 1957, when he returned from his detention in the Seychelles and was acclaimed as a hero in Athens, there were reports of a plot by certain army officers to overthrow the Greek government and install the Ethnarch as Prime Minister.

100. Mayes, *op. cit.,* pp. 22–23. In May 1952, rebuffed by the Greek government, in his effort to get it to sponsor a recourse to the UN, Makarios taunted the Greek government for believing that "the door was still open for friendly talks with Britain." The doors would open only when they were forced open "by moving the lever of the UN." For Makarios' reported views on self-government, see *GPD,* April 25, 1956, p. 293 (Kartalis); February 25, 1959, p. 321 (Stefanopoulos). Kranidiotis, *op. cit.,* p. 80. For his fear of British measures in the field of education, *Agon,* November 24, 1964. This source refers to British measures enacted after the 1931 uprising in Cyprus and mentions a decree of July 16, 1952, to which the Greek Cypriot secondary school authorities had objected, at the Ethnarch's instigation. Eden, *op. cit.,* p. 445, writes he favored the establishment of a university in Cyprus linked to English universities, which "would help to wean the Cypriots away from the cultural attraction of Athens."

101. *GPD,* February 28, 1959, p. 427 (Maniadakis). "Listen, Your Beatitude," Plastiras was said to have told Makarios, "had you come to my poor hut and asked me to fight for Cyprus, I would have accepted gladly, because I am a soldier. But you come to the office of the Premier of Greece and you ask me to set Greece on fire, without being able to be of any help to Cyprus. Stay quiet there." Also April 25, 1956, p. 289 (Karamanlis). Karamanlis also revealed (*ibid.,* p. 288) that Papandreou on June 20, 1950, had informed the Mayor of Nicosia Dervis that Greece could not help in the Cyprus cause." "Greece," he wrote, "breathes with two lungs, a British and an American one. It cannot therefore risk suffocating because of the Cyprus question." In 1950, on the other hand, when Plastiras was Prime Minister, after ascertaining, through Venizelos, the negative U.S. attitude toward any raising of the Cyprus issue, he advised the Cypriots to wait for a better moment but also to organize a struggle. No blood, he said, had yet been shed. The Tree of freedom was watered with blood. "Shed your blood and we will help." (*Ibid.,* December 13, 1958 [N. Zorbas], 356–57.)

102. *Ibid.*, April 25, 1956, p. 306 (Venizelos); p. 289 (Karamanlis). Venizelos, both as Premier, in 1951, and as Foreign Minister, in 1952, withstood strong pressure from Makarios.

103. See Introduction, pp. 7–8.

104. See above, Chapter II, pp. 69–70.

105. 571 H.C. Deb. (5th ser.), pp. 66–69, both for Makarios' letter and Macmillan's reply. For the Colonial Secretary's statement on self-determination of December 19, 1956, 562 H.C. Deb. (5th ser.), p. 1268.

106. *Grivas Memoirs*, pp. 180, 182–83.

107. 572 H.C. Deb. (5th ser.), p. 22.

108. Averoff-Tossizza speech in the Political Committee at the twelfth Assembly, 927th meeting, December 9, 1957, *Cyprus before the United Nations*, p. 54. Also Royal Greek Embassy, Washington, press release (cited hereafter as "Embassy Press Releases") July 20, 1957. Makarios had made a similar statement in an interview with Lord Lambton, 573 H.C. Deb. (5th ser.), pp. 776–77, July 15, 1957.

109. "News from Turkey," June 5, 1957, pp. 2–3.

110. *New York Times*, June 6, 1957. The earlier-mentioned "Isaakios" letter to Grivas of that same date also referred to a possible new recourse to the United Nations.

111. *GPD*, May 20, 1957, p. 13.

112. The *Observer*, August 15, 1957, reported that Spaak, in June, had prepared a note proposing an independent Cyprus under international guarantee. The U.S. State Department was said to favor this proposal but did not believe that the United Nations could play the role of guarantor. According to press reports of July 6, the plan called for the creation of a dominion within the Commonwealth, the transfer of part or of the whole island to NATO control, and negotiations between the U.S. and Britain concerning Cyprus as a military base. (*Grivas Memoirs*, p. 190.)

113. *Ibid.*, p. 183–84. Grivas charges that the British were now getting ready to co-operate with the Communists, the leaders of AKEL, against EOKA. On May 18, 1957, he had issued directives to counteract this situation.

114. See above, p. 137.

115. In 1954 both the General Assembly and the Economic and Social Council condemned forced labor and appealed to governments to re-examine their laws and administrative practices, *Everyman's United Nations* (N.Y.: United Nations), Seventh edition, 1964, p. 319. The U.S.S.R. was the primary target though it was not named.

116. This rule provides that all items proposed for inclusion on the agenda shall be accompanied by an explanatory memorandum and, if possible, by basic documents or by a draft resolution.

117. "Embassy Press Releases" August 5, 1957.

118. *Ibid.*, August 5, 1957.

119. See above, Chapter I, p. 40. On December 19, 1956, the Permanent Mission of Greece to the UN had transmitted to the Secretary-General a new series of documents, pursuant to the sixteen transmitted to Hammarskjöld on April 26, 1956, "containing full evidence of continuing violations by the British authorities and forces of fundamental human rights and relative principles of international law in Cyprus." British repression, it was charged, was mainly directed against the civilian population "with complete disregard for certain legal and moral standards . . . respected even

in times of full belligerency and war." Earlier, through the diplomatic channel, protests had been incidentally registered. (*White Book,* p. 11.) The idea of resorting to the Human Rights Commission went back to October 1955, *GPD,* December 13, 1958, pp. 352–53 (Merkouris).

120. Copy in author's files. Also *Keesing's 1955–56,* X, 14222.

121. Article 24 of the Convention provides that "any High Contracting Party may refer to the Commission, through the Secretary-General of the Council of Europe, any alleged breach of the provisions of the Convention by another High Contracting Party."

122. Article 15 of the Convention provides that "In time of war or other public emergency threatening the life of the nation any High Contracting Party may take measures derogating from its obligations under this Convention to the extent strictly required by the exigencies of the situation, provided that such measures are not inconsistent with its other obligations under International Law." This Article also mentions certain obligations from which no party can derogate even in case of emergency and war. Finally, it provides that any party that "avails itself of this right of derogations shall keep the Secretary-General of the Council of Europe fully informed on the measures which it has taken and the reasons therefor. It shall also inform the Secretary-General when such measures have ceased to operate and the provisions of the Convention are again being fully executed."

123. *International Organization,* X (1956), 502, 655; XI, 195, 558. *Council of Europe News,* November, 1957, p. 2; January 1957, p. 4.

124. See above, p. 134.

125. *Grivas Memoirs,* p. 186. *New York Times,* June 15, 1957.

126. *International Organization,* XI, 681.

127. *RIIA Memo. 1958,* p. 31. *Grivas Memoirs,* p. 187. In the Foreword to this *White Paper,* Governor Harding said that this document gathered together incontrovertible evidence that the allegations were part of a deliberate and organized conspiracy and that Grivas acknowledged this. In his campaign, he had at his disposal the power of propaganda of the Church as well as the support of the Greek and Greek-Cypriot press and the official publicity organs of the Greek government. The systematic repetition of allegations of torture had started mainly at the beginning of 1956. The specific allegations of brutality had been based initially on an isolated case of ill-treatment—the only case of deliberate ill-treatment that had ever been established during the emergency. The government and military authorities had carried out inquiries on each allegation and a total of seven prosecutions had been instituted between September, 1955, and June, 1956. Many of the allegations had been, however, in such vague terms that the only possible reply was a plain denial. In seven other cases, the allegations had been disproved on the basis of evidence supplied by Greek Cypriots. If brutality was as widespread as was alleged, it might have been expected that there would have been a large number of private prosecutions against individual police or military officers for assault or similar actions. The *White Paper* defended the respective roles of the police and the judiciary in the anti-EOKA campaign. A public inquiry into the conduct of the security forces would, however, "impair their ability to deal effectively with fresh outbreaks of terrorism." (*Keesing's 1956–1957,* XI, 15650.)

128. *Grivas Memoirs,* p. 188. Mayes, *op. cit.,* pp. 135–37.

129. *Cyprus before the United Nations,* pp. 294–95.

130. *Grivas Memoirs,* p. 188.

131. *International Organization,* XI, 693. *Council of Europe News,* August 1957, p.

3. Article 3 of the Convention provides that no one shall be subjected to torture or to inhuman or degrading treatment or punishment.

132. *Ibid.*, XII, 241. *Council of Europe News*, November 1957, p. 2.

133. *Grivas Memoirs*, pp. 189–90. *Times* (London), July 15, 1957.

134. See again below, Chapter V, p. 258, and Epilogue, p. 526.

135. See below, p. 150. After visiting Cyprus from April 23–25, Duncan Sandys, Minister of Defense, emphasized not only that Cyprus, by becoming a base for nuclear weapons, could make a great contribution to the deterrence of war and communism but that special problems would arise if the political deadlock continued in the island and it should be necessary to consider partitioning Cyprus. (*Keesing's 1957–1958*, XI, 15651.) Partitioning would mean the maintenance of British bases in Cyprus, because value still was attached to the island's location.

136. The six other major Cyprus debates in the House of Commons took place on May 5 and December 5, 1955, and on March 14, May 14, July 19, and December 19, 1956.

137. 573 H.C. Deb. (5th ser.), p. 891.

138. *Ibid.*, pp. 771–86.

139. *Ibid.*, pp. 776–77. One of the questions dealt with Makarios' insistence on bipartite talks between Cyprus and Britain, to the exclusion of Greece and Turkey. Two others dealt with the question of the participation of Turkish Cypriots in such talks. Makarios made it clear he was not opposed to such participation but thought they should take part in proportion to their ratio in the whole population of Cyprus and should not have "the same say as ourselves as they would veto all our suggestions."

140. *Ibid.*, p. 779. The British government's *White Paper on Defence, Outline of Future Policy* (London: H.M. Stationery Office, April, 1957); Cmd. 124, p. 4, mentioned that in the event of emergency, British forces in the Middle East would be made available to support the Baghdad Pact alliance. These forces would include bomber squadrons based in Cyprus capable of delivering nuclear weapons. The paper also noted that, apart from its own importance, the Middle East guarded NATO's right flank and was the gateway to the African continent. Thirdly, it pointed out that as a result of the termination of Britain's treaty with Jordan, Britain had been relieved of the responsibility of defending that country in the event of attack; and British forces were being withdrawn. The British troops in Libya would also be reduced. Soviet and Soviet bloc representatives attacked these strategic considerations of Britain during the debate on the Cyprus question in the Political Committee of the twelfth Assembly. (See below, Chapters VIII, IX, X, pp. 351, 370, 381, 391. The representatives of Egypt and Syria likewise referred with anxiety to the use of Cyprus as a "springboard for aggression," during the Suez crisis of 1956. (See below, Chapters IX and X, pp. 370, 390.)

141. Between December 1, 1954, and June 30, 1957, the British military expenditures in Cyprus totaled approximately £28 million of which about £9 million represented capital expenditures. (573 H.C. Deb. [5th ser.], pp. 1119–20 [July 17, 1967].) It should be noted that after the Anglo-Italian talks of April, 1938, the British government, while accepting Fascist fortifications in the Mediterranean, agreed not to fortify Cyprus without prior consultation with the Italian government, A. Eden, *The Reckoning* (Boston: Houghton Mifflin, 1965), p. 14.

142. 571 H.C. Deb. (5th ser.), p. 142. Lennox-Boyd stated that 1,140 persons were in detention on May 28, 1957. It was not possible to say, he added, when they would be released.

143. 573 H.C. Deb. (5th ser.), pp. 784–786.

144. *Ibid.*, 797–98. On February 5, 1957, Callaghan, it should be noted, had inquired from the Greek chargé d'affaires in London what number of years did the Greek government have in mind for the conduct of a plebiscite in Cyprus and whether the Greek government would accept the result of such a plebiscite if it favored the establishment of Cyprus as an autonomous state within the Commonwealth. The Greek diplomat replied that a period of five to seven years would be acceptable and that his government would recognize any result of a freely conducted plebiscite. Said Callaghan: "If Labour were in power and I were Colonial Secretary, we would be able to conclude an agreement with you today." On this occasion, Callaghan drew the Greek diplomat's attention to the danger lest the British government go ahead with partition of the island because, in his view, conservative circles were concluding that the maintenance of the entire island no longer served any military purpose and the intention was to cut back their military commitments. Cyprus, he said, was costing the British government £20–30 million a year. He, being an Irishman, had told an unnamed Turkish constitutional specialist that he was opposed to partition. He urged the Greeks to seek the maintenance of the status quo and a statement with regard to self-determination; the freeing of Makarios, for the purpose of re-examining the Radcliffe constitutional proposals, which, if amended, could constitute a framework for self-determination; and the cessation of EOKA's armed activities.

145. *Ibid.*, p. 796.

146. *Ibid.*, p. 817.

147. British Information Services release T32, July 25, 1957.

148. *Grivas Memoirs*, p. 199.

149. *Ibid.*, pp. 191, 199. Late in August 1957, the Greek Foreign Minister wrote to Grivas that independence with a perpetual guarantee of this status might be acceptable to the Allies.

150. *Ibid.*, 191–92.

CHAPTER IV

1. See above, Chapter III, p. 143.

2. Sir Roger Allen had presented his credentials on May 6, 1957, *Times* (London), May 7, 1957.

3. See above, Chapter II, pp. 73–74.

4. See above, Chapter III, p. 114, n. 30.

5. *The Tripartite Conference*, p. 3.

6. This conference of the main Greek party leaders took place in August prior to the London Tripartite Conference. It was chaired by Acting Foreign Minister Kanellopoulos. (*GPD*, April 5, 1956, p. 35 [Kanellopoulos].) Papandreou, after orally expressing his views, sent in a written statement. (*Ibid.*) Venizelos, on the other hand, dictated his views to a secretary during the conference itself. (*Ibid.*) He favored attendance of the tripartite conference, but Greek withdrawal from it if the British refused a request for recognition of the principle of self-determination for Cyprus. (*Ibid.*, April 5, 1956, 57 Venizelos]; November 30, 1956, 114 [Venizelos].) Papapolitis brought with him an entire memorandum. (*Ibid.*, April 5, 1956, p. 35 [Kanellopoulos].) Markezinis refused to voice an opinion and had nothing to sign. None, except for Papapolitis, recommended non-attendance of the conference. Papapolitis said that attendance should be conditioned on Britain's acceptance that the

principle of self-determination should be applied to Cyprus. (*Ibid.*) With regard to the substance of the Cyprus question, only Papandreou and Markezinis formulated the demand for self-determination within a reasonable and fixed time limit, (*ibid.*, November 30, 1956, p. 113 [Karamanlis].) Venizelos and Papapolitis said this was a matter for discussion. Thus, at that time (August, 1955), there had been no unanimity among Greek party leaders over a demand for self-determination for Cyprus within a reasonable and fixed time limit. In his long memorandum (*ibid.*, November 30, 1956, pp. 113–14), Papapolitis contended, among other things, that the right of self-determination could not be the object of discussion, because it was a rule of law based on the UN Charter and two UN resolutions, of 1952 and 1953, respectively. Only the procedure of the right's implementation was, in his view, discussable. He also proposed that the Cypriots (Makarios) should be invited to the conference, and argued that Turkey's attendance would be legitimized only through Turkish recognition that self-determination should be applied to Cyprus.

7. *Keesing's 1955–1956*, IX, 14396.

8. Eden, *op. cit.*, p. 446.

9. *The Tripartite Conference*, p. 37. In emphasizing the British strategic need for Cyprus, to enable Britain to meet its commitments under NATO, the Baghdad Pact, the Tripartite Declaration of 1950 regarding the Middle East, the Special Agreement with Iraq, the treaty of Alliance with Jordan (1948), Macmillan declared that Britain had to have the necessary facilities to carry out these obligations. "For a number of different reasons, geographical, historical, and legal, the only satisfactory site for these facilities is Cyprus. . . . It has sometimes been said that the United Kingdom only needs a base in Cyprus. This . . . can be misleading, for the term 'base' implies that our needs can be satisfied by some self-contained unit, bounded, perhaps, by a perimeter of barbed wire. . . . But for our special needs and to carry out our special duties this is not enough."

10. *Ibid.*, pp. 15, 17.

11. *Ibid.*, pp. 25, 28, 38–39. About possible Turkish counterclaims, see Eden, *Full Circle*, p. 447.

12. *Ibid.*, pp. 41–42, 43.

13. Eden, *op. cit.*, p. 447.

14. *Ibid.*, pp. 448–49.

15. For text of this note and for the State Department's announcement concerning Greek-Turkish tension, see *Department of State Bulletin*, XXXIII (September 26, 1955), 496.

16. The Athens newspaper, *Ta Nea*, on August 5, quoting a NATO source in Paris, reported that the British government had invited the Greek and Turkish governments to a conference and that Ambassador Seferiadis in London had explained the reasons why the Greek government could not accept this proposal. It added that the Greek government's attitude was to reject such a tripartite conference unless this was based in advance on a plan acceptable in principle to the Cypriots. The entourage of Makarios was said to have no news of any fresh developments. A Foreign Office spokesman in London, asked to comment on such reports, said that the British government had been in touch over a number of weeks about possible ways of making progress on the Cyprus issue but that no formal invitation to a conference had been issued. (*Times* [London], August 6, 1957.)

17. *Times* (London), August 9, 1957, reported that a Greek government spokesman had given the following terms for Greek participation in the suggested conference: First, the right of self-determination should be recognized by all in advance. Second, the outline of the planned settlement should be submitted in advance and

acceptable to the Greeks and the Cypriots. Third, the conference should aim at elaborating the details of the accepted settlement. By these terms, Greece was trying to insure the conference's success, it was added.

18. At the House of Commons debate mentioned above (see above, Chapter III, p. 150), Secretary of Defense Sandys, on his return from the Middle East, had indicated that Britain was no longer interested in Cyprus as a base but wanted merely bases in Cyprus.

19. See above, Introduction, pp. 6–7. *GPD,* December 13, 1958, pp. 353–54 (G. Lychnos).

20. See above, Chapter III, p. 118 n. 49. *The Tripartite Conference,* p. 14.

21. The diplomatic correspondent of the *Times* (London), August 12, reported that the British government was hopeful that a conference would take place to settle at least temporarily the Cyprus problem and disclosed many of the points made in this note and in the earlier conversations. It revealed that British strategic interests no longer required sovereignty over the island but that Britain wished to retain there certain bases and other facilities, could not entertain any threat to its military security through the establishment of a Communist regime there or communal war, would insist on an acceptable solution before surrendering its sovereignty; also that the British government would enter into no prior commitments to a solution known to be unacceptable to the other parties.

22. See above, Chapters I and II, pp. 43, 49.

23. According to a Washington dispatch in the *Times* (London), August 12, 1957, Dulles had been informally invited during his London conversations to send observers to this conference, and the final decision depended on the nature of the advances made by the British government and more specially on the attitude of Greece, which was showing little enthusiasm.

24. *Keesing's 1957–1958,* XI, 15701. Nearly half of the emergency regulations (33 out of 76) were revoked on August 9, 1957. Among the measures revoked were: those relating to "consorting with terrorism" under which persons found in the company of armed terrorists were subject to the death penalty or to life imprisonment or lesser prison terms in less serious cases; the powers to detain suspected EOKA members without trial, to control lines of communication, and to appoint press and radio censors. All processions and assemblies, except those organized by illegal bodies, were no longer banned, and certain curfew regulations were relaxed. Among emergency regulations still maintained were those making the death penalty mandatory for carrying or discharging arms and throwing bombs, those authorizing search and arrest without a warrant, and those sanctioning the control of publications. On September 11, 1957, a new relaxation of certain emergency measures was announced so that persons convicted of discharging firearms or throwing bombs would no longer be liable to mandatory death penalty but might be sentenced to imprisonment for life or a lesser period; and life imprisonment, not death, would be the maximum penalty for carrying bombs or firearms. (*Ibid.,* p. 15778.) As mentioned above, see Chapter III, p. 144, coincident with a meeting of the relevant subcommission of the Commission of Human Rights at Strasbourg and on the eve of the announcement of the Radcliffe proposals, some of the emergency measures introduced by Governor Harding in November 1955 and 1956, had been relaxed on December 18, 1956, and the subcommission had taken cognizance of this decision. On that occasion, there had been a revocation of: (1) emergency regulations under which males under the age of 18 could be sentenced to whipping for certain specified offenses; (2) collective punishment regulations under which fines would be levied collectively on the inhabitants of particular areas, and stores and dwelling houses in such areas closed; (3) places of public resort or entertainment would not be closed in future, except temporarily as part of a particular anti-terrorist operation in a given area or for the

purpose of denying the use of particular premises to the terrorists. It was also decided then to review the cases of all persons detained either under the Detention of Persons law or under the emergency regulations "with a view to releasing any who can be set at liberty without serious prejudice to the conduct of security operations"; to relax the regulations requiring persons to obtain exit permits whenever they left the colony; and to introduce new press control regulations and abolish the earlier ones, of November 22, 1956, which enabled the Governor to suspend newspapers without prior notification and without appeal to a court of law. A month after Grivas' truce offer, a further relaxation of the emergency regulations was announced on April 14, 1957. (*Ibid.*, pp. 15476–77.)

25. The entire Athens press was most reserved. Both *Kathimerini* and *To Vima* had seen in this move a maneuver of British propaganda on the eve of the UN General Assembly. They noted that the rights restored were minor in comparison with those that Governor Harding still denied the Cypriots. Makarios, too, said that the relaxation of measures of only secondary importance were involved. *"Embassy Press Release,"* August 12, 1957.

26. Syria and Egypt, in particular, see above, Chapter I, p. 43. Also below, Chapters IX and X, pp. 370 and 390.

27. See above, p. 156.

28. See above, pp. 166.

29. Heléne Vlachos, director of *Kathimerini*, was evidently being referred to here. See also below, Epilogue, p. 513.

30. Menelaos Alexandrakis, appointed Ambassador in Nicosia in summer, 1964.

31. The date of October 27 for the elections was decided by the Grand National Assembly on September 2, 1957.

32. According to an Athens dispatch of August 26, *Times* (London), August 27, 1957, in a day of unusual diplomatic activity that included a one-hour talk between Averoff-Tossizza and Makarios. Greek diplomatic circles denied that any concrete British proposals had been made and had said that the British soundings did not seem to offer grounds for further negotiations.

33. For high tension in Greek-Turkish relations at that time, see above, Chapter II, pp. 78 ff.

34. Since 1955, the Soviet bloc had started supplying arms, technicians, and political backing to several Arab nations, Syria included, and a crisis had occurred in the area which led to the enunciation of the "Eisenhower Doctrine" early in 1957. There appeared to be a major buildup of Soviet arms in Syria, on Turkey's southern border, with Turkey responding by concentrating troops there. A "war scare" resulted that involved heated charges and countercharges between the United States and the U.S.S.R. In October, 1957, Syria resorted to the Assembly with a request for the dispatch of an investigation commission on the spot, see below, Chapters V and VI, pp. 225 and 276.

35. *Grivas Memoirs*, pp. 196–97. The rest of the letter is here published for the first time.

36. Indeed, elections took place on May 11 of the following year and revealed an increase in power of extreme left EDA, which was ascribed to popular discontent with Western policies in the Cyprus question. See also below, Epilogue, pp. 512–13.

37. *Grivas Memoirs*, pp. 193–94.

38. *Ibid.*, p. 191.

39. *Ibid.*, pp. 197–98,

40. See above, Chapter II, pp. 77–78.

41. The British recourse to the UN had contained such charges, *GAOR, Eleventh Session,* Annexes Item 55, pp. 6–7.

42. On September 5 the Greek Ministry for Foreign Affairs issued a release saying that there was no need publicly to inquire into the purpose of reports, coming from London, about soundings or even pressures for holding a tripartite conference on Cyprus. It was necessary, however, to state that the Greek government's position on this particular matter had been clearly defined and no modification of this position was to be expected under the circumstances. That certain press and semiofficial quarters mistook routine contacts for diplomatic soundings did not alter the substance of the question nor affect the Greek government's position. The Foreign Ministry would not deal in future with any such reports published in the foreign press, "Embassy Press Release," September 6, 1957.

43. The discussion had centered around a Turkish government note handed to the Greek Ambassador in Ankara which contained a complaint against inscriptions that had appeared in certain towns of Western (Greek) Thrace visited by Premier Karamanlis and called the Turks to leave Greece, otherwise they would be killed. Averoff-Tossizza complained about the rather stiff tone of the Turkish note and expressed surprise at it. The Premier had heard of no such complaint during his tour in Thrace and, having learned that Ambassador Vergin had mentioned such a thing to another diplomat in Athens, had ordered an investigation. He had also instructed the Greek Ambassador in Ankara to express surprise and regret about the Turkish *démarche.* The Greek Foreign Minister also observed that it was Greek policy to try to improve relations with Turkey in spite of provocations, such as the Istanbul events, the burglary at the Greek Embassy in Ankara, and inflammatory speeches by Menderes. He added that some months earlier Greece had stated it no longer intended silently to acquiesce in such provocations. (See above, Chapter I, p. 44.) Vergin explained that the information about the wall inscriptions together with photographs had been given to him by the Turkish Consul in Komotini. The inscriptions were in Turkish but with words not usually used by Turks. Averoff-Tossizza made various hints about the expediency of such denunciations on the eve of the debate in the UN, while the Turkish envoy expressed fear of greater tension during the debates there. He was not optimistic about a solution either before or after the Assembly. The Foreign Minister told him his government would do its best not to exacerbate the debate. About a solution, he too, was not optimistic. With regard to the Turkish diplomat's suggestion to his Greek colleague in Ankara about the usefulness of a meeting between the Greek and Turkish Premiers, Averoff-Tossizza said such a meeting would be harmful were it to end by recording the existing disagreements. It would be another matter, however, if a probable solution had been explored beforehand and the conclusion had been reached through the diplomatic channel that a solution existed to which both parties were agreed. For the Greek government, the question remained one between the Cypriot people and the British government. Of course, if the Greek government, knowing the views of the Cypriots, were to reach a solution acceptable to them, then any sort of talks would be useful. Thus, if the general outline of a solution were agreed upon explicitly, then and only then Premier Karamanlis would have no difficulty in going to Ankara in order to discuss with Premier Menderes in detail the problem and ratify, as it were, the agreement.

44. See above, Chapter II, pp. 79 ff.

45. See above, p. 166.

46. For text, see *Documents on American Foreign Relations 1957* (New York: Harper & Bros., 1958), pp. 195 ff. The President proclaimed the "Doctrine" in a message to Congress on January 5, 1957. That same day Congress formulated a joint

resolution which was adopted with amendments by the Senate on March 5, 1957, and by the House of Representatives two days later.

47. *To Vima*, August 30, 1957.

48. *New York Times*, August 31, 1957. "Embassy Press Release," August 30, 1957.

49. *Grivas Memoirs*, p. 200. "Embassy Press Release," August 28, 1957.

50. *New York Times*, September 6, 1957. "Embassy Press Release," August 30, 1957. *To Vima*, September 6, 1957.

51. *New York Times*, September 6, 1957. Dr. Kuchuk, the Turkish Cypriot leader, was reported to have said in Istanbul that Menderes had told him clearly that agreeing to the partition of the island in the event of a change in its status constituted the limit of the concessions the Turkish government was prepared to make. Turkish Information Office, N.Y. "News from Turkey," September 4, 1957, p. 2.

52. See above, Chapter III, p. 140.

CHAPTER V

1. See above, Chapter IV, p. 156.

2. On June 20, 1957, the permanent representative of Greece to the UN, in a press release, had stated, with regard to the UN report on Hungary, that inhuman practices such as those described in that document were being resorted to in Cyprus by the British Colonial authorities and referred to the Foreign Minister's statement at the eleventh Assembly about the evidence at hand. The same Committee set up for investigating the Hungarian case might, it was suggested, be entrusted with the task of finding out the truth in the case of Cyprus, *Cyprus Before the United Nations*, pp. 294–95.

3. See above, Chapter III, pp. 143 ff.

4. *Ibid.*, p. 148.

5. Article 60 of the European Convention on Human Rights and Fundamental Freedoms provides that "nothing in this present Convention shall be construed as limiting or derogating from any of the human rights or fundamental freedoms which may be ensured under the laws of any High Contracting Party or under any other agreement to which it is a party."

6. See above, Chapter III, pp. 145–46.

7. See above, Chapter I, p. 50. Also below, Chapter VI, p. 261.

8. This concept, it will be recalled, was developed at the Nuremberg trials of Nazi leaders in 1946.

9. Together with Premier Karamanlis, the Foreign Minister had made an official visit to Egypt from August 17–21, 1957, at a time of tension in U.S.-Arab relations. The primary purpose of this visit was the question of the future of the Greeks in Egypt. Although the Cyprus question was not mentioned in the Anglo-Egyptian communiqué published during this visit, Karamanlis told a press conference in Cairo that the matter had been discussed with President Nasser who agreed that the right of self-determination for the people of Cyprus should be recognized. In private, the Egyptian Foreign Minister assured his Greek colleague that the Egyptian Delegation at the UN should be regarded as an extension of the Greek Delegation in the Cyprus question. However, as seen below, the Egyptian Delegation did not prove willing to

appear before the General Committee to state its views on the issue as a party concerned in it. The Egyptian press, on the other hand, played up the statement by Karamanlis that the "air bridge" to Jordan would not pass over Greece, namely that the Greek government would not allow American transport planes to use Greek air fields on their way to Jordan.

10. See above, Chapter IV, p. 162.

11. *Cyprus Before the United Nations*, pp. 2–27 (verbatim proceedings).

12. S. D. Bailey, *The General Assembly of the United Nations* (New York: Frederick A. Praeger, 1964, paperback), p. 85.

13. See above, Introduction, pp. 13, 22.

14. See above, Chapter III, p. 101.

15. See above, Chapter IV, pp. 154 ff.

16. See above, Chapter I, p. 52. Note his avoidance of any analogy with Hungary.

17. Article 2, paragraph 7, of the Charter provides: "Nothing contained in the present Charter shall authorize the United Nations to intervene in matters which are essentially within the domestic jurisdiction of any state or shall require the Members to submit such matters to settlement under the present Charter; but this principle shall not prejudice the application of enforcement measures under Chapter VII.

18. In the House of Commons, on July 15, 1957, Profumo, Undersecretary of State for the Colonies, had mentioned this case. 573 H.C. Deb. (5th ser.), p. 788.

19. Lloyd was quoting himself from the official but summary UN record. *GAOR, Ninth Session*, General Committee, 93d meeting, September 23, 1954, p. 9. For full text of his speech, *Report on the Inscription of the Cyprus Item on the Agenda of the Ninth Session of the General Assembly of the United Nations held at New York on September 23/24, 1954* (London: H.M. Stationery Office, October, 1954), Cmd. 9300, p. 7. "The tension which would follow United Nations intervention," he had warned, "would merely delay political progress in the island." In general, he had predicted that inscription of the item might gravely endanger political, social, and military stability in the Middle East.

20. On that occasion, the Turkish government did not request representation at the preliminary hearing on the Cyprus question in the General Committee. The Turkish representative, however, made a long statement on his government's views on the question in the Political Committee on December 14, 1954. (*GAOR, Ninth Session*, First Committee, pp. 551–54. Full text in Turkish Information Office, *Turkish Views on Cyprus* [New York, n.d.].)

21. On that occasion, the Turkish representative spoke in the General Committee, Turkey being a member of it that year. (*Ibid., Tenth Session*, General Committee, 102d meeting, September 21, 1955, p. 4.)

22. *GAOR, Eleventh Session*, General Committee, 107th meeting, November 14, 1956, p. 7. Plenary Meetings, 578th meeting, November 15, 1956, pp. 41–42.

23. Article 73 of the UN Charter provides, in part, that "Members of the United Nations which have or assume responsibilities for the administration of territories whose peoples have not yet attained a full measure of self-government recognize the principle that the interests of the inhabitants of these territories are paramount, and accept as a sacred trust the obligation to promote to the utmost . . . the well-being of the inhabitants of these territories, and, to this end:

"a. to ensure, with due respect for the culture of the peoples concerned, their political, economic, social, and educational advancement, and their protection against abuses;

"b. to develop self-government, to take due account of the political aspirations of the peoples, and to assist them in the progressive development of their free political institutions, according to the particular circumstances of each territory and its peoples and their varying stages of advancement.

24. The reference here is to an incident during the battle of Fontenoy, 1745, waged during the War of the Austrian succession between Maurice de Saxe, leading the French, and the Duke of Cumberland, leading the British.

25. Around the use of this word—in French *"bouleversement,"*—by the Foreign Minister, there was a discussion in the Greek Parliament. (*GPD*, October 24, 1957, p. 77 [Papandreou]) p. 82 [Averoff-Tossizza].)

26. Articles 34 and 35 of the Charter refer to the Security Council's competence to investigate any international dispute or situation that may lead to international friction or give rise to a dispute and to the right of UN members or non-members to bring any dispute or such situation to the attention of the Security Council or the General Assembly.

27. For such proposals, see above, Chapter IV, p. 162.

28. See also above, Chapter V, p. 165.

29. In an effort to pave the way for improved relations with Turkey as well as for a settlement of the Cyprus question, Pesmazoglou, a non-career diplomat, had been appointed to Ankara at the end of June, 1957, while on the Turkish side Iksel was replaced by Vergin. Both Ambassadors were to play an important role in the diplomatic exchanges that led to the Zürich agreement of February 11, 1959. In an article of June 20, 1957, in *Kathimerini*, Pipinelis had urged efforts to improve Greek-Turkish relations and to re-establish Greek-Turkish friendship. The new international perspectives in the Mediterranean and the Balkans made such efforts imperative, he wrote, regardless, even, of NATO obligations, because of the failure to implement the Lisbon 1952 decision of the NATO Ministerial Council, the delay in German rearmament, and the French embroilment in Algeria. These developments had led to a great reliance on the nuclear deterrent, hence to changes in the strategy of the alliance. The British decision to cut down their forces in Germany added to the alliance's problems. There was a trend, he felt, toward greater reliance on local (conventional) forces, and the likelihood of local wars had increased, with the great powers being hesitant to intervene in them (to avoid escalation into nuclear warfare).

30. *Cyprus before the United Nations*, pp. 28–29.

31. *Ibid.*, 29–31.

32. Rule 73 of the rules of procedure provides that during the discussion of any matter, a representative may rise to a point of order, and the point of order shall be immediately decided by the President in accordance with the rules of procedure. A representative may appeal against the ruling of the President. The appeal shall be immediately put to the vote and the President's ruling shall stand unless overruled by a majority of the members present and voting. A representative rising to a point of order may not speak on the substance of the matter under discussion.

33. See above, Chapter IV, p. 162.

34. See above, Chapter I, p. 40.

35. *GAOR, Twelfth Session*, 680th plenary meeting, pp. 20–21.

36. *Ibid.*, 681st meeting, pp. 28–29, 35–37.

37. *Ibid.*, 685th meeting, pp. 99–100.

38. *Ibid.*, pp. 97–98.

39. *Ibid.*, p. 98.

40. See Chapter II, pp. 79–81. In the general debate at the previous Assembly, Karamanlis had urged the creation of a special UN police force. (*GAOR, Eleventh Session*, 588th plenary meeting, November 21, 1956, p. 209.)

41. The statement was somewhat of an exaggeration. The Arabs emerged in the Mediterranean in the seventh century A.D.

42. *Ibid., Twelfth Session*, 689th plenary meeting, pp. 164–67.

43. The National Pact, drafted initially in Erzurum in July, 1919, and rephrased at Sivas in January, 1920, provided that the destinies of the predominantly Arab portions of the Ottoman Empire, plus western Thrace, should be settled by a free vote.

44. *GAOR, Twelfth Session*, Plenary Sessions, 692d meeting, pp. 198–99.

45. *Ibid.*, 682d meeting, p. 48; 688th meeting, pp. 146, 149, 150; 691st and 692d meetings, pp. 193, 198.

46. *Ibid.*, 694th meeting, pp. 216.

47. *Ibid.*, 697th meeting, pp. 237, 247.

48. *Ibid.*, 699th meeting, p. 260.

49. *Ibid.*, 702d meeting, pp. 300–301, 305; 703rd meeting, pp. 316, 322.

50. Speaking to the Parliament at the end of 1956, Averoff-Tossizza reported that fifty-nine journalists had been brought to Greece, on the Greek government's invitation, and that booklets on the Cyprus question had been published in nineteen languages. (*GPD*, November 27, 1956, p. 85.) It should be added that special efforts were exerted to influence U.S. public opinion with regular bulletins, such as "Hellenic News," and the Cyprus question, which were released by the Greek Information Services in the U.S., since 1954.

51. See above, Chapter I, p. 50, and below, Chapter VI, p. 261.

52. See above, Chapter I, p. 51.

53. *Grivas Memoirs*, pp. 201–2.

CHAPTER VI

1. On September 8, 1957, an EOKA leaflet threatening imminent resumption of violence was issued in Nicosia, signed by "Dighenis." It was the second signed by him since March 14 when he had offered a truce, *Daily Telegraph* (London), September 9, 1957.

2. Spaak went to Washington late in October and took part, to a certain extent, in the Eisenhower-Macmillan three-day meeting (October, 22–25), which ended in a "Declaration of Common Purpose." (*Documents on American Foreign Relations 1957* [New York: Harper & Bros., 1958], pp. 132–36.) During his stay in the United States, he met Makarios and, according to a Greek diplomatic source, was favorably impressed by the Ethnarch.

3. *Report of the 56th Annual Conference of the Labour Party* (Brighton: 1957), p. 196. Premier Karamanlis greeted this resolution as an important step. (*To Vima*, October 6, 1957.) That same paper, on October 9, published a report about a BBC talk by C. M. Woodhouse, who dampened the high expectations which the Labour party resolution had aroused among the Greeks. About the Parliamentary Labour party's embarrassment. (Mayes, *op. cit.*, p. 196.)

4. Mayes, *op. cit.*, pp. 187–88, points out that Ramsay MacDonald, who in 1919

had stated at the International Socialist Conference that the Labour party would apply the principle of self-determination to Cyprus, sent the Bishops in exile after the disturbances of 1931, when he was Prime Minister. After World War II, the Cypriots several times appealed to the Labour government in vain. (Kranidiotis, *op. cit.*, pp. 60, 73.) It had been a Labour government in 1951 that firmly rebuffed the Greek government's new *démarches* about Cyprus. (See above, Introduction, p. 51, n. 11.) On the other hand, the Cyprus question, as already indicated, see above, Chapter II, p. 79, was very valuable when the Labour party was in the Opposition. The left-wingers in the party—Aneurin Bevan, Tom Driberg, R. H. S. Crossman—were particularly vociferous on this issue, while Barbara Castle was to be the mid-wife, as it were, of Cyprus' independence because of her interview with Makarios on September 22, 1958. A precedent for the Brighton resolution was that of Scarborough (September, 1954) in which the Labour conference deplored the policy adopted by the government and urged the Parliamentary Labour party to oppose this policy on every occasion. Resolutions of the Labour conferences were, however, not binding on the Parliamentary group. The value of these resolutions was psychological for the Greeks, who either as government officials or in the Opposition exploited them abundantly, e.g., by Papandreou. (*GPD*, October 24, 1957.)

5. In this interview of September 20, 1957, with the newspaper *Kathimerini*, Allen had said that self-determination was an excellent principle but there were occasions when it ran counter to the equally good basic principle of friendly neighborly relations. "Moreover, there are many places in the world, including Greece itself," he had added, "where a national minority is the majority in a certain locality. How far should this principle of self-determination be carried? Common sense must be the guide in all such matters." Allen also said the U.S. might decline any UN offer of trusteeship over Cyprus as a transitional step. He also paid tribute to Britain's record as a colonial power. Noting that Soviet influence in the Middle East was disquieting, he advocated good neighborly relations between Greece and Turkey. Greece, he said, did not want a threat at her back door or outside domination any more than the U.S. did. Allen said he hoped the Cyprus problem would be solved in corridors or through diplomatic channels before public discussions took place. "Everyone would prefer to avoid bitter public controversy if possible." He hinted, though, that "open debate might be useful in mobilizing public opinion behind the principles on which the United Nations was founded." Another formal conference would run the risk of failure, unless careful preparations were made beforehand. The U.S. would be willing to attend such a conference as an observer. It hoped "to see achieved in Cyprus a solution which the people of Cyprus can accept and which countries most directly concerned are willing to live with. The people of the area are not likely to try very hard to make a solution work if it is pushed down their throats by the positive policy of the United States or anybody else." *Daily Telegraph*, September 21, 1957. An exchange of letters followed between Acting Foreign Minister C. Tsatsos and Allen (September 25 and 29, respectively). In his reply to Minister Tsatsos, Allen pointed out there was no justification for interpreting his remarks as applicable to Western Thrace or precluding self-determination for Cyprus. ("Embassy Press Release," October 1, 1957.)

6. *Keesing's 1957–1958*, XI, 15825. Premier Karamanlis publicly justified this rejection on the grounds of the hostility which certain Balkan countries had shown toward Greece either by their own will or as instruments of others, invading Greece or proclaiming their intention of appropriating certain Greek territories, or allowing their border areas to be used as hide-outs and bases for persons who secretly entered into Greek territory with the intention of destroying Greece's independence or undermining its regime.

7. See above, p. 245.

8. See above, Chapter IV, p. 154.

9. *SDB*, vol. XXXVII (October 28, 1957), 674. In this statement it was said among other things that Khrushchev should be under no illusion that the U.S., Turkey's friend and ally, took lightly its obligations under NATO and was not determined to carry out the national policy expressed in the joint resolution of Congress on the Middle East (the "Eisenhower Doctrine").

10. For instance, L. Akritas, in an article in *To Vima*, October 27, 1957, wrote that Allen's recall was evidence of Washington's unfavorable attitude toward the Cyprus question, and indicative of pressures on the Greek government.

11. Allen had arrived in Athens in early October, 1956. On October 26, at the Propeller Club in Athens, he had spoken about the Eastern Mediterranean and had stressed that the only way of reaching a solution to the Cyprus problem was through negotiations. No organization, he said, could impose a permanent solution, and the United States could take no such initiative. Commenting on this statement, Premier Karamanlis expressed appreciation of Allen's realism and Greece's awareness that UN resolutions were not enforceable. They did not lack, however, moral force. Greece was resorting to the UN because the British government was not offering solutions such as Allen suggested. Surely negotiations were more useful, but these presupposed the appropriate person with whom to negotiate—an allusion to Makarios in exile. Opposition leader Papandreou, in a statement in Thessaloniki, struck a similar note. ("Embassy Press Release," October 27, 1956.)

12. *Kathimerini*, October 17, 1957. Averoff-Tossizza refused to comment on this report. He knew, he said, of no Greek personality having made that statement.

13. The items discussed at this important conference were: (1) NATO; (2) Cyprus; (3) the Balkan Pact; (4) U.S. military aid to Greece; (5) U.S. economic aid to Greece. With regard to Cyprus, Murphy, responding to a question by Karamanlis, said that the U.S. had no opinion on the question but was trying to find a solution that was satisfactory to all concerned. It recognized and fully appreciated the Greek government's moderation in this question and its efforts but did not see what it could do now. "Our position is clear," he said later during the conversation on Cyprus. "We support the view that the people of Cyprus have the right to self-government." Having in mind especially the fact that the U.S.S.R. could exploit the situation, the U.S. government, Murphy reiterated, would seek by all means for a solution to be found. When NATO was discussed, Murphy, in response to a remark of Karamanlis that NATO should find a mechanism through which it would be possible to resolve differences occurring among members, said that it was more useful for inter-allied differences to be examined in informal and friendly conversations and not brought up in formal and rigid procedures.
On the Greek side, Karamanlis emphasized his government's moderation in spite of violence, threats, and insults, as well as the justice of the cause, which many Americans recognized, he said, though they had doubts about the timeliness of raising the question. Greece, Karamanlis argued, did not seek something that went against the interests of Turkey and Britain. The Greek government was confident that it could fully guarantee the strategic importance of the island and the protection of the Turkish minority. The Turks, however, were the very last people who had a right to talk about Cyprus. First came the Cypriot people; second, Britain, which occupied the island; third, came Greece, because the majority of the inhabitants were Greek; and Turkey came last.
Karamanlis also drew attention to the harmful effects of the Cyprus question on the Balkan Pact and NATO. He predicted worse to come. A solution therefore should be found at the earliest. The best procedure would be for the plebiscite, by which the Cypriot people would decide about their future, to be determined through direct talks between the British and the Cypriots, or through NATO. If no U.S. help were forthcoming, the Greek government would have to wage a battle during the UN

debate on the substance of the Cyprus question and would be obliged to flatter foes and fight friends. He was convinced that if the question was placed in a purely political framework, it would be solved in twenty-four hours. The U.S. was in a position to help by telling the British that if they did not give a solution, it would support Greece in the debate on the substance of the question. In conclusion, he urged the U.S. government to try to achieve the liberation of Makarios. No negotiation could succeed in the absence of the Ethnarch. If the British wished to show good faith, they would free Makarios. That same day, in his conversation with Eisenhower, Karamanlis urged him to intercede with the British in the matter of freeing Makarios from his detention in the Seychelles. (See above, Chapter II, p. 75.) Attending this conference of November 15, 1956, were on the Greek side, in addition to the Premier, Ambassador G. V. Melas; Embassy Counsellor Kavalieratos; Brigadier-General Yeroyannopoulos, Head of the Greek Armed Forces Mission; and A. Sismanidis, Head of the Office of Foreign Trade at the Greek Embassy in Washington. On the American side were Herbert Hoover, Jr., Acting Secretary of State (Dulles being sick); Rountree; Burke Elbrick; Murphy; Jacob Beame, acting Assistant Secretary of State for East European Affairs; Walter Walmsley, acting Assistant Secretary of State for International Organizations; Owen Jones, Director of the Bureau of Greek-Turkish-Iranian Affairs; Benson Timmons, Director of Regional European Affairs (NATO); Murat Williams, Assistant Director of Greek-Turkish-Iranian Affairs; Chalmers Wood, Director of the Greek Desk; Gordon Gray, Undersecretary of Defense for Economic Affairs (External Military Aid); Willis, Director of the Treasury (aid matters); and Cedric Seager, Director of Middle Eastern Affairs (ICA).

14. See above, Chapter III, p. 147.

15. In extensive comments on this news, Athens newspapers were unanimous in their assessment that this move would have no bearing on British policy toward Cyprus. "Embassy Press Release," October 23, 1957.

16. The estimated population of Greece in 1956 was 8,031,000. (*The New Inter-National Yearbook 1958* [New York: Funk and Wagnalls, 1958], p. 190.)

17. *GPD*, October 24, 1957, pp. 77–79.

18. *Ibid.*, October 24, 1957, pp. 79–81.

19. *Ibid.*, October 24, 1957, p. 81.

20. See above, Chapter V, pp. 200–202.

21. *Ibid.*, pp. 193–97.

22. *GPD*, October 24, 1957, pp. 81–83.

23. *Ibid.*, October 24, 1957, pp. 84–86.

24. *Ibid.*, October 24, 1957, pp. 87–88 (D. Stratis).

25. *Ibid.*, October 24, 1957, p. 90 (Passalidis).

26. *Ibid.*, October 24, 1957, p. 95 (S. Pistolakis, of the Party of Peasants and Toilers).

27. See above, Chapter IV, p. 181.

28. *Grivas Memoirs*, pp. 207–8.

29. *Keesing's*, 1958, XII, 16219.

30. *Grivas Memoirs*, p. 203.

31. It is not clear to what statement of G. V. Allen "Isaakios" was referring. In a farewell speech at the Propeller Club on October 25, 1957, Allen expressed regret at leaving Greece before the accomplishment of his task but pointed out he regarded his

departure as a suspension rather than termination of his duties in Greece. After speaking on the startling new developments in pure science, he referred to the campaign of enlightenment which Makarios was carrying out in the U.S. and said this could be fruitful, since the American people, regardless of their political views, were persuaded by arguments based on logic and sound principles. In the forthcoming debate in the UN he added, delegates of the member states would vote freely and only their votes would be of lasting significance. Democratic processes were slow, and reason often had to contend with strong emotions or with indifference. However, with persistence and confidence, justice would prevail. Colonialism was going through a steady transformation during the past decade, and it would be strange if the coming year did not bring further, and perhaps startling progress in this area.

32. See below, Chapter VII, pp. 276–78.

33. See below, p. 269.

34. *To Vima*, October 30, 1957, had attacked the Stratos speech and its implications. The Athens newspaper *Ta Nea*, October 31, 1957, editorially sought to allay fears expressed in certain unnamed American quarters to the effect that Greece might undergo a change in policy. ("Embassy Press Release," October 31, 1957.)

35. This letter is not from Grivas' *Memoirs*.

36. *Grivas Memoirs*, pp. 208–9.

37. *RIIA Memo, 1959*, p. 40. *Eleftheria*, November 11, 1957. (Text of Greek government statement.)

38. See above, Chapter IV, p. 181.

39. *Grivas Memoirs*, p. 212. Grivas omits the passages that follow in this "Isaakios" letter.

40. At the conference of November 15, 1956, mentioned above in note 13, Premier Karamanlis observed that, although the defensive position of Greece had improved since Greece had joined NATO in 1952, this position had improved only very slightly since then. If one took into account the most immediate foe in case of a clash, Bulgaria, according to sure estimates, had 700 medium tanks. Against these, Greece had only some antiquated light tanks. As a result of this inferior position, the Greek Army would be forced to abandon a substantial section of its own territory from the first moment of gunfire (eastern Macedonia and western Thrace) and would try to hold the Strymon line. The link between the Greek and the Turkish forces would be severed, with harmful effects for the cohesion of NATO. The defense of the Turkish Straits would then become problematic because the Turkish forces in eastern Thrace had only a limited defensive value, since the territory in which they were located did not permit much movement. The conclusion, he said, was that the Greek forces would have to bear the brunt of an attack from Bulgaria. Therefore a full armored division together with modern anti-tank artillery should be furnished to Greece. As far as the Greek navy was concerned, Karamanlis requested that for insuring the defensive capabilities of Greece, it was necessary to get modern and battleworthy naval units which, at any rate, would be placed within the framework of NATO naval forces and would be used for the common defense. He felt that the U.S. government had overlooked the Greek factor in these matters and had exaggerated the significance of the Turkish factor. He said SHAPE had supported a memorandum on Greek defense needs, and, he hoped, these recommendations would be realized.

41. See below, Chapter VII, p. 286.

42. *To Vima*, December 1, 1957. The Turkish newspaper *Hurriyet* had published a series of articles calling for the deportation of Greek students studying at the Theological School of Halki on Heybeli Ada. It also invoked law 2007 of 1932 prohibiting aliens from practicing certain professions and trades.

CHAPTER VII

1. *I.O.*, XII, 1958, 229.

2. On that occasion, the Greek government had been the only one to refuse to attend the Canal Users' Conference in London. Moreover, it had asked the 730 Greek pilots of the Canal (out of a total of 900) to remain at their posts. (*GPD*, June 24, 1958, p. 190 [Averoff-Tossizza].) Of course, aside from the Cyprus question there was the matter of the important Greek community in Egypt and their interests, which the Greek government had to keep in mind.

3. See above, Chapter V, p. 230.

4. *GAOR, Ninth Session*, Plenary, 477th meeting, September 24, 1954, p. 51.

5. *New York Times*, December 26, 1957.

6. "Embassy Press Release," December, 1957.

7. In an exclusive interview with the Athens newspaper *Ethnos*, August 24, 1957, the Syrian Foreign Minister, Salah al-Bittar, had said that Syria always stood and would continue to stand on the Greek side in the Cyprus question. (*Ibid.*, August 24, 1957.)

8. See above, pp. 272-73.

9. *GAOR, Twelfth Session*, 711th plenary meeting, October 28, 1957, pp. 403-4.

10. *Ibid.*, First Committee, 898th meeting, November 17, 1957, pp. 168-69.

11. Kyrou, *op. cit.*, p. 283. See above, Introduction, p. 13.

12. *To Vima*, November 19, 1957 (dispatch of its UN correspondent).

13. See above, Chapter III, p. 145.

14. See above, Chapter V, p. 215.

15. See above, Chapter II, pp. 77-78.

16. The Foreign Minister had argued this way in his conversation with Allen, on October 7, 1957, see Chapter VI, p. 248.

17. See above, Chapter VI, p. 268.

18. Rule 132 of the rules of procedure provides that "if two or more proposals relate to the same question, a committee shall, unless it decides otherwise, vote on the proposals in the order in which they have been submitted. A committee may, after each vote on a proposal, decide whether to vote on the next proposal."

19. The Turkish government had been alarmed by the Brighton statement on Cyprus of the Labour party as well as by another statement that the same party had issued in November. In the latter statement the Labour party insisted that the people of Cyprus should have the right to determine their own future after an agreed interim period of self-government. The British government should, for that purpose, invite representatives of the Greek and Turkish communities to take part in discussions for defining the functions and powers of the interim government, the arrangements for its election, and the safeguards of minority rights. The major responsibility of the affairs of the island should rest in the hands of the Greek Cypriots, but the legitimate rights of the Turkish minority should be safeguarded. *RIIA Memo 1958*, p. 33.

20. See above, Chapter V, p. 270.

21. *Hurriyet* accused the Patriarch, among other things, of conspiring in the Cyprus question and of acting as an agent of the "Megali Idea"—the defunct

"Manifest Destiny" of Greece in the nineteenth century until 1922. (*To Vima*, December 1, 1957.) This Treaty of Establishment of 1930 was denounced by the Turkish government on March 12, 1964. As a result, the majority of the 12,000 Greek nationals established in Istanbul under the provisions of the Treaty were deported. This instrument was part of the 1930 Greek-Turkish agreements, which set up the basis for Greek-Turkish friendship. The Greek government waived all claims to indemnization for the property abandoned by the Greeks evacuated to Greece under the 1923 agreement on the compulsory and mutual exchange of populations, which involved over one million Greeks as against half a million Turks.

22. See above, Chapter III, p. 117.

23. The full text of the draft resolution was as follows: "The General Assembly, *having examined* the question of Cyprus, *expressing its concern* that no progress has been made toward the solution of the problem in compliance with the operative paragraph of resolution 1013 (XI), considering *further* that the situation in Cyprus is still fraught with danger and that a solution in conformity with the principles of the Charter of the United Nations and at the earliest possible time is required to preserve peace and stability in that area, *expresses the wish* that the people of Cyprus will be given the opportunity to determine their own future by the application of their right to self-determination."

CHAPTER VIII

1. All the debates as rendered in this and the following chapters, are based on *Cyprus before the United Nations,* which is a reproduction of verbatim proceedings of the UN concerning Cyprus. The official but summary records have also been taken into account. The texts of the British, Greek, Turkish, and U.S. set statements were obtained from the respective delegations or official publications.

2. Document A/C.1/803, *GAOR, Twelfth Session,* Annexes, Agenda Item 58, pp. 3–7.

3. See above, Chapter IV, p. 170.

4. *Keesing's 1958*, XII, 16219–20.

5. Reports, the Chairman reminded the Committee, had to be prepared by the rapporteur for the Assembly's consideration.

6. See above, Chapter VII, p. 287.

7. See below, Chapter XII, p. 506, for the handling of the Cyprus question at this summit NATO council of December 16–19, 1957.

8. See above, Chapter V, p. 203. This had been the British position from the very outset, *GAOR, Ninth Session,* General Committee, 93d meeting, p. 8. On that occasion, the British representative had stated that, though some delegations might hold that discussion did not constitute intervention, his delegation could not accept this argument.

9. In October, 1946, the Colonial Secretary stated he intended to ask the Governor to convoke a consultative Assembly for framing proposals for constitutional reform, including the setting up of a centralized legislature. The Ethnarchic Council, however, categorically rejected any solution that did not grant national liberty by union with Greece. After the laws of 1937 controlling the election of the Archbishop were repealed and a new such high official was elected, the British proposals were again rejected—with the new constitution being put forward in May, 1948. With the end of the mandate over Palestine on May 15, 1948, preparations began then for the arrival

of British troops from Palestine and the setting up of a radar-equipped airbase in Cyprus. *RIIA Memo 1958*, pp. 7–8.

10. On July 28, 1954, the British government proposed a new constitution providing for a legislature with both official and nominated members—forming together a majority—and elected members. Some unofficial members of the legislature would take part in the executive council which would be in charge of the administrative departments. On this occasion, Henry Hopkinson, Minister of State for Colonial Affairs, made clear that the British contemplated no change in sovereignty over the island. (See Introduction, p. 10.) The previous month, the government had announced the transfer to Cyprus of the Middle East land and Air Headquarters. (*RIIA Memo 1958*, p. 10.)

11. See above, Introduction, p. 9, n. 16, but see also Chapter III, p. 130, n. 89, n. 90

12. A Greek deputy, Kassimatis, had criticized the handling of the Cyprus question at the early stage, see above, Chapter I, p. 54. There seems to be no doubt that this aspect of the problem was neglected at the time. Yet, in spite of the purely legal fact of the cession of Cyprus by Turkey to Britain under Article 20 of the Treaty of Lausanne, there were early signs that Turkey was interested in the island's status and in the maintenance of that status. At the seventh General Assembly, in 1952, in the Third Committee, when the Greek representative made a reference to Cyprus, his Turkish colleague countered by expressing his government's interest in the island. Adil Derinsu pointed out that Cyprus was not inhabited entirely by Greeks. Consequently any consultation which might be arranged by the administering power should be so organized that the inhabitants of Turkish origin would have an opportunity to express their view. Turkey would support their rights in that respect. (*GAOR, Seventh Session*, Third Committee, 454th meeting, November 24, 1952, p. 223.) By early 1954, as already mentioned (see above, Introduction, pp. 10–11, n. 21) there had been additional indications of Turkey's interest in Cyprus.

13. *GAOR, Ninth Session*, Supplement 21, p. 5. See above, Introduction, pp. 13–14.

14. The night of March 31–April 1, 1955, several explosions near government, police, and military installations rocked Nicosia, Famagusta, Larnaca, and Limassol, and Grivas circulated his first proclamation to the people of Cyprus as leader of EOKA. (*Grivas Memoirs*, p. 35.) In this, he called upon the Cypriots to throw off the British yoke and to emulate the heroes of ancient Greece and of the Greek war of independence. He also appealed to the "diplomats of the world" to do their duty with regard to this struggle. March 25, Greek Independence Day, the Archbishop had suggested as the appropriate opening date for Grivas' operations. (British Information Services release T40, August 28, 1956, giving the text of a statement issued by the Colonial Office, on the Grivas Diaries, which Grivas himself [*op. cit.*, p. 127] acknowledged as genuine.) See also above, Chapter II, p. 71.

15. *Verbatim Record*, 847th meeting, February 18, 1957, pp. 72–77. Athens Radio, in accordance with law 2312 of 1953, was under Greek government control. It transmitted two special programs on Cyprus, containing commentaries. In the British analysis, see Appendix D, these contained incitements to insurrection, and praise for terrorists and for the murder of those who opposed *enosis*.

16. See above, Chapter IV, p. 160.

17. At the General Committee meeting of September 21, 1955, Anthony Nutting, Minister of State for Foreign Affairs, had argued that it was when passions were highest and divisions most acute that direct diplomatic contact and negotiations were most needed and could achieve success. Britain would persevere in its efforts. "If we are able to do this away from the atmosphere of political debate, of charge and counter-charge, I am convinced that, in time, with good will all around, we shall succeed." For these reasons, he had to oppose the inscription of the item proposed by

Greece. (A/BUR/102.) Lodge, too, had taken a similar attitude, saying that a fresh debate might be acrimonious and would not be conducive to a peaceful settlement of the question. (*Ibid.*) By seven votes to four, with four abstentions, the General Committee, on September 23, 1955, decided not to recommend the inclusion of the Cyprus item in the agenda. (See also above, Introduction, p. 22.)

18. See above, Chapter III, p. 123.

19. *Ibid.*, p. 127, for EOKA's response.

20. See above, Chapter III, p. n. 81.

21. See above, Chapter III, n. 90 on *enosis* and self-determination. At the time of the first Greek recourse, in 1954, Lloyd had voiced this charge. The Greek government, he said, appeared to be endeavoring to acquire for itself sovereignty over Cyprus by means of *enosis* between the island and the territory of Greece. It was asking the UN to interfere in the domestic affairs of a foreign power in order to make territorial gains. (*GAOR, Ninth Session*, General Committee, 93d meeting, September 23, 1954, p. 8.) At the Assembly's eleventh session, Noble asserted that it was the pursuit of *enosis* which had caused havoc in British-Greek relations and had also dangerously threatened the defenses of the world in southeast Europe. (*Verbatim Record*, 847th meeting, February 18, 1957, p. 56.)

22. This was the famous Lennox-Boyd formula of "double self-determination," presented to the House of Commons together with the Radcliffe draft Constitution on December 19, 1956. (See above, Chapter II, p. 89.)

23. Lord Radcliffe, *Constitutional Proposals for Cyprus* (London: H.M. Stationery Office, 1956), Cmd. 42. For details, see above, Chapter I, n. 13.

24. See above, Chapter I, p. 13, and below, Chapter IX, p. 312 for reasons of the Greek government's rejection of these proposals.

25. See above, Chapter II, p. 75–75.

26. *Ibid.*, p. 73.

27. See above, Chapter III, pp. 109–11, for Whitehall's view about the deadlock in May 1957.

28. The summary but official record (*GAOR, Twelfth Session*, First Committee, 927th meeting, December 9, 1957, p. 346, paragraph 11), gives the impression that what the verbatim record clearly shows to be a recapitulation of British policy in Cyprus since the end of World War II, describes efforts to reach a settlement since Lord Ismay's proposal of early 1957. The effect is to magnify British efforts to comply with Resolution 1013 (XI), regardless of the origin of the distortion of the summary but official record.

29. The Labour Opposition, it will be recalled, accused the British government of allowing matters to drift, see above, Chapter III, p. 149.

30. See above, Chapter IV, p. 154.

31. These, it will be recalled, included the maintenance of bases under British sovereignty in Cyprus, see above, Chapter IV, pp. 154, 168.

32. See also below Noble's reversion to the theme of the recrudescence of terrorism in Cyprus, which the Greek Foreign Minister was finding politically counterproductive and Grivas regarded mainly as reprisals against brutal behavior on the part of the local authorities. (See above, Chapter VI, 265, and *Grivas Memoirs*, p. 204.) On one occasion, Greek Cypriot villagers sent a protest to the UN about the behavior of British troops in their village. (*Ibid.*, Annex, p. 28). Between September 27 and November 27 there had been eight deaths attributed to EOKA violence, including those of a Turkish Cypriot policeman and of a British serviceman—the first British subject to be assassinated since Grivas' cease-fire of March 14,

1957. (*Keesing's 1958*, XII, 16219.) The assassinations of Greek Cypriots were, as mentioned earlier, regarded as warnings against would-be defectors from EOKA's ranks, or traitors of EOKA.

33. See above, Chapter VI, p. 258, for the British approach to the Greek government. Noble's remark suggests that a similar *démarche* was made with the Turkish government as well.

34. After the Suez fiasco of 1956, the number of British treaty obligations in the Middle East had been limited to the Baghdad Pact of 1955 and the tripartite declaration of May 1950 by Britain, France, and the United States. Article 51 of the Charter provides: "Nothing in the present Charter shall impair the inherent right of individual or collective self-defense if an armed attack occurs against a member of the United Nations, until the Security Council has taken the measures necessary to maintain international peace and security. Measures taken by members in the exercise of this right of self-defense shall be immediately reported to the Security Council and shall not in any way affect the authority and responsibility of the Security Council under the present Charter to take at any time such action as it deems necessary in order to maintain or restore international peace and security."

35. See above, Chapter VII, 294.

36. *GAOR, Eleventh Session*, Annexes, Agenda Item 55, pp. 10–16. It should be noted, in this connection, that the Greek Foreign Minister did not circulate at the twelfth session the pamphlet on undercover British intelligence activities mentioned in Chapter II, pp. 77–78.

37. *Verbatim Record*, 849th meeting, February 19, 1957, p. 16.

38. See also, Chapter I, n. 13.

39. On June 28, 1956, in an oral answer, Eden said he had no statement to make on Cyprus. He referred to the offers made during the Harding-Makarios talks (555 H.C. Deb. [5th ser.], pp. 692–93). Then, on July 12, 1956, outlining a new approach to the problem, he stated that the British government had accepted the principle of self-determination. The problem was, however, whether a solution concerning its application would be devised which would provide fully for the protection not only of Britain's interests in Cyprus and the eastern Mediterranean but also those of Turkey and other countries to whom Britain had treaty obligations. This, unfortunately, he added, had not been found possible. It had become plain, he said, that steps to create conditions which might lead to the application of self-determination would raise far wider issues for Turkey as a party to the Lausanne settlement. Thus, the British government had accepted that unilateral steps that would create conditions leading to self-determination could not be realized. Certain steps, however, could be taken within the island itself. Britain intended to proceed with the development of internal self-government and for this purpose had decided to send Lord Radcliffe to Cyprus for a preliminary visit without any terms of reference, for the time being. (556 H.C. Deb. [5th ser.], pp. 595–97.) Eden's statement had been made after Cypriot constitutional problems had been discussed in London by Governor Harding, British ministers, and service chiefs, between June 3–23, 1956. During the discussions, the British government had consulted with the Turkish government on matters relating to the Turkish Cypriot minority and Turkey's strategic interests in Cyprus. (*Keesing's, 1955–1956*, X, 15064). In a Commons debate on July 19, James Griffiths, Labour M.P., charged that Turkish objections had led to the dropping of an approach based on self-determination (*Ibid.*, 1398.)

In response, Lloyd made it quite clear that as a result of exchanges with the Turkish government, the British government had decided that progress could not be achieved along the line of self-determination and that it was better—indeed necessary—to pursue the alternative line of constitutional development. There would have been very grave dangers if the Turkish views were not taken into account, he added.

(*Ibid.*, pp. 405–6.) Griffiths, he went on to say, had failed to understand the position of the Turks, for whom Cyprus was an offshore island that covered the approaches to Turkey's southern ports. In support of the government position, he referred to a U.S. statement of July 14, 1956, that the United States welcomed the intention of the British government, as announced by Eden, to proceed with the development of self-government on the island of Cyprus. (*Ibid.*, 1409, 1412). It was during this debate, in response to Lloyd's statement that he had never heard the most virulent supporters of self-determination suggest that the Turkish Cypriots should have the right to self-determination, that Elliott came up with the suggestion of just that. Lord Radcliffe, he said, should have the power to consider partition of the island as one of the possible solutions. (*Ibid.*, 1422, see also above, Chapter II, p. 88.) Eden, at this time, regarded the alliance with Turkey as the first consideration "in our policy in that part of the world" and in a message to Eisenhower stressed the violent determination of the Turkish government against *enosis*. He asserted that there was in Turkey a pressure group of perhaps a quarter of a million Turkish Cypriots who played a part in molding Turkish opinion. "If anything in the nature of widespread communal disturbances were to break out," he added, "this would put a heavy and most disagreeable task upon our forces which would have to try to keep the parties apart and restore order." (Eden, *op. cit.*, p. 462.)

40. 562 H.C. Deb. (5th ser.), p. 1272. (Lennox-Boyd statement of December 19, 1956.)

41. See above, Chapter IV, p. 178.

42. *Verbatim Record*, 847th meeting, February 18, 1957, pp. 11–12. For 3,000 years, he had stressed then, that the ethnic character of the island had remained Greek, with foreign occupations constituting mere episodes which had not seriously altered the population's ethnic composition.

43. As will be seen below, the Turkish representative insisted on the term "Greek-speaking Cypriots."

44. Treaty of Peace Signed at Lausanne on July 24, 1923, League of Nations, *Treaty Series*, Vol. XXVIII, 1924.

45. For Turkish arguments about "encirclement," see below, p. 91, and note 344.

46. In the Aegean islands of Mytilene, Chios, Nikaria, and Samos, the Greek government undertook to observe the following restrictions under Article 13 of the Treaty of Lausanne of 1923:
(1) No naval base and no fortifications would be set up on the above islands.
(2) Greek military aircraft would be forbidden to fly over the Turkish coast, with Turkey reciprocally undertaking a similar obligation with regard to overflights over the Greek islands.
(3) The Greek military forces in the above islands would be limited to the normal contingent called up for military service, which could be trained on the spot, as well as to a force of gendarmerie and police in proportion to the force of gendarmerie and police existing in the whole of the Greek territory.
Under Article 14 of the Italian Peace Treaty of 1947, by which Italy ceded to Greece the Dodecanese islands, "these islands shall be and remain demilitarized." (U.S. Department of State, *Treaties and Other International Acts*, Series 1648). At the Assembly's twelfth session, Averoff-Tossizza did not couple this proposal for the demilitarization of Cyprus with a status of independence for the island as he had done at the previous session of the Assembly. (*Verbatim Record*, 854th meeting, February 21, 1957, pp. 98–100).

47. This formula about the people of Cyprus owning the island had been put forward during the Committee debate of the Cyprus question at the eleventh Assembly by the Greek Foreign Minister who had maintained that the territory belonged to the people; hence, though a transfer of sovereignty might be involved

should the right of self-determination be exercised, there was no "secession" of territory. (*Verbatim Record*, 854th meeting, February 21, 1957, p. 92.) This concept was connected with ideas Krishna Menon had expressed earlier, at the time of the first Greek recourse over Cyprus in 1954. (*GAOR*, Plenary Meetings, 477th meeting, p. 19), with Kyrou then presenting this idea in his statement before the Political Committee on December 14, 1954.

48. In the view of the Greek government, the Assembly's adoption, at its ninth session, on December 17, 1954, of Resolution 814 (IX) constituted a recognition of the "international character of the question of Cyprus, and the implementation of the right of self-determination of the Cypriot population—of the whole population of the island, whatever its racial, ethnic, historical, or linguistic origin or its religious belief—became a matter of United Nations concern." *GAOR, Ninth Session*, 514th Plenary Meeting, December 17, 1954, p. 540. (See also above, Introduction, p. 14.)

49. See above, Chapter I, p. 57, n. 64; Chapter V, p. 234.

50. This was Makarios' interpretation as well, see above, Chapter II, p. 74.

51. See above, Chapter II, p. 68.

52. See above, p. 309.

53. Charles Foley was founder and editor of the *Times of Cyprus*. He has written since several books on Cyprus and, together with Grivas, published an English version of the latter's memoirs, see below, Bibliography.

54. See above, Chapter II, p. 74.

55. The text of Lord Home's statement was as follows: "The Indian delegate also made a most constructive intervention. Indeed a welcome breath of realism came into the United Nations Assembly and carried the day, that the British Government and the people of Cyprus should be left to settle between themselves the future of the island of Cyprus, without external pressures and intervention." (202 H.L. Deb. [5th ser.], pp. 114–15, February 27, 1957.)

56. 566 H.C. Deb. (5th ser.), p. 1109.

57. For the Greek Foreign Minister's statement on the occasion, see *Cyprus before the United Nations*, p. 280. Barker, *op. cit.*, pp. 142–45 tells the Pallicaridis story, stressing that he had been convicted after trial for having killed a sixty-year-old Greek villager, who was said to collaborate with a Turkish policeman. *Keesing's 1957–1958*, XI, 15475, on the other hand, writes that Pallicaridis was hanged for carrying firearms in contravention of the emergency regulations, and that he had been the first to be executed for this offense. This emergency regulation had been introduced in November, 1956.

58. For his misgivings, see above, Chapter V, and pp. 279–80.

59. During the last few months of his governorship, Sir John Harding had commuted the death sentences of five convicted EOKA members—in four cases to life imprisonment and in one case to fifteen years' imprisonment. The commutations brought the total number of reprieves granted by Sir John to twelve. (*Keesing's 1958*, XII, 16219).

60. During this curfew, he said, no one was authorized to leave his house, and troops were liable to enter at all hours to search. Some victuals had been distributed to the villagers by the British authorities during the first two days, but they were quite inadequate, and the people of the neighboring villages were obliged to come to their assistance and feed them. But the crops had been lost and the cattle decimated. The sick, children, and elderly were completely isolated from the outside world. Doors and windows were closed to the light of day, and the souls of men were cut off from light and liberty. (See also above, Chapters III and V, pp. 101 and 199.)

61. One might suppose, he said, that those who applied these tortures were sexual perverts, since the tortures usually consisted of attacks on the genital organs. Not even priests had been spared the tortures of this variety.

62. These involved Pandelis Katemaris and Theodoros Papandreas, tortured on October 27 and November 9, respectively—the latter "by two abnormal characters, Linwood and Dear, torturers who have become notorious in Cyprus." The latter was shot by two EOKA members on April 14, 1958, dying of the wounds inflicted (*Keesing's 1958–1959*, XII, 16221).

63. See above, Chapter V, p. 201.

64. See above, Chapter III, p. 134. Both the verbatim and the official records mention the date of May 26. The correct date, however, is May 28, 1957.

65. See above, Chapter III, pp. 127.

66. See above, Chapter III, pp. 117, 121, for various versions of the British draft statement, starting with the one of November 21, 1955.

67. *Grivas Memoirs*, pp. 120–21; Foley edition of Grivas' *Memoirs*, pp. 87–88. Here is the story of this first truce offer in brief: On August 16, 1956, Grivas, in a leaflet signed "Dighenis," announced the suspension of EOKA operations, to test the sincerity of the British authorities who stated the EOKA's activities had created a situation in which it was impossible to achieve a just solution of the Cyprus problem. The government of Cyprus responded on August 22 by offering in great detail terms of surrender to EOKA members, giving them a choice either to leave Cyprus for Greece or to remain in Cyprus. To both choices certain conditions were attached. Next day, Grivas in a second "Dighenis" leaflet rejected this offer. (*Keesing's 1956*, X, 15061.) He ordered that operations be resumed on August 28. (*Grivas Memoirs*, p. 128). In the view of Averoff-Tossizza, as expressed to Counsellor Raymond Thurston, of the U.S. Embassy in Athens, on August 24, 1956, EOKA's truce offer had been a brave and bold act. It was surely no coincidence that it had occurred the day on which the Suez Canal Users' Conference was held in London. He supposed, he said, that the day had been chosen in order to show that the Greeks, old and faithful allies of the West, wished to stop war in order to facilitate matters. But the West, through the mouth of the British, had replied not only in an idiotic way because it had not availed itself of the opportunity that could save face for Britain, but also in an insulting way, because its tone was one that was used toward routed foes. The British attitude toward "Dighenis'" offer had doubly and deeply disappointed him. On the one hand it proved that Britain was not disposed to give a solution of any sort to the Cyprus problem but, on the contrary, wished to render the question more acute and perhaps even create difficulties for the Greek government so that internally a dangerous political situation should arise. On the other hand, it also proved for the first time the powerlessness of U.S. policy in this matter (he never doubted American good will). For, surely, the U.S. on this occasion must have sought to exert pressure on, or at least to advise the British government, and the results had demonstrated this impotence. On this occasion, the Greek Foreign Minister could not refrain from expressing to the U.S. diplomat his unpleasant surprise at the fact that Secretary of State Dulles had not seen fit to reply to a personal message of his, sent the day after the truce offer in which he suggested U.S. mediation in the Cyprus question at this point.

68. See above, Chapter III, p. 135.

69. A reference to the unfortunate remark of Secretary of State for Colonies Hopkinson in the House of Commons on July 28, 1954, which the Greeks, having in mind Eden's earlier categorically negative attitude in the Cyprus question, regarded as meaning that Cyprus, in spite of Hopkinson's later qualification, was, indeed, among those territories of the Commonwealth which could "never" expect to become

fully independent. (531 H.C. Deb. [5th ser.], p. 508.) See also above, Introduction, p. 10.

70. It will be recalled that Ambassador Seferiadis, in August, 1957, in a conversation at the Foreign Office, had used this phrase, see above, Chapter IV, p. 157.

71. The Opposition had frequently attacked the Greek government for not having published and exploited this information. (See above, Chapter I, p. 50.) It was to do so again after the twelfth General Assembly. (See below, Chapter XII, pp. 504-5.)

72. An analysis of this problem is contained in a lecture delivered in 1957 by C. Eustathiades, "Autodisposition, plébiscites internationaux et la these du partage de Chypre," *Etudes de Droit International 1929–1959* (Athens, 1959), II, 663 ff.

73. *Verbatim Record*, 856th meeting, February 22, 1957, p. 58.

74. The full statement is given below, with the passages in parentheses indicating the parts which the Greek Foreign Minister did not cite in his statement: (The Labour party calls attention to the critical situation again developing in Cyprus. The present stalemate between the British government and the Cypriot people exposes the failure of the Conservative policy there.) The Labour party has insisted, since the crisis began in 1954, that the people of Cyprus, like all other peoples, have a right to determine their own future. We have also emphasized our view that this right should be exercised after an agreed interim period of self-government. Such a procedure obviously requires the creation of representative institutions in which both Greek and Turkish Cypriots would play their respective parts; but the proposals for a constitution have hitherto been unacceptable in Cyprus because they have not included firm guarantees of self-determination after an agreed period, and we now call on Her Majesty's government to give such guarantees. We do not include partition within our definition of democratic self-determination.

(Although there have been international exchanges on the future status of the island, the British government has vacillated for three years on the central issue of self-determination.) The National Executive Committee of the Labour party demands that the government now break the deadlock by inviting representatives, chosen by the Greek and Turkish communities in Cyprus, to take part in discussions. The object of such discussions should be to reach agreement on the functions and powers of the interim government, the arrangements for its election, and the safeguarding of minority rights. In entering such discussions the British government must recognize that the major responsibility for the affairs of the island will rest in the hands of the Greek Cypriots, but that the legitimate rights of the Turkish minority must be safeguarded. The establishment of representative government in Cyprus is a necessary first step toward the fulfilment of the principle of self-determination in a democratic way. (We would therefore urge the British government to take a new initiative now, and the people of Cyprus to respond to such an invitation. We hope that the possibility of such discussions will not be impeded by any further outbreaks of violence.) (Text issued by the Labour party Press and Publicity Department, November 27, 1957.)

75. See above, Chapter VI, p. 250 for the Foreign Minister's discussion with the British Ambassador about the political significance of these Labour party statements.

76. *Ibid.*, p. 248.

77. See above, Chapter I, p. 42.

78. Greece lost about one tenth of its population or 700,000 lives during the period 1940–1949, Averoff-Tossizza stated.

79. The distinction of the two roles which speakers often assume at various points of their statements in the UN debates is made by Nicholas, *op. cit.*, p. 121. The one role is that of the representative of the nation; the other, that of a representative of

the international community. That other roles are played, too, is proposed in Conclusions, see below, p. 542.

80. The distances are those of the island from respective mainlands. However, the distance of Cyprus from the nearest Greek island territory, as Averoff-Tossizza was to point out, is 135 not 700 miles.

81. In his set statements in the Political Committee both at the ninth and eleventh sessions of the Assembly, Sarper had expounded at far greater length the Turkish geographical and historical arguments. At the former, he had stated that from the viewpoint of physical geography, Cyprus was part of Turkish territory as indicated by geological research. It had once been a peninsula attached to the Anatolian mainland. From the climatic viewpoint, too, he stressed then, Cyprus was a continuation of the southern regions of Anatolia. (For full text of this speech of December 14, 1954, Turkish Information Office, N.Y., *Turkish Views on Cyprus* [New York; n.d.], p. 8.) No such detailed analysis of the geographic argument was presented at the eleventh session. On this occasion, he laid great emphasis on the historic factor and on the theme that Cyprus had never belonged to Greece but to the various empires which had ruled Asia Minor. In remote history, Sarper acknowledged, there had been minor Greek colonies in Cyprus as there had been elsewhere in the Mediterranean—in Sicily, Marseilles, the Spanish coast. Yet the fate of the island had always been with Asia Minor. Thus, Cyprus had belonged to the Assyrian, Persian, and Arab empires, and to the Eastern Roman Empire, only as long as those empires ruled over Asia Minor. Even Alexander the Great held Cyprus not because Greece was under his rule but as a temporary conqueror of Asia Minor. And the Crusaders, with their kingdoms in Asia Minor (*sic*), had seen the necessity of ruling Cyprus. To call the Eastern Roman Empire a "Greek Empire" was, Sarper thought, a singular idea, and to bring in this argument as proof that Cyprus should belong to Greece seemed to him even more peculiar. The Greeks had been but one of the many subject peoples in the Eastern Roman Empire, which was no more Greek than the Western Roman Empire was Spanish or French. That many nations had shared a common destiny under the same Roman rule could not make one of them the sole heir of the Eastern Roman Empire. Of course, Sarper noted that from 1571 to 1923 Cyprus had been an integral part of Turkey (the Ottoman Empire). (*Verbatim Record*, 848th meeting, February 18, 1957, pp. 41–42.)

82. In his set statement at the Assembly's ninth session, Sarper had argued that just as he had demonstrated that Cyprus had no geographical or historical connection with Greece, so were the inhabitants of Cyprus not Greeks. In addition to 100,000 Turks, there were about 380,000 people who were of the Greek Orthodox Church and spoke Greek in a dialect that was peculiar to the island. This "Greek-speaking group" had no racial connection whatever with Greece, and belonged, he maintained, "to a race which historians describe as Mediterranean, or Mediterranean 'Levantine.'" Like many other races, this agglomeration, he said, had merits and characteristics of its own. For some reason, and in order to differentiate them they were called "Levantines." (Turkish Information Office, *op. cit.*, pp. 8–9.) Sarper then went on to underline that it was to the tolerant Ottoman administration that the "Greek-speaking people of Cyprus" owed not only their religious freedom but their freedom of language as well. At the Assembly's eleventh session, Sarper did not use in his set speech the term "Levantine" to denote the Greek Cypriots, but again stressed that this group had essentially no racial connection with the Greeks. By this time, it would seem, the Turkish government felt it was desirable to counter Krishna Menon's concept of a separate Cypriot nation, which raised problems for Turkish as well as Greek debaters.

83. Note the use of German terms loaded with Nazi connotations to denigrate Greek policy in the Cyprus question. (See also above, Chapter III, n. 21.) Sarper had again used this term in his set statement at the eleventh General Assembly where he

ad said that the Greek government was abusing the principle of self-determination in rder to impose a "Diktat" upon others, (*Ibid.*, p. 86.) At the ninth session, he even nore explicitly drew a parallel between Greek policy toward Cyprus and Nazi policy vith regard to Austria or Czechoslovakia's Sudetenland by using the word "Anchluss." (Turkish Information Office, *op. cit.*, pp. 14–15.) See also below, p. 342.

84. The concern of Turkey in the UN to dissociate itself from colonialism had been pparent at the Assembly's eleventh session, when Sarper had reacted sharply to the ;reek explanatory memorandum (see Appendix D), which contained many charges f "colonial oppression" or "colonial justice" against the British authorities in Cyprus. *Verbatim Record*, 848th meeting, February 18, 1957, pp. 25–26.) The agitation rganized in Greece over Cyprus, Sarper maintained, had nothing to do with colonialism" or "the principle of self-determination."

85. The lengthiest Turkish dissertation on self-determination is found in Sarper's tatement at the ninth Assembly. Its tenor was that, although self-determination ·estowed the benefits of freedom and independence on peoples and nations when ·roperly applied, it was a principle that threatened peace and tranquility and thereby lrove innocent people to anarchy when it was misused. Applied to the agglomeration alled a "nation," the theory of self-determination contradicted the principle of the sovereignty of the state" and thereby created problems that were difficult to resolve. ²o neglect self-determination in favor of exclusive adherence to the theory of the sovereignty of the state" paved the way to tyranny and despotism, whereas to hold elf-determination as more valuable than the "sovereignty of the state" gave rise to narchy (Turkish Information Office, *op. cit.*, pp. 11, 13). By the end of 1956, it hould be recalled, the Turkish government had accepted the concept of double elf-determination for the Greek and Turkish communities on the island. Accordingly, t set aside the theory about a conflict between the concepts of self-determination and overeignty.

86. *Verbatim Record*, 848th meeting, February 18, 1957, pp. 47–51; 53–55. The ·rinciple of self-determination, Sarper stated then, was not applicable in the case of he Greek claim to Cyprus. The case before the Committee was a claim for the evision of frontiers established by international treaty.

87. At the previous Assembly, too, Sarper had cited this statement. (*Ibid.*, pp. ;1–52.)

88. Sarper said that the Delegation of China at the United Nations Conference on nternational Organization (UNCIO) at San Francisco had furnished the draft for ·aragraph (b) of Article 73 of the Charter which referred to "the particular ircumstances of each territory and its people." However, on June 17, 1945, the)rafting Committee recommended the use of the plural "peoples" in the above ·hrase. Then, on June 19, Committee 4 of Commission II had recommended the .doption of this final text which was finally incorporated in the Charter.

89. See above, Chapter I, pp. 41–42.

90. Under the Treaty of Frederikshamn of 1809, Sweden ceded to Finland and the λland islands to Russia, so that both areas, in spite of a great degree of autonomy, ·ecame integral parts of the Russian Empire, with Russian sovereignty over them ·eing in no way affected by the non-fortification provisions agreed to by Russia, ¡ngland, and France in the Treaty of Paris of 1856. When early in December, 1917, he Finns declared their independence, the Alander members of the Finnish Diet ·oined in this declaration of independence, i.e., opted for joining the new Finnish state, ·r in Greek Cypriot terms, for *enosis*, regardless of their ethnic character. In January, ₁918, Sweden recognized the independence of Finland without making any reserva ions about the territorial extent of the new state. Thus, its silence could be construed ₁s a sort of acquiescence to the Finnish claim that the Aland islands were an integral ·art of the new and independent Finland. The Finns used this argument with great

effect during the negotiations on the Aland islands in the League of Nations and the Swedes had great difficulty in rebutting it. The population of the islands is 99 per cent Swedish, and in a series of unofficial plebiscites it opted overwhelmingly for union with Sweden. For the Swedes, however, the islands were separated from them by a large and deep channel. On the other hand, from the Finnish side, the island seemed like an extension of the mainland. Like Finland, Turkey, with regard to the Cyprus question, emphasized a similar geopolitical argument of propinquity. However, like Sweden in 1918, Turkey in 1923 had recognized British sovereignty over Cyprus without attaching any conditions. Hence, in 1954, it had no legal, as against a political, basis for arguing that it had a right to discuss the status of Cyprus if this matter were raised by other parties.

91. *Verbatim Record*, 848th meeting, February 18, 1957, p. 43-45. On that occasion, Sarper stressed that Turkey had only two open areas of communication with the rest of the world. If the country that held all the islands on the western approaches of Turkey—as was the case with Greece—were at the same time to hold Cyprus, which controlled all the remaining routes of communication, which were those of the south, then it would have encircled Turkey. "No country can allow itself to be so completely encircled and to leave its entire security at the mercy of one country, no matter how great a friend and ally the latter may be." This was a direct quotation from Zorlu's statement at the Tripartite London Conference (August 29–September 6, 1955). On that occasion, the Turkish Foreign Minister had described as follows the strategic reasons "that bind Cyprus to Turkey": Cyprus, of necessity, from the military point of view, should belong either to Turkey proper or to a country that was as closely interested as Turkey was in the fate of Eastern countries in the vicinity of Turkey. Namely, if Turkey or one of the countries of the Middle East which were bound to Turkey by military commitments should be involved in war, Cyprus, too, should be at war. The defense and logistics of the area, he maintained, could not be conceived otherwise. In the case of war, outside assistance to the war potential of Turkey could only come through its western and southern ports in the Mediterranean. Unfortunately, the western ports within the effective operations area of the potential enemy and Turkey at war could only be supplied through its southern ports. All these southern ports were under cover of Cyprus. Whoever controlled the island was in a position to control Turkish ports. If the power that controlled this island was also in control of the western islands (i.e. the Greek islands), it would have effectively surrounded Turkey. (*The Tripartite Conference*, pp. 22–23.) In a memorandum of August 19, 1954, to the UN, the Turkish government had stressed that, from the strategic standpoint, Cyprus was of prime importance for the defense of southern Turkey in particular and of the northeastern Mediterranean in general. Accordingly, it had to be in a position to be defended with the utmost effectiveness; it had to be maintained in a position to be able to fulfil its role as a point of great strategic value in all directions; finally, in order to attain the above-mentioned ends, complete order and stability should prevail on the island. (Turkish Information Office, *op. cit.*, pp. 26–27.)

92. 562 H.C. Deb. (5th ser.), p. 1272. See above, Chapter II, p. 89.

93. At the Assembly's previous session, Noble told the Committee that since Grivas started its activities on April 1, 1955, there had been 265 victims of the EOKA campaign. Of these, 131 were Greek Cypriots (119 civilians, the remainder members of the security forces); 101 British subjects (85 servicemen and police, and 16 civilians); most of the remainder were Turkish Cypriots, of whom nine belonged to the police force. (*Verbatim Record*, 847th meeting, February 18, 1957, p. 63–65.) During the four years of Cyprus troubles (1954–1959), some 506 were killed, more than half of them Greeks, and 1,260 people were wounded. Of those killed, there were 142 British (104 servicemen, 26 civilians, 12 policemen); 84 Turkish Cypriots (22 policemen, 62 civilians, of whom 55 were victims of intercommunal strife); and 278 Greek Cypriots (15 policemen, 236 civilians, of whom 60 were victims of

intercommunal strife). (*Keesing's 1959*, XIII, 16833.) To the number of Greek Cypriots must be added 150 who lost their lives fighting for EOKA, the victims of the Cypriot fight for freedom, as Grivas calls them, in a list of 204 names which also includes 54 Greek Cypriots killed by Turkish Cypriots in intercommunal strife. (*Grivas Memoirs*, XIII–XVIII.) Of these, 112 were killed by British servicemen or members of the security forces. Eight were hanged by the British authorities. Twenty-four were killed in accidents while engaged in EOKA activities, for instance through accidental explosions. Thus, during the period 1955–59, a total of 428 Greek Cypriots were killed.

94. *Verbatim Record*, 848th meeting, February 18, 1957, pp. 53–63.

95. See above, Chapters II and IV, pp. 73 and 177.

96. See above, Chapter III, p. 134.

97. For the Greek response to this sort of interpretation, see below, p. 348.

98. At the previous session of the Assembly, Sarper had stated, "in the case of Cyprus . . . an integral part of the Turkish mainland, the 380,000 Greek-speaking Cypriots should not be cast against the more than 100,000 Turkish Cypriots but should be taken into account in conjunction with the 25,000,000 Turks who compose the overall Turkish nation on the mainland." (*Verbatim Record*, 848th meeting, February 18, 1957, p. 51.) This argument, too, is found in Foreign Minister Zorlu's speech at the tripartite London conference of 1955, *The Tripartite Conference*, p. 22.

99. See above, Chapter IV, pp. 158–61.

100. See above, Chapter III, pp. 114 ff.

101. *White Book*, p. 1.

102. See especially Noble's opening statement, *Verbatim Record*, 847th meeting, February 18, 1957, pp. 62–77. Some of the information given by the British representative may have been based on the wiretapping activities mentioned above, Chapter II, pp. 77–78.

103. Probably a reference to the *Black Book* distributed by the Ethnarchy at the General Assembly's twelfth session, see above, Chapter VII, 281.

104. *Verbatim Record*, 848th meeting, February 18, 1957, pp. 37–38.

105. This is not correct. See above, Introduction, p. 6. Since early 1945 the Communist party of Greece had been clamoring for Cyprus as it was, too, for Eastern (Turkish) Thrace. (Xydis, *op. cit.*, pp. 88–93.) In 1945, Kyrou, at the other extreme, did not favor raising publicly the Cyprus problem lest this harm the cause. (*Ibid.*, p. 99, note 80.) And in 1941 and 1942, the Greek government raised this question, see above, Introduction, p. 6.

106. See above, note 83.

107. See above, Introduction, pp. 6–7.

108. In the *New York Times*, September 13, 1955, Kennett Love reported that Makarios had told him that "self-determination has become the battlecry of Cypriot Greeks in recent months, instead of *enosis* by which is meant unity with Greece. But this is a change in tactics not in ultimate aims."

109. *Verbatim Record*, 848th meeting, February 18, 1957, pp. 38–40.

110. Turkish Information Office, *op. cit.*, pp. 7–8.

111. See above, Chapter I, p. 54.

112. See above, Chapter I, pp. 42, 53. *GPD*, March 14, 1957, p. 102.

113. See above, Chapter III, p. 112.

114. See above, p. 327.

115. See above, Chapter III, p. 114, note 30.

116. See above, Chapter VII, p. 291.

117. *The Tripartite Conference*, pp. 24 (regarding the "Megali Idea"), 37–38. Perhaps more acrimonious remarks were made in the unpublished speeches of the Turkish Foreign Minister at that conference.

118. The Treaty of Sèvres was signed on August 10, 1920. The Greek troops had landed in Izmir (Smyrna) in May of the previous year, with the approval of the British, French, Italian, and U.S. governments. N. X. Rizopoulos, "Greece at the Paris Peace Conference," Doctoral Dissertation, Yale University, 1963, pp. 209–10.

119. *Grivas Memoirs*, p. 29. *Keesing's 1955*, X, 14221. On December 18, 1954, a twenty-four hour strike took place in protest against the UN's decision not to consider self-determination for Cyprus, and demonstrations occurred in Nicosia and other cities. In the capital, students and schoolboys stoned the windows of British-owned stores and bars as well as of the U.S. Consulate. The police, in efforts to disperse the crowds, made repeated truncheon charges and used tear gas. Before the situation was brought under control, some fifty persons were arrested. In Limassol, students hauled down the Union Jack from the District Commissioner's office and in its place hoisted the Greek flag, while stone-throwing crowds defied repeated appeals to disperse. British troops, then, fired three shots, wounding two of the demonstrators. Casualties totaled twenty-three. Some of the older demonstrators were sentenced to three or four months' imprisonment.

120. See above, Chapter III, p. 125.

121. *Ibid.*, p. 127.

122. *Ibid.*, p. 148.

123. *Ibid.*, pp. 134–35.

124. For Spaak's interest in the Cyprus question, see above, Chapters III, IV, and VI, 137, 186, 242, respectively. Toward mid-September, 1957, Governor Harding, in an interview with a Yugoslav journalist, said he visualized a solution of "independence" with dual power, i.e., of the Cypriot people and of a Council appointed by NATO and consisting of a Briton, a Greek, and a Turk. The Governor was opposed to UN interference because of the possible infiltration of the U.S.S.R. in the island. Only NATO was acceptable to Britain, for exerting supervision over the regime of Cyprus through the proposed Council. The solution should ensure a British base on the island that would be subject to no restrictions. It should exclude any Communist infiltration. It should also ensure internal peace. These were the same points the British government had emphasized in its soundings of the Greek government in August, see above, Chapter IV, p. 154.

125. See above, Chapter III, p. 150.

126. See above, Chapter VII, p. 296.

127. The verbatim proceedings of the Foreign Minister's speech contains no such word. On the other hand, he frequently used the term "atrocities."

CHAPTER IX

1. See above, Introduction, pp. 22–23; Chapter I, n. 61.

2. See above, Chapter I, pp. 41–42.

3. For earlier threats, through the diplomatic channel, see above, Chapter II, pp. 79–80.

4. See above, Chapter V, p. 219.

5. See above, Chapter VIII, p. 338.

6. See above, Chapter II, p. 84.

7. See above, Chapter VIII, p. 335.

8. The Greek Foreign Minister's reference to the questions of Morocco, Tunisia, Algeria, and West Irian reveals the extent to which these cases influenced Greek foreign policy–makers in dealing with the Cyprus question. Here is a summary of these questions up to 1958.

i. The Moroccan Question. At the sixth Assembly in 1951, six Arab states complained that the French had violated the principles of the Charter in Morocco and asked the Assembly to consider the matter. However, the Assembly postponed the question's consideration "for the time being," as it would with regard to the Cyprus question at its ninth session in 1954. The Moroccan question again came up at the Assembly's seventh session, in 1952, and on December 19 a resolution sponsored by eleven Latin American States expressed "confidence" that France would "endeavor to further the fundamental liberties" of the Moroccan people and that the parties would "continue negotiations toward developing the free political institutions of the people of Morocco." The eighth, ninth, and tenth Assemblies again discussed the Moroccan issue, and on December 3, 1955, the latter Assembly adopted a resolution, whereby, in view of the imminent negotiations between France and Morocco, it decided to postpone further consideration of the item. On March 2, 1956, representatives of France and Morocco signed a joint declaration by which the former recognized the latter's independence. (*Everyman's United Nations* [sixth edition], pp. 136–37).

ii. The Tunisian Question. Eleven Asian and African UN members, on April 2, 1952, asked the Security Council to consider "the present grave situation in Tunisia." However, on April 14, the Security Council refused to include the question in its agenda. Then, on July 30, the same eleven states asked that the question be included in the agenda of the seventh Assembly, with the Assembly deciding to consider the question on October 16. On December 17, 1952, the Assembly adopted a resolution in which it expressed "the hope" that the parties would continue negotiations with a view to bringing about self-government for the Tunisians and appealed to the parties to settle their disputes in accordance with the spirit of the Charter. The eighth and ninth General Assemblies likewise included the question in their agenda. The latter failed to adopt a draft resolution introduced by thirteen of the sponsoring states which the First Committee had adopted and which had been amended in the Assembly. On December 17, 1954, on the other hand, it adopted a resolution under which the Assembly, noting with satisfaction that the parties concerned had entered into negotiations, expressed "confidence" that the negotiations would bring about a satisfactory solution and decided to postpone further consideration of the question. Finally, agreement was reached between France and Tunisia on March 20, 1956, and Tunisia applied for membership in the UN on July 14, being admitted on November 12, 1956. (*Ibid.*, pp. 156–57.)

iii. The Algerian Question. This question was first raised in the eleventh Assembly in 1956 by fifteen Asian and African states. On February 15, 1957, the Assembly expressed the hope that in a spirit of co-operation a peaceful, democratic, and just solution would be found, in conformity with the principles of the UN Charter. At the next Assembly, twenty-two Asian and African states requested inclusion of the Algerian question in the agenda. On December 10, 1957, the Assembly expressed its concern over the situation in Algeria, took note of the offer of good offices made by the King of Morocco and the President of Tunisia, and expressed the wish that in a spirit of effective co-operation, *pourparlers* would be entered into and other appropriate means utilized with a view to a solution in conformity with the purposes and principles of the Charter. (*Ibid.*, p. 141.)

iv. The Question of West Irian (West New Guinea). On August 17, 1954, Indonesia asked for the inclusion of this question in the agenda of the ninth Assembly. On November 30, 1954, the First Committee adopted a draft resolution which provided that the Assembly would "express the hope" that Indonesia and the Netherlands would pursue their endeavors to find a solution to the dispute in conformity with the principles of the UN Charter, and request the parties to report progress to the Assembly's next session. However, in the Assembly, the required two-thirds vote was not forthcoming for any of the parts of this draft resolution, which was not put to the vote as a whole. Afghanistan and fourteen other members introduced the question at the tenth Assembly in 1955, and on December 16 the Assembly adopted a resolution expressing "the hope" that the negotiations which would commence shortly between Indonesia and the Netherlands would be fruitful. This hope not being realized, the question appeared again in the agenda of the eleventh Assembly at the request of sixteen Asian and African states. The First Committee adopted a thirteen-power draft resolution whereby the Assembly would request its President to appoint a good offices commission to assist in negotiations between Indonesia and the Netherlands in order that a "just and peaceful solution" might be achieved in conformity with the principles and purposes of the Charter. The Assembly, however, failed to adopt this draft resolution, which did not obtain the required two-thirds majority. At its twelfth session, the Assembly again included the question in its agenda on September 18, 1957, but again failed to adopt a draft resolution recommended by the First Committee. Under the terms of this draft resolution, the Assembly would invite both parties to pursue their endeavors to find a solution of the dispute in conformity with the principles of the UN Charter, and would request the UN Secretary-General to assist the parties concerned in the implementation of the Assembly resolution. (*Ibid.*, p. 114–15.)

9. On the basis of proposals submitted by a special mission of the Trusteeship Council to British Togoland, the Assembly, at its tenth session in 1955, resolved that a plebiscite should be conducted there to determine whether the people desired union with neighboring Gold Coast (later Ghana) or wished to continue under trusteeship, pending on ultimate settlement of the territory's future. On May 9, 1956, a plebiscite under UN supervision revealed that 93,365 favored union; 67,422 supported the alternative choice. The Assembly decided to interpret these plebiscite results as a whole. Accordingly, the territory was united with the Gold Coast to form the new independent state of Ghana on March 6, 1957. (*Ibid.*, p. 370).

10. In this speech before the General Committee, on September 23, 1954, Lloyd had predicted such disturbances in Cyprus. (*GAOR, Ninth Session*, General Committee, 93d meeting, 9.) And earlier that year, in a conversation with the Greek Ambassador in London, he had predicted trouble. (See above, Introduction, p. 9.)

11. As of December 31, 1956, there were 697 Greeks and 1,135 Turks in the Cypriot police; 1,475 special Turkish gendarmes and 1,417 Turkish auxiliary police on a population ratio of 80 per cent Greek Cypriots and 18 per cent Turkish Cypriots. (*Grivas Memoirs*, p. 211.) On May 14, 1957, Lennox-Boyd, in the House of Commons, stated that the strength of the auxiliary police was 1,399. Of these, 46 were Greek Cypriots and 1,335 Turkish Cypriots. (570 H.C. Deb. [5th series], 14.)

12. See above, Chapter VIII, pp. 331, 341–42.

13. *Ibid.*, p. 334.

14. *Ibid.*, p. 340.

15. *Ibid.*, p. 316.

16. *Ibid.*, p. 317.

17. *Ibid.*, p. 306.

18. The *Verbatim Record* omitted the last paragraph of Lodge's statement, unlike the official summary record or the text published in the *Bulletin of the Department of State*, XXXVIII (January 6, 1958), 31–32. If this omission actually was the result of Lodge's not having read this paragraph of the official U.S. statement, and if this omission had been intentional, perhaps it was due to an effort to spare the susceptibilities of the Greek Delegation, which was so anxious that U.S. statement should not influence other Committee members.

19. Convention of Defensive Alliance between Great Britain and Turkey, signed at Constantinople on June 4, 1878 (*British and Foreign State Papers*, LXIX, 1877–78, 744.)

20. Order in Council Relative to the Annexation of the Island of Cyprus to His Majesty's Dominions, London, November 5, 1914. (*Ibid.*, CVIII (1914) Part II, 165.)

21. *New York Times*, December 10, 1957, reported that disorders had erupted all over Cyprus and seventy-five had been hurt and eighty arrested. Also, *Grivas Memoirs*, pp. 210–11. See also above, Chapter VIII, p. 302.

22. Grivas himself mentions two leaflets of November 5 and 7, 1957. A quotation from the former said that it was the duty of any enslaved people to kill as many invaders as possible and all those who warmed their hands at the hearth of conquerors. On December 4, 1957, Grivas had circulated an order in which he wrote that EOKA would never cease its struggle unless it received guarantees that the principle of self-determination would be applied. (*Grivas Memoirs*, pp. 204–5.) Papageorgiou, *op. cit.*, pp. 88–91, publishes the texts of two defiant leaflets circulated on the eve of the UN debate but gives them no date.

23. See above, Chapter V, 203.

24. See above, Chapter VIII, pp. 301–2.

25. *Ibid.*, p. 321.

26. *Ibid.*, pp. 305 ff.

CHAPTER X

1. Lord Radcliffe, *Constitutional Proposals for Cyprus* (London: H.M. Stationery Office, 1956), Cmnd. 42 For details and Greek reaction, see above, Chapter I n. 13; and Chapter VIII, 312.

2. The plebiscite had taken place on January 15, 1950. The Ethnarchy, under Makarios' predecessor, had organized it. As Bishop of Kition, however, Makarios had played an important role in its organization; 95.7 per cent voted for union—*enosis*—with Greece. The results were communicated to the British and Greek governments as well as to the UN. In the plebiscite, all Greek Cypriots of age eighteen and over, of both sexes, were allowed to vote by signing their name on sheets provided in the churches throughout the island. An Archiepiscopal encyclical of December 8, 1949, had urged voters to vote for *enosis*. Out of 224,747 Greek Cypriots eligible to take part in the plebiscite, 215,108 actually did so. Civil servants and other government employees did not take part. (Mayes, *op. cit.*, p. 19.)

3. *Verbatim Record*, 848th meeting, February 18, 1957, pp. 66–72.

4. See above, Chapter VIII, p. 302.

5. *New York Times,* December 12, 1957, reported that the Turkish government had urged Britain to prevent the murder of Turkish Cypriots.

6. See above, Chapter IX, p. 365.

7. In 647-49 A.D. the Amir of Syria, Mu'awiyia, attacked Cyprus for the first time. The Arabs overran Cyprus again in 653 A.D. and established a garrison which was withdrawn after 680. Then, until Emperor Nicephorus Phocas, in 965, took over Cyprus, the island was neither under Arab nor under Byzantine control. (*Encyclopaedia Britannica* [1963 ed.], VI, 952.)

8. Cyprus, the Syrian observed, had been used as a base in the Anglo-French attack on Egypt in 1956.

9. For Averoff-Tossizza's proposal of demilitarization, see above, Chapter IX, pp. 358-59. Evidently, because of the Syrian-Turkish crisis, Zeineddine did not revert to the suggestion he had made at the previous Assembly that Greece and Turkey negotiate together to relieve the tensions affecting them because of the Cyprus dispute. (*Verbatim Record,* 852d meeting, February 22, 1957, p. 4.)

10. *Defense: Outline of Future Policy* (London: H.M. Stationery Office, 1957) Cmd. 124.

11. See above, Chapter VIII, p. 336.

12. See above, Chapter III, p. 133.

13. See above, Introduction, p. 8.

14. On April 24, 1953, Makarios had requested the Governor of Cyprus, in accordance with UN Resolution 637 (VII) of December 16, 1952, to respect the result of the plebiscite of 1950 or to facilitate the realization of the right of self-determination through a new plebiscite to be held as soon as possible. Royal Greek Embassy Information Service, *Cyprus Demands Self-Determination* (Washington, D.C.: October, 1954), p. 7.

15. *Ibid.,* pp. 21-36 (Appendices A and B).

16. *GAOR, Eighth Session,* plenary meetings, 439th meeting, September 21, 1953, pp. 66-67. See Introduction, p. 5.

17. See above, Chapter IX, p. 371.

18. *Disturbances in Cyprus, 1931* (London: H.M. Stationery Office, 1932), Cmd. 4045, p. 22, refers to Loizidis as one of the agitators.

19. His brother Socrates had been seized when the British authorities intercepted the sailing vessel "Aghios Georghios" which was bringing arms and munitions to Cyprus in January, 1955 (*Grivas Memoirs,* p. 31). Mayes, *op. cit.,* pp. 32 and 231.

20. Mayes, *op. cit.,* pp. 83-86, on the other hand, gives several examples, the earliest one of 1893, of Turkish Cypriot protests against suggestions by Britishers or Greek Cypriots that the island be united to Greece.

21. Article 20 of the Treaty of Lausanne provided that "Turkey hereby recognizes the annexation of Cyprus proclaimed by the British Government on 5th November, 1914."

22. Since the establishment of an independent Greece, wars with Turkey occurred in 1897, 1912-13, and 1917-1922.

23. On January 11, 1956, a Turkish police sergeant who had given evidence at the trial of *EOKA* members was shot dead. This precipitated Turkish Cypriot attacks against Greek stores in Nicosia. The Turkish underground organization *Volkan* issued on that occasion leaflets threatening reprisals—five Greek lives for every Turk killed. Dr. Kuchuk protested to Governor Harding and in a message to Makarios demanded that the Greek community should condemn the murder. On March 19, 1956, fighting

broke out between Greek and Turkish Cypriots at the village of Vassilia, near Nicosia, and about twenty people were hurt. Next day, in reprisal, some 500 Turks smashed the windows of Greek-owned shops and offices in the Turkish quarter of Nicosia. On April 23, 1956, fighting broke out in Nicosia between Turkish and Greek Cypriots after a Turkish policeman had been shot dead by terrorists. Communal rioting broke out next day and continued on April 25. Then, on May 25, in revenge for the murder of Police Constable Ahmed, crowds of Turkish Cypriots attacked and smashed Greek stores and premises in Nicosia, Limassol, Larnaca, and Paphos. Kuchuk, in cables to Premier Menderes, Hammarskjöld, Lennox-Boyd, and John Foster Dulles, denounced the terrorists and declared that the Turkish Cypriots were determined never to live under Greek rule. (*Keesing's 1957-1958*, XI, 14694, 14762, 14901, 14902.) There were Turkish riots again in January and February, 1957. (*Ibid.*, 15478-79.)

24. Omer Sami Gosar, of the Turkish newspaper *Cumhuriet*, had written this letter.

25. The full citation, as given by Loizidis, reads as follows: "We were in Istanbul when Nansen proposed that a treaty of exchange should be drawn up at Lausanne. Within a week, we had a deputation of a dozen Turks from Greece, and this is what they said—this is what the Turks said to this Committee: 'Dr. Nansen, we have just lived through ten years of war between Greece and Turkey. Terrible events have happened in Asia Minor in the last two months. In all that time, no Greek has ever raised a hand against us. Our persons, our rights, our churches and our schools have been respected. Please leave us now in our homes among our brother Greeks.'"

26. See above, Chapter V, p. 216.

27. The journalist was Iris Russell of the *Sunday Dispatch*. She reported, among other things, that an emergency regulation had been introduced to prevent the prosecution of any member of the security forces without the consent of the Attorney-General. More than one hundred cases of complaints had been sent to the Governor, but in all cases the reply had been that the allegations were unfounded, grossly exaggerated, or completely untrue.

28. See above, Chapter III, p. 146, about the Greek application to the Human Rights Commission of the Council of Europe.

29. This was a reference to what became Resolution 1188 (XII) entitled "Recommendations Concerning International Responsibility for the Right of Peoples and Nations to Self-Determination." (*GAOR, Twelfth Session*, Annexes, Agenda Item 32, p. 4.) The U.S. voted in favor of this resolution. Britain, on the other hand, voted against its first operative clause and abstained on the whole.

30. *GAOR, Eleventh Session*, Fourth Committee, 553d meeting, November 23, 1956, pp. 13-14.

31. Loizidis was evidently referring to press reports about demonstrations in Cyprus.

32. It had been Sir Leslie Munro, head of the New Zealand Delegation, who, speaking on a point of order, had moved at the ninth Assembly in 1954 that the Assembly should not consider further the Cyprus question. (*GAOR, Ninth Session*, First Committee, 748th meeting, December 14, 1954, p. 543.) See Introduction, p. 13.

33. 531 H.C. Deb. (5th ser.), p. 508. See Introduction, p. 10.

34. See above, Chapter VIII, pp. 303-4.

35. For text, see above, Chapter VII, p. 296.

36. See above, Chapter VIII, pp. 322-23.

37. In a letter of March 13, 1897, to the Duke of Westminster, Gladstone had

written the following: "I subjoin the satisfaction I should feel were it granted me, before the close of my long life, to see the population of that Hellenic island placed by a friendly arrangement in organic union with their brethren of the Kingdom of Greece." (Greek Government, Press and Information Department, Prime Minister's Office, *Documents and Press Comments on the Cyprus Question,* Athens, 1954, p. 7.) In a letter of November 14, 1919, Prime Minister D. Lloyd George had written to the Archbishop of Cyprus that "the wishes of the inhabitants of Cyprus for union with Greece will be taken into a most careful and sympathetic consideration by the government when they consider its future." (*Ibid.,* p. 7.) In an address to the Legislative Council in Nicosia, in 1907, Churchill had said: "I think it is only natural that the Cypriot people, who are of Greek descent, should regard their incorporation with what may be called their mother country as an ideal to be earnestly, devoutly, and fervently cherished. Such a feeling is an example of patriotic devotion which so nobly characterizes the Greek nation." (*Ibid.,* p. 7.). Mayes, *op. cit.,* p. 84, points out that Churchill went on to mention "the opinion held by the Moslem population of the island." He also asserts that *enosis* propagandists frequently insert a comma after the words "Cypriot people" which makes the relative non-restrictive. As may be seen above, the Greek government publication mentioned in this note used the comma.

38. See above, Chapter III, pp. 114 ff.

39. *Ibid.,* pp. 117, 119.

40. Arenales Catalan had stated then that the Cyprus problem had two aspects which had to be taken into consideration when the draft resolutions were being considered. There was, first, the internal aspect, with the people of Cyprus being the main party concerned; and the external aspect, with Greece, Britain, and Turkey being the main parties concerned. "The position of Guatemala vis-à-vis the draft resolutions is to be based on the following. First, the United Kingdom does not state that Cyprus is to be an integral part of its metropolitan territory. . . . [it] simply proclaims that it has sovereignty over Cyprus, whether it be called a colony or a non-self-governing territory." Guatemala, he had then said, had always denied that an administering authority had sovereignty over the administered. The British government itself had admitted the application of the principle of self-determination in Cyprus and had merely conditioned it as to time. Therefore, it was accepted by the Guatemalan Delegation that Britain did not have sovereignty over Cyprus. Secondly, Greece had declared it did not want sovereignty over Cyprus. Thirdly, Turkey had stated it had ceded sovereignty, which implied it did not intend to re-establish sovereignty. If none of these states had sovereignty over Cyprus, who had? Who, then was to decide on the fate of its inhabitants? It appeared then that one was faced with a typical case of the application of the principle of self-determination. "If in a case of this nature we do not apply it, then why was it proclaimed in the Charter?" (*Verbatim Record,* 855th meeting, February 22, 1957, pp. 61-62.) It should be added that the verbatim proceedings of Arenales Catalan's speech at the twelfth Assembly contain an entire section that precedes this reference to his speech at the eleventh session. This large section of the Guatemalan's speech mentions views supposedly expressed by him at the ninth session as well, and contains comments on the tenth session's decision not to include the Cyprus item on the Assembly's agenda. However, the official record of the ninth session indicates that no Guatemalan representative spoke on that occasion. The official (summary) record of his speech at the twelfth session makes no reference to this supposed Guatemalan intervention at the Assembly's ninth session—which indicates that the Guatemalan Delegation corrected this error. Arenales Catalan was evidently referring to his remarks in the General Committee on September 18, 1957. (See above, Chapter V, pp. 211-12. *GAOR, Twelfth Session,* First Committee, 931st meeting. December 11, 1957, p. 379.)

41. The verbatim proceedings indicate that Entezam had said "the two parties," and this which suggested an acceptance of the Greek viewpoint. However, the official

record, evidently corrected by the Iranian Delegation, uses the expression "all parties"—which was more neutral or closer to the British and Turkish views (*GAOR, Twelfth Session,* First Committee, 931st meeting, December 11, 1957, p. 380.)

42. In this Greek government explanatory memorandum of June 13, 1956, sent to the Secretary-General (see Appendix D), it was stated, on the one hand, that free men and free peoples always considered that the only possible answer to violence was violence. On the other hand, it was said that on the British side violence was being used against freedom, whereas on the Cypriot side violence was used in favor of freedom, and that in neither case violence should be praised. Greece, it was maintained, was against violence and favored a peaceful approach. In taking the Cyprus issue to the UN in 1954, it had tried to prevent violence.

43. Rule 116 provides that "during the course of a debate the Chairman may announce the list of speakers and, with the consent of the committee, declare the list closed. He may, however, accord the right of reply to any member if a speech delivered after he has declared the list closed makes this desirable."

44. See above, Chapter I, p. 40.

45. Under Resolution 421 D (V), the Assembly, after considering that the list of human rights in the first eighteen articles of the Universal Declaration of Human Rights did not contain some of the most elementary rights, and that in drafting the Convention, the purposes and principles of the Charter would in the future have to be taken into account, and that these purposes and principles should be implemented and applied logically and assiduously protected, called upon the Economic and Social Council to request the Commission on Human Rights to study ways and means of guaranteeing to peoples and to nations the right of self-determination and to prepare recommendations for consideration by the General Assembly at its sixth session. (*GAOR, Fifth Session,* Resolutions adopted, 42–43.)

46. Under Resolution 545 (VI), the Assembly, taking into account that, because of lack of time, neither the Economic and Social Council nor the Commission of Human Rights had been able to fulfil the request formulated in part D of Resolution 421 (V), and that the violation of the right to self-determination had resulted in bloodshed and war in the past, and was considered a continuous threat to peace, decided to include in the Universal Declaration of Human Rights an article on the right of peoples and nations to self-determination, thus reaffirming the principle contained in the UN Charter. (*GAOR, Sixth Session,* Resolutions adopted, p. 36–37.) See also above, Introduction, p. 7.

47. See above, Chapter VII, p. 294.

48. See above, Chapter III, pp. 154 ff.

49. See above, Chapter IX, p. 369.

50. *Ibid.,* p. 371.

51. See above, Chapter I, p. 47.

52. The official record does not contain the criticism of Lodge and of U.S. policy contained in this paragraph. It is, therefore, of no use for understanding the U.S. protest through the diplomatic channel which this statement triggered. (See below, Chapter XII, 483.) It is possible that the Greek Delegation saw to it that the gist of these critical remarks was expunged from the record.

53. See above, Chapter VIII, 320.

54. See above, Chapter IX, p. 374.

55. *Verbatim Record,* 849th meeting, February 19, 1957, 17.

56. *New York Times,* December 12, 1957, reported that after two days of rioting,

Cyprus had returned to relative calm, and that Sir Hugh Foot had appealed to Mayor Dervis for the latter's co-operation in halting this violence.

57. See above, statements by the representatives of the U.S.S.R., Chapter VIII, p. 352; Ceylon, Yugoslavia, the Ukrainian S.S.R., Romania, Colombia, Chapter IX, pp. 358, 370, 371, 372, 376; Czechoslovakia, Bolivia, Federation of Malaya, Syria, Nepal, Byelorussian S.S.R., Hungary, Sudan, Ethiopia, Ireland, Guatemala, Uruguay, and Panama, Chapter X, pp. 382 ff.

58. See above, statements by the representatives of the U.S., Afghanistan, Belgium, France, New Zealand, Australia, Netherlands, Pakistan, Portugal, and Iran, Chapter IX, pp. 371, 384, 385, 400, 403-5, 407, 409.

59. See above, Chapter VIII, p. 345.

60. Averoff-Tossizza probably had in mind Secretary of State Dulles.

61. In the Greek Parliament, on November 29, 1956, the Foreign Minister had declared that Greece did not recognize that Turkey should have a right of veto about the future of the island, namely that Turkey had basic and general interests with regard to the island's future. Greece, however, did recognize that Turkey had a number of special interests which had to be covered. (*GPD*, November 29, 1956, p. 88.)

62. See above, Chapter VIII, p. 306.

63. See above, p. 402.

64. See above, p. 415.

65. See above, Chapter III, p. 120, for a similar approach during the Harding-Makarios talks.

66. Rule 119 of the rules of procedure provides that "during the discussion of any matter, a representative may move the suspension or the adjournment of the meeting. Such motions shall not be debated, but shall be immediately put to the vote. The President may limit the time to be allowed to the speaker moving the suspension or adjournment of the meeting."

CHAPTER XI

1. Rule 121 of the rules of procedure provides, among other things, that "as a general rule, no proposal shall be discussed or put to the vote at any meeting of the committee unless copies of it have been circulated to all delegations not later than the day preceding the meeting."

2. *GAOR, Twelfth Session*, Annexes, Agenda Item 58, p. 8.

3. See above, Chapter VIII, 340.

4. See above, Chapter X, pp. 422-23.

5. *Ibid.*, p. 390.

6. Rule 131 of the rules of procedure provides that, "when an amendment is moved to a proposal, the amendment shall be voted on first. When two or more amendments are moved to a proposal, the committee shall first vote on the amendment furthest removed in substance from the original proposal and then on the amendment next furthest removed there from, and so on, until all the amendments have been put to the vote. Where, however, the adoption of one amendment necessarily implies the rejection of another amendment, the latter amendment shall not be put to the vote. If one or more amendments are adopted, the amended

proposal shall then be voted upon. A motion is considered an amendment to a proposal if it merely adds to, deletes from or revises part of that proposal."

7. See above, n. 6.

8. Peru, together with the Philippines and Sweden, had been a member of the standing Committee the Assembly had set up in 1950 to deal with the matter of the 5,000 Greek children who had been removed from Greece and retained in the territories of the northern neighbors of Greece. (*Everyman's United Nations*, pp. 66.)

9. The Spanish subamendment read as follows: "*expresses the wish* that further negotiations and discussions between those concerned will be promptly undertaken" instead of "*expresses its earnest hope.* . . ." *GAOR, Twelfth Session*, Annexes, Agenda Item 58, p. 8.

10. At the time of the Paris Peace Conference and its aftermath in the Council of Foreign Ministers in 1946, when the Greek government had expressed similar fears about the public Greek reaction to the negative attitude of the U.S. toward the Greek territorial claims against Bulgaria and Albania, the State Department had responded in a similar way. (Xydis, *op. cit.*, p. 415.)

11. See above, Chapter X, p. 408.

12. Uruguay had voted for the seventeen-state draft resolution on Algeria (*GAOR, Twelfth Session*, Annexes, Item 62, p. 5).

13. The first passage from the speech of Mariano J. Drago, of Argentina, quoted by the Spanish representative was the following: "Thus, the words 'self-determination of peoples,' as used in Article 1, paragraph 2, of the Charter, refer only to the freedoms of sovereign peoples to choose a government. There would be no sense to this principle of the Charter if the intention was that one of the conditions of the development of friendly relations among nations should be the right of peoples to self-determination." (A/C.1/PV.921, p. 26.) The second passage was the following: 'The erroneous interpretation of paragraph 2 of Article 1 has given rise to the slogan the right of peoples to self-determination'—a slogan so often cited during this debate. But nothing of the kind exists. Neither paragraph of Article 1 nor any other provision of the Charter incites non-self-governing peoples to rebellion—that is, those peoples who, under the definition contained in article 73 of the Charter, have not yet attained full measure of self-government.'"

14. See above, p. 440.

15. The Turkish invocation of Article 33 as well as the unfounded charge that the Greek subamendment had contained no reference to "negotiations" were dropped from the official but summary record. (*GAOR, Twelfth Session*, First Committee, 34th meeting, 394.) Article 33 of the Charter provides that (1) the parties to any dispute, the continuance of which is likely to endanger the maintenance of international peace and security, shall, first of all, seek a solution by negotiation, inquiry, mediation, conciliation, arbitration, judicial settlement, resort to regional agencies or arrangements, or other peaceful means of their own choice; (2) the Security Council shall, when it deems necessary, call upon the parties to settle their dispute by such means.

16. See above, p. 431.

17. See above, Chapters VI, 248, 250; VIII, 327, for Averoff-Tossizza's emphasis on the importance of the Labour party's resolutions.

18. For Article 131 of the rules of procedure, see n. 6, above.

19. See above, p. 461.

20. The Chairman gave no indication of which delegation or delegations asked for

a roll-call vote. Rule 128 of the rules of procedure provides that "the committee shall normally vote by a show of hands or by standing, but any representative may request a roll-call. The roll-call shall be taken in the English alphabetical order of the names of the members, beginning with the member whose name is drawn by lot by the Chairman. The name of each member shall be called in any roll-call and he shall reply 'Yes,' 'No' or 'Abstention.' The result of the voting shall be inserted in the record in the English alphabetical order of the names of the members."

21. "The destiny of Cyprus is the attainment of self-government and independence," Menon had said at the previous session. *Verbatim Record* 856th meeting, February 22, 1957, p. (54–55).

22. Noble had said so repeatedly, see above, Chapters VIII and IX, pp. 303 and 375. So had Premier Macmillan, see above, Chapter III, p. 152.

23. For text, see Dischler *op. cit.,* pp. 82–86.

24. The Greeks noted with slight dismay the omission of this passage from the official record but do not seem to have ascertained whether this omission was due to British and/or Turkish intervention with the Indian Delegation or to self-censorship on the part of that delegation. The latter hypothesis is not to be rejected. The theory of first setting up an independent state and then allowing it to determine its own future could have undesirable results from the Indian viewpoint, if applied to Kashmir.

25. Rule 90 of the rules of procedure provides that "the President shall not permit the proposer of a proposal or of an amendment to explain his vote on his own proposal or amendment."

26. "Embassy," *Press Release,* December 13, 1957. *New York Times,* December 14, 1957, reported that the Cypriots hailed the UN result.

CHAPTER XII

1. See above, Chapter X, pp. 417–18.

2. *Ibid.,* pp. 379–80.

3. *Keesing's 1954–1955,* XI, 14221.

4. See below, p. 491. Mayes, *op. cit.,* pp. 138–39, it should be noted, gives an incorrect account of this, saying that Ghana abstained in the voting in the Assembly, whereas the official records indicate that Ghana voted for the Greek draft resolution recommended by the Political Committee. (*GAOR, Twelfth Session,* 731st plenary meeting, December 14, 1957, p. 623.)

5. *GAOR, Twelfth Session,* 731st plenary meeting, December 14, 1957, pp. 618–23.

6. *New York Times,* December 14, 1957.

7. See above, p. 486.

8. See above, Chapter XI, p. 455.

9. Alker and Russett, *op. cit.,* pp. 25–26, 257–58, speculate about the meaning of absence, and see deviancy from Arab group behavior on the part of Jordan, Lebanon, and Tunisia, because of the Western source of their economic aid.

10. See above, Chapter I, p. 42. At the ninth Assembly, in 1954, the Greek representative had likewise committed his government to a new recourse to the United Nations. (See above, Introduction, p. 14.)

11. *Keesing's 1958*, XII, 16220.

12. *Grivas Memoirs*, Annex, p. 29.

13. *Eleftheria*, December 24, 1957. *RIIA Memorandum, 1959*, p. 42.

14. See above, Chapter X, pp. 294, 379.

15. See above, Chapter VII, p. 283.

16. See above, Chapter XI, p. 428.

17. What is meant here is that the seventeen-state draft resolution on the Algerian question—item 59—introduced by Indonesia and cosponsored by Afghanistan, Burma, Ceylon, Egypt, Ghana, Iraq, Jordan, Lebanon, Libya, Morocco, Nepal, Saudi Arabia, Sudan, Syria, Tunisia, and Yemen had not been put to the vote in the General Assembly. The Political Committee had been unable to recommend that resolution to the General Assembly because of a tie vote (37 in favor; 37 against, with 6 abstentions). This, however, did not prevent the plenary body from adopting Resolution 1184 (XII), sponsored by seven states—Argentina, Brazil, Canada, Cuba, the Dominican Republic, India, Iran, Ireland, Italy, Japan, Mexico, Norway, Peru, Spain, and Thailand. Unlike the other draft resolution, however, this one contained no reference at all to self-determination. In it, the General Assembly expressed concern about the Algerian situation, took note of the good offices offer of the King of Morocco, and expressed "the wish" that in a spirit of effective co-operation, *pourparlers* would be entered into, and other appropriate means utilized, with a view to a solution, in conformity with the purposes and principles of the Charter. (*GAOR, Twelfth Session*, Annexes, Item 59, p. 3.)

18. See above, Chapter V, p. 219, for the conversation between Foreign Minister Zorlu and the Greek Ambassador in Ankara.

19. *GPD*, January 20, 1958, 453–58. The subcommission had arrived in Cyprus on January 12 and remained there until January 29, 1958.

20. This summit NATO Council session took place on December 16–19, 1957. To meet the new Soviet challenge, the Council decided to organize its political and economic strength on the principle of interdependence and to take into account developments outside its own area. It also confirmed its support of the independence and sovereignty of states in the Middle East and its interest in the economic well-being of its peoples. The U.S. declared itself prepared to take part in a NATO nuclear stockpile, in which nuclear weapons would be deployed under U.S. custody. And it would be prepared to make IRBM's available to other states through bilateral agreements. For the Cyprus question at this NATO session, see below, p. 506.

21. See above, Chapter XI, p. 432.

22. See above, Chapter X, pp. 419–20.

23. *Ibid.*, p. 423.

24. *GPD*, January 21, 1958, 465–68. Privately, on the other hand, Venizelos had spoken with favor about a solution involving the guaranteed independence of Cyprus, see above, Chapter II, p. 87.

25. See above, Chapter X, pp. 415–16.

26. *GPD*, January 21, 1958, pp. 469–72.

27. *Ibid.*, pp. 473–75.

28. *Ibid.*, pp. 479–82.

29. *Ibid.*, pp. 487–88.

30. 580 H.C. Deb. (5th series), 150. On January 30, 1958, in an oral answer on the situation in Cyprus, Lennox-Boyd observed that the Labour party statements

concerning Cyprus at Brighton had added to the tension because of Turkish fear of the attitude of an alternative (Labour) government toward the Cyprus question (*Ibid.*, 502). Then, on February 6, he reiterated that he had no statement to make on the future of Cyprus. (*Ibid.*, p. 205. *Grivas Memoirs,* pp. 218–19.)

31. See above, Chapter II, p. 89.

32. *Grivas Memoirs,* p. 222.

33. During this NATO Council session, the Greek government was reported to have tried to get Chancellor Konrad Adenauer's good offices toward a solution but in vain. (*Le Monde,* December 19, 1957.) Spaak reportedly continued his explorations. (*To Vima,* December 19, 1957.) It was also said that he would go to Ankara. (*Eleftheria,* December 20, 1957.) According to Grivas, the Cyprus question was discussed between Eisenhower, Karamanlis, and Menderes, also between Karamanlis, Menderes, and Lloyd, with Spaak reiterating his offer of good offices. (*Grivas Memoirs,* p. 218.)

34. For the plan of Sir Hugh Foot, see above, p. 505. It was based on the idea of self-government for a period of five or seven years before any final decision about the island's status was taken. It included an end to the state of emergency and Makarios' return to the island; negotiations with the leaders of the two communities in order to work out a system of self-government; and an assurance that at the end of the interim period no final decision would be taken that the Greeks and Turks did not accept. (R. Stephens, *Cyprus, A Place of Arms* [New York: Praeger, 1966], pp. 152, 53.)

35. 572 H.C. Deb. (5th series), 1051. *Grivas Memoirs,* p. 228.

36. See above, Chapters III, IV, and VI, pp. 103, 180–81, 264, respectively.

37. *Grivas Memoirs,* p. 220.

38. *Ibid.,* p. 221.

39. See below, Epilogue, p. 513.

40. *Grivas Memoirs,* pp. 223, 219–20, 239; Appendix, p. 30.

41. *Keesing's 1958,* XII, 16220.

EPILOGUE

1. *GPD,* December 13, 1958, p. 327 (Karamanlis); December 11, 1958, p. 256 (Averoff-Tossizza).

2. *Keesing's, 1958,* XII, 16220.

3. *The Last Battle* (in Greek) (Athens, 1961), p. 11. This book is evidently based on sources provided by Averoff-Tossizza himself, if it was not written by him, for his 1961 election campaign.

4. 589 H.C. Deb. (5th ser.), pp. 1315–18. The plan's outline, as presented in an *aide-mémoire* conveyed by the British to the Greek government in a message of June 10, 1958, was as follows: (1) Association of Cyprus not only with Britain, and thus with the British Commonwealth, but also with Greece and Turkey. (2) Co-operation and participation by the Greek and Turkish governments with the British government in a joint effort to achieve the peace, progress, and prosperity of the island. (3) The appointment of a representative of the Greek government and a representative of the Turkish government to co-operate with the Governor. (4) Arrangements for the Greek and Turkish Cypriots to have Greek or Turkish nationality as well as their British nationality. (5) A new constitution providing for representative government

and communal autonomy, prepared in consultation with representatives of the two communities and the Greek and Turkish government. (6) Main provisions of the new Constitution: (a) A separate House of Representatives for each community, with final legislative authority in communal affairs. (b) A Council presided over by the Governor and including the representatives of the Greek and Turkish governments and six elected Ministers drawn from the two Houses of Representatives (four Greek Cypriots and two Turkish Cypriots), to exercise authority over internal affairs, other than communal affairs and internal security. (c) Reserve powers for the Governor acting after consulting the Greek and Turkish governments' representatives to ensure protection of community interests. (d) Authority for external affairs, defense, and internal security reserved to the Governor, acting after consulting the Greek and Turkish governments' representatives. (e) Provision for the representatives of Greek and Turkish governments to have any legislation which they think discriminatory reserved for consideration by an impartial tribunal. (7) No change, under the plan, in the international status of the island (i.e. maintenance of British sovereignty) for seven years. (8) Subject to an end of violence, progressive steps to relax the emergency regulations and eventually to end the state of emergency (this process to include the return of Cypriots at present excluded from the island under the emergency regulations). (Royal Ministry of Foreign Affairs, *The Cyprus Question, Correspondence exchanged between Mr. Constantine Karamanlis, Prime Minister of Greece, and the Right Honourable Harold Macmillan, Prime Minister of the United Kingdom* [June 10, 1958–August 19, 1958] [Athens, 1958], pp. 7–8. [Cited hereafter as *Karamanlis-Macmillan correspondence*.].)

The Greek government rejected this plan, *ibid.*, pp. 12–14, as it had rejected the last Macmillan plan in September, 1955. The participation of the three governments in the administration of the island, the separate assemblies for each segment of the population, and dual nationality, would divide rather than unite the island. If applied, it would lead to an intense antagonism both between the majority and the minority of the population and among the governments of the countries it involved in the island's administration. (*Ibid.*, p. 19 [message of Karamanlis to Macmillan, of July 31, 1958].) Makarios likewise rejected this plan. As for the Turkish Foreign Minister, he continued to maintain the conviction in a statement of June 19, 1958, that the best possible solution was partition and proposed that the principles of partnership and partition should be fused in a perfected plan, at a tripartite conference that would determine the final international status of Cyprus. At such a conference, the Macmillan plan would be acceptable as a conference paper (*Keesing's, 1958*, XII, 16451). After visits to Ankara and Athens, Macmillan, on August 15, 1958, announced some slight revisions in this plan. The representatives of the Greek and Turkish governments, he stated, would not actually sit on the Governor's Council, although their functions would remain unchanged. The proposals concerning dual nationality would be deferred, and some form of representative institution involving the co-operation and joint action of the two communities might be established later, in the light of the two communities' experience in operating separately through their Houses of Representatives and jointly in the Governor's Council, (*Karamanlis-Macmillan Correspondence*, p. 21 [Macmillan message of August 14, 1958, to Karamanlis]; pp. 23–24 [Macmillan statement of policy, August 15, 1958].)

5. *RIIA Memorandum 1959*, pp. 51–52.

6. *GPD*, December 11, 1958, pp. 254, 255–56 (Averoff-Tossizza). On September 7, 1958, Makarios had told the Greek government privately that he was now willing to accept independence for Cyprus under UN auspices after a period of self-government. (Stephens, *op. cit.*, p. 155.)

7. *The Last Battle*, pp. 15–16.

8. *GAOR, Thirteenth Session*, Annexes, Agenda item 68, 3–5 (cited hereafter as *Agenda Item 68*).

9. *Ibid.*, 5-14. The jurists were Professors Maurice Bourquin and Alejandro Alvarez. For Turkish arguments about Article 73 (b) of the Charter, see above, Chapter VIII, 332.

10. *RIIA Memorandum 1959*, pp. 46-47.

11. *Agenda Item 68*, pp. 15-16.

12. *Ibid.*, p. 16.

13. See above, Chapter VIII, p. 332.

14. See above, Chapter II, p. 89.

15. *Agenda Item 68*, p. 16.

16. *The Last Battle*, pp. 7, 19, 21, 23.

17. *Agenda Item 68*, p. 16.

18. *Ibid.*, pp. 16-17.

19. See above, Chapter VI, p. 243. For British reaction, p. 246.

20. Ethiopia had not been among the original sponsors.

21. *Agenda Item 68*, p. 17.

22. *Ibid.*, p. 17.

23. *GPD*, December 11, 1958, p. 256 (Averoff-Tossizza).

24. *GAOR, Thirteenth Session*, 782d plenary meeting, p. 457-58 (statement of the Rapporteur of the First Committee, Franz Matsch).

25. *GAOR, Thirteenth Session*, First Committee, 1009th meeting, December 4, pp. 312-13; 1010th meeting, p. 316.

26. *GPD*, December 11, 1958, pp. 256-57.

27. *GAOR, Thirteenth Session*, First Committee, 1003d meeting, December 1, 1958, p. 283.

28. *GPD*, December 11, 1958, p. 257. *The Last Battle*, p. 72. The British representative had made a similar though less vibrant warning at the Assembly's previous session, see above, Chapter X, p. 414, and as early as 1954, Lloyd had predicted "toil and moil" in Cyprus. (See above, Introduction, p. 9.)

29. *GPD*, December 12, 1958, p. 304.

30. *Ibid.*, December 11, 1958, p. 257.

31. *Ibid.*

32. In the first of these amendments, Greece proposed the deletion of the third paragraph of the preamble of the Iranian draft resolution which read: "*Noting* the efforts which have been made in furtherance of this resolution (Resolution 1013 [XI]), and in particular the efforts to bring about a conference between the three governments concerned and representatives of the Cypriots, at which there would be discussion not only of the interim arrangements for the administration of Cyprus but also for a final solution." In the second of these amendments, Greece proposed that the fourth paragraph of the preamble of the Iranian draft resolution should be replaced by the following: "*Believing* that a conference at which there would be discussion, not only of the interim arrangements for the administration of Cyprus, but also of a final solution, with the assistance, if desired, of governments and personalities acceptable to the interested parties, offers the best hope for peaceful progress toward an agreed solution of the Cyprus problem." In the third of its amendments, Greece proposed the replacement of the fifth paragraph of the preamble of the Iranian draft resolution by the following: "*Considering* that self-government of Cyprus should be

established in accordance with the Charter of the United Nations." The fifth paragraph of the Iranian draft resolution read: "*Considering* that self-government and free institutions should be developed in accordance with the Charter of the United Nations to meet the legitimate aspirations of the Cypriots." (*Agenda Item 68*, pp. 16–17.)

33. In the first of these subamendments, Turkey proposed that in the amendment proposed by Greece to the fourth preambular paragraph of the Iranian draft resolution, the words "between the three governments directly concerned and the representatives of the Cypriots" should be inserted after the words "*Believing* that a conference." In the second of these subamendments, Turkey proposed that in the Greek amendment to the fifth preambular paragraph of the Iranian draft resolution the words "self-government of Cyprus should be established" should be replaced by the words "self-government by the Cypriots should be developed." In the third of its subamendments, Turkey proposed that in the text of the third Greek amendment to the Iranian draft resolution, the words "in accordance with the Charter of the United Nations" should be replaced by the words "in accordance with the purposes and principles of the Charter of the United Nations." (*Ibid.*, p. 17.)

34. GPD, December 12, 1958, pp. 282 (Venizelos); 304 (Markezinis). The latter noted that, as compared with the previous Assembly, the votes of the seven additional countries—Indonesia, Haiti, Ghana, Ecuador, El Salvador, Costa Rica—had been lost through their abstaining from the vote on the Iranian draft resolution or, in the case of Liberia, through its vote in favor of the Colombian draft resolution.

35. See above, pp. 516–17.

36. *Agenda Item 68*, 18.

37. *Ibid.*, pp. 18–19.

38. GPD, December 12, 1958, p. 279 (Passalidis). The EDA spokesman said that at the head of the most intransigent enemies of Greece was the "imperialist" United States.

39. GAOR, *Thirteenth Session*, First Committee, 1000th meeting, November 28, 1958, p. 268.

40. *Ibid.*, 1010th meeting, December 4, 1958, p. 312.

41. GPD, December 11, 1958, p. 257.

42. *Ibid.*, p. 258–59.

43. *The Last Battle*, pp. 127–78.

44. *Ibid.*, pp. 116–17. H. Foot, *A Start in Freedom* (New York: Harper & Row, 1964), p. 176. *Times* (London), December 6, 1958. The latter two sources represented the British view of optimism.

45. *The Last Battle*, p. 117.

46. GPD, December 11, 1958, p. 258–59.

47. *The Last Battle*, pp. 119–21.

48. GAOR, *Thirteenth Session*, 782d plenary meeting, December 5, 1958, pp. 458–59.

49. *Agenda Item 68*, p. 19.

50. GPD, December 11, 1958, p. 259.

51. Foot, *op. cit.*, p. 176.

52. *The Last Battle*, p. 129.

53. Foot, *op. cit.*, p. 179.

54. *Grivas Memoirs,* p. 341. The parenthetical information is not from this source.

55. *Keesing's, 1959,* XIII, 16833.

56. See above, Chapter VI, p. 257.

57. *Ibid.,* p. 258.

58. *Conference on Cyprus* (London: H.M. Stationery Office, February 1959), Cmd. 679 and 680 (Miscellaneous Nos. 5 and 6, 1959).

59. *GAOR, Tenth Session,* 521st plenary meeting, September 23, 1955, p. 62.

60. See above, Chapters I and XI, pp. 41–42 and 469, respectively.

61. See above, Chapter I, p. 53.

62. See above, Chapter III, p. 137.

63. See above, Chapter IV, pp. 162–63.

64. See above, Chapter X, p. 380.

65. See above, pp. 514 and 516.

CONCLUSIONS

1. Article 23 of the Italian Peace Treaty provided an interesting example of an agreement to resort to the General Assembly over the question of the disposal of the former Italian colonies, should the United States, Britain, France and the Soviet Union be unable to reach a solution by negotiations within a specified time. (L. M. Goodrich and Anne P. Simons, *The United Nations and the Maintenance of International Peace and Security* [Washington: The Brookings Institution, 1955], pp. 88 and 239.)

2. H. Sprout and M. Sprout, *Foundations of International Politics* (Princeton, N.J.: Van Nostrand Co., 1962), p. 143, refer to human and non-human instruments of statecraft but without considering international agencies as such.

3. *Ibid.,* pp. 143, 155–56, refer to targets of action in discussing techniques of statecraft.

4. J. G. Stoessinger, *The United Nations and the Superpowers* (New York: Random House, 1965), p. 168.

5. E. G. Riggs, *op. cit.,* p. 106.

6. Iklé, *op. cit.,* p. 21.

7. *Ibid.*

8. I. L. Claude, Jr., "Conflict, Cooperation, and Consensus—the Role of the UN: a Review," *Journal of Conflict Resolution* (hereafter cited as *JCR*), VI, 1962, 166.

9. See above, Introduction, pp. 15–16.

10. See above, Chapter IV, pp. 158–61.

11. See above, Chapter III, pp. 115 ff. and 120.

12. See above, Chapters II, p. 72; III, p. 134.

13. See above, Chapter IV, pp. 154 ff.

14. See above, Epilogue, p. 524.

15. C. A. McClelland, *Theory and the International System* (New York: Macmillan Co., 1966), p. 79, introduces this type of relationship which, he acknowledges, resembles Morgenthau's policy of the status quo and David Singer's perpetuation or reinforcement type of relationship.

16. See above, Chapter V, pp. 196–97.

17. C. R. Shepherd, *Small Groups* (San Francisco: Chandler, 1964), pp. 42–43, refers to the theory of E. Goffman, *The Presentation of Self in Everyday Life* (New York: Doubleday, 1959) about two types of small-group behavior: upstage and backstage.

18. S. K. Bailey, *Congress Makes a Law* (New York: Columbia University Press, 1950), p. vii.

19. A. W. Cordier, "Diplomacy Today," *Journal of International Affairs*, XVII, 1963, 6.

20. See above, Chapter V, pp. 197, 218, and Epilogue, p. 525.

21. See above, Chapter VII, p. 283.

22. Alker and Russett, *op. cit.*, p. 150.

23. Rules 15 and 16 of the rules of procedure of the General Assembly.

24. Goodrich and Simons, *op. cit.*, p. 79.

25. *Ibid.*, p. 103.

26. Rule 40 of the rules of procedure of the General Assembly. The postponement of the consideration of the question of placing the item on the agenda has been ruled to be in accordance with the Assembly's rules of procedure. (Goodrich and Simons, *op. cit.*, p. 102.)

27. Rule 24 of the rules of procedure of the General Assembly.

28. Goodrich and Simons, *op. cit.*, p. 105, write that it is difficult to see how the General Committee can perform any useful function unless it is given considerable latitude in the range of its discussions and recommendations.

29. See above, Chapter V, pp. 193, 197, 207.

30. Krech and others, *op. cit.*, p. 279, for "denotational" and "connotational" words.

31. *GAOR, Ninth Session,* General Assembly, 477th plenary meeting, September 24, 1954, pp. 51–52.

32. Goodrich and Simons, *op. cit.*, p. 113, mention three other arguments besides lack of competence that are put forward in support of non-inclusion of an item in the Assembly's agenda: (1) that no dispute or situation on the nature described in the recourse exists; (2) that the Assembly should not take up the item because other procedures of settlement are available, have been agreed upon, or are being used for seeking a solution to the problem; and (3) that the item's consideration would serve no useful purpose and might obstruct rather than help a settlement.

33. See above, Introduction, p. 5.

34. See above, Chapter V, p. 227.

35. *Ibid.*, p. 217.

36. As Goodrich and Simons, *op. cit.*, p. 147, put it, the item then is not likely to receive careful consideration.

37. See above, Introduction, p. 13.

38. See above, Chapter I, pp. 51–52.

39. See above, Chapter VII, p. 279.

40. Article 18 of the UN Charter.

41. At the twelfth Assembly the three parties charged their opponents with non-compliance with Resolution 1013 (XI), i.e., with disregard for the moral authority of the UN and, while the Greek representative charged the British authorities in Cyprus with violations of human rights, the British representative charged EOKA with terrorism and, to a lesser extent than at the previous Assembly, the Greek government with providing material and moral aid to EOKA. As for the Turkish representative, he used the German word *Anschluss* with its strong negative connotation because of its association with Hitler and his take-over of Austria, to characterize the claim for *enosis*. The Greek representative, on the other hand, often used the term "colonialism" which likewise has a negative connotation.

42. For example, the Greek representative denied that the Radcliffe draft constitution was a liberal document; that his government was giving aid to EOKA; that EOKA was a terrorist organization, and that Makarios was its leader. He also denied that the Cypriots were Levantines; that Greece was seeking for a treaty revision; or that Cyprus was of strategic importance. The British and Turkish representatives, on their side, denied that they opposed self-determination, that they were colonialists or favored colonialism, etc.

43. For example, the Greek representative predicted and warned, that if colonialism persisted in Cyprus, the struggle of EOKA might be resumed. He also threatened to publish data on violations of human rights in Cyprus. The British representative, at the time of the first recourse over Cyprus, predicted that communal strife was likely to break out if the Greeks persisted in the campaign for *enosis*, and at the last recourse he warned that not only communal strife would start again but that a wider conflict in the area might occur. Iklé, *op. cit.*, pp. 63–64, observes that in both warnings and threats, the menacing party tries to dissuade the opponent from making a certain move or from refusing to comply with a certain demand. In a warning, however, the menacing party points out to the opponent the natural consequences that are likely to follow from his non-compliance whereas in a threat he asserts that he will make a special effort to cause the opponent to suffer the predicted loss, should he fail to comply. As the above Greek and British examples indicate, the distinction between the two may be really quite blurred.

44. The Greek representative, for example, appealed to the United Nations that it act to abolish colonialism and to remove this evil which was a dangerous threat to world peace. He also appealed to it not to support anything less than what the Labour party had proposed as a solution of the Cyprus problem.

45. Iklé, *op. cit.*, pp. 197 ff.

46. For example, the Greek representative's proposals to his Turkish colleague concerning the safeguards the Greek government would be prepared to grant with regard to certain "legitimate" Turkish interests in Cyprus (see above, Chapter X, pp. 419–20). Another example of such a proposal, at the eleventh Assembly, had repercussions in Greek domestic politics and was exploited by the Turkish government as evidence of Greek maneuvering. (See above, Chapters I and III, pp. 42 and 112, respectively.)

47. See above, Chapter XI, p. 455, for the Turkish representative's misconstruction of the Greek draft resolution.

48. See above, Chapter XI, p. 442, for certain remarks of the Peruvian representative. The author of *The Last Battle*, p. 109, recounts how the Greek Foreign Minister, at one point during the Cyprus debate in the Committee at the thirteenth Assembly, deliberately resorted to what the French call *bafouillement* (rambling) in order to gain thinking time.

49. Alker and Russett, *op. cit.*, p. 157.

50. See above, Chapter VIII, p. 346.

51. See above, Chapter II, p. 77. Also Chapter IV, p. 183.

52. See above, Chapter VIII, p. 340.

53. See above, Chapter II, pp. 79–80.

54. See above, Chapter IX, p. 369.

55. See above, Chapter X, p. 415.

56. *Ibid.*, pp. 419–20.

57. *Ibid.*, p. 424.

58. McGrath and Julian, *op. cit.*, pp. 4–5.

59. See above, Chapter XI, pp. 435, 439.

60. *Ibid.*, pp. 454–55.

61. *Ibid.*, pp. 437, 441.

62. G. Schubert, *The Public Interest* (Glencoe, Ill.: Free Press, 1960), pp. 199–200, 204, on the rationalist and idealist view of the public interest.

63. Schubert, *ibid.*, p. 204, notes that the approach of psychological realists to the public interest is conservative in its general overtones.

64. F. J. Sorauf, "The Public Interest Reconsidered," *Journal of Politics*, XIX, 639 (cited in Schubert, *op. cit.*, p. 203).

65. See above, Chapter XI, pp. 454, 475.

66. See above, Chapter IX, p. 369, and Chapter XI, p. 435.

67. Burke, *op. cit.*, p. 50.

68. A former member of the U.S. Delegation to the UN, Ernest A. Gross, *The United Nations: Structure for Peace* (New York: Harper & Bros., 1962), p. 67, deplores the fact that non-aligned smaller nations often press for "negotiation" between the great powers while remaining non-committal about the merits of issues in dispute between them, and tend to regard "talks" between disputants as ends in themselves. As this case study has revealed great powers act in the same fashion if they wish to remain non-committal or unaligned about the merits of an issue between parties to a dispute.

69. See above, Chapter IX, pp. 359, 376.

70. *GPD*, December 11, 1958, 256.

71. See above, Chapter XI, p. 466.

72. See above, Chapter X, p. 425.

73. Riggs, *op. cit.*, pp. 34–37, writing about the U.S. practices, observes that negotiation, compromise, log-rolling, and accommodation are not scorned by the United States. If consultation is not enough, he adds, then "pressure" is made—"the attempt to persuade a delegate or his government to support the United States by methods which extend beyond a factual exposition of the merits of the case." Pressure, he points out, springs from insistence rather than from the content of the message, and predictions may be made, but threats may not. Non-influential states may use the same methods but without effect.

74. *GAOR, Twelfth Session*, Annexes, Agenda Item 59, p. 3.

75. See above, Introduction, Chapters I, and VII, pp. 11–12, 60 ff, 273, respectively.

76. At the ninth Assembly, while the Greek Delegation voted for Resolution 814 (IX), the Soviet bloc states abstained, *GAOR, Ninth Session,* First Committee, 752d meeting, December 15, 1954, p. 567.

77. Alker and Russett, *op. cit.,* p. 264.

78. See above, Chapter VII, p. 273.

79. Goodrich and Simons, *op. cit.,* p. 267.

80. As Hadwen and Kaufman write, *op. cit.,* pp. 35–36, after a delegation has made a preliminary decision to put forward a proposal, "great activity is required."

81. See above, pp. 139, 197, 217, 223.

82. See above, Chapter VII, p. 283.

83. See above, Introduction, p. 13, and Chapters I and VII, pp. 39–40, 287.

84. See above, Introduction, p. 21.

85. Hadwen and Kaufman, *op. cit.,* pp. 36–37.

86. Sometimes, a delegation presses its viewpoint regardless of whether it expects to get a majority and sometimes even with the express purpose of being defeated, Hadwen and Kaufman, *op. cit.,* 35–36.

87. See above, Introduction, p. 20.

88. Hadwen and Kaufman, *op. cit.,* p. 40.

89. S. Bullitt, *To Be a Politician* (New York: Garden City, 1959), p. 90, cited in E. S. Redford, D. B. Truman, A. Hacker, A. F. Westin, R. C. Wood, *Politics and Government in the United States* (national edition) (New York: Harcourt, Brace & World, 1965), p. 282.

90. Iklé, *op. cit.,* pp. 87 ff., and 204, emphasizes the *esprit communautaire* often invoked at meetings of European international institutions, but the community spirit—the UN spirit—is also frequently invoked in the General Assembly and other U.N. organs.

91. See above, Chapter X, p. 424, for the Greek Foreign Minister's angling for an amendment acceptable to him, under which the term "right" of self-determination would be replaced by the term "principle" of self-determination.

92. See above, Chapter XI, p. 431.

93. F. C. Iklé, in collaboration with Nathan Leites, "Political Negotiations as a Process of Modifying Utilities," *JCR,* VI, 1962, 21. These categories can be tested on the various Greek proposals concerning the Cyprus question in the United Nations, and their dynamic development from one range to the other is what the author of this Cyprus study calls "the process of shifting goals."

94. The Greek Foreign Minister introduced a draft resolution for setting up a commission to investigate both the British charges of material aid to EOKA on the part of the Greek government and the Greek charges of violations of human rights by the British authorities in Cyprus. This draft resolution, however, was not put to the vote, see above, Chapter I, p. 40.

95. See above, Introduction, p. 13.

96. See above, Chapter I, p. 41.

97. S. D. Bailey, *op. cit.,* p. 147.

98. See above, Chapter I, p. 39.

99. See above, Epilogue, p. 523.

100. See above, Chapter XII, p. 479. J. G. Peristiany, "Honor and Shame in a Cypriot Highland," in J. G. Peristiany (ed.), *Honor and Shame: The Values of Mediterranean Society* (Chicago: University of Chicago Press, 1966), p. 188, writes that the Greek is a keen gambler attracted more powerfully by the risk than by the gain, more, namely, by the opportunity of proving himself than by the prize. And in his introduction (*ibid.*, p. 11) he puts forward as a tentative exploratory answer to the matter referred to in the book's title that honor and shame is the constant preoccupation of individuals in small scale, exclusive societies where face to face personal, as opposed to anonymous, relations are of paramount importance and where the social personality of the actor is as significant as his office. Perhaps these sociological hypotheses help understand Makarios' behavior not only in this instance but in others too. Similar motivations may have prompted some of the sponsoring states of draft resolutions on West Irian (at the eleventh and twelfth Assemblies), on Algeria (at the thirteenth), and on Oman (at the sixteenth), to press for a vote in the Assembly of their resolutions which the appropriate committee had recommended for adoption. In all the above four cases no other draft resolutions had been tabled, and the voting in the Committee had revealed a less than two-thirds majority required for adoption by the Assembly. Thus, at the eleventh Assembly, the Political Committee, by 39 votes to 25, with 9 abstentions, adopted a resolution on West Irian sponsored by thirteen states—Bolivia, Burma, Ceylon, Costa Rica, Ecuador, Ethiopia, India, Iraq, Pakistan, Saudi Arabia, Sudan, Syria, and Yugoslavia (*GAOR, Eleventh Session, Annexes,* Agenda Item 63, 3.) At the Assembly's next session, it did likewise, adopting by 42 votes to 28, with 11 abstentions, a draft resolution on West Irian, sponsored by nineteen states—Afghanistan, Bolivia, Burma, Ceylon, Egypt, Ethiopia, India, Indonesia, Iraq, Jordan, Lebanon, Libya, Morocco, Nepal, Saudi Arabia, Sudan, Syria, Tunisia, and Yemen (*GAOR, Twelfth Session,* Annexes, Agenda Item 65, 3.) At the Assembly's thirteenth session, the Political Committee adopted, by 36 votes to 18, with 25 abstentions, a draft resolution on Algeria, sponsored by seventeen states—Afghanistan, Burma, Ceylon, Ghana, Indonesia, Iraq, Jordan, Lebanon, Liberia, Libya, Morocco, Nepal, Saudi Arabia, Sudan, Tunisia, United Arab Republic (*GAOR Thirteenth Session,* Annexes, Agenda Item 63, 3.) At the Assembly's sixteenth session the Special Political Committee adopted by 38 votes to 21, with 29 abstentions, a draft resolution on Oman sponsored by sixteen states—Afghanistan, Guinea, Indonesia, Iraq, Jordan, Lebanon, Libya, Morocco, Saudi Arabia, Sudan, Syria, Tunisia, United Arab Republic, Yemen, Yugoslavia, and Mali (*GAOR, Sixteenth Session,* Annexes, Agenda Item 23, 3.)

101. Kyrou, *op. cit.*, p. 303, asserts that New Zealand's Leslie Munro was knighted by Queen Elizabeth II in her Christmas list of 1954 as a reward for his sponsorship of Resolution 814 (XI). This suggests that rewards of a personal character may be a factor in the behavior of national representatives in "Parliamentary diplomacy" and raises the extremely indelicate and unanswerable question that is justified, however, from the viewpoint of the political scientist, of whether, to put the matter most crudely, votes can be "bought" in the United Nations. Use of such techniques for exerting influence is not unknown in international politics, as witness the cases of Talleyrand in the Napoleonic and post-Napoleonic era, or of Lord Burghley in the times of Elizabeth I. Representatives of third-party states, the national interests of which are not directly involved in a particular case being considered by the United Nations, would seem, a priori, to be particularly vulnerable in this respect, with the economically powerful states having an advantage over the economically weaker states in successfully pursuing such activities.

102. Hadwen and Kaufman, *op. cit.*, p. 65. These authors mention that the *Economist* had coined the term "fire brigade" for the mediators during the UN consideration of the Suez crisis in 1956.

103. See above, Epilogue, p. 518.

104. See above, Chapter I, p. 41.

105. Iklé, *op. cit.*, p. 15, distinguishes three types of ambiguity: (1) the parties have an honest misunderstanding about the implications that the agreement does not spell out; (2) one party, though knowing what the opponent expects from bargain, pretends he has a different understanding of it—in which case he may exploit ambiguity to cover up deliberate violations of the agreement; and (3) the parties are aware that the ambiguous terms mean different things to each of them. Resolution 1013 (XI) would fall in this latter category. Unlike Iklé, who calls this third type of ambiguity "equivocality," this author prefers to stick to the term "ambiguity," qualifying it with the adjective "deliberate" because, "equivocality" may connote deception, which cannot be the case when both parties are fully aware that the ambiguity means different things to each.

106. B. Gross, *op. cit.*, p. 177.

107. See above, Chapter I, p. 43. Rule 129 of the Assembly's rules of procedure provides, among other things, that the President shall not permit the proposer of a proposal or of an amendment to explain his vote on his own proposal or amendment. Yet Krishna Menon did exactly this. See also Chapters VIII, p. 326; IX, p. 368.

108. C. F. Alger, "Nonresolution Consequences of the U.N. and their Effect on International Conflict," *JCR*, V, 1961, 142. Iklé, *op. cit.*, points out that negotiations may be a substitute for violent action. L. A. Coser, *The Functions of Social Conflict* (Glencoe, Ill.: Free Press, 1956), p. 136, writes that if alternative means are not available or are believed to be not available, the only way to a reappraisal of the contending parties is to use the "weapon of last resort."

109. See above, Chapter I, p. 57. Also *GPD*, April 25, 1956, p. 285, and December 13, 1958, p. 326, when Premier Karamanlis said that there were only three ways toward solving the Cyprus question: the United Nations; direct negotiations; and war. Since the latter course could not be taken, only the other two remained.

110. Alger, *op. cit.*, p. 142. B. Gross, *op. cit.*, p. 67, quite correctly observes that history shows that negotiation is not in itself an alternative to war or other forms of violence. Bombs fell on Pearl Harbor, he notes, while discussions were taking place.

111. Coser, *op. cit.*, pp. 155–56.

112. B. Gross, *op. cit.*, p. 149.

113. V. Aubert, "Competition and Dissensus," *JCR*, VIII, 1963, 26, refers to Simmel, Kurt Wolff (ed.), *The Sociology of Georg Simmel* (Glencoe, Ill.: Free Press, 1950), pp. 135 ff.

114. I. L. Claude, Jr., "Implications and Questions for the Future," *IO*, XIX, 844–45.

115. Coser, *op. cit.*, p. 139, citing Simmel.

116. Hovet, *op. cit.*, pp. 30–46. He distinguishes six types of groups in the United Nations: blocs, caucusing groups, geographic distribution groups, regional groups, common interest groups, and temporary groups.

117. B. Gross, *op. cit.*, p. 148, refers to this sort of action in the legislative struggle in the U.S. Congress.

118. M. Barkin, "Conflict Resolution through Implicit Mediation," *JCR*, VIII, 1964, 121.

119. See above, Introduction, pp. 33–34.

120. Barkin, *op. cit.*, p. 122.

121. See above, Introduction, p. 34.

122. R. Falk, *Law, Morality, and War in the Contemporary World* (New York: Praeger, 1963), pp. 67–69. Also cited by Barkin, *op. cit.*, p. 123.

123. Barkin, *op. cit.*, p. 126.

124. I. L. Claude, "The Containment and Resolution of Disputes," F. O. Wilcox and H. Field Haviland, Jr. (eds.), *The United States and the United Nations* (Baltimore: Johns Hopkins Press, 1961), p. 108. He points out the need for *relatively disinterested* third parties for mediation (italics added).

125. This is the term used by Alger, who observes that the creation of international organizations may have a two-level effect. On the first there is the organization's success at attaining the goals for which it was established; on the second, are the basic changes in the international system in which the organizations were established, *op. cit.*, p. 144. He mentions six types of non-resolution consequences; (1) The impact of the Assembly experience of the representatives. (2) The possible friendship across national boundaries. (3) The participation of experts. (4) Shifting majorities. (5) The expansion of national concern. (6) The availability of new information for representatives of member states (*ibid.*, p. 132-37).

126. See above, Chapter I, pp. 60-61. C. M. Woodhouse, "Modern Greece, 1939-1964," in W. A. Heurtley and others, *A Short History of Greece* (Cambridge: Cambridge University Press, 1965), pp. 171-172, notes, in his account of the Cyprus affair, that during 1958 Greece concluded trade agreements with the Soviet Union and Poland, and relaxed controls on trade with Communist China which had been imposed to please the U.S. government.

127. R. Tanter, "Dimensions of Conflict Behavior, 1958-1960," *JCR*, X, 1966, p. 60 (theories of Simmel and Coser).

128. *Ibid.* (theory of Muzaffer Sherif).

129. *Ibid.*, pp. 60-61.

130. *Ibid.*, p. 60 (theory of P. Sorokin).

131. Woodhouse, *op. cit.*, p. 166.

132. T. A. Couloumbis, *Greek Political Reaction to American and NATO Influences* (New Haven: Yale University Press, 1966), pp. 93 ff. The election statistics are taken from this book, Appendix E, pp. 230-32.

133. *GPD*, May 22, 1956, 355 (Mavros); pp. 423-424 (Papaspyrou). On December 13, 1958, Karamanlis justified the government's measures against public demonstrations over Cyprus. The demonstrations could create the impression that Greece was in a state of anarchy. Hence they could cause harm rather than good for the national question. He noted that in 1951 when the opposition was in power, a demonstration over Cyprus had been prohibited, *ibid.*, December 13, 1958, p. 327.

134. During the elections of February 19, 1956, the Center campaigned jointly with the Left, so that it is difficult to estimate the total pro-Western percentage of the votes.

135. Woodhouse, *op. cit.*, p. 172, believes that this increase of ERE's Parliamentary strength was a sort of vote of confidence in Karamanlis' Cyprus policy and enabled him to proceed to the "final liquidation of the Cyprus problem."

136. Tanter, *op. cit.*, p. 60.

137. Foot, *op. cit.*, p. 151.

138. *Ibid.*

139. *Ibid.*, pp. 153, 170, 156.

140. *Grivas Memoirs*, pp. 217-18.

141. *Ibid.*, pp. 63-65.

142. Sir John Harding, "Terrorism in Cyprus," *The Daily Telegraph*, January 3, 1958.

143. See above, Introduction, p. 9.

144. *Ibid.*, p. 10.

145. *Ibid.*, p. 19.

146. See above, Chapter III, pp. 125–26.

147. *Ibid.*, p. 127.

148. See above, Chapters I and III, pp. 42, 112–13.

149. Foot, *op. cit.*, p. 150.

150. *Ibid.*, p. 152.

151. E. R. Haas and A. S. Whiting, *Dynamics of International Relations* (New York: McGraw-Hill, 1956), pp. 21–22, 126. More recently, the human personality factor in international politics is stressed in I. D. Duchacek, *Nations and Men* (New York: Holt, Rinehart & Winston, 1966), pp. 9–30.

Bibliography

BIBLIOGRAPHY

UNPUBLISHED DOCUMENTATION

Personal Files of Mr. E. Averoff-Tossizza, Athens.

OFFICIAL PUBLISHED DOCUMENTATION

Great Britain

British and Foreign State Papers, Vol. LXIX (1877–78); Vol. CXXI (1920).

Conference on Cyprus. Documents Signed and Initialled at Lancaster House, Cmnd. 679 (Miscellaneous No. 4), H.M. Stationery Office, 1959.

Conference on Cyprus. Final Statements at the Closing Plenary Session at Lancaster House on February 19, 1959, Cmnd. 680 (Miscellaneous No. 5), H.M. Stationery Office, 1959.

Cyprus 1956. H.M. Stationery Office, 1957 (Colonial Office).

Cyprus, Cmnd. 1093, H.M. Stationery Office, July, 1960.

Cyprus. Correspondence Exchanged Between the Governor and Makarios, Cmd. 9708, H.M. Stationery Office, March, 1956.

Cyprus. Statement of Policy, Cmnd. 455, H.M. Stationery Office, June, 1958.

Defence, Outline of Future Policy, Cmd. 124, H.M. Stationery Office, April, 1957.

Discussion on Cyprus in the North Atlantic Treaty Organization, September–October, 1958, Cmnd. 566 (Miscellaneous No. 14), 1958.

Disturbances in Cyprus in October 1931, Cmd. 4045, H.M. Stationery Office, 1932.

House of Commons Debates, 5th series, 1951–58.

RADCLIFFE, LORD. *Constitutional Proposals for Cyprus,* Cmnd. 42, H.M. Stationery Office, December, 1956.

Report on the Inscription of the Cyprus Item on the Agenda of the Ninth Session of the General Assembly of the United Nations held at New York on September 23/24, 1954, Cmd. 9300, H.M. Stationery Office, October, 1954.

Report on the Proceedings of the Twelfth Session of the General Assembly of the United Nations held at New York, Cmnd. 417, H.M. Stationery Office, April, 1958.

Terrorism in Cyprus. The Captured Documents, H.M. Stationery Office, 1956 (translated extracts issued by authority of the Secretary of State for the Colonies).

The Tripartite Conference on the Eastern Mediterranean and Cyprus, Cmd. 9594, H.M. Stationery Office, October, 1955.

Greece

Cyprus before the United Nations, Discussion of the Cyprus Question before the Twelfth General Assembly of the United Nations 1957–1958, Washington, Royal Greek Embassy Information Service, 1958.

Cyprus Demands Self-Determination, Washington, Royal Greek Embassy Information Service, October, 1954.

The Cyprus Question. Correspondence Exchanged between Mr. Constantine Karamanlis, Prime Minister of Greece, and the Right Honorable Harold Macmillan, Prime Minister of the United Kingdom (June 10, 1958–August 19, 1958), Athens, Royal Ministry of Foreign Affairs, 1958.

The Cyprus Question. Discussion at the North Atlantic Treaty Organization, September–October, 1958, Athens, Royal Ministry of Foreign Affairs, 1958.

The Cyprus Question. Negotiations, October 4, 1955 to March 5, 1956, Athens, Royal Ministry of Foreign Affairs, 1956.

Documents and Press Comments on the Cyprus Question, Athens: Press and Information Department, Prime Minister's Office, 1954.

"Hellenic News," Royal Greek Embassy Information Service, Washington, D.C., 1954–55.

Journal of the Debates of the Parliament, 1955–59 (in Greek).

Press Releases of the Royal Greek Embassy Information Services, Washington, D.C., 1954–58.

The Question of Cyprus, Reply to the Arguments Advanced by the British Delegation during the Ninth Session of the Assembly of the United Nations (September 23–24, 1954), Royal Ministry of Foreign Affairs, Athens, November, 1954.

Turkey

Proceedings of the Grand National Assembly (in Turkish), Vol. X (1956), and Vol. XVII (1957).

Turkish Views on Cyprus, New York: Turkish Information Office, n.d.

"News from Turkey," 1957; New York, Turkish Information Office.

United States

ARMOUR, NORMAN, *Greece, Turkey, and Iran,* U.S. Senate Special Committee to Study the Foreign Aid Program, 85th Cong., 1st sess., Washington, D.C.: Government Printing Office, February, 1957.

Council of Europe

Consultative Assembly, Seventh Ordinary Session, 22d sitting, October 21, 1955.

NATO

Non-Military Cooperation in NATO, Text of Report of the Committee of Three, December, 1956.

United Nations

General Assembly, Official Records, Sixth, Seventh, Eighth, Ninth, Tenth, Eleventh, Twelfth, and *Thirteenth Sessions* (debates on, and references to, the Cyprus question).

UNOFFICIAL PUBLISHED DOCUMENTATION

Council on Foreign Relations, *Documents of American Foreign Relations, 1954;* same for 1957, New York: Harper & Bros., 1955 and 1958.

Royal Institute of International Affairs, *Documents on International Affairs 1957,* London: Oxford University Press, 19.)

PAPAGEORGIOU, S. (ed.). *Archive of Illegal Documents of the Cypriot Struggle 1955–1959* (in Greek), Athens: Olympic Publications, 1961.

BOOKS

ALASTOS, D. *Cyprus Guerrilla.* London: Heinemann, 1960.

ALKER, H. R. and RUSSETT, B. M. *World Politics in the General Assembly.* New Haven: Yale University Press, 1965.

BAILEY, S. D. *The General Assembly of the United Nations.* New York: F. A. Praeger, 1964.

BAILEY, S. K. *Congress Makes a Law.* New York: Columbia University Press, 1950.

BARKER, D. *Grivas: Portrait of a Terrorist.* New York: Harcourt, Brace & Co., 1959.

BURKE, K. *A Rhetoric of Motives.* New York: Prentice Hall, 1950.

COSER, L. A. *The Functions of Social Conflict.* Glencoe, Ill.: The Free Press, 1956.

COULOUMBIS, T. A. *The Greek Political Reaction to American and NATO Influences,* New Haven: Yale University Press, 1966.

DAKIN, D. *The Greek Struggle in Macedonia 1897–1914.* Thessaloniki: Institute for Balkan Studies, 1966.

DISCHLER, L. *Die Zypernfrage.* Frankfurt-am-Main, Berlin: Alfred Metzner Verlag, 1960.

DUCHACEK, I. D. *Nations and Men.* New York: Holt, Rinehart & Winston, 1966.

EDEN, A. *Full Circle.* Boston: Houghton Mifflin, 1960.

———. *The Reckoning.* Boston: Houghton Mifflin, 1965.

FALK, R. *Law, Morality, and War in the Contemporary World.* New York: F. A. Praeger, 1963.

FOLEY, C. (ed.). *Grivas Memoirs.* New York: F. A. Praeger, 1964.

———. *Island in Revolt.* London: Longmans, 1962.

FOOT, H. *A Start in Freedom.* New York: Harper & Row, 1964.

GOODRICH, L. M., and SIMONS, ANNE P. *The United Nations and the Maintenance of International Peace and Security.* Washington: The Brookings Institution, 1955.

GRIVAS-DIGHENIS. *Memoirs of the EOKA Struggle 1955–59* (in Greek). Athens, 1961.

GROSS, B. *The Legislative Process.* New York: McGraw-Hill, 1953.

GROSS, E. A. *The United Nations: Structure for Peace.* New York: Harper & Bros., 1962.

HAAS, E. B., and WHITING, A. S. *Dynamics of International Relations.* New York: McGraw-Hill, 1956.

HADWEN, G. and KAUFMAN, J. *How UN Decisions Are Made.* Leiden: A. W. Sythoff, 1960.

HAVILAND, H. FIELD, JR. *The Political Role of the General Assembly.* New York: Carnegie Endowment for International Peace, 1951.

HOVET, T. JR. *Bloc Politics in the United Nations.* Cambridge, Mass.: Harvard University Press, 1960.

———. *Africa and the United Nations.* Evanston, Ill.: Northwestern University Press, 1963.

IKLÉ, F. C. *How Nations Negotiate.* New York: Harper & Row, 1964.

KALOGEROPOULOS-STRATIS, S. *La Grèce et les Nations Unies.* New York: Manhattan Publishing Co., 1957.

KONIDARIS, G. I. *Historical Reminiscences About the Preparation of the Struggle for the Freedom of Cyprus and March 7, 1953* (in Greek). Athens, 1964.

KRANIDIOTIS, N. *Cyprus in the Struggle for Freedom* (in Greek). Athens, 1958.

KRECH, D., CRUTCHFIELD, R. S. and BALLACHEY, E. L. *Individual in Society.* New York: McGraw-Hill, 1962.

KYROU, A. A. *Greek Foreign Policy* (in Greek). Athens, 1955.

MAYES, S. *Cyprus and Makarios.* London: Putnam, 1960.

McLELLAND, C. A., *Theory and the Interstate System.* New York: Macmillan, 1966.

McGRATH, J. E. and JULIAN, J. W. *Negotiation and Conflict: An Experimental Study.* Technical Report No. 16. University of Illinois, July, 1962.

MUNRO, L. *United Nations: Hope for a Divided World.* New York: Holt, Rinehart & Winston, 1960.

NICHOLAS, H. G. *The United Nations as a Political Institution.* London: Oxford University Press, 1959.

RIGGS, R. S. *Politics in the United Nations: A Study of U.S. Influence in the General Assembly.* Urbana, Ill.: Illinois University Press, 1958.

RUSSELL, R. B. *A History of the United Nations Charter.* Washington, D.C.: Brookings Institution, 1958.

SCHUBERT, G. *The Public Interest.* Glencoe, Ill.: Free Press, 1960.

SHEPHERD, C. R. *Small Groups.* San Francisco: Chandler Publishing Co., 1964.

SPROUT, H., and SPROUT, M. *Foundations of International Politics.* Princeton, N.J.: Van Nostrand Co., 1962.

STEPHENS, R. *Cyprus: A Place of Arms.* New York: F. A. Praeger, 1966.

STOESSINGER, J. G. *The United Nations and the Superpowers.* New York: Random House, 1965.

THAYER, C. W. *Guerrilla.* New York: Harper & Row, 1963.

WOODHOUSE, C. M., "Greece 1939–1964," in W. A. HEURTLEY, H. C. DARBEY, C. W. CRAWLEY, and C. M. WOODHOUSE, *A Short History of Greece.* Cambridge: Cambridge University Press, 1965.

XYDIS, S. G. *Greece and the Great Powers 1944–1947.* Thessaloniki: Institute for Balkan Studies, 1963.

ZOTIADIS, G. B., *The Idea of the Partition of Cyprus* (in Greek). Athens, 1959.

ARTICLES

ALGER, C. F. "Nonresolution Consequences of the United Nations and Their Effect on International Conflict," *Journal of Conflict Resolution,* Vol. V, 1961.

AUBERT, V. "Competition and Dissensus, *Journal of Conflict Resolution,* VII, 1963, 26–42.

BARKIN, M., "Conflict Resolution through Implicit Mediation," *Journal of Conflict Resolution,* VIII, 1964, 121–30.

CLAUDE, I. L., JR. "Conflict, Cooperation, and Consensus—The Role of the UN: A Review," *Journal of Conflict Resolution,* VI, 1962, 166–68.

———. "Implications and Questions for the Future," *International Organization,* Vol. XIX, 1965.

———. "The Containment and Resolution of Disputes," in F. O. WILCOX and H. FIELD HAVILAND, JR. (eds.), *The United States and the United Nations.* Baltimore: Johns Hopkins Press, 1961.

EUSTATHIADES, C. "Autodisposition, plébiscites internationaux et la thèse du partage de Chypre," in *Etudes de Droit International 1929–1959,* II, Athens, 1960, 663 ff.

HAAS, E. B. "Dynamic Environment and Static System: Revolutionary Regimes in the United Nations," in M. A. KAPLAN (ed.), *The Revolution in World Politics,* New York: J. Wiley & Sons, 1962, pp. 267–309.

IKLÉ, F. C., in collaboration with N. Leites, "Political Negotiation as a Process of Modifying Utilities," *Journal of Conflict Resolution,* VI, 1962, 19–28.

CORDIER, A. W. "Diplomacy Today," *Journal of International Affairs,* XVII, 1963, pp. 1–8.

KALLIGAS, C. P. Articles on Makarios. *Agon* (Cyprus) (in Greek), November 17–December 13, 1964.

MANIADAKIS, C. Letter to *Kathimerini,* March 8, 1959 (in Greek).

PIPINELIS, P. Articles on the Cyprus Question. *Kathimerini,* February 26–March 7, 1959 (in Greek).

SORAUF, F. J. "The Public Interest Reconsidered," *Journal of Politics*, XIX, 1957, 616–39.

TANTER, R. "Dimensions of Conflict Behavior, 1958–1960," *Journal of Conflict Resolution*, X, 1966, pp. 41–64.

XYDIS, S. G. "Toward 'Toil and Moil' in Cyprus," *Middle East Journal*, XX, 1966, 1–19.

———. "Where Greece Stands Today," *Perspective of Greece, Atlantic Monthly, Supplement*, June, 1955, pp. 17–20.

Index

INDEX

Abdoh, Djalal, 207–8, 302, 352, 394, 424–25, 430, 436, 442, 444–47, 458–59, 461, 463–65, 475

Aegean, 80, 82

Aegean islands, 80, 229

Afghanistan, 39, 59, 381, 384, 466–67, 493

Africa, 286, 359

African states, 13, 58, 495

Afro-Asian group, 58–59, 392, 397, 447, 452, 495, 548

Afxendiou, Grigoris, 68

Agha Shahi, 487–88

Ahmed, G., 407

AKEL, 105

al-Bittar, Salah

al-Shabandar, Mousa, 273, 486–87

Aland islands, 334, 347, 367

Albania, 59, 60, 62, 273, 440, 466–67, 493, 498, 544

Alexander the Great, 229

Alexandretta, 268, 368; see also Hatay

Algeria, 363–64, 370, 448–49, 530; European minority in, 364

Algerian question, 27, 33, 58, 59, 166, 233, 273–74, 278, 297, 302, 322, 356–57, 408, 420, 432, 436, 451–52, 474, 495, 502, 517, 545

Allamanis, S., 504

Allen, George V. 77, 78–83, 84–87, 94–96, 101, 136–40, 156–57, 184, 193, 246–50, 253–56, 264, 483, 548

Allen, Sir Roger, 76, 134, 154–56, 161, 164–66, 167, 169–72, 172–75, 182, 246, 258–60, 321–22, 375

Anatolia, 45, 231

Anglo-Egyptian agreement, 70

Ankara, 11, 44, 80, 84, 89–91, 109–11, 120, 127, 186, 218, 219, 224, 259, 345, 383, 504, 505, 525

Ankara Pact, 8

Annexation of Cyprus, 111, 113–14, 127, 130, 340–41, 342–44, 361, 414

Ano Panagia, 131

Anthimos, Bishop of Kition, 67

Anti-Greek riots; see Istanbul and Izmir

ANZUS, 399

Arab League, 272–73, 466, 556

Arab Legion, 128, 563

Arab states, 58, 75, 77, 181, 186, 229, 231, 236, 263–64, 267, 273, 277, 278, 381, 455, 469, 480, 493, 495

Aranha, Osvaldo, 275

Araujo, Alfonso, 489

Arenales Catalan, Emilio, 208, 211–12, 215, 406–7, 464, 480

Areopagus, 458

Argentina, 59, 275, 451, 466–67, 489–90, 493

Armour, Jr., Norman, 191, 482

Armour Report, 261

Asia Minor, 330, 346–437, 420, 504

Asian states, 13, 53, 58, 278, 476, 495

Atatürk, Kemal, 91, 314, 331

Athens, 6, 9, 76, 90, 107, 117, 127, 131–32, 194, 238, 243, 246, 248, 263,

Athens—*Continued*
266, 271, 375, 453, 475, 476, 478, 482–83, 498, 500, 506–7, 514–15, 525, 548, 559; Archbishop of, 342, 526; British Embassy in, 253; Turkish Embassy in, 253; U.S. Embassy in, 253; University of, 132

Athens Radio, 40, 126, 133, 144–45, 305, 307

Atlantic Charter, 34, 69

Australia, 14, 59, 260, 275, 394, 401–4, 413, 416, 422, 461, 466–67, 480, 492–93

Austria, 59, 275, 466–67, 480, 485, 493

Averoff-Tossizza, Evangelos, xi, 28–29, 339–40, 344–46, 358–59, 373–75, 383, 386–89, 393, 403, 415, 423, 436, 439, 443–46, 450, 452–53, 454, 477–83, 485–86, 495, 498, 504, 506, 514, 518, 521, 524, 526, 534–35, 540, 544, 548–51, 560–61, 563; and Athens explosions, 483; biographical sketch of, 45–47; and Cyprus (atrocities in, 42, 44, 52, 187, 200–202, 210, 235–36, 285, 318–20, 418; and Britain, 42–43, 52, 137, 139, 162, 165–66, 168, 170–71, 179, 183–84, 199–200, 209–10, 218, 229, 235, 247, 250–52, 258, 266, 280, 282, 284–85, 287, 290, 295, 297, 311–12, 314, 316–18, 320–28, 360–61, 366, 368–69, 416, 421, 494, 500–501, 504, 521; and Commonwealth membership, 48, 163, 166, 244; and Dominion status, 48, 186, 218; and Egypt, 43–49; and *enosis*, 42, 53, 110–13, 209, 324, 366; and independence, 42, 48, 50–51, 53, 107, 139, 162, 166, 179, 186, 192, 217–18, 237–39, 241, 244, 248, 251–52, 265–66, 268, 291, 324, 380, 491, 518; and Lebanon, 49, 325; and NATO, 48, 82, 95, 97, 107, 193, 250, 252, 255, 259, 263, 265, 268, 285, 297, 378, 503; and Parliamentary debates, 44, 49, 51–53, 110, 112, 113, 137, 262–63, 344, 500–502, 518, 520–21, 524, 544; and partition, 43, 51, 88–89, 93, 107, 137, 169, 179, 291, 322, 324, 422, 504; plebiscite in, 48, 186, 218, 325; policy toward, as seen from Ankara, 111–12; policy toward, as seen from Whitehall, 109–11; and self-determination, 47, 51–53, 162–63, 166, 187, 200, 216, 219, 224, 227–37, 239–41, 244, 248–49, 251, 262, 265–66, 282–85, 287–88, 290–91, 297, 311–12, 321, 324–25, 328, 353, 363–64, 369, 419, 421–24, 431–32, 456–58, 478, 481, 490–91, 494, 501–2, 504; and self-government, 42, 162, 166, 218, 294, 312, 369; strategic aspects of, 48, 314–15, 324, 420, 521;

and Syria, 49, 325, 420; and Turkey, 42, 46, 48, 53, 79–84, 86–88, 91–92, 95, 138–39, 162, 170, 179–80, 184, 187, 197, 209, 217–19, 229, 234, 237–39, 241, 245, 247–48, 251–55, 257–62, 264–68, 282, 284–85, 288, 290–92, 295, 297–98, 359–68, 418–21, 424, 428–29, 456, 481, 502, 504, 521, 524; and the U.S.S.R., 48); and European Commission of Human Rights, 145, 194; and G. Grivas (Dighenis), 66–68, 71, 101, 103, 109, 179–80, 240–41, 264–67, 507, 526 (*see also* "Isaakios"); and C. Karamanlis, 233 ff., 301; and Labour party, 240–41, 248–49, 253, 256, 283, 285, 290, 327; meetings with (Allen, G. V., 78–84, 86–87, 94–96, 98–101, 136–40, 156–57, 172–74, 183–84, 185, 246–50, 253–55; Allen, Sir Roger, 154–56, 164–66, 169–72, 258–59; Dulles, J. F., 47–49, 197–98, 286; Eden, A., 7, 47, 417; Hammarskjöld, D., 42–43; Herter, C. A., 223; Iksel, S., 80–81, 88–93; Kohler, F. D., 80–81; Krishna Menon, V. K., 41, 293, 380–81; Kuznetsov, V., 61–63; Lloyd, S., 217–19, 514–15; Lodge, H. C., 283–84, 353–54, 481–82, 522–23; Makarios, 161–63, 280–81, 478–79; Noble, A. H. P., 284, 286–87, 302–3; Pavicevic, M., 87, 260–61; Peake, Sir Charles, 77; Penfield, J. K., 174, 255–57; Rountree, W. M., 89; Sarper, S., 290–92; Sergeev, M., 96–98; Spaak, P.-H., 186–87, 243–45, 268–69; Wadsworth, J. J., 41, 56–57; Zoli, A., 193; Zorlu, F. R., 521–22, 525); and the United Nations, 228, 233 ff., 315, 456–57 (and recourse to the General Assembly, 57–58, 136–37; and Resolution 1013 [XI], 42–44, 50, 52, 157, 162, 199–201, 263, 313, 315–19, 321–22, 326, 328, 368; and Resolution 1287 [XIII], 524; rhetorical style in, 34–35; and statements in the First Committee, 311–29, 346–48, 359–69, 416–22, 429–30, 431–33, 442, 455–58, 475; and statements in General Assembly, 220–22, 227–30, 490–91, 494; statements in the General Committee, 198–202, 209–11, 214, 216, 262–63; Thailand proposal in, 41, 53, 238, 254, 256; U.S. proposal in, 56–57)

Axis, 96, 132

Azkoul, Karim, 446

Baghdad Pact, 51, 54, 58, 77, 99, 128–29, 136, 150–52, 180–81, 186, 232, 264, 266, 273, 382, 399, 407, 409, 481, 505, 512

Bakalbassis, George, 11
Baku, 225
Balkan Pact, 17, 250
Balkan Treaty of Alliance, Political Co-operation, and Mutual Assistance, 11
Balkans, 45, 266
Balkans custom union, 46
Bandung Conference, 133
Bandung resolution, 397
Barco, James W., 223–24, 520
Batum, 255
Baxter, William Oliver, 18–20
Bayar, Celal, 219, 223
Bayur, Hikmet, 87
Bedford, 152
Beirut, 512
Belaunde, V. A., 52, 392, 440–41, 451–52, 458–59, 488–89
Belgium, 14, 59, 90, 381, 384–85, 466–67, 493, 515, 518
Belgrade, 266
Benedict, Patriarch of Jerusalem, 480
Berlin crisis, 36, 525
Bermuda, 67, 75
Bevan, Aneurin, 512
Birgi, Nuri, 79, 89, 91, 116, 152, 157
Black Book, 281, 320, 396
Blanqui, L. A., 70
Bled, 11
Boczaada (Tenedos), 94
Boeotia, 8
Boland, Frederick H., 426
Bolivia, 59–60, 368, 381–84, 407, 442, 447, 450–51, 466–67, 480, 493, 520, 546
Bonn, 19, 76, 82, 107, 274
Boston University, 132
Brazil, 275, 466–67, 476, 493
Brentano, Heinrich von, 107
Brighton statement, 250, 252, 253, 256, 261, 290, 512
Britain, 4, 6–7, 14–15, 17, 23, 27, 35, 40, 52, 57–60, 64, 72–73, 79–80, 93, 97, 99, 108, 111, 113, 116, 130, 139, 144, 151–52, 155, 158–60, 166, 168, 185–86, 200–203, 205, 207, 209, 218, 235–37, 245, 263, 269, 272, 276, 280, 285–86, 289–90, 303–4, 306–7, 310, 314, 318, 323–26, 328–30, 335–39, 347, 349, 351, 353–54, 359–61, 364–65, 368, 370, 372, 374, 376–77, 382–85, 387, 390–91, 393, 400–410, 414–16, 421, 428, 441–42, 449, 451–52, 469, 472–74, 482, 486, 488,

494–95, 498–99, 515, 518, 521, 523–26, 529–30, 533, 540, 542, 545, 553, 558, 560; *see also* United Kingdom
British Delegation to the UN, 9, 43, 281, 283–84, 287–88, 293–94, 302–11, 329, 364, 443, 469, 479–80, 484, 520, 522, 541, 549
British Empire, 103, 382, 471
British-Greek relations, 360
Brussels, 109
Buenos Aires, 275
Bulganin, Nikolai A., 99
Bulgaria, 59–60, 62, 266, 273, 466–67, 493
Bulgars, 69
Burma, 12, 14, 33, 272, 466–67, 476, 493
Bursa, 107–8
Byelorussian S.S.R., 59, 381, 391, 466–67, 493
Byzantine political theory, 131
Byzantines, 469

Caccia, Sir Harold, 117, 120
Cairo, 266
Callaghan, James, 148–51, 505
Cambodia, 33, 466–67, 476, 493
Canada, 59, 275, 425, 430–31, 433, 436, 442–44, 446–47, 452–53, 459, 465, 466–67, 488–89, 492–93, 498
Canberra, 275
Canellopoulos, Panayotis, 19
Cannon, Cavendish W., 18, 21, 115
Casablanca, 230
Casals, Pablo, 527
Castle, Barbara, 249, 514
Central Powers, 469
Ceylon, 33, 59, 208, 232, 272, 358–59, 368, 376, 407, 466–67, 469, 473–74, 476, 493, 517, 520, 544
Chapman, Daniel A., 485–86
Chile, 14, 275, 425, 430, 433, 436, 442–44, 446, 453, 459, 465, 466–67, 488–89, 492–93, 546
China, 59, 213, 225, 424, 428, 466–67, 493
"Chronicle of a Secret Organization," 46
Chryssanthopoulos, Themistocles, 354, 356, 379–80
Churchill, Winston S., 10, 72, 227, 404
Cilicia, 512
Colina, Rafael de la, 468, 477, 481, 522–23
"College News Conference" (ABC), 266

Colombia, 12, 13, 41, 54, 59, 372, 376–77, 382, 392, 466–67, 489, 515, 544

Colombo, 253

Colonial Office, 209, 364

Cominform, 12

Commission of Human Rights, xi, 127, 144–47, 194, 239, 263, 280–82, 297, 396, 503

Common Market, 94

Commonwealth, 10, 12, 48, 58, 72, 141, 148, 163, 272, 275, 303–4, 306, 382, 384, 399, 404, 466

Communist China, 521

Communist party of Greece (KKE), 6, 98, 266

Conservative government, 93, 148, 282

Constantinople, 46, 360, 366

Constantinople, Patriarchate of, 81, 129, 292

Constantinople Agreement (1878), 330, 372, 382, 394

Convention for the Protection of Human Rights and Fundamental Freedoms, 144, 146–47, 194, 503

Cooper, Henry Ford, 461

Copais, 8

Copenhagen, 274

Corfu Straits, 63

Costa Rica, 275, 466–67, 493, 546

Council of Europe, x, 47, 108, 280–81

Council of Foreign Ministers, 6

"Courier," 250

Cretan problem, 138

Crete, 6, 388, 396

Crosthwaite, P. M., 479

Cuba, 466, 493

Cyprus: airways in, 495; Archdiocese of, 316 (see also Church of); atrocities in, 40, 50, 52, 142–46, 187, 193–97, 200–204, 210, 230, 235, 261–63, 274, 279–83, 287–88, 295, 297, 318, 339, 350, 354, 375, 381, 396, 400, 418, 505, 541; auxiliary police of, 365, 419; British administration of, or authorities in, 5, 76, 126, 130, 134, 142, 145, 209, 232, 350; British bases in, 6–8, 10–11, 89, 111, 150, 168, 179, 253; British-Cypriot negotiations concerning, 60, 73–74, 87, 104, 107, 114, 116, 134–46, 149, 272, 283, 285, 287, 290, 295, 312, 316, 322, 336–38, 351, 354, 377, 382, 390, 408, 500, 518, 525; cession of, to Turkey, 87, 95, 160; Christian Orthodox Union of Youth, 130; Church of,

90, 93, 129, 132, 304, 331, 333, 349, 375; Communist party in, 11, 304; condominium, 176, 246, 308; Constitution for, 8, 10, 11, 16, 126; Crown Colony of, xi, 469, 474; demilitarization of, 315, 416, 434, 521–22; Dominion status for, 148, 163, 186, 218, 245–46; Emergency measures, 108, 113, 122, 125, 134–35, 144–45, 147, 301–2, 322, 350, 385, 401, 500, 503; enosis (union), 4, 6, 26, 43, 50, 54, 64, 71, 83, 108, 110, 114, 130–32, 142, 147, 152, 159–60, 166, 242–43, 246, 272, 304–8, 324, 331, 333, 341–43, 346, 366, 374, 383–84, 388, 391, 404, 415, 443, 486, 505, 527, 549; Ethnarchy, 25, 31, 54, 71, 75, 129–30, 281, 316, 336, 396; Greek community in, 333, 362, 376, 386, 395; Greek-British negotiations over, 8, 9, 15–17, 28, 57, 87, 392–93; independence for, 3, 26, 42, 50, 54, 87, 107, 108, 113, 137, 139–41, 152, 162, 166, 167, 179, 185, 186–87, 217, 240–41, 242–44, 248, 251, 272, 291, 293, 324, 334, 344, 351, 380–81, 384, 389, 391, 413, 469–70, 472, 474, 485–86, 491, 516, 525, 527–28; Macmillan Plan for, 160, 176, 514–15, 525; mayors of, 316; NATO membership, 252; partition of, 51, 87–89, 92–93, 107–8, 111, 136, 137, 140, 147, 156, 166, 170, 179, 186, 208, 242, 246, 248–49, 254, 259, 268, 270, 291, 308, 322, 324–25, 335, 351, 383, 385, 391, 404, 408, 422, 473, 482, 504–5, 511, 514, 518–19, 522, 528; plebiscite in, 4, 7–8, 48, 54, 64, 93, 132–33, 186, 218, 325, 383, 390, 397, 549; self-determination for, 3, 4, 7, 13, 15, 26, 27–28, 33, 35, 39–40, 50–54, 60, 92, 94, 104, 108, 110, 115–16, 118–22, 124, 132, 135, 137, 143, 147, 151, 158–60, 162–63, 166, 178–79, 181, 187, 194, 197, 199, 202, 206–8, 213, 219, 224, 228, 230, 237, 239–40, 248–49, 252, 261–62, 266, 272, 275, 280, 282–85, 287, 288, 290–96, 306, 309, 312, 321, 323–25, 328, 331–32, 341–43, 346, 351–53, 363–64, 368–69, 372, 376–77, 380, 382, 387, 390–92, 396–400, 411–15, 419–22, 424, 428, 431–35, 437, 440, 442–43, 445–46, 448–58, 468, 473, 478, 481, 485–91, 494, 497–505, 513, 516, 523, 527, 541–43, 547, 549; self-government for, 9, 28, 53, 74, 87, 92, 108, 115–16, 119, 121–23, 132, 151, 166, 218, 239, 293, 294, 304–6, 308, 321, 342, 385, 400, 403, 414, 505, 516–18, 520, 541; tripartite negotiations over, 10, 43–44, 78, 87, 154 ff., 193, 196, 200, 218, 238, 243, 245–46, 267, 286–87, 293–94, 308–10, 336, 377, 401, 403–5, 409,

482, 500, 523, 551; Turkish base in, 506; Turkish community in, 306, 330, 333, 362, 376, 395, 429 (*see also* Turkish Cypriots); Turkish minority in, 18, 48, 111, 122, 126, 151, 160, 162, 175, 179, 187, 219–20, 224, 239, 242, 246, 252, 253, 268, 295, 324–25, 347, 354, 362, 365, 377, 384, 391, 394, 398, 404, 406, 414, 416, 420, 453, 474, 478, 489, 502, 514, 516, 518, 522; Turks in, 110, 135, 137, 287, 381; UN trusteeship for, 108, 109, 141; violations of human rights in, 52, 193, 416 (*see also* Cyprus, atrocities in, and Terrorism, governmental); violence in, 14, 305, 316, 370, 373–74, 411 (*see also* Terrorism)

"Cyprus is Turkish," 366

Cyprus radio, 264, 505

Czech-Egyptian arms deal, 128

Czechoslovakia, 59, 212, 381–82, 466–67, 493

Dardanelles, 94

Denktash, Rauf, 131

Denmark, 193, 274, 425, 430, 433, 436, 442–44, 446, 453, 459, 465–67, 488–89, 492–93, 498, 544

Dervis, Themistocles, 429

"Dighenis," 55–56, 66, 69, 137–38, 144, 262, 317, 319, 322, 373, 562 (*see also* Grivas, George)

Disarmament question, 224–25, 231, 481, 496

Dixon, Sir Pierson, 109, 284, 286, 479, 522, 524

Dodecanese, 68, 79, 160; Turks in, 360

Dominican Republic, 89, 466–68, 476, 493

Dorotheos, Archbishop of Athens, 89, 342

Drago, Mariano J., 489–90

Drakos, Markos, 68

Dulles, Allen, 265–66

Dulles, John Foster, 17, 19–22, 36, 47, 116, 118, 128, 152, 161, 172, 191, 197, 224–26, 231, 252, 255, 257, 284, 286, 354, 445, 523, 548, 563

Dutch New Guinea; *see* West Irian

East-West conflict, xii, 128, 547

Eastern bloc, 58, 280, 505; *see also* Soviet bloc

Eastern Orthodox Church, 131

Ecuador, 59–60, 232, 237, 275, 368, 466–67, 493, 546

EDA (United Democratic Left), 51, 55, 98–99, 263–64, 460, 504, 513

Eden, Anthony, 6–7, 9, 15, 22, 47, 72, 117–18, 120, 125, 128, 158–61, 257, 417, 561–62

Egypt, 10–11, 43, 49, 59–60, 77, 80–81, 99, 111, 197, 230, 233, 236, 264, 272, 277, 350, 369–70, 433, 447, 460–61, 463, 466–67, 493, 495

Egyptians, 469

Eisenhower, Dwight D., 20, 67, 75, 99, 128, 166, 191

Eisenhower-Macmillan meeting, 75

"Eisenhower Doctrine," 99–100, 185, 225, 229, 277, 352, 381

El Salvador, 13, 59, 275, 442, 447, 463, 466–67, 493, 546

Eleftheria, 152

Elizabeth II, 147

Elliniko airbase, 483

Engen, Hans, 274, 436–38, 446–47, 462, 466, 498

Enosis; see Cyprus and *enosis*

Entezam, Nasrollah, 41, 392, 409–10, 447, 454

EOKA (National Organization of Cypriot Fighters), ix, 23–24, 36, 43, 55–56, 64, 66–76, 78, 92–93, 101–4, 106, 110, 115, 117, 126–27, 130, 135, 137, 142, 144, 149, 152–53, 162, 181, 233, 239, 264, 266, 311, 316–17, 319, 321–22, 333, 346, 348, 370, 373, 375, 391, 408, 422, 429–30, 500, 507, 511, 514–15, 519, 525, 530, 541

EPEK, 505

"Epic of Albania," 69

ERE (National Radical Union), 47, 561

Esin, Seyfullah, 205–7, 214, 220–21, 230–32, 292

Eskishehir, 345

Ethiopia, 59, 272, 394, 405, 466–67, 493, 517, 520

Ethnarchic Bureau, 52, 129–30

Ethnarchy, Council of the, 129

European countries, 58, 59, 397

European Defense Community, 19

Falkland islands, 275

Far East, 225

Fascist Italy, 383, 405
Fawzi, Mahmoud, 370
Finland, 193, 334, 466–67, 493
Foot, Sir Hugh (later Lord Caradon), 260, 280, 290, 302, 309, 318, 359, 405, 429, 476, 490, 505–6, 525, 561–63
Foreign Office, 110, 164, 169, 223, 259, 286
France, 14, 58–59, 70, 257, 347, 364, 381, 384–85, 466–67, 471, 493, 495
Free World, 51, 98, 280, 407, 521
Freitas-Valle, Cyro de, 275
Frydas, A.; see Nicosia, Greek Consul in
Fulton, James J., 316

Gallipoli, 340
Garin, Vasco Vieira, 408–9
Garoufalias, P., 271
Gaulle, Charles de, 27, 562
Geneva Conference, 128
Genoa, 469
George, Prince of Greece, 388
Georges-Picot, Guillaume, 212, 385
Germany, 232
Ghana, 229, 237, 261, 303, 359, 466–67, 485–86, 491, 492–93
Gibraltar, 10
Gladstone, William E., 404
Glubb, John Bagot, 128, 563
Greece, 14, 23, 286, 466–67, 471, 553; cabinet, 73, 296, 507, 550–51; Chamber of Deputies, 112; see also Parliament; Church of, 93, 130; Communist insurrection in, 341, 374; Delegation to the UN, 12–13, 19, 21, 27, 33, 40–41, 48, 51, 55, 60, 62, 234 ff., 272–73, 276, 279 ff., 281–83, 286–88, 293–94, 296–98, 302, 311 ff., 338, 343, 345–46, 353, 355–56, 364, 369, 372, 377, 382, 389, 394, 396, 402, 404, 410–12, 414, 416, 425, 428, 433–34, 437–38, 443, 444, 446–47, 451–54, 457–59, 461–63, 465, 469, 472, 475–76, 478–81, 486, 489, 492, 496–97, 500, 505, 511, 515–16, 519–20, 522–23, 537–38, 541, 546–49, 552; elections, 117, 124, 560–61; Government, 4, 503, 506–7, 512, 526, 556–59; London Embassy of, 117, 281; Parliament, 6, 14, 16, 24, 31, 50, 111, 113, 114, 343–44, 520; Permanent Mission to the UN, 11, 112, 144, 155, 191, 234, 282, 288, 301, 495 ff., 502; Washington Embassy, 57, 62, 95, 117, 118, 281, 292, 301, 379, 444, 483
Greek Air Force, 526
Greek Army, 340, 345, 348

Greek Cypriot Communists, 71
Greek Cypriots, 71, 75, 106, 264, 334–35, 359, 373, 375, 381, 390, 392, 395, 399, 404, 407, 429, 441–42, 450, 487, 505–6, 511–12, 518, 530
Greek General Staff, 110
"Greek question," 529
Greek Rally party, 8, 560
Greek War of Independence, 69
Greek-Albanian relations, 61, 62, 63
Greek-American relations, 62
Greek-Bulgarian relations, 63
Greek-British relations, 360
Greek-Soviet relations, 61, 63
Greek-Turkish relations, 10–11, 45, 78, 84, 91–93, 95, 158, 177, 192, 218–19, 239, 245, 246, 253, 261, 290, 292, 305, 323, 367, 502
Greek-Turkish wars, 347
Grivas, George, 14, 24–25, 27, 29–30, 49, 64–65, 67, 68–72 (biography), 78, 101–6, 109, 111, 125, 126–27, 130–33, 135, 137–38, 151–53, 180–81, 240, 263–66, 282, 335–36, 348, 506, 525–26, 553–55, 561–63; see also "Dighenis"
Gromyko, Andrei, 224–26, 231, 255
Guatemala, 41, 59, 208, 211, 275, 382, 394, 406–7, 438–39, 464, 466–67, 480, 493, 520
Gunewardene, R. S. S., 358–59, 389, 473–74

Hague, The, 274
Haiti, 89, 434–35, 439, 466–67, 493, 517, 546
Halifax, Lord, 8
Hammarskjöld, Dag, 109, 112–14, 226, 229
Harding, Sir John, 24, 43–44, 66–67, 72, 74, 103, 106, 108, 114–18, 127, 144–48, 150, 152, 199, 260, 279–80, 306, 317–18, 322, 338, 395, 405, 500, 512, 562–63
Harding-Makarios talks, 24, 28, 43, 64, 113–28, 294, 306, 321, 338, 404
Hayter, Sir William, 259
Hatay, 368; see also Alexandretta
"Heads of Agreement," 10
Hellenism, 507
Henderson, Loy W., 185
Hephaistus, 70
Herter, Christian A., 172
Hispaniola, 89

Hitler, 225
Home, Lord, 317, 368
Honduras, 466–67, 476, 493
Hood, J. D. L., 461–62
Hopkinson, Henry (Lord Colyton), 10, 17, 364, 400, 561–62
House of Commons, 15, 17, 67, 72, 74, 88, 117, 126, 158, 317, 322, 332, 393, 396, 400, 505–6; Cyprus debate in, 148–52
House of Lords, 67, 368
Hoyer-Millar, Frederick (Lord Inchyra), 157
Hughes, John C., 20
Hull, Cordell, 34
Human rights, violations of; *see* Cyprus, atrocities in
Hungarian question, 191, 197, 217, 224, 408, 529
Hungary, 59, 146, 191, 232, 394, 400–401, 448, 449, 466–67, 493, 541
Hussein, King of Jordan, 128, 563

Iceland, 25, 30, 59, 193, 392, 442, 453–54, 466–67, 470, 493, 517, 520, 545
Iksel, Settar, 79, 80–81, 84, 90–93
Iliou, I., 504
Illueca, Jorge H., 413–14, 480
Imroz (Imbros), 94
India, 12, 33, 39, 59, 87, 233, 236–37, 254, 359, 394, 399, 466–73, 476, 493, 515, 517, 520, 527–28, 552
Indians in South Africa, question of, 13, 222, 472
Indochina, 225
Indonesia, 278, 466–67, 493
Intelligence Service (British), 31, 77–78
ICBM, 98–99, 263, 269, 289
IRBM, 98, 269
International Court of Justice, 337, 452
International Labor Office (ILO), 145
Iran, 59, 272, 302, 392, 409–10, 442, 444, 447, 454, 466–67, 493, 515, 522–23, 553
Iraq, 59, 128, 185, 272–73, 466–67, 473, 476, 481, 487, 493, 512, 537, 547
Ireland, 59, 223, 394, 405–6, 408, 466–67, 493, 517, 520, 546
Iron Curtain, 62, 281
Irwin, Henry F. 356
"Isaakios," 102, 109, 179–80, 240, 264, 507; *see also* Averoff-Tossizza

Ismay, Lord, 72–74, 94, 107, 109, 175, 262, 336
Israel, 58, 273, 466–67, 493, 495
Istanbul, 84, 86, 186, 395; Greeks in, 81–82, 85, 95, 113, 179, 270, 292–93; riots of 1955 in, 50, 84–85, 112, 114, 116, 158, 161, 179, 257, 292, 323, 345, 353, 366, 505
Italian government, 56
Italian Peace Treaty, 334
Italy, 46, 59, 274, 334, 347, 367, 466–67, 471, 493, 553
Izmir, 84, 86, 114, 116, 161, 257; Greek Consulate in, 161

Jamali, Fadil, 273
Japan, 58, 59, 466–67, 471, 493
Jawad, Hashim, 273, 474
Jewish minority in Greece, 420
Jordan, 36, 59, 128, 185, 272–73, 466–67, 480–81, 512, 520
"Justice for Cyprus Committees," 133

Karachi, 136
Karamanlis, Constantine, xi, 24, 29, 31, 46–47, 54, 62, 63–64, 72–73, 75–77, 83, 84–86, 90, 93, 115, 118–20, 143, 157, 165, 180, 185–86, 196, 218, 227, 233, 235, 253, 257, 267, 282, 287, 296, 301, 482–83, 502, 506–7, 512–13, 525, 550–51, 561–62
Kardelj, Edvard, 267
Kartalis, George, 343
Kashmir, 33, 272, 380, 407, 473, 563
Kassimatis, Gregory, 7, 53–55, 112, 271
Kathimerini, 249, 476
Kavalieratos, Phaidon A., 18–19, 44–45, 483–84
Kenya, 147, 370
Khrushchev, Nikita S., 36, 255, 525
Kition, 129
KKE; *see* Communist party of Greece
Knights Templars, 469
Kohler, Foy D., 80
Kokkinou, Loulla, 203–4
Köprülü, Fuat, 116, 122
Korea, 30, 161, 225, 328
Korean Armistice, 8
Korean Question, 54, 529
Kranidiotis, Nikos, 124
Krishna Menon, V. K., 12, 41–42, 50, 53–55, 142, 158, 254, 271–72, 293,

Krishna Menon, V. K.—*Continued*
326, 358–59, 368, 380–81, 468–73,
497, 517, 527, 548, 563
Kuchuk, Fazil, 76, 108, 114, 429, 511
Kuznetsov, V., 61–63, 208, 215, 278
Kykko, Abbot of, 131; monastery of, 131
Kyprianos, Bishop of Kyrenia, 342–43,
346
Kyrenia, 129, 395
Kyrou, Achilles A., 69
Kyrou, Alexis A., 7–9, 11–12, 14–15,
17–18, 20–22, 29–31, 33–34, 69, 134,
274, 480, 555, 560–61, 563

Labour government, 129
Labour party, 10, 52, 73, 78–79, 93, 106,
108, 135, 147, 148, 151, 235, 240–41,
248–51, 253, 256, 261–62, 280–83,
285, 290, 297, 327, 344, 396, 398, 505,
512, 514, 562
Laingen, Bruce Lowell, 354, 356, 380
Lall, Arthur S., 293, 380, 446
Lambton, Lord, 149
Lancaster House, 526
Lange, Halvard, 498
Laos, 33, 466–67, 476, 493
Larkin, T. C., 399–400
Latin America, 455
Latin American group, 58, 466, 522
Latin American rebellions, 383
Latin American states, 13, 54, 59, 194,
275, 377, 379–80, 397, 399, 407, 447,
448, 476, 495, 521, 546, 556
Latvian S.S.R., 349
Lausanne, 46, 231, 334; Conference, 331;
Treaty of, 45, 80, 94, 160, 313–14,
329, 337, 354, 367–68, 370, 372, 382,
394, 418, 470–71
League of Nations, 231, 409
Lebanon, 36, 133, 185, 233, 325, 379,
446, 461, 463–64, 493, 512, 520, 552
Lenin, Vladimir I., 70
Lennox-Boyd, Alan, 72–75, 89, 101, 108,
125, 126, 136, 147–49, 151, 157–58,
317, 322, 335, 505, 516, 561, 563
Leonidas, 69
Lequerica, José Felix de, 451–52, 473
Liatis, Alexis, 121, 271, 521
Liberal party (Greek), 98, 261
Liberia, 59, 461, 466–67, 493
Libya, 272–73, 466, 481, 493
Lionaes, Aase, 207, 212
Lisbon, 274
Lloyd, Selwyn, 9, 12, 107, 117, 152, 157,

202–5, 213, 217–19, 221, 224, 226–27,
231–32, 258, 262, 374, 505–6, 515,
525, 548, 561
Lloyd George, D., 404
Lodge, Henry Cabot, 20–22, 223, 278,
283–84, 293–94, 353–54, 356, 370,
377, 380, 416–17, 424–25, 445, 466,
473, 481–84, 492, 497, 521, 522–23,
549
Loizidis, Savvas, 55, 58–60, 77, 347,
380–81, 391–99
Loizidis, Socrates, 393
London, 19, 76, 106, 110, 162, 281
London Agreement, 4, 53–527
London Conference of 1959, 267, 524,
554
London Tripartite Conference on the
Eastern Mediterranean and Cyprus,
24, 43, 64, 114, 115, 155–57, 158–61,
168, 170, 176–77, 196, 257, 305–6,
323, 333, 337–38, 346, 357
Louis XV, 210
Loutfi, Omar, 433, 446–47, 463
Luns, Joseph M. A. H., 274
Luxembourg, 14, 59, 466–67, 493

Macedonia, 69
Macmillan, Harold, 67, 72, 75, 118, 135,
145, 147, 152, 159, 174, 251, 562; first
plan of, 160; second plan of, 176,
514–15, 525
Madagascar, 76
Madrid, 275
Mahé, 76
Makarios III, Archbishop and Ethnarch,
5, 8, 24, 26, 29, 43–44, 47, 49, 52, 54,
68, 70–71, 73–76, 78–79, 83–84, 87,
90–94, 101–11, 114–27, 130, 135–36,
137–39, 144–46, 149, 151–52, 157,
159, 161–63, 166, 179–81, 185, 191,
194–95, 199, 203–4, 217, 219, 235,
240, 243, 246, 252, 261–64, 266, 272,
276, 279, 280–83, 289, 291, 295, 297,
301, 306–7, 311, 316, 320–22, 336,
338, 342, 346, 348–51, 361, 366, 375,
380, 384–85, 392, 400–401, 408, 443,
478–79, 481, 494, 500, 502, 505–6,
511, 513, 514, 525–27, 541, 552–54,
561, 563; biography of, 131–34
Makhaira, Abbot of, 374–75; Monastery
of, 68
Makins, Sir Roger, 127
Makivchuk, F. Y., 370
Malaya, 33, 229, 232, 237, 261, 303, 359,
381, 389–90, 407, 431, 466–68, 476,
493
Malvinas islands; *see* Falkland islands

Manchester Guardian, 108
Mangasha, Ato Yawand-Wossen, 405
Maniadakis, Constantine, 15
Manuilsky, D., 440
Mao Tse-tung, 512
Marathassa, 76
Marathon, 69
Markezinis, Spyros, 16
Marshall Plan, 225
Massachusetts, 417
Matsch, Franz, 485, 523
Mau-Mau, 317
Mediterranean, 72, 213, 230, 314, 373, 398, 441, 470; eastern, xi, 17, 45, 49, 118, 120–21, 170, 208, 263, 266, 277, 306, 370, 417
"Meet the Press" (NBC), 266
"Megali Idea," 45, 46, 69
Melas, George V., 116, 143, 159, 167, 192, 197, 257, 271, 283, 286, 289
Melas, Michel C., 163, 175, 242, 245–46
Melas, Pavlos, 69
Menderes, Adnan, 11, 76, 79, 81, 87, 90–92, 108, 112, 136, 140, 186, 291–92, 506, 525, 562
Menemencioglou, Turgut, 291
Merkouris, S., 145
Metaxas, John, 15, 69
Mexico, 59, 60, 275, 379, 466–68, 472, 481, 493, 522–24, 552–53
Mezincescu, Edouard, 372–73
"Micrasiatic catastrophe," 45
Middle East, 9, 10, 17, 100, 128–29, 147, 150, 181, 195, 224–26, 229–32, 236, 253–55, 263, 265, 277, 286, 290, 350, 353, 487, 525, 529
Middle East Command, 10, 36, 70, 147
Milikouri, 72, 319
Milliet, 504
Minerva, 453
Mitsada, 388
Mod, Peter, 400–401
Moore, A. R., 284, 286
Moroccan question, 13
Moroccan resolution, 13–14
Morocco, 59, 273, 363, 466–67, 493, 529
Morphou, 495
Morrison, Herbert S., 7
Moscow, 77, 117
Mostras, Vassili, 9, 76, 78
Mouskos, Michael C., 131; *see also* Makarios

Munro, Sir Leslie, 22, 198, 208–9, 211–12, 214–17, 220–23, 492
Murphy, Robert D., 89, 223, 257, 284
Muslim heritage, 517

Najib-Ullah, Dr., 384
Nairobi, 76
Nasser, 267
National Pact, 231
Nazi army, 345, 383
Nazi-Soviet pact, 97
Nepal, 33, 59, 140, 381, 390–91, 407, 466–68, 493
Nervo, Padilla, 481
Nesbitt, Wallace, 430–31, 454
Netherlands, 12, 59, 208, 274, 394, 404–5, 466–67, 493
New Delhi, 272, 557
New York, 107, 193, 219, 246, 261, 266, 268, 271, 276, 279, 302, 338, 347, 354, 444–45, 550
New York Times, 255, 490
New Zealand, 13, 22, 24, 59, 198, 275, 394, 399, 401, 466–67, 480, 493
Niarchos, Stavros, 260
Nicaragua, 466–68, 476, 493
Nicosia, 30, 71, 107, 117, 121, 125, 129, 131, 144, 152, 252, 264, 302, 375, 429, 490, 495; Greek Consul General in, 100, 418 (*see also* Vlachos, A.); Greek Consul in, 100–3, 153, 281; Mayor of, 430; Turkish Consulate in, 388
Nikolareizis, Dimitri, 43
Nisot, Joseph, 385
Nobel Prize, 77
Noble, Allan H. P., 43–44, 184, 193–94, 284, 286, 311–12, 318, 321, 323, 358, 368–69, 372, 384, 396, 401, 405, 420, 485, 491–92, 494, 518–19, 549; speeches in the Political Committee by, 302–11, 373–76, 414–16, 442–43, 474–75, 479
Noel-Baker, Philip, 396
Nordic Council, 274
Norstad, Lauris, 98
NATO, x, xi, 8, 10–12, 17, 25–26, 30, 36, 47, 49, 51, 58, 72–73, 75–76, 80, 82–83, 87, 89–90, 94–95, 97–100, 107–10, 112–13, 116, 118, 120, 127–28, 133, 135, 150–52, 154, 158, 161, 163, 164, 166, 169, 175, 186–87, 191, 193, 204, 216, 225, 232, 242 ff., 250, 252–53, 255, 259, 263–69, 274, 280, 285, 289, 292, 297, 303, 307, 341–51, 370, 372, 378, 381–82, 384, 399, 404, 415, 429, 444, 466, 482–83,

NATO—*Continued*
497–98, 503, 506, 515, 523, 527, 542, 545, 559
"Northern tier," 9
Norton, Sir Clifford, 6–7
Norway, 59, 193, 208, 211–12, 274, 425, 430, 433, 436–38, 442–44, 446, 453, 455, 459, 461–63, 465–67, 488–89, 492–93, 498
Nosek, Jiri, 212, 216
Novitsky, G. K., 391
Nuclear bases, 96–97, 150, 352
Nuclear war, 96–99
Nuri es Said, 273
Nutting, Anthony, 14

O'Brien, Conor Cruise, 405–6
Observer, The, 43, 67
OHEN (Christian Orthodox Union of Youth), 130
Olympic Thunder, 76
Oman, 370, 495
Onassis, Aristotle, 76
Organization of American States (OAS), 275, 382, 399
Orly, 186–87
Oslo, 193, 274
Osman, Yacoub, 404
Ottoman Empire, 10, 69, 138, 330, 434
Oxford Union, 563

Pacific Charter, 117, 119, 121
Pakistan, 33, 59, 87, 232, 272, 359, 394, 407, 466–68, 487–88, 493
Palamas, Christian X., 74, 113, 143, 193, 198, 274–75, 278, 283–84, 286, 289–90, 378, 447, 477–79, 481–82
Palestine, 409, 421
Pallicaridis, Evagoras, 317, 319, 393–94
Panama, 39, 59, 275, 382, 394, 399, 413–14, 466–67, 480, 493, 517, 520
Pan-Arab nationalism, 230
Pan-Cyprian Gymnasium, 131, 302
Pan-Cyprian National Assembly, 133, 152
Pan-Cyprian Youth Organization (PEON), 130
Pan-Hellenic Committee for Self-Determination for Cyprus, 89, 342
Papagos, Alexander, 8–11, 14–15, 17, 19–21, 28–30, 54, 64, 70, 72, 115, 133, 161, 559–63

Papandreou, George, 16, 51, 64, 86–87, 98, 261–62, 343, 513
Papapolitis, S., 504–5
Paphos, 131, 367
Paraguay, 466–68, 476, 493
Paris, 19, 186, 263, 392, 444, 482, 525
Paris Peace Conference, 6
Parliament (British), 470
"Parliamentary diplomacy," 6, 16, 24, 28, 69, 133, 533–34, 540, 555
Patriarchate of Istanbul, 81–82, 84–86, 113, 292; *see also* Patriarchate of Constantinople
Paul I, King of Greece, 6, 476, 507, 513
Pavicevic, Miso, 87, 260–61
"Peaceful coexistence," 278, 479
Peake, Sir Charles, 8, 47, 76–77, 115, 119, 120, 157, 560
Pearl Harbor, 97
Peive, Y. V., 349–52, 391
Penfield, James K., 174, 255–57, 301, 482–84, 513
Persia, Great King of, 229
Persian Gulf, 225, 230
Persians, 469
Peru, 279, 392, 440–41, 451, 452, 458–59, 461–62, 468, 476, 488–89, 493, 552
Pesmazoglou, George, 219, 264, 293, 361, 504, 525
Philippines, 59, 237, 272, 392, 466–68, 493
Pipinelis, Panayotis, 15
Plastiras, Nicholas, 47, 133
Poland, 59, 63, 466–67, 493
Polaris, 99
Politis, Jean, 7
Portugal, 58, 59, 274, 394, 408–9, 466–67, 493
Potomac Charter, 117, 119, 121
Prica, Srja, 370
Profumo, John, 135, 151, 322
Protitch, Dragoslav, 296, 394
"Pseudo-agreements," 532
Pyla, 264

Quai D'Orsay, 274
Quiroga Galdo, German, 382–84, 450–51, 480

Radcliffe constitution, 43, 51, 53, 64, 67, 73–76, 87, 89, 92, 105, 108–10, 135,

151, 167, 175, 196, 218, 262, 306, 312, 351, 381, 401, 416, 516
Reddaway, John, 124, 127
Rendis, Constantine, 107
Republican party, 51, 504
Resolution 290 (IV), 225–26
Resolution 421 (V), 413
Resolution 545 (VI), 396, 413
Resolution 637 (VII), 4, 8, 16, 26, 392, 396
Resolution 742 (VIII), 9
Resolution 814 (IX), 3, 13–16, 22–23, 545, 551
Resolution 1013 (XI), 3, 26–28, 39, 41, 50, 52, 55, 66, 68, 73–75, 78–79, 104, 107–8, 112–14, 127, 134, 136, 142, 151, 157, 162, 164, 167, 168, 178, 192, 195, 199–200, 206, 208, 221, 232, 238, 261–62, 264, 269, 281, 284, 291, 296, 301, 304, 307, 310–11, 313, 315–19, 322, 326, 328, 335–39, 350–51, 368, 370, 372, 376–77, 381–82, 384–85, 388, 390–91, 393, 400–402, 405–15, 428, 430, 433–35, 439–40, 468, 485, 488, 491, 493, 497, 499–500, 504, 513, 516, 520, 523–24, 527, 532–33, 545, 551, 554
Resolution 1287 (XIII), 3, 26, 28, 524–25, 527, 532–33, 545, 551, 554
Resolution 1573 (XV), 27
Reuters, 366
Rhodes, 80, 250
Rizk, Edward A., 463–64
Roberts, Sir Frank, 246
Rodriguez Fabregat, Enrique, 407–8, 448–49
Rolin, Henri A., 144
Romania, 59, 250, 372–73, 381, 466–67, 471, 493
Romans, 469
Rome, 186, 193
Romulo, Carlos, 237, 392
RAF airfield (Nicosia), 264, 507
Ross, A. D. M., 172, 175, 267
Rossides, Zenon, 135, 284, 375, 395
Rountree, William M., 89, 167, 192, 197, 223, 254–55, 284, 286, 379–80, 444–45, 483–84
Rousseau, Douanier, 69
Russian danger, 10

Saint Cyr, 562
St. Irene, Church of, 132
Saint-Lot, Emile, 434–35
Salamis, 69

San Francisco Conference (UNCIO), 332, 547
Sandys, Duncan, 150
Santiago, 275
Sarper, Selim, 27, 112–13, 243, 285, 289–91, 346–48, 360–64, 366, 395, 397, 398, 419–20, 424, 430, 447, 456, 458, 481, 485, 489, 492, 504, 511; speeches by, in the Political Committee, 329–46, 385–89, 410–12, 423, 428–30, 435–36, 454–55, 458, 467
Saudi Arabia, 59, 232, 466–67, 520
Scandinavian states, 193
Schurmann, C. W. A., 404–5
Selim II, 394
Serbs, 69
Sergeev, Mikhail, 96–99
Serrano, José, 488
Sèvres, Treaty of, 46, 347
Seychelles islands, 24, 26, 31, 45, 49, 54, 64, 75–76, 127, 133, 145, 179, 316, 336, 349, 362, 563
Shaha, Rishikesh, 390–91
Shepilov, Dimitri T., 61
Sisco, Joseph J., 356–58
Slav expansionism, 218
Slavophobia, 131
Slim, Mongi, 212–13, 215–16, 449–50
Solomon, judgment of, 383
Somaliland, 272
South Tyrol, 275
Southeast Asia Treaty Organization (SEATO), 51, 225, 275, 399, 407
Southern Albania; see Northern Epirus
South-North alignment, 528, 547
Soviet bloc, 11, 25, 51, 59–63, 97, 186, 273, 288, 291, 390, 400, 466, 498, 520, 556
Soviet Delegation to the UN, 495–96
Soviet satellites, 36
Spaak, Paul-Henri, 107, 109, 136–37, 139–40, 147, 152, 155, 163, 165, 169–70, 174–77, 186–87, 242 ff., 252, 421, 494, 500–501, 504, 521; an 263, 265, 267–70, 276, 286, 292, 482, 506, 517, 527
Spain, 59, 274, 447, 451–52, 459, 466–68, 473
Sparta, 69
Spectator, The, 351
Sputnik, 97, 263, 286, 289, 496
Stadium street, 483
Stalin, Joseph V., 8
Stefanopoulos, Stefanos, 9, 11, 15, 19–20, 22, 24, 159

Stockholm, 274, 480

Stoica, Chivu, 273

Strasbourg, 106, 108, 144, 194, 262, 396

Strategic Air Command (SAC), 163

Stratos, Andreas, 54–55, 265, 277–78, 343, 480

Sudan, 59, 394, 404, 466–67, 517, 520

Suez, 36, 49, 58, 70, 81, 129, 147, 224, 229, 236, 255, 273

Swaraj, 527

Sweden, 193, 274, 334, 467

Syria, 36, 43, 59, 99, 133, 179, 186, 225, 229, 233, 236, 242, 268, 272, 325–26, 368, 381, 390, 398, 420, 433–34, 447, 460–67

Syrian complaint, 2, 266–68, 480

Syrian war scare (crisis), 49, 185, 257, 265, 267, 273, 286, 289, 495–96, 512

Taiwan straits, 512, 525

Taksim; see Cyprus, partition of

Terrorism, agitational, 24, 32, 40, 135–36, 305, 307, 309, 335–36, 339–41, 350–51, 388, 400, 404, 408, 518, 555

Terrorism, governmental, 24, 40, 134, 143, 233

Thailand, 40–41, 50, 52–53, 59–60, 158, 208, 238, 254, 272, 276, 392, 468, 493, 553

Thames, 382

Theophilos, 69

Theotokis, Spyros, 31, 45, 115–20

Thermopylae, 69

Theseion, 70

Thessaloniki, 63, 484; farm school of, 167

Thessaly, 45

Thors, Thor, 392, 453–54

Thrace, Western, 160, 184, 332, 334; Turks in, 48, 79, 95–96, 184, 360, 387, 419

Times (London), 114

Times of Cyprus, 316, 419, 476

TMT (Turkish Defense Organization), ix, 511

To Vima, 476

Togoland, 364, 397

Treaty of Establishment (1930), 293

Tribune, 147

Trieste, 334, 367

Troodos, 69

Trujillo, José Vicente, 237

"Truman Doctrine," 6

Tsatsos, Constantine, 55, 57, 63, 86

Tsiang, T. F., 213–14

Tsouderos, Emmanuel J., 6

Tunisia, 59, 212, 233, 273, 363, 442, 447, 449–50, 466–67, 493, 520

Tunisian question, 529

Tunisian resolution, 13–14

Turkey and Cyprus, 9, 11, 17, 23, 29, 54, 58–59, 78–79, 286, 289, 381, 394, 466–67, 493, 495, 498, 516, 541–43, 553, 557–58; elections in, 164, 175, 177, 181, 217, 223, 242–43, 259, 279, 309; Grand National Assembly of, 44, 177

Turkish Cypriots, 71, 74, 76, 81, 83, 106, 114, 127, 134, 149, 166–67, 252, 264, 302, 307, 321, 333, 335, 339, 358–59, 367, 373, 375, 381, 383, 386–90, 395, 404, 429, 441, 442, 487, 505–6, 511–12, 518; *see also* Cyprus, Turkish community in, or Turkish minority in

Turkish Delegation to the UN, 284, 289, 479, 481, 482, 489, 517, 519–20, 522–23, 541

Turko-Syrian dispute, 246

Turks, 69

Turks in northern Greece; *see* Western Thrace, Turks in

Tyler, William R., 283

Tylliria, 72, 76

Ukrainian S.S.R., 59, 369, 372, 381, 391, 440, 466–67, 493

Ullrich, Josef, 381–82

Unden, Osten, 274

Union of South Africa, 58–59, 466, 484–85, 493

U.S.S.R., 11, 16, 34, 36, 59, 60–62, 75, 96, 97, 99, 150, 225–26, 231, 242, 263, 266–67, 269, 278, 289, 349, 372, 425, 495–96, 520, 523–24, 529, 531

United Arab Republic, 517, 520

United Democratic Left; *see* EDA

United Kingdom, 145, 375, 394, 443, 467, 480, 492–94

United Nations, xii, 3, 6, 7, 20, 126, 132–34, 136–37, 139–43, 157, 162, 164, 177–78, 180–83, 187, 193, 196, 219, 226–28, 232, 243–44, 246, 280, 285, 289, 290, 291, 315, 320, 328, 335, 355, 359, 361, 377–78, 382, 384, 392, 395, 398–99, 401–2, 406, 409, 413, 420, 433, 436–42, 445–46, 449–52, 456–57, 460, 462, 469, 470, 472–73, 476, 480, 486–87, 490–92, 499–500, 529–30; *ad hoc* Political Committee, 12, 13, 61; Charter of, 195, 336, 352, 412, 431,

433–434, 439, 441, 450, 453, 458, 469, 472–73, 492, 517 (Article 1 of, 5, 117, 131; Article 2 of, 11, 194, 203, 209, 212–13, 217, 221, 303, 385; Article 10 of, 5, 16; Article 14 of, 5, 16; Article 27 of, 547; Article 33 of, 22, 371, 455, 521, 534; Article 34 of, 212; Article 35 of, 5; Article 51 of, 310, 555; Article 52 of, 26, 555; Article 55 of, 210, 376, 402; Article 73 of, 16, 209, 272, 293, 332; Article 74 of, 332; Article 98 of, 530; Article 99 of, 530; Article 103 of, 370; purposes and principles of, 5, 178, 230, 238, 283, 285, 295–96, 350, 354, 370, 382, 393, 397, 430, 437–38, 440–42, 448, 454, 485, 488, 516); and Commission on Human Rights, 448; Economic and Social Council of, 232, 447; Fourth Committee of, 7, 8, 13, 363; General Assembly of, 3, 4, 53, 171, 228, 296, 354, 371, 373, 400, 411, 414–15, 432, 436, 439, 442, 446, 448, 450, 465, 469, 470, 475, 477 ff., 498, 501, 506, 532 ff. (Fifth Session of [1950], 7, 392; Sixth Session of [1951], 7, 47, 133, 392; Seventh Session of [1952], 8, 133, 392; Eighth Session of [1953], 4, 9, 133, 392; Ninth Session of [1954], 3–4, 54, 57, 304, 349, 393, 404, 537, 551; Tenth Session of [1955], 3, 22, 28, 161, 306, 349, 537; Eleventh Session of [1956–57], 3, 27, 47, 51–64, 127, 137, 261, 276, 305, 312, 334, 350, 413, 453, 504, 527, 537–38, 551, 558; Twelfth Session of [1957], 3, 23, 28, 33, 35, 39–44, 63, 78, 154, 495–96, 499, 511, 513, 516, 520, 527, 533, 537–38, 540, 541–42, 544–47, 553, 557; Thirteenth Session of [1958], 3, 4, 33, 36, 511, 513 ff., 526, 546, 553); General Committee of, 12, 19, 22, 194, 198 ff., 220, 236–37, 261, 272, 279, 303, 374, 396, 466, 536–37, 542; Political Committee of, 12–13, 19, 22, 28, 33, 39, 47, 53, 60, 66, 112, 113, 231, 237, 239, 262, 271, 273, 276, 278, 279, 281–82, 287–89, 293–98, 301 ff., 356, 380, 381 ff., 428 ff., 445–46, 478–79, 481, 484–85, 488–94, 498, 499, 504, 506, 511, 513, 516 ff.; Rules of procedure in, 143, 198, 206, 211, 222, 278, 288, 297, 339, 412, 424, 431, 433, 438, 457, 460–61, 465, 535–37; Secretariat of, 12, 288, 444, 462, 530, 534; Secretary-General of, 24, 52, 56, 61, 74, 112, 114, 127, 143–144, 195, 213, 232, 238, 344, 392, 429, 515, 530, 534–35, 537, 548 (see also Hammarskjöld); Security Council of, 26, 34, 85, 228, 232, 435, 512, 530, 547, 555; Third Committee of, 7, 8, 13, 143, 397; and United States, 8, 12, 14, 16–17, 20–21, 35–36, 40–41, 47, 49, 51, 55–57, 59,

115, 118, 127–28, 139–41, 156, 163, 166, 169, 172, 174, 176–77, 185, 191–93, 216, 223, 236, 246, 248, 252–53, 256, 269, 272, 275–76, 283–84, 286, 288, 353–57, 370–71, 379–80, 382, 416, 466, 468, 473, 476, 493, 496–97, 501, 505, 520–21, 526–27, 544, 547, 553–54 (bases of, in Greece, 6; Congress of, 128, 556; Consul of, in Nicosia, 119; Delegation of, to the UN, 13, 18–19, 21, 41, 140, 283–84, 294, 355, 357–58, 372, 378, 414, 425, 444–46, 496, 519; Department of State of, 18, 41, 57, 62, 89, 127, 139–40, 166, 174, 184, 193, 197, 223–24, 246, 249, 253–54, 257, 269, 283–84, 292, 354–58, 372, 378–80, 444–46, 482–83, 521, 523, 563; Marines, 512; Sixth Fleet of, 99, 137)

UNEF, 229;

UNOGIL, 512

U.S.–Greek Agreement, October 12, 1953, 8

USIA, 256, 483–84, 559

Urquia, Miguel Rafael, 463

Uruguay, 14, 275, 294, 407–8, 442, 448–49, 466–67, 493, 546

Vafiadis, Markos, 8

Vassilia, 395

Vela, David, 438–39

Venezuela, 59, 208, 466–68, 476, 493

Venice, 469

Venizelos, Eleftherios, 47, 132, 314, 331

Venizelos, Sophocles, 6, 8, 46, 64, 83, 86–87, 133, 342–43, 503–4, 513

Vergin, Nuredin, 185

Vietnam, 529

Vlachos, Angelos, 66, 103, 106, 152 (see also Nicosia, Greek Consul-General in)

Voice of America, 250

Volkan, ix, 511

Vyshinsky, A. J., 11–12

Wadsworth, James J., 41, 56–57

Walker, E. Ronald, 401–4

Wang, Yun-wu, 428

Washington, 247, 253–54, 271, 280, 355, 465, 521

Wathayakon, Prince, 392

West Germany, 257

West Irian, question of, 13, 33, 58, 59, 233, 262, 274, 278, 357, 363, 493

Western Alliance, 17, 176, 187, 263, 266, 444, 497
Western bloc, 186, 496
Western group, 58
White, Lincoln, 127–28
White Paper (British), 145, 275, 391
Whitehall, 78, 109, 110–11
Wilcox, Francis O., 286
Williams, E. R., 89, 354–55
World Council of Churches, 132
World Peace Council, 352
World War I, 46, 314, 340, 346, 404, 469, 504
World War II, 46, 49, 69, 131, 255, 304–5, 322, 345, 348, 401, 542

Yemen, 59, 232, 466–67, 493, 520
Yugoslavia, 11, 14, 58, 59, 60, 233, 264, 266, 274, 334, 367–69, 440, 446, 466–67, 493, 520

Zeineddine, Farid, 390, 433–34, 447, 460–61, 465
Zeno, Emperor, 129
Zoli, A., 193
Zorlu, Fatin Rustu, 27, 79, 91, 116, 159–60, 176, 219, 259, 292–93, 346, 361, 506, 517–18, 421–22, 524–25, 563
Zuleta Angel, Alberto, 376–77, 382
Zürich Agreement, 4, 53, 524–27, 554
Zweig, Stefan, 432